MW00784960

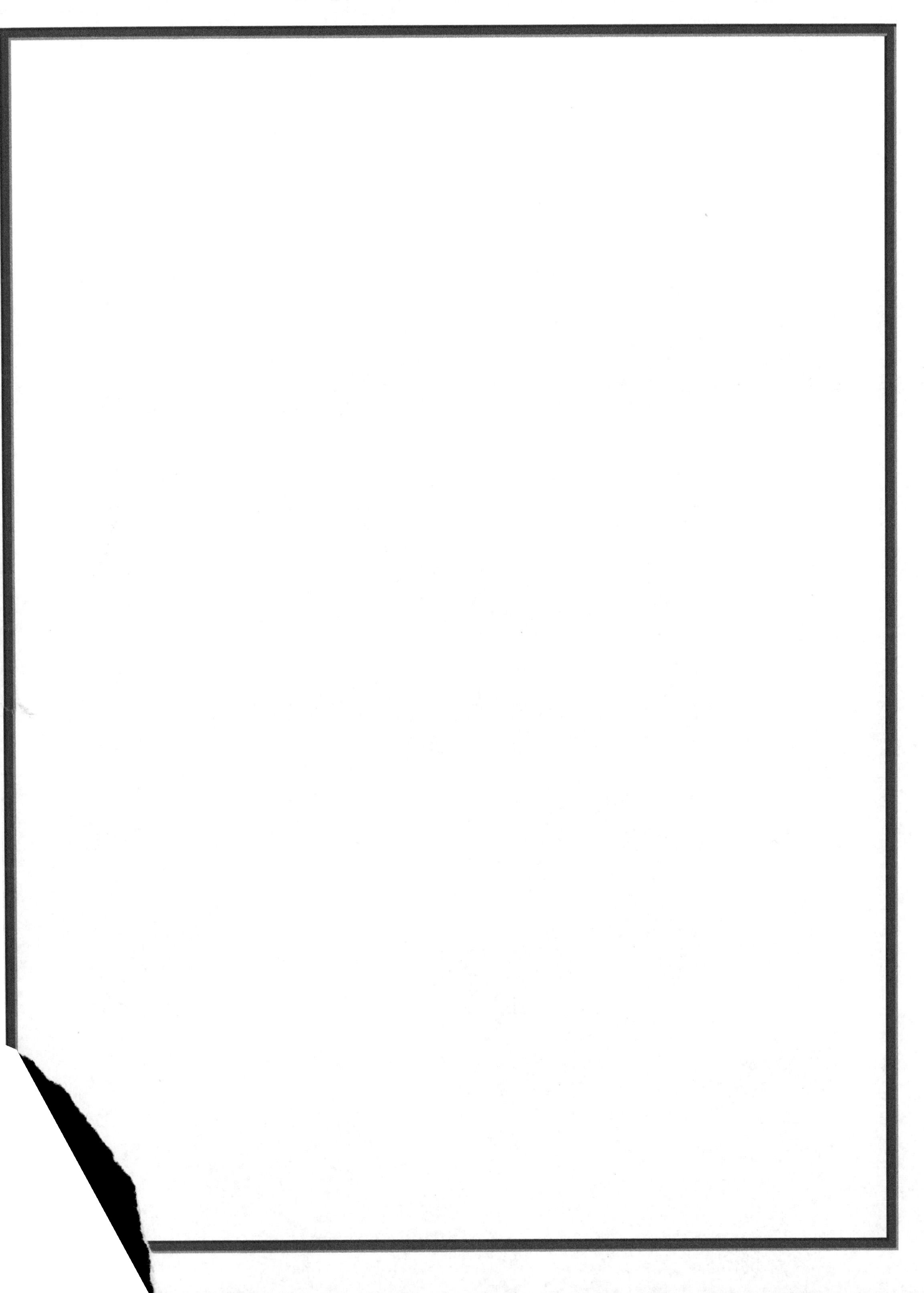

Lightning over the West Rocky Mountains

The Almond Tree
Aaron's Rod
The Messiah King of Israel

A Message of Revelation to my heart from
the Word of the God of Israel
Regarding the identity of the Messiah
The Davidic Dynasty Returns

Official Shroud Face Photograph

By Kimberly Kay Ballard

Published and Printed in 2015 by Olive Press Publisher Lowville New York in the United States of America

Photograph & Rendering Credits & Copyrights:

All Scripture quotations from; The Holy Bible Containing the Old and New Testaments Translated out of the original tongues; And with the former translations diligently compared and revised by His Majesty's Special Command Appointed to be read in Churches as well as Synagogues. King James. The Authorized King James Version of the Bible 1897 Oxford Printed at the University Press London: Humphrey Milford, Amen House, E.C.4 – New York 35 West 32nd Street

All original Photographs, scenes and the original Artist renderings of the Cherubim Angel's at the Garden Tomb pg 718 & The Jesus Boat Rendering pg 352 ©2013 by Kimberly Kay Ballard, All Rights Reserved, with the exception of the following photographs and Cherubim Artist Renderings:

A very Special thank you for the Photograph of the Miracle budding Almond Tree on Mount Moriah on front cover and page 75, Courtesy of LV ©2007, Jerusalem Israel & The Olive Branch & Olives from the Mount of Olives with rocks and the cut stone from Solomon's quarry and the marble & Roman glass, Pool of Siloam & Jordan water.

The original Artist rendering of the Ark of the Covenant on the front cover was adapted from its original black background, to glow on a snow background and adapted to B&W in the interior to be on water and in smaller edited photos on pages 108, 109, 110, 111, 703, 720 by Kimberly K Ballard and was based upon the Ron Wyatt discovery ©2010 Anchor Stone International - A special thank you Mr. Jerry Bowen, Director of Anchor Stone International, for permission to use the original Artist rendering.

A very special heartfelt thank you to the generous Official Professional Shroud Photographer & friend, Mr. Barrie M. Schwortz of the State of Colorado USA, for permission to use the Official Shroud of Turin Photographs ©1978 Barrie M. Schwortz Collection, STERA, Inc. All Rights Reserved, pages 4, 91, 107, 206, 220, 235, 246, 276, 309, 316, 368, 378, 379, 380, 382, 384, 385, 387, 546, 602, 613, 618, 668, 681, 760, 776, 840.

A very special heartfelt thank you to the generous Dr. Petrus Soons of Panama and the Netherlands, for permission to use the Official 3D Hologram Shroud face image of Messiah Yeshua in grayscale. Used with permission granted May 9th 2013 © Dr. Petrus Soons Based upon images taken by Giuseppe Enrie ©1931 All Rights Reserve on pages 111, 170, 310, 319, 323, 341 (adapted on water), 461, 462, 550, 551, 552, 567 (adapted glow line), 680, 727, 728.

A very heartfelt thank you to the generous, El Centro Español de Sindonologia for permission to use the Official photograph of the Sudarium of Oviedo SPAIN, permission granted May 8th 2013, by Mr. Mark Guscin, LaCoruna, SPAIN and Jorge Manuel Rodriguez, Valencia SPAIN - The Official Sudarium of Oviedo Spain Photograph ©2013 El Centro Español de Sindonologia (CES) All Rights Reserved on pages 220, 674, 681, 684, 688, 726.

A very heartfelt thank you to the generous Dr. Avinoam Danin, Professor Emeritus of Botany from The Hebrew University of Jerusalem Israel, for photographs from www.flora.huji.ac.il ©2013 Dr. Avinoam Danin, Fig Tree Photos on pg 322, 380, 386, 388, 398, 401, 403, 404. Acacia trees pg 613 & 628 & Pistacia lentiscus pg 689, 690.

A very special heartfelt thank you to the generous Marina Banai for the photographs of, "THE JESUS BOAT" ©2013 the Yigal Allon Center, Ginosar Israel on pg 322, 329, 334, 336, 836.

A heartfelt thank you for use of Mount Nebo Great Rolling Stone, Garden tomb, Golgotha, rock sample, TM photos ©2011 Courtesy of Simon Brown England pg 94, 97, 98, 143, 146, 152, 154, 155, 156, 159, 160, 161, 215, 221, 233, 234, 276, 277, 426, 457, 459, 460, 476, 501, 502, 504, 505, 506, 512, 514, 515, 606, 607, 665, 692, 693, 697, 717, 719, 765, 838.

The Holy Almond Tree Menorah rendering on page 254 & the Molten Brazen Sea rendering on pg 786 adapted from an Artist rendering in the ©1887 book; "Biblical Archaeology Volume I," by Dr. Carl Friedrich Keil Professor of Theology from; "The Foreign Theological Library; Printed by Morrison and Gibb for T&T Clark, 38 George Street, Edinburgh, Scotland ©1887 & Photographed & Modified with flames & other artistic effects into this updated adaptation 2013, by Kimberly K. Ballard

A special heartfelt thank you to Jim and Penny Caldwell of (splitrockresearch.org), for their photographs of the fruiting Fig Tree on the Real Mount Sinai in Arabia pg 837, the Split Rock at Horeb 207, 211, 214, 837 & the burnt peak of Mount Sinai in Arabia pg 521, 837 ©1992 Jim & Penny Caldwell, All Rights Reserved

A very heartfelt special thank you to Eduardo Guerra Fausti & Eliane Abdinnour for the Official Dec. & Oct. ©2009 Magdala Center Excavation photos the Magdala Stone pg 259, 332, 469, 706, 836. The Magdala Synagogue 331, 348, 470, 836 & for the Aerial Photo of the Magdala Synagogue ©2013 David Silverman & Yuval Nadel for Magdala Center Excavations Israel pg 330, 836.

A heartfelt thank you to Leon Mauldin for the photos ©2014 of Mount Nebo on pg 94 & 159 & Jordan River pg 854

A very heartfelt thank you to my friend Gershon Salomon of The Temple Mount & Land of Israel Faithful Movement for the ©2003, ©2007-2014 Photos of the model of the Second Holy Temple on pg 779 & 855 & the Third Temple schematic model in Jerusalem Israel pg 855. (Edited to B&W, some cropped, faded, & flipped by KK Ballard).

The Almond Tree
Aaron's Rod
The Messiah King of Israel

Royal Dedications and Acknowledgments

To His Highest Royal Majesty in Heaven
To the Most Honourable KING of KINGS AND LORD of LORDS
God of Israel, You are the KING of the Universe
I dedicate this book to Your honour with all my heart, so that Your glory
and Majesty will be shown, revealing Your Eternal Testimony,
by the Rod of Your power, Your might, Your beauty
and Eternal Royal Divine Majesty and Sovereignty,
as the glorious Saviour of the World
All Kingdoms pale in comparison to Your Eternal Kingdom
Blessed be the Name of our LORD and Saviour
Yeshua HaMashiach, who gives us the key of King David of Israel

Lion & Crown in the Snow

Dedications

Dedicated to my beautiful beloved Mother Lynda, I love you so much! May you obtain great blessing from this book from the KING, and receive a crown of righteousness for teaching me about Him, and for our computer to write this book for His eternal glory through your kindness and love! You are a precious eternal jewel in the Crown of the KING & a blessing to my heart forever. With the LORD we have overcome! To My Israeli friend LV, I thank you with all my heart for sending me the Almond Tree budding in Jerusalem on Holy Mount Moriah! Without the LORD directing you, this miracle from the LORD would never have happened between us and this book would not have transpired! Thank you to my dear friend Brenda for your loving support over the years, especially during the very hard times and for always supporting my musical endeavors. You are always the everlasting kind, gentle, loyal friend and faithful sister to me and the most incredible pianist! Love to my sisters Laura & Melinda, Karen & Melanie & Dad, my grandparents Mary & Maurice Carroll thank you for the Fruiting Fig Tree photos ©2013 pg 389 & 390. My love to grandparents Elizabeth & Percy Farris for the Bible & Irvin holly, Irvin fine linen from County Cork Ireland & for your King David painting! Love to my nieces & nephews & extended family members, including those in Heaven. I miss you! May the LORD inscribe your names in the Book of Life! Love to my darling Jasmine who is always in my heart! Love to the Dallas Malloy family. To my faithful college friends Laura and Maria, thank you for many years of true loyal friendship. You have blessed my life through so much kindness with your words and deeds! Special thanks to Dr Avinoam Danin, Emeritus Professor of Botany at The Hebrew University in Jerusalem Israel for his friendship & photos! Special thanks to my friend & Official Shroud Photographer Mr. Barrie M. Schwortz for speaking with me about the Shroud so many times, for your photographs, and thank you for sharing my article with the, "Scholars!" Thank you to Jeff A Benner for use of his Semitic charts on pg 170 on the ancient Hebrew letter Shin ©1999-2013. A very special heartfelt thank you to Gershon Salomon in Jerusalem Israel with The Temple Mount & Land of Israel Faithful Movement for the photos of the Holy Temple pg 779 & 855! Thank you to everyone that so graciously contributed to the photographs within this book!!! A very special thank you to the DeRieux family for their rooster & hen photos pg 437-443 & my sister Melinda's Magnolia Tree seed pod pg 750 & 753 & Persimmon Tree pg 753 & to my sister Laura for the Gardenia! Special thanks to Cheryl Zehr at Olive Press Publisher in Lowville New York for additional editing, finalizing the book cover and for printing this book. The Artistic Design, Layout, Editing & Artistic Direction of this book & its cover is the work of Kimberly Kay Ballard.

Dedication Malloy Palm Tree & Jasmine Cat

Contents

Chapter 3

79 THE BRANCH THE ROD MESSIAH

Chapter 4

109 MOSES THE TABERNACLE THE ARK OF THE COVENANT

Chapter 5

163 THE YAD THE RIGHT HAND ON THE ROD THE FINGER OF GOD

Chapter 6

Chapter 7

Chapter 8

Chapter 9

Chapter 10

Chapter 11

All Roses, Iris, Peony, Gardenia, Daffodil, Columbine, Cat Jasmine, Ranunculus flower, praying Rabbit on the Contents pages

  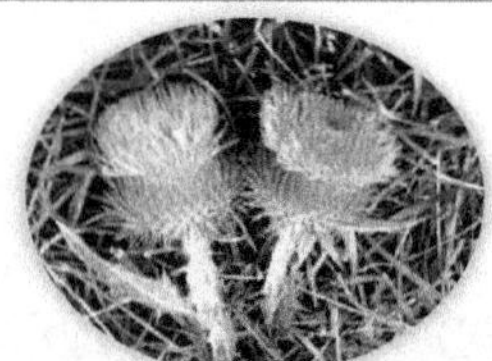  

Chapter 12

731 THE ALMOND TREE OF LIFE ALPHA & OMEGA THE FIRST AND THE LAST THE BEGINNING AND THE END

Snare Drum, Crown, Shield & Dedication Elizabeth Irvin Farris Holly Family Crest Irvin House of Drum Castle & Bonshaw Tower, Scotland Photos ©2013 Kimberly K Ballard All Rights Reserved

Scripture and Invitation

Snow on branch Photo ©2013 Kimberly K Ballard All Rights Reserved

At that time Yeshua answered and said, I praise Thee O Father, LORD of Heaven and earth that Thou didst hide these things from the wise and intelligent and didst reveal them to babes. Yes, Father, for thus it was well-pleasing in Thy sight. All things have been handed over to Me by My Father; and no one knows the Son, except the Father; nor does anyone know the Father, except the Son, and anyone to whom the Son wills to reveal Him. Matthew 11:25-27

The LORD revealed Himself to me and I have written every detail within this book that took 7 years after it started!

Everlasting life is a gift of the LORD God of Israel
You must repent of your sins, believe in the LORDS Eternal Testimony and turn to Him with all of your heart.
Go and be Baptized in the living water, in Name of the LORD, who is the Father, Son and Holy Spirit.
He is the Eternal KING OF KINGS AND LORD OF LORDS.
Then Eternal life and Eternal Salvation will be yours forever!
I hope that this book of the revelation of the Messiah and the Eternal King of Israel,
Will bless everyone that reads it, all over the world!
Shalom With Love! The King is coming! Get ready!
Kimberly K Ballard

For the everlasting glory of my Beautiful KING!

The initial writing of this book was completed on September 7th 2010 at 5:17PM, just before the Eve of Rosh HaShanah & more revelations came through 2011! The First Editing was completed on June 1st 2012 7:12 PM. The 5th Editing was finished at the time of the High Holy Days of Rosh HaShanah & Yom Kippur, September 27th 2012.

The Final Manuscript was completed during the Feast of Tabernacles October 3rd 2012. Finished 7th Editing January 17th 2013 one week before Tu B' Shevat! Manuscript was finalized on Tu B' Shevat January 26th 2013. Book Cover finished at Passover 2013. Final Editing completed December 30th, 2013 & pdf in Shevat! I love You KING Yeshua!

Lamentations 5:18 Because of the mountain of Zion, which is desolate, the foxes walk upon it. Thou, O LORD, remainest forever; thy throne from generation to generation. Wherefore dost thou forget us forever, and forsake us so long time? Turn thou us unto thee, O LORD, and we shall be turned; renew our days as of old.

Luke 9:57-58 And it came to pass, that, as they went in the way, a certain man said unto him, Lord, I will follow thee whithersoever thou goest. And Yeshua said unto him, Foxes have holes, and birds of the air have nests; but the Son of man hath not where to lay his head.

Psalm 42:1 As the deer panteth after the water brooks, so panteth my soul after Thee, O God.

Introduction

On February 16th 2007, in the middle of winter, I was awakened from my sleep at 4AM. I was given a very clear and orderly message from the LORD. It flooded my mind and heart, as I wrote down every detail that was being shown to me, by the Holy Spirit. This message was the key that unlocked the door to the mystery of the Messiah of Israel. It was without a doubt, the key of King David. To my astonishment, the LORD used this key to unveil His mysteries to me and He gave me some earth shattering revelations for the last days. I was not expecting the first miracle to happen, nor did I expect it to lead to so many Divine revelations and other true miracles, over the course of six years. As it began to unfold, the LORD impressed me to write down every detail and to put it in a book! As I turned His key in the lock, I stepped through the opened door before me and I saw the LORD face to face. Without any expectations, a true miracle came back to me from Jerusalem. This was the beginning of the unveiling of the Messiah of Israel. It was as if a fire was burning inside my heart and mind, as the LORD unveiled His mystery to me. The first time that I perceived God's message, I wept and sobbed from the depths of my heart. It was extremely touching, that the LORD had chosen to give this miracle to me, at this historical moment in Israel's redemption. I was keenly aware, that this knowledge was hidden by the LORD through many centuries. Perhaps this precious gift for Israel was hidden by the LORD, within the Scriptures, until the time of the end. The LORD therefore, encoded His Eternal Testimony in such a way, that in the last days, the world would never again doubt His Everlasting glory, as the details began to emerge from His secret vault. In my heart, I know that the Messiah is coming soon. I believe that as time draws near to His return, He is allowing the blessings to be manifested and broadcast, as a final warning to all people, telling them to turn to Him. The Bible was precisely and accurately written by the power of God's Holy Spirit, as He impressed it upon the hearts of His faithful Jewish Prophets and Apostles. The Word of God is like an Almond Blossom! When the bud of an Almond blossom is closed tightly, you can only discern the outer petals. You are not able to see that there are hidden petals within the bud, because the flower has not yet fully opened to your gaze. So the flower in a sense is veiled to you, because at first, it is hidden from your view. Then suddenly, at just the right moment in time, the Almond blossom begins to unfurl and a breathtaking picture emerges. The winter is over like the Diaspora and spring arrives with a flurry of new life budding forth. The beauty of the blossoming Almond Tree is magnificent and the fragrance is exhilarating! We watch in amazement, as the Almond blossoms begin to unfurl their soft delicate petals and gently cascade open, in a full array of pale pink. This is how I describe the Testimony of the LORD. He is the beautiful Tree of Life. I invite you to come and see the heart of the LORD in full bloom! Can you hear the footsteps of KING Messiah?

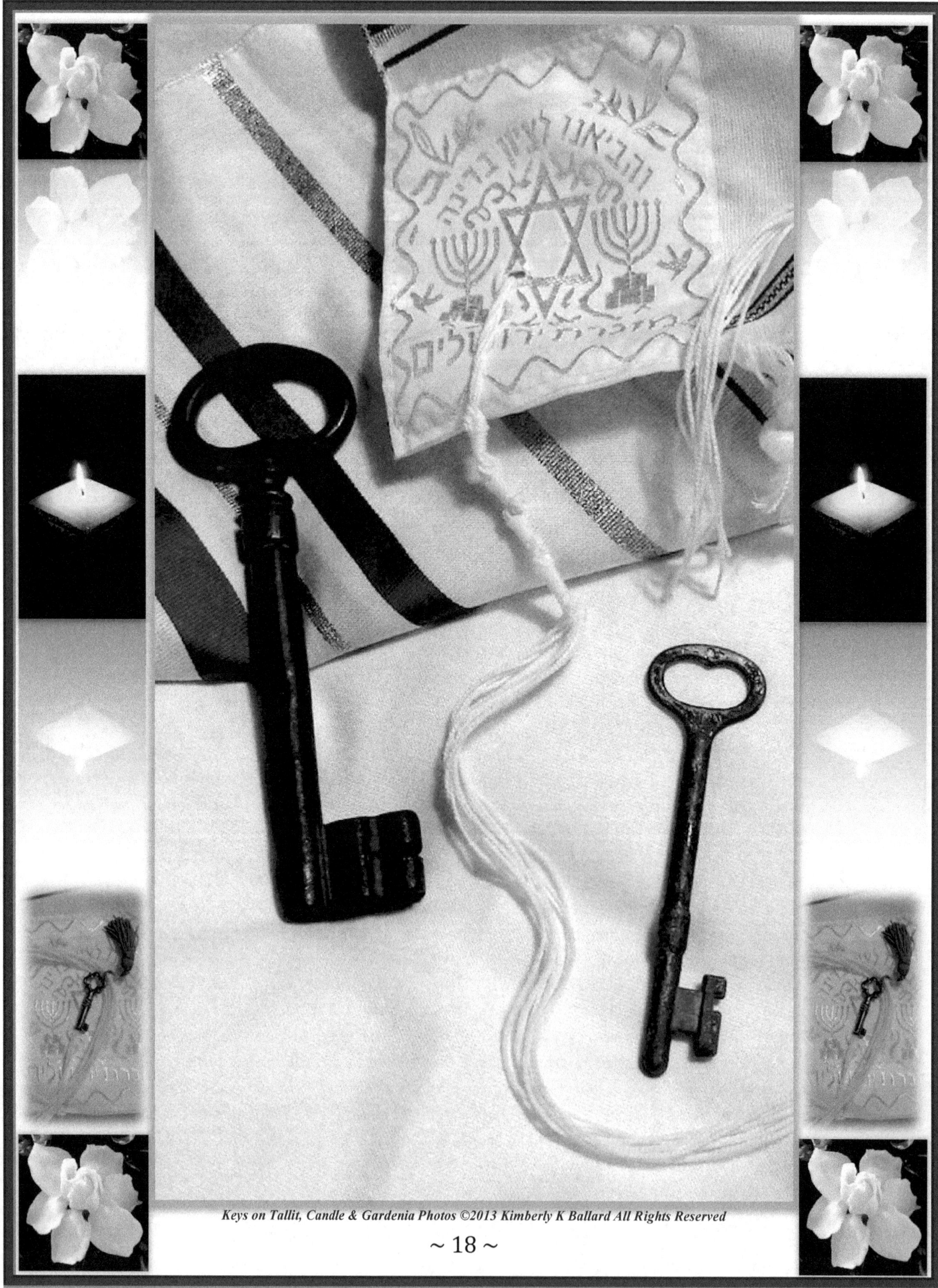

Keys on Tallit, Candle & Gardenia Photos ©2013 Kimberly K Ballard All Rights Reserved

Chapter 1

MESSIAH IS A MYSTERY

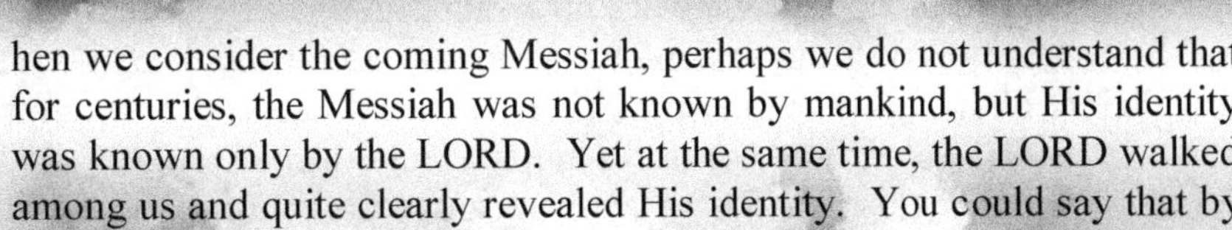

Lock & Key & Snow
Photos ©2013 Kimberly K Ballard All Rights Reserved

When we consider the coming Messiah, perhaps we do not understand that for centuries, the Messiah was not known by mankind, but His identity was known only by the LORD. Yet at the same time, the LORD walked among us and quite clearly revealed His identity. You could say that by His fruits we should know Him. His works stand as a profound Testimony of the LORD. The elements of His Testimony were written and recorded in the ancient text of the Holy Scriptures of the Bible centuries ago. The ancient Prophets of Israel, who were chosen by God, were given these hidden mysteries to write in a book. Because these secrets are still being revealed to us today, this book called, *"The Holy Bible,"* is like no other book on earth. It is literally *the Word of God* revealed. What I have to show you in my book, is the final Testimony of the LORD, as it was revealed to me. Believe me when I say that it is miraculous! I was so deeply touched when the LORD opened my understanding to see this Testimony. We will discover that the Messiah is called, *"The Sar HaPanim."* This Hebrew phrase is translated as, *"The Prince of the face of the LORD God."* The Messiah is intriguing. He is a mystery that was to be revealed at the right moment in time, like an Almond Tree that buds when the winter is over and the first tender sprouts of spring burst forth with new life and you stand there transfixed, gazing at its beauty. I love a great mystery. The LORD wrote the most astonishing hidden mystery in His Testimony of the Torah, that was to be revealed at the end of days and now it is time to reveal it. It is time to honour the one true Messiah, who is indeed, the majestic and glorious everlasting KING of Israel!

Now it is interesting to analyze the definition of the word, *"mystery,"* because by definition, *"a mystery,"* is any truth unknowable, except by Divine revelation. A mystery is something *secret* that is connected to the life and death of the Messiah! The conclusion therefore, is to say that it is only by the LORD'S Divine revelation, through His Holy Spirit, that the Messiah is revealed to us. Without the Holy Spirit, it is impossible to discern the mysteries of the LORD and it is impossible to completely understand the Messiah's identity.

Mystery;

1. *Something that is secret or impossible to understand.*
2. *Something that arouses curiosity through its obscure nature.*
3. *Secrecy, of the quality of being obscure or enigmatic.*
4. *Any truth unknowable except by Divine revelation.*
5. *An incident or scene in connection with the life or passion of Messiah.*

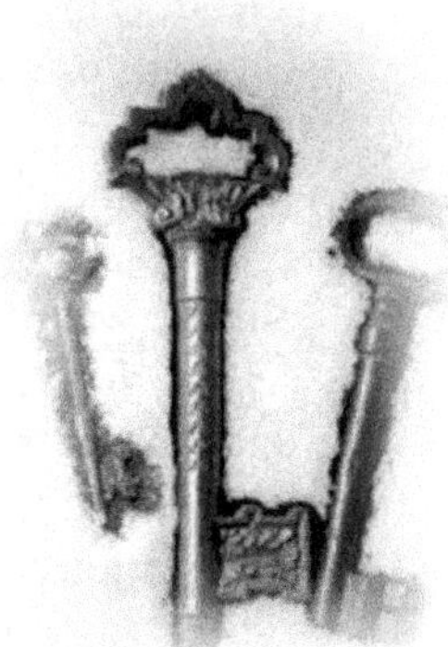

Keys in the snow & Key on Tallit
Photos ©2013 Kimberly K Ballard
All Rights Reserved

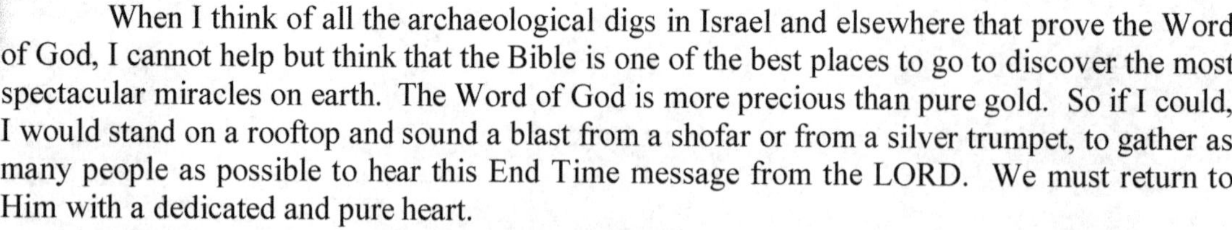

When I think of all the archaeological digs in Israel and elsewhere that prove the Word of God, I cannot help but think that the Bible is one of the best places to go to discover the most spectacular miracles on earth. The Word of God is more precious than pure gold. So if I could, I would stand on a rooftop and sound a blast from a shofar or from a silver trumpet, to gather as many people as possible to hear this End Time message from the LORD. We must return to Him with a dedicated and pure heart.

I must say, that many aspects of the Messiah have been discovered over the course of 2,000 years, but so much of His Divine Covenant still remains to be exhibited before the world. The LORD chooses to reveal these facts and sometimes the LORD chooses someone as simple as a shepherd or a musician to relay His message to His people. Over the course of six years, by Divine Revelation, I have faithfully written this book, as the LORD directed me through His Holy Spirit. It has been a long labor of love that I will miss when I am finished!

Psalm 25:14 *The secret of the LORD is with them that fear Him; and He will show them His Covenant.*

I believe that because we are now living in the time frame called, *"The end of days,"* the LORD is breaking the seal of the prophecy in the book of Daniel and in the book of Revelation, allowing us for the first time, to view these end time mysteries. Our minds are about to be captivated, as these truths are suddenly opened and revealed to our understanding for the first time in history. This book is meant to both glorify the LORD God of Israel and to reveal Him as the Eternal KING OF KINGS. In chapter one, I must first lay the groundwork, before I begin relaying the story of the astonishing miracle that happened to me, that prompted me to write this book in the first place. I believe that you are going to be thunderstruck, when you read every element of the LORD'S Testimony, as I have outlined every Divine detail of this masterpiece. For years I read the text of the entire Bible, but specifically from the year 2007 onward, the LORD began to open my understanding to see things within the text of the Bible, that I had never seen or understood before in my entire life. So I was nevertheless shocked, speechless and quite frankly overwhelmed to tears, when the LORD suddenly gave me the ability to discern these truths for the first time, when I contemplated the LORD and searched for Him with all my heart. I was studying the Scriptures diligently and sincerely with a humbled heart, in a different way than I had ever studied them before. So why did the LORD send these incredible messages of hope to me? I believe this happened, because I told the LORD that I was giving my entire life to Him and I wanted to follow Him in complete sincerity. I became quite a dedicated and diligent student of the Bible and at this time, I literally requested favor from the LORD, so that He would indeed reveal to me, the unfathomable meaning within particular events within the Bible. My desire was to fully know Him, in order to perceive the depths of His glory. Loving the LORD is all about having a close relationship with Him. So I was intently asking the LORD questions, as I would of my closest friend. This relationship with the LORD became like a daily walk in the refreshing rain. When He manifested Himself by His Spirit to me, I began to realize that He is very close to us and not far away as we would ordinarily assume Him to be, although in Proverbs 15:29, the LORD is said to be far from the wicked, but He is close to the righteous. To the righteous, His ears are open to their prayers. His desire is for us to love Him and to take an interest in Him, just as anyone wants to be truly loved and cherished.

The LORD became my closest friend and after this first miracle happened, I began to understand the way that He thinks and speaks. To my astonishment, He gave me so many answers to my questions. He gave me answers that were far above and beyond any expectations that I had in my heart. The LORD God of Israel is staggeringly brilliant, because He encoded the Messiah deep within the text of His Holy Scriptures from the very beginning and this is the secret! So let me say right here, that because the LORD touched my heart in such

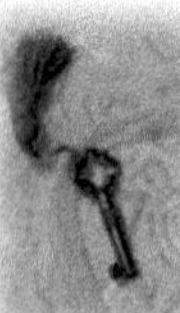

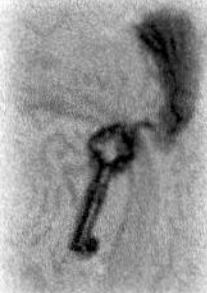

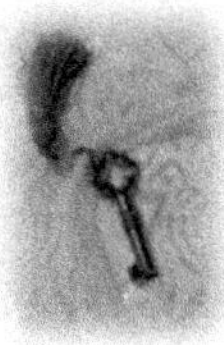

a fantastic and deeply moving way with His Testimony, I am inspired to say to Him that, *"I love you LORD forever and even more than I could possibly imagine!"* At the time of *the end of days,* the Messiah will be revealed to Israel and they will certainly see His face as, *"The Sar HaPanim, the Prince of the face of the LORD God."* So I proclaim that the last and final KING of Judah, of the Davidic Dynasty, will now open the eyes of the blind!

Proverbs 16:15 *In the light of the KING'S countenance is life; and His favour is as a cloud of the latter rain.*

He is coming to reign as our KING OF KINGS, so we should get to know His Royal Majesty now, before He arrives. His glory and honour is far greater than anything in this life that we have known. We should long for Him as our beautiful Eternal KING, full of grace, love, righteousness, truth, light, and life. I stand as a witness and I can say that knowing the LORD'S heart, has brought me such excitement and hope in my life. Sometimes I close my eyes and imagine the beauty of the face of the LORD God. I ponder the magnificence of dwelling in His midst, as it was in the Garden of Eden, before corruption, sin, and death entered the world. As a musician and a composer, I can imagine that the music of Heaven is far superior to any that we have ever heard. Although to me, Barbra Streisand's voice is as close to musical Heaven as I have ever heard on this earth! Her voice is a symphony, a wall of sound that wraps itself around your heart and vibrates to the inner core of your being. So I hope the music of Heaven is something like this sound! Below I have written a few of the Scriptures that confirm that the Messiah is a mystery, who is to be revealed in due time.

Romans 16:25-27 *Now to Him that is of power to stablish you according to my gospel, and the preaching of Jesus Christ, according to the revelation of the mystery, which was kept secret since the world began, But now is made manifest, and by the scriptures of the prophets, according to the commandment of the everlasting God, made known to all nations for the obedience of faith: To God only wise, be glory through Jesus Christ forever. Amen.*

The Holy Spirit of the LORD also gave Spiritual discernment of the mysteries of God, to the Jewish Apostle Paul. Remember that Saul/Paul was from the tribe of Benjamin and he was a Pharisee and a son of a Pharisee. Saul was a dedicated Torah Scholar, a student of the famed Rabbi Gamaliel and He was a devout Hebrew of Hebrews. The mysteries were also revealed to at least three of the twelve Jewish disciples of Yeshua and to the ancient Prophets of Israel, who foreshadowed the Jewish Messiah in their writings.

I Corinthians 2:7-16 *But we speak the wisdom of God in a mystery, even the hidden wisdom, which God ordained before the world unto our glory; Which none of the princes of this world knew; for had they known it, they would not have crucified the LORD of glory. But as it is written, Eye hath not seen, nor ear heard, neither have entered into the heart of man, the things which God hath prepared for them that love Him. But God hath revealed them unto us by His Spirit; for the Spirit searcheth all things, yea, the deep things of God. For what man knoweth the things of a man, save the spirit of man which is in him? Even so the things of God knoweth no man, but the Spirit of God. Now we have received, not the spirit of the world, but the Spirit which is of God; that we might know the things that are freely given to us of God. Which things also we speak, not in the words which man's wisdom teacheth, but which the Holy Spirit teacheth; comparing spiritual things with spiritual. But the natural man receiveth not the things of the Spirit of God; for they are foolishness unto him; neither can he know them, because they are spiritually discerned. But he that is spiritual judgeth all things, yet He Himself is judged of no man. For who hath known the mind of the LORD, that He may instruct him? But we have the mind of Messiah.*

The mystery of the Messiah was revealed at the proper moment in history, at the time of the Second Temple period. The Biblical Archaeological digs have slowly revealed the historical record of ancient Israel, but Messiah Yeshua is the most extraordinary part of this revealed history, as we will soon discover.

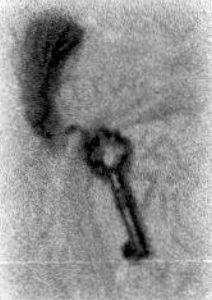

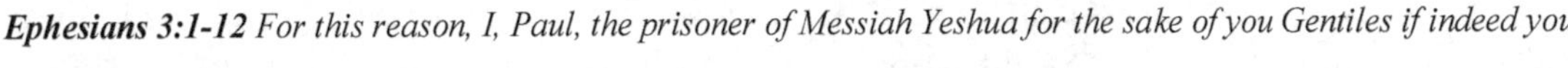

Ephesians 3:1-12 *For this reason, I, Paul, the prisoner of Messiah Yeshua for the sake of you Gentiles if indeed you*

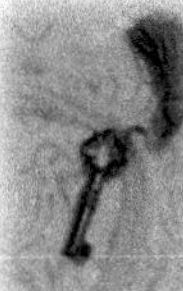

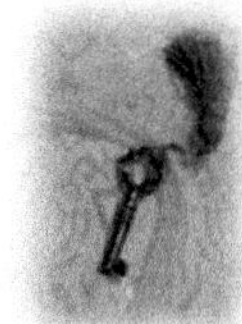

have heard of the stewardship of God's grace which was given to me for you that by revelation there was made known to me the mystery, as I wrote before in brief. And by referring to this, when you read you can understand my insight into the mystery of Messiah, which in other generations was not made known to the sons of men, as it has now been revealed to His Holy Apostles and Prophets in the Spirit; To be specific, that the Gentile's are fellow heirs and fellow members of the body, and fellow partakers of the promise in Messiah Yeshua through the Gospel, of which I was made a minister, according to the gift of God's grace which was given to me according to the working of His power. To me, the very least of all Saints, this grace was given, to preach to the Gentile's the unfathomable riches of Messiah, and to bring to light what is the administration of the mystery which for ages has been hidden in God, who created all things; In order that the manifold wisdom of God might now be made known through the Church to the rulers and authorities in the Heavenly places. This was in accordance with the eternal purpose which He carried out in Messiah Yeshua, our LORD, In whom we have boldness and confident access through faith in Him.

Colossians 4:2-4 *Devote your selves to prayer, keeping alert in it with an attitude of thanksgiving; praying at the same time for us as well, that God may open up to us a door for the Word, so that we may speak forth the mystery of Messiah, for which I have also been imprisoned; in order that I may make it clear in the way I ought to speak.*

It was predetermined by the will of God that the Jewish disciples of the Messiah, were to be sent forth by the LORD, to boldly proclaim this mystery to the world. This was the mystery that was previously unknown by mankind, until the LORD descended from Heaven to earth, to fulfill the ancient prophecies of His own Living Testimony. Are there other prophecies that are yet to be fulfilled by the Messiah? The answer is yes, because His time is in the past, in the present and in the future. Just as He fulfilled His works in the past, He will also fulfill them in the future. So He will come to the earth from Heaven in the future, to restore the earth and He will reign as KING OF KINGS AND LORD OF LORDS. The fact is however, that if we have believed in His Name and have put our faith and trust in Him, we will immediately go into His Divine Presence when we die. We have the wonderful promise of Eternal life in Him. When we die, we are absent from our earthly body, but immediately present with the LORD and this is our greatest comfort. By His grace we are saved and not by our own works or performance.

When the LORD came to His beloved Israel during the Second Temple period, He fulfilled the good news of Eternal salvation. This gift of Eternal life is not only for Israel, but it is a gift to all people in every Nation, to anyone that places their trust in the LORD God of Israel, in Messiah Yeshua. The LORD expects us all to turn from wickedness and from living a sinful life. We must be cleansed in the LORD'S baptism of Living Water, to be filled with the LORD'S Spirit that breathes Eternal life into us. The Eternal Testimony of the Heavenly Covenant of the LORD God is this Gospel message of Eternal life.

I Timothy 3:16 *And without controversy great is the mystery of godliness; God was manifest in the flesh, justified in the Spirit, seen of angels, preached unto the Gentiles, believed on in the world, received up into glory.*

To solve any great mystery, a detective must gather all the facts of the case, along with the Testimony of many witnesses, to prove the case beyond a doubt. In our case, the Bible contains the Testimony of thousands of witnesses, over many centuries of history. As we will see, these witnesses verify the facts of the identity of the Messiah and His works speak of His greatness and glory. If we can establish a timeline fitting all the clues and pieces of the puzzle together, into one cohesive picture, then this will tell the whole story from beginning to end. It will prove to be a solid Testimony, from Genesis to Revelation, because the LORD is the First and the Last, the Beginning and the End. Then we will see the full picture in a panorama before our eyes and the truth will emerge victoriously and triumphantly. Therefore, the mystery of the Messiah will be solved once and for all, proving the LORD is faithful and true, in every sense of the Word. With this idea in mind, I have gathered the evidence from His Holy works and from the Testimony of thousands of eyewitnesses. Armed with these undeniable truths, we will solve the mystery of the Messiah! Only the KING of Glory will

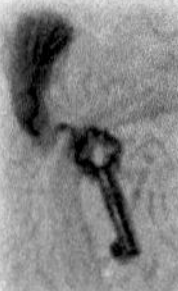

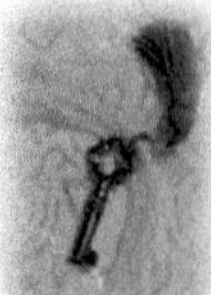

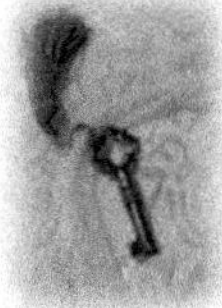

remain standing forever, as an Eternal banner that is the Standard of love over Israel and over all of us in every Nation, as well as over the place where the LORD God said that His Name will dwell forever, in the Eternal City of Jerusalem.

MESSIAH IS FROM THE ANCIENT OF DAYS

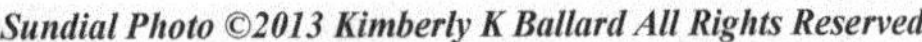

Sundial Photo ©2013 Kimberly K Ballard All Rights Reserved

A wonderful place to begin seeking the truth is to look within the well known Messianic prophecy given to us by the LORD, through the ancient Prophets of Israel, regarding the coming of the Messiah out of Bethlehem. It contains a hidden revelation.

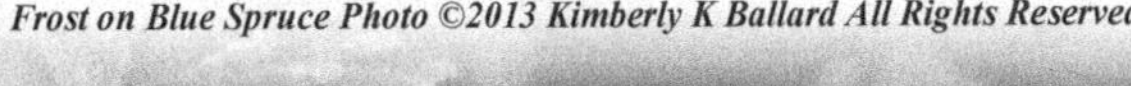

Frost on Blue Spruce Photo ©2013 Kimberly K Ballard All Rights Reserved

Micah 5:2 *But you, Bethlehem Ephrata, though you are little among the thousands of Judah, yet out of you shall come forth to Me the one to be Ruler in Israel, Whose goings forth are from of old, from everlasting.*

This prophecy clearly says that the Messiah is not only out of Bethlehem, but most importantly that, *"His goings forth are from everlasting."* This indicates that Messiah Yeshua always existed in eternity past and He is from, *"The Ancient of Days."* We already know that *the LORD God of Israel* is the only one with the title, *"The Ancient of Days."* Therefore, since the Messiah is from everlasting, He absolutely must be the LORD God of Israel, as well as the Messiah. *He is one God.* The LORD would miraculously come from Heaven to Bethlehem as the Messiah, to fulfill His Living Testimony of the Torah on the earth. The only Jewish Messiah to ever come out of Bethlehem is Yeshua of Nazareth. His earthly parents were chosen by the LORD to fulfill His will. Both parents were direct descendants of King David of the tribe of Judah, the beloved musician and composer! Joseph and Mary were *Royalty* and they were Torah abiding Jews of ancient Israel, who visited the Holy Temple in Jerusalem, on all the special Holy Convocations of the LORD. Joseph's line through Jeconiah was cursed *(Jeremiah 22:28-30)* and Mary's through Nathan was not. The Messiah reconciled this breech! The little town of Bethlehem, formerly called, *"Ephrata,"* was their family town of origin. They were sent back to Bethlehem for the census. Mary gave birth to Messiah Yeshua, in the place that fulfilled the ancient Prophecy that was written in the book of Isaiah.

Doves on Maple tree
Photo ©2013
Kimberly K Ballard

Isaiah 7:13-14 *And he said, Hear ye now, O house of David; Is it a small thing for you to weary men, but will ye weary my God also? Therefore the LORD Himself shall give you a sign; Behold, a virgin shall conceive, and bear a son, and shall call His Name Immanuel.*

In the Gospel of Luke, the Heavenly Hosts appeared with the angel of the LORD, to announce the birth of Yeshua. They were heralding the Heavenly message, telling the people of Israel that, *"On this day in the city of David, the Saviour, which is Messiah the LORD, was born."* The text clearly says that the LORD God of Israel is the Messiah, the Saviour of Israel!

Luke 2:10-11 *And the angel said unto them, Fear not; for, behold, I bring you good tidings of great joy, which shall be to all people. For unto you is born this day in the city of David a Saviour, which is Messiah the LORD.*

The LORD therefore, came in the flesh, down from Heaven as Immanuel, *"God with us."* The Messiah was sent to fulfill the prophecies of the LORD, because He is from *everlasting.* We are not at the end of the book of the redemption of Israel at the moment and He will return to fulfill more of His prophecy in the future. He came specifically from Heaven to earth, to fulfill His Living Testimony. This was exactly the same Testimony that the LORD showed to Moses on Mount Sinai. Moses then made the parallel or mirror image of the Heavenly things in earthly form.

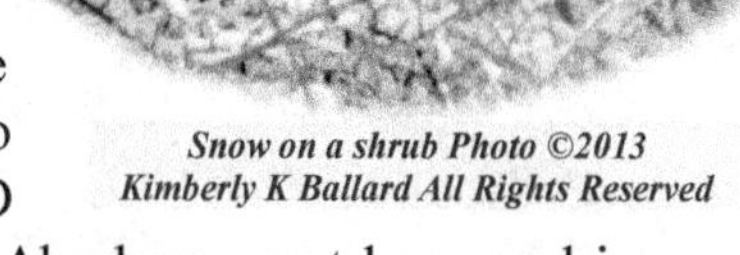
Snow on a shrub Photo ©2013
Kimberly K Ballard

In another Scripture, Yeshua reveals His identity, when He tells the people of Israel that, *"He existed before Abraham was born."* Messiah Yeshua clearly says that He is, *"I AM."* So it is obvious in the story, that Abraham saw the future days of Messiah Yeshua in a vision, before the Messiah came to the earth, to fulfill the LORD'S Living Testimony. The LORD had revealed Himself to Abraham *as the Messiah* and this gave Abraham great hope and joy. Armed with this knowledge, Abraham was excited for the day to come, when the LORD would dwell with us as the Messiah, at the proper time in history.

John 8:56-58 *Your father Abraham rejoiced to see My day; and he saw it, and was glad. Then said the Jews unto Him, Thou art not yet fifty years old, and hast Thou seen Abraham? Yeshua said unto them, Verily, verily, I say unto you, Before Abraham was, I AM.*

John the Jewish disciple, revealed Messiah Yeshua as, *"The Word of God."* He declared that, *"The Word of God was in the beginning with God and the Word was God."* Messiah Yeshua is not only from, *"The Ancient of Days, from everlasting,"* but He existed forever as, *"The Word of God."* When you have the Bible in your hand, the Word is with you, just as the Word is with God, in His hand and it is life!

John 1:1-5 *In the beginning was the Word, and the Word was with God, and the Word was God. The same was in the beginning with God. All things were made by Him; and without Him was not anything made that was made. In Him was life; and the life was the light of men. And the light shineth in darkness; and the darkness comprehended it not.*

I John 1:1-7 *That which was from the beginning, which we have heard, which we have seen with our eyes, which we have looked upon, and our hands have handled, of the Word of life; For the life was manifested, and we have seen it, and bear witness, and shew unto you that eternal life, which was with the Father, and was manifested unto us; That*

which we have seen and heard declare we unto you, that ye also may have fellowship with us; and truly our fellowship is with the Father, and with His Son Yeshua Messiah. And these things write we unto you, that your joy may be full. This then is the message which we have heard of Him, and declare unto you, that God is light, and in Him is no darkness at all. If we say that we have fellowship with Him, and walk in darkness, we lie and do not the truth; But if we walk in the light, as He is in the light, we have fellowship one with another and the blood of Yeshua Messiah His Son cleanseth us from all sin.

Frost on Lilac bush Photo ©2013 Kimberly K Ballard All Rights Reserved

In the beginning the LORD separated the light from the darkness and this was the first day of creation. So the first thing that the LORD created was the light. He is visible within His creation as the light, *"The First,"* the, *"Aleph,"* in Hebrew, or in Greek, *"The Alpha,"* in this context. Now in the beginning, in Genesis, *wherever the light was there was life.* This is why we have life in the Messiah, because He is the light, *the Prince of the face of the LORD God.* This means that Yeshua is *the light of the LORD'S countenance.* This explains why it is that when we are genuinely abiding in the LORD, who is the source of the light, no darkness can abide in us. This explains why the LORD is close to the righteous who have the light, but He is far from the wicked who remain in the darkness.

Psalm 34:14-18 *Depart from evil, and do good; seek peace, and pursue it. The eyes of the LORD are upon the righteous, and His ears are open unto their cry. The face of the LORD is against them that do evil, to cut off the remembrance of them from the earth. The righteous cry, and the LORD heareth, and delivereth them out of all their troubles. The LORD is nigh unto them that are of a broken heart; and saveth such as be of a contrite spirit.*

The light does not abide with the darkness they are separate from each other. If one claims to know God and yet they do wicked evil deeds, then they do not know the LORD God at all. The light always puts out the darkness, like a lamp lights up a room. Proverbs 16:15 says, *"In the light of the king's countenance is life."* When you have seen the face of Messiah and believe in the light, then you have Eternal life, because life can only grow and flourish in the light, as it was in the beginning, just like a seed can only flourish where there is light, as it comes up from the darkness of the soil, into the brightness of light to have life!

Where there is no light there is only darkness and death. To have Eternal life is to behold the face of the LORD God. To die without the LORD is to be separated from Him forever in darkness. Without the light of the LORD God, there can be no Eternal life in us. Our only other option would be, to be cast into the outer darkness and separated from God. This is why only the LORD could give us Eternal life, *because the life is in the KINGS countenance!* So when the Messiah came down from Heaven as the true light and *the express image of God,* the LORD was temporarily dwelling in the midst of the Land of Israel, until He completed His Living Testimony of Eternal life. Then He ascended into Heaven from the Mount of Olives and His glory departed.

Genesis 1:1-5 *In the beginning God created the Heaven and the earth. And the earth was without form, and void; and darkness was upon the face of the deep. And the Spirit of God moved upon the face of the waters. And God said, Let there be light; and there was light. And God saw the light, that it was good; and God divided the light from darkness. And God called the light Day, and the darkness He called Night. And the evening and the morning were the first day.*

John 12:46-47 *I AM come a light into the world, that whosoever believeth on Me should not abide in darkness. And if any man hear My Words, and believe not, I judge him not; for I came not to judge the world, but to save the world.*

The Light is the key of our salvation Photo ©2013 Kimberly K Ballard All Rights Reserved

Daniel 2:22 *He revealeth the deep and secret things; He knoweth what is in the darkness, and the light dwelleth with Him.*

There is a description of the Ancient of Days that was written by Daniel. The Ancient of Days is identical in appearance to the Apostle John's description of Messiah Yeshua, as He was seen in Heaven in the book of Revelation. In Revelation, Messiah the LORD declares that He is the First and the Last and that He lived, then died and is alive forevermore. His death and the darkness of the tomb, could not keep the light from shining forth out of the sepulchre. The Messiah, who is the seed of life, came to life, because the Word of God was inside of Him. The light of the LORD cannot be extinguished, even though men did try to do it! In Daniel and in Revelation, we can see the description comparison of the Ancient of Days. He is pure and clean!

Daniel 7:9-10 *I beheld till the thrones were cast down, and the Ancient of Days did sit, whose garment was white as snow, and the hair of His head like the pure wool; His throne was like the fiery flame, and His wheels as burning fire. A fiery stream issued and came forth from before Him; thousand thousands ministered unto Him, and ten thousand times ten thousand stood before Him; the judgment was set, and the books were opened.*

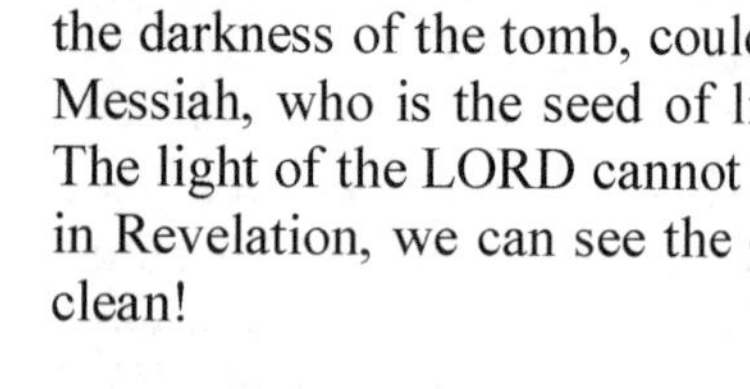

Snow on Maple Photo ©2014 Kimberly K Ballard All Rights Reserved

Revelation 1:13-18 *And in the midst of the seven candlesticks one like unto the Son of man, clothed with a garment down to the foot, and girt about the paps with a golden girdle. His head and His hairs were white like wool, as white as snow; and His eyes were as a flame of fire; And His feet like unto fine brass, as if they burned in a furnace; and His voice as the sound of many waters. And He had in His right hand seven stars; and out of His mouth went a sharp two edged sword; and His countenance was as the sun shineth in His strength. And when I saw Him, I fell at His feet as dead.*

And He laid His right hand upon me, saying unto me, Fear not; I AM the First and the Last. I AM He that liveth, and was dead; and, behold, I AM alive forevermore, Amen; and have the keys of hell and of death.

Another factor to consider is that Daniel also told us *"that thousand thousands ministered unto the Ancient of Days and ten thousand times ten thousand stood before Him."* This is exactly what we see in the book of Jude and Revelation when John gave the description revealing that Messiah Yeshua is the LORD God in Heaven. In Revelation, *"There are ten thousand times ten thousand and thousands of thousands who are saying that the Lamb is worthy to receive many honours!"* We all know that Messiah Yeshua is *"The Lamb."* In Genesis 22:8, Abraham told Isaac that *"God would provide, Himself a Lamb."* The Perfect God became *"The Perfect Lamb!"*

Heavy Snow on Bristle Cone Pine & Juniper & Snow on Old Windows Photos ©2013 Kimberly K Ballard All Rights Reserved

***Genesis 22:8** And Abraham said, My son, God will provide Himself a lamb for a burnt offering; so they went both of them together.*

***Revelation 5:11-12** And I beheld, and I heard the voice of many angels round about the throne and the beasts and the elders; and the number of them was ten thousand times ten thousand, and thousands of thousands; Saying with a loud voice, Worthy is the Lamb that was slain to receive power, and riches, and wisdom, and strength, and honour, and glory, and blessing.*

When the LORD comes to reign on earth, He comes with, *"Ten thousands of His Saints!"*

***Jude 1:14** And Enoch also, the seventh from Adam, prophesied of these, saying, Behold, the LORD cometh with ten thousands of His Saints.*

***Exodus 18:21** Moreover thou shalt provide out of all the people able men, such as fear God, men of truth, hating covetousness; and place such over them, to be rulers of thousands, and rulers of hundreds, rulers of fifties, and rulers of tens.*

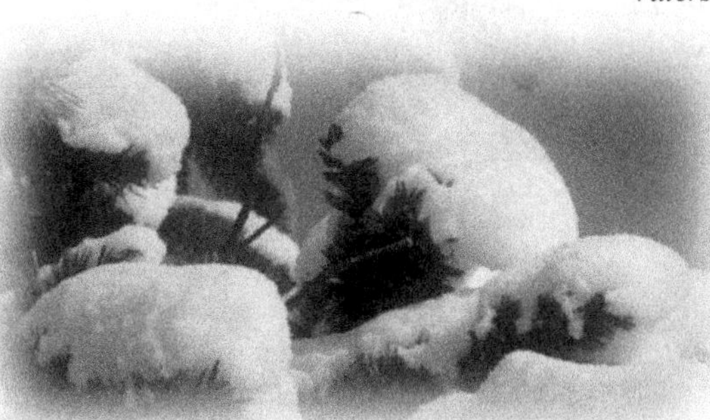

In the book of the Acts of the Jewish Apostles, we see that, *"Thousands of Jews believed Yeshua was the Messiah and they were all zealous of the law of God."*

***Acts 21:20** And when they heard it they glorified the LORD, and said unto Him, Thou seest, brother, how many thousands of Jews there are which believe; and they are all zealous of the law.*

Now with all this information about the Messiah having existed from everlasting and by observing the words of the Prophet Isaiah, we can see that the LORD God who *"Hides His face," is the Saviour.* Therefore, when we see the face of Messiah, *"The Sar HaPanim,"* then the LORD'S face is unveiled to us *as the KING of Glory.* The God of Israel is called, *"The Saviour!"* Here are a few Scriptural references, verifying that *God is the Saviour and the Redeemer of Israel.*

He is the Messiah or *the liberator* of His people and the one Messiah who liberates the whole world from the tyranny of Satan's curse. All of us should be forever grateful and thankful to Him!

Isaiah 45:15 *Verily Thou art a God that hidest Thyself, O God of Israel, the Saviour.*

Snow on branches & Snow on Juniper

Isaiah 54:8 *In a little wrath I hid My face from thee for a moment; but with everlasting kindness will I have mercy on thee, saith the LORD thy Redeemer.*

Isaiah 43:3 *For I AM the LORD thy God, the Holy One of Israel, thy Saviour; I gave Egypt for thy ransom, Ethiopia and Seba for thee.*

Jude verse 25 *To the only wise God our Saviour, be glory and Majesty, dominion and power, both now and ever, Amen.*

The LORD God of Israel, *the Saviour,* is therefore the one who performed great miracles, not only in Egypt, but also when He came to dwell on the earth as the Messiah of Israel.

Psalm 106:21 *They forgot God their Saviour, which had done great things in Egypt.*

The truth is then, that the miracles of the LORD God of Israel are absolutely and positively visible in the miracles of Messiah Yeshua. King David wrote that the LORD God is the one who heals diseases and clearly Yeshua healed the sick and the diseased and they were regenerated to perfection. Yeshua also many times forgave sins and raised the dead from their corrupted flesh. The following Scriptures verify this.

Psalm 103:2-3 *Bless the LORD, O my soul, and forget not all His benefits; Who forgiveth all thine iniquities; who healeth all thy diseases.*

Matthew 4:23 *And Yeshua went about all Galilee, teaching in their Synagogues, and preaching the Gospel of the Kingdom, and healing all manner of sickness and all manner of disease among the people.*

The Saviour Messiah LORD God is, *"the hope"* that saves Israel in time of trouble, as Jeremiah wrote.

Jeremiah 14:8 *Oh the hope of Israel, the Saviour thereof in time of trouble, why shouldest thou be as a stranger in the land, and as a wayfaring man that turneth aside to tarry for a night?*

I Thessalonians 2:19 *For what is our hope, or joy, or crown of rejoicing? Are not even ye in the presence of our Lord Jesus Christ at his coming?*

After the LORD God of Israel chose Mary to bring forth the Messiah, she gave a beautiful prayer, after the angel Gabriel appeared to her and revealed that the Messiah would come to earth through her Davidic line. Mary said *"the LORD God had remembered Israel in His mercy, as He had promised her forefathers."*

Luke 1:46-55 *And Mary said, My soul doth magnify the LORD, And my spirit hath rejoiced in God my Saviour, For He hath regarded the low estate of his handmaiden; for, behold, from henceforth all generations shall call me blessed. For He that is mighty hath done to me great things; and Holy is His Name. And His mercy is on them that fear Him from generation to generation. He hath shewed strength with His arm; He hath scattered the proud in the imagination of their hearts. He hath put down the mighty from their seats, and exalted them of low degree. He hath filled the hungry with good things; and the rich He hath sent empty away. He hath holpen His servant Israel, in remembrance of His mercy; As He spake to our fathers, to Abraham, and to his seed forever.*

Zechariah the Prophet wrote that *the LORD said, "For lo, I come, and I will dwell in the midst of thee and that you will know that the LORD of Hosts has sent Me to you!"* The LORD of Hosts is speaking as Messiah here, stating He inherits Judah as His portion.

Zechariah 2:10-13 *Sing and rejoice, O daughter of Zion; for, lo, I come, and I will dwell in the midst of thee, saith the LORD. And many Nations shall be joined to the LORD in that day, and shall be my people; and I will dwell in the midst of thee, and thou shalt know that the LORD of Hosts hath sent Me unto thee. And the LORD shall inherit Judah His portion in the Holy Land, and shall choose Jerusalem again. Be silent, O all flesh, before the LORD; for He is raised up out of His Holy habitation.*

Snowflakes, Snow Dove, Frost on branches & Rose bushes
Photos ©2014 Kimberly K Ballard All Rights Reserved

Now we can comprehend from this Scripture why Messiah Yeshua repeatedly told the children of Israel that *"He was sent"* from Heaven to Israel to dwell in their midst, during the Second Temple period. He is the LORD of Hosts.

John 8:42 *Yeshua said unto them, If God were your Father, ye would love Me; for I proceeded forth and came from God; neither came I of Myself, but He sent Me.*

John 7:33 *Then said Yeshua unto them, Yet a little while am I with you, and then I go unto Him that sent Me.*

Whoever sees Messiah Yeshua is seeing the one who sent Him.

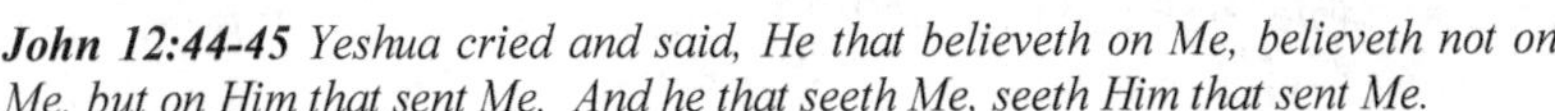

John 12:44-45 *Yeshua cried and said, He that believeth on Me, believeth not on Me, but on Him that sent Me. And he that seeth Me, seeth Him that sent Me.*

I Timothy 2:3-6 *For this is good and acceptable in the sight of God our Saviour; Who will have all men to be saved, and to come unto the knowledge of the truth. For there is one God, and one mediator between God and men, the man Messiah Yeshua; Who gave Himself a ransom for all, to be testified in due time.*

Now a believer in Messiah, who was named *Titus,* specifically stated that through God's loving kindness, *"He appeared to mankind as the Saviour,"* to bring about everlasting salvation, *as Yeshua.* His appearance on the earth to dwell in our midst was to renew us by the washing of regeneration, to bring us everlasting life through His Holy Spirit. According to the LORD'S mercy He saved us. The Testimony of Yeshua *would be testified in due time,* just as it is now about to be revealed to the world in a new way through the Torah. This is a final witness and everlasting Testimony, revealing His glorious Eternal Covenant.

Heavy Snowflakes falling

Titus 2:4-7 *But after that the kindness and love of God our Saviour toward man appeared, not by works of righteousness which we have done, but according to His mercy He saved us, by the washing of regeneration, and renewing of the Holy Spirit; Which He shed on us abundantly through Yeshua Messiah our Saviour; That being justified by His grace, we should be made heirs according to the hope of Eternal life.*

Now that we have carefully examined the facts and have fit the clues together, there is only one conclusion that is clear. *The LORD God of Israel is Messiah Yeshua the KING. He is one God and His Name is one. There is no other Name by which we must be saved, but by the LORD'S Name of salvation which is, "Yeshua."*

The mystery of the Messiah is now beginning to unfurl. The LORD God of Israel is the Messiah, who appeared to mankind and dwelt here in human form. The LORD was manifested in the flesh, to save us from the curse of death in the flesh, from the Garden of Eden.

MESSIAH THE LORD IN A TEMPORARY SUKKAH

Sukkah & Red Berries, Strawberries & Pomegranates

With God all things are possible, because the LORD has absolutely no limitations. The LORD'S works are mighty.

There was a time in the wilderness when the children of Israel tested the LORD. In the Psalms, the LORD said that, *"They limited Him"* and this upset the LORD greatly. The LORD also said, *"That they trusted not in His salvation."* If His salvation in Hebrew is called,

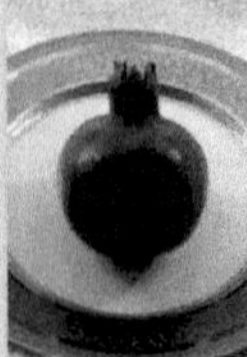
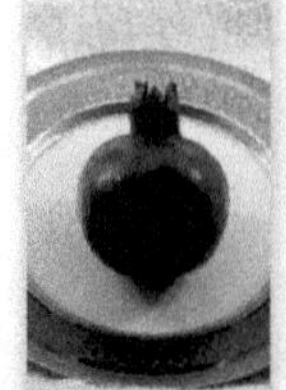

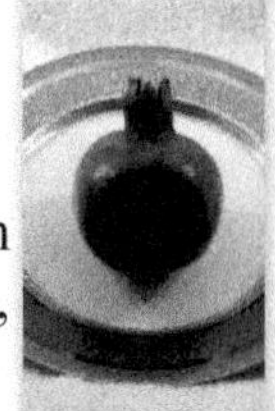

"Yeshua," then we must not deny Him and test the LORD again. When they put limitations on the LORD and did not believe in the power of the one who created everything in the universe, this angered the LORD.

Psalm 78:41 *Ye, they turned back and tempted God, and limited the Holy One of Israel.*

Because God has no limits, it is absolutely perfectly possible for the LORD to come to earth to dwell with us in *a temporary sukkah.* If we deny that this is possible for the LORD to accomplish His Testimony on earth, by manifesting Himself in the flesh, then we have sinfully limited the LORD'S power. The fact remains that He alone is more than capable of providing for the salvation of Israel and for everyone that He created. There are no limits to His unimaginable power and therefore, *it is not impossible for God to manifest Himself in the flesh as the second perfect Adam, in order to save us from the curse of death. All of the LORD'S magnificent works miraculously reveal His profound identity.*

Psalm 145:3-4 *Great is the LORD, and greatly to be praised; and His greatness is unsearchable. One generation shall praise Thy works to another, and shall declare Thy mighty acts.*

Mark 10:27 *And Yeshua looking upon them saith, With men it is impossible, but not with God; for with God all things are possible.*

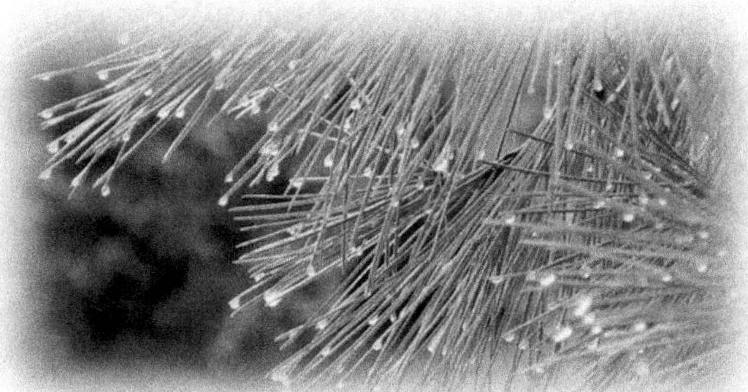

Inside the sukkah you pray for rain for the next year - Rain on Pine Needles
Photos ©2014 Kimberly K Ballard All Rights Reserved

So how is it possible for the Messiah to be from everlasting and yet come into the line of Judah and come in the body of a man? *Just as the Ark of the Covenant is a vessel and the LORD abode upon it, likewise, the temporary body of a man is also a vessel.* The LORD was therefore abiding in a vessel of human flesh, as the Saviour Messiah Yeshua, *"The Fruitful Branch."* The Scripture's tell us that, *"The LORD made a body prepared for the Messiah."* The key to understanding how He did this, is found in the fact that the human body is indeed a type of sukkah, a temporary dwelling. In the sukkah we pray for rain for the coming year.

Blackberries in my Sukkah Photo ©2013
Kimberly K Ballard All Rights Reserved

When we go to be with the LORD, we give up our temporary bodies or dwellings and we receive our permanent Eternal bodies with the LORD in Heaven, in the Eternal Holy Temple with God. Now remember that the God of the universe came down to dwell in the Temple of King Solomon, in the Holy of Holies, upon the Ark of the Covenant. It was not impossible for the LORD to descend from Heaven to abide upon the Ark. If God accomplished descending into the Holy of Holies on earth, then it is absolutely true that He came down to dwell in a temporary sukkah of human flesh, as our Messiah. Even though the Heavens themselves could not contain Him, the LORD God of Israel came to dwell in *the earthly House* that was built for Him on the earth. So Messiah was the LORD God, living in a temporary dwelling of the flesh. As the permanent body of the Heavenly Temple, *He is the Ark of His own Living Testimony in Heaven.*

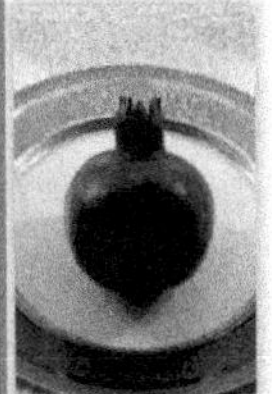

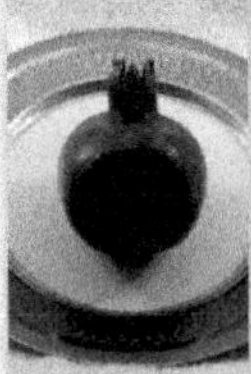

We have limitations here, but the LORD does not have any limitations and with Him all things are possible. Messiah is *the Branch bearing Fruit,* so He is clearly represented in the sukkah. A sukkah is made of living leafy green branches and fruit adorns the ceiling and walls of the sukkah. The roof is kept opened in the sukkah to see the universe expanse above us. There is only one door to the sukkah and only one door into the permanent dwelling in Heaven, which is Messiah Yeshua, who is the Eternal sukkah! In the temporary earthly sukkah, we are looking up to the Heavens towards our permanent home, because the LORD is up there! His Living Testimony, as the Fruitful Living Branch, became our permanent shelter in Heaven. When we sit in our temporary sukkah's out under the stars, we are testifying that He is our Eternal home! The fact is Messiah Yeshua came in the flesh as the second Adam, because He had no sin. Death came upon all the descendants of Adam and Eve, from their sin of rejecting the LORD as their KING OF KINGS and by their defiance of His Word. Messiah the LORD therefore, had to come to earth in the flesh temporarily, to destroy sin in the flesh, so that restoration could take place between the LORD God and mankind, so that the entire earth would be restored to an Eden like state.

Red Berries Photo ©2013 Kimberly K Ballard All Rights Reserved

This is exactly what happened with Moses when he lifted up the serpent on a pole and all those who looked at it, were saved from the serpents, because the rod was made in the image of the thing that was causing them death. Now mankind could once again dwell in the Divine Presence of the LORD because of the Testimony of the Messiah. After Yeshua was resurrected from the dead, He ascended up to Heaven in His permanent dwelling, because He is alive forevermore. His living resurrected body is therefore, the Eternal Heavenly Temple made without human hands. Upon Him, the incorruptible Heavenly Temple is built and He is the Chief Cornerstone of this Eternal Temple. When Yeshua descends from Heaven, He will indeed be the permanent Heavenly Temple resting in Jerusalem. If you think about it, there will be seven Temples in total. There was the Tabernacle of Moses in the wilderness, the Tabernacle at Shiloh, the First Temple of King Solomon, the Temple of Zerubabbel, the Second Temple of Herod, the Third Temple and the LORD descends as the Eternal Temple number 7!

Red Berries Photos ©2013 Kimberly K Ballard All Rights Reserved

John 2:20-21 *Then said the Jews, Forty and six years was this Temple in building, and wilt Thou rear it up in three days? But He spake of the Temple of His body.*

Messiah Yeshua is truly represented in the sukkah of the Feast of Tabernacles, because He became the First Fruits of the resurrection. He was specifically raised to life on the LORD'S Feast of First Fruits as the perfect flesh.

I Corinthians 15:20-23 *But now is Messiah risen from the dead, and become the First Fruits of them that slept. For since by man came death, by man came also the resurrection of the dead. For as in Adam all die, even so in Messiah shall all be made alive. But every man in his own order; Messiah the First Fruits; afterward they that are Messiah's at His coming.*

The following Bible verses, verify the LORD God of Israel is the Messiah.

I Corinthians 15:47 *The first man is of the earth, earthy; the second man is the LORD from Heaven.*

Exodus 6:2-3 *And God spake unto Moses, and said unto him, I AM the LORD; And I appeared unto Abraham, unto Isaac, and unto Jacob, by the Name of God Almighty, but by My Name YHVH {the LORD} was I not known to them.*

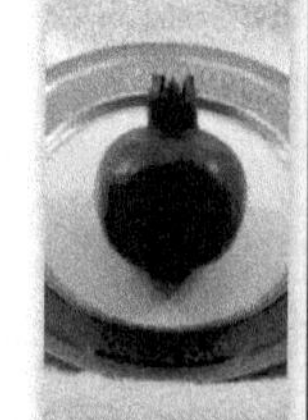

These two verses again, tell us plainly, that the second Adam or the man Messiah is quite literally, *"The LORD from Heaven."* Almighty God, who appeared to the Patriarch's of Israel, had not revealed Himself to them yet as, *"YHVH,"* or by the Name, *"The LORD."* The fact is that He had only appeared to them as, *"God Almighty,"* but later He revealed to Moses, that He is known by the Name, *"YHVH, the LORD."* This means that the LORD and Almighty God are one in the same. These are not two different Gods. *This is one God who has different Names.* Now the LORD has another Name which is, *"Yeshua."*

Red Berries Photo ©2013 Kimberly K Ballard All Rights Reserved

Matthew 1:20-23 *But while he thought on these things, behold, the angel of the LORD appeared unto him in a dream, saying, Joseph, thou son of David, fear not to take unto thee Mary thy wife; for that which is conceived in her is of the Holy Spirit. And she shall bring forth a Son, and thou shalt call His Name Yeshua; for He shall save His people from their sins. Now all this was done, that it might be fulfilled which was spoken of the LORD by the Prophet, saying, Behold, a virgin shall be with child, and shall bring forth a Son, and they shall call His Name Immanuel, which being interpreted is, God with us.*

It is written that this, *"Yeshua, shall save His people Israel, from their sins."* We will soon see that Eternal life is in His flesh and in His life blood atonement for our sins. This is the life blood of the Living Covenant in Heaven. Now here is one of my special sukkah's that is opened through the branches of its roof to look toward Heaven!

If the Feast of Tabernacles lands in October, your sukkah can suddenly be covered with heavy snow in one day! The friendly wild rabbits and birds came to dwell inside my snow sukkah! I love to read and sing inside it!
Photos ©2013 Kimberly K Ballard All Rights Reserved

THE LAND OF ZEBULON THE LAND OF NAPHTALI

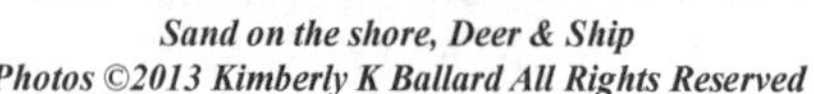

Sand on the shore, Deer & Ship

The ancient Prophet Isaiah declared that Messiah the Word would be, *"A light that shines in the darkness, in the land of Zebulon and the land of Naphtali, beyond Jordan, in Galilee of the Nations."* Naphtali's emblem is the deer and Zebulon's the ship. The Messiah is called a, *"Son"* and *"The Mighty God."* He is the everlasting Father and the Prince of Peace or Shalom. He will be KING OF KINGS over all the earth and the LORD OF LORDS!

Isaiah 9:1-8 *Nevertheless the dimness shall not be such as was in her vexation, when at the first He lightly afflicted the land of Zebulon and the land of Naphtali, and afterward did more grievously afflict her by the way of the sea, beyond Jordan, in Galilee of the Nations. The people that walked in darkness have seen a great light; they that dwell in the land of the shadow of death, upon them hath the light shined. Thou hast multiplied the Nation, and not increased the joy; they joy before thee according to the joy in harvest, and as men rejoice when they divide the spoil. For Thou hast broken the yoke of his burden, and the staff of his shoulder, the rod of his oppressor, as in the day of Midian. For every battle of the warrior is with confused noise, and garments rolled in blood; but this shall be with burning and fuel of fire. For unto us a child is born, unto us a Son is given; and the government shall be upon His shoulder; and His Name shall be called Wonderful, Counsellor, The mighty God, The everlasting Father, The Prince of Peace. Of the increase of His government and peace there shall be no end, upon the throne of David, and upon His Kingdom, to order it, and to establish it with judgment and with justice from henceforth even forever. The zeal of the LORD of Hosts will perform this. The LORD sent a Word into Jacob, and it hath lighted upon Israel.*

Messiah Yeshua is the light that descended from Heaven to live in Galilee, in the land of Zebulon and the land of Naphtali. Messiah Yeshua was baptized *beyond the Jordan* and He brought the Kingdom of God to earth, to proclaim liberty to the captives, as it is written in Isaiah 61. He came to remove our bondage of death, from the curse of Eden. When the Messiah came during the Second Temple period, this prophecy was fulfilled before all the people of Israel, as He declared it in the Synagogues and in the Holy Temple in Jerusalem. Yeshua proclaimed that the Kingdom of God had come upon them, but sadly, many within His generation were unable to discern the times and seasons of the Messiah's arrival. Just as Isaiah had prophesied, Messiah the LORD, the Greatest Rabbi, had broken the yoke of Israel's burden. The LORD sent *the Word* into Jacob as the light of the world.

Yeshua fulfilled the Living Testimony of the LORD. So now, they would also be given Eternal life through the power of the LORD'S own Living Testimony. Isaiah wrote that *"The Son is the Mighty God, the Prince of Peace."* The Prince of Peace is the countenance of the face of God, which proves again that He is *"The Sar HaPanim and the Sar Shalom."* Yeshua told us, *"No one knows who the Son is and no one knows who the Father is, unless the LORD reveals it to them!"* The hidden truth is that they are one in the same, but He only reveals this to whomever He chooses.

Matthew 11:27-30 *All things are delivered unto Me of My Father; and no man knoweth the Son, but the Father; neither knoweth any man the Father, save the Son, and He to whomsoever the Son will reveal Him. Come unto Me, all ye that labour and are heavy laden, and I will give you rest. Take My yoke upon you, and learn of Me; for I AM meek and lowly in heart; and ye shall find rest unto your souls. For My yoke is easy, and My burden is light.*

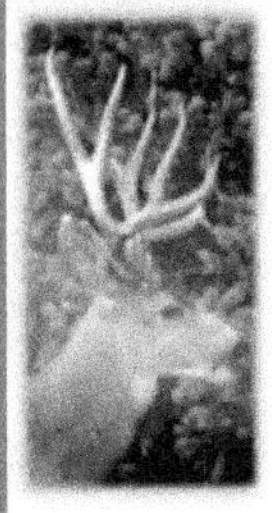
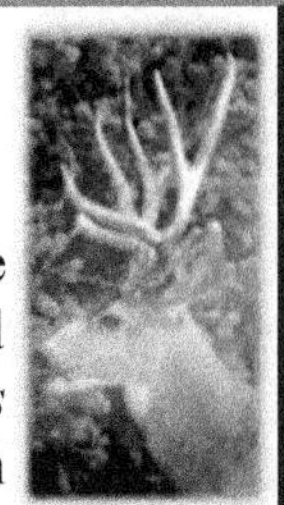

It is also written in Proverbs, *"that the Almighty has a Son."* Obviously the Son is the one who inherits the Kingdom of God, as the second perfect Adam. Only the LORD could come save us from death and give us Eternal life, *thereby making His inheritance as a Son, His own.* When the LORD descended to earth as the Messiah and ascended back into Heaven again, He thereby established forever, the Heavenly Davidic Kingdom, which is the permanent restoration of the Davidic Dynasty. Yeshua said that He ascended and descended from Heaven before.

Proverbs 30:4-5 *Who hath ascended up into Heaven, or descended? Who hath gathered the wind in His fists? Who hath bound the waters in a garment? Who hath established all the ends of the earth? What is His Name, and what is His Son's Name, if thou canst tell? Every Word of God is pure; He is a shield unto them that put their trust in Him.*

John 6:62 *What then if you should behold the Son of Man ascending where He was before.*

John 16:28 *Yeshua said, I came forth from the Father and have come into the world; I am leaving the world again and going to the Father.*

Yeshua also told the Jewish leaders in the Holy Temple, that He is not from the earth and that He came down from Heaven. The LORD had revealed this from the beginning to them, because He is written within His creation, in the separation of the light from the darkness. Therefore, we can conclude that the light from Heaven came to Galilee of the Nations, who lived in darkness and the LORD would remove this darkness forever.

When the Jewish leaders in the Holy Temple intently asked Yeshua who He was, He told them, *"That He is the same who was with them from the beginning."* In other words, He was telling them that *He is the same one LORD God that created the universe in Genesis, in the beginning and they knew Him, but could not even recognize Him, as He stood in their midst performing miracles!*

John 8:23-32 *And He said unto them, Ye are from beneath, I AM from above; Ye are of this world; I AM not of this world. I said therefore unto you, that ye shall die in your sins; for if ye believe not that I AM He, ye shall die in your sins. Then they said unto Him, Who art Thou? And Yeshua saith unto him, even the same that I said unto you from the beginning. I have many things to say and to judge of you; but He that sent me is true; and I speak to the world those things which I have heard of Him. They understood not that He spake to them of the Father. Then said Yeshua unto them, When ye have lifted up the Son of man, then shall ye know that I AM He, and that I do nothing of Myself; but as my Father hath taught Me, I speak these things. And He that sent Me is with Me; the Father hath not left Me alone; for I do always those things that please Him. As He spake these Words, many believed on Him. Then said Yeshua to those Jews which believed on Him, If ye continue in My Word, then are ye My disciples indeed; And ye shall know the truth, and the truth shall make you free.*

In the book of Hebrews, we see that, *"The Messiah is the radiance of God's glory."* So the Messiah is the heir of all things and when we see His face, we are truly seeing the LORD God of Israel with our own eyes, as it is revealed to us!

Hebrews 1:1-10 *God, who at sundry times and in divers manners spake in time past unto the fathers by the Prophets, Hath in these last days spoken unto us by His Son, whom He hath appointed heir of all things, by whom also He made the worlds; Who being the brightness of His glory, and the express image of His person, and upholding all things by the Word of His power, when He had by Himself purged our sins, sat down on the right hand of the Majesty on High; Being made so much better than the angels, as He hath by inheritance obtained a more excellent name than they. For unto which of the angels said He at any time, Thou art My Son, this day have I begotten Thee? And again, I will be to Him a Father, and He shall be to Me a Son? And again, when He bringeth in the firstbegotten into the world, He saith, And let all the angels of God worship Him, And of the angels He saith, Who maketh His angels spirits, and His ministers a flame of fire. But unto the Son He saith, Thy throne, O God, is forever and ever; a Sceptre of Righteousness is the Sceptre of Thy Kingdom. Thou hast loved righteousness, and hated iniquity; therefore God, even Thy God, hath anointed Thee with the oil of gladness above Thy fellows. And, Thou LORD, in the beginning hast laid the foundation of the earth; and the Heavens are the works of Thine hands.*

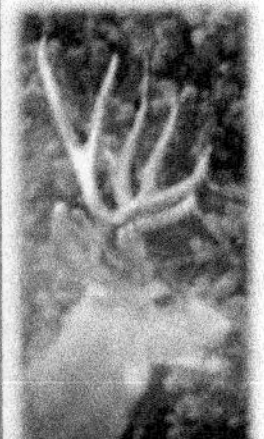
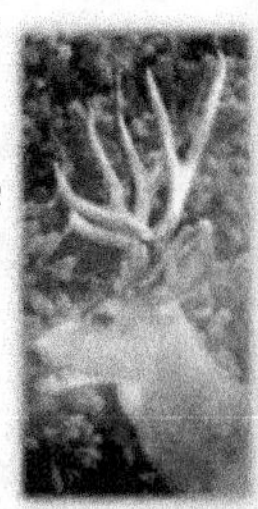

The Messiah who has always existed is a mystery, because we have never seen Him to know what His appearance looks like, from the beginning of time. Can anyone other the LORD, calm the wind and the waves as Yeshua did, when He spoke the Word and it was accomplished? The LORD God alone has the Words to speak that control His creation! He will be revealed at the end of time and He is being revealed to us right now! So open your eyes and see and let the scales fall from your eyes! The Saviour Messiah Yeshua is indeed the LORD God of Israel. He is our Eternal Redeemer!

People have debated for centuries, pondering the identity of the Messiah. Of course they would attempt to say that a certain person was not the Messiah, based upon their own bias, but how could they know for certain who He was, without any doubt? Even if the Messiah came and fulfilled all the prophecies written in the Bible about Him, there would still be some very stubborn people that would continue questioning whether or not this man was qualified to be the Messiah of Israel. Now many have come and gone who claimed to be the Messiah and even some of the devoted Rabbi's selected their own Messiah and they got it very wrong, but the LORD knew this in advance that many would come in His Name saying, *"I am the Messiah!"* The LORD already made preparations for this because He knew long ago that in the last days *men would not see it or believe it, unless He gave them a sign.* The LORD said that the Jews *require a sign.* So this sign that God provided had to be so certain and specific that it could never be denied again. So the LORD hid it within His Torah, in the Ark of His Heavenly Covenant. So you see, the LORD wants us to believe in Him with our hearts without having to see signs, miracles, and wonders. Even so, He is willing to give us many signs and wonders just to prove Himself to our stubborn hearts. He is so compassionate that He made sure that we would know the identity of the Messiah of Israel for certain and never ever doubt Him again! I believe that you will be so astounded by this revelation that you will weep in your heart, when you see the truth and understand what the LORD has done for you. Our God is a LORD of love. He is so beautiful to have hidden Himself in the divine design, so our curious hearts could find Him. He is so full of love for you, my friend! Many people from all Nations will come to Him and be His people, but Israel is His beloved forever and He is revealing that her redemption is extremely close!

I find it hard to express how exciting it is to see the chilling secret details of the LORD, for the very first time. The further you read in this book, the more you will see the miracles that are revealed that will absolutely astonish you. They came from God. The Prophets were chosen, not based upon their own merits, but the LORD specifically revealed Himself to those that He loved. Many of them did not even believe that they were worthy to be used of God. The LORD used those who searched diligently for Him and had a humbled heart. I wrote down every single detail of His Testimony, within the following chapters and it took six years to write everything down, as these revelations came to me in different stages. This first chapter prepares the way for the story and the Eternal Testimony of the LORD that proclaims His Majestic Glory.

Revelation 1:1-3 *The Revelation of Yeshua Messiah, Which God gave Him to show to His bond-servants, the things which must shortly take place; and He sent and communicated it by His angel to His bond-servant John, who bore witness to the Word of God and to the Testimony of Yeshua Messiah even to all that he saw. Blessed is he who reads and those who hear the words of the prophecy, and heed the things which are written in it; for the time is near.*

Now the LORD says that *when the seventh angel is about to sound, the mystery of God is finished.* This is the mystery He showed to all His Jewish Prophets and Apostles. They wrote it down and inscribed the mystery onto the Hebrew scrolls that became our Bible.

Revelation 10:7 *But in the days of the voice of the seventh angel, when he is about to sound, then the mystery of God is finished, as He preached to His servants the Prophets.*

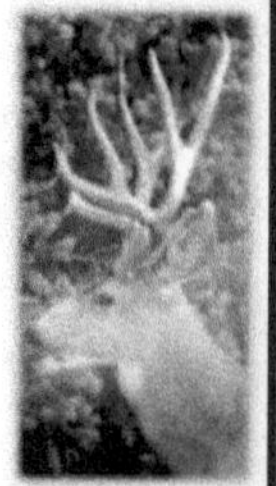

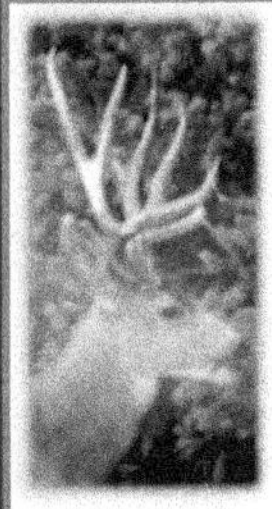

No one understood this mystery, since the beginning of time. The LORD was only going to reveal it through the Prophets of Israel and through the Jewish Apostles of Israel. Clearly, when the final revelation of the mystery of the Messiah is revealed, then the secrets of God will be finished and this will happen in the days of the voice of the seventh angel, when he is about to sound. *The seven trumpets were blown before the Ark to scatter the enemies of God when the Israelites took possession of the Promised Land with Joshua and this will happen again in the future, as the seven trumpets of Revelation sound, before Israel enters the Eternal Promised Land with Messiah Yeshua!* This is chilling! The time of the mystery of God may very well be close at hand, because the LORD has opened up the door of understanding to me in so many incredible ways and what I have written in this book, by the power of God's Spirit, is the revelation of this mystery. It is truly astonishing that for centuries, no one understood this mystery that was predestined before the ages or the wisdom of God. In other words, it was God's plan from of old, from everlasting and it is to our glory, because He gave us Eternal life with the promise of a new glorified body in His Heavenly Kingdom. Messiah Yeshua accomplished all that He was sent to accomplish, so we could finally be reconciled to God. The sins stemming from the curse of Eden would be removed by the Messiah once and for all, through the blood of the Lamb of God. The crucifixion of the Messiah was therefore, predestined from the beginning of the ages. His Testimony is the Living Testimony of the LORD. This means that the LORD God, had absolute control over the entire situation, during His condemnation and crucifixion and His Testimony had to happen according to the predetermined plan of God, *according to the pattern that the LORD showed to Moses.* Yeshua accomplished it and on the cross He declared, *"It is finished."* In the following story, it will become astonishingly clear, why these events had to happen exactly in this manner. The mist on the glass that prevents you from seeing the whole picture will soon be wiped away. You will then be looking at the LORD face to face. In the history of the world, I can tell you that some of these revelations have never been seen before by anyone! In ancient times, the Gentiles had not searched for the LORD God, but they do search for the LORD now, because of Yeshua's Living Testimony. You must know that a promise was also given to the righteous Gentiles who believe in the LORD God of Israel and they will also come and be His people in the Holy city of Jerusalem. This was part of the LORD'S Eternal plan. He wanted to bring every person back to Him, as it was in the Garden, in the beginning.

Romans 10:20 *And Isaiah is very bold and says, I was found by those who sought Me not, I became manifest to those who did not ask for Me.*

Isaiah 65:1 *I permitted Myself to be sought by those who did not ask for Me; I permitted Myself to be found by those who did not seek Me. I said, "Here AM I, here AM I," to a Nation which did not call on My Name.*

The LORD who is the First and the Last manifested Himself to Israel *First* and to the Gentile Nations *Last.* So it was the LORD'S plan that the entire world from the First to the Last, from beginning to end, would come to love and worship Him. This then, forms a complete picture of His redemption. He is the one true God of Israel, who created the whole universe from beginning to end. The Synagogue is the Church and it was originally all Jewish, before it ever went to Rome. When Paul, the master Torah Scholar and Jew from the tribe of Benjamin, speaks of the Church, he is referring to both Jews and Gentiles, who would come to the God of Israel, through the LORD, manifested as the Messiah. The Messiah came and brought the message of Eternal salvation to the Jews *First,* because Messiah Yeshua is Jewish. By His grace, He brought the knowledge of the wisdom of God, through the Gospel of the Messiah to the Gentiles *Last.* The message of the Testimony of the LORD will continue to be told throughout all the Nations, until the time of the end, when the times of the Gentiles are fulfilled. After the last people have been brought to the LORD, then Israel, who came *First,*

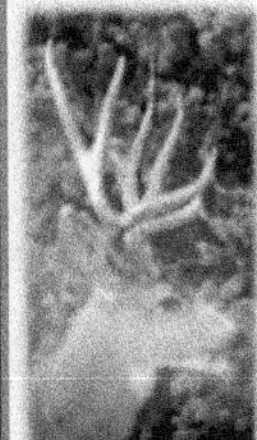

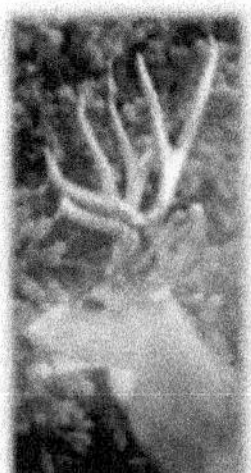

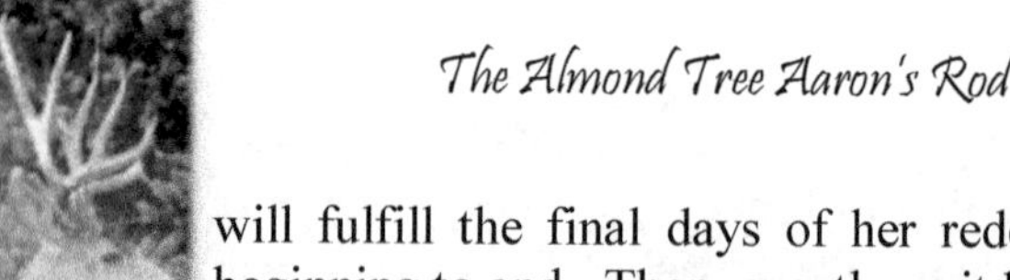

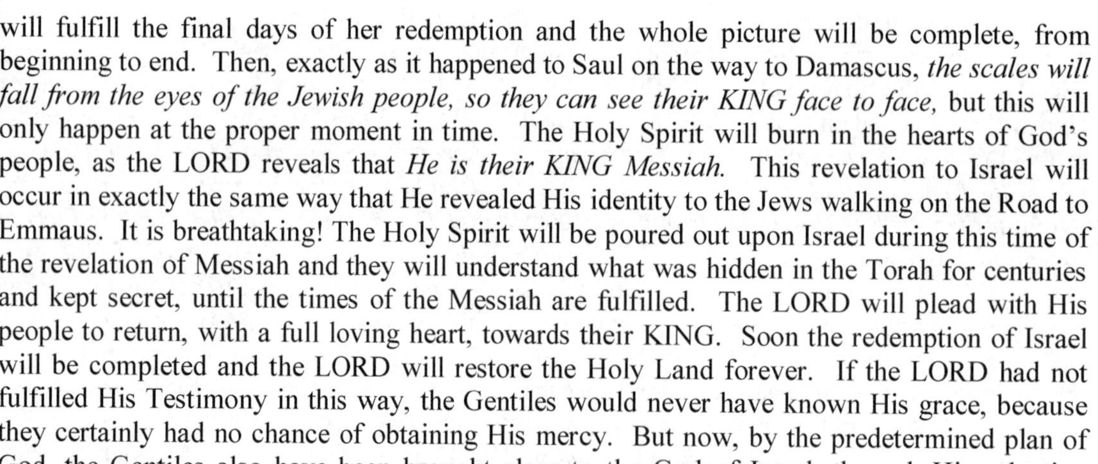

will fulfill the final days of her redemption and the whole picture will be complete, from beginning to end. Then, exactly as it happened to Saul on the way to Damascus, *the scales will fall from the eyes of the Jewish people, so they can see their KING face to face,* but this will only happen at the proper moment in time. The Holy Spirit will burn in the hearts of God's people, as the LORD reveals that *He is their KING Messiah.* This revelation to Israel will occur in exactly the same way that He revealed His identity to the Jews walking on the Road to Emmaus. It is breathtaking! The Holy Spirit will be poured out upon Israel during this time of the revelation of Messiah and they will understand what was hidden in the Torah for centuries and kept secret, until the times of the Messiah are fulfilled. The LORD will plead with His people to return, with a full loving heart, towards their KING. Soon the redemption of Israel will be completed and the LORD will restore the Holy Land forever. If the LORD had not fulfilled His Testimony in this way, the Gentiles would never have known His grace, because they certainly had no chance of obtaining His mercy. But now, by the predetermined plan of God, the Gentiles also have been brought close to the God of Israel, through His salvation Named, *"Yeshua."*

The promise of Eternal life not only includes Jews, but also the righteous Gentiles, who love the LORD and want to serve Him with all their heart. It is the Holy Spirit of God, who reveals the Messiah to the hearts of men. The Jews, who believed that Messiah Yeshua came to save them, were given the understanding of this mystery of the Messiah. They understood that His identity was the LORD of Hosts and they went to great lengths and suffered incredible persecution, to bring this Testimony to the entire world, so that everyone on the earth could be saved and live forever!

Mark 4:11-12 *And He was saying to them, To you has been given the mystery of the Kingdom of God; but those who are outside get everything in parables, in order that while seeing, they may see and not perceive; and while hearing, they may hear and not understand lest they return and be forgiven.*

I Peter 1:20 *He was foreknown before the foundation of the world but has appeared in these last times for the sake of you who through Him are believers of God.*

John 8:14-18 *Yeshua answered and said to them, Even if I bear witness of Myself, My witness is true; for I know where I came from, and where I am going; but you do not know where I came from, or where I am going. You people judge according to the flesh; I AM not judging anyone. But even if I do judge, My judgment is true; for I AM not alone in it, but I and He who sent Me. Even in your law it has been written that the Testimony of two men is true. I AM He who bears witness of Myself, and the Father who sent Me bears witness of Me.*

Ephesians 5:32 *This mystery is great; but I am speaking with reference to Messiah and the Church.*

Ephesians 1:9 *He made known to us the mystery of His will, according to His kind intention which He purposed in Him.*

Gold Key on Tallit
Photo ©2014 Kimberly K Ballard All Rights Reserved

All things that are hidden will come to light and all the LORD'S secrets will be revealed regarding the Messiah, exhibiting the Eternal mystery of God.

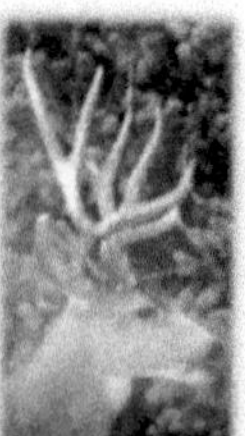

Isaiah 48:5-6 *I have even from the beginning declared it to thee; before it came to pass I shewed it thee; lest thou shouldest say, Mine idol hath done them, and my graven image, and my molten image, hath commanded them. Thou hast heard, see all this; and will not ye declare it? I have shewed thee new things from this time, even hidden things, and thou didst not know them.*

THE NAME MESSIAH THE NAME YESHUA

Gold Key on Tallit & Fragrant Cloud Rose & Snow
Photo ©2013 Kimberly K Ballard All Rights Reserved

Before I tell my incredible story, I want to share that throughout this book, I will be using the original Hebrew Name of the Messiah and not the translation of the Greek or Latin form of His Name. Therefore when the Bible says, *"Jesus,"* I will refer to Him by His God-given Hebrew Name, *"Yeshua."* This as we have already seen, is extremely important and will also be extremely significant in the coming chapters. Within this book I will use the Hebrew word, *"Messiah,"* instead of the translated word, *"Christ."* They mean exactly the same thing, but I feel that the change of the Messiah's Name into the Greek and Latin forms, taken from the original Hebrew, has been the cause of great confusion. Clearly understand that the words, *"Jesus Christ,"* are a translation of, *"Yeshua the Messiah,"* In Hebrew this is the phrase, *"Yeshua Ha Mashiach or Moshiach."* The word, *"Messiah,"* was translated into the Greek word, *"Christos"* and then into, *"Christ,"* in English. This can cause confusion to some people, especially to the Jewish community. The LORD sent the angel Gabriel to tell Mary to Name the Messiah, *"Yeshua." The Hebrew form of Yeshua's Name has great significance and there is incredible meaning within His Name that I feel has been lost in the translation.* I suppose though, that this in itself has contributed greatly to the mystery of the Messiah! The Hebrew name, *"Yehoshua," is, "Joshua"* and was later shortened to, *"Yeshua."* Now looking at the true meaning of the name, *"Joshua=Yehoshua=Yeshua=Jesus,"* we find that the Name means, *"YHVH is salvation," or, "YHVH rescue's," or, "YHVH saves."* As I stated already, the Name, *"Yeshua," is the Hebrew word, "Yeshuah" which means "salvation" and it means, "God saves."* If you have never heard about the meaning of the Name *Yeshua,* which is His true Biblical Name, then you must realize this truth, before reading further in this book, or you will miss everything!

The Name, *"Yeshua,"* is indeed the name, *"Joshua"* and I will share with you why this is so significant later on. When Messiah Yeshua began His ministry, He told us that He came in His Father's Name and because His Name means, *"YHVH is Salvation,"* then He was being truthful and completely honest. So now I just want to show you exactly what was inscribed on the cross in the Hebrew language! Unfortunately, the Roman Church later abbreviated what was really on the cross and they changed it into four Latin initials. These Latin Roman initials are on all the paintings of the Roman Church, depicting the crucifixion, but in reality, *there were never initials placed upon the cross of the Jewish Messiah Yeshua. In reality, there was a full inscription written above Yeshua on the cross.* This full inscription was written in three different languages. It was inscribed in Hebrew, Greek and Latin. When you see the full inscription in Hebrew, that was inscribed above Messiah Yeshua, you will see that a shocking truth emerges. I believe that the words in Hebrew were so significant that Rome wanted to hide this information, and keep it from our knowledge about the Jewish Messiah of Israel. It is already true that the Romans wanted to disconnect Yeshua from His Jewishness. As you will see every single detail about Him is so significant, and this inscription is profoundly important.

Roses Photo ©2013 Kimberly K Ballard

The Hebrew was written as;
Y H V H
Yeshua` **H**aNotsri **V**'Melech **H**aYehudim and this was later translated to;
"Jesus of Nazareth, the KING of the Jews"
Written in Hebrew letters, the phrase reads from right to left and spells out the letters;

Yod **H**ey **V**av **H**ey = which is **YHVH**

This is the inscription as it appeared on the cross in Hebrew, reading from right to left;

ישוע הנצרי ומלך היהודים

Do you see that a shocking discovery is written before your eyes, as you take the first letter from each one of these Hebrew words about Yeshua and it reveals that the KING came in His Father's Name, in the Hebrew YHVH? The four letters in the Hebrew language make up the Tetragrammaton, which is the unpronounceable Name of God. This is likely why the Priests in the Holy Temple wanted the inscription to be changed!

John 19:21-22 *Then said the Chief Priests of the Jews to Pilate, Write not, The KING of the Jews; but that He said, I AM KING of the Jews. Pilate answered, What I have written I have written.*

When the Jewish Priests saw that the Hebrew letters of Yeshua's inscription, spelled out, *"YHVH,"* which appeared on the cross before their eyes, obviously they objected to the phrase being spelled the way that it was written. However, it was the will of the LORD and it was written by the predetermined plan of God, the KING. This was part of the fulfillment of the Testimony of the LORD and so this truth was declared upon the cross that was lifted up for all to see it. The Name on the cross written as, **Y**eshua **H**aNotsri **V**'Melech **H**aYehudim, proves that when you pray in Yeshua's Name, *you are actually praying in the Name of the God of Israel* and in the Name of the KING'S Salvation, which of course is the Hebrew word, *"Yeshuah."*

John 5:43-47 *I AM come in My Father's Name, and ye receive Me not; if another shall come in his own name, him ye will receive. How can ye believe, which receive honour one of another, and seek not the honour that cometh from God only? Do not think that I will accuse you to the Father; there is one that accuseth you, even Moses in whom ye trust. For had ye believed Moses, ye would have believed Me; for he wrote of Me. But if ye believe not his writings, how shall ye believe My Words?*

This means that all the letters and words in Yeshua's Name boldly declare that He is the LORD and the Eternal KING of the Jewish people. He is the LORD, who inherits Judah as His portion. It is very important to grasp the meanings of the words and letters in their original language in the Hebrew, because the Messiah is Jewish! The LORD God clearly encoded His Name in the spelling of, *"Yeshua HaNotsri V'Melech HaYehudim."* For this reason, Yeshua is indeed, *"God with us,"* as, *"Immanuel or Emmanuel."* If we look at the Title Name *Immanuel or Emmanuel,* we can see the following truth.

Immanu/Emmanu עמנו means, "with us" and El אל means, "God" = עמנואל

There is only one true Messiah and only one Messiah who is encoded from the very beginning, *in the Torah of God.* This one Messiah is the only one qualified to be the true Messiah of Israel. I ask you to let the scales fall from your eyes.

I found out that when you ask the LORD to show you His truths and if you ponder Him with all of your heart and if you seek His face, He will tell you the secrets of this long held mystery of the Messiah of Israel. The God of Israel is the revealer of secrets! So we are going to be looking at the unveiling of the face of God in the Mystery of the Messiah! *This is truly the glory of the LORD that shall be revealed and testified in due time!*

Daniel 2:47 *The king answered unto Daniel and said, Of a truth it is, that Your God is a God of gods, and LORD of Kings, and a revealer of secrets, seeing Thou couldest reveal this secret.*

Isaiah 40:5 *And the glory of the LORD shall be revealed, and all flesh shall see it together; for the mouth of the LORD hath spoken it.*

We are the ones who are about to witness this together. Believe me, things get so exciting, that sometimes I stop writing and start weeping from the joy of the LORD, who touched my heart by revealing this mystery to me for the very first time in my life!

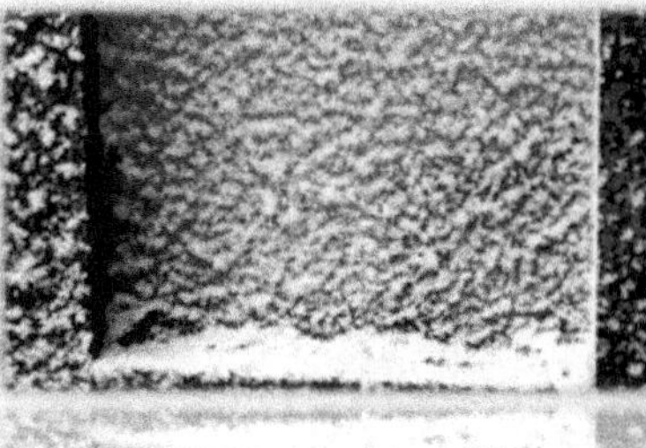

THE ALMOND BLOSSOM BEGINS TO OPEN!

Frosted Snow Windows & Heavy Snow falling
Photos ©2013 Kimberly K Ballard All Rights Reserved

The frosted snow coats the window pane in winter, like a glass that covers the mystery in Jerusalem, that is about to be unveiled from centuries past. As it was in ancient times, when Yeshua walked through the land of Israel with His people, they understood what we are about to see in all the chapters of this book that you are about to read. Remember that God's anointed will bud and will be a Lamp. So the Almond bud begins to open, as the flower petals slowly unfurl to our gaze. We have barely touched the surface of the astounding story that I have to tell you. This chapter was meant to lay the foundation of the mystery of Messiah. With this understanding now, I will tell the story of all the revelations that the LORD gave to me, *regarding the Almond Tree, Aaron's rod and the Messiah KING of Israel!*

So what exactly did the Jews see 2,000 years ago, when Yeshua revealed Himself to them in the Torah? I can hardly wait to tell you my astounding miracles. What follows is the first true miracle that I wrote down as it transpired in 2007! It all began in the middle of the bitter snowy winter, but without my knowledge, something was about to bud in Jerusalem and it was the key that would change my life forever!

Keys on Tallit Photo ©2013 Kimberly K Ballard All Rights Reserved

Snow Branch Lantern Photo ©2013 Kimberly K Ballard All Rights Reserved

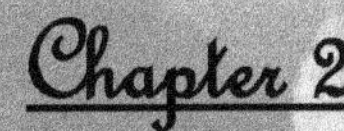

Chapter 2

THE MIRACLE OF THE ALMOND TREE AND AARON'S ROD

While the snow fell outside and all the trees were asleep, taking a deep winter rest, it was almost as if they slumbered in a sepulchre of stillness that would never end. There was no sign of life within the trees, yet they eagerly awaited a resurrection to life, that would soon come, at the glorious arrival of spring. Not even a tiny sprig was sprouting leaves. In this snow covered landscape, there was not even the hint of a single flower preparing to unfurl to the gaze, so that one could delight in the pleasant fragrance of the fruiting trees. Only the bare brown branches were on display on the trees, except for a few evergreens that remained vivid green, throughout the long winter. It was cold and wintery in Colorado and I was not even thinking of spring arriving any time soon, as it does not make an appearance, until late April or early May. In fact, it was the middle of February and not much was happening, with the exception of daily making my appearance at the local library. There were two elements that kept me inside for much of the time and they were the cold temperatures, combined with the early sunset, at 4:30 pm. There was not much to do after the sun disappeared behind the Rocky Mountains. It was during this time, that I was diligently reading my Bible. I was studying it with complete dedication and as I pensively concentrated on it, I remained in the deepest form of contemplation. Entire days were spent pondering the text. At night, I relished placing the Gospel of John movie in my DVD player, so I could listen to the Scripture's come alive, while I relaxed in the dark, before going off to sleep.

It was wonderful to close my eyes and concentrate on the words being spoken from the Bible, without having to experience the eye strain from constantly reading. I have never been to Israel. This movie however, took me to Jerusalem in a sense and I felt as if I was experiencing it from 2,000 years ago. Jerusalem is such a deeply historical and Biblical place. This was the city where the LORD walked among His people, Israel. I did not have the slightest idea about the seasons as they occur in Israel and I had no knowledge of the plants or trees that grow in that climate. At the time of my Almond Tree miracle, I only knew about the olive trees in the Garden of Gethsemane. To grow anything in Colorado is rather difficult, but we managed to grow two lovely cherry trees. Fruiting trees are not in abundance at home. For the first time, I was about to encounter the most beautiful tree that would change my life and my heart forever. As I pulled my covers up close and snuggled down into the warmth, I listened intently to the fascinating movie.

MY STORY FOR THE GLORY OF THE LORD

Old Book, Snow & Frost on window pane
Photos ©2013 Kimberly K Ballard All Rights Reserved

One particular night, as I lay under the covers, quietly listening to the Gospel of John movie, there was a certain scene that captivated me. I would stop the DVD to rewind it up to this point and then I would listen carefully to the words as they were spoken, in order to ponder them again. The outstanding performance of actor Henry Ian Cusack, in his portrayal of Yeshua of Nazareth, was perhaps one of the greatest contributing factors to having my miracle happen in the first place. Each time this certain scene came up, I would ponder the meaning in my heart and read it from the text the next morning, from my Bible. I had such a deep sense that there was so much more to the events that took place in this scene, then we have previously discovered. So I began to talk to the LORD about it in my prayers and I would mention this specific scene to Him, explaining that I wanted to understand it from His perspective. I was walking with the LORD with all my heart every day and I knew He heard my prayers. I was keenly aware that He was listening to my heart. I felt His Presence and I knew the LORD was absolutely alive and very close at hand and that He was with me day and night.

The scene I mentioned, takes place at night in Jerusalem, between Yeshua of Nazareth and Nicodemus. He was a man of the Pharisee's and a ruler of the Jews, who served in the Holy Temple in Jerusalem. He was a deeply dedicated and devout righteous Jewish man who believed with all his heart that Yeshua was the Messiah of Israel. Nicodemus had to secretly visit Yeshua by night because it was not safe to follow Him openly. As I repeatedly pondered the meaning of this scene, I had no idea that the LORD was about to reveal the profound meaning of it to me in vivid detail. A miracle was about to take place and the LORD was preparing my heart to see it for the first time.

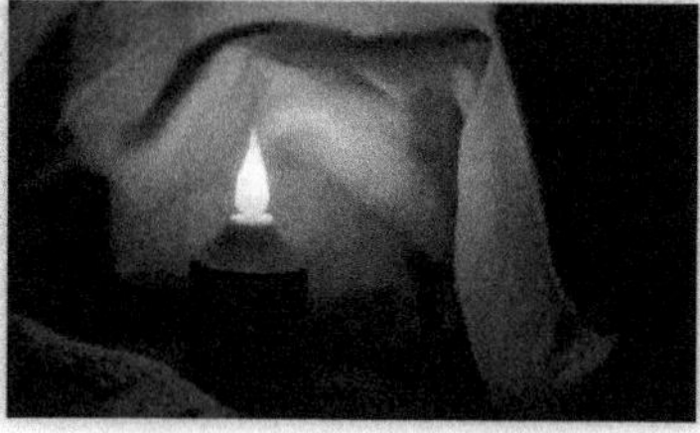

Candle light in the covers Photo ©2013 Kimberly K Ballard All Rights Reserved

I would like to describe the scene for you in the Gospel of John that captivated me. It was night, the crickets were chirping, the small clay lamps flickered and burned from their wicks in the cool night air on the porch, in the heart of Jerusalem. There was a slight breeze upon the fabric curtains that billowed softly from their rods, as they hung down, flowing loosely behind them, in this quiet Jerusalem neighborhood. Yeshua spoke the gentle words, as He gazed up to Heaven, looking into the glimmering night sky. Yeshua revealed that He had come down from Heaven and Nicodemus, who was pensive and puzzled, considered His Words carefully.

John 3:1-17 *There was a man of the Pharisees, named Nicodemus, a ruler of the Jews; The same came to Yeshua by night, and said unto him, Rabbi, we know that thou art a teacher come from God; for no man can do these miracles that thou doest, except God be with him. Yeshua answered and said unto him, Verily, verily, I say unto thee, except a man be born again, he cannot see the Kingdom of God. Nicodemus saith unto Him, how can a man be born when he is old? Can he enter the second time into his mother's womb, and be born? Yeshua answered, Verily, verily, I say unto thee, except a man be born of water and of the Spirit, he cannot enter into the Kingdom of God. That which is born of the flesh is flesh; and that which is born of the Spirit is spirit. Marvel not that I said unto thee, ye must be born again The wind bloweth where it listeth, and thou hearest the sound thereof, but canst not tell whence it cometh, and whither it goeth; so is every one that is born of the Spirit. Nicodemus answered and said unto Him, how can these things be? Yeshua answered and said unto him, Art thou a master of Israel, and knowest not these things?*

Verily, verily, I say unto thee, We speak that we do know, and testify that we have seen; and ye receive not our witness. If I have told you earthly things, and ye believe not, how shall ye believe, if I tell you of Heavenly things? And no man hath ascended up to Heaven, but He that came down from Heaven, even the Son of man which is in Heaven. And as Moses lifted up the serpent in the wilderness, even so must the Son of man be lifted up; That whosoever believeth in Him should not perish, but have eternal life. For God so loved the world, that He gave His only begotten Son, that whosoever believeth in Him should not perish, but have everlasting life. For God sent not His Son into the world to condemn the world; but that the world through Him might be saved.

Moses lifted up that serpent on a pole and somehow this pertained to the Messiah! Nicodemus must have known what these words meant because Nicodemus believed that Yeshua had come from God and was the long awaited Messiah of Israel. A little while later in the story, it is Nicodemus who helps Joseph of Arimathaea to take the body of Yeshua to the tomb for His burial, during the Feast of Unleavened Bread. We can simply gather that Nicodemus recognized the profound significance that this was the Messiah of Israel and therefore, he took great care of Yeshua's earthly body during His burial, as we see later in the Gospel of John.

John 19:38-42 *After this, Joseph of Arimathaea, being a disciple of Yeshua, but secretly, for fear of the Jews, asked Pilate that he might take away the body of Yeshua; and Pilate gave him permission. So he came and took the body of Yeshua. And Nicodemus, who at first came to Yeshua by night, also came, bringing a mixture of myrrh and aloes, about a hundred pounds. Then they took the body of Yeshua, and bound it in strips of linen with the spices, as the custom of the Jews is to bury. Now in the place where He was crucified there was a garden, and in the garden a new tomb in which no one had yet been laid. So there they laid Yeshua, because of the Jews' Preparation Day, for the tomb was nearby.*

All the Jewish sages, the great Prophets of Israel, had foretold that the Messiah was coming in the future and now the time had come for His arrival. The book of Daniel, chapter nine, tells us that the Messiah would come within a certain number of years, based upon the decree to rebuild the Temple in Jerusalem. When the exact amount of days had passed from this decree and on the exact day that was foretold by Daniel the Prophet, Yeshua rode into Jerusalem on a donkey and the people of Israel waved palm branches proclaiming, *"Blessed is He who comes in the Name of the LORD, Hoshanna in the Highest!"* It must have been so exciting at that moment to be there in Jerusalem!

Heavy Snow on Lilac bushes
Photo ©2014 Kimberly K Ballard All Rights Reserved

It was the middle of winter here and the candlelight was soothing, as the Words poured forth from Yeshua in the scene. This created the air of mystery within His Words and the atmosphere that captivated me! Nicodemus was only one of thousands of righteous Jews from the Temple who believed that Yeshua was the Messiah. I watched as I pondered it all and finally shut off the lights. Under the warmth of my covers, I soon fell fast asleep, but it was bitter cold outside in the frosty elements. I had no idea that something magnificent was about to bud in Israel and the LORD was preparing the way to show it to me!

"AWAKENED" FROM MY SLEEP!

Snow falling on Lanterns & Snow on Bristle Cone Pine Tree
Photos ©2013 Kimberly K Ballard All Rights Reserved

At 4 AM, I suddenly was awakened from my sound sleep. It was still and as dark as night outside. It was as if the Holy Spirit had awakened me. I was extremely alert and there was electricity about me. It felt as if the LORD Himself was standing there speaking to my mind and heart about Himself. It was February 16th 2007 and no one else was awake. I felt the Presence very strongly of the Holy Spirit of God upon me. I sat upright and flicked on the light switch near my bed. Suddenly, a revelation of the meaning of this saying of Yeshua, about Moses and the serpent on the pole, came rushing into my thoughts. All at once the LORD was revealing the true meaning of this to my heart! The thoughts came so fast into my mind and heart that I literally said out loud, *"Wait a minute, wait a minute, let me get some paper!"* I searched my covers and found a tiny scrap of paper on the side of my bed. I grabbed a pencil with the scrap of paper and I began to write as fast as possible, in a sort of intensely focused state. I was alert, but deep in thought, and I was hearing the words to my heart, from the Holy Spirit of God. I wrote the details down, so I would not miss anything that was being shown to my heart, by the LORD. The message was given to me in a clear precise order and I was to write it down on the paper. It was very clear to me that the answer was not coming from me or from my mind. It was rushing into my heart and into mind through the Presence of the Holy Spirit of the LORD God of Israel. I knew immediately, the LORD wanted me to send this message to Jerusalem.

Only later did I realize just how profound this message was going to be for the entire world. It was incredibly exciting, because instantly, I knew that it was the LORD'S own Testimony being revealed, at a time when the Messiah of Israel is getting ready to return! It was impressed upon me that I was supposed to take this message and show it to someone specific in Jerusalem. In 2004, I was privileged to meet this gentleman from Jerusalem, who had come to the United States to speak. I knew he was preparing for the coming of the Messiah and was interested in building the prophesied Third Holy Temple. I knew in my heart, that I was to send it specifically to him, via email, at his office in Jerusalem. It was so profound that I knew with certainty, that I was clearly being directed by the LORD very early that morning, to deliver it to Jerusalem and that is exactly what I did! The Holy Spirit impressed it upon me that this was to be my sole mission and I must not hesitate to send it there at once!

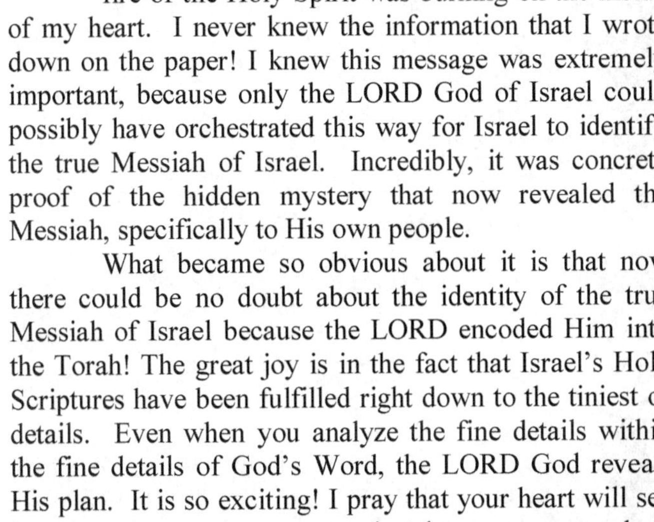

The God of Israel is a God of order and this message was in perfect order without me thinking of organizing it. It was a very clear and concise short message that revealed the great depth of God and His Messiah through the history of the Nation of Israel.

I finished writing the message down so quickly, that I did not have time to think about what I was writing down. I did not even really see the words. It really was as if I was just taking notes or dictation from the LORD. I only saw what was written on the page, when I finished writing what was spoken to my heart.

As I stopped writing, I was deeply touched and moved as I read the message to myself for the first time, and tears began streaming down my face. I realized the profound truth that stared back at me from the paper. It revealed the answer to my question in Yeshua's words that said, *"That He must be lifted up like the serpent on the pole of Moses."* I would get midway through reading it and a chill would run through me. The fire of the Holy Spirit was burning on the inside of my heart. I never knew the information that I wrote down on the paper! I knew this message was extremely important, because only the LORD God of Israel could possibly have orchestrated this way for Israel to identify the true Messiah of Israel. Incredibly, it was concrete proof of the hidden mystery that now revealed the Messiah, specifically to His own people.

Heavy Snow on Bristle cone Pine & Snow on glass Photos ©2013 Kimberly K Ballard All Rights Reserved

What became so obvious about it is that now there could be no doubt about the identity of the true Messiah of Israel because the LORD encoded Him into the Torah! The great joy is in the fact that Israel's Holy Scriptures have been fulfilled right down to the tiniest of details. Even when you analyze the fine details within the fine details of God's Word, the LORD God reveals His plan. It is so exciting! I pray that your heart will see it too, as your eyes are opened and your ears now hear that the Messiah of Israel loves you! I urge everyone, especially in Israel, to return to the God of Israel and repent for having not trusted the LORD and in His salvation. The message is to tell the world, that the Messiah is coming soon from Heaven and the KING OF KINGS will reign forever in the New Jerusalem.

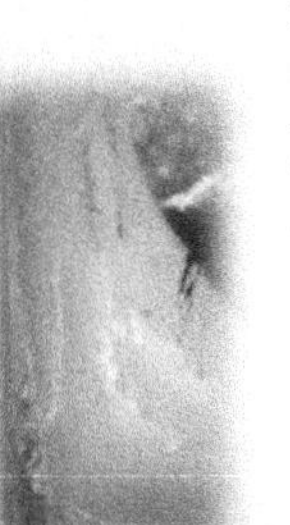

Now, regarding Moses lifting up the serpent on the pole in the wilderness, if you asked any modern pastors what this Scripture means, they would tell you that it means that if we look to the Messiah who was lifted up on the cross, as the children of Israel looked to Moses lifting up the serpent on the pole, then we will live and not die. Those who trusted and believed Moses, as he lifted up the rod, would live and not die. However, if they would not look at the serpent on the pole as it was lifted up, then they would surely die from the biting serpents and death for them was a certainty. I quickly realized though, that there was a much deeper meaning to this event. No one had ever seen what the LORD had just revealed to me by His Holy Spirit, about this specific Scripture and I say this with a completely gentle, loving, and humbled heart. The interpretation from the pastors on this subject was minimal at best and was only a surface explanation. They never knew the depth of what it meant in all of history, but what I understood now, through this revelation, was the fact that the LORD had hidden His secret within this prophecy!

I mentioned earlier that there was a prophecy spoken by the LORD to Moses in Deuteronomy that the LORD would raise up a Prophet from among His people and the people were to listen to Him. Messiah Yeshua was literally, *"raised up"* from among His people and He came in the Name of the LORD God of Israel.

Heavy Snow on Street Lamp
Photo ©2013 Kimberly K Ballard All Rights Reserved

Deuteronomy 18:15-22 *The LORD your God will raise up for you a Prophet from among your own people, like myself; Him you shall heed. This is just what you asked of the LORD your God at Horeb, on the day of the Assembly, saying, Let me not hear the voice of the LORD my God any longer or see this wondrous fire any more, lest I die. Whereupon the LORD said to me, They have done well in speaking thus. I will raise up a Prophet for them from among their own people, like yourself; I will put My Words in His mouth and He will speak to them all that I command Him; and if anybody fails to heed the Words He speaks in My Name, I Myself will call him to account. But any Prophet who presumes to speak in My Name an oracle that I did not command him to utter, or who speaks in the name of other gods, that prophet shall die. And should you ask yourselves, How can we know that the oracle was not spoken by the LORD? If the Prophet speaks in the Name of the LORD and the oracle does not come true, that oracle was not spoken by the LORD; the Prophet has uttered it presumptuously; do not stand in dread of him.*

The Jewish John the Baptist was a messenger from God who was sent to prepare the way of the LORD to travel. John was sent to prepare the people of Israel to meet the LORD when the Messiah arrived. So the people were to repent and be cleansed in the river of living water. The same thing happened with the children of Israel, with Moses. The LORD told Moses to prepare Israel to meet Him. They were instructed to wash their clothes and to prepare to meet the LORD on the third day, at the base of Mount Sinai. John was sent to tell Israel that the Kingdom of Heaven was at hand, but many did not see the signs of the times and the KING was rejected again.

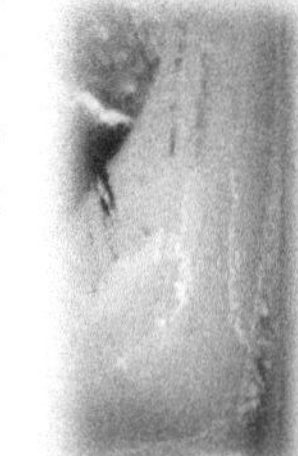

A SCRAP OF PAPER CONTAINED THE MESSAGE

Scrap of paper with message & the Oval at CSU & Snow Photos ©2013 Kimberly K Ballard All Rights Reserved

As I sat there staring at the message on the scrap of paper, I could not believe what I was reading. It was so powerful. Tears were streaming down my face, and I gently sobbed as I read it repeatedly. My heart was instantly illuminated by the glory of God and it burned within me. It was the most incredible event that I have ever experienced. This brought to mind, the story of the Jewish men walking on the road to Emmaus in *Luke 24:13-53.* As they walked along talking to each other, suddenly Yeshua appeared in their midst after His resurrection. Yeshua acted as if He had never heard of the miraculous events that had just unfolded in Jerusalem.

Their hearts burned within them as Yeshua revealed to them all the Scriptures that pertained to His Eternal Testimony that had to be fulfilled, that had been written down by the ancient Jewish Prophets of Israel. Suddenly the scales fell from their eyes and the Jewish men suddenly understood something new *within the Torah* that had previously been hidden from their understanding until this miraculous moment. The secrets of God were suddenly made visible to them. As the Holy Spirit filled their hearts, they were astonished with this new knowledge and it was life-changing. It is interesting that the Jewish men had never seen or understood these mysteries before because the mystery of the Messiah was meant to be revealed at the right moment in time. How exciting it must have been for the LORD to appear to them alive, after they knew that He had died, as they talked about His appearance to His disciples. I have always been amused by the fact that Yeshua has a sense of humor. As their Creator, He knows everything that they are thinking and feeling at that moment! He wants to inspire their hearts more with the revelation that He is giving to them, as He is walking in their midst. Yeshua then vanished out of their sight and the Scriptures came alive within their hearts. These men were never the same again, I assure you!

Now I know that what I wrote down on the tiny scrap of paper at 4AM was the same revelation *from the Torah* that they received nearly 2,000 years ago on the Road to Emmaus. Just as their hearts burned within them with the fire of the Holy Spirit, I could feel my heart burn within me, by the light and power of God's Spirit. He miraculously showed me the secrets of God, for the very first time. It was the key to the door that revealed the face of God. It is so exciting to read this account!

Luke 24:13-53 *And, behold, two of them went that same day to a village called Emmaus, which was from Jerusalem about three-score furlongs. And they talked together of all these things which had happened. And it came to pass, that, while they communed together and reasoned, Yeshua Himself drew near, and went with them. But their eyes were holden that they should not know Him. And He said unto them, What manner of communications are these that ye have one to another, as ye walk, and are sad? And the one of them, whose name was Cleopas, answering said unto Him, Art thou only a stranger in Jerusalem, and hast not known the things which are come to pass there in these days? And He said unto them, What things? And they said unto Him, Concerning Yeshua of Nazareth, which was a Prophet mighty in deed and word before God and all the people; And how the Chief Priests and our rulers delivered Him to be condemned to death, and have crucified Him. But we trusted that it had been He which should have redeemed Israel; and beside all this, today is the third day since these things were done. Yea, and certain women also of our company made us astonished, which were early at the sepulchre; And when they found not His body, they came, saying, that they had also seen a vision of angels, which said that He was alive. And certain of them which were with us went to the sepulchre, and found it even so as the women had said; but Him they saw not.*

Then He said unto them, O fools, and slow of heart to believe all that the Prophets have spoken; Ought not Messiah to have suffered these things, and to enter into His glory? And beginning with Moses and all the Prophets, He expounded unto them in all the Scriptures the things concerning Himself. And they drew nigh unto the village, whither they went; and He made as though He would have gone further. But they constrained Him, saying, Abide with us; for it is toward evening, and the day is far spent. And He went in to tarry with them. And it came to pass, as He sat at meat with them, He took bread, and blessed it, and brake, and gave to them. And their eyes were opened , and they knew Him; and He vanished out of their sight. And they said to one another, Did not our heart burn within us, while He talked with us by the way, and while He opened to us the Scriptures? And they rose up the same hour, and returned to Jerusalem, and found the eleven gathered together, and them that were with them, Saying, the LORD has risen indeed, and hath appeared to Simon. And they told what things were done in the way, and how He was known of them in breaking of bread. And as they thus spake, Yeshua Himself stood in the midst of them, and saith unto them, Peace be unto you. But they were terrified and affrighted, and supposed that they had seen a spirit. And He said unto them, Why are ye troubled? And why do thoughts arise in your hearts? Behold My hands and My feet, that it is I Myself; handle Me, and see; for a spirit hath not flesh and bones, as ye see Me have. And when He had thus spoken, He shewed them His hands and feet. And while they yet believed not for joy, and wondered, He said unto them, Have ye here any meat? And they gave Him a piece of broiled fish, and of an honeycomb. And He took it, and did eat before them. And He said unto them, These are the Words which I spake unto you, while I was yet with you, that all things must be fulfilled, which were written in the law of Moses, and in the Prophets, and in the Psalms, concerning Me. Then opened He their understanding, that they might understand the Scriptures, And said unto them, Thus it is written, and thus it behoved Messiah to suffer, and to rise from the dead the third day; And that repentance and remission of sins should be preached in His Name among all Nations, beginning at Jerusalem. And ye are witnesses of these things. And, behold, I send the promise of my Father upon you; but tarry ye in the city of Jerusalem, until ye be endued with power from on high. And He led them out as far as to Bethany, and He lifted up His hands, and blessed them. And it came to pass, while He blessed them, He was parted from them, and carried up into Heaven. And they worshipped Him, and returned to Jerusalem with great joy; And were continually in the Temple, praising and blessing God. Amen.

Eurasian Ring-necked Dove in the Snow Photo ©2014 Kimberly K Ballard All Rights Reserved

On the third day, *Yeshua revealed to them, that He is the LORD God of Israel.* They understood that Yeshua was encoded within Genesis in the very beginning. Yeshua had also said that John the Baptist was a burning and shining light because He was filled with the Holy Spirit of God and was sent to prepare Israel to meet the LORD on the third day! You will soon understand what I am referring to specifically regarding this topic, because it is superbly shocking!

Eurasian Ring-necked Dove perched on the trellis in the snow
Photo ©2014 Kimberly K Ballard All Rights Reserved

John 5:31-40 *If I bear witness of Myself, My witness is not true. There is another that beareth witness of Me; and I know that the witness which He witnesseth of Me is true. Ye sent unto John, and he bare witness unto the truth. But I receive not Testimony from man; but these things I say, that ye might be saved. He was a burning and a shining light; and ye were willing for a season to rejoice in his light. But I have greater witness than that of John; for the works which the Father hath given Me to finish, the same works that I do, bear witness of Me, that the Father hath sent me. And the Father Himself, which hath sent Me, hath borne witness of Me. Ye have neither heard His voice at any time, nor seen His shape, And ye have not His Word abiding in you; for whom He hath sent, Him ye believe not. Search the Scriptures; for in them ye think ye have eternal life; and they are they which Testify of Me. And ye will not come to Me, that ye might have life.*

I suddenly realized that what I had written down by the power of the Holy Spirit, onto the paper, was actually the LORD'S own Testimony of the heart. It touched me deeply. It was extraordinary and it was like the finest gift you could ever receive from someone that you love with all your heart. I felt the Holy Spirit's Presence in the room and it was so powerful that I could not stop reading it over and over again. How is it possible that I had read my Bible all my life and listened to thousands of sermons, yet this had been hidden, not only from my view, but obviously it had been hidden from thousands of Biblical Scholars throughout the centuries? Was this a revelation for the Last Days? Had I really only been looking at things through a glass darkly all those years? I was walking with Him in my heart now, so full of thankfulness and *I specifically spoke to the LORD and began telling Him that I love Him.* So was this His way of showing me that He loves me back? Is this why He manifested Himself to my heart? He opened the Almond blossom in the middle of winter and told me to gaze upon it! He knew that I would write this message down and send it to the right person, in the right place, at the right time in Jerusalem. Yes, He knew every extraordinary thing that was about to happen to me!

I thought about *I Kings 19:11-13.* Elijah heard the LORD speak to him in a still small voice! The KING came to me silently in the winter snow like a majestic deer. I perceived His message, and I understood what I was supposed to accomplish for Him.

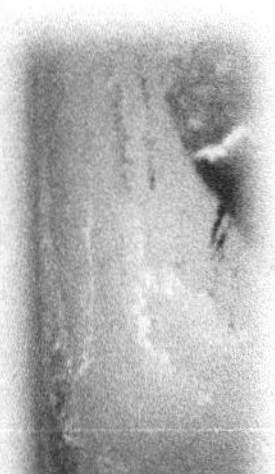

I Kings 19:11-13 *And he said, Go forth, and stand upon the mount before the LORD. And, behold, the LORD passed by, and a great and strong wind rent the mountains, and brake in pieces the rocks before the LORD; but the LORD was not in the wind: and after the wind an earthquake; but the LORD was not in the earthquake: And after the earthquake a fire; but the LORD was not in the fire: and after the fire a still small voice. And it was so, when Elijah heard it, that he wrapped his face in his mantle, and went out, and stood in the entering in of the cave. And, behold, there came a voice unto him, and said, What doest thou here, Elijah?*

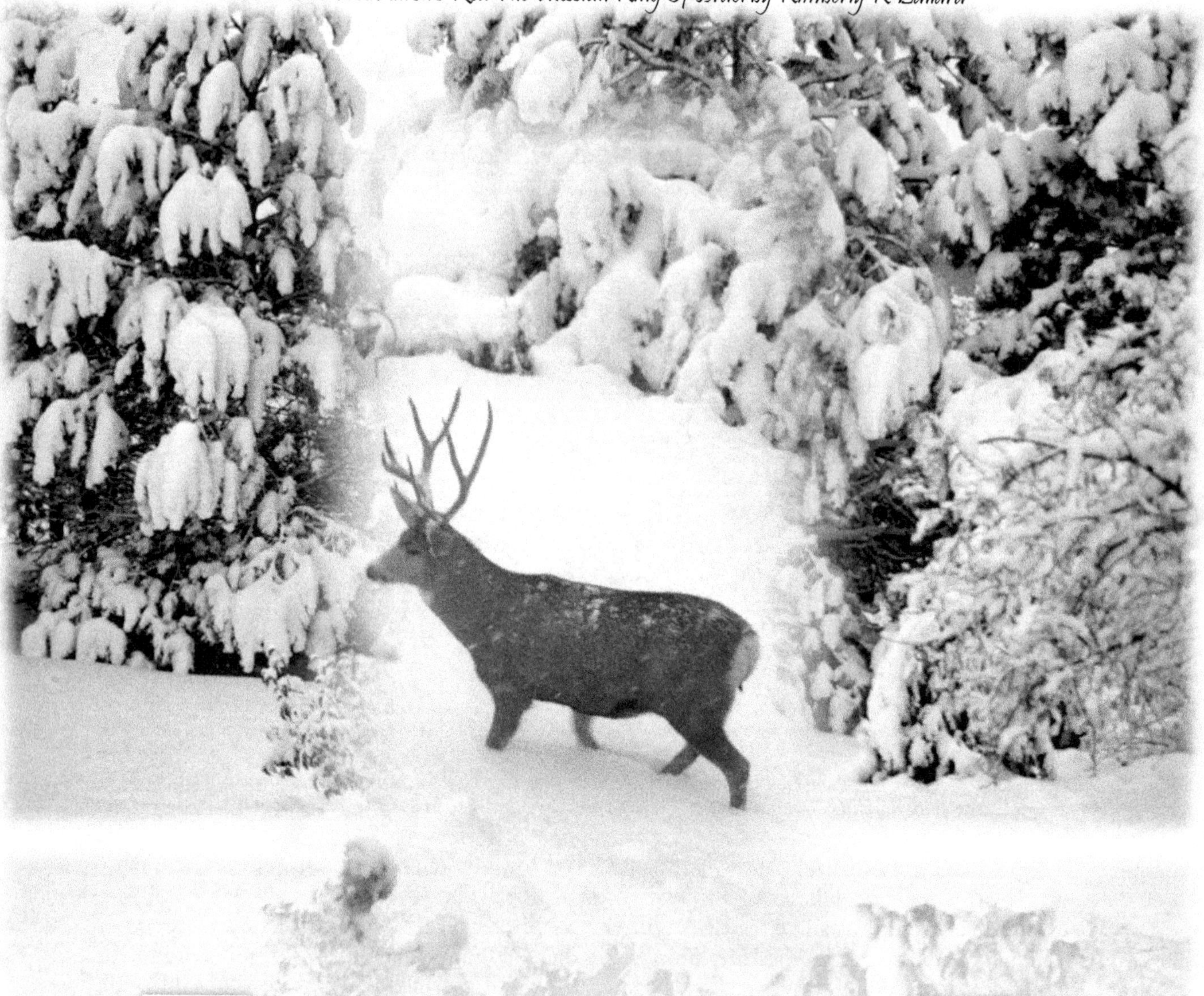

THE MESSAGE I SENT TO JERUSALEM

Jerusalem Lion Emblem & Snow Scene with Majestic Deer

I was so thrilled in my heart from this message of the LORD. Believe me, it was all I could do to put my head on my pillow and go back to sleep. The truth is that it was much too early to get up yet. I managed to lie down again while pondering it all, wiping the tears from my eyes with lots of tissues. I slept a couple more hours. I knew that when I woke up, I was going to take this message to the library to email it to Jerusalem to this gentleman. When the sun barely appeared over the eastern horizon, I got up and dressed and started the day.

I knew that Jerusalem was in the same direction in the east as the rising sun. I could not help but think about Jerusalem and about the LORD. I kept looking up at the eastern sky and toward the direction of Jerusalem, as I drove to the public library to do some work on the computer. Since I did not own a computer at home at the time, I had to drive into town to the library to use their computers and their email service. I was so excited and in a hurry when I

left the house, that I actually forgot to take the scrap of paper with me that had the revelation from the LORD on it! I did not realize that I did not have it with me until I was almost in the library parking lot! *Oh no!* Now I could not go back home to retrieve it because my appointed time was set up on the hour. Although it was a very short concise message, it was very precise and it was given to me in a specific order that was so important.

As I arrived at the library, I went inside and sat down at the computer that was assigned to me for one hour. When I realized that I did not bring the scrap of paper with me, I just thought to myself, *"Oh well, I'll have to do it another time."* I was not happy with myself for leaving it at the house, but I had other business to do on the computer that I thought I would do first anyway. I was working away on other things, when suddenly I had the strongest impression in my heart to hurry. I was supposed to remember what was on the scrap of paper that the LORD had revealed to me at 4AM. My heart was telling me to quickly write it in an email and, in that moment, the LORD was again directing me to send it to Jerusalem immediately! When I looked down at my watch, I realized to my surprise that my time was almost up! I only had 25 minutes left to be on the computer. Again I said the words, *"Oh no!"* So I said a little prayer in my heart. *"LORD, please help me to remember what you had me write down on that scrap of paper, so I can send it to Jerusalem to my new friend, if this is Your will."* To my surprise, all the words came flooding back to me in an instant with no confusion and I had no problem remembering it in perfect order! It was a race against time at this point. I did not know how they would take this message in Jerusalem. The message from the LORD was so exciting and it was so unlike anything that they had ever heard before from the Torah, regarding the Messiah. So I knew in my heart that this message was for Israel and they just had to hear this secret about Yeshua that had never been revealed before.

I had a feeling that they would not accept what the LORD had shown to me, but I knew for a fact that the LORD had spoken it to my heart. With only 25 minutes remaining, I felt strongly that the LORD did not want me to wait to send it another day.

BACK AT THE LIBRARY

Old Book & Snow Photos ©2013 Kimberly K Ballard All Rights Reserved

It was astonishing to me, when I realized that the Testimony of the Messiah that started in Jerusalem centuries ago had made its way to me. Now this final Testimony of the LORD was going to return to Jerusalem! The Testimony had come full circle and now it was returning home again, to the place where the LORD said that His Name would be written forever. This was unbelievable and thrilling to me!

Now I understood why Yeshua said the following words about the disciple John. He said, *"If I want him to live until I come, what is that to you?"* I realized that I was sending John's message back to Jerusalem after 2,000 years, at a time when we are very close to the

return of Yeshua. So John in a sense is still living here, because he wrote down the Living Testimony of the LORD, as an eyewitness of His Majesty. The message is still alive, so John is still alive! John's message was now about to return home to Jerusalem, where it all started!

Meanwhile, back at the library…. As I sat there with very little time left on the clock, I hurriedly typed it, read it and hit the send button. I debated whether or not to send it, but because I had such a strong impression to email it that exact moment, I went ahead with sending the message. I listened to the Holy Spirit of God, prompting me to accomplish His will and I was obedient in sending it on February 16, 2007. Just when the hands on the clock were straight up on the hour, the librarian came to tell us to get off the computers immediately, so others could use them. They literally came over to where we were sitting at the computers in the lab and said, *"Stop! Time is up!"* This happened the same split second that I hit the send button! It was done! It was accomplished and I said in my heart, *"Yes, LORD!"* In a flash, with one last quick glance, I saw it go to Jerusalem and I was thrilled! I quickly turned away from the computer and headed out to my car to return home! That was a miracle in itself that I had exactly the right amount of time to write it out. I was out of time and I thought, *"Well, let the chips fall where they may, I can't take the email back."* In the twinkling of an eye, it went to Jerusalem and it arrived across the ocean to its destination! How exciting it was to send a message to Jerusalem, that the LORD had given to me to send! Honestly, I really did not think anything would happen after that. Inside I felt a huge sense of relief at having accomplished this task for the LORD. In my heart I gave a sigh of joy and said, *"Ahhhh…now your message is in Jerusalem, LORD! It is done!" "It is in Your hands, LORD!"* When I think about it, I could easily have not paid any attention to this strong impression that spoke to my heart. I was happy that I had been obedient to the LORD, even though certain things could have prevented it from happening at all! The reason I say this is because of what happened next. I was not expecting a reply at all, let alone a miracle to happen in Jerusalem! I did not know I was about to receive a miracle of Biblical proportions from Jerusalem, in response to my email! The LORD had totally orchestrated everything to happen! All I could say was, *"Wow, how incredible!"* If I had not hit the send button when I did, in that split second, then the next events would not have happened at all, or perhaps not in their proper time.

The blessing came the following day on Saturday, February 17, 2007, which was a Shabbat in Israel.. However, since I did not go back to the library until Monday February 19th, the message sat all weekend waiting for me to come back to the library. I was unaware that anything special had happened in Jerusalem with my message.

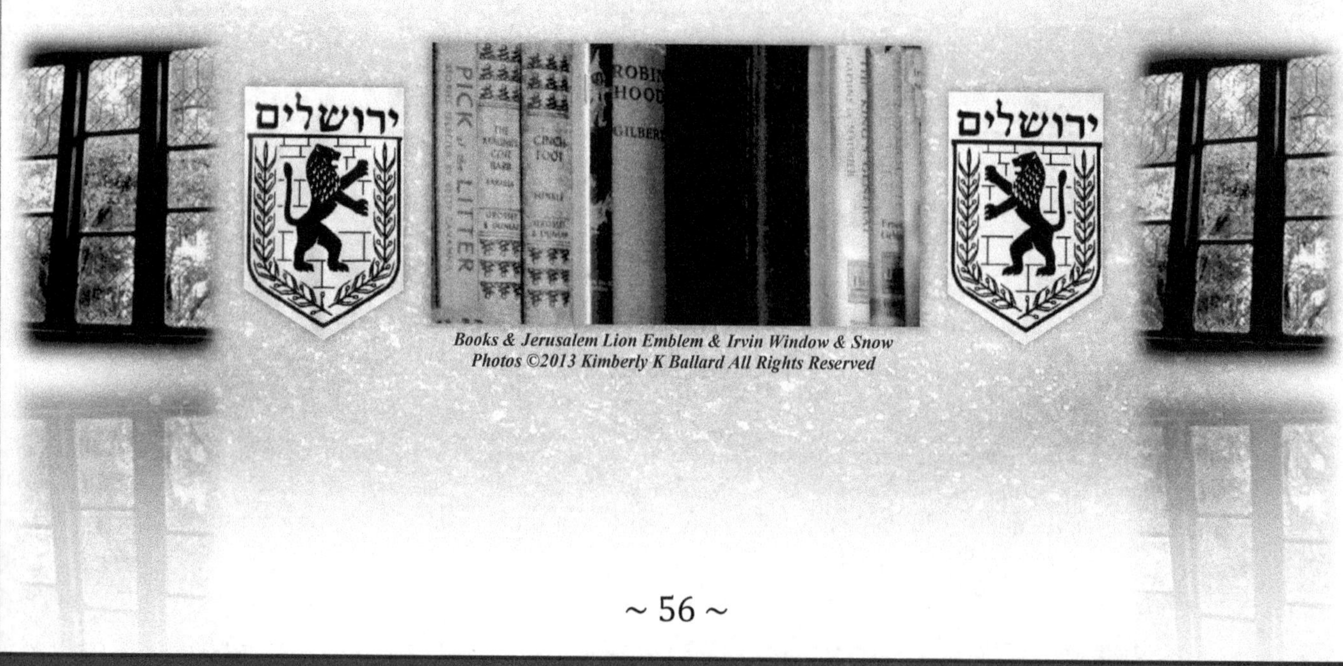

Books & Jerusalem Lion Emblem & Irvin Window & Snow

When Monday arrived, I opened my email and saw a reply from someone in Jerusalem, who was affiliated with the person that I had sent my message to on Friday! I was so excited. I did not know the person who wrote a letter back to me. In my inbox there was a response to my letter, but there was something incredible attached to this letter. When I reflect on it now, I think of how profound this miracle is, because Messiah Yeshua walked the streets of the Old City of Jerusalem on Holy Mount Moriah! This is incredibly where my miracle took place! It was as if the LORD was sending me an unbelievable verification back from Jerusalem, regarding the message that He had told me to write down and send there. I was so astonished by this event. I truly believe that this was a sign of His approval and His perfect timing! I could not believe the picture that was attached to the email and now this miraculous picture is on the cover of this book, thanks to my new Israeli friend, verifying the LORD'S Eternal Testimony!

As I was pondering this miracle, I realized that on the very same day that I had emailed this office in Jerusalem and at the very same hour that I was typing the email about an Almond Tree, the LORD was leading this person in Jerusalem to take a photograph of an Almond Tree coming to life! *This particular Almond Tree was just budding on Holy Mount Moriah!* This person had no idea that she was going to be receiving a letter from the United States or reading a special message from a stranger in a little town in Colorado who had received a revelation from the LORD about the Almond Tree. I am forever grateful that the LORD appointed her to be the one to receive my email! The LORD appointed her to take a walk that day in the Old City of Jerusalem, on Holy Mount Moriah. There is a nine hour difference in the time on the clock between Colorado and Jerusalem Israel, but in spite of this difference, the LORD was still doing something extraordinary with her at the very same time that He was with me, across the ocean. The LORD had chosen this beautiful person and He made sure that she was the one who received my message the following day. Instead of the message going to the person who I thought would receive it, she received it first and she was the one who read it! I had prayed that whoever read it would have the Holy Spirit reveal the truth to their heart. The LORD chose to manifest Himself that day to her heart! She told me in her response that what I had written was a true revelation from the LORD, who she called in Hebrew, *"HaShem!"* I had no way of knowing what she was doing in Jerusalem. I was on the other side of the ocean far away in cold wintery Colorado. She had no idea that I even existed.

When I left the library that Friday, on February 16, 2007, after having sent my message to the office in Jerusalem, in my own mind I began to question whether I had made a mistake sending the message. I started to think to myself, *"Well, I wonder if I overstepped the LORD'S time table and maybe I should not have sent it?"* I did not know how a Jewish person would receive the message that the LORD had given to me about the Messiah's identity. I also discovered that anytime you are revealing something about the LORD'S Messiah to the chosen people of Israel, it seems as if the evil one tries to take it away from them by any means possible, so they will not receive what was promised to them. *The Messiah's Testimony is a promise given to Israel, as a blessing forever.*

So without any further hesitation, let me share the revelation that the LORD gave to me that I wrote down on that tiny scrap of paper at 4AM.

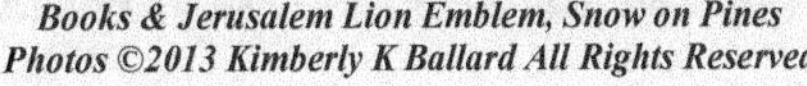
Books & Jerusalem Lion Emblem, Snow on Pines

MY LETTER TO JERUSALEM

February 16th 2007 Friday

Shalom Friends!

Let me share what the LORD showed me. It has to do with Aaron's rod. I was reading in Josephus *(historical book written by the Jewish Historian)*. When the people rebelled and they were trying to find out who God had chosen as the High Priest, every head of each tribe had a rod of wood. Moses took the rods and laid them in the Tabernacle and the next day went and retrieved them. Only Aaron's rod had sprouted leaves and bloomed and grew the fruit of almonds because his rod was a branch cut off of an Almond Tree. So this was God's way of saying Aaron is the High Priest of the tribe of Levi. I forgot to mention that each tribe's name was inscribed on the rod…so Aaron's rod said Levi on it. While reading this story, it came to me, (at 4AM), that this is a picture of Messiah!!! Let me explain:

Aaron's rod was a branch cut off of an Almond Tree
Messiah was a branch of King David

Aaron's rod was dead after being cut off the Almond Tree
Messiah was dead after being cut off

Aaron's rod was given life from being dead
Messiah was raised to life from being dead

Aaron's rod was the wood of a tree
Messiah was crucified on a tree

Aaron's rod had the tribe name inscribed upon it
Messiah's tree (the cross) had His name inscribed upon it;
Jesus of Nazareth KING of the Jews Pilate said, *"What I have written stays written."* Messiah will always be KING of the Jews

Aaron's rod sprouted to life and produced fruit, Almonds. Messiah was resurrected to life and was the First Fruits of those who die unto Salvation

Aaron's rod made him the High Levitical Priest (A picture of the Heavenly Priesthood) Messiah Yeshua is the High Priest of Heaven after the Order of Melchizedek!!!

Yeshua/Jesus said, *"As Moses lifted up the serpent on a pole, so too the Son of Man must be lifted up, so that those who believe will have Eternal life."*

Heavy Snow on Maple tree Branches & white dove
Photos ©2013 Kimberly K Ballard All Rights Reserved

The Rod is a picture of death coming to life and a picture or type and shadow of Heaven's High Priest, the Messiah of Israel!!!

I burst into tears and cried when this was shown to me by the Holy Spirit. I could not believe it because this revelation proved the identity of the Messiah of Israel to be Yeshua. It was a story of absolute truth revealed. This is incredible!
Shalom with love…K

==================================

A RESPONSE FROM JERUSALEM

The next day after I emailed that letter, the person responded to my email on the 17th of February, but as I said, I did not actually see it until Monday. The response letter from Jerusalem and the miracle photograph that came with it was so spectacular! My heart was blessed forever, by the following letter that proved that God's timing was stunningly accurate and perfect!

Email Response from Jerusalem,
February 17, 2007,
On Saturday the Sabbath.
Time 15:22:56+0200

Dear Kim,

What you write here is just incredible! It took me a while to compose myself after reading it. It is a true revelation and HaShem has done a beautiful thing to allow you to see this. Yesterday, *(February 16th Friday 2007),* I was walking to the Old City of Jerusalem and I saw my first Almond Tree this year starting to flower. I am attaching that picture for you and hope it brings you joy from the Holy Land. HaShem strongly directed me to take it and now I know it was for you. G. has not looked at your email yet, but they are on his desk. Shabbat Shalom & love from Jerusalem, LV.

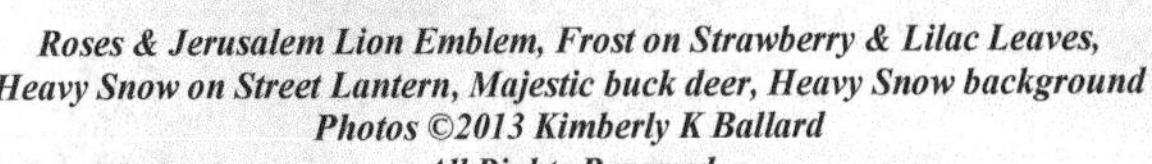

Roses & Jerusalem Lion Emblem, Frost on Strawberry & Lilac Leaves, Heavy Snow on Street Lantern, Majestic buck deer, Heavy Snow background

AN ALMOND TREE BUDDING

An Almond Tree budding on Holy Mount Moriah Jerusalem Israel
Photo by LV & Snow Dove on Snow Photos ©2013 Kimberly K Ballard All Rights Reserved

There in front of my eyes, attached to her email was this photograph she took the same day that I sent my revelation of the Almond Tree to her office. The photograph was a picture of the first Almond Tree beginning to flower that she had seen that day. Suddenly it occurred to me that this Almond Tree was acting just like Aaron's rod! It was budding to life and beginning to flower before her eyes, just before she got my message! *This really shocked me because, unbelievably, this tree was blooming in the Old City of Jerusalem on Holy Mount Moriah where the LORD dwells forever and where Yeshua came to life!* I was stunned and blessed and tears welled up in my eyes. I realized that something very powerful was taking place at this very moment in both of our lives! The LORD had done an astonishing thing that proved that my revelation was truly from the LORD God of Israel! The LORD was proving Himself to be faithful and true! In my heart I knew that it was the LORD who had guided her to photograph that Almond Tree on the very same day and at the very same hour, that I was typing the urgent message in Colorado! We were so excited! It was a true miracle! I copied off the email and the photograph of that Almond Tree from the library computer and returned home with it. *I was like a little kid in my heart.* I cannot even express how my heart was leaping for joy, because she told me that, *"HaShem,"* had strongly directed her to take the picture of that Almond Tree that ironically was just coming to life, from the death of winter in Israel!

Me at age five, I was like a little kid in my heart 1968 Photo ©2013 KK Ballard All Rights Reserved

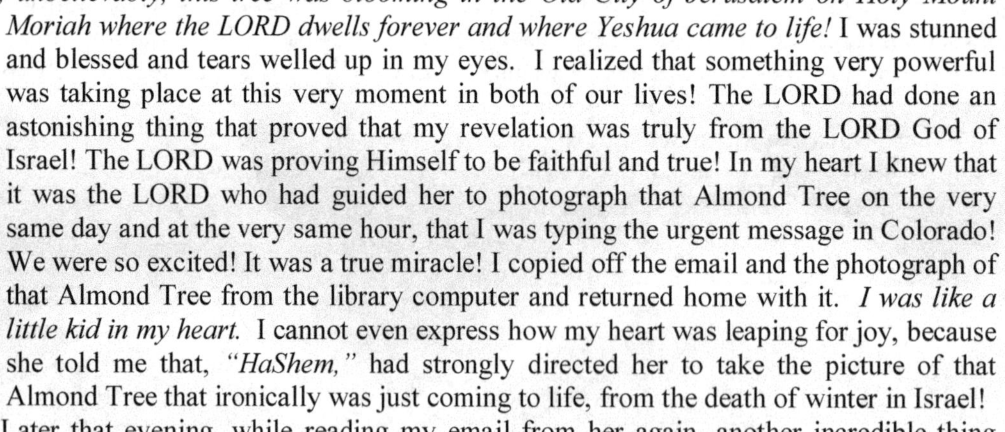

Later that evening, while reading my email from her again, another incredible thing happened. I walked over to my wall to look at my Biblical Jewish calendar. It was only at that moment, that I realized something even more spectacular had taken place that I had not noticed right away. I suddenly remembered that she had opened and read my email on the 17th. I must explain that I had read the account of Aaron's rod during that time, not from the Bible, but from a book called, *"The Antiquities of the Jews," by Flavius Josephus, who was a First Century Jewish Historian.* Of course at this time, I was viewing and pondering the Gospel of John DVD and asking the LORD to show me the deeper meaning of Yeshua's Words that declared that He must be lifted up like Moses' serpent on the pole.

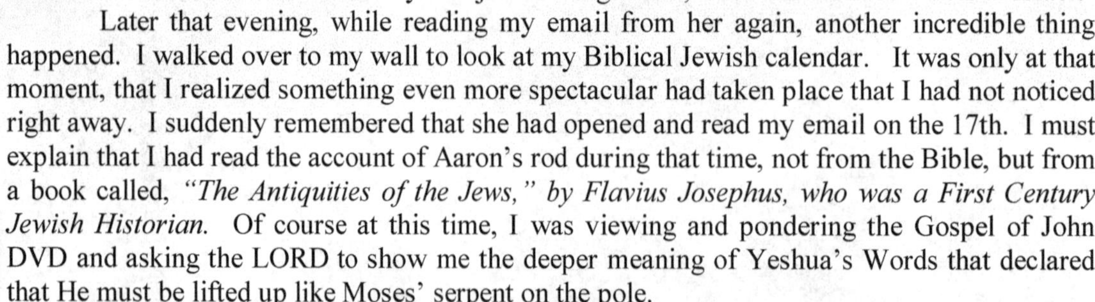

That night as I was looking at my Biblical calendar and thinking of my message being opened by my new Israeli friend on the 17th, I decided to go get my Bible to find out specifically where the story of Aaron's rod is recorded in the Scriptures. The Bible fell open to Numbers and I was absolutely stunned when I discovered that the story of Aaron's rod is recorded in

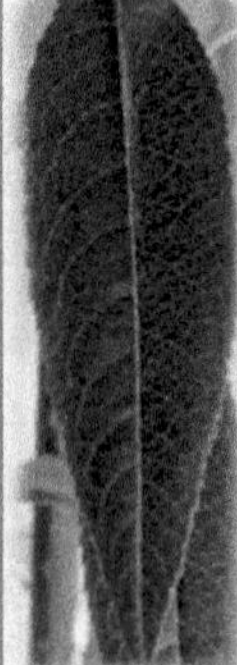

Numbers 17! It had been a while since I had read the Biblical account from Numbers, because I was studying other Scriptures, so I did not remember exactly where it was located. Nothing but the hand of the LORD could have made everything fall into place like this. The timing was exactly perfect, right down to an Almond Tree budding in Israel on the 17th and the message of Aaron's rod and the Messiah going to Jerusalem. I knew it was much more than just a simple coincidence. We both knew and felt in our hearts that something Divine had taken place! A real true miracle had transpired and I could not believe it. The LORD had timed this perfectly to reveal His Messiah to both of us! Just when I thought about how spectacular this was, I remembered another miraculous connection to the number 17. I had forgotten about it! You will find that the next connection is chilling, because, as I thought about Aaron's rod coming to life in Numbers 17, suddenly I remembered that Messiah Yeshua, *"The Branch,"* came to life on the Jewish Biblical calendar on Nisan 17**!** He produced the Fruit of Eternal life on the Feast of First Fruits on Nisan 17 and Aaron's rod budded and bore fruit in Numbers 17! Also, Noah's flood waters burst forth on the 17th day of the 2nd month and the Ark rested on the Mountains in the 7th month, on the 17th day.

Yeshua died as the Passover Lamb, on Nisan 14. However, Nisan 17 comes 3 days after Passover. Ironically, I was born to life in this world on the 17th of the 3rd month! Yeshua was raised to life as the Living Branch, on the 3rd day on Nisan 17. Amazing! So literally, Aaron's rod that was the branch cut off from the Almond Tree, budded and bore fruit on the 17th and Messiah Yeshua, the cut off Branch from Israel, budded and bore fruit on the 17th. Both of them were rods from the Almond Tree. My friend to told me that she tried to pass the Almond Tree *3 times* and she opened my Almond Tree revelation on the 17th, and sent the picture on the 17th! Her Almond Tree was the first Almond Tree flowering and Messiah was the First Fruit that came to life as the Rod of the Almond Tree. It is astonishing to think about it! That night as I was still observing the Jewish Biblical calendar and pondering these things, her words really struck me for the first time that she had said, *"Yesterday, I was walking to the Old City and I saw my first Almond Tree this year starting to flower."* Incredibly my revelation of the Almond Tree in Colorado *happened the same day* she past that Almond Tree in Jerusalem and photographed it by Divine appointment! If I had not felt that sudden urgency at the library, to type the message and get it there immediately to Jerusalem, this miracle never would have happened. When the LORD woke me up from my sleep with the message at 4AM in Colorado, it was approximately, 1PM in Jerusalem (a nine hour difference). Miraculously the LORD was bringing these events together through the miles! Just think, she could have photographed any kind of tree in the world, but she was directed to photograph *the first Almond Tree budding to life at that moment in the Old City of Jerusalem, on Holy Mount Moriah!* Meanwhile, I was hitting the send button and was out of time, as she was taking the picture in Israel! Now do you believe in miracles? The answer is yes, because it was the Holy Spirit of the LORD at work! Again tears welled up in my eyes, because the LORD was showing me, that not only had I not overstepped His will, but He proved that His timing was impeccably perfect. How else can you explain it? He made the Almond Tree come to life in the Old City of Jerusalem in February and proved it with the number 17 and the number 3 and these numbers reveal the exact days that the Messiah fulfilled, in the very place where He budded to life! This special message that the LORD had given me, was so true and it was obvious that no one could deny it anymore, that Yeshua is the Living budded Almond Branch who is encoded in the Torah of God.

Snow Scene & Almond Leaf
Photos ©2014 Kimberly K Ballard All Rights Reserved

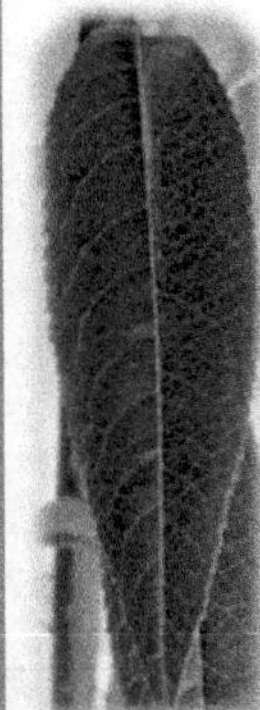

MY RESPONSE TO MY FRIEND IN JERUSALEM

After my first letter to Jerusalem to my new friend, we continued our correspondence. What follows, is the next letter that I sent to Jerusalem, after receiving the picture of the beautiful Almond Tree. On Monday February 19th 2007, I wrote the following email to her.

Jerusalem Lion Emblems & Snow Dove Photos ©2013 Kimberly K Ballard All Rights Reserved

Shalom Friend,

I am amazed at your email that I just opened today. This revelation about the Messiah is not the only one that I have had. I wanted to tell you that I have had three dreams about the Messiah. In the first dream, I was standing at the base of the Holy Temple facade. I was looking up at the height of it and I saw the columns on either side of it. I saw the Temple doors. It was at a slight angle and it was high up, so that I was looking straight up at it. The only thing that happened was a message that said, "*The Temple is rising before my eyes.*" Dream two came on the 3rd of January and I saw Messiah coming in the night sky. He was sitting upon a throne and I could see His robe. There were no stars, just black sky and He was clothed in light, sitting with a sceptre in His hand. I was looking upward standing in my sister's kitchen, where it was daylight. We were both looking up. My message was clear and simple, *"Tell them I AM coming soon."* I had another dream that I will have to go back and recall that happened on the 12th of January. This message was also amazing. I noticed the dates of 3 and 12 as they are numbers HaShem, the God of Israel uses!! Your email touched me beyond anything you can imagine. When the LORD showed this about Aaron's rod, I cried too. I did not know this before. I had prayed that your hearts would be open to the truth of this, as it is amazing and blows me out of the water. Are you telling me that you took this beautiful picture of the Almond Tree before you got my email? That is mind blowing, because I had no idea that any Almond Trees would be blooming at this time. I am touched to the heart!!!! HaShem is working also in you to send that picture to me!!! Funny, I just planted some Almond seeds and pomegranate seeds yesterday to see if they would grow. It is the middle of winter here, so why I would have this message from HaShem about Aaron's rod is beyond me. I had a similar thing happen with a realization that Messiah may come in a Jubilee year. I asked another friend in Israel when the next Jubilee was and she at that time said, *"next year"* which was going to be 2007. I found some books on-line after this and they confirmed my hypothesis about Messiah returning in a Jubilee year. I was reading Dead Sea Scroll 11Q13 which speaks of the Messiah as coming in a Jubilee year. This could be at Trumpets in the fall. Yeshua fulfilled all the Feasts of Israel at His first coming. I was not sure how you would feel about the Aaron's rod revelation. I prayed that your hearts would see it too. It shows that this was all HaShem's plan, right down to the fact that Messiah had to be crucified on a tree. This is why every time they tried to stone Him, it says that He slipped away as, *"His time had not yet come."* This is why Yeshua came and was crucified on a tree. He was dead, then was raised to life like Aaron's rod of the Almond Tree and by doing this, Yeshua has become the High Priest of Heaven after the Order of Melchizedek. In this way, He has brought glory to the LORD of Hosts, God of Israel. Messiah is the Heavenly version or the type and shadow of the Levitical

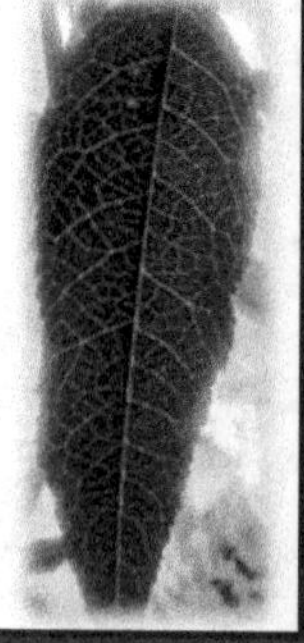

earthly version of the Rod of Aaron! Thank you for the glorious photo!!! I love it and I am blessed to know that HaShem is working!
K.

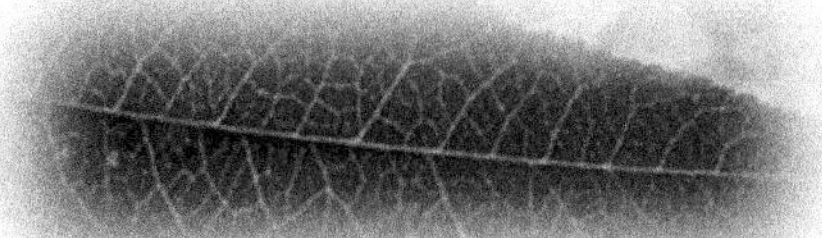

Later I remembered that the third dream that I had about the Messiah was unusual. I was standing on a porch and there were impressions of His feet on the ground, just off the edge of the porch. I wanted to see how small my feet were, compared to His big feet. So I stepped off the porch and turned around to face the footprints. Then all at once, just as I was going to place my foot in the impression of His footprint, I was startled by this very loud booming voice that came out of nowhere and said, *"I AM going to make a place for you, that where I AM, there you may be also!"* I jumped, startled at the voice!

NEXT LETTER FROM JERUSALEM

This was my friend's next response to my email on Monday, which I received on Wednesday, 21 February 2007 Time: 14:31:21+0200

Kim, With HaShem all things are perfect. Yes, I took the picture before I read your email. I tried to walk past that tree three times but it was like an angel was pulling my arm saying, *"Take a picture of the BEAUTIFUL tree."* With your permission, I would like to share your Branch insight with some others. Is that OK? And I also believe it is VERY possible that this could be the year. I pray non-stop that we are ready. Shalom, Shalom and love from Jerusalem! LV

Wow! OK, I said to myself, she tried to pass the Almond Tree three times? Allow me to show you a few of the connections of the number 3 and how it pertains to the LORD God of Israel. The LORD set the earth as the 3rd planet from the sun

(Exodus 19:11-17)

On the 3rd day the LORD came down on Mount Sinai and the people met God

On the 3rd day Messiah Yeshua was resurrected as the Living Branch and the people met Him.

The 3rd cup of wine at the Passover Seder is the one that honors Messiah Yeshua.

(Exodus 25:32)

3 Almond branches of the Lamp stand from one side

3 Almond branches of the Lamp stand on its other side

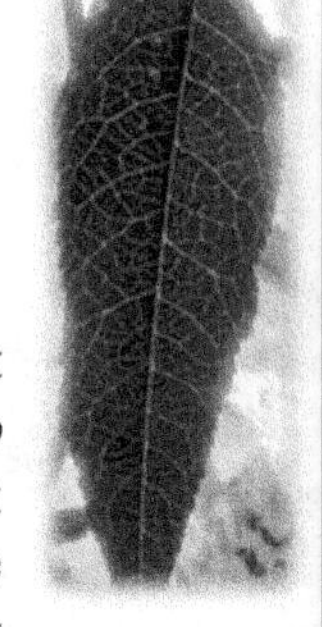

3 cups shaped like Almond blossoms in one branch of the Lamp stand (Ex 25:33).
3 cups shaped like Almond blossoms in the other branch of the Lamp stand
3 The whorl on the Lamp stand is a three-in-one organ or node, a knot, a joint in a stem.
3 The sign of Jonah which was the only sign that Yeshua gave to Israel that reveals to them that He is their Messiah. He said, *"As Jonah was 3 days and 3 nights in the belly of the fish, so too will the Son of Man be 3 days and 3 nights in the tomb or the heart of the earth."* These are just a few of the signs of the LORD that have to do with the number 3. If I told you all of the connections of the LORD that have to do with the number 3, then I would be here for a long time in this chapter! As we get further into the book, I will reveal more about how the number 3 is connected to the LORD, our Messiah Yeshua and you will be completely speechless!

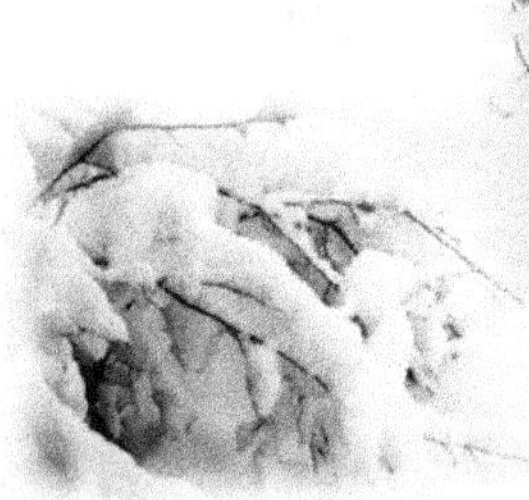

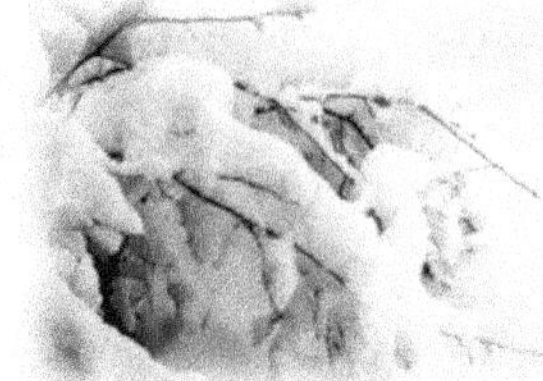

THE INVISIBLE ASSISTANT

There is something unique and quite astounding about my friend passing the Almond Tree three times in the very place where Messiah Yeshua performed His miracles. When she told me that someone very powerful had pulled her to the tree and impressed her to take the photograph of this Almond Tree, this was so incredible to think about. I was thinking to myself, *"Why did she happen to have a camera with her that day?"* It was probably a camera in her cell phone, but what if she had not taken it with her that day? Why did she take the picture in the first place, on the very same day, when I was in Colorado typing out the miracle of the Almond Tree revelation? What if she had waited to take the picture later? What if she had just ignored the message to her heart to take the picture at all? Why didn't she just ignore it and keep walking, which obviously she tried to do three times until she was totally drawn to take the photograph by an unexplained force or power? She had told me that HaShem was leading her to take the photo of the, *"Beautiful tree."* Why did she take the picture at all?

Frosty winter scene with Icicles

She had no idea that anyone was going to write to her about Aaron's rod from the Almond Tree! We had never met or spoken to each other before. I did not know her at all! I had never seen or touched an Almond Tree in my entire life! Why did I suddenly feel the urgency to email that message as fast as I could type it out, with only 25 minutes to spare? Why did I even listen to the tugging at my heart to fulfill this for the LORD, at that exact moment? I kept on thinking about all the factors involved in this miracle and how one small thing could have altered this miracle from ever happening. The LORD had orchestrated this event. I believe He was revealing Himself to us by the power of His Holy Spirit at this time, because He is very near to His return. We are living in the last days and at this time, we see very little hope in the world. It was quite apparent that the LORD was with us, making all these events come together into one astonishing miracle. When my friend sent the Almond Tree photo to me, my heart was so touched. When this miracle happened, I understood the LORD in my heart in a way I never had before. I wanted to proclaim just how much I love the LORD with all my heart and so I

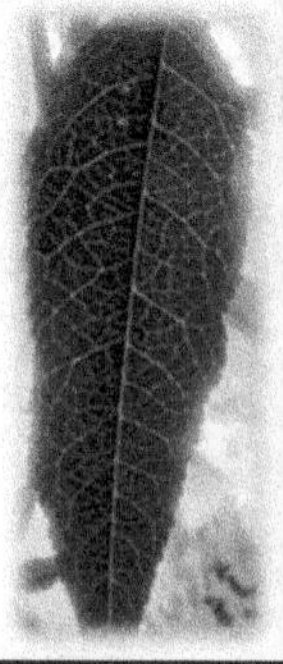

began writing this down in a book, as I felt the LORD was instructing me to do! When my Israeli friend tried to pass that Almond Tree three times and she was pulled to it by a force that was not visible, this reminded me of a story that I remembered about King David and his *"Invisible Assistant!"*

Flavious Josephus wrote the following regarding David and Goliath. **Quote:** "But the youth (David) met his antagonist, (Goliath) being accompanied with an Invisible Assistant, who was no other than God, the LORD Himself! David also carried his staff with him! David said, "All men shall learn that God is the protector of the Hebrews and that our armor and our strength are in His Providence; and that without God's assistance all other warlike preparations and power are useless." ***(Josephus 1737, Copyright 1998)***

I believe without a doubt, that this *Invisible Assistant,* who accompanied David, is the same *Invisible Assistant* who accompanied my Israeli friend and pulled her by the arm to the Almond Tree to photograph it. The LORD God manifested Himself as the *Invisible Assistant,* to both of us at the same time, even though we were in two different places on the earth. He revealed Himself to both of us as the Branch of the Almond Tree that came to life, as the Rod and Staff of God that budded!

When I realized that David had the LORD as his *Invisible Assistant,* I suddenly understood who it was we were dealing with here, when my friend said that HaShem had strongly directed her to take a picture of the Beautiful tree, the third time she tried to pass it! It became obvious that her *Invisible Assistant* was the same *Invisible Assistant* that was urging me to send His message to the right person, in the right place, at the right time across the ocean. This was also His Divine Providence, just as it was with David and we both knew it in our hearts! As He pulled her to the Almond Tree, the LORD was saying, *"Look inside the flowering Almond blossom and you will find My heart and see My face as the Sar HaPanim!"* He was telling her, *"I AM your Messiah, the Living Branch of the Almond Tree of Life and this is the place on Holy Mount Moriah, where I budded and bore the First Fruit!"*

Lion Statue in the Snow
Photo ©2014 Kimberly K Ballard All Rights Reserved

Well, just when it appears as though the story ends with this first miracle, I can assure you that the miracles did not stop with this one incredible event. I have many more surprises within the following chapters that reveal our *Invisible Assistant.* After all these incredible events happened the LORD manifested Himself to me again. I was so astonished by this, and for having so much revealed to me. It was clear that He was revealing His identity and He was showing me, *His Heavenly Eternal Testimony* that is hidden and is encoded within the Almond Tree of Life. This was truly going to be an end time message for the entire world.

I Timothy 1:16-17 *Howbeit for this cause I obtained mercy, that in me first Yeshua Messiah might shew forth all longsuffering, for a pattern to them which should hereafter believe on Him to life everlasting. Now unto the KING eternal, immortal, invisible, the only wise God, be honour and glory forever and ever. Amen.*

SUMMARY
AARON'S ALMOND ROD MESSIAH THE ALMOND ROD MY REVELATION WITH THE SCRIPTURES

Icicle Photos & Frost on Pine Needles

I felt it was most fitting to go back and view each portion of the Almond Tree revelation as it was given to me in order, by the power of the Holy Spirit. In this summary, I want to go over each of the seven points that the LORD gave me. I did not realize until this moment there were seven (the number of perfection), but this time I will show the specific corresponding Scriptural references from the Word of God, that verifies His Testimony. I will also include a portion of Josephus' account of Aaron's rod.

1. AARON'S ROD WAS A BRANCH CUT OFF AN ALMOND TREE:

Quote from; Antiquities of the Jews - Book IV CHAPTER 4 section 2;

2. Now Moses, upon his hearing for a good while that the people were tumultuous, was afraid that they would attempt some other innovation, and that some great and sad calamity would be the consequence. He called the multitude to a congregation, and patiently heard what apology they had to make for themselves, without opposing them and this lest he should embitter the multitude; he only desired the heads of the tribes to bring their rods, (3.) with the names of their tribes inscribed upon them, and that he should receive the priesthood in whose rod God should give a sign. This was agreed to. So the rest brought their rods, as did Aaron also, who had written the tribe of Levi on his rod. These rods Moses laid up in the Tabernacle of God. On the next day he brought out the rods, which were known from one another by those who brought them, they having distinctly noted them, as had the multitude also; and as to the rest, in the same form Moses had received them, in that they saw them still; but they also saw buds and branches grown out of Aaron's rod, with ripe fruits upon them; they were almonds, the rod having been cut out of that tree. The people were so amazed at this strange sight, that though Moses and Aaron were before under some degree of hatred, they now laid that hatred aside, and began to admire the judgment of God concerning them; so that hereafter they applauded what God had decreed, and permitted Aaron to enjoy the priesthood peaceably. And thus God ordained him priest three several times, and he retained that honor without further disturbance. And hereby this sedition of the Hebrews, which had been a great one, and had lasted a great while, was at last composed.

1. MESSIAH WAS A ROD, A BRANCH OF KING DAVID:

***Isaiah 11:1-10** And there shall come forth a Rod out of the stem of Jesse, and a Branch shall grow out of His roots; And the Spirit of the LORD shall rest upon Him, the spirit of wisdom and understanding, the spirit of counsel and might, the spirit of knowledge and of the fear of the LORD; And shall make Him of quick understanding in the fear of the LORD; and He shall not judge after the sight of His eyes, neither reprove after the hearing of His ears; But with righteousness shall He judge the poor, and reprove with equity for the meek of the earth; and He shall smite the earth with the Rod of His mouth, and with the breath of His lips shall He slay the wicked. And righteousness shall be the girdle of His loins, and faithfulness the girdle of His reins. The wolf also shall dwell with the lamb, and the leopard shall lie down with the kid; and the calf and the young lion and the fatling together; and a little child shall lead them. And the cow and the bear shall feed; their young ones shall lie down together: and the lion shall eat straw like the ox. And the sucking child shall play on the hole of the asp, and the weaned child shall put his hand on the cockatrice' den. They shall not hurt nor destroy in all My Holy Mountain; for the earth shall be full of the*

knowledge of the LORD, as the waters cover the sea. And in that day there shall be a root of Jesse, which shall stand for an ensign of the people; to it shall the Gentiles seek; and His rest shall be glorious.

2. AARON'S ROD WAS DEAD AFTER BEING CUT OFF THE ALMOND TREE

Quote from Josephus chapter 4, book 4, Section 2: "Moses had received them, in that they saw them still; but they also saw buds and branches grown out of Aaron's rod, with ripe fruits upon them; they were almonds, the rod having been cut out of that tree."

2. MESSIAH YESHUA WAS DEAD AFTER BEING CUT OFF

Daniel 9:26 *And after threescore and two weeks shall Messiah be cut off, but not for Himself; and the people of the prince that shall come shall destroy the City and the Sanctuary; and the end thereof shall be with a flood, and unto the end of the war desolations are determined.*

Daniel clearly revealed that the Messiah would come during the Second Temple period, just before the Second Temple was to be destroyed by Titus and his Roman Soldiers. This destruction of the House of God, happened 40 years after the Messiah became the cut off Branch of Israel. The Scripture tells us that He was not cut off for Himself. As we know, Joseph was also cut off from his own brothers. The LORD had a purpose for this temporary separation. The Branch from the Almond Tree of Life was cut off from Israel, to save many people alive to Eternal life! We know that Joseph revealed Himself to his brothers at the proper time according to God's will and Messiah Yeshua will reveal Himself to His brothers and sisters of Israel at the proper time.

Isaiah 53:8 *He was taken from prison and from judgment; and who shall declare His generation? For He was cut off out of the land of the living; for the transgression of My people was He stricken.*

3. AARON'S ROD WAS GIVEN LIFE FROM BEING DEAD

Numbers 17:8 *And it came to pass, that on the morrow Moses went into the Tabernacle of witness; and, behold, the rod of Aaron for the house of Levi was budded, and brought forth buds, and bloomed blossoms, and yielded almonds.*

3. MESSIAH WAS RAISED TO LIFE AFTER BEING DEAD

Messiah the Rod came to life on the 7th day, the Sabbath of the LORD. *I will later discuss the* details of the women coming to the tomb just as morning arrived on the third day after Passover. They found that Yeshua was already resurrected to life.

Matthew 28:1-7 *In the end of the Sabbath, as it began to dawn toward the first day of the week, came Mary Magdalene and the other Mary to see the sepulchre. And, behold, there was a great earthquake; for the angel of the LORD descended from Heaven, and came and rolled back the stone from the door, and sat upon it. His countenance was like lightning, and his raiment white as snow; and for fear of him the keepers did shake, and became as dead men. And the angel answered and said unto the women, Fear not ye, for I know that ye seek Yeshua, which was crucified. He is not here; for He is risen, as He said. Come, see the place where the LORD lay. And go quickly, and tell His disciples that He is risen from the dead; And, behold, He goeth before you into Galilee; there shall ye see Him; lo, I have told you.*

All Robins & Nest with Robin eggs Photos ©2013 Kimberly K Ballard All Rights Reserved

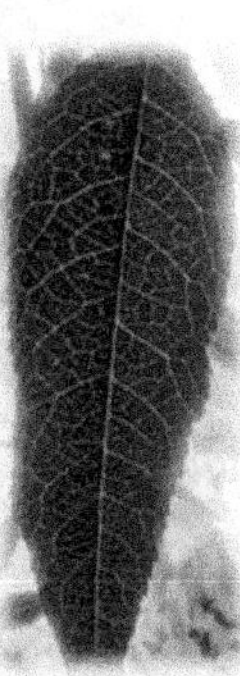

4. AARON'S ROD WAS THE WOOD OF A TREE

Again, Josephus wrote that Aaron's rod was the wood of an Almond Tree.

Josephus chapter 4, book 4, and section 2 again; "Moses had received them, in that they saw them still; but they also saw buds and branches grown out of Aaron's rod, with ripe fruits upon them; they were almonds, the rod having been cut out of that tree."

4. MESSIAH WAS CRUCIFIED ON A TREE

Yeshua was crucified on a tree bearing the curse of Adam, so the Gentiles could now be part of the promise and the blessing of Abraham. They would receive the Spirit of God through faith, by baptism in Messiah Yeshua, through the Holy Spirit.

Galatians 3:13-14 *Messiah hath redeemed us from the curse of the law, being made a curse for us; for it is written, Cursed is every one that hangeth on a tree; That the blessing of Abraham might come on the Gentiles through Yeshua Messiah; that we might receive the promise of the Spirit through faith.*

Mark 15:32-33 *Let Messiah the King of Israel descend now from the cross that we may see and believe. And they that were crucified with Him reviled Him. And when the sixth hour was come, there was darkness over the whole land until the ninth hour.*

John 19:16-17 *Then delivered he Him therefore unto them to be crucified. And they took Yeshua and led Him away. And He bearing His cross went forth into a place called the place of a skull, which is called in the Hebrew Golgotha.*

Chickadee Photo ©2013 Kimberly K Ballard

Matthew 27:32-35 *And as they came out, they found a man of Cyrene, Simon by name; him they compelled to bear His cross. And when they were come unto a place called Golgotha, that is to say, a place of a skull, They gave Him vinegar to drink mingled with gall; and when He had tasted thereof, He would not drink. And they crucified Him, and parted His garments, casting lots; that it might be fulfilled which was spoken by the Prophet, They parted My garments among them, and upon My vesture did they cast lots.*

Luke 23:31-34 *For if they do these things in a green tree, what shall be done in the dry? And there were also two other, malefactors, led with him to be put to death. And when they were come to the place, which is called Calvary, there they crucified Him, and the malefactors, one on the right hand, and the other on the left.*

5. AARON'S ROD HAD THE TRIBE NAME INSCRIBED UPON IT LEVI

Numbers 17:2-3 *Speak unto the children of Israel, and take of every one of them a rod according to the house of their fathers, of all their princes according to the house of their father's twelve rods; write thou every man's name upon his rod. And thou shalt write Aaron's name upon the rod of Levi; for one rod shall be for the head of the house of their fathers.*

5. MESSIAH THE ROD HAD HIS TREE THE CROSS WITH HIS NAME INSCRIBED UPON IT *"THE KING OF THE JEWS."*

John 19:19-22 *And Pilate wrote a title, and put it on the cross. And the writing was, YESHUA OF NAZARETH THE KING OF THE JEWS. This title then read many of the Jews; for the place where Yeshua was crucified was nigh to the City; and it was written in Hebrew, and Greek, and Latin. Then said the Chief Priests of the Jews to Pilate, Write not, The KING of the Jews; but that He said, I AM KING of the Jews. Pilate answered, what I have written I have written.*

Luke 23:38 *And a superscription also was written over Him in letters of Greek, and Latin, and Hebrew, THIS IS THE KING OF THE JEWS.*

Matthew 27:37 *And set up over His head His accusation written, THIS IS YESHUA THE KING OF THE JEWS.*

Notice that Messiah Yeshua was crucified the third hour! This is just another miracle of the number 3, having significance to the Branch who was cut off, that plainly declares that Yeshua is the Messiah of Israel! *This Rod was according to the House of His Father and His Name was written on His own Rod!* This Rod was laid before the House of the Heavenly Tabernacle of God (Moses' Tabernacle of witness), and it was here, that Messiah Yeshua met with us on Holy Mount Moriah where my miracle Almond Tree budded in 2007! I have seen the budding Rod of an Almond Tree!

Mark 15:25-28 *And it was the third hour, and they crucified Him. And the superscription of His accusation was written over, THE KING OF THE JEWS. And with Him they crucify two thieves; the one on His right hand, and the other on His left. And the Scripture was fulfilled, which saith, And He was numbered with the transgressors.*

Blue jay & Robin Photos ©2014 Kimberly K Ballard All Rights Reserved

6. AARON'S ROD SPROUTED TO LIFE AND PRODUCED FRUIT OF ALMONDS

The Rod sprouting to life, bearing the fruit of Almonds, was *the Testimony* that Aaron placed within the Ark. The Rod Messiah is the Branch from the Tree of Life, that bore the First Fruit of Eternal life and His Eternal Testimony is in Heaven.

Numbers 17:1-11 *And the LORD spake unto Moses, saying, Speak unto the children of Israel, and take of every one of them a rod according to the house of their fathers twelve rods; write thou every man's name upon his rod. And thou shalt write Aaron's name upon the rod of Levi; for one rod shall be for the head of the house of their fathers. And thou shalt lay them up in the Tabernacle of the congregation before the Testimony, where I will meet with you. And it shall come to pass, that the man's rod, whom I shall choose, shall blossom; and I will make to cease from me the murmurings of the children of Israel, whereby thy murmur against you. And Moses spake unto the children of Israel, and every one of their princes gave him a rod a piece, for each prince one, according to their fathers' houses even twelve rods; and the rod of Aaron was among their rods. And Moses laid up the rods before the LORD in the Tabernacle of witness. And it came to pass, that on the morrow Moses went into the Tabernacle of witness; and, behold, the rod of Aaron for the house of Levi was budded, and brought forth buds, and bloomed blossoms, and yielded almonds. And Moses brought out all the rods from before the LORD unto all the children of Israel; and they looked, and took every man his rod. And the LORD said unto Moses, Bring Aaron's rod again before the Testimony, to be kept for a token against the rebels; and thou shalt quite take away their murmurings from Me that they die not. And Moses did so; as the LORD commanded him, so did he.*

Let me share what I see in this account of the LORD. The Rod that is laid before the Testimony is the Covenant of the God of Israel, to the twelve tribes. Just as there was one rod for each fathers household, so too *the Father God has a Rod of His own and His Name is written on it.* He holds the Rod out towards us for salvation which is, *"Yeshua"* and this Rod of the Eternal Testimony of the LORD, gives us Eternal life. Moses put the rod in the Tabernacle of *witness (Numbers 17:7)*. So *Moses is an eternal witness* to this resurrection pattern of the Testimony of the LORD God. The dead cut off Almond Branch of Aaron is the rod that sprouted to life over night. When this rod budded, it blossomed and bore the fruit of almonds. This was the sign that God gave to Israel, that Aaron was His anointed one, chosen as the High Priest. Aaron's earthly rod was placed before the Testimony, just as Messiah the Rod was placed before the KING OF KINGS own Living Eternal Testimony, in the Heavenly Tabernacle. Both are chosen and both are the, *"anointed one."* Both rods are living branches and both are High Priests! Messiah gave us the Covenant of His heart which is full of love for everyone of us!

Yeshua of Nazareth is the only person, whose life, death, burial and resurrection, are the mirror image and exact parallel pattern of Aaron's rod that budded in the Torah. This is according to all the Biblical accounts.

The first fruits were to be brought to the LORD God. Messiah Yeshua, the First Fruit of the Almond Tree of Life ascended back into Heaven. The LORD gave special instructions to Israel for *the first fruits* and for every *first born son.* Yeshua was the *first born Son* of Mary and is the Redeemer of Israel. He is the First Fruit of the Tree of Life. If we eat this Fruit, we are cleansed in His baptism. The LORD said that Israel could eat the first fruits if they were clean. The blood of this Lamb was the Testimony of the true meat on the LORD'S own altar. When we think of the thigh that is mentioned in Numbers, we can see that this pertains also to Messiah Yeshua.

Revelation 19:16 *And He hath on His vesture and on His thigh a Name written, KING OF KINGS AND LORD OF LORDS.*

Numbers 18:13-18 *The first fruits of everything in their land, that they bring to the LORD, shall be yours; everyone of your household who is clean may eat them. Everything that has been proscribed in Israel shall be yours. The first issue of the womb of every being, man or beast, that is offered to the LORD, shall be yours; but you shall have the first-born of man redeemed, and you shall also have the firstling of unclean animals redeemed. Take as their redemption price from the age of one month up, the money equivalent of five shekels by the sanctuary weight, which is twenty gerahs. But the firstlings of cattle, sheep, or goats may not be redeemed; they are consecrated. You shall dash their blood against the altar, and turn their fat into smoke as an offering by fire for a pleasing odor to the LORD. But their meat shall be yours; it shall be yours like the breast of elevation offering and like the right thigh.*

Israel was supposed to bring *the first fruits of all the trees* to the House of the LORD, during the appointed time. Yeshua became the First Fruit of the Tree of Life on Nisan 17.

Nehemiah 10:34-37 *And we cast the lots among the Priests, the Levites, and the people, for the wood offering, to bring it into the House of our God, after the houses of our fathers, at times appointed year by year, to burn upon the altar of the LORD our God, as it is written in the law; And to bring the first fruits of our ground, and the first fruits of all fruit of all trees, year by year, unto the House of the LORD; Also the firstborn of our sons, and of our cattle, as it is written in the law, and the firstlings of our herds and of our flocks, to bring to the House of our God, unto the Priests that minister in the House of our God; And that we should bring the first fruits of our dough, and our offerings, and the fruit of all manner of trees, of wine and of oil, unto the Priests, to the chambers of the House of our God; and the tithes of our ground unto the Levites, that the same Levites might have the tithes in all the cities of our tillage.*

6. MESSIAH WAS RESURRECTED TO LIFE AND WAS THE FIRST FRUITS OF THOSE WHO DIE UNTO SALVATION

Singing Robin
Photo ©2014 KK Ballard

I Corinthians 15:20-23 *But now is Messiah risen from the dead, and become the First Fruits of them that slept. For since by man came death, by man came also the resurrection of the dead. For as in Adam all die, even so in Messiah shall all be made alive, But every man in his own order; Messiah the First Fruits; afterward they that are Messiah's at His coming.*

Colossians 2:9-17 *For in Him dwelleth all the fullness of the Godhead bodily. And ye are complete in Him, which is the head of all principality and power; In whom also ye are circumcised with the circumcision made without hands, in putting off the body of the sins of the flesh by the circumcision of Messiah; Buried with Him in baptism, wherein also ye are risen with him through the faith of the operation of God, who hath raised Him from the dead. And you, being dead in your sins and the uncircumcision of your flesh, hath He quickened together with Him, having forgiven you all trespasses; Blotting out the handwriting of ordinances that was against us, which was contrary to us, and took it out of the way, nailing it to His cross; And having spoiled principalities and powers, he made a shew of them openly, triumphing over them in it. Let no man therefore judge you in meat, or in drink, or in respect of an holy day, or of the new moon, or of the Sabbath days; Which are a shadow of things to come; but the body is of Messiah.*

The body of Messiah is the Heavenly Fruit of Heaven. If we eat this Fruit, we will live forever. The First Fruit from the Tree of Life is the Living Eternal Testimony of God.

Proverbs 8:19-23 *My fruit is better than gold, yea, than fine gold; and My revenue than choice silver. I lead in the way of righteousness, in the midst of the paths of judgment; That I may cause those that love Me to inherit substance; and I will fill their treasures. The LORD possessed me in the beginning of His way, before His works of old, I was set up from everlasting, from the beginning, or ever the earth was.*

7. AARON'S ROD MADE HIM THE HIGH LEVITICAL PRIEST A PICTURE OF THE HEAVENLY PRIESTHOOD

Numbers 17:5 *And it shall come to pass, that the man's rod, whom I shall choose, shall blossom; and I will make to cease from me the murmurings of the children of Israel, whereby they murmur against you.*

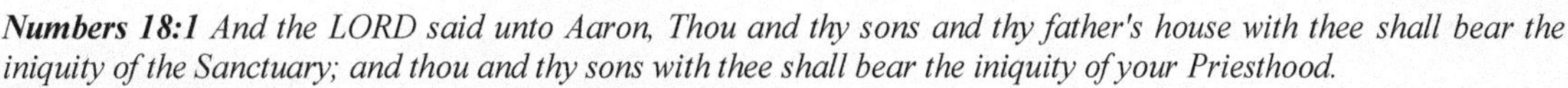

Numbers 18:1 *And the LORD said unto Aaron, Thou and thy sons and thy father's house with thee shall bear the iniquity of the Sanctuary; and thou and thy sons with thee shall bear the iniquity of your Priesthood.*

Numbers 18:7-8 *Therefore thou and thy sons with thee shall keep your Priest's office for everything of the altar, and within the veil; and ye shall serve; I have given your Priest's office unto you as a service of gift; and the stranger that cometh nigh shall be put to death. And the LORD spake unto Aaron, Behold, I also have given thee the charge of mine heave offerings of all the hallowed things of the children of Israel; unto thee have I given them by reason of the anointing, and to thy sons, by an ordinance forever.*

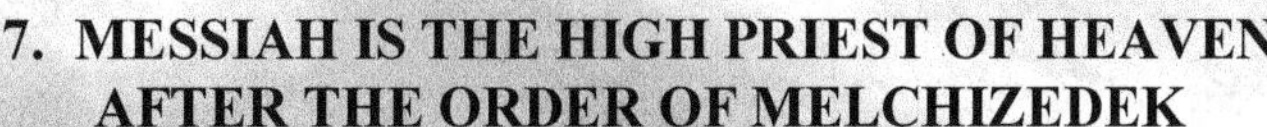

The High Priesthood is a position appointed by the LORD. Aaron was proven to be the LORD'S choice, the anointed one. The LORD caused Aaron's rod to come to life, to prove Aaron was chosen. Aaron was of the order of the earthly Levitical Priesthood and he was from the tribe of Levi.

Blue jay & Finch Photos ©2014 KK Ballard All Rights Reserved

7. MESSIAH IS THE HIGH PRIEST OF HEAVEN AFTER THE ORDER OF MELCHIZEDEK

Messiah Yeshua is the chosen High Priest of Heaven and is God's anointed one. The Heavenly Priesthood differs from the earthly Levitical Priesthood in the fact that the Heavenly is after the Order of Melchizedek. This is why those who have been baptized in Messiah are now living under His Heavenly Priesthood and not living under the earthly Levitical Priesthood. This is what the Scripture means when it says that we are not under the old law. The Messiah's Priesthood under the Order of Melchizedek is the new and better Priesthood because it comes from the Eternal Kingdom of God. The Levitical Priesthood is only a type and shadow or mirror image of the Heavenly Eternal Priesthood of the LORD.

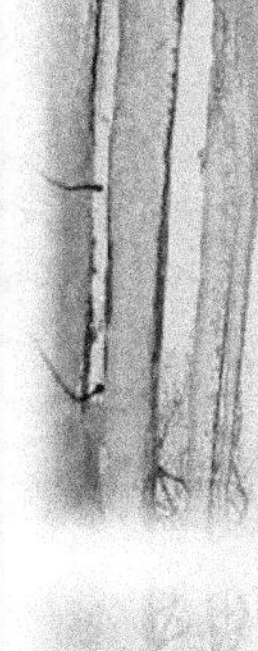

Hebrews 2:17 *Therefore, He had to be made like His brethren in all things, that He might become a merciful and faithful High Priest in things pertaining to God, to make propitiation for the sins of the people.*

Now because there is a change in the Priesthood there is also a change in the law and this is why the Gentiles are not under the Levitical law. They are under the Messiah, the LORD'S Priesthood, and His Eternal law. *The LORD sprang out of Judah,* which is past tense. Messiah the LORD had already come to earth for this purpose.

Hebrews 7:11-28 *If therefore perfection were by the Levitical Priesthood, for under it the people received the law, what further need was there that another Priest should rise after the order of Melchizedek, and not be called after the order of Aaron? For the Priesthood being changed, there is made of necessity a change also of the law. For He of whom these things are spoken pertaineth to another tribe, of which no man gave attendance at the altar. For it is evident that our LORD sprang out of Judah; of which tribe Moses spake nothing concerning Priesthood. And it is yet far more evident; for that after the similitude of Melchizedek there ariseth another Priest, Who is made, not after the law of a carnal commandment, but after the power of an endless life. For He testifieth, Thou art a Priest for ever after the order of Melchizedek. For there is verily a disannulling of the commandment going before for the weakness and unprofitableness thereof. For the law made nothing perfect, but the bringing in of a better hope did; by the which we draw nigh unto God. And inasmuch as not without an oath He was made Priest; For those Priests were made without an oath; but this with an oath by Him that said unto Him, The LORD sware and will not repent, Thou art a Priest for ever after the order of Melchizedek; By so much was Yeshua made a surety of a better Testament. And they truly were many Priests, because they were not suffered to continue by reason of death; But this man, because He continueth ever, hath an unchangeable Priesthood. Wherefore He is able also to save them to the uttermost that come unto God by Him, seeing He ever liveth to make intercession for them. For such an High Priest became us, who is Holy, harmless, undefiled, separate from sinners, and made higher than the Heavens; Who needeth not daily, as those High Priests, to offer up sacrifice, first for his own sins, and then for the people's; for this He did once, when He offered up Himself. For the law maketh men High Priests which have infirmity; but the Word of the oath, which was since the law, maketh the Son, who is consecrated forevermore.*

Aaron's rod brought Israel temporary salvation, but Messiah Yeshua, the Heavenly Rod brings Israel Eternal salvation. Melchizedek means, *"KING of Righteousness."* In Dead Sea Scroll 11Q13, it speaks about this KING of Righteousness, coming to bring an end of the transgression and to bring in everlasting righteousness. He came to declare the favorable year of the LORD. This is exactly what Yeshua did when He stood up in the Synagogue and read the scroll in Isaiah 61. Yeshua declared that this prophecy was being fulfilled in their hearing and all Israel was astonished. Messiah is also the Bridegroom who returns to be married to His Bride.

Isaiah 61:1-11 *The Spirit of the Lord GOD is upon me; because the LORD hath anointed me to preach good tidings unto the meek; he hath sent me to bind up the brokenhearted, to proclaim liberty to the captives, and the opening of the prison to them that are bound; To proclaim the acceptable year of the LORD, and the day of vengeance of our God; to comfort all that mourn; To appoint unto them that mourn in Zion, to give unto them beauty for ashes, the oil of joy for mourning, the garment of praise for the spirit of heaviness; that they might be called trees of righteousness, the planting of the LORD, that he might be glorified. And they shall build the old wastes, they shall raise up the former desolations, and they shall repair the waste cities, the desolations of many generations. And strangers shall stand and feed your flocks, and the sons of the alien shall be your plowmen and your vinedressers. But ye shall be named the Priests of the LORD: men shall call you the Ministers of our God: ye shall eat the riches of the Gentiles, and in their glory shall ye boast yourselves. For your shame ye shall have double; and for confusion they shall rejoice in their portion: therefore in their land they shall possess the double: everlasting joy shall be unto them. For I the LORD love judgment, I hate robbery for burnt offering; and I will direct their work in truth, and I will make an everlasting covenant with them. And their seed shall be known among the Gentiles, and their offspring among the people: all that see them shall acknowledge them, that they are the seed which the LORD hath blessed. I will greatly rejoice in the LORD, my soul shall be joyful in my God; for he hath clothed me with the garments of salvation, he hath covered me with the robe of righteousness, as a bridegroom decketh himself with ornaments, and as a bride adorneth herself with her jewels. For as the earth bringeth forth her bud, and as the garden causeth the things that are sown in it to spring forth; so the Lord GOD will cause righteousness and praise to spring forth before all the nations.*

Blue jay Photo ©2014 Kimberly K Ballard

The name Melchizedek is of the Hebrew word, *"Tzadik,"* which is translated as, *"Zadok,"* in English. It means, *"Righteous."* To be a *Tzadik* is to be a *"Righteous Saint."* During the time of King David and King Solomon's reign, one of the High Priest's was Zadok.

Zadok was more than just a faithful and loyal High Priest. I soon realized that Zadok was also the most loyal of the Mighty men of Valor, who remained faithful to King David, when the other Priest Abiathar turned against him. Zadok was appointed and sent by King David to take his son Solomon to the Gihon Spring, to anoint him as David's successor. Solomon was the LORD'S chosen one, who was appointed by the LORD, to sit on the throne of David. This was to be done before Solomon's brother could steal the throne from him. One can trace Zadok's line to see that he was of the family of Phineas. This family served as God's anointed Priestly line, generation after generation. It was this true Priestly line that was passed down from father to son for centuries, down the same family tree. However, this line apparently was changed during the Roman rule in the Second Temple period, when Yeshua lived among His people. It was never supposed to be changed! The Jewish Historian Flavious Josephus tells us that when Rome ruled Jerusalem, they selected and appointed their own High Priests to perform the duties of the Priesthood in the Holy Temple in Jerusalem. The Priests, who were usurpers, preferred to trust and follow Caesar, rather than the LORD. Now this is quite interesting, and the reason I bring this to the forefront, is because, according to Josephus' account, the Jews who had been appointed by Rome as the replacement High Priests in the Holy Temple in Jerusalem, during the trial of Yeshua, were the only two Priests in the history of the lineage of the Priesthood in Jerusalem who were not in succession. In other words, this information indicates that the two Priests, *Caiaphas and Annas,* who served at Yeshua's trial, were not descendants of the true Priestly line of Phineas and Zadok. So they were not appointed by God to have the Priesthood. In order for Rome to manipulate and control Jerusalem and the Holy Temple, they apparently broke the line of succession and appointed others that they chose, for their own political gain. By giving these positions to others, who would do their bidding, the Priesthood became corrupted. The formerly unbroken genetic chain of the Priestly line of Phineas and Zadok was usurped. This explains why Yeshua said that they were a perverse and wicked generation, and John the Baptist called them a brood of vipers. They were not being good shepherds to their own people in Israel. They were bowing to Rome instead of bowing to the LORD God. These were the leaders that wanted Yeshua to die. They were afraid that if they did not appease Caesar, then Rome would take away the Holy Temple and their high positions all together. Then they feared that they would no longer be a nation if the center and heart of their religious system was taken away. Instead of turning to God for their help, and trusting in His faithfulness to their forefathers, they were clinging to whatever earthly political power they had left in Jerusalem. So this Temple was destined to be destroyed.

So now we can understand that the Holy Temple was corrupted because the Priesthood was corrupted. We can verify this because it was just before Passover when Messiah Yeshua went into the Holy Temple, and began to drive out the money changers. Yeshua was doing exactly what every Jewish person does before Passover. The LORD Messiah was, *"getting the leaven out of His Father's House!"* Leaven is a symbol for sin. So Yeshua overturned the tables spilling their corrupted worldly money, and He drove out the animals, because they were turning God's House into their own ventures for profit. Yeshua was saying, in essence, that this was the Holiest House of the LORD God Almighty. They were corrupting it by profiting off of it. They were sinning at the Father's House! The God of Israel, who is Holy, could not have any leaven in His House before Passover! Every single Jewish person gets the leaven out of their house before Passover! This ritual is still performed at Passover to this day in every observant Jewish home. Yeshua was not doing anything unusual or radical, just removing the sin and corruption from the House of God. The Bible states that even though this corruption had infiltrated Jerusalem and the Holy House of God, the LORD still used the people and circumstances to bring about His Divine will. Caiaphas (the High Priest) prophesied that, *"It was better for one man to die for all the people, instead of all of them dying."* This was because Messiah the Branch was to die for all His people, by being cut off, as part of the Eternal Covenant. The LORD, the second perfect Adam, was going to save Israel forever, along with the righteous Gentiles of the nations.

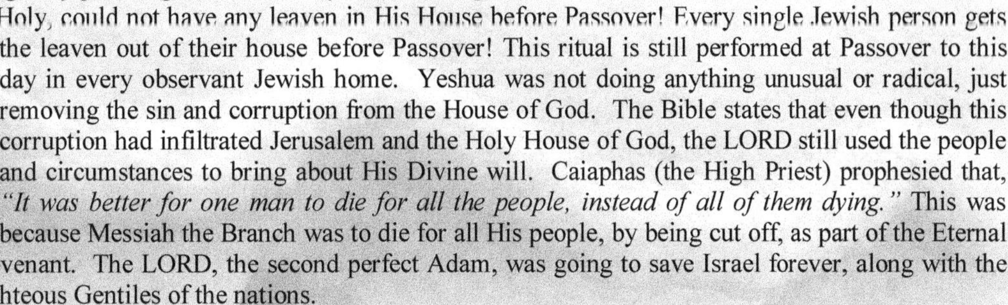

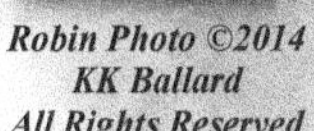

Robin Photo ©2014
KK Ballard
All Rights Reserved

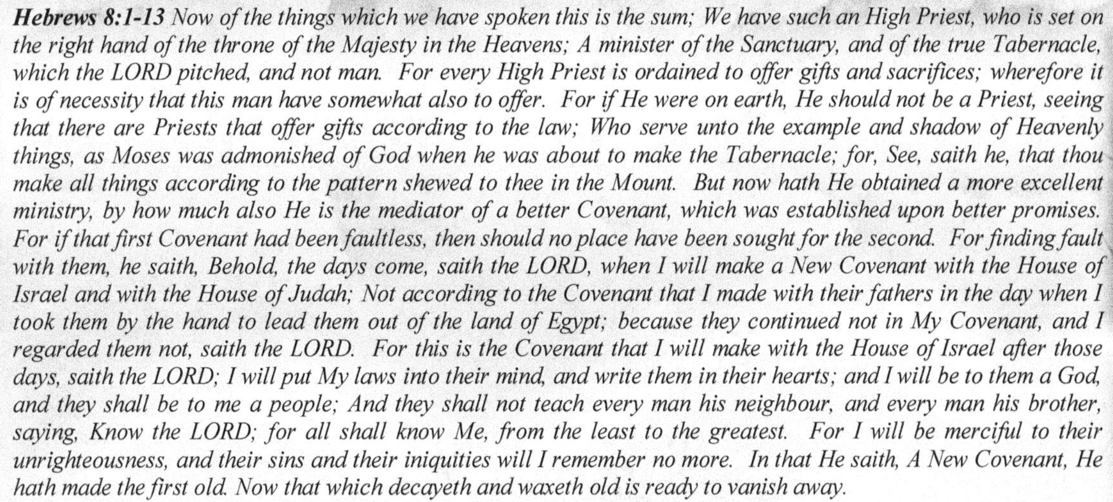

Hebrews 8:1-13 *Now of the things which we have spoken this is the sum; We have such an High Priest, who is set on the right hand of the throne of the Majesty in the Heavens; A minister of the Sanctuary, and of the true Tabernacle, which the LORD pitched, and not man. For every High Priest is ordained to offer gifts and sacrifices; wherefore it is of necessity that this man have somewhat also to offer. For if He were on earth, He should not be a Priest, seeing that there are Priests that offer gifts according to the law; Who serve unto the example and shadow of Heavenly things, as Moses was admonished of God when he was about to make the Tabernacle; for, See, saith he, that thou make all things according to the pattern shewed to thee in the Mount. But now hath He obtained a more excellent ministry, by how much also He is the mediator of a better Covenant, which was established upon better promises. For if that first Covenant had been faultless, then should no place have been sought for the second. For finding fault with them, he saith, Behold, the days come, saith the LORD, when I will make a New Covenant with the House of Israel and with the House of Judah; Not according to the Covenant that I made with their fathers in the day when I took them by the hand to lead them out of the land of Egypt; because they continued not in My Covenant, and I regarded them not, saith the LORD. For this is the Covenant that I will make with the House of Israel after those days, saith the LORD; I will put My laws into their mind, and write them in their hearts; and I will be to them a God, and they shall be to me a people; And they shall not teach every man his neighbour, and every man his brother, saying, Know the LORD; for all shall know Me, from the least to the greatest. For I will be merciful to their unrighteousness, and their sins and their iniquities will I remember no more. In that He saith, A New Covenant, He hath made the first old. Now that which decayeth and waxeth old is ready to vanish away.*

The first Covenant was under the Levitical law, but the New Eternal Covenant from the Kingdom of God that the LORD Messiah is from, is after the Heavenly Order of Melchizedek.

Hebrews 5:4-11 *And no man taketh this honour unto himself, but he that is called of God, as was Aaron. So also Messiah glorified not Himself to be made an High Priest; but He that said unto Him, Thou art My Son, today have I begotten thee. As He saith also in another place, Thou art a Priest forever after the order of Melchizedek. Who in the days of His flesh, when He had offered up prayers and supplications with strong crying and tears unto Him that was able to save Him from death, and was heard in that He feared; Though He were a Son, yet learned he obedience by the things which He suffered; And being made perfect, He became the author of eternal salvation unto all them that obey Him; Called of God an High Priest after the order of Melchizedek. Of whom we have many things to say, and hard to be uttered, seeing ye are dull of hearing.*

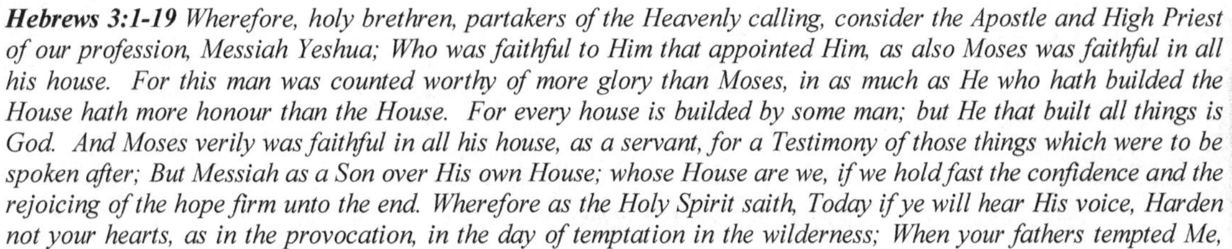

Hebrews 3:1-19 *Wherefore, holy brethren, partakers of the Heavenly calling, consider the Apostle and High Priest of our profession, Messiah Yeshua; Who was faithful to Him that appointed Him, as also Moses was faithful in all his house. For this man was counted worthy of more glory than Moses, in as much as He who hath builded the House hath more honour than the House. For every house is builded by some man; but He that built all things is God. And Moses verily was faithful in all his house, as a servant, for a Testimony of those things which were to be spoken after; But Messiah as a Son over His own House; whose House are we, if we hold fast the confidence and the rejoicing of the hope firm unto the end. Wherefore as the Holy Spirit saith, Today if ye will hear His voice, Harden not your hearts, as in the provocation, in the day of temptation in the wilderness; When your fathers tempted Me,*

proved Me, and saw My works forty years. Wherefore I was grieved with that generation, and said, They do always err in their heart; and they have not known My ways. So I sware in My wrath, They shall not enter into My rest. Take heed, brethren, lest there be in any of you an evil heart of unbelief, in departing from the Living God. But exhort one another daily, while it is called Today; lest any of you be hardened through the deceitfulness of sin. For we are made partakers of Messiah, if we hold the beginning of our confidence steadfast unto the end; While it is said, Today if ye will hear His voice, harden not your hearts, as in the provocation. For some, when they had heard, did provoke: howbeit not all that came out of Egypt by Moses. But with whom was He grieved forty years? Was it not with them that had sinned, whose carcasses fell in the wilderness? And to whom sware He that they should not enter into His rest, but to them that believed not? So we see that they could not enter in because of unbelief.

Hebrews 4:14-16 *Seeing then that we have a great High Priest, that is passed into the Heavens, Yeshua the Son of God, let us hold fast our profession. For we have not an High Priest which cannot be touched with the feeling of our infirmities; but was in all points tempted like as we are, yet without sin. Let us therefore come boldly unto the throne of grace that we may obtain mercy, and find grace to help in time of need.*

Blue jay
Photo ©2014 Kimberly K Ballard All Rights Reserved

In this summary, I showed many Scriptures that detail the *seven* points of my Divine Almond Tree revelation. Messiah is the Rod that budded and He bore the First Fruit of salvation. This is all part of the mystery of the Messiah that is encoded in the Torah, from the beginning. After my fantastic letters of correspondence with my new friend in Jerusalem, the LORD continued to manifest Himself to me. He is the magnificent Almond blossom from the Tree of Life, that is about to open in full bloom. My Almond Tree miracle made me an eyewitness of the power of the Living God. He is very much alive right now and I know that He longs for you to see His heart and His face, as the Heavenly Eternal KING OF GLORY

Almond Blossoms on Snow with Jerusalem Lions Photos ©2013 Kimberly K Ballard All Rights Reserved

MY MIRACLE ALMOND TREE BUDDING ON HOLY MOUNT MORIAH JERUSALEM!

February 16th 2007 and shown in color on the Front Cover of this book,
As it appeared by the guidance of the Invisible Assistant!
Courtesy of LV my beautiful Israeli Friend Photo ©2013 Kimberly K Ballard All Rights Reserved

Budding Almond Rods with rays ©2015 & heavy snow
Photos ©2014 Kimberly K Ballard All Rights Reserved

Isaiah 59:19 So shall they fear the Name of the LORD
from the west,
and His glory from the rising of the sun.
When the enemy shall come in like a flood,
the Spirit of the LORD
shall lift up a standard against him.

IN THE ARMS OF A TREE

A Poem by Kimberly K. Ballard

I found serenity in the arms of a Tree
In its shelter and shade
I came searching for me
Lost here - alone...returning to find
An old friend to recognize or hug me
To give me peace of mind
In its might it stood strong...unchanged and unmoved
It had shared all my days
Only it, understood
Every moment contained in its rings of wood
It was then that I realized God was just like the Tree
He was there with His Angel's to set my heart free
I found serenity in the arms of a Tree
It was God Himself...Comforting me

Written November 27th ©2000
7 Years before My Almond Tree Revelation!

The Branch Photo ©2013 Kimberly K Ballard All Rights Reserved

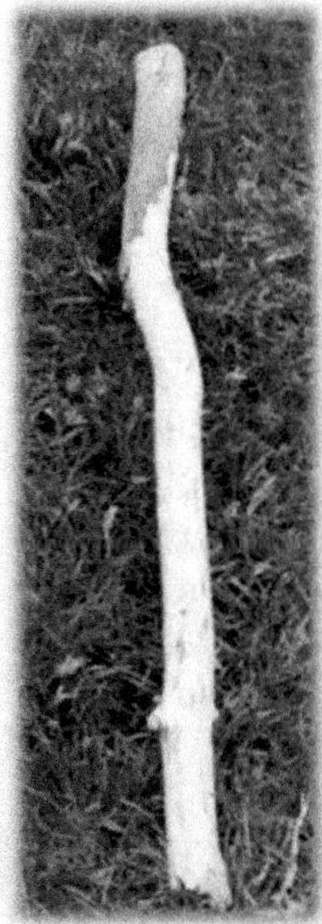

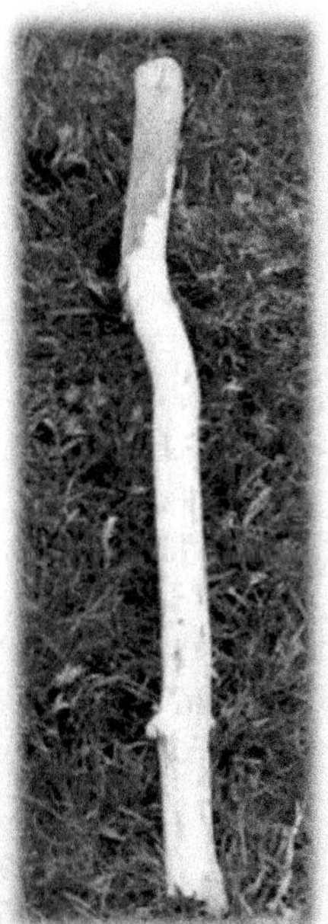

Chapter 3

THE BRANCH THE ROD MESSIAH

The Almond Rod & Snow on Junipers

The Almond tree miracle in Jerusalem made me ponder *the bitterness* of winter in Colorado while *the sweet* blossoms in Israel released their fragrant scent. It was so profound that *this tree* was resurrecting itself from winter dormancy. The ancient Jewish Prophets of Israel wrote about Messiah who was to come and they called Him, *"The Branch."* He was cut off from Israel but He was, *"raised up,"* from death to life, inside Holy Mount Moriah in Jerusalem. The depth of this story was unfolding.

Jeremiah 23:5-6 *Behold the days are coming, declares the LORD, When I shall raise up for David a righteous Branch. And He will reign as KING and act wisely, and do justice and righteousness in the land. In His days Judah will be saved, and Israel will dwell securely; and this is His Name by which He will be called, The LORD is our Righteousness.*

Yeshua taught the Torah, *the Law of Moses and the Prophets* in the Holy Temple and the surrounding synagogues around the Holy Land of Israel. Yeshua has the title, *"The LORD, the Rabbi of Righteousness."* During His earthly visitation, *the Branch* revealed to the children of Israel that the Scriptures were fulfilled within their hearing. They were eyewitnesses of His Divine miracles. Yeshua entered the Holy Temple on Holy Mount Moriah on the LORD'S Feast Days and revealed His identity to them as, *"The God of the Living."* Every sign and miracle Messiah Yeshua performed proved He is the Eternal Almond Rod of the God of Israel. So it became apparent that when *the Branch* was cut off, the LORD was able to graft Himself back into the tree, as though He had never died, thus proving He is not the god of the dead.

The First Almond Branch

Isaiah 11:1-10 *And there shall come forth a Rod out of the stem of Jesse, and a Branch shall grow out of His roots; And the Spirit of the LORD shall rest upon Him, the spirit of wisdom and understanding, the spirit of counsel and might, the spirit of knowledge and of the fear of the LORD; And shall make Him of quick understanding in the fear of the LORD; and He shall not judge after the sight of His eyes, neither reprove after the hearing of His ears; But with righteousness shall he judge the poor, and reprove with equity for the meek of the earth; and He shall smite the earth with the rod of His mouth, and with the breath of His lips shall He slay the wicked. And righteousness shall be the girdle of His loins, and faithfulness the girdle of His reins. The wolf also shall dwell with the lamb, and the leopard shall lie down* *with the kid; and the calf and the young lion and the fatling together; and a little child shall lead them. And the cow and the bear shall feed; their young ones shall lie down together; and the lion shall eat straw like the ox. And the sucking child shall play on the hole of the asp, and the weaned child shall put his hand on the cockatrice' den. They shall not hurt nor destroy in My entire Holy Mountain; for the earth shall be full of the knowledge of the LORD, as the waters cover the sea. And in that day there shall be a root of Jesse, which shall stand for an ensign of the people; to it shall the Gentiles seek; and His rest shall be glorious.*

As I pondered the leaves of the trees whirling in the wind to the ground in the fall, I could see how our earthly bodies perish like they do, yet new leaves sprout to life the following spring. This Heavenly Almond Tree was apparently allowing us to be *grafted into it* so we can become one with it. We inherit resurrected bodies like newly sprouted leaves that never die. This is an Eternal Living Tree in the Garden of God. Even the Gentiles would seek *"The Branch, the Rod raised up." I believe Isaiah wrote of* Messiah Yeshua as *the Almond Branch bearing the beautiful fruit that is glorious.* He is the pride and adornment of Israel.

Isaiah 4:2 *In that day the Branch of the LORD will be beautiful and glorious, and the fruit of the earth will be the pride and the adornment of the survivors of Israel.*

Job wrote that *God has a Rod* that He uses upon men! This Rod, the Messiah of Israel, brings salvation and correction through the Living Torah.

Job 21:9 *Their houses are safe from fear, neither is the Rod of God upon them.*

NAZARETH, NAZARENE, NAZARITE

A Nazarite who takes a vow to God does not cut his hair
Hair Photos ©2013 Kimberly K Ballard All Rights Reserved

Jesse was the father of King David. As a descendant of King David, Messiah Yeshua is Royalty, the Sovereign of Israel. He is *the green shoot of Jesse,* raised in Nazareth.

"Nazareth," is derived from the Hebrew word, *"Nêtser,"* which also happens to mean, *"A green shoot, a branch, a descendant."* The primary root word of, *"Nêtser"* is, *"Natsar"* and it means, *"A hidden thing, to conceal."* In other words, the Messiah of Israel is revealed as *a hidden mystery,* concealed within the Torah of God.

A green Shoot of Jesse – A Second Almond Branch
Photo ©2013 Kimberly K Ballard All Rights Reserved

From Strong's Concordance; #5342 **Nêtser,** ***nay'-tser;*** from 5341 in the sense of greenness as a striking color; a shoot; fig. a descendant; Branch. #5341 **NÂtsar,** ***naw-tsar;*** a prim. Root; to guard, in a good sense (to protect, maintain, obey, etc.) or a bad one (to conceal, etc.):- besieged, hidden thing, keep (-er, -ing), monument, observe (-r), subtil, watcher (-man). ***(Source: ©1995 Strong's Exhaustive Concordance).***

Zechariah the Prophet reveals that Messiah, called *"The Branch," will come as a humble servant.* Yeshua removed the iniquity of the Land of Israel in one day, just as it is written. A Nazarite does not cut his hair when he is *set apart* for the LORD.

***Zechariah 3:8-10** Hear now, O Joshua the High Priest, thou, and thy fellows that sit before thee; for they are men wondered at; for, behold, I will bring forth My servant the BRANCH. For behold the stone that I have laid before Joshua; upon one stone shall be seven eyes; behold, I will engrave the graving thereof, saith the LORD of Hosts, and I will remove the iniquity of that land in one day. In that day, saith the LORD of Hosts, shall ye call every man his neighbor under the vine and under the fig tree.*

The Second Branch
Photo ©2013 Kimberly K Ballard

***Matthew 2:23** And he came and dwelt in a city called Nazareth; that it might be fulfilled which was spoken by the Prophets, He shall be called a Nazarene.*

Within the Holy Temple of the LORD in Jerusalem, a special place was designated for the *Nazarite. I believe this is because it pertains to the LORD God as* Messiah Yeshua. The Nazarite must bring *the sin offering and the elevation offering.* Yeshua became the Lamb of the sin offering as He was elevated. Yeshua abstained from drinking wine again until He drinks it in the Kingdom of Heaven. There will never be another Branch *raised up* for David that will bring Eternal salvation to the children of Israel. Yeshua the Rod gives Eternal life to all that believe in Him by faith. He is the power of God.

THE NAME OF MESSIAH THE BRANCH WAS FORETOLD

Branches & Sugar-Pinecones
Photos ©2013 Kimberly K Ballard All Rights Reserved

Before it was fulfilled, Zechariah the Prophet revealed the name of, *"The Branch."* The LORD said, *"To place the Crown on the one named Joshua."* So Messiah Yeshua was a vision and a prophetic Word from the LORD. God became our Joshua/Yeshua! He would one day wear the Royal Crown, as Israel's final KING of Judah, and restore the Davidic Dynasty into an everlasting Sovereignty.

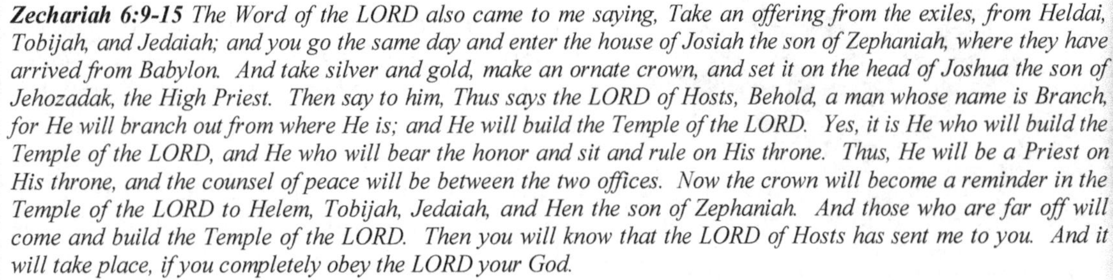

***Zechariah 6:9-15** The Word of the LORD also came to me saying, Take an offering from the exiles, from Heldai, Tobijah, and Jedaiah; and you go the same day and enter the house of Josiah the son of Zephaniah, where they have arrived from Babylon. And take silver and gold, make an ornate crown, and set it on the head of Joshua the son of Jehozadak, the High Priest. Then say to him, Thus says the LORD of Hosts, Behold, a man whose name is Branch, for He will branch out from where He is; and He will build the Temple of the LORD. Yes, it is He who will build the Temple of the LORD, and He who will bear the honor and sit and rule on His throne. Thus, He will be a Priest on His throne, and the counsel of peace will be between the two offices. Now the crown will become a reminder in the Temple of the LORD to Helem, Tobijah, Jedaiah, and Hen the son of Zephaniah. And those who are far off will come and build the Temple of the LORD. Then you will know that the LORD of Hosts has sent me to you. And it will take place, if you completely obey the LORD your God.*

In the history of Israel, a King never served in the role of High Priest. Even King David appointed Zadok and Abiathar as his righteous High Priests, and they were great Mighty Man of Valour. The Rod of God reigns forever as a KING, a High Priest, and as a *Mighty Man of Valour* in the Heavenly Holy Temple, in the Eternal Kingdom of God. The Mighty Men were renowned for their skill in battle. They were loyal to the extreme. I believe the LORD miraculously showed me exactly where Zadok is buried, and I sent this information to Israel.

This grave reveals the true location of King David's grave. Ironically the day before I sent it (June 3rd 2014), in the city of David, they anointed the place near the Gihon where Zadok anointed Solomon as the King of Israel! The LORD was telling me to send the information!

The prophecy proclaims that Messiah will *"Branch out"* and descend from Heaven. His Saints, are like bricks of living stone in the Heavenly Temple that the LORD God built without the hands of men. Messiah Yeshua is the cornerstone who returns to dwell in our midst forever, reigning in Jerusalem that will be restored to Paradise. Stones are placed on Jewish graves but one day the graves will be opened, and the Saints like living stones, will rise to dwell with the LORD God forever. Soon Zadok the Priest and King David will rise!

THE BRANCH FROM THE ALMOND TREE OF LIFE

Almond Tree & Almond Rods & Meyer Lemon Blossoms
Photos ©2013 & 2014 Kimberly K Ballard All Rights Reserved

If you study the structure of a tree, you will find that the LORD God is hidden within the fine details of the various elements of the tree. This is what I discovered later while I was researching the details about the Almond Tree after my miracle transpired in Jerusalem.

Cherry Tree Blossoming
Photo ©2013 Kimberly K Ballard All Rights Reserved

By definition, *the branch* of a tree *divides and makes the tree cleft.* As we will see, this is the LORD'S signature on all His works. Now that Yeshua is revealed in the Fruitful Branch, from the Almond Tree of Life, there is more!

The circular growth rings on a tree show *the life cycle* of a tree and the rings are symbolic of *Eternal life.* Messiah, *the Jewish Tree of life*, gives us Eternal life, and He creates *the life cycle that is considered so sacred that it is revered in Judaism.*

On Rosh HaShanah, the Challah bread is shaped like a crown to honour the LORD God as the KING of Israel. It represents *the circle of life.* I will prove to you later that Yeshua is the Royal Jewish KING, who was born on Rosh HaShanah, and He wears this Royal crown. The Messiah is the Bread of Life, and the Bread offering of Heaven. It is interesting that sometimes instead of a crown the Challah Bread is made into the shape of a bird. This reminds me of the Holy Spirit descending in the form of a dove upon KING Yeshua in the Jordan River, when Heaven was opened. The Branch from the Tree of Life is also *the Bridegroom,* who gives His bride *a betrothal ring of Eternal life,* as a gift. So Yeshua is pictured in *"the crown"* of the tree which is the portion of the tree from *"the first branch"* to the top of the tree. Messiah Yeshua is *the first Branch* that allows us to ascend up into Heaven.

The crown of an Almond Tree & leaves
Photo ©2013 Kimberly K Ballard
All Rights Reserved

Next, at the center core of the wood of a tree is what is known as *"the heartwood."* This brings to mind that the LORD'S heart is deep within His Word, the Living Torah, which is the Tree of Life. Yeshua's Eternal Testimony is *the Covenant of the heart.* Whoever diligently seeks the KINGS heart will find it at *the core* of the Almond Tree of Life. The secret of God is revealed within this tree.

Now there is another part of a tree called the *"cambium"* and it helps to heal any wounds on the tree. Yeshua performed many miracles in Israel healing the sick and the wounded. Remember that Isaiah prophesied that by the Messiah's wounds or stripes, we are healed.

The outer portion of a tree called the *"sapwood"* stores water and minerals. It sustains the tree keeping it alive and healthy. As water rises up through the main trunk of the tree, it spreads out into all its branches and nourishes every leaf, feeding them the proper amount of water and minerals. Likewise, the Almond Tree of Life contains *the Living Water that sustains us.* We are the branches and the leaves of His Almond Tree of Life. He causes us to flourish with His *vibrant life.* Yeshua actually declared that this is what He came to do for us!

John 10:10 *The thief cometh not, but for to steal, and to kill, and to destroy; I AM come that they might have life, and that they might have it more abundantly.*

The most remarkable feature in the structure of a tree is found in the *surface of the bark.* This part of the tree is *decay resistant.* King David had prophesied that the Messiah's body would not see decay. King David died and his own body decayed, as it is written in the book of the Acts of the Jewish Apostles (Acts 13:36). However, Messiah Yeshua's body did not see decay proving that He is indeed the Living Branch from the Almond Tree of Life.

A Cherry Tree Blossoming Photo ©2013 Kimberly K Ballard All Rights Reserved

Needless to say, it was impossible to keep Him in the grave because the Holy Spirit of Life was inside Him. He had the power to resurrect Himself to life again, offering us the First fruit from the Almond Tree of Life. We could then dwell forever with Him in the Garden of Heaven!

Psalm 16:10 *For Thou wilt not leave my soul in hell; neither wilt Thou suffer Thine Holy One to see corruption.*

Acts 13:33-37 *God hath fulfilled the same unto us their children, in that He hath raised up Yeshua again; as it is also written in the second Psalm, Thou art My Son, this day have I begotten Thee. And as concerning that He raised Him up from the dead, now no more to return to corruption, He said on this wise, I will give you the sure mercies of David. Wherefore He saith also in another Psalm, Thou shalt not suffer Thine Holy One to see corruption. For David, after he had served his own generation by the will of God, fell on sleep, and was laid unto his fathers, and saw corruption; But He, whom God raised again, saw no corruption.*

Jeremiah prophesied that Yeshua would spring forth. The day this was to be fulfilled, Jeremiah said, *"He shall be called; the LORD is our righteousness."*

Jeremiah 33:15 *In those days and at that time I will cause a righteous Branch of David to spring forth; and He shall execute justice and righteousness on the earth, In those days Judah shall be saved, and Jerusalem shall dwell in safety; and this is the Name by which He shall be called; the LORD is our righteousness.*

By definition the word *"spring"* means *"to come or to appear suddenly."* When Yeshua appeared to Israel, He was suddenly in the Holy Temple in Jerusalem declaring His identity to them, but many were not prepared or ready to meet Him. They did not know the hour of their visitation. John the Baptist, the son of the true High Priest, was sent as the messenger by the LORD God to prepare the way before His arrival as our *Yeshua/Joshua.*

Spring A Cherry Tree Blossoming Photo ©2013 Kimberly K Ballard All Rights Reserved

Malachi 3:1-3 *Behold, I will send My messenger, and he shall prepare the way before Me; and the LORD, whom ye seek, shall suddenly come to His Temple, and even the messenger of the Covenant, whom ye delight in; behold, He shall come, saith the LORD of Hosts. But who may abide the day of His coming? And who shall stand when He appeareth? For He is like a refiner's fire, and like fuller's soap; And He shall sit as a refiner and purifier of silver; and He shall purify the sons of Levi, and purge them as gold and silver, that they may offer unto the LORD an offering in righteousness.*

A Cherry Tree Blossoming Photo ©2013 Kimberly K Ballard All Rights Reserved

Isaiah prophesied that *"the Branch, would bear fruit and that the Spirit of the LORD would rest upon Him."* This was fulfilled when Yeshua was baptized in the Jordan River by John the Baptist. When John said to Yeshua, *"You come to me to be baptized?"* Yeshua replied, *"We must fulfill all righteousness."* The Holy Spirit rested and remained in Yeshua whose body was *a sacred holy vessel to expiate our sins.* If a rooster can become *a sacred holy vessel* in the Jewish Kapparot ceremony to expiate the sins of man, then surely *the Messiah's body is a far greater sacred holy vessel for this same Divine purpose!* This was just one more miraculous sign that *the LORD God had indeed arrived in Israel!*

John 1:32-34 *And John bare record, saying, I saw the Spirit descending from Heaven like a dove, and it abode upon Him. And I knew Him not; but He that sent me to baptize with water, the same said unto me, upon whom thou shalt see the Spirit descending, and remaining on Him, the same is He which baptizeth with the Holy Spirit. And I saw, and bare record that this is the Son of God.*

Thousands of Hebrews listened and obeyed this Word from the LORD. They prepared themselves to meet Him as He came to dwell in their midst but many did not listen. So they were not ready when the LORD *suddenly appeared* as their Yeshua, teaching Torah in His Holy Temple. Yeshua revealed that He is far greater than Jonah who brought the Gentiles to repentance, so they would only worship the one true Living God of Israel instead of false gods.

Matthew 12:41 *The men of Nineveh shall rise in judgment with this generation, and shall condemn it; Because they repented at the preaching of Jonah; and, behold, a greater than Jonah is here.*

Messiah the Rod of God justifies every believer. *The LORD alone fulfills the complete and perfect righteousness of His Law.* Why could we not be justified to Eternal Life by the Law of Moses? Every person tried to obtain righteousness through their own earthly deeds, by trying to keep the whole Law. However, no matter how hard mankind tried to keep every single aspect of the Law in righteousness, they could not ever achieve it. The sin of failing to keep the entire Law *perfectly* only guarantees you death. Therefore, no one could ever be justified by human self–righteousness. However, through the LORD'S Holy Spirit abiding in us, we can obtain *His righteousness that is perfection of the Law that gives us life,* through grace and mercy. This is why the New Testament says that the Law of Moses brought death. If you were circumcised and yet failed to keep the Law, then it rendered this Covenant useless. The circumcised Messiah circumcises our hearts with His Holy Spirit, the perfection of the Law.

A Cherry Tree Blossoming Photo ©2013 Kimberly K Ballard All Rights Reserved

Acts 13:38-42 *Be it known unto you therefore, men and brethren, that through this man is preached unto you the forgiveness of sins; And by Him all that believe are justified from all things, from which ye could not be justified by the Law of Moses. Beware therefore, lest that come upon you, which is spoken of in the Prophets; Behold, ye despisers, and wonder, and perish; for I work a work in your days, a work which ye shall in no wise believe, though a man declare it unto you. And when the Jews were gone out of the Synagogue, the Gentiles besought that these words might be preached to them the next Sabbath.*

Since there was no person on earth that could keep the Law perfectly, the LORD God of Israel had to intervene by sending His Rod, the Messiah from Heaven. Yeshua had no sin and was *perfect in righteousness* as the Son, in the vessel of flesh, as the second perfect Adam. *The true circumcision is of the heart, as He writes the Living Torah upon our hearts.* In this way, He restores us to the Garden like it was in Eden. The Living Branch from the Almond Tree of Life is the Covenant that saved us from the curse of death, through the sinless and spotless Lamb, God provided. All of us have failed as human beings to keep the whole Law of God. We are renewed to His righteousness, by the power of His Holy Spirit in baptism. If we abide in Him, through the washing of His baptism, then we have obtained the forgiveness of our sins. Therefore, the Law of the LORD stands to perfection, *but it is only obtained through the Righteous Branch.* Through Him we are saved and forgiven and thereby restored into a relationship with the LORD God forever. This is *the grace* of God's heart whereby He saved us. We are instructed to turn away from sin and from all unrighteousness and we are to repent before the LORD. We are then to be baptized and washed in the Living Water of His baptism. In this way, our filthy garments are purified and this prepares us to meet the LORD face to face. There is absolutely no other way on earth to obtain true righteousness and Eternal life, except through the LORD'S Living Almond Rod that budded! Yeshua made it clear that we can only go to the Father through Him, *the Righteous Rod of God.*

John 14:6 *Yeshua saith unto him, I AM the way, the truth, and the life; no man cometh unto the Father, but by Me.*

John 1:17-18 *For the Law was given by Moses, but grace and truth came by Yeshua Messiah. No man hath seen God at any time; the only begotten Son, which is in the bosom of the Father, He hath declared Him.*

John 1:12-14 *But as many as received Him, to them gave He power to become the sons of God, even to them that believe on His Name; Which were born, not of blood, nor of the will of the flesh, nor of the will of man, but of God. And the Word was made flesh, and dwelt among us, and we beheld His glory, the glory as of the only begotten of the Father, full of grace and truth.*

THE ROD PERFORMED SIGNS AND MIRACLES

The Almond Rod & Rappahannock River Virginia with Tree Photo ©2013 Kimberly K Ballard All Rights Reserved

The Almond rod of Aaron and Moses came to life because the power of God's Spirit or Ruach was upon it. It truly represents our resurrection through His Holy Spirit.

Now it is interesting that the LORD God declared unto Moses that *it was with the rod in his hand that he would perform signs of the LORD* before the children of Israel at the Red Sea and in the wilderness. In this way, they would recognize the identity of the only true Living LORD God who created the entire universe.

Exodus 4:17 *And thou shalt take this rod in thine hand, wherewith thou shalt do signs.*

Deuteronomy 6:22 *And the LORD shewed signs and wonders, great and sore, upon Egypt, upon Pharaoh, and upon all his household, before our eyes.*

Aaron's earthly rod would be a sign of the future fulfillment of Messiah Yeshua the Heavenly Rod in the hand of God who saved Israel in the past. Many times He used His Rod to bring them salvation. So it was evident that the everlasting salvation of the LORD would come to all of us, as *God manifested Himself to us in His own Rod of salvation called, "Messiah Yeshua, the Branch."* With this Heavenly Rod, He had a preordained plan to save Israel and the world forever. The power of His Testimony was so strong Satan could not prevail against it.

The Rod that was stretched out over the Red Sea saved Israel from Pharaoh and his mighty army and the Rod also provided bread for them when they were hungry and provided living water to drink, when they were thirsty. The LORD guided Israel with this Rod in His outstretched arm. His glorious right hand held His Rod and went before the children of Israel. The Rod that Moses used in his hand was in truth referred to as, *"The Rod of God."*

Exodus 4:20 *And Moses took his wife and his sons, and set them upon an ass, and he returned to the land of Egypt; and Moses took the Rod of God in his hand.*

This Rod was specifically for the purpose of performing *the signs of the LORD* before men, so they could see the mighty works of the LORD and understand that He alone is God. Messiah the Rod was sent from Heaven to dwell with us, to perform the signs, miracles, and wonders before men, so we would also understand that He alone is God who saved us forever.

The Messiah was therefore glorified through His mighty works, because they reveal that He is genuinely, the one and only LORD God of Israel.

John 13:31-32 *Therefore, when he was gone out, Yeshua said, Now is the Son of man glorified, and God is glorified in Him. If God be glorified in Him, God shall also glorify Him in Himself, and shall straightway glorify Him.*

This Rod was used for the same reason as a *Testimony* before the Pharaoh of Egypt, so he would believe that there is only one true Living God. Through the Rod in the hand of the Good Shepherd, all the flocks of Israel and the righteous Gentiles will be gathered to the LORD. This gives us new understanding when we read the following Proverb.

Proverbs 13:24 *He that spareth his rod hateth his son; but he that loveth him chasteneth him betimes.*

The Rod is the instrument of love that God uses to correct His people and it is *the Word of God.* The Good Shepherd keeps His flocks on the right path with His Rod. He directs all their steps, so they do not fall, and because the LORD loved Israel, He did not spare His Rod, *Yeshua* on them. This is the purpose of the death of the Messiah. The Messiah, the cut off Almond Branch, had to die to save us, demonstrating His love for all His creation. God has chastened us in love with His Rod, to bring His entire flock back to Him. The LORD also used His Rod to create the Heavens and the earth and every living thing. If we abide in the Rod of God that is full of His Ruach/Holy Spirit, then the life of the LORD abides inside us and we will be raised from death to life, like Yeshua.

The Rod of Moses Photo ©2013 Kimberly K Ballard All Rights Reserved

Now the truth is that when Yeshua was here, He performed all the signs, miracles and wonders revealing that He is the Rod in the right hand of the God of Israel. The signs and miracles that Yeshua performed not only reveal that He is the LORD God, but they uniquely qualify Yeshua to be the Eternal *KING Messiah of Israel.* As we believe in the power of the Rod of God and are baptized in His Mikveh of Living Water, we receive His Holy Spirit of Life by faith. After being purified in this way, we then have His power abiding within us to perform miracles and signs in His Name. This is only possible if we truly abide in Him in righteousness and walk with the LORD, like Noah walked with God. By faith, Noah was given salvation by the LORD! Although the Kingdom of God had come to Israel at the time of the Second Temple, many in Israel did not believe these signs and miracles of the LORD that Yeshua performed before their eyes. The undeniable truth is, however, that all the signs that Aaron performed with the Rod of God are *the very same signs* that Yeshua performed *as the Rod of God.* The LORD is the only one with the power to heal the sick and raise the dead. Yeshua gave sight to those born blind. He made the deaf hear, healed the lame, and raised the dead. The Rod of God restored their corrupted flesh and brought life to it again. So what did Messiah Yeshua tell the unbelieving in Israel about this? He told them that, *"Unless they saw signs and wonders they would not believe Him!"* Even though He was repeatedly performing the miracles of the LORD of Hosts before their eyes, they still questioned whether or not He was *sent* from Heaven. They had been given *the Torah* by God.

So above everyone else in the world, they should have recognized that this was *the sign* that the LORD had given to Moses. *This was His Living Rod! They should have seen that Rabbi Yeshua was the LORD God of Israel!* It was so evident in the miracles and signs that they were witnessing with their own eyes!

John 4:48 *Then said Yeshua unto him, Except ye see signs and wonders, ye will not believe.*

Luke 11:16 *And others, tempting Him sought of Him a sign from Heaven.*

John 6:25-26 *And when they had found Him on the other side of the sea, they said unto Him, Rabbi, when camest thou hither? Yeshua answered them and said, Verily, verily, I say unto you, Ye seek me, not because ye saw the miracles, but because ye did eat of the loaves, and were filled. Labour not for the meat which perisheth, but for that meat which endureth unto everlasting life, which the Son of Man shall give unto you; for him hath God the Father sealed. Then said they unto Him, What shall we do, that we might work the works of God? Yeshua answered and said unto them, This is the work of God, that ye believe on Him whom He hath sent. They said therefore unto Him, What sign shewest Thou then, that we may see, and believe Thee? What dost Thou work?*

In the following Scripture, there is a profound and overlooked statement. As Yeshua raised the young man from death to life, the people of Israel witnessed it and they said that *"God hath visited His people,"* verifying that they understood that Yeshua is the Rod of God that performs the mighty works of God.

Luke 7:12-16 *Now when He came nigh to the gate of the city, behold, there was a dead man carried out, the only son of his mother, and she was a widow; and much people of the city was with her. And when the LORD saw her, He had compassion on her, and said unto her, Weep not, And He came and touched the bier; and they that bare him stood still. And He said, Young man, I say unto thee, Arise. And he that was dead sat up, and began to speak. And He delivered him to his mother. And there came a fear on all; and they glorified God, saying, That a great Prophet is risen up among us; and, <u>That God hath visited His people.</u>*

Cherry Blossoms Photo ©2014 Kimberly K Ballard All Rights Reserved

Psalm 30:2-3 *O LORD my God, I cried unto Thee, and Thou hast healed me. O LORD, Thou hast brought my soul from the grave; Thou hast kept me alive, that I should not go down to the pit.*

On another occasion, Messiah Yeshua resurrected a young damsel and they laughed at Him to scorn, because they were in disbelief that He was *the Rod of God,* until the moment that she arose and walked before them alive again! They saw this *sign* as eyewitnesses and understood that this miracle was performed by the hand of God!

Mark 5:38-6:2 *And He cometh to the house of the ruler of the Synagogue, and seeth the tumult, and them that wept and wailed greatly. And when He was come in, He saith unto them, Why make ye this ado, and weep? The damsel is not dead, but sleepeth. And they laughed at Him to scorn. But when He had put them all out, He taketh the father and the mother of the damsel, and them that were with Him, and entereth in where the damsel was lying. And He took the damsel by the hand, and said unto her, Talitha cumi; which is, being interpreted, Damsel, I say unto thee, arise. And straightway the damsel arose, and walked; for she was of the age of twelve years. And they were astonished with a great astonishment. And He charged them straightly that no man should know it; and commanded that something should be given her to eat. And He went out from thence, and came into His own country; and His disciples follow Him. And when the Sabbath day was come, He began to teach in the Synagogue; and many hearing*

Him were astonished, saying, From whence hath this man these things? And what wisdom is this which is given unto Him, that even such mighty works are wrought by His hands?

As this elaborate work was *wrought by the hand of the Rod of God,* they were all astonished. The people wondered at these marvelous things that Yeshua did before them. So it was evident in all these miracles that Yeshua is the Rod embodying the power of God.

MOSES AND AARON'S ROD TURNED WATER TO BLOOD MESSIAH THE ROD THE WATER AND THE BLOOD

The Almond Rod of Aaron & blood red water

One of the most powerful miracles of the LORD was observed when the rod struck the waters and turned them to blood, in the sight of Pharaoh of Egypt. The LORD had said, *"That by this sign you will know that, I AM the LORD."* These signs were also performed by the LORD'S Ruach/Spirit on the Rod. In this specific miracle, the LORD revealed Himself as the creator of the universe, simply by changing the elements of life. The water that sustains life on the earth could only be changed into the element of blood that gives life by the one that created life in the first place, by the LORD God Almighty. The life blood already contains a high percentage of water. Pharaoh saw this miracle with his own eyes, but his heart was hardened and he would not accept it. Pharaoh thought of himself as a god, but neither he nor his magicians, could copy the mighty powerful works of the one true Living God of Israel. This would be a bit like man trying to create a beautiful flower and all he can create is an artificial silk flower that has *no life* in it. That was Pharaoh at his best! Pharaoh was only a cheap imitator. The LORD God could create all the elements needed to give the flower life. His glory was revealed when He gave the flower beauty, fragrance, and the ability to reproduce by the seed of life that He placed inside them. Because the LORD said, *"That by this sign, we would know that He is, I AM, the LORD,"* then it should not surprise us that Yeshua performed this very sign when He turned water into wine in Cana of Galilee, *that represented His own life blood of the Eternal Covenant.* Remember that when Moses used the rod, the power of God was upon the rod in his hand. Here is the account of Moses turning the water into blood.

Exodus 7:13-25 *And he hardened Pharaoh's heart that he hearkened not unto them; as the LORD had said. And the LORD said unto Moses, Pharaoh's heart is hardened; he refuseth to let the people go. Get thee unto Pharaoh in the morning; lo, he goeth out unto the water; and thou shalt stand by the river's brink against he come; and the rod which was turned to a serpent shalt thou take in thine hand. And thou shalt say unto him, The LORD God of the Hebrews hath sent me unto thee, saying, Let my people go, that they may serve me in the wilderness; and, behold, hitherto thou wouldest not hear. Thus saith the LORD; in this thou shalt know that I AM the LORD; behold, I will smite with the rod that is in mine hand upon the waters which are in the river, and they shall be turned to blood. And the fish that is in the river shall die, and the river shall stink; and the Egyptians shall loathe to drink of the water of the river. And the LORD spake unto Moses, Say unto Aaron, Take thy rod, and stretch out thine hand upon* *the waters of Egypt, upon their streams, upon their rivers, and upon their ponds, and upon all their pools of water, that they may become blood; and that there may be blood throughout all the land of Egypt, both in vessels of wood, and in vessels of stone. And Moses and Aaron did so, as the LORD commanded; and he lifted up the rod, and smote the waters that were in the river, in the sight of Pharaoh, and in the sight of his servants; and all the waters that were in the river were turned to blood. And the fish that was in the river died; and the river stank, and the Egyptians could not drink of the water of the river; and there was blood throughout all the land of Egypt. And the magicians of Egypt did so with their enchantments; and Pharaoh's heart was hardened, neither did he hearken unto them; as the LORD had said. And Pharaoh turned and went into his house, neither did he set his heart to this also. And all the Egyptians dug round about the river for water to drink; for they could not drink of the water of the river. And seven days were fulfilled, after that the LORD had smitten the river.*

River Photo ©2013 Kimberly K Ballard

In this historical record, the LORD actually revealed that He is the God of creation, by *allowing the water to remain blood for seven days*. Although both the water and the blood give life, *the LORD took the element of life away* by turning one element of His creation into another element of His creation, and through this act, *He revealed that He has the power over death and life, through His Rod!* The Holy Spirit breathes life into us. The water and the blood have God's breath of life in them, but the *oxygen, the breath of life in this sign,* was removed by the power of *the Holy Spirit* on the Rod of God! So all the fish died when the water turned to blood and everything decayed.

Yeshua performed His first miracle in Cana of Galilee. Now there is more to the wedding in Cana in a later chapter, but it is mentioned here, because it pertains to the specific sign that was given to Moses by the LORD. It is interesting that in this miracle, there were six stone water jars filled with water. When the wedding guests had run out of wine, *Yeshua turned the water in the six stone vessels, into wine.* Remember that when Moses struck the river with the rod, not only did the water in the river turn to blood, *but all the water in the stone vessels also turned to blood* and the people could not drink it. The six stone vessels in Cana represented that Yeshua is the Rod of God who created all things in six days and on the seventh day, He rested. Yeshua was the seventh vessel of Living Water in this miracle and they all drank the best wine that He created, as they attended the wedding. *The seventh day will be like our wedding feast with the LORD.* Messiah is the Bridegroom of Israel. Yeshua's first miracle at the wedding feast in Cana, took place on the third day. He brought us Eternal life on the third day and during the Passover Seder, the wine in the third cup, represents the betrothal of the LORD'S bride to Himself, through Messiah's *life blood* Covenant. This is why the first miracle that Yeshua performed as the Rod of God was to change the water into wine.

Yeshua said that He will raise Israel up on the third day to live in His Presence and this is when the wedding will take place. Remember that Messiah Yeshua told the Priests in the Holy Temple that He is the one who will build the Temple in three days. *The prophecy in Hosea said that the LORD would revive Israel in two days and on the third day He would raise her up and usher in the Kingdom of God.* This truth was revealed in the wedding in Cana. It was during this first miracle on the third day, that the Israelites, who were at the wedding in Cana, declared that *the Bridegroom had saved the best wine for last.* This indicated that when the LORD Messiah comes in His glory, He will serve the best wine at the marriage supper of the Lamb. The Scripture tells us that this miracle in Cana was the *"beginning"* of all the miracles that Yeshua performed. The LORD Messiah is the *beginning and the end* of all things. This is absolutely amazing isn't it, because Yeshua revealed *the beginning* of creation by performing the miracle of the Rod turning the water into wine in the six stone vessels. Yeshua paid the Bride's price for Israel. At the wedding, He manifested His glory and they believed on Him. They understood that all these *signs* pertained to what Moses had written thousands of years ago when he revealed that the rod performs the work of the one called, *"I AM, the LORD."* He is the Living Water that purifies us, containing His breath of life and His life blood that causes us to live forever. In the chapter on Yeshua's miracles, we will look at more facts pertaining to this miracle in Cana.

John 2:1-11 *And the third day there was a marriage in Cana of Galilee; and the mother of Yeshua was there; and both Yeshua was called, and His disciples, to the marriage. And when they wanted wine, the mother of Yeshua saith unto Him, they have no wine. Yeshua saith unto her, Woman, what have I to do with thee? Mine hour is not yet come. His mother saith unto the servants, Whatsoever He saith unto you, do it. And there were set there six water pots of stone, after the manner of the purifying of the Jews, containing two or three firkins apiece. Yeshua saith unto them, Fill the water pots with water. And they filled them up to the brim. And he saith unto them, Draw out now, and bear unto the governor of the feast. And they bare it. When the ruler of the feast had tasted the water that was made wine, and knew not whence it was; but the servants which drew the water knew; the governor of the feast called the bridegroom, And saith unto him, Every man at the beginning doth set forth good wine; and when men have well drunk, then that which is worse; but thou hast kept the good wine until now. This beginning of miracles did Yeshua in Cana of Galilee, and manifested forth His glory; and His disciples believed on Him.*

John 4:46 *So Yeshua came again into Cana of Galilee, where He made the water wine. And there was a certain nobleman, whose son was sick at Capernaum.*

Mark 14:24-25 *And He said unto them, This is My blood of the New Testament, which is shed for many. Verily I say unto you, I will drink no more of the fruit of the vine, until that day that I drink it new in the Kingdom of God.*

There was another time that the Rod Yeshua performed the miracle of *turning water to blood.* It happened in the Garden of Gethsemane, upon the Mount of Olives.

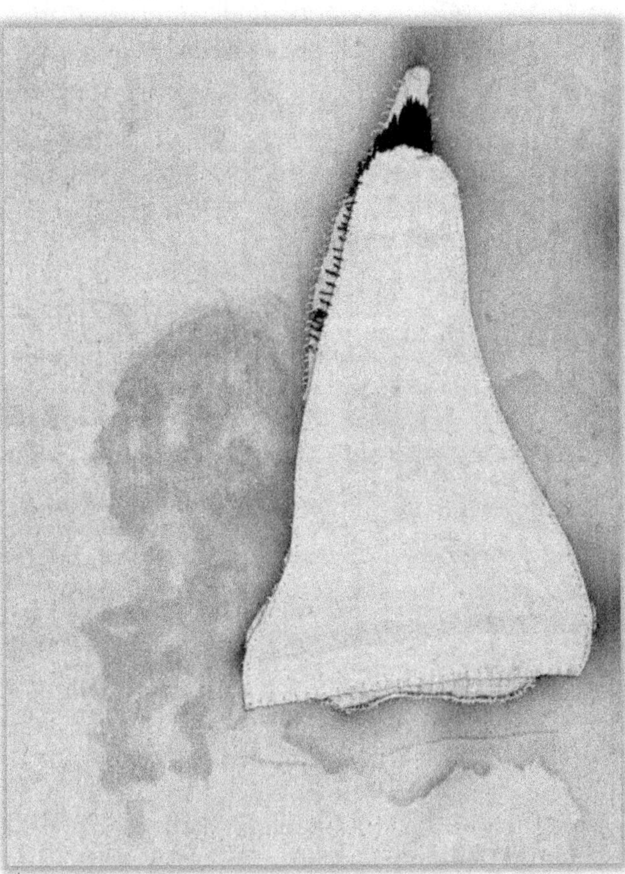

Official Shroud Sword Wound
Photograph ©1978 Barrie M. Schwortz Collection, STERA Inc., All Rights Reserved

Luke 22:39-44 *And He came out, and went, as He was wont, to the Mount of Olives; and His disciples also followed Him. And when He was at the place, He said unto them, Pray that ye enter not into temptation. And He was withdrawn from them about a stone's cast, and kneeled down, and prayed, Saying, Father, if Thou be willing, remove this cup from Me; nevertheless not My will but Thine, be done. And there appeared an angel unto Him from Heaven, strengthening Him. And being in an agony He prayed more earnestly; <u>and His sweat was as it were great drops of blood falling down to the ground.</u>*

When Yeshua the Rod of God prayed, His sweat, the Living Water coming from within Him, turned to blood and fell to the ground! In Deuteronomy, the LORD told Israel, *"To pour the blood out on the ground as water."* Even this fine detail, reveals Yeshua's identity as the LORD God of Israel.

Deuteronomy 15:23 *Only thou shalt not eat the blood thereof; thou shalt pour it upon the ground as water.*

After this, the *water and the blood*

that mingled together, poured out of the heart of Messiah Yeshua at the crucifixion. As soon as the Roman Soldier pierced His side with the lance and punctured His heart, at once *life blood and living water came out and fell to the ground*, because the Rod had been struck. This was written that we might believe, according to the eyewitness named John, the son of Zebedee.

John 19:32-37 *Then came the soldiers, and brake the legs of the first, and of the other which was crucified with him. But when they came to Yeshua, and saw that He was dead already, they brake not His legs; But one of the soldiers with a spear pierced His side, and forthwith came there out blood and water. And he that saw it bare record, and his record is true; and he knoweth that he saith true, that ye might believe. For these things were done, that the Scripture should be fulfilled, A bone of Him shall not be broken. And again another Scripture saith, They shall look on Him whom they pierced.*

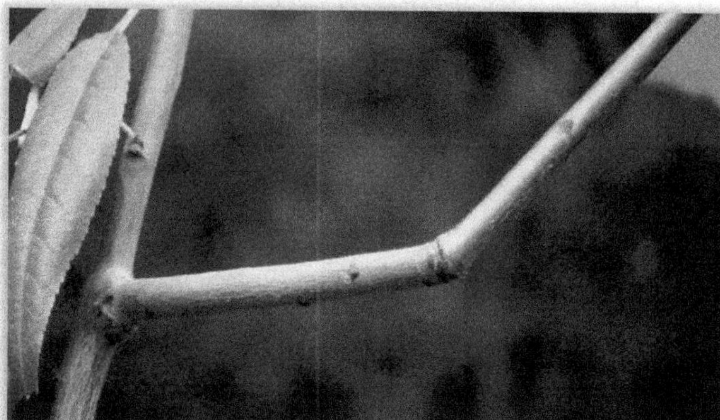

Almond Rod Photo ©2014 Kimberly K Ballard All Rights Reserved

One of the great miracles of Yeshua, the Living Rod of God, took place when a woman touched Him and *power went out from Him.* At that moment the woman, who had *an issue of blood,* was immediately healed and the blood stopped. Because the power of the Holy Spirit is on the Rod of God, on the Messiah, *He healed her from the blood issue, just as He stopped the plague of the blood with Moses in Egypt.* There was no earthly physician that could heal this woman and stop her blood from flowing, except the LORD. The power of the Rod of God that touched this woman, verified that Messiah is the true physician. He heals and restores completely, and brings great comfort to us under the wings of His Priestly Jewish tallit. This woman was trembling before the LORD because of His mighty power. *This miracle also verifies that during Yeshua's resurrection as the Living Branch, the power of God was inside Yeshua and radiated outward from Him, leaving His photographic image on His burial Shroud!*

Luke 8:43-48 *And a woman having an issue of blood twelve years, which had spent all her living upon physicians, neither could be healed of any, Came behind Him, and touched the border of His garment; and immediately her issue of blood stanched, And Yeshua said, Who touched Me? When all denied, Peter and they that were with Him said, Master, the multitude throng Thee and press Thee, and sayest Thou, Who touched Me? And Yeshua said, Somebody touched Me; for I perceive that virtue is gone out of Me. And when the woman saw that she was not hid, she came trembling, and falling down before Him, she declared unto Him before all the people for what cause she had touched Him, and how she was healed immediately. And He said unto her; Daughter, be of good comfort; thy faith hath made thee whole; go in peace.*

Living Almond Rod Photo ©2014 Kimberly K Ballard All Rights Reserved

John recorded that *Yeshua the LORD,* came not by water only, *but by water and blood.* As I said, the Spirit of God is on the Rod, so in the following passage, we see that there are three that bear witness on earth and they are, *"The Spirit, the water, and the blood."* When Yeshua performed this particular sign, *He revealed the Spirit, the water, and the blood.* These were the same signs that were given as a Testimony to Pharaoh centuries earlier, that proved this was the LORD God that created the universe. *The*

Spirit, the water and the blood, are one and the same. The three that bear witness in Heaven are also one and the same. So the Father, Messiah the Son, who is the second perfect Adam, the Lamb, who is the Rod and the Word of God, full of His Holy Spirit are one LORD God called, *"I AM." He reveals Himself to us in these various ways.*

I John 5:1-13 *Whosoever believeth that Yeshua is the Messiah is born of God; and every one that loveth Him that begat loveth Him also that is begotten of Him. By this we know that we love the children of God, when we love God, and keep His commandments. For this is the love of God, that we keep His commandments; and His commandments are not grievous. For whatsoever is born of God overcometh the world; and this is the victory that overcometh the world, even our faith. Who is he that overcometh the world, but he that believeth that Yeshua is the Son of God? This is He that came by water and blood, even Yeshua Messiah; not by water only, but by water and blood. And it is the Spirit that beareth witness, because the Spirit is truth. For there are three that bear record in Heaven, the Father, the Word, and the Holy Spirit; and these three are one. And there are three that bear witness in earth, the Spirit, and the water, and the blood; and these three agree in one. If we receive the witness of men, the witness of God is greater; for this is the witness of God which he hath testified of His Son. He that believeth on the Son of God hath the witness in himself; he that believeth not God hath made Him a liar; because he believeth not the record that God gave of His Son. And this is the record, that God hath given to us eternal life, and this life is in His Son. He that hath the Son hath life; and he that hath not the Son of God hath not life. These things have I written unto you that believe on the Name of the Son of God; that ye may know that ye have eternal life, and that ye may believe on the Name of the Son of God.*

Living Almond Rod Photo ©2014 Kimberly K Ballard All Rights Reserved

I Peter 1:18-23 *Forasmuch as ye know that ye were not redeemed with corruptible things, as silver and gold, from your vain conversation received by tradition from your fathers; But with the precious blood of Messiah, as of a lamb without blemish and without spot; Who verily was foreordained before the foundation of the world, but was manifest in these last times for you, Who by Him do believe in God, that raised Him up from the dead, and gave Him glory; that your faith and hope might be in God. Seeing ye have purified your souls in obeying the truth through the Spirit unto unfeigned love of the brethren, see that ye love one another with a pure heart fervently; Being born again, not of corruptible seed, but of incorruptible, by the Word of God, which liveth and abideth forever.*

Living Almond Rod Photo ©2014 Kimberly K Ballard All Rights Reserved

This Scripture says that the Messiah was *foreordained as the Lamb* before the foundation of the world and that He was only made *manifest* in the last days for us! This shows us that *Messiah is the LORD God in Heaven* clearly made visible as reality to us. It is through the Living Rod, the Messiah, that the glory of God is made manifest, as He foreordained it. In every one of Messiah Yeshua's miracles, signs, and wonders, He manifested *the glory* of God, revealing He is without a doubt *the Rod of God who performs the miracles of God,* even turning the water into blood and the water into wine that represented His life blood of the Heavenly Covenant of His heart!

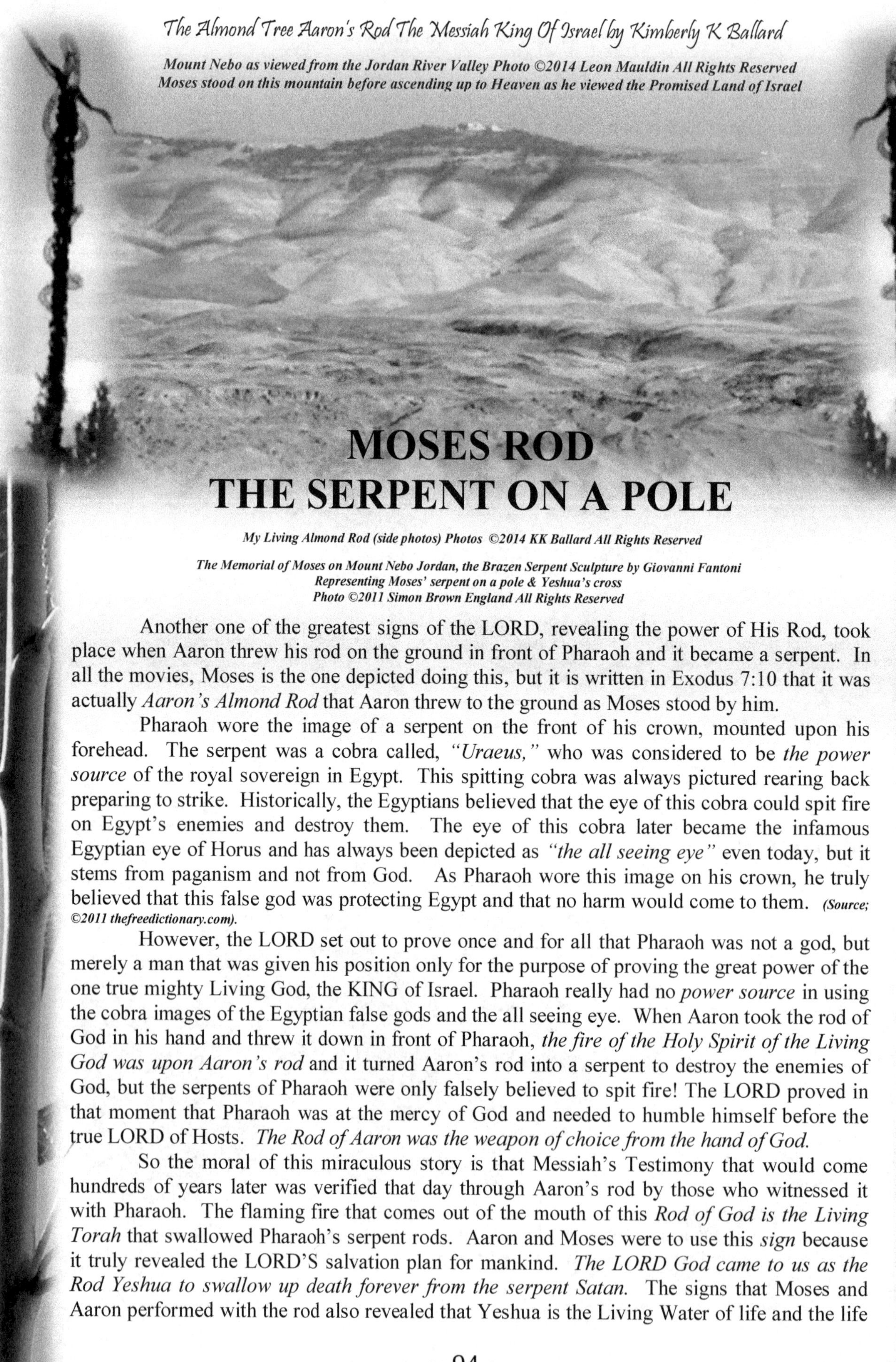

Mount Nebo as viewed from the Jordan River Valley Photo ©2014 Leon Mauldin All Rights Reserved
Moses stood on this mountain before ascending up to Heaven as he viewed the Promised Land of Israel

MOSES ROD THE SERPENT ON A POLE

My Living Almond Rod (side photos) Photos ©2014 KK Ballard All Rights Reserved

The Memorial of Moses on Mount Nebo Jordan, the Brazen Serpent Sculpture by Giovanni Fantoni
Representing Moses' serpent on a pole & Yeshua's cross
Photo ©2011 Simon Brown England All Rights Reserved

Another one of the greatest signs of the LORD, revealing the power of His Rod, took place when Aaron threw his rod on the ground in front of Pharaoh and it became a serpent. In all the movies, Moses is the one depicted doing this, but it is written in Exodus 7:10 that it was actually *Aaron's Almond Rod* that Aaron threw to the ground as Moses stood by him.

Pharaoh wore the image of a serpent on the front of his crown, mounted upon his forehead. The serpent was a cobra called, *"Uraeus,"* who was considered to be *the power source* of the royal sovereign in Egypt. This spitting cobra was always pictured rearing back preparing to strike. Historically, the Egyptians believed that the eye of this cobra could spit fire on Egypt's enemies and destroy them. The eye of this cobra later became the infamous Egyptian eye of Horus and has always been depicted as *"the all seeing eye"* even today, but it stems from paganism and not from God. As Pharaoh wore this image on his crown, he truly believed that this false god was protecting Egypt and that no harm would come to them. ***(Source; ©2011 thefreedictionary.com).***

However, the LORD set out to prove once and for all that Pharaoh was not a god, but merely a man that was given his position only for the purpose of proving the great power of the one true mighty Living God, the KING of Israel. Pharaoh really had no *power source* in using the cobra images of the Egyptian false gods and the all seeing eye. When Aaron took the rod of God in his hand and threw it down in front of Pharaoh, *the fire of the Holy Spirit of the Living God was upon Aaron's rod* and it turned Aaron's rod into a serpent to destroy the enemies of God, but the serpents of Pharaoh were only falsely believed to spit fire! The LORD proved in that moment that Pharaoh was at the mercy of God and needed to humble himself before the true LORD of Hosts. *The Rod of Aaron was the weapon of choice from the hand of God.*

So the moral of this miraculous story is that Messiah's Testimony that would come hundreds of years later was verified that day through Aaron's rod by those who witnessed it with Pharaoh. The flaming fire that comes out of the mouth of this *Rod of God is the Living Torah* that swallowed Pharaoh's serpent rods. Aaron and Moses were to use this *sign* because it truly revealed the LORD'S salvation plan for mankind. *The LORD God came to us as the Rod Yeshua to swallow up death forever from the serpent Satan.* The signs that Moses and Aaron performed with the rod also revealed that Yeshua is the Living Water of life and the life blood. He is the only one who can give us Eternal Life and *the Almond Rod of Aaron proved this before Pharaoh.* The cut off Almond Branch bore the curse of Eden at the cross and redeemed us to Eternal life, when He was resurrected. So we rejoice in our Yeshua!

Isaiah 25:8 *He will swallow up death in victory; and the LORD GOD will wipe away tears from off all faces; and the rebuke of His people shall He take away from off all the earth; for the LORD hath spoken it. And it shall be said in that day, Lo, this is our God; we have waited for Him, and He will save us; this is the LORD; we have waited for Him, we will be glad and rejoice in His salvation.*

When the LORD sent the ten plagues upon the Egyptians as judgment, the plagues were representative, in living color, of all their so called gods. These false gods included insects, reptiles, birds, and other fake planet gods that they worshipped. The frog was one of the false gods in Egypt, but the LORD made them sick of the frogs by sending millions of them in a huge plague! The LORD gave them so many frogs that they could no longer stand it. The LORD with His Rod was exhibiting in living color that He is Almighty God who controls all living things, including the water, the blood, the fire, the weather, life, and death. The Egyptians received more than their fill of the plagues of their false gods! This is how the LORD gives His Royal Divine judgment. Pharaoh refused to repent or believe in the one true Living God who created all of these things in the universe and who shows *signs and wonders with His Rod.* Pharaoh wanted to worship and rule by these created things, but the LORD created them all. The LORD never intended for mankind to worship anything that He created. Now the LORD God also called Pharaoh *"the great dragon!"* We find that in the book of Revelation the dragon is judged!

My Garden Frog amongst cucumbers ©2013 Kimberly K Ballard All Rights Reserved

Ezekiel 29:3 *Speak, and say, Thus saith the LORD GOD; Behold, I AM against thee, Pharaoh King of Egypt, the great dragon that lieth in the midst of his rivers, which hath said, My river is mine own, and I have made it for myself.*

Revelation 12:9-17 *And the great dragon was cast out, that old serpent, called the Devil, and Satan, which deceiveth the whole world; he was cast out into the earth, and his angels were cast out with him. And I heard a loud voice saying in Heaven, Now is come salvation, and strength, and the Kingdom of our God, and the power of His Messiah; for the accuser of our brethren is cast down, which accused them before our God day and night. And they overcame him by the blood of the Lamb, and by the Word of their Testimony; and they loved not their lives unto the death. Therefore rejoice, ye Heavens, and ye that dwell in them. Woe to the inhabiters of the earth and of the sea! For the devil is come down unto you, having great wrath, because he knoweth that he hath but a short time. And when the dragon saw that he was cast unto the earth, he persecuted the woman which brought forth the man child. And to the woman were given two wings of a great eagle, that she might fly into the wilderness, into her place, where she is nourished for a time, and times, and half a time, from the face of the serpent. And the serpent cast out of his mouth* *water as a flood after the woman, that he might cause her to be carried away of the flood. And the earth helped the woman, and the earth opened her mouth, and swallowed up the flood which the dragon cast out of his mouth. And the dragon was wroth with the woman, and went to make war with the remnant of her seed, which keep the Commandments of God, and have the Testimony of Yeshua Messiah.*

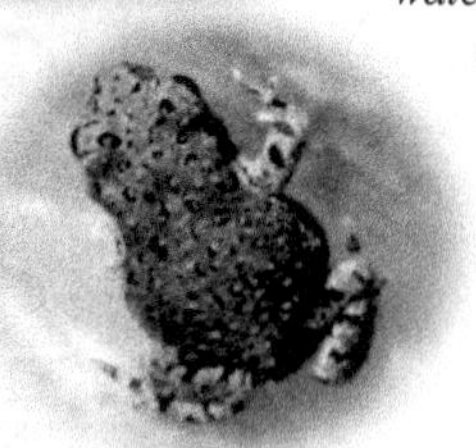

Revelation 20:2-3 *And he laid hold on the dragon, that old serpent, which is the Devil, and Satan, and bound him a thousand years, And cast him into the bottomless pit, and shut him up, and set a seal upon him, that he should deceive the Nations no more till the thousand years should be fulfilled; and after that he must be loosed a little season.*

Isaiah 27:1 *In that day the LORD with His sore and great and strong sword shall punish leviathan the piercing serpent, even leviathan that crooked serpent; and He shall slay the dragon that is in the sea.*

In Exodus, the LORD God showed Moses what signs to perform with His Almond Rod that would reveal His *"Yeshua."* This was to be *a sign* that was to prove that the God of Abraham, Isaac, and Jacob had truly appeared to Moses.

Exodus 4:1-9 *And Moses answered and said, but, behold, they will not believe me, nor hearken unto my voice; for they will say, The LORD hath not appeared unto thee. And the LORD said unto him, what is that in thine hand? And he said a rod. And He said, Cast it on the ground. And he cast it on the ground, and it became a serpent; and Moses fled from before it. And the LORD said unto Moses, Put forth thine hand, and take it by the tail. And he put forth his hand, and caught it, and it became a rod in his hand; That they may believe that the LORD God of their fathers, the God of Abraham, the God of Isaac, and the God of Jacob, hath appeared unto thee. And the LORD said furthermore unto him, Put now thine hand into thy bosom. And he put his hand into his bosom; and when he took it out, behold, his hand was leprous as snow. And he said, put thine hand into thy bosom again. And he put his hand into his bosom again; and plucked it out of his bosom, and, behold, it was turned again as his other flesh. And it shall come to pass, if they will not believe thee neither hearken to the voice of the first sign, that they will believe the voice of the latter sign. And it shall come to pass, if they will not believe also these two signs, neither hearken unto thy voice, that thou shalt take of the water of the river, and pour it upon the dry land; and the water which thou takest out of the river shall become blood upon the dry land.*

Now it's fascinating that the LORD gave *three signs* to Moses to reveal Himself to the people of Israel so they would believe that He was in fact the God of their fathers, who had appeared to Moses, *revealing His redemption plan of the future with the Messiah.* The LORD showed Moses sign one, the rod becoming a serpent and then turning back into a Rod or a Branch because the LORD was going to use this Rod, *the Branch,* in His own hand in the future to save us. The second sign involves the hand being cursed with leprosy or disease and then being healed from disease. This also reveals that the flesh saw corruption. This signified that Messiah at the right hand of God, in the future, was going to resurrect our bodies from corruption and restore us to Eternal life and there would be no more decay. This reveals that Messiah Yeshua, who died and was raised to life, whose body saw no corruption, is the powerful Rod of God that gives life to the dead and He is the mighty hand of God. Now if they would not listen to the first two signs with the Rod, the LORD gave them a third sign in order that they might believe Him. The living water of the river was to be poured out on the dry land. It would then turn to blood on the dry land. Messiah Yeshua proved by His miracles that He is the Living Water, the source of power on the Rod. It is from this *Living River* of the water of Life, that we must drink to have Eternal life. Yeshua did fulfill this sign in the Garden of Gethsemane. This was incredibly, the fulfillment of the third sign of the LORD, that He performed with the Rod. Yeshua was therefore, truly verified to be the Rod, the Branch of the LORD, that was to be *raised up* to life the third day.

Remember that Pharaoh sent forth an order to slay all the Hebrew baby boys when Moses was born? The plan was to prevent *the redeemer* of Israel from coming into the world to save Israel. Likewise, when Yeshua was born, Herod sent forth an order to slay all the Hebrew baby boys, to prevent the Redeemer of Israel from coming to save Israel. In both cases however, it was not possible to stop the LORD'S plan of redemption for Israel and the world! The LORD God controls the events and rulers on the world stage, whether they know it or not. *They have never prevented the LORD'S plan of salvation from coming to pass.* The LORD had not forgotten the blood of the Hebrew babies that cried out of the Nile. When the LORD told Moses to take the water from the river and pour it out on the dry ground and it became blood, Pharaoh was confronted with His own evil. The life was in the blood. *This is why Yeshua, the Living Water, has the life blood that redeems us because the life is in His blood.* Remember, when Cain killed Abel? Abel's blood cried out from the ground for justice! The LORD was going to bring justice for the death of the precious Hebrew babies. The Messiah's life blood was also poured out on the ground for us on Holy Mount Moriah, *in the place of the Garden of Eden.* The Living Water, the life blood, and the Spirit of God's Rod bore witness there that we were redeemed. This was the third sign of the LORD that was given to Moses. On the third day, Yeshua was raised up as the Living Branch, as the Living Water that saved us with His Life blood and we receive His Holy Spirit, as we are made pure in Him. The serpent that Moses set upon a pole in the wilderness was made in the likeness of the fiery serpents that were killing them. It was made of brass (Numbers 21:9). Messiah *the Rod of God* has feet like burnished bronze, like fine brass. The serpent brings certain death, but *the Rod of God lifted up* is the *true power source* that brings life! Today on Mount Nebo there is a memorial to Moses and the brazen serpent is wrapped around the cross of Messiah Yeshua. It represents what Moses and Aaron demonstrated. *God's Eternal power is in His Rod.* God therefore, came to us *in the likeness of the flesh* as our Messiah to destroy Satan's curse on all flesh. In this way, we would have life forever and no longer experience the bitterness of death. So the Rod Yeshua forever destroyed the corruption of the flesh because this is exactly how Satan was killing us. The LORD *bore the curse for us* to bring us back to His Garden called *"Heaven"* where we can dwell with Him forever. Messiah Yeshua had to be lifted up like Moses Rod, so that all who look upon Him as *the Rod of God* and believe will live forever and not die.

I Corinthians 15:53-57 *For this corruptible must put on incorruption, and this mortal must put on immortality. So when this corruptible shall have put on incorruption, and this mortal shall have put on immortality, then shall be brought to pass the saying that is written, Death is swallowed up in victory. O death, where is thy sting? O grave, where is thy victory? The sting of death is sin; and the strength of sin is the law. But thanks be to God, which giveth us the victory through our LORD [Yeshua] Messiah.*

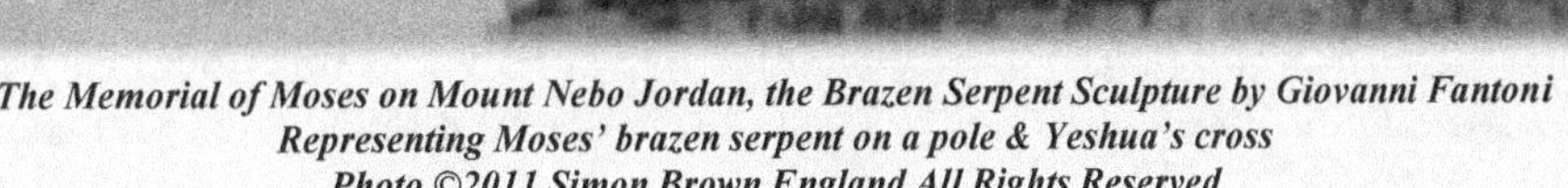

The Memorial of Moses on Mount Nebo Jordan, the Brazen Serpent Sculpture by Giovanni Fantoni
Representing Moses' brazen serpent on a pole & Yeshua's cross
Photo ©2011 Simon Brown England All Rights Reserved

So now if we go back to the Scripture that Yeshua declared to Nicodemus on that starlit night in Jerusalem, we can understand Yeshua's Words when He said, *"As Moses lifted up the serpent in the wilderness, even so must the Son of man be lifted up so that whosoever believeth in Him should not perish but have Eternal life."* Yeshua made *the way* for us to enter into His Heavenly Paradise. No one else would die for us but the LORD God who restores life!

John 3:13-17 *And no man hath ascended up to Heaven, but he that came down from Heaven, even the Son of man which is in Heaven. And as Moses lifted up the serpent in the wilderness, even so must the Son of man be lifted up; That whosoever believeth in Him should not perish, but have eternal life. For God so loved the world, that He gave His only begotten Son, that whosoever believeth in Him should not perish, but have everlasting life. For God sent not His Son into the world to condemn the world; but that the world through Him might be saved.*

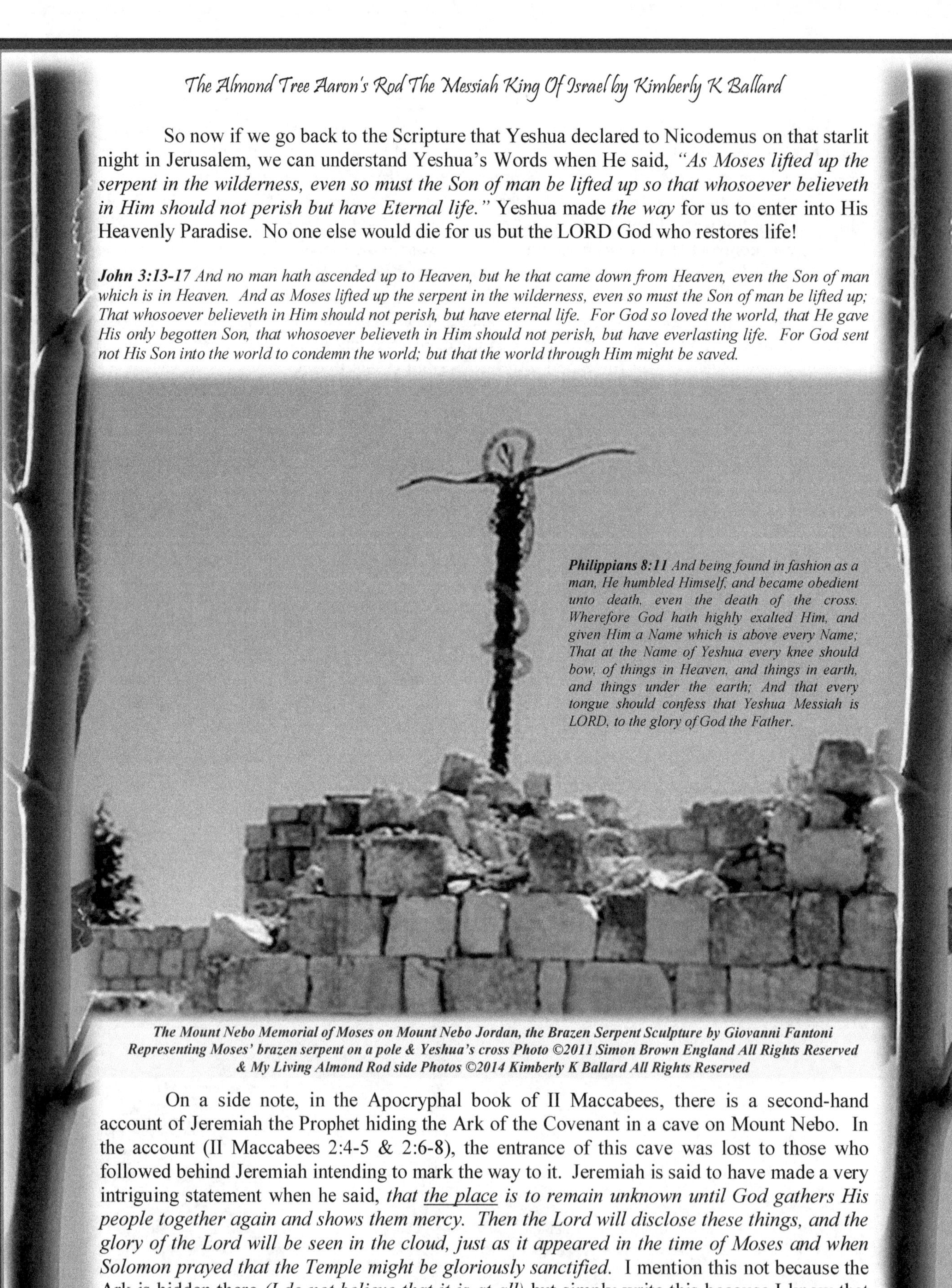

Philippians 8:11 *And being found in fashion as a man, He humbled Himself, and became obedient unto death, even the death of the cross. Wherefore God hath highly exalted Him, and given Him a Name which is above every Name; That at the Name of Yeshua every knee should bow, of things in Heaven, and things in earth, and things under the earth; And that every tongue should confess that Yeshua Messiah is LORD, to the glory of God the Father.*

The Mount Nebo Memorial of Moses on Mount Nebo Jordan, the Brazen Serpent Sculpture by Giovanni Fantoni Representing Moses' brazen serpent on a pole & Yeshua's cross Photo ©2011 Simon Brown England All Rights Reserved & My Living Almond Rod side Photos ©2014 Kimberly K Ballard All Rights Reserved

On a side note, in the Apocryphal book of II Maccabees, there is a second-hand account of Jeremiah the Prophet hiding the Ark of the Covenant in a cave on Mount Nebo. In the account (II Maccabees 2:4-5 & 2:6-8), the entrance of this cave was lost to those who followed behind Jeremiah intending to mark the way to it. Jeremiah is said to have made a very intriguing statement when he said, *that <u>the place</u> is to remain unknown until God gathers His people together again and shows them mercy. Then the Lord will disclose these things, and the glory of the Lord will be seen in the cloud, just as it appeared in the time of Moses and when Solomon prayed that the Temple might be gloriously sanctified.* I mention this not because the Ark is hidden there *(I do not believe that it is at all)* but simply write this because I know that the LORD is about to disclose these things! The LORD showed it to me and I will show you!

THE LIVING BRANCH IN THE BURNING BUSH

Flaming Fire on Almond Rod & Blossoms on Branch

After the LORD showed me all these things, another amazing truth came to light and I shared it with my friend in Jerusalem. The most astonishing truth was shown to me by the LORD. This verified again, *my miracle of the Almond Branch.* The LORD spoke to Moses out of the burning bush and there was something quite special about this burning bush. It was no ordinary bush! The branches on the burning bush were actually *living branches* in flaming fire and they were not consumed. The most astonishing thing about the burning bush is the fact that *its living branches were bearing leaves, blossoms and fruit!* By the LORD'S revelation, I saw that this describes Yeshua the Living Fruitful Branch, the Rod full of the fire of the Holy Spirit, who came to life, bearing leaves, flowers, and fruit! Although a fierce fire was raging upon this burning bush, it was not consumed by the fire, because this was the Holy Spirit of God. The Scripture says that *"The Word" of the LORD came to Moses out of the burning bush.* Messiah Yeshua is *"The Word of God"* as it is written by the Jewish disciple, John. The Living Branch bore Fruit because the Holy Spirit was abiding in Him and He sprouted to life. So within the burning bush, *the fire of His Holy Spirit/Ruach was upon its fruitful branches.* The fire of the Holy Spirit/Ruach was upon Yeshua, the Fruitful Branch, as He performed the signs and miracles of the LORD God. Within the details of the burning bush, we plainly see that the LORD God of Israel is the Messiah. *The Word of God is a Tree of Life. The burning bush is a picture of the Divine design of the Holy Almond Tree Menorah in the Heavenly Temple!* The LORD spoke His Word, out of the living branches that were full of the flaming fire of His Holy Spirit. The gold Menorah bears fruitful leafy Almond Branches and oil with a fire burning in its lamps. All of these represent Messiah, the Word, the LORD, and this is why we have no need of a lamp in Heaven, because the LORD is the light.

In the Jewish Historian Josephus' account of the Burning Bush, we see that the branches were full of leaves, flowers, and fruit, yet it was not consumed.

Antiquities of the Jews - Book II Chapter 12 section 1 Flavious Josephus; CONCERNING THE BURNING BUSH AND THE ROD OF MOSES.

1. NOW Moses, when he had obtained the favor of Jethro, for that was one of the names of Raguel, staid there and fed his flock; but some time afterward, taking his station at the mountain called Sinai, he drove his flocks thither to feed them. Now this is the highest of all the mountains thereabout, and the best for pasturage, the herbage being there good; and it had not been before fed upon, because of the opinion men had that God dwelt there, the shepherds not daring to ascend up to it; and here it was that a wonderful prodigy happened to Moses; for a fire fed upon a thorn bush, yet did the green leaves and the flowers continue untouched, and the fire did not at all consume the fruit branches, although the flame was great and fierce. Moses was affrighted at this strange sight, as it was to him; but he was still more astonished when the fire uttered a voice, and called to him by name, and spake Words to him, by which it signified how bold he had been in venturing to come into a place whither no man had ever come before, because the place was divine; and advised him to remove a great way off from the flame, and to be contented with what he had seen; and though he were himself a good man, and the offspring of great men, yet that he should not pry any further; and he foretold to him, that he should have glory and honor among men, by the blessing of God upon him.

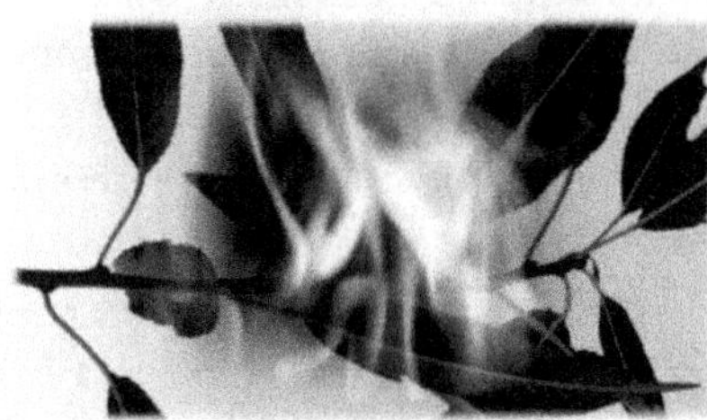

Living Almond Rod with flaming fire & Menorah

Now what the LORD showed me about this is a profound Testimony. Josephus wrote that the burning bush was a thorn bush. The incredible fact is that botanically, the Almond Tree is from *the Rosaceae* plant species. This is the rose family! Although an Almond Tree does not have thorns, roses are bushes with thorns from the same plant family as the Almond Tree. There is also the shrub called the *"dwarf flowering Almond or Prunus Glandulosa."* The Rosaceae plant species bears much fruit! Yeshua the Living Branch also wore the Crown of Thorns, to bear much fruit! It is said that from *the Rosaceae* plant species come all of the following trees and bushes bearing many fruits. They include but are not limited to, *"almonds, blackberries, peaches, pears, apples, cherries, raspberries, plums and strawberries,"* just to name a few. The Rosaceae species is one of the most productive fruitful plant species known to mankind. So is it any wonder that the LORD was seen in this variety of thorn bush, in *the Rosaceae* family? Messiah Yeshua is sometimes called *"The Rose of Sharon."*

The burning bush is a picture of the Messiah, our First Fruits from the Almond Tree of Life. When the Word of God spoke to Moses out of this bush, it means that Moses saw the Testimony of the Messiah, before Yeshua's arrival hundreds of years later. *Yeshua is the burning bush!* This account in Josephus is interesting, because it says, *"That when the LORD spoke, the fire uttered a voice."* We see that this same thing happened on Shavuot (Pentecost) when the Holy Spirit descended in cleft flaming tongues of fire and rested upon each of the disciples of Yeshua. The Biblical account of the burning bush is written in the book of Exodus.

Exodus 3:1-6 *Now Moses kept the flock of Jethro his father in law, the Priest of Midian; and he led the flock to the backside of the desert, and came to the mountain of God, even to Horeb. And the angel of the LORD appeared unto him in a flame of fire out of the midst of a bush; and he looked, and, behold, the bush burned with fire, and the bush was not consumed. And Moses said, I will now turn aside, and see this great sight, why the bush is not burnt. And when the LORD saw that he turned aside to see, God called unto him out of the midst of the bush, and said, Moses, Moses. And he said, Here am I. And he said, Draw not nigh hither; put off thy shoes from off thy feet, for the place where on thou standest is Holy ground. Moreover he said, I AM the God of thy father, the God of Abraham, the God of Isaac, and the God of Jacob. And Moses hid his face; for he was afraid to look upon God.*

In this account, the angel of the LORD appeared to Moses in the flame of fire, out of the burning bush. The angel of the LORD is also the one that appeared at the Garden tomb in Holy Mount Moriah and rolled the Great Stone from Yeshua's sepulchre. The angel of the LORD declared that Yeshua was not dead, but alive. *This was the Living Testimony of the Rod of God, full of the fire of the Holy Spirit of God and He came to life the third day, as the Fruitful Living Branch on the LORD'S Feast of First Fruits.* So the LORD God of Israel had already revealed His identity to Moses, *"As the Fruitful Branch from the Almond Tree of Life!"*

Now when I thought about this burning bush that was not consumed by the fire, because the LORD was in the midst of it, it occurred to me that this is exactly what happened when the LORD delivered the three Israelites from the fiery furnace in Babylon. I should mention here that the number three is also connected to the following story of salvation from the LORD! In Babylon they said, *"One like the Son of God, was in the midst of the fire, so they were not consumed."* Yeshua's title is *"the Son of God, the Word of God."* So once again, we see that the Word of God, in the midst of the fire, kept them from being consumed, just like the Word of God was in the midst of the burning bush and it was not consumed. Here is the account.

Daniel 3:14-30 *Nebuchadnezzar spake and said unto them, Is it true, O Shadrach, Meshach, and Abed-nego, do not ye serve my gods, nor worship the golden image which I have set up? Now if ye be ready that at what time ye hear the sound of the cornet, flute, harp, sackbut, psaltery, and dulcimer, and all kinds of musick, ye fall down and worship the image which I have made; well; but if ye worship not, ye shall be cast the same hour into the midst of a burning fiery furnace; and who is that God that shall deliver you out of my hands? Shadrach, Meshach, and Abed-nego, answered and said to the king, O Nebuchadnezzar, we are not careful to answer thee in this matter. If it be so, our God whom we serve is able to deliver us from the burning fiery furnace, and He will deliver us out of thine hand,*

O king. But if not, be it known unto thee, O king, that we will not serve thy gods, nor worship the golden image which thou hast set up. Then was Nebuchadnezzar full of fury, and the form of his visage was changed against Shadrach, Meshach, and Abed-nego; therefore he spake, and commanded that they should heat the furnace one seven times more than it was wont to be heated. And he commanded the most mighty men that were in his army to bind Shadrach, Meshach, and Abed-nego, and to cast them into the burning fiery furnace. Then these men were bound in their coats, their hosen, and their hats, and their other garments, and were cast into the midst of the burning fiery furnace. Therefore because the king's commandment was urgent, and the furnace exceeding hot, the flame of the fire slew those men that took up Shadrach, Meshach, and Abed-nego. And these three men, Shadrach, Meshach, and Abed-nego, fell down bound into the midst of the burning fiery furnace. Then Nebuchadnezzar the king was astonied, and rose up in haste, and spake, and said unto his counselors, Did not we cast three men bound into the midst of the fire? They answered and said unto the king, True, O king. He answered and said, Lo, I see four men loose, walking in the midst of the fire, and they have no hurt; and the form of the fourth is like the Son of God. Then Nebuchadnezzar came near to the mouth of the burning fiery furnace, and spake, and said, Shadrach, Meshach, and Abed-nego, ye servants of the Most High God, come forth, and come hither. Then Shadrach, Meshach, and Abed-nego, came forth of the midst of the fire. And the princes, governors, and captains, and the king's counselors, being gathered together, saw these men, upon whose bodies the fire had no power, nor was an hair of their head singed, neither were their coats changed, nor the smell of fire had passed on them. Then Nebuchadnezzar spake, and said, Blessed be the God of Shadrach, Meshach, and Abed-nego, who hath sent His angel, and delivered His servants that trusted in Him, and have changed the king's word, and yielded their bodies, that they might not serve nor worship any god, except their own God. Therefore I make a decree, That every people, nation, and language, which speak anything amiss against the God of Shadrach, Meshach, and Abed-nego, shall be cut in pieces, and their houses shall be made a dunghill; because there is no other God that can deliver after this sort. Then the king promoted Shadrach, Meshach, and Abed-nego, in the province of Babylon.

The form of *the fourth man* walking in the midst of the flaming fire *was like the Son of God.* It is the same miracle that happened at the burning bush. When the LORD was in the midst of the fire, upon the fruitful living branches, the fire did not consume the bush. It was alive by the Divine Holy Spirit of God.

English Rose "Heritage" Flaming Fire & Living Almond Rod
Photos ©2013 & 2014 Kimberly K Ballard All Rights Reserved

The One like the Son of God was the Fruitful Living Branch, *the Living Torah* who was in the midst of the flaming fire with the three Hebrew men in the fiery furnace. They were not harmed or consumed because *the Living Branch from the Almond Tree of Life was in their midst!* The LORD gave them *Yeshua,* which is salvation! The smell of smoke was not on them, nor was it on their clothing. The hair of their heads was not singed. Why were they saved by the Rod of God? They had refused to worship the pagan gods of Babylon, so the LORD rescued and saved them with His Rod in the midst of the flaming fire. *The Son of God appeared in the form of a man in the fiery furnace and He came to save the sons of Israel.* This is the ultimate purpose of the Rod of God! This is why the Messiah was sent to Israel in the form of a man, to save them. So Aaron's rod and Messiah the Rod, full of the fire of the Ruach/Holy Spirit, are represented in the incredible burning bush, *in the Holy Almond Tree Menorah* and in the fiery furnace of Babylon! As I said before, it is interesting to note that the voice of the LORD came out of the consuming fire in the burning bush. Scripture tells us that the voice of the LORD divideth the flames of fire. This explains why Yeshua told the disciples to tarry in Jerusalem until they were endued with power from on high which was His Ruach/Spirit. The LORD'S Word out of His mouth speaks with the sword of His Divine Spirit. This is clearly the flaming fire out of the mouth of *the Almond Rod, the Messiah.* Incredible!

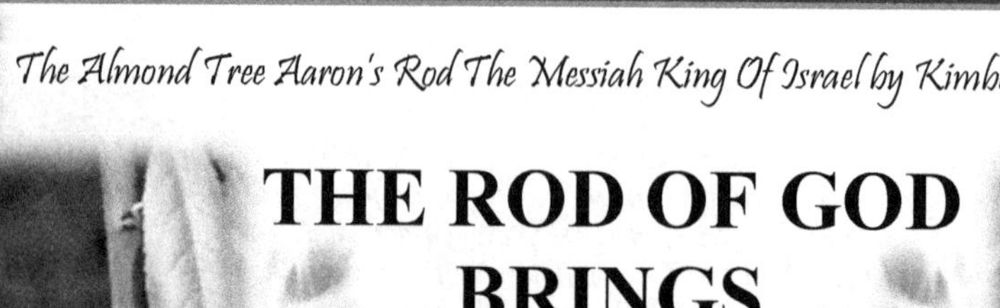

THE ROD OF GOD BRINGS SALVATION

Living Almond Rod Branch forming a right arm

The more I studied this truth that Yeshua is the Rod of God, the more I began to realize that whenever the rod is *lifted up* or held out in the outstretched arm of the LORD God, it always brings salvation to Israel. *The LORD saves with His Rod.* When Moses held out the rod in his hand, as he was instructed to by the LORD, *salvation came to Israel.* When I understood that *it is only the Rod of God that saves,* then I understood why *Yeshua is absolutely, the only way to ever obtain Eternal life.*

One of the greatest stories ever told, is the story of the Red Sea crossing. The Rod of God divided the waters and the Hebrews were told by Moses *"To stand still and see the Yeshua of the LORD."* Remember that the Branch makes things cleft! The breath of the Holy Spirit blew back the waters all that night, as *the Rod* made a pathway before them to be saved.

Exodus 14:10-31 *And when Pharaoh drew nigh, the children of Israel lifted up their eyes, and, behold, the Egyptians marched after them; and they were sore afraid; and the children of Israel cried out unto the LORD. And they said unto Moses, Because there were no graves in Egypt, hast thou taken us away to die in the wilderness? Wherefore hast thou dealt thus with us, to carry us forth out of Egypt? Is not this the word that we did tell thee in Egypt, saying, Let us alone, that we may serve the Egyptians? For it had been better for us to serve the Egyptians, than that we should die in the wilderness. And Moses said unto the people, Fear ye not, stand still, and see the salvation of the LORD, which He will shew to you today; for the Egyptians whom ye have seen today, ye shall see them again no more forever. The LORD shall fight for you, and ye shall hold your peace. And the LORD said unto Moses, Wherefore criest thou unto Me? Speak unto the children of Israel, that they go forward; But lift thou up thy rod, and stretch out thine hand over the sea, and divided it; and the children of Israel shall go on dry ground through the midst of the sea. And I, behold, I will harden the hearts of the Egyptians and they shall follow them; and I will get me honour upon Pharaoh, and upon all his host, upon his chariots, and upon his horsemen. And the Egyptians shall know that I AM the LORD, when I have gotten Me honour upon Pharaoh, upon his chariots, and upon his horsemen. The angel of God, which went before the camp of Israel, removed and went behind them; and the pillar of the cloud went from before their face, and stood behind them; And it came between the camp of the Egyptians and the camp of Israel; and it was a cloud and darkness to them, but it gave light by night to these; so that the one came not near the other all the night. And Moses stretched out his hand over the sea; and the LORD caused the sea to go back by a strong east wind all that night, and made the sea dry land, And the waters were divided. And the children of Israel went into the midst of the sea upon dry ground; and the waters were a wall unto them on their right hand, and on their left. And the Egyptians pursued, and went in after them to the midst of the sea, even all Pharaoh's horses, his chariots, and his horsemen. And it came to pass, that in the morning watch the LORD looked unto the host of the Egyptians through the pillar of fire and of the cloud, and troubled the host of the Egyptians, And took off their chariot wheels, that they drave them heavily; so that the Egyptians said, Let us flee from the face of Israel; for the LORD fighteth for them against the Egyptians. And the LORD said unto Moses, Stretch out thine hand over the sea, that the waters may come again upon the Egyptians, upon their chariots, and upon their horsemen. And Moses stretched forth his hand over the sea, and the sea returned to his strength when the morning appeared; and the Egyptians fled against it; and the LORD overthrew the Egyptians in the midst of the sea. And the waters returned, and covered the chariots, and the horsemen, and all the host of Pharaoh that came into the sea after them; there remained not so much as one of them. But the children of Israel walked on dry land in the midst of the sea; and the waters were a wall unto them on their right hand, and on their left. Thus the LORD saved Israel that day out of the hand of the Egyptians; and Israel saw the Egyptians dead upon the sea shore. And Israel saw that great work which the LORD did upon the Egyptians; and the people feared the LORD, and believed the LORD, and his servant Moses.*

Like the Hebrews - Canadian Geese in flight

Again, the power of the Ruach/Holy Spirit was on the Rod as the hand was stretched out over the sea. As soon as the power left and went back to Moses' strength, then the Egyptian army drowned in the sea. As Moses held the rod up in his hand with the Holy Spirit's power on it, Israel was saved, but when he let down his hands, destruction came upon Pharaoh and his army. *It is always the lifting up of the Rod that brings salvation from death. This is the profound reason that Messiah Yeshua had to be lifted up on the cross.*

Another miraculous story shows us that *the Rod lifted up*, also brings victory over the enemies of the LORD. Moses sat upon a stone, lifting the rod up in the air with his hands and as the rod was lifted up, the Hebrews were given victory over their enemies. When Moses arms became tired, he lowered the rod that was in his hands and the Hebrews began to lose the battle. Suddenly Aaron and Hur intervened and lifted up Moses arms. When the rod was again lifted up in the hands of Moses, the Hebrews not only prevailed, but obtained victory and they were given *"Yeshua"* because the rod was lifted up! *This story details for us that the Rod Messiah Yeshua must be lifted up on the cross for Israel's salvation and for her to have the victory over her enemies and over all the enemies of God.* So think about this fact for a moment. As Yeshua was lifted up, there was one man on one side of the Rod and another man on the other side of the Rod lifted up on the cross as the arm of the LORD stretched out His hands to save us, just as Aaron and Hur stood on either side of Moses while he lifted up the rod! This explains why Yeshua obtained a better victory for Israel as their Eternal KING of Glory, because Yeshua has destroyed the workings of Satan forever! The LORD is also the Rock, and Moses sat upon the stone while he lifted up the rod in his hands with his arms outstretched to bring *Yeshua* to Israel. The Name, *"YHVH nissi,"* means *"The LORD is my banner and a place of refuge."* The banner of God lifted up, is His Rod which is our Saviour Messiah! The people of Israel are His vassals that are granted land rights and protection for allegiance to Him.

Exodus 17:9-16 *And Moses said unto Joshua, Choose us out men, and go out, fight with Amalek; tomorrow I will stand on the top of the hill with the Rod of God in mine hand. So Joshua did as Moses had said to him, and fought with Amalek; and Moses, Aaron, and Hur went up to the top of the hill. And it came to pass, when Moses held up his hand, that Israel prevailed; and when he let down his hand, Amalek prevailed. But Moses hands were heavy; and they took a stone, and put it under him, and he sat thereon; and Aaron and Hur stayed up his hands, the one on the one side, and the other on the other side; and his hands were steady until the going down of the sun. And Joshua discomfited Amalek and his people with the edge of the sword. And the LORD said unto Moses, Write this for a memorial in a book, and rehearse it in the ears of Joshua; for I will utterly put out the remembrance of Amalek from under Heaven. And Moses built an altar, and called the name of it YHVH nissi; For he said, Because the LORD hath sworn that the LORD will have war with Amalek from generation to generation.*

John 19:17-18 *And He bearing His cross went forth into a place called the place of a skull, which is called in the Hebrew Golgotha; Where they crucified Him, and two other with Him, on either side one, and Yeshua in the midst.*

John 8:28 *Then said Yeshua unto them, When ye have lifted up the Son of man, then shall ye know that I AM HE, and that I do nothing of Myself; but as My Father hath taught Me, I speak these things.*

John 5:39-40 *Search the Scriptures; for in them ye think ye have eternal life; and they are they which Testify of Me. And ye will not come to Me, that ye might have life.*

The voice of the LORD was heard from Heaven *as Yeshua declared that He must be lifted up on the cross, so He could draw all mankind back to Himself, as it was in the beginning, in the Garden of Eden.* He said that the prince of this world will then be cast out. This Scripture also reveals that He is the light, represented in the Almond Tree of Life, in the Holy Almond Tree Menorah. *The light and fire of the Holy Spirit comes out of the Rod of God. The LORD laid down His life for us and no one took it from Him.*

John 10:17-18 *Therefore doth My Father love Me, because I lay down My life, that I might take it again. No man taketh it from Me, but I lay it down of Myself. I have power to lay it down, and I have power to take it again, This Commandment have I received of My Father.*

John 12:27-35 *Now is My soul troubled; and what shall I say? Father, save Me from this hour; but for this cause came I unto this hour. Father, glorify Thy Name. Then came there a voice from Heaven, saying, I have both glorified it, and will glorify it again. The people therefore, that stood by, and heard it, said that it thundered; others said, An angel spake to Him. Yeshua answered and said, This voice came not because of Me, but for your sakes. Now is the judgment of this world; now shall the prince of this world be cast out. And I, if I be lifted up from the earth, will draw all men unto me. This He said, signifying what death He should die. The people answered Him, We have heard out of the law that Messiah abideth forever; and how sayest Thou, The Son of man must be lifted up? Who is this Son of man? Then Yeshua said unto them, Yet a little while is the light with you. Walk while ye have the light, lest darkness come upon you; for he that walketh in darkness knoweth not whiter he goeth.*

John 17:1-3 *These words spake Yeshua and lifted up His eyes to Heaven, and said, Father, the hour is come; glorify thy Son, that Thy Son also may glorify Thee; As Thou hast given Him power over all flesh, that He should give eternal life to as many as Thou hast given Him. And this is life eternal, that they might know Thee the only true God, and Yeshua Messiah, whom Thou hast sent.*

Luke 19:9-11 *And Yeshua said unto him, This day is salvation come to this house, forsomuch as he also is a son of Abraham. For the Son of man is come to seek and to save that which was lost. And as they heard these things, He added and spake a parable, because He was nigh to Jerusalem, and because they thought that the Kingdom of God should immediately appear.*

In Hebrew the following Scripture also says, *"I have waited for Thy Yeshuah, O LORD!"*

Genesis 49:18 *I have waited for Thy salvation, O LORD.*

Now it is interesting to look at the words that the Chief Priests declared about Yeshua.

Matthew 27:39-43 *And they that passed by reviled Him, wagging their heads, And saying, Thou that destroyest the Temple, and buildest it in three days, save thyself. If Thou be the Son of God, come down from the cross. Likewise also the Chief Priests mocking Him, with the Scribes and Elders, said, He saved others; Himself He cannot save. If He be the King of Israel, let Him now come down from the cross, and we will believe Him. He trusted in God; let Him deliver Him now, if He will have Him; for He said, I AM the Son of God.*

Now it is very obvious exactly why Messiah Yeshua could not come down from the cross and save Himself even though He had the power to do so. Just like it was with Moses, if the Rod was lowered and not lifted up, then Israel would not be saved and have the Eternal victory from their Eternal KING. The KING Yeshua will build the Temple in three days, but first the Rod had to be lifted up for salvation to draw all mankind back to the Garden of God, and to fulfill His Living Testimony as the Almond Rod of God that budded. It is clear that Messiah Yeshua did not come to save Himself, but to save Israel and the entire world from the curse of death. So Yeshua refused to listen to them taunting Him, and telling Him to come down from the cross if He was the KING of Israel. The truth is that the LORD loved us so much, that He gave His only begotten Son, *Himself in a temporary vessel of flesh, as the second perfect Adam, the Rod of God, to reverse the curse of Adam,* so that whosoever believes in Him should not perish, but have everlasting life! This is the reason why it is written that whoever has the Son has the Father also, but whoever does not have the Son, does not have the Father either. *This is one God manifesting Himself in the flesh to redeem us back to Himself!*

This takes us back to the original Scripture that produced my Almond Tree miracle in 2007. Messiah Yeshua proclaimed that after He was *lifted up* then we would understand His identity! This was all part of the mystery of God that was to be revealed in the last days. When the LORD reigns in Jerusalem on the Temple Mount it will be a house of prayer for all nations.

John 3:14-17 *And as Moses lifted up the serpent in the wilderness, even so must the Son of man be lifted up; That whosoever believeth in Him should not perish, but have eternal life. For God so loved the world, that He gave His only begotten Son, that whosoever believeth in Him should not perish, but have everlasting life. For God sent not His Son into the world to condemn the world; but that the world through Him might be saved.*

When Messiah Yeshua was lifted up, we were to know for certain that He is the LORD God of Israel, *"I AM HE,"* the Eternal Royal Sovereign KING of Israel. He is the only KING OF KINGS AND LORD OF LORDS. The Almighty power is forever in the Rod of God lifted up! Psalm 59:16 says; *"But I will sing of Thy power; yes, I will sing aloud of Thy mercy in the morning; for Thou hast been my defence and refuge in the day of my trouble."*

Flower Blossoms Crabapple Tree Photo ©2013 Kimberly K Ballard All Rights Reserved

Flower Blossoms Crabapple Tree and Almond Rod Budding Photos

And the Almond Rod of God budded to life!

Isaiah 33:10 Now will I rise, saith the LORD; now will I be exalted; now will I lift up Myself.

Acts 4:33 And with great power gave the Apostles witness of the resurrection of the LORD Yeshua; and great grace was upon them all.

Psalm 21:13 Be Thou exalted, LORD, in Thine own strength; so will we sing and praise Thy power.

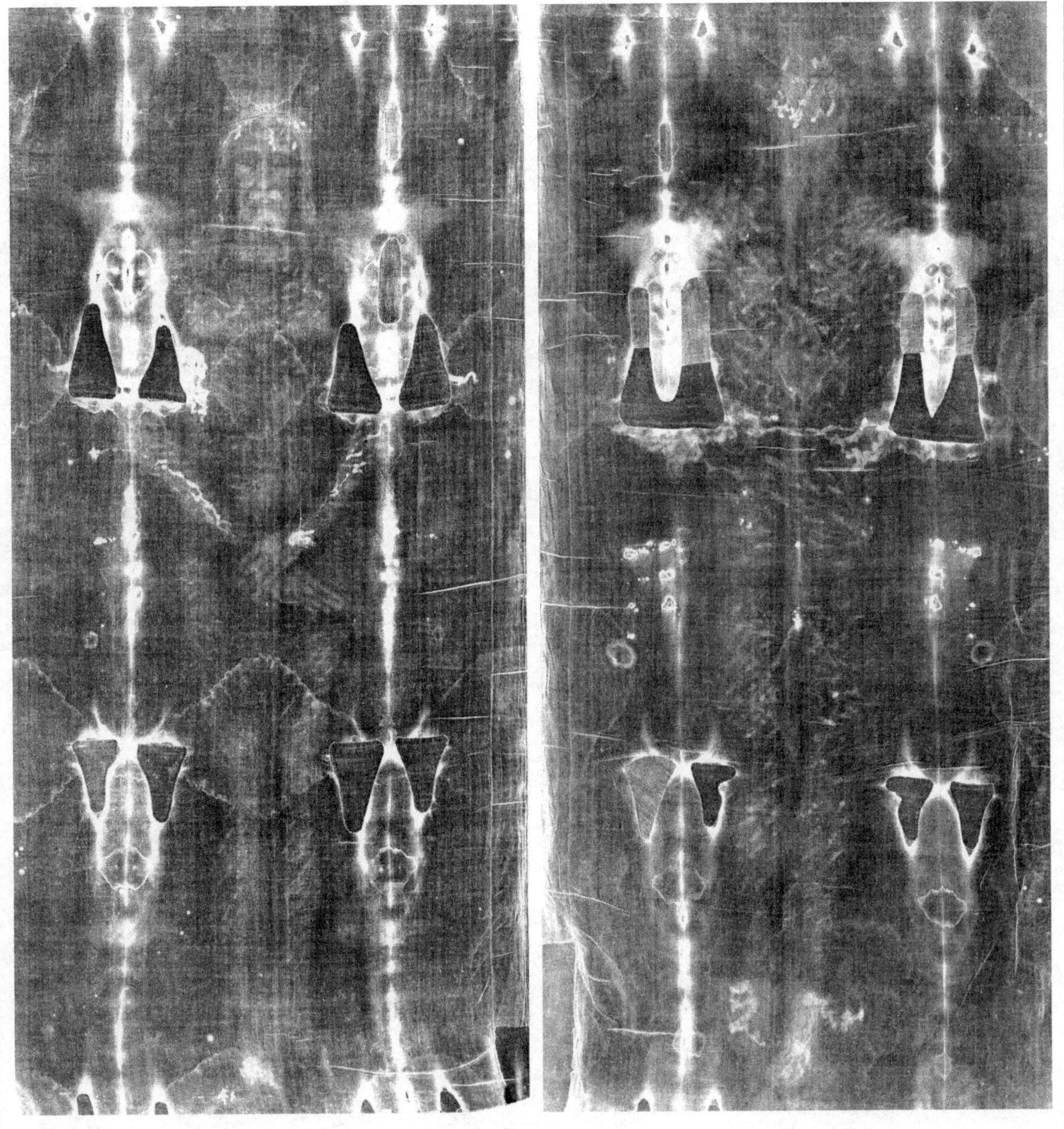

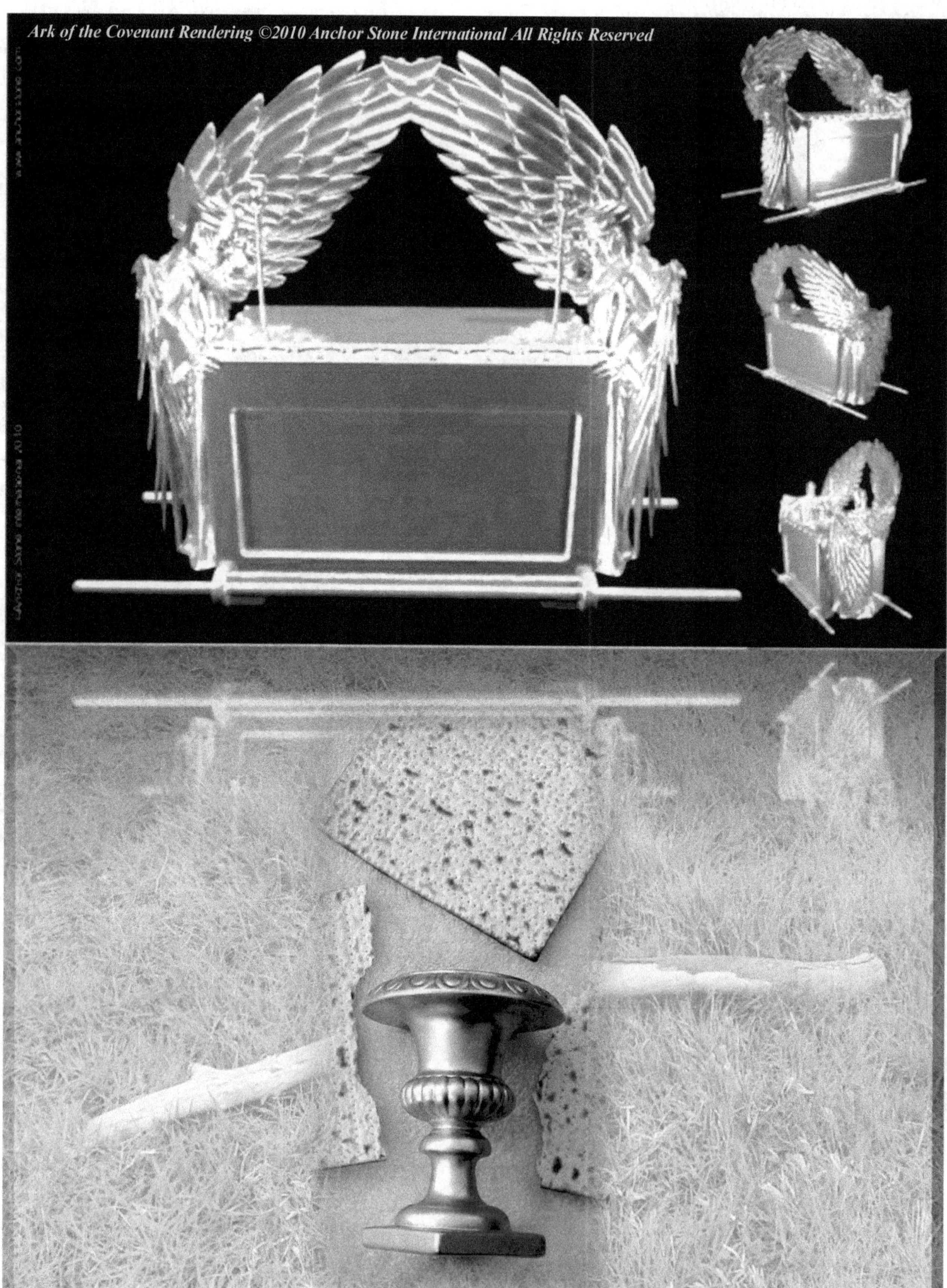

The Almond Rod is laid before the Testimony & Matzah Photo ©2013 Kimberly K Ballard All Rights Reserved

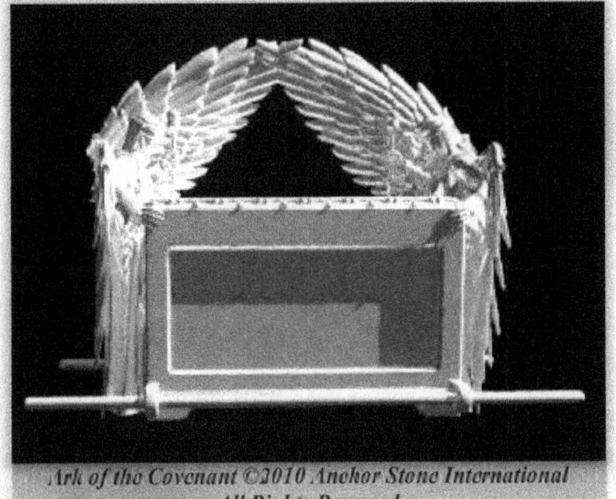

Chapter 4

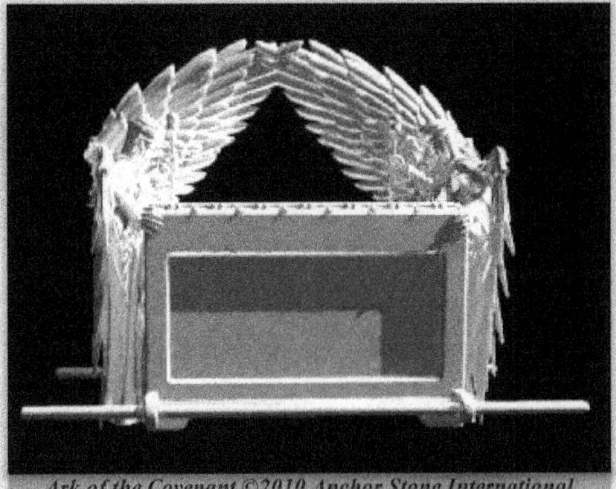

MOSES THE TABERNACLE THE ARK OF THE COVENANT

In the Biblical story of the Exodus, the LORD instructed Moses to build an earthly Tabernacle, with all of its furniture, furnishings, and vessels. The fine details were to be carefully observed by Moses. In essence, Moses was to copy the Heavenly Tabernacle, so the Tabernacle on the earth was an exact replica of it. This is why it was extremely important for Moses to follow God's instructions precisely. Within the fine details, the identity of the Messiah of Israel would be revealed, at the end of days. The LORD encoded Himself within His own design, so it contains the hidden mysteries of God. The LORD then showed King David His plans to build the Holy Temple in Jerusalem. Of course this Holy Temple was based upon the Tabernacle that Moses built. King David gathered all the materials necessary to complete this great task, and he gave the pattern to his son Solomon. King Solomon followed the pattern when he built the First Holy Temple in Jerusalem. Every element contained within and without this Tabernacle and Temple is therefore the parallel of the Heavenly Temple, where the LORD dwells in Heaven. Moses was also instructed by the LORD to record the Word of God and save it in an Ark, for future generations. The Torah is the direct Divine revelation of the LORD and this makes it more valuable than anything on earth. His Word is Eternal. Moses even understood that one day, the Messiah of Israel would be revealed through the design of the LORD. So we do not have to guess at the identity of the true Messiah of Israel. We only have to read the Word that Moses preserved in order to see and understand His identity.

So what if we have never paid attention to the design that the LORD showed to Moses? What if we never saw the pattern because we never thought to lean in and look at it, like the Almond blossom that conceals its inner petals? What if every single day, for centuries, it was right there in front of us, but no one saw it? What if generation after generation, everyone strolled by the beautiful blossoming Almond Tree that was standing in the center of the garden, admiring it from afar, but never bothered to get up close enough to observe its delicate flowers?

It stands to reason that the only person who would qualify to be the true Messiah of Israel would be the only one who matches the pattern that was given to Moses on Mount Sinai, and part of this pattern is the rod of Aaron! If we understand this, then we should comprehend that the Messiah was present throughout the entire history of Israel, and that He indeed goes back to the Ancient of Days. I know and believe that the LORD manifested Himself to me when He gave me the key to the mystery of the Messiah that is found in Aaron's rod that budded and I know this was the key that allowed me to see God face to face.

John 14:21 *He that hath My Commandments, and keepeth them, he it is that loveth Me; And he that loveth Me shall be loved of My Father, and I will love him, And will manifest Myself to him.*

In *the pattern,* we should see that *Messiah Yeshua is written in the Bible from the very beginning.* So the bottom line is that there is only one Messiah who fits every element of the LORD'S Divine design and now I want to show you the staggering truth!

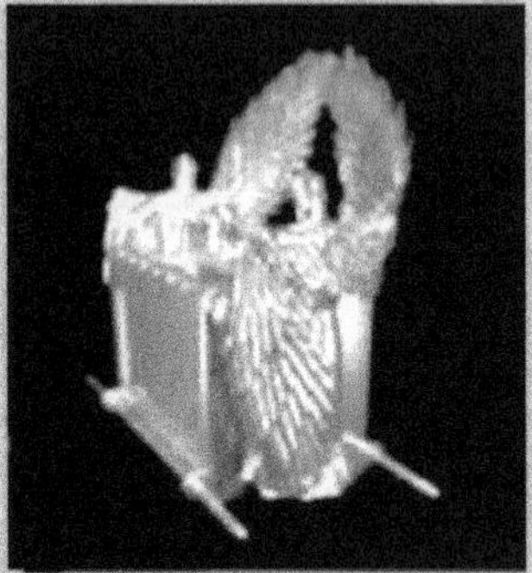

Ark of the Covenant

INSIDE THE ARK OF THE COVENANT OF MOSES THE TESTIMONY

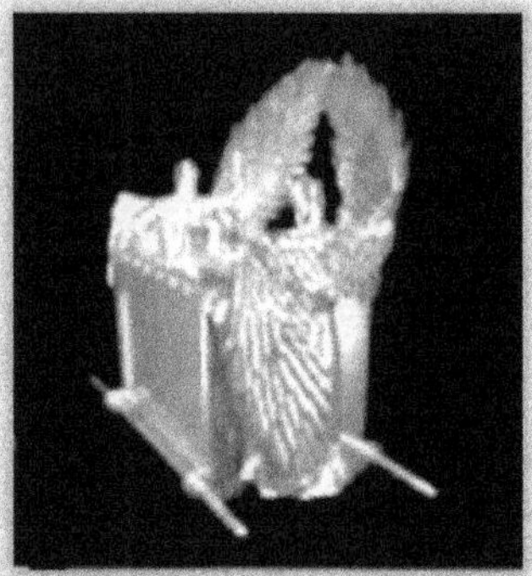

Ark of the Covenant

After my miracle of the Almond Tree occurred, the LORD opened the gates of His knowledge of revelation to my understanding, and I suddenly began to discern some of the greatest secrets never known before this time in history! I was literally stunned by everything!

The Jerusalem Almond Tree budding on Holy Mount Moriah was only the beginning. Many more miraculous revelations were yet to come in this story. I knew then, that the LORD was trying to show me the deeper secrets of His Eternal Testimony because we are truly living in the last days. The *Testimony* is placed inside the Ark.

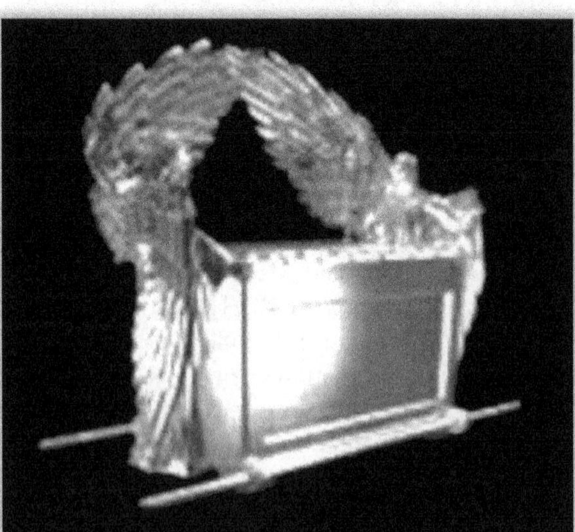

Ark of the Covenant ©2010 Anchor Stone International
All Rights Reserved

Exodus 25:16 *And thou shalt put into the Ark the Testimony which I shall give thee.*

There were three elements that the LORD told Moses to put inside the Ark of the Covenant, as the Testimony.

1. The golden jar of Manna, containing the bread from Heaven.

2. The rod of Aaron that was a branch cut off from an Almond Tree. This was the dead branch that came to life and bore flowers, buds, leaves and the fruit of almonds.

3. The Tablets of Stone, written by the finger of God, containing His Laws and Commandments.

These items were the contents of the Testimony of the Ark on earth, *but the Ark in Heaven contains the same three elements and the Heavenly versions are living! The Ark is symbolic of God's Presence among His people!*

INSIDE THE ARK OF HEAVEN THE LORD'S TESTIMONY

By the power of the Holy Spirit, I came to understand that this is precisely the reason why *Yeshua told the Pharisees to study the Scriptures. It was because Moses wrote of Him!*

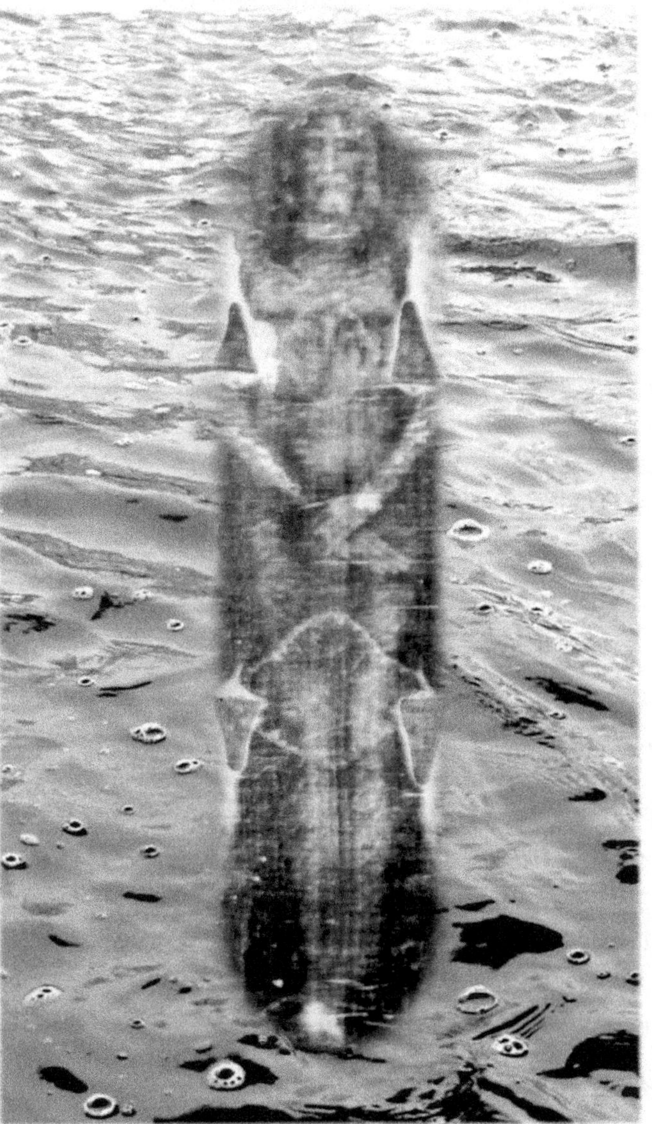

Shroud 3D Photo ©2013 Dr Petrus Soons All Rights Reserved
Edited to be on water by KK Ballard All Rights Reserved

John 5:45-46 *Do not think that I will accuse you to the Father; there is one that accuseth you, even Moses, in whom ye trust. For had ye believed Moses, ye would have believed Me; for he wrote of Me.*

You are about to see how Moses wrote of Messiah Yeshua with your own eyes, for the first time! *Moses wrote the hidden details about Messiah Yeshua in the Torah, so there would be no doubt of the Messiah's identity* and I will show you the proof, according to the Scriptures! It is astonishing!

KING Messiah, the LORD, is encoded in the Ark of the Living Covenant in Heaven in the same three items.
1. Messiah Yeshua is the unleavened Bread from Heaven, which is the Bread of Life.
2. Messiah Yeshua is the Almond Rod of God, the Branch cut off the Almond Tree. Yeshua was resurrected from death to life like Aaron's rod and He bore the First Fruit of Eternal life, from the Almond Tree of Life.
3. Messiah Yeshua is the Word of God, sitting at the right hand of the Ark of the LORD because He is the hand and finger of God, who wrote the Laws and Commandments. He is the Rock, the Living Chief Cornerstone of the Heavenly Temple. The Messiah wrote His Eternal Covenant, not upon stone this time, but upon the hearts of all women and all men.

Every item within the Ark of the throne of God is *the Living Testimony of Messiah, the LORD.* Now if we look at each one of the three elements contained within the Ark of the Covenant that abides in Heaven, with the corresponding Scriptures, we can see exactly how Moses revealed that Messiah Yeshua is the LORD God of Israel.

MESSIAH YESHUA THE LIVING BREAD FROM HEAVEN

Matzah & Cup, Snow on Maple Tree & broken Matzah

1. Messiah Yeshua is the Bread that came down from Heaven. The Word of God is *"The Living Torah,"* and He is the unleavened Bread of Heaven. So Messiah Yeshua is the Bread of Life! Yeshua told the people in Israel this truth when they asked Him for a sign!

John 6:30-35 *They said therefore unto Him, What sign shewest Thou then, that we may see, and believe Thee? What dost Thou work? Our fathers did eat manna in the desert; as it is written, He gave them bread from Heaven to eat. Then Yeshua said unto them, Verily, verily, I say unto you, Moses gave you not the bread from Heaven; but My Father giveth you the true Bread from Heaven. For the Bread of God is He which cometh down from Heaven, and giveth life unto the world. Then said they unto Him, LORD, evermore give us this Bread. And Yeshua said unto them, I AM the Bread of Life; he that cometh to Me shall never hunger; and he that believeth on Me shall never thirst.*

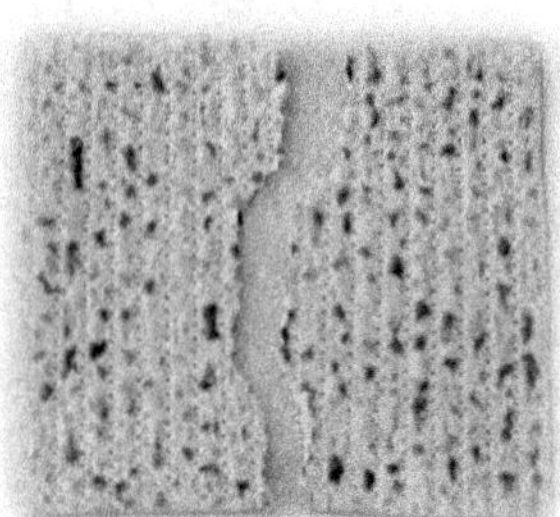

John 6:45-51 *It is written in the Prophets, And they shall be all taught of God. Every man therefore that hath heard, and hath learned of the Father, cometh unto Me. Not that any man hath seen the Father, save He which is of God, He hath seen the Father. Verily, verily, I say unto you, He that believeth on Me hath everlasting life. I AM the Bread of Life. Your fathers did eat manna in the wilderness, and are dead. This is the Bread which cometh down from Heaven, that a man may eat thereof, and not die. I AM the Living Bread which came down from Heaven; if any man eat of this Bread, he shall live forever; and the Bread that I will give is My flesh, which I will give for the life of the world.*

I Corinthians 11:23-29 *For I have received of the Lord that which also I delivered unto you, That the Lord Yeshua the same night in which He was betrayed took bread; And when He had given thanks, He brake it, and said, Take, eat; this is My body, which is broken for you; this do in remembrance of Me. After the same manner also He took the cup, when He had supped saying, this cup is the New Testament in My blood; this do ye, as oft as ye drink it, in remembrance of Me. For as often as ye eat this bread, and drink this cup, ye do shew the Lord's death till He come. Wherefore whosoever shall eat this bread, and drink this cup of the Lord, unworthily, shall be guilty of the body and blood of the Lord. But let a man examine himself, and so let him eat of that bread, and drink of that cup. For he that eateth and drinketh unworthily, eateth and drinketh damnation to himself, not discerning the Lord's body.*

Luke 22:7-22 *Then came the day of Unleavened Bread, when the Passover must be killed. And He sent Peter and John, saying, Go and prepare us the Passover, that we may eat. And they said unto Him, Where wilt Thou that we prepare? And He said unto them, Behold when ye are entered into the city, that shall a man meet you, bearing a pitcher of water; follow him into the house where he entereth in. And ye shall say unto the good man of the house, The Master saith unto thee, Where is the guest chamber, where I shall eat the Passover with my disciples? And he shall show you a large upper room furnished; there make ready the Passover. And when the hour was come, He sat down, and the twelve apostles with Him. And He said unto them, With desire I have desired to eat this Passover with you before I suffer; For I say unto you, I will not anymore eat thereof, until it be fulfilled in the Kingdom of God. And He took the cup, and gave thanks, and said, Take this, and divide it among yourselves; For I say unto you, I will* *not drink of the fruit of the vine, until the Kingdom of God shall come. And He took bread, and gave thanks, and brake it, and gave unto them, saying, This is My body which is given for you; this do in remembrance of Me. Likewise also the cup after supper, saying, This cup is the New Testament in My blood, which is shed for you. But, behold, the hand of him that betrayeth Me is with Me on the table. And truly the Son of man goeth, as it was determined; but woe unto that man by whom He is betrayed!*

Matthew 15:24-29 *But He answered and said, I am not sent but unto the lost sheep of the House of Israel. Then came she and worshipped Him, saying, Lord, help me. But He answered and said, It is not meet to take the children's bread, and to cast it to dogs. And she said, Truth, Lord; yet the dogs eat of the crumbs which fall from their Masters table. Then Yeshua said unto her, O woman, great is thy faith; be it unto thee even as thou wilt. And her daughter was made whole from that very hour. And Yeshua departed from thence, and came nigh unto the sea of Galilee; and went up into a Mountain, and sat down there.*

We must also remember that Messiah Yeshua was born in Bethlehem and this name means *"House of Bread."* The *hidden manna from Heaven* came to dwell in our midst.

Acts 2:42-47 *And they continued steadfastly in the Apostle's doctrine and fellowship, and in breaking of bread, and in prayers. And fear came upon every soul; and many wonders and signs were done by the Apostles. And all that believed were together, and had all things in common; And sold their possessions and goods, and parted them to all men, as every man had need. And they, continued daily with one accord in the Temple, and breaking bread from house to house, did eat their meat with gladness and singleness of heart, Praising God, and having favour with all the people. And the LORD added to the church daily such as should be saved.*

Now the Living Torah is the hidden manna, the mystery of Messiah revealed! The LORD is, of course, our Spiritual food in Heaven.

Revelation 2:17 *He that hath an ear, let him hear what the Spirit saith unto the churches; To him that overcometh will I give to eat of the hidden manna, and will give him a white stone, and in the stone a new name written, which no man knoweth saving he that receiveth it.*

MESSIAH YESHUA THE ALMOND ROD OF GOD

We have already seen this part of the Testimony but here it is pertaining to the Ark.

2. Messiah is the Almond Rod of God that is the exact parallel of Aaron's rod in the Heavenly Ark. Yeshua was cut off from His people Israel and He died, bearing the curse of Eden. He came to life as the Living Fruitful Branch on the third day, bearing the First Fruit of Eternal salvation, from the Almond Tree of Life.

The power of God is inside the Rod, the Messiah, as I will point out in the last chapter! Here are a few Scriptures proclaiming Yeshua's resurrection to life!

A Living Almond Rod of God Photos

Matthew 28:5-11 *And the angel answered and said unto the woman, Fear not ye; for I know that ye seek Yeshua, which was crucified. He is not here; for He is risen, as He said, Come, see the place where the LORD lay. And go quickly, and tell His disciples that He is risen from the dead; and, behold, He goeth before you into Galilee; there shall ye see Him; lo I have told you, And they departed quickly from the sepulchre with fear and great joy; and did run to bring His disciples word. And as they went to tell His disciples, behold, Yeshua met them, saying, All hail. And they came and held Him by the feet, and worshipped Him. Then said Yeshua unto them, Be not afraid; go tell my brethren that they go into Galilee, and there shall they see Me. Now when they were going, behold some of the watch came into the City, and shewed unto the Chief Priests all the things that were done.*

Mark 16:4-6 *And when they looked, they saw that the stone was rolled away; for it was very great. And entering into the sepulchre, they saw a young man sitting on the right side, clothed in a long white garment; and they were affrighted. And he saith unto them, Be not affrighted; Ye seek Yeshua of Nazareth, which was crucified; He is risen; He is not here; behold the place where they laid Him.*

John 20:8-9 *Then went in also that other disciple, which came first to the sepulchre, and he saw and believed. For as yet they knew not the Scripture, that He must rise again from the dead.*

Mark 14:27-28 *And Yeshua saith unto them, all ye shall be offended because of Me this night; for it is written, I will smite the Shepherd, and the sheep shall be scattered. But after that I AM risen, I will go before you into Galilee.*

Luke 24:33-34 *And they rose up the same hour, and returned to Jerusalem, and found the eleven gathered together, and them that were with them, Saying, The LORD is risen indeed, and hath appeared to Simon.*

Luke 14:25 *When once the Master of the House is risen up, and hath shut to the door, and ye begin to stand without, and to knock at the door, saying, LORD, LORD, open unto us; and He shall answer and say unto you, I know you not whence ye are.*

Acts 3:18-26 *But those things, which God before had shewed by the mouth of all His Prophets, that Messiah should suffer, He hath so fulfilled. Repent ye therefore, and be converted, that your sins may be blotted out, when the times of refreshing shall come from the Presence of the LORD; And He shall send Yeshua Messiah, which before was preached unto you; Whom the Heaven must receive until the times of restitution of all things, which God hath spoken by the mouth of all His Holy Prophets since the world began. For Moses truly said unto the fathers, A Prophet shall the LORD your God raise up unto you of your brethren, like unto me; Him shall ye hear in all things whatsoever He shall say unto you. And it shall come to pass, that every soul, which will not hear that Prophet, shall be destroyed from among the people. Yea, and all the Prophets from Samuel and those that follow after, as many as have spoken, have likewise foretold of these days. Ye are the children of the Prophets, and of the Covenant which God made with our fathers, saying unto Abraham, And in thy seed shall all the kindred's be blessed, Unto you first God, having raised up His Son Yeshua, sent Him to bless you, in turning away every one of you from his iniquities.*

Colossians 3:1 *If ye be risen with Messiah, seek those things which are above, where Messiah sitteth on the right hand of God.*

Isaiah told us that Messiah the Branch would bear fruit.

Isaiah 11:1 *Then a shoot will spring from the stem of Jesse, And a Branch from His roots will bear fruit.*

Messiah Yeshua's parents traveled to Bethlehem for the census of the Royal House and lineage of King David. Bethlehem the, *"House of Bread,"* was previously called *"Ephratah,"* the *"Place of Fruitfulness" and it was here that* Messiah Yeshua came to this earth to restore us to Heaven, as the Living Almond Branch. This is the Testimony of the LORD in Heaven.

I Corinthians 15:20-23 *But now is Messiah risen from the dead, and become the First Fruits of them that slept. For since by man came death, by man came also the resurrection of the dead. For as in Adam all die, even so in Messiah shall all be made alive. But every man in his own order; Messiah the First Fruits; afterward they that are Messiah's at His coming.*

In the book of II Kings, *the bread was the bread of the first fruits!* So Messiah Yeshua is the Bread from Heaven who was laid in the tomb, during the Feast of Unleavened Bread. Then Yeshua was raised to life as the First Fruits, on the Feast of First Fruits, on Nisan 17. This makes *Yeshua the Bread of the First Fruits* that is given to all the people that they may eat and become *the first fruits of His creatures.* In Luke 22 they heard Yeshua's Testimony!

II Kings 4:42 *And there came a man from Baalshalisha, and brought the man of God bread of the first fruits, twenty loaves of barley, and full ears of corn in the husk thereof. And he said, Give unto the people, that they may eat.*

Living Almond Tree of the Testimony of witness

James 1:18 *Of His own will begat He us with the Word of truth, that we should be a kind of first fruits of His creatures.*

Luke 22:66-71 *And as soon as it was day, the elders of the people and the chief priests and the scribes came together, and led him into their council, saying, Art thou the Messiah? Tell us. And he said unto them, If I tell you, ye will not believe: And if I also ask you, ye will not answer me, nor let me go. Hereafter shall the Son of man sit on the right hand of the power of God. Then said they all, Art thou then the Son of God? And he said unto them, Ye say that I am. And they said, What need we any further witness? For we ourselves have heard of his own mouth.*

Living Almond Tree of the Testimony Photo ©2013 Kimberly K Ballard All Rights Reserved

The Chief Priests heard *the Testimony of witness* from Messiah Yeshua's own Words. When Yeshua was asked if He was the Messiah, the Son of God, He told the Chief Priests and the Scribes that it was true. Then He told them that in the future, they would see Him sitting at the right hand of *the power* of God, because He is the *Royal Rod of God.*

Matthew 26:63-64 *But Yeshua kept silent, and the High Priest said to Him, I adjure You by the Living God, that You tell us whether You are the Messiah the Son Of God. Yeshua said to Him, You have said it yourself; nevertheless I tell you, hereafter you shall see The Son of Man sitting at the right hand of power and coming on the clouds of Heaven.*

THE WORD OF GOD WRITTEN IN STONE WITH THE FINGER OF GOD

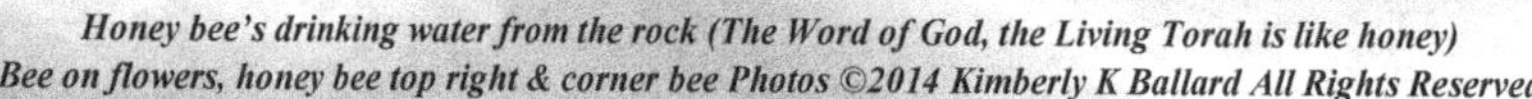

Honey bee's drinking water from the rock (The Word of God, the Living Torah is like honey)
Bee on flowers, honey bee top right & corner bee Photos ©2014 Kimberly K Ballard All Rights Reserved

3. Messiah is the Word of God. *Yeshua is the Living Torah* and the Chief Cornerstone laid in Zion and He is the stone that the builder's rejected, the Rock of offense. *The Rod in the right hand of God has the finger that writes the Laws and Commandments of God.* The Word of God was written in stone by the finger of God on Mount Sinai, *but Messiah Yeshua the LORD would write His Living Torah Covenant Testimony on the hearts of mankind forever in the Garden in Jerusalem.* From the time of the destruction of the Second Temple, after Yeshua departed and ascended into Heaven in the glory cloud, the Living Testimony of the *"Living Torah"* was forever written upon the heart, because the sheep of the House of Israel were scattered, no longer having a Holy Temple in Jerusalem. The Scriptures below verify this.

John 1:1-5 *In the beginning was the Word, and the Word was with God, and the Word was God. The same was in the beginning with God. All things were made by Him; and without Him was not anything made that was made. In Him was life; and the life was the light of men. And the light shineth in darkness; and the darkness comprehended it not.*

I Peter 1:18-23 *Forasmuch as ye know that ye were not redeemed with corruptible things, as silver and gold, from your vain conversation received by tradition from your fathers; But with the precious blood of Messiah, as of a lamb without blemish and without spot; Who verily was foreordained before the foundation of the world, but was manifest in these last times for you. Who by Him do believe in God, that raised Him up from the dead, and gave Him glory; that your faith and hope might be in God. Seeing ye have purified your souls in obeying the truth through the Spirit unto unfeigned love of the brethren, see that ye love one another with a pure heart fervently; Being born again, not of corruptible seed, but of incorruptible, by the Word of God, which liveth and abideth forever.*

Revelation 19:13 *And He was clothed with a vesture dipped in blood; and His Name is called The Word of God.*

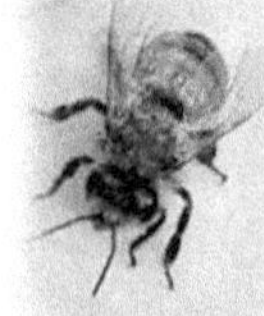

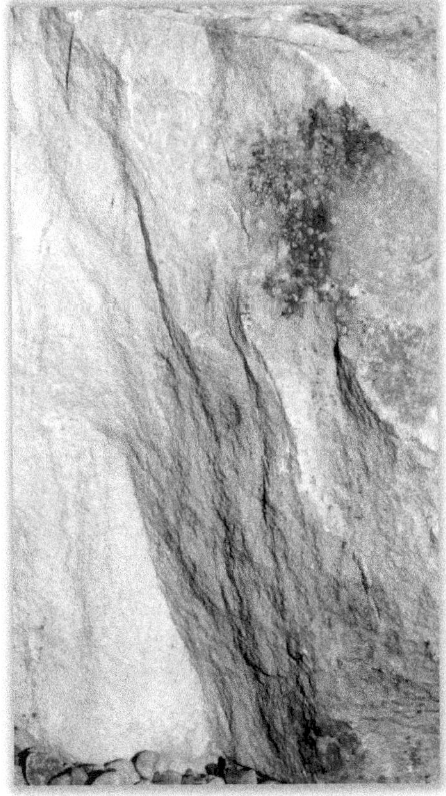

Stone Photo ©2014

Isaiah 28:16 *Therefore, thus saith the LORD God, Behold, I lay in Zion for a Foundation a Stone, a tried Stone, a precious Cornerstone, a sure Foundation; he that believeth shall not make haste.*

I Peter 2:6-8 *Wherefore also it is contained in the Scriptures, Behold, I lay in Zion a Chief Cornerstone, elect, precious; and he that believeth on Him shall not be confounded. Unto you therefore which believe He is precious; but unto them which be disobedient, the Stone which the builders disallowed, the same is made the head of the corner, And a Stone of stumbling, and a Rock of offense, even to them which stumble at the Word, being disobedient; whereunto also they were appointed.*

At the end of the age, Messiah Yeshua is the Stone that will crush the corrupted kingdoms of this world that originated in ancient Babylon, just like Moses burned the golden calf with fire, crushed it into dust and threw it into the brook of living water. Yeshua will pour forth the fire of God's wrath with the Word from His mouth, crushing the pagan Babylonian kingdoms of this world and the fire of His Spirit will purify the earth from these abominations. Then Messiah Yeshua, the Stone out of Holy Mount Moriah, will set up the Eternal Kingdom of Heaven in the New Jerusalem, in Israel and there will be no more sin or evil. The LORD will dwell in our midst upon the Ark of His Living Testimony in the Heavenly Temple, in the Eternal city of Jerusalem. Yeshua stayed in the wilderness forty days and nights and did not eat bread or drink water, just like Moses did not eat bread or drink water. *The Living Torah is written upon this Stone, the LORD God.*

Matthew 21:42-44 *Yeshua said to them, Did you never read in the Scriptures, The Stone which the builders rejected, This became the Chief Cornerstone; This came about from the LORD, And it is marvelous in our eyes? Therefore I say to you, the Kingdom of God will be taken away from you, and be given to a nation producing the fruit of it. And he who falls on this Stone will be broken to pieces; but on whomever it falls, it will scatter him like dust.*

Deuteronomy 9:21 *And I took your sin, the calf which ye had made, and burnt it with fire, and stamped it, and ground it very small, even until it was as small as dust; and I cast the dust thereof into the brook that descended out of the Mount.*

Yeshua is the Stone cut out of the Mountain of God, made without hands, that crushes the kingdoms of the great statue in Daniel's prophecy.

Daniel 2:31-36 *Thou, O king, sawest, and behold a great image. This great image, whose brightness was excellent, stood before thee; and the form thereof was terrible. This image's head was of fine gold, his breast and his arms of silver, his belly and his thighs of brass, His legs of iron, his feet part of iron and part of clay. Thou sawest till that a Stone was cut out without hands, which smote the image upon his feet that were of iron and clay, and brake them to pieces. Then was the iron, the clay, the brass, the silver, and the gold, broken to pieces together, and became like the chaff of the summer threshing floors; and the wind carried them away, so that no place was found for them; and the Stone that smote the image became a great Mountain, and filled the whole earth. This is the dream; and we will tell the interpretation thereof before the king.*

The great Mountain that fills the whole earth with righteousness is the Mountain called Moriah where Messiah the LORD will reign forever, after He crushes these corrupted kingdoms of the earth and blows away the chaff with the breath of His Holy Spirit/Ruach.

Daniel believed that the LORD was his KING and he understood the meaning of the secrets and mysteries of Messiah Yeshua, *the Stone and the Word of God.*

Daniel 2:44-47 *And in the days of these kings shall the God of Heaven set up a Kingdom, which shall never be destroyed; and the Kingdom shall not be left to other people, but it shall break in pieces and consume all these kingdoms, and it shall stand forever. Forasmuch as thou sawest that the Stone was cut out of the Mountain without hands, and that it brake in pieces the iron, the brass, the clay, the silver, and the gold; the great God hath made known to the king what shall come to pass hereafter; and the dream is certain, and the interpretation thereof sure. Then the king Nebuchadnezzar fell upon his face, and worshipped Daniel, and commanded that they should offer an oblation and sweet odours unto him. The king answered unto Daniel, and said, Of a truth it is, that your God is a God of gods, and a LORD of kings, and a revealer of secrets, seeing thou couldest reveal this secret.*

In the book of Revelation, we see the fulfillment of this prophecy. Here, Messiah Yeshua is the KING OF KINGS who comes to rule with a Rod of iron and to dash them to pieces because they have corrupted the earth with their abominations.

Revelation 2:25-27 *Nevertheless what you have, hold fast until I come. And he who overcomes, and he who keeps My deeds until the end, To him I will give authority over the Nations; And He shall rule them with a Rod of iron, as the vessels of the potter are broken to pieces, as I also have received authority from My Father.*

When the veil is taken away from our eyes, we can see that Yeshua is the Messiah of Israel, *who is the Living Heavenly Ark of the Covenant.* Every single Scripture proves that *Yeshua is the Almond Rod that budded* and that He is *the Living Bread from Heaven* and *the Living Torah* Word of God. *He is the Stone and the finger of God,* who writes His Living Testimony upon our hearts, so they are no longer hard like tablets of stone, but sealed with His life blood through His love for us upon the tender tablets of our hearts, and this Living Covenant gives us Eternal life.

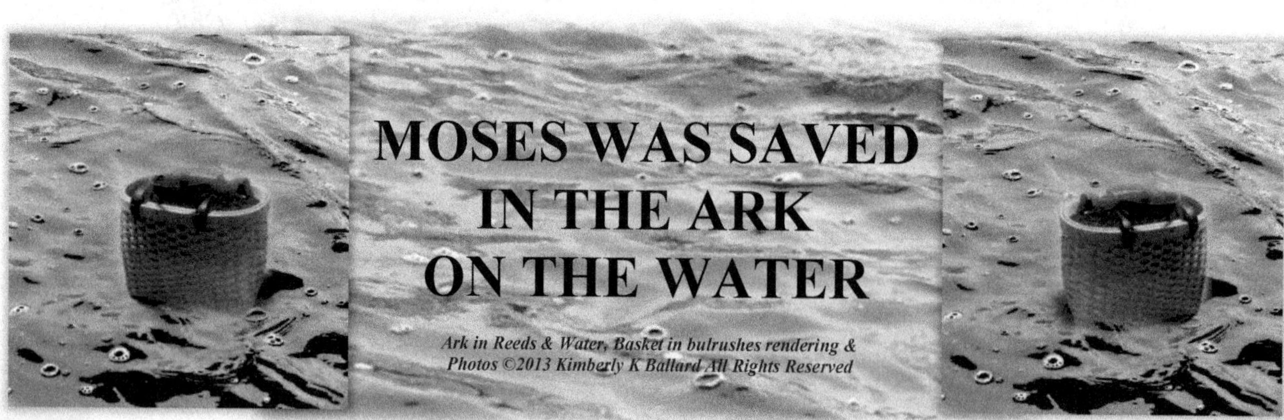

Ark in Reeds & Water, Basket in bulrushes rendering & Photos ©2013 Kimberly K Ballard All Rights Reserved

An Ark is a chest or box, *symbolizing the Divine Presence of God.* As a baby, Moses was saved in a type of Ark, as it floated upon the surface of the waters, while other babies perished. The mother of Moses hid him for three months, before she put Moses inside the Ark of bulrushes lined with pitch, to save him from death by the decree of Pharaoh. Now the most interesting detail about the Ark is the fact that throughout history, the Ark always saved people from certain death, even though *the Ark came in different forms, shapes and sizes. The Ark was a place or haven of salvation.* In Hebrew the name, *"Moses,"* is, *"Moshe."* His mother named him this, because he was, *"Drawn out of water."*

Exodus 2:1-3 *And there went a man of the house of Levi, and took to wife a daughter of Levi. And the woman conceived, and bare a son; and when she saw him that he was a goodly child, she hid him three months.*

And when she could not longer hide him, she took for him an Ark of bulrushes, and daubed it with slime and with pitch, and put the child therein; and she laid it in the flags by the river's brink.

Moses Ark & Bulrushes
Photos ©2014

Moses, who was a *redeemer* of Israel, *was representative of Messiah Yeshua,* the deliverer and Saviour, who was to come. We know that the Divine Presence of the LORD was upon the Ark of Moses, because in the beginning, the Spirit of the LORD God moved upon the face of the waters. Moses moved on the face of the waters, in the Ark.

Genesis 1:2 *And the earth was without form and void; and darkness was upon the face of the great deep. And the Spirit of God moved upon the face of the waters.*

NOAH WAS SAVED IN THE ARK ON THE WATER

Noah's Ark Rendering
Photos ©2013 by Kimberly K Ballard All Rights Reserved

The Ark of Noah, floated on the surface of the waters. By the Divine intervention of the LORD, He gave *the righteous* salvation in the Ark and gave them protection from the apocalyptic flood waters. The Divine Presence of the LORD was with Noah in the Ark because Noah walked with God. *When the time was right for the judgment of the wicked, Noah went into the Ark with his family, with the clean and unclean animals and birds and every living thing.* Then the LORD shut the door of the Ark. The Ark became a Divine refuge of salvation and protection from the judgment that came upon the wicked who perished because they were not in the Ark of God's salvation. If the wicked had repented and turned to the LORD God and believed in His salvation plan, then perhaps they would not have perished when the waters overtook the earth. Instead of believing, they mocked the Ark, while it was being built by righteous Noah. So when the flood came, they were left outside the door of the Ark. Noah completed everything that God had commanded him to do before *"the great day"* when the rains began to fall.

Flood Waters of September 2013 remembering the Ark of Noah
Photos ©2013
Kimberly K Ballard All Rights Reserved

In Genesis, we can see how the Great flood came upon the earth.

Genesis 6:12-22 *And God looked upon the earth, and, behold, it was corrupt; for all flesh had corrupted his way upon the earth. And God said unto Noah, The end of all flesh is come before Me; for the earth is filled with violence through them; and, behold, I will destroy them with the earth. Make thee an Ark of gopher wood; rooms shalt thou make in the Ark, and shalt pitch it within and without* *with pitch. And this is the fashion which thou shalt make it of; The length of the Ark shall be three hundred cubits, the breadth of it fifty cubits, and the height of it thirty cubits. A window shalt thou make to the Ark, and in a cubit shalt thou finish it above; and the door of the Ark shalt thou set in the side thereof; with lower, second, and third stories shalt thou make it. And, behold, I, even I, do bring a flood of waters upon the earth, to destroy all flesh, wherein is the breath of life, from under Heaven; and everything that is in the earth shall die. But with thee will I establish My Covenant; and thou shalt come into the Ark, thou, and thy sons, and thy wife, and thy sons' wives with thee. And of every living thing of all flesh, two of every sort shalt thou bring into the Ark, to keep them alive with thee; they shall be male and female. Of fowls after their kind, and of cattle after their kind, of every creeping thing of the earth after his kind, two of every sort shall come unto thee, to keep them alive. And take thou unto thee of all food that is eaten, and thou shalt gather it to thee; and it shall be for food for thee, and for them. Thus did Noah; according to all that God commanded him, so did he.*

Genesis 7:1-24 *And the LORD said unto Noah, Come thou and all thy house into the Ark; for thee have I seen righteous before Me in this generation. Of every clean beast thou shalt take to thee by sevens, the male and his female; and of beasts that are not clean by two, the male and his female. Of fowls also of the air by sevens, the male and the female; to keep seed alive upon the face of all the earth. For yet seven days, and I will cause it to rain upon the earth forty days and forty nights; and every living substance that I have made will I destroy from off the face of the earth. And Noah did according unto all that the LORD commanded him. And Noah was six hundred years old when the flood of waters was upon the earth. And Noah went in, and his sons, and his wife, and his son's wives with him, into the Ark, because of the waters of the flood. Of clean beasts, and of beasts that are not clean, and of fowls, and of everything that creepeth upon the earth, There went in two and two unto Noah into the Ark, the male and the female, as God had commanded Noah. And it came to pass after seven days, that the waters of the flood were upon the earth. In the six hundredth year of Noah's life, in the second month, the seventeenth day of the month, the same day were all the fountains of the great deep broken up, and the windows of Heaven were opened. And the rain was upon the earth forty days and forty nights. In the selfsame day entered Noah, and Shem, and Ham, and Japheth, the sons of Noah, and Noah's wife, and the three wives of his sons with them, into the Ark; They, and every beast after his kind, and all the cattle after their kind, and every creeping thing that creepeth upon the earth after his kind, and every fowl after his kind, every bird of every sort. And they went in unto Noah into the Ark, two and two of all flesh, wherein is the breath of life. And they that went in, went in male and female of all flesh, as God had commanded him; and the LORD shut him in. And the flood was forty days upon the earth; and the waters increased, <u>and bare up the Ark, and it was lift up above the earth.</u> And the waters prevailed, and were increased greatly upon the earth; and the Ark went upon the face of the waters. And the waters prevailed exceedingly upon the earth; and all the high hills that were under the whole Heaven, were covered. Fifteen cubits upward did the waters prevail; and the mountains were covered. And all flesh died that moved upon the earth, both of fowl, and of cattle, and of beast, and of every creeping thing that creepeth upon the earth, and every man; All in whose nostrils was the breath of life, of all that was in the dry land, died. And every living substance was destroyed which was upon the face of the ground, both man, and cattle, and the creeping things, and the fowl of the Heaven; and they were destroyed from the earth; and Noah only remained alive, and they that were with him in the Ark. And the waters prevailed upon the earth an hundred and fifty days.*

Remembering Noah's flood
the Rushing Waters of Boulder Creek

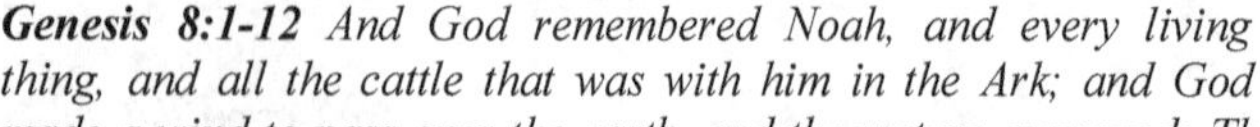

Genesis 8:1-12 *And God remembered Noah, and every living thing, and all the cattle that was with him in the Ark; and God made a wind to pass over the earth, and the waters asswaged; The fountains also of the deep and the windows of Heaven were stopped, and the rain from Heaven was restrained; And the waters returned from off the earth continually; and after the end of the hundred and fifty days the waters were abated. And the Ark rested in the*

A Dove wading in water in the birdbath
Photo ©2014 Kimberly K Ballard

seventh month, on the seventeenth day of the month, upon the mountains of Ararat. And the waters decreased continually until the tenth month; in the tenth month, on the first day of the month, were the tops of the mountains seen. And it came to pass at the end of forty days, that Noah opened the window of the Ark which he had made; And he sent forth a raven, which went forth to and fro, until the waters were dried up from off the earth. Also he sent forth a dove from him, to see if the waters were abated from off the face of the ground; But the dove found no rest for the sole of her foot, and she returned unto him into the Ark, for the waters were on the face of the whole earth; then he put forth his hand, and took her, and pulled her in unto him into the Ark. And he stayed yet other seven days; and again he sent forth the dove out of the Ark; And the dove came in to him in the evening; and, lo, in her mouth was an olive leaf pluckt off; so Noah knew that the waters were abated from off the earth. And he stayed yet other seven days; and sent forth the dove; which returned not again unto him anymore.

As I thought about the dove of Noah in the Ark, I thought of a few beautiful doves that seem to thrive in my yard since my Almond Tree revelation and I have often noticed that the doves do not like to set the sole of their feet down in unclean water. If I scrub the birdbath and wash it clean with fresh water, the doves will come to wade in the clean water. Noah's dove could not find anywhere to alight and she returned to set her feet in the Ark. Doves also feed on the ground. So Noah's dove could not find any ground where she could feed because the waters were not yet abated. *Now when I saw this, I suddenly realized that the LORD cleanses the earth by the two elements that are representative of His Holy Spirit/Ruach!* The Holy Spirit moved on the surface of *the waters* in the beginning, and the Holy Spirit is given to us through our baptism in *the Living Water.* The Holy Spirit was the all consuming *fire* on the burning bush, and the Holy Spirit in *flaming tongues of fire* alighted upon the Jewish disciples of Yeshua, in Jerusalem on Shavuot.

1. The LORD cleansed the earth the first time with *water* in the Great Flood.
2. The LORD will cleanse the earth the second time with *fire* at the end of the age. The two witnesses, who will come in the power of God's Holy Spirit during the tribulation, will have the power to control the rain, which is *the water,* and *the fire* proceeds out of their mouths to devour their enemies, like a consuming fire! *The two witnesses are speaking and prophesying the Living Torah Testimony of Messiah the LORD.* When Elijah was on the earth, the Holy Spirit was upon him and he shut the Heavens so it did not rain and there was no *water.* When Moses was on the earth, the power of the Holy Spirit of the LORD was upon him and upon his rod, so he was able to turn the *water* into blood and he brought forth the plagues of Egypt. The LORD spoke *the Living Torah* to Moses out of the consuming *fire* on the burning bush and out of the consuming *fire* upon Mount Sinai. When the Holy Spirit is abiding upon the two witnesses, they will cleanse through these two elements. We will look at them later!

Remembering Flood Waters of Noah
Photos ©2013 Kimberly K Ballard

Once I understood that the LORD cleanses with *water* first and *fire* second, I realized this was a profound revelation because it directly connects to our baptism. This is exactly what happened to the Jewish disciples of Yeshua who were first baptized in the Jordan River. Later when they waited in Jerusalem to be endued with power, it came about on Shavuot or Pentecost seven weeks after Passover, they received the fire of the Holy Spirit. He appeared with a mighty rushing wind in flaming cleft tongues of fire and rested and abode upon each one of Yeshua's Jewish disciples. After they received the Holy Spirit of the LORD, they were suddenly filled with the power to perform the mighty miracles of the Rod of God. Our baptism in the LORD is symbolic of Messiah Yeshua's resurrection because our sins are put to death in the Living Water. We are then raised up out of the Living Water in the power and fire of the Holy Spirit that now abides within us and gives us new life. Therefore, we are sealed and have the promise of Eternal life in the LORD. So with this truth, I suddenly realized that this explains why the believers in Messiah Yeshua, who have already been cleansed and purified in the LORD through the two elements that represent the Holy Spirit of the LORD, are not destined for the wrath of God that comes with His judgment. *We have already been saved in the Ark of Heaven.* God was the support for Noah's Ark and His hand of protection was always upon it. When the family of Noah disembarked from the Ark, all life was given a fresh start to begin again on the right path, leading us to the LORD of glory.

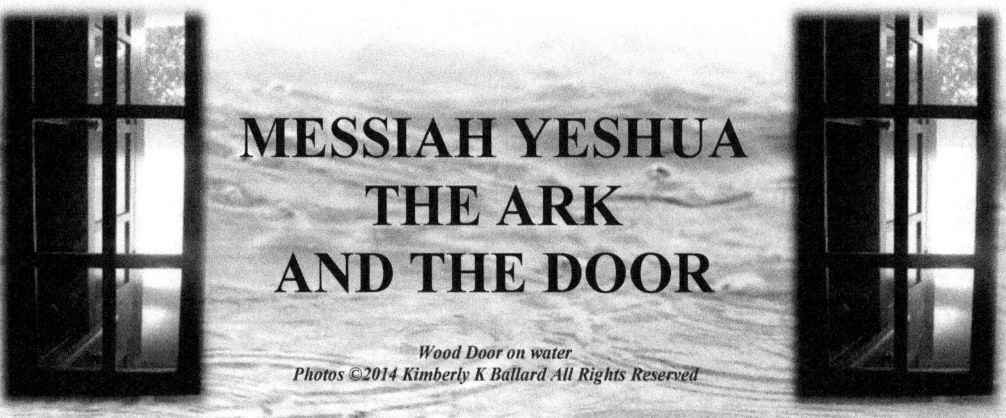

Wood Door on water
Photos ©2014 Kimberly K Ballard All Rights Reserved

Noah's Ark was a type of barn. A barn is a place for storing animals and grain for later use. The Ark had a door and it was through this door that all the cargo was loaded before the door of the Ark was shut. In order to be preserved and saved from the coming flood, everything had to enter in through the door. The Ark of Noah protected the grain and all the living beings inside the Ark. They were kept for later use by the LORD. They were in a haven of protection from the violent storm of judgment because they listened to the LORD when He directed them to enter into the Ark through the door. They did not even see the flood because they were divinely kept secure in the Ark made of Acacia wood and pitch. The flood waters suddenly burst forth from the depths of the ocean as the tectonic plates shifted and the earth's crust was made cleft. Water rose from the middle as the earth parted to the right and to the left. The rains of the Heavenly canopy poured down from Heaven and covered the whole earth.

By definition the Ark is like a barn;

Barn *- A large building, as on a farm for storing hay, grain, etc. and often for housing livestock.* ***(Source: Random House College Dictionary, revised edition 1975 Copyright 1975 By Random House, Inc.).***

Flood waters & uprooted Tree Photo ©2013 Kimberly K Ballard All Rights Reserved

The good grain of wheat is kept inside the barn, like the righteous Saints are kept inside the Ark of God. So Noah, his family, and the living creatures were also like good grain, stored in the barn of the LORD.

The believers of the LORD God are like manna that is stored in the Heavenly Ark of the Covenant. They are gathered into the LORD'S barn.

Matthew 13:24-30 *Another parable put He forth unto them, saying, The Kingdom of Heaven is likened unto a man* *which sowed good seed in his field; But while men slept, his enemy came and sowed tares among the wheat, and went his way. But when the blade was sprung up, and brought forth fruit, then appeared the tares also. So the servants of the householder came and said unto him, Sir, didst not thou sow good seed in thy field? From whence then hath it tares? He said unto them, an enemy hath done this. The servants said unto him, Wilt thou then that we go and gather them up? But He said, nay; lest while ye gather up the tares, ye root up also the wheat with them. Let both grow together until the harvest; and in the time of harvest I will say to the reapers, Gather ye together first the tares, and bind them in bundles to burn them; but gather the wheat into my barn.*

Messiah Yeshua declared that He is the door of the sheep. He said *"No one goes in through the door, except through Me."* The Good Shepherd sits at the door with His Rod and He guides only His sheep through the door where they are kept safe. He closes the door behind them to protect them from any predators, and He saves them from any evil that would befall them by keeping every evil outside and away from His flock. He is concerned about their welfare and He provides everything for them to thrive.

John 10: 7-9 *Then said Yeshua unto them again, Verily, verily, I say unto you, I AM the door of the sheep. All that ever came before me are thieves and robbers; but the sheep did not hear them. I AM the door; by Me if any man enter in, he shall be saved, and shall go in and out, and find pasture.*

Wood Door with glass panels
Photo ©2014 Kimberly K Ballard

Messiah Yeshua also told the parable of the ten virgins. This parable speaks of Yeshua returning from Heaven for those that have accepted the *Living Covenant* that He made with the unleavened bread and the cup of wine at His last Passover Seder. It symbolized His Jewish payment of the Bride's price. Yeshua revealed Himself as the Bridegroom from Heaven who will come to take His Bride at some future date. It will be just like it was in the days of Noah. The five wise virgins had the five books of Moses and they had the oil in their lamps, the Spirit of the Living God. So they went through the door when the Bridegroom came and the door was shut behind them. The five foolish virgins had five pillars that they thought was the voice of God but it was not. Having been deceived they were left outside the door yelling, *"LORD, LORD, let us in didn't we do things in Your name, and in Your name cast out demons?"* He said to them *"Depart from Me, I never knew you!"* They had performed their deeds *"In the name of"* Satan who has been elevating *himself above the Living God. It was* Satan inspiring them to murder with terrors *"in his name!"* They received eternal death! They did not have *The Living Torah,* Messiah the Living God. Without a pure wedding garment, they could not enter the inner court of the KING!

Matthew 25:1-13 *Then shall the Kingdom of Heaven be likened unto ten virgins, which took their lamps, and went forth to meet the Bridegroom. And five of them were wise, and five were foolish. They that were foolish took their lamps, and took no oil with them; But the wise took oil in their lamps. While the Bridegroom tarried, they all slumbered and slept. And at midnight there was a cry made, Behold, the Bridegroom cometh; go ye out to meet Him, Then all those virgins arose, and trimmed their lamps. And the foolish said unto the wise, Give us of your oil; for our lamps are gone out. But the wise answered, saying, Not so; lest there be not enough for us and you; but go ye rather to them that sell, and buy for yourselves. And while they went to buy; the Bridegroom came; and they that were ready went in with Him to the marriage; and the door was shut. Afterward came also the other virgins, saying, LORD, LORD, open to us. But He answered and said Verily, verily I say unto you, I know you not. Watch therefore, for ye know neither the day not the hour wherein the Son of Man cometh.*

It is through *the power of the Holy Spirit abiding upon Messiah the Rod,* that we have obtained salvation. We can only be saved and protected if we come into *The Living Ark* of the LORD, before the wrath of God's final judgment comes upon the earth. Getting into Yeshua's Ark before the judgment reminds me of a song by the musician, Prince, that tells us to *"Get on the boat, people!"* I could not have said it better myself! We must abide in the Eternal Testimony of the Living Ark of the LORD Yeshua who is the Bread, the Almond Rod, the Living Torah and the Rock. Just as the LORD made His Covenant with us with the rainbow after the flood of Noah, Yeshua made a Covenant with us and the rainbow is over the Ark of His Living Covenant in Heaven. Yeshua said that He will cleanse the earth by fire at the end of the age. Those who have not been cleansed by the LORD'S baptism in *the Living Water* and in *the fire* of His Holy Spirit will experience the judgment of God.

Matthew 25:37-39 *But as the days of Noah were, so shall also the coming of the Son of man be. For as in the days that were before the flood they were eating and drinking, marrying and giving in marriage, until the day that Noah entered into the Ark, And knew not until the flood came, and took them all away; so shall also the coming of the Son of man be.*

II Thessalonians 1:6-8 *Seeing it is a righteous thing with God to recompense tribulation to them that trouble you; And to you who are troubled rest with us, when the LORD Yeshua shall be revealed from Heaven with His mighty angels, In flaming fire taking vengeance on them that know not God, and that obey not the Gospel of our LORD Yeshua Messiah.*

Life will be going on as usual, just like it did with righteous Noah and then suddenly the end will come. I mentioned before, that when Noah was preparing the Ark, the people all around him were mocking the Ark and laughing at it. They were scoffers who ridiculed righteous Noah, because he believed God and trusted by faith in His Word of salvation. This is exactly what is happening in our generation. Yeshua, *the Living Ark of God,* has been preparing us for centuries to meet Him face to face. So it is interesting that throughout the centuries, the unbeliever's in the world have continually mocked Messiah Yeshua, the only Ark of Eternal salvation. The LORD is giving the believer's fair warning now, like He did with Noah, to get ready and to prepare ourselves to enter the Ark of salvation before the judgment comes upon the scoffers who will not believe in God's salvation plan. The time right now is our preparation period before the judgment comes upon the earth! The LORD also gave fair warning to Noah to prepare and to get ready to enter the Ark before the flood waters of judgment came. *Noah went into the Ark that was prepared ahead of time, before the flood came.* As soon as Noah was safely through the door of the Ark and tucked away inside for protection, the LORD shut the door behind his family and it was too late for anyone else that remained outside the Ark of His protection and salvation. This is why it is so important to turn your heart to the LORD right now and obey the Commandments and Words of the LORD because this is the only way to Heaven. This is how it will be when Yeshua gathers us suddenly in the rapture. He will close the door of Heaven behind Him after we are safely tucked away for protection in Heaven, in the true Ark of God. Many on the earth will suddenly and quite tragically realize that they have been left outside of the Ark! They will scream to the LORD to let them in, but He will say to them, *"Depart from me, I never knew you!"* Anyone that continues to live in sin, mocking Yeshua, and any who secretly plot to bring forth evil plans against the LORD will be burned up as chaff off the LORD'S threshing floor, because they are disobedient to God and did not trust Him to save them.

Rain Flood Waters sitting on the leaves of a Peony Tree
Photo ©2013 KK Ballard
All Rights Reserved

They also believed in their hearts that they could achieve a very evil plan. In essence, we have all been given a choice. We can prepare ahead of time and choose to be saved in the Ark of the LORD, or we can choose to reject the LORD and mock the only Ark that saves us. If anyone is foolish enough to choose that route, they will not only be foolish, but they will surely perish. The LORD will save those who walk closely with Him, just like He saved Noah who daily walked with God. We will be kept safe in His Heavenly Ark, until the indignation of the tribulation is overpast. The earth must be cleansed a second time, in order to purify it for the LORD'S return to the earth to reign forever, and now we know that the cleansing of the earth is completed by the two elements that represent the Holy Spirit of God. After the earth has been cleansed by the LORD, the Kingdom of God will come to earth. At the end of Tribulation or seven years of *"Jacob's Trouble,"* Yeshua will come back to the earth with all the Saints, who have been purified or made white, because they were ready as His Bride to enter the Ark before the fire. He will usher in the Kingdom of God and establish His reign for 1,000 years and Messiah will reign forever in the Eternal city of Jerusalem. The truth is that in every recorded case in the Bible, it is *the Ark* that saves! This is why every item that is contained in the Ark is for our salvation and it is the food for our souls. There is still time to believe and trust Messiah the LORD, the Heavenly Ark. We must prepare ourselves ahead of time to enter the Ark, while the door is opened, in order to be counted as one of the righteous remnant of the LORD. Then we will be stored in His barn, as the righteous manna or grain of His Living Testimony, until the indignation is overpast. The LORD will use us later as the good grain from His storehouse. Moses and Noah were preserved in the Ark from death and likewise we are saved and preserved in the Ark of salvation, in Messiah Yeshua. We can have assurance that we will be protected from certain death, by entering through the door. However, when the LORD closes the door, it will be too late to be saved from the fire. Now is the time for salvation! Messiah Yeshua fulfills every detail of the Living Testimony of the LORD inside the Heavenly Ark of the Covenant. There is much more to this story and it begins with Joshua!

JOSHUA CROSSES THE JORDAN RIVER WITH THE ARK OF THE COVENANT

Reflecting on the Jordan River crossing River (Lancaster PA) & Stones Photos ©2013
Budding Almond Rod Photos ©2015 Kimberly K Ballard All Rights Reserved

One day, I was reading a book on Biblical Archaeology. It was showing pictures of the Jordan River. I was not familiar with it at all, but at once, by the power of the Holy Spirit, I figured out that the location where Joshua crossed the Jordan River with the High Priests holding the Ark of the Covenant, was the exact same location where Messiah Yeshua stood with John the Baptist, when Yeshua was baptized in the Jordan River.

I remembered that this was a fulfillment of the Prophecy in Isaiah Chapter 40. After I figured this out, about two or three years went by and suddenly people were allowed to go to visit this particular location in the Jordan River, without a special military escort, after something like 40 years. I was floored by this because no one had been allowed to go to this location to visit it. The LORD had revealed this to me before anyone could visit this place!

Isaiah 40:3-5 *The voice of him that crieth in the wilderness, Prepare ye the way of the LORD, make straight in the desert a highway for our God. Every valley shall be exalted, and every mountain shall be made low; and the crooked shall be made straight, and the rough places plain; And the glory of the LORD shall be revealed, and all flesh shall see it together; for the mouth of the LORD hath spoken it.*

The question is exactly how was *Messiah Yeshua's baptism in the Jordan River,* a fulfillment of this prophecy with John the Baptist? The glory of the LORD God was to be revealed in this place. Before I *shock you with the astounding truth*, we first must go back to review two important stories in the history of Israel that took place in this same location in the Jordan River. In the first story, Joshua crossed the Jordan River. The High Priests held the Ark of the LORD that contained the Testimony and they lifted it up and carried it, going before the people, as the LORD led the way before them, into the Promised Land. The children of Israel did not know the way to go, so the LORD had to go before them to show them the way into the Promised Land.

White Stones Photo ©2014 Kimberly K Ballard All Rights Reserved

The Divine Presence of the LORD was in their midst, abiding upon the Ark. The children of Israel came out of the wilderness and they had to cross over the Jordan River, in order to enter into the Promised Land. Joshua then took the children of Israel across the Jordan River and into the Promised Land. At that time, the river was swollen. The LORD left them there *three days,* in order to say, *"Trust Me, I AM with you, I AM the LORD and I will show you the way, as I go before you across the Jordan River and into the Promised Land."*

Joshua 3:1-17 *And Joshua rose early in the morning; and they removed from Shittim, and came to Jordan, he and all the children of Israel, and lodged there before they passed over. And it came to pass after three days, that the officers went through the host; And they commanded the people, saying, When ye see the Ark of the Covenant of the LORD your God, and the Priests the Levites bearing it, then ye shall remove from your place, and go after it. Yet there shall be a space between you and it, about two thousand cubits by measure; come not near unto it, that ye may know the way by which ye must go; for ye have not passed this way heretofore. And Joshua said unto the people, Sanctify yourselves; for tomorrow the LORD will do wonders among you. And Joshua spake unto the Priests, saying, Take up the Ark of the Covenant, and pass over before the people. And they took up the Ark of the Covenant, and went before the people. And the LORD said unto Joshua, This day will I begin to magnify thee in the sight of all Israel, that they may know that, as I was with Moses, so I will be with thee. And thou shalt command the Priests that bear the Ark of the Covenant, saying, When ye are come to the brink of the water of Jordan, ye shall stand still in Jordan. And Joshua said unto the children of Israel, Come hither, and hear the Words of the LORD your God. And Joshua said, Hereby ye shall know that the Living God is among you, and that He will without fail drive out from before you, the Canaanites, and the Hittites, and the Hivites, and the Perizzites, and the Girgashites, and the Amorites, and the Jebusites. Behold, the Ark of the Covenant of the LORD of all the earth passeth over before you into Jordan. Now therefore take you twelve men out of the tribes of Israel, out of every tribe a man. And it shall come to pass, as soon as the soles of the feet of the Priests that bear the Ark of the LORD, the LORD of all the earth, shall rest in the waters of Jordan, that the waters of Jordan shall be cut off from the waters that come down from above; and they shall stand upon an heap. And it came to pass, when the people removed from their tents, to pass over Jordan, and the Priests bearing the Ark of the Covenant before the people; And as they that bare the Ark were come unto Jordan, and the feet of the Priests that bare the Ark were dipped in the brim of the waters, for Jordan overfloweth all his banks all the time of harvest, That the waters which came down from above stood and rose up* *upon an heap very far from the city Adam, that is beside Zaretan; and those that came down toward the sea of the plain, even the salt sea, failed and were cut off; and the people passed over right against Jericho. And the Priests that bare the Ark of the Covenant of the LORD stood firm on dry ground in the midst of Jordan, and all the Israelites passed over on dry ground, until all the people were passed clean over Jordan.*

What I am about to say is very important! The Ark of the Covenant is the throne of the LORD God of Israel, the Sovereign of the entire universe!

The Ark had the Divine Presence of the LORD abiding upon it and the LORD Himself was actually leading the way across the Jordan River into the Promised Land. Only the LORD knew the way into the Promised Land! Israel had never traveled this way before! This is also very important to Israel's future! They do not know the way into the Eternal Promised Land, but remember the LORD has always guided them like a Good Shepherd, using His Rod to direct the steps of His sheep.

As the Ark of the Testimony was carried by the Priests, they stopped and stood still in the middle of the Jordan River with the Ark. The people were to stay back and follow, to see where the LORD would lead them. The LORD would drive out their enemies from before them and this is what the LORD will do in the future *because He is about to show them the way across the Jordan River and into the Eternal Promised Land!* After all the people of Israel had crossed over the Jordan River, the Priests were to set up 12 stones in the middle of the river where their feet had stood, while holding the Ark of God, as well as set up an eternal memorial of twelve stones in Gilgal that represented the twelve tribes of Israel. It is absolutely chilling! *The marks from their feet may still be underneath these stones and I believe that they are there to this day!* The waters of the Jordan were cut off because the Ark of God's Covenant passed through the Jordan River, as the LORD was abiding upon the Ark.

Joshua 4:1-24 *And it came to pass, when all the people were clean passed over Jordan, that the LORD spake unto Joshua, saying, Take you twelve men out of the people, out of every tribe a man, And command ye them, saying, Take you hence out of the midst of Jordan, out of the place where the Priests feet stood firm, twelve stones, and ye shall carry them over with you, and leave them in the lodging place, where ye shall lodge this night. Then Joshua called the twelve men, whom he had prepared of the children of Israel, out of every tribe a man; And Joshua said unto them, Pass over before the Ark of the LORD your God into the midst of Jordan, and take you up every man of you a stone upon his shoulder, according unto the number of the tribes of the children of Israel; That this may be a sign among you, that when your children ask their fathers in time to come, saying, What mean ye by these stones? Then ye shall answer them, That the waters of Jordan were cut off before the Ark of the Covenant of the LORD; when it passed over Jordan, the waters of Jordan were cut off; and these stones shall be for a memorial unto the children of Israel forever. And the children of Israel did so as Joshua commanded, and took up twelve stones out of the midst of the Jordan, as the LORD spake unto Joshua, according to the number of the tribes of the children of Israel, and carried them over with them unto the place where they lodged, and laid them down there. And Joshua set up twelve stones in the midst of Jordan, in the place where the feet of the Priests which bare the Ark of the Covenant stood; and they are there unto this day. For the Priests which bare the Ark stood in the midst of*

Jordan, until everything was finished that the LORD commanded Joshua to speak unto the people, according to all that Moses commanded Joshua; and the people hasted and passed over. And it came to pass, when all the people were clean passed over, that the Ark of the LORD passed over, and the Priests in the presence of the people. And the children of Reuben, and the children of Gad, and half the tribe of Manasseh, passed over armed before the children of Israel, as Moses spake unto them; About forty thousand prepared for war passed over before the LORD unto battle, to the plains of Jericho. On that day the LORD magnified Joshua in the sight of all Israel; and they feared him, as they feared Moses, all the days of his life. And the LORD spake unto Joshua, saying, Command the Priests that bear the Ark of the Testimony, that they come up out of Jordan. Joshua therefore commanded the Priests, saying, Come ye up out of Jordan. And it came to pass, when the Priests that bare the Ark of the Covenant of the LORD were come up out of the midst of Jordan, and the soles of the Priests feet were lifted unto the dry land, that the waters of Jordan returned unto their place, and flowed over all his banks, as they did before. And the people came up out of Jordan on the tenth day of the first month, and encamped in Gilgal, in the east border of Jericho. And those twelve stones which they took out of Jordan, did Joshua pitch at Gilgal, And he spake unto the children of Israel, saying, When your children shall ask their fathers in time to come, saying What mean these stones? Then ye shall let your children know, saying, Israel came over this Jordan on dry land. For the LORD your God dried up the waters of Jordan from before you, until ye were passed over, as the LORD your God did to the Red Sea, which He dried up from before us, until we were gone over; That all the people of the earth might know the hand of the LORD, that it is mighty; that ye might fear the LORD your God forever.

White Stone Photo ©2014 Kimberly K Ballard All Rights Reserved

So the question is, was the LORD also going to show Israel the way into the Eternal Promised Land? Of course He was going to show them the way! This historical event with Joshua bearing the Ark of the LORD'S Testimony with the High Priests was only a type and shadow of what was to come in Israel's future! This historical event took place so that we might know for certain that this was the work of the hand of the LORD! I realized that there was a parallel between Messiah Yeshua and what happened with Joshua when the people of Israel went in to possess the Promised Land. In the book of Revelation, the seven trumpets are blown, the harpers are harping and Yeshua is arriving, bringing the Ark of Heaven down to dwell in the Eternal Land of His possession. In Joshua chapter six, the armies, the Priests and musicians all played and seven trumpets were blown before the Ark, after it was led across the Jordan River in a procession. The LORD went before the people in His power to scatter His enemies, to remove them from His Land. So in Revelation, Yeshua is coming with the armies of Heaven, with the seven trumpet judgments and to dwell upon the throne of His Ark forever in His Holy Land called, *"Israel,"* as Israel's redemption is finally complete. Fantastic!

When the children of Israel ask their fathers in a time to come *what these twelve stones mean,* they will surely be astonished when they see the truth. This is what I am about to show you that the LORD revealed to me by His Holy Spirit and it is so chilling and fantastic that I could not believe it myself! Nothing will bless them like this stunning Divine revelation!

ELIJAH AND ELISHA IN THE JORDAN RIVER

The second story is the crossing of Elijah and Elisha in the Jordan River. Elijah and Elisha crossed over the Jordan River in the exact same location where Joshua crossed over the Jordan River with the High Priests, carrying the Ark of the Covenant. The second story is found in the book of II Kings and it is important to read this Scripture, to understand what was happening during this historical event.

II Kings 2:1-22 *And it came to pass, when the LORD would take up Elijah into Heaven by a whirlwind, that Elijah went with Elisha from Gilgal. And Elijah said unto Elisha, Tarry here, I pray thee; for the LORD hath sent me to Bethel. And Elisha said unto him, As the LORD liveth, and as thy soul liveth, I will not leave thee. So they went down to Bethel. And the sons of the Prophets that were at Bethel came forth to Elisha, and said unto him, Knowest thou that the LORD will take away thy master from thy head today? And he said, Yea, I know it; hold ye your peace. And Elijah said unto him, Elisha, tarry here, I pray thee; for the LORD hath sent me to Jericho. And he said, As the LORD liveth, and as thy soul liveth, I will not leave thee. So they came to Jericho. And the sons of the Prophets that were at Jericho came to Elisha, and said unto him, Knowest thou that the LORD will take away thy master from thy head today? And he answered, Yea, I know it; hold ye your peace. And Elijah said unto him, Tarry, I pray thee, here; for the LORD hath sent me to Jordan. And he said, As the LORD liveth, and as thy soul liveth, I will not leave thee. And they two went on. And fifty men of the sons of the Prophets went, and stood to view afar off; and they two stood by Jordan. And Elijah took his mantle, and wrapped it together, and smote the waters, and they were divided hither and thither, so that they two went over on dry ground. And it came to pass, when they were gone over, that Elijah said unto Elisha, Ask what I shall do for thee, before I be taken away from thee. And Elisha said, I pray thee, let a double portion of thy Spirit be upon me. And he said, Thou hast asked a hard thing; nevertheless, if thou see me when I am taken from thee, it shall be so unto thee; but if not, it shall not be so. And it came to pass, as they still went on, and talked, that, behold, there appeared a chariot of fire, and horses of fire, and parted them both asunder; and Elijah went up by a whirlwind into Heaven. And Elisha saw it, and he cried, My father, my father, the chariot of Israel, and the horsemen thereof. And he saw him no more; and he took hold of his own clothes, and rent them in two pieces. He took up also the mantle of Elijah that fell from him, and smote the waters, and said, Where is the LORD God of Elijah? And when he also had smitten the waters, they parted hither and thither; and Elisha went over. And when the sons of the Prophets which were to view at Jericho saw him, they said the Spirit of Elijah doth rest on Elisha. And they came to meet him, and bowed themselves to the ground before him. And they said unto him, Behold now, there be with thy servants fifty strong men; let them go, we pray thee, and seek thy master; lest peradventure the Spirit of the LORD hath taken him up, and cast him upon some mountain, or into some valley. And he said, Ye shall not send. And when they urged*

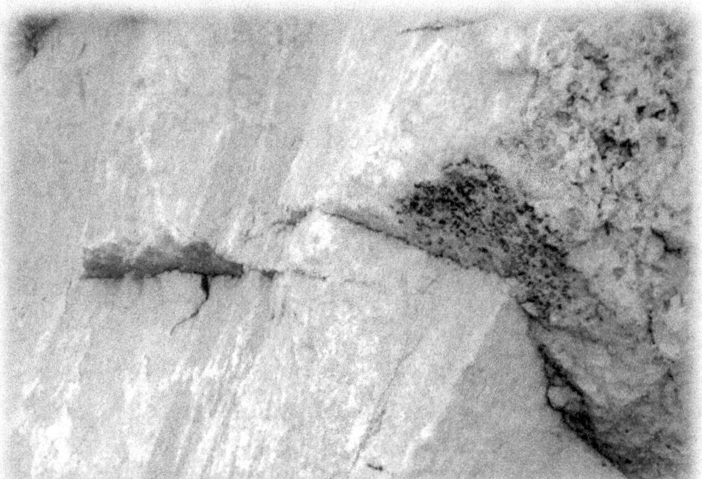

White Stone Photo ©2013 Kimberly K Ballard All Rights Reserved

him till he was ashamed, he said, Send. They sent therefore fifty men; and they sought three days, but found him not. And when they came again to him, for he tarried at Jericho, he said unto them, Did I not say unto you, Go not? And the men of the city said unto Elisha, Behold, I pray thee, the situation of this city is pleasant, as my lord seeth; but the water is naught, and the ground barren. And he said, Bring me a new cruse, and put salt therein. And they brought it to him. And he went forth unto the spring of the waters, and cast the salt in there, and said, Thus saith the LORD, I have healed these waters; there shall not be from thence any more death or barren land. So the waters were healed unto this day, according to the saying of Elisha which he spake.

So the Spirit of God was upon Elijah and then Elisha as they crossed over and stood in the Jordan River, *in the very same place where Joshua stood hundreds of years earlier* when the Divine Presence of the LORD was abiding upon the Ark. In this same location, Elisha received a *double portion of the Spirit of Elijah* after Elijah was carried up into Heaven in the whirlwind in the chariots of Israel. Then Elisha touched the Mantle of Elijah to the waters of the Jordan and they were parted in this place. This was the proof that the Holy Spirit of the LORD was now abiding upon Elisha in a double portion in the Jordan River. When Elisha touched the Mantle to the water, it was made cleft, just like the Red Sea was made cleft when the rod was lifted up and the waters stood up in a heap on either side of them and just like the earth was made cleft in the flood of Noah. Within the definition of the word *"Mantle,"* I found the Mollusk of the High Priest!

Mantle;
1. A loose sleeveless cloak
2. In Zoology; a single or paired outgrowth of the valves of the shell in mollusks and brachiopods. ***(Source: Random House College Dictionary, revised edition 1975 Copyright 1975 By Random House, Inc.).***

Murex mollusk Photo ©2014 Kimberly K Ballard All Rights Reserved

It is fascinating that the second definition of the word *"Mantle"* pertains to mollusk shells, because the mollusk happens to be the source of the dye that was used for the Jewish Priestly garments of the High Priest. This special dye is called, *"tekhelet blue"* and it comes from the mollusk called *"Murex Trunculus."* The source for this special Priestly dye was only rediscovered in Israel within the last 20 years, after it was lost for 2,000 years. The expensive royal purple dye also came from the gland of the same mollusk. They discovered by Divine Providence that if the fabric was dyed and left in the sunshine, the color would turn from royal purple into a rich indigo tekhelet blue color for the fringes of the Priestly garments. Reuven Prager of *Beged Ivri* in Jerusalem remakes the dye and Biblical garments. So I find it interesting that Elisha touched the Mantle to the water and it was made cleft, because Elijah's Mantle was obviously dyed with the tekhelet blue of the High Priest! Therefore, it is obvious why the Mantle is a piece that goes on the outside of a Torah scroll. This means that Elijah was wearing a Jewish Priestly garment with the tekhelet color on his Mantle when he parted the waters with his Mantle. As the Jordan River was made cleft with Elijah's Mantle, it was a sign of the Rod of God, parting the Red Sea, so the children of Israel could cross over on dry ground and enter the Promised Land. Elisha then *received the double portion of the Spirit of Elijah,* and again he crossed over the Jordan River. Elijah was taken up into Heaven alive from this same location. This was an example of the rapture.

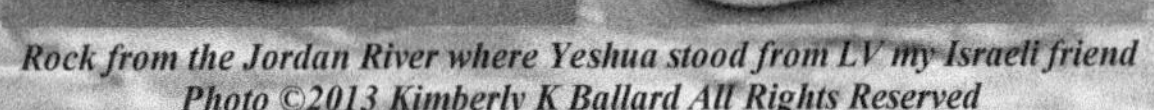

Rock from the Jordan River where Yeshua stood from LV my Israeli friend
Photo ©2013 Kimberly K Ballard All Rights Reserved

MESSIAH YESHUA THE ARK IN THE JORDAN RIVER

Snow white Dove Photos ©2013 Kimberly K Ballard All Rights Reserved

What I have to show you next is an extremely exciting revelation and this is what the LORD showed my heart about Joshua and Messiah Yeshua. I suddenly figured out that *John the Baptist was standing in the Jordan River baptizing in the Name of the LORD in the same exact location where Elijah, Elisha, and Joshua had previously stood, when the Divine Presence of the LORD was abiding with them on the Ark.* This is why the Priests came to this location from the Holy Temple and they asked John if he was the Messiah! John declared, *"No, I am not."* Then they asked if he was Elijah and John declared again, *"No, I am not."*

John 1:21-23 *And they asked him, What then? Art thou Elijah? And he saith, I am not, Art thou that Prophet? And he answered, No. Then said they unto him, Who art thou? That we may give an answer to them that sent us. What sayest thou of thyself? He said, I am the voice of one crying in the wilderness, Make straight the way of the LORD, as said the Prophet Esaias.*

John was *the messenger sent in the Spirit and power of Elijah.* He was standing in the same location where Elisha received *the double portion of Elijah's Spirit.* John was sent to declare to Israel that soon one was coming, who was far greater than he. John also declared that he was a voice crying in the wilderness *to make straight the way of the LORD.* Remember that the LORD showed Israel *the way* to enter the Promised Land? John's father was the High Priest Zacharias who officiated in the Divine service of the LORD in the Holy Temple in Jerusalem. Zacharias was lifting up prayers and incense in the Holy Temple and as he was standing before the Holy of Holies, the angel of the LORD appeared to him on the right side of the incense altar and he said that the prayers of Zacharias had been heard and that he would soon have a son, *who would go before* ***the face*** *of the LORD in the Spirit and Power of Elijah.*

Luke 1:16-17 *And many of the children of Israel shall he turn to the LORD their God. And he shall go before Him in the Spirit and power of Elijah, to turn the hearts of the fathers to the children, and the disobedient to the wisdom of the just; to make ready a people prepared for the LORD*

John came preaching repentance *in the wilderness* and he was telling the children of Israel to be baptized in the Jordan River, in the Living Water and in the fire of the Holy Spirit, so they would be ready and prepared to meet the LORD. Then they would be ready to enter the Promised Land, as soon as the Messiah arrived. The people were to wash their garments and purify themselves in preparation for meeting the LORD face to face. This is exactly what the children of Israel were commanded to do at Mount Sinai before meeting the LORD. Now it is interesting that John came out of *the wilderness,* just like Israel came out of *the wilderness* just before they were about to enter the Promised Land. John was not just preparing Israel to meet the Messiah, He was preparing them to meet *THE LORD* face to face, who was dwelling in their midst as their Messiah! John was preaching that the Kingdom of God was at hand. As I mentioned before, some were ready and were obedient and they repented of their sins and washed their garments in the Living Water and in the LORD'S Holy Spirit, but others among the people of Israel ignored the call to repent and to prepare before the Messiah arrived. John was truly the messenger sent from God to prepare *His way* and He was about to arrive! Then one day, Yeshua came to John to be baptized in the Jordan River. So *Yeshua came to the exact location of the crossing of Joshua, Elijah, and Elisha to be baptized there.* I was so excited when the LORD inspired my heart to see that *Yeshua was the Heavenly Ark of the Living Testimony and the High Priest of Heaven, who was standing with the son of the High Priest, where the earthly Ark had once stood with the High Priests and Joshua!* Suddenly the LORD brought it into my mind that *"it is one Joshua who took Israel into the earthly Promised Land and it is another greater Joshua, Messiah Yeshua, the LORD Himself as a man of His tribe that leads Israel into the Eternal Promised Land!* This is why Yeshua told His Jewish disciples that now they know ***the way*** into the Eternal Promised Land!

White Stone Photo ©2013 Kimberly K Ballard All Rights Reserved

John 14:3-9 *And if I go and prepare a place for you, I will come again, and receive you unto Myself; that where I AM, there ye may be also. And whither I go ye know, and the way ye know. Thomas saith unto Him, LORD, we know not wither Thou goest; and how can we know the way? Yeshua saith unto him, I AM the way, the truth, and the life; no man cometh unto the Father but by Me. If ye had known Me, ye should have known My Father also; and from henceforth ye know Him, and have seen Him. Phillip saith unto him, LORD, shew us the Father, and it sufficeth us. Yeshua saith unto him, Have I been so long time with you, and yet hast thou not known Me Phillip? He that hath seen Me hath seen the Father; and how sayest thou then, Shew us the Father?*

Now remember that the road leading into the Promised Land was a road that Israel had never traveled before. So the LORD went before them to show them the way. *Yeshua was the Heavenly Army Commander parallel of the earthly Joshua.* When Messiah Yeshua declared that He is *The Way,* He meant that He is *The Way* into the Eternal Promised Land! The One who declared this is the One who gives Eternal life through His Living Covenant Testimony in Heaven. One account of Yeshua's baptism is written here in the Gospel of Mark.

Mark 1:1-20 *The beginning of the Gospel of Yeshua Messiah, the Son of God; As it is written in the Prophets, Behold I send My messenger before Thy face, which shall prepare Thy way before Thee. The voice of one crying in the wilderness, Prepare the way of the LORD, make His paths straight. John did baptize in the wilderness, and preach the baptism of repentance for the remission of sins. And John was clothed with camel's hair, and with a girdle of a skin about his loins; and he did eat locusts and wild honey; And preached, saying, There cometh one mightier than I after me, the latchet of whose shoes I am not worthy to stoop down and unloose. I indeed have baptized you with water; but He shall baptize you with the Holy Spirit. And it came to pass in those days, that Yeshua came from Nazareth of Galilee, and was baptized of John in the Jordan. And straightway coming up out of the water, he saw the Heavens opened, and the Spirit like a dove descended upon Him; And there came a voice from Heaven, saying, Thou art My beloved Son, in whom I AM well pleased. And immediately the Spirit driveth Him into the wilderness. And He was there in the wilderness forty days, tempted of Satan; and was with the wild beasts; and the angels ministered unto Him. Now after that John was put in prison, Yeshua came into Galilee, preaching the Gospel of the Kingdom of God. And saying, The time is fulfilled, and the Kingdom of God is at hand; repent ye, and believe the Gospel. Now as he walked by the Sea of*

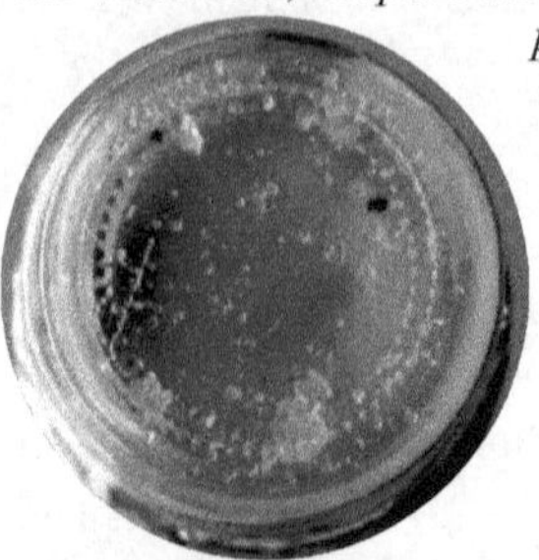

Water from the Jordan River from the place where Yeshua stood when He revealed He was the Presence of God among His people leading the way before them into His Eternal Garden! Photo ©2013 KK Ballard All Rights Reserved

Galilee, He saw Simon and Andrew his brother casting a net into the sea; for they were fishers. And Yeshua said unto them, Come ye after Me, and I will make you to become fishers of men. And straightway they forsook their nets, and followed Him. And when He had gone a little farther thence, He saw James the son of Zebedee, and John his brother, who also were in the ship mending their nets. And straightway He called them; and they left their father Zebedee in the ship with the hired servants, and went after Him.

The LORD'S Divine Presence abode and stayed upon the Ark that Moses built when Joshua's Priests carried it across the Jordan River, but this Ark was an *earthly copy* of the Heavenly Ark! The Divine Presence again abode upon Elijah and Elisha in the same place in the Jordan River. Then hundreds of years later, Messiah Yeshua came to John, *the son of the High Priest,* and they stood in the Jordan River in the place where Joshua stood with the High Priests. Suddenly Heaven was opened and the Holy Spirit of God descended like a dove from Heaven and it abode and stayed upon Yeshua, the High Priest of Heaven. This was fantastic! Messiah's body was the perfect vessel that the Divine Presence was dwelling in, as He stood in the Jordan River! Therefore, standing in the Jordan River was the Eternal Living Testimony of the LORD because *Yeshua is the Living Torah* who sits on *the Ark* of His throne in Heaven.

Our proof of this truth is found in the fact that Messiah Yeshua is the Rod of the Almond Tree that was cut off that came to life, bearing the First Fruit of Eternal life. Yeshua was the Unleavened Bread from Heaven, the hidden Manna. Yeshua was the Rock, the Word of God, and the finger of the right hand of God. He is the life blood, as the perfect Lamb that God provided for us, to atone for our sins and the LORD'S life blood is sprinkled upon the true Ark in Heaven. Remember that I previously told you on page 150 that a dove does not like to set her feet on anything unclean? This time with Messiah Yeshua, instead of *the Jordan River parting, the Heavens were opening and parting* as the Holy Spirit descended like a dove from Heaven and abode upon Messiah Yeshua because He was pure and clean and had no sin! So Yeshua was the Living Ark of the LORD'S Living Testimony, dwelling in our midst and guess what? I realized that the reason why the Holy Spirit came to Yeshua in the form of a dove and abode upon Him in the Jordan River is because the dove returned to Noah and rested upon his hand and he pulled the dove back inside the Ark! So the Holy Spirit came down from Heaven in the form of a dove and *rested upon the hand of God,* upon Messiah Yeshua, *because the Holy Spirit was returning to abide in the Heavenly Ark of GOD'S Eternal Testimony that was now dwelling in our midst upon the earth! At that moment I realized to my astonishment that the Holy Spirit in the form of a dove was returning to the LORD, the true Heavenly Ark, as the LORD God now stood on the earth, in the place of Joshua's crossing, as Yeshua, in the body of a man of His tribe, so that the LORD will inherit Judah as His portion forever!* When the dove of God's Spirit rested upon the hand of God, it went back inside *the Living Ark*, to rest inside Messiah Yeshua! Then a voice was heard from Heaven proclaiming that Yeshua was the beloved Son with whom the LORD was well pleased. *The voice came from the Mercy Seat of the Ark as He abode there,* as we see in the book of Numbers. Messiah Yeshua is the Ark of Salvation and the LORD came as the *second Joshua* who was now showing us *the way to Heaven, as the*

Eurasian ring-necked Dove Photo ©2013 Kimberly K Ballard All Rights Reserved

Heavens were parted, because *He is the Living Water.* Yeshua is therefore going before us, leading *the way* to the Eternal Promised Land!

Numbers 7:89 *And when Moses was gone into the Tabernacle of the congregation to speak with Him, then he heard the voice of one speaking unto him from off the Mercy Seat that was upon the Ark of Testimony, from between the two Cherubim's; and he spake unto Him.*

John 1:29-36 *The next day John seeth Yeshua coming unto Him, and saith, Behold the Lamb of God, which taketh away the sin of the world. This is He of whom I said, After me cometh a man which is preferred before me; for He was before me. And I knew Him not; but that He should be made manifest to Israel, therefore am I come baptizing with water. And John bare record, saying, I saw the Spirit descending from Heaven like a dove, and it abode upon Him. And I knew Him not; but He that sent me to baptize with water, the same said unto me, Upon whom thou shalt see the Spirit descending, and remaining on Him, the same is He which baptizeth with the Holy Spirit. And I saw, and bare record that this is the Son of God. Again the next day after John stood, and two of his disciples; And looking upon Yeshua as He walked, he saith, Behold the Lamb of God!*

So Messiah Yeshua the LORD was *the Divine Presence* standing in the Jordan River and Messiah Yeshua was the Heavenly Joshua, leading the way before Israel into the Eternal Promised Land. The LORD manifested Himself as the Living Rod to give Israel and all who believe in Him Eternal life. Yeshua is the High Priest of Heaven and *the Rod* that made the waters cleft and *the Heavens cleft,* just like Elijah's Mantle of the High Priest with the Spirit abiding upon it parted the Jordan. After the Divine Presence of the Holy Spirit abode upon Yeshua, He was driven out into the wilderness for 40 days, and returned to proclaim the Living Torah with His voice. This is parallel to Israel having been in the wilderness for 40 years before entering the Promised Land with the LORD speaking to Joshua. It represents the flood of Noah that was upon the earth for 40 days and 40 nights. *The Ark of Salvation was here!*

Now if John came to make the Messiah known to Israel, then how were they to see it? They were to recognize the Rod from the crossing of the Red Sea! The Rod parted the Red Sea, and in this very place where Yeshua stood in the Jordan River, the waters were parted by the Living Ark. *This time the Heavens parted, showing us that He is the way to enter into Heaven!* The Rod of God brought salvation to Israel! When the Rod stood in the Jordan River, the Divine Presence was abiding on Him. Israel should have recognized that He was the Rod of God who made *the way* before them to bring them salvation. Another interesting thing about this is that when Israel crossed over the Red Sea, with the LORD going before them with the power on His Rod, all the children of Israel were baptized in the midst of the Sea, as the children of God. Then the Messiah was baptized in the midst of the Jordan River, *as the Rod of the Testimony of the LORD.* This is why John stated that in order to make the Messiah manifested to Israel, he came baptizing with water.

Sea Photo ©2013 Kimberly K Ballard

The baptism of water was to remind the children of Israel that their Messiah KING is the LORD God of Israel and His Rod has saved them once again. So John was making the Messiah known to Israel through the baptism in water because the children of Israel had been baptized in the Red Sea. The LORD led the way before them with His Ruach/Spirit abiding on His Rod and they were all baptized in the Sea. When we are baptized, we declare that we are children of God. This is *The Way* that leads to Eternal life and this is how the LORD leads us into the Eternal Promised Land!

The LORD told Moses that by the Rod performing miracles, signs, and wonders, Israel would know for certain that He is the LORD of Hosts! So it is exciting to see what happened after Yeshua stood in the Jordan River. After being in the desert forty days, *Yeshua immediately went out and performed signs, miracles, and wonders for three years!* All

Yeshua's miracles were *the signs of God's Rod,* and so Israel can be certain that their Messiah is the LORD of Hosts! Another sign that I discussed earlier that I will mention again is that Messiah will raise Israel up after three days, just as He was raised to life on the third day. Messiah Yeshua will build the Eternal Temple in three days. The twelve baptized disciples were also given the power of the LORD'S Ruach/Spirit, abiding on this Living Heavenly Rod, to go out and perform the LORD'S signs, miracles, and wonders in His Name.

In order for Israel to enter into the Eternal Promised Land called *"Heaven," they must follow behind the Heavenly Ark with Yeshua leading the way.* Only the LORD knows *The Way* how to enter the Eternal Promised Land and right now the LORD is showing them how to enter in! This is a fabulous and marvelous work of God and I am so grateful to the LORD that He allowed my eyes to see Him manifested in these truths! When *Elijah* comes in the future or one is anointed to come in the Spirit and power of Elijah, they will again prepare *the way* of the LORD to travel. Joshua prepared the way with the Priests and *the Ark* for the children of Israel to enter the Promised Land. John the Baptist, the son of the High Priest, came to prepare the way of the LORD with *Messiah the Ark,* so Israel could enter the Eternal Promised Land. This is why the Jewish disciples dropped everything that they were doing at once and immediately followed behind *the Heavenly Ark,* and they went forth to show others *the way*! As I said before, the two witnesses in the future will be Elijah and Moses, who have the power of God abiding upon them. I will talk a lot more about them later but this will be accomplished soon!

Marble & Limestone from the Holy Temple & quarry

THE 12 STONES

Marble & Limestone from the Holy Temple & quarry

Believe it or not, this was not the end of the story! Remember that I said the Priests placed twelve stones, one for each of the twelve tribes of Israel, in the Jordan River in the place where their feet were standing with the Ark, and this was to be *a memorial* to Israel forever? The Holy Spirit made me shiver again and I was shocked! Immediately after Messiah Yeshua came out of the wilderness, like the children of Israel with the Ark, *He chose the twelve Jewish disciples* and it was after this that He performed the signs, miracles, and wonders of the LORD as the Rod of God! Wow, this was incredible because it came into my heart *that the twelve Jewish disciples, who were chosen by Messiah Yeshua after His feet stood in the Jordan River, were actually the twelve Jewish Living Stones that Yeshua laid as the Foundation Stones of the*

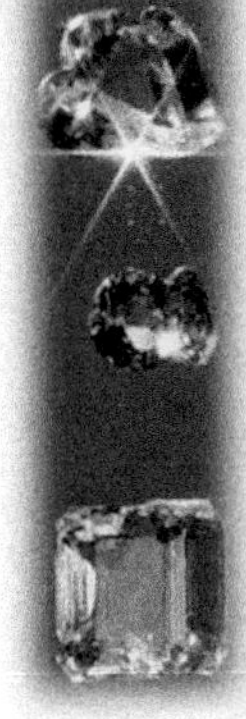

Heavenly Temple, in the Eternal Promised Land called "Heaven!" These twelve Living Stones were to be a permanent Eternal memorial to Israel! I was so excited when the LORD revealed this to my heart by His grace. This was simply a breathtaking Divine revelation!

In the book of Revelation, the Jewish disciples that were chosen by Messiah Yeshua are indeed called *"the Foundation Stones of Heaven,"* while the twelve tribes of Israel are called *"the Gates of the Heavenly Temple!"* Each gate is a Pearl of great price! I did not understand why *Yeshua's disciples were the Foundation Stones of the Heavenly Temple* until this exciting moment! The reason was so simple. The Messiah chose the twelve Living Stones from the twelve tribes of Israel to set as the Living Foundation Stones in His Heavenly Temple, after He stood in the Jordan River with the son of the High Priest, showing Israel *the way* to enter the Eternal Promised Land! They had to follow behind Yeshua, the LORD'S Living Ark of the Testimony! This was so fantastic! I was given the most incredible answer to this question by the LORD. I never expected to discover something so wonderful, but the LORD opened my eyes to see it! So Joshua laid the twelve stones in the Jordan as a memorial forever in the earthly Promised Land, but Messiah Yeshua the LORD laid the twelve Living Stones in Heaven, as an Eternal memorial to the children of Israel forever! Now I could see why the twelve stones that Joshua set in the Jordan River were such an important memorial and were to be kept for Israel to remember these stones forever. Remember that Joshua said, *"When your children shall ask their fathers in time to come, saying, What mean these stones? Then ye shall let your children know, saying, Israel came over this Jordan on dry land."* Then Joshua said, *"For the LORD your God dried up the waters of Jordan from before you, until ye were passed over, as the LORD your God did to the Red Sea, which He dried up from before us, until we were gone over; That all the people of the earth might know the hand of the LORD, that it is mighty; that ye might fear the LORD your God forever."* This was the Rod of God who performed this and *Yeshua the Ark is showing them the way.* Surely this is their God and this is their KING! Every sign that Yeshua performed was in perfect agreement with His Scriptures! It is also incredible to realize that the twelve Living Stones that the LORD chose are alive today in Heaven because He is the Living God and they rest upon Him as the Chief Cornerstone! When we believe on the Word of God, *the Living Torah Messiah,* we also become Living Stones that are built upon this very Foundation! So Messiah Yeshua came to earth as the Son of a Carpenter who worked with stone, from the Royal House and lineage of King David! So of course Messiah builds the permanent *Heavenly Temple* out of these *Living Stones that are fashioned by Him, made without the hands or tools of mankind!*

White Stone Photo ©2014 Kimberly K Ballard All Rights Reserved

Matthew 13:54-58 *And when He was come into His own country, He taught them in their Synagogues, insomuch that they were astonished, and said, Whence hath this man this wisdom, and these mighty works? Is not this the Carpenter's son? Is not His mother called Mary? And His brethren, James, and Joses, and Simon and Judas? And His sisters, are they not all with us? Whence then hath this man all these things? And they were offended in Him. But Yeshua said unto them, A Prophet is not without honour, save in His own country, and in His own House. And He did not many mighty works there because of their unbelief.*

Now the LORD revealed to me that this is why Messiah Yeshua said in the book of Revelation to the Churches, *"To him that overcomes, I will give to eat of the hidden manna and give him a white stone with a new name written on it."* As I showed before, Yeshua is indeed the hidden Manna, in *the Ark of the Testimony of the LORD* that we will be given. He chisels away and removes our rough exterior, so that we shine with His radiance. It is interesting too, remember, that it is still a Jewish custom to place stones as a memorial upon Jewish graves, and on Rosh HaShanah these graves will be opened to raise the dead!

Revelation 2:17 *He that hath an ear, let him hear what the Spirit saith unto the churches; To him that overcometh will I give to eat of the hidden manna, and will give him a white stone, and in the stone a new name written, which no man knoweth saving he that receiveth it.*

Limestone
from the quarry in Jerusalem
Photo ©2013
Kimberly K Ballard
All Rights Reserved

As soon as I saw all of these amazing details by Divine Providence, I remembered that the Holy Temple in Jerusalem was built from the beautifully polished white marble stones that King Solomon quarried, upon King David's direction. As the sunshine fell upon its glimmering polished white marble stones, the reflection of the Holy Temple was radiant. At night the light from the torches, surrounding the walls of Jerusalem, reflected a beautiful shimmering glow on the Temple's exterior. The Holy Temple was awe inspiring and magnificent. King David prepared the white marble stones, as well as the precious gem stones, for the first Holy Temple that his son Solomon built, specifically to House the Ark of the Covenant, containing *the Testimony.* When the Ark was placed inside the special Sanctuary, in the House of the LORD, the LORD descended into the midst of the Holy of Holies and He abode there. The LORD was seated between the two Cherubim Angels, upon the Mercy Seat. The Holy Temple shimmered like pure white snow!

Psalm 99:1 *The LORD reigneth; let the people tremble; He sitteth between the Cherubim's; let the earth be moved.*

All of David's preparations for the Holy Temple were recorded in the book of the Chronicles.

I Chronicles 29:1-2 *Furthermore David the King said unto all the congregation, Solomon my son, whom alone God hath chosen, is yet young and tender, and the work is great; for the palace is not for man, but for the LORD God. Now I have prepared with all my might for the House of my God the gold for things to be made of gold, and the silver for things of silver, and the brass for things of brass, the iron for things of iron, and wood for things of wood; onyx stones, and stones to be set, glistering stones, and of diverse colours, and all manner of precious stones, and marble stones in abundance.*

Now with the knowledge that the Temple itself was made from these beautifully polished white marble stones, we can see that Yeshua was revealing that if we overcome, we are given one of these *polished white stones* in Heaven and our name is inscribed upon it forever where it will remain as an Eternal memorial in His Royal Heavenly Pavilion. The word *"polished"* means *"refined, elegant, cultured, having no imperfections, flawless."* ***(Source: ©2010 thefreedictionary.com).***

White Stone Photo ©2014
Kimberly K Ballard All Rights Reserved

Psalm 127:1 *Except the LORD build the house, they labour in vain that build it; except the LORD keep the city, the watchman waketh but in vain.*

Isaiah 66:1 *Thus saith the LORD, The Heaven is My throne, and the earth is My footstool; where is the house that ye build unto Me? And where is the place of My rest?*

The twelve gemstones on the Breastplate of the High Priest, that are set over his heart, are inscribed with the names of the twelve tribes of Israel. A new name is inscribed upon the *Living Stones* in the Heavenly Temple to remind us that Yeshua is the High Priest of Heaven and His Living Torah Testimony is forever written upon the heart of mankind! Yeshua's Jewish disciples are an Eternal memorial to Israel, set as the Foundation Stones, in the Eternal Holy Temple of God.

There were also twelve white marble memorial stones placed at Mount Sinai after the Hebrews crossed over the Red Sea!

Revelation 21:14 *And the wall of the city had twelve Foundation Stones, and on them were the twelve names of the twelve Apostles of the Lamb.*

White Stone
Photo ©2014 Kimberly K Ballard
All Rights Reserved

The *twelve gates* in Heaven, are inscribed with the names of the twelve tribes of Israel, just as it states also in Ezekiel 48:31-35, because they were actually *the gate keepers of the city.*

Revelation 21:12 *It had a great and high wall, with twelve gates, and at the gates twelve angels; and names were written on them, which are those of the twelve tribes of the sons of Israel.*

Now if we go back and read what Simon Peter said about the Living Stones, *He said that the Living Stones are precious and chosen of the LORD!* Yeshua is the precious Living Stone that was disallowed of men, but chosen of God. The term, *"disallowed,"* has a very interesting meaning. The Messiah was rejected of men, because they refused to believe the truth and to validate the KING OF KINGS. They stumble at *the Word, at the Living Torah!*

My stone from the place in the Jordan River where Yeshua stood
Where Joshua crossed over
Photo ©2013 Kimberly K Ballard All Rights Reserved

Disallow or Disallowed;

To refuse to admit the truth or validity of. To refuse to allow; reject.
(Source: ©1975 The Random House College Dictionary).

I Peter 2:4-10 *To whom coming, as unto a Living Stone, disallowed indeed of men, but chosen of God, and precious, Ye also, as Lively Stones, are built up a Spiritual House, an Holy Priesthood, to offer up Spiritual sacrifices, acceptable to God by Yeshua Messiah. Wherefore also it is contained in the Scripture, Behold, I lay in Zion a Chief Corner Stone, elect, precious; and he that believeth on Him shall not be confounded. Unto you therefore which believe He is precious; but unto them which be disobedient, the stone which the builders disallowed, the same is made the head of the Corner, And a Stone of stumbling, and a rock of offence, even to them which stumble at the Word, being disobedient; whereunto also they were appointed. But ye are a chosen generation, a Royal Priesthood, an Holy Nation, a peculiar people; that ye should shew forth the praises of Him who hath called you out of darkness into His marvelous light; Which in time past were not a people, but are now the people of God; which had not obtained mercy, but now have obtained mercy.*

One of the amazing things that I noticed in Simon Peter's statement is the term, *"Lively Stones."* Lively means *"full of life, vigorous, animated, cheerful, full of energy and full of Spirit!"* This is what we will become in the Heavenly Kingdom of God! We will be forever full of vigorous life, cheerful and energetic, full of His Spirit! This is truly exciting to comprehend! The Lively Stones are built upon this Spiritual House and Holy Priesthood. Now this is what was meant in the following Scripture. As John was baptizing the children of Israel in the Jordan River, in the location where Joshua crossed into the Promised Land with the Ark of the

LORD, John said, *"All flesh shall see the salvation of God."* This is exactly what Moses declared at the Red Sea crossing (Exodus 14:13) before the Rod was lifted up and the waters parted before them, bringing them salvation. John declared to them, *"That God was able to raise up of these Stones, children unto Abraham!"* John was revealing to the children of Israel that they would all become the Eternal white polished memorial Stones of the Heavenly Spiritual Temple, made without hands, as they were baptized and purified white in the Testimony of the LORD'S baptism. The Jewish people that were standing there with John were all about to witness *the salvation of the LORD* through His Living Rod of Yeshua, who was about to be lifted up to show them *the way* that leads into the Eternal Promised Land, but would they have faith enough to follow Him across the River?

Luke 3:6-8 *And all flesh shall see the salvation of God. Then said he to the multitude that came forth to be baptized of him, O generation of vipers, who hath warned you to flee from the wrath to come? Bring forth therefore fruits worthy of repentance, and begin not to say within yourselves, We have Abraham to our father; for I say unto you, That God is able of these stones to raise up children unto Abraham.*

Stone Photo ©2014 Kimberly K Ballard

When John said this, he was standing in the location of the Jordan River where Joshua crossed over and set the memorial stones and he was telling them that salvation was not based upon their own merits, rather it was based on the salvation that the Rod of God provided, through Messiah's Living Testimony, that would purify them to Eternal life, *as Living Stones* of the Heavenly Temple. Remember that the earthly Tabernacle and the Temple were only copies of the true Eternal Temple that is built in Heaven, where Messiah is the High Priest and the minister of the Sanctuary. As I said, it is the LORD who builds this Sanctuary and not man!

Hebrews 8:1-2 *Now of the things which we have spoken this is the sum; We have such an High Priest, who is set on the right hand of the throne of the Majesty in the Heavens; A Minister of the Sanctuary, and of the true Tabernacle, which the LORD pitched, and not man.*

As Messiah the Rod of God, performed His signs, miracles, and wonders, the people of Israel rejoiced in the LORD and praised God with a loud voice for all the mighty works they witnessed by the hand of Yeshua. Some of the Pharisees told Yeshua to rebuke these disciples for declaring Him KING, but, if you will notice, in the reply that Yeshua gave to the Pharisees, His Words reveal that *His disciples are the Living Stones that are chosen by the LORD. Yeshua declared that these Stones would cry out if they stopped praising God for all His magnificent works! Their lives are an Eternal memorial to Israel laid in Heaven!*

Luke 19:37-42 *And when He was come nigh, even now at the descent of the Mount of Olives, the whole multitude of the disciples began to rejoice and praise God with a loud voice for all the mighty works that they had seen; Saying, blessed be the KING that cometh in the Name of the LORD; peace in Heaven, and glory in the Highest. And some of the Pharisees from among the multitude said unto Him, Master rebuke thy disciples. And He answered and said unto them, I tell you that, if these should hold their peace, the stones would immediately cry out. And when he was come near, He beheld the city, and wept over it, Saying, If thou hadst known, even thou, at least in this thy day, the things which belong unto thy peace! But now they are hid from thine eyes.*

When the people at the Temple refused to believe the Messiah and His mighty works, that were *the signs of the LORD God,* the LORD hid these things from their eyes, so they could no longer see the truth. One day, their eyes will be opened and they will see that Yeshua is the Messiah, the LORD God of Israel. When Yeshua stood in the Holy Temple in Jerusalem, speaking to His people, He prophesied and said, *"Tear down this Temple and in three days I will build it again."* The Rod of God was literally telling them that He is the one who builds the

Heavenly Temple of the LORD. They were amazed at *the signs* Yeshua was performing and they asked Him to show them *a sign* and He gave them more than one, but they missed it!

John 2:18-25 *The Jews therefore answered and said to Him, What sign do You show to us, seeing that You do these things? Yeshua, answered and said to them, Destroy this Temple, and in three days I will raise it up. The Jews therefore said, It took forty-six years to build this Temple, and will You raise it up in three days? But He was speaking of the Temple of His body. When therefore He was raised from the dead, His disciples remembered that He said this; and they believed the Scripture, and the Word which Yeshua had spoken. Now when He was in Jerusalem at the Passover, during the Feast, many believed in His Name, beholding His signs which He was doing. But Yeshua, on His part, was not entrusting Himself to them, for He knew all men, and because He did not need anyone to bear witness concerning man for He Himself knew what was in man.*

Since Messiah Yeshua's body is the perfect vessel of the Ark of the LORD'S Living Testimony, He would come to life Eternally the third day and show Israel the way to Heaven. Messiah is the Stone that the builders rejected on the earth because they refused to validate Him as their KING. As I thought about all these things and pondered why the Rod of God is also called the Word of God, *the Living Torah,* it suddenly came into my heart that the Rod is used for correction (which I mentioned before). Now if you think about it, *Yeshua was actually standing upon Joshua's memorial stones as He was baptized by John,* who was declaring that all flesh shall see *"The Yeshua"* of the LORD, where Heaven parted and the dove descended in the place where Elijah ascended into Heaven in the chariot of Israel in II Kings 2:12!

Elijah cloud Photo ©2013

Jeremiah 3:23 *Truly in vain is salvation hoped for from the hills, and from the multitude of mountains; truly the LORD our God is the salvation of Israel.*

The Torah, written down by the power of the LORD'S Ruach/Holy Spirit by the Prophets, the Sages of Israel, was meant to convict us of our sins. The Word of God teaches us to turn from evil and to go down the right path of righteousness, following behind the LORD, the true Heavenly Ark. When Yeshua ascended back into Heaven, His sheep were scattered into all nations, but He has been gathering them for two thousand years, back to Jerusalem. This is where He calls us!

Another very interesting aspect of this is the fact that *the Rod of God is the voice of the LORD, The Living Torah.* We see that this is true in the following Scripture that is written in the book of Micah.

Micah 7:9 *The LORD'S voice crieth unto the city, and the man of wisdom shall see Thy Name; Hear ye the Rod, and who hath appointed it.*

This explains why *the Living Torah and the Living Rod* are contained within the Ark of the LORD'S Eternal Testimony in Heaven and His voice comes from His throne. The LORD'S voice comes out of the Shechinah glory cloud between the two Cherubim Angels. Since God is the Messiah of Israel, the Temple of Heaven is the Messiah's body, the Holy vessel that contains the Eternal resurrection Testimony of the LORD because He is the polished Rock! The LORD alone is perfection and completion, so therefore, He is the Heavenly Temple built without the hands of mankind.

Ephesians 2:18-22 *For through Him we both have access by one Spirit unto the Father. Now therefore ye are no more strangers and foreigners, but fellow citizens with the Saints, and of the Household of God; And are built upon the foundation of the Apostles and Prophets, Yeshua Messiah Himself being the Chief Cornerstone; In whom all the* *building fitly framed together growth unto an Holy Temple in the LORD; In whom ye also are builded together for an habitation of God through the Spirit.*

I Corinthians 3:9-17 *For we are labourers together with God; ye are God's husbandry, ye are God's building. According to the grace of God which is given unto me, as a wise Master builder, I have laid the foundation, and another buildeth thereon. But let every man take heed how he buildeth thereupon. For other foundation can no man lay than that is laid, which is Yeshua Messiah. Now if any man build upon this foundation gold, silver, precious stones, wood, hay, stubble; Every man's work shall be made manifest; for the day shall declare it, because it shall be revealed by fire; and the fire shall try every man's work of what sort it is. If any man's work abide which he hath built thereupon, he shall receive a reward. If any man's work shall be burned, he shall suffer loss; but he himself shall be saved; yet so as by fire. Know ye not that ye are the Temple of God, and that the Spirit of God dwelleth in you? If any man defile the Temple of God, him shall God destroy; for the Temple of God is Holy, which Temple ye are.*

The Scriptures tell us that Messiah Yeshua will return after a Third Holy Temple is built on the Temple Mount in Jerusalem. This Third Holy Temple will exist during the time of Jacob's trouble or the great tribulation period. After this seven year period of time is complete, the LORD will return and descend from Heaven, coming with great power and glory, bringing with Him the Kingdom of God, the Eternal Spiritual Temple and the believer's, who will descend with Him, to dwell forever in Jerusalem. The Third Temple is ready to be built! The Third Temple in Jerusalem prepares the way for the return of the KING OF KINGS AND LORD OF LORDS to come reign! It is interesting that in reality, as I mentioned in chapter 1 (page 35) the Third Temple is really the sixth Temple. *The Heavenly Temple of the LORD is the seventh Temple of perfection and completion.* Allow me to explain what I mean. The first Temple was the Tabernacle of Moses in the Wilderness. The second Temple was the Tabernacle at Shiloh. The third Temple was the Temple of King Solomon. The fourth Temple was the Temple of Zerubbabel. The fifth Temple was Herod's Temple. The sixth Temple is the so called Third Temple or the Jacob's Trouble Temple and the final seventh perfect Temple is the Heavenly Temple that descends with the LORD'S arrival in Jerusalem! As the KING arrives, rivers of Living Water will flow out from the Holy Temple Mount before Him in Jerusalem Israel. The LORD is the River of Life-Giving Waters! So the Scripture about the rushing Living Waters, flowing out from the Eternal Temple, is both Spiritual as well as literal. Just recently it was discovered that there is a rushing raging river underneath Holy Mount Moriah, which is the Temple Mount of the LORD. Remember that a great river came out of the Garden of Eden? When we enter His Eternal Kingdom, He will provide us with Life-Giving Living Water and the hidden manna, so we will never thirst or be hungry again!

There is a prophecy in Zechariah that reveals that the LORD God will make those who are of His flock, *as the Stones of a crown.*

Dedication Mom's Gemstone Photo

Zechariah 9:16 *And the LORD their God shall save them in that day as the flock of his people; for they shall be as the Stones of a crown, lifted up as an ensign upon His land.*

The Stones of a crown prophecy is very interesting because the book of Revelation says that *the Foundation Stones of Heaven's Temple are made of gorgeous precious gemstones. The Jewish disciples are these precious gems!* In the Kingdom of Heaven, the Shechinah glory of the LORD shines and reflects His light off everything. The Eternal Heavenly Temple will shimmer with this radiance, *as the LORD'S glory light reflects off of us!* The streets of Heaven are made of pure gold, so they are transparent. Only very pure gold is transparent like glass and the pure white marble stones, together with the brilliantly refracting pure gemstones, make this Heavenly Temple more spectacular than we can ever imagine! This is a place you never want to leave!

We have no concept of the beauty of the Temple that the Messiah is building, but we can be a part of His Eternal Temple! Can you imagine just how breathtaking Heaven will be with His fiery glory light refracting from these gemstones? This makes you want to go to Heaven! These precious gemstones of His Crown make up the Bride of Messiah, *the Bride of the LORD.*

Refracting Gemstones & beautiful purple Columbine
Photo ©2013 Kimberly K Ballard

Revelation 21:2-3 *And I John saw the Holy city, New Jerusalem, coming down from God out of Heaven, prepared as a bride adorned for her husband. And I heard a great voice out of Heaven saying, Behold, the Tabernacle of God is with men, and He will dwell with them, and they shall be his people, and God Himself shall be with them, and be their God.*

The next Scripture in Revelation tells us that in Heaven, the LORD and the Lamb is *the Temple* of it!

Revelation 21:19-20 *And the foundations of the wall of the city were garnished with all manner of precious stones. The first foundation was jasper; the second, sapphire; the third, a chalcedony; the fourth, an emerald; The fifth, sardonyx; the sixth, sardius; the seventh, chrysolyte; the eighth, beryl; the ninth, a topaz; the tenth, a chrysoprasus; the eleventh, a jacinth; the twelfth, an amethyst. And the twelve gates were twelve pearls; every several gate was of one pearl; and the street of the city was pure gold, as it were transparent glass. <u>And I saw no Temple therein; for the LORD God Almighty and the Lamb are the Temple of it.</u>*

I leave you with one lasting heartfelt impression of the Heavenly Temple of the LORD. If you are at this time missing someone very precious to your heart that you have loved dearly that has died, the LORD wants you to know that He is your Comforter. His Heavenly Kingdom is more beautiful, loving, and full of vigorous life than we can ever imagine. Think of life on earth as a huge drought, void of God! Then picture the Majesty and glory of the LORD in Heaven, as the refreshing rain that makes everything come alive. Heaven is not a place of death at all. It is a lush, vivid, colorful place of life with Eternal beauty and flowers! The LORD is not the God of the dead, He is the God of the Living! These images of Heaven give me such great comfort. So the true Living God of Eternal life does not ever call us to martyr ourselves deliberately, rather, *He sent His Rod to die for us,* so that we might be saved through Him by His love because He wants us to live forever in His glorious Kingdom, through His beautiful grace!

I know that my loved ones that have died, including my Father, his brother, my Aunt, and Grandparents are experiencing this spectacular place. I know that they are waiting to see me again, when I cross over into the Eternal Promised Land! So I will follow behind the Ark of Messiah Yeshua forever and love Him with all of my heart!

Gemstones refracting the light – Notice the light on the heart shape!
Photo ©2014 Kimberly K Ballard

Matthew 23:29-33 *Yeshua answered and said unto them, Ye do err, not knowing the Scriptures, nor the Power of God. For in the resurrection they neither marry, nor are given in marriage, but are as the angels of God in Heaven. But as touching the resurrection of the dead, have ye not read that which was spoken unto you by God, saying, I AM the God of Abraham, and the God of Isaac, and the God of Jacob? God is not the God of the dead, but of the living. And when the multitude heard this, they were astonished at His doctrine.*

Mark 16:5-6 *And entering into the sepulchre, they saw a young man sitting on the right side, clothed in a long white garment; and they were affrighted. And he saith unto them, Be not affrighted; Ye seek Yeshua of Nazareth, which was crucified; He is risen; He is not here; behold the place where they laid Him.*

Yeshua is the Living Almond Branch Testimony of the Tree of Life because Yeshua is the LORD God of the Living, not the God of death, and Eternal Life is inside Yeshua!

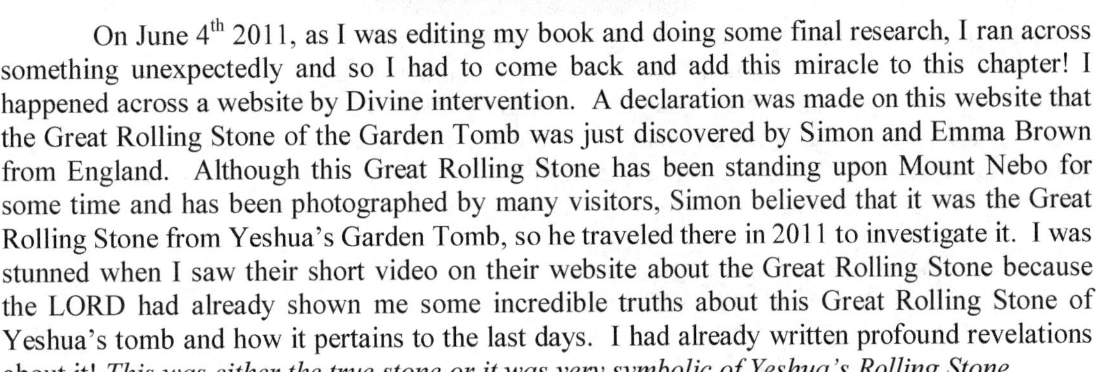

THE GREAT ROLLING STONE STANDING ON MOUNT NEBO

The Great Rolling Stone on Mount Nebo Photos ©2011 Simon Brown England All Rights Reserved
British Union Jack Flag Photos ©2013 Kimberly K Ballard All Rights Reserved

On June 4th 2011, as I was editing my book and doing some final research, I ran across something unexpectedly and so I had to come back and add this miracle to this chapter! I happened across a website by Divine intervention. A declaration was made on this website that the Great Rolling Stone of the Garden Tomb was just discovered by Simon and Emma Brown from England. Although this Great Rolling Stone has been standing upon Mount Nebo for some time and has been photographed by many visitors, Simon believed that it was the Great Rolling Stone from Yeshua's Garden Tomb, so he traveled there in 2011 to investigate it. I was stunned when I saw their short video on their website about the Great Rolling Stone because the LORD had already shown me some incredible truths about this Great Rolling Stone of Yeshua's tomb and how it pertains to the last days. I had already written profound revelations about it! *This was either the true stone or it was very symbolic of Yeshua's Rolling Stone.*

Now the LORD was about to show me that this was all written in stone! In their short video, they showed that the Great Rolling Stone of Yeshua's Garden tomb was now standing upon Mount Nebo. The stone was definitely extremely aged and somewhat damaged.

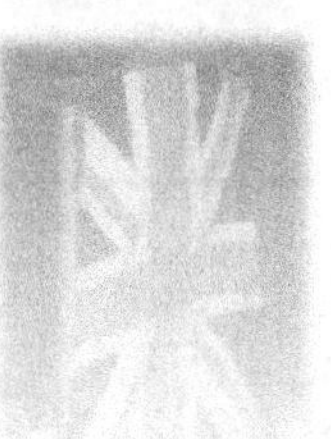

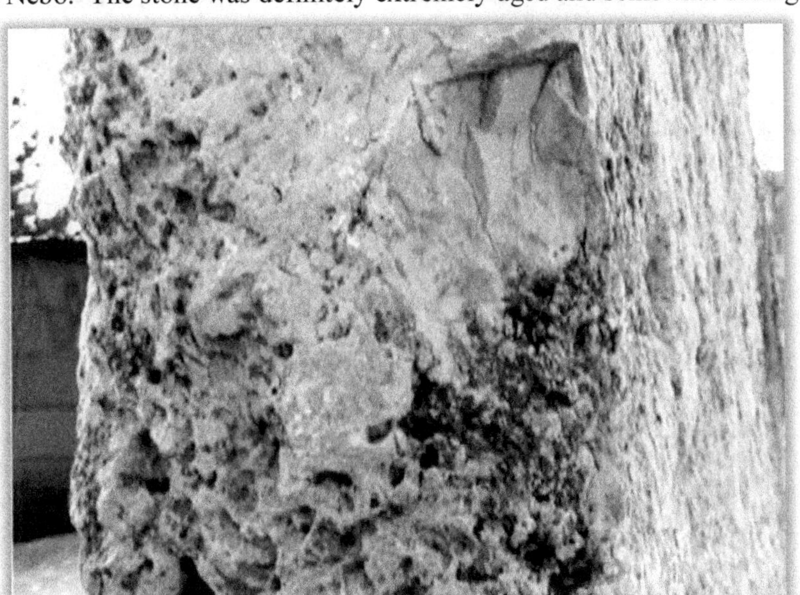

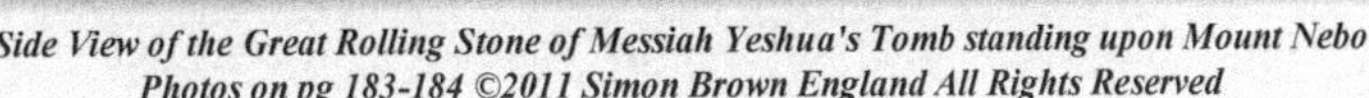

Side View of the Great Rolling Stone of Messiah Yeshua's Tomb standing upon Mount Nebo
Photos on pg 183-184 ©2011 Simon Brown England All Rights Reserved

Simon Brown had gone to Israel and he had filmed at the Garden tomb, showing that he had measured the track of the Great Rolling Stone at Yeshua's tomb and he had taken other measurements in and around the entrance of the tomb. Simon had ascended Mount Nebo in order to measure this Great Rolling Stone. He measured the height and width of the stone. He said that he had obtained tiny test samples of the stone from the two locations and had them analyzed by a scientist in England to see if the two samples matched each other. The analysis that he received back verified that the two samples were the same rock. This means that the Great Rolling Stone on Mount Nebo was a perfect match to the hewn stone at Yeshua's Garden tomb in Mount Moriah. Simon compared *the measurements* that he had taken at the Garden tomb to those of the Great Rolling Stone on Mount Nebo. Even more shocking to me though, was the fact that they declared with this discovery, that this Great Rolling Stone came with a prophecy, but they did not know what the meaning of the prophecy was that went with it. I was stunned because the Scripture they gave as the prophecy was the very Scripture that had started my Almond Tree revelation three years earlier that I had already written was a prophecy! So I already knew the meaning of the prophecy by Divine Providence! They did not know what the Rolling Stone was doing up on Mount Nebo, but they were just certain that this was Yeshua's Rolling Stone because of its size, color, and texture. It was through another Divine miracle of God, that I had miraculously been writing the meaning of this very Scripture in my book, for a little over three years before being introduced to Simon, as the LORD had revealed all the things to me that you have been reading. Incredibly, the prophecy they said went with the Rolling Stone was the exact same Scripture from the Gospel of John that I had pondered in 2007 when I received the revelation of the Almond Tree, but they did not know this yet! This was so exciting and I could not believe this was now happening on top of everything else!

John 3:14-15 *And as Moses lifted up the serpent in the wilderness, even so must the Son of man be lifted up; That whosoever believeth in Him should not perish, but have eternal life.*

Since they do not know me, they had no knowledge that the LORD had given me the miracle of the Almond Tree in 2007 and that He had manifested Himself to my heart, through a very unusual set of circumstances. They still do not know yet, that in February 2007, the LORD had awakened me out my sleep at 4AM and had revealed the meaning of this very Scripture to me! For three and a half years, I had written every detail down in the form of this book. So it was due to everything the LORD had revealed to me about the Rolling Stone of Yeshua's Garden tomb (which is later in this book) that *I knew exactly why the Great Rolling Stone of the Garden Tomb was standing upon Mount Nebo, even though I did not know, when I wrote it, that it was in existence and was standing upon Mount Nebo!* I believed it was the true stone because of its profound meaning. I was so thrilled by this incredible connection that I just had to write to them to tell them this incredible news. They said on their website that you could email your comments to them. So I immediately wrote to them in England to let them know that a huge miracle had just occurred and they were not even aware of it yet!

I could not give them all the details that I had written in my book yet because the LORD showed me that this Testimony goes in a certain order and it was already well over 1,200 pages long. It was impossible to relay every detail in this book to someone yet. This book was already in the editing stage when this all came about. I wanted them to know as soon as possible that I believed this was the Great Rolling Stone of the Garden tomb that was standing on Mount Nebo. In a later chapter of this book, you will find the magnificent revelation that the LORD revealed to me about *Yeshua's Great Rolling Stone* and due to this, I was quite certain that this had to be the Great Rolling Stone of Yeshua's Garden tomb that was now standing upon Mount Nebo. This archaeological piece of Messiah Yeshua's Testimony is part of the greatest story that was never told! One day soon, the LORD will show them the

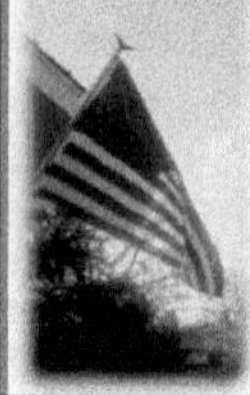

details in this book and they will be absolutely floored when they realize the full impact of the miracle that was happening now. Everyone will see that the mighty hand of God brought all these things together, for such a time as this, *to proclaim the power and glory of the LORD God of Israel!* We were connected by the LORD'S Divine will, on June 4th 2011, four days before Shavuot or Pentecost, (when the Torah was given at Mount Sinai)! This all unfolded so unexpectedly while I was first editing and it was truly as if the LORD was unveiling the depth of His incredible end time Testimony. So now I would like to share the letters of my first correspondence with Simon and Emma Brown from England. The following letter is the first letter that I sent to them, upon finding their website at realdiscoveries.com. Even if I did not agree with everything on the website, Simon and his friend had a documentary film already about the Garden Tomb that had previously aired on TBN, the Trinity Broadcasting Network.

Sent to England, on Saturday, June 4th 2011 at 7:18pm

Blessings Simon and Emma,

I just ran across your video about the Rolling Stone and was shocked by it. You see, I have been writing a book, because the LORD showed me an end time Testimony and it includes the Rolling Stone! The time of my writing to you in England, landed on the 400th Anniversary of the King James Bible. The miracle happened, when the LORD gave me a message to send to Jerusalem. When I did send it to Jerusalem, I was not expecting a miracle back, but it happened. After this happened, the Holy Spirit opened my understanding to see things in the Bible, that I had never seen before. Some of them are chilling and astonishing. Now I know what they saw on the road to Emmaus. I wanted to tell you something I noticed that I am not sure you saw on Mount Nebo. You know the map that points toward the directions of the towns of Israel upon Mount Nebo? Well I think the Rolling Stone is depicted on that map and the Rolling Stone is standing at an angle, meaning that the Stone itself is acting like a compass. On the map, I believe that the circular center point, is the Rolling Stone and it has a cross and the letters M & N on it, for Mount Nebo. So I am telling you that the Rolling Stone is depicted on the map and is the compass point from which, you can line up the different places that make up the Promised Land! It has the cross on it, thereby proving that it is in fact the Rolling Stone. Also in my book, which I wish to at some point make into a film, I show that the Rolling Stone is extremely significant, for reasons that I explain in detail in my book. By some strange coincidence, I found your website without looking for it. So there is more than meets the eye about the Rolling Stone and the LORD has preserved it I believe, as part of His final Testimony. I wish I could tell you more about it, but I am currently editing my book and soon it will be ready. I think the fact that the cross is pictured on that map on Mount Nebo and the Stone is set at an angle, proves this is ***the way*** into the Promised Land. You would truly be astonished by what the LORD has shown my heart about this, but for now, I believe you are right and that it is the Rolling Stone of Yeshua. I send you many blessings and positive verification that you are correct.

Shalom and blessings Kimberly Ballard

I was excited, because a response came back quickly to my letter from England.

Saturday, To: Colorado, June 4, 2011, 12:43 PM

Dear Kimberly,

This is amazing I believe this is indeed God's will for you to be telling me this absolutely amazing story. PLEASE tell me what you can, as you have made me very excited. Please can I add this email to the comments on my article? And also I make Christian films and I would love to help you make one for free. (Right!) God Bless you Kimberly, Simon

Wow! This was definitely Divine intervention and Divine Providence. It was thrilling as we exchanged a few more emails about Mount Nebo. Then suddenly, something even more incredible happened and it slowly unfolded in the most astonishing fashion. The next letter came to me from his wife Emma. I could hardly contain my enthusiasm.

Saturday, To: Colorado, June 4, 2011 3:34 PM
Dear Kimberly, Simon and I, are looking at the picture that you described to us on the map at Mount Nebo, which we do find interesting, as you have stated, but we are still trying to understand if there is a connection with the picture of the stone and the cross facing the Holy cities. Can you shed any more light on this matter? Do you believe the round circle with the cross inside represents the stone and are you saying that the stone is facing Jerusalem? Any more help would be greatly appreciated.
God Bless, Emma and Simon

I was thrilled to get this letter while the LORD was helping me finish the work on my book, and this took longer than expected! Because of what I had written, without ever having been up to Mount Nebo, I knew that *the Great Rolling Stone had to be facing Jerusalem like a compass and was directly facing Holy Mount Moriah, the Holy Mountain of God, and the Garden Tomb itself.* The Great Rolling Stone that had been rolled away by the angel of the LORD was now pointing *the way* into the Eternal Promised Land, because as I said earlier, *Yeshua is the vessel, the Ark of God's Divine Presence,* that is leading *the way* for Israel to enter into the Heavenly Promised Land, across the Jordan River. Moses stood upon Mount Nebo and took his last view of the Promised Land, but Moses was not allowed to enter the Promised Land. It was *Joshua* that took the Hebrews across the Jordan River and into the Promised Land. I began to research to see if I could find a video or at least another photograph that might show a glimpse of the Rolling Stone on Mount Nebo. I thought that some visitor to Mount Nebo likely photographed it and did a video of the area and I thought that if by chance the cameraman panned the camera around on Mount Nebo, he may well have captured a view that would show me where the Great Rolling Stone was actually standing, compared to where the map was overlooking the valley below. I told them that I believed it had to be standing at an angle, overlooking the Promised Land. The view from Mount Nebo towards Israel (the Promised Land) is shown in the following picture taken by Simon Brown in 2011!

Moses view of the Promised Land from on top of Mount Nebo Photo ©2011 Simon Brown All Rights Reserved

I was trying to determine where the map was, compared to where the Great Rolling Stone was standing, because I believed the Rolling Stone was depicted on this map with the cross of Yeshua in the middle of it.

This huge Rolling Stone was nearly ten feet tall (nine feet eight inches I believe he said). It was hand hewn, exactly like the Garden tomb of Joseph of Arimathaea. Simon said that the chisel marks on the Garden Tomb match the chisel marks on the Great Rolling Stone on Mount Nebo. Suddenly I realized that what I had said to them appeared to be correct. The Great Rolling Stone, even though it appeared to be in a different place from where the map was on Mount Nebo, was still angled and facing what the LORD promised to Israel! I knew that it had to be overlooking the valley, just like the map was overlooking the valley. This proved that it was in fact standing like a compass, as if it was a key that unlocked the door that shows that Messiah *Yeshua* leads the way into the Eternal Promised Land! Since everything was coming together in such a miraculous and spectacular fashion, after having written about Yeshua being the second Joshua, I really started thinking that these were very clear signs, that our beloved Messiah Yeshua is about to return to the earth, because these things were now beginning to be revealed at the same time! I wrote to them again and I tried to explain all the things that I believed the LORD was showing me about the Rolling Stone on Mount Nebo.

Sent To England: Saturday, June 4th 2011 22:50

Hi Emma & Simon!

Well, yes, I am saying that I believe the map shows the Rolling Stone and the cross is depicted on the half circle, because it is the Garden tomb Rolling Stone. I do believe it is angled, based on another video I found. Although I have never been there, I can't say where it is in proximity to the map, but I feel that it is connected to the map, even if the map is in a different location from the Stone. I just go by what the LORD reveals to my heart. Is it possible the Stone was moved? Or which direction is it facing? Based on what my heart says, I believe the Stone is pictured on that map and I think it is pointing to what the LORD Promised to Israel forever!

My next letter to them, mentioned why the cross was depicted on the arch on the Mount Nebo Map.

Sent To England: Saturday, June 4th 2011

Dear Simon and Emma,

There would be no reason for that cross to be etched on the arch on the Mount Nebo map, unless the cross was specifically referring to the Great Rolling Stone of Yeshua's tomb. Why is there a cross on the map on the rounded arch? Because that is the Rolling Stone that sealed the tomb of Yeshua. I have things in my book pertaining to it. So to answer your question, yes I believe the map is depicting the Rolling Stone and the cross on it proves that it came from Yeshua's tomb! I could not tell where the Stone is located, but even if it is in a different place than the map, it has to be the arch on the map that has the cross on it. Thanks for your emails it's exciting! God Bless…Kimberly Ballard

---

I also noticed that the shape of the arch with a line across the bottom of it, as it was depicted on the Mount Nebo map, matched the shape of the Garden tomb itself. So it was like a key, pointing to where the resurrection had occurred. *This Stone was pointing to the Testimony of the LORD, in His Holy Mount Moriah. Again, it was pointing like a key to the Almond Branch that came to life, bearing the First Fruit of Eternal life. I therefore knew that*

the Great Rolling Stone was also pointing the way to the Almond Tree of Life! It was pointing to the location of the Garden of God! The Great Rolling Stone was truly standing on the highest point of Mount Nebo, overlooking the Promised Land that the LORD had promised to Israel forever!

Simon sent me a reply without knowing anything that I had written by the Divine revelation of the LORD. He did not know that I had written that Yeshua was the one leading Israel into the Eternal Promised Land, just like Joshua led Israel with the Ark. This is why I knew that I was not jumping to a conclusion when I declared that I knew it was pointing *the way* toward the Eternal Jerusalem. The Holy Spirit was revealing this to me and the LORD was verifying it all! Simon wrote to me again.

==

Saturday, To Colorado: June 4, 2011, 4:26 PM

Hello Kimberly,

What you are saying is very interesting however, we must not jump to conclusions and pray that the Holy Spirit will lead us to the truth. Now there is a possibility that the Great Stone could be facing Jerusalem, however, until I do more research, I will not know that for sure and remember I said in my article that there is a prophecy that connects Mount Nebo to the crucifixion site which is John 3:14, which could be why the cross is drawn in the map by the monastery staff at Mount Nebo. However, there is something very familiar, as it is set in a certain position. I will just use some small parts of yours emails discussing what you believe about the Great Stone, which may I hope, be more evidence. And the stone is so badly marked, it is hard to say about any notches that link up with the lines you see on the map, yes there could be. God Bless Simon and Emma

==

I needed proof that what the LORD had impressed upon me was indeed true. I needed to see for certain, that the Great Rolling Stone was facing what God had Promised to Israel. I emailed Simon and Emma to tell them where to look on this particular video, to verify the locations of the map and the Great Rolling Stone.

Sent to England: Saturday, June 4, 2011 4:09 PM

Hi Simon and Emma! Watch this video clip and you will see the angle of the stone come into the frame from the right side at the 3:22 mark. Then the map is shown later near the 5:40 mark, but wait until the 6:23 mark and it shows that map. The half circle depicts the Rolling Stone with the cross. Ok, look at the angle of that Rolling Stone...it appears to be angled toward the cities that God Promised to Israel. You have been there to film, so where is that map in connection to the stone? Is it possible they are both angled, even if not together in the same place? What do you think friends? Yes, I know by the power of the Holy Spirit, exactly why that Stone is there on Mount Nebo. I do have an outstanding answer to that mystery. Is the map near the Rolling Stone? Or is the Rolling Stone angled to face towards where the map is located. And does the Rolling Stone overlook the valley towards Jerusalem? What do you think friends? God Bless...Kimberly

I later saw some of Simon's photographs of the Great Rolling Stone that I had not seen before and much to my excitement, I found out that it was standing exactly as I thought! *It was, majestically and incredibly, facing the Promised Land!* It was absolutely a key of Yeshua leading the children of Israel to unlock *the door* of Eternal life! The next letter contained the following statements from Simon.

To Colorado: Sunday, June 5, 2011 5:47 AM

Dear Kimberly,

Thanks for your very interesting emails. YES I do believe you and I do believe God is revealing all this to you. Kimberly at the moment I believe you have brought something very amazing to my attention AND IT IS THIS. The Great Stone at Mount Nebo is a Christian site, built in honor of Moses with one prophecy told by Yeshua. The Great Stone at Mount Nebo has no recorded history, as to who made it, why it was made, when it was made, or how it got there in the beginning. All we know, is that it was found near Mount Nebo and put there to protect and show it. So to many, the Great Stone at Mount Nebo is also shrouded in mystery as to its true identity. The Great Stone at Mount Nebo also stands at one of the highest points of the Holy Land and is as you say pointing towards what the LORD Promised Israel, with Jerusalem in the middle. I believe there are also mysterious marks and maybe writing also on the Great Stone. As you say, the Great Stone at Mount Nebo also has a map facing the Promised Land of Israel and in the map, there is half a circle with the cross of Yeshua right in the middle of it. The half circle on the map, could be the Great Stone. It is also a message from God. Now what is also interesting here is that my good friend told me the Great Stone at Mount Nebo has a prophecy. There is a Bible prophesy and it is this; *"Just as Moses lifted up the snake in the wilderness, so the Son of Man must be lifted up, that everyone who believes may have eternal life in Him."* John 3:14. Is this all a coincidence? THE SITE and The Great Stone at Mount Nebo is a prophecy BY GOD. Simon

===

What Simon did not know was just how profound this truly was because the stone has a far greater meaning than meets the eye and I had not revealed this yet to anyone. In my heart, I knew that the LORD did not want me to reveal it yet, but there were so many things that I had miraculously written in my book by Divine Providence, before ever knowing that this stone was actually now standing upon Mount Nebo, facing the Promised Land of Israel, and this proof was quite astonishing! So I wrote back hoping to convince him that my hypothesis was not simply based upon my own thoughts about it, but it was Scriptural and the LORD had proven to me, through His Holy Spirit, that this was going to be extraordinarily historic!

===

Sent to England: Saturday, June 4, 2011 11:52 pm

Hi again,

Yes one should never jump to a conclusion Simon, but if it all points to the Testimony that the LORD revealed to me, then I believe it is there for a reason. You know you mentioned that prophecy in John? Well, I did not tell you this, but that is the very verse that started my miracle and revelation. This exact verse of the prophecy is in the first chapters of my book. That is why it is even more of a coincidence and I don't believe that I am jumping to any conclusions, but only that the LORD will prove it in due time. If this prophecy, which is the very verse that made my miracle happen in Jerusalem, is the very one you mention, then that is very strange. It is all connected. My miracle began while watching the Gospel of John DVD and particularly the same verse that you declared on your webpage, is a prophecy. Well in 2007, this is the very verse that I had pondered and the LORD opened my understanding to it. Therefore, my whole book is based on that verse! A miracle that came back to me from Jerusalem is based upon that one Scripture, although my book uses many Scriptures to prove that each thing is accurate according to the Bible. When I saw that you had declared to have found the Rolling Stone, I was even more shocked that you happened to say something also about that verse. It is like the LORD is verifying to me, what I have written is absolutely true. It is so strange, but exciting! If you had not mentioned the very verse in John, that was the basis

for my first miracle and revelation of the LORD, then I would not think that stone was anything on Mount Nebo. That was the verse that opened the door and it is the key of David. *The LORD has an end time Testimony and I believe that Stone is revealed as part of it.* It is too lengthy to go into detail, but trust me, I know the LORD'S heart. Do they not know why, the Rolling Stone is on Mount Nebo? Blessings Kimberly

I was so encouraged, because on his website was the Gospel of John DVD! He had the movie clip that was my favorite, showing the scene that had brought about my Almond Tree revelation and miracle a little over three years ago. So I thought I would show him the scene that was the starting point of my book about this prophetic Scripture.

==

Sent to England: Saturday, June 4, 2011 5:30 PM

Shalom Simon, this is the movie and scene that I mention in my book that leads to the greatest revelation that will ever be told. The Holy Spirit woke me up and gave me a detailed message to send to Jerusalem about this particular verse, the one where Yeshua is standing out on the porch talking to Nicodemus. One thing I mentioned to you that I had thought about doing was eventually either making a documentary of my book or creating a feature film about it. I have been praying for the LORD to open the right door. If you look at that Mount Nebo clip I sent you, notice at the 6:22 mark, the map and then later, around 10:06 in the distance on the right hand side and center right, is the Rolling Stone and it does appear to be facing the valley from where he just panned. And the map was in the direction from where he just panned. The Stone is angled toward that valley, I think...see what I mean at 10:06 and it shows it quickly. The Stone was visible in the 9 minute and something mark, as I stated earlier. If you had not shown both the serpent on the pole on Mount Nebo and the Rolling Stone, I would not think that this is a miracle, but due to the fact that I have been writing what the LORD showed me for three and a half years having to do with these exact things, then that is no coincidence, but the hand of the LORD God! Plus this is happening between us, on the 400th year of the publishing of the King James Bible in England! Talk to you soon I hope! Thanks for blessing me today...Kimberly

==

The next astonishing verification came, after the LORD reminded me when I woke up the next morning, *that a year earlier, I had discovered this Jewish Priestly Angel in the rock formation at the Garden tomb.* So I went to sleep that night and I woke up realizing that I still had this photograph in my files, of a Jewish Priestly Angel that I had discovered at the Garden Tomb in the rock formation and had outlined in blue ink so I could remember where I saw it. The LORD impressed it upon my heart to send it that morning to Simon and Emma. So I sent it to them, just to see what they would say. It was not until 2013 that I just realized I sent this to Simon on Shavuot on Pentecost, the very day the disciples were endued with power!

==

Sent To England: Wed, June 8, 2011 5:01 pm
Subject: I want to show you an Angel!

Dear Simon - Thanks for your emails and info! For a long time I have seen something at the Garden tomb that no one has ever seen. At first I thought it was an optical illusion, but I absolutely know for certain now, that it is indeed in the rock formation. I was not sure if I should show it to you or not, but I decided to show it to you because I feel the Holy Spirit revealed it to me. Now for the exciting thing I saw at the Garden tomb that the Holy Spirit caused my eyes to see, I am going to attach a picture for you of the Garden tomb. In this

picture, I have drawn a line around the figure of what I think is an Angel! I clearly see the face of a man with a simple Jewish kippah on. He has a mustache and I can see the eyes, nose, mouth and beard and I believe perhaps two wings coming off it with an extended arm pointing. I have outlined it and I pray that you will see what I see. All of a sudden, while I was writing in my book about the Garden tomb, I was looking at a photograph of the Garden tomb one day and suddenly my eyes saw this figure of an Angel. Please look at what I have outlined. I believe part of the wall is missing where the wings are. Please by the grace of God have a look and by the power of the Holy Spirit, tell me you see it too? I hope the LORD will show you that I am being truthful when I say that the LORD gave me a Testimony for the end times, that He wants me to do something with. This is proof...be blessed! KB - Please let me know if you see it.

==

REPLY Sent To Colorado:

Wednesday, June 8, 2011 10:53 AM

Yes Kimberly **BRILLIANT!** I can clearly see a face at the top. Well done. Here is a photo of how the Great stone fits perfectly on the Tomb.
God Bless, Simon

==

Right after I sent this picture of the Garden tomb Angel to Simon *he replied by sending me a photograph.* Simon sent a picture showing three different views of the Garden tomb blended together into one picture. In this photograph, Simon was trying to show me the measurements that he took of the Rolling Stone and how the Stone fits perfectly at the Garden tomb like a glove. He had drawn a perfect white circle in the size and shape of the Great Rolling Stone that stands on Mount Nebo and he had superimposed this white circle and placed it at the door of the Garden tomb. Wow! It did fit so perfectly, that it was unbelievable! I barely had time to look at it for very long though, because I had to leave soon after I received his photograph in my email. It was only later that afternoon that the thought came to me to go back and study the photograph that he just emailed to me, to see if my Jewish Priestly Angel by any chance appeared in his photograph. When I did this, I just about gasped out loud when I saw the truth! The Angel was not only in Simon's photograph too, but the Angel, much to my astonishment, fit perfectly over the Great Rolling Stone, as if the Angel was sitting over it! It was a perfect fit! I could barely type out an email to them because I was so excited by this discovery! Here is the letter I sent to them, although I had originally typed it all in capital letters, because I was so unnerved by this astonishing sight! As I said…the day just happened to be Pentecost or Shavuot the same day the Jewish disciples were sent the fire of the Holy Spirit!

Sent To England: Wednesday, June 8, 2011 6:13 PM

LOOK!!

Simon & Emma, Bless the LORD! If you are not sitting down, you better get ready to! I have something astonishing to tell you and it is going to astound you, my friends. It is definitely the Rolling Stone of the Garden tomb! Do you know how I know for certain? Does it look like I'm shouting? I am shouting it from the roof top! Ha, Ha! The LORD has done something incredible. This afternoon, I went back into my email and opened the picture of the Rolling Stone that you sent me this morning, after I sent you the photograph of the Garden tomb and the Angel that the LORD showed me, to the right side of the door. I wondered to myself this afternoon, if the Angel might show up in the picture that you sent to me too? So what did I do? I looked and you are not going to believe it! *The Angel fits perfectly with the wing around the Rolling Stone on both sides with the Mantle touching the top of the Stone!* I recognized the kippah or mitre from a website about the Third Temple, because they just

commissioned the Priestly garments to be remade in Jerusalem and this Angel is wearing the Jewish Priestly mitre!!! You must take a look at the mitre, to see what I mean. The Angel fits perfectly on top of the Great Rolling Stone! I then took your photograph and drew around the Angel again, as it appeared on top of the Rolling Stone that you had superimposed in your picture. *My Angel fits perfectly on the top of your Rolling Stone and this proves that it is the Great Rolling Stone of the Garden tomb!* Yeshua, the LORD, has brought us together can you believe this!!! How incredible! Take a look and I wish I could see your reaction when you see it for the very first time! Keep in mind that the wing of the Angel is where the rock is chunked out, just as the center of the blocked part, was once repaired. Wow! Praise the LORD! This is the most astonishing thing ever to happen! Please take a look for yourselves. One more incredible thing is that the wing stops just above the window on the Garden tomb! This is astonishing! And look at your picture of the white circle on the photo to the right, you can see the wing of the Angel is perfectly aligned, even with the white circle line you drew, *without having ever seen the Angel!* I believe for certain now, that the LORD is continuing to show me another aspect of His Testimony so this will be more verification in my book about the LORD. It is incredible, just stunning! It is the Great Rolling Stone and the LORD has provided this proof, because I had outlined that Angel when the LORD showed it to me, wearing the Jewish mitre on his head, which is the Priestly garment of Israel. I cannot believe it sat in my photos with the blue line around it until this morning when the LORD put it in my heart to show it to you. As I went back this afternoon (on Pentecost) to look at your photo that you sent me, after I sent you the Angel picture, then that I saw that the Angel is sitting on top of the Rolling Stone perfectly, as if it is guarding the tomb!! What do you say my friends? Love Kimberly

---

All Iris, Clematis, Rose Peony, Gardenia, Banana Tree, Lilac, Daffodil, Pansy, Dove & Carnation
Photos ©2013 Kimberly K Ballard
All Rights Reserved

The Angel at the Garden Tomb & the Great Rolling Stone lined up perfectly as you can see in this photograph!
Photo ©2011 Simon Brown England
All Rights Reserved

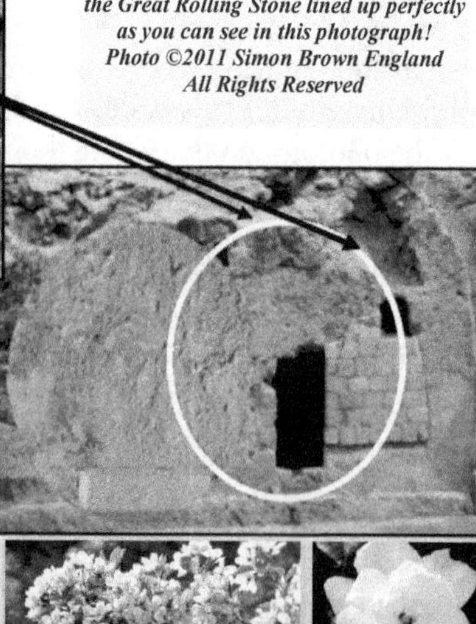

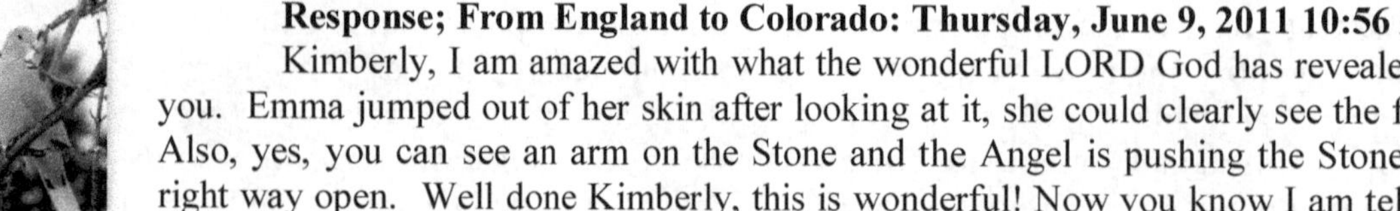

Response; From England to Colorado: Thursday, June 9, 2011 10:56 AM

Kimberly, I am amazed with what the wonderful LORD God has revealed to you. Emma jumped out of her skin after looking at it, she could clearly see the face. Also, yes, you can see an arm on the Stone and the Angel is pushing the Stone the right way open. Well done Kimberly, this is wonderful! Now you know I am telling the truth. It is the Great Stone as I believed it to be. Can I write a little article about

what you have just found or even better can you write me a little article about what you have found and I will send it to 1000's of people to see what they say about this? Blessings Simon and Emma

How could I not write the article about this, it was so fantastic? I also asked them if they would mind if I wrote this in my book, because it was a verification of the Testimony that the LORD had shown to me. They said, *"Sure we would be honored!"* So Simon kept looking at the Jewish Angel and was amazed and I could not believe that this miracle happened on Shavuot, on Pentecost! How incredible!

==

Sent To Colorado: Thursday, June 9, 2011, 4:36 PM
Hello Kimberly! Yes I have been looking at the Angel for some time. I look forward to your article of the Angel and the map with the cross in the middle. Try not to make it too long. It is late here now, 11:30 PM good night! Talk to you tomorrow.
Blessings Simon

==

Of course I was so excited, that I could not sleep. I was pondering all these events and thinking about how marvelous the works of the LORD are, that are being unveiled in our generation and so I wrote another email to them. It was funny that Simon said that Emma just about jumped out of her skin when she saw the Jewish Angel, because she was in a video about the Garden tomb but she had no idea she was standing next to it, and had no idea it was there! Fantastic LORD! It reminded me how the invisible assistant works!

==

Sent To England: later that night; Hi Simon and Emma! That is so funny Emma! Can you imagine that thousands of people have been to the Garden tomb and yet this Angel has never been seen before by anyone! Isn't it incredible? When the LORD first showed it to me, I was working on my book in a section about the Garden tomb so I was looking at photos of the tomb. All of a sudden I saw this Angel with the Jewish Priestly mitre and wings. Yes the Angel is facing the right direction to roll the stone away! It is absolutely astonishing.

So I pasted the one photo of the Garden tomb into my files, so I could go in and draw a line around what I saw, which was an Angel wearing a Mantle and the Priestly mitre. He is looking down towards the door! Did you see the wing curves up just above the window? It is a perfect fit. Because I went back to look at your picture these two separate archaeological objects completely came together, only because I felt the LORD prompting me to contact you from the United States. I had to tell you that the reason I believe you that Rolling Stone on Mount Nebo, is the one from the Garden tomb, is because since 2007, the Holy Spirit revealed details to me about Yeshua's Rolling Stone and these things are in a book I am writing. Yes, if you want, I will write a brief article for you! This is so astonishing! Just think I put that photo of the Garden tomb Angel in my folder with my blue outline, saving it for a year, to eventually show to someone. When I woke up this morning on Shavuot/Pentecost, the LORD brought it to my mind and I thought He wanted me to show it to you. At that time, I was not thinking about where my Angel would fit in connection to your Mount Nebo Rolling Stone. But yesterday, when I went to observe your photo with the white circle, it just happened to outline where the wing of the Angel is, and that is not a coincidence, but another miracle. This is so astonishing and the LORD said not to hide His light under a bushel, but to put it on a lamp stand so it shines forth! So if you would like for me to write an article to put on your website I will do it!!! I was hoping that the LORD would wake you up in the middle of the night over

there in England, so you could see my emails!!! I wish I could have seen your reaction when you saw it! Awesome! And now the LORD sent me rain and it NEVER rains here. It was so hot that you could barely stand it the other day. Is there anything you would like for me to say in my article about it? The LORD has given me many miracles. It was from one of these astonishing miracles that I started writing my book in 2007. Thanks friends! Kimberly

==

After the joy of having had this happen, I woke up the next morning to another exciting event. I began telling my Mother that the LORD had shown me that there is a river that runs underneath Jerusalem and I had written the meaning of it in my book. That morning to my surprise, a Pastor on the radio, happened to mention that when he was in Israel, he heard a river rushing underneath the Temple Mount, when he placed his ear to the rocks. I was telling my Mother what I had written about it and I told her the reason why the river is there. I was completely shocked because later that same afternoon, out of nowhere, I got this email from my Israeli friend in Jerusalem and I had not heard from her in a long time. She was the one who sent me the Almond Tree photograph, after the LORD gave me the revelation and told me to send it to Jerusalem! Without her knowing anything I had been talking about or writing in my book, she suddenly the same day sent me an article that was in the Jerusalem newspaper that morning. The article said that a river, which is the longest ever found in Israel, was just discovered running under the city! I had written about a river being beneath Jerusalem and here was the proof again and that morning I was telling my Mother that a river runs underneath Jerusalem! This all happened the same week! Remember that when Yeshua comes that the rushing Living Water will flow out from the Heavenly Temple on the Temple Mount.

After all these things happened, I felt that the Messiah must be returning very soon! So I worked on the article for Simon and Emma Brown and sent it to them. They posted my article on their *"realdiscoveries.com"* website in England. The article shows all the photos of my Jewish Priestly Angel in Holy Mount Moriah with their Great Rolling Stone from Mount Nebo. It was a miracle that the LORD opened all these doors at the same time proving everything, and I believe He poured out His Holy Spirit on us on Shavuot, just like He did with His disciples 2,000 years ago! The LORD was revealing something astonishing at the Garden tomb in Holy Mount Moriah of all places on this day!

Later, after all these things happened, I sent some old photographs of the Garden Tomb that I had saved in my files to Simon to show him that there were other stones that used to be sitting in the rolling track and a slab of stone out of the sepulchre. They have since been removed. I told him that I believed that they were likely the original stopper for the rolling stone at Yeshua's Garden tomb. I thought I should send this information with the old pictures I had saved in my files. What I believed to be the original stopper stones were visible in the old photographs that I had saved in my files from my own research, before meeting Simon and Emma. Simon then wrote an article about this after he obtained the picture from the original archived source. Simon also showed me the following photos of his rock samples taken from the Garden tomb and from the Great Rolling Stone.

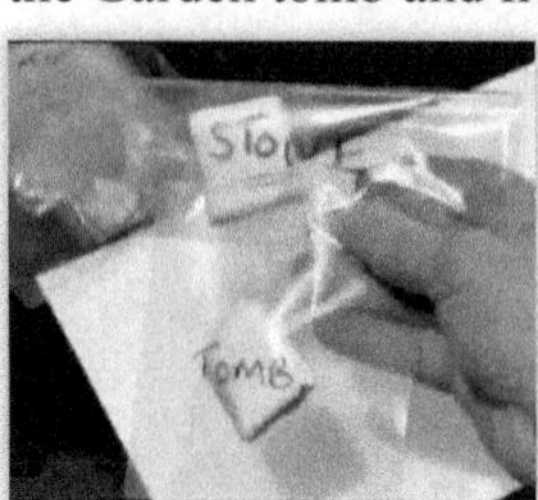

Simon's Rolling Stone & Garden Tomb rock samples Photo ©2011 Simon Brown England All Rights Reserved

The mighty hand of God was now unfolding this stunning part of His final Testimony that was to be revealed in the last days! So I wrote the following article for them to post on their website in England (including details that I said here) about my Jewish Priestly Angel discovery.

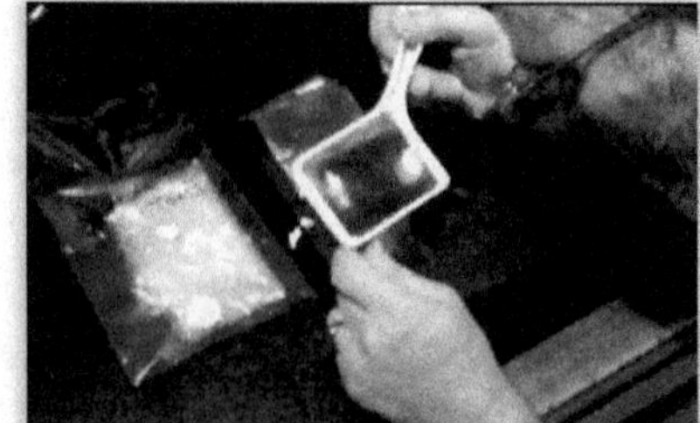

Simon Brown observing his rock samples Photo ©2011 Simon Brown England All Rights Reserved

THE JEWISH PRIESTLY ANGEL AT THE GARDEN TOMB AND THE GREAT ROLLING STONE ON MOUNT NEBO

My Article for Simon's Website in England
Written © June 9th 2011 by Kimberly K. Ballard
The article contains part of the above information

Face of the Jewish Priestly Angel Photo ©2013 extracted from Simon Brown's Garden Tomb Photo ©2011 All Rights Reserved

In 2007, a great miracle came to me from Jerusalem when the LORD gave me a message and impressed it upon my heart to send it to Jerusalem. When I did this I was not expecting a miracle to occur, but it did and it was incredible to say the least. From this point on the LORD opened my understanding to see things in the Bible that I had never seen before, so I began to write them down in a book. I have been working on it for three and a half years and I am currently editing it so it can soon be published. About a year ago I was writing about the Garden tomb and I began to look at photographs of it. I was researching for my book and not looking for anything specific in the photographs. The LORD had shown me many astonishing things about Himself that I have yet to tell the world. When this happened to me, I understood what the LORD meant in the following Scripture.

Matthew 11:25-27 *At that time Jesus answered and said, I thank Thee, O Father, LORD of Heaven and earth, because Thou hast hid these things from the wise and prudent, and hast revealed them unto babes. Even so, Father; for so it seemed good in Thy sight. All things are delivered unto Me of My Father; and no man knoweth the Son, but the Father; neither knoweth any man the Father, save the Son, and he to whomsoever the Son will reveal HIM.*

I knew from this Scripture, that the LORD loved me enough, to reveal some of His deepest revelations to my heart. Even my friend in Jerusalem who was part of my miracle in 2007, told me that my message was a true revelation from *HaShem,* the Hebrew Name for the LORD. When the LORD revealed more to me, I was both astonished and excited. It is because of what has just occurred that I would like to share one of these miracles with you!

One day as I was looking at Garden tomb photos, the LORD brought to my attention this image of a Jewish Priestly Angel above the door and to the right of the Garden tomb. Part of the wing was chunked out of the rock and damaged, but you could make out the shape of it and I saw this incredible face looking down over the door of the tomb, as if guarding it! I was completely shocked when I saw this face, because I never expected anything like this to appear before my eyes! I recognized the head covering as the Jewish mitre that is worn by the Priests of the Holy Temple in Jerusalem. They recently began remaking this mitre for the garments of the Priest's to be used in the coming Third Temple in Jerusalem. The Angel appeared to have a mantle like a collar and a beard or mustache. I could clearly make out the eyes, nose, beard, the mitre, the mantle and two wings with an outstretched arm and pointing finger. One wing faced downward toward the window of the tomb and the other went out and was lifted up above, toward the door. I was so amazed by what I saw that day. I wondered if it was really there or if it was an optical illusion (because of the light and shadow effects of the sun shining on the rocks). I knew I saw this (masculine) face so clearly. So I searched for another photograph of the Garden tomb that was taken at another angle to see if the Angel still appeared to be there.

To my surprise the Angel appeared, even when the photograph was taken from a different location. This time I saw that the Angel, taken at this other angle was clearer than before. I said, Wow, there must really be something to this if I can see it from two different angles! It appeared to be a Jewish Priestly Angel based upon the garments. I could see it from two completely different angles. So I saved the picture, so I could outline the Angel in blue ink. Then I could remember where I saw it. I was going to contact someone with this information in Israel, but I was not sure if I should, so I held onto the photo. So for a year I did nothing with this picture, except keep it in my file. I thought about it from time to time, as I continued writing my book. There is actually more to this story than I can write in this brief space.

The Angel at the Garden Tomb discovered by Kimberly Kay Ballard in 2010
Simon blurred the Angel for me in this Photo ©2011 Simon Brown England All Rights Reserved

In my book I had written some truths about the LORD and I had talked about Mount Nebo. So just recently, I was looking online for something completely unrelated to the Garden tomb or the Rolling Stone. Suddenly this website came up in front of me and it said that the Great Rolling Stone of the Garden tomb was just discovered on Mount Nebo. The discovery came from Simon and Emma Brown from England. I pondered this discovery. I knew in my heart, based upon what I had been shown by the LORD and written by the power of the Holy

Spirit, that this was in fact the Great Rolling Stone of Yeshua's tomb. It was now on Mount Nebo. I immediately contacted Simon and Emma Brown to say that I believed that they were correct that this was the Great Rolling Stone of Yeshua's tomb. Later I noticed that the map that was on Mount Nebo, faces the valley and shows the various cities of Israel. This was the view of the Promised Land. This was the last scene that Moses looked upon. The LORD put it in my heart that the Rolling Stone was actually depicted on this map and was the center point from which, all the cities of Israel are viewed. I had never been there before, so I had to find videos online, to see where the Rolling Stone was located, based upon where the map was located on Mount Nebo. I knew that the LORD was showing me, that the arched object on the Mount Nebo map with the cross in the middle of it, pointing to the various cities of Israel, was in fact, the Great Rolling Stone. I knew that the Rolling Stone, even if it was not near the map, must be standing like a compass, facing the Promised Land. Then sure enough, after researching some videos, I saw that the Rolling Stone appeared to be facing at an angle, which meant that it was directly pointing to Jerusalem. The LORD revealed this to me. It had to be the Great Rolling Stone. Also this Rolling Stone was hewn stone, not smooth, like many of the other Rolling Stones in Israel. Joseph of Arimathaea had hand hewn the tomb of Yeshua, so the Rolling Stone had a rough texture, like the walls of the Garden tomb. The map showed the Rolling Stone with the cross and the letters M & N for Mount Nebo on it. Why would the map on Mount Nebo have a cross on the rounded arch, unless it was the Great Rolling Stone of Yeshua's sepulchre, which is the Garden tomb? I sent this information to Simon and Emma Brown, saying that I believed the Rolling Stone was standing facing the valley of the Promised Land at an angle, like a compass. They kindly wrote me back asking me, *"Are you saying this and saying this?"* Yes, I wrote back, that is exactly what I am saying and I know why the stone is there! So we exchanged some exciting emails about this and then the next morning the LORD reminded me that I had that photograph of the Jewish Angel at the Garden tomb. I felt impressed by the Holy Spirit, to send it to Simon & Emma Brown. I told them that when they saw this picture, they would understand that I was telling the truth that the LORD had revealed things to me. I wanted to show them the Angel at the Garden tomb, which is something that I never imagined would exist, but it was really there! I sent it to Simon and asked him to tell me if he saw it too. It was the photo of the Garden tomb with the blue line that I had drawn around the Jewish Angel. To my excitement, Simon wrote back and said, *"Brilliant!"* Yes I see the face clearly! Wow! It was wonderful to know that he saw it too! We were thrilled! It was such a blessing that the LORD had brought us together in such an incredible way! So then I asked Simon to show it to Emma to see what she thought about it. This morning Simon wrote to me saying that Emma just about jumped out of her skin when she saw it! Simon sent me a picture of the Garden tomb, showing how the Rolling Stone that is up on Mount Nebo fits the Garden tomb perfectly. The photo included the measurements of the Stone that he took. So I briefly looked at the three pictures that he sent. Then I had to leave and did not return until the afternoon. Later that day, it occurred to me to go back and look at Simon's photograph, to see if by chance, my Angel appeared in his photograph. In the photograph that he sent to me that morning, he had superimposed the Rolling Stone, based upon the measurements that he had taken, of the Rolling Stone upon Mount Nebo and he showed me how the stone fits perfectly at the site of the Garden tomb, both in height and in width. Simon had drawn a white circle, showing where the Rolling Stone would fit, when it was rolled in front of the door of the Garden tomb in Jerusalem. So I had gone back to look for my Angel to see if it appeared in Simon's photograph. Suddenly, I saw the incredible truth! I was astonished, because at once, I saw in his photograph, that my Jewish Angel was perfectly lined up over the Rolling Stone that Simon had placed in front of the tomb of Yeshua. In other words, I saw that the Angel's wings, curved with the Rolling Stone perfectly in alignment. The mantle of the Angel, was touching the top of the Rolling Stone. The Angel was looking down toward the door of the tomb in the

direction, as Simon said, that the Stone would have been rolled away! Wow it was thrilling! My Jewish Priestly Angel was looking down over the door of the tomb with one wing on top of the Rolling Stone and the other going downward perfectly lined up with the edge of Simon's Rolling Stone. The tip of the wing ended just a couple of inches above the window of the tomb! This was just astounding! The Angel was not covered by the Rolling Stone at all, but it was literally perfectly sitting above the Rolling Stone, *as if it was guarding the tomb!* Absolutely astonishing! I never expected the LORD to show His mighty works to me, but these are true miracles being revealed before our eyes. I have many more astounding things to reveal about the LORD as soon as I publish my book! For us to have come from two different places in the world with photographs that line up perfectly on Pentecost was a miracle! Not only was my Jewish Angel positioned above and over Simon and Emma's Rolling Stone, it was a perfect fit! It was as if the two pictures meshed into one. I asked my Mother to come have a look at this photograph to see if she saw the Angel and if she could see how it was in perfect alignment with Simon's Rolling Stone. She saw it immediately, as soon as she entered the room and she was astonished by this amazing sight! I knew that this was proof that it had to be Messiah Yeshua's Great Rolling Stone from the Garden tomb, because of this miracle of the Angel that the LORD had revealed to me, that was now perfectly positioned over it. In my heart, I felt that this Stone was the very one that the Angel of the LORD rolled away, when Yeshua was resurrected. Yeshua said, *"Blessed are those who have not seen and yet believe."* By the LORD'S Holy Spirit, His truths and mighty works are made known. These are only a few of the wondrous works of the LORD and He is revealing them to our generation. His truths still stand. We only need to open our hearts to the LORD to see them. Soon I will be revealing many more exciting end time revelations of the LORD. Be blessed and may you be inscribed in the Lamb's Book of life! KB *(Posted in England at realdiscoveries.org and .com)*

Once again, the LORD'S timing for this miracle to be revealed on the very day that the Holy Spirit descended in flaming tongues of fire upon the Jewish disciples 2,000 years ago just boggles the mind! The deep meaning of the Rolling Stone was in my book already and I was finished writing my book at this point! He verified it! This is not the end of this miracle yet!

A little while after writing about the Jewish Priestly Angel, I was watching a movie about King David and I was astonished to see that King David wore a Jewish mitre that was identical to the mitre on the head of the Jewish Priestly Angel at *the Garden tomb in Holy Mount Moriah,* and King David purchased this Mountain of God to honour the KING forever!

Hibiscus Flower & Gardenia blossom
Photos ©2013 Kimberly K Ballard

Mount Nebo as viewed from the Jordan River Valley (Mount Nebo at center in the distance) Photo ©2014 Leon Mauldin All Rights Reserved
Moses stood on this mountain before ascending up to Heaven as he viewed the Promised Land of Israel

The Great Rolling Stone called the Abu Badd standing on Mount Nebo facing the Promised Land toward the LORD'S Garden in Holy Mount Moriah, Jerusalem Israel Photo ©2011 Simon Brown England All Rights Reserved

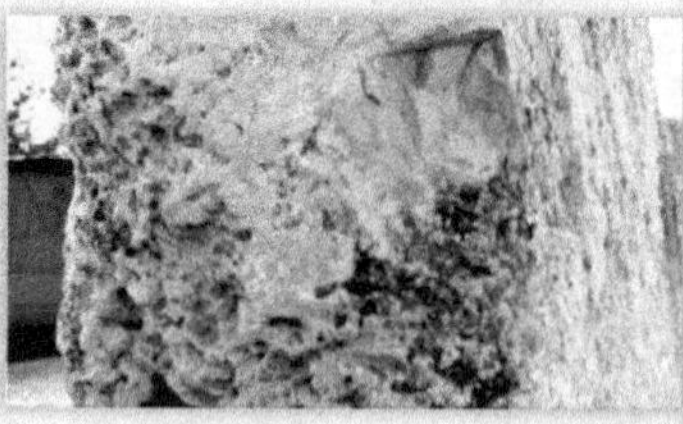

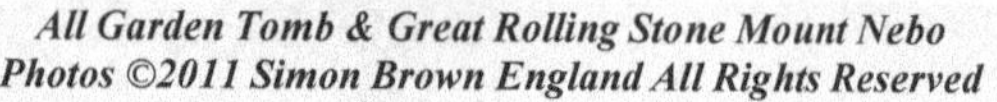

All Garden Tomb & Great Rolling Stone Mount Nebo

Simon Brown of England & his friend measuring the Rolling Stone & the Garden Tomb

The Angel is pointing to the
opened flower above
the niches
This signet shaped object
in the Garden of the KING,
is etched in
the Royal Stone of Kings,
in the rock face of
Holy Mount Moriah, where the
LORD said that His Name
would dwell forever,
with the lower case letters,
"Alpha & Omega!"
MY JEWISH PRIESTLY ANGEL AT THE GARDEN TOMB
& SIMON BROWN'S MOUNT NEBO ROLLING STONE
FIT PERFECTLY TOGETHER
WITH THE ANGEL SITTING ABOVE THE ROLLING STONE
AS SHOWN IN SIMON'S ©2011 PHOTOGRAPHS All Rights Reserved
(SIMON VERIFIED THE WIDTH OF THE STONE TO THE TRENCH)
9.8 Hi

Introduction
On February 16th 2007, in the middle of winter, I was awakened from my sleep at
4AM. I was given a very clear and orderly message from the LORD. It flooded my
mind and heart, as I wrote down every detail that was being shown to me, by the Holy
Spirit. This message was the key that unlocked the door to the mystery of the Messiah
of Israel. It was without a doubt, the key of King David. To my astonishment, I found
that this key was now unbelievably in
hands. I was not expecting this miracle to
me to write down every detail and
happen. As it began to unfold, the
epped through the opened door
to put it in a book! As I turned the key
y expectations, a true miracle
before me and I saw the LORD face to
ning of the unveiling of the
came back to me from Jerusalem.
my heart and mind, as the
Messiah of Israel. It was as if a fire
perceived God's message, I
LORD unveiled His mystery to me.
extremely touching, that the
wept and sobbed from the depths of
storical moment in Israel's
LORD had chosen to give this miracle
dden by the LORD through
redemption. I was keenly aware, that this know
ared alive and He walked
many centuries. On the Road to Emmaus, the
the Scriptures. Now I
with them, as the Holy Spirit opened their
Holy Spirit opened my
believe that what they understood that day is exactly
hidden by the LORD,
eyes to see in 2007. Perhaps this precious gift for
refore, encoded His
within the Scriptures, until the time of the end.
would
Eternal Testimony in such a way, that in the last days
doubt His Everlasting glory, as the details began to
my heart, I know that the Messiah is coming soon.
His return, He is allowing the blessings to be
warning to all people, telling them to turn to Him.
accurately written by the power of God's Holy Spirit, as
hearts of His faithful Jewish Prophets and Apostles.
Almond Blossom! When the bud of an Almond
discern the outer petals. You are not able to see
bud, because the flower has not yet fully opened to
is veiled to you, because at first, it is hidden from your view.
right moment in time, the Almond blossom begins to unfurl and
emerges. The winter is over like the Diaspora and spring arrives
life budding forth. The beauty of the blossoming Almond
fragrance is exhilarating! We watch in amazement, as
unfurl their soft delicate petals and gently
This is how I describe the Testimony of the
and see
and the Almond Tree is His Testimony. I
LORD in full bloom! Can you hear the footsteps

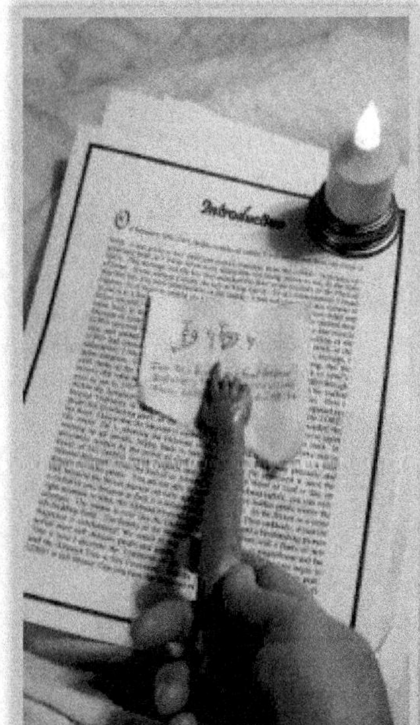

Chapter 5

THE YAD
THE RIGHT HAND
ON THE ROD
THE FINGER OF GOD

The way to read a Torah Scroll is by using a Torah pointer called a, *"Yad,"* which is the Hebrew word for *"hand."* This instrument is *a rod or arm,* with a right hand at the end of it. The index finger of the hand at the end of the rod is extended and is pointing. The way to use a Yad is to hold the rod portion of the Yad in your own hand, while pointing with the index finger on the Yad to the words of the text on the Torah Scroll. This is the Jewish way to read *the Word of God.* The rod of the Yad actually appears as an outstretched arm. This reveals that Messiah Yeshua is the Rod of God in the outstretched arm of God. Messiah Yeshua is therefore, consequently, the right hand of God and He writes the Word of God with His own finger. *The finger of God always points to the Word of God.* So the finger of Yeshua, who is *the Word of God,* points to Himself as *the Living Torah.* When the LORD revealed this to me after my miracle of the Rod of the Almond Tree, I saw that truly the mystery of God as the Messiah was beginning to be revealed a little at a time. The LORD was unveiling to me, the most astonishing Jewish picture of Yeshua that no one had ever seen before, and I was stunned by this truth! We have never understood the full picture of the Messiah's identity as the God of Israel, but now we can see it. From this profound truth alone, we can see that God is one with His Rod. The Bible tells us that *the Messiah is "the arm of the LORD revealed."* Now Yeshua is revealed because we already know for certain He is the budded Almond Rod of God. *So Yeshua, the one who brings salvation, is the arm, hand, and finger of God!*

We know that according to Scripture, Yeshua ascended back into Heaven and was seated at *the right hand* of the Majesty on High. It all makes perfect sense and it becomes so clear, that *Yeshua is revealed as the Yad, pointing to Himself as the Word of God, as the LORD God of Israel.* Probably the most shocking element of this is the understanding that Yeshua is indeed *the finger of God.* At the first revelation of this, it may come as a shock, but it is Scripturally accurate. So the brilliant truth is that when the LORD stretched out His arm with the Rod in His right hand, He wrote *His Word, the Living Torah,* with His finger upon the tablets of stone on Mount Sinai and when Yeshua came to the earth, He wrote His Living Testimony as the Word of God, as the Living Torah, with His finger upon the tablets of our hearts. It is important to notice that the two tablets of the Law of God that were inscribed with the LORD'S own finger were placed inside the Ark of the Testimony. *This means that Yeshua, the Word of God, the finger of God, abides in the Ark of the LORD'S own Living Testimony in Heaven.* We can now see that the budded Almond Rod is the Living Branch, the Living Torah, and the Yad of God. Now we know why KING Messiah sits at the right hand of the Majesty on High because He is the Living Testimony of the Ark of the LORD in Heaven, and the Ark of this Living Testimony is the LORD'S throne, guarded by two Living Cherubim Angels. Yeshua is now perfectly revealed in the last days, as the Living Rod of salvation, the LORD'S own outstretched arm or His Jewish Yad. *This Living Yad will always point the way to the Living Torah that abides in the Heavenly Ark.* So Yeshua is not only leading Israel into the Eternal Promised Land, *He is literally pointing the way!* The Ark goes before them into the Eternal Kingdom of God. Yeshua declared seven statements on the cross and this was a picture of the completion and perfection of the Living Torah salvation of the LORD. When Messiah Yeshua ascended back into Heaven, He sent the Holy Spirit to His disciples seven weeks after Passover on Shavuot (or Pentecost.) Remember that the Holy Spirit was sent to dwell within those who had been purified in the baptism of the Living Water, in Messiah the LORD. When we are baptized in His Mikveh, our sins are washed away and *our heart* is cleansed. *Then He sends the power of His Holy Spirit to abide within our heart and He inscribes the Living Torah, the Word of God upon the tablets of our heart.*

On Mount Sinai, in the earthly copy of the Ark, it was written in hard stone, but now *Messiah writes it upon the tender fleshly heart of mankind forever, so we will love Him as the Living Ark!* Remember the Scripture in the book of Jeremiah that says, the LORD will make a New Covenant with the House of Israel that is not like the old one that was written on tablets of stone? *This New Eternal Living Covenant takes away the hardness of our hearts! It is therefore the true circumcision of the flesh that takes away our uncleanness. This Eternal Covenant of the Living Torah, Messiah Yeshua's Living Testimony, abides as the Heavenly Ark forever.* This is the New Covenant that the LORD told us *"would cause us to know Him!"* The LORD is the only one that could take away our sins through His own Living Testimony and we are forgiven! This is exactly what the LORD declared through the Prophet Jeremiah.

Jeremiah 31:31-34 *Behold, the days come, saith the LORD, that I will make a New Covenant with the House of Israel, and with the House of Judah; Not according to the Covenant that I made with their fathers in the day that I took them by the hand to bring them out of the land of Egypt; which My Covenant they brake, although I was an husband unto them, saith the LORD; But this shall be the Covenant that I will make with the House of Israel; After those days, saith the LORD, I will put My law in their inward parts and write it in their hearts; and will be their God, and they shall be My people. And they shall teach no more every man his neighbour, and every man his brother, saying, Know the LORD; for they shall all know Me, from the least of them unto the greatest of them, saith the LORD; for I will forgive their iniquity, and I will remember their sin no more.*

WRITTEN ON THE TABLETS OF THE HEART

Yad writing upon the heart, a heart in the hand of God & a hand holding a heart of roses
Heavy snow Photos ©2013 Kimberly K Ballard All Rights Reserved

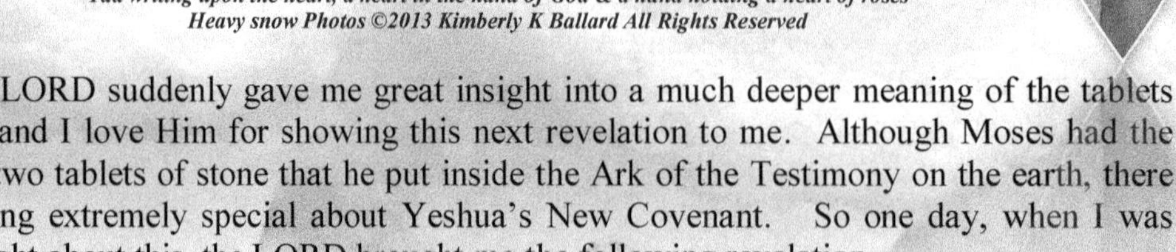

The LORD suddenly gave me great insight into a much deeper meaning of the tablets of the heart and I love Him for showing this next revelation to me. Although Moses had the copy of the two tablets of stone that he put inside the Ark of the Testimony on the earth, there was something extremely special about Yeshua's New Covenant. So one day, when I was deep in thought about this, the LORD brought me the following revelation.

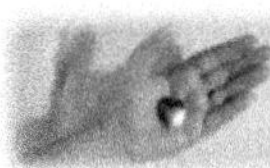

THE HEART HAS TWO SIDES JUST LIKE TWO TABLETS OF STONE!

On the right side of the human heart, there is the right atrium and the right ventricle. On the left side of the heart, there is the left atrium and the left ventricle. The most thrilling part of this, though, is the fact that the heart is actually cleft in the middle! I realized that the main artery that is supplying the life blood is coming out of the middle of the heart, between the two tablets of the heart! Wow! This is like the Red Sea crossing and the cleft rock of Horeb! I just realized that this is a picture of Messiah Yeshua, the Rod, because we know that when His feet stand upon the Mount of Olives, the land will be made cleft under His feet. Half of the land will go to *the left side* and the other half of the land will go to *the right side.* Then rivers of life giving water will flow out from *the middle,* from His throne, because He is the source of life! This is so astonishing! The LORD told Israel that, *"the life of the flesh is in the blood!"* So *the life blood* flows through the main artery, between the two sides of the heart, and *the LORD is our life blood.* Consequently, *it is only through the LORD'S life blood* that we could we have Eternal life, and this is how the Messiah has written the Living Testimony of God upon the two tablets of our heart. The Rod is the central source of life, the Living Water that purifies our hearts and gives us Eternal life through the breath of His Holy Spirit!

Valentine heart
Photo ©2014 Kimberly K Ballard All Rights Reserved

Leviticus 17:11 *For the life of the flesh is in the blood; and I have given it to you upon the altar to make an atonement for your souls; for it is the blood that maketh an atonement for the soul.*

No one else can ever give us Eternal life, but the LORD Himself. Therefore, *His life blood* is *the Living Torah Testimony* that flows through the two tablets of our hearts, causing us to *love* Him! As the High Priest of Heaven, Yeshua has sprinkled His own Living life blood, with His own finger, upon the Mercy Seat of the Ark of His own Living Testimony in Heaven. This means that the LORD has sealed the New Covenant in His own life blood, *as the Eternal source of life.* There is more to this and it is even more exciting! Our hearts contain, *"plasma,"* which is, *"55% of the blood volume and is 92% water!"* **(Source: ©2003 thefreedictionary.com).** So you could say that *the Living Water is in the life blood* and it flows through the main vein, into the two tablets of the human heart. This miraculous truth proves that the LORD God created our hearts and that He is the Living Water! In the beginning, the Holy Spirit of God moved on the surface of the waters and brought them to life. The Spirit of God breathed the breath of life into us and mankind became a living soul. The breath of life comes from God, through His Holy Spirit, so this is truly profound because oxygen is carried in the life blood through the carrier called *"hemoglobin."* It is the *"hemoglobin that binds the oxygen to the blood."* ***(Source: ©1975 The Random House Inc., College Dictionary).***

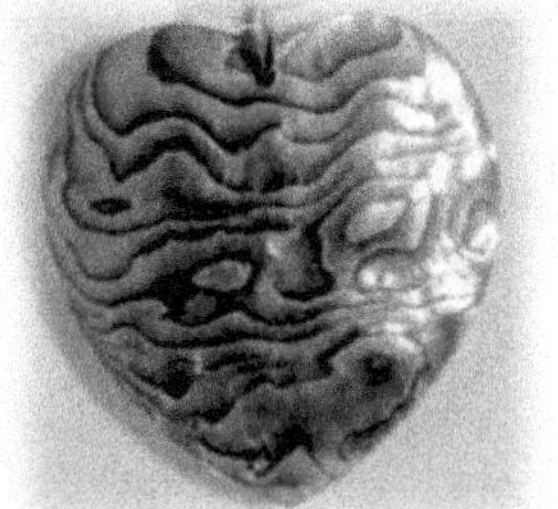

Abalone heart Photo ©2014
Kimberly K Ballard All Rights Reserved

So the Holy Spirit, who breathes the breath of life into us, *binds us to the LORD who* is the Living Water and the life blood full of oxygen and therefore the breath of His Holy Spirit gives us Eternal life. Now with this incredible knowledge, I completely comprehended the Scripture about the three that bear witness on the earth the water, the blood, and the Spirit. As I stated earlier, these three testify on earth, that the LORD'S Testimony is true. The LORD said

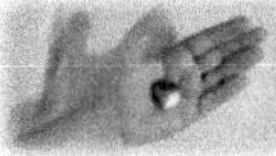

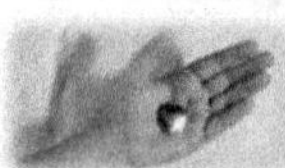

that these three are one. The Father, the Word, and His Holy Spirit are one. This means again, that the Father is the Messiah who saves us, and His Ruach/Holy Spirit from His heart breathes Eternal life into us. This verifies He is one God who is performing all things, by His Royal Majesty and mighty Divine power.

I John 5:7-8 *For there are three that bear record in Heaven, the Father, the Word, and the Holy Spirit and these three are one. And there are three that bear witness in earth, the Spirit, and the water, and the blood; and these three agree in one. If we receive the witness of man, the witness of God is greater; for this is the witness of God which He hath testified of His Son. He that believeth on the Son of God hath the witness in himself; he that believeth not God hath made Him a liar; because he believeth not the record that God gave of His Son. And this is the record that God hath given to us eternal life, and this life is in His Son. He that hath the Son hath life; and he that hath not the Son of God hath not life.*

The LORD God provided Himself the Lamb, just as Abraham said that He would!

Genesis 22:8 *And Abraham said; God will provide Himself the Lamb for a burnt offering my son. So they went both of them together.*

Yeshua is the perfect Lamb's life blood of the pure sin offering of a much better sacrifice and Yeshua did seal this New Covenant in His life blood.

Valentine heart Photo ©2014 Kimberly K Ballard All Rights Reserved

Matthew 26:28 *For this is My blood of the New Testament, which is shed for many for the remission of sins.*

I Corinthians 11:25 *After the same manner also He took the cup, when He had supped, saying, This cup is the New Testament in My blood; this do ye, as oft as ye drink it, in remembrance of Me.*

Hebrews 9:14 *How much more shall the blood of Messiah, who through the eternal Spirit offered Himself without spot to God, purge your conscience from dead works to serve the Living God?*

Colossians 1:13-14 *Who hath delivered us from the power of darkness, and hath translated us into the Kingdom of His dear Son; In whom we have redemption through His blood, even the forgiveness of sins; Who is the image of the invisible God, the firstborn of every creature; For by Him were all things created, that are in Heaven, and that are in earth, visible and invisible, whether they be thrones, or dominions, or principalities, or powers; all things were created by Him, and for Him; and He is before all things, and by Him all things consist.*

Ephesians 2:13 *But now in Messiah Yeshua ye who sometimes were far off are made nigh by the blood of Messiah.*

Now when we have the Messiah in the center of our heart, we receive the Law of God on the two tablets of our heart, not on tablets of stone, like the split rock of Horeb that was cleft and water flowed down the middle of it! His life giving Holy Spirit now dwells within us and this is why those who have died in the Messiah will be raised to life first, as the first fruits of His creation. Our High Priest in Heaven made the Eternal life blood atonement for the remission of our sins forever. When we are given the pureness of heart through the Messiah's Living Testimony, *the Water, blood, and Spirit,* then in the future, we will be resurrected by His Spirit, who breathes the breath of life into us. I suddenly realized that this is another reason why Yeshua declared that, *"those who are pure in heart will see God!"* This is what He meant!

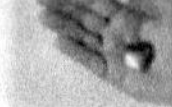

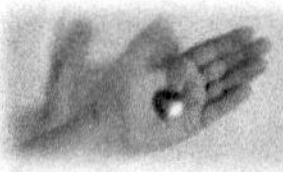

When you have allowed Him to enter into your heart, He allows you to see His face and to know Him. He is very beautiful!

Robins in the Birdbath Photo ©2014 Kimberly K Ballard All Rights Reserved

Matthew 5:8 *Blessed are the pure in heart; for they shall see God.*

The LORD said in Ezekiel, that He will sprinkle His clean water on us and cleanse us and *put a new heart full of His Spirit within us.*

Ezekiel 36:25-27 *Then will I sprinkle clean water upon you, and ye shall be clean; from all your filthiness, and from all your idols, will I cleanse you. A new heart also will I give you, and a new Spirit will I put within you; and I will take away the stony heart out of your flesh, and I will give you a heart of flesh. And I will put My Spirit within you, and cause you to walk in My statutes, and ye shall keep My judgments, and do them.*

So the purpose of baptism is to create a new heart within us, so that once it is purified, it is inscribed with *the Living Torah by the finger of God.* This makes me love the LORD so much more, as I ponder the depth of the mighty deeds of the LORD who did all things to draw us back to Him in love. This section alone shows us how much the LORD loves each one of us because it is so obvious that He encoded Himself within His creation and *within the heart* of every single one of His living creatures. He loves you and He loves me! God has a huge heart where His Holy Spirit resides!

Proverbs 21:1 *The king's heart is in the hand of the LORD, as the rivers of water; he turneth it whithersoever he will.*

Psalm 34:11 *The counsel of the LORD standeth forever, the thoughts of His heart to all generations.*

THE OUTSTRETCHED ARM OF GOD

The outstretched Arm & Yad of God the Almond Tree & Abalone heart Photos ©2014 Kimberly K Ballard All Rights Reserved

One day, as I was pensively thinking about my miracle of the Almond Tree, the LORD gave me this understanding, that Yeshua was the Yad of God. So now I want to relate to you, how the Holy Spirit helped me to understand this truth. This was shown to my heart by the Holy Spirit, only a couple of weeks after the LORD gave me the Almond Tree revelation and the miracle from Jerusalem on Holy Mount Moriah.

The Holy Spirit brought it into my mind, that the branch of a tree is also called a *"limb."* By definition a *"limb" is the arm of a tree. The limb of the tree is where the fruit is found!* I had no idea the profound meaning of this at the time. What I was about to discover about the Messiah's identity, that was hidden within the definition of the word *"Branch,"* was stunning. The Holy Spirit connected the dots within my heart and I realized that there are many Scriptures that verify that Messiah the Branch is *"the Arm of the LORD revealed." So Messiah therefore, has to be the Yad of God.* It was after my revelation of this that I wrote that whenever the Rod of God was held out in His outstretched arm, Israel was saved! At this point, I thought it would be quite interesting to get the dictionary out and read the definition of the simple word *"arm."* I knew that if the Messiah was in fact *"the Arm of the LORD revealed,"* then there had to be more within the definition of the word *"arm"* that reveals that He is the LORD. What I discovered was truly magnificent! The Messiah is actually hidden within each one of the definitions and descriptions of the word *"arm."*

The Right Arm of an Almond Tree
Photo ©2014 Kimberly K Ballard All Rights Reserved

Definition; Arm;
1. A limb connected to a body with a hand attached.
2. The arm of a tree
3. A branch of the military of a combatant unit. Like a rampant leopard going face to face with an enemy. ***(Source: Webster's New Twentieth Century Dictionary Unabridged Second Edition Copyright ©1970 By The World Publishing Company).***

This was even more revealing! Now when I analyzed each of the descriptions of the word *"arm,"* individually, as I will show, they all apply to Yeshua as the Yad of God!

Description: 1. "A Limb connected to a body with a hand attached."

Messiah the Branch is the Limb attached to the same body of the LORD, He is the LORD'S own Arm revealed. Messiah is the Rod in the right hand of the LORD God of Israel. A Branch makes a tree cleft, which is the signature of the hand of the LORD. Messiah was made cleft from the Almond Tree of Life, as the Branch cut off. *A limb sticks out from the main tree trunk, but they are both part of the same tree.* It is one tree with different parts! The Almond Tree of Life is one tree whose Branches come out from the main trunk of the tree. The Branch Messiah comes out of the main trunk of the Almond Tree of Life, like an outstretched arm or limb, bearing the Heavenly Fruit. The Living Torah is the Almond Tree of Life and this tree is the LORD, our Messiah. Remember, even when a Branch gets cut off from this tree, God is able to bring it to life again and graft it in, as if it was never cut off and never dead!

Hebrews 1:1-4 *God, who at sundry times and in divers manners spake in time past unto the fathers by the Prophets, hath in these last days spoken unto us by His Son, whom He hath appointed heir of all things, by whom also He made the worlds; Who being the brightness of His glory, and the express image of His person, and upholding all things by the Word of His power, when He had by Himself purged our sins, sat down on the right hand of the Majesty on High; Being made so much better than the angels, as He hath by inheritance obtained a more excellent name than they.*

The LORD commanded Israel *to bind the Word of God to the arm, the hand, and the fingers.* It is written in Deuteronomy 6 and 11 and also in Exodus 13. This binding of the Word is done symbolically with the Jewish *"Tefillin."* The Word of God is bound to the arm, hand, and fingers in the *"shel Yad,"* which is *the hand Tefillin.* Messiah the Word of God, the Living Torah, is the arm, hand, and finger of God, who was bound for our salvation and we are to remember Him and bind ourselves to Him through His Ruach/Spirit. Messiah Yeshua is the *"shel Yad"* of Heaven. In the Gospel of John, *the Word of God was bound* and sent to Caiaphas the High Priest.

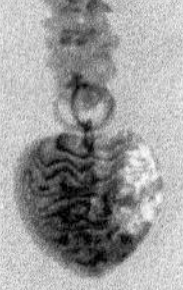

John 19:24 *Now Annas had sent Him bound unto Caiaphas the High Priest.*

There is also the head *Tefillin* called *"the shel Rosh."* The *Tefillin* are also called *"Phylacteries."* The Word of God is placed inside a small square box that is bound to the upper part of the forehead. The Word of God is placed on the front of the brain. *This should cause one to think about the meaning of the Word of God and what this ritual really means.* A strap is wrapped around the head and it goes down the shoulders. The strap going around the arm, hand, and fingers is wrapped and knotted in a very special manner, as is the strap going around the head. The Hebrew letter *"shin"* is wrapped around the hand. There are two Hebrew *"shin"* letters on *the shel Rosh, on the forehead.*

There is one three-digit shin on one side and one four digit shin on the other side of the *shel Rosh.* The fourth digit on *the shin* is associated with the future revelation of the Messiah! *The Word of God is in the middle, inside the box!* This three-digit and four-digit shin, completes a perfect number 7, which indicates that the Word of God is perfect and complete. The Word of God, Yeshua, gave us this perfect number 7 on the cross when He declared His final Words to us. The box is a type of Ark that contains the Word of God. The five books of Moses and the two tablets of the Law of God make a perfect complete 7 and it gives us a picture of *the Living Torah, the Messiah,* who is the Word of God. *This brings back that profound picture of the heart, with the life blood and Living Water of the LORD in the middle as the Rod of God, with the tablets of the heart on either side.* It brings back that picture of Messiah Yeshua's feet standing on the Mount of Olives in the middle, making the land cleft under His feet. Yeshua is the in middle as the Living Almond Rod of the Heavenly Ark, the Word of God with His Living Testimony. He is the Living Torah, the number 7 of perfection and completion of the LORD'S Divine Living Testimony. Of course the Name Yeshua is spelled as *"Yod Shin Vav Ayin"* in Hebrew and I believe these letters are on the Shroud under Yeshua's neck. So the Tefillin actually contain the first two letters of Yeshua's Name. *The arm Tefillin, points to the heart!* Now isn't this incredible? This means that *the Word of God* is pointing toward the heart. Yeshua is the Yad pointing to *the Living Torah,* which is the LORD'S Divine Testimony of the heart! This all reveals the Messiah as the God of Israel!

One incredible connection to Messiah Yeshua is in the winding of the hand Tefillin. The strap is wound around the hand and goes between the thumb and index finger. It is then wound around the middle joint of the middle finger and twice around the lower joint. It is symbolic of a betrothal to the LORD, like a wedding ring. This is so amazing, because the strap is wound *three times,* which is not only representative of the resurrection of Yeshua on the third day, but also represents that His cup was the third cup of wine in the Passover Seder, sealing His betrothal to Israel, which binds them to the LORD because He is the Rod, Arm, Hand, and Finger of God! So in this symbolic act of putting on the Tefillin, without fully knowing it, Israel is betrothing themselves as the Bride, to Messiah Yeshua, to the Yad of God!

The letter *"shin"* is wrapped around the hand across the palm of the hand. There is a special knot that is tied on *the shel Rosh* called *"a double dalet."* This knot is set on the back of the head. I find this fascinating because it is connected to Yeshua. The Messiah is not seen or understood fully by Israel yet, and therefore the back of the head is the appropriate place for this knot! When I get to the end of this book, I will show you an incredible connection to Yeshua and this double dalet. The LORD showed me that the double dalet has to do with the Great Rolling Stone of Yeshua's Garden Tomb from Holy Mount Moriah that is now standing upon Mount Nebo. I had written about the double dalet and the Great Rolling Stone of Yeshua's sepulchre before knowing that it was actually a knot on the shel Rosh! *By Divine Providence, I was stunned when I discovered in 2013 that the blood stain, that looks like a number three with a line coming down from it on Yeshua's forehead on the Shroud of Turin, is an ancient form of the Hebrew letter "shin" that incredibly means, "Thorn, pierced, and Shepherd that acts as a shield to protect against predators!" I was mesmerized and stunned when I found this ancient form of the letter shin and noticed to my astonishment that it matched the blood stain on Yeshua's forehead on His fine linen burial Shroud because it is on the hand*

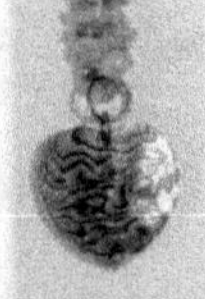

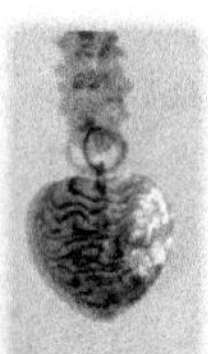

of God! It is on the one whose Name is Shaddai. It is on the one Living God! ***(Source: The ancient Hebrew letter shin and its meaning Ancient Hebrew Research Center ©1999-2013 Jeff A. Benner - ancient-hebrew.org/3_sin.html).***

The following Semitic charts on the ancient Hebrew letter Shin are ©1999-2013 Jeff A. Benner and are viewable at the website: ancient-hebrew.org/3_sin.html & the Shroud in 3D by Dr. Petrus Soons is viewable at the website: shroud3d.com & Photos of the Shroud by Photographer Barrie M. Schwortz are viewable at the website: Shroud.com

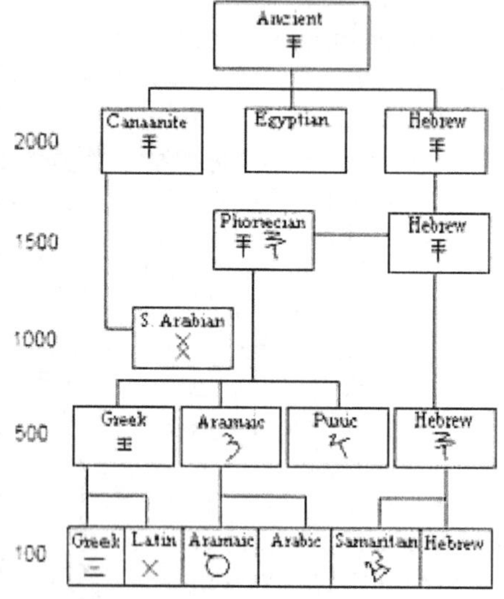

In this Semitic chart we can see the ancient Hebrew letter shin as it appears in Hebrew & Phoenician in the form of a number 3 with a line coming down from it and you can see this letter shin in the blood stain that is on Messiah Yeshua's forehead on His burial Shroud!

3D Hologram of the Shroud face Photo ©2013 Dr Petrus Soons taken from Enrie Photos All Rights Reserved

Look at Messiah Yeshua's forehead and notice the ancient Hebrew letter shin on His forehead in blood.

	2000	1500	1000	500	100
Egyptian					
Canaanite	[illegible]	[illegible]	[illegible]		
Hebrew		[illegible]	[illegible]	[illegible]	
Phonecian		[illegible]	[illegible]	[illegible]	
Aramaic		[illegible]	[illegible]	[illegible]	[illegible]
Greek			[illegible]	[illegible]	[illegible]
S. Arabian			X		
Punic				[illegible]	
Latin					X
Samaritan					[illegible]
Arabic					

In this Semitic chart we can also see the ancient Hebrew letter shin as it appears in Hebrew & Phoenician in the same form of the number 3 with a line coming down from it and you can compare this letter shin to the blood stain on Messiah Yeshua's forehead on the Shroud of Turin!

Now there is more to the wrapping and knotting technique of the Tefillin, including the knot called the *"Yod"* that is on the *shel Yad* strap. Together, the Shin, Dalet, and Yod form the Name for *"Almighty,"* in Hebrew which is *"Shaddai."* The point that I want to make here is that these Commandments, of binding the Word of God to the forehead and the hand, were not simply to be some ritual for Israel to keep. These Commandments of the binding of the Word of God to the hand and forehead were intended by the LORD to be *a sign* for Israel!

Deuteronomy 6:8 *And thou shalt bind them for a sign upon thine hand, and they shall be as frontlets between thine eyes.*

The sign that is hidden in this memorial has to do with *the revelation that the Messiah is the Rod of God, the Yad or hand of God, and miraculously He is wearing the "shin" on His forehead on His burial Shroud!* The LORD binds His *Living Torah* to us through His Yad in His life blood, Living Water, and Holy Spirit for Eternal life. This is *the signature* of the hand of God. The Messiah is, therefore, always *bound to us* so that the LORD'S Name is forever bound to us for Eternal life.

Remember that in the book of Exodus, it was the life blood of the lamb that served as a *"token"* upon the doorposts of the houses, and the LORD said that when He saw the life blood of the lamb on the doorposts that He would Passover the Israelites and they would not be harmed by the plague of death! The word *"token"* means several things. First of all it is *"a sign, a symbol, an emblem, or a distinguishing mark."* The Hebrew letter *"dalet"* on *the shel*

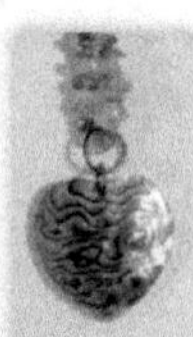
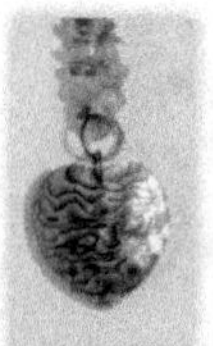

Rosh means *"door."* So the life blood of the LORD, the Messiah, is our *distinguishing mark.* The blood of the true Lamb of God sealed us from death and we remember Yeshua's blood and body, which is the unleavened bread from Heaven in the Passover Seder. In the Passover from Egypt, the lamb's blood was placed upon the lintel and side posts of the doors and death passed over the Israelites. The lintel is the *headpiece* of the door. Messiah is the door of Heaven and his head dripped with the life blood from the wounds He received as the Lamb, and his arms were outstretched with the life blood dripping from His wrists, representing the side posts of the door of Heaven. They were instructed by the LORD *to eat the Passover with their **Staff** in their hand* because ultimately this Passover reveals *the LORD as Messiah, the Rod* and the Lamb, who saves us with His life blood, so that death passes over us.

Because we are sealed with the LORD God's seal, we are never to take the mark of the Anti-Christ, the number of Satan, who the LORD said is only a man *(Ezekiel 28:2). His* name is represented by *666 the number of the beast* which is written in Greek in the New Testament as *Chi xi stigma.* ***(Sources: www.youtube.com/watch?v=vFw2KrI3mng) AND (www.biblestudytools.com/lexicons/greek/nas/chi-xi-stigma.html).*** The LORD showed me something profound about this and it is about to be revealed. So I pray that you will be saved by the LORD Yeshua. In II Thessalonians it is written *that the coming of the LORD Yeshua Messiah will not come until the "man of sin is revealed."*

***II Thessalonians 2:1-12** Now we beseech you, brethren, by the coming of our Lord Jesus Christ, and by our gathering together unto him, That ye be not soon shaken in mind, or be troubled, neither by spirit, nor by word, nor by letter as from us, as that the day of Christ is at hand. Let no man deceive you by any means: for that day shall not come, except there come a falling away first, and that man of sin be revealed, the son of perdition; Who opposeth and exalteth himself above all that is called God, or that is worshipped; so that he as God sitteth in the temple of God, shewing himself that he is God. Remember ye not, that, when I was yet with you, I told you these things? And now ye know what withholdeth that he might be revealed in his time. For the mystery of iniquity doth already work: only he who letteth will let, until he be taken out of the way. And then shall that Wicked be revealed, whom the Lord shall consume with the spirit of his mouth, and shall destroy with the brightness of his coming: Even him, whose coming is after the working of Satan with all power and signs and lying wonders, And with all deceivableness of unrighteousness in them that perish; because they received not the love of the truth, that they might be saved. And for this cause God shall send them strong delusion, that they should believe a lie: That they all might be damned who believed not the truth, but had pleasure in unrighteousness.*

The LORD God of Israel, the Almighty, is most offended when people worship false gods, because He alone created heaven and earth. In my research I found that *the crescent moon-god,* the ancient Sumerian pagan god was known by the name *"Sin." He was the chief deity of Babylon.* ***(Sources: www.britannica.com/EBchecked/topic/545523/Sin) and (en.wikipedia.org/wiki/Sin_%28mythology%29).*** *The LORD God of Israel said that Satan tried to elevate himself above Him and tried to sit on the LORD'S Holy Mountain in Jerusalem elevating himself there. One of the names of this pagan god is the "deceiver." This is historical fact revealed that can readily be researched. I realized that the son of perdition, "the man of sin," is therefore, the moon-god "Sin," and a false prophet makes people believe a strong delusion about him that he is God so they will perish. It is interesting to read what the LORD said about a false prophet.*

***Deuteronomy 13:1-5** If there arise among you a prophet, or a dreamer of dreams, and giveth thee a sign or a wonder, And the sign of the wonder come to pass, where of he spake unto thee, saying, Let us go after other gods, which thou hast not known, and let us served them; Thou shalt not hearken unto the words of that prophet, or that dreamer of dreams: for the LORD your God proveth you, to know whether ye love the LORD your God with all your heart and with all your soul. Ye shall walk after the LORD your God, and fear him, and keep his commandments, and obey his voice, and ye shall served him, and cleave unto him. And that prophet, or that dreamer of dreams, shall be put to death; because he hath spoken to turn you away from the LORD your God, which brought you out of the land of Egypt, and redeemed you out of the house of bondage, to thrust thee out of the way which the LORD thy God commanded thee to walk in. So shalt thou put the evil away from the midst of thee.*

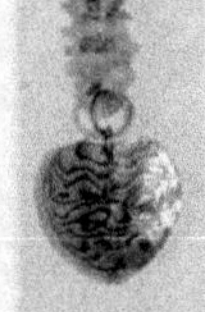
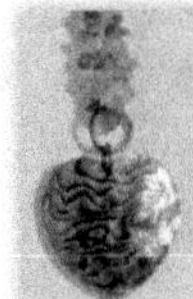

Now that the *"man of sin"* has been revealed, this means that the LORD Yeshua is coming quickly! Prepare yourself and never take the mark of the beast or the number of his name that comes from Satan. To accept it is like signing a Covenant of death, and it will bring about God's complete condemnation upon any person who takes it because they are worshipping a pagan false god. Satan cursed the world with death. He performs his wickedness through terrors so they kill themselves. This Anti-Christ mark is in total denial of the one true Living God of Israel that gives us Eternal life through His Rod, Messiah Yeshua, who created the universe. If we belong to the LORD God Almighty of Israel, He has forever sealed us with His own Name and we never take a badge of servitude to a pagan god. In the world to come, Israel will certainly know the hidden secret of HaShem that reveals that the face of God is the face of the Jewish Messiah who saved the world from Satan's bondage of death.

Revelation 22:4 *And they shall see His face; and His Name shall be in their foreheads.*

Deuteronomy 11:18 *Therefore shall ye lay up these My Words in your heart and in your soul, and bind them upon your hand, that they may be as frontlets between your eyes.*

The word *"frontlets,"* used in the Scripture, means *the forehead.* The Scriptures that are kept inside the Phylacteries declare that the LORD brought Israel out of Egypt with the strength of His strong hand! *In the hand is the Rod,* Messiah the Saviour!

Exodus 13:9 *And it shall be for a sign unto thee upon thine hand, and for a memorial between thine eyes, that the LORD'S Law may be in thy mouth; for with a strong hand hath the LORD brought thee out of Egypt.*

Israel was to remember this forever that the strength of God's Arm is the Rod of salvation, *Yeshua!* We now understand that the LORD is one and His Name is one because *"The Branch"* is the limb from the Almond Tree of Life.

The arm of an Almond Tree
Photo ©2014 Kimberly K Ballard
All Rights Reserved

Description: 2. "The Arm of a Tree."

Messiah Yeshua is clearly God's own Arm revealed and this Arm is the Living Branch, *the limb* of the Almond Tree of Life that was made cleft for us. This is the signature of the hand, the Yad of God. The Almond Tree Menorah has 7 branches that represent the Almond Tree of Life, the perfect Living Testimony of Messiah the LORD.

Description: 3. "An Arm is a branch of the military of a combatant unit. Like a rampant leopard going face to face with an enemy."

This definition of the word *"arm"* is profound because Yeshua is represented by the Rampant Lion of the Tribe of Judah. *The emblem of the Rampant Lion of Judah is the military ensign of the Messiah.* As the Prophecy declares, *the Messiah, the Lion of the Tribe of Judah, will go face to face against the enemies of God, in the last day's battle (Zechariah 14:3).* Yeshua told us that He will come again to slay the wicked with the Sword of His mouth *(Revelation 2:16).* This Sword is the Word of God that is breathed by His Spirit out of His mouth. The armies of Heaven return to earth with Yeshua,

Almond Rod ©2014 Kimberly K Ballard All Rights Reserved

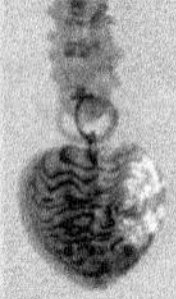

riding upon white horses, to possess the Eternal Promised Land in Jerusalem. The horses of the LORD are made pure and white, like the Priestly white linen garments of the Saints.

White Horse coming in the clouds Photo ©2013 KK Ballard All Rights Reserved

The armies of Heaven are the combat units that follow behind the strong Arm of Messiah. The Rod of God leads them, as He goes before them, as our Royal Ensign and Emblem of the Rampant Lion of Judah and as the Ark of our Eternal salvation. The Rod of God is known as the Son of God because He holds the book of the inheritance of the earth and the universe in His hand. The seven trumpets are blown before the Heavenly Ark when Messiah routes His enemies from His Eternal Promised Land in the future battle of Armageddon. This is precisely what transpired with Joshua when the Israelites went in to possess the Promised Land. The Priests blew *the seven trumpets before the Ark* and the army marched ahead of them with the rear guard behind the Ark of the LORD in Joshua 6. The Lion of Judah has prevailed!

Revelation 5:5 *And one of the elders saith unto me, Weep not; behold, the Lion of the tribe of Judah, the Root of David, hath prevailed to open the book, and to loose the seven seals thereof.*

Revelation 19:13-14 *And He was clothed with vesture dipped in blood; and His Name is called The Word of God. And the armies which were in Heaven followed Him upon white horses, clothed in fine linen, white and clean.*

When Yeshua declared the Words, *"I and the Father are one,"* and the Words, *"I AM in the Father and the Father is in Me,"* He was revealing He is the limb, the Branch that is attached to the main body of the Almond Tree of Life. All things were created through the Rod of God and by the hand of God.

At the time of creation in Genesis, the LORD said, *"Let us make man in Our image."* The LORD was not speaking to the angels when He said this because we were made in the image of God and not in the image of the angels. It is also true that angels have wings and the last time I checked in the mirror, I did not have any wings! So who was the LORD speaking to? *The LORD revealed to me that He was looking at His own reflection, in His own reflective Rod, when He proclaimed His creation.* This is one God who does all His works through His Rod, through His Yad. The LORD goes forth and proclaims the Name of the LORD with His own Rod.

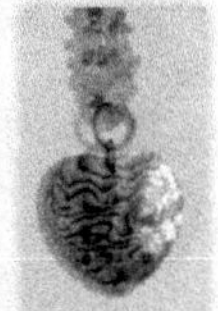

MOSES THE ROD AND THE RED SEA THE ARM OF GOD

Pacific Ocean waves & Almond Rod

One day I was observing a map of Israel and I noticed that when the children of Israel crossed over the Red Sea, they actually crossed over *the right arm* or *the right branch* of the Red Sea. On the map, the Gulf of Suez is the left arm or branch, and the Gulf of Aqaba is the *right arm or right branch* of the Red Sea. ***(Sources for this Exodus crossing site: splitrockresearch.org – Jim & Penny Caldwell) AND (Book- The Exodus Case by Dr Lennart Moller).*** In this detail, the LORD revealed His identity in *the right arm, the Branch,* when He saved Israel through the midst of the Red Sea, at the crossing in the Gulf of Aqaba. The LORD led the children of Israel toward the Promised Land with *the Rod "The Branch" in His right hand.*

Exodus 14:21-22 *Then Moses stretched out his hand over the sea; and the LORD swept the sea back by a strong east wind all night, and turned the sea into dry land, so the waters were divided. And the sons of Israel went through the midst of the sea on the dry land, and the waters were like a wall to them on their right hand and on their left.*

Notice that the Word of God, the Rod was in the middle, while either side was made cleft, just like the heart and just like Yeshua on the Mount of Olives, in the future.

Exodus 14:26-31 *Then the LORD said to Moses, Stretch out your hand over the sea so that the waters may come back over the Egyptians, over their chariots and their horsemen. So Moses stretched out his hand over the sea, and the sea returned to its normal state at daybreak, while the Egyptians were fleeing right into it; then the LORD overthrew the Egyptians in the midst of the sea. And the waters returned and covered the chariots and the horsemen, even Pharaoh's entire army that had gone into the sea after them; not even one of them remained. But the sons of Israel walked on dry land through the midst of the sea, and the waters were like a wall on their right hand and on their left. Thus the LORD saved Israel that day from the hand of the Egyptians, and Israel saw the Egyptians dead on the seashore. And when Israel saw the great power which the LORD had used against the Egyptians, the people feared the LORD, and they believed in the LORD and in His servant Moses.*

Isaiah's prophecy mentions that *"the arm of the LORD should awake as in the days of old."* By saying this, Isaiah was indicating that the Rod Messiah actually fought the battles of the LORD from the beginning because Messiah is the Rod of salvation in the strong and powerful outstretched arm of the LORD God of Israel. The term *"Strong Arm"* means *"to use physical force or coercion."* It is interesting that *coercion* can mean *"a government of force."* In this case, *the LORD'S Kingdom was fighting against the forces of spiritual darkness.* When the LORD created the wall of water on either side and held it back with His *strong arm, the mighty power abiding on the Rod gave Israel their Yeshua.* You can see that the LORD used His *strong arm* to bring salvation to Israel within the following Scriptures.

Psalm 89:10 *Thou hast broken Rahab in pieces, as one that is slain; Thou hast scattered Thine enemies with Thy strong arm.*

Psalm 136:11-12 *And brought Israel out from their midst, For His loving-kindness is everlasting. With a strong hand and an outstretched arm, For His loving-kindness is everlasting.*

When a person wears *"the helmet of salvation,"* they are binding the Word of God to their head and mind, like the *Tefillin,* so they do not forget all the great things that the LORD has done, *as the Living Torah and as their Messiah.*

Isaiah 59:16-17 *And He saw that there was no man, And was astonished that there was no one to intercede, Then His own arm brought salvation to Him; And His righteousness upheld Him. And He put on righteousness like a breastplate, and a helmet of salvation on His head; And He put on garments of vengeance for clothing, And wrapped Himself with zeal as a mantle.*

The LORD, *who wraps Himself with zeal as a mantle,* is the one who rights the age old wrong of slavery in Egypt and slavery to the bondage of Satan's curse of death from Eden. This tells us that He is diligent with fervor toward His cause, to redeem us with His Rod in His outstretched arm. The hand of God reaches out to save us.

Exodus 13:3 *And Moses said to the people, Remember this day in which you went out from Egypt, from the house of slavery; for by a powerful hand the LORD brought you out from this place, And nothing leavened shall be eaten.*

Exodus 6:6 *Say, therefore, to the sons of Israel, I AM the LORD, and I will bring you out from under the burdens of the Egyptians, and I will deliver you from their bondage. I will also redeem you with an outstretched arm and with great judgments.*

Moses said that Israel was to remember that *"by a powerful hand the LORD brought you out from this place and nothing leavened shall be eaten."* Why did Moses say this to Israel? Because the powerful hand Messiah, *the Living Torah,* is also the unleavened Bread from Heaven. So Israel was to remember this mighty work of the LORD'S hand by eating only unleavened bread. Of course, Messiah Yeshua was put in the tomb on the Feast of unleavened Bread, and this powerful hand of God had the power to come to life again because the Spirit of life was inside Him.

The Heavens and the earth were created by the powerful Rod in the LORD'S outstretched arm.

Jeremiah 32:17 *Ah LORD God! Behold, Thou hast made the Heavens and the earth by Thy great power and by Thine outstretched arm! Nothing is too difficult for Thee...*

Remembering the power of the Red Sea crossing
Ocean Photo ©2013 Kimberly K Ballard

Yeshua also revealed Himself to Israel through His miracles when *He stretched out His arm and hand* and instantly healed the lame, the blind, the sick, and the dead because the mighty power of the Holy Spirit was on the Yad. Isaiah the Prophet of God tells us that *the arm of the LORD revealed is the very one who will justify many and pay the price for the sins and iniquities of His people.* He reveals that the arm of the LORD will be cut off from the land of the living, referring to Messiah Yeshua, *the Branch.*

Isaiah 53:1-12 *Who hath believed our report? And to whom is the arm of the LORD revealed? For He shall grow up before Him as a tender plant, and as a root out of a dry ground; He hath no form nor comeliness; and when we shall see Him, there is no beauty that we should desire Him. He is despised and rejected of men; a man of sorrows, and acquainted with grief; and we hid as it were our faces from Him; He was despised, and we esteemed Him not. Surely He hath borne our griefs, and carried our sorrows; yet we did esteem Him stricken, smitten of God, and afflicted. But He was wounded for our transgressions, He was bruised for our iniquities; the chastisement of our peace was upon Him; and with His stripes we are healed. All we like sheep have gone astray; we have turned everyone to his own way; and the LORD hath laid on Him the iniquity of us all. He was oppressed, and He was* *afflicted, yet He opened not His mouth; He is brought as a lamb to the slaughter, and as a sheep before her shearers is dumb, so He opened not His mouth. He was taken from prison and from judgment; and who shall declare His generation? For He was cut off out of the land of the living; for the transgression of My people was He stricken. And He made His grave with the wicked, and with the rich in His death; because He had done no violence, neither was any deceit in His mouth. Yet it pleased the LORD to bruise Him; He hath put Him to grief; when Thou shalt make His soul an offering for sin, He shall see His seed, He shall prolong His days, and the pleasure of the LORD shall prosper in His hand. He shall see the travail of His soul, and shall be satisfied; By His knowledge shall My righteous Servant justify many; for He shall bear their iniquities. Therefore will I divide Him a portion with the great, and He shall divide the spoil with the strong; because He has poured out His soul unto death; and He was numbered with the transgressors; and He bare the sin of many, and made intercession for the transgressors.*

Technically speaking, when the LORD bared His Holy arm in the sight of all the nations, they saw the Hebrew *"Yeshua"* of God.

Isaiah 52:10 *The LORD has bared His Holy arm in the sight of all the nations, that all the ends of the earth may see the salvation of our God.*

Isaiah 40:10-11 *Behold, the LORD God will come with might, with His arm ruling for Him. Behold His reward is with Him, And His recompense before Him. Like a Shepherd He will tend His flock, In His arm He will gather the lambs, And carry them in His bosom; He will gently lead the nursing ewes.*

Sometimes a limb is *cut off a tree,* so the tree produces the very best fruit. So Messiah, *"The Branch,"* was cut off from the Almond Tree of Life, so that this Heavenly tree would bear only the very best fruit for the Heavenly Kingdom of God. This reminded me of something.

When I was in college I had a prophetic dream that I was cut off and I told my mentor *(my favorite person)* about this dream. We discussed it as meaning I was going to be cut off from singing at the college. Later my mentor, without warning, cut me off. My heart was broken, and my soul and spirit were crushed. It took me years to see that the dream was actually revealing that the hand of God, Messiah the Branch, was cut off. The LORD made my life parallel to His through this time of testing. Yeshua was cut off but it happened for the Glory of God. Likewise, if I had not been cut off by someone so close to me *(shedding many tears over it),* I never would have written this book. I realize now that this was also for the Glory of God. When someone hurts you, God can use these events to bring you closer to Him.

♫ THE SONG OF MOSES ♫

Djembe drum, Egyptian Tambourine (similar to timbrels) & my Percussion Mallets Briefcase

A song was written by Moses after the Red Sea crossing, during the Exodus from Egypt. Moses wrote this *song of deliverance, called "The Song of the Sea,"* after the LORD saved the Hebrews with the Rod in His hand. It is the same power that raised the dead Rod Yeshua as the Living Almond Branch like Aaron's rod. I believe the LORD showed me that *"The Song of Moses" was a prophecy of the Messiah.* When we get to the end of this book, I will show you how the Messiah was to be made known and recognized by Israel, in the pattern of salvation *that Moses wrote about in this song* that declares the mighty works of the Yad of God. I will show you a new song of Moses! Here is the old song that Moses wrote.

Exodus 15:1-19 *Then sang Moses and the children of Israel this song unto the LORD, and spake, saying, I will sing unto the LORD, for He hath triumphed gloriously; The horse and his rider hath He thrown into the sea. The LORD is my strength and song, and He is become my salvation; He is my God, and I will prepare Him an habitation; my Father's God, and I will exalt Him. The LORD is a man of war; The LORD is His Name. Pharaoh's chariots and his host hath He cast into the sea; His chosen captains also are drowned in the Red Sea. The depths have covered them; they sank into the bottom as a stone. Thy right hand, O LORD, is become glorious in power, Thy right hand, O LORD, hath dashed in pieces the enemy. And in the greatness of Thine excellency Thou hast overthrown them that rose up against Thee; Thou sentest forth Thy wrath, which consumed them as stubble. And with the blast of Thy nostrils the waters were gathered together, the floods stood upright as an heap, and the depths were congealed in the heart of the sea. The enemy said, I will pursue, I will overtake, I will divide the spoil; My lust shall be satisfied upon them; I will draw My sword, My hand shall destroy them. Thou didst blow with Thy wind, the sea covered them; They sank as lead in the mighty waters. Who is like unto Thee, O LORD, among the gods? Who is like Thee, glorious in holiness, fearful in praises, doing wonders? Thou stretchedst out Thy right hand, the earth swallowed them. Thou in Thy mercy hast led forth the people which Thou hast redeemed; Thou hast guided them in Thy strength unto Thy holy habitation. The people shall hear, and be afraid; sorrow shall take hold on the inhabitants of Palestina. Then the dukes of Edom shall be amazed; the mighty men of Moab, trembling shall take hold upon them; all the inhabitants of Canaan shall melt away. Fear and dread shall fall upon them; by the greatness of Thine arm they shall be as still as a stone; till Thy people pass over, O LORD, till the people pass over, which Thou hast purchased. Thou shalt bring them in, and plant them in the mountain of Thine inheritance, in the place, O LORD, which Thou hast made for Thee to dwell in, in the Sanctuary, O Lord, which Thy hands have established. The LORD shall reign forever and ever. For the horse of Pharaoh went in with his chariots and with his horsemen into the sea, and the LORD brought again the waters of the sea upon them; but the children of Israel went on dry land in the midst of the sea.*

My Percussion Mallets Briefcase for playing the March of Moses Photos ©2013 Kimberly K Ballard All Rights Reserved

By observing the cadence of the *Song of Moses,* we can figure out the original rhythm of this song. The cadence is the rhythmic flow of sounds within the song through the syllables of each word. It gives indicators where the song comes to a pause at the end of an idea. By speaking the syllables while clapping a rhythm, you can discern the beat of the song. The opening line says, *"I will sing unto the LORD, for He hath triumphed gloriously; The horse and the rider hath He thrown into the sea."* So for example, if I clapped in 6/8 time sounding like triplet notes we would then be able to sing the lines to this beat with pauses in the correct places at the end of each line. We could therefore sing a melody that matches this beat with the syllables of the words and use pauses where necessary, thus creating the melody line. Ironically, the song with this time signature, allows for the blowing of trumpets or the shofar before the first line begins. With tight drum rolls played on the & beats, we can visualize this *"Song of the Sea"* as a type of *March* in 6/8 time.

My Snare Drum Photos ©2013 KK Ballard All Rights Reserved

While tapping out this beat, I can now imagine a Scottish bagpiper's snare drum line, tapping out the rhythm of *The Song of the Sea, by Moses.* Now if the melody line is accentuated with the sound of a Jewish melody, then we might come very close to actually hearing *The Song of Moses, The Song of the Sea!* In this case, the song may very well sound like a Scottish sailor song in 6/8 time as a joyful and jubilant *March,* proclaiming the great things the LORD did through the sea, as the Hebrews *marched! God went before His people to march through the wilderness (Psalm 68:7).*

The opening line glorifies the LORD for giving the Israelites salvation. Moses provides the details of the awesome power of the hand of God, in providing a way of escape from their enemies. *There was nowhere to turn, because the enemy had shut them in.* There was a wall of jagged cliffs to their right and to their left. So they were forced to look straight into the path that the LORD provided and to *trust in His power* to lead them across through the sea. The song details how *the LORD is a man of war.* Moses explains how it was *the hand of the LORD that saved them* when there was no way of escape. Moses refers to *"The Excellency of the LORD,"* which provides us a glimpse of the LORD'S Royal status. Moses goes on and on about the mighty strength of the LORD and how He makes His enemies tremble. Nothing can stop the LORD from guiding His children across the sea toward the Promised Land. Until the people Passover into the Land of their inheritance, into the Land that the hand of the LORD has established where His Sanctuary is set forever, *the plan of the LORD can never be foiled by the enemies of God.* They are said to be in dread as the LORD brings His people into the Land of their inheritance. The LORD is able to put to shame every enemy that says with pride in their heart that they will come to divide the spoil and lust after God's Holy Land. While the sea has covered their enemies like a sinking stone, they *march* forward in the pathway of the LORD into great victory. The prophetic nature of *The Song of Moses* indicates that, at the time of Messiah Yeshua's arrival, the Israelites will once again be given a Divine victory by the powerful hand of God as He is coming to *march* before them to cross over the Jordan River, taking them into the Eternal Promised Land. The victorious people standing with the LORD God Almighty will sing *"A New Song of Moses"* that is not yet known, but soon we shall see, I believe, that this song is now revealed at the end of this book! This victorious song is going to be a joyful and jubilant *March* with harpers going before *the Living Ark! The singers went before the players on instruments, and the damsels playing timbrels followed in Psalm 68:25!*

Like Moses I am a songwriter and this is the Music Building with the Arched Window at CSU, Where I stood many years playing Timpani in the CSU Symphony Orchestra, Percussion Ensemble & Marimba Ensemble and the place where my dream finally came to an end Photo ©2013 Kimberly K Ballard All Rights Reserved

THE RIGHT HAND OF GOD

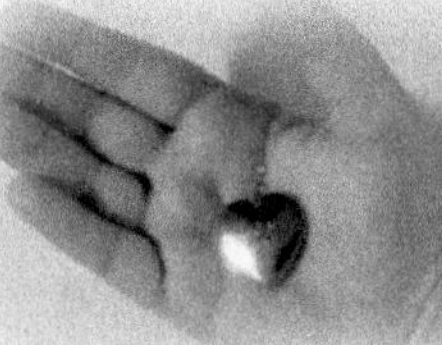

Right hand pointing to the Almond Tree & corner lifting up the Almond Rod & Torah of the heart in the Right hand of God Photos ©2014 Kimberly K Ballard All Rights Reserved

The definition of the word *"Hand" or "Yad"* in Hebrew has some interesting connotations that reveal the works of the LORD. First of all, *the hand leads and gives guidance.* When you take someone by the hand, you *hold them up or you hold onto them* and you *lead them in the right path,* so they will not fall, sink, or trip on any hindrance. It is written, that the LORD'S hand leads and holds us.

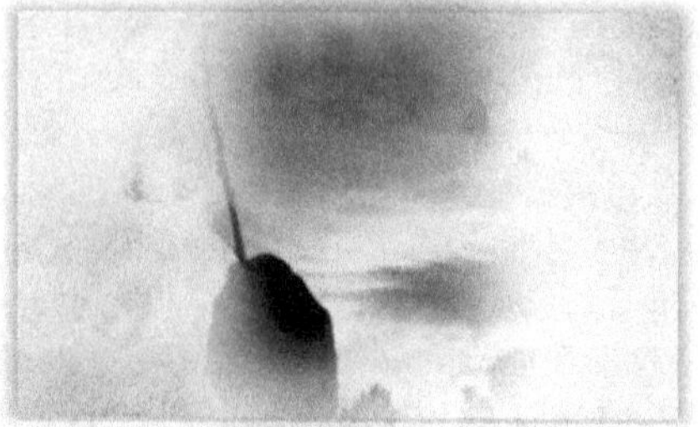

Right Hand lifting up the Almond Rod & Snow print Photos ©2014 KK Ballard All Rights Reserved

Psalm 139:9-10 *If I take the wings of the morning, and dwell in the uttermost parts of the sea; Even there shall Thy hand lead me, and Thy right hand shall hold me.*

As I was thinking about how the Israelites crossed the Red Sea, I thought about the fact that the LORD made a straight path in front of them as He guided them with His hand. *The Living Torah went before their face.* They were to *follow the LORD* in this path with the LORD'S Rod leading *the way.* The Israelites were not to look to the right or to

the left, they were to follow *the Rod of salvation* and put their complete trust in Him! The LORD was the guiding light that went before them. Now the LORD brought another story to mind that was similar to this one.

King Josiah was only eight years old when he began to reign in Jerusalem and he did what was right in the sight of the LORD. Why did Josiah do what was right in the sight of the LORD? *Josiah did not look to the right or to the left. Josiah looked only to the LORD for His guidance!* This is exactly what King David did that was right in the sight of the LORD. David never turned from worshipping the one true Living God. David looked straight to the LORD for guidance, so he would know which way to go. Even though David himself was a King, David still humbled himself before the Great KING OF KINGS and asked for His advice and help in sincerity and truth. He never took the advice of earthly political figures!

II Chronicles 34:1-2 *Josiah was eight years old when he began to reign, and he reigned in Jerusalem one and thirty years. And he did that which was right in the sight of the LORD, and walked in the ways of David his father, and declined neither to the right hand, nor to the left.*

II Kings 22:1-2 *Josiah was eight years old when he began to reign, and he reigned thirty and one years in Jerusalem. And his mother's name was Jedidah, the daughter of Adaiah of Boscath. And he did that which was right in the sight of the LORD, and walked in all the way of David his father, and turned not aside to the right hand or to the left.*

Follow the path of the LORD – Sidewalk Boulder Creek & Dove tracks in the snow

I came to a great understanding of the significance of this truth. We are to trust the LORD'S *path* which He prepares before us. Trusting His *path* means to allow the LORD to lead us with His Rod in His hand. We are to trust the Messiah. When we do this, we are like the children of Israel, who crossed the Red Sea. We are saved. The Rod, the Messiah, goes before us shining His light in our *pathway* before our feet ever take a step. I also thought about the fact that if you did look to the right or to the left, then your eyes would be focused elsewhere and not on the right *path* where the LORD was leading you. If you think about it this way, *the LORD is in the center* of the *path,* and looking to the right or to the left would cause you to look at the wall of water that is on either side of you, that is held back by the hand of God and by the breath of His Spirit. *So the truth is that if the Israelites had looked to the right or to the left and focused on the wall of water surrounding them, fear easily would have gripped them and paralyzed them from going in the right direction under the guidance of the mighty Rod in the hand of God.* Now if this did happen and you did look to the right or to the left, then fear would overtake you and you might turn back! Turning back would therefore reveal that you do not trust the LORD or trust in the power of His Rod with your whole heart. As *the Heavenly Living Ark, the LORD always leads you in the path straight ahead!* In the following Proverb, the LORD instructed us to ponder *the path* that He provides *and to look right on* and not to the right or to the left.

Proverbs 4:25-27 *Let thine eyes look right on, and let thine eyelids look straight before thee. Ponder the path of thy feet, and let all thy ways be established. Turn not to the right hand nor to the left; remove thy foot from evil.*

The LORD said to ponder the path of your feet! So the LORD wants us to focus on the Rod that goes before us, shining His light on the pathway that guides us to the Eternal Promised Land. It is quite easy for the problems of this life to take our focus off the LORD'S Divine path. Suddenly, I had a realization, that this explains why Lot's wife turned into a pillar of salt!

Genesis 19:26 *But his wife looked back from behind him, and she became a pillar of salt.*

The LORD sent His angels to deliver Lot's family. The angels took Lot and his family by the hand out of the corrupted city of Sodom. They were to be obedient and follow the path that the LORD was showing them to go. By following the path of the LORD, they would be saved from the destruction of the city. However, Lot's wife did not trust the path of the LORD that was before her. Lot's wife turned back and she looked behind her to see what was happening. Maybe relatives were left behind! Now I realized that in order for Lot's wife to look behind her, *she first had to look to the right or to the left!* That was her sin! *The LORD'S path was in front of her, but she did not put complete trust in the hand of the LORD and therefore she was not saved, but she was punished with the rest of the city that perished.* The LORD is always leading us into paths of righteousness. *So, it is the powerful Holy Spirit on the Rod Yeshua that leads the children of Israel across the Jordan River and into the Eternal Promised Land in the future.* This is a wonderful promise not only for Israel, but for the entire world and, since God is our Shepherd, we must follow behind Him to reach our destination, into the Heavenly green fields of Eternity, into the Heavenly Jerusalem! His Holy Spirit shows us what to do!

Zechariah 4:5-6 *Then the angel that talked with me answered and spake unto me, Knowest thou not what these be? And I said, No, my LORD. Then he answered and spake unto me, saying, This is the Word of the LORD unto Zerubbabel, saying, Not by might, nor by power, but by My Spirit, saith the LORD of Hosts.*

The LORD'S right hand is *the hand that grasps His possession* and upholds us. He *sets us in a good place. The hand keeps you from falling.* When something is *in your hand,* you control it. Messiah the Yad, has all power and authority to control our destiny. If you say you have *a hand in the work, you mean that you are actively taking part in it or you have a share in it.* The LORD is actively working His miracles, signs, and wonders before us. The Testimony of the LORD, involves the use of His hand to give us Eternal life.

Psalm 63:8 *My soul clings to Thee; Thy right hand upholds me.*

Psalm 18:35 *Thou hast also given me the shield of Thy salvation; and Thy right hand hath holden me up, and Thy gentleness hath made me great.*

***Coin of Israel 1969 Photo ©2014 Kimberly K Ballard**

When you have something of value, it is often *handed down from father to son.* Yeshua is called *"The Son of the Father."* He is Yeshua ha-Ben (Yeshua the Son) the firstborn of the redeemed of Israel. He was redeemed with thirty pieces of Shekel (silver) given to Caiaphas the High Priest! The Jewish Messiah Yeshua is revealed in the Jewish Pidyon ha-ben ceremony according to Israeli Rabbi Simcha Pearlmutter of blessed memory, and I will show you this in part of Rabbi Pearlmutter's Testimony about Yeshua, in the following excerpts from the text. ***(Source: biblesearchers.com/yahshua/rabbipearlmutterprint.shtml).***

Rabbi Simcha Pearlmutter, Rabbi Testimony of Jesus, Yeshua, Messiah from Part Nine of Nine:
I am running out of time, but I want to show you one more thing—another book. This very large book that I have here contains many, many words from the Talmud and from the holy books. It's completely a Jewish lexicon. And over here, we have, notice it carefully, "Yeshua ha-Ben." If you see all the columns, this is a Jewish book. There is not a word of English in it, not that I know of. I haven't seen it yet, and the word "Yeshua ha-Ben." Now what is Yeshua ha-Ben? Notice, it's "Yeshua," the name of the

person Yeshua, and then "ha-Ben" means "the Son." Yeshua, the Son. But, what does it say? I am going to read it. It is very short. It says, kinui latekis, meaning "a shortened form," or "a nickname of the ceremony," shel pidyon ha-ben, "of the redeeming of the firstborn." You see, in Judaism when a mother gives birth to a first child, and that child is a male and it passes the womb, that child then thirty days later must be redeemed because he doesn't belong to the mother or the father. He belongs to HaShem, and he must be redeemed. How do we redeem him? With thirty pieces of shekel, thirty pieces of silver. And who is it paid to? The kohen, the High Priest. And then he is redeemed. And that ceremony by the way is called "Yeshua ha-Ben," because he is the redemption of our firstborn sons. Every firstborn son who is a Jew is redeemed by the name of Yeshua the Son at the thirty day ceremony after his birth. I will finish the sentence. *Shel pidyon ha-ben, ha-bachor, ha-n'eiras [words missing in transcript] sheloshim yom [words missing in transcript],* which is conducted 30 days after the time of his birth. We call it "Yeshua ha-Ben." ***(Source: Rabbi Simcha Pearlmutter, Rabbi Testimony of Jesus, Yeshua, Messiah Part Nine of Nine. Full text: jerusalemcalling.org/Rabbi_Simcha_Pearlmutter.htm.)***

Silver Shekel coin of Israel 1985
Photo ©2014 Kimberly K Ballard
All Rights Reserved

The Jews redeemed the Messiah, Yeshua ha-Ben or Yeshua the Son, with thirty pieces of silver, and it was given to the High Priests in the Holy Temple in Jerusalem. This happened in the following accounts, just before Messiah Yeshua became the Passover Lamb, the firstborn of the redeemed of the whole earth.

Silver Shekel coin of Israel 1985
Photo ©2014 Kimberly K Ballard
All Rights Reserved

Matthew 26:14-15 *Then one of the twelve, called Judas Iscariot, went unto the chief priests, And said unto them, What will ye give me, and I will deliver Him unto you? And they covenanted with him for thirty pieces of silver.*

Matthew 27:1-11 *When the morning was come, all the chief priests and elders of the people took counsel against Jesus to put him to death: And when they had bound him, they led him away, and delivered him to Pontius Pilate the governor. Then Judas, which had betrayed him, when he saw that he was condemned, repented himself, and brought again the thirty pieces of silver to the chief priests and elders, Saying, I have sinned in that I have betrayed the innocent blood. And they said, What is that to us? See thou to that. And he cast down the pieces of silver in the temple, and departed, and went and hanged himself. And the chief priests took the silver pieces, and said, It is not lawful for to put them into the treasury, because it is the price of blood. And they took counsel, and bought with them the potter's field, to bury strangers in. Wherefore that field was called, The field of blood, unto this day. Then was fulfilled that which was spoken by Jeremy the prophet, saying, And they took the thirty pieces of silver, the price of him that was valued, whom they of the children of Israel did value; And gave them for the potter's field, as the Lord appointed me. And Jesus stood before the governor: and the governor asked him, saying, Art thou the King of the Jews? And Jesus said unto him, Thou sayest.*

Coin of Israel 1969
Photo ©2014 Kimberly K Ballard
All Rights Reserved

Rabbi Simcha Pearlmutter, Rabbi Testimony of Jesus, Yeshua, Messiah from Part Eight of Nine:

So you see with all that, we talk about the same thing, a Mashiach who has been forcibly taken away and bound in chains and kept in chains by the non-Jewish world for all these years while they have upheld, not him, but someone who is not really a defender of Israel as Moses was to be, and as the one who would be like Moses was to be, but the accuser of Israel. And so, we are to rescue him. We Jews are to redeem the Mashiach, can you imagine that? We Jews have a job of redeeming the Mashiach! Yes, in good Jewish eschatology in midrashim written by our Rabbis, we are told that the Mashiach has been sitting in the exile together with us and suffering every death that we have suffered because Isaiah 53 talks about, b'motav, "in his many deaths." ***(Source: Rabbi Simcha Pearlmutter, Rabbi Testimony of Jesus, Yeshua, Messiah Part Nine of Nine. Full text: jerusalemcalling.org/Rabbi_Simcha_Pearlmutter.htm.)***

Coin of Israel 1969
Photo ©2014 Kimberly K Ballard

The only one who could redeem the world was God Himself. So He came to dwell on earth as *"Yeshua ha-Ben, and the son of the Father & Son of David"* in the perfect body of the second Adam to restore our flesh. He inherits the Kingdom of God, *the Eternal Davidic Dynasty.* Messiah/Mashiach the Rod is *the right hand* of the Father. God gave us His *"hand of mercy."* This hand of God sits with Him on the throne of the Ark of the LORD, on the Mercy Seat. *This is one God who redeemed us as the firstborn, Yeshua ha-Ben.*

Matthew 25:31 *When the Son of man shall come in His glory, and all the Holy angels with Him, then shall He sit upon the throne of His glory.*

Silver Holy half shekel coin from Israel set in the Walls of Jerusalem Minted by Beged Ivri
Photo ©2014 Kimberly K Ballard

Holy half shekel coin from Israel Minted by Beged Ivri
Photo ©2014 Kimberly K Ballard

The silver Holy half shekel coin was given to the treasury at the Holy Temple in Jerusalem, and it is currently minted in Israel for the first time in 2,000 years by Beged Ivri. The reverse of one of the silver Holy half shekel coins depicts the Holy fire of God descending upon the Holy Mount over the walls of Jerusalem. The front of this coin depicts the harp of King David, and it is set in the walls of Jerusalem. The purchase of this coin goes to help repair the walls of Jerusalem. ***(Source: begedivri.com).***

A hand that is skillful has dexterity to accomplish great artistic masterful works of elegance revealing the brilliance of the mind behind the one performing the works. The highest skill level makes you a *"Master."* Yeshua was also called *"Master"* and *"Rabbi"* by His Jewish disciples. A Rabbi is not simply a *"Teacher" but is also a "Master or Lord."* The Rabbi is an ordained teacher of Jewish Law and ritual. *This means that the Rabbi, in essence, is a Master of the Torah and Yeshua is the Living Torah, which makes Him LORD, Rabbi and Master!* A Rabbi also performs marriages and is considered to be the Spiritual head of the Congregation. What a grand title for the Messiah, who is ordained to marry those who have put their trust in Him.

Coin of Israel 1969
Photo ©2014 Kimberly K Ballard

Yeshua betrothed the believers to Himself in marriage during His Last Passover Seder. As I mentioned before, the *"shel Yad"* is wrapped three times around the finger, as a sign of betrothal to the LORD. Now if you say that you join hands with someone, you become associates or enter into partnership with that person. This is precisely what we have done as believers when we *join the hand of the LORD* and we enter into His Eternal Covenant. The *joining of hands* simply refers to the connection of a husband to his wife in marriage.

There is another exciting definition of the word *"hand"* and it literally comes from the root word *"hinthan"* which means *"to seize."* This is remarkable because it is *the hand of God that seizes! The word "seize" means to take suddenly!* This connects it to the rapture of believers into the glory cloud to meet Messiah the LORD in the air. The origin of the word for *"rapture"* is the Greek word *"harpazo"* which also means *"to seize!"* Now this gives us an exciting picture of the rapture. *Yeshua is the hand that will seize us up, grasping us with the hand of God as His possession, in the rapture!* It is the hand of God that gives aid or help to a person and Yeshua will be saving us from the wrath to come. In this situation, the hand of God will quickly seize us up as His possession with all the resurrected Saints. Then we will see the LORD face to face and enter the Kingdom of Heaven. We are solely dependent on the LORD for our help.

Matthew 15:25 *Then came she and worshipped Him, saying, LORD, help me.*

When I discovered this connection between the hand of the LORD and the seizing up *as a possession*, I was so inspired. This insight into the rapture came from the Holy Spirit. The seizing up is actually the term *"caught up"* in the following rapture passage in I Thessalonians.

I Thessalonians 4:16-18 *For the LORD Himself shall descend from Heaven with a shout, with the voice of the archangel, and with the trump of God; and the dead in Messiah shall rise first; Then we which are alive and remain shall be caught up together with them in the clouds, to meet the LORD in the air; and so shall we ever be with the LORD. Wherefore comfort one another with these words.*

We are to wait for Yeshua's return, because *He is the Ark* that delivers us from the wrath to come.

I Thessalonians 1:9-10 *For they themselves shew of us what manner of entering in we had unto you, and how ye turned to God from idols to serve the Living and true God; And to wait for His Son from Heaven, whom He raised from the dead, even Yeshua, which delivered us from the wrath to come.*

As the Yad, the hand of the LORD, *points to the Living Torah* with His Holy Spirit, He helps us to learn the depth of His Word. Then we can discern His identity and come closer to Him. It is *the hand of God* that feeds us! He gives us the Living Water to drink for our thirst and the unleavened Bread from Heaven. So Yeshua, *the Living Torah,* is the source of our Eternal food from the Almond Tree of Life. He abides on the Ark in the center of Heaven that contains the hidden Manna.

The hand is also sometimes called *"the source or origin."* So the hand of God is our source of origin. It was the hand of God that created us. The Messiah was therefore in existence in the very beginning, creating the Heavens and the earth. This means that no one is a mistake, we are all made in the image of God and He wishes to commune with His entire creation forever. We are the subjects of His Majesty!

Clock Hands Photo ©2014 Kimberly K Ballard All Rights Reserved

The *hands* of a clock are *an indicator of time.* They serve as pointers of the *times and seasons* of the LORD, and we are under the timetable of the LORD. For this reason, technically, we are not under the Roman calendar, the Gregorian calendar. Messiah Yeshua is the hand of the LORD making Him our Biblical clock that fulfills everything.

After I sent my first revelation letter to Jerusalem, I began to realize that *Yeshua fulfilled all seven Feast days of the LORD at His first coming*, and He fulfills more of His plans on these same Feast days in the future. This is verified in Yeshua's statement on the cross *"it is finished."* Since all *seven* were precisely accomplished on time, this is another indication that *His Living Testimony* is perfect. Many people are wrongly saying that Yeshua only fulfilled the spring Feasts at His first coming, and fulfills the fall Feasts at His second coming. In this book I will show you exactly how Yeshua already fulfilled all seven of them already!

Israel was commanded by the LORD *to keep the seven Feasts of the LORD forever* and these are based upon Leviticus 23. The prophecies of the Messiah were woven into the fabric of Israel, and written in the Torah of Moses long ago. Yeshua's intricate Jewish identity has been stripped from Him over the centuries. When we restore His Jewish identity to see that He is a Jewish Rabbi, then, incredibly, the Scripture's open to us like never before. The Word of God draws us in and we see the Almond flower in full bloom like never before.

The seven Feasts of the LORD include *Passover, the Feast of Unleavened Bread, the Feast of First Fruits, Shavuot which is the Feast of weeks or Pentecost.* These are the four spring feasts. The Fall Feasts include, *Rosh HaShanah which is the Feast of Trumpets or Yom Teruah, Yom Kippur which is The Day of Atonement, and finally Sukkot, also called the Feast of Tabernacles.* The Messiah came according to the LORD'S Biblical calendar and not according to the pagan Roman calendar. This leads me to truthfully say that the Jewish Messiah Yeshua was not born on an ancient pagan Roman holiday that was renamed *"Christmas,"* although it is true that Yeshua is the light of the world and that *He was conceived at Hanukkah in December or Kislev which very well could have landed on the day of Christmas.* So it is indeed extremely appropriate to celebrate Him as the Heavenly light, but I have written, in one of the coming chapters, exactly what the LORD revealed to me about the timing of *the birth* of our Saviour Yeshua, and it is outstanding to say the least! We should take a serious look at the truth.

Another point I must make regarding the appointed times of the Messiah is the fact that *Yeshua was not resurrected on a pagan Babylonian Roman holiday known as "Easter"* which in name alone, written in I King's 11, is historically an abomination to the LORD. The gate of Babylon was the *"Ishtar"* gate, the name of a so-called pagan goddess! These traditions are not accurate according to the Jewish Gospel accounts. *God's calendar accurately reveals the Jewish Messiah!* It is Yeshua's Jewishness that enables us to understand Him completely. The *"Last Supper"* was Yeshua's *Last Jewish Passover Seder.* The Messiah told us to remember Him in the breaking of the Matzah *(the unleavened bread)* and in *the wine during the Jewish Passover Seder.* He was placed in the tomb during *the Feast of Unleavened Bread. Yeshua was resurrected during the Jewish Feast of First Fruits.* Yeshua returns in all His glory to celebrate the Feast of Tabernacles with us. Israel will see Him again when they say in their hearts, *"Blessed is He who comes in the Name of the LORD."* Then He will come to heal their land and restore all things under the Kingdom of God.

In ancient times, if a person was in the military, their *right hand* was called *"the weapon hand."* The Rod of God, *the Lion of Judah, is the weapon hand* of the LORD that goes against the enemies of God.

Yad, Candle & Bible Photo ©2014 Kimberly K Ballard All Rights Reserved

Psalm 21:8-9 *Your hand will find out all your enemies; <u>Your right hand</u> will find out those who hate you. You will make them as a fiery oven in the time of your anger; The LORD will swallow them up in His wrath, And fire will devour them.*

Psalm 98:1-3 *O sing to the LORD a new song, For He has done wonderful things, <u>His right hand</u> and His Holy Arm have gained the victory for Him. The LORD has made known His salvation, He has revealed His righteousness in the sight of the Nations. He has remembered His loving kindness and His faithfulness to the House of Israel, All the ends of the earth have seen the salvation of our God.*

John 5:24-29 *Verily, verily, I say unto you, He that heareth My Word and believeth on Him that sent Me, hath everlasting life, and shall not come into condemnation; but is passed from death unto life. Verily, verily, I say unto you, The hour is coming, and now is, when the dead shall hear the voice of the Son of God; and they that hear shall* *live. For as the Father hath life in Himself; so hath He given to the Son to have life in Himself; And hath given Him authority to execute judgment also, because He is the Son of man. Marvel not at this; for the hour is coming, in the which all that are in the graves shall hear His voice, and shall come forth; they that have done good, unto the resurrection of life; and they that have done evil, unto the resurrection of damnation.*

When the LORD said that Israel was *inscribed upon the palms of His hands,* this meant that they are inscribed upon Messiah Yeshua, the High Priest of Heaven. *The hand is used in tenderness to express loving kindness by touch and sensitivity. He is the God of life!*

Isaiah 49:16 *Behold, I have graven thee upon the palms of My hands; thy walls are continually before Me.*

Psalm 36:7 *How excellent is Thy loving-kindness, O God! Therefore the children of men put their trust under the shadow of Thy wings.*

Psalm 42:8 *Yet the LORD will command His loving-kindness in the daytime, and in the night His song shall be with me, and my prayer unto the God of my life.*

The Yad pointing to Yeshua Sculpted by & Photo ©2013 Kimberly K Ballard All Rights Reserved

The Psalms declare in Hebrew *that the hand of God is our Yeshua,* as we can see in the following Biblical examples. The Messiah went forth into battle and gained *"His Holy Land"* by His mighty strength. *His Holy Land is the Land of Israel,* the hill country that exists forever in eternity because the LORD dwells there.

Snow on the Rocky Mountains Colorado - our hill country with super moon Photo ©2014 Kimberly K Ballard All Rights Reserved

Boulder Colorado Flatirons Photo ©2013 Kimberly K Ballard All Rights Reserved

Psalm 78:52-54 *But He led forth His own people like sheep, and guided them in the wilderness like a flock; And He led them safely, so that they did not fear; But the sea engulfed their enemies. So He brought them to His Holy Land, To this hill Country which His right hand had gained.*

Psalms 108:4-6 *For Thy mercy is great above the Heavens; and Thy truth reacheth unto the clouds. Be thou exalted, O God, above the Heavens; and Thy glory above all the earth; That Thy beloved may be delivered; save with Thy right hand, and answer me.*

Mark 16:19 *So then when the LORD Yeshua had spoken to them, He was received up into Heaven, and sat down at the right hand of God.*

Matthew 26:63-64 *But Yeshua kept silent, And the High Priest said to Him, I adjure You by the Living God, that You tell us whether You are the Messiah, the Son of God. Yeshua said to him, You have said it yourself; nevertheless I tell you, hereafter you shall see the Son of Man sitting at the right hand of power, and coming on the clouds of Heaven.*

THE MAN'SHAND WROTE ON THE WALL

The Yad of God writing on the wall
Photo ©2013 Kimberly K Ballard All Rights Reserved

Finally, it is the hand that writes! The *man's hand* that wrote on the wall in the plaster came out of Heaven. This was the hand, Yeshua. The judgment fell upon those that had stolen the gold vessels from the LORD'S Temple in Jerusalem and they had defiled the LORD'S vessels by eating and drinking out of them. Those who stole the vessels from the LORD'S House were flaunting themselves in arrogance and pride, as they worshipped many pagan false gods, and in doing so, insulted the LORD of Glory, as they committed these abominable deeds! This event took place in the book of Daniel. The hand of a man appeared from Heaven and wrote a judgment on the wall as Belshazzar was blatantly feasting, using the stolen Holy Temple vessels. This was the Yad, the finger of God, that wrote on the wall and Messiah Yeshua is the Yad who brings the judgment of God's wrath upon an unbelieving world in the last days. The same hand that wrote this judgment belongs to the Rod of God and it was this hand that wrote the Ten Commandments with His finger on stone tablets at Mount Sinai. This hand appeared opposite from the Lamp stand in the place where the Bread of the Presence stands, in the Heavenly Temple and Yeshua is the hidden Manna depicted on the Lamp stand.

Daniel 5:1-6 *Belshazzar the king made a great feast to a thousand of his lord's, and drank wine before the thousand. Belshazzar, whiles he tasted the wine, commanded to bring the golden and silver vessels which his father Nebuchadnezzar had taken out of the Temple which was in Jerusalem; that the king, and his prince's, his wives, and his concubines might drink therein. Then they brought the golden vessels that were taken out of the Temple of the House of God which was at Jerusalem; and the king, and his prince's, his wives, and his concubines, drank in them. They drank wine, and praised the gods of gold, and of silver, of brass, of iron, of wood, and of stone. In the same hour came forth finger's of a man's hand, and wrote over against the candlestick upon the plaster of the wall of the king's palace; and the king saw the part of the hand that wrote. Then the king's countenance was changed, and his thoughts troubled him, so that the joints of his loins were loosed, and his knees smote one against another. The king cried aloud to bring in the astrologers, the Chaldeans, and the soothsayers. And the king spake, and said to the wise men of Babylon, Whosoever shall read this writing, and shew me the interpretation thereof, shall be clothed with scarlet, and have a chain of gold about his neck, and shall be the third ruler in the kingdom. Then came in all the king's wise men; but they could not read the writing, nor make known to the king the interpretation thereof. Then was King Belshazzar greatly troubled, and his countenance was changed in him and his lord's were astonied. After these things, Daniel was brought in to interpret the writing on the wall. The fingers of the man's hand which had appeared and wrote on the wall had written the words, ME'NE, ME'NE, TE'KEL, U-PHAR'-SIN.*

The writing on the wall was the judgment against King Belshazzar. Basically the days of his kingdom were numbered and it was finished. The king had been weighed in the balances and he was he found guilty. His kingdom was to be divided and given to others. Belshazzar was horrified when this hand appeared out of nowhere and proclaimed the judgment and his legs went slack! I suspect that Yeshua will appear suddenly out of nowhere and the judgment and wrath of God will be poured out on all the ungodly sinners in the future judgment because they have refused to believe in the LORD Messiah. Ironically, Yeshua told the Jewish leaders, before the Second Temple was destroyed, that a kingdom divided against itself cannot stand. God's punishment to King Solomon was also the division of his kingdom. This judgment came because they were worshipping false gods. *The kingdom was made cleft by the hand holding the Rod of God!* Solomon's kingdom was divided into the northern kingdom of Israel and the kingdom of Judah in the south.

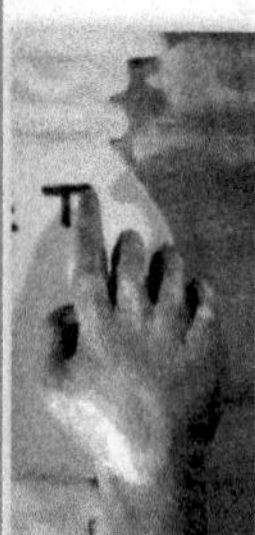

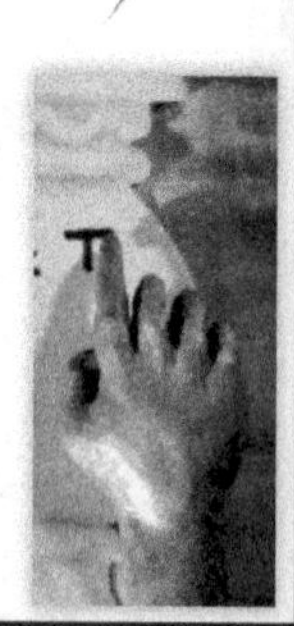

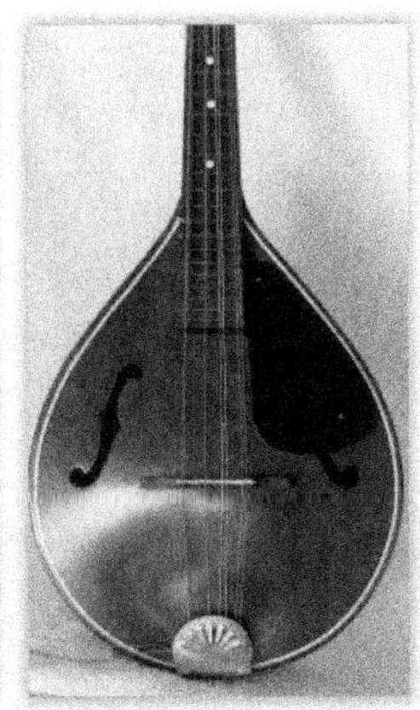

THE FINGER OF GOD

Mandolin I bought from my friend Marion in 1983 in Fort Collins Colorado & my Darbuka Drum Photos ©2014 Kimberly K Ballard All Rights Reserved

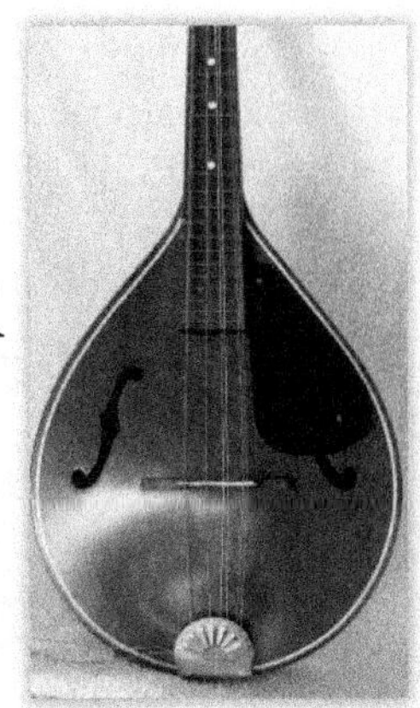

By definition, a finger includes *"any of the five extreme parts of the hand."* In reference to music, *"finger"* specifically refers *"to the ability of the musician to play skillfully upon a musical instrument and to exhibit excellent execution and dexterity during a musical performance, using the fingers of the hands."* It is said that when God created the universe, *music* was involved in the Divine artwork, and each Hebrew letter corresponded to a musical note. Every living thing vibrates to a frequency which gives a tonal quality to the sound of life. The title of my first CD of original music in 2006 was therefore called, *"My Frequency!"*

As I thought about this, as it pertains to the LORD, I recognized that each hand has five fingers, and the five fingers of the LORD represent the five books of Moses, *the Torah,* written by the hand and finger of God. The two hands together add up to ten fingers, representing the two tablets of stone containing the Ten Commandments of God written with the finger of God. Should it surprise us then that Yeshua is the Yad, the hand of God, and *He is the Living Torah* who created everything in the universe? The Jewish disciple, John, wrote that nothing was made without *the Word of God.* The *Word of God* existed in the beginning and *the Word was God. The Word is the Living Torah.* To the Jewish people, *the Torah that was written down by Moses* is very precious, as it was translated to him by the LORD, but to Jewish and Gentile Christians and Messianic believers, *Messiah the Living Torah,* is the most precious and dear because He fulfills it all. So the truth is that the Jews and the Gentiles both have *the Torah* and we both love it and keep it! *Music is the sound of life given to us by the Living God!*

Mandolin Photo ©2014 KK Ballard All Rights Reserved

So the LORD is once again represented in the hands because He created them! There is a saying that *if you have your finger in something,* it means that you are interested in it or you have a concern and share in the matter. You are deeply focused on what you love. Of course the LORD has concern for us and He is very interested in our lives, and the LORD beckons to us with Messiah, His finger. The LORD calls us to come closer to Him, to discover that He is the Living fulfillment of the Torah of Moses. It is His desire that we seek Him with a loving and kind heart.

The LORD is the creator of music. The LORD gave us the ability to create music on musical instruments using our hands and fingers and to sing with the voice that He gave us. This was made possible, through sound waves and vibrations. *When the sound waves vibrate, they hit our ear drum and we hear what the sound waves produce.* When Yeshua performed the miracle of healing the deaf mute, *Yeshua put His fingers* in the man's ears and he could suddenly hear! *The Word of God* put His skillful fingers in the ears of the man, and the hand of the LORD produced the sound waves in the inner ear of the man and his hearing was completely restored! As I stated earlier, when the LORD spoke the creation

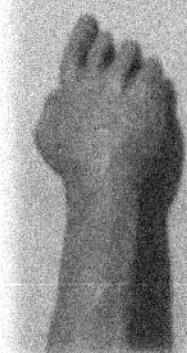

into being, it is said that a melody came forth through His Words, as He spoke the sacred Hebrew letters of the alphabet. In this miracle, *Yeshua was revealed as the finger of God creating the sound waves, the vibration of life into the man's ear, as he was healed instantly.*

Mark 7:32-33 *And they bring unto him one that was deaf, and had an impediment in his speech; and they beseech Him to put His hand upon him. And He took him aside from the multitude, and put His fingers into his ears, and He spit, and touched his tongue; And looking up to Heaven, He sighed, and saith unto him, Ephphatha, that is, Be opened. And straightway his ears were opened, and the string of his tongue was loosed, and he spake plain. And He charged them, so much the more a great deal they published it; And they were beyond measure astonished, saying, He hath done all things well; He maketh both the deaf to hear, and the dumb to speak.*

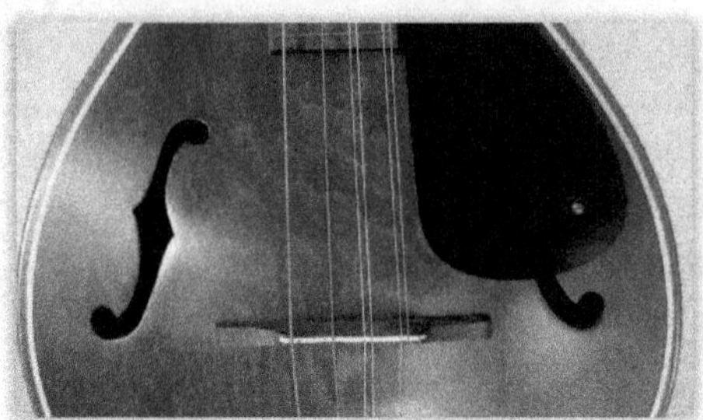

Mandolin with new strings

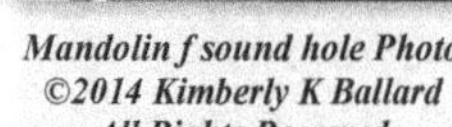

Mandolin f sound hole Photo

In this miracle, I also realized that when Yeshua spit and touched the man's tongue, *Yeshua's spit was the Living Water and He was the Rod of God that divided and made cleft the string of the man's tongue and it was loosed.* The LORD God is our physician. Incredibly, I read that, medically, this is exactly how a surgeon fixes the tongue of a person who has a string under their tongue that is too short or too tight from birth. The string of the tongue is the skin underneath the tongue and if it is too short or tight, the tongue cannot move, and speech is impossible. So this man in the miracle was mute. A surgeon actually *divides* the piece of skin under the tongue, *making this piece of skin cleft* and the tongue is then free to move. When the string under the tongue is loosed through this method, the person can suddenly speak! Even this miracle proved that Yeshua performed the signature of the hand of the LORD. We make the strings of an instrument speak! We do everything with our hands and our fingers and so does the LORD. His hands and His fingers declare His mighty works as the Rod of God and we should take notice of all the beauty that He has created around us and genuinely love other people!

The next realization that came to me by the revelation of the LORD was a bit shocking at first. *I am showing you that the miracles of Messiah Yeshua actually do reveal that He is the finger of God who inscribed the Word of God on the two tablets of stone on Mount Sinai before Moses and later upon our hearts as His Eternal Covenant with His entire creation.*

With Moses, we can see in the following three passages that *"the Testimony is written by the finger of God."*

Exodus 31:17-18 *It is a sign between me and the children of Israel forever; for in six days the LORD made Heaven and earth, and on the seventh day He rested, and was refreshed. And He gave unto Moses, when He had made an end of communing with him upon Mount Sinai, two tables of Testimony, tables of stone, <u>written with the finger of God.</u>*

Deuteronomy 9:9-11 *When I was gone up into the Mount to receive the tables of stone, even the tables of the Covenant which the LORD made with you, then I abode in the Mount forty days and forty nights, I neither did eat bread nor drink water; And the LORD delivered unto me two tables of stone <u>written with the finger of God</u>; and on them was written according to all the Words, which the LORD spake with you in the Mount out of the midst of the fire in the day of the assembly. And it came to pass at the end of forty days and forty nights, that the LORD gave me the two tables of stone, even the tables of the Covenant.*

Remember that after Yeshua was baptized in the Jordan River, He was driven out into the wilderness for forty days and forty nights. Yeshua ate no bread and drank no water in the

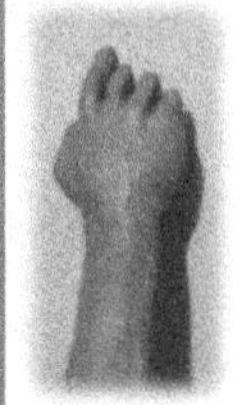

wilderness, exactly as Moses ate no bread and drank no water *before he received the tablets of the Word of God from the LORD, while standing in His Divine Presence.* When the LORD Yeshua came out of the wilderness, *He immediately began His ministry of taking the Living Torah* to the people of Israel. *The Living Word of God was dwelling in our midst, inscribing His Living Testimony with His finger upon the tablets of our hearts, so He would forever be our God in Jerusalem and we would forever be His people.* Yeshua's miracle of not eating bread or drinking water emphasizes that He is the LORD God Almighty, the Living Bread from Heaven, the Living Water that came to love us and to give Himself as our Bridegroom.

Exodus 34:1-10 *And the LORD said unto Moses, Hew thee two tables of stone like unto the first: and I will write upon these tables the words that were in the first tables, which thou brakest. And be ready in the morning, and come up in the morning unto Mount Sinai, and present thyself there to Me in the top of the mount. And no man shall come up with thee, neither let any man be seen throughout all the mount; neither let the flocks nor herds feed before that mount. And he hewed two tables of stone like unto the first; and Moses rose up early in the morning, and went up unto Mount Sinai, as the LORD had commanded him, and took in his hand the two tables of stone. And the LORD descended in the cloud, and stood with him there, and proclaimed the Name of the LORD. And the LORD passed by before him, and proclaimed, The LORD, The LORD God, merciful and gracious, longsuffering, and abundant in goodness and truth, Keeping mercy for thousands, forgiving iniquity and transgression and sin, and that will by no means clear the guilty; visiting the iniquity of the fathers upon the children, and upon the children's children, unto the third and to the fourth generation. And Moses made haste, and bowed his head toward the earth, and worshipped. And he said, If now I have found grace in Thy sight, O LORD, let my LORD, I pray thee, go among us; for it is a stiffnecked people; and pardon our iniquity and our sin, and take us for Thine inheritance. And he said, Behold, I make a covenant; before all thy people I will do marvels, such as have not been done in all the earth, nor in any nation; and all the people among which thou art shall see the work of the LORD; for it is a terrible thing that I will do with thee.*

The LORD descended in a cloud and stood there proclaiming His own Name. *This is the Rod of God proclaiming the Name of the LORD and He forgives sins.* Messiah Yeshua declared that *He had the authority to forgive sins.* So the following verse proves that Yeshua is *the Rod and Yad of God* that has power on earth to forgive sins. Yeshua healed the man who was sick, as He forgave his sins.

Mark 2:10-12 *But that ye may know that the Son of man hath the power on earth to forgive sins, He saith to the sick of the palsy, I say unto thee, Arise, and take up thy bed, and go thy way into thine house. And immediately he arose, took up the bed, and went forth before them all; insomuch that they were all amazed, and glorified God, saying, We never saw it on this fashion.*

The Messiah wrote the Ten Commandments of the Testimony, first in stone and later upon the hearts of women and men, beginning in Jerusalem! How do we know this for certain? In Exodus, the LORD told Moses to tell Aaron to stretch out his hand with the rod in it to reveal the miracles of the LORD. *When Pharaoh's magicians saw the miracles of Aaron's rod, they proclaimed "This is the finger of God!"*

Exodus 8:16-19 *And the LORD said unto Moses, Say unto Aaron, Stretch out thy rod, and smite the dust of the land, that it may become lice throughout all the land of Egypt. And they did so; for Aaron stretched out his hand with his rod, and smote the dust of the earth, and it became lice in man, and in beast; all the dust of the land became lice throughout all the land of Egypt. And the magicians did so with their enchantments to bring forth lice, but they could not; so there were lice upon man, and upon beast. Then the magicians said unto Pharaoh, <u>This is the finger of God;</u> and Pharaoh's heart was hardened, and he hearkened not unto them; as the LORD had said.*

Pharaoh was an eyewitness of the power of God, but instead of believing the works that God's Rod performed before him, Pharaoh hardened his heart like a rock, refusing to validate the Great KING! *Now Messiah Yeshua actually told the people of Israel that He casts out devils with the finger of God.* Yeshua told them, *"That the Kingdom of God is come upon you."* So did they *harden their hearts like a rock* and not hearken unto the LORD *to see that*

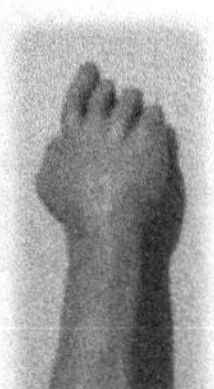
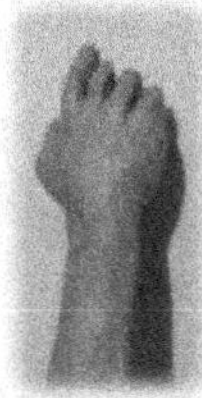

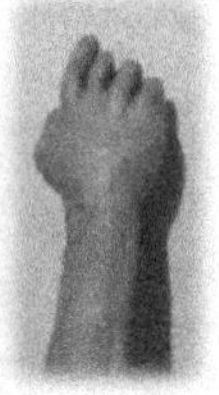

Messiah Yeshua is the Almond Rod and the finger of God who was performing mighty miracles, signs, and wonders in their midst before their eyes, just as He had done with Pharaoh centuries earlier? Did they not allow His Holy Spirit to soften their hearts towards their KING?

Luke 11:20-23 *But if I with the finger of God cast out devils, no doubt the Kingdom of God is come upon you. When a strong man armed keepeth his palace, his goods are in peace; But when a stronger than he shall come upon him, and overcome him, he taketh from him all his armour wherein he trusted, and divideth his spoils. He that is not with Me is against Me; and he that gathereth not with Me scattereth.*

The children of Israel were scattered because they could not see that Messiah Yeshua was the Rod of God performing the works of the Creator in their midst. Let our generation not harden our hearts! *Validate the KING!* Yeshua, the High Priest of Heaven after the Order of Melchizedek, is the anointed finger of God who placed His own life blood with His own finger *upon the Heavenly Ark.* The LORD became the pure and perfect sin offering for His people.

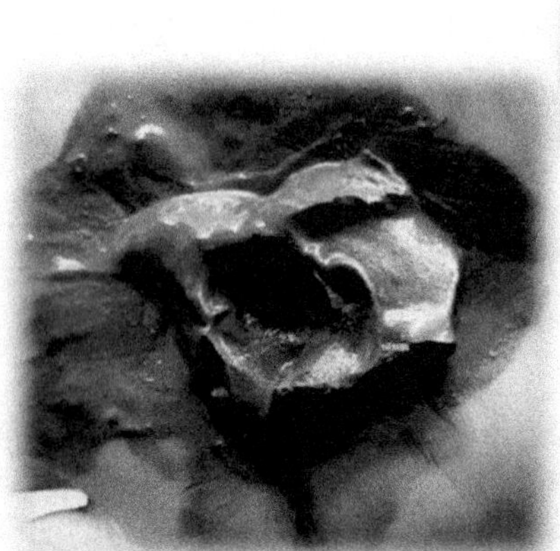

YESHUA HEALS THE BLIND MAN

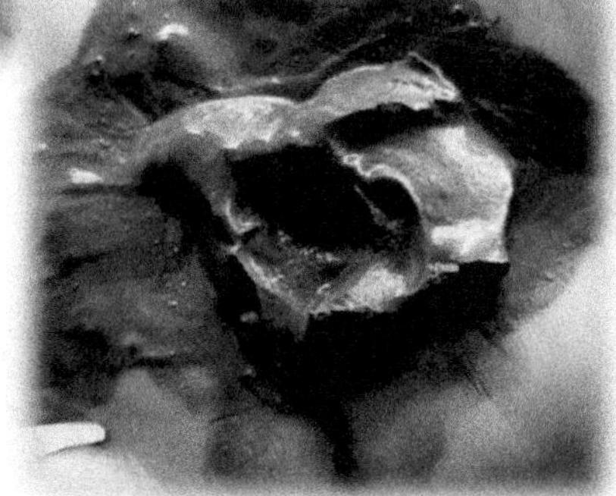

Yad & Dead Sea Mud from Israel
Photos ©2014 Kimberly K Ballard All Rights Reserved

The incredible miracle of Yeshua healing the blind man is so shocking and fantastic and that I want to show you how this miracle proves that Yeshua is the finger of God! In Jerusalem there was a blind man who was born blind and Yeshua came to heal this man. Yeshua specifically told the Jewish disciples that this man was *born blind,* not because of any of his own sins or because of the sins of his parents. Yeshua declared that this man was *born blind, so the works of God should be made manifest in him!* Yeshua was about to reveal His true identity and the people were about to be astonished at this great miracle. Yeshua goes on to say that He must work *the works of the one who sent Him.* Now the story of the healing of the blind man is found in John Chapter 9 and is written as follows.

John 9:1-41 *And as Yeshua passed by, He saw a man which was blind from his birth. And His disciples asked Him, saying, Master, who did sin, this man or his parents, that he was born blind? Yeshua answered, Neither hath this man sinned, nor his parents; but that the works of God should be made manifest in him. I must work the works of Him that sent Me, while it is day; the night cometh, when no man can work. As long as I AM in the world, I AM the light of the world. When He had thus spoken, He spat on the ground, and made clay of the spittle, and He anointed the eyes of the blind man with the clay, And said unto him, Go, wash in the Pool of Siloam, which is by interpretation, Sent. He went his way therefore, and washed, and came seeing. The neighbors therefore, and they which before had seen him that he was blind, said, Is not this he that sat and begged? Some said, This is he; others said, He is like him; but he said, I am he. Therefore said they unto him, How were thine eyes opened? He answered and said, A man that is called Yeshua made clay, and anointed mine eyes, and said unto me, Go to the Pool of Siloam, and wash; and I went and washed, and I received sight. Then they said unto him, Where is He? He said, I know not. They brought to the Pharisees him that aforetime was blind. And it was the Sabbath day when Yeshua made the clay, and opened his eyes. Then again the Pharisees also asked him how he had received his sight. He said unto them, He put clay upon mine eyes, and I washed, and do see. Therefore said some of the Pharisees, This man is not of God, because He keepeth not the Sabbath day. Others said, How can a man that is a sinner do such* *miracles? And there was a division among them. They say unto the blind man again, What sayest thou of Him, that He hath opened thine eyes? He said, He is a Prophet. But the Jews did not believe concerning him, that he had been blind, and received his sight, until they called the parents of him that had received his sight. And they asked them, saying, Is this your son, who ye say was born blind? How then doth he now see? His parents answered them and said, We know that this is our son, and that he was born blind; But by what means he now seeth, we know not; or who hath opened his eyes, we know not; he is of age; ask him; he shall speak for himself. These words spake his parents, because they feared the Jews; for the Jews had agreed already, that if any man did confess that He was Messiah, he should be put out of the Synagogue. Therefore said his parents, He is of age; ask him. Then again called they the man that was blind, and said unto him, Give God the praise; we know that this man is a sinner. He answered and said, Whether He be a sinner or no, I know not; one thing I know, that, whereas I was blind, now I see. Then said they unto him again, What did He to thee? How opened He thine eyes? He answered them, I have told you already, and ye did not hear; wherefore would ye hear it again? Will ye also be His disciples? Then they reviled him, and said, Thou art His disciple; but we are Moses disciples. We know that God spake unto Moses; as for this fellow, we know not from whence He is. The man answered and said unto them, Why herein is a marvelous thing, that ye know not from whence He is, and yet He hath opened mine eyes. Now we know that God heareth not sinners; but if any man be a worshipper of God, and doeth His will, him He heareth. Since the world began was it not heard that any man opened the eyes of one that was born blind. If this man were not of God, He could do nothing. They answered and said unto him, Thou wast altogether born in sins, and dost thou teach us? And they cast him out. Yeshua heard that they had cast him out; and when He had found him, He said unto him, Dost thou believe on the Son of God? He answered and said, Who is He, LORD, that I might believe on Him? And Yeshua said unto him, Thou hast both seen Him, and it is He that talketh with thee. And he said, LORD, I believe. And he worshipped Him. And Yeshua said, For judgment I am come into this world, that they which see not might see; and that they which see might be made blind. And some of the Pharisees which were with Him heard these Words, and said unto Him, Are we blind also? Yeshua said unto them, If ye were blind, ye should have no sin; but now ye say, We see; therefore your sin remaineth.*

Now the astounding truth of this miracle was also revealed to me by the Holy Spirit. In order to heal the eyes of the blind man, Yeshua gathered some dirt in His hand and He spit in it. He mixed the dirt *with His finger* and made clay from it and put it on the eyes of the blind man. To recognize exactly who is performing this miracle, we need to go back to the beginning, to Genesis! What happened when the LORD created mankind in the book of Genesis?

Water from the Pool of Siloam in Israel in a jar
Photo ©2013 Kimberly K Ballard
All Rights Reserved

Genesis 2:7 *And the LORD God formed man of the dust of the ground, and breathed into his nostrils the breath of life; and man became a living soul.*

The LORD God created Adam from the dust of the ground! So Yeshua made clay out of the dust of the ground with His own spittle, in His own hand. *When Yeshua spit into His hand, the Living Water was mixed with the dust of the earth!* Yeshua mixed the clay with *His finger* and Yeshua put the clay mixture upon the eyes of the blind man with *His finger*. He then told the man to go wash his eyes in the Pool of Siloam. The Pool of Siloam was the pool of *"living water"* where the Priests washed in a Mikveh bath before going up to the Holy Temple to perform their sacred duties. The word *"Siloam"* means *"sent."* So the man was sent to wash the clay off his eyes in the living water. *The Messiah was demonstrating that He is the Living Water who was sent to us. He is the finger of God who created mankind out of the dust of the earth with His own hand, in the beginning.* Yeshua, therefore, had the power to create new eyes for the blind man out of the clay. Only the hand of God could mix dirt with His own saliva and make it into clay in His hand and with His finger, and create new eyes from the clay for the man who was born blind. *God is the Potter and we are the clay!* The man was cleansed in the baptism of the Messiah, as He was

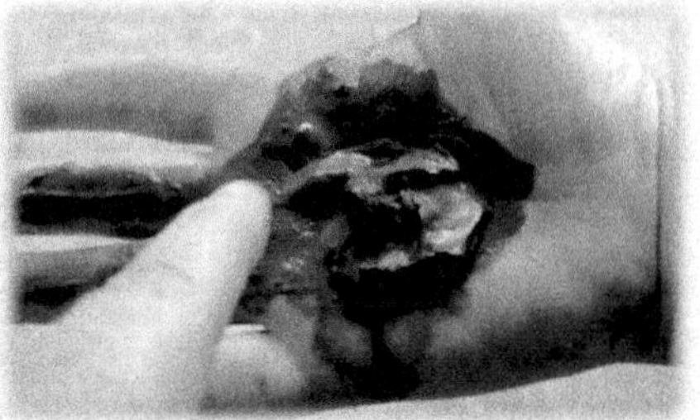

Dead Sea mud from Israel
Photo ©2014 Kimberly K Ballard All Rights Reserved

sent by the hand of God to wash off the clay in the living water of the Pool of Siloam. *This entire miracle reveals that Yeshua is the hand and finger of God.* Yeshua is again proven here to be the Yad of God who created everything in the universe. In this miracle, Messiah Yeshua revealed that He was God dwelling with us. *The miracle was not just to show that Yeshua healed the eyes of this blind man, but was to show that Yeshua was involved in creation, when He formed Adam out of the dust of the ground from this location.*

Jeremiah the Prophet wrote *the Word of the LORD,* revealing that *Yeshua the Yad of God is the Potter and so did the Prophet Isaiah.*

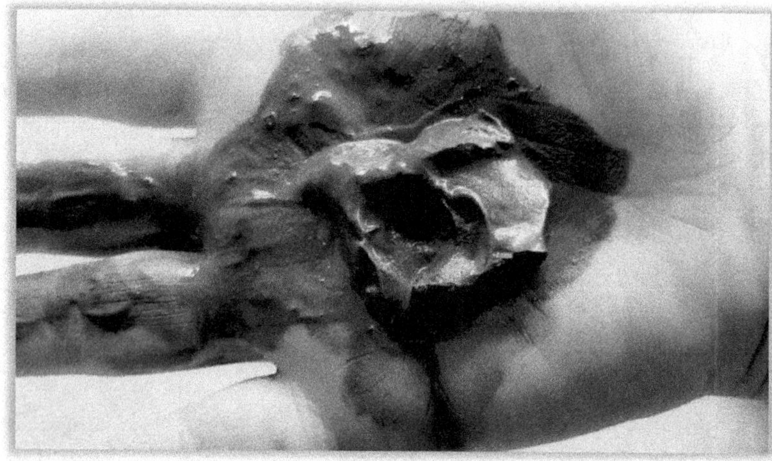

Dead Sea mud from Israel
Photo ©2014 Kimberly K Ballard All Rights Reserved

Jeremiah 18:5-6 *Then the Word of the LORD came to me, saying, O House of Israel, cannot I do with you as this potter? Saith the LORD. Behold, as the clay is in the potter's hand, so are ye in Mine hand, O House of Israel.*

Isaiah 64:8 *But now, O LORD, Thou art our Father; we are the clay, and Thou our Potter; and we all are the work of Thy hand.*

Isaiah 45:9-13 *Woe unto him that striveth with his Maker! Let the potsherd strive with the potsherds of the earth. Shall the clay say to Him that fashioneth it, What makest Thou? Or Thy work, He hath no hands? Woe unto him that saith unto his Father, What begettest Thou? Or to the woman, What hast thou brought forth? Thus saith the LORD, the Holy One of Israel, and His Maker, Ask Me of things to come concerning My sons, and concerning the work of My hands command ye Me. I have made the earth, and created man upon it; I, even My hands, have stretched out the Heavens, and all their hosts have I commanded. I have raised Him up in righteousness, and I will direct all His ways; He shall build My city, and He shall let go My captives, not for price nor reward, saith the LORD of Hosts.*

Lamentations 4:2 *The precious sons of Zion, comparable to fine gold, how are they esteemed as earthen pitchers, the work of the hands of the Potter!*

So we see that the LORD God of Israel is *the Messiah and the Saviour* of the world. This is the revelation of the mystery of Messiah. Yeshua performed so many miracles that proved He is the Yad and the finger of God and Yeshua even said that He was *the finger of God performing all these miracles*. The man who had been born blind had lived in total darkness all of his life, *but by the power of God's Spirit on the Rod,* this man saw the true light, Messiah the LORD, on the seventh day Sabbath of the LORD. The Messiah took away the darkness and gave the man the light from Heaven. Yeshua commanded the blind man *by His Word* to go wash. The blind man then had the eyes to see the light of the glory of God in the face of Messiah, the reflective Rod. Yeshua was sent to the earth, to take away the sins of darkness and to heal us, so we could be brought into the marvelous light and glory of His countenance.

It is also very interesting that when *the Rod of God* was speaking to the Pharisees, a *division* rose up among them. The Rod was making the Pharisees cleft! This is the signature of the work of the LORD God. In this miracle, Yeshua also revealed that He is the light of the world and that in Him there is no darkness at all! When the blind man saw and believed that this was the work of the LORD God of Israel, He knelt down to the ground and worshipped Yeshua! *In a later chapter about Yeshua's birth you will see that there is a far greater revelation to this miracle of healing the blind man! This was the Messiah who would restore the Davidic Dynasty! Yeshua was proven to be the Potter working the clay in His hand!* This Jewish man could now see as if he had never been born blind, and he confronted the Jewish leaders when he said to them, *"Never in the history of the world was there anyone that could ever heal the eyes of the blind."* He was trying to get them to see that *Yeshua was the LORD God of Israel,* but they refused to hear and they closed their eyes to the truth. *So they became blind, as the blind man could now see! One day their eyes will also see the light!*

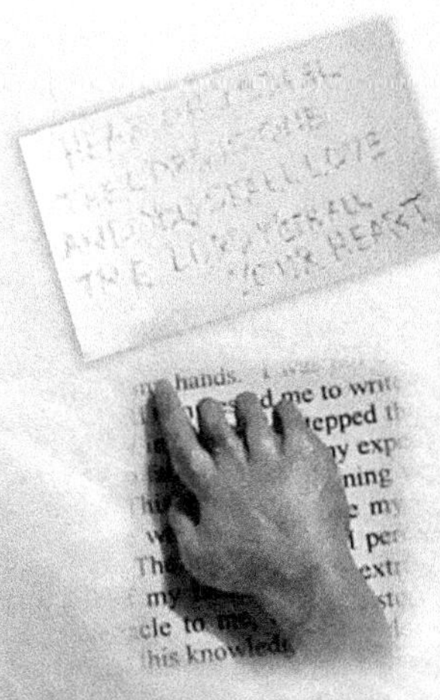

TEMPLE TEST YESHUA WRITES ON THE GROUND WITH HIS FINGER

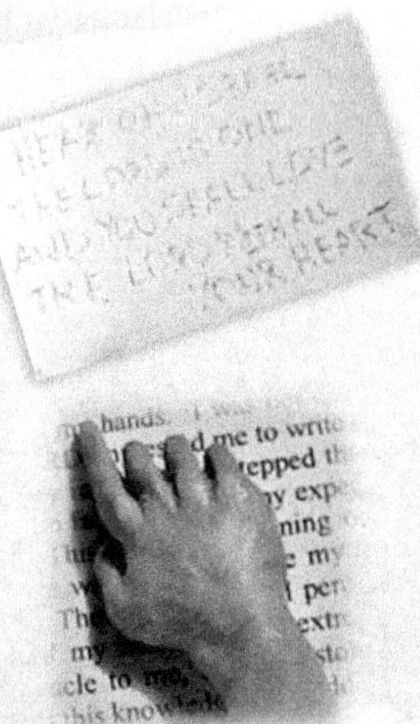

Yeshua writes on the ground
Photo ©2013 Kimberly K Ballard All Rights Reserved

Yeshua was in the Holy Temple in Jerusalem when a harlot was brought before Him by the Scribes and the Pharisees. *Yeshua stooped down and wrote on the ground with His finger. Yeshua was writing on stone!* They were testing Him about one of the Ten Commandments. However, the true Temple test was given back to them in the form of a question, in typical Rabbinical fashion, by Rabbi Yeshua! Now the question is did the forefathers of the Scribes and Pharisees ever break this Commandment against the LORD before? *The Messiah was answering them as the Rod, the hand and the finger of God. He convicted them that their forefathers had broken the LORD'S heart by playing the harlot, when they were considered to be married to the LORD God of Israel.* This was the true Temple Test and the Jewish Messiah turned it around, so they were convicted in their own hearts. They knew the truth about the sins of their forefathers.

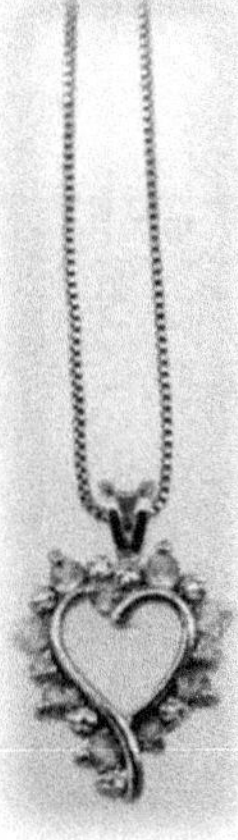

John 8:1-20 *Yeshua went unto the Mount of Olives. And early in the morning He came again into the Temple, and all the people came unto Him; and He sat down, and taught them. And the Scribes and Pharisees brought unto Him a woman taken in adultery; and when they had set her in the midst, They say unto Him, Master, this woman was taken in adultery, in the very act. Now Moses in the Law commanded us, that such should be stoned; but what sayest Thou? This they said, tempting Him, that they might have to accuse Him. But Yeshua stooped down, and with His finger wrote on the ground, as though he heard them not. So when they continued asking Him, He lifted up Himself, and said unto them, he that is without sin among you, let him first cast a stone at her. And again He stooped down, and wrote on the ground. And they which heard it, being convicted by their own conscience, went out one by one, beginning at the eldest, even unto the last; and Yeshua was left alone, and the woman standing in the midst. When Yeshua had lifted up Himself, and saw none but the woman, He said unto her, Woman, where are those thine accusers? Hath no man condemned thee? She said, No man, LORD. And Yeshua said unto her, Neither do I condemn thee; go, and sin no more. Then spake Yeshua again unto them, saying, I AM the light of the world; he that followeth Me shall not walk in darkness, but shall have the light of life. The Pharisees therefore said unto Him, Thou bearest record of Thyself; Thy record is not true. Yeshua answered and said unto them, Though I bear record of Myself, yet My record is true; for I know whence I came, and whither I go; but ye cannot tell whence I come, and whither I go. Ye judge after the flesh; I judge no man. And yet if I judge, My judgment is true; for I AM not alone, but I and the Father that sent me. It is also written in your Law, that the Testimony of two men is true. I AM one that bear witness of Myself, and the Father that sent Me beareth witness of Me. Then said they unto Him, Where is Thy Father? Yeshua answered, ye neither know Me, nor My Father; if ye had known Me, ye should have known My Father also. These Words spake Yeshua in the treasury, as He taught in the Temple; and no man laid hands on Him; for His hour was not yet come.*

In order to fully understand this confrontation with Messiah Yeshua in the Holy Temple in Jerusalem, we must go back to the Prophet Jeremiah and take a look at what was happening between the LORD God and His people Israel, at that time. It was during the time period of the Prophet Jeremiah that Israel had turned their hearts away from the LORD God. In that generation, they had greatly sinned against the LORD by setting up pagan idols from Babylon in the LORD'S Land. On every high hill they set up a pagan shrine and they turned from the LORD to worship false gods and idols. Therefore, the LORD'S judgment, which He spoke through the mouth of the Prophet Jeremiah, was to come upon them. *The warning came in the form of an Almond Tree!* The First Holy Temple was destroyed because of their sins against the LORD, *"playing a harlot."* The Israelites were taken into captivity to Babylon for seventy years as a punishment for committing these sins and for not giving His Holy Land the Shmittah rest that it deserved. In this story, in that generation, *the LORD said that Israel had played the harlot against Him!*

Jeremiah 2:19-20 *Thine own wickedness shall correct thee, and thy backslidings shall reprove thee; know therefore and see that it is an evil thing and bitter, that thou hast forsaken the LORD thy God, and that My fear is not in thee, saith the LORD God of Hosts. For of old time I have broken thy yoke, and burst thy bands; and thou said, I will not transgress; when upon every high hill and under every green tree thou wanderest, playing the harlot.*

Heart Photo ©2014 Kimberly K Ballard All Rights Reserved

Israel was supposed to be *the wife of the LORD God,* but they had turned, in their hearts, away from Him. *The LORD'S heart was greatly grieved because He loved them with all His heart.* So for seventy years, the Israelites were in Babylon, taken into captivity, until the time of their punishment was fulfilled. Then the LORD restored the Israelites back to Jerusalem out of His loving kindness and mercy toward them. The LORD spoke the following Words *to His wife, Israel. He wanted her to return to Him!*

Jeremiah 3:1-4 *They say, If a man put away his wife, and she go from him, and become another man's, shall he return unto her again? Shall not that land be greatly polluted? But thou hast played the harlot with many lovers; yet return again to Me, saith the LORD. Lift up thine eyes unto the high places, and see where thou hast not been lien with. In the ways hast thou sat for them, as the Arabian in the wilderness; and thou hast polluted the land with thy whoredoms and with thy wickedness. Therefore the showers have been withholden, and there hath been no latter rain; and thou hadst a whore's forehead, thou refusedst to be ashamed. Wilt thou not from this time cry unto me, My Father, thou art the guide of my youth?*

Jeremiah 2:7-9 *And I brought you into a plentiful country, to eat the fruit thereof and the goodness thereof; but when ye entered; ye defiled My Land, and made Mine heritage an abomination. The Priests said not, Where is the LORD? And they that handle the Law knew Me not; the Pastors also transgressed against Me, and the Prophets prophesied by Ba'al, and walked after things that do not profit. Wherefore I will yet plead with you, saith the LORD, and with your children's children will I plead.*

These were very strong words from the LORD. The test in the Holy Temple was astonishing really *because the ancestors of the Scribes and Pharisees had played the harlot against the LORD.* Then the Scribes and Pharisee's brought a harlot to the LORD Yeshua, accusing her of being caught in adultery, saying that she was caught in the very act! This was total hypocrisy since their own ancestors had been caught in the very act while playing the harlot against Him! It was all so hypocritical and they were immediately convicted in their hearts. After the miracles, signs, and wonders that the LORD performed in the midst of the children of Israel, they had turned from Him. After all the miracles of the LORD that Yeshua was performing before their eyes, they were refusing to believe in Him. Even though the LORD had revealed Himself to their ancestor's, they began worshipping false gods instead of worshipping the one and only true Living God. *She had a whore's forehead because the Word of God in her mind had been polluted.*

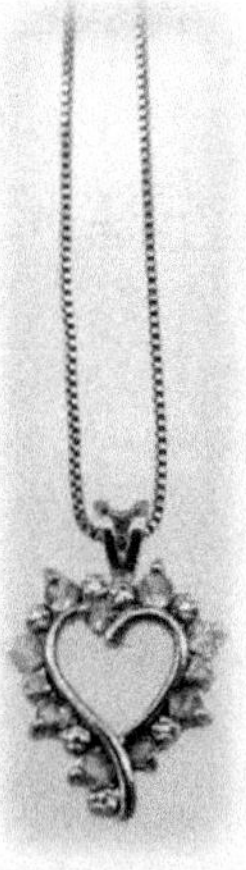

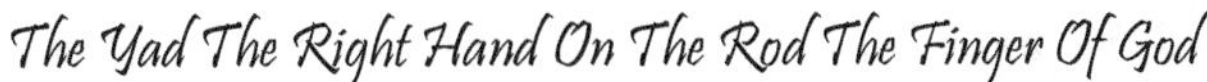

Now when the Scribes and Pharisee's brought the harlot before Messiah Yeshua and they were condemning her for playing the harlot, they thought that she should die for this sin. This harlot was standing before *the Rod of God and the very finger of God who had written this Law on tablets of stone*, and she was being condemned by these hypocrites. *When Yeshua stooped down and wrote on the ground with His finger, He was writing "the Word of God" on the ground, upon stone! He stood up again and told them, "Whoever among you is without sin, to let him cast the first stone at her."* At once, they were astonished and convicted in their hearts! The Scribes and Pharisees knew that their ancestors had been given the Commandments of God, written by the LORD'S own finger in stone and yet they had gone against them. One by one they left, older ones first, because they knew the history of their ancestors who had paid the price in Babylon for seventy years for playing *the harlot* against the LORD. They also paid the very high price of their Holy Temple being destroyed because they had turned away from God. The older ones were the first to be convicted in their hearts. The truly interesting part of this story is that the LORD could have condemned His people for playing *the harlot* against Him. The LORD could have given them a death sentence, like the one they were about to meter out to this harlot. Instead of total condemnation and death, the LORD was forgiving and merciful to their ancestors. *The loving LORD God exiled His wife and then He brought His beloved wife back to Him hoping she would love Him! Yeshua told this harlot to go and sin no more.* This is exactly the same message that the LORD gave to Israel when they were allowed to return from their captivity in Babylon! *They were to go back to Jerusalem and sin no more!* The LORD also expected the Scribes and Pharisees, who were the descendants of the Babylonian exiles, to go and sin no more against the LORD! The LORD required that His people return to Him in repentance, to never sin against Him again. *The LORD wanted Israel's total love and devotion to Himself.* This Temple test proves that even though we sin, if we turn from sinning against the LORD and return to Him with all our heart, He will forgive us.

Yeshua was basically telling the Scribe's and Pharisee's that they had been shown *mercy*. They were the ones that had been given the Law of God directly by Moses. They realized at that moment that perhaps their ancestor's should have died, but just as the LORD did not condemn them for playing *the harlot* against Him, so He did not condemn this harlot who was cast before Him for condemnation. The LORD was demonstrating to them that He had shown their ancestor's this mercy, after they were punished. The LORD did restore and forgive Israel for her sins. What is truly interesting, though, is that Israel's punishment for playing *the harlot*, with the idols and gods of Babylon, was their exile of seventy years in Babylon living with *"the Mother of harlots"* because they were worshipping the pagan gods of Babylon on every high hill in the Land of Israel. The LORD'S judgment was righteous, as He gave them a long dose of what they wanted! He basically said, *"Ok, if you want to worship "the Mother of harlots" and all the pagan gods of Babylon, then I will send you to live among these abominations!"* When the LORD saw how much they enjoyed playing *the harlot,* He gave them over to their desire. So this is a very interesting judgment because suddenly Israel was in Babylon and they were forced to cling to the LORD God of Israel, as they grieved for the Holy Temple of the LORD in Jerusalem! After seventy long years of yearning for the LORD while desperately praying to be restored and returned to Jerusalem, the LORD finally allowed them to return from their captivity and they were released from *"the Mother of harlots."* After their punishment and return, the LORD allowed the Holy Temple in Jerusalem to be rebuilt and dedicated again to the one true God of Israel. Even after all that happened, we find later on, in the book of Jeremiah, that the LORD had mercy upon His people and He still loves them with all His heart. *God brought them into "Israel."* So you see, there are no *"Land for peace"* deals here *because the LORD said that this Land belongs to Him and He gave it to Israel as an inheritance forever.* The LORD God declared it! Now we should heed this truth or face the Divine judgment of God!

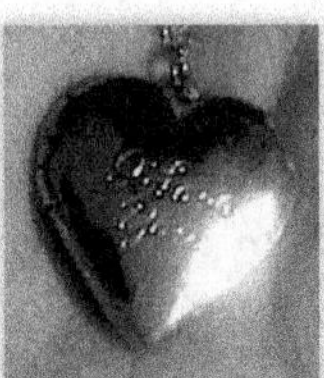
Heart Photo ©2013 Kimberly K Ballard All Rights Reserved

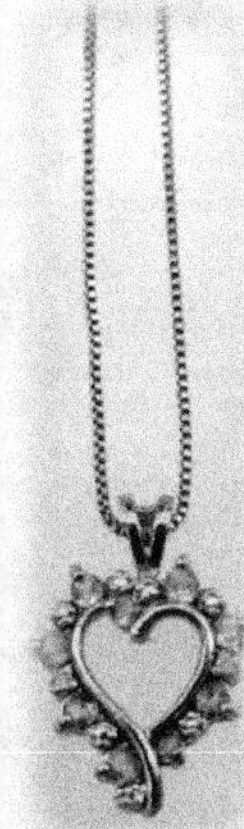

Jeremiah 3:18 *In those days the House of Judah shall walk with the House of Israel, and they shall come together out of the land of the north to the Land that I have given for an inheritance unto your fathers.*

The LORD clearly states that He will gather His people into the Land that they have been given, by Him, as an inheritance. This is the Land of Israel. Anyone who denies this truth is in total opposition to the LORD and to *the Word of God.*

Now one question that remains is what did Yeshua write with His finger on the ground when the harlot was brought before Him? Perhaps He wrote the very Commandment that He wrote with His finger on the tablets of stone on Mount Sinai before Moses. Perhaps Messiah Yeshua's finger wrote the Words, *"Thou shalt not commit adultery!" No, I believe, however, that Yeshua wrote the greatest Commandment of all with His finger, "The Shema," so they would understand His Eternal love for them! Yeshua wrote, "Hear O Israel, the LORD your God is one, and you shall love the LORD your God with all your heart and with all your soul and with all your might!"*

Matthew 22:36-38 *Master, which is the great Commandment in the Law? Yeshua said unto him, Thou shalt love the LORD thy God with all thy heart, and with all thy soul, and with all thy mind. This is the first and great Commandment.*

The Jews in the Holy Temple saw Yeshua *writing this love message from Him* on the ground in the Holy Temple with His finger. Suddenly their memories were refreshed and they were emotionally affected within their hearts. So they departed without casting a single stone against the harlot. *They were trying to test the LORD, but instead He tested them within their hearts, as their Rabbi of Righteousness, as He wrote with His finger on the ground on the stone in the Holy Temple of the LORD!* This is stunning! *He wanted them to love Him with all their hearts and to return to Him!* When Yeshua was here, He repeatedly told us to follow *"His Commandments."* Yeshua's finger did not pronounce judgment upon this woman because the LORD said that He is forgiving and will forgive wickedness, rebellion, and sin, as long as true repentance comes from the heart and the person never returns to commit evil or live in it. When we love Him, He manifests Himself to us, and He shows us His heart!

The Shema written in the snow on the pavement on a Snow heart
Photos ©2014 Kimberly K Ballard All Rights Reserved

John 14:15-21 *If ye love Me, keep My Commandments. And I will pray the Father and He shall give you another Comforter, that he may abide with you forever; Even the Spirit of truth; whom the world cannot receive, because it seeth Him not, neither knoweth Him; but ye know Him; for He dwelleth with you, and shall be in you. I will not leave you comfortless; I will come to you. Yet a little while, and the world seeth Me no more; but ye see Me; because I live, ye shall live also. At that day ye shall know that I AM in My Father, and ye in Me, and I in you. He*

that hath My Commandments, and keepeth them, he it is that loveth Me; and he that loveth Me shall be loved of My Father, and I will love him, and will manifest Myself to him.

Yeshua, *the Yad of God,* sealed *His Commandments and Covenant* upon the tablets of our heart forever, so we would love Him Eternally as His Bride! I believe, with astonishment, that the Scribes and Pharisee's understood something incredible was happening the moment that they saw Yeshua writing on the ground on stone with His finger in the Holy Temple of God in Jerusalem. When they *saw this sign and the message of love from the Shema,* they knew immediately He was the Yad of God and they knew their ancestors were guilty of betraying the LORD, so they could no longer condemn this harlot. The Temple test is a demonstration, showing us that the LORD is a merciful God, who does not wish for any to perish, but for all people to return to Him and completely love Him in holiness and truth because He loves us so much! The depth of His love for us cannot be measured!

John 3:16 *For God so loved the world, that He gave His only begotten Son, that whosoever believeth in Him should not perish, but have everlasting life.*

This Temple test is actually a Rabbinical lesson for Israel today, teaching them to return to the God of Israel, *Messiah the KING,* with all their hearts and to love Him only! He is the Bridegroom of Israel who is always drawing Israel back to His own heart. He draws everyone in the world who loves Him back to Himself, allowing us to love Him forever. This is such a beautiful truth and merciful blessing from the LORD God. Let me be the first to say, *"I love you KING Yeshua with all my heart!"*

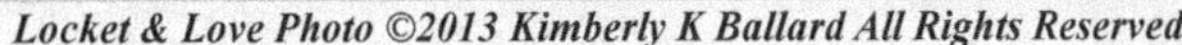

Locket & Love Photo ©2013 Kimberly K Ballard All Rights Reserved

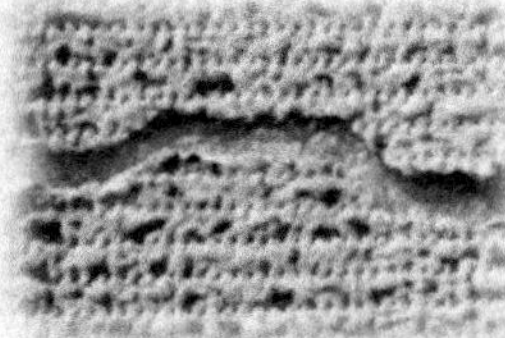

THE SIGNATURE OF THE HAND OF THE LORD TO MAKE CLEFT

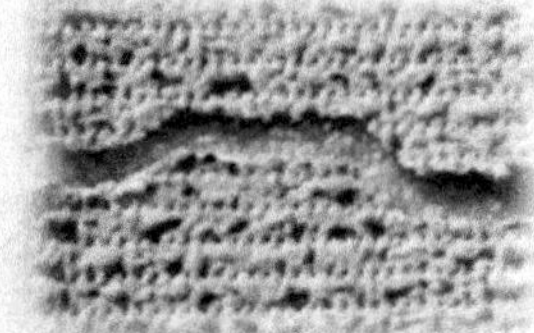

The Yad of God, with His finger, signs and seals the signature of God upon all His Divine works, as the Yad writes the Word of God. The Divine signature is to make things cleft. This Divine signature should also be apparent in the mighty works of Messiah Yeshua, as the hand that seals us with His Holy Spirit.

Ephesians 4:30 *And grieve not the Holy Spirit of God, whereby ye are sealed unto the day of redemption.*

When the LORD revealed His signature to us, this allowed us to clearly identify His works, so there would be no doubt that He is the LORD of Hosts performing the miracles. When we see this sign, we must pay attention to it, and when He tells us to honour and remember Him by making something cleft, we must not ignore His sign. We must focus on it, as we come to understand the deep significance of it.

In the book of Psalms, we find that the LORD'S voice, speaking with His Holy Spirit of fire, makes the flames cleft, which is the sword of His mouth, *the Living Torah.*

Psalm 29:7 *The voice of the LORD divideth the flames of fire.*

The signature of the hand of God Photo ©2014 Kimberly K Ballard All Rights Reserved

Remember that on Shavuot, the LORD'S Feast of Weeks which is Pentecost, when the Jewish disciples tarried in Jerusalem until they were endued with power from on high from the Holy Spirit of God, the cleft tongues of fire descended upon them. This was perhaps actually the powerful voice of God resting upon them.

II Samuel 22:14 *The LORD thundered from Heaven, and the most High uttered His voice.*

Acts 2:1-5 *And when the day of Pentecost was fully come, they were all in one accord in one place. Suddenly there came a sound from Heaven as of a rushing mighty wind, and it filled all the house where they were sitting. And there appeared unto them cloven tongues like as of fire, and it sat upon each of them. And they were all filled with the Holy Spirit, and began to speak with other tongues, as the Spirit gave them utterance. And there were dwelling at Jerusalem Jews, devout men, out of every Nation under Heaven.*

The definition of *"cleave"* reveals Messianic facts that are remarkable pertaining to Yeshua.

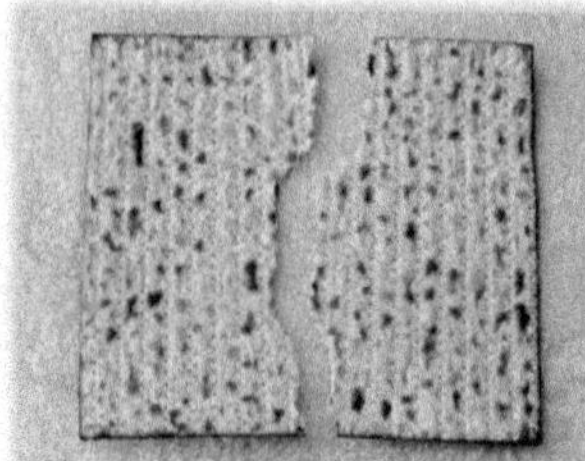

Broken cleft Matzah Photo ©2013 Kimberly K Ballard All Rights Reserved

Cleave, cleft, cleaved, cloven, cleaving.
1. To split or divide by or as by a cutting blow, esp. along a natural line of division, as the grain of wood.
2. To make by or as by cutting: to cleave as path through the wilderness.
3. To cut off; sever; to cleave a branch from a tree.
4. To part or split, esp. along a natural line of division.
5. To penetrate or advance by or as by cutting; To cleave through the water. **(Source: Definition from the Random House College Dictionary, revised edition 1975 Copyright ©1975 By Random House, Inc.).**

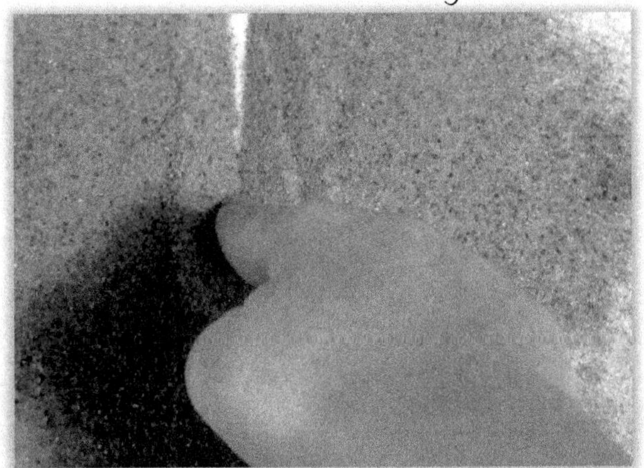

Making the sand cleft Photo ©2014 Kimberly K Ballard All Rights Reserved

In definition #3 of the word *"cleave,"* we can clearly see that the Rod of God, *the Branch Messiah Yeshua,* would indeed be *"cut off"* from the Almond Tree of Life, *as the Limb and the Arm of God.* So clearly we can see that the Messiah reveals the signature of God. The Rod of God lifted up, that made the waters cleft, is evident in definition #5. The Rod of God made a pathway through the wilderness, in definition #2. In order for the Messiah to fulfill the Word of God, He absolutely had to be *cut off* in this manner, *as the Branch,* in order to be the cleft work of the signature of God.

Now it is interesting that the LORD told us that all the clean animals that had *cloven* hooves, were for our food.

Deuteronomy 14:6 *And every beast that parteth the hoof, and cleaveth the cleft into two claws, and cheweth the cud among the beasts, that ye shall eat.*

Remember that the Jewish disciples recognized Messiah Yeshua the LORD in *the breaking* of bread when He appeared to them after His resurrection and ate bread with them! This happened as they sat down at *"meat."*

Broken Matzah & Gold cup Photo ©2014 Kimberly K Ballard All Rights Reserved

Luke 24:30-35 *And it came to pass, as He sat at meat with them, He took bread, and blessed it, and brake, and gave to them. And their eyes were opened, and they knew Him; and He vanished out of their sight. And they said one to another; Did not our heart burn within us, while He talked with us by the way, and while He opened to us the Scriptures? And they rose up the same hour, and returned to Jerusalem, and found the eleven gathered together, and them that were with them, saying The LORD is risen indeed, and hath appeared to Simon. And they told what things were done in the way, and how He was known of them in breaking of bread.*

Yeshua is the *kosher,* pure, cleft meat of the Passover Lamb of God that we are to eat as our meat, *as the Living Torah!* In the definition of the word *"meat,"* we find that it is defined as *"the edible part of a fruit or nut, or the flesh of animals."* Another definition of the word *"meat"* is *"the essential point or part; gist; crux."* By definition, *"crux"* means *"a cross!"* It is defined as *"something that torments by its puzzling nature and a basic or decisive point."* **(Source: Random House College Dictionary, revised edition ©1975 Random House, Inc.).**

The, *"decisive point,"* refers to *"having the power or quality of determining; putting an end to controversy." So Yeshua's power put an end to the controversy of whether or not we could have Eternal life.* The true Unleavened Bread from Heaven, *the pure meat* that was nailed to the cross, *"the crux,"* was *the decisive point* in the history of mankind for all flesh. *Inside Holy Mount Moriah, the true meat from the Almond Tree of Life literally came out of God's Garden on the Feast of First Fruits to give us the Living Bread from Heaven so that we may eat this fruit and never die.*

John 6:51 *I AM the Living Bread which came down from Heaven; if any man eat of this bread, he shall live forever; and the bread that I will give is My flesh, which I will give for the life of the world.*

THE STAFF OF LIFE THE BREAD OF HEAVEN IS CLEFT

Broken or cleft Matzah on Gold Cup
Almond Branch
Photos ©2013 Kimberly K Ballard

Now that it is perfectly clear that *Yeshua is the cleft Branch from the Almond Tree of Life,* is there more to the mystery of Yeshua calling Himself *"the Bread that came down from Heaven"?* The exciting truth is yes, because *the Rod* is also called, *"The Staff of Life!"*

For centuries, bread has always been known as *"the Staff of Life."* This gives us a vivid picture of *Messiah Yeshua as the raised up "Staff of Life!"*

In Psalm 23, David prophesied and wrote about Messiah the LORD when he declared, *"Thy Rod and Thy Staff, they comfort me."* The hope of having Eternal life through *the raised up Staff of Life* is a great promise of hope because the Rod of God put an end to the contention between God and human flesh, and now we can have Eternal Life because the LORD fulfilled His Testimony with us.

In ancient times, bread contained all the vital nutrients and minerals to sustain life, and *Yeshua is the Living Torah that is our sustaining life.* The Good Shepherd feeds His flock with *the meat from His hand!* When *the Living Torah speaks,* He raises us up from death to life, and this is the comfort of the Rod and Staff of God.

Now I have to point out something that is extremely important. The unleavened bread of Messiah Yeshua was never supposed to be eaten as a whole wafer! *The unleavened bread that the Jewish Messiah instructed us to eat was always made cleft by Him, thus symbolizing that it was the signature of God's work. Yeshua instructed us* to *break the unleavened bread, the Matzah, when we partake of the Jewish Passover Seder.* This is also how we know whether or not we are taking the LORD'S Passover in the proper manner. This is such a significant part of the LORD'S Testimony. So we should follow the LORD'S instructions exactly when we remember Him in His Divine Testimony. Yeshua said that anyone who comes to Him, He will in no wise cast out. This signature or sign of *breaking* the bread represents the power of the Rod of God parting the Red Sea and thus saving Israel and that He saves us. Yeshua also instructed us to take and eat His unleavened bread, *"in a worthy manner,"* which means there is no other way of eating the LORD'S unleavened bread that represents the God of Israel. By making the unleavened bread *cleft,* this testifies that *Messiah Yeshua is the cleft Branch that was cut off from the Almond Tree of Life.* This testifies that He is the *clean meat* of the Lamb, *the Word of God from Heaven that* we are to eat. This cleft unleavened bread represents the fact that Messiah Yeshua had no leaven or sin *as the pure Living Torah from Heaven.* This sign signifies the hidden manna in the LORD'S Living Testimony that dwells in the Heavenly Ark of God. Yeshua never did His work in any other way.

The Messiah's true communion is therefore, found within the Jewish Passover Seder, in the cleft Matzah! Yeshua is remembered in the third cup, the cup of Redemption, which is *the sign of the life blood of His Living Covenant of the heart,* because Yeshua was the First Fruit of salvation and the grapes of this wine came from God's Garden on Holy Mount Moriah.

I Corinthians 11:23-29 *For I have received of the LORD that which also I delivered unto you, that the LORD Yeshua the same night in which he was betrayed took bread; And when He had given thanks, He brake it, and said, Take, eat; this is My body, which is broken for you; this do in remembrance of Me. After the same manner also He took the cup, when He had supped, saying, This cup is the New Testament in My blood; this do ye, as oft as ye drink it, in remembrance of Me. For as often as ye eat this bread, and drink this cup, ye do shew the LORD'S death till He come. Wherefore whosoever shall eat this bread, and drink this cup of the LORD, unworthily, shall be guilty of the body and blood of the LORD. But let a man examine himself, and so let him eat of that bread, and drink of that cup. For he that eateth and drinketh unworthily, eateth and drinketh damnation to himself, not discerning the LORD'S body.*

So it is true that there was never a single instance of Messiah Yeshua eating a whole wafer or an unbroken cracker because this does not represent the work of the LORD God of Israel. *I believe that the LORD'S signature must be visible upon His communion.* Also, it would be utterly wrong for us to use any type of bread that is full of leaven for the communion service! *Yeshua had no sin, so only the unleavened bread of the Passover is the bread that truly represents Him.* One should never eat the Passover Matzah of the Messiah *without breaking it first because the Branch was broken for us and was made cleft from the Almond Tree of Life!* If you think about it, a whole piece of bread (with yeast) or a whole unbroken wafer would likely be considered unclean, simply because it does not represent the LORD'S Divine works or reveal His Living Testimony. I believe that this is what Yeshua was telling us when He said, *"Do not eat the Passover in an unworthy manner."* We were told to follow Yeshua's example exactly *because it is the sign and signature of the Testimony of the LORD.* As I pondered the Apostle Paul's words that declare that those who take this bread and wine in an unworthy manner bring damnation upon themselves, I discovered something interesting about the KING when I looked up the definition of the words *"unworthy," or "unworthily."*

Unworthy; *Of a kind not worthy. Lacking worth or excellence. Not commendable or creditable. Not of adequate merit or character. Beneath the dignity, (usually fol. by of) behavior unworthy of a King.* **(Source: Random House College Dictionary, revised edition ©1975 Random House, Inc.).**

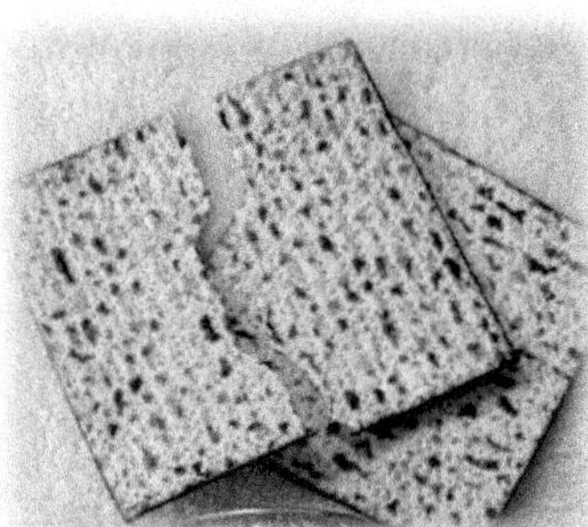

Cleft broken Matzah of Passover
Photo ©2013 Kimberly K Ballard

Yeshua is the KING OF KINGS AND LORD OF LORDS. So when one does not make cleft His unleavened bread, this would be *"of a kind that is not worthy." This is a kind that is beneath the dignity of the Great KING!* If it does not reveal His Divine character, then it would *have no commendable or creditable application.* The cleaving of the bread is a significant visual mark or symbol of the LORD. The KING of KINGS is pure and holy, so we must give the LORD the Highest possible degree of acknowledgement, praise, respect, and honour for His Divine Eternal glorious Living Testimony. Even earthly Monarch's require this dignity in their kingdoms!

The definition of the word *"character"* means *"a significant visual mark or symbol, to engrave or inscribe, graving tool, its mark. Moral qualities, ethical standards, principles and the like."* **(Source: Random House College Dictionary, revised ed. ©1975 Random House, Inc.).**

If anyone has been misguided to partake of a kind not worthy out of ignorance through a lack of true understanding, or has partaken of a kind that does not represent the LORD God of Israel, who was broken for us, then it is important to realize the true meaning of it now and repent with all your heart before the LORD. God looks upon the heart in mercy. Now that we know the truth, we should remember the LORD in the correct manner at the Passover Seder table. The Bible says that if anyone brings to you another Gospel or Yeshua, other than the one preached in the Gospels, *"Let them be accursed."* Do not allow the Jewishness of our Messiah to be removed from Him!

Galatians 1:6-12 *I marvel that ye are so soon removed from him that called you into the grace of Messiah unto another gospel; Which is not another; but there be some that trouble you, and would pervert the gospel of Messiah. But though we, or an angel from Heaven, preach any other gospel unto you than that which we have preached unto you, let him be accursed. For do I now persuade men, or God? Or do I seek to please men? For if I yet pleased men, I should not be the servant of Messiah. But I certify you, brethren, that the gospel which was preached of me is not after man. For I neither received it of man, neither was I taught it, but by the revelation of Yeshua Messiah.*

The Apostle Paul proclaims that He did not receive this gospel from men, but He was given the Divine revelation by Messiah Yeshua Himself! Remember also that *"Ishtar"* was one of the reasons that the LORD judged Jerusalem. Yeshua was historically and truthfully resurrected three days after Passover on Nisan 17 on the holiday known as the Jewish *"Feast of First Fruits"* on the Biblical Jewish calendar. We should celebrate Yeshua's resurrection by the title, *"The Feast of First Fruits!"* We must return to the origins of the truth and learn the true Jewish appointed days of the Jewish Messiah because the LORD fulfilled them Himself. The Rod of God made the sea cleft in order to save Israel that day! Messiah made the bread cleft in order to save Israel that day and then when He was broken and lifted up for our salvation, He saved us that day! *So the Jewish Apostle's continued to break bread!*

Acts 2:42-43 *And they continued steadfastly in the Apostle's doctrine and fellowship, and in breaking of bread, and in prayers. And fear came upon every soul; and many signs were done by the Apostle's.*

The Feast of Shavuot or Pentecost, written in Leviticus 23, is *the day of offering a new meat offering unto the LORD!* Therefore, Messiah Yeshua, *the Living Torah,* sent His Holy Spirit to His Jewish disciples on *the day of the new meat offering!* It is incredible because *He is the Living Torah, the true meat!* Yeshua, the Lamb, without spot or blemish, was offered as *the new meat offering* on this day in Heaven.

Leviticus 23:15-16 *And ye shall count unto you from the morrow after the Sabbath, from the day that ye brought the sheaf of the wave offering; seven Sabbaths shall be complete; Even unto the morrow after the seventh Sabbath shall ye number fifty days; and ye shall offer a new meat offering unto the LORD.*

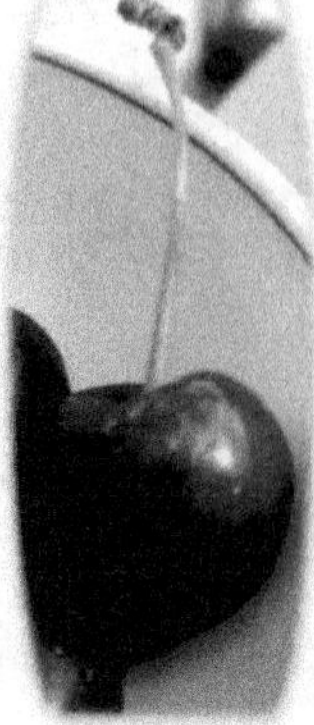

Let us always remember Messiah Yeshua at the right time and in the right way that honours the majesty, glory, and dignity of the Great KING for His mighty works are astounding! Happy Feast of First Fruits, He is risen!

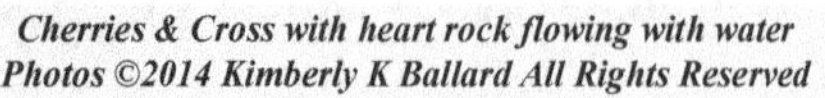
Cherries & Cross with heart rock flowing with water

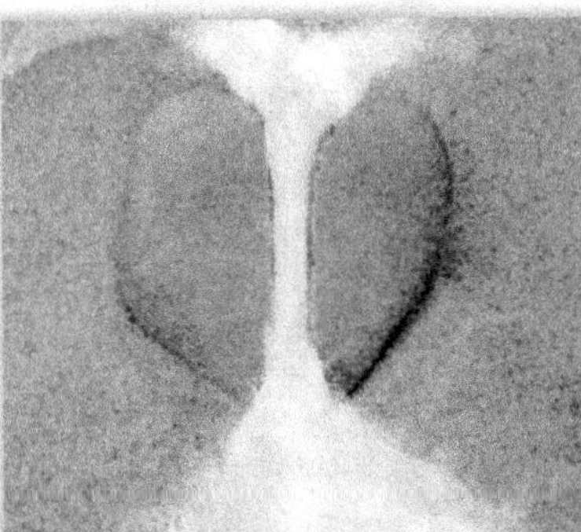
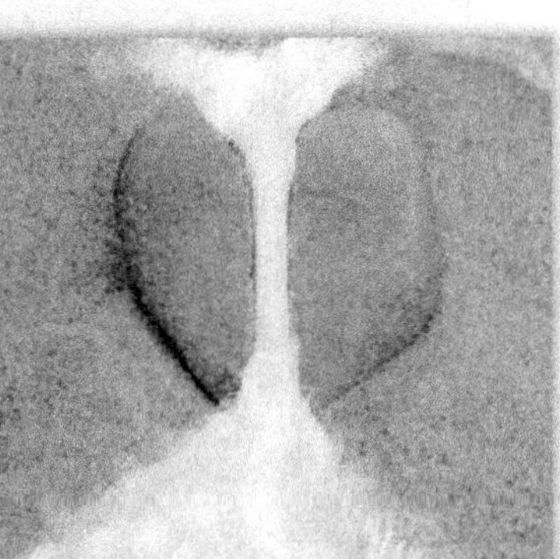

THE CLEFT ROCK IN HOREB THE HEART AND THE LIVING WATER

Living Water flowing through the heart not the rock!

In the wilderness, the Israelites murmured because they were thirsty, so the LORD provided water in abundance for them to drink to quench their thirst. The LORD told Moses to strike the rock with the rod in his hand. It was made *cleft* in the middle and living water gushed out for people to drink, *and on either side of the gushing water, there was a tablet of stone* (Numbers 20:11, Psalm 78:20, Exodus 17:6). I have already shown how this describes the human heart and represents the Tefillin containing the Word of God with *the Rod of God in the middle of it.* The Rod of God is the Rock Messiah, and the Living Water flows out from Him. Remember that as the LORD gives us life, the life blood that contains the plasma of the heart that is 92% living water gushes up the main vein of the heart in the middle. It pumps the *life blood* into the two tablets of the heart on either side. *As I stated before, the cleft rock at Horeb is a symbol of the heart and specifically God's heart!* When Moses stood in the cleft of this rock in Horeb, the LORD covered him with his Yad and His glory passed by. *The LORD was symbolically placing Moses in the middle of his heart for protection and the Yad of God covered him with salvation (Yeshua) so that the full glory of the LORD would not kill him as it passed by!* It symbolizes Messiah Yeshua's Living Covenant of the heart that is written on two tablets of tender flesh, rather than on hard stone. In the beginning, it grieved the LORD when mankind hardened his heart toward God, and the whole process of our salvation by the Yad of God was designed to send the Rod Messiah to us to remove this hardness of our hearts, so we would once again soften our hearts to love God. *Now we know this is the true circumcision, when the LORD takes away our stony hearts in the wilderness and He writes His Living Torah Covenant upon our hearts for Eternal life in His Heavenly Garden on Holy Mount Moriah, which is freedom from Sinai's stony bondage. Yeshua, the Rock and the Rod lifted up on the cross, was struck with the Roman lance. As the Living Water and life blood gushed out from the heart of the LORD God and fell onto the ground on Holy Mount Moriah, we would never thirst again for the LORD!*

John 19:33-35 *But when they came to Yeshua, and saw that He was dead already, they break not His legs; But one of the soldiers with a spear pierced His side, and forthwith came there out blood and water. And he that saw it bare record, and his record is true; and he knoweth that he saith true, that ye might believe.*

John 18:22-23 *And when He had thus spoken, one of the officers which stood by struck Yeshua with the palm of his hand, saying, Answerest Thou the High Priest so? Yeshua answered him, If I have spoken evil, bear witness of the evil; but if well, why smitest thou Me?*

I must come back to add here that the real rock of Horeb that was discovered by Jim & Penny Caldwell and their children in 1992 in Arabia, is also elevated and lifted up! This is a perfect picture of Messiah Yeshua, the Rock, who was elevated and lifted up to fulfill all righteousness of the Law and the Prophets as the final Testimony of the LORD in the Heavenly Ark. Moses struck the rock in Horeb so the people could drink the living water that flowed out

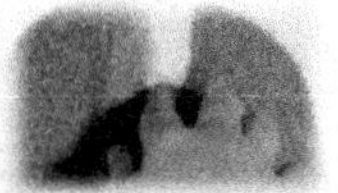

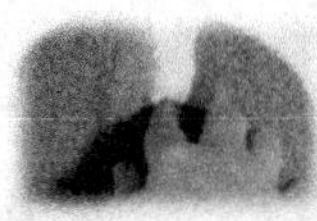

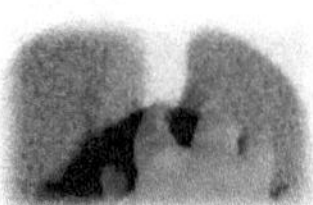

from it in great abundance. *I was shocked, though, when the LORD showed me that Yeshua, the Rod of God, was actually standing on top of this rock in Horeb with His feet (Exodus 17:6), and then I knew it was the power of God's Rod that made the rock underneath His feet cleft, so that Living Water came gushing out like rivers of Living Water from Him!* Moses stood down below at the base of this rock before the LORD and he hastily smote the rock with the earthly copy of the rod in his hand, because the people were scolding him, *but the LORD was actually standing above him on top of the rock in Horeb and the Rod of God split the rock under His feet, so the people of Israel could drink.* The *power* therefore, did not come from the rod of Moses and Aaron. The power came from Messiah, *the Rod of God, standing on the rock!* This is exactly how the Rod made the Red Sea cleft as the Rod carved a pathway in the middle, creating a wall of water on the right and on the left. It is rumored that maybe Moses, who struck the rock twice because he was not patient for the LORD, may have struck the rock once horizontally and once vertically with his rod, thereby making the shape of the Hebrew letter Tav, a signature mark that stood for *"the Covenant of Truth." It was the sign of the cross, but the LORD, the Heavenly Rod, only split the rock once under His feet!* Moses did not cross into the earthly Promised Land because of this incident. He went directing into Heaven!

Exodus 17:1-6 *And all the congregation of the children of Israel journeyed from the wilderness of Sin, after their journeys, according to the commandment of the LORD, and pitched in Rephidim; and there was no water for the people to drink. Wherefore the people did chide with Moses, and said, Give us water that we may drink. And Moses said unto them, Why chide ye with me? Wherefore do ye tempt the LORD? And the people thirsted there for water; and the people murmured against Moses, and said, Wherefore is this that thou hast brought us up out of Egypt, to kill us and our children and our cattle with thirst? And Moses cried unto the LORD, saying, What shall I do unto this people? They be almost ready to stone me. And the LORD said unto Moses, Go on before the people, and take with thee of the elders of Israel; and thy rod, wherewith thou smotest the river, take in thine hand, and go. <u>Behold, I will stand before thee there upon the rock in Horeb</u>; and thou shalt smite the rock, and there shall come water out of it that the people may drink. And Moses did so in the sight of the elders of Israel.*

Water from the rock Photo ©2014 Kimberly K Ballard All Rights Reserved

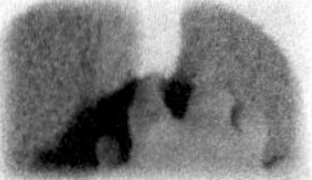

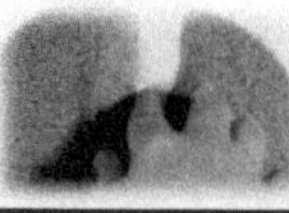

The Heart of flesh is like the cleft rock at Horeb
One heart is soft and the other is hard like a flinty rock
The LORD is the refreshing rain that takes away the hard heart of a person
and He turns it into a loving heart of tenderness

II Corinthians 3:3 *Forasmuch as ye are manifestly declared to be the epistle of Messiah ministered by us, written not with ink, but with the Spirit of the living God; not in tablets of stone, but in fleshy tablets of the heart.*

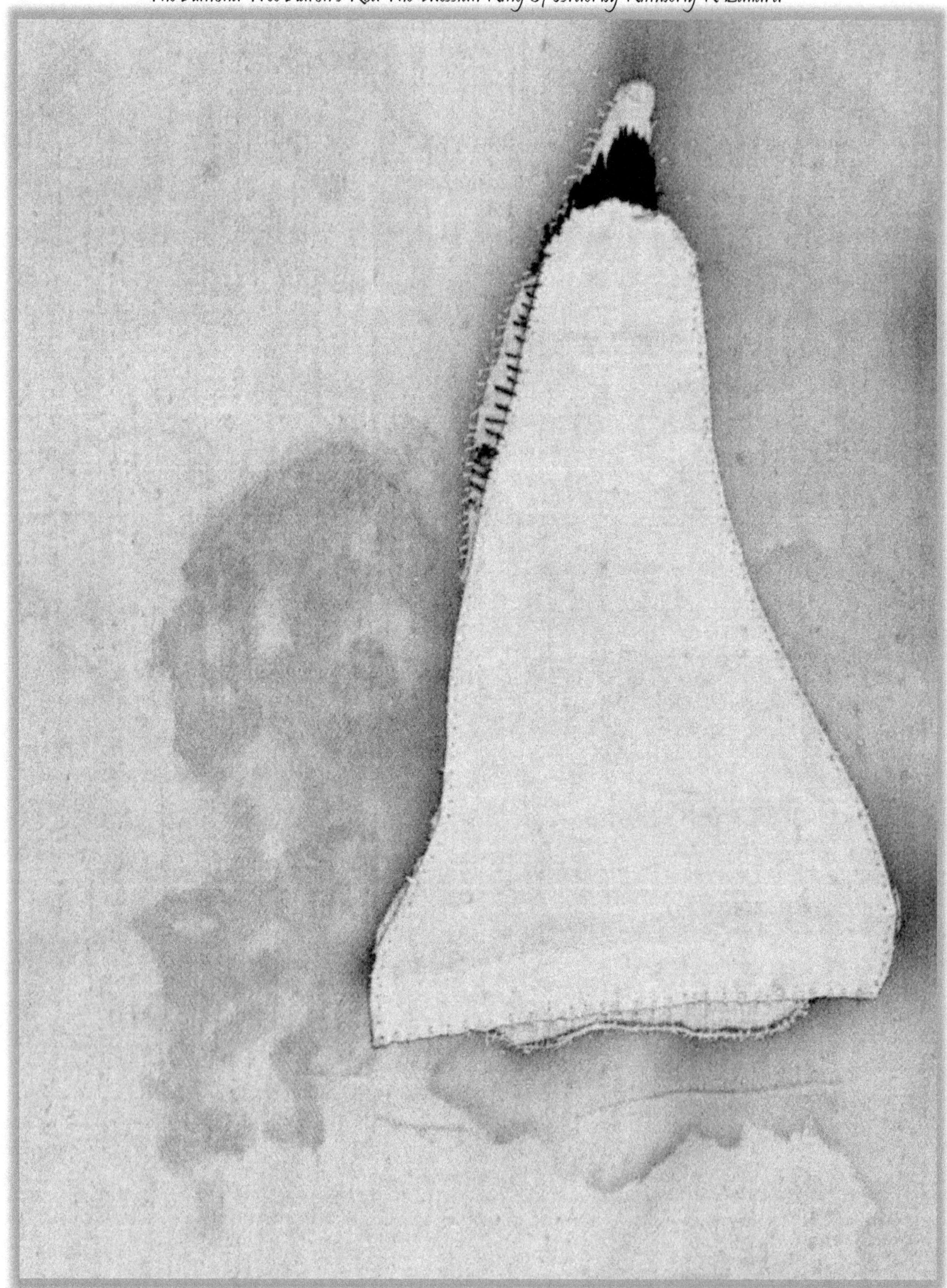

The Living Water & Life blood came out of "The Rock" Messiah's tender heart to give us Eternal Life!

The Official Split Rock of Horeb
discovered near Mount Sinai in Arabia
By Jim & Penny Caldwell

Edited to Black & White Photo
by KK Ballard with permission

The Living Water came out of the Rock in Horeb
when the LORD stood on the top of this rock with His feet.
He was demonstrating His tender loving heart that gives us life!
The hardness of the heart is like this rock in the wilderness.

As the powerful Rod of God stood on top of this rock in Horeb and made the rock cleft, the people were not only drinking living water, *but they were also drinking from the Spiritual Rock, the Messiah, who is the Word of God, the Living Torah. The Rod of God was their Living Water, Spiritual Bread, and meat in the wilderness.*

I Corinthians 10:1-4 *For I do not want you to be unaware, brethren, that our fathers were all under the cloud, and all passed through the sea; and all were baptized into Moses in the cloud and in the sea; and all drank the same spiritual food; and all drank the same spiritual drink, for they were drinking from a Spiritual Rock which followed them; and the Rock was Messiah.*

Psalm 78:15-20 *He split the rocks in the wilderness, and gave them abundant drink like the ocean depths. He brought forth streams also from the rock, and caused waters to run down like rivers. Yet they still continued to sin against Him, To rebel against the Most High in the desert, And in their heart they put God to the test by asking food according to their desire. Then they spoke against God; they said, Can God prepare a table in the wilderness? Behold, He struck the rock, so that waters gushed out, and streams were overflowing; Can He give bread also? Will He provide meat for His people?*

Example: Living Water River gushing between the rocks Boulder Falls Colorado Photo ©2013 Kimberly K Ballard All Rights Reserved

This reminds me of Satan tempting Yeshua in the wilderness, asking Him to turn the stones into bread if He was truly the Son of God. *Moses was told to speak to the Rock who was standing on top of the rock, so that **the Rod of God** would cause the waters to come forth as the LORD made it cleft before Him and all the people of Israel.* In the Numbers passage it says, *"It shall give forth His water," as Moses spoke to the Rock!* In other words, the LORD was the Rock of Living Water he was speaking to!

Numbers 20:7-11 *And the LORD spake unto Moses, saying, Take the rod, and gather thou the assembly together, thou, and Aaron thy brother, and speak ye unto the rock before their eyes; and it shall give forth His water, and thou shalt bring forth to them water out of the rock; so thou shalt give the congregation and their beasts drink. And Moses took the rod from before the LORD, as he commanded him. And Moses and Aaron gathered the congregation together before the rock, and he said unto them, Hear now, ye rebels; must we fetch you water out of this rock? And Moses lifted up his hand, and with his rod he smote the rock twice; and the water came out abundantly, and the congregation drank, and their beasts also.*

In creation, the LORD also made the earth cleft with rivers of living water, by His Word!

Habakkuk 3:8-9 *Was the LORD displeased against the rivers? Was Thy wrath against the sea, that Thou didst ride upon Thine horses and Thy chariots of salvation? Thy bow was made quite naked, according to the oaths of the tribes, even Thy Word. Se'lah. Thou didst cleave the earth with rivers.*

At the Rock of Horeb, the LORD also gave Living Water for the animals to drink to quench their thirst in the wilderness. This reveals that they will also drink *the Living Water* of the LORD, when His Eternal Kingdom comes. It comforts me knowing just how much the LORD cares for His beautiful animals, birds, and entire creation. He supplies all their needs and refreshes them, too. The LORD was so kind hearted that He saved the animals and birds in the Ark of Noah. *As the Living Ark,* He will also deliver the animals, birds, and all creation from the curse of Adam. Every living thing that was first created in the Garden of Eden will be brought into the glorious liberty of the children of God, into the Eternal Garden. The animals and birds will dwell with us. This is so comforting and it is such a peaceful, beautiful picture of paradise! The next Scripture in the book of Romans is one of my favorite verses concerning this. It comforted my heart, when my beloved cat Jasmine, passed away after 18 years and 4 months. He spent half my life with me! I had such great joy in my heart knowing that I have a promise from the LORD in this Scripture that one day we will be reunited in the Heavenly Kingdom of God. The LORD made all the precious animals and birds for His Divine pleasure.

Romans 8:18-23 *For I reckon that the sufferings of this present time are not worthy to be compared with the glory which shall be revealed in us. For the earnest expectation of the creature waiteth for the manifestation of the sons of God. For the creature was made subject to vanity, not willingly, but by reason of him who hath subjected the same in hope. Because the creature itself also shall be delivered from the bondage of corruption into the glorious liberty of the children of God. For we know that the whole creation groaneth and travaileth in pain together until now. And not only they, but ourselves also, which have the first fruits of the Spirit, even we ourselves groan within ourselves, waiting for the adoption, to wit, the redemption of our body.*

Yeshua told the Samaritan woman at Jacob's well that the water He would give her, would be in her a well of water springing up to Eternal life.

John 4:13-14 *Yeshua answered and said unto her, Whosoever drinketh of this water shall thirst again; But whosoever drinketh of the water that I shall give him shall never thirst; but the water that I shall give him shall be in him a well of water springing up into Eternal life.*

The cleft rock at Horeb proves that the protection of the LORD was in His hand that provided the Living Water. God is *the Rock* of our salvation, *He is our Yeshua.*

Psalm 62:1-2 *Truly my soul waiteth upon God; from Him cometh my salvation. He only is my Rock and my salvation; He is my defense; I shall not be greatly moved.*

Rivers of Living Water from the cleft rock at Boulder Falls Colorado Photo ©2013 Kimberly K Ballard All Rights Reserved

When I read this verse, I think of Yeshua who was laid in the tomb that was hewn out of the rock in Holy Mount Moriah because He is the Rock of our salvation! This brings up another fascinating truth. Yeshua said that *He would build His Church upon this Rock and the Rock that He was referring to was Himself!* Yeshua was not referring to Simon Peter as *the Rock. Simon Peter was a Living Stone!* The LORD Messiah is *the Rock* of our salvation! When Yeshua declared this truth, He was asking the Jewish disciples, *"Who do the people say that I AM?"* They told Him, *"Some say that you are one of the Prophets or Elijah,"* and then Simon Peter said the following true words.

Matthew 16:13-20 *When Yeshua came into the coasts of Caesarea Philippi, He asked His disciples, saying, Whom do men say that I the Son of man AM? And they said, Some say that thou art John the Baptist; some Elijah; and others, Jeremiah, or one of the Prophets. He saith unto them, But whom say ye that I AM? And Simon Peter answered and said, Thou art the Messiah, the Son of the Living God. And Yeshua answered and said unto Him, Blessed art thou, Simon Bar Jonah; for flesh and blood hath not revealed it unto thee, but My Father which is in Heaven. And I say also unto thee, That thou art Peter, and upon this Rock I will build My Church; and the gates of hell shall not prevail against it. And I will give unto thee the keys of the Kingdom of Heaven; and whatsoever thou shalt bind on earth shall be bound in Heaven; and whatsoever thou shalt loose on earth shall be loosed in Heaven. Then charged He His disciples that they should tell no man that He was Yeshua the Messiah.*

When Simon Peter answered saying, *"You are the Messiah, the Son of the Living God,"* Yeshua blessed Simon Peter because the Holy Spirit had revealed this to him, and Yeshua looked at Simon Peter and He said to him, *"Upon this Rock, I will build my Church." Yeshua was talking about Himself as the Rock of salvation!* The Rock was not in reference to Simon Peter, it was in reference to Messiah the LORD who is our salvation which in Hebrew is *"Yeshua,"* and this was verified in Psalm 62 that we just read. *The Living Water comes out of this Rock by the Rod of God.* So clearly, Messiah Yeshua is *the Rock* upon which the true Church or Synagogue is built.

My Jordan River rock from Joshua's crossing site, where Yeshua stood during His baptism

II Samuel 22:32 *For who is God, save the LORD? And who is a rock, save our God?*

When Yeshua said, *"I will give unto thee the keys of the Kingdom,"* He was giving them *the Living Testimony of the LORD in Heaven* and this key was the key of David. *The keys of the Kingdom reveal that Yeshua's Living Testimony is the Covenant of the Heavenly Ark of the LORD God of Israel.* So this Living Testimony was to be sent forth by the Holy Spirit, the breath of God that was abiding upon the Spirit-filled Jewish disciples to gather a multitude of Saints for the LORD'S Eternal Kingdom. *The Rock was therefore never Simon Peter.* Remember I said that Simon Peter is a *Living foundation stone* of the Heavenly Spiritual Temple. The evidence of this is on the Rock of Horeb and the cleft Matzah of the Passover Seder. The truth is in Yeshua's baptism at Joshua's crossing site. *So the true Church or Synagogue is built upon the Rock of Holy Mount Moriah in Jerusalem, which is Yeshua, the LORD God of Israel. He is the freedom from the bondage of sin and death at Mount Sinai, at Horeb!*

Psalm 89:26-27 *He shall cry unto Me, Thou art my Father, my God, and the Rock of my salvation, Also I will make Him my firstborn, higher than the kings of the earth.*

Psalm 61:2 *From the end of the earth will I cry unto Thee, when my heart is overwhelmed; lead me to the Rock that is higher than I.*

MESSIAH'S FEET WILL MAKE THE MOUNT OF OLIVES CLEFT THE SECOND TO THIRD DAY OF CREATION

Olive Sprig & Olives from The Mount of Olives in Jerusalem, from LV my Israeli friend Photo ©2013 Kimberly K Ballard All Rights Reserved

I have something to share with you now that is absolutely fantastic! Zechariah the Prophet wrote about the coming of the Messiah of Israel in the future.

Zechariah 14:1-9 *Behold, the day of the LORD cometh, and thy spoil shall be divided in the midst of thee. For I will gather all nations against Jerusalem to battle; And the city shall be taken, and the houses rifled, and the woman ravished; and half of the city shall go forth into captivity, and the residue of the people shall not be cut off from the city. Then shall the LORD go forth, and fight against those nations, as when He fought in the day of battle. And His feet shall stand in that day upon the Mount of Olives, which is before Jerusalem on the east, and the Mount of Olives shall cleave in the midst thereof toward the east and toward the west, and there shall be a very great valley; and half of the mountain shall remove toward the north, and half of it move toward the south. And ye shall flee to the valley of the mountains; for the valley of the mountains shall reach unto Azal; yes, ye shall flee, like as ye fled from before the earthquake in the days of Uzziah the king of Judah; and the LORD my God shall come, and all the Saints with thee. And it shall come to pass in that day, that the light shall not be clear, nor dark; but it shall be one day which shall be known to the LORD, not day, nor night; but it shall come to pass, that at evening time it shall be light. And it shall be in that day, that Living Waters shall go out from Jerusalem; half of them toward the former sea, and half of them toward the hinder sea; in summer and in winter shall it be. And the LORD shall be KING over all the earth; in that day shall there be one LORD, and His Name one.*

All of the truths that I have written about so far lead to the fact that in the future, when Messiah Yeshua returns from Heaven and sets His feet down upon the Mount of Olives, the land will be made cleft underneath His feet because Yeshua is the Rod of God, the hand of God!

Whenever the Heavenly Ark stood in the midst;

1. *The Sea was cleft by the Rod.*
2. *The Jordan River was cleft by the Rod.*
3. *The Rock at Horeb was cleft by the Rod.*
4. *The land will be made cleft by Yeshua the Rod. Living Water will gush from Him as He stands in the middle, with the water flowing on either side of Him, as He carves a pathway toward the Holy Temple Mount. He will usher in the everlasting refreshing from His Heavenly Kingdom forever, as He is the Living Ark standing in its midst!*

The Official Split Rock of Horeb
Photo ©1992 Jim & Penny Caldwell
All Rights Reserved
Edited to Black & White by KK Ballard

Micah prophesied about this future event with Messiah Yeshua.

Micah 1:4 *And the mountains shall be molten under Him, and the valleys shall be cleft, as wax before the fire, and as the waters that are poured down a steep place.*

Revelation 7:17 *For the Lamb which is in the midst of the throne shall feed them, and shall lead them unto living fountains of waters; and God shall wipe away all tears from their eyes.*

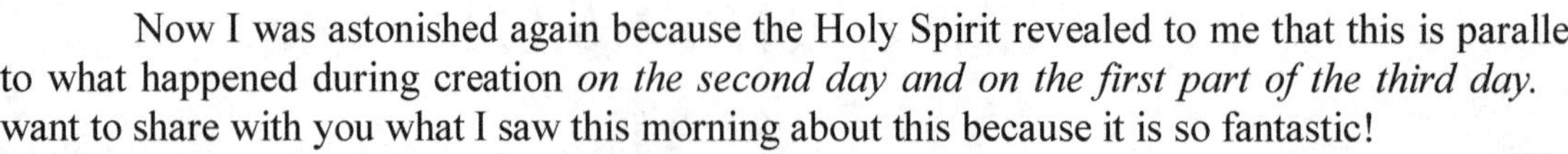

Now I was astonished again because the Holy Spirit revealed to me that this is parallel to what happened during creation *on the second day and on the first part of the third day.* I want to share with you what I saw this morning about this because it is so fantastic!

Genesis 1:6-8 *And God said, Let there be a firmament in the midst of the waters, and let it divide the waters from the waters. And God made the firmament, and divided the waters which were under the firmament from the waters which were above the firmament; and it was so. And God called the firmament Heaven. And the evening and the morning were the second day.*

After the waters of the firmament were divided, *the second day* was completed. Then we begin with all the things that happened on *the third day* of creation. Keep in mind that God said that *this firmament was in the midst of the waters.* The word *"firmament"* means *"support and vault."* It is interesting that the word *"support"* means *"something that bears the weight and holds the position, so it does not sink, fall or slip."* It is very important that this firmament was in the midst of the waters.

During creation, the LORD divided the waters, making them *cleft,* revealing from *the very beginning* that this was the LORD'S signature on His work. When *the third day* began in Genesis, we see some of the same details that happened later with Moses and the children of Israel at the Red Sea crossing, and again later with Joshua, Elijah, and Elisha at the Jordan River crossing! Now keep in mind what happened to them as you read the following passage in Genesis.

Genesis 1:9-10 *And God said, Let the waters under the Heaven be gathered together unto one place, and let the dry land appear; and it was so. And God called the dry land Earth; and the gathering together of the waters called He seas; and God saw that it was good.*

Monterey California Ocean Waves
Photo ©2013 Kimberly K Ballard All Rights Reserved

I realized that when Joshua crossed the Jordan River, *the waters were gathered into one place and the dry land appeared, exactly as it happened during creation in Genesis! Remember that with Joshua, the Ark of the Presence of the LORD was in the midst of the waters and He was the support for Israel as He went before them, guiding their path, so they would not fall, sink, or slip, as they entered the Promised Land.* He supports them with *the Rod of His Yeshua,* full of the Holy Spirit of God, standing in the midst of the waters. This is again why all the children of Israel were baptized in the midst of the Red Sea as they crossed over *because the LORD was in their midst with His Spirit on the Rod as the firmament!*

Joshua 3:15-17 *And as they that bare the Ark were come unto the Jordan and the feet of the Priests that bare the Ark were dipped in the brim of the water, for Jordan overfloweth all his banks all the time of harvest. That the waters which came down from above stood and rose up upon an heap very far from the city Adam, that is beside Zaretan; and those that came down toward the sea of the plain, even the salt sea, failed, and were cut off; and the people passed over right against Jericho. And the Priests that bare the Ark of the Covenant of the LORD stood on firm ground in the midst of Jordan, and all the Israelites passed over on dry ground, until all the people were passed clean over Jordan.*

Remember that Joshua actually declared that this happened, so that the world might know *the hand* of the LORD! The hand is Messiah!

Dry sandy seashore Photo Monterey California
Photo ©2013 Kimberly K Ballard

Joshua 4:22-24 *Then shall ye let your children know, saying, Israel came over this Jordan on dry land. For the LORD your God dried up the waters of Jordan from before you, until ye were passed over, as the LORD your God did to the Red Sea, which He dried up from before us, until we were gone over; That all the people of the earth might know the hand of the LORD, that it is mighty; that ye might fear the LORD your God forever.*

The LORD gathered the waters together in one place in a heap and the dry land appeared *as the Ark of the LORD stood firm as the firmament in the midst of the waters until they crossed over with salvation by the Rod, the Yad of God.* So in the creation, the LORD divided the waters, making them cleft, and on the third day, the LORD gathered together the waters in one place and the dry land appeared!

Do you realize that Messiah the LORD is coming and His feet will divide the land and the Living Waters will flow out from His Temple, *as His Divine Presence is with us, because His Spirit and the Heavenly Ark will be standing in our midst forever as the firmament?* This means that His Holy Spirit/Ruach is on the Rod as the firmament in the midst of the waters. *So Messiah Yeshua stood as the firmament in the midst of the Jordan River and the Heavens were cleft when the Holy Spirit returned to the Heavenly Ark, in the form of a dove, and lighted upon the hand of God!* In the midst of the waters, *Yeshua the Rod of God* was leading the children of Israel in the path to the Heavenly Eternal Promised Land! This is exactly what happened to the children of Israel at the Red Sea crossing. Compare what the Rod did in creation to Moses at the Red Sea crossing and note well the descriptive words correlating to creation on *the second and third day*! It is *the Rod* that makes the Sea cleft! It is *the Rod* that divided the waters and made the dry land appear. It is *the Rod* that made Israel to cross over on the dry land after He divided the waters. *The signature of God is all over this miracle, revealing that Messiah Yeshua is the LORD God of Israel, from the very beginning of creation.*

Exodus 14:15-16 *And the LORD said unto Moses, Wherefore criest thou unto Me? Speak unto the children of Israel, that they go forward; But lift thou up thy rod, and stretch out thine hand over the sea, and divide it; and the children of Israel shall go on dry ground through the mist of the sea.*

Skipping forward in the same chapter, verses 19-22 incredibly begin like the first section of Genesis when the LORD divided the light from the darkness, on the first day of creation. Then as we just noted *on the second and third day of creation,* the LORD divided the waters and made the dry land appear, just as He did later with Moses, Joshua, Elijah, and Elisha! *The wind is the breath of the Presence of the LORD'S Ruach/Holy Spirit that was in the midst of the sea, going before them on the Rod of salvation.* With Moses, the waters were gathered into one place and they crossed over on dry land as *the Presence of the LORD* was going before them, making *the way* exactly as the LORD performed it on *the second and third day of creation! The LORD was their support. He was the firmament in their midst!*

Exodus 14:19-22 *And the Angel of God, which went before the camp of Israel, removed and went behind them; and the pillar of cloud went from before their face, and stood behind them; And it came between the camp of the Egyptians and the camp of Israel; and it was a cloud and darkness to them, but it gave light by night to these; so that the one came not near the other all the night. And Moses stretched out his hand over the sea; and the LORD caused the sea to go back by a strong east wind all that night, and made the sea dry land, and the waters were a wall unto them on their right hand, and on their left.*

The LORD had separated the Egyptians from the Israelites, by giving one darkness and the other light and this is exactly what the LORD did in the beginning when *He separated the darkness from the light* and this is what the LORD did with Moses at the Red Sea crossing. After the light and darkness were separated, then the LORD divided the waters on one side from the waters on the other side and dry land appeared.

Psalms 78:13 *He divided the sea, and caused them to pass through; and He made the waters to stand up as an heap.*

It is astounding to see that the Rod of God, the hand and finger of God, was in every detail of the history of Israel and Messiah Yeshua was revealed from the beginning of creation.

So now, incredibly, I have to tell you that the LORD just revealed to me that when Yeshua was resurrected *the third day, later the same evening on the first day of the week,* Yeshua appeared to the Jewish disciples who were *gathered together in one place. The LORD Yeshua came and stood in their midst when the door was shut. Yeshua was at that moment the firmament, the Heavenly Ark of the Living Testimony standing in their midst as their support, bearing the weight of their burdens, so they would not sink, fall, or slip, and He showed them His hands and His side. Then He breathed His Spirit upon them and the breath of life went into them, so they would know the way to cross over into the Heavenly Eternal Promised Land, following behind Him as the Living Ark of the Covenant.* The LORD has miraculously woven this entire story together into something spectacular!

John 20:19-22 *Then the same evening, being the first day of the week, when the doors were shut where the disciples were assembled for fear of the Jews, came Yeshua and stood in the midst, and saith unto them, Peace be unto you, And when He had so said, He shewed unto them His hands and His side. Then were the disciples glad, when they saw the LORD. Then said Yeshua to them again, Peace be unto you; as My Father hath sent Me, even so send I you. And when He had said this He breathed on them, and saith unto them, Receive ye the Holy Spirit.*

Luke 24:36-45 *And as they thus spake, Yeshua Himself stood in the midst of them, and saith unto them, Peace be unto you. But they were terrified and affrighted, and supposed that they had seen a spirit. And He said unto them, Why are ye troubled? And why do thoughts arise in your hearts? Behold My hands and My feet, that it is I Myself; handle Me, and see; for a spirit hath not flesh and bones, as ye see Me have. And when He had thus spoken, He shewed them His hands and His feet. And while they yet believed not for joy, and wondered, He said unto them, Have ye here any meat? And they gave Him a piece of a broiled fish, and of an honey-comb. And He took it, and did eat before them. And He said unto them, These are the Words which I spake unto you, while I was yet with you, that all things must be fulfilled, which were written in the law of Moses, and in the prophets, and in the psalms, concerning Me. Then opened He their understanding, that they might understand the Scriptures.*

Throughout the entire history of Israel, the LORD was gradually revealing His identity and revealing His face to us. Now we know why the land will be made cleft and the waters will flow out from one place *when Yeshua, the Heavenly Ark, the Living Rod, sets His feet on the Mount of Olives, leading us to His Heavenly Garden forever!*

Gardenia Garden
Photo ©2013 Kimberly K Ballard

The Official Split Rock of Horeb
Photo ©1992 Jim & Penny Caldwell

Gardenia Garden
Photo ©2013 Kimberly K Ballard

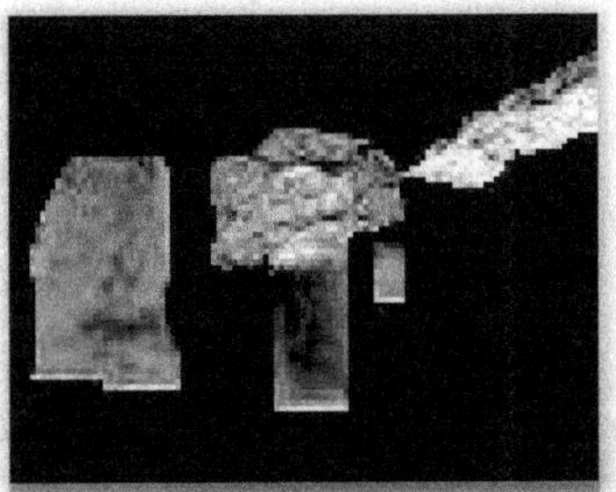
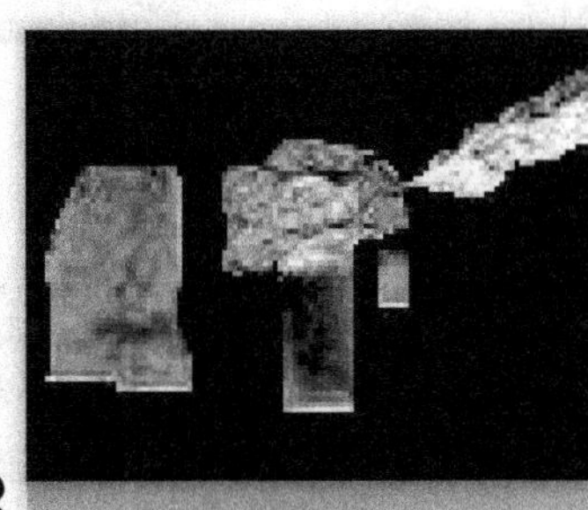

THE YAD OF THE JEWISH ANGEL THE NICHES AT THE GARDEN TOMB

Before I leave the subject of *the Yad of God,* the LORD showed me another wonderful miracle that pertains to His Testimony. There are many more details about this that I will share later within the depths of this book and when you read them, you will see why I have come to this remarkable conclusion. What you are about to read, unveils one of the final mysteries of the Messiah and the works of the Yad of God that He performed with His mighty hand.

When a Divine miracle occurred and I discovered the Jewish Priestly Angel at the Garden tomb, I noticed that the Angel has a Yad. By this I mean that the Angel has a right arm that is outstretched. His hand and index finger are extended. The index finger of the Angel is pointing to a specific place in the exterior rock wall of the Garden tomb in Holy Mount Moriah. This Holy Mountain of God is the location of the Garden tomb of Messiah Yeshua. When I thought about this Angel, I suddenly remembered that *Angels are messengers that are sent by God, and they come to us heralding specific messages about the LORD. This tells me that the Angel at the Garden tomb is pointing to something extraordinary pertaining to the LORD.* I truly believe that this Angel is pointing to *the Testimony of the LORD,* whether it was left in Word or in tangible evidence at the Garden tomb by Messiah the LORD. It was meant to be discovered in Holy Mount Moriah in the last days just before Yeshua returns from Heaven to reign. Within the astounding details I am about to discuss, I believe the LORD gave us a miracle that is to be revealed in our generation. *Angels act as guardians of the Ark!* As I pondered this Jewish Priestly Angel, pointing with his Yad, I saw that the Angel was pointing to three niches that are hewn out of the rock high up in the exterior wall of the Garden tomb. I researched the earliest photographs of the Garden tomb so I could discern exactly how the tomb appeared when it was first excavated. This is when I found the original stopper stones.

I was specifically researching the photographs so I could try to determine whether or not the three niches and the Angel existed at the time of the first excavation of the tomb. I could see where the wing of the Angel came down above the window of the tomb and I could see the niches. The earliest photographs proved exactly what I suspected. So the niches and the Angel were buried under the dirt for hundreds of years with the sepulchre, and this can only mean that the carvings are original to the earliest history of Yeshua's tomb. Therefore, the three niches and the Jewish Priestly Angel existed in the earliest years of Jewish Christianity, which tells me they were Jewish in origin. Keep in mind that the first Christians were Jewish worshiping at the Holy Temple in Jerusalem. The three niches consist of one large niche and to the right of that niche, there is a smaller niche. Then to the right of the smaller niche, there is a very tiny rectangular niche that is cut out in the rock face. I had pondered these niches for a long time, but nothing came to my mind except that perhaps a Torah scroll had been placed within the larger niche, but this did not explain why there were three niches in the face of the wall. As I pondered this, I woke up one day and before I came upstairs to edit this portion of the book I was startled, because the LORD suddenly gave me a vision of what was once placed inside the three niches! Whatever had been set inside the three niches was so important that the Jewish Priestly Angel was pointing to it in Mount Moriah, the Holy Mountain of God, and the

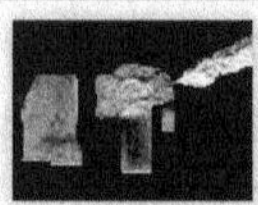

Angel was still trying to get our attention. The Angel was declaring and heralding a very important piece of the Testimony of the LORD! I had already written the following chapters, so when this happened and it verified everything that I had said, I was so completely shocked and astonished. The LORD was now showing me that His Testimony is again written in stone, and He was incredibly verifying everything I had written through His Divine revelation! Now I felt very strongly when I woke up that the LORD was opening my mind and He was showing me exactly what the three niches held at the Garden tomb. Then I understood that the Jewish Priestly Angel was pointing, not only to the Name of the LORD that was inscribed in a signet shaped object, but also to three elements of the LORD'S Eternal Testimony that I believe were once displayed in the exterior wall of the Garden tomb. In my vision, I could see that the three elements were displayed and stored inside clay jars and they were set inside the three niches in the exterior wall of the Garden tomb. Just above the middle niche, where the Angel is pointing, there is an interesting chiseled out area that is shaped like an opened flower, which at first glance looked like a cloud shape. In the center of this opened flower, there is a raised oval convex part of the stone and the petals go around it. I believe that this oval convex stone is inscribed with the *Alpha & Omega* letters because I can see two letters inscribed upon the signet shaped object and, ironically, the letters *Alpha and Omega* are also written inside the Garden tomb with the Name Yeshua and the cross. The way that the letters appear on this oval make it look exactly like a signet ring and you will see why this is so important in another chapter when I discuss the KING because I had already written about His signet ring before this unexpected miracle happened! *All I can say in this section is that finding the KING'S signet ring, in the Holy Mountain of God is like finding a marriage proposal to Israel.* Because I have only discovered this in photographs and have not visited the Garden tomb yet, I am not certain of the exact inscription. It could say the Name *"Yeshua"* in Hebrew, or it could be inscribed with *"YHVH"* in Hebrew, but based upon what I have already written in this book, my personal opinion is that the inscription appears to be a shorter inscription of the two letters *"Alpha and Omega"* in Greek (lowercase letters), and this is how the letters also appear inside the tomb. The inscription is in the center of the raised opened flower that has the appearance of an oval shaped signet ring and the Angel is pointing directly towards this object with the extended index finger of his Yad, and this flower sits just above the middle niche. Now in order to fully understand exactly why I am saying this, you must continue to read the rest of the chapters. You should spend time studying my chapter on Yeshua's resurrection, otherwise you might think that this is only a speculation. I am basing my vision, upon every single amazing detail and upon all the evidence that the LORD has already presented to me and these things are extremely significant to the LORD'S Divine Testimony. When I thought about the LORD'S *Alpha and Omega* on the convex oval signet, this made me think that the very tiny rectangular niche to the right of it was a place for a Jewish mezuzah.

Now ordinarily the mezuzah is placed to the right side of the entrance to a door, but because I believe that what was contained within the two clay jars that stood next to it pertained to the LORD'S Living Testimony, I believe that this tiny niche, once held a Jewish mezuzah. The mezuzah would therefore have been placed on the far right side of the two larger niches, and, as I stated, the Angel is pointing to the signet ring containing the inscription and it is bordered by a flower that is chiseled into the rock face. The mezuzah is a piece of parchment that contains the Scriptures from the Torah that include Deuteronomy 6:4-9 and 11:13-21. The Jewish blessing called *"The Shema"* is contained within these specific verses, which again, states the profound Words of God, *"Hear, O Israel, the LORD our God, the LORD is One."*

Deuteronomy 6:4-9 *Hear, O Israel; The LORD our God is One LORD; And thou shalt love the LORD thy God with all thine heart, and with all thy soul, and with all thy might. And these Words, which I command thee this day, shall be in thine heart; and thou shalt teach them diligently unto thy children, and shalt talk of them when thou sittest in thine house, and when thou walkest by the way, and when thou liest down, and when thou risest up. And thou shalt*

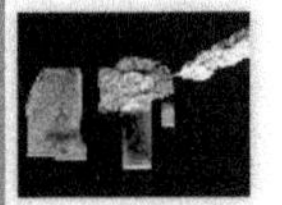

bind them for a sign upon thine hand, and they shall be as frontlets between thine eyes. And thou shalt write them upon the posts of thy house, and on thy gates.

Remember *The Shema* is what Yeshua wrote with His finger! The absolutely astonishing thing about this verse is the fact that the Garden of God in Mount Moriah is in fact *"The gate of Heaven." This is the doorpost of the House of God. Yeshua told us that He is the door into Heaven. This is where the Living Heavenly Ark rested in our midst in Holy Mount Moriah. The LORD'S Eternal House will stand in this place forever and Messiah Yeshua is the door in this Garden and He is the gate into the Eternal Promised Land! This Garden is the location of the former Garden of Eden and Yeshua's Living Testimony that occurred in this place, in His Holy Mountain, reveals the way back to His paradise Garden to dwell with the LORD forever! So the Great Rolling Stone on Mount Nebo points to this Garden that was once Eden!* The LORD told us *"to pay attention to His Testimonies, so Israel will obtain the Land."*

Deuteronomy 11:13-21 *And it shall come to pass, if ye shall hearken diligently unto My commandments which I command you this day, to love the LORD your God, and to serve Him with all your heart and with all your soul, That I will give you the rain of your land in his due season, and the first rain and the latter rain, that thou mayest gather in thy corn, and thy wine and thine oil. And I will send grass in thy fields for thy cattle, that thou mayest eat and be full. Take heed to yourselves, that your heart be not deceived, and ye turn aside, and serve other gods, and worship them; And then the LORD'S wrath be kindled against you, and He shut up the Heaven, that there be no rain, and that the land yield not her fruit; and lest ye perish quickly from off the good land which the LORD giveth you. Therefore shall ye lay up these My Words in your heart and in your soul, and bind them for a sign upon your hand, that they may be as frontlets between your eyes. And ye shall teach them your children, speaking of them when thou sittest in thine house, and when thou walkest by the way, when thou liest down, and when thou risest up. And thou shalt write them upon the door posts of thine house, and upon thy gates; That your days may be multiplied, and the days of your children, in the land which the LORD sware unto your fathers to give them, as the days of Heaven upon the earth.*

Now the message is perfectly clear. The Angel is trying to point our attention to *the Living Testimony of Messiah Yeshua* because he is pointing to the Name of the LORD that is inscribed in this place, *on a signet shaped object,* and to the right of it where, I believe, there was the Jewish blessing that declared that *the LORD God is the Messiah, one God.* After *The Shema* in Deuteronomy, we find something that it is quite interesting! Within this verse, the LORD says *"that it is with a mighty hand, that He has brought Israel out of Egypt and that in generations to come, the children will ask about the LORD'S Testimonies!"* This is the place of His Eternal Testimony and part of this is being revealed to us right now, in this book, to our generation. *This is the tomb of the Rod of God, the Yad or hand of God!* So think about the fact that I am about to send forth the message that the LORD gave me, revealing His Eternal Divine Testimony and then this Scripture *tells Israel, to pay attention to and keep His Testimonies!* The Messiah is about to bring Israel into the Heavenly Eternal Promised Land that He promised their forefathers forever and He tells them that if they diligently keep *His Testimonies,* then their enemies will be cast off the Land from before them!

Deuteronomy 6:10-25 *And it shall be, when the LORD thy God shall have brought thee into the land which He sware unto thy fathers, to Abraham, to Isaac, and to Jacob, to give thee great and goodly cities, which thou buildest not, And houses full of all good things, which thou fillest not, and wells digged, which thou diggedst not, vineyards and olive trees, which thou plantedst not; when thou shalt have eaten and be full; Then beware lest thou forget the LORD, which brought thee forth out of the land of Egypt, from the house of bondage. Thou shalt fear the LORD thy God, and serve Him and shalt swear by His Name. Ye shall not go after other gods, of the gods of the people which are round about you; For the LORD thy God is a jealous God among you lest the anger of the LORD thy God be kindled against thee, and destroy thee from off the face of the earth. Ye shall not tempt the LORD your God, as ye tempted Him in Massah. Ye shall diligently keep the commandments of the LORD your God, and His Testimonies, and His statutes, which He hath commanded thee. And thou shalt do that which is right and good in the sight of the LORD; that it may be well with thee, and that thou mayest go in and possess the good land which the LORD sware unto thy fathers, To cast out all thine enemies from before thee, as the LORD hath spoken. And when thy son asketh*

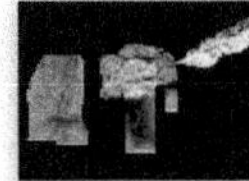

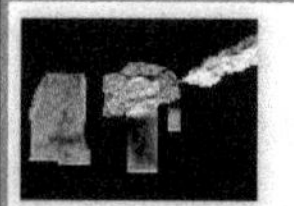

thee in time to come, saying, What mean the Testimonies, and the statutes, and the judgments, which the LORD our God hath commanded you? Then thou shalt say unto thy son, We were Pharaoh's bondmen in Egypt; and the LORD brought us out of Egypt with a Mighty hand; And the LORD shewed signs and wonders, great and sore upon Egypt, upon Pharaoh, and upon all his household, before our eyes; And He brought us out from thence, that He might bring us in, to give us the land which He sware unto our fathers. And the LORD commanded us to do all these statutes, to fear the LORD our God, for our good always, that He might preserve us alive, as it is at this day. And it shall be our righteousness, if we observe to do all these commandments before the LORD our God, as He hath commanded us.

These Words should ring in the ears of Israel today, telling them to return to the LORD thy God and to do all His Commandments and to open their eyes to *His incredible Testimonies* and *to believe that the LORD, the Messiah, is one God and His Name is one. The Messiah is God because He is one KING who is coming to reign forever in Jerusalem.*

Now you tell me, could there be a more profound Scripture placed in the wall of the Garden tomb on the right side of *the Testimony of the Living Branch of the Almond Tree of Life?* This is the place where Adam and Eve brought forth the curse of death and Yeshua took the curse away in this place and He leads us to Heaven through *this gate, as the Living Ark of the Eternal Covenant!*

So, now that I have discussed that part of the story, what on earth was placed inside the other two mysterious niches and set inside the exterior wall of the Garden tomb inside the clay jars? First of all, I believe that there has been a great archaeological misunderstanding of the Garden tomb. I believe that thousands of people have been told information that is simply not accurate regarding the niches. The truth is, when the tomb was excavated, nobody really had any idea why the niches were set in the exterior wall of the tomb. So speculation began and people came up with their own ideas about it. Now I absolutely believe that all the speculation is completely wrong. Some of these people say it is *"the idea"* of the tomb that matters.

It has been assumed and claimed that the niches in the exterior wall were put there to support the beams of an ancient Byzantine Church that was built centuries ago in front of the Garden tomb, but, honestly, I think that no one really has any idea what they were used for and someone just made a suggestion that was based solely upon a hunch. After this idea was suggested by someone, then everyone else followed this circulated idea, and they went with it as if it was the true answer. Then after a while, they kept on telling this false information as if it was a fact. I believe though, that this explanation is totally wrong. *I believe that the niches held something extremely precious and deeply significant pertaining to the LORD'S Testimony* and you will understand why I say this when you read my chapter on *the KING. The pieces of His Testimony were kept inside clay jars for some time and set inside the niches in the exterior wall and the Jewish Priestly Angel was proclaiming this Eternal Testimony to us.* Therefore, this tomb is far greater than anyone knows right now!

One morning, as I was still pondering the niches, after I realized that the very tiny niche looked like it was the size fit for a mezuzah, I was still wondering about the Torah Scroll idea. Was there a Torah Scroll set inside the larger niche? No, because there were two niches left. Then when I had the vision in the morning, incredibly, the LORD put it in my heart that the two niches contained two extremely significant items that were kept and preserved inside two clay jars, similar to the clay jars that preserved the Dead Sea Scrolls. *What entered my heart that morning is that inside the larger clay jar, they preserved the burial Shroud of Messiah Yeshua that bore His miraculous image! It was displayed in the exterior wall of the rock hewn tomb as a sign of the Eternal Living Covenant because it verified the Eternal Testimony of Messiah Yeshua, the LORD. I remind you once again that this is Holy Mount Moriah where the LORD said that His Name dwells forever, and His Name is literally inscribed at the Garden tomb in the opened flower where Messiah, the Almond Branch, came to life! The Rod of God was set before the Testimony, just as Aaron's rod was set before the Testimony of witness, but this was in God's Garden and the Angel is pointing to it! The next*

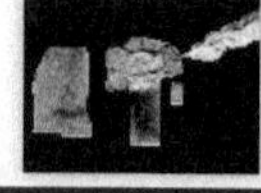

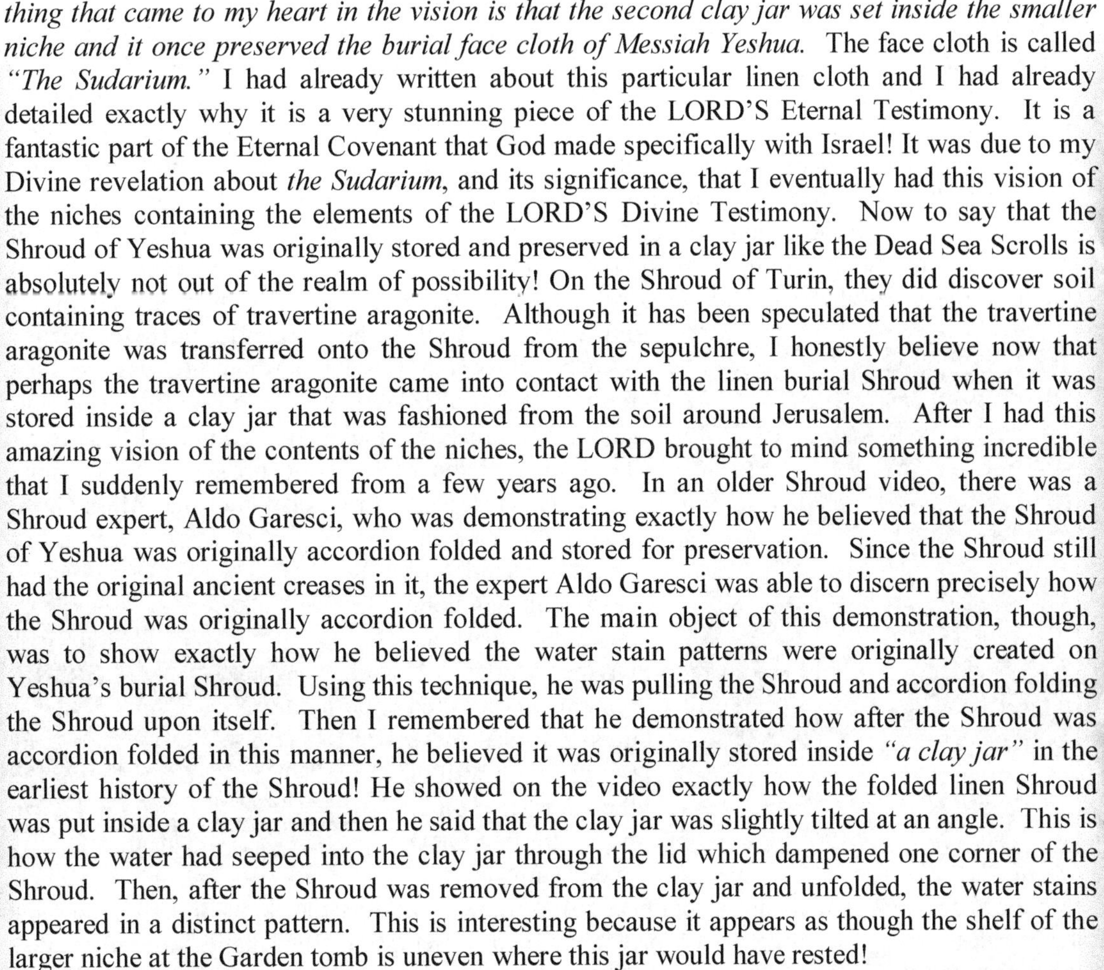

thing that came to my heart in the vision is that the second clay jar was set inside the smaller niche and it once preserved the burial face cloth of Messiah Yeshua. The face cloth is called *"The Sudarium."* I had already written about this particular linen cloth and I had already detailed exactly why it is a very stunning piece of the LORD'S Eternal Testimony. It is a fantastic part of the Eternal Covenant that God made specifically with Israel! It was due to my Divine revelation about *the Sudarium*, and its significance, that I eventually had this vision of the niches containing the elements of the LORD'S Divine Testimony. Now to say that the Shroud of Yeshua was originally stored and preserved in a clay jar like the Dead Sea Scrolls is absolutely not out of the realm of possibility! On the Shroud of Turin, they did discover soil containing traces of travertine aragonite. Although it has been speculated that the travertine aragonite was transferred onto the Shroud from the sepulchre, I honestly believe now that perhaps the travertine aragonite came into contact with the linen burial Shroud when it was stored inside a clay jar that was fashioned from the soil around Jerusalem. After I had this amazing vision of the contents of the niches, the LORD brought to mind something incredible that I suddenly remembered from a few years ago. In an older Shroud video, there was a Shroud expert, Aldo Garesci, who was demonstrating exactly how he believed that the Shroud of Yeshua was originally accordion folded and stored for preservation. Since the Shroud still had the original ancient creases in it, the expert Aldo Garesci was able to discern precisely how the Shroud was originally accordion folded. The main object of this demonstration, though, was to show exactly how he believed the water stain patterns were originally created on Yeshua's burial Shroud. Using this technique, he was pulling the Shroud and accordion folding the Shroud upon itself. Then I remembered that he demonstrated how after the Shroud was accordion folded in this manner, he believed it was originally stored inside *"a clay jar"* in the earliest history of the Shroud! He showed on the video exactly how the folded linen Shroud was put inside a clay jar and then he said that the clay jar was slightly tilted at an angle. This is how the water had seeped into the clay jar through the lid which dampened one corner of the Shroud. Then, after the Shroud was removed from the clay jar and unfolded, the water stains appeared in a distinct pattern. This is interesting because it appears as though the shelf of the larger niche at the Garden tomb is uneven where this jar would have rested!

I remember being amazed that the water pattern that he recreated in this demonstration was identical to the water stain pattern on the Shroud of Turin! This expert Aldo Garesci said that he believed that the Shroud had been stored in a clay jar that was like the clay jars that preserved the Dead Sea Scrolls. In his demonstration, he actually placed the replica Shroud into a clay jar of this type. I could not believe that the LORD brought this to mind and it was eventually going to be my proof later on, that my vision was true. This remarkable demonstration verified the reason why the Jewish Priestly Angel is pointing to the niches with his finger, like a Yad. *Now I believe more than ever that the Angel is pointing to the Living Testimony of the LORD, in Holy Mount Moriah.* This expert was exactly correct in every way! The incredible thing is that I did not come to this conclusion by watching his video demonstration of the water stain pattern several years ago. I only came to this conclusion recently when I discovered that the Angel was pointing with his Yad to the niches at the Garden tomb and I thought about the fact that the word *"Angel" means "messenger," or one who is sent to declare the truths of the LORD.* This is how I knew for certain that the Angel was pointing to part of Yeshua's Living Testimony *where the Rod of God came to life!* The Angel is pointing to the glorious resurrection of the LORD in His Holy Mountain, and he is pointing to the true Yad Messiah and pointing *the way* to Eternal life. Now, remarkably, you know how I said that at first I thought that perhaps a Torah scroll was kept and put inside one of the niches? *A chill went through me when I suddenly realized, that the Angel is really pointing to the Living Torah that was placed inside the Garden of God, in the LORD'S Holy Mount Moriah!* So why would the Mezuzah be to the right of this Testimony and not placed next to the door of the tomb? *Yeshua is the door and gate into the Eternal Promised Land because He is the LORD!*

He is the Ark of the Covenant and Angels are guardians of the Ark! Remember that the Scriptures pertaining to *The Shema* tell us that the generations to come are to observe *His Testimonies* and that they are to be kept in the hearts of their children, so He would bring them into the Land and He would remove their enemies! The Shroud was folded in the middle lengthwise and pulled back on itself. After the Shroud was folded, it became no larger than a folded bed sheet. It definitely fit into the clay jar in Aldo Garesci's demonstration! The Sudarium and the Shroud, both originated in Jerusalem. The two cloths remain preserved today, revealing the incredible truth of *the Testimonies of the LORD'S resurrection as the Branch of the Almond Tree of Life in His Garden.* I also believe that the mezuzah was placed in the exterior wall of the Garden tomb by the earliest Jewish believers in Messiah Yeshua, because the niche for *The Shema* blessing is in the wall on the upper right side of the other two niches that contained the Eternal Testimony of the LORD who proves that He is one God. All of this is to remind Israel that Messiah the Rod is the Yad, the mighty hand of God, who has done these marvelous Divine works. I remain astonished myself to see these things in the wall of the Garden Tomb, but the LORD opened my eyes to see them for such a time as this! I believe that *the Testimony* was first kept in the Garden, but later it had to be removed for safety, protection, and preservation from many foreign invaders who infiltrated the Holy Land. I think the message for us today is that the *Alpha & Omega* ascended back into Heaven in the glory cloud and He will return exactly the same way that He went into the cloud. I know that the two witnesses who stand on either side of Him will come before Him to prepare His way! I mentioned before that I will show you at the end of this book exactly why the two witnesses are Moses and Elijah! The Jewish Priestly Angel is sending a message to our generation because he is pointing with his Yad to the Living Testimony of God that saves us and *the Angel is pointing to the Living Torah, which is the Almond Tree of Life!* When a Jewish Priest gives the Priestly blessing, he stands before the congregation and faces them. He holds his arms outward in an outstretched manner and puts his hands into a formation. He parts his four fingers in the middle, making them cleft. On some ancient Jewish tombstones, a crown is placed above the cleft hands of the High Priest. Yeshua is the High Priest of Heaven and the hand of God, the Rod who parted the Red Sea and made it cleft. The Yad of God, who is the High Priest of Heaven, makes the work of His hands cleft! When He returns, He will make the Land cleft before Him, so that we may enter into the Eternal Kingdom of God, into His paradise Garden on Holy Mount Moriah in Jerusalem. This is the sign of the LORD our God and it is a signature on all His Works. These signs are not simply rituals of Israel, but the Jewish people are constantly expressing and revealing, in every sense of the Word, the identity of their own Saviour Messiah who is, without a doubt, the LORD God of Israel, our KING Yeshua. We must pay attention to His marvelous Testimonies!

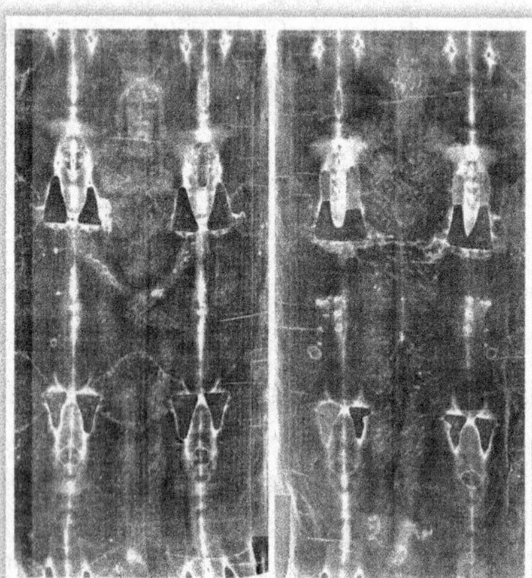

Official Shroud Pair Photograph ©1978 Barrie M. Schwortz Collection, STERA Inc., All Rights Reserved

The Sudarium of Oviedo Spain Official Photograph ©2013 El Centro Español de Sindonologia (CES) All Rights Reserved

What an exciting way to end this chapter on *the Yad of God* and it was all possible by the LORD'S Divine Providence and through His revelation in the last days! What a gift that He choose to reveal this to me after my Almond Tree miracle! He was cut down but came to life!

Job 14:7 *For there is hope of a tree, if it be cut down, that it will sprout again, and that the tender branch thereof will not cease.*

Our cut off Branch Yeshua will not cease as our Living Almond Tree of Life! The Jewish Priestly Angel at the Garden Tomb, points to the signet shaped opened Almond flower bearing the letters *"Alpha & Omega" and points to the three niches! Notice the uneven shelf in the large niche on the left where the Shroud would have been kept in the clay jar in this Garden tomb photo!*

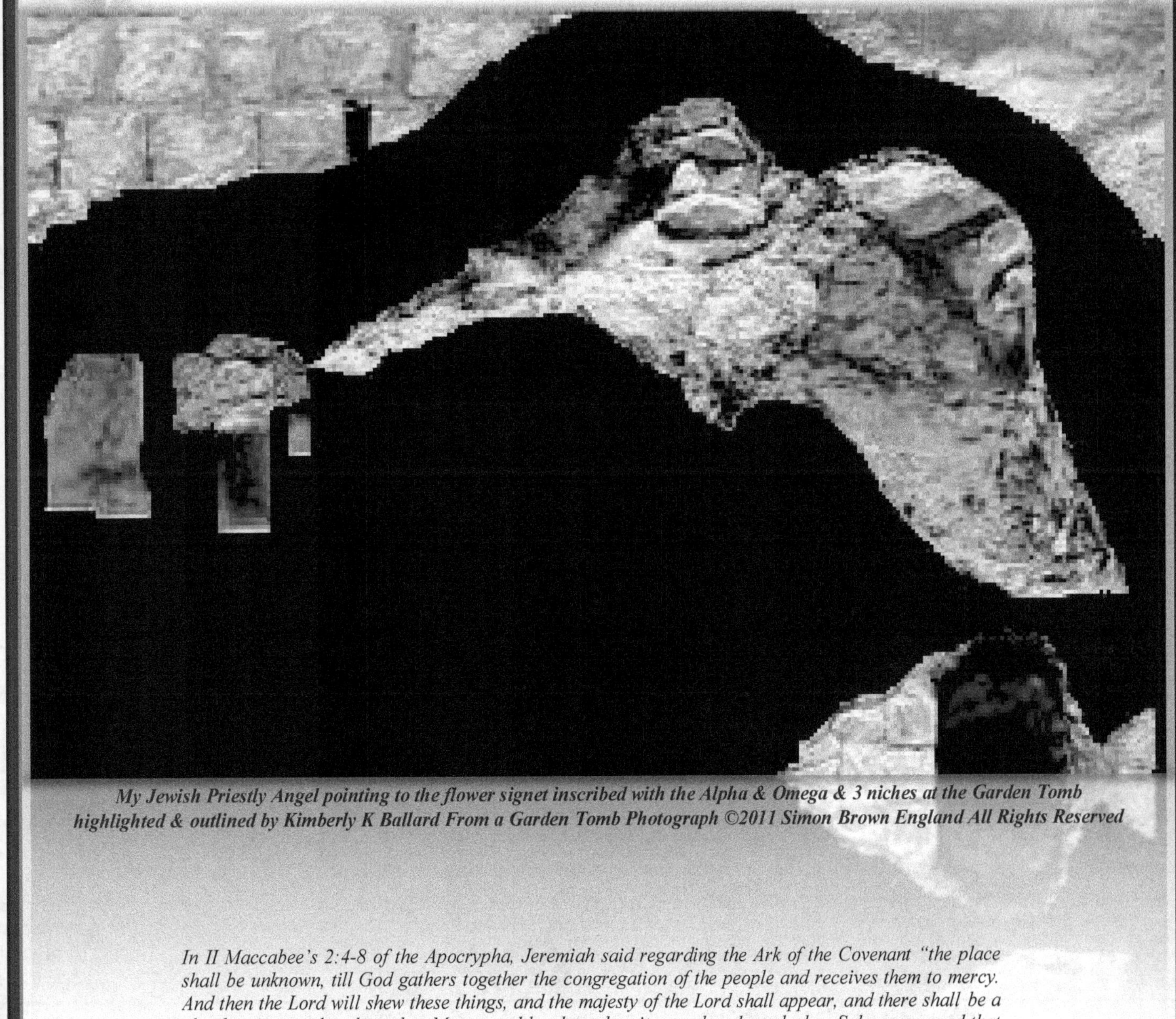

My Jewish Priestly Angel pointing to the flower signet inscribed with the Alpha & Omega & 3 niches at the Garden Tomb highlighted & outlined by Kimberly K Ballard From a Garden Tomb Photograph ©2011 Simon Brown England All Rights Reserved

In II Maccabee's 2:4-8 of the Apocrypha, Jeremiah said regarding the Ark of the Covenant "the place shall be unknown, till God gathers together the congregation of the people and receives them to mercy. And then the Lord will shew these things, and the majesty of the Lord shall appear, and there shall be a cloud as it was also shewed to Moses, and he shewed as it was also shewed when Solomon prayed that the place might be sanctified to the great God." The Ark symbolized God's Presence among His people.

The Yad with Candle & Branch Scripture, Crowns, Icicles, Snow on Street Light Photos ©2013 Kimberly K Ballard All Rights Reserved

Sheep, Lambs & Miniature horse from Ollin Farms, Harp, Five smooth stones, Shepherds bag & the Rod Photos

Chapter 6

THE GOOD SHEPHERD HIS ROD AND HIS STAFF THE MILITARY STANDARD OF GOD

Mother sheep with her lamb,
The Rod of the Good Shepherd & Living Almond Rod
Photos ©2013 & ©2015 KK Ballard All Rights Reserved

King David wrote one of the most memorable songs in Psalm 23.

A Psalm of David – Psalm 23:1-6 *The LORD is my Shepherd; I shall not want. He maketh me to lie down in green pastures; He leadeth me beside the still waters, He restoreth my soul; He leadeth me in the paths of righteousness for His Name's sake. Yea, though I walk through the valley of the shadow of death, I will fear no evil; for Thou art with me; Thy Rod and Thy Staff they comfort me. Thou preparest a table before me in the presence of mine enemies; Thou anointest my head with oil; my cup runneth over. Surely goodness and mercy shall follow me all the days of my life; and I will dwell in the House of the LORD forever.*

King David was comforted by the Rod and Staff of the LORD, so he wrote the words of Psalm 23 and played it on his harp made of *Algum wood.* Just before David wrote, *"Thy Rod and Thy Staff, they comfort me,"* David wrote the words, *"Yea though I walk through the valley of the shadow of death, I will fear no evil."* The Rod and Staff brought comfort from the shadow of death. David was prophesying about the coming Messiah on his harp, as the Holy Spirit gave him utterance. When Yeshua died, the cut off Branch was resting in the shadow of death, in the darkness of the sepulchre, inside Holy Mount Moriah. Then miraculously, the Rod of God budded to life and the darkness of the shadow of death, was overcome by the light of the glorious resurrection of the LORD God of Israel. King David knew long ago that when the Messiah would come through his Royal line and fulfill His Living Testimony, it would eternally bring comfort to Israel and to everyone that would believe in His Living Covenant.

This is how He was going to gather the scattered people from all Nations and bring them back to His Holy Mountain, to His Garden. *So God revealed the power of His Heavenly Rod through the miracles that were performed with the earthly rod of Aaron and Moses.* This is exactly the reason why Yeshua declared that we should at least believe in His works. The works alone testify to the Majesty of the Great KING and to the fact that Yeshua is indeed *the Heavenly Rod* in the hand of God the Father.

John 10:37-38 *If I do not the works of My Father, believe Me not. But if I do, though ye believe not Me, believe the works; that ye may know, and believe, that the Father is in Me, and I in Him.*

The works performed with this mighty Rod, reveal that Messiah Yeshua is *"The Royal Military Standard,"* of God's Army and His image was miraculously imprinted upon His burial Shroud after He was lifted up on the pole, which was the cross. The Rod was sent from Heaven to guide Israel and all believers into the Eternal Promised Land, and the LORD would send forth His Living Testimony to the nations, so they would come back to Him from Eden's eviction long ago. It was for this reason that the Rod and Staff brought great comfort to Israel because, through the Jewish Messiah, they were given the promise that we would be restored to the Kingdom of Heaven. The sons of darkness will be separated from the sons of light when the LORD returns, sending His *"Royal Standard"* to go before His Heavenly Army. As I thought more about this, I realized that the Good Shepherd uses His Rod and Staff for another astonishing purpose that also correlates to part of Yeshua's Living Testimony! Whenever a shepherd was walking along the hills of Bethlehem with his flock, the rod or staff in his hand was the instrument he would use to keep the snakes away from his flock of sheep! From this perspective, it is obvious why the LORD sent His Living Rod, *"The Standard of His Heavenly Army,"* to rescue His flock from Satan! The LORD had to intervene to save us. The LORD God actually referred to Pharaoh as the great dragon, whose emblem was, of course, that fiery cobra serpent. This dragon serpent moved from Egypt, Persia, and Babylon (or Shinar) to Rome and it was a symbol of a few other ancient kingdoms. This is why the dragon is depicted on the base of the Menorah that was carried off to Rome by the Army of Titus in 70AD.

In the annals of history, many of the ancient Emperors deified themselves as gods. Pharaoh and the Roman Emperors all believed that they should be worshipped like a god.

Ezekiel 29:3-6 *Speak, and say, Thus saith the LORD GOD; Behold, I AM against thee, Pharaoh king of Egypt, the great dragon that lieth in the midst of his rivers, which hath said, My river is mine own, and I have made it for myself. But I will put hooks in thy jaws, and I will cause the fish of thy rivers to stick unto thy scales, and I will bring thee up out of the midst of thy rivers, and all the fish of thy rivers shall stick unto thy scales. And I will leave thee thrown into the wilderness, thee and all the fish of thy rivers; thou shalt fall upon the open fields; thou shalt not be brought together, nor gathered; I have given thee for meat to the beasts of the field and to the fowls of the heaven. And all the inhabitants of Egypt shall know that I AM the LORD; because they have been a staff of reed to the House of Israel.*

I have written a few interesting historical facts here about the use of *the ancient Roman Army Military Standards.* The Roman legions used the dragon, the flying serpent, and other pagan symbols. One source I found said the following about these *Standards.*

"This Roman dragon serpent had a metal head, depicting sharp teeth and scale body armour. The Roman Standard was made of limp fabric, so that as they rode on their horses into battle, it filled with air, flew back and slithered in the wind like a windsock. It appeared to be alive as it moved and it was constructed to make a loud hissing sound to create fear, as the Roman troops galloped on horseback, charging forward to slay their perceived enemies. It was carried into battle by the designated Roman dragon bearer. This dragon serpent emblem that was referred to as the, "Draconarius," was depicted on ancient coins and drawings of very early battle scenes." It is interesting that the Thracian Soldiers who also used this emblem called it, "bel, beast and monster." Sometimes it was depicted with seven heads. Sometimes the head resembled a wolf or a fish." ***(Source: Legion XXIV– Imperial Standards ©2010 Imperial Aquila–Signums–Vexillium–Imago–Draco–Standards; legionxxiv.org/signum/).***

Another source that I researched reveals more about the *Roman Standards.* I suddenly remembered that Flavious Josephus, the first century Jewish Historian, wrote about the Roman soldiers carrying these pagan images into Jerusalem. This act was abhorrent to the Jewish Priests on the Holy Temple Mount. This caused an enormous rebellion! When I read that these *Standards* included emblems of the planets, such as Jupiter, which represents the abomination of desolation and included the emblem of a woman that had the moon at her feet, otherwise known as *"The lady of victory,"* and images of the crescent moon, the sun, the bull, and the eagle on their standards, sometimes even depicting a hand at the top of them as they marched, caused me to understand that this was all meant to be a parallel mockery of *God's Royal Military Standards.* Another source gave me even more details about these pagan *standards showing how they were used and worshipped by the pagan soldiers who carried them.*

"The Roman Soldiers would march into battle carrying a metal dragon head on the end of a pole, as a type of military standard, but they would also use what was called the, "Imago," on a pole. Often this pole was stuck into the ground at the tent of the Army camp. This was a 3 dimensional image and portrait of the face and head of the Emperor of Rome on the end of a pole and it was framed by a metal backing, to ever display the deified Roman Emperor. The Army would look to the Emperor on the Standard and commit their loyally to him. They were important in the fact that they were used as, "signaling posts." **(Source: "Army Standards – The Roman Empire," ©2008 roman-empire.net/army/leg-standards.html).**

"Imagines," the Latin word for, "Images," were said to be, "medallions, statues or busts of the Emperors that were in the camps of the soldiers." **(Source: "Signa Militaria," - A Dictionary of Greek and Roman Antiquities. William Smith, LLD. William Wayte. G. E. Marindin. Albemarle Street, London. John Murray. ©1890 All Rights Reserved) - (perseus.tufts.edu/hopper/text?doc=Perseus:text:1999.04.0063:entry=signa-militaria-cn)**

One of the most interesting details about this Roman Military Army Standard that parallels to Messiah Yeshua, who will be used in battle as *"The Royal Standard of God's Army"* against the enemies that try to attack His flock in the future, is the fact that *the standards* of the Roman legions were kept in their own tent in the heart of the camp. A trumpeter would sound a blast of the trumpet to draw attention to the *Standard,* so the soldiers would loyally look to the Emperor. Remember that when Yeshua *the Royal Standard* comes from Heaven, the trumpet will sound and this will get the attention of His loyal Saints! This also reminds me of *the Ark of the Covenant, containing the Testimony.* It was also placed inside its own tent at the heart of the camp of the Israelites, as the emblem of their *Royal Standard.* The Rod of Aaron that budded was part of this *Royal Standard* of the earthly Ark of the Covenant, but *Yeshua is the Royal Standard of the Heavenly Ark,* as the Almond Rod that budded to life. Remember that whenever the Divine Presence moved from the camp with the Ark, the Israelites would march, but whenever *the LORD'S Standard* was firmly resting and abiding in the tent of meeting, the Army did not march and did not go forward, until the LORD was leading the way before them as their *Official Royal Military Standard.*

Model Tent of the camp Photo ©2014 Kimberly K Ballard All Rights Reserved

Since the Roman scenario was literally a pagan copy of *the LORD'S Military Standards,* I now comprehended why the Roman soldiers put Yeshua's name on the top of His pole as *"THE KING OF THE JEWS!" He was the hand of God lifted up on a pole!* Notice in the following quote how the Roman's revered these *Standards,* put them into their own tent and even anointed them with oil and encircled them with laurel crowns! Yeshua is the anointed Jewish Messiah, having the oil of the Holy Spirit of God abiding upon Him and he was encircled with a Crown of Thorns to bear the curse of death from Eden! I am astonished that I have already written about Yeshua's Crown of Thorns in a later chapter and there, I reveal why the Roman's mocked Yeshua with this emblem, but the following quote stunned me with a verification of this truth! The *Roman Army standard* quote says the following, *that they really worshipped their standards!*

"The Standards were important in pitching and striking camp. The first act of setting up camp was to stake the Standards into the ground. The Standards were afforded their own tent, at the very heart of the camp itself, next to the tent of the commanding officer. When striking camps the Standards were drawn from the ground. For the Standards to remain stuck fast within the earth was deemed a serious omen and the soldiers, ever superstitious, might even refuse their orders to move, lest they offend the will of the gods. The Standards also played key roles at religious festivals. On these occasions, they would be anointed with precious oils and decorated with garlands, (laurel crowns). So revered were the Standards during such ceremonies, that it might be argued the Standards themselves were worshipped by the troops." **(Source: "Army Standards – The Roman Empire," ©2008 roman-empire.net/army/leg-standards.html).**

"Simple commands were relayed in tandem through the trumpeters by the cornicines and the Standard bearers. A blast from the trumpet (cornu) would draw attention to the Standard. A number of prearranged command signals, such as up and down movements, or swaying movements, then visually relayed the order to the ranks." **(Source: "Army Standards – The Roman Empire," ©2008 roman-empire.net/army/leg-standards.html).**

It is interesting that when the Bible speaks about the Anti-Christ, the opposition to God, he is given his power by the great dragon that has seven heads and ten horns and he worships a god of fortresses, which is the Tower of Babel. It is also interesting that in Revelation 13 whoever does not worship the *"image"* of the Beast is killed. In the book of Revelation, this image, or *"Imago"* is given breath so that it can speak, just like the Dragon that was full of wind or breath and hissed loudly to cause fear.

When the Dead Sea Scrolls were discovered in the twentieth century, a scroll was found in 1947 that was called, *"The War Scroll."* I remembered that this scroll goes into vivid detail about how the end time apocalyptic battle, otherwise known as *"Armageddon,"* the war to end all wars, will be fought between the sons of darkness and the sons of light. Passages that speak of this final battle give intricate details of God's Army assembling with their trumpets and banners to perform maneuvers.

"The sons of light will prepare the battle trumpets in (2:15-3-11). They carry specific banners for their tribes in (3:12-5-2). It goes into detail about the Military movements of the troops in (5:3-9:16) and it reveals prayers that the Priests give throughout the seven phases of battle engagement in (9:17-15:3). **(Source: The Dead Sea Scrolls: A New Translation ©1996 by: Michael Wise, Martin Abegg, Jr. and Edward Cook, Harper San Francisco. An Imprint of HarperCollins Publishers, Inc.).**

The Roman Standard that had the hand on the end of the pole mimics Yeshua as the Messianic Jewish hand of God and the War Scroll seems to indicate that in this final future end time battle *"The Great hand of God shall overcome Belial (Satan) and all the angels of his dominion and all the angels of his dominion shall be destroyed forever." (IQM 1:14-15) The War Scroll is, "A text that describes the eschatological last battle in gory detail as righteousness is fully victorious and evil is forever destroyed."* **(Source: The Dead Sea Scrolls: A New Translation ©1996 by: Michael Wise, Martin Abegg, Jr. & Edward Cook, Harper San Francisco. An Imprint of HarperCollins Publishers, Inc.).**

A KINGS Royal Crown Emblem
Photo ©2014 Kimberly K Ballard

Joshua's military movements with *the Ark and the Priests blowing the seven trumpets* as they went in to possess the Promised Land, is finalized with Yeshua and the seven trumpets of the wrath judgments against God's enemies, as *the military Saints of God's Army, prepare with the Heavenly Ark, to lead them into the everlasting Promised Land.* It is the final battle that *Yeshua will lead as the Royal Standard of God.* What I find astonishing about the War Scroll is that it says, *"And when the banners of the infantry cause their hearts to melt, then the strength of God will strengthen the hearts of the sons of light."* **(The Dead Sea Scrolls: A New Translation ©1996 by: Michael Wise, Martin Abegg, Jr. & Edward Cook, Harper San Francisco. An Imprint of HarperCollins Publishers, Inc.).**

It becomes obvious that the infantry of the sons of light are strengthened when *the Rod of God* is standing in their midst as *the Heavenly Ark of God goes before them,* to melt the hearts of their enemies. Isaiah 59:19 says, *"When the enemy shall come in like a flood, the Spirit of the LORD shall lift up a Standard against Him."* So it is written and so shall it be done! *The Royal Standard of God shall return and the 144,000 of each of the tribes of Israel shall assemble for the work of the LORD!* The LORD will reveal to them that we were made in *His image* alone and this is why KING Messiah Yeshua's image was left inside Holy Mount Moriah on His burial Shroud as *the Royal Standard of God!*

KING DAVID'S HARP MUSICAL INSTRUMENTS OF THE HOLY TEMPLE

Lamb, Gold Lyre on snow & Peacock Feather
Photos ©2015 KK Ballard All Rights Reserved

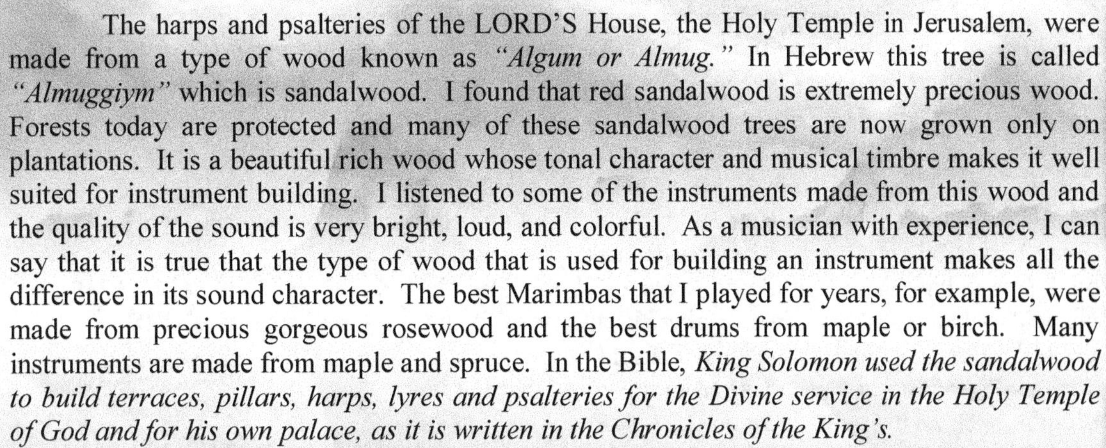

The harps and psalteries of the LORD'S House, the Holy Temple in Jerusalem, were made from a type of wood known as *"Algum or Almug."* In Hebrew this tree is called *"Almuggiym"* which is sandalwood. I found that red sandalwood is extremely precious wood. Forests today are protected and many of these sandalwood trees are now grown only on plantations. It is a beautiful rich wood whose tonal character and musical timbre makes it well suited for instrument building. I listened to some of the instruments made from this wood and the quality of the sound is very bright, loud, and colorful. As a musician with experience, I can say that it is true that the type of wood that is used for building an instrument makes all the difference in its sound character. The best Marimbas that I played for years, for example, were made from precious gorgeous rosewood and the best drums from maple or birch. Many instruments are made from maple and spruce. In the Bible, *King Solomon used the sandalwood to build terraces, pillars, harps, lyres and psalteries for the Divine service in the Holy Temple of God and for his own palace, as it is written in the Chronicles of the King's.*

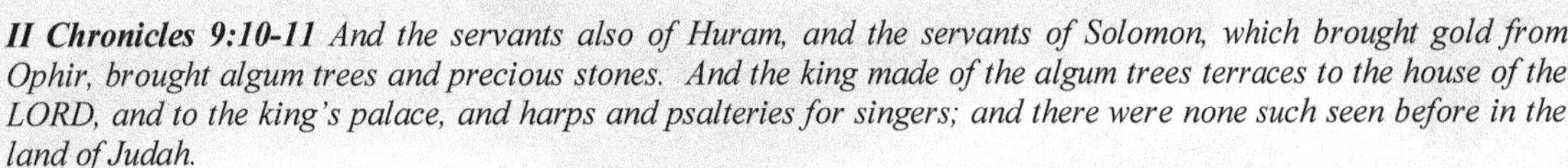

II Chronicles 9:10-11 *And the servants also of Huram, and the servants of Solomon, which brought gold from Ophir, brought algum trees and precious stones. And the king made of the algum trees terraces to the house of the LORD, and to the king's palace, and harps and psalteries for singers; and there were none such seen before in the land of Judah.*

King David was the harpist and sweet singer of Israel and his son Solomon traded with merchants by ship. When Solomon began his building of the Holy Temple, he hired Hiram King of Tyre who had a navy fleet of ships, and traveled with his servants to different lands to harvest exotic woods, precious gemstones, ivory, gold, silver, peacocks, and apes from Ophir and Tarshish.

II Chronicles 2:7- 9 *Send me now therefore a man cunning to work in gold, and in silver and in brass, and in iron, and in purple, and crimson, and blue, and that can skill to grave with the cunning men that are with me in Judah and in Jerusalem, whom David my father did provide. Send me also cedar trees, fir trees, and algum trees, out of Lebanon; for I know that thy servants can skill to cut lumber in Lebanon; and, behold, my servants shall be with thy servants. Even to prepare me timber in abundance; for the House which I am about to build shall be wonderful great.*

Ophir I believe was located at the Southern end of Arabia near Mount Sinai. It is interesting that the Bible mentions *Tarshish in Lebanon* as the source for some of the wood, but upon researching the gold from Ophir, I also found that there is a Mount Ophir in the Straits of Malacca in Malaysia and it was also known for all of the precious items that Hiram acquired and it is interesting that it was called *"The farthest mountain."* Some facts about sandalwood and Malaysia that I gathered stated that *"Peacocks originate in the area of Malaysia, in Southeast Asia and ivory was plentiful there. From ancient times this Mount Ophir in Malaysia was said to have an abundance of pure gold and sandalwood grew abundantly in the moist forests of its tropical climate. One of the facts about Malaysia is that it is considered to have*

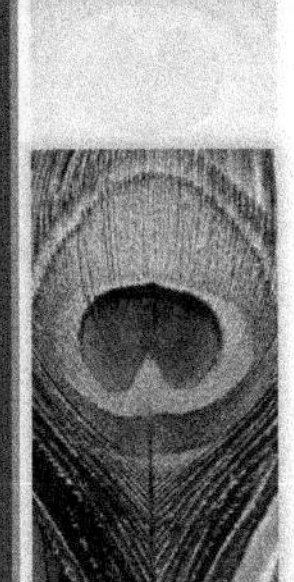

the most Flora or types of flowers of almost any place in the world and was often visited by traders and merchants. Some of the traders apparently came from as far away as Greece, to enjoy the lush tropical flowers, unusual plants, animals and waterfalls. In Malaysia, the gold and precious gemstones are considered to be very clear and pure." ***(Source: ©2013 Malaysia Wikipedia, the free encyclopedia).***

King David and King Solomon spared no expense in the building of the House of God! Sandalwood is still used today to build musical instruments, especially the *zither and erhu* which are Asian stringed instruments. The *erhu* is made of gorgeous ebony sandalwood. The *"guzheng or zither"* is also made from a variety of different types of sandalwood, usually ebony, red, or purple sandalwood. The psalteries of King Solomon that are mentioned in the Bible are indeed in the *zither or harp* family. The ancient *Israeli harp* had 22 strings and the sandalwood *guzheng* of Asia has between 18 and 23 strings. Sandalwood, which also came from Arabia, produces a superb rich sound that is stunning and surprisingly loud. An Israeli harpist friend of mine once told me that *"the Jewish Talmud indicates, that the harps that were played in the Holy Temple in Jerusalem on the Festival Days of the LORD, could be heard all the way to the city of Jericho."* ***(Quote from Shoshanna Harrari from House of Harrari Israel).*** Sandalwood which of course is known for its long lasting fragrance was always prized for its beautiful wood grain and because it was resistant to wood rot, this would have made it an excellent choice for building in the LORD'S Holy Temple. The following Scriptures also indicate that the *Algum Trees* harvested by Hiram, were brought back to Jerusalem on his merchant navy ships and were used to build the musical instruments, the harps, psalteries, and lyres for the LORD'S Divine service in the Holy Temple.

The trumpets were made from the silver that Hiram brought back on his trade excursions.

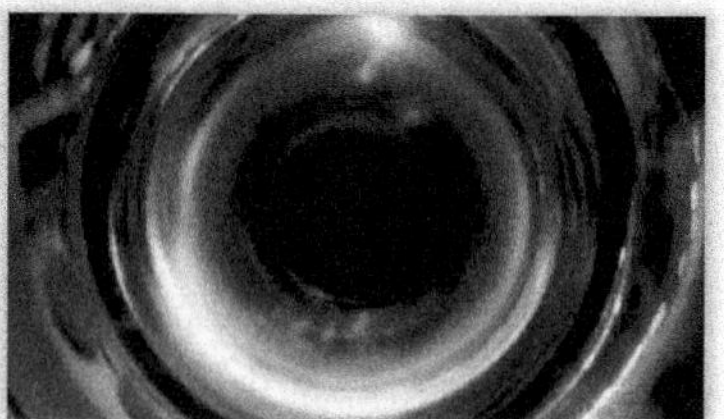

All Trumpet & Cymbal Photos
©2013 Kimberly K Ballard
All Rights Reserved

I Kings 10:10-15 *And she gave the king an hundred and twenty talents of gold, and of spices very great store, and precious stones; there came no more such abundance of spices as these which the queen of Sheba gave to king Solomon. And the navy also of Hiram, that brought gold from Ophir, brought in from Ophir great plenty of almug trees, and precious stones. And the king made of the almug trees pillars for the House of the LORD, and for the king's house, harps also and psalteries for singers; there came no such almug trees, nor were seen unto this day. And King Solomon gave unto the queen of Sheba all her desire, whatsoever she asked, beside that which Solomon gave her of his royal bounty. So she turned and went to her own country, she and her servants. Now the weight of gold that came to Solomon in one year was six hundred threescore and six talents of gold. Beside that he had of the merchantmen, and of the traffick of the spice merchants, and of all the kings of Arabia, and of the governors of the country.*

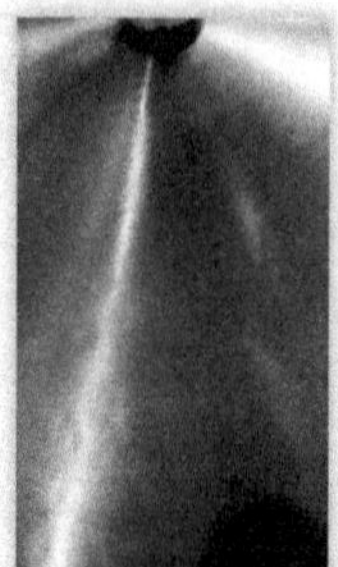

II Chronicles 9:21 *For the king's ships went to Tarshish with the servants of Huram; every three years once came the ships of Tarshish bringing gold, and silver, ivory, and apes, and peacocks.*

The ships only returned to Jerusalem every three years with the goods. With all of this knowledge coming to light, we can be sure that the Messiah is coming soon. If the harps for the LORD'S Temple are built from this gorgeous heavenly sandalwood from Havilah which is NW Arabia near Mount Sinai, then we will be closer to Heaven! God was praised with high sounding cymbals made of bronze! I believe that the gold for the Holy Temple also came from this region and it was all in abundance to glorify the KING OF KINGS AND LORD OF LORDS in Jerusalem.

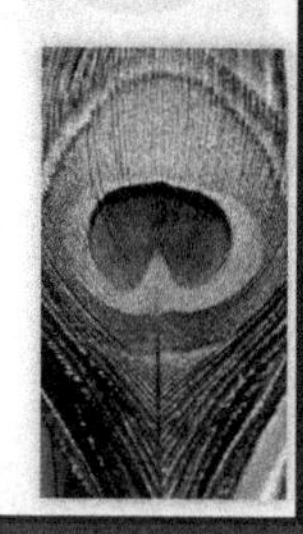

THE DOOR OF THE SHEEP WOUNDS IN THE HANDS OF THE LORD THE NAILS

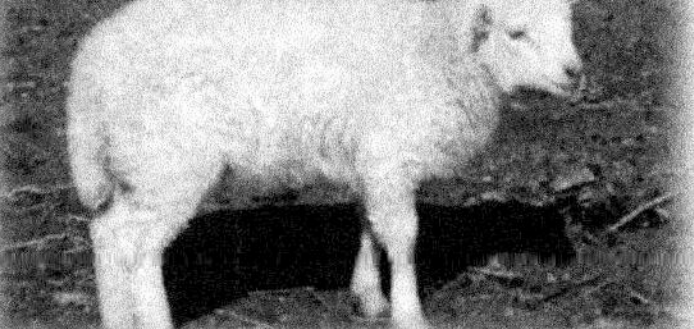

The Rod and Staff guides us into green pastures and leads us beside still waters. King David prophesied in Psalm 23 about the Heavenly Garden of God.

When Yeshua spoke the following Words, He declared that He is the one who has *the key of David*, and He is the one who opens and shuts the door of Heaven. No one else has this power and no one else has *the key of David* that unlocks the door, but He reveals the key that unlocks the door to us, if we abide in Him. He manifests Himself to those who love Him!

Revelation 3:7-8 *And to the angel of the church in Philadelphia write; These things saith He that is Holy, He that is true, He that hath the key of David, He that openeth, and no man shutteth; and shutteth, and no man openeth; I know thy works; behold, I have set before thee an open door, and no man can shut it; for thou hast kept My Word, and hast not denied My Name.*

John 10:9 *I AM the door; by Me if any man enter in, he shall be saved, and shall go in and out, and find pasture.*

John 10:7 *Then said Yeshua unto them again, Verily, verily, I say unto you, I AM the door of the sheep.*

As we think about this in a deeper way, we find that Isaiah prophesied about Messiah Yeshua, using these exact words and it is quite remarkable.

Isaiah 22:22-25 *And the key of the House of David will I lay upon His shoulder; so He shall open, and none shall shut; and He shall shut, and none shall open. And I will fasten Him as a nail in a sure place; and He shall be for a glorious throne to His Father's House, And they shall hang upon Him all the glory of His Father's House, the offspring and the issue, all vessels of small quantity, from the vessels of cups, even to all the vessels of flagons. In that day, saith the LORD of Hosts, shall the nail that is fastened in the sure place be removed, and be cut down, and fall; and the burden that was upon it shall be cut off; for the LORD hath spoken it.*

Now Messiah Yeshua, the Branch of David, was cut off for the sins of His people and this was *"the burden that was removed."* Since Yeshua alone holds this key of David, it is true that He shall open and none shall shut because He is the door of the Heavenly Ark of the Testimony of the LORD in Heaven. The outstanding part of this prophecy in Isaiah, though, is the proclamation that the LORD gave when He said *"that He will fasten Him as a nail in a sure place and that they shall hang upon Him all the glory of His Father's House."* Not only was Yeshua nailed with wrought iron nails to the cross, but He was glorified in Golgotha, which is Holy Mount Moriah. The place where Yeshua was nailed and fastened in a *"sure place"* is the sacred Mount, where the LORD'S House was built. This door and gate of Heaven has the nails in it! *The LORD fastened Himself as a nail in a "sure place" where the LORD'S Name dwells forever in Jerusalem Israel!*

If we think about the promise of Messiah's glorious resurrection in this place, then it pertains directly to the words *"sure place."*

By definition the word *"sure"* means; *"Impossible to doubt or dispute. Not hesitating or wavering, Confident as of something awaited or expected, Bound to come about, or happen, inevitable. Having one's course directed, destined or bound. Worthy of being trusted or depended on, reliable and marked by freedom from doubt."* By definition the word *"place"* means *"An area with definite or indefinite boundaries. A building or area set aside for a specified purpose; A place of worship. A dwelling or a house."* **(Source: ©2010 thefreedictionary.com).**

Yeshua was therefore nailed in a *"sure place"* because we are *"awaiting and expecting"* the promise of Eternal life and it is *"inevitable."* It is *"impossible to doubt or dispute"* what Yeshua accomplished as the Divine Testimony of the LORD and this means that our course as believers is *"directed, destined and bound"* to be eternally with Him in the Kingdom of Heaven. We can depend on Messiah Yeshua because He is *trustworthy and reliable*. This *"sure place"* that was set aside for the KING to reign is the *"place,"* of *"The House"* of the Living God in Jerusalem.

After Yeshua was fastened on the cross with the wrought iron nails, the Branch was cut off, precisely as the LORD proclaimed it in the book of Isaiah. So Messiah Yeshua's Living Testimony is a sure thing and it cannot be moved because He was nailed to the cross to specifically bear the burden of His people in the secure place of God's Holy Mountain. He was also resurrected to life in the hand hewn tomb that was cut out of the rock in Holy Mount Moriah. *So this Living Testimony of the Ark of Heaven is "The glory of His Father's House."*

The Romans secured the Great Rolling Stone that served as the door of Yeshua's sepulchre with at least one huge iron spike. The remains of this ancient iron spike can still be seen embedded in the stone to the left of the exterior entrance to the door in Holy Mount Moriah. It remained fastened in the *"sure place"* in the Holy Mountain where Yeshua fulfilled the Eternal Testimony of the Heavenly Ark of God as it is written in Matthew's Gospel, and this is without a doubt *"the gate of Heaven at the House of God."* Twice Pontius Pilate told his Roman Soldiers *"to go make the Garden sepulchre in Mount Moriah as 'sure' as possible!"*

Matthew 27:65 *Pilate said unto them, Ye have a watch; go your way, make it as sure as ye can. So they went, and made the sepulchre sure, sealing the stone, and setting a watch.*

A door is fastened securely with iron nails so that it cannot be moved. The Great Rolling Stone of Yeshua's sepulchre was fastened with at least one iron spike in Holy Mount Moriah so it could not be moved, but it was rolled back only by the Angel of the LORD.

When King David gathered all the materials to build the Holy Temple in Jerusalem, he prepared *wrought iron nails for the doors of the gates.*

I Chronicles 22:3 *And David prepared iron in abundance for the nails for the doors of the gates, and for the joinings; and brass in abundance without weight.*

Hand forged Iron Nails Photo ©2013 Kimberly K Ballard All Rights Reserved

So we can say with absolute certainty that the *"sure place"* where Yeshua was nailed with *hand forged iron nails* and where His Great Rolling Stone was secured with an *iron spike* is *the gate of Heaven*, and in this place, in God's Garden in Holy Mount Moriah, the Good Shepherd with His Rod laid down His life for His sheep and defeated the serpents curse of death. Here in this *place,* the Almond Rod of God budded to life and became the Eternal Covenant of everlasting life!

In Ecclesiastes, we read something interesting about *"the Words of the wise that are like goads."* A goad is a rod with a point on one end and it is used to urge the sheep into action and to prod them along. *This description clearly fits Messiah Yeshua, who is the wise Word of God, the Rod or the goad that is urging and prodding the sheep of Israel into action!*

When Saul was blinded by Yeshua's Shechinah glory on the road to Damascus, Yeshua said the following words to Saul about *the goads* because Yeshua was about to prod him into action!

Acts 9:5-6 *And he said, Who art Thou, LORD? And the LORD said, I AM Yeshua whom thou persecutest; it is hard for thee to kick against the goads. And he trembling and astonished said, LORD, what wilt Thou have me to do? And the LORD said unto him, Arise, and go into the city, and it shall be told thee what thou must do.*

Hand forged Iron Nail
Photo ©2013 Kimberly K Ballard

Ecclesiastes 12:11 *The Words of the wise are as goads, and as nails fastened by the Masters of assemblies, which are given from one Shepherd.*

The goad in this Heavenly encounter is *the Rod of God, the Messiah* who was speaking to Saul of Tarsus from Heaven and Saul was astonished at Yeshua's profound Words! Now we can see that the Word, the Rod, was fastened with iron nails by *"the Master of assemblies,"* and this was given to us *"by one Shepherd"* called *"KING Messiah the LORD."*

Now it is fascinating that Ezra told us that the LORD will give Israel *a nail in His Holy Place* and that their eyes will be lightened and they would be revived from bondage.

Ezra 9:8 *And now for a little space grace hath been shewed from the LORD our God, to leave us a remnant to escape, and to give us a nail in His Holy Place, that our God may lighten our eyes, and give us a little reviving in our bondage.*

The Messiah, who was nailed there and gloriously resurrected to life, is the one *who lighted the eyes of Israel* as the light of His Living glory shined forth out of the darkness of the sepulchre in God's Garden. Yeshua is the radiant light of the world. *Yeshua revived Israel when He lighted their eyes because they were no longer under the bondage of death.* The Gentiles that also believed in Him were delivered from the bondage of death. Yeshua said *"that the time was coming, when everyone would worship God in Spirit and in truth."* This is realized in the fact that *Yeshua is the Living Torah and the Almond Tree of Life.* Yeshua's Words are therefore *Spirit and life.* So grace and truth came through Yeshua the Messiah, the LORD God of Israel.

John 6:63 *It is the Spirit that quickeneth; the flesh profiteth nothing; the Words that I speak unto you, they are Spirit, and they are life.*

John 1:17 *For the law was given by Moses, but grace and truth came by Yeshua Messiah.*

Simon Brown pointing to the hand forged Iron Spike at the Garden Tomb
Photo ©2011 Simon Brown England

So it is by the Divine Providence of God that Messiah Yeshua was fastened in a *"sure place"* at the gate of Heaven with the iron nails because He is the secure door of the sheep in the place where He fulfilled His Eternal *Testimony,* and there is no other way to enter the Heavenly Promised Land, to dwell in God's Eternal Garden.

Psalm 93:5 *Thy Testimonies are very sure; holiness becometh Thine House, O LORD, forever.*

Colossians 2:8-15 *Beware lest any man spoil you through philosophy and vain deceit, after the tradition of men, after the rudiments of the world, and not after Messiah. For in Him dwelleth all the fullness of the Godhead bodily. And ye are complete in Him, which is the head of all principality and power; In whom also ye are circumcised with the circumcision made without hands, in putting off the body of the sins of the flesh by the circumcision of Messiah; Buried with Him in baptism, wherein also ye are risen with Him through the faith of the operation of God, who hath raised Him from the dead. And you, being dead in your sins and the uncircumcision of your flesh, hath He quickened together with Him, having forgiven you all trespasses; Blotting out the handwriting of ordinances that was against us, which was contrary to us, and took it out of the way, nailing it to His cross; And having spoiled principalities and powers, He made a shew of them openly, triumphing over them in it.*

The Prophet Zechariah wrote down the following Words of the LORD.

Zechariah 10:3-4 *Mine anger was kindled against the shepherds, and I punished the goats; for the LORD of Hosts hath visited His flock the House of Judah, and hath made them as His goodly horse in the battle. Out of Him came forth the corner, out of Him the nail, out of Him the battle bow, out of Him every oppressor together.*

The LORD visited His flock, and specifically *The House of Judah.* Yeshua is from the tribe of Judah. He is God who visited His people. Remember that *Messiah Yeshua is the Chief Cornerstone of the Heavenly Temple and the nail came out of Him!* This brings to mind something that is profound, that we find in the following story. This story takes place just after Yeshua is resurrected. I was floored when the LORD revealed this to me. The Jewish disciples were discussing the nail prints in Yeshua's hands. Then after eight days, they were together again with Thomas. Now Thomas, who had doubted that they had seen the Messiah alive, told them *"that unless he saw the nail prints in His hands and put his finger into the print of the nails and thrust his hand into His side, he would not believe."* So now they were together with Thomas again and Yeshua appeared suddenly and stood in their midst while the door was shut! He then immediately told Thomas to believe and to stop doubting, as He showed them the nail marks in His hands! *Yeshua was at that very moment revealing that He is the door nailed in a secure place at the gate of Heaven in God's Garden in Jerusalem Israel!*

The Garden Tomb, "The sure place"
Measuring the Garden Tomb Photo ©2011 Simon Brown England

John 20:25-29 *The other disciples therefore said unto him, We have seen the LORD, but he said unto them, Except I shall see in His hands the print of the nails, and put my finger into the print of the nails, and thrust my hand into His side, I will not believe. After eight days again His disciples were within, and Thomas with them; then came Yeshua, the doors being shut, and stood in the midst, and said, Peace be unto you. Then saith He to Thomas, Reach hither thy finger, and behold My hands; and reach hither thy hand, and thrust it into My side; and be not faithless, but believing. and Thomas answered, My LORD and My God. Yeshua saith unto him, Thomas, because thou hast seen Me, thou hast believed; blessed are they that have not seen, and yet have believed.*

Thomas suddenly grasped the meaning and truth that *Yeshua was the door of Heaven* and Thomas proclaimed at once, *"My LORD and My God."* Now of course you may wonder why I am saying all of this about Thomas. When you read what the Prophet Zechariah wrote, you will understand why Thomas said to Yeshua, *"My LORD and My God."* You must read the Words of the LORD God of Israel! *Remember that Yeshua is the hand of God, the Yad who has the wounds in His hands at the wrist, which is evident on the burial Shroud of Yeshua!*

Zechariah 13:1-9 *In that day there shall be a fountain opened to the house of David and to the inhabitants of Jerusalem for sin and for uncleanness. And it shall come to pass in that day, saith the LORD of Hosts, that I will cut off the names of the idols out of the land, and they shall no more be remembered; and also I will cause the prophets and the unclean spirit to pass out of the land. And it shall come to pass, that when any shall yet prophesy, then his father and his mother that begat him shall say unto him, Thou shalt not live; for thou speakest lies in the Name of the LORD; and his father and his mother that begat him shall thrust him through when he prophesieth. And it shall come to pass in that day, that the prophets shall be ashamed every one of his vision when he hath prophesied; neither shall they wear a rough garment to deceive; But he shall say, I am no Prophet, I am an husbandman; for man taught me to keep cattle from my youth. And one shall say unto Him, What are these wounds in thine hands? Then He shall answer, Those with which I was wounded in the House of My friends. Awake, O sword, against My Shepherd, and against the man that is my fellow, saith the LORD of Hosts; smite the Shepherd, and the sheep shall be scattered; and I will turn mine hand upon the little ones. And it shall come to pass, that in all the land, saith the LORD, two parts therein shall be cut off and die; but the third shall be left therein. And I will bring the third part through the fire, and will refine them as silver is refined, and will try them as gold is tried; they shall call on My Name, and I will hear them; I will say, It is my people; and they shall say, The LORD is my God.*

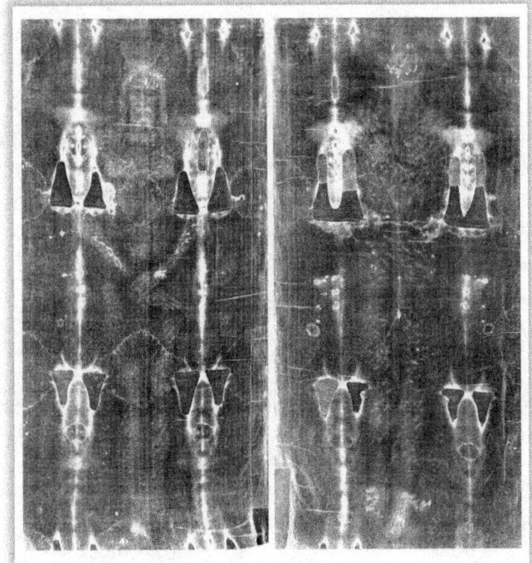

Official Shroud Pair Photo showing the wrist wounds
Photograph ©1978 Barrie M. Schwortz Collection, STERA Inc., All Rights Reserved

The LORD of Hosts is speaking these Words! *The LORD God of Israel is declaring that He is the one who has the wounds in His hands that He got in the House of His friends in the "sure place" of Holy Mount Moriah!* The House I believe He is referring to is the Holy Temple of the LORD that was in Jerusalem during the Second Temple period, when Messiah Yeshua was crucified and bore the wounds in His hands. Without a doubt, the wounds that the LORD of Hosts is speaking about here in this Scripture are *the wounds in His own hands caused by the wrought iron nails during the crucifixion.* Now the wounds are at the base of His hands at *the wrist* where the *"median"* nerve was damaged, as seen on the Shroud of Turin. Coincidentally, Moses dwelt in the land of *"Median or Midian," in the wilderness of death,* before guiding the Israelites to the Promised Land! I am astonished at this connection that the LORD showed me! *The LORD was struck through the median nerve to hasten His death, so that He could bring us the Living Covenant of Eternal life at the gate of Heaven in Jerusalem! Median* was the ancient land of the Medes. Remember that I just said that *the Rod Messiah is the Yad the right hand of God*, and the wounds are in His hands or wrists through the *median* nerve! Thomas declared, *"My LORD and My God,"* because Thomas already knew this Scripture in Zechariah about the LORD of Hosts saying that He has the wounds in His hands! Thomas was startled when He suddenly grasped the full meaning of what He was witnessing with his own eyes! It was a fulfilled Scripture! It was completely shocking! Now Thomas understood that *this was the LORD God of Israel, the LORD of Hosts* who appeared in the room and stood in their midst while the door was shut! This was proof that the LORD God of Israel had indeed visited His people! This becomes quite clear in the Gospel of Luke. The Jewish people declared the following statement about Yeshua after they witnessed His miracles.

Luke 7:16-17 *And there came a fear on all; and they glorified God, saying, That a great Prophet is risen up among us; and, That God hath visited His people. And this rumour of Him went forth throughout all Judea, and throughout all the region round about.*

The Jewish High Priest Zacharias, who was John the Baptists father, declared the same words. Zacharias was prophesying that the Messiah was about to arrive to redeem His people Israel, and He refers to *the Messiah as "the LORD God of Israel."*

Luke 1:67-68 *And his father Zacharias was filled with the Holy Spirit and prophesied, saying, Blessed be the LORD God of Israel; for He hath visited and redeemed His people.*

It is very interesting that even the words spoken by Judas Iscariot tell us that he betrayed the innocent blood of the Messiah. This was written to reveal that Yeshua was the perfect spotless innocent Lamb that God provided for us to atone for the sins of His people on Passover on Nisan 14! Remember, Judas Iscariot *betrayed Yeshua ha-Ben for the redeeming price of thirty pieces of silver.* Messiah was redeemed! The LORD God of Israel also declared in the book of Zechariah that *He was betrayed for thirty pieces of silver and that this was the price He said "I was prized at of them."* Now the LORD God of Israel spoke these Words that foretold the above events and they were to happen when He visited His people and yet they did not recognize Him. In both cases, the silver was cast down in the Holy Temple and the Potter's field was purchased with the silver. The Scriptures prove again that Messiah Yeshua is the LORD God of Israel. This is another reason Thomas declared *"My LORD and My God." The LORD of Hosts said that He had the wounds in His hands and that they shall say, "The LORD is my God."* Thomas fulfilled this prophecy when He suddenly grasped the identity of the one who was standing alive in their midst when the door was shut. Messiah Yeshua was valued at thirty pieces of silver. These are the Prophetic Words that were spoken by the LORD God of Israel and they clearly say that He will be betrayed for thirty pieces of silver. Notice that it says in Zechariah that this was *"the Word of the LORD!" His Staff was cut off!*

Zechariah 11:10-17 *And I took My Staff, even Beauty, and cut it asunder, that I might break My Covenant which I had made with all the people. And it was broken in that day; and so the poor of the flock that waited upon Me knew that it was the Word of the LORD. And I said unto them, If ye thing good, give Me My price; and if not, forbear. So they weighed for My price thirty pieces of silver. And the LORD said unto me, Cast it unto the potter; a goodly price that I was prized at of them. And I took the thirty pieces of silver, and cast them to the potter in the House of the LORD. Then I cut asunder mine other Staff, even Bands, that I might break the brotherhood between Judah and Israel. And the LORD said unto me, Take unto thee yet the instruments of a foolish shepherd. For, lo, I will raise up a shepherd in the land, which shall not visit those that be cut off, neither shall seek the young one, nor heal that that is broken, nor feed that that standeth still; but he shall eat the flesh of the fat, and tear their claws in pieces. Woe to the idol shepherd that leaveth the flock! The sword shall be upon his arm, and upon his right eye; his arm shall be clean dried up, and his right eye shall be utterly darkened.*

When Messiah, *the first born son, the Living Torah,* visited His people Israel, this Scripture was fulfilled and Matthew, the Levite, recorded it in his Gospel account.

Matthew 27:3-11 *Then Judas, which had betrayed Him, when he saw that he was condemned, repented himself, and brought again the thirty pieces of silver to the Chief Priests and Elders, Saying, I have sinned in that I have betrayed the innocent blood. And they said, What is that to us? See thou to that. And he cast down the pieces of silver in the Temple, and departed, and went and hanged himself. And the Chief Priests took the silver pieces, and said, It is not lawful for to put them into the treasury, because it is the price of blood. And they took counsel, and bought with them the potter's field, to bury strangers in. Wherefore that field was called, The field of blood, unto this day. Then was fulfilled that which was spoken by Jeremiah the Prophet, saying, And they took the thirty pieces of silver, the price of Him that was valued, whom they of the children of Israel did value; And gave them for the potter's field, as the LORD appointed me. And Yeshua stood before the governor; and the governor asked Him, saying, Art thou the KING of the Jews? And Yeshua said unto him, Thou sayest.*

After the LORD was betrayed for thirty pieces of silver and the Potter's field was purchased, Yeshua stood before the governor and they asked Yeshua, *"Are you the KING of the Jews?" He declared that this was the truth!* Yeshua was and is the KING OF KINGS. He not only is the LORD God of Israel betrayed for thirty pieces of silver, but He has the wounds in

His hands to prove it. The Good Shepherd clearly left the photographic evidence of this miracle on Yeshua's burial Shroud image. The LORD said that there would come a time, and this time has already passed, that the shepherds of Israel would not care for the flock of Israel, and that this would be a great sin against the LORD. So the LORD came down from Heaven as the Rod of the Good Shepherd of Israel, to save His flock from the bad shepherds and to shine forth the light of the glory of God upon them for Eternal salvation. The LORD used His Rod to eventually draw His entire flock, including Gentile believers, back to Jerusalem.

Matthew 9:36 *But when He saw the multitudes, He was moved with compassion on them, because they fainted, and were scattered abroad, as sheep having no shepherd.*

The Good Shepherd was *cut off with His Staff*, and the Holy Temple was burned exactly 40 years later. The sheep of Israel were scattered all over the world and the LORD'S flock wandered into all the nations, but the Testimony of the resurrected Living Messiah would draw them all back home again!

Jeremiah 50:17 *Israel is a scattered sheep; the lions have driven him away; first the king of Assyria hath devoured him; and last this Nebuchadnezzar king of Babylon hath broken his bones.*

Isaiah 53:6 *All we like sheep have gone astray; we have turned everyone to his own way; and the LORD hath laid on Him the iniquity of us all.*

The word *"smite"* means *"to strike down with deadly blows and to injure and slay with weapons or with the hands."* So the phrase, *"Smite the Shepherd and the sheep will be scattered,"* is referring to the injuries that Yeshua received from the deadly blows. The *smiting* of the Messiah happened as He was killed with weapons and slapped and punched in the face with the fists and opened hands of the Roman Soldiers. Remember that when Moses struck the rock with the rod twice, the LORD was angry at Moses, so Moses could not enter the Promised Land. Remember the Rock was Messiah, the Rod of the Good Shepherd, who was struck. Yeshua only had to pay the Bride's price one time. Yeshua was *struck* again with the Roman lance, which pierced His heart and caused the life blood and living water to drain out from His heart and onto the ground in God's Garden. His life blood saved us. When the nails were driven into Yeshua's wrists and feet, He was *struck* again. His head was pierced with thorns, as the Roman Soldiers *struck* the Crown of Thorns with the reeds in their hands.

Now Yeshua was in Galilee preaching in the Synagogues and He proclaimed that He had come to take the yoke of the oppressing bad shepherds off the neck of His people Israel. Yeshua declared that He is the one who truly loves them enough to bear *the bitterness of the curse,* in order to bring them Eternal life. As Yeshua stood in the midst of the Synagogue, He spoke the Words that brought freedom and liberty to the sons and daughters of Israel. It must have been incredible when Yeshua told the Jews that day that the Scriptures were being fulfilled in their hearing! One of the interesting things that I noticed right away about the following passage of Scripture, is the fact that *the Jewish people in the Synagogues were all speaking well of Yeshua* and they were amazed at the gracious Words that were proceeding from Yeshua's lips because *the Living Torah* coming from His lips was very soothing to their Jewish souls! Yeshua fulfilled the prophesy from *Isaiah 61:1-11.*

Luke 4:14-22 *And Yeshua returned to Galilee in the power of the Spirit; and news about Him spread through all the surrounding district. And He began teaching in their Synagogues and was praised by all. And He came to Nazareth, where He had been brought up; and as was His custom, He entered the Synagogue on the Sabbath, and stood up to read. And the book of the Prophet Isaiah was handed to Him. And He opened the book, and found the place where it was written, The Spirit of the LORD is upon Me, Because He anointed Me to Preach the Gospel to the poor. He has sent Me to proclaim release to the captives, And recovery of sight to the blind, To set free those who are downtrodden, To proclaim the favorable year of the LORD. And He closed the book, and gave it back to the* *attendant, and sat down; and the eyes of all in the Synagogue were fixed upon Him. And He began to say to them, Today this Scripture has been fulfilled in your hearing. And all were speaking well of Him, and wondering at the gracious Words which were falling from His lips; and they were saying, Is this not Joseph's son?*

Isaiah 61 says that the LORD turns our garments snow white, as wedding garments of salvation, and the bride is given a garland as a crown. We have been cleansed by the Living Water and the fire of His Holy Spirit, and *we are wrapped in a robe of the Living Torah of salvation, as His Bride. We are literally wrapped in His robe of light, like a Heavenly Tallit!*

The Jewish Messiah was *the seed* that sprouted to life that makes all the other seeds that are sown in Him, to sprout up to everlasting life. This is the idea behind the word *"Torah."* The Torah is meant to be dispersed like seeds. *So Yeshua was the seed of the Living Torah that sprouted and was to be dispersed into all the nations of the world to draw us back to His Heavenly Kingdom.* The sheep of Israel will be gathered in the arms of the LORD by Yeshua because He holds us in His heart and He cared enough to go searching for His lost sheep. Yeshua revealed that He is the Jewish Bridegroom, who wears the garland for His wedding day, to His beloved. The following verses reveal that the Messiah will gather His sheep.

Ezekiel 34:*6 My sheep wandered through all the mountains, and upon every high hill; yea, My flock was scattered upon all the face of the earth, and none did search or seek after them.*

I Peter 2:25 *For ye were as sheep going astray; but are now returned unto the Shepherd and Bishop of your souls.*

Isaiah 40:10-11 *Behold, the LORD God will come with might, With His Arm ruling for Him. Behold, His reward is with Him, Like a Shepherd He will tend His flock, In His Arms He will gather the lambs, And carry them in His bosom; He will gently lead the nursing ewes.*

Let us always remember that a Good Shepherd is concerned when His sheep go astray and He will do whatever it takes to bring us safely back to Him. He was even willing to lay down His life, to be nailed in the *"sure place"* to bring Eternal life to His sheep, so they could live with Him forever in paradise, not in the land of Median! Messiah Yeshua has accomplished this for Israel, and for everyone in every nation that comes to the true and Living God. He sustains His lambs forever in His loving arms and that sounds very comforting to me!

Sheep & Lambs, Snow on Junipers & Jerusalem Lion Emblem

SING THE HALLEL

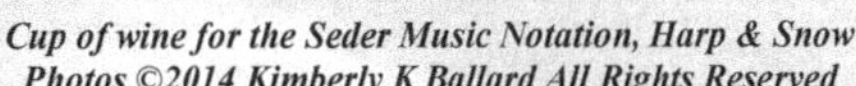

Cup of wine for the Seder Music Notation, Harp & Snow

It was Passover when the Jewish disciples were partaking of the Jewish Passover Seder when Messiah Yeshua made the New Covenant with Israel. Just after He sealed the New Covenant of the heart with His Bride by partaking of the broken unleavened bread and the third cup of wine, immediately the Jewish disciples went out *singing a hymn* and they ascended up to the Mount of Olives. Yeshua told them that after He was raised to life, *He would go before them. He meant as the Living Testimony of the Heavenly Ark of the LORD'S Eternal Covenant.*

Mark 14:26-28 *And after singing a hymn, they went out to the Mount of Olives. And Yeshua said to them, You will all fall away, because it is written, I will strike down the Shepherd, and the sheep shall be scattered, But after I have been raised, I will go before you to Galilee.*

This is such an overlooked Scripture. It is so important because the hymn that Yeshua and the Jewish disciples were singing after the Passover Seder was called *"The Hallel."* The prayers of *"The Hallel"* are found in Psalm 113-118. Why is this set of Psalms important? Right after Yeshua sealed the New Covenant with them, with the Passover wine, the Jewish disciples sang the following words with the Messiah!

Passover Seder cups & Matzah

Psalm 116:13 *I will take the cup of salvation, and call on the Name of the LORD.*

The cup of salvation they were singing about is the very cup of salvation that Yeshua had just offered His precious chosen Jewish disciples! Yeshua proclaimed at this Passover Seder that this was the cup that He would not drink again until He comes to usher in the Kingdom of God and restores Israel and Jerusalem forever as the place of His Eternal throne. This will fulfill the final piece of Israel's redemption. Another passage from *"The Hallel"* that is found in Psalm 118 contains the following phrases that pertain to Yeshua's Covenant as the Messiah. In this part of *the Hallel,* it mentions *the opening of the gates of righteousness, so that we may enter in because the LORD has "Become our salvation!"* This Psalm *mentions the stone that the builders rejected that has become the head of the corner.* The song speaks of *"binding the sacrifice to the horns of the altar" and Yeshua was about to be bound and taken away* to become the perfect spotless Lamb that was offered by the LORD for us, and He fulfilled this at the gate of Heaven!

Psalm 118:19-28 *<u>Open to me the gates of righteousness</u>. I will enter into them. I will give thanks to God. <u>This is the gate of the LORD; the righteous will enter into it</u>. I will give thanks to you, for you have answered me, and have become my salvation. The stone which the builders rejected has become the head of the corner. This is the LORD'S doing. It is marvelous in our eyes. This is the day that the LORD has made. We will rejoice and be glad in it! Save us now, we beg you, LORD! LORD, we beg you, send prosperity now. Blessed is He who comes in the Name of the LORD! We have blessed you out of the House of the LORD. The LORD is God, and He has given us light. <u>Bind the sacrifice with cords, even to the horns of the altar</u>. You are my God, and I will give thanks to you. You are my God, I will exalt you. Oh give thanks to the LORD, for He is good, for His loving kindness endures forever.*

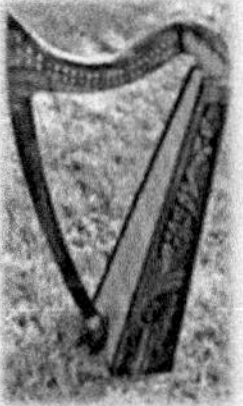

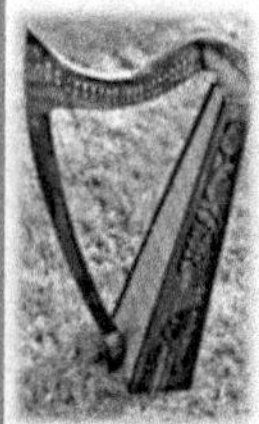

Yeshua declared that when Israel once again proclaims with all their heart the words, *"Blessed is He who comes in the Name of the LORD,"* then He will hear and return for them! *In Hebrew this is "Baruch Haba B'shem Adonai."* In Psalm 118:25 of the Hallel they are also calling out, *"Save now, I beseech Thee, O LORD: O LORD, I beseech Thee, send now prosperity."* Yeshua mentions *"Baruch Haba B'shem Adonai"* pertaining to His return for the virgins in Matthew 23.

Matthew 23:38-39 *Behold, your House is left unto you desolate. For I say unto you, Ye shall not see Me henceforth, till ye shall say, Blessed is He that cometh in the Name of the LORD.*

The opening of the gates in *the Hallel,* is speaking of the Messiah, since of course Yeshua is the door and the gate into Heaven in Holy Mount Moriah. At the crucifixion, when *the veil was made cleft by the Rod of God lifted up,* Yeshua our Great High Priest made the way through the veil to *the Holiest Place,* so we could enter in forever into His Divine rest in the KINGS inner court!

Resembling the Gates of the Holy Temple in Jerusalem
Dedicated to the Malloy Family

Mark 15:38 *And the veil of the Temple was rent in twain from the top to the bottom.*

Psalm 28:8-9 *The LORD is their strength, And He is a saving defense to His anointed. Save Thy people, and bless Thine inheritance; Be their Shepherd also, and carry them forever.*

Psalm 80:1-3 *Oh, give ear, Shepherd of Israel, Thou who dost lead Joseph like a flock; Thou who art enthroned above the Cherubim, shine forth! Before Ephraim and Benjamin and Manasseh, stir up Thy power, And come to save us! O God, restore us, And cause Thy face to shine upon us, and we will be saved.*

The LORD describes Himself as *the Deliverer* in Ezekiel, proclaiming that *He* will care for His people. Messiah the Redeemer wants all the scattered sheep of Israel to be gathered under *His Rod and Staff.* For two thousand years He has been gathering them from every nation where they were scattered on a gloomy and cloudy day! Remember that with God a thousand years is like one day!

Ezekiel 34:10-12 *Thus saith the LORD God; Behold, I am against the shepherds; and I will require My flock at their hand, and cause them to cease from feeding the flock; neither shall the shepherds feed themselves anymore; for I will deliver My flock from their mouth, that they may not be meat for them. For thus saith the LORD God; Behold, I, even I, will both search My sheep, and seek them out. As a shepherd seeketh out his flock in the day that he is among his sheep that are scattered; so will I seek out My sheep, and will deliver them out of all places where they have been scattered in the cloudy and dark day.*

Ezekiel 34:15 *I will feed My flock, and I will cause them to lie down saith the LORD God.*

Ezekiel 34:22-24 *Therefore will I save My flock, and they shall no more be a prey; and I will judge between cattle and cattle. And I will set up one Shepherd over them, and He shall feed them even My servant David; He shall feed them, and He shall be their Shepherd. And I the LORD will be their God, and My servant David a Prince among them; I the LORD have spoken it.*

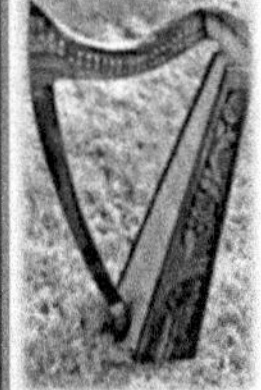

As I was studying this, I noticed that it was the third time that Yeshua appeared to the Jewish disciples, after He was raised to life, that He revealed that He would come back on the third day to feed His flock forever. The third time Yeshua appeared He asked Simon Peter three times if he loved Him, and then Yeshua told Peter three times to feed His sheep. *Yeshua was telling Simon Peter to feed His sheep with the Living Testimony of the Living Torah of the Heavenly Ark, which is the key of David!*

John 21:13-17 *Yeshua then cometh, and taketh bread, and giveth them and fish likewise. This is now the third time that Yeshua shewed Himself to His disciples, after that He was risen from the dead. So when they had dined, Yeshua saith to Simon Peter, Simon, son of Jonah, lovest thou Me more than these? He saith unto Him, Yea, LORD; Thou knowest that I love Thee. He saith unto Him, Feed my lambs. He saith to Him again the second time, Simon, son of Jonah, lovest thou Me? He saith unto Him, Yea, LORD; Thou knowest that I love Thee. He saith unto Him, Feed My sheep. He saith unto him the third time, Simon, son of Jonah, lovest thou Me? And he said unto Him, LORD, Thou knowest that I love Thee, Yeshua saith unto Him, Feed My sheep.*

Yeshua also told the following parable that revealed that He was going to seek out the lost sheep of the House of Israel. This Good Shepherd was prepared to go to the ends of the earth to bring His beloved flocks back to Him! Even if only one lamb wandered away, the LORD cared enough to search for that one lost lamb to carry it back in His arms to His Holy city where He could tend to it forever.

Lamb Photo ©2015 Kimberly K Ballard

Luke 15:3-7 *And He told them this parable, saying, What man among you, if he has a hundred sheep and has lost one of them, does not leave the ninety-nine in the open pasture, and go after the one which is lost, until he finds it? And when he has found it, he lays it on his shoulders, rejoicing, And when he comes home, he calls together his friends and his neighbors, saying to them, Rejoice with me, for I have found my sheep which was lost! I tell you that in the same way, there will be more joy in Heaven over one sinner who repents, than over ninety-nine righteous persons who need no repentance.*

Matthew 10:5-7 *These twelve Yeshua sent out after instructing them, saying, Do not go in the way of the Gentiles, and do not enter any city of the Samaritans; But rather go to the lost sheep of the House of Israel. And as you go preach, saying, The Kingdom of Heaven is at hand.*

Jeremiah also prophesied that the LORD would not only gather His sheep, but He would also deliver them by paying a price for them!

Jeremiah 31:10-11 *Hear the Word of the LORD, O Nations, And declare in the coastlands afar off, And say, He who scattered Israel will gather him, And keep him as a Shepherd keeps his flock. For the LORD has ransomed Jacob, And redeemed him from the hand of him who was stronger than he.*

Harp Shepherds Rod & five smooth stones
Photo ©2013 Kimberly K Ballard

After Yeshua ascended into Heaven, the Jewish disciples who were dispersed from Jerusalem, *now having the seed of the Living Torah,* began to take *the Word of God* to the entire world. So *the Rod and Staff of the LORD God* has literally been gathering all the lost sheep for two thousand years, and very soon the Good Shepherd will return to reign over His flock forever and to establish the Eternal throne of David.

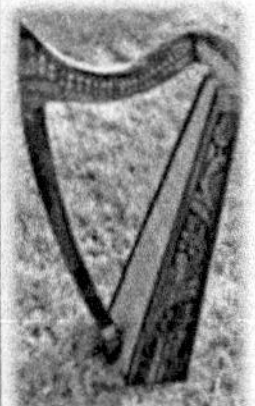

DAVID FIGHTS GOLIATH WITH HIS STAFF IN HIS HAND!

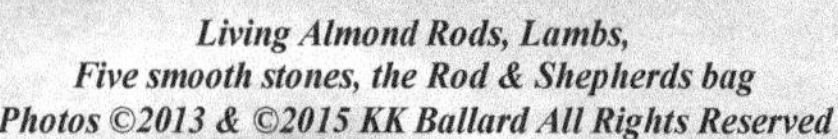

Living Almond Rods, Lambs,
Five smooth stones, the Rod & Shepherds bag

In the story of David and Goliath that is recorded in I Samuel 17, the LORD revealed some astounding details to me of the Messiah that have never been revealed before. I absolutely had the chills! Do you realize that something unique happened when David fought against Goliath and won? Goliath came with a sword and a javelin against David. King Saul offered the use of his armour and weapons to David, so he would stand a chance fighting against Goliath, but David put them off, saying that he could not use them. The reason why he put them off is because David said that he had not *proved* them! I realized that instead David took with him the things that had been *proven* to be reliable by him. David took the very symbolic items that related to the one that had saved Israel through the midst of the Red Sea, and David used these weapons to fight against Goliath. Everyone is focused on the amazing work of the sling shot that David used on Goliath, but the truth is that David actually took something far greater with him that he used as his weapons of choice. I realized that the weapons that David took with him that day that were *proven* reliable *all represented the LORD God of Israel!* Before I explain this in detail, I first want to show you the story of David and Goliath as it is written in I Samuel 17, and then I will detail the profound hidden secrets of this battle that I discovered by Divine revelation, in David's weapons of choice!

I Samuel 17:38-50 *And Saul armed David with his armour, and he put an helmet of brass upon his head; also he armed him with a coat of mail. And David girded his sword upon his armour, and he assayed to go; for he had not proved it. And David said unto Saul, I cannot go with these; for I have not proved them. And David put them off him. And he took his staff in his hand, and chose him five smooth stones out of the brook, and put them in a shepherd's bag which he had, even in a scrip; and his sling was in his hand; and he drew near to the Philistine. And the Philistine came on and drew near unto David; and the man that bare the shield went before him. And when the Philistine looked about, and saw David, he disdained him; for he was but a youth, and ruddy, and of a fair countenance. And the Philistine said unto David, Am I a dog, that thou comest to me with staves? And the Philistine cursed David by his gods. And the Philistine said to David, Come to me, and I will give thy flesh unto the fowls of the air, and to the beasts of the field. Then said David to the Philistine, Thou comest to me with a sword, and with a spear, and with a shield; but I come to thee in the Name of the LORD of Hosts, the God of the armies of Israel, whom thou hast defied. This day will the LORD deliver thee into mine hand; and I will smite thee, and take thine head from thee; and I will give the carcasses of the host of the Philistines this day unto the fowls of the air, and to the wild beasts of the earth; that all the earth may know that there is a God in Israel. And all this assembly shall know that the LORD saveth not with sword and spear; for the battle is the LORD'S, and He will give you into our hands. And it came to pass, when the Philistine arose, and came and drew nigh to meet David, that David hasted, and ran toward the army to meet the Philistine. And David put his hand in his bag, and took thence a stone, and slang it, and smote the Philistine in his forehead, that the stone sunk into his forehead; and he fell upon his face to the earth. So David prevailed over the Philistine with a sling and with a stone, and smote the Philistine, and slew him; but there was no sword in the hand of David.*

Now my eyes were suddenly opened to see exactly why David took five smooth stones from the brook! Moses wrote the Word of God, *the Torah,* the five books of Moses, and the five books are like *living stones.* So David took *"five smooth stones"* out of the brook of *"living water."* The five smooth stones represent *"The Word of God, the Living Torah" who is* Messiah the LORD, *our Living Water!* David then placed them into his shepherd's bag, which represents the LORD Messiah as our Good Shepherd. Then I noticed that in David's hand was his *Staff!* Now the Scripture tells us that *when Goliath saw David with the Staff in his hand, Goliath cursed against David by his gods.* Goliath therefore knew without a doubt that *the Staff or the Shepherd's Rod* stood for *the power* of the LORD God of Israel, who is the Saviour Yeshua! The hidden secret in this battle is truly that David's weapons were all symbolic of the LORD who saved Israel with *His Rod, the Living Torah!* It is so fantastic! David took only the protection of the LORD as his weapons of choice to fight against Goliath, and this meant that *the LORD was going to fight this battle for David by His powerful Rod.* So therefore, David's weapons were not like Saul's earthly armour and weapons! *David took the Rod of God with him! This was Heavens proven armour!* The most stunning detail about this, though, is the fact that David only took *one smooth stone* out of his Shepherd's bag to strike Goliath in the forehead. The *one smooth stone* was a *living stone* that represented *the Messiah, the Living Torah, the Word of God,* and it sank deep into the forehead of Goliath! This brings to mind that *the Word of God* sank deep into Goliath's brain, like the *Tefillin* containing *the Word of God* that is mounted on the forehead so that it can sink deep into the brain to remind us of God!

Goliath was forced to fall on his face to the ground *before the one true Living God,* who fought this battle for David. Now David specifically told us that the LORD does not *"save"* with the sword and spear! How does the LORD save?

THE LORD SAVES WITH THE ROD MESSIAH,
THE STAFF OF THE GOOD SHEPHERD,
HIS WORD, THE LIVING TORAH,
THE LIVING WATER,
AND WITH THE ONE TRUE ROCK!

The one true Rock & Living Almond Rod
Lamb Photos ©2015 KK Ballard

It only took *one rock* to do the job because the LORD is *the Rock* bearing the Word of God! Everything David had in his hands represented the LORD God as the Messiah of Israel! Because David had the symbols of *the Rod of God* with him, David was saved by the ever faithful LORD in this battle! Goliath was coming to use earthly worldly weapons against David, but David already knew that *the Rod of God from Heaven had proven faithful* in saving Israel in the wilderness and through the midst of the Red Sea. David said to Goliath, *"You come to me with a sword and spear, but I come to you in the Name of the LORD of Hosts!"* The words spoken by David prove that he was *allowing* the LORD to fight this battle! David also said, *"That all the earth may know that there is a God in Israel." These are the very words I placed on the back cover of this book!* David declared, *"The battle is the LORD'S and He will deliver you into our hands!"* So this was simply incredible that the LORD revealed all of this to my heart! Saul had been trying to fight the Philistines in his own earthly strength, but David knew that *the Rod, the Word of God*, always saved Israel before and was his Heavenly strength. This strength to fight the enemy was always in *the Yad* of the LORD God of Israel, *the one true Rock, proven to be the Heavenly armour of God.* So it only took *one smooth stone of the Living Torah* to strike Goliath and win the battle! It is upon *this Rock* that the true Church is built! Just like the power of the Rod of Almighty God was David's Heavenly protection and armour, it is also our Heavenly protection and armour and we are instructed to *"Put on the full armour of God."* The *LORD'S salvation or Yeshua* was therefore certain for David because He was willing in his heart, to take only the proven weapons of God that are His Royal Standard!

It is written in the Psalms that the Israelites had proven the work of *the Rod of God* in the wilderness! Remember that the Ark and the Rod were their military Standards of God!

Psalm 95:7-9 *For He is our God; and we are the people of His pasture, and the sheep of His hand. Today if ye will hear His voice, Harden not your heart, as in the provocation, and as in the wilderness; When your fathers tempted Me, proved Me, and saw My work.*

We are reminded of the fact that when Messiah Yeshua stood in the living water of the Jordan River as *the Living Torah, He was the one true Rock* standing in the very spot where the Priests and Joshua had placed the twelve stones centuries before, with the Ark of the Covenant in the midst of the Jordan River. The Scriptures declare that the stone that the builders rejected has become the Chief Cornerstone and it was miraculously this *one Rock Messiah* that took the life of Goliath. Obviously David knew that the power of the God of Israel was on His *Staff.* David knew with absolute certainty that *the power of the Staff of God,* would save him from Goliath and from any useless worldly weapons. For this reason, David was not afraid when he came before Goliath. He was very confident when He came in the Name of the LORD of Hosts, allowing the *Royal Commander of the Heavenly Army* to go before him in this battle. It was for the same reason that Jacob worshipped the LORD by leaning on the top of His *Staff! Jacob knew the Rod and Staff represented the LORD God of Israel and His Yeshua.*

Hebrews 11:21 *By faith Jacob, when he was a dying, blessed both the sons of Joseph; and worshipped, leaning upon the top of his staff.*

Lion of Judah Ensign Photo ©2014 Kimberly K Ballard All Rights Reserved

The Staff or Rod is an emblem and ensign of authority! Notice in the following definition of the word *"Staff"* it says that it is *"a rod used as a weapon."* So Messiah *the Rod* is proven to be the weapon that fights the battles for Israel. In the future, it is this same weapon that will be used against the enemies of God when *the Rod* returns from Heaven to destroy Satan forever! The Rod is our aid in walking the right path!

Definition of Staff or Staves; *1. A stick, pole, or rod for aid in walking or climbing for use as a weapon, etc.*
2. A rod or wand serving as an ensign of office or authority.
(Source: Definition Random House College Dictionary, revised edition © 1975 By Random House, Inc.).

If the Rod is an ensign of authority and *Yeshua is the Rod,* then we can understand the Scriptures that tell us that there will be a root of Jesse that will stand for an *ensign.* Isaiah wrote that the Messiah comes a second time to recover the remnant of His people Israel. Isaiah prophesied that the Gentiles will seek this ensign and this has been fulfilled, because they have done this for two thousand years! Yeshua came once already and is coming a second time to recover the remnant of Israel! God's *Royal ensign* is His Rod, KING Messiah. Remember this *Royal ensign* was sent to gather a righteous remnant out of all the Gentile nations.

Isaiah 11:10-12 *And in that day there shall be a root of Jesse, which shall stand for an ensign of the people; to it shall the Gentiles seek; and His rest shall be glorious. And it shall come to pass in that day, that the LORD shall set His hand again the second time to recover the remnant of His people, which shall be left, from Assyria, and from Egypt, and from Pathros, and from Cush, and from Elam, and from Shinar, and from Hamath, and from the islands of the sea. And He shall set up an ensign for the Nations, and shall assemble the outcasts of Israel, and gather together the dispersed of Judah from the four corners of the earth.*

Isaiah 5:26 *And He will lift up an ensign to the nations from far, and will hiss unto them from the end of the earth; and, behold, they shall come with speed swiftly.*

Yeshua was lifted up on the cross on Holy Mount Moriah, on Golgotha, and people from all nations have been drawn to the LORD God of Israel because of this *Majestic Royal ensign which is a Branch of the Armed forces indicating the Jewish Nationality!*

Isaiah 18:3-5 *All ye inhabitants of the world, and dwellers on the earth, see ye, when He lifteth up an ensign on the mountains; and when He bloweth a trumpet, hear ye. For so the LORD said unto me, I will take my rest, and I will consider in My dwelling place like a clear heat upon herbs, and like a cloud of dew in the heat of harvest. For afore the harvest, when the bud is perfect, and the sour grape is ripening in the flower, He shall both cut off the sprigs with pruning hooks, and take away and cut down the branches.*

The children of Israel were to *pitch their own Standard with the ensign* of their father's house, far off about the Tabernacle. So if Messiah is the *ensign* of the LORD God, then *the Rod Yeshua is the ensign of His Father's House, who is always about the Heavenly Temple or Tabernacle of God. So He must be about His Father's business as He stated at age twelve!*

Numbers 2:2 *Every man of the children of Israel shall pitch by his own standard, with the ensign of their father's house; far off about the Tabernacle of the congregation shall they pitch.*

The Lion of Judah Ensign
Photo ©2014
Kimberly K Ballard

This is revealed in Luke 2:49 when Yeshua's parents found the young twelve year old *teaching Torah* to the Rabbis in the Holy Temple! Yeshua proved that He is *the ensign* of His Father's House. The Temple was not living up to *His Royal Standard because it was to be a house of prayer for all nations!*

Matthew 21:12 *And Yeshua went into the Temple of God, and cast out all them that sold and bought in the Temple, and overthrew the tables of the moneychangers, and the seats of them that sold doves, And said unto them, It is written, My House shall be called the House of prayer; but ye have made it a den of thieves. And the blind and the lame came to Him in the Temple; and He healed them.*

With great might, we can proclaim like King David, that *the Rod of God is our ensign* and Messiah Yeshua is our Divine weapon of choice! The *ensign* of the Living Torah lifted up is *"The Royal Standard"* of His Majesty, THE KING OF KINGS for all nations!

Isaiah 59:19 *So shall they fear the Name of the LORD from the west, and His glory from the rising of the sun. When the enemy comes in like a flood, the Spirit of the LORD shall lift up a Standard against him. And the Redeemer shall come to Zion, and unto them that turn from transgression in Jacob, saith the LORD.*

I thank the LORD He revealed this secret to me. King David trusted in the power of God's Rod to defeat the enemy and save him. David was young, but he did not attempt to battle Goliath in his own strength or with Saul's heavy earthly armour. David was loved by the LORD. He trusted with pure faith when he put on the full armour of God! What a fantastic story! David and Goliath revealed the Messiah! This brings to mind the Scripture in Ephesians about putting on the full armour of God that is *"the power and strength"* of His might.

Ephesians 6:10-20 *Finally, my brethren, be strong in the LORD, and in the power of His might. Put on the whole armour of God, that ye may be able to stand against the wiles of the devil. For we wrestle not against flesh and blood, but against principalities, against powers, against the rulers of the darkness of this world, against spiritual wickedness in high places. Wherefore take unto you the whole armour of God, that ye may be able to withstand in the evil day, and having done all, to stand. Stand therefore, having your loins girt about with truth, and having on the breastplate of righteousness; And your feet shod with the preparation of the Gospel of peace; Above all, taking the shield of faith, wherewith ye shall be able to quench all the fiery darts of the wicked. And take the helmet of salvation, and the sword of the Spirit, which is the Word of God; Praying always with all prayer and supplication in the Spirit, and watching thereunto with all perseverance and supplication for all Saints; And for me, that utterance may be given unto me, that I may open my mouth boldly, to make known the mystery of the Gospel, For which I am an ambassador in bonds; that therein I may speak boldly, as I ought to speak.*

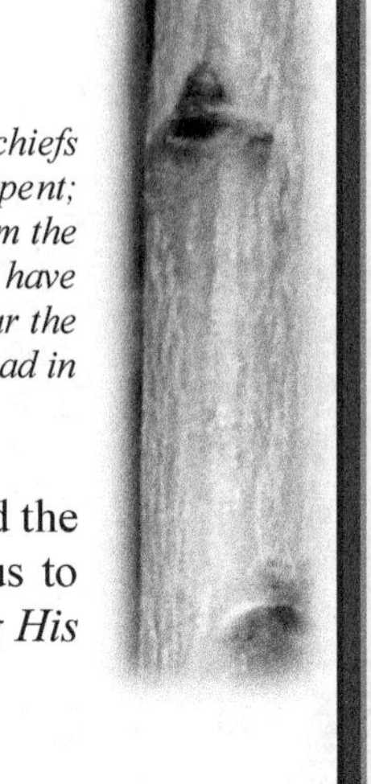

***Psalm 140:1-7** Deliver me, O LORD, from the evil man; preserve me from the violent man; Which imagine mischiefs in their heart; continually are they gathered together for war. They have sharpened their tongues like a serpent; adder's poison is under their lips. Se'lah. Keep me, O LORD, from the hands of the wicked; preserve me from the violent man; who have purposed to overthrow my goings. The proud have hid a snare for me, and cords; they have spread a net by the wayside; they have set gins for me. Se'lah. I said unto the LORD, Thou are my God; hear the voice of my supplications, O LORD. O GOD the LORD, the strength of my salvation, Thou hast covered my head in the day of battle.*

The battle is the LORD'S and He will fight it for His people! Never forget that God the LORD, *the strength of our Yeshua lifted up,* is our weapon of choice. He goes before us to fight the battles in His power and might and *this is the Royal Standard of His Army bearing His image!*

Jerusalem Lion Emblem
Snow & Crown Photos ©2013
Budding Almond Rod ©2015
Kimberly K Ballard
All Rights Reserved

Official Shroud Pair Photograph ©1978 Barrie M. Schwortz Collection, STERA Inc., All Rights Reserved

DAVID'S COMFORT WAS THE STAFF OF LIFE IN THE RIGHT HAND OF GOD

Dedication Painting of King David
In Monochromatic color
By My Grandmother Elizabeth Irvin Farris
Fine Arts Degree CU Boulder Colorado Class of 1930
Photo of her painting in B& W & Almond Rod & leaf

King David had the hope of Messiah in his heart. David knew that the LORD would send forth *the Branch,* who would come to life and defeat Satan's curse of death. David had the hope of being resurrected one day by *the Rod of God,* who was to come in the flesh to dwell among us in His Davidic line. David saw the LORD sitting at the right hand of the LORD. This is the face of God, as it is seen reflected in His Rod. David knew that the Messiah would raise him to life from the grave. David took great comfort in this hope. David had the wisdom and knowledge of God because he walked with God. The Living Branch Testimony of Messiah is our comfort and hope for Eternal life. When our loved ones die, we do not have to mourn for them as others do who have no hope, but as believer's, we can have joy in our hearts, knowing that the Messiah has defeated death and Satan. The reunion that we will experience with our loved ones will truly be a glorious event. We can know for certain that our precious loved ones are alive in the Heavenly realm with the LORD and that they are abiding in His glorious Heavenly Temple Garden. This promise removes any fear of death out of our hearts. The sorrow that can overcome us for years after a loved one dies can be greatly eased in our minds and hearts because the LORD is faithful to fulfill everything that He has promised to us. Yeshua promised Eternal life to all who would call upon His Name. So the *Staff* in the right hand of the LORD God is the comfort that takes away our deepest sorrows.

John 16:22 *And ye now therefore have sorrow; but I will see you again, and your heart shall rejoice, and your joy no man taketh from you.*

Colossians 2:2-3 *That their hearts might be comforted, being knit together in love, and unto all riches of the full assurance of understanding, to the acknowledgement of the mystery of God, and of the Father, and of Messiah; In whom are hid all the treasures of wisdom and knowledge.*

Isaiah 40:1 *Comfort, O comfort My people, says your God.*

When Simon Peter stood in the Holy Temple in Jerusalem, he spoke the following words of hope to Israel and this hope was in Messiah Yeshua, who was delivered to death by the foreknowledge of the LORD God. Simon Peter said, *"Death could not keep Messiah in the grave."* Simon Peter then talked about King David, who was a Prophet of Israel, and he said that David saw this event of the Messiah long ago. Simon Peter also declared that Messiah Yeshua is the LORD God of Israel.

Acts 2:22-39 *Ye men of Israel, hear these words; [Yeshua] of Nazareth, a man approved of God among you by miracles and wonders and signs, which God did by Him in the midst of you, as ye yourselves also know; Him, being delivered by the determined counsel and foreknowledge of God, ye have taken, and by wicked hands have crucified and slain; Whom God hath raised up; having loosed the pains of death; because it was not possible that He should be holden of it. For David speaketh concerning Him, I foresaw the LORD always before my face, for He is on my right hand, that I should not be moved; Therefore did my heart rejoice, and my tongue was glad; moreover also my flesh shall rest in hope; Because thou wilt not leave my soul in hell, neither wilt thou suffer thine Holy one to see corruption. Thou hast made known to me the ways of life; Thou shalt make me full of joy with Thy countenance. Men and brethren, let me freely speak unto you of the Patriarch David, that he is both dead and buried, and his sepulchre is with us unto this day. Therefore being a Prophet, and knowing that God had sworn with an oath to him, that of the fruit of his loins, according to the flesh, He would raise up Messiah to sit on his throne; He seeing this before spake of the resurrection of Messiah, that His soul was not left in hell, neither His flesh did see corruption. This [Yeshua] hath God raised up, whereof we all are witnesses. Therefore being by the right hand of God exalted, and having received of the Father the promise of the Holy Spirit, He hath shed forth this, which ye now see and hear. For David is not ascended into the Heavens; but he saith himself, The LORD said unto my LORD, Sit thou on My right hand, Until I make Thy foes Thy footstool. Therefore let all the House of Israel know assuredly, that God hath made that same Yeshua, whom ye have crucified, both LORD and Messiah.*

King David saw the Messiah before He came to the earth! David was given this foreknowledge through the Ruach/Holy Spirit, and he prophesied in the Psalms regarding *Messiah Yeshua's Living Testimony as the Staff of Life* and this was revealed as David's comfort. It was the key of David and if we understood it, we would have the key to open the hidden mystery of Messiah Yeshua. This is the mystery of God that is finished!

In the Sermon on the Mount, *Yeshua the Rod of God* revealed that those who mourn will be comforted by Him.

Matthew 5:4 *Blessed are they that mourn; for they shall be comforted.*

John 5:24-29 *Verily, verily, I say unto you, He that heareth My Word, and believeth on Him that sent Me, hath everlasting life, and shall not come into condemnation; but is passed from death to life. Verily, verily, I say unto you, the hour is coming, and now is, when the dead shall hear the voice of the Son of God; and they that hear shall live. For as the Father hath life in Himself; so hath He given to the Son to have life in Himself; And hath given Him authority to execute judgment also, because He is the Son of man. Marvel not at this; for the hour is coming, in the which all that are in the graves shall hear His voice, And shall come forth; they that have done good, unto the resurrection of life; and they that have done evil, unto the resurrection of the damnation.*

When Yeshua speaks the Word of life, then life comes to those who hear His voice. *This is exactly what happened when Yeshua performed the miracle of raising Lazarus in front of all the very loving Jewish people, who stood faithfully with Mary and Martha after their brother Lazarus died.* In the story of Yeshua raising Lazarus, you will notice that *when the Rod lifted up His eyes and spoke the Word of life,* then Lazarus came forth alive out of the grave and this was part of the Living Testimony of the LORD. He has the power to give life from death because the Rod lifted up always saves and breathes forth the Word of life, *the Living Torah of perfection.* All the Jews in Israel witnessed Yeshua raising the dead on this occasion with Lazarus, as well as on numerous other occasions. So they believed that this was the LORD who would bring about the resurrection of the dead in the last day. The restoration of the corrupted flesh was a miracle that only the LORD God of Israel could perform with His Rod to reveal His glory. The Holy Spirit/Ruach was groaning inside Yeshua, inside His heart!

John 11:30-45 *Now Yeshua was not yet come into the town, but was in that place where Martha met Him. The Jews then which were with her in the house, and comforted her, when they saw Mary that she rose up hastily and went out, followed her, saying, she goeth unto the grave to weep there. When Mary was come where Yeshua was, and saw Him, she fell down at His feet, saying unto Him, LORD, if Thou hadst been here, my brother had not died. When Yeshua therefore saw her weeping, and the Jews also weeping which came with her, He groaned in the Spirit, and was troubled, And said, Where have ye laid him? They said unto Him, LORD, come and see. Yeshua wept. Then said the Jews, Behold how He loved him! And some of them said, Could not this man, which opened the eyes of the* *blind, have caused that even this man should not have died? Yeshua therefore again groaning in Himself cometh to the grave. It was a cave, and a stone lay upon it. Yeshua said, Take ye away the stone. Martha, the sister of him that was dead, saith unto Him, LORD, by this time he stinketh; for he hath been dead four days. Yeshua saith unto her, Said I not unto thee, that, if thou wouldest believe, thou shouldest see the glory of God? Then they took away the stone from the place where the dead was laid. And Yeshua lifted up his eyes, and said, Father, I thank Thee that Thou hast heard Me. And I know that Thou hearest Me always; but because of the people which standby I said it, that they may believe that Thou hast sent Me. And when He thus had spoken, He cried with a loud voice, Lazarus, come forth. And he that was dead came forth, bound hand and foot with grave clothes; and his face was bound about with a napkin. Yeshua saith unto them, Loose him, and let him go. Then many of the Jews which came to Mary, and had seen the things which Yeshua did, believed on Him.*

When the resurrection of the dead occurs in the future, they will return to Jerusalem, singing and praising God for this marvelous blessing.

Isaiah 51:11-12 *Therefore the redeemed of the LORD shall return, and come with singing unto Zion; and everlasting joy shall be upon their head; they shall obtain gladness and joy; and sorrow and mourning shall flee away. I, even I, AM He that comforteth you; who art thou, that thou shouldest be afraid of a man that shall die, and of the son of man which shall be made as grass.*

II Corinthians 1:3-4 *Blessed be God, even the Father of our LORD Yeshua Messiah, the Father of mercies, and the God of all comfort; Who comforteth us in all our tribulation, that we may be able to comfort them which are in any trouble, by the comfort wherewith we ourselves are comforted of God. For as the sufferings of Messiah abound in us, so our consolation also aboundeth by Messiah.*

When the Messiah descends from Heaven in the future, He will give a shout and blow the shofar at the Last Trump. At that exact moment, the dead will hear His voice and they will come up out of their graves exactly like Lazarus came up out of his grave at the sound of Yeshua's bold voice. The minute that we are absent from this body, we are instantly present with the LORD! Yeshua was very compassionate and He wept over the pain that others were experiencing. He loves us so much in His heart that He saves every tear that we cry in His bottle, and He inscribes our tears in His book of life!

Psalm 56:8 *Thou tellest my wanderings; put Thou my tears into Thy bottle; are they not in Thy book?*

Heaven is a beautiful place with no curse and there will be no more tears or sorrow there. The LORD says that He will wipe every tear from our eyes and perhaps there will be tears of joy when we realize everything that the LORD accomplished to save us from the bondage of corruption.

PASSING UNDER THE ROD OF THE GOOD SHEPHERD

If the Messiah is the door and gate of the sheep, then this gate serves a very specific purpose. In ancient times, a shepherd took his rod in his hand and marked his sheep with the rod as they passed through the sheep gate and went into the sheep pen. When we receive the baptism of Messiah, we are sealed with the LORD'S Holy Spirit and we become His sheep, bearing the LORD'S mark that is given to us, only by *the Rod of God.* We are then sealed with the Name of the LORD God of Israel and sealed within our hearts spiritually for Eternal life.

All the Holy vessels in the LORD'S Temple and all the animals bear the Name of the LORD upon them and they are marked, *"Holy to the LORD or Holiness to the LORD!"*

Zechariah 14:20-21 *In that day shall there be upon the bells of the horses, HOLINESS UNTO THE LORD; and the pots in the LORD'S house shall be like the bowls before the altar. Yea, every pot in Jerusalem and in Judah shall be holiness unto the LORD of Hosts; and all they that sacrifice shall come and take of them, and seethe therein; and in that day there shall be no more the Canaanite in the House of the LORD of Hosts.*

The LORD'S seal is a heavenly mark of ownership. It means that we belong to the Living God, and there is no enemy who can steal us from the flock. When Messiah Yeshua said that He would gather His sheep and that He is the door of Heaven, He said that not one of His sheep would be lost. Every single sheep is precious in His sight. He goes looking for any that stray from Him. In Leviticus, we find something remarkable about the marking of the flock for the LORD, with the rod.

Leviticus 27:30-34 *And all the tithe of the land, whether of the seed of the land, or of the tree, is the LORD'S; it is holy unto the LORD. And if a man will at all redeem ought of his tithes, he shall add thereto the fifth part thereof. And concerning the tithe of the herd, or of the flock, even of whatsoever passeth under the rod, the tenth shall be holy unto the LORD. He shall not search whether it be good or bad, neither shall he change it; and if he change it at all, then both it and the change thereof shall be holy; it shall not be redeemed. These are the commandments, which the LORD commanded Moses for the children of Israel in Mount Sinai.*

The LORD specifically said that the seed of the land or of the fruit tree, is the LORD'S and it is Holy to Him! This is the Living Testimony of Messiah Yeshua, the seed that bore Fruit on the third day. It is Holy to the LORD because it reveals His Living Testimony that abides in the Ark of Heaven. Now, I want to point out that this Scripture specifically tells us that the LORD said, *"Every tenth one of the sheep that passes under the rod shall be Holy to the LORD."*

When Melchizedek came, Abram gave *a tenth* of all that he had to the Priest of God Most High. God Most High delivered his enemies into his hand!

Genesis 14:18-19 *And Melchizedek king of Salem brought forth bread and wine; and he was Priest of God Most High. And he blessed him, and said; Blessed be Abram of God Most High, Maker of Heaven and earth; and blessed be God Most High, who hath delivered Thine enemies into thy hand. And he gave a tenth of all.*

Melchizedek, the Priest of God Most High, brought the bread and the wine. These are the two elements of Yeshua's Passover Covenant with Israel and He is the Priest of God Most High in Heaven, after the Order of Melchizedek! So the shepherd would stand at the sheep gate or the door of the sheep pen, and in his hand, he held *a rod or staff.* As the sheep went through the door of the gate, the shepherd would *mark every tenth one as "Holy to the LORD"* with the dye on his rod. The passage in Leviticus says that this is what it means to *"pass under the rod."* Now when I saw this, I suddenly understood what was taking place in the book of Revelation! First let us look at what the Prophet Jeremiah said about the coming Messiah and about the flocks of Israel that pass under the hands of the one who numbers them. *This is only the LORD who does this and it is Messiah the Branch, the Rod of God!*

Jeremiah 33:12-16 *Thus says the LORD of Hosts, There shall again be in this place which is waste, without man of beast, and in all its cities, a habitation of shepherds who rest their flocks. In the cities of the hill country, in the cities of the lowland, in the cities of the Negev, in the land of Benjamin, in the environs of Jerusalem, and in the cities of Judah, the flocks shall again pass under the hands of the one who numbers them, says the LORD. Behold, days are coming; declares the LORD, when I will fulfill the good Word which I have spoken concerning the House of Israel and the House of Judah. In those days and at that time I will cause a righteous Branch of David to spring forth; and He shall execute justice and righteousness on the earth. In those days Judah shall be saved, and Jerusalem shall dwell in safety; and this is the Name by which He shall be called; the LORD is our righteousness.*

So the LORD is the Good Shepherd who seals His sheep with His own Name because they only belong to Him. He counts them as they pass under the Rod, Messiah. This is the only door or gate of the sheep. The LORD'S sheep must come through the door of the Good Shepherd and they must pass under *the Living Rod* to enter into the sheep pen through the gate of Heaven because, in this case, the sheep pen represents Heaven, *the Eternal Promised Land.* When I understood this, I knew that it revealed something astounding in the book of Revelation! When the Messiah returns to the earth to reign, He will be on Mount Zion with this *select, elite group of Israelites known as the 144,000 that are taken out of the 12 tribes of Israel.* In the book of Romans chapter 11, in the New Testament, it says, *"That all Israel will be saved."*

Romans 11:26 *And so all Israel shall be saved; as it is written, There shall come out of Zion the Deliverer, and shall turn away ungodliness from Jacob.*

I was astonished when I realized that the elite 144,000 Israelites that are standing on Mount Zion with the Messiah are *"a tenth"* of the whole flock that are *"set apart,"* and they are marked by *the Rod of God* as *"HOLY TO THE LORD!"* They will serve God day and night in His Heavenly Temple and in His Kingdom forever. *They are Jewish firstborn males who have gone through the Yeshua ha-Ben redeeming ceremony at birth, and are dedicated to God!* This is why they are called *"the redeemed from the earth"* in the Scripture in Revelation 14:3-4! They are the only ones who will know the new song of Moses! The LORD will wipe away every tear from their eyes. Now I have to mention that some have falsely claimed that the 144,000 are the only ones saved out of Israel, but this is not true. We can clearly understand *they have been redeemed for thirty pieces of silver* as I mentioned on pages 180-181. Also I must mention that the 144,000 only refer to the 12 tribes of Israel and not to anyone else, just as it is written! It does not have anything to do with any Church. The tenth of the flock is an elite group of Jewish people, virgins that are sealed as *"HOLY TO THE LORD,"* and they will be given a special Divine service to perform for the LORD forever in His Eternal Temple. I want to reiterate that the Scriptures tell us that *"ALL ISRAEL IS SAVED."* The Priests are set apart for the Divine service in the Holy Temple and so are the 144,000 elite Jews that are selected by the Rod and taken out of each of the 12 tribes of Israel for this special Divine service. They will serve the LORD as Priests to Him forever. They are called *"The first fruits,"* and therefore they have that title placed upon them that says, *"HOLY TO THE LORD!"* In the book of Revelation, the Lamb is standing on Mount Zion with this group of 144,000 select lambs out of each of the twelve tribes of Israel and they are sealed with Yeshua, the LORD'S Name only!

Revelation 14:1-5 *And I looked, and behold, the Lamb was standing on Mount Zion, and with Him one hundred and forty-four thousand, having His Name and the Name of His Father written on their foreheads. And I heard a voice from Heaven, like the sound of many waters and like the sound of loud thunder, and the voice which I heard was like the sound of harpists playing on their harps. And they sang a new song before the throne and before the four living creatures and the elders; and no one could learn the song except the one hundred and forty-four thousand who had been redeemed from the earth. These are the ones who have not been defiled with women, for they have kept themselves chaste. These are the ones who follow the Lamb wherever He goes. These have been redeemed from among men, as first fruits to God and to the Lamb. And no lie was found in their mouth; they are blameless.*

Revelation 7:1-4 *And after these things I saw four angels standing on the four corners of the earth, holding the four winds of the earth, that the wind should not blow on the earth, nor on the sea, nor on any tree. And I saw another angel ascending from the east, having the seal of the living God; and he cried with a loud voice to the four angels, to whom it was given to hurt the earth and the sea, Saying, Hurt not the earth, neither the sea, nor the trees, till we have sealed the servants of our God in their foreheads. And I heard the number of them which were sealed; and there were sealed an hundred and forty and four thousand of all the tribes of the children of Israel.*

Revelation 7:13-17 *And one of the elders answered, saying unto me, What are these which are arrayed in white robes? And whence came they? And I said unto him, Sir, thou knowest. And he said to me, These are they which* *came out of great tribulation, and have washed their robes, and made them white in the blood of the Lamb. Therefore are they before the throne of God, and serve Him day and night in His Temple; and he that sitteth on the throne shall dwell among them. They shall hunger no more, neither thirst anymore; neither shall the sun light on them, nor any heat. For the Lamb which is in the midst of the throne shall feed them, and shall lead them unto Living fountains of Waters; and God shall wipe away all tears from their eyes.*

So the 144,000 are the first fruits unto God from the twelve tribes of Israel, just as Messiah Yeshua was the First Fruit from the Almond Tree of Life that gives us Eternal life. All Israel will pass under the Rod, at the door of the Good Shepherd, *but a tenth will be selected out of the whole group for performing the Divine service,* as He counts them and none will be lost, just as Yeshua said! Having seen this truth by the power of the Holy Spirit, I know that the 144,000 of the twelve tribes of Israel have been greatly misunderstood for centuries! Not only will they have a very special Divine Eternal purpose to serve, but the LORD said that they are blameless! They will not be harmed during the judgment. Not only are they are saved by Messiah the Rod, the power of God, in the time of Jacob's trouble *"the great tribulation"* but the 144,000 are appointed to always stay close to the KING as His faithful nobles. The KING keeps His ministers close to discuss His Law with them. Noah was saved out of the flood waters of tribulation by entering in through the door of the Ark, and Israel will be saved in the time of Jacob's trouble by going through the door that will be opened to them by Messiah, who is the door of the Heavenly Ark. This gate or door of the sheep is *Yeshua,* and they will enter through this door because they are sealed with the LORD'S Name and protected from the destruction of the tribulation, and after that they perform the Eternal Divine service of the KING OF KINGS in the Heavenly Kingdom of God, and so shall it be forever and ever!

Ezekiel 34:30-31 *Thus shall they know that I the LORD their God am with them, and that they, even the House of Israel, are My people, saith the LORD GOD. And ye My flock, the flock of My pasture, are men, and I AM your God, saith the LORD GOD.*

Ezekiel 34:12-14 *As a shepherd seeketh out his flock in the day that he is among his sheep that are scattered; so will I seek out My sheep, and will deliver them out of all places where they have been scattered in the cloudy and dark day. And I will bring them out from the people, and gather them from the countries, and will bring them to their own land, and feed them upon the mountains of Israel by the rivers, and in all the inhabited places of the country. I will feed them in a good pasture, and upon the high mountains of Israel shall their fold be; there shall they lie in a good fold, and in a fat pasture shall they feed upon the mountains of Israel. I will feed My flock, and I will cause them to lie down, saith the LORD GOD.*

In 2004, when the Cave of John the Baptist was discovered by Dr. Shimon Gibson, he described the figure of John that was etched in the plaster as having a *staff* in his hand. Ironically, his other hand was lifted up and cut off. This does not mean that his tomb was desecrated, as was stated at that time! *The LORD has made it clear to me, through the revelations in this book, that John's hand was lifted up and cut off in this inscription to proclaim that Messiah Yeshua is the Branch, the Arm of the LORD revealed, that was lifted up and cut off to save us!* It depicts the fact that John was sent as a messenger to proclaim to Israel, by baptizing them in water, that Messiah the LORD is *the Staff of Life in the hand of the Good Shepherd,* who is none other than the LORD God of Israel. I am now sharing this new information that the LORD has revealed to me about that cave in Israel and it only confirms that this was indeed the cave of John the Baptist, proclaiming the Messiah of Israel to be *Yeshua, the Rod of God cut off!* There is also a cross etched in the plaster in this cave along with this inscription of John the Baptist! What a beautiful loving LORD KING Messiah we have and after discovering this truth, like King David, I feel the LORD'S comfort in my heart. He is faithful and true and you can always count on the Good Shepherd to love you and to keep you safe! Put on the full armour of God with His powerful Rod. The Rod lifted up has been proven and He is our one true Rock, to stand against the Goliath we face today!

Lambs, Harp with Shepherds Rod & five smooth stones, Lyre, Crown & Cloud Photos ©2015 KK Ballard All Rights Reserved

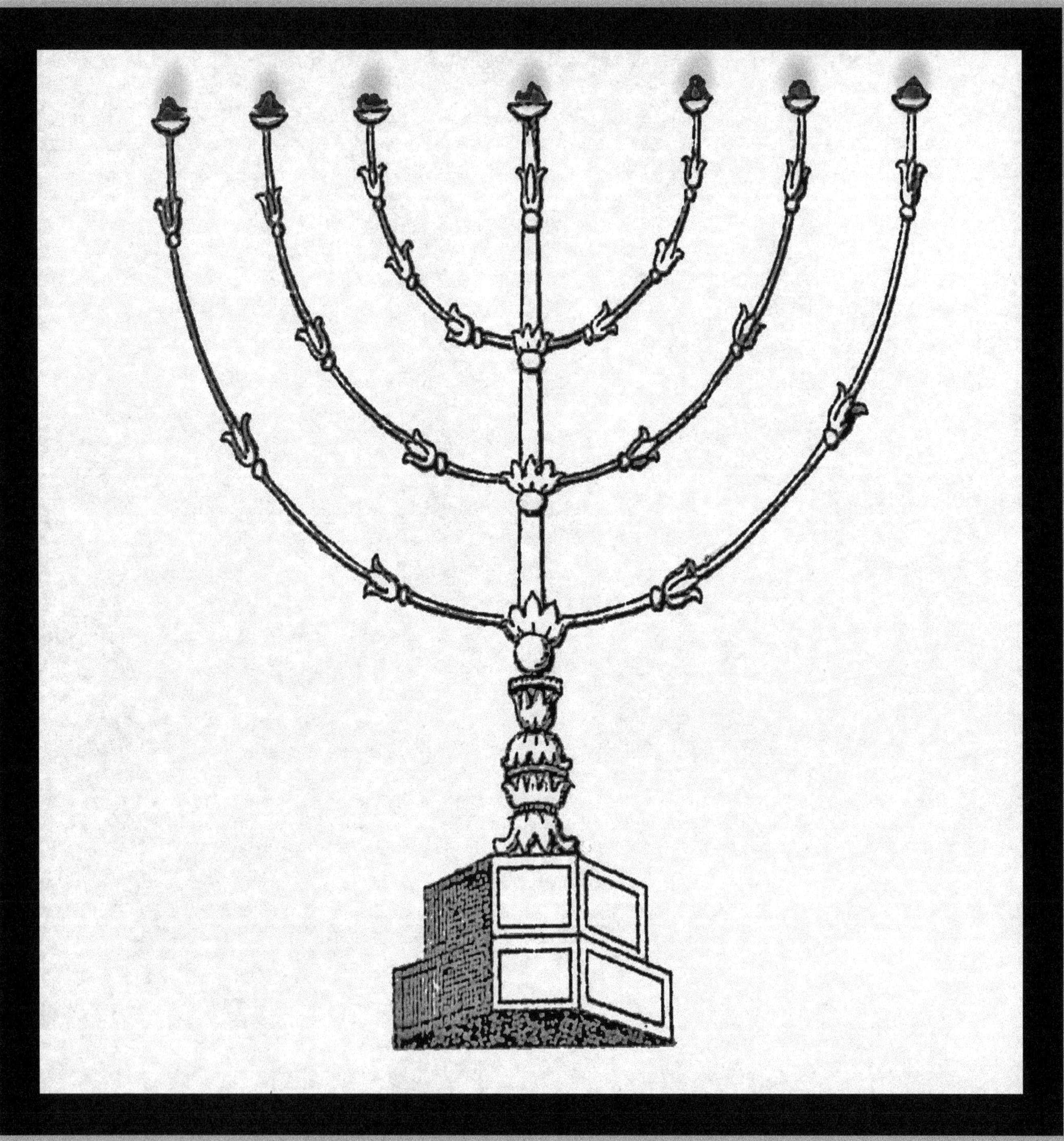

The Holy Almond Tree Menorah an Artist rendering from the ©1887 book, "Biblical Archaeology Volume 1," by Dr. Carl Friedrich Keil Professor of Theology Edinburgh, Scotland
Modified with flames & effects Photo Rendition ©2013 Kimberly K Ballard All Rights Reserved

Chapter 7

THE HOLY ALMOND TREE MENORAH

The Holy Menorah in the Snow with candles & flames, Icicles & Snow
Photos ©2013 Kimberly K Ballard All Rights Reserved

On the seventh night of Hanukkah, in the year 2007, for the first time in 2,000 years, the bronze Menorah electroplated with 95 pounds of pure gold that was built for use in the coming Third Temple in Jerusalem was presented before the people with great excitement. This was a very special ceremonial dedication! As the night progressed, the enthusiasm mounted. All eyes joyfully watched with wonder as the purple veil came down from around the glass enclosure containing the beautiful gold Menorah of the LORD. The unveiling was accompanied by the glorious sounding blasts of a blazing fanfare that was resonating from two Holy silver trumpets. It was a chilling moment in history. The gold Menorah was moved, on the second night of Hanukkah, from the Cardo of the Jewish Quarter where it had previously stood for seven years, to a new location on the stairs leading to the western wall plaza. This profoundly exciting event marked a turning point in history. This was a sure sign that the Messiah was soon to come. On December 22nd 2014, they had pure olive oil to light it. The Israeli people clapped their hands while dancing in the streets. The air was filled with Israeli's singing praises unto the LORD of Hosts as the gold Menorah was finally restored and rededicated for use in the coming Third Temple in Jerusalem, after 2,000 years of exile. The LORD'S Divine design is intricately woven into this Holy Almond Tree Menorah that stands in the Holy Place in the Holy Temple of the LORD.

Moses was shown the Divine design by the LORD on Mount Sinai, and he replicated the design through a master craftsman named, *"Bezaleel."* The LORD inspired me with the fact that He is the Master Designer, who gives us the gift of creating and designing. Bezaleel was from the tribe of Judah, like Messiah Yeshua. Bezaleel was the grandson of Hur.

I Chronicles 2:19-20 *And when Azubah was dead, Caleb took unto him Ephrath, which bare him Hur. And Hur begat Uri, and Uri begat Bezaleel.*

The Great Grandmother of Bezaleel was *"Ephrath."* This name is like the original city name of Bethlehem, where Messiah Yeshua would come into the world. Ephrathah, which is the same as *"Ephrath"* means *"Fruitful."* It was Aaron and Hur that held up the arms of Moses to save Israel by the power of God on the rod in Moses hands. Bezaleel from the tribe of Judah was called by name by the LORD to construct the Tabernacle and everything it contained. He was highly skilled as an engraver of precious metals. Bezaleel was also highly skilled in embroidery and in carving wood. Bezaleel also had apprentices that worked under his authority to accomplish all that the LORD God had commanded Moses to do. The Holy pure gold

Almond Tree Menorah was one of the finest works of art, that Bezaleel was commissioned to create. The building of the Tabernacle furnishings is recorded here in the book of Exodus.

Exodus 31:1-11 *And the LORD spake unto Moses, saying, See, I have called by name Bezaleel the son of Uri, the son of Hur, of the tribe of Judah; And I have filled him with the Spirit of God, in wisdom, and in understanding, and in knowledge, and in all manner of workmanship. To devise cunning works, to work in gold, and in silver, and in brass, And in cutting of stones, to set them, and in carving of timber, to work in all manner of workmanship. And I, behold, I have given with him Aholiab, the son of Ahisamach, of the tribe of Dan; and in the hearts of all that are wise hearted I have put wisdom, that they may make all that I have commanded thee. The Tabernacle of the congregation, and the Ark of the Testimony, and the Mercy seat that is thereupon, and all the furniture of the Tabernacle, And the table and his furniture, and the pure Candlestick with all his furniture, and the altar of incense, And the altar of burnt offering with all his furniture, and the laver and his foot, And the cloths of service, and the holy garments for Aaron the Priest, and the garments of his sons, to minister in the Priest's office, And the anointing oil, and sweet incense for the Holy Place; according to all that I have commanded thee shall they do.*

Exodus 35:30-35 *And Moses said unto the children of Israel, See, the LORD hath called by name Bezaleel the son of Uri, the son of Hur, of the tribe of Judah; And He hath filled him with the Spirit of God, in wisdom, in understanding, and in knowledge, and in all manner of workmanship; And to devise curious works, to work in gold, and in silver, and in brass, And in the cutting of stones, to set them, and in carving of wood, to make any manner of cunning work. And He hath put in his heart that he may teach, both he, and Aholiab, the son of Ahisamach, of the tribe of Dan. Them hath he filled with wisdom of the heart, to work all manner of work, of the engraver, and of the cunning workman, and of the embroiderer, in blue, and in purple, in scarlet, and in fine linen, and of the weaver, even of them that do any work, and of those that devise cunning work.*

Since I am a musician and composer of music, I felt so inspired when I read about Bezaleel who was the highly skilled artistic craftsman in all manner of artistic design! This study gave me a whole new perspective. The LORD is the one who gives us wisdom and knowledge, by the power of His Holy Spirit, to design and create works of art and music! Another example of this would be found in the harp playing and songs of King David who was anointed by the LORD. As David played the music upon his harp, he prophesied through the Holy Spirit of God as he wrote the lyrics to his Psalms. It is written in the book of Chronicles that the musicians and singers, who were appointed to perform the songs of the LORD for the Divine service in the Holy Temple, were also very cunning artists, praising God with high sounding cymbals!

I Samuel 16:13 *Then Samuel took the horn of oil, and anointed him in the midst of his brethren; and the Spirit of the LORD came upon David from that day forward. So Samuel rose up, and went to Ramah.*

I Chronicles 25:1 *Moreover David and the captains of the host separated to the service of the sons of Asaph, and of Héman, and of Jeduthun, who should prophesy with harps, with psalteries, and with cymbals...)*

I Chronicles 25:7 *So the number of them, with their brethren that were in instructed in the songs of the LORD, even all that were cunning, was two hundred fourscore and eight.*

Cymbal
Photo ©2014 Kimberly K Ballard

The word *"cunning"* means that their artistic work *"exhibited ingenuity."* The word *"ingenuity"* reveals that their designs were *"clever and inventive, ingenious and imaginative."* So all the artisans of the LORD were highly skilled because the Holy Spirit had anointed them, and, when His Spirit filled their hearts, they prophesied the Word's of the LORD, and they had the ability to design the Holy vessels of the LORD as the Spirit of God gave them the knowledge and skill to accomplish the great

masterpieces for His glory. These cunning artists and musicians were exhibiting fine ingenuity and creativity as they crafted the excellent designs of the LORD.

The work was sometimes delicate, like the designs they created in the embroidery work that was sewn upon the veil and upon the garments of the Priests. The work was quite pleasing to the eye. It took the skilled hand of a jeweler to bevel the gemstones and to mount them upon the breastplate of the High Priest. Bezaleel was not only gifted in these things, he was also a Master craftsman in working with gold and silver. He could take any idea or design and fashion it exactly how they wanted it to look. Some of the designs that Bezaleel worked were fine lacy filigree designs that were intricate ornamental works of art. Bezaleel was also skillful in carving scroll designs upon wood or upon precious metals. His apprentices also helped with the construction of all the Holy vessels and furniture of the LORD. Bezaleel was responsible for crafting the two Cherubim angels upon the Ark of the Covenant, along with the decorative moulding that was mounted upon the sides of the Ark. So Bezaleel created the Holy Almond Tree Menorah for the Tabernacle of the LORD as the Holy Spirit guided his hands and equipped him with this Divine knowledge.

For centuries, the secret mysteries of the LORD'S Living Testimony were kept hidden within the Divine design of Bezaleel's Almond Tree Menorah. As I began to study the details within this tree, it began to blossom and then it started unveiling its secrets. My Jerusalem Almond Tree that blossomed miraculously by the Invisible Assistant was a pure representation of the Holy Almond Tree Menorah. The hidden story that it told was truly an expression of the Testimony of Yeshua's Divine resurrection inside the Foundation Stone of Holy Mount Moriah in Jerusalem Israel. The LORD was now beginning to unveil the connection of Yeshua to the Divine design of the pure gold Almond Tree Menorah crafted by Bezaleel. I soon discovered that in Botanical terms, the hidden petals within the Divine design are called *"Corolla."* This word is one of the elements that we will investigate further in this study.

Almond Blossoms on Holy Mount Moriah
Photo by LV ©2007 by Kimberly K Ballard
All Rights Reserved

The Holy Almond Tree Menorah that was crafted out of pure gold by Bezaleel, by the power of the Holy Spirit, is a lamp stand that has seven lamps upon each one of its seven Almond branches. The seven Almond branches shoot forth out of the main trunk of the solid gold Tree.

King David wrote, *"That the Word of the LORD was a lamp and a light unto his feet, unto his path."* So Messiah Yeshua was revealed in the prophetic words of King David because Yeshua is *the Living Torah Word of God,* thereby making Him the Living Lamp or the pure Almond Tree Menorah, our Eternal radiant light. This would therefore indicate that *the Living Torah* is the pure Holy Almond Tree Menorah of life!

Psalm 119:105 *Thy Word is a lamp unto my feet, and a light unto my path.*

II Samuel 22:29 *For Thou art my lamp, O LORD; and the LORD will lighten my darkness.*

The most exciting truth, though, that I have discerned by the power of the Holy Spirit is the fact that Yeshua's beautiful Living Testimony is mysteriously concealed and discovered within the Divine design of the pure gold Almond Tree Menorah that was originally constructed by the LORD'S artistic craftsman, Bezaleel.

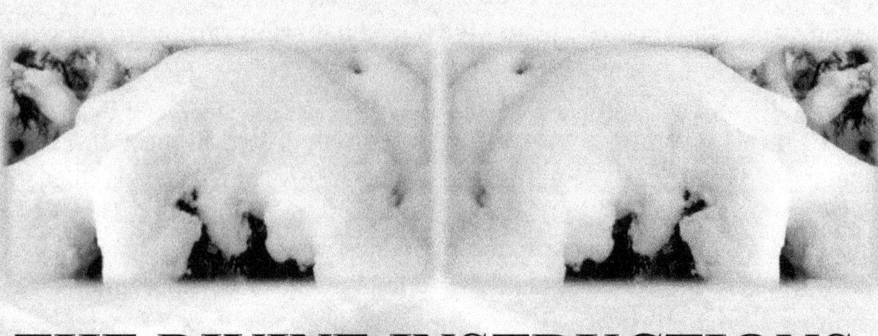

THE DIVINE INSTRUCTIONS

The Holy Menorah in the snow & Snow on Juniper Photos ©2013 Kimberly K Ballard All Rights Reserved

It was a matter of paramount importance that Moses, and ultimately Bezaleel, precisely follow the Divine design instructions of the LORD during the construction of the Holy Almond Tree Menorah and also for everything else pertaining to the Holy Tabernacle of the LORD. In the Torah, we find the detailed instructions for building the pure gold Holy Almond Tree Menorah that is also called *"the candlestick"* or the *"lamp stand."* I must reiterate that it is extremely important to observe the details within this design.

Exodus 25:31-40 *You shall make a lamp stand of pure gold; the lamp stand shall be made of hammered work; its base and its shaft, its cups, calyxes, and petals shall be of one piece. Six branches shall issue from its sides; three branches from one side of the lamp stand and three branches from the other side of the lamp stand. On one branch there shall be three cups shaped like almond-blossoms, each with calyx and petals, and on the next branch there shall be three cups shaped like almond-blossoms, each with calyx and petals; so for all six branches issuing from the lamp stand. And on the lamp stand itself, there shall be four cups shaped like almond-blossoms, each with calyx and petals; a calyx, of one piece with it, under the second pair of branches, and a calyx, of one piece with it, under the last pair of branches; so for all six branches issuing from the lamp stand. Their calyxes and their stems shall be of one piece with it, the whole of it a single hammered piece of pure gold. Make its seven lamps-the lamps shall be so mounted as to give the light on its front side-and its tongs and fire pans of pure gold. Note well, and follow the patterns for them that are being shown to you on the mountain.*

Numbers 8:4 *And this work of the candlestick was of beaten gold, unto the shaft thereof, unto the flowers thereof, was beaten work; according to the pattern which the LORD had shewed Moses, so he made the candlestick.*

Exodus 37:17-24 *And he made the candlestick of pure gold; of beaten work made he the candlestick; his shaft, and his branch, his bowls, his knops, and his flowers, were of the same; And six branches going out of the sides thereof; three branches of the candlestick out of the one side thereof, and three branches of the candlestick out of the other side thereof; Three bowls made after the fashion of almonds in one branch, a knop and a flower; and three bowls made like almonds in another branch, a knop and a flower; so throughout the six branches going out of the candlestick. And in the candlestick were four bowls made like almonds, his knops, and his flowers; And a knop under two branches of the same, and a knop under two branches of the same, and a knop under two branches of the same, according to the six branches going out of it. Their knops and their branches were of the same; all of it was one beaten work of pure gold. And he made his seven lamps, and his snuffers, and his snuffdishes, of pure gold. Of a talent of pure gold made he it, and all the vessels thereof.*

The Holy, pure gold Almond Tree Menorah was to stand *in the Holy Place* in the Sanctuary of the LORD opposite from the Table of the Shewbread or Showbread.

Hebrews 9:1-2 *Then verily the first Covenant had also ordinances of Divine service, and a worldly Sanctuary. For there was a Tabernacle made; the first, wherein was the candlestick, and the table, and the shewbread; which is called the Sanctuary.*

Exodus 40:24-25 *And he put the candlestick in the tent of the congregation, over against the table, on the side of the Tabernacle southward. And he lighted the lamps before the LORD; as the LORD commanded Moses.*

So Bezaleel, was about to encode the Living Testimony of the Messiah, upon the Holy Almond Tree Menorah. For this reason, Bezaleel had to make the Menorah *exactly according to the pattern* that the LORD showed to Moses upon Mount Sinai.

THE DIVINE DESIGN A LIVING TESTIMONY

Almond Blossoms LV on Mount Moriah Israel & Snow
Photos ©2013 Kimberly K Ballard All Rights Reserved

The base that Bezaleel constructed for the original Almond Tree Menorah is the principal or essential starting place of the Divine design. The base of the Menorah must be analyzed first because it is the foundation upon which the entire Almond Tree is resting. The Living Testimony of Messiah Yeshua, the Living Almond Branch, the Rod of God, is resting upon this foundation. Upon this base, the Almond Tree of Life is set forever as a sure foundation. There is quite a bit of archaeological evidence showing that the original Menorah was set upon a base bearing three legs. This was the original design of the Holy Menorah of the LORD. Images of this type of Menorah have been discovered all over the Land of Israel, Mount Sinai, and many other locations. It is depicted this way in the excavations of many ancient Synagogues. It is also artistically pictured as having three legs on many of the ancient mosaics, etched onto Jewish graves, and depicted upon the ancient Hasmonean coins. One of the recent archaeological excavations took place in the ancient city of Magdala, in 2009. The ancient Synagogue of Magdala was unearthed for the first time in nearly 2,000 years. I know Mary Magdalene attended this particular Synagogue in Magdala and that Yeshua taught here because the LORD revealed this to me. I have proof that I will show you! A large rectangular stone was discovered resting in the center of the Synagogue and it was etched with an ancient Menorah bearing a tripod base.

Official Photograph of, "The Magdala Stone,"
taken in October 2009
Courtesy of and ©2009 Magdala Center Excavations, Israel
All Rights Reserved

I have written more about this in the chapter on Messiah Yeshua's miracles. The archaeologists who discovered it and unearthed it said *"that whoever etched this Menorah, must have been an eyewitness to the original Menorah that once stood in the Holy Temple."*

This base is very different from the base that is on the Menorah that was carried off by the Romans in 70AD, and is depicted on the triumphal Arch of Titus in Rome. That particular Menorah on the Arch is a corrupted version of the original because the base relief contains depictions of dragons and other pagan creatures and this was against Jewish Law. Many Jewish Rabbis have also declared that the Menorah that was carried off to Rome was indeed a corrupted version and was not made according to the original Divine design that Moses and Bezaleel replicated. I might also mention that I noticed that there are some hearts that are etched upon the stone in the Synagogue at Magdala, and the hearts are beside the Almond Tree Menorah. *To me, this is a striking reminder that Messiah Yeshua's Testimony as the Living Almond Branch from the Almond Tree of Life is the loving Eternal Covenant of the heart.*

The three legs on the Holy Menorah go out from the base of the shaft and run down to the ground, like the roots of a firmly planted tree. The base supports the Living Testimony of the Branch that is encoded within the Divine design. I discovered, surprisingly, that some Jewish Rabbi's actually believed that the three legs on the original design stood for *"the Messianic hope of Israel!"* You will understand the importance of this later. Then as I was doing final editing in September of 2013, Eilat Mazar, a very distinguished Archaeologist in Israel, discovered some fantastic ancient jewelry that was buried near the Temple Mount that miraculously depicted the Menorah with a three legged base! What timing for such a find! Now, within the definitions of the word *"base"* we find that this is the point of establishing Yeshua's Testimony. It is the beginning point and the foundation of the Holy Menorah.

A brass base in the snow with four legs
Photo ©2013 Kimberly K Ballard
All Rights Reserved

Definition Base,

1. To lay the base or foundations.
2. To put a thing on a base or foundation.
3. To establish or found.
4. The bottom of a thing, considered as its support, or the part of the thing on which it rests; foundation.

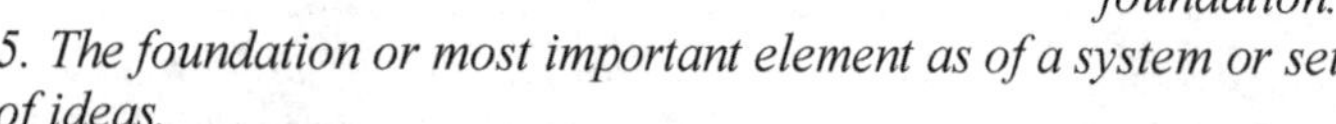

5. The foundation or most important element as of a system or set of ideas.
6. Anything from which a start is made; basis
7. The principal or essential ingredient.
8. The point of attachment of a part of the body.
9. Goal, starting place.
10. In geometry the lowest side of the perimeter of a figure, on which it is thought of as resting.
11. In Botany, the part of fruit where it is united with the peduncle; the part of a leaf next to the stem.
12. In dyeing, a substance used for fixing colors.
13. In heraldry, the lower portion of a shield.
14. In mathematics, a constant figure upon which a mathematical table is computed. ***(Source: Webster's New Twentieth Century Dictionary Unabridged Second Edition Copyright ©1970 The World Publishing Company).***

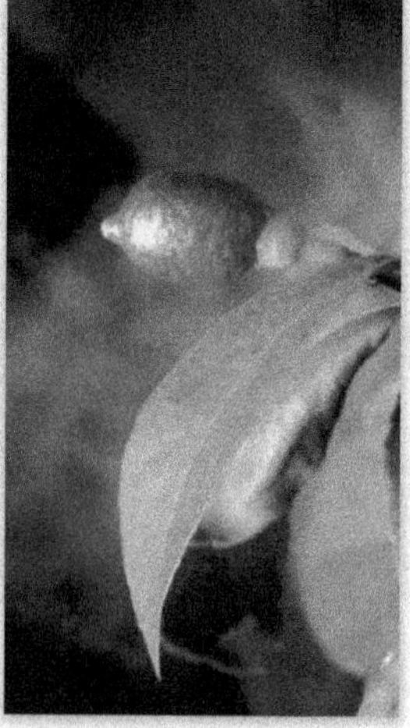

A Meyer Lemon fruit
Showing the base where the fruit forms
Photos ©2013
Kimberly K Ballard
All Rights Reserved

The base serves as the resting place for the seven lamps and the branches. This design elaborates the fact that *the seventh day is the LORD'S day of rest.* Yeshua's Testimony rests because He fulfilled the LORD'S Eternal Covenant in Holy Mount Moriah at Golgotha which

is said to be standing at 777 meters, according to the topographical map. This is a completely perfect Testimony of Messiah Yeshua. So the *three legs* on the Holy Almond Tree Menorah that go down to the ground like the roots of the tree reveal that *Yeshua is the Almond Tree that sprouted to life on the third day,* and this base confirms our firm foundation. Now this Almond tree is forever firmly rooted in a *sure place* on Holy Mount Moriah in God's Garden where His Testimony is eternally set upon this reliable foundation, and this is where my miracle Almond tree budded! This is *the principal or essential ingredient that is our constant, and it depicts the light* which is the LORD in all His glory. This refers to the steadfast faithfulness of the LORD. The LORD never changes and His light never goes out. The Temple Menorah was to stay lit.

Genesis 2:2 *And on the seventh day God ended His work which He had made; and He rested on the seventh day from all His work which He had made.*

II Chronicles 6:41-42 *Now therefore arise, O LORD God, into Thy resting place, Thou, and the Ark of Thy strength; let Thy Priests, O LORD God, be clothed with salvation, and let Thy Saints rejoice in goodness. O LORD God, turn not away the face of Thine anointed; remember the mercies of David Thy servant.*

Jeremiah 50:6 *My people hath been lost sheep; their shepherds have caused them to go astray, they have turned them away on the mountains; they have gone from mountain to hill, they have forgotten their resting place.*

The Bible says that no other foundation can be laid that firmly establishes the Living Testimony of Messiah Yeshua. This Almond Tree is built of pure gold and in the end we will see that His work is faithful and true. It will endure forever because He is the KING of Glory who takes us into His Eternal resting place.

I Corinthians 3:11-13 *For other foundation can no man lay than that is laid, which is Yeshua Messiah. Now if any man build upon this foundation gold, silver, precious stones, wood hay, stubble; Every man's work shall be made manifest; for the day shall declare it, because it shall be revealed by fire; and the fire shall try every man's work of what sort it is.*

Romans 15:20-21 *Yea, so have I strived to preach the Gospel, not where Messiah was named, lest I should build upon another man's foundation; But as it is written, To whom He was not spoken of, they shall see; and they that have not heard shall understand.*

Isaiah 48:13 *Mine hand also hath laid the foundation of the earth, and My right hand hath spanned the Heavens; when I call unto them, they stand up together.*

Isaiah 28:16 *Therefore thus saith the LORD GOD, Behold, I lay in Zion for a foundation a stone, a tried stone, a precious corner stone, a sure foundation; he that believeth shall not make haste.*

One of the most astonishing fragments of the Dead Sea Scrolls that was documented as *"Fragment 7 of 4Q285"* speaks of *"The Branch of David"* (which according to my Israeli friend is the word *"Tzemach"* in Hebrew) that would be slain and pierced by the Romans! This little known fact that was discovered in the Dead Sea Scrolls has been kept quiet, subdued, and left out of some of the translations of the Holy Scriptures, but it was found in the book of Isaiah in the Messianic passage of the Dead Sea Scrolls. By definition *"the base is the most important element of this set of ideas"* because the entire *Testimony* of the LORD rests upon it. The third day of His resurrection is represented in the base bearing three legs as *the anchor* of the soul.

Anchor Photo ©2014 Kimberly K Ballard All Rights Reserved

Hebrews 6:17-18 *Wherein God, willing more abundantly to shew unto the heirs of promise the immutability of his counsel, confirmed it by an oath; That by two immutable things, in which it was impossible for God to lie, we might have a strong consolation, who have fled for refuge to lay hold upon the hope set before us; Which hope we have as*

an anchor of the soul, both sure and stedfast, and which entereth into that within the veil; Whither the forerunner is for us entered, even Yeshua, made an High Priest forever after the order of Melchizedek.

In the definition of the word *"base"* we see that it can also refer to *"part of a shield."* The Scriptures tell us many times that *the LORD is our shield* and that our hope is in *His Word* which is a reference to the Messiah! We must place our trust in Him *because this shield is soaked in the Living Water which quenches Satan's arrows!*

Shield
Photo ©2014 Kimberly K Ballard

Psalm 119:114 *Thou art my hiding place and my shield; I hope in Thy Word.*

Proverbs 30:5 *Every Word of God is pure; He is a shield unto them that put their trust in Him.*

Psalm 84:11 *For the LORD God is a sun and shield; the LORD will give grace and glory; no good thing will He withhold from them that walk uprightly.*

The Royal shield is our salvation and the right hand of the Rod of God holds us up!

Psalm 18:35 *Thou hast also given me the shield of Thy salvation; and Thy right hand hath holden me up, and Thy gentleness hath made me great.*

A Meyer Lemon Blossom
With fruit forming at the base
Photo ©2013 Kimberly K Ballard

In Botany *"the base is the part of the fruit, where it connects to the peduncle."* This is fascinating because *"the peduncle is part of the shoot of seed plants where the flower is formed."* Yeshua blossomed to life as the First Fruits of salvation and, of course, the Almond flowers are blossoming upon the pure gold Holy Almond Tree Menorah. Within every detail of the Divine design, the Messiah's Living Testimony is suddenly made visible to us as we observe it closely!

Moving up from the base, in the center of the Menorah is *the Rod known as the main Shaft.* It serves as the solid core or trunk of the Almond Tree. By definition the *"shaft"* is the stem of a spear. Within this detail of the Divine design is the proof that Yeshua was going to be pierced in the side and in the heart with the Roman spear. When this Scripture was fulfilled, the three elements that were present that testify of the LORD God are the Spirit, the water, and the blood, and these three testify that Yeshua's Testimony is true. So *the number three* for the Rod of God is indeed the solid base of His Testimony. The spear pierced Yeshua's heart because His Testimony as the Living Branch is the New Covenant of the heart that was made with the life blood and Living Water of the LORD. Each element within the definition of the word *"shaft"* vividly testifies that the LORD is the Messiah. In the following section, I have broken this down with many Scriptural proofs. *The Shaft of the Almond Tree Menorah is the Rod and the main Branch or stem that comes up out of the stump.*

Definition;
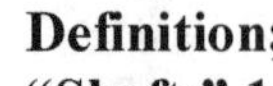
"Shaft;" 1. The stem of an arrow or spear.

Arrow
Photo ©2014 Kimberly K Ballard

John 19:34 *But one of the soldiers with a spear pierced His side, and forthwith came there out blood and water.*

2. A missile or something compared to a missile; bolt; as, shafts of lightning.

Luke 17:24 *For as the lightning, that lighteneth out of the one part under Heaven, shineth unto the other part under Heaven; so shall also the Son of man be in His day.*

Lightning
Photo ©2013 Kimberly K Ballard

II Samuel 22:14-15 *The LORD thundered from Heaven, and the most High uttered His voice. And He sent out arrows, and scattered them; lightning, and discomfited them.*

3. A cone or column of light, a ray, a beam.
The LORD sent His pillar of light to lead the children of Israel in the wilderness.

Nehemiah 9:19 *Yet Thou in Thy manifold mercies forsookest them not in the wilderness; the pillar of the cloud departed not from them by day, to lead them in the way; neither the pillar of fire by night, to shew them the light, and the way wherein they should go.*

4. A long slender part or objects specifically,
(a) The trunk of a tree or the stem of a plant.

The Shaft of the Holy Menorah is the trunk of the Almond Tree of Life.

Our First Fruit of salvation is the KING of Righteousness. Yeshua has saved our souls and He is the Tree of Life that is written in Proverbs!

Proverbs 11:30 *The fruit of the righteous is a Tree of Life; and he that wins souls is wise.*

The roots of the tree are connected to the stump. The stump is connected to the Rod, which is the stem or *Shaft* in the center of the Menorah. Some translations in Isaiah 11 render the stem of Jesse as *"the stump of Jesse," and the Branch grows out of the roots.* This root of Jesse is mentioned in Fragment 4Q285 of the Dead Sea Scrolls!

Isaiah 11:1-5 *And there shall come forth a Rod out of the stem of Jesse, and a Branch shall grow out of his roots; And the Spirit of the LORD shall rest on Him, the Spirit of wisdom and understanding, the Spirit of counsel and might, the Spirit of knowledge and of the fear of the LORD; And shall make Him of quick understanding in the fear of the LORD; and He shall not judge after the sight of His eyes, neither reprove after the hearing of His ears; But with righteousness shall He judge the poor, and reprove with equity for the meek of the earth with the Rod of His mouth, and with the breath of His lips shall He slay the wicked. And righteousness shall be the girdle of His loins, and faithfulness the girdle of His reins.*

"Shaft, item #4;" continued; **(b) The mid section of a long bone;**
Another incredible piece of the Testimony of Messiah Yeshua that I discovered concealed within the *Shaft* of Holy Menorah, is *the Lamb shank bone!* This is known as, *"The shaft of the arm."* In Hebrew, this bone is called, *"Zeroa."* It is unbelievable that this word happens to refer to the *"mighty arm,"* of the LORD. This detail shows us, that Yeshua the Rod of God is the Passover Lamb and He is the arm of the LORD revealed! Not one of His legs was broken in fulfillment of the Holy Scriptures. Yeshua died as the Passover Lamb of God, on Nisan 14.

(c) The supporting stem of a branched candlestick.
"The Branch" of the Almond Tree Menorah is mentioned again, in the definition of *Shaft.*

The Branch will grow up out of His place, which is Heaven, and He will build the Temple of the LORD. Yeshua told the Jewish leaders to tear down the Temple and He will build it again in three days. This is more evidence that the *three legs* of the Holy Almond Tree Menorah testify that *Yeshua did grow up out of His place and sprout to life during His resurrection on the third day.*

Zechariah 6:12 *And speak unto him, saying, Behold, the man whose Name is The BRANCH; and He shall grow up out of His place, and He shall build the Temple of the LORD; Even He shall build the Temple of the LORD; and He shall bear the glory, and shall sit and rule upon His throne; and He shall be a Priest upon His throne; and the counsel of peace shall be between them both.*

Jerusalem Flag
Photo ©2014 Kimberly K Ballard
All Rights Reserved

(d) A flag pole, etc.
The flag pole definition brings to mind that Messiah Yeshua is *the ensign* that all the Gentiles seek, *and His rest shall be glorious* which is visible on the Divine design of the Menorah. The base of this Eternal Almond Tree is the place of rest for us if we abide in the Tree of Life. The flag pole again reveals *"the Royal Standard"* and Yeshua's image was lifted up on the pole, revealing that He alone is the God of Israel.

Isaiah 11:10 *And in that day there shall be a root of Jesse, which shall stand for an ensign of the people; to it the Gentiles seek; and His rest shall be glorious.*

These truths have all *been kept secret from the foundation of the world* by the LORD.

Matthew 13:34-35 *All these things spake Yeshua unto the multitude in parables; and without a parable spake He not unto them; That it might be fulfilled which was spoken by the Prophet, saying, I will open My mouth in parables; I will utter things which have been kept secret from the foundation of the world.*

Extending outward from the Rod or Shaft of the Menorah, there is an amazing detail. This is a critical part of the Living Testimony of Messiah Yeshua. We find that *the Rod* is in the center of the Holy Menorah and the arms are budding flowering Almond branches that are outstretched and lifted up from the Rod! Astonishing! This is a pure representation of Messiah Yeshua, the Rod lifted up in the outstretched arm of God that budded to life to save us. *The Royal Standard rises up from the stump!*

Isaiah 52:13 *Behold, My Servant shall deal prudently, He shall be exalted and extolled, and be very high.*

John 3:14 *And as Moses lifted up the serpent in the wilderness, even so must the Son of man be lifted up; That whosoever believeth in Him should not perish, but have eternal life.*

Isaiah 26:11 *LORD, when Thy hand is lifted up, they will not see; but they shall see, and be ashamed for their envy at the people; yea, the fire of Thine enemies shall devour them.*

Isaiah 6:1 *In the year that king Uzziah died I saw also the LORD sitting upon a throne, high and lifted up, and His train filled the Temple.*

The amazing thing is that there are *three sets of branches blossoming* with Almond flowers and buds on the Holy Menorah. The buds are referred to as *"knops."* This detail speaks clearly of Messiah Yeshua budding to life on the third day and it boldly declares and reveals that the LORD Messiah is one God who is indeed the Almond Tree of Life! This Eternal Living Testimony of the Messiah is proven to forever rest upon the Holy Almond Tree Menorah and can never be removed from it!

Exodus 25:35 *And there shall be a knop under two branches of the same, and a knop under two branches of the same, and a knop under two branches of the same, according to the six branches that proceed out of the candlestick. Their knops and their branches shall be of the same; all shall be one beaten work of pure gold.*

As Bezaleel began hammering out the Divine design for the Holy Almond Tree Menorah (by the power of God's Ruach/Holy Spirit) he was actually beating the Living Testimony and Eternal Covenant of Messiah Yeshua into the Holy Divine design. The entire work of art was beaten out of one piece of pure solid gold. Now at the birth of Messiah Yeshua, the wise men of the east brought the gift of pure gold to the Jewish KING who was born. The pure gold truly represented the LORD in the solid gold Menorah because the true light was coming into the world to dwell among us as our Saviour Messiah. The Holy Spirit was abiding inside Him, making His light evident to all who saw it. When Yeshua the Branch was cut off, this KING was beaten, like the pure gold branches of the Menorah that were beaten out of one solid piece.

Luke 22:63-65 *And the men that held Yeshua mocked Him, and smote Him. And when they had blindfolded Him, they struck Him on the face, and asked Him, saying, Prophesy, who is it that smote Thee? And many other things blasphemously spake they against Him.*

Mark 14:65 *And some began to spit on Him, and to cover His face, and to buffet Him, and to say unto Him, prophesy; and the servants did strike Him with the palms of their hands.*

Matthew 27:30 *And they spit upon Him, and took the reed, and smote Him on the head.*

The Almond branches on the Holy Menorah testify that Yeshua was in the tomb for three days and three nights before He blossomed and budded to life as the Living Fruitful Almond Branch on the third day, on *the Feast of First Fruits.* There are three flowering Almond branches on one side of the Menorah and there are three flowering Almond branches on the other side of the Menorah. So basically the Shaft, the main Stem of the Holy Menorah *is the "Ascending Rod"* that serves as the axis of the tree. Yeshua is *the Ascending Rod* that *ascended* in the glory cloud into Heaven after fulfilling His Eternal Living Testimony of the Heavenly Ark.

By definition a *"stem"* is also *"the rod that is in the center of a lock!"* A key goes into *the rod* and when the key is turned, the door is unlocked. So incredibly, *Yeshua, the Stem of Jesse, the Rod of God, holds the key of David and He unlocks the door of Heaven* and shows us *"the way"* to enter into the Eternal Garden of God! It is absolutely remarkable!

Old Lock Photo ©2014 Kimberly K Ballard All Rights Reserved

Isaiah 22:22 *And the key of the house of David will I lay upon His shoulder; so He shall open, and none shall shut; and He shall shut, and none shall open.*

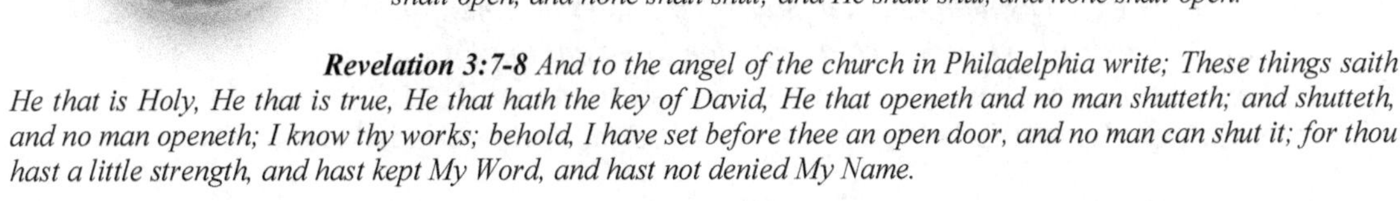

Revelation 3:7-8 *And to the angel of the church in Philadelphia write; These things saith He that is Holy, He that is true, He that hath the key of David, He that openeth and no man shutteth; and shutteth, and no man openeth; I know thy works; behold, I have set before thee an open door, and no man can shut it; for thou hast a little strength, and hast kept My Word, and hast not denied My Name.*

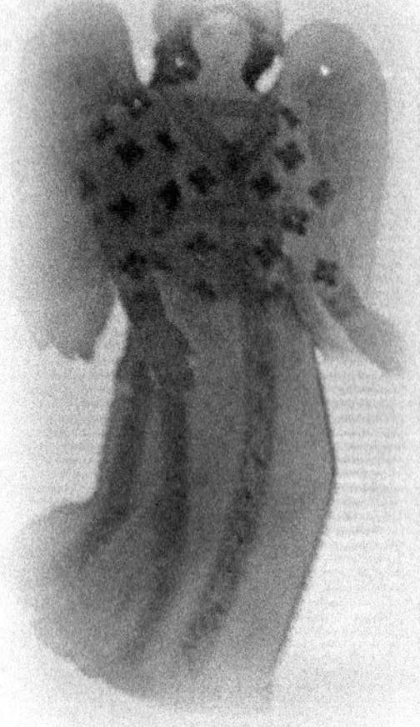

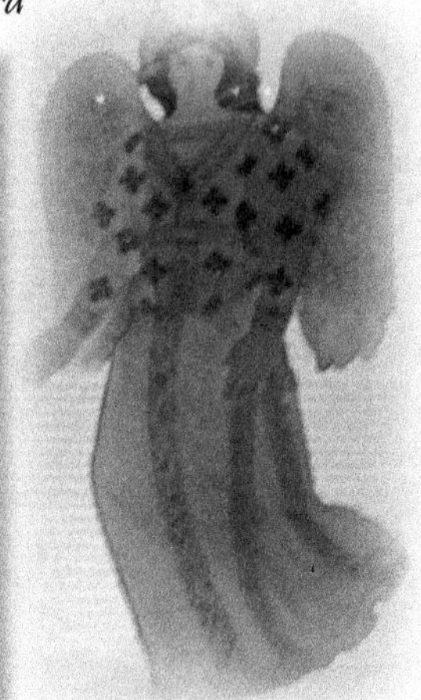

A Menorah in the pure snow & Angel Photos

THE HIDDEN DETAILS WITHIN THE DIVINE DESIGN THE CALYX – THE VEIL – THE COROLLA - THE FINGERPRINT THE CORONA - THE CROWN – THE HALO –THE ECLIPSE

Blue Moon Photos

Now we know that the LORD is so brilliant that He encoded hidden elements that are not visible to the human eye within His Divine design on the Holy Menorah. The hidden petals I mentioned before found on the Menorah are called *"Corolla."* So now I want to show you each element of the astonishing detail that is encoded in the design, as the LORD revealed it to me. The arms lifted up are the Almond branches that are bearing the Almond flowers and the *"Calyx"* that is sometimes referred to as the *"Knop,"* is the bud. In researching the meaning of the word *"Calyx"* in the dictionary, I could not believe what I discovered! The Messiah's identity is concealed within the *"Calyx"* on the Almond Branch, on the Holy Menorah. In Psalm 132, David wrote that the Messiah would be the horn of David that would *"bud"* to life, and He would give us Eternal salvation, as the anointed Lamp. It is true, then, that *this verse* also verifies that Yeshua is depicted and prophesied to be the Holy Almond Tree Menorah.

Psalm 132:16-17 *I will also clothe her Priests with salvation; and her Saints shall shout aloud for joy. There will I make the horn of David to bud; I have ordained a Lamp for Mine anointed.*

In Hebrew, salvation is, of course, *"Yeshuah."* So the Psalm actually says, *"I will clothe her Priests with Yeshuah and her Saints shall shout aloud for joy! There will I make the horn of David to bud; I have ordained a lamp for Mine anointed."*

The truth is, since our garments are made pure in the Messiah, we are literally clothed with Yeshua, exactly as it is written in David's Psalm. We are indeed *wrapped in a robe of*

light! By delving deeper into the word definitions within the word *"Calyx,"* we find more incredible details. It just so happens that the *"Calyx"* is *"the veiled part of a flower."* It is the part of the flower that we do not see, as it remains hidden!

Calyx*; An outer covering (veiled part) of a flower external to the corolla, which encloses, and consisting of a whorl of leaves or sepals, usually of a green color, and less delicate texture than the corolla.* ***(Source: Webster's New Twentieth Century Dictionary Unabridged Second Edition Copyright ©1970 The World Publishing Company).***

If we extract each one of the Botanical elements within the *"Calyx,"* we find that there are more Messianic revelations. Within the *"Calyx,"* there is the part called the *"Whorl,"* and I find this part to be so fascinating!

Whorl; *1. Botany; An arrangement of three or more parts, a leaves or petals; radiating from a single organ or node. 2. One of the circular ridges or convolutions of a fingerprint.*

Now the LORD manifests Himself like *the Whorl in the Calyx!* The LORD radiates His glory through His Rod Messiah, who is the Yad and Finger of God. He accomplishes His works by the power of His Spirit on the Rod. *He is the Lamb shank of the Passover Seder.* The Whorl on the Menorah reflects the fact that the LORD God of Israel is one God who manifests Himself as the Father God, as our Messiah Yeshua the Son (Yeshua ha-Ben) the second perfect Adam, and through His Holy Spirit. Like the Whorl, the LORD God of Israel manifests Himself three ways, and these three are radiating out of a single node as one! He is one KING! Israel was required by God to keep three special Feasts and to go up to Jerusalem three times a year to celebrate them. The three chosen Feasts include, *Shavuot, Passover, and Tabernacles.* Shavuot speaks of the giving of the Holy Spirit by Messiah Yeshua, the Word of God. Passover speaks of the blood of the Covenant of the heart, fulfilled by Messiah Yeshua the Lamb. The Third Feast is Tabernacles or Sukkot, which speaks of us Eternally dwelling in the LORD'S Temple, in the Heavenly Kingdom of God because Yeshua fulfilled the Living Testimony as the Fruitful Branch of the Almond Tree of Life. All three of these Feasts are pictured on the pure gold Almond Tree Menorah, and all three represent *one God,* manifesting Himself three ways, like the *Whorl.* The three main parts of this tree are: first the roots, the base that serves as the solid foundation; second the trunk that is the Shaft, the ascending Rod that is the central or main part of the tree; and the third part of the tree are the arms lifted up that are flowering Almond branches. Although life is flowing through the three different parts of the tree, this is still only one Holy tree! So we can see that *the Almond Tree Menorah* represents the LORD God manifesting Himself in three ways, like the *Whorl.*

The LORD God of Israel is Messiah Yeshua and His Ruach/Holy Spirit abides in Him, inside His heart. The Holy Spirit groans within and the Holy Spirit groaned inside Yeshua's heart when Lazarus died! The LORD God of Israel is the Almond Tree of Life and in this one tree, we see the budding Branch that came to life, having the Holy Spirit of life inside Him. As we abide in this Almond tree, we become grafted into the main Shaft, into the Rod Yeshua, the Lamb of God, and the breath of His Holy Spirit in Him gives us Eternal life. It is so fantastic that His everlasting Testimony of the Heavenly Ark is clearly and secretly woven into the Divine design of the Holy Almond Tree Menorah!

The next element of the Menorah that I want to discuss is the part called the *"Corolla"* that is found within the *"Calyx."* In Botanical terms, the *"Corolla"* consists of the inner petals or leaves that are hidden from view within the Almond flowers. This is the part that hides the secrets of the Messiah until the flower is fully visible. It is truly astounding that the *"Corolla"* reveals the one who wears the Crown as *"THE KING OF KINGS AND LORD OF LORDS!"*

Corolla; *n. [L. corolla, a little crown, dim. of corona, a crown, wreath.] In Botany, the petals or inner leaves of a flower. It is distinguished from the perianth by its fine texture and bright colors.*

Incredibly, we find that within the *"Calyx,"* the veiled petals or inner leaves are called *"Corolla."* Within the *"Corolla,"* we find a *"Crown" that is hidden from view.* Messiah Yeshua wears many Royal Crowns as the Royal Sovereign of the universe. Within the definition of the word *"Crown,"* we find the *"Corona" and the "Wreath."* These both have special significance to the Testimony of Messiah Yeshua, and I will analyze them further. Within the definition of the words *"Crown"* and *"Wreath"* are all the secrets that reveal Yeshua is the KING of Israel.

Meyer Lemon Blossom
Photo ©2013 Kimberly K Ballard All Rights Reserved

Now I think it is a fabulous coincidence that within the word *"Crown,"* we find the word *"Bezel."* There is no doubt in my mind now that the word *"Bezel"* comes from the Master craftsman of the LORD named *"Bezaleel,"* because He was the fine jeweler, chosen by the LORD God of Israel to make all the Holy vessels for the Tabernacle of Moses. So Bezaleel ironically appears to be encoded within the Divine design of the Holy Almond Tree Menorah and maybe this was God's special gift to him after he worked the design into the Menorah, according to the LORD'S Divine pattern! *"The KING of the Jews"* is Yeshua's title as the Messiah. As the High Priest of Heaven, Yeshua wears a *golden girdle* with a *Royal gold Crown and the Jewish mitre.* The High Priest in the Holy Temple wears the gold *"Tzitz,"* the Hebrew word for *"Crown."* Encoded in the *"Crown,"* we find the special knotted fringes that the High Priest wears on his garment called *"tzitzit."* Within the word *"Crown,"* the secret details of Yeshua's Testimony are found. This is so incredible! Within the definition of the word *"Crown,"* we find the leaves and Living Branches of a Tree! This tells us that Yeshua, the Living Branch, wears the Crown! Within the detail of the *Crown* is the Passover Lamb, *in the shank bone, which is the shaft!* It is so exciting and remarkable to see this!

Ornamental Wreath
Photo ©2014 Kimberly K Ballard
All Rights Reserved

Crown or Wreath;
n. 1. Any of various types of symbolic headgear worn by a King, Queen, Emperor etc, as a symbol of Sovereignty.
2. An ornamental wreath or circlet for the head, conferred by the ancients as a mark of victory, athletic or military distinction, etc.
3. The distinction that comes from a great achievement.
4. The Crown, the Sovereign as head of the state, or the Supreme power of a Monarch.
9. Something having the form of a crown, as the "corona" of a flower.
10. Botany; a. the leaves and living branches of a tree.

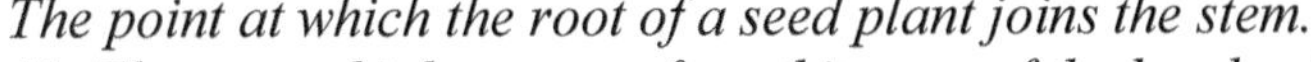

The point at which the root of a seed plant joins the stem.
11. The top or highest part of anything, as of the head, a hat, a mountain, etc.
16. The highest or most nearly perfect state of anything.
17. An exalting or chief attribute.
19. Also called head. Nautical; The part of an anchor at which the arms join the shank.
20. Also called bezel, top, jewelry. The part of a cut gem above the girdle.
22. Knots, a knot made by interweaving the strands at the end of a rope.
23. To place a crown or garland upon the head of.
24. To invest with or as with a regal crown or with regal dignity and power.
25. To surmount as with a crown.
26. To complete worthily; bring to a successful or triumphant conclusion;
31. Knots. To form a crown on the (end of a rope).

Now I am going to analyze the definitions even further and look at the word *"Corona."* Remember that within the *"Corolla,"* the veiled part is a *"Crown"* and within the *"Crown,"* is the *"Corona."* The most astonishing evidence that declares that Yeshua is the Messiah of Israel is found concealed within this particular part of the Divine design. *I was completely astonished when I discovered that the Crown of Thorns, as well as the location and events of Yeshua's crucifixion, are encoded in the part of the Holy Menorah called the "Corona!"*

Corona, n. pl. coronas, coronae, [L. a crown]
1. A crown; especially, one bestowed by the Romans as a reward for distinguished military service.
2. In architecture, the top of a cornice situated between the bed molding and the cymatium.
3. In anatomy and Zoology,
(a) Any crown or crown like part;
(b) The upper part of a skull or tooth etc.
4. In Botany; (a) The circle of florets of a composite flower;
(b) A cuplike appendage of the corolla or petals attached to the stem, as the daffodil, milkweed, etc;
(c) The appendage at the top of seeds enabling them to disperse.
5. In astronomy,
(a) A luminous circle around the sun, or moon;
(b) The halo around the sun, seen only during a total eclipse.
6. In ecclesiastical usage, the stripe passing horizontally about the lower edge of a mitre.

Corona ring visible around the Moon
Photo ©2013 Kimberly K Ballard

So within the *"Corona and the Crown,"* I found all of the following pieces of Yeshua's outstanding Testimony. I will list each of them now! The Jewish Messiah Yeshua was given *a Roman Crown of Thorns in mockery.* Yeshua was crucified in the place called *"skull hill"* which is *"the upper part of the hill of Golgotha, on Holy Mount Moriah."* Yeshua prayed in the Garden of Gethsemane, *"Take this cup away from Me."* Yeshua said that, *"Except a corn of wheat fall into the ground and die, it bringeth forth much fruit."* In other words, Yeshua is *the seed* that must die in order to produce many more seeds that are *dispersed* from Him because He is *the Living Torah* of the Heavenly Kingdom.

During the crucifixion a total eclipse may have occurred creating a *"Corona"* with a halo around the sun. As the High Priest of Heaven, Yeshua wears the *Crown and the Jewish mitre* of His High Priesthood. I could not believe it when the LORD allowed me to see this astonishing detail within His Divine design! Each of these elements is woven into the Almond Tree Menorah that sits in the Holy Temple in the Holy Place, before the Holy of Holies!

Now let me explain more about this discovery that was shown to me, by the Divine revelation of the LORD! Within the definition of the word *"Corona,"* we find that there is *"a crown that the Romans give as a reward for distinguished military service."* I was profoundly touched when I saw this detail, because my heart suddenly understood the astonishing truth about the Crown of Thorns! The Roman soldiers were deliberately mocking Yeshua who was *the Jewish KING Messiah.*

This shed new light on the fact that because the soldiers were Romans and the Romans controlled Jerusalem, as well as the Jewish Temple, they thought that it was laughable that they had total control over what was about to happen to the Jewish KING Messiah. The Romans knew that the Jewish people were anticipating the arrival of their Messiah, who they believed would come and rescue them out of the hands of the Romans. Yeshua was expected to defeat the Romans by some type of military victory, if He was truly the Messiah of Israel. The fact is, however, that Yeshua was now at their mercy, or so it seemed and appeared to them. They felt that they had the power to destroy the Jewish KING Messiah. Suddenly, I had this picture in my mind of what really happened. *They were forcing the Crown of Thorns upon Yeshua because the Roman Soldiers were performing in mockery the Roman gesture of placing a Crown upon the head of a Roman for distinguished military service!* They were reenacting this gesture in mockery with a Crown of Thorns, instead of a real Crown, because Yeshua was the Jewish KING, *the Royal Standard of God.* So as they pushed the Crown of Thorns upon Yeshua's head, they laughed and bowed the knee saying, *"Hail, KING of the Jews,"* as they drove the Thorns of the Crown into His tender head and skull and they beat upon it with the reeds in their hands. They even placed a reed in Yeshua's hand like a Rod or Royal Sceptre, and the Roman Soldiers beat His face and spit in it. They whipped Yeshua with the Roman flagrum, but He was innocent as a Lamb! Yeshua opened not His mouth because, as the Lamb of God, His life blood was going to save Israel forever and draw righteous Gentiles to worship the one true God. This time, the Romans were using a Crown of Thorns instead of their usual, *"Roman crown of victory for distinguished military service."* This was meant to be a very spiteful and hateful act on the part of the Roman legion. Yeshua had already been declared as the KING of the Jewish people.

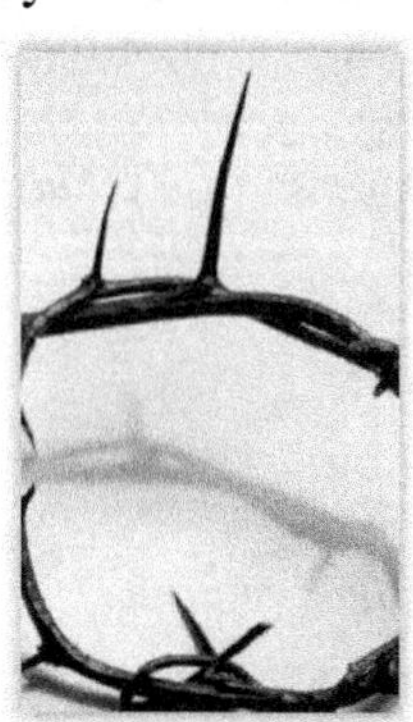

Crown of Thorns
Photo ©2013
Kimberly K Ballard
All Rights Reserved

Pagan Rome was not only in complete control over the entire Land of Israel, but Caesar controlled the Jewish Temple, and Jewish religious system. So it was corrupted. The Romans believed that they were unconquerable, as their Emperor was a god to them. So they felt that they had achieved a great victory over Israel and over the God of Israel! Caesar, whose image was pictured on *the Roman Standard,* thought of himself as a god and of course this was an abomination to the LORD God of Israel.

To the Romans, it appeared that this Jewish KING could not save Himself from their evil deeds, so they did not believe that Yeshua was a KING or a Messiah. It was all meant to mock *the Jewish KING.*

With a Royal drum roll, I can say, however, that this was indeed the Jewish KING Messiah, but Yeshua was no ordinary earthly KING! Yeshua's Kingdom was not of this world, just as He told the Jewish leaders in the Holy Temple. The Romans were clueless to the fact, that the LORD was in complete control over this situation. The truth is that this KING Messiah was going to die as the cut off Branch in order to bear the Eternal Fruit to save Israel forever and to draw everyone back to the Eternal Garden of the LORD God! What the Romans did not know is the fact that the Messiah did not come to save Himself. The Messiah came to save Israel forever. So we see that Yeshua came as the Ark of the Living Covenant to the Jordan River and the dove returned to the Ark and rested and stayed upon Him! The LORD was

literally showing Israel *the way,* by leading them into the Eternal Promised Land. This Joshua/Yeshua was their Righteous leader. *As the Rod of God was lifted up, as God's Royal Military Standard, Yeshua the image of God was saving Israel for Eternity.* So without realizing it, what the Romans meant for evil, the LORD turned into something extraordinary for Israel and for the entire world. Hidden from the eyes of the Roman Soldiers was Israel's *Invisible Assistant!* Yeshua had total power and the ultimate victory over Rome, but they did not know it yet! The Roman's also thought that they were in absolute control, but the reverse is what actually happened! God sent forth His Rod to be lifted up, with the arm of the LORD outstretched, to save Israel and reverse the curse of death from Eden. Instead of bringing Israel *temporary victory,* Messiah Yeshua, the Jewish KING, brought Israel *Eternal victory,* because the kingdoms of this world will one day perish. Yeshua will return to set up His Eternal Kingdom of Heaven upon the earth and inherit Judah as His portion. This great military victory of the Jewish KING Messiah was far more astounding than anything the Roman's could imagine or dream up! The Jewish people would be astonished to understand this now! Yeshua said He would return in the future and fight the enemies of God. Rome never could have predicted that Yeshua would rise from the dead, as the all powerful Rod of God, as the Living Branch from the Almond Tree of Life! This truth was hidden from their eyes.

What the Romans could not see is the fact that the very one that they were mocking with a Crown of Thorns is the very one who they will face in the judgment, when the wicked are resurrected and given a sentence of Eternal condemnation for their evil. They will see Yeshua again face to face when He comes in the future, wearing the solid gold Crown of the precious KING OF KINGS AND LORD OF LORDS. Yeshua/Joshua will lead the Jewish Saints in the greatest military victory against Satan that was ever waged in the history of the universe. When Yeshua comes, He will usher in the Kingdom of God and He will wear many *Royal Crowns* of glory during His Eternal reign because *He is the Rod of God, the Royal Heavenly Standard* who achieved the Eternal victory forever and ever. Amen!

The Romans did not know that the Testimony of Messiah Yeshua was already encoded within the Divine design of God's Holy Almond Tree Menorah that sits in the Holy Place in Heaven. This Crown of Thorns was hidden upon the Menorah by the LORD, centuries before Yeshua came to the earth, to fulfill the Living Testimony of the Heavenly Ark, and it was the exact, perfect Divine design that was given to Moses that Bezaleel worked. So this mocking Roman Crown that was forced upon the Messiah was already encoded in the Almond Tree of Life by God! This is proof that Yeshua's Testimony had to be fulfilled, exactly the way that it was fulfilled, because the Torah of truth clearly declares and proclaims it! Every detail of the LORD'S Living Testimony was in the LORD'S hands. The elements of the LORD'S Living Testimony were only waiting to be fulfilled at the right moment in time. This is also true about the future. Yeshua will return to accomplish and fulfill the final pieces of this Testimony, but they will only take place at the proper moment in time. I now believe that the LORD hid these secrets within the pure Holy Almond Tree Menorah, so that one day, when this was discovered in the last days, Israel would be able to recognize and honour their true Messiah, *Yeshua the KING.*

WITHIN THE DEFINITION OF THE "CORONA," IS THE JEWISH "MITRE."

It is the ancient Jewish High Priest's *"Ceremonial Crown."* I recognized this Jewish mitre on the Jewish Priestly Angel in the rock formation in Holy Mount Moriah at the Garden tomb. I had written about the mitre already before I discovered the Angel by Divine Providence!

Mitre;

1. Judaism, the official headdress of the High Priest.

2. the official headdress of a bishop in the Western Church, a tall cap having an arch like outline in the front and back.

3. And oblique surface formed on a piece of wood or the like so as to butt against an oblique surface on another piece to be joined with it.
4. To bestow a miter upon, or raise to a rank entitled to it.

As you can see, the word definitions contain many words. When you investigate the words within the words, you discover that Messiah Yeshua is revealed within them. *The Words on the tree, therefore, are the beautiful flowers on the Almond Tree of Life.* As the flowers unfurl, you begin to see the glorious KING who was concealed within them. Each one of these words will take you deeper into the Living Testimony of the LORD, *into the Living Torah,* and into His Heavenly Ark. This Testimony is absolutely astonishing!

WITHIN THE DEFINITION OF THE "CORONA," IS THE "HALO."
A HALO IS A THRESHING FLOOR
ON WHICH THE WHEAT SEED IS THRESHED
A HALO APPEARS AROUND THE SUN DURING A SOLAR ECLIPSE
THIS PHENOMENON MAY HAVE OCCURRED AT THE CRUCIFIXION!

Halo, *n.; pl. halos, haloes,*
1. A threshing floor on which oxen trod in a circular path, the round disk of the sun or moon, a halo around them, from halein, to grind.
2. A ring of light that seems to encircle the sun, moon, or other luminous body; it results from the refraction of light through vapor.
3. A symbolic ring of disk of light shown around the head of a saint, etc., as in pictures; nimbus; often used as a symbol of virtue or innocence.
4. The splendor of glory attributed to a person or thing famed or idealized in legend or history.

When I researched the word *"Halo,"* I discovered that a *"Halo"* is the circular pattern that is made by the oxen on a threshing floor as they tread down the grain while going around in a circle. The wheat seed must be threshed or beaten. Of course, I instantly thought about Araunah the Jebusite's threshing floor. King David purchased this threshing floor and he set up an altar for the LORD in this place and the plague was stayed. The destroying angel was standing by this threshing floor. Araunah was threshing wheat with oxen on Mount Moriah, when this astounding event took place. Araunah is a word that means *"The LORD."* David paid Araunah 600 shekels of gold for the land and he built an altar in this place on Mount Moriah in Jerusalem. *Eventually this became the resting place for the Ark of the Covenant.* David's son Solomon later built the Holy Temple in this exact location where his father David built the original altar. The Ark was later housed within this Holy Temple in Jerusalem on Holy Mount Moriah. Due to the fact that King David paid Araunah in full, with 600 shekels of gold, for this threshing floor for the glory of the LORD, the land rightfully still belongs first of all to God and second to Israel because David was the King of Israel! Araunah's threshing floor definitely showed the halo pattern that was left by the oxen, as they threshed the grain seed on Mount Moriah. This is where the Holy Temple was built. Today this place is referred to as the *"Temple Mount"* in Jerusalem, and of course this is the place where God said that His Name would dwell forever. Now before I tell this story, I want to point out that Yeshua is the seed of David! The seed is the Word of God, which is Messiah, the Living Torah of life. *I have much more to say about this threshing floor, in the last chapter of this book.* Yeshua is the seed of Abraham, the seed of Isaac, and the seed of Jacob. There was another ancient form of threshing the wheat seed and this involved beating it with rods. Yeshua was beaten on the Crown of Thorns with the rods in the hands of the Roman Soldiers. We know that there was indeed a *halo* from the oxen on Mount Moriah, because Araunah allowed David to purchase the

oxen, along with the wooden threshing boards. *Yeshua died in the location of this Holy Mountain. He was placed in the earth in the LORD'S Holy Mount Moriah, as the seed, as the Living Torah Word of God that sprouted and within this seed is Eternal life!*

The following is the account of King David purchasing this threshing floor of Araunah the Jebusite on Holy Mount Moriah.

I Chronicles 21:1-30 *Satan arose against Israel and incited David to number Israel. David said to Joab and to the commanders of the army, Go and count Israel from Beer-sheba to Dan and bring me information as to their number. Joab answered, May the LORD increase His people a hundredfold; my lord king, are they not all subjects of my lord? Why should my lord require this? Why should it be a cause of guilt for Israel? However, the king's command to Joab remained firm, so Joab set out and traversed all Israel; then he came to Jerusalem. Joab reported to David the number of the people that had been recorded. All Israel comprised 1,100,000 ready to draw the sword, while in Judah there were 470,000 men ready to draw the sword. He did not record among them Levi and Benjamin, because the king's command had become repugnant to Joab. God was displeased about this matter and He struck Israel. David said to God, I have sinned grievously in having done this thing; please remit the guilt of your servant, for I have acted foolishly. The LORD ordered Gad, David's seer; Go and tell David; Thus said the LORD; I offer you three things; choose one of them and I will bring it upon you. Gad came to David and told him, Thus said the LORD; Select for yourself a three-year famine; or that you be swept away three months before your adversaries with the sword of your enemies overtaking you; or three days of the sword of the LORD, pestilence in the land, the angel of the LORD wreaking destruction throughout the territory of Israel. Now consider what reply I shall take back to Him who sent me. David said to Gad, I am in great distress, Let me fall into the hands of the LORD, for His compassion is very great; and let me not fall into the hands of men. The LORD sent a pestilence upon Israel, and 70,000 men fell in Israel. God sent an angel to Jerusalem to destroy it, but as He was about to wreak destruction, the LORD saw and renounced further punishment and said to the destroying angel, Enough! Stay your hand! The angel of the LORD was then standing by the threshing floor of Araunah the Jebusite. David looked up and saw the angel of the LORD standing between Heaven and earth, with a drawn sword in his hand directed against Jerusalem. David and the elders, covered in sackcloth, threw themselves on their faces. David said to God, Was it not I alone who ordered the numbering of the people? I alone am guilty, and have caused severe harm; but these sheep, what have they done? O LORD my God, let Your hand fall upon me and my father's house, and let not Your people be plagued! The angel of the LORD told Gad to inform David that David should go and set up an altar to the LORD on the threshing floor of Araunah the Jebusite. David went up, following Gad's instructions, which he had delivered in the name of the LORD. Araunah too saw the angel; his four sons who were with him hid themselves while Araunah kept on threshing wheat. David came to Araunah; when Araunah looked up, he saw David and came off the threshing floor and bowed low to David, with his face to the ground. David said to Araunah, Sell, me the site of the threshing floor, that I may build on it an altar to the LORD, Sell it to me at the full price, that the plague against the people will be checked. Araunah said to David, Take it and let my lord the king do whatever he sees fit. See, I donate the oxen for burnt offerings, and the threshing boards for wood, as well as wheat for a meal offering, I donate all of it. But King David replied to Araunah, No, I will buy them at the full price. I cannot make a present to the LORD of what belongs to you, or sacrifice a burnt offering that has cost me nothing. So David paid Araunah for the site 600 shekels worth of gold. And David built there an altar to the LORD and sacrificed burnt offerings of well-being. He invoked the LORD, who answered him with fire from Heaven on the altar of burnt offerings. The LORD ordered the angel to return his sword to his sheath. At that time, when David saw that the LORD answered him at the threshing floor of Araunah the Jebusite, then he sacrificed there for the Tabernacle of the LORD, which Moses had made in the wilderness, and the altar of burnt offerings, were at that time in the shrine at Gibeon, and David was unable to go to it to worship the LORD because he was terrified by the sword of the angel of the LORD.*

When David looked up, he saw the angel of the LORD standing there between Heaven and earth *at the gate of Heaven*, and he was terrified by the sword of the angel of the LORD. This is the same angel of the LORD that came down from Heaven and rolled away the great stone from Yeshua's sepulchre in the Garden *at the same gate to Heaven!* In the last chapter of this book, I have written some more spectacular revelations about this threshing floor, so I hope you will read to the end! The LORD has shown me something thrilling for the last days!

Now a *"Halo"* is not only the pattern left in the threshing floor by the oxen, a *"Halo"* is also the bright ring of light that appears around the sun during a total solar eclipse when the sky is completely darkened. It is speculated that this is what took place when Yeshua was crucified at Golgotha on Holy Mount Moriah. The crucifixion took place near the place of Araunah's threshing floor, and if it was a solar eclipse that darkened the sky, the *halo* would

have appeared around the sun as the sky was turned to darkness. Others have speculated that the moon turned to blood in a lunar eclipse. Messiah Yeshua is always artistically depicted in paintings wearing a *Halo* around His head. It is interesting that *Yeshua, the seed, the Word of God, was threshed on Araunah's threshing floor in the place where David built the original altar.* It is a powerful piece of the LORD'S Testimony. Threshing floors were always located on the highest point of a hill, and today Golgotha is said to be the highest point of Mount Moriah at the 777 meter mark above sea level, and remarkably, the Holy Menorah has *seven branches, seven lamps, and seven wicks*. The design of the Holy Almond Tree Menorah is the complete and perfect Testimony of the LORD Yeshua, the Tree of Life!

During the crucifixion a miraculous event occurred that proved that the signature and fingerprint of God was upon this Testimony. The *veil* of the Most Holy Place called *"the Holy of Holies"* was *made cleft by the Rod of God, the hand of God,* as Yeshua was *lifted up* on the cross. *There was no earthly ark of Moses behind this veil! Instead, the Heavenly Ark, Yeshua, the Royal Standard of God was in our midst!* The Living Almond Rod of God parted the two embroidered Cherubim angels on the veil, thus making *the way* for us to return through them to the Garden of God like Eden. This was fantastic! Now we could return to dwell with Him as it was in the beginning without the curse! *The veiled part of the Calyx on the Holy Menorah is where I discovered the events of the crucifixion.* The following Scriptures give us an account of these events. When the sky became dark there could have been a *"Corona"* visible or a *"blood red moon."* As the earth shook, the rocks were also made cleft during the crucifixion. This Eternal Testimony is encoded upon the Divine design of the Holy Almond Tree Menorah.

Rare Blood Red Moon
Photos ©2010 December 13 & April 14 ©2014 Passover
Kimberly K Ballard All Rights Reserved

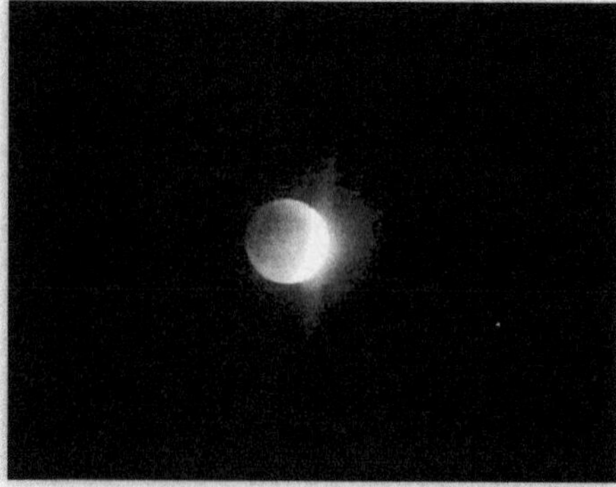

Account #1; *Matthew 27:45-54* *Now from the sixth hour darkness fell upon all the land until the ninth hour. About the ninth hour Yeshua cried out with a loud voice, saying, Eli, Eli, lama sabachthani? That is, My God, My God, why hast Thou forsaken Me? And some of those who were standing there, when they heard it began saying, This man is calling for Elijah. And immediately one of them ran, and taking a sponge, he filled it with sour wine, and put it on a reed, and gave Him a drink. But the rest of them said; Let us see whether Elijah will come to save Him. And Yeshua cried out again with a loud voice, and yielded up His Spirit. And behold, the veil of the Temple was torn in two from top to bottom, and the earth shook; and the rocks were split, and the tombs were opened; and many bodies of the Saints who had fallen asleep were raised; and coming out of the tombs after His resurrection they entered the holy city and appeared unto many. Now the centurion, and those who were with him keeping guard over Yeshua, when they saw the earthquake and the things that were happening, became very frightened and said, Truly, this was the Son of God!*

Account # 2; *Mark 15:33-39* *And when the sixth hour had come, darkness fell over the whole land until the ninth hour. And at the ninth hour Yeshua cried out with a loud voice, Eloi, Eloi, lama sabachthani? Which is translated, My God, My God, why hast Thou forsaken Me? And when some of the bystanders heard it, they began saying, Behold, He is calling for Elijah. And someone ran and filled a sponge with sour wine, put it on a reed, and gave Him a drink, saying, Let us see whether Elijah will come to take Him down. And Yeshua uttered a loud cry, and breathed His last. And the veil of the Temple was torn in two from top to bottom. And when the centurion who was standing right in front of Him, saw the way He breathed His last, he said, Truly this man was the Son of God!*

This was a fulfillment of Psalm 22!

Partial Solar Eclipse
3PM on Oct 23rd 2014
Photo ©2014
Kimberly K Ballard
All Rights Reserved

There were so many earthly and Heavenly disturbances that occurred during the crucifixion. Everything that the LORD created in the universe reacted to it.

The Blood Red Moon Lunar Eclipse of Passover night April 14, 2014 (4/14/14) after the Passover Seder Photographs ©2014 Kimberly K Ballard All Rights Reserved Edited to B&W from full color photos & video clip

Blood Red color is completely covering the surface of the Moon at its peak Edited to B&W Photo ©2014 Kimberly K Ballard All Rights Reserved

Blood Red color leaving the surface of the Moon Edited to B&W Photo ©2014 Kimberly K Ballard All Rights Reserved

Aaron's rod that budded was part of the Covenant within the Holy of Holies. So Messiah Yeshua, *the Living Rod of God that budded to life,* is the Covenant within the Heavenly Holy of Holies.

Hebrews 9:1-5 *Now even the first Covenant had regulations of Divine worship and the earthly Sanctuary. For there was a Tabernacle prepared, the outer one, in which were the Lamp stand and the table and the sacred bread; this is called the Holy Place. And behind the second veil, there was a Tabernacle which is called the Holy of Holies, having a golden altar of incense and the Ark of the Covenant covered on all sides with gold, in which was a golden jar holding the manna, and Aaron's rod which budded, and the tables of the Covenant. And above it were the Cherubim of glory overshadowing the Mercy seat; but of these things we cannot now speak in detail.*

When this Hebrews passage was written they could not speak in detail of these things yet dealing with the Ark, because the *Heavenly* versions of them were not yet disclosed. For the first time in history, I am speaking of these things in detail! I am proclaiming that *Messiah Yeshua's Living Testimony is the Covenant of the Ark and all it contains in Heaven.* He is sitting on His throne in the Most Holy Place in Heaven. This Heavenly Ark will return to the earth in the future with two witnesses to prepare the way for His final arrival. This Heavenly Ark will rest forever in Jerusalem Israel, and the time of His return is quickly approaching! We are given signs that this time is near.

After the Roman centurion witnessed the strange phenomena that occurred, after Yeshua was pierced with the spear, he proclaimed, *"Surely this man was the Son of God!"* After Yeshua gave up His Spirit on the cross, *the Rod,* which is the Rock of Heaven, was struck with a Roman lance and the life blood and Living Water of the LORD gushed out from the heart of the Messiah, from the spear wound in Yeshua's side. John wrote in His Gospel account that he was a witness to this phenomenon. I wrote earlier that the LORD used this sign with Moses in times past, *saying that with the Rod, the water would be turned to blood and all would know that He is the LORD of Hosts.* Yeshua's life blood mixed with the Living Water from His heart and it fell to the ground on Holy Mount Moriah, revealing He is the LORD of Hosts. Remember that this life blood and this Living Water of the LORD, is the Covenant that is written on the tablets of our heart and therefore, it gives us Eternal life through the breath of His Holy Spirit. This life-giving Living Water gushed out from Yeshua's heart, as the Rod and the Rock were struck, *as the Royal Military Standard of God was lifted up on His Holy Hill!!*

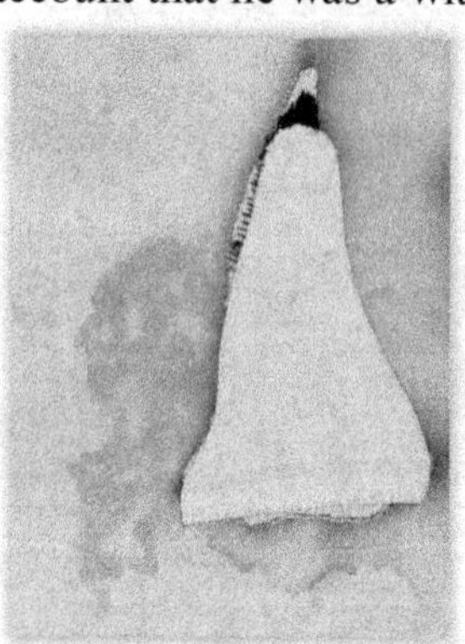

Official Shroud Sword Wound Photograph ©1978 Barrie M. Schwortz Collection, STERA Inc., All Rights Reserved

Partial Solar Eclipse at 3PM Oct 23rd 2014 Photo ©2014 Kimberly K Ballard All Rights Reserved

Simon Brown (above) pointing to the Earthquake crack that happened at the Garden Tomb during Yeshua's resurrection. The rocks were rent (cleft) in another earthquake nearby at the crucifixion site of Messiah Yeshua in Jerusalem Israel. Photo ©2011 Simon Brown England All Rights Reserved

Cross in the Clouds with Almond Trees & Aerial Cloud
Photos ©2013 Kimberly K Ballard All Rights Reserved

Golgotha Holy Mount Moriah Jerusalem Israel
Photo ©2011 Simon Brown England All Rights Reserved

A GRAIN OF WHEAT SEED AND THE ALMOND SEED

Shema Prayer Scroll with Wheat Grain & Snow Menorahs

As I was researching the seed for this book, I ran across something that was totally amazing and so I wanted to share this profound knowledge about a grain of wheat. Yeshua the seed, the Word of God, is now revealed as the Living Torah full of Eternal life. Now this also pertains to the fact that Yeshua is the Staff of Life, the Unleavened Bread, or Manna, from Heaven. As I said, Yeshua the seed was threshed on Araunah's threshing floor where David built the altar. This wheat seed, the Messiah, provides the pure flour of the Unleavened Bread in Heaven in the House of the LORD. Remember that *"the Corona"* that is depicted on the Holy Menorah is *"an appendage that allows the seeds to be dispersed."* The Almond seed is the *"KING"* of nuts and it is the fruit or meat of the Almond Tree Menorah. So it was by pure coincidence that I happened to run across an amazing photograph of this little grain of wheat. The wheat seed was shown frame by frame in its various stages of growth from the beginning until it reached maturity. When I looked at this picture, I suddenly noticed something spectacular! *I saw that the signature of the LORD was on the wheat seed!* I noticed that even from the beginning, from the very earliest stage of growth, the grain of wheat appears as if it is cleft on one side. There is of course a distinct split down the center of the grain of wheat on the front of the seed going down the full length of it, just like the split rock of Horeb! The seed is cleft in the middle and the life is inside the seed. What struck me about this picture is that the wheat grain has the appearance of a tiny Torah scroll! At every stage of the development of the wheat seed, it continues to look like a Torah scroll. As I was pondering this amazing sight, I took notice of the fact that the wheat seed is wrapped and hidden in a husk for protection. So what I saw in this truth was remarkable. *This picture of the wheat seed was a picture of Yeshua, the seed, the Living Torah, who was wrapped in a fine linen Shroud like the wheat husk, and He was hidden in the tomb in God's Holy Mount Moriah, on the Feast of Unleavened Bread, like the hidden Matzah at Passover.* He was the Rod, the Rock and the Living Water, just what we saw in Horeb. When He came to life, He allowed the other seeds to be dispersed, so they would have life in them and then grow to eventually produce the best possible fruit. The wheat seed is cleft because the signature of God is on it and the life is inside the seed, just as it was with Messiah Yeshua because He invented the seed of life! The Manna that the LORD sent to the children of Israel in the wilderness was like Coriander *seed.* It was not exactly Coriander *seed,* but the Bible says it was similar to it and the color was like *bdellium.*

Numbers 11:7 *And the Manna was as coriander seed, and the colour thereof as the colour of bdellium.*

Exodus 16:31 *And the House of Israel called the name thereof Manna; and it was like coriander seed, white; and the taste of it was like wafers made with honey.*

The coriander is considered to be *"an herbaceous plant bearing seeds and seed like fruit."* The Manna was a Spiritual food given by the LORD. *Bdellium* is thought to be similar to myrrh or a type of resin. It is also said to be crystal in color or very white in color, and it

melts in the sun. Contained within the Heavenly Living Ark of the Covenant, Yeshua is again revealed as the hidden Manna, the seed threshed as the Unleavened Bread of Heaven. It is quite amazing how accurate the Scriptures are, even down to the smallest details. The LORD is very detail oriented and He is the greatest artist of all time! *God gives to each of the seeds a body of its own* and we know that Messiah Yeshua came in a pure body of flesh that was prepared for Him. The LORD showed us His creation as the seed of life from Heaven. Yeshua came in the state of perfection, manifested in the flesh to dwell with us in His earthly body, as it was before the fall of mankind, so that He could abolish death in the flesh from the curse of Adam. John called Yeshua the Word of God. The Word was with God in the beginning and the Word was God. He further told us that *the Word became flesh* and dwelt among us. Yeshua told us that *the Word is the seed.* If the *Word is the seed,* then the Torah, or in this case *the Living Torah is the seed,* that once planted, *brings forth many seeds to be dispersed from it,* as the *"Corona"* reveals on the Holy Menorah. The Living Torah, the Tree of Life, could only disperse more seeds and bear more fruit for the Kingdom of Heaven *if the Branch was cut off from the Almond Tree of Life.* This would bring to pass the destruction of the workings of Satan. This body of Messiah was the Fruitful leafy Branch of life which was the LORD'S temporary sukkah. For this reason, Messiah Yeshua's body is a wheat seed of hidden Manna *in the Ark of the Testimony in Heaven. This is why we will never use the earthly Ark again because it was only a type and shadow of the true Living Ark of the LORD that contains the Living Testimony of Messiah Yeshua.*

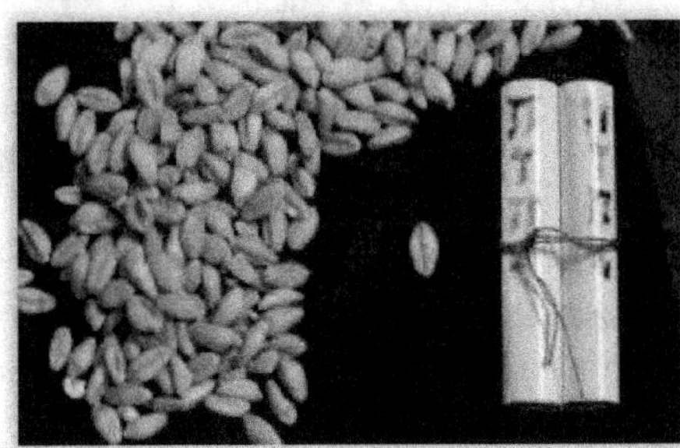

Shema Prayer Scroll with Wheat Grain
Photo ©2013 Kimberly K Ballard All Rights Reserved

Luke 8:11-12 *Now the parable is this; The seed is the Word of God. Those by the way side are they that hear; then cometh the devil, and taketh away the Word out of their hearts, lest they should believe and be saved.*

When we have *the Living Torah,* His seed of life remains inside us and this seed gives us life because *His Holy Spirit breathes the resurrection life into us,* just as His Ruach/Holy Spirit made the water come to life in the beginning in Genesis, as He overshadowed it. He is the perfect Matzah. So His mighty Ruach/Holy Spirit breathed life inside Mary's womb with His Word, as it overshadowed her. *As the Living Torah, the LORD is the giver of life, and, in the case of Mary, He fashioned a human body without the help of a man. Remember that Adam, the first man, was not born of a woman and a man. Adam was formed by God and His Ruach/Holy Spirit breathed life into Adam's human body and he became a living soul. Messiah Yeshua's human body was, therefore, also formed by God as the second Adam, as a temporary vessel, to destroy the curse of death in the flesh, and the LORD GOD lived in this body, returning His life-giving Spirit to us so we could live forever!*

I John 5:9-12 *If we receive the witness of men, the witness of God is greater; for this is the witness of God which He hath testified of His Son. He that believeth on the Son of God hath the witness in himself; he that believeth not God hath made him a liar; because he believeth not the record that God gave of His Son. And this is the record that God hath given to us eternal life, and this life is in His Son. He that hath the Son hath life; and he that hath not the Son of God hath not life.*

I Corinthians 15:35-49 *But some man will say, How are the dead raised up? And with what body do they come? Thou fool, that which thou sowest is not quickened, except it die: And that which thou sowest, thou sowest not that body that shall be, but bare grain, it may chance of wheat, or of some other grain: But God giveth it a body as it hath pleased Him, and to every seed his own body. All flesh is not the same flesh: but there is one kind of flesh of men, another flesh of beasts, another of fishes, and another of birds. There are also celestial bodies, and bodies terrestrial: but the glory of the celestial is one, and the glory of the terrestrial is another. There is one glory of the*

sun, and another glory of the moon, and another glory of the stars: for one star differeth from another star in glory. So also is the resurrection of the dead. It is sown in corruption; it is raised in incorruption: It is sown in dishonour; it is raised in glory: it is sown in weakness; it is raised in power: It is sown a natural body; it is raised a spiritual body. There is a natural body, and there a spiritual body. And so it is written, The first man Adam, was made a living soul; the last Adam was made a quickening spirit. Howbeit that was not first which is spiritual, but that which is natural; and afterward that which is spiritual. The first man is of the earth, earthy: the second man is the Lord from heaven. As is the earthy, such are they also that are earthy: and as is the heavenly, such are they also that are heavenly. <u>And as we have borne the image of the earthy, we shall also bear the image of the heavenly</u>.

Yeshua's burial Shroud reveals exactly how He bore the image of the earthy, while at the same time, it reveals His miraculous resurrection to bear the image of the Heavenly. Yeshua was literally meant to be threshed on the threshing floor of Araunah and *to be buried as the pure wheat seed during the Feast of Unleavened Bread in Holy Mount Moriah.* The LORD God sprouted to life in His garden, to be the finest First Fruit of Eternal life. Eating this seed from *the Staff of Life,* becomes our Heavenly Bread, our Eternal Manna, made from the purest, finest wheat grain in the Heavenly Kingdom of God. He is the pure and holy kosher Matzah of God! After the LORD has purified and circumcised our hearts of stone and given us hearts of flesh that are inscribed with *His Living Torah* of the Eternal Ark of God, we also become *new wheat seeds that disperse this Living Torah to the world.* We can bear much fruit, just as the Jewish disciples bore the best fruit for the Kingdom of God, only after the oil and fire of His Ruach/Holy Spirit comes to dwell within us. This then, is how we are resurrected to life, as He places His *seed of life from the Living Torah with the breath of His Ruach/Spirit,* within our hearts.

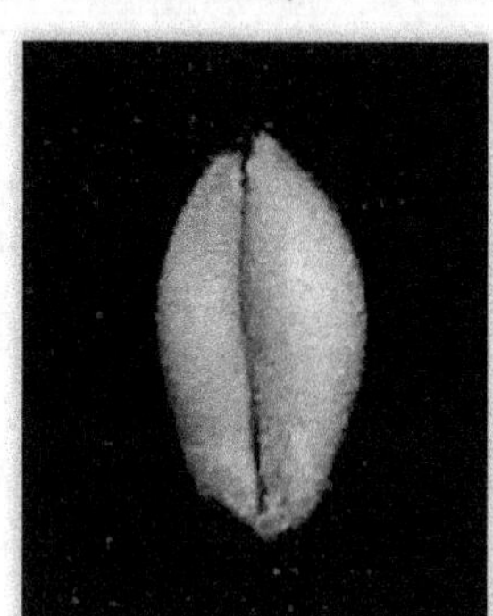

Cleft Wheat Grain looks like a tiny Torah Scroll Photo ©2013 KK Ballard All Rights Reserved

Yeshua told several parables about the seed being the Word of God and He explains how this would bring forth fruit in the earth. Yeshua said that the wheat is the good seed that will be saved to Eternal life. The Messiah will return to gather His wheat into His barn, at the harvest in the future and I discuss this further in the final chapter.

Yeshua speaks of the seed as *the Living Torah* and if we have ears to hear this, we are to hear it! The one that *receives the seed in the good ground* is the one that *hears the Living Torah and understands it!*

Matthew 13:3-9 *And He spake many things unto them in parables, saying, behold, a sower went forth to sow; And when He sowed, some seeds fell by the way side, and the fowls came and devoured them up; Some fell upon stony places, where they had not much earth; and forth with they sprung up, because they had no deepness of earth; And when the sun was up, they were scorched; and because they had no root, they withered away. And some fell among thorns; and the thorns sprung up, and choked them; But other fell into good ground, and brought forth fruit, some an hundredfold, some sixtyfold, some thirtyfold. Who hath ears to hear, let him hear.*

The parable that Messiah Yeshua taught says that *the seed of the Living Torah* does not take root in some places where it is sown. It is often the case that as soon as this seed is sown, Satan attempts to remove it from *the heart* of the believer by burdening them with the cares of this life and with the deception that the riches of this world are what matter. Truly, however, we only become rich when we obtain this *seed of the Living Torah that gives us Eternal life.* The *"way side" that He mentioned in the parable is land that is immediately adjacent to a road, highway, or path.* We can therefore veer off the path and highway to Heaven quite easily if we do not follow the road or pathway behind the Living Heavenly Ark of the Covenant.

Matthew 13:18-23 *Hear ye therefore the parable of the sower. When any one heareth the Word of the Kingdom, and understandeth it not, then cometh the wicked one, and catcheth away that which was sown in his heart. This is he which received seed by the way side. But he that received the seed into stony places, the same is he that heareth the*

Word, and anon with joy receiveth it; Yet hath he not root in himself, but dureth for a while; for when tribulation or persecution ariseth because of the Word, by and by he is offended. He also that received seed among the thorns is he that heareth the Word; and the care of this world, and the deceitfulness of riches, choke the Word, and he becometh unfruitful. But he that received seed into the good ground is he that heareth the Word, and understandeth it; which also beareth fruit, and bringeth forth, some an hundredfold, some sixty, some thirty.

As we come to understand *the Living Torah, the Messiah,* and His Ruach/Spirit comes to live inside our hearts, we become branches grafted into the main *Branch, into the central Rod or Stem of Jesse,* abiding in the Holy Menorah of Heaven. We become one piece of pure gold with the Almond Tree of Life! God is our Lamb shank bone of Passover! What a beautiful picture the LORD has hidden within the details of His Holy design. Not abiding in the LORD, the Tree of Life, causes us to wither like dead branches to be cast into the fire in His judgment. The Almond Tree Menorah artistically shows us the Almond seed, with the flowering and budding branches, depicting the Messiah's Living Testimony of witness of the Heavenly Ark.

John 15:6 *If a man abide not in Me, he is cast forth as a branch, and is withered; and men gather them, and cast them into the fire, and they are burned.*

John 15:4 *Abide in Me, and I in you. As the branch cannot bear fruit of itself, except it abide in the vine; no more can ye, except ye abide in Me.*

Almonds on Matzah Photo ©2013 Kimberly K Ballard All Rights Reserved

It is very interesting to consider then that Almond seeds are very beneficial to heart health! They contain vitamin E, essential vitamins and minerals, and they are low in certain fats. The Almond seed is said *"to reduce the risk of heart disease, even as much as 50% when they are eaten 5 days of the week."* So if *the Almond seed* gives us heart health, *is it any wonder that the Living Testimony of Messiah in the Almond Tree is the Covenant of the heart, which is depicted on (page 259) on the Magdala Synagogue Stone?* When you think about eating Almonds for *five days of the week,* this really does represent Messiah Yeshua as *the Living Torah*, our true meat! The LORD repairs our stony hearts! The LORD fixes our broken hearts!

Ezekiel 36:26 *A new heart also will I give you, and a new Spirit will I put within you; and I will take away the stony heart out of your flesh, and I will give you an heart of flesh.*

Jeremiah 24:7 *And I will give them an heart to know Me, that I AM the LORD; and they shall be My people, and I will be their God; for they shall return unto Me with their whole heart.*

Deuteronomy 30:6 *And the LORD thy God will circumcise thine heart, and the heart of thy seed, to love the LORD thy God with all thine heart, and with all thy soul, that thou mayest live.*

Ezekiel 11:17-20 *Therefore say, Thus saith the LORD GOD; I will even gather you from the people, and assemble you out of the countries where ye have been scattered, and I will give you the Land of Israel. And they shall come thither, and they shall take away all the detestable things thereof and all the abominations thereof from thence. And I will give them one heart, and I will put a new Spirit within you; and I will take the stony heart out of their flesh, and will give them an heart of flesh; That they may walk in mine ordinances, and do them; and they shall be My people, and I will be their God.*

Remember Yeshua said the greatest Commandment is to love the LORD with all your heart!

MESSIAH'S CUP ON THE ALMOND BRANCHES OF THE HOLY MENORAH

Gilded Cup Photo ©2013 Kimberly K Ballard All Rights Reserved

The LORD showed me that in Genesis 40 of the Torah, the dream interpretations of Joseph are actually prophetic interpretations that foreshadow the coming events of the crucifixion and resurrection of Messiah Yeshua.

Genesis 40:8-23 *And they said unto him, We have dreamed a dream, and there is no interpreter of it. And Joseph said unto them, do not interpretations belong to God? Tell me them, I pray you. And the chief butler told his dream to Joseph, and said to him, In my dream, behold, a vine was before me; And in the vine were three branches; and it was as though it budded, and her blossoms shot forth; and the clusters thereof brought forth ripe grapes; And Pharaoh's cup was in my hand; and I took the grapes, and pressed them into Pharaoh's cup, and I gave the cup unto Pharaoh's hand. And Joseph said unto him, This is the interpretation of it; The three branches are three days; Yet within three days shall Pharaoh lift up thine head, and restore thee unto thy place; and thou shalt deliver Pharaoh's cup into his hand, after the former manner when thou wast his butler. But think on me when it shall be well with thee, and shew kindness, I pray thee, unto me, and make mention of me unto Pharaoh, and bring me out of this house; For indeed I was stolen away out of the land of the Hebrews; and here also have I done nothing that they should put me into the dungeon. When the chief baker saw that the interpretation was good, he said unto Joseph, I also was in my dream, and behold, I had three white baskets on my head; And in the uppermost basket there was all manner of bake-meats for Pharaoh; and the birds did eat them out of the basket upon my head. And Joseph answered and said, This is the interpretation thereof; The three baskets are three days; Yet within three days shall Pharaoh lift up thy head from off thee, and shall hang thee on a tree; and the birds shall eat thy flesh from off thee. And it came to pass the third day, which was Pharaoh's birthday, that he made a feast unto all his servants; and he lifted up the head of the chief butler and of the chief baker among his servants. And he restored the chief butler unto his butlership again; and he gave the cup into Pharaoh's hand; but he hanged the chief baker; as Joseph had interpreted to them. Yet did not the chief butler remember Joseph, but forgat him.*

In the story, we have *the Cupbearer or Butler and the Baker.* Joseph said that *"the three branches are three days,"* and because of Joseph's dream interpretation, we know for certain that the three branches, flowering and fruiting on either side of the Holy Menorah also represent *three days.* In Messiah's case, the three branches on one side of the Holy Menorah are three days and the three branches on the other side of the Holy Menorah are three nights. Yeshua gave this sign to Israel *as the sign of Jonah* to reveal that He is their KING Messiah. This is the exact length of time that Yeshua said He would be in the sepulchre before budding to life as the perfect Almond Branch, bearing the Eternal fruit on the third day, on the LORD'S Feast of First Fruits. On one branch of the Holy Menorah, we find three cups that are shaped like Almond flowers with buds and blossoms on each branch. So these flowering and fruiting Almond branches perfectly represent the Rod that budded on the third day.

In the Garden of Gethsemane, Yeshua spoke of drinking *the cup* that was prepared for Him. So the grapes of the Cupbearer represent Yeshua's Covenant in the third cup of wine in the Passover Seder. The grapes of the Cupbearer foreshadow the cup of redemption representing Yeshua's life blood as the Lamb, dashed upon the Ark of Heaven, the Covenant of the heart from the LORD God of Israel. Now the LORD showed me something else about the dream interpretation of Joseph. In the story, *the Baker represents the loaves of bread and the meat!* The Baker was not simply hung on a tree, but he was *crucified,* just like Messiah Yeshua!

Flavious Josephus wrote this in his book, *Antiquities of the Jews.* Book 2, Chapter V, Section 3: But Joseph, considering about the dream, said to him that he would willingly be an interpreter of good events to him, and not of such as his dream denounced to him; but he told him that he had only *three days* in all to live, for that *the three baskets signify that on the third day he should be crucified,* and devoured by fowls, while he was not able to help himself.

The Baker represents the bread and the meat and he was crucified on a tree. So incredibly the dream interpretation of Joseph to the Baker reveals that Yeshua is the Living Bread and the true meat, *the Living Torah,* who would be crucified on a tree and resurrected the third day! The Cupbearer also reveals the cup of wine from *the First Fruit of the vine.* Yeshua was resurrected in the LORD'S vineyard. This represents the Eternal betrothal cup of the Covenant of Messiah Yeshua. It is no coincidence then that the two elements of the Cupbearer and the Baker, are the two elements that Yeshua used during His Last Passover Seder to seal His Eternal Covenant when He gave this cup and this bread to His Bride Israel and sealed the deal for His future marriage to her. Yeshua told the Jewish disciples to remember Him in the breaking of the unleavened bread and in the third cup of wine. It is so profound and exciting to see this connection, by the power of the Holy Spirit! The Passover of Israel was always about the freedom from the bondage of Egypt where Pharaoh was of course called by the LORD *"the great dragon, the serpent Satan"* (Ezekiel 29:3). Now Messiah Yeshua brought deliverance from the bondage of death and corruption. So the second deliverance by the Messiah was the freedom from the great and heavy bondage of the serpent from the Garden of Eden. Now when Yeshua broke the bread at His Last Supper, the blessing that is typically said is this, *"Blessed are you, O LORD our God, KING of the Universe, who brings forth bread from the earth."* In the tomb *Yeshua was actually in the earth resting during the Feast of Unleavened bread and He was brought forth from the earth in Holy Mount Moriah as the Living Bread, the Living Torah, on the Jewish Feast of First Fruits.* Remember that part of the curse of Eden included the bondage of mankind who now would have to get bread by toiling and tilling the earth by the sweat of the brow. God was no longer dwelling with us providing the true Bread from Heaven, until Yeshua returned from Heaven to dwell with us and give us this Eternal Bread as a gift, without us having to struggle for it anymore under the curse. Messiah freed us from this bondage forever. After Yeshua, the grain seed, was threshed on the LORD'S threshing floor, *He was placed in the earth in the Garden of God.* Yeshua rested in the earth on the Feast of Unleavened Bread and came forth alive *from the place where Adam was created,* on the Feast of First Fruits. Yeshua therefore, removed the bondage of death from this place where the original sin had occurred. He brought about the healing of the breech between God and mankind in this place. The Passover became a greater freedom when the Messiah set the captives free, once and for all, from the bondage of the corruption of the flesh. For this reason, Yeshua sealed His Living Covenant of this freedom in the breaking of the unleavened bread during the Passover Seder. So the Baker in Joseph's story is foreshadowing Messiah as the true Bread of Heaven brought forth from the earth, and if we eat this Bread, we will live forever.

When Yeshua sealed the Covenant with the third cup of wine, it was during the time of Passover when this blessing is spoken *"Blessed are you, O LORD our God, KING of the Universe who creates the Fruit of the vine."* The grapes of the Cupbearer revealed that the Messiah would be raised up on the Feast of First Fruits on the third day *where the LORD God planted His vineyard in the very beginning,* and He would bring *the Branch*, bearing the First Fruit, to life. The end of toiling for *the fruit* from the ground came about in spiritual terms and Yeshua sealed His Living Testimony in the cup of wine made from grapes. Yeshua is the Bread, meat, and the true drink. So the truth is Yeshua drank, the second cup, the cup of judgment for the sins of His people and for all who would accept His cup of redemption, the third cup, representing the life blood of the LORD as the Eternal Covenant. This cup is

obviously depicted on the Holy Almond Tree Menorah on the branches and this cup is the LORD'S marriage proposal!

Now if we go back to look at the word *"Calyx"* which is on *the Branch* of the Holy Almond Tree Menorah, we find that by definition it is *"a cup-like part of the plant."* It is clearly the Messiah's cup of the Living Testimony. Yeshua asked three times for this cup to be taken from Him, but then He declared to His Father, *"Not as I will, but as You will."* Yeshua knew that it was His destiny to fulfill it. It was His will!

Concord Grapes Photo ©2013 Kimberly K Ballard All Rights Reserved

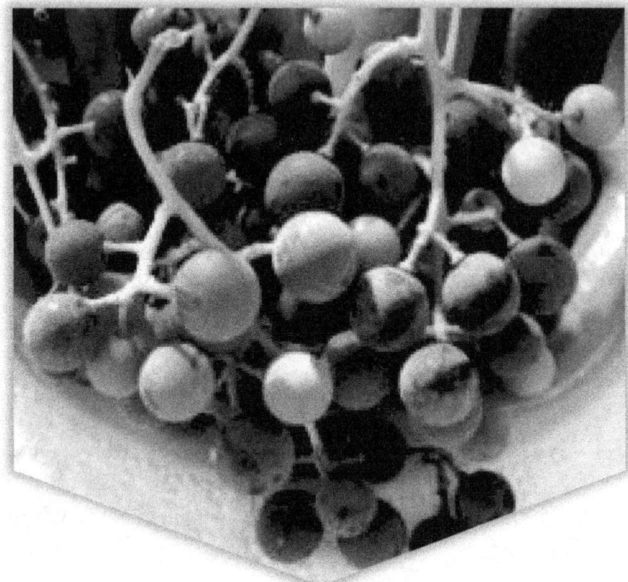

Matthew 20:23 *Yeshua said to them, you will indeed drink from My cup, but to sit at my right or left is not for me to grant. These places belong to those for whom they have been prepared by My Father.*

Matthew 26:39 *Going a little farther, He fell with His face to the ground and prayed, My Father, if it is possible, may this cup be taken from Me. Yet not as I will, but as You will.*

Matthew 26:42 *He went away a second time and prayed, My Father, if it is not possible for this cup to be taken away unless I drink it, may Your will be done.*

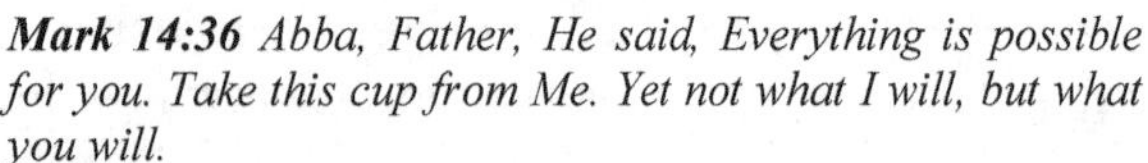

Mark 14:36 *Abba, Father, He said, Everything is possible for you. Take this cup from Me. Yet not what I will, but what you will.*

Luke 22:42 *Father, if you are willing, take this cup from Me; yet not My will, but yours be done.*

John 18:11 *Yeshua commanded Peter, Put your sword away! Shall I not drink the cup the Father has given Me?*

Grape Leaf from my vineyard Photo ©2014 Kimberly K Ballard All Rights Reserved

The Rod of God had to fulfill the Father's will because this is one God fulfilling His Living Testimony through His Rod lifted up. It had to happen this way in order for Yeshua to become the Living Almond Branch of the Testimony of the LORD bearing the *"Calyx"* design on the pure gold Almond Tree Menorah! In the definition of the word *"Calyx"* we see that it is also *"the green outer covering."* This is incredible since Yeshua is *"the green shoot of Jesse."* The most astonishing connection to this, however, is in the fact that Messiah Yeshua is the Living Testimony of the Ark in Heaven. The Ark is the throne where the Rod of God sits, and around the throne, there is a rainbow of emerald green! Ironically, it is this part of the Almond Tree Menorah that is veiled or covered. I believe this is because it has not yet been revealed to Israel! This veil is taken away in Messiah Yeshua!

Calyx or Calyxes; *Botany; 1. The outer covering, outermost group of floral parts, Usually green; the sepals. Anat. Zool. 2. a cuplike part. Husk, covering, akin to kalyptein to veil, cover!*

The fine Divine design details that we have looked at so far on the Holy Menorah that reveal Messiah Yeshua include all the following elements; *"The Calyx, the Corona, the Corolla, the Crown, the Veil, the Halo, the Threshing Floor, the Almond Rod or Branch that budded to life which is the Lamb shank bone, and the Cup of the Covenant."* On the Menorah we also saw *"the Rod that struck the Rock, the blood and water that flowed from Yeshua's side signifying that His blood and Living Water is our life blood. He provided the Living Water at Horeb when the Rod struck the Rock. We also found on the Holy Menorah, the Crown of Thorns that was given by the Romans for a great military victory, that was done in mockery of the Jewish KING because Yeshua, the image of God, was lifted up as the Royal Military Standard of God!* It is absolutely impossible that anyone other than the LORD God of Israel could possibly have encoded all of these hidden design details upon the Almond Tree Menorah. So the Holy Menorah represents *the crucifixion* and more importantly *the resurrection* of the Living Messiah, the budded Living Almond Branch. The only person to ever fulfill every single one of these precious details of the Divine design of God's Menorah is Messiah Yeshua of Nazareth. Amen!

THE MENORAH SEVEN LAMPS AND SEVEN WICKS

The Holy Menorah in the Snow
Photo ©2013 Kimberly K Ballard All Rights Reserved

The Holy Menorah has a center Rod with six other branches attached to it. Upon those seven Almond branches are *seven lamps* filled with pure olive oil.

Numbers 8:2-4 *Speak unto Aaron, and say unto him, When thou lightest the lamps, the seven lamps shall give light over against the candlestick. And Aaron did so; he lighted the lamps thereof over against the candlestick, as the LORD commanded Moses. And this work of the candlestick was of beaten gold, unto the shaft thereof, unto the flowers thereof, was beaten work; according unto the pattern which the LORD had shewed Moses, so he made the candlestick.*

The flaming fire representing the Holy Spirit shines forth the light and fills the Holy Place. Yeshua's eyes burn with flaming fire because He is *the Word of God,* full of the pure oil of the Ruach/Holy Spirit of God.

Revelation 19:12 *His eyes were as a flame of fire, and on His head were many crowns; and He had a Name written, that no man knew, but He Himself. And He was clothed with vesture dipped in blood; and His Name is called The Word of God.*

Daniel 10:6 *His body also was like the beryl, and His face as the appearance of lightning, and His eyes as lamps of fire, and His arms and His feet like in colour to polished brass, and the voice of His Words like the voice of a multitude.*

Yeshua told us that the light or lamp of the body is the eye, revealing that He is the Holy Menorah of Heaven, full of light. The flaming fire and light shines through His eyes as our Heavenly Menorah. This *light* is the Word of God that shines into our hearts. Those who abide in the LORD also have His light shining through our eyes as His Holy Spirit burns within us. We are instructed not to hide this light. Yeshua told us to put this light on a candlestick or lamp stand, so that all can see it and absorb the light, as He dwells in our hearts, shining through us.

Luke 11:33-36 *No man, when he hath lighted a candle, putteth it in a secret place, neither under a bushel, but on a candlestick, that they which come in may see the light. The light of the body is the eye; therefore when thine eye is single, thy whole body also is full of light; but when thine eye is evil, thy body also is full of darkness. Take heed therefore that the light which is in thee be not darkness. If thy whole body therefore be full of light, having no part dark, the whole shall be full of light, as when the bright shining of a candle doth give thee light.*

Matthew 6:22-23 *The light of the body is the eye; if therefore thine eye be single, thy whole body shall be full of light. But if thine eye be evil, thy whole body shall be full of darkness. If therefore the light that is in thee be darkness, how great is that darkness!*

With the knowledge that Yeshua's eyes burn like lamps of fire, we can now truly picture the meaning of the Aaronic Blessing, when it speaks of the LORD'S countenance.

Street Lamps Monterey CA
Photo ©2014 Kimberly K Ballard

Numbers 6:22-27 *And the LORD spake unto Moses, saying, Speak unto Aaron and unto his sons, saying, On this wise ye shall bless the children of Israel, saying unto them, The LORD bless thee, and keep thee; The LORD make His face shine upon thee, and be gracious unto thee; The LORD lift up His countenance upon thee, and give thee peace. And they shall put My Name upon the children of Israel; and I will bless them.*

The light and radiance of the Shechinah glory of God, shines from Yeshua. The Jewish disciples saw and witnessed this on the Mount of transfiguration, when He was changed before their eyes into His glorified state. Messiah's face is called *"the Sar HaPanim, the Prince of the face of the LORD God."* This means that because Yeshua is the Rod lifted up, He is *the countenance* that is lifted up upon us, that brings us peace in the Aaronic Blessing. Yeshua is the *"Prince of Peace."* Yeshua's name contains the Hebrew letter *"ayin"* meaning eye. The LORD looks down from heaven upon the children of men, to see if there are any that understand, and seek God (Psalm 14:2).

In Heaven, there is no need of the sun or the moon or the light of a lamp because *the Lamb* is the Eternal light of the Heavenly Menorah! The Shank bone, the Shaft of the Menorah, testifies of Him.

Revelation 21:22-23 *And I saw no Temple therein; for the LORD God Almighty and the Lamb are the Temple of it. And the city had no need of the sun, neither of the moon, to shine in it; for the glory of God did lighten it, and the Lamb is the light thereof.*

Revelation 22:5 *And there shall be no night there; and they need no candle, neither light of the sun; for the LORD God giveth them light; and they shall reign forever and ever.*

If the LORD is the Holy Almond Tree Menorah and His eyes burn the flaming fire of pure oil, then we can understand why it is that the following Scriptures tell us that *"the Branch,"* the LORD, has seven eyes. These are the *seven lamps* that light the earth.

Zechariah 3:8-9 *Hear now, O Joshua the High Priest, thou, and thy fellows that sit before thee; for they are men wondered at; for, behold, I will bring forth My servant the BRANCH. For behold the stone that I have laid before Joshua; upon one stone shall be seven eyes; behold, I will engrave the graving thereof, saith the LORD of Hosts, and I will remove the iniquity of that land in one day.*

Zechariah 4:10 *For who hath despised the day of small things? For they shall rejoice, and shall see the plummet in the hand of Zerubbabel with those seven; they are the eyes of the LORD, which run to and fro through the whole earth.*

Now the seven lamps have another meaning! Resting in the *seven lamps* on the Holy Menorah, there are *seven wicks*. The wicks absorb the pure oil of the Holy Spirit. When the wicks become saturated with the pure oil, they are touched by a spark and the wicks ignite into a flaming fire. The flaming fire emits the light, from each one of the seven lamps on the Holy Menorah. The LORD said that the seven candlesticks are the seven Churches of God. They shine the light of Messiah through His Ruach/Holy Spirit.

The LORD gave a warning that if the Churches do not repent and follow all His Commandments that He would put their lamp out. The first and foremost of these Commandments is to love the LORD God of Israel with all your heart and *to never worship any other god or gods*. The seven Churches need to *remain pure,* as they abide in the one solid piece of pure gold of the Living Holy Almond Tree Menorah.

The Priestly garments were made of pure white linen, and pure white was a requirement for the Divine service of the LORD. If these garments became unclean, they were no longer worn or washed, but they were utilized again as strips of cloth. *The Priests in the Holy Temple would place the strips of the unclean cloth into the seven oil-filled lamps to be used as the wicks of the Holy Menorah.* This opens my mind to understand that the seven Churches represent the wicks of the seven lamps. It came to me, that the Gentiles, who were once considered unclean, are like the soiled garments. So the only way that we could be made clean was for the LORD to provide us with His Life Blood of the Covenant, and with the pure oil of His Holy Spirit, through the baptism of Messiah Yeshua, *the Living Torah* and Living Water. Now because of the fact that our garments have become saturated in the pure oil of the Ruach/Holy Spirit, our garments have become clean and white through *the purification of the flaming fire that burns inside us,* by the power of God's Spirit because we have saturated ourselves in Him. When our wick is full of the LORD'S oil of the Spirit, He lights the spark within us and now we shine brightly as a flaming fire, shining forth God's light because the fire of His Ruach/Holy Spirit burns in us and shines through us. After this happens, we can bear much fruit in the Name of the LORD. This is exactly what happened with the Jewish disciples on Shavuot or Pentecost when the LORD sent His Holy Spirit in cleft tongues of fire upon each one of them and they could *suddenly perform miracles.* Remember that when Yeshua appeared alive on the road to Emmaus after His resurrection, the Jews said that their hearts *burned* within them as Yeshua spoke to them! He suddenly opened their eyes to see His identity in the Torah!

So the seven Churches that are the seven candlesticks are the *soiled wicks* that have been washed and purified white by the Word of God and through the saturation of the baptism in the pure oil of His Ruach/Holy Spirit. Now we have this life-giving seed dwelling inside of us, that is the seed of life from the Almond Branch that raises us from death to life at the sound of the Last Trump. The LORD will give a shout with His voice and He will breathe the breath of life into the dead and they will be raised to Eternal life because *His life-giving seed, the Living Torah of life* abides inside them.

In the book of Revelation, the one standing in the midst of the seven candlesticks in the Holy Temple of the LORD is called *"the Son of man."* This is Yeshua and He is wearing the garments of the Jewish High Priest. Yeshua also gives us garments or white robes of purification to wear. The *"golden girdle"* made of fine linen that Yeshua is wearing is said *"to be 32 cubits long."* According to the Temple Institute in Jerusalem, *"This number is very significant pertaining to the golden girdle!"* The Jewish disciple named John saw one standing in the Holy Temple in Heaven, holding the *seven golden candlesticks* in His right hand. John saw Yeshua the LORD, wearing this *golden girdle.* I wanted to mention this because it reveals that the Messiah is the High Priest of Heaven who has made atonement for our sins. As we saw earlier, the Jewish *Priestly mitre* is hidden in the Divine design of the Holy Menorah. This is the linen *mitre* worn by the High Priest. Knowing that Yeshua is the Branch of the Almond Tree on the Holy Menorah who holds *the seven candlesticks* in His right hand explains why He is the one wearing the *golden girdle* in Heaven as part of His garment. Now what I find astonishing is that this *golden girdle*, mentioned as part of Aaron's Priestly garment and mentioned in Revelation as part of Yeshua's Heavenly garment, is the fact that it is worn over the heart. The measurement of this so called *"curious golden girdle" is declared to be 32 cubits in length. The golden girdle is said to "atone for the sins of the heart,"* according to the Temple Institute in Jerusalem, and *"this is seen even in the detail of its measurement, 32 cubits: For 32 is the gammatria (the numerical equivalent; from the Greek gamma, the third letter of the Greek alphabet, equals tria, number 3) of the Hebrew word lev, meaning heart."* ***(Source: The Golden Girdle Temple Institute Jerusalem Israel ©2008 templeinstitute.org/beged/priestly_garments-11.htm).***

The most astonishing part of this mystery is that the Messiah, who atoned for our sins with the Covenant of heart, was raised up from death to life on *the third day* as the Almond Branch from the Tree of Life. This is no coincidence! This special golden girdle that Yeshua is wearing in the book of the Revelation, revealing Messiah as the LORD God of Israel, is mentioned in the book of Exodus.

Exodus 29:5-6 *And thou shalt take the garments, and put upon Aaron the coat, and the robe of the ephod, and the ephod, and the breastplate, and gird him with the curious golden girdle of the ephod; And thou shalt put the mitre upon his head, and put the holy crown upon the mitre. Then shalt thou take the anointing oil, and pour it upon his head, and anoint him.*

Exodus 28:8 *And the curious girdle of the ephod, which is upon it, shall be of the same, according to the work thereof; even of gold, of blue, and purple, and scarlet, and fine twisted linen.*

Yeshua is not only wearing the *golden girdle* in Heaven, He is also wearing *the tunic,* which is the robe of the High Priest that goes down to the feet.

Revelation 1:13-20 into 2:1 *And in the midst of the seven candlesticks one like unto the Son of man, clothed with a garment down to the foot, and girt about the paps with a golden girdle. His head and His hairs were white like wool, as white as snow; and His eyes were as a flame of fire; And His feet like unto fine brass, as if they burned in a furnace; and His voice as the sound of many waters. And He had in His right hand seven stars; and out of His mouth went a sharp two edged sword; and His countenance was as the sun shineth in His strength. And when I saw Him, I fell at His feet as dead. And He laid His right hand upon me, saying unto me, Fear not; I AM the first and the last; I AM He that liveth, and was dead; and, behold, I AM alive forevermore, Amen; and have the keys of hell and of death. Write the things which thou hast seen, and the things which are, and the things which shall be hereafter; The mystery of the seven stars which thou sawest in My right hand, and the seven golden candlesticks. The seven stars are the angels of the seven churches; and the seven candlesticks which thou sawest are the seven churches. Unto the angel of the church of Ephesus write; These things saith He that holdeth the seven stars in His right hand, who walketh in the midst of the seven golden candlesticks.*

Messiah Yeshua is also wearing the *golden girdle* in Heaven, when He declares to John, *"I AM the First and the Last."* He is our High Priest of Heaven after the Order of Melchizedek. The mysteriousness of the *"curious golden girdle"* speaks clearly of Yeshua's

Living Testimony of the Heavenly Ark of the Covenant that was fulfilled *on the third day*, on the Feast of First Fruits. King David knew that the Messiah was encoded on the Holy Almond Tree Menorah when he wrote the following Psalm.

Five lights for the Torah of Moses – Brass Chandelier Photo ©2013 Kimberly K Ballard All Rights Reserved

Psalm 119:105 *Thy Word is a lamp unto my feet, and a light unto my path.*

Yeshua, the Yad of God, wrote the Commandments and Laws of God with His finger. So *Yeshua the Living Torah* showed us *"the way"* of life as *the Lawgiver!*

Proverbs 6:23 *For the Commandment is a Lamp; and the Law is Light; and reproofs of instruction are the way of life;*

According to The Temple Institute in Jerusalem, *"The garments of ordinary Priests were used as wicks for the Holy Menorah," and "The tunics are used as the Menorah wicks and the pants and belts are used as the wicks for the oil lamps of the Festival of the Water Libation, during Sukkot. When the High Priest's garment was worn out, it was hidden away, so no other man could wear it."* ***(Source: The Garments of the Priests Temple Institute Jerusalem Israel ©2008 templeinstitute.org/priestly_garments.htm).***

It is interesting that the wicks of the oil lamps for Sukkot and the oil lamps of the Festival of the Water Libation ceremony pertain to this particular Feast of the LORD. Ironically, on the eighth day of the Feast of Sukkot, during the Water Libation ceremony, Yeshua stood in the Holy Temple in Jerusalem and declared that He is the Living Water.

John 7:37-41 *In the Last day, that great day of the Feast, Yeshua stood and cried, saying, If any man thirst, let him come unto Me, and drink. He that believeth on Me, as the Scripture hath said, out of his belly shall flow rivers of Living Water. But this spake He of the Spirit, which they that believe on Him should receive; for the Holy Spirit was not yet given; because that Yeshua was not yet glorified. Many of the people therefore when they heard this saying, said, Of a truth this is the Prophet. Others said, This is the Messiah, But some said, Shall Messiah come out of Galilee?*

The Jewish disciples told Yeshua not to go *in secret* to this Feast, but to reveal His identity to the Jews in the Holy Temple. The Messiah went in secret. He was hidden and *no man will ever wear His garments,* because He is the High Priest of Heaven!

John 7:2-4 *Now the Jews Feast of Tabernacles was at hand, His brethren therefore said unto Him, Depart hence, and go into Judaea, that Thy disciples also may see the works that Thou doest. For there is no man that doeth anything in secret, and he himself seeketh to be known openly. If Thou do these things, shew Thyself to the world.*

So now I understand the profound words of the Prophet Isaiah. He wrote that we are all as *an unclean thing,* and that all our righteousness's are as filthy rags. The wicks of the Menorah are the filthy rags! Remember that long ago the LORD hid His face from Israel because of her iniquities (Isaiah 59:2). This was only a temporary condition.

Isaiah 64:6 *But we are all as an unclean thing, and all our righteousness's are as filthy rags; and we all do fade as a leaf; and our iniquities, like the wind, have taken us away. And there is none that calleth upon Thy Name, that stirreth up himself to take hold of Thee; for Thou hast hid Thy face from us, and hast consumed us, because of our iniquities.*

Since we are as filthy rags, we must be purified by the LORD God, while resting in the Lamp stand and absorbing the pure oil of His Holy Spirit, day and night. Because *Yeshua is the Living Torah,* His Commandments are a Lamp and His Laws are a light to us and He shines this light before our feet, showing us the pathway into Eternal life. As the *seven purified lamps* of the LORD, we can now reflect the light of the LORD *because we have all the Laws and Commandments in Messiah the LORD from the Ark of His Living Testimony that abides in Heaven which is perfection.* In this way, our once soiled garments become pure, clean and white, like the new linen garments of the ordinary Priests, who serve in the LORD'S Holy Temple in Heaven. It is only when our garments have been made clean and white by the LORD that we can perform the Divine service of the LORD. We really have no true righteousness through ourselves. Our Heavenly righteousness can only come to us by the perfect Holy Spirit of the LORD through the baptism in His Living Water and in the fire of His Ruach, through the Rabbi of Righteousness.

Luke 3:16 *John answered, saying unto them all, I indeed baptize you with water; but one mightier than I cometh, the latchet of whose shoes I am not worthy to unloose; He shall baptize you with the Holy Spirit and with fire.*

John 1:29-34 *The next day John seeth Yeshua coming unto him, and saith, Behold the Lamb of God, which taketh away the sin of the world. This is He of whom I said, After me cometh a man which is preferred before me; for He was before me. And I knew Him not; but that He should be manifest to Israel, therefore am I come baptizing with water. And John bare record, saying, I saw the Spirit descending from Heaven like a dove, and it abode upon Him. And I knew Him not; but He that sent me to baptize with water, the same said unto me, Upon whom thou shalt see the Spirit descending, and remaining on Him, the same is He which baptizes with the Holy Spirit. And I saw, and bare record that this is the Son of God.*

The Holy Menorah made of one piece of pure gold has many parts, yet this is still only one Living Tree called *"The LORD God!"* As we are grafted into this tree, all the parts function together as one beautiful Menorah shining light! All the elements of the Holy Menorah are one. So we abide in the *Almond Tree of Life* that is one solid piece of pure gold. We then become heirs of the promise of Abraham.

Galatians 3:26-29 *For ye are all the children of God by faith in Messiah Yeshua. For as many of you as have been baptized into Messiah have put on Messiah. There is neither Jew nor Greek, there is neither bond nor free, there is neither male nor female; for ye are all one in Messiah Yeshua. And if ye be Messiah's, then are ye Abraham's seed, and heirs according to the promise.*

Acts 11:15-18 *And as I began to speak, the Holy Spirit fell on them, as on us at the beginning. Then I remembered I the Word of the LORD, how that He said, John indeed baptized with water; but ye shall be baptized with the Holy Spirit. For as much then as God gave them the like gift as He did unto us, who believed on the LORD Yeshua Messiah; what was I, that I could withstand God? When they heard these things, they held their peace, and glorified God, saying, Then hath God also to the Gentiles granted repentance unto life.*

In Revelation, it is clear that those who have washed their robes to be white in the blood of the Lamb will serve the LORD day and night in His Holy Temple, in the Eternal Kingdom of Heaven.

Revelation 7:14-15 *And I said unto him, Sir, thou knowest. And he said to me, These are they which came out of the Great Tribulation, and have washed their robes, and made them white in the blood of the Lamb. Therefore are they before the throne of God, and serve Him day and night in His Temple; and He that sitteth on the throne shall dwell among them.*

Revelation 3:5 *He that overcometh, the same shall be clothed in white raiment; and I will not blot out his name out of the book of life, but I will confess his name before My Father, and before His angels.*

Ecclesiastes 9:8 *Let thy garments be always white; and let thy head lack no ointment.*

The Holy Menorah made of beaten work from pure gold, according to the pattern of the LORD, is quite significant. The Saints, the Jews and followers of Messiah Yeshua have been persecuted so badly over the centuries, and every blow has welded them deeper into this solid tree. Truly they have been purified as pure gold to remove their impurities. They have become one with the Almond Tree of Life. The seven lamps of the LORD speak of a fulfillment of the LORD'S Testimony through His people. This gold must be *refined* perfectly in the LORD.

Flaming Fire

Exodus 37:23-24 *And he made his seven lamps, and his snuffers, and his snuff dishes, of pure gold. Of a talent of pure gold made he it, and all the vessels thereof.*

Revelation 4:5 *And out to the throne proceeded lightning's and thundering and voices; and there were seven lamps of fire burning before the throne, which are the seven Spirits of God.*

Exodus 26:37 *And thou shalt make the seven lamps thereof; and they shall light the lamps thereof, that they may give light over against it.*

Zechariah 4:2 *And said unto me, What seest thou? And I said, I have looked, and behold a candlestick all of gold, with a bowl upon the top of it, and his seven lamps thereon, and seven pipes to the seven lamps, which are upon the top thereof.*

Revelation 4:4 *John to the seven churches which are in Asia; Grace be unto you, and peace, from Him which is, and which was, and which is to come; and from the seven Spirits which are before His throne.*

Deuteronomy 4:36 *Out of Heaven He made thee to hear His voice, that He might instruct thee; and upon earth He shewed thee His great fire; and thou heardest His Words out of the midst of the fire.*

A fire must have oxygen, air or wind, in order to burn and grow. So it is fascinating that Yeshua declared that *everyone who is born of God's Holy Spirit is like this wind.* The lamps of the Holy Almond Tree Menorah give light as the wind causes the flame to burn brightly and constantly. It was the wind of the Holy Spirit that caused the waters to divide in the beginning when the dry land appeared. It was the wind of the Holy Spirit that dried the land before Israel at the Red Sea crossing when the LORD was in their midst. The disciples of Yeshua, on Shavuot, heard the sound of a rushing mighty wind as the Ruach/Holy Spirit descended upon them in flaming tongues of fire. In the future, it is the Holy Spirit of God, who breathes His Word in the final judgment, and He separates or divides the wheat from the chaff and burns the chaff from off His threshing floor with the breath of His mouth.

John 3:5-8 *Yeshua answered, Verily, verily, I say unto thee, Except a man be born of water and of the Spirit, he cannot enter into the Kingdom of God. That which is born of the flesh is flesh; and that which is born of the Spirit is spirit. Marvel not that I said unto thee, Ye must be born again. The wind bloweth where it listeth, and thou hearest the sound thereof, but canst not tell whence it cometh, and whither it goeth; so is every one that is born of the Spirit.*

You must be born of the LORD'S Ruach/Holy Spirit to have Eternal life. In order to have Eternal life, you must be *a branch* that is grafted into the main Almond Tree of Life through the central Branch Messiah, the Rod who is the Passover Lamb, and now we know this Lamb shank bone is remarkably encoded forever on the Holy Menorah in the Almond Rod!

IN THE BEGINNING THE LIGHT AND THE DARKNESS

The light in the darkness
Photo ©2013 Kimberly K Ballard

In the beginning, the LORD created the light. He separated the light from the darkness. Since we know that Yeshua is the light represented in Almond Tree Menorah of Life and in the Divine design, we can be absolutely positive that He created the universe. He is the light and in Him is no darkness or shifting shadow. If we walk in His light, we can no longer walk in the darkness because He has separated the darkness from the light. He did this at creation, making the darkness and the light cleft with His Rod, with His Yad. The Word Messiah is a light unto our path, if we choose to walk in it. *There is no darkness that can overtake the children of God because we have the LORD as our Eternal light.* In the LORD is the brightness of the Shechinah glory that burns brighter than the sun shining in its strength. Where the LORD abides with the light, there is no darkness that abides there at all. This is why there is no night in Heaven. This is how we know whether or not we are children of the light!

I Thessalonians 5:5 *Ye are all the children of light, and the children of the day; we are not of the night, nor of darkness.*

Colossians 1:10-23 *That ye might walk worthy of the LORD unto all pleasing, being fruitful in every good work, and increasing in the knowledge of God; Strengthened with all might, according to His glorious power, unto all patience and longsuffering with joyfulness; Giving thanks unto the Father, which hath made us meet to be partakers of the inheritance of the Saints in light; Who hath delivered us from the power of darkness, and hath translated us into the Kingdom of His dear Son; In whom we have redemption through his blood, even the forgiveness of sins; Who is the image of the invisible God, the firstborn of every creature; For by Him were all things created, that are in heaven, and that are in earth, visible and invisible, whether they be thrones, or dominions, or principalities, or powers; all things were created by Him, and for Him; And He is before all things, and by Him all things consist. And He is the head of the body, the church; who is the beginning, the firstborn from the dead; that in all things He might have the preeminence. For it pleased the Father that in Him should all fullness dwell; And, having made peace through the blood of His cross, by Him to reconcile all things unto Himself; by Him, I say, whether they be things in earth, or things in Heaven. And you, that were sometime alienated and enemies in your mind by wicked works, yet now hath He reconciled, In the body of His flesh through death, to present you holy and unblameable and unreproveable in His sight; If ye continue in the faith grounded and settled, and be not moved away from the hope of the Gospel, which ye have heard, and which was preached to every creature which is under Heaven; whereof I Paul am made a minister.*

Remember that the Living Torah from Heaven came to dwell with us, as the light that shined in the darkness of the Land of Zebulon and the Land of Naphtali, in Galilee.

I John 2:8 *Again, a new Commandment I write unto you, which thing is true in him and in you; because the darkness is past, and the true light now shineth.*

I John 1:1-10 *That which was from the beginning, which we have heard, which we have seen with our eyes, which we have looked upon, and our hands have handled, of the Word of Life; For the Life was manifested, and we have seen it, and bear witness, and shew unto you, that eternal life, which was with the Father, and was manifested unto*

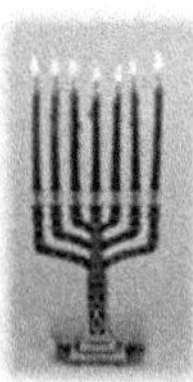

us; That which we have seen and heard declare we unto you, that ye also may have fellowship with us; and truly our fellowship is with the Father, and with His Son Yeshua Messiah. And these things write we unto you, that your joy may be full. This then is the message which we have heard of Him, and declare unto you, that God is light, and in Him is no darkness at all. If we say that we have fellowship with Him, and walk in darkness, we lie, and do not the truth; But if we walk in the light, as He is in the light, we have fellowship one with another, and the blood of Yeshua Messiah His Son cleanseth us from all sin. If we say that we have no sin, we deceive ourselves, and the truth is not in us. If we confess our sins, He is faithful and just to forgive us our sins, and to cleanse us from all unrighteousness. If we say that we have not sinned, we make Him a liar, and His Word is not in us.

I was sitting here writing about the light and the darkness in creation and something happened to me that was unexpected. I am using an old King James Bible for my reference to the Scriptures. This Bible was given to my Grandfather on June 12, 1931 and printed in 1897. My Grandfather passed away about three or four months before I was born, so I never had the pleasure of meeting him. He was a wonderful and beautiful father to my Mother and to her sister and a wonderful husband to my Grandmother. This was his little Bible. So I could not help but think about the fact that my Grandfather had no idea that one day his little Bible would be in my hands and would be used for the purpose of writing this astounding Testimony of the LORD. This just goes to show you, that if you have a Bible, you never know how it will be used in the future by the LORD. This proves that the LORD is in every detail of our lives. *Even if we experience sorrow, tragedy, or great rejection, the LORD works everything to His glory.* I believe the LORD is using my Grandfather in my life at this moment in time, through his Bible, to bring honour and glory to the LORD God of Israel. What a blessing this is to my heart! As I was just sitting here typing the above paragraph about the light and the darkness, all of a sudden the fan that is circulating the air in the room turned the pages of this little Bible. I could not believe this happened because the fan blew the pages to the very front of the Bible to the opening dedication page that I have never seen before. On this page, there was cursive writing. So I stopped what I was doing to read the dedication that was written in blue ink in 1931 by a woman named *"Mrs. Rosamond."* She wrote the following statement to my Grandfather Percy Farris, as she dedicated this little Bible to him. The page said the following words.

"May all the truths learned from the study of this Bible be as songs in the night and as lamps in the darkness to light your pathway from sense to soul."

Forget-me-not flowers & Snow
Photos ©2013 Kimberly K Ballard
All Rights Reserved

Wow what an incredible coincidence. I do believe the LORD works in mysterious ways! I never saw that page until just now when the fan blew the pages open to it. I was so dazzled by this because the pages turned to the very front of the Bible, which I find to be quite strange because the fan usually blows the pages to the middle of the book. So I stopped writing in amazement and I was going to return later to continue my work. Just out of curiosity though, I thought I would look to see what page the dedication was written on. I could not believe it! The fan turned the Bible to *the third page*. Can you believe that? It is chilling to think that as I am writing this, the LORD is watching me. I believe He caused the fan to turn this Bible to the third blank page at the beginning of the book, because the number three verifies His Living Testimony on the Holy Menorah! It is difficult for the fan to turn the page to the third page

because the cover of this Bible is old heavy leather. When you flip so far to the front of the book, the Bible easily flips closed if too many pages go forward toward the cover. So now I was a little curious and I wondered if her surname *"Rosamond"* had any significant meaning. This was also a surprise because I soon discovered that it originated from the Latin phrase *"Rosa Munda."* Now believe it or not I found that this phrase in Latin means *"pure rose"* and it is an epithet for the Virgin Mary! I just find it so hard to believe that this is another strange coincidence! Mrs. Rosamond's name is an epithet for Yeshua's Mother! Wow! This made me wonder if the Holy Spirit and not the fan actually blew upon the pages so they fell open to the third page, so I would find this dedication about the lamp lighting our pathway. *I was also just mentioning that it is the Holy Spirit that breathes the wind.* I believe the LORD wanted me to see the words from Mrs. Rosamond because they verify the Testimony of Yeshua in the Almond Tree Menorah on the third page! Everything the LORD had revealed to me about the number three is depicted on the Holy Menorah regarding Yeshua. This was a special blessing and gift to my heart. Mrs. Rosamond wrote that she hoped that all the truths from this Bible would be as songs in the night. At the time when this occurred, I was not only writing this book, I was composing music for the LORD'S glory, from the Bible. This was simply amazing. *I was in the process of writing songs in the night and writing about the light!* I believe that my Grandfather Percy Farris and Mrs. Rosamond would be shocked and greatly blessed if they knew how this little Bible from 1931 was now being used today for the LORD'S glory. The LORD'S Word never comes back void, it remains the most remarkable Testimony. My Grandfather's Bible is now 80 years old in June 2011! God bless Mrs. Rosamond for this little Bible. God bless my beloved Grandfather Farris for leaving this gift behind.

There is one more thing I would like to mention here in this place! In the year 1983, the movie, *"Yentl,"* with Barbra Streisand playing the lead role had great meaning in my life and I loved the music soundtrack. There were some Jewish prayers in this movie and it was released when I was in college studying music. I was a Percussion Performance major and voice major at CSU. So I would play this soundtrack relentlessly and sing the prayers in it in the basement of my beloved friend, mentor, and graduate student Professor Marion's house where I lived. I would belt out, *"A Piece of Sky,"* and play the dramatic ending timpani part up in the air! I displayed the vinyl album cover on my floor in my room as art. Singing the prayers blessed me deeply. Oddly enough the other day, when I watched the newly released DVD of Yentl for the first time since I saw it in the theater in 1983, I was so surprised to discover that almonds were mentioned three times! Twice they mentioned almond cookies and once they mentioned almond cakes, in my favorite Jewish movie of all time! I could not believe that the LORD was using this in my life, without me being aware of it until I was editing my book about the miracle of the Almond Tree. ***(Movie references – Yentl ©1983 MGM Metro-Goldwyn-Mayer Studios Inc. TM).*** When my Israeli friend and I experienced the Almond Tree miracle in 2007, she just happened to send me recipes for almond cookies and for almond cakes on the first anniversary of our miracle in Jerusalem! It was so neat! I had never encountered the Almond Tree so much and I had no idea of this connection to *Yentl* before yesterday. Three times they mentioned the almond! *It is the sign of the Messiah in the Holy Almond Tree Menorah!* One more astonishing thing that happened as I was working on editing this part of my book is the fact that my emails from Barbra Streisand's charity in 2012 were about heart health, and almonds are excellent for heart health because the LORD is the Covenant of the heart! Then I discovered by Divine Providence that Emanuel, her beloved father, is in a way connected to the *"Corona"* on the Holy Menorah that gives Eternal life! Yeshua is Emmanuel, God with us! These are *three* more astounding coincidences about the Jewish Messiah's Covenant of the heart and the *"Corona"* that is hidden in the Holy Almond Tree Menorah of Eternal Life! This is astonishing to say the least, and I believe that it is the LORD'S Divine blessing and that it was shown to me for a very special reason that maybe one day I will understand!

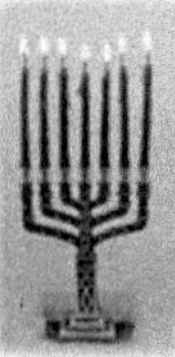

THE EVENING AND THE MORNING WERE THE FIRST DAY

Sun in the evening on Snow

I will now carry on with what I was going to say about the light and the darkness, in the previous section! In the beginning God divided the light from the darkness. We know that where the LORD dwells, there is no darkness at all because He is the Eternal light of the Holy Menorah. The light always puts out the darkness, so the two do not dwell together. He made them cleft and this was the LORD'S signature on His creation.

When God separated the light from the darkness, the evening and the morning were the first day. The days on the Jewish Biblical calendar, for this reason, *begin at sundown. So a new Biblical day begins at sundown and it continues until the following sundown.* This is not like the Roman calendar that begins in the morning and then continues until midnight. The Roman calendar is the opposite of the Biblical calendar. The Jewish Biblical calendar that I discussed before is the true calendar of God.

Genesis 1:3-5 *And God said, Let there be light; and there was light. And God saw the light, that it was good; and God divided the light from the darkness. And God called the light day, and the darkness He called night. And the evening and the morning were the first day.*

Now the next time that the LORD separated the light from the darkness was when Messiah Yeshua the Branch was being cut off, as He was lifted up on the cross. *As the light of the LORD was departing from the earth, suddenly the earth became dark.* Yeshua gave up His Spirit when He breathed His last breath and when the Roman Centurion saw how Yeshua breathed His last breath, the Roman soldier proclaimed, *"That surely this was the Son of God!"* The Holy Spirit is the breath of life and the Spirit departed and ascended back into Heaven. Now incredibly, from this moment forward, the Holy Almond Tree Menorah that was standing in the Second Jewish Temple would no longer light. It failed to light from that moment on, up to the destruction of the Second Temple 40 years later in 70 AD (*Talmud Bavli Yoma 39b). The light was separated from the darkness at the moment of the Messiah's death* because *the Rod of God* made them cleft, when the Rod was lifted up on the cross. This means that when the veil in the Holy Temple was made cleft by the Rod during the crucifixion, the Holy Place that we could now enter through the veil *was the throne room of the Temple of God in Heaven*, where the LORD truly resides, because the LORD is our Great High Priest and KING OF KINGS. Yeshua was going to go back to Heaven and He was leaving the darkness upon the earth as His light was departing, but He gave us a gift! He sent His Ruach/Holy Spirit from Heaven seven weeks after this event was fulfilled, and it descended to rest upon His Jewish disciples. Now the light and power of the Living Torah of the LORD was inside them and they had the power of the Rod of God to go forth proclaiming the Messianic hope of Eternal salvation, which would gather all the lost sheep together into one place, in Jerusalem.

Darkness was over all the land from the sixth hour to the ninth hour. This means there were *three* hours of darkness. The LORD showed me something about this that is absolutely

fantastic and it is going to be a game changer! In the Gospel account of Matthew, written in Chapter 28, there is the story of the resurrection of Messiah, the Living Rod of God. What I am about to show you is an astonishing revelation! *Suddenly, the LORD opened my eyes to see that when Mary Magdalene and Mary came to Yeshua's Garden sepulchre in Holy Mount Moriah, it was the seventh day Sabbath before the dawn had occurred of the first day of the week, and Messiah Yeshua was already resurrected to life, as the Living Rod of God during the seventh day, the Jewish Sabbath of the LORD!* ***As evening was becoming morning, of the first day of the week,*** the women saw the angel of the LORD, who had descended from Heaven with a great earthquake. The angel of the LORD came and rolled the Great Stone from the door of the sepulchre in God's Garden in Holy Mount Moriah and he sat upon it. The angel of the LORD appeared to the Jewish women and he said, *"Fear not ye; for I know that ye seek Yeshua, which was crucified. He is not here; for He is risen as He said. Come, see the place where the LORD lay. And go quickly, and tell His disciples that He is risen from the dead; and, behold, He goeth before you into Galilee; there shall ye see Him, lo, I have told you."* (Matthew 28:5-7) Wow! As I thought about these words the LORD gave me a very chilling and astounding revelation! I realized this was identical to the LORD'S creation in the very beginning, *as the evening was becoming morning the first day of the week!*

At the moment of Yeshua's glorious resurrection inside Holy Mount Moriah, *the Living Almond Rod of God budded.* So the *darkness* of Messiah's death and burial in the Garden of God, bearing Adam's curse of death in the former Garden of Eden, *was separated and made cleft from the light* of the LORD'S glorious living resurrection Testimony, *as evening was becoming morning, the first day of the week.* So Yeshua, the Living Branch from the Almond Tree of Life, was already alive on *the seventh day Sabbath,* before the angel of the LORD appeared and proclaimed this miraculous Living Testimony of the LORD'S glory. This means that Yeshua was resurrected on the seventh day Sabbath that the LORD consecrated at the beginning of His creation.

The truth is then, that the angel of the LORD, the Heavenly messenger, had come to declare that the light had been separated from the darkness, as the evening was becoming morning on the first day of the week, as they were seeking the LORD in the Garden! So the darkness and the light were made cleft by the Rod of God, and the angel of the LORD proclaimed it on the first day of the week! Therefore, the LORD God of Israel revealed that He is Messiah Yeshua during His resurrection in Holy Mount Moriah, because this is exactly what the Rod of God did in the beginning during the creation, when He separated the light from the darkness, as evening was becoming morning on the first day, from this very place!

Now this is not all that happened that is so miraculous! On the same day that the angel of the LORD appeared to Mary Magdalene and Mary at the Garden tomb, but later, as evening came on, which is toward the second day of the week, Yeshua appeared to His disciples and this is when He stood in their midst when the doors were shut.

John 20:19-22 *Then the same day at evening, being the first day of the week, when the doors were shut where the disciples were assembled for fear of the Jews, came Yeshua and stood in the midst, and saith unto them, Peace be unto you. And when He had so said, He shewed unto them His hands and His side. Then were the disciples glad, when they saw the LORD. Then said Yeshua to them again, Peace be unto you; as My Father hath sent Me, even so send I you. And when He had said this, He breathed on them, and saith unto them, Receive ye the Holy Spirit.*

Now Yeshua came and stood in their midst, as the evening of the first day was about to become the second day. In the beginning, the LORD created *the firmament in the midst of the waters on the second day* and He made the waters cleft from the waters.

Genesis 1:6-8 *And God said, Let there be a firmament in the midst of the waters, and let it divide the waters from the waters. And God made the firmament, and divided the waters which were under the firmament from the waters*

which were above the firmament; and it was so. And God called the firmament Heaven. <u>And the evening and the morning were the second day.</u>

As I said earlier, *the firmament is a support that strengthens,* but I did not yet connect one important part of this, that I will now share! Of course it is also the vault of Heaven. *So the incredible truth is that Yeshua appeared to the Jewish disciples as the firmament, who was standing in their midst, as the Living Water, as the evening of the first day of the week, was becoming morning of the second day!* It is absolutely chilling and astounding to see this for the first time in history! *When Yeshua breathed on the disciples, He told them to receive the Holy Spirit and the Spirit of life from the Living Water, went into them.* So the truth is that as the firmament, the LORD who was standing in their midst, strengthened the Jewish disciples and He gave them the power to go remit sins. The firmament is considered to be the sky, and as I will show you later, under the LORD'S feet the pavement is like sapphire blue sky. *Messiah Yeshua was at that moment strengthening and supporting the Jewish disciples by breathing His Holy Spirit upon them, as He stood as the firmament in their midst, as the evening and the morning were the second day, just as it was with the LORD'S Rod during His creation!* Now because the LORD strengthened them with the breath of His Holy Spirit, this was their *support* to go fulfill the will of the LORD God. The LORD God of Israel was once again revealing that He is Messiah Yeshua who performed this same work on the second day of creation! It is very clear in the following Scriptures that the resurrection of the Living Almond Rod of God, the Messiah, is the light that takes away the darkness. *Messiah Yeshua, who is the light of the Heavenly Almond Tree Menorah of Life, is the light that did arise in the darkness of the Garden tomb, bathed in the glorious Shechinah light of the LORD, in His Garden in Holy Mount Moriah.* Now this is very interesting because the following Psalm *refers to the light that arises in the darkness as "He."* This Psalm reveals the Messiah, who is gracious and full of compassion. The Rabbi of Righteousness is the greatest Rabbi of all time, for Eternity!

Psalm 112:4 *Unto the upright <u>there ariseth light in the darkness; He</u> is gracious and full of compassion, and righteous.*

The Living Branch from the Almond Tree of Life therefore, took the darkness of death away forever and replaced it with *Eternal life* in the LORD'S Eternal light, in His Garden in Jerusalem, at the gate of Heaven! This is where the LORD'S House dwells forever in eternity on His Holy Mount! Here, in Jerusalem, He brings us out of the shadow of death! Light is life and where the light exists, all life flourishes! There is no death!

Psalm 107:13-15 *Then they cried unto the LORD in their trouble, and He saved them out of their distresses. He brought them out of darkness and the shadow of death, and brake their bands in sunder. Oh that men would praise the LORD for His goodness, and for His wonderful works to the children of men!*

John 12:44-46 *Yeshua cried and said, He that believeth on Me, believeth not on Me, but on Him who sent Me, and He that seeth Me seeth Him that sent Me. I AM come a light into the world, that whosoever believeth on Me should not abide in darkness.*

John 9:5 *As long as I AM in the world, I AM the light of the world.*

John 8:12 *Then spake Yeshua again unto them, saying, I AM the light of the world; he that followeth Me shall not walk in darkness, but shall have the light of life.*

Messiah Yeshua radiates His glorious light in the center of Heaven where He stands in the midst of it (Revelation 5:6 & 7:17). He brings us there to dwell with Him in the never ending-light of this Living Almond Tree Menorah in Heaven. He is the Holy Lamp stand.

So Messiah Yeshua, who lifted up His outstretched arms, was the light of the budding Almond Branch of the Holy Menorah in Heaven, who was walking in the midst of Israel, but soon He departed and the light departed. He did not leave us alone however. He sent the light of His Living Spirit to dwell inside us, so we would glow with His radiance, like His Temple lamps in this dark world.

John 12:35-38 *Then Yeshua said unto them, Yet a little while is the light with you. Walk while ye have the light, lest darkness come upon you; for he that walketh in darkness knoweth not whither he goeth. While ye have light, believe in the light, that ye may be the children of light. These things spake Yeshua, and departed, and did hide Himself from them. But though He had done so many miracles before them, yet they believed not on Him; That the saying of Esaias the Prophet might be fulfilled, which he spake, LORD, who hath believed our report? And to whom hath the arm of the LORD been revealed?*

Isaiah 2:5 *O house of Jacob, come ye, and let us walk in the light of the LORD.*

II Samuel 22:29 *For Thou art my Lamp, O LORD; and the LORD will lighten my darkness.*

John 3:19-22 *And this is the condemnation, that light is come into the world, and men loved darkness rather than light, because their deeds were evil. For every one that doeth evil hateth the light, neither cometh to the light, lest his deeds should be reproved. But he that doeth truth cometh to the light, that his deeds may be made manifest, that they are wrought in God. After these things came Yeshua and his disciples into the land of Judaea; and there he tarried with them, and baptized.*

At the end of the age, when *the Day of the LORD* comes, it is a time of God's wrath. *The Day of the LORD is a day of great darkness, with no light in it at all.*

Now as I thought about this, I began to understand why the Messiah would rapture the believers out of this world, before *the day of the LORD'S wrath* is poured out. The LORD has placed His Holy Spirit of life in those who have the baptism of Messiah Yeshua. *When Yeshua descends from Heaven with a shout and with the voice of the archangel, the Rod of God will again, make cleft the light from the darkness!* The believers who are called *"the sheep"* are at that moment separated from the unbelieving wicked people who are called *"the goats."* In order for the LORD to *separate the light from the darkness, as it was in the beginning,* He will have to take the light completely out of this earth and those who have the light, like the virgins who had the oil in their lamps, will ascend up to Heaven to be with the Heavenly Menorah light of Messiah while He leaves behind the darkness in this sin cursed world. Then His wrath will be poured out on the earth and those who have chosen not to believe the LORD'S Living Testimony will die. We must be separated from one another at this time because the darkness cannot come to dwell and abide with the light, and the light can no longer dwell and abide with the darkness as the age of God's grace comes to an end. This is precisely why we are living in the age of grace right now. The LORD is graciously giving us the age of grace before Messiah Yeshua returns, so we can humble ourselves in repentance before Him, preparing ourselves to meet the LORD face to face, by washing our garments in His baptism of Living Water and in the fire of His Holy Spirit. When the age of grace is over, it will then be too late for those who refuse to believe. This is why the rapture will happen and the LORD will gather the good wheat into His Heavenly Temple. Those who have spiritually soaked their garments in the oil of His Ruach/Holy Spirit and have washed their garments in the life blood and Living Water of Messiah, the Lamb of God, will be caught up with the LORD, to meet Him in the air in the glory cloud of Heaven where we will always be with the LORD. The rapture will happen in the twinkling of an eye, at the Last Trump, during Rosh HaShanah, and we will be with the LORD forever. This is the blessed hope we have been given by Messiah Yeshua's Living Testimony. It is faithful and true and Yeshua is the shining reflecting Rod that saves us from the darkness of death. In the rapture, the Rod of God will separate the light from the darkness, as He did in the beginning, making them cleft. *Only the darkness will be prevailing on the earth when the*

LORD brings His judgment in flaming fire upon the wicked. The Scriptures tell us that *the days of darkness* will be cut short for the sake of the elect. The reason for this is that during this time, it will be quite difficult for anyone to be saved because the light has departed, and so only evil will be prevailing! Right now, though, there is still time, as the Rod of God is held out to us now, in favor, but soon the Rod of God will not be held out to us anymore, and it will be like when Israel was fighting the Amalekites. As soon as the Rod was not held out in favor, death came.

Matthew 24:22 *And except those days should be shortened, there should no flesh be saved; but for the elect's sake those days shall be shortened.*

It is extremely important to believe the Living Testimony of Messiah Yeshua now, *before the Day of the LORD comes.*

The Light in the Darkness Photo ©2013 Kimberly K Ballard All Rights Reserved

Amos 5:18-20 *Woe unto you that desire the day of the LORD! To what end is it for you? <u>The day of the LORD is darkness, and not light.</u> As if a man did flee from a lion, and a bear met him; or went into the house, and leaned his hand on the wall, and a serpent bit him. <u>Shall not the day of the LORD be darkness, and not light? Even very dark and no brightness in it</u>?*

Since the LORD said that *the Day of the LORD is even very dark with NO brightness in it,* this will be the most frightening event that this world has ever seen since the Great Flood of Noah. We are truly saved in *the Living Ark of the Covenant,* through Messiah Yeshua.

I Peter 3:18-22 *For Messiah also hath once suffered for sins, the just for the unjust, that He might bring us to God, being put to death in the flesh, but quickened by the Spirit; By which also He went and preached unto the spirits in prison; Which sometime were disobedient, <u>when once the long-suffering of God waited in the days of Noah, while the Ark was a preparing, wherein few, that is, eight souls were saved by water. The like figure whereunto even baptism doth also now save us</u> not the putting away of the filth of the flesh, but the answer of a good conscience toward God, by the resurrection of Yeshua Messiah. Who is gone into Heaven and is on the right hand of God; angels and authorities and powers being made subject to Him.*

The Light in the darkness Hannukiah & Servant Candle Photos

Light in the darkness Hannukiah & Snow Menorah Photos ©2013 Kimberly K Ballard All Rights Reserved

Psalm 119:129-130 *Thy testimonies are wonderful: therefore doth my soul keep them. The entrance of Thy words giveth light; it giveth understanding unto the simple. I opened my mouth, and panted: for I longed for Thy commandments. Look Thou upon me, and be merciful unto me, as thou usest to do unto those that love Thy Name.*

Psalm 36:9 *For with Thee is the fountain of life: in Thy light shall we see light.*

Luke 11:36 *If thy whole body therefore be full of light, having no part dark, the whole shall be full of light, as when the bright shining of a candle doth give thee light.*

The LORD is called *"the Father of Lights"* who gives us every good gift. The LORD says in Psalm 84 that there is no good thing that He will withhold from those who love Him and walk in His way. The LORD has no variation or shifting shadow. He is gloriously radiant and beautiful to behold to the extreme.

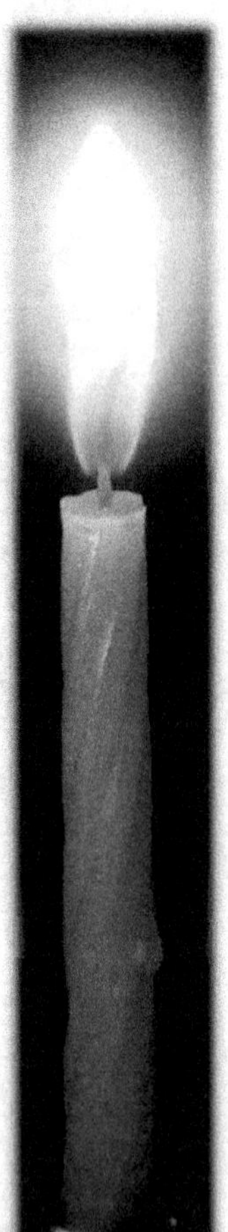

James 1:17-18 *Every good thing bestowed and every perfect gift is from above, coming down from the Father of lights; with whom there is no variation, or shifting shadow. In the exercise of His will He brought us forth by the Word of truth, so that we might be, as it were, the first fruits among His creatures.*

Yeshua revealed that the Lamp was the Word of God and His Testimony. The light of *the Living Torah* will be revealed and it will not be kept secret. Therefore, it must be put upon a lamp stand, so that everyone receives the light of the Living Almond Tree Menorah of Life!

Mark 4:21-23 *And He was saying to them, A lamp is not brought to be put under a peck-measure, is it, or under a bed? Is it not brought to be put on the lamp stand? For nothing is hidden, except to be revealed; nor has anything been secret, but that it should come to light. If any man has ears to hear, let him hear.*

Isaiah 60:1-3 *Arise and shine; for your light has come, And the glory of the LORD has risen upon you. For behold, darkness will cover the earth, And deep darkness the peoples; but the LORD will rise upon you, And His glory will appear upon you. And nations will come to your light, And Kings to the brightness of your rising.*

II Corinthians 4:6 *For God, who commanded the light to shine out of darkness, hath shined in our hearts, to give the light of the knowledge of the glory of God in the face of Yeshua Messiah.*

Acts 26:22-23 *And so, having obtained help from God, I stand to this day testifying both to small and great, stating nothing but what the Prophets and Moses said was going to take place; that the Messiah was to suffer, and that <u>by reason of His resurrection from the dead He should be the first to proclaim light</u> both to the Jewish people and to the Gentiles.*

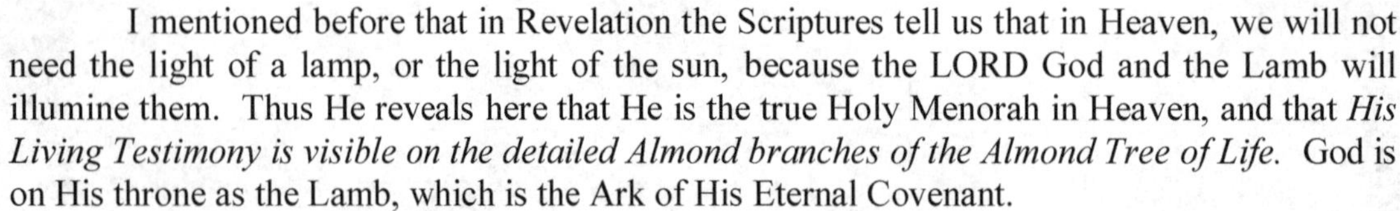

I mentioned before that in Revelation the Scriptures tell us that in Heaven, we will not need the light of a lamp, or the light of the sun, because the LORD God and the Lamb will illumine them. Thus He reveals here that He is the true Holy Menorah in Heaven, and that *His Living Testimony is visible on the detailed Almond branches of the Almond Tree of Life.* God is on His throne as the Lamb, which is the Ark of His Eternal Covenant.

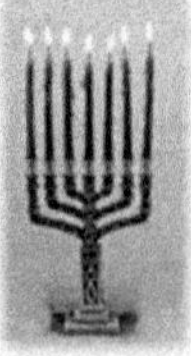

Revelation 22:3-6 *And there shall no longer be any curse; and the throne of God and of the Lamb shall be in it, and His bond-servants shall serve Him; and they shall see His face and His Name shall be written on their foreheads. And there shall no longer be any night; and they shall not have need of the light of a lamp nor the light of the sun, because the LORD God shall illumine them; and they shall reign forever and ever.*

In Luke's Gospel account, Yeshua revealed something else to me that is truly incredible. Yeshua spoke six words that will cause us to discover His true identity, if we follow the six words leading to the seventh. *Remember that I said that Yeshua, as the "Stem" of Jesse, reveals that He is the rod in the center of a lock!* It is the key of David! Now I noticed that if you place the six words of Yeshua on the top of the seven lamps of the Holy Menorah and direct His Words toward the central Rod, or the main Stem or Branch at the center of the Almond Tree that is the shaft, the Lamb shank, you will see that the sixth word is *"opened"* and it points to the seventh Branch in the center of the Menorah! So this perfect Almond Branch in the *number seven* is the key to unlock the door that swings opened, revealing the face of the LORD God, the *Sar HaPanim,* and the Messiah, who is the perfect Rod or Branch *number seven,* at the center of the Almond Tree of Life. It is only when we have diligently searched for Him that will we see who He is within the Living Testimony of the Tree of Life.

I will give you a bit of an illustration to show you what I mean. There are seven candles or lamps on the Holy Menorah. Yeshua's six Words are placed on each candle or lamp of the Almond Tree Menorah. Number 1 is, *"Ask,"* 2 is, *"Given,"* 3 is, *"Seek,"* 4 is, *"Find,"* 5 is, *"Knock,"* and 6 is, *"Opened,"* thus *revealing the seventh behind the door that you have just knocked upon!* You are in essence knocking upon the door after asking and seeking the LORD, so that He, *the Rod who has the key in His hand will open the lock of the seventh door to you,* so you can now see Him face to face! The secret mystery of Messiah is now opened to you as the Rod opens the door!

When the sixth is opened to you, then the seventh, the central Rod, is revealed showing that Messiah Yeshua, the Living Almond Branch, is the LORD God of Israel, the Passover Lamb, and He alone has the key of David that unlocks this door!

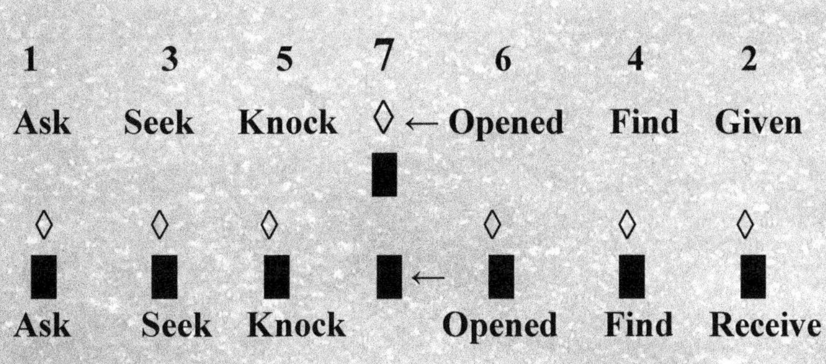

Menorah in the Snow Photo ©2013 Kimberly K Ballard All Rights Reserved

In this simple illustration of *the Holy Almond Tree Menorah,* you are drawn to the central Rod, the main Shaft of the solid gold Menorah. You can clearly see that the Messiah turns the key of David in the lock, and after the door is opened to you, it is now possible to see the LORD'S hidden identity within the Lamp stand. The seventh is the LORD'S number of perfection and completion. Yeshua fulfilled the seven Holy Feasts of the LORD as *the perfect Living Torah.*

Now to further explain this, you can only see Him in the Almond Tree Menorah if you *"ask"* Him. Then it will be *"given"* to you. If you *"seek"* Him, then you will *"find"* Him. If you *"knock,"* the door will be *"opened"* unto you, revealing the face of the LORD God of Israel at the center, which is the central Rod, the face of Messiah, the Sar HaPanim, which is the Prince of the face of the LORD God. His Eternal Living Testimony is now revealed on the Holy Almond Tree Menorah in Heaven. It is true then, that if we follow His command, then His Holy Spirit guides us to see the LORD'S face because it has been hidden from us. He then gives us the Bread from Heaven and the true meat, *the Living Torah, which is Himself!*

Luke 11:9-13 *And I say unto you, Ask, and it shall be given you; seek, and ye shall find; knock, and it shall be opened unto you. For every one that asketh receiveth; and he that seeketh findeth; and to him that knocketh it shall be opened. If a son shall ask bread of any of you that is a father, will he give him a stone? Or if he ask a fish, will he for a fish give him a serpent? Or if he shall ask an egg, will he offer him a scorpion? If ye then, being evil, know how to give good gifts unto your children; how much more shall your Heavenly Father give the Holy Spirit to them that ask Him?*

Now I might also mention here that the three cups on the Holy Menorah also represent *"Faith, Hope, and Love."* This is because of the fact that we must have *faith* to believe that Messiah Yeshua's Living Testimony is accurate and true. Then His Living Testimony brings us the *hope* of salvation. Messiah *Yeshua said that the greatest of these is love.* I honestly comprehend now what this means! When we truly *"love Him,"* then we will *"ask"* of Him and it will be *"given"* to us. When we honestly *"love Him,"* then we will *"seek"* Him and we will *"find"* Him. When we *"love Him"* with all our heart, then we will *"knock"* and it will be *"opened"* to us, revealing His face as the LORD God of Israel in *the center* of the seventh lamp. *Yeshua is the hidden face of the LORD God of Israel.* His face is now clearly revealed behind the opened door of number seven, at the center of the Holy Almond Tree Menorah and this is the main tree trunk of the Almond Tree of Life! From this time forward, because the LORD has revealed the details of His Divine design to my heart, Yeshua's identity will no longer be hidden on the Holy Menorah. The glory of the Royal Sovereign of the entire universe will shine forth from the budding and blossoming Almond Tree of Life from the Holy Lamp stand. He has now revealed His Eternal glory to our gaze. This tells us, that all of the elements in His Divine design that we have seen on the Holy Menorah are a beautiful Testimony of Messiah the LORD. This day I boldly declare that we should desire to spiritually soak in the oil of His Holy Spirit, so we can burn brightly, as the shining lamps that reflect the LORD'S light. The LORD will remove the darkness from this earth forever with His glorious light. The Romans in mockery of this threw the Jewish disciple John into a vat of burning oil, but John, full of the oil of the Holy Spirit of God, was not harmed, and everyone that witnessed this miracle in the coliseum believed in the LORD because John was full of Yeshua's light! Matthew 5:14-16 says we are the light of the world, and to put this light on a candlestick.

Candle Photo ©2014 Kimberly K Ballard All Rights Reserved

THE ELECTRICAL PHOTOGRAPHIC CORONA DISCHARGE

Zoom Lens
Photo ©2013 Kimberly K Ballard All Rights Reserved

There is an extremely thrilling aspect of the word *"Corona"* that pertains to Messiah Yeshua, hidden within the Divine design of the Holy Menorah. In the definition of the word *"Corona,"* we find that there is a phenomenon known as the *"Electrical Photographic Corona Discharge."* This involves *photographic elements* of science!

THE CORONA DISCHARGE IS AN ELECTRICAL DISCHARGE THAT IS USED IN PHOTO COPYING AND IN OTHER SPONTANEOUS HIGH VOLTAGE EVENTS TO CREATE AN IMAGE!

This phenomenon occurs with an Electrical Photographic Corona Discharge *"when there is a burst of energy, as an electrical charge of high voltage fires, thereby producing a spark. This energy creates a discharge and leaves behind an image."* ***(Source: The Electrical Photographic Corona Discharge ©2010 en.wikipedia.org/wiki/Corona_discharge).***

This is what happens in a photo copy machine that produces the image and makes it appear on paper! I found a few images that were created this way using a spark plug, along with an explanation of how this *Corona* occurs in a scientific context. This becomes a bit more scientific, so I will not endeavor to write about it in a lot of detail, but immediately, when I saw that the *Corona* was encoded within the Divine design of the Holy Menorah, I was stunned. I thought that surely this must be exactly how the image of Yeshua came to be imprinted on His linen burial Shroud. Of course I am referring to the famous Shroud of Turin that originated in Jerusalem. The image was *undeniably encoded in the Holy Menorah* within the word *"Corona,"* and this was chilling! I tell you the truth when I say that I only found this on the Holy Menorah, by the Divine revelation of the Holy Spirit, as it was shown to my heart. The truly incredible part of it is the fact that I never had any previous knowledge about this phenomenon before discovering it on the Divine design of the Holy Menorah.

I also had no idea at the time that a few scientists actually believed already that the image was formed on the Shroud by none other than a *"Corona."* Due to the fact that I was so excited when I discovered that it was *hidden in the Holy design of the Heavenly Menorah,* I decided to call the expert photographer for the Shroud of Turin. I wanted to ask the honorable Barrie M. Schwortz if he could answer this question for me because we had spoken on numerous occasions on the phone before. I wanted to find out from him if this was a possibility that Yeshua's image was imprinted upon His burial Shroud *through the process of an Electrical Photographic Corona Discharge!* At the time, I did not tell him that was I asking this because I found this *Corona* in the hidden details of the design on the Holy Menorah while writing my book! I was anxious to see what this professional, world renowned photographer's point of view was about it, without telling him how I came to this conclusion. I knew that if anyone would know the answer to my question, it would be Barrie Schwortz because he is a photographic expert! So I called him up and we

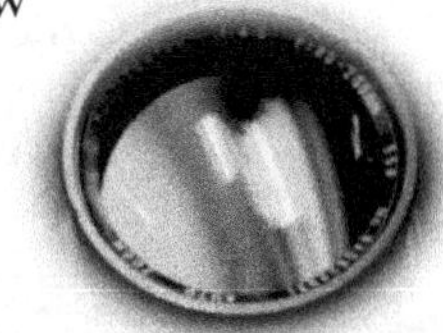

had a wonderful conversation and I finally asked Barrie my question about *the Electrical Photographic Corona Discharge.* When he told me that it might be possible, I was truly floored! At that moment, I wanted to tell him how I came to this conclusion, without coming from a scientific point of view, but I wanted to wait and see if this was even a possibility first. I was quite surprised when Barrie told me that some of the scientists, who had studied the Shroud, had already theorized that a *Corona* created Yeshua's image on the Shroud. Can you imagine how I felt when he said this to me? It was shocking, since I had not even known what an *Electrical Photographic Corona Discharge* was before this moment, and I only came across it while writing my chapter about the design of the Holy Menorah! The scientists were coming from a purely scientific study on the Shroud, but I was coming from a purely spiritual study on the Holy Menorah of the Jewish Temple. I was not even studying the Shroud! I was only studying my Bible and asking the LORD to show me how He was encoded in the Almond Tree. At this point, I knew that if the image was encoded on the Holy Menorah of the LORD, then it was highly probable that the image occurred through this phenomenon on the Shroud of Turin. Every little detail so far, for the design on the Menorah, had been proven Biblically and was clearly part of Yeshua's Living Testimony, so I knew that this was likely no exception.

This has to be strikingly true when we consider that the resurrection of *"The Branch,"* the Messiah, is the highlight of the Living Testimony of the LORD. This shows us even more that the image of Yeshua on His burial Shroud is a stunning and unfathomable miracle of Biblical proportions. *After all, this Almond Rod is the Covenant of Life that abides in the Ark of Heaven.* Let us not forget that Yeshua is the Rod, parallel to Aaron's rod that budded to life. On the Shroud itself, we find the Living proof of the death, burial, and resurrection of Messiah Yeshua. This really made me shiver! The LORD created this incredible image on His Shroud before photography ever existed and before the photo copy machine was ever invented. This miraculous aspect alone should prove that this miracle was only produced by the hand of God. *If Yeshua is the Rod in the hand of God, performing His mighty works, then God's signature is all over this miracle.* This is *the fingerprint* of God because, if you think about it, the moment that Messiah was resurrected from death to life, the light that was inside Yeshua separated from the darkness of death, thereby making the Branch cleft at the resurrection! In that split second, life and death, the light and the darkness, were made cleft as it was in the beginning, and this reveals that Yeshua is the Rod of God who came to life in Holy Mount Moriah, the Mountain where God said that His Name would dwell forever, in Jerusalem! It was interesting that during the course of my conversation with Barrie, he stated that although it was possible that an *Electrical Photographic Corona Discharge* could cause the image, he thought it was probably unlikely, for one reason. When I asked him why, I was profoundly struck by his answer. Barrie said that it was possible but *"it would take an extremely high voltage!"* I was shocked by this answer and I wanted to say something to him right then about how I came up with this idea, and I hope that one day soon I will be able to tell him. I knew that I had to wait until the LORD showed me every detail about it before I revealed it, and it is all part of Messiah Yeshua's Living Testimony. When Barrie said this to me, I was smiling in my heart and I had a huge grin on my face! The truth is, He unknowingly gave me a confirmation. The moment Barrie said that it was possible, but probably unlikely because it would take an *"extremely high voltage,"* I sat there on the stairs in amazement, pondering his words. In my mind I was joyfully thinking *"The Holy Spirit of God is as high a voltage as you can get!"*

So Barrie basically verified it, without realizing it! What he said to me was profound! Since I knew that *the Holy Spirit inside Yeshua radiated outward,* the image was created when the spark of life burst forth from inside Yeshua, like a seed coming to life, as *the Living Torah.* It was *the extremely high voltage of the Holy Spirit inside Yeshua that created the high voltage charge that fired* the exact moment of His resurrection. Remember that the Word of God is the seed and the seed has the life inside itself! When the high voltage came from inside Yeshua, *the*

Word of God, the Living Torah, He sprouted to life as the Almond Rod of God that budded. *At this exact moment, a flash of light, "the spark," occurred with the spontaneous high voltage of God's Spirit, and the Electrical Photographic Corona Discharge spark of life occurred, thereby leaving His image behind!* So the truth is that Yeshua's image was quite literally photo copied onto His fine linen burial Shroud. This means that this produced *a photographic negative image of Yeshua,* as if someone snapped a picture of Him at the moment of His resurrection. Since *the spark of life* came from inside Yeshua, this image is a virtual x-ray of His entire being. This explains the reason why we can see the wounds and bruises in His flesh and why His skeletal structure is visible. Clearly, *the life came from within and radiated outward.* When you ponder this statement, consider the Words of Yeshua when a woman touched Him and she was healed from her blood issue, as *the Rod of God* stopped her plague of blood!

Luke 8:46 *And Yeshua said, Somebody hath touched Me; for I perceive that virtue is gone out of Me.*

Yeshua said, *"Virtue is gone out of Me,"* and the word *"virtue"* in this context was transcribed from the Greek word *"dynamin,"* and it refers to *"the power of God."* The term *"gone out"* is rendered in Greek, *"exelelythuian,"* and it means *"to go or come out of." The power of the God of life was inside Yeshua, the Rod of God, and the power radiated outward onto the Shroud.* The LORD revealed *His resurrection* through the creation *when He made the seed with the life inside it.* A seed sprouts to life in just the right conditions with the help of the light and the water! So *the light* of this seed came from within Yeshua because the LORD is *the light and the Living Water.* Yeshua declared this to the woman at Jacob's well when He offered her a drink of this life-giving water. He revealed Himself to her as Israel's Messiah!

This seed sprouted to life inside the dark tomb, inside God's Holy Mountain! The image of Yeshua on the burial Shroud left us with so much undeniable proof that He is the Living Rod of God. As Barrie said, *"It would take an extremely high voltage!" So therefore, we can truly say that this image could only occur through the extremely high voltage of the glory of God!* When the Shroud is photographed, it becomes a positive image from a photographic negative. Although my conversation with Barrie appeared to have been answered in a negative, it actually turned out to be a positive, just like the Shroud of Turin! How amazing is that? The Shroud image is therefore an actual photograph of Messiah Yeshua who died and came to life 2,000 years ago. The Shroud is a remarkable relic of the Living Testimony of the LORD that has been preserved over the centuries. This conversation with Barrie Schwortz was such an affirmation and it gave me the chills again! So with this knowledge, perhaps *the Electrical Photographic Corona Discharge* theory should be reinvestigated. *All I can say for now is that the Corona is definitely encoded within the details of the Divine design on the Holy Menorah of the LORD. The Corona is hidden under the "Calyx" on the Almond branches of the Holy Menorah.* I have shown that Messiah Yeshua is undeniably depicted as *the budding and blossoming Almond Branch with the Corona* on the Holy Menorah of the LORD. If Yeshua's image was created by the fire of the Holy Spirit within Him, *when the spontaneous spark of life occurred,* then this is a truly thrilling and profound discovery!

One more astonishing fact about this is the fact that the Bible declares that Messiah Yeshua is *"the express image of God!"* This takes us back to what I declared at the beginning of this book. Messiah Yeshua is the *"Sar HaPanim, the Prince of the face of the LORD God."* So when we are looking upon the face of Messiah Yeshua, upon His Shroud, this means *we are seeing the face of God,* as it is revealed to our gaze! It is quite fascinating that the Bible tells us *that the veil that hides the face of God is taken away in Messiah Yeshua!* Now how do I know that this is the absolute truth? In the following Scripture that is recorded in the book of Luke, it is written that John the Baptist was called, *"The Prophet of the Highest."* We can easily

overlook the extremely important words within the text that boldly declare something astonishing! It is incredible that this passage tells us that John the Baptist, who was the messenger sent by God (in the spirit and power of Elijah), is the one who would go before *"the face of the LORD, to prepare His way!"*

Luke 1:76-80 *And thou, child, shalt be called the Prophet of the Highest; for thou shalt go before the face of the LORD to prepare His ways; To give knowledge of salvation unto His people by the remission of their sins, Through the tender mercy of our God; whereby the dayspring from on high hath visited us, To give light to them that sit in darkness and in the shadow of death, to guide our feet into the way of peace. And the child grew, and waxed strong in spirit, and was in the deserts till the day of his shewing unto Israel.*

It is also written that *"Life is in"* Messiah Yeshua and this means *"The spark of life!"*

John 1:4 *In Him was life; and the life was the light of men.*

Remember that the book of Revelation is actually *the revelation* that the LORD God of Israel is in fact Messiah Yeshua, the Eternal KING of glory!

Now recently there was a Shroud documentary that aired. On this documentary, there was a gentleman who stated that, *"the man on the Shroud appears to have white hair,"* but he said that *"this man was not old enough to have white hair."* So he figured that there must be some mistake and that perhaps His hair was darker in real life than it appears on the Shroud. He had no explanation for this strange phenomenon. When I thought about this, I remembered the Scripture in Revelation that says that when the Jewish disciple John saw the vision of Yeshua in Heaven, He appeared to have *"White hair that was, as white as wool, white as snow."* This is the appearance of the Ancient of Days. No one has ever thought about the fact that this feature alone appearing on the Shroud reveals the glory of the LORD'S resurrection within the image. The Shroud is a prophetic piece of the Living Testimony of the face of the LORD God and He left it here for us to gaze upon and to ponder His marvelous works. There is a prophecy in the book of Zechariah that declares, *"People will look upon Me whom they have pierced."* The LORD God of Israel is the one speaking these Words and *Yeshua gave us the Spirit of grace, through the Living Torah!*

Zechariah 12:10 *And I will pour upon the House of David, and upon the inhabitants of Jerusalem, the Spirit of grace and of supplications; and they shall look upon Me whom they have pierced, and they shall mourn for Him, as one mourneth for his only Son, and shall be in bitterness for His firstborn.*

Zechariah chapter 12, beginning with verse 1, verifies that this passage was spoken by the mouth of the LORD God of Israel.

Zechariah 12:1 *The burden of the Word of the LORD for Israel, saith the LORD, which stretcheth forth the Heavens, and layeth the foundation of the earth, and formeth the Spirit of man within him.*

In summary, the following elements of Yeshua's Testimony are visible on the Shroud. Yeshua's legs were not broken because He is the Lamb of God, the shank bone of the Rod of God. Yeshua's side was pierced, causing the Living Water and life blood to gush out from the LORD'S heart, giving us Eternal life as it flows through the two tablets of our heart and breathes His Spirit of life into us. Yeshua was pierced with nails because He is the door of Heaven, nailed in a *sure place.* Yeshua was the *cut off* Branch of the Almond Tree of life that budded in Holy Mount Moriah. Yeshua wore the Crown of Thorns of the curse because the Messiah came to life and destroyed the curse of death, winning the victory for Israel and the earth forever, as the KING of glory! Yeshua was *beaten* like the pure gold of the Almond Tree Menorah because He is the central Rod, the Branch that supports all the other branches.

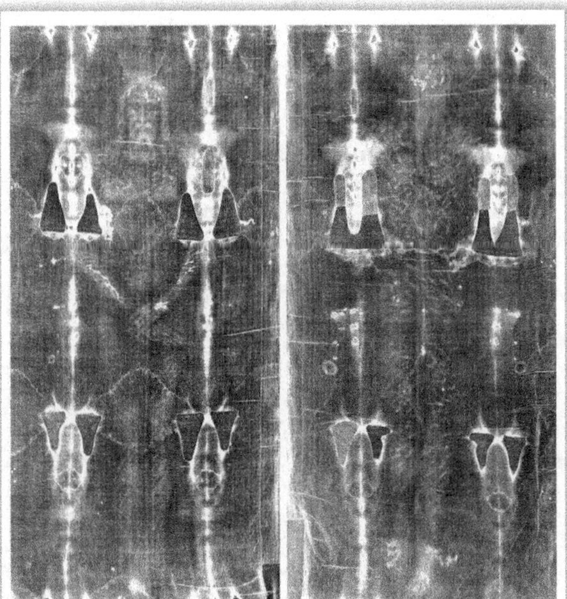

Official Shroud Pair
Photograph ©1978 Barrie M. Schwortz Collection, STERA Inc., All Rights Reserved

When we look upon the Shroud of Messiah Yeshua, we see the one who was pierced, and we are actually seeing the face of the LORD God of Israel (made without hands) as it is revealed behind the key of David. In the last chapter of this book, I have elaborated more on this subject of the face of God in Messiah the Rod. The LORD works through people sometimes without their knowledge and the LORD was definitely working through Barrie Schwortz in my conversation that day! I used to look at Barrie's photos in books at the library and I asked the LORD to meet him one day. Within months of saying this in my prayers, Barrie moved to Colorado!

John 19:33-37 *But when they came to Yeshua, and saw that He was dead already, they brake not His legs; But one of the soldiers with a spear pierced His side, and forthwith came there out blood and water. And he that saw it bare record, and his record is true; and he knoweth that he saith true, that ye might believe. For these things were done, that the Scripture should be fulfilled, A bone of Him shall not be broken. And again another Scripture saith, They shall look upon Him whom they pierced.*

He is the Light of the resurrection glory - Brass Candlestick Photo ©2014 Kimberly K Ballard All Rights Reserved

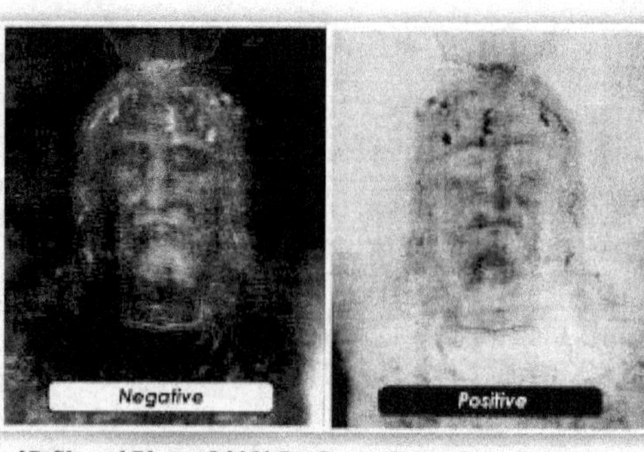

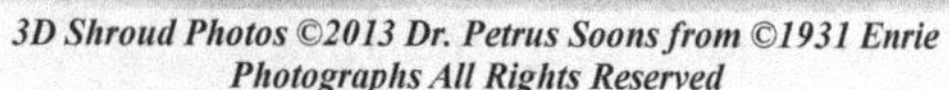
3D Shroud Photos ©2013 Dr. Petrus Soons from ©1931 Enrie Photographs All Rights Reserved

THE THIRD DAY

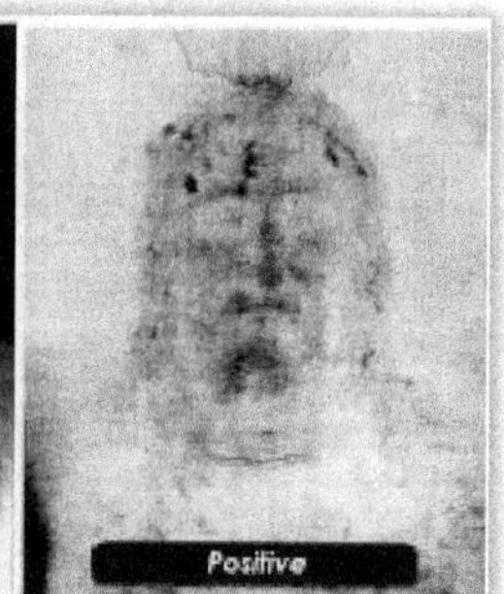

3D Shroud Photos ©2013 Dr. Petrus Soons from ©1931 Enrie Photographs All Rights Reserved

I was overwhelmed when the LORD showed me exactly why Yeshua was raised to life on the third day on the Feast of First Fruits, which occurs on Nisan 17 of the Biblical calendar. One important aspect of what I am about to show you pertains to the Words that were spoken by Yeshua. Remember that Yeshua said, *"The seed is the Word of God."* This was written in Luke 8:11 and we have already talked about this Almond seed. So before I continue to reveal Yeshua in the Holy Menorah, I have to show you the shocking truth that reveals why Yeshua was resurrected on the third day! I wept when the LORD revealed this to my heart because it was such a miracle. I thought that my miracle of the Almond Tree in Jerusalem was so spectacular, but I had no idea at the time that the LORD was not finished showing me the most astonishing part of His hidden Testimony within the Almond Tree. The LORD just opened my eyes to see why Yeshua was resurrected to life on the third day and it is written in *the Torah.* Before I share this with you, though, I just want to verify that Yeshua was historically resurrected on the third day. Yeshua told the Jewish disciples many times before it came to pass that He would die and be raised to life on the third day, and now it is clear to me that He was telling them this for a very profound reason!

Matthew 16:21 *From that time forth began Yeshua to show unto His disciples, how that He must go unto Jerusalem, and suffer many things of the elders and Chief Priests and Scribes, and be killed and be raised again the third day.*

Acts 10:40-41 *Him God raised up the third day and shewed Him openly; Not to all the people, but unto witnesses chosen before of God, even to us, who did eat and drink with Him after He rose from the dead.*

Luke 24:44-46 *And He said unto them, These are the Words which I spake unto you, while I was yet with you, that all things must be fulfilled, which were written in the Law of Moses, and in the Prophets, and in the Psalms concerning Me. Then opened He their understanding, that they might understand the Scriptures, And said unto them, thus it is written, and thus it behoved Messiah to suffer, and to rise from the dead the third day.*

I Corinthians 15:3-7 *For I delivered unto you first of all that which I also received, how that Messiah died for our sins according to the Scriptures; And that He was buried, and that He rose again the third day according to the Scriptures; And He was seen of Cephas, then of the twelve; After that, He was seen of above five hundred brethren at once; of whom the greater part remain unto this present, but some are fallen asleep. After that, He was seen of James; then of all the apostles.*

Matthew 12:38-40 *Then certain of the Scribes and of the Pharisees answered, saying, Master, we would see a sign from Thee. But He answered and said unto them, An evil and adulterous generation seeketh after a sign; and there shall no sign be given to it, but the sign of the Prophet Jonah; For as Jonah was three days and three nights in the whale's belly; so shall the Son of man be three days and three nights in the heart of the earth.*

Matthew 20:19 *And shall deliver Him to the Gentiles to mock, and to scourge, and to crucify Him; and the third day He shall rise again.*

Luke 24:7 *Saying, the Son of man must be delivered into the hands of sinful men, and be crucified and the third day rise again.*

As I pondered *the third day* of the resurrection of Yeshua, suddenly the Holy Spirit breathed in me and showed me the astonishing truth. I was so shocked and amazed as I was given this Divine revelation by the LORD! This is going to open your heart and mind like you cannot imagine! Mary Magdalene and Mary, who came to the sepulchre *as evening was becoming morning the first day*, were also involved in another simply incredible miracle! It came into my heart that Mary Magdalene and Mary also came to the sepulchre of Yeshua *as evening was becoming morning the third day after Passover.* As they approached the sepulchre, it was nearing the end of the seventh day Sabbath of the LORD, but the Fruitful Branch Yeshua had already come to life as the parallel of Aaron's rod that budded and He was the First Fruit of salvation. It was still dark, but the dawn was arriving at the sepulchre. *This was the third day and it was the Feast of First Fruits which is Nisan 17.*

Matthew 28:1 *In the end of the Sabbath, as it began to dawn, toward the first day of the week, came Mary Magdalene and the other Mary came to see the sepulchre.*

John 20:1 *The first day of the week cometh Mary Magdalene early, when it was yet dark, unto the sepulchre, and seeth the stone taken away from the sepulchre.*

Luke 24:1-2 *Now upon the first day of the week, very early in the morning, they came unto the sepulchre, bringing the spices which they had prepared, and certain others with them. And they found the stone rolled away from the sepulchre. And they entered in, and found not the body of the LORD Yeshua.*

Mark 16:1-4 *And when the Sabbath was past, Mary Magdalene, and Mary the Mother of James and Salome, had bought sweet spices, that they might come and anoint Him. And very early in the morning the first day of the week, they came unto the sepulchre at the rising of the sun. And they said among themselves, Who shall roll us away the stone from the door of the sepulchre? And when they looked, they saw that the stone was rolled away; for it was very great.*

It is so significant that this event took place at the Garden tomb, in Holy Mount Moriah, *where the Garden of Eden was originally located in Jerusalem!* You must keep in mind everything that Yeshua told His Jewish disciples before it came to pass. He must die and be resurrected to life the third day, as the seed that is the Word of God. It had to fall into the earth and be buried in order to sprout to life, bearing fruit from the Almond Tree of life inside God's Holy Mount. Yeshua was supposed to be threshed on the LORD'S threshing floor, to fulfill His own Testimony.

Blossoming Cherry tree Photo

John 12:24-41 *Verily, verily, I say unto you, Except a corn of wheat fall into the ground and die, it abideth alone; but if it die, it bringeth forth much fruit.*

The Living Torah has the seed of life inside Himself. Yeshua manifested Himself as *the Tree of Life,* pictured in the Holy Almond Tree Menorah. The LORD opened my eyes to see the most incredible secret of Messiah Yeshua that is ever to be revealed in history! Again, we find that the mystery of Messiah *"the Fruitful Branch,"* is encoded in creation from the very beginning in Genesis in *the Torah.*

Blossoming Cherry tree
Photo ©2011
Kimberly K Ballard

When a seed is planted in the ground in the earth, this is a type of sepulchre. It appears as though there is no life in the seed. However, at the right moment in time, the seed suddenly comes to life because *the life was inside the seed itself.* So this is a perfect representation of how Messiah Yeshua, *the Word of God the seed,* having the Holy Spirit of life inside Himself, came to life at the right moment in time on the third day. Now I revealed in the last section that at the exact moment that this seed burst forth with the light of life, Yeshua left His image imprinted upon His fine linen burial Shroud. *Keep in mind that the LORD Messiah is the Living Branch of the Almond Tree bearing the First Fruit of Eternal Life.* So what does this have to do with creation in Genesis? *I discovered the fact that the LORD encoded the Messiah's resurrection in the third day of creation, and this is the reason that Yeshua came to life on the third day, on the Feast of First Fruits!* This is, without a doubt, the most fantastic news for all of us! The shocking secret that reveals why Messiah Yeshua was resurrected on the third day is found *in the very first chapter of creation in the Torah!*

Genesis 1:11-13 *And God said, Let the earth bring forth grass, the herb yielding seed, and the fruit tree yielding fruit after his kind, whose seed is in itself upon the earth and it was so. And the earth brought forth grass, and herb yielding seed after his kind, and the tree yielding fruit whose seed was in itself, after his kind; and God saw that it was good. And the evening and the morning were the third day.*

Blossoming tree like the cross of
Messiah Yeshua
Photo ©2014 Kimberly K Ballard

The astonishing revelation is that God created the fruit trees yielding fruit with the seed of life inside of them, and they came to life as the evening was becoming morning, the third day! Then God said that it was good! Suddenly I saw the connection that Mary Magdalene went to the Garden tomb with the other Mary ***as the evening was becoming morning the third day***, and the Fruitful Branch had already budded with Fruit because the seed of Life from the Living Torah was inside Yeshua the LORD! The seed placed in the earth in the Holy Mountain of God had already sprouted to life in God's Garden before the Jewish seventh day Sabbath of the LORD ended. The Branch from the Almond Tree of Life, bearing Eternal Fruit, came to life *as the evening was becoming morning the third day* on the LORD'S Feast of First Fruits! Fantastic!

I was stunned when all of this came together before my eyes and I knew that no one could ever deny again that the LORD God of Israel is Messiah Yeshua, who existed in the very beginning, during creation. Yeshua's Divine Testimony was therefore Eternally encoded in the Torah and testified to in the Holy Almond Tree Menorah of God!

When I was pondering this, I thought about the fact that the wine of Yeshua's Eternal Covenant was from the Fruit of the LORD'S vineyard and the LORD told us that He is the vinedresser. So in the place where Yeshua came to life as the Living Fruitful Branch, there was

at one time a huge vineyard that was planted by the LORD in His Garden in the very beginning in Holy Mount Moriah. Now this miracle suddenly gave me the knowledge that revealed why Yeshua the Branch is specifically represented *in the third cup of wine* at the Passover Seder!

Grape leaves in vineyard Photo ©2014 Kimberly K Ballard All Rights Reserved

Messiah is pictured in the third cup because He is *the Eternal Fruit* of the LORD'S Living Testimony in Heaven. Therefore, this profound truth reveals why the Holy Almond Tree Menorah of the LORD represents His Living Testimony in the *three cups* that are on each branch of the Almond Tree of Life *because we now understand that He came to life as the evening was becoming morning, the third day.* By drinking the third cup of wine in the Passover Seder, which is profoundly called *"the cup of redemption,"* we are accepting the Covenant and marriage proposal of the Bridegroom of Heaven, and of course, this wine of the marriage Covenant represents Yeshua's life blood as the perfect Lamb of God. This was the LORD'S own life blood, shed for us, to restore us to Eternal life in Him. So Yeshua instructed us to remember the Living Branch that bore the Eternal fruit by drinking *the third cup* of wine at the Passover Seder and now we can understand why partaking of *the third cup* truly honours the KING! After I made the connection of Messiah Yeshua, *the Fruitful Branch, to the third day of creation* through God's kind heart of revelation, I began to understand exactly why Yeshua asked Simon Peter *three times* if He loved Him. Three times Yeshua told Simon Peter, *"Feed My sheep."* Simon Peter was to take *the Living Torah,* the Almond Tree of Life to the Jews first and then to the Gentiles because Messiah the LORD is the true meat of the Almond and the pure meat of the perfect Lamb, without spot or blemish and He is the Unleavened Bread from Heaven. Yeshua wanted those who love Him to feed His sheep with *His Word, the Living Torah,* until He returns to the earth on the third day to raise up Israel and to usher in the Eternal Kingdom of God!

John 21:15-17 *So when they had dined, Yeshua said to Simon Peter, Simon, son of Jonah, lovest thou Me more than these? He saith unto Him, Yea, LORD; Thou knowest that I love Thee. He saith unto him, feed My lambs. He saith to him again the second time, Simon, son of Jonah, lovest thou Me? He saith unto him, Yea, LORD; Thou knowest that I love Thee. He saith unto him, feed My sheep. He saith unto him the third time, Simon, son of Jonah, lovest thou Me? Peter was grieved because He said unto him the third time, Lovest thou Me? And he said unto Him, LORD, Thou knowest all things; Thou knowest that I love Thee, Yeshua saith unto him, feed My sheep.*

In this verse, Yeshua was actually *revealing to Simon Peter,* that He is the Branch from the Almond Tree of Life, who bore Fruit with the seed of life of *the Living Torah inside Himself, as evening was becoming morning on the third day* after Passover. He was *revealing to Simon Peter* that He divided the darkness of death from the light of life in Holy Mount Moriah in the Garden of God, *as the evening was becoming morning on the first day of the week,* but He had come down from Heaven to feed the sheep of the House of Israel with the Heavenly Manna for Eternity. He was the Unleavened Bread brought forth from the earth in the Garden of God in Holy Mount Moriah during the Feast of Unleavened Bread! So the seed of life was to be taken to the lost sheep of the House of Israel first and then to the Gentiles.

So now I have to take you back to my original Almond Tree miracle because this revealed another miracle that I did not know about until I wrote this. I want to live in that moment again and revel in the words of my Israeli friend. When she answered my email, after I sent her the Almond Tree revelation that the LORD had spoken to my heart, she photographed the Almond Tree *as it was coming to life* in the Old City of Jerusalem and she said that it was *"the first" Almond Tree that she saw that was beginning to flower."* Do you remember what else she told me? *She tried to pass that Almond Tree "three times," and that is when "the Invisible Assistant" took her by the arm to the tree and impressed it upon her to photograph it!* What I simply cannot get over, is the fact that she told me these things back in 2007 without ever knowing this part of the story of the Almond Tree miracle because this part of the miracle had not happened yet, until about a year after the Jerusalem miracle! Now I will put it all together into one paragraph in summary. *Yeshua came to life on the Seventh day Sabbath of the LORD, as the evening was becoming morning the first day of the week, bringing the light of God's glory out of the darkness of the sepulchre in the Garden in Holy Mount Moriah, from the Foundation Stone. It was like the separation of the light and the darkness that occurred on the first day of creation in the Torah in this same location and He left His image in the tomb to prove it, in the place where Adam and Eve were created in God's image! Then it was also revealed to me at this point, that Mary Magdalene and Mary came to the sepulchre in the Garden of the LORD God, in Holy Mount Moriah, as the evening was becoming morning the third day. This means that Yeshua was the Fruitful Almond Branch from the Almond Tree of Life, who came to life like the Fruit trees in the third day of creation in the Torah. As the women arrived at the Garden sepulchre, the Fruitful Branch had already come to life because the seed of life, the Living Torah, was inside Yeshua!* So now you can understand why I quietly wept with joy over this astonishing blessing of Divine revelation. The LORD performed this marvelous miracle before my eyes! My Almond Tree miracle was so thrilling that I could never imagine how spectacular this miracle was going to be in my life. I wonder how this profound discovery will affect the world when they see it for the first time in history, and finally understand the loving heart of our KING!

Blossoming Cherry tree
Photo ©2014 Kimberly K Ballard
All Rights Reserved

Now I want to show you another event that took place with the LORD on the third day! ***THE LORD GOD TOLD MOSES TO GET THE PEOPLE READY TO MEET HIM ON THE THIRD DAY!*** It was *the third day* when the LORD descended upon Mount Sinai to meet the people face to face! It was *the third day* when Yeshua appeared alive and met Mary in the Garden and then later met with the Jewish disciples and the 500 at one time! It was *the third day* when Moses went up to be with the LORD on top of Mount Sinai. It was *the third day* when the LORD blew the trumpet. It was *the third day* when the people saw the LORD with their own eyes! It is incredible because the LORD told Moses to make the people ready for *the third day* and the men were not to touch a woman or their wife. So when Yeshua was raised to life on *the third day*, I realized that He told Mary not to touch Him yet, since He had not yet ascended to the Father! Mary Magdalene was one of many who would one day become the Jewish wife and Bride of Messiah!

John 20:17 *Yeshua saith unto her, Touch Me not; for I AM not yet ascended to My Father; but go to My brethren, and say unto them, I ascend unto My Father, and your Father; and to My God, and your God.*

The people were to wash their garments before meeting the LORD face to face and this is what the baptism of Messiah Yeshua is all about! It is to prepare us before hand, so we are ready to meet the LORD face to face! This explains why John the Baptist came proclaiming the message to the people of Israel saying, *"Repent, prepare the way of the LORD to travel."* John was baptizing in water to make the Messiah known to Israel! John was preparing the Jewish people and he was getting them ready to meet the LORD face to face! They were to wash their garments in the Jordan River, so they would be clean and white before He arrived! Messiah was the vessel, the Ark of God's Testimony, standing in the Jordan River as our Yeshua, leading the way across the Jordan River and into the Eternal Promised Land. Messiah the Ark of the Living Covenant holds the key of David and reveals the great mystery of the Heavenly Rod, the Living Almond Branch, from the Tree of Life. This is exactly what the people did at Mount Sinai when they were told to prepare and to get themselves ready to meet the LORD! The LORD came to them in a thick cloud! This is how Yeshua will return from Heaven, in a thick cloud! The trumpet sounded long! Yeshua will come at the Last Trump and sound the trumpet long! Moses went up!

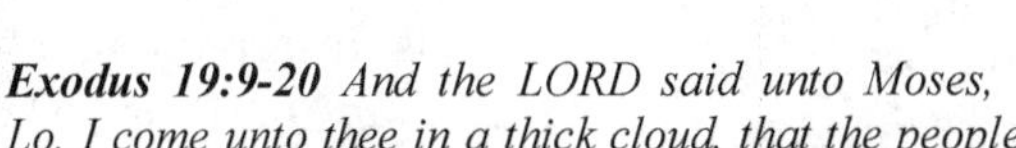

Exodus 19:9-20 *And the LORD said unto Moses, Lo, I come unto thee in a thick cloud, that the people may hear when I speak with thee, and believe thee forever. And Moses told the words of the people unto the LORD. And the LORD said unto Moses, Go unto the people, and sanctify them today and tomorrow, and let them wash their clothes, And be ready against the third day; for the third day the LORD will come down in the sight of all the people on Mount Sinai. And thou shalt set bounds unto the people round about, saying, Take heed to yourselves, that ye go not up into the Mount, or touch the border of it; whosoever toucheth the Mount shall be surely put to death; There shall not an hand touch it, but he shall surely be stoned, or shot through; whether it be beast or man, it shall not live; when the trumpet soundeth long, they shall come up to the Mount. And Moses went down from the Mount unto the people, and sanctified the people; and they washed their clothes. And he said unto the people, Be ready against the third day; come not at your wives. And it came to pass on the third day in the morning, that there were thunders and lightnings, and a thick cloud upon the Mount, and the voice of the trumpet exceeding loud; so that all the people that was in the camp trembled. And Moses brought forth the people out of the camp to meet with God; and they stood at the nether part of the Mount. And Mount Sinai was altogether on a smoke, because the LORD descended upon it in fire; and the smoke thereof ascended as the smoke of a furnace, and the whole Mount quaked greatly. And when the voice of the trumpet sounded long, and waxed louder and louder, Moses spake, and God answered him by a voice. And the LORD came down upon Mount Sinai, on the top of the Mount; and the LORD called Moses up to the top of the Mount; and Moses went up.*

The third day involves meeting the LORD KING face to face! Incredibly, the Jewish disciples saw Yeshua's face imprinted on His fine linen burial Shroud on *the third day* after He budded to life in Mount Moriah in God's Holy Garden! This explains why the LORD will come to raise up Israel on the third day at His second coming and they will see Him face to face! The people met the resurrected Messiah face to face *on the third day* after they had prepared themselves previously by washing in John's Mikveh or baptism. Yeshua did not appear to everybody after His resurrection, as the Scriptures tell us. He only appeared to those that had washed their garments in the Jordan River and were ready to meet Him *the third day! Because Messiah Yeshua is depicted in the third day of creation, we can now understand why Yeshua is Emmanuel or Immanuel which is the title "God with us."* The Word of God came in the flesh to dwell among us as the Fruitful Branch of the Almond Tree of Life.

Official Photograph of the Shroud Face of Messiah Yeshua
Photograph ©1978 Barrie M. Schwortz Collection, STERA Inc., All Rights Reserved

From the day that Messiah Yeshua ascended back into Heaven, we have also been instructed to get ready to meet Him face to face and to wash our garments. Yeshua will descend from Heaven with a shout, with the voice of the archangel and with the trump of God in the cloud. This is exactly what they heard on Mount Sinai when the LORD descended upon the Holy Mount in flaming fire. The trumpet was exceedingly loud and it became louder and louder. Instead fading off like a normal trumpet blown by a human, this trumpet became exceedingly loud because the Ruach/Holy Spirit was breathing into the shofar of God! Making our garments white in the LORD is called *"the righteousness of the Saints."* Yeshua will only come for those who have prepared their garments and made themselves ready before His arrival.

Since it is becoming exceedingly clear that Yeshua is coming back soon, this message is urgent. I am telling everyone to get ready to meet the LORD face to face! Is it any wonder then why the LORD encoded Himself within the Divine design of His Holy Almond Tree Menorah? *After the LORD showed me that the Shroud image was within the Corona on the Holy Menorah, I understood exactly why the Shroud was such an important piece of the Living Testimony of the LORD and the reason why the disciples saw Yeshua's face on the Shroud on*

the third day because they were going to meet Him face to face. Now you can understand how I know that this is the reason why the LORD showed me in a vision that the Jewish Priestly Angel at the Garden Tomb in Mount Moriah is pointing to three niches in the wall of the sepulchre with his Yad. The items that were placed inside the three niches of the exterior wall of Yeshua's Garden tomb reveal the proof of His Living Testimony. This place in the Garden is the gate and door of Heaven *and it was the location of the Garden of Eden.* If you think about it, *the contents of the three niches* reveal that Yeshua was raised to life on *the third day,* as the Fruitful Living Branch of the Heavenly Ark. I realized when I saw the Angel pointing and heralding something of great importance that the angel was really pointing to *the Living Torah! The Living Torah is the Tree of Life and Messiah is the Branch of this tree bearing the Eternal First Fruit.* Yeshua is the light of the Holy Almond Tree Menorah that leads us through the door and gate of Heaven, into the Eternal Promised Land, into the Heavenly Garden of God. This is one reason why the Great Rolling Stone from this Garden sepulchre is facing this Garden now from Mount Nebo like a door because this is *"the way"* across the Jordan River into Heaven! This means that the Mezuzah that was declaring *"the LORD our God is one,"* was placed on the right side of the door of the gate of Heaven, just as I said earlier, where Yeshua's Living Testimony was written in stone in Holy Mount Moriah. The LORD'S Name is written inside and outside of this Garden sepulchre! As I said before, I believe the letters *"Alpha and Omega"* are inscribed upon this rock at the Garden tomb where Yeshua came to life and the Angel is pointing directly to it in the signet shaped stone and he is trying to get our attention as a messenger of God! These words are faithful and true. Yeshua is the light of the world and His flaming fire of the Holy Spirit burns with the pure oil of anointing in this solid gold Menorah of Heaven. It is a fabulous image that I will never forget it!

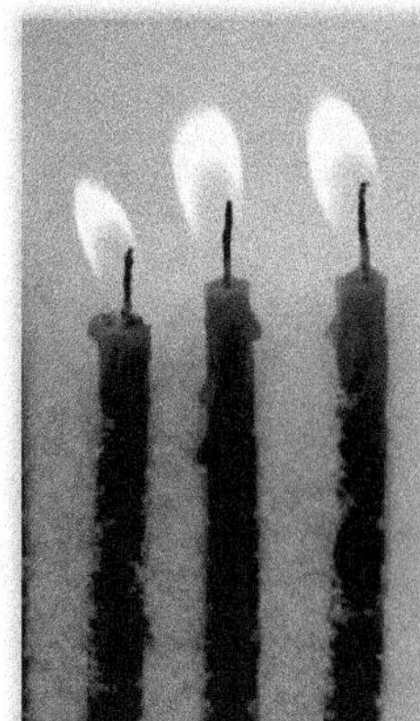

The light in the snow
Photo ©2014
Kimberly K Ballard

II Samuel 22:29 *For Thou art my Lamp, O LORD; and the LORD will lighten my darkness.*

Psalm 119:105 *Thy Word is a lamp unto my feet, and a light unto my path.*

No one comprehended the profound Testimony of Messiah Yeshua that was revealed from *the Torah,* as it was shown to Moses, but now we can understand this glorious miracle through the power of the Word of God and the meaning behind the marvelous works of our Royal KING! Now if you go back and read John chapter one, you will see the meaning of these words in a totally new light!

John 1:1-19 *In the beginning was the Word, and the Word was with God, and the Word was God. The same was in the beginning with God. All things were made by Him; and without Him was not anything made that was made. In Him was life; and the life was the light of men. And the light shineth in darkness; and the darkness comprehended it not. There was a man sent from God, whose name was John. The same came for a witness, to bear witness of the Light, that all men through Him might believe. He was not that Light, but was sent to bear witness of that Light. That was the true Light, which lighteth every man that cometh into the world. He was in the world, and the world was made by Him, and the world knew Him not. He came unto His own, and His own received Him not. But as many as received Him, to them gave He power to become the sons of God, even to them that believe on His Name; Which were born, not of blood, nor of the will of the flesh, nor of the will of man, but of God. And the Word became flesh, and dwelt among us, and we beheld His glory, the glory as of the only begotten of the Father, full of grace and truth. John bare witness of Him, and cried, saying, This was He of whom I spake, He that cometh after me is preferred before me; for He was before me. And of His fullness have all we received, and grace for grace. For the Law was given by Moses, but grace and truth came by Yeshua Messiah. No man hath seen God at any time; the only begotten Son, which is in the bosom of the Father, He hath declared Him. And this is the record of John, when the Jews sent Priests and Levites from Jerusalem to ask him, Who art thou?*

Holy Menorah lit in the snow & Majestic Deer Scene

Until this moment in history, we could not perceive the full nature and meaning of Yeshua's stunning Almond Tree Testimony and Eternal Covenant of life. The Living Torah is the true Heavenly Light of the world and He is the Heavenly Lamp stand that came to dwell among us! With His Shechinah glory, He guides our pathway to Eternal life, but we must follow in the light behind the Ark after Yeshua, who is leading us across the Jordan River and into the Heavenly Promised Land!

3D Hologram Shroud face positive & negative images Photos ©2013 Dr. Petrus Soons from Enrie Photographs ©1931 All Rights Reserved

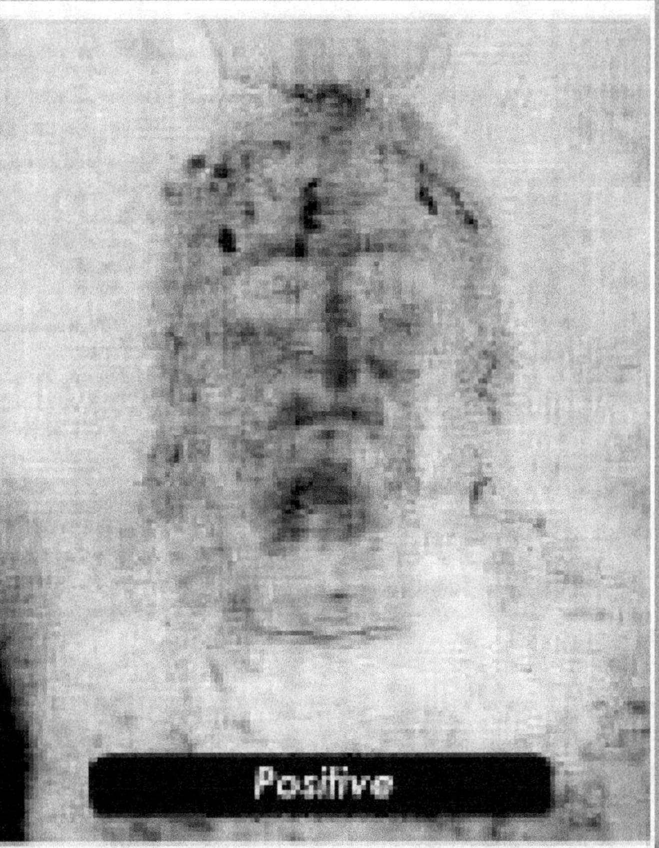

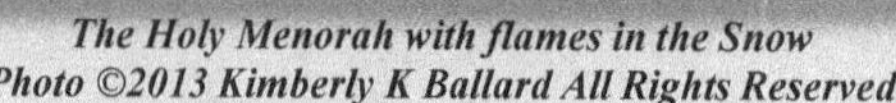

The Holy Menorah with flames in the Snow

The KING is coming! Majestic Deer by Fence & Snow Photos ©2014

Fig Tree ©2013 A. Danin Jerusalem Israel

Official Photograph of "THE JESUS BOAT"

3D Shroud Photo ©2013 Dr Petrus Soons from ©1931 Enrie All Rights Reserved

3D Shroud Photo ©2013 Dr Petrus Soons from ©1931 Enrie All Rights Reserved

Chapter 8

MESSIAH'S IDENTITY REVEALED IN HIS MIRACLE'S

Snow on Junipers Photo
©2014 Kimberly K Ballard All Rights Reserved

It was winter in Jerusalem during the time of Hanukkah called *"the Feast of Dedication,"* and Messiah Yeshua was walking in the Holy Temple in the Portico of Solomon. It was the Festival of lights and it was the time for celebrating the miracle of the oil of the Holy Menorah. Yeshua was walking along, talking to the children of Israel, and He was telling them to believe His works. The people were pondering Him in their hearts and they were asking Yeshua if He was the Messiah. Yeshua told them that they should at least believe in His miracles and works because the works verify and testify that He is in the Father and that the Father is in Him. They would not believe this even though Yeshua's miracles revealed the works of the LORD God of Israel. They could not comprehend or understand that it was true.

John 10:22-25 *And it was at Jerusalem the Feast of Dedication, and it was winter. And Yeshua walked in the Temple in Solomon's porch. Then came the Jews round about Him, and said unto Him, How long dost Thou make us doubt? If Thou be the Messiah, tell us plainly. Yeshua answered them, I told you, and ye believed not; the works that I do in My Father's Name, they bear witness of Me.*

So the works reveal that Messiah Yeshua is the Rod of God. It was winter in 2007, when the LORD gave me the Almond Tree revelation. Soon after this happened, within the next year, the LORD began to open my understanding to see things within *the miracles* of Yeshua that I had never seen before and I was so astonished by them!

As the LORD revealed these amazing details about His works and miracles to me, I began to write down every detail within this book. The Rod of God was sent for this purpose, to fulfill the Scriptures. The works of *the God of Israel in the Old Testament* are visible in the powerful miracles of Messiah Yeshua. The Rod of God that was sent to perform the miracles, signs and wonders of God, has no limitations. He can perform anything, even if it is beyond our human comprehension.

John 5:36-40 *But I have greater witness than that of John; for the works which the Father hath given Me to do, bear witness of Me, that the Father hath sent Me. And the Father Himself, which hath sent Me, hath borne witness of Me. Ye have neither heard His voice at any time, nor seen His shape. And ye have not His Word abiding in you; for whom He hath sent, Him ye believe not. Search the Scriptures; for in them ye think ye have eternal life; and they are they which testify of Me. And ye will not come to Me, that ye might have life.*

Since the Scriptures testify of Messiah Yeshua, this means that *the Torah* itself testifies of Him and we should understand Yeshua's works and miracles from *the Torah.* The follow sections include many of the fantastic Divine revelations that I received from the LORD about Yeshua's works and miracles as I worked on this project for His glory. I pray that you will be thrilled and shiver when you see them for the first time, as I did by Divine Providence!

THE MIRACLE OF FEEDING 5,000 WITH 5 LOAVES AND TWO FISH

5 Loaves & 2 Fish
Photos ©2013 Kimberly K Ballard All Rights Reserved

One of the greatest miracles that Messiah Yeshua performed took place in the wilderness, in a desert place. This is when Yeshua fed over 5,000 people of Israel with only 5 barley loaves and 2 small fish. The 5,000 men of Israel, plus the women and children, sat down to eat miraculously from the 5 loaves and two fish. Yeshua fed all of the people until they were content and full. The pieces or fragments that were left over from this Feast were gathered up into 12 baskets. The account of this miracle that I will show you is written in the Gospel of John and in the Gospel of Matthew.

John 6:1-15 *After these things Yeshua went over the Sea of Galilee, which is the sea of Tiberias. And a great multitude followed Him, because they saw His miracles which He did on them that were diseased. And Yeshua went up into a mountain, and there He sat with His disciples. And the Passover, a Feast of the Jews was nigh. When Yeshua then lifted up His eyes, and saw a great company come unto Him, He saith unto Philip, Whence shall we buy bread, that these may eat? And this He said to prove him; for He Himself knew what He would do. Philip answered Him, Two hundred pennyworth of bread is not sufficient for them, that every one of them may take a little. One of His disciples, Andrew, Simon Peter's brother, saith unto Him, There is a lad here, which hath five barley loaves and two small fishes; but what are they among so many? And Yeshua said, Make the men sit down. Now there was much grass in the place. So the men sat down in number about five thousand. And Yeshua took the loaves; and when He had given thanks, He distributed to the disciples, and the disciples to them that were set down; and likewise of the fishes as much as they would. When they were filled, He said unto His disciples, Gather up the fragments that remain, that nothing be lost. Therefore they gathered them together, and filled twelve baskets with the fragments of the five barley loaves, which remained over and above unto them that had eaten. Then those men, when they had seen the miracle that Yeshua did, said, This is of a truth that Prophet that should come into the world. When Yeshua therefore perceived that they would come and take Him by force, to make Him a King, He departed again into a mountain Himself alone.*

In this miracle, it was near Passover and the time of the barley harvest was at hand. The first wave sheaf of the barley harvest was cut, presented, and waved to the LORD, as the First Fruits offering, before the entire crop was harvested. Messiah lay in the tomb as the grain sacrifice on Nisan 16, when the wave sheaf was presented to the LORD God, as the First Fruits offering. He was glorified on the Feast of First Fruits on Nisan 17, while the rest of Messiah's crop would be harvested later. The Israelites, who miraculously ate from the five barley loaves

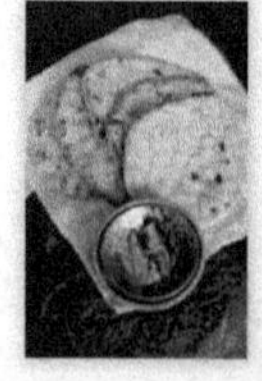

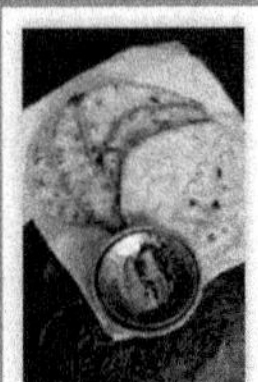

and the two fish by the hand of Yeshua, were also called *"first fruits"* unto God. To understand exactly what was happening in Yeshua's miracle, one must look in *the Torah!*

In the book of Numbers, in chapter 11, it speaks of *the fish* that the Israelites were longing to eat while they were in the wilderness. The situation was dire, so the Israelites were begging God to give them meat because they were sick and tired of eating the manna that the LORD had given to them to eat! Of course the manna was ground in mills, and with mortars, then used to make bread in the wilderness.

Numbers 11:4-6 *The riffraff in their midst felt a gluttonous craving; and then the Israelites wept, and said, If only we had meat to eat? We remember the fish, that we used to eat free in Egypt; the cucumbers, the melons, the leeks, the onions, and the garlic. Now our gullets are shriveled. There is nothing at all! Nothing but this manna to look to!*

So as we can see, the Israelites desired the flesh and meat of *fish* from the LORD. Again, in Numbers chapter 5, the Israelites complained to the LORD about not having flesh of meat to eat, and again they remembered *the fish* that they used to eat so freely in Egypt. This Scripture also speaks of the LORD, providing the manna for them to eat.

Numbers 5:1-18 *And when the people complained, it displeased the LORD; and the LORD heard it; and His anger was kindled; and the fire of the LORD burnt among them, and consumed them that were in the uttermost parts of the camp. And the people cried unto Moses; and when Moses prayed unto the LORD, the fire was quenched. And he called the name of the place Taberah; because the fire of the LORD burnt among them. And the mixt multitude that was among them fell a lusting: and the children of Israel also wept again, and said, Who shall give us flesh to eat? We remember the fish, which we did eat in Egypt freely; the cucumbers, and the melons, and the leeks, and the onions, and the garlic; But our soul is dried away; there is nothing at all, beside this manna, before our eyes. And the manna was as coriander seed, and the colour thereof as the colour of bdellium. And the people went about, and gathered it, and ground it in mills, or beat it in a mortar, and baked it in pans, and made cakes of it; and the taste of it was as the taste of fresh oil. And when the dew fell upon the camp in the night, the manna fell upon it. Then Moses heard the people weep throughout their families, every man in the door of his tent; and the anger of the LORD was kindled greatly; Moses also was displeased. And Moses said unto the LORD, Wherefore hast thou afflicted thy servant and wherefore have I not found favour in thy sight, that thou layest the burden of all this people upon me? Have I conceived all this people? Have I begotten them, that thou shouldest say unto me, Carry them in thy bosom, as a nursing father beareth the sucking child, unto the land which thou swarest unto their fathers? Whence should I have flesh to give unto all this people? For they weep unto me, saying, Give us flesh, that we may eat. I am not able to bear all this people alone, because it is too heavy for me. And if thou deal thus with me, kill me, I pray thee, out of hand, if I have found favour in thy sight; and let me not see my wretchedness. And the LORD said unto Moses, Gather unto me seventy men of the elders of Israel, whom thou knowest to be the elders of the people, and officers over them; and bring them unto the Tabernacle of the congregation, that they may stand there with thee. And I will come down and talk with thee there; and I will take of the Spirit which is upon thee, and will put it upon them; and they shall bear the burden of the people with thee, that thou bear it not thyself alone. And say thou unto the people, Sanctify yourselves against tomorrow, and ye shall eat flesh; for ye have wept in the ears of the LORD, saying, Who shall give us flesh to eat? For it was well with us in Egypt; therefore the LORD will give you flesh, and ye shall eat.*

Notice the Scripture says that, *"The LORD will give the children of Israel the flesh of meat to eat."* Moses also said, *"Whence should I have flesh to give unto all this people?"* Moses spoke these words just before the LORD fed the Israelites. The words of Moses are the same words that Yeshua spoke to Philip just before He fed the 5,000 plus Israelites with the flesh of fish, and with the 5 barley loaves of bread. So they should have recognized Yeshua and known exactly who it was that was feeding them! In this miracle, Yeshua revealed to Israel *that He is the hand of God* who provided the bread and meat for the children of Israel in the wilderness! Yeshua proclaimed the words of Moses and *He said this to prove Philip.* After Yeshua spoke these words, Yeshua miraculously fed the multitude until they were content.

John 6:5-6 *When Yeshua then lifted up His eyes, and saw a great company come unto Him, He saith unto Philip, Whence shall we buy bread, that these may eat? And this He said to prove him; for He Himself knew what He would do.*

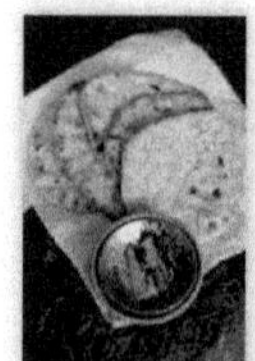

Incredibly, the LORD gave me a great revelation showing me the deep hidden meaning of this miracle, and I want to share it with you now! This miracle is not simply about Yeshua providing and multiplying enough food for everyone in a miraculous way from some child's lunch! I am so thrilled to say that the Holy Spirit has revealed the astonishing truth that is found within this miracle and I have presented what He showed me in the following words!

The five loaves of barley bread in Yeshua's miracle represent the Torah—the bread, the five books of Moses—given to the children of Israel by the LORD. The two fish represent the two tablets of the Law written in stone by the finger of God. They represent the meat and flesh given to the children of Israel by the LORD. So Yeshua was feeding the Israelites upon a mountain in a desert place with the elements of the Torah and the Law because Yeshua the LORD is the complete Living Torah and the Law of God. He is the true Spiritual Bread from Heaven and He is the pure flesh of meat. Messiah is the Yad and the finger of God as the Rod outstretched. In Yeshua's miracle, the five barley loaves and two fish add up to the number 7 and this is, of course, God's number of perfection and completion. The Israelites were being fed by the hand of the Good Shepherd, by the Rod of God, the Messiah, on the mountain in the desert place until they were content.

Five Loaves & Two Fish = the Living Torah & the Law of God - Photo ©2013 Kimberly K Ballard All Rights Reserved

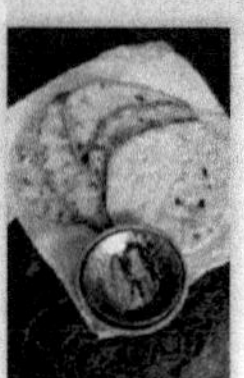
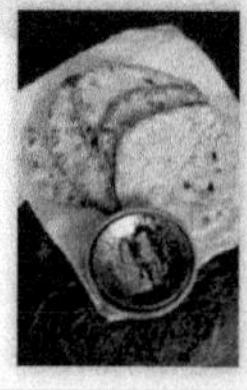

There is another hidden truth in this miracle. *The five barley loaves in Yeshua's miracle reveal that He is the Word of God, the Living Torah. So Yeshua is the Bread that came down from Heaven and this Bread is His flesh which is the true meat. This is the perfect Testimony that abides in the Ark of God in Heaven.* The finger of God, *Messiah Yeshua,* has written this Living Testimony upon our hearts and Yeshua said that if we eat this Living Bread of His flesh, *the true meat,* we will live forever.

Five Loaves & two fish = The Living Torah, Messiah the LORD

John 6:47-51 *Verily, verily, I say unto you, He that believeth on Me hath everlasting life. I AM that Bread of life. Your fathers did eat manna in the wilderness, and are dead. This is the Bread which cometh down from Heaven, that a man may eat thereof, and not die. I AM the Living Bread which came down from Heaven; if any man eat of this Bread, he shall live forever; and the Bread that I will give is My flesh, which I will give for the life of the world.*

They tempted God saying, *"Can He give bread and flesh of meat in the wilderness?"*

Psalm 78:18-20 *And they tempted God in their heart by asking meat for their lust. Yea, they spake against God; they said, Can God furnish a table in the wilderness? Behold, he smote the rock, that the waters gushed out, and the streams overflowed; can He give bread also? Can He provide flesh for His people?*

Yeshua spoke the Words that declare that He is the true kosher meat and the true kosher Living Bread that came down from Heaven, *the Living Torah* that gives Eternal life!

John 6:55-63 *For My flesh is meat indeed, and My blood is drink indeed. He that eateth My flesh, and drinketh My blood, dwelleth in Me, and I in him. As the Living Father hath sent Me, and I live by the Father; so he that eateth Me, even he shall live by Me. This is that Bread which came down from Heaven; not as your fathers did eat manna and are dead; he that eateth of this Bread shall live forever. These things said He in the Synagogue, as He taught in Capernaum. Many therefore of His disciples, when they had heard this, said, This is an hard saying; who can hear it? When Yeshua knew in Himself that His disciples murmured at it, He said unto them, Doth this offend you? What and if ye shall see the Son of man ascend up where He was before? It is the Spirit that quickeneth; the flesh profiteth nothing; the Words that I speak unto you, they are Spirit, and they are life.*

So when Yeshua performed this miracle, *the Bread from Heaven, the Staff of Life, the Rod of God,* prepared a table for His people in the wilderness and His identity was obvious. He was feeding the children of Israel from only five barley loaves and two small fish, a perfect number seven! After the 5,000+ were content and full, Yeshua had them collect all the left over pieces and there were twelve baskets full of fragments that were gathered up. The LORD showed me that the twelve baskets represent the remnant or the fragment of people that are leftover from the 12 tribes of Israel that have been scattered all over the world. In this miracle, Yeshua revealed that He is the Messiah who will gather up the 12 tribes of Israel and not one of them will be lost! This proves that the Good Shepherd is going to gather and feed His flock forever with His Rod Messiah Yeshua and not one of His sheep will be lost under the hand of the Good Shepherd of Israel! The Rod that saves the children of Israel will eternally provide them with the Living Torah, which is the true Spiritual meat and the true Spiritual hidden manna. He is a picture of completeness and perfection. In Him we are content and full. Death could not keep the Word of God in the grave because the seed of life from the Almond Tree of Life, which is the true Spiritual meat, was inside Him. This is an astonishing hidden truth that the LORD revealed miraculously to my heart! It is another key, revealing that Messiah Yeshua is the LORD God of Israel! The Messiah of Israel was the one who the LORD said *that He would raise up like unto Moses.* Yeshua was *raised up* as the Living Branch, fulfilling the Word of God.

At the end of this miracle, *after Yeshua fed the children of Israel in the wilderness*, lo and behold, *the Messiah, the LORD went up into a mountain to pray alone.* This is precisely what happened when the LORD was on Mount Sinai. On Mount Sinai He gave the Israelites the five books of Moses and the two tablets of the Law, the Ten Commandments written in stone with His finger. Then the LORD remained upon the mountain after giving them His Spiritual food. In our miracle, the LORD Messiah Yeshua, is upon the mountain alone after giving the Israelites the five loaves and the two fish. Yeshua's miracle was intended to reveal His identity to the children of Israel, *as the Living Torah.* As He said before, *"to see Him is to see the Father because this is one God who saves and feeds His sheep with His Rod!"*

Now in another miracle that was similar to this one, Yeshua fed the children of Israel with seven loaves and a few fishes. It is astonishing to see that this miracle also reveals the LORD God of Israel, working through His Rod, as Messiah Yeshua. This time, the Jewish disciples asked the same question that Moses asked the LORD. They wanted to know where they would get enough bread to feed all these people.

Matthew 15:33-39 *And His disciples say unto Him, Whence should we have so much bread in the wilderness, as to fill so great a multitude? And Yeshua saith unto them, How many loaves have ye? And they said, seven, and a few fishes. And He commanded the multitude to sit down on the ground. And He took the seven loaves and the fishes, and gave thanks, and brake them, and gave to His disciples to the multitude. And they did all eat, and were filled; and they took up of the broken meat that was left seven baskets full. And they that did eat were four thousand men, besides woman and children. And He sent away the multitude, <u>and took ship, and came into the Coasts of Magdala</u>.*

Starfish in the water Photo

Now I have to tell you that it is absolutely outstanding that the LORD showed me that *Yeshua took the ship and went to the Coasts of Magdala* after performing this miracle! Magdala was known for its fishing industry and *Yeshua went there after performing the miracle of the few fishes and the seven loaves! In Magdala, they just discovered and excavated the ancient Synagogue of Mary Magdalene!* Mary would have attended this particular Synagogue on Shabbat and this is the place where she went to listen to the Torah being preached! It is incredible to read that *Yeshua came to the Coasts of Magdala in a ship* and now I will show you the incredible reason why in the following pages!

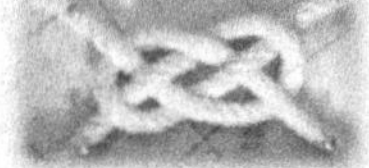

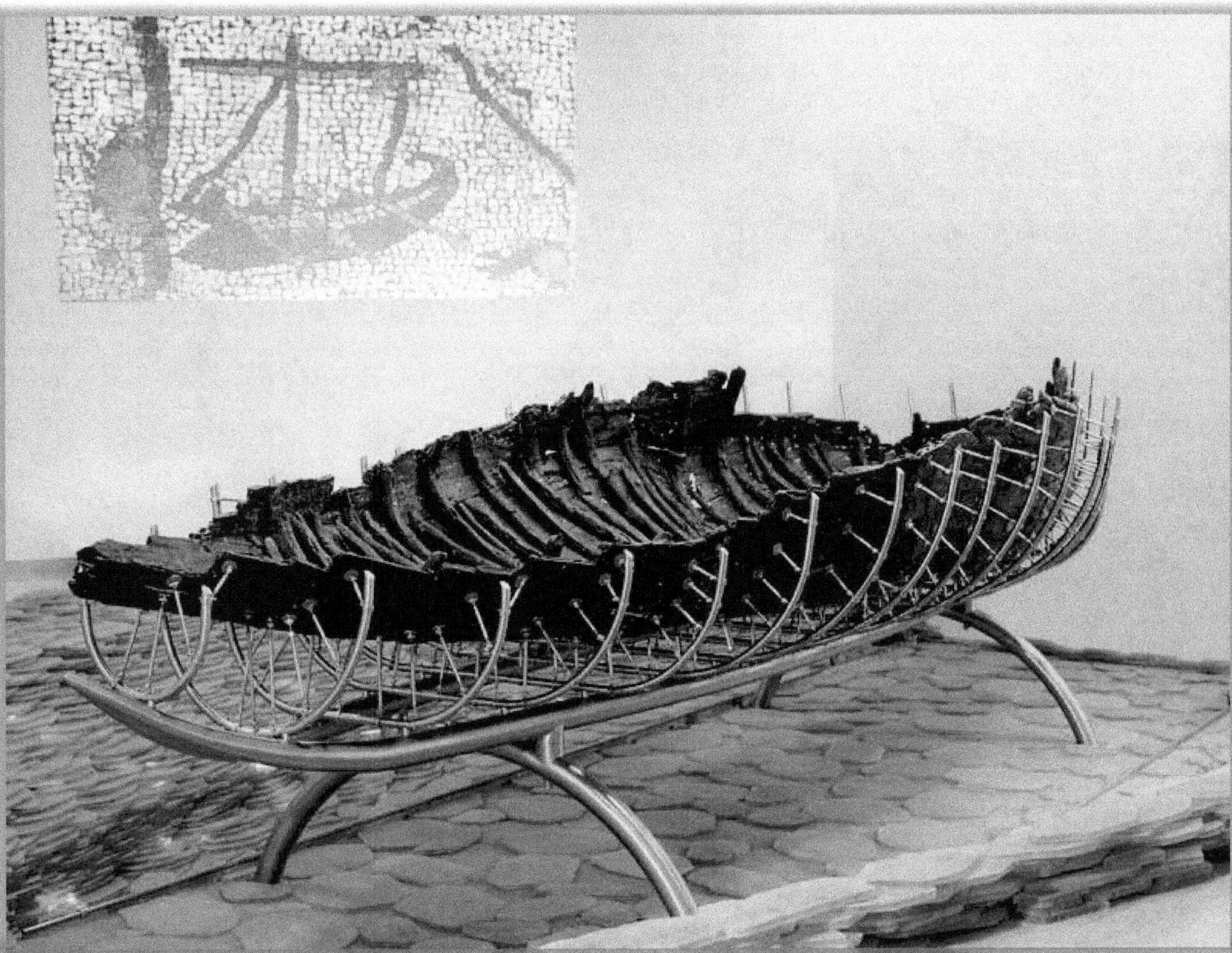

Official Photograph of "THE JESUS BOAT,"
©2013 The Yigal Allon Center, Ginosar Israel
All Rights Reserved

By a miracle of God, this ship was discovered & excavated
On the Coast of the Sea of Galilee,
Between Magdala and Ginosar Israel!

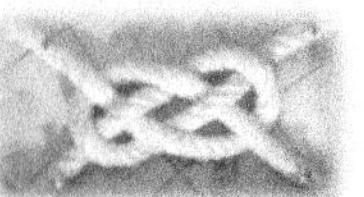

Messiah Yeshua was indeed speaking in this Synagogue that was just excavated in Magdala where they found the depiction of the *seven branched menorah beside the hearts etched on a stone,* revealing His Eternal Covenant of the heart! Incredibly, this place is also known as *"Migdol,"* which is the Hebrew root of *Magdala.*

The Official First Century Synagogue of Magdala that was recently excavated in Israel On the Coast the Sea of Galilee, where Yeshua came in, "THE JESUS BOAT" It was here that Yeshua was confronted by the Pharisees & Sadducees. This is where Yeshua gave them the sign of Jonah, proving that He is Israel's Messiah! Aerial photograph By David Silverman & Yuval Nadel For Magdala Center Excavations, Israel ©2013 All Rights Reserved

I just realized that *Messiah Yeshua was between Migdol and the Sea* when all of this transpired, when He miraculously fed the Israelites with the seven loaves and a few fishes. Right after this, Yeshua came walking towards the Jewish disciples in the ship on the water in the midst of the Sea at night! In Exodus 14:2, *the LORD God of Israel* told Moses to encamp *between Migdol and the Sea* with the Israelites, just before the Rod parted the Red Sea and they walked through the midst of the Sea and then the LORD gave them the flesh of meat and bread to eat until they were full in Exodus 16:8! We know for certain that Yeshua was in the

Synagogue in Magdala or Migdol because the Scripture goes on to tell us that it was here in this place that the Pharisees and Sadducees came and tempted Him, and this is where they desired that Yeshua would show them *a sign* from Heaven! It was here in *Magdala or Migdol* that Yeshua gave them the sign of Jonah, who was swallowed up by the great fish!

Official Photograph of, "The Magdala Synagogue," ©2009 Magdala Center Excavations Israel All Rights Reserved taken December 2009

It was here that Yeshua warned the disciples about the leaven of the Pharisees and the Sadducees. Then the disciples reasoned among themselves saying, *"It is because we have taken no bread."* The Scripture goes on to say the following about it. The Pharisees and Sadducees had a doctrine, but they did not yet have *the true Bread from Heaven, the Living Torah or the LORD God of Israel in the flesh, as their true meat!* Miraculously, the LORD had given me the revelations in this book (many about Mary Magdalene), while Mary Magdalene's Synagogue was being unearthed at the same time! He showed me *that Hezekiah's pool on Holy Mount Moriah, was also known as the "Amygdalon pool"* which is Greek for *"Almond Tree"* and means *Magdala or Migdol! So Mary Magdalene, who saw the budded Almond Tree of Life first at the Garden tomb, is named miraculously after the Almond Tree! The amygdala are also an almond shaped part of the limbic system of the brain connected to the emotions!*

Official Photograph taken October 2009, "The Magdala Stone" ©2009 Magdala Center Excavations Israel All Rights Reserved

The LORD revealed to me that the Magdala Stone would likely have been the Jewish "bimah," platform that stood in the center of the Synagogue. The Rabbi, in this case, would have been Messiah Yeshua, and I am now revealing that as He stood upon this platform to read the Torah Scroll in the *Synagogue of Magdala "the Living Torah was speaking to them" teaching them His Eternal life Covenant of the heart, as He fed them spiritually with the true Living Bread from Heaven, as the Living Almond Tree Menorah!* It is therefore the most astonishing find after nearly 2,000 years, and the fact that my revelations about it and Mary Magdalene came at the same time to tell this story, is a huge miracle of Biblical proportions!

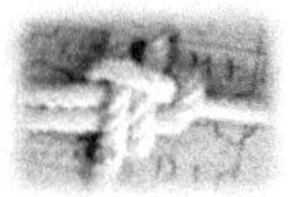

Matthew 16:8-12 *Which when Yeshua perceived, He said unto them, O ye of little faith, why reason ye among yourselves, because ye have brought no bread? Do you not yet understand, neither remember the five loaves of the five thousand, and how many baskets ye took up? Neither the seven loaves of the four thousand, and how many baskets ye took up? How is it that ye do not understand that I spake it not to you concerning bread that ye should beware of the leaven of the Pharisees and of the Sadducees? Then understood they how that He bade them not beware of the leaven of bread, but of the doctrine of the Pharisees and of the Sadducees.*

Then after all these things transpired, Yeshua went to the Coast of Caesarea Philippi and He asked the disciples who they believed that He was and Simon Peter declared that Yeshua was the Messiah, the Son of the Living God.

Now in the miracle, before Yeshua went in the ship to the Coasts of Magdala, He was in the wilderness area with the Israelites and He fed them with *the seven loaves, the bread and from a few fishes, the meat!* In both miracles, Yeshua made the bread and meat cleft, which is the LORD'S signature on all His works. Now this time, they ate until they were full and then they took up of the broken meat that was left, seven baskets full. In Genesis, during creation, the LORD spoke the following Words concerning the fishes.

Fish in reef with starfish Photo ©2013 Kimberly K Ballard All Rights Reserved

Genesis 9:2-3 *And the fear of you and the dread of you shall be upon every beast of the earth, and upon every foul of the air, upon all that moveth upon the earth, and upon all the fishes of the sea; into your hand are they delivered. Every moving thing that liveth shall be meat for you; even as the green herb have I given you all things.*

So the fishes represent *the meat* in Genesis. What this means is incredible! Job also revealed more to us about *the meaning of the fishes.*

Job 12:7-11 *But ask now the beasts, and they shall teach thee, and the fowls of the air, and they shall tell thee; Or speak to the earth, and it shall teach thee; <u>and the fishes of the sea shall declare unto thee; Who knoweth not in all these that the hand of the LORD hath wrought this?</u> In whose hand is the soul of every living thing, and the breath of all mankind. Doth not the ear try Words? And the mouth taste His meat?*

The Word of God is the meat, the Living Torah! *So in Yeshua's miracle, the few fishes of the sea are declaring unto you that this work is wrought from the hand of the LORD and as these events took place, Yeshua was between Migdol and the Sea with the Israelites!* This is where *"THE JESUS BOAT"* from the first century was discovered near Magdala, complete with a lamp and cooking pot. When they touched this boat for the first time, with Yeshua's permission in prayer, it began to rain from Heaven after a four year drought and a rare rainbow appeared in the sky over them! *(jesusboatmovie.com)*

Fish reef Photo ©2013 Kimberly K Ballard All Rights Reserved

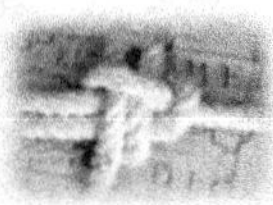
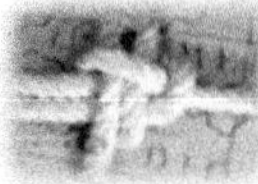

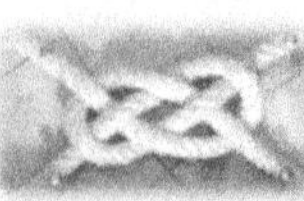

Official Photo "THE JESUS BOAT," ©2013 the Yigal Allon Center, Ginosar Israel All Rights Reserved

So how do we know for certain that this was the hand of the LORD in Yeshua's miracle that wrought this? *It says that the fishes shall tell you!*

In another miracle, *the fishes were miraculously given in abundance to the Jewish disciples of Yeshua!* After He performed this miracle, Yeshua fed them on the shore with the bread and with the meat of the flesh of fish, and it was waiting for them to eat after they returned to the shore in the ship. This occurred *the third time* that Yeshua appeared to them alive after He was raised to life, *and they knew it was the LORD* when they saw this miracle!

John 21:1-14 *After these things Yeshua shewed Himself again to the disciples at the Sea of Tiberius; and on this wise shewed He Himself. There were together Simon Peter, and Thomas called Didymus, and Nathanael of Cana in Galilee, and the sons of Zebedee, and two other of His disciples. Simon Peter saith unto them, I go fishing. They say unto him, We also go with thee. They went forth, and entered into a ship immediately; and that night they caught nothing. But when the morning was now come, Yeshua stood on the shore; but the disciples knew not that it was Yeshua. Then Yeshua saith unto them, Children, have ye any meat? They answered Him, No. And He said unto them, Cast the net on the right side of the ship, and ye shall find. They cast therefore, and now they were not able to draw it for the multitude of fishes. Therefore that disciple whom Yeshua loved saith unto Peter, It is the LORD. Now when Simon Peter heard that it was the LORD, he girt his fisher's coat unto him, for he was naked, and did cast himself into the sea. And the other disciples came in a little ship; for they were not far from land, but as it were two hundred cubits, dragging the net with fishes. As soon then as they were come to land, they saw a fire of coals there, and fish laid thereon, and bread. Yeshua saith unto them, Bring of the fish which ye have now caught. Simon Peter went up, and drew the net to land full of great fishes, an hundred and fifty and three; and for all there were so many,*

yet was not the net broken. Yeshua saith unto them, Come and dine. And none of the disciples durst ask Him, Who art Thou? Knowing that it was the LORD. Yeshua then cometh, and taketh bread, and giveth them, and fish likewise. This is now the third time that Yeshua shewed Himself to His disciples, after that He was risen from the dead.

Model Ship Photo ©2014 Kimberly K Ballard All Rights Reserved

In this miracle, Yeshua appeared alive on the shore and He called out to the children of Israel, *"Children, have ye any meat?"* So what did Yeshua do? When they said, *"No,"* Yeshua told them to put their net on the right side of the ship. When they followed His command, a multitude of fishes were caught in their net and they realized it was the LORD. Remember that the Rod is in the right hand of God and so Messiah Yeshua produced a multitude of fishes on the right side of the ship. Yeshua provided a table in the wilderness on the shore with the bread and with the meat of fishes and He told them to come and dine with Him. So Yeshua's miracle confirmed the words of Job that declared *"The fishes of the sea shall declare unto thee, who knoweth not in all these that the hand of the LORD hath wrought this?"* This miracle revealed that Yeshua is the Yad, the right hand of God, who miraculously fed His sheep with all the fishes and bread that they desired that day! They pulled up a multitude of fishes in their net from the right side of the ship and they brought it to the shore. In the hand of the LORD is the soul of every living thing and the breath comes from Him by His Ruach/Holy Spirit. Messiah Yeshua, who is the Word that became flesh and dwelt among us, revealed again in this miracle that He is the true Bread and the true flesh of meat in the miracle of the multitude of fishes. So He asked them to come and dine with Him because He is *the Living Torah* and the Good Shepherd who feeds them. *So I was astonished then that "THE JESUS BOAT" was actually saved by a few gold fishes that protected it from destruction after it was removed from the Sea of Galilee! The fishes saved "THE JESUS BOAT" for this revelation!*

Ship Photo ©2014 Kimberly K Ballard All Rights Reserved

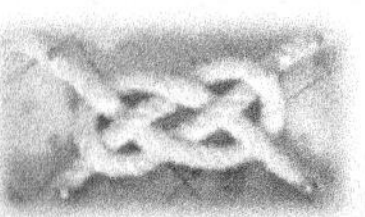

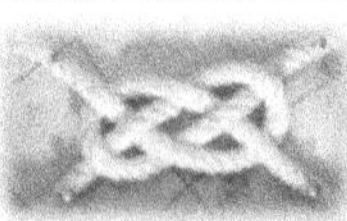

Official Photo of, "THE JESUS BOAT," ©2013 the Yigal Allon Center, Ginosar Israel All Rights Reserved

In another astonishing miracle, the people of Israel came to hear the Word of God spoken *by Yeshua as He sat in the ship.* The people sat on the land, but Yeshua was sitting in the boat. The thrilling part of this miracle is that I realized that the ship Yeshua was sitting in was a type of Ark. Noah was saved in the ship, the Ark, and Moses was saved in a type of Ark, in a basket of reeds that floated upon the surface of the waters of the Nile River. *I suddenly understood that Yeshua was the Living Torah sitting inside an Ark, floating on the surface of the waters, while preaching the Word of God to the children of Israel who were standing upon the dry land!* After the people listened to Yeshua speaking the Word of God from the ship, Yeshua then immediately told Simon Peter to launch out into the deep and to let his nets down for a draught. Simon Peter explained that they had toiled all night and had caught nothing. *Nevertheless, Simon Peter said, "But at Your Word, I will let down the net." As Simon Peter said this to the Living Torah, suddenly the nets were so full that a second ship had to be brought near to hold all the multitude of the fishes that they had caught.* When Simon Peter realized that this was the LORD, he fell at Yeshua's knees and begged Him for forgiveness for

not believing and for being a sinful man. *After the two ships began to sink from the vast multitude of the catch of fishes, they brought the ships to the shore* and the Scripture says *"They forsook it all and followed Yeshua," I realized that they forsook it all to follow the Heavenly Ark!* The account of this miracle is written in the Gospel of Luke. This is one more miraculous event that proves Job's statement that declared, *"The fishes of the sea shall declare unto you that the hand of the LORD hath wrought this."* Yeshua was the Rod in the right hand of God, performing this elaborate work with the multitude of fishes when He spoke the Word, *the Living Torah* out of His mouth! *Perhaps Simon Peter's boat was left in place as it sank!*

Luke 5:1-11 *And it came to pass, that, as the people pressed upon Him to hear the Word of God, He stood by the lake of Gennesaret, And saw two ships standing by the lake; but the fishermen were gone out of them, and were washing their nets. And He entered into one of the ships, which was Simon's, and prayed him that he would thrust out a little from the land. And He sat down, and taught the people out of the ship. Now when He had left speaking, He said unto Simon, Launch out into the deep, and let down your nets for a draught. And Simon answering said unto Him, Master, we have toiled all night, and have taken nothing; nevertheless at Thy Word I will let down the net. And when they had this done, they inclosed a great multitude of fishes; and their net brake. And they beckoned unto their other ship, that they should come and help them. And they came, and filled both the ships, so that they began to sink. When Simon Peter saw it, he fell down at Yeshua's knees, saying, Depart from me; for I am a sinful man, O LORD. For he was astonished, and all that were with him, at the draught of the fishes which they had taken; And so was also James, and John, the sons of Zebedee, which were partners with Simon. And Yeshua said unto Simon, Fear not; from henceforth thou shalt catch men. And when they had brought their ships to land, they forsook all, and followed Him.*

So now that we understand the deeper meaning of all the miracles of the fishes, we can now understand the miracle of the seven loaves and the meat of a few fishes. The LORD revealed to me that this miracle actually reveals the LORD'S Passover. *The seven loaves that they ate in Yeshua's miracle represent the seven days of eating only unleavened bread, during the LORD'S Passover.* Messiah Yeshua would be placed inside Holy Mount Moriah on the Feast of Unleavened Bread and raised to life as the First Fruits of the harvest of those who are given Eternal life in God's Garden. Remember that Yeshua is the second Adam full of the Ruach/Holy Spirit, *the Living Torah*, who had no leaven or sin in Him.

Exodus 12:15-27 *Seven days shall ye eat unleavened bread; even the first day ye shall put away leaven out of your houses; for whosoever eateth leavened bread from the first day to the seventh day, that soul shall be cut off from Israel. And in the first day there shall be an holy convocation, and in the seventh day there shall be an holy convocation to you; no manner of work shall be done in them, save that which every man must eat, that only may be done of you. And ye shall observe the feast of unleavened bread; for in this selfsame day have I brought your armies out of the land of Egypt; therefore shall ye observe this day in your generations by an ordinance forever. In the first month, on the fourteenth day of the month at even, ye shall eat unleavened bread, until the one and twentieth day of the month at even. Seven days shall there be no leaven found in your houses; for whosoever eateth that which is leavened, even that soul shall be cut off from the congregation of Israel, whether he be a stranger, or born in the land. Ye shall eat nothing leavened; in all your habitations shall ye eat unleavened bread. Then Moses called for all the elders of Israel, and said unto them, Draw out and take you a lamb according to your families, and kill the Passover. And ye shall take a bunch of hyssop, and dip it in the blood that is in the bason, and strike the lintel and the two side posts with the blood that is in the bason; and none of you shall go out at the door of his house until the morning. For the LORD will pass through to smite the Egyptians; and when He seeth the blood upon the lintel, and on the two side posts, the LORD will pass over the door, and will not suffer the destroyer to come in unto your houses to smite you. And ye shall observe this thing for an ordinance to thee and to thy sons forever. And it shall come to pass, when ye be come to the land which the LORD will give you, according as He hath promised, that ye shall keep this service. And it shall come to pass, when your children shall say unto you, What mean ye by this service? That ye shall say, It is the sacrifice of the LORD'S Passover, who passed over, the houses of the children of Israel in Egypt, when He smote the Egyptians, and delivered our houses. And the people bowed the head and worshipped.*

Now Yeshua took the seven loaves and a few fishes and made them cleft, the signature of the LORD. They ate until they were filled and it says that they took up of the broken meat

that was left, seven baskets full. In order to understand the deeper meaning that is hidden in Yeshua's miracle, we first have to look at the following Scripture.

I Corinthians 11:23-24 *For I have received of the LORD that which also I delivered unto you, That the LORD Yeshua the same night in which He was betrayed took bread; And when he had given thanks, He brake it, and said, Take, eat; this is My body, which is broken for you; this do in remembrance of Me.*

So in the miracle of feeding the 4,000, Yeshua revealed Himself as *the broken meat in the seven baskets,* meaning that He is the number seven. He is the Lamb that God provided for us, full of completion and perfection, because this was the final Living Testimony of God, and this is why Yeshua declared on the cross as He was lifted up, *"It is finished."* Messiah's body is the broken meat that is given to us and this is the Unleavened Bread that is broken in the Passover Seder. As many of us know, His body is wrapped as the hidden Manna that is secreted away and buried in linen at the Passover Seder. *This piece of Matzah is special, and after it is found and removed from the linen Shroud, everyone rejoices and partakes of it!* It represents the Living Torah made cleft. We are to remember that it is the sacrifice of the LORD'S Passover. *Perhaps the most astonishing truth in Yeshua's miracle of the seven loaves of bread and the seven baskets of broken meat is the fact that the two sevens in this miracle add up to a complete number 14. Nisan 14, on the Hebrew Biblical Calendar, is the very day that Yeshua became the perfect meat as the Passover Lamb who was sacrificed as the offering for us on Mount Moriah, and this took place during the Feast of Unleavened Bread.* The miracles that Yeshua performed are indeed the works of the hand of God. *It is true that as the Living Torah, He is the Heavenly Unleavened Bread, a perfect seven, and He is the Heavenly Spiritual meat, another perfect seven. His Testimony therefore adds up to 14, and He sealed His Covenant with his disciples on Nisan 14, during the Passover Seder.* His Living Testimony is a complete and perfect Covenant that is sealed upon the doorposts of the two tablets of our heart with His life blood as the Lamb of God, and death passes over us, so that we will have Eternal life in the Heavenly Kingdom of God. For this reason, the wrath of God passes over us!

This is the Rod in the right hand of God that completed the work and performed this miracle and they ate and they were content. In this miracle, *the LORD God of Israel was dwelling in their midst as the Messiah of Israel* and He was feeding the children of Israel!

Now there are three more connections to the Messiah regarding the number 14, and they emerge in the genealogical record of Yeshua. The number 14 pertains three times to the generations that lived before the arrival of the Messiah. These three testify that Yeshua is the Lamb who died on Nisan 14 and was resurrected the third day, as the Fruitful Branch from the Almond Tree of Life. It represents the three cups on the Holy Menorah with seven branches.

Matthew 1:17 *So all the generations from Abraham to David are <u>fourteen</u> generations; and from David until the carrying away into Babylon are <u>fourteen</u> generations; and from the carrying away into Babylon unto Messiah are <u>fourteen</u> generations.*

Matzah Unleavened Bread
Photo ©2014

Yeshua told the children of Israel that they should work for the Bread that does not spoil. The manna in the wilderness that the LORD provided was only temporary so it did spoil. They could not store it for any length of time. The children of Israel were given the earthly manna that perished because it was only a shadow of the true Bread from Heaven. The Word of God that comes down out of Heaven, the Messiah, *is the permanent Living Torah* that Israel and all believers eat because He is the Bread that never perishes. In the following Scripture, Yeshua reveals that His flesh is *the Living Torah,* the Bread and flesh of meat, sealed as the Eternal Covenant with His life blood on Passover.

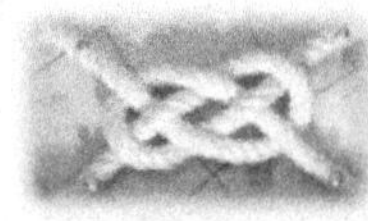

John 6:53-59 *Yeshua therefore said to them, Truly, truly, I say to you, unless you eat the flesh of the Son of Man and drink His blood, you have no life in yourselves. He who eats My flesh and drinks My blood has eternal life, and I will raise him up on the last day. For My flesh is true food, and My blood is true drink, He who eats My flesh and drinks My blood abides in Me, and I in him. As the living Father sent Me, and I live because of the Father, so he who eats Me, he also shall live because of Me. This is the Bread which came down from Heaven; not as the fathers ate, and died, he who eats this Bread shall live forever. These things He said in the Synagogue, as He taught in Capernaum.*

The seven loaves also remind us that the LORD is the LORD of the 7th day Sabbath when He rested from all His work that He created.

The seven baskets of broken meat of *the fishes* of Yeshua's miracle tell us again that *"the hand of the LORD has wrought this work!"* In Exodus, it was the LORD who had given Israel both the meat and the manna and they saw the glory of God in it. *The LORD said that He heard the murmurings of the children of Israel and at evening, they should eat flesh and in the morning, they should be filled with bread. When Yeshua died on the cross it was evening and when He was resurrected as the Living Branch, the women came to the tomb very early in the morning, only to discover that the Living Branch had already come to life. The LORD had told them that in the morning, "You shall see the glory of the LORD," and at the Garden tomb in Mount Moriah, in the morning, the women did see the glory of the LORD!* At Mount Sinai, after they ate the flesh in the evening and the bread in the morning, the LORD said, *"And you shall know that I AM the LORD your God!"* So Yeshua was clearly revealing, *"I AM the LORD your God,"* when He fulfilled these miracles!

Exodus 16:7-12 *And in the morning, then ye shall see the glory of the LORD; for that he heareth your murmurings against the LORD; and what are we, that ye murmur against us? And Moses said, This shall be, when the LORD shall give you in the evening flesh to eat, and in the morning bread to the full; for that the LORD heareth your murmurings which ye murmur against Him; and what are we? Your murmurings are not against us, but against the LORD. And Moses spake unto Aaron, Say unto all the congregation of the children of Israel, come near before the LORD; for He hath heard your murmurings. and it came to pass, as Aaron spake unto the whole congregation of the children of Israel, that they looked toward the wilderness, and, behold, the glory of the LORD appeared in the cloud. And the LORD spake unto Moses saying, I have heard the murmurings of the children of Israel; speak unto them, saying, At even ye shall eat flesh, and in the morning ye shall be filled with bread; and ye shall know that I AM the LORD your God. As the LORD commanded Moses, so Aaron laid it up before the Testimony, to be kept, And the children of Israel did eat manna forty years, until they came to a land inhabited; they did eat manna, until they came to the borders of the land of Canaan. Now an omer is the tenth part of an ephah.*

An omer, which is a tenth part of an ephah of this manna, was laid up before the Testimony to be kept. It was only a pattern of the true Living Bread and meat that is laid up before the Living Testimony of Messiah Yeshua in the Eternal Heavenly Ark. The same question that Yeshua asked Philip, about where they would get bread enough for all the people, is also the same question that is asked in II Kings 4 with Elisha.

II Kings 4:42-44 *And there came a man from Ba'al-shalisha, and brought the man of God bread of the first fruits, twenty loaves of barley, and full ears of corn in the husk thereof. And he said, Give unto the people, that they may eat. And his servitor said, What, should I set this before and hundred men? He said again, Give the people, that they may eat; for thus saith the LORD, They shall eat, and shall leave thereof.*

In this case, the barley bread of the first fruits was their bread. Yeshua was raised to life on the Feast of First Fruits, and in this case, the LORD said to let them eat and leave what was left over, and this is what happened in Yeshua's miracle when they ate until they were full. Yeshua had them collect all the left over pieces of the barley bread and the meat. The fragments were gathered up in the 12 baskets and in the seven baskets. Clearly those who ate the bread and meat in Yeshua's miracle were to be the *first fruits* unto the God of Israel. The LORD'S intervention in the wilderness, by providing the Israelites with the meat, the two

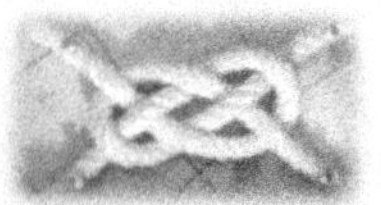

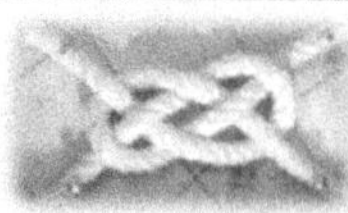

tablets of the Law of God, and with the manna, the unleavened bread, the five books of Moses, were only a shadow of the Messiah. The LORD God of Israel is the Messiah, who is represented in the five loaves and in the two fish that add up to seven, the number of completion and perfection!

Now the LORD also showed me that this was revealed when Martha received Yeshua into her house, and this story is found in Luke's account.

Luke 11:38-42 *Now it came to pass, as they went, that He entered into a certain village; and a certain woman named Martha received Him into her house. And she had a sister called Mary, which also sat at Yeshua's feet, and heard His Word. But Martha was cumbered about much serving, and came to Him, and said, LORD, dost Thou not care that my sister hath left me to serve alone? Bid her therefore that she help me. And Yeshua said unto her, Martha, Martha, thou art careful and troubled about many things; But one thing is needed; and Mary hath chosen that good part, which shall not be taken away from her.*

What did Mary have that was the one thing that was needed, that Martha did not have yet? Mary sat at Yeshua's feet and she heard His Word. *Mary had chosen the Living Torah, the true Spiritual food from Heaven, but Martha was busy serving earthly food!* Mary had chosen the Unleavened Bread from Heaven, the pure meat, but Martha was too busy serving earthly food to pay Spiritual attention to the Words that were coming from *the Living Torah!* It is astonishing to see this truth for the first time, but the miracle did not end with this one! Next, there is another miracle that proved the identity of the LORD even further.

In 1973, the ossuary of Mary and Martha was discovered in a first century Jewish Christian burial cave near Bethany, near Jerusalem, on the Mount of Olives. Their brother Lazarus was also found buried in this location, as well as Simon Bar Jonah or Simon Peter, who was buried only meters away from the other believers in Messiah Yeshua. The ossuaries that were found in this location were dated to the first century and some of the ossuaries were etched with the sign of the cross and with the Name *"Yeshua"* because they knew that one day they would be resurrected by Him in the future! They were His faithful friends!

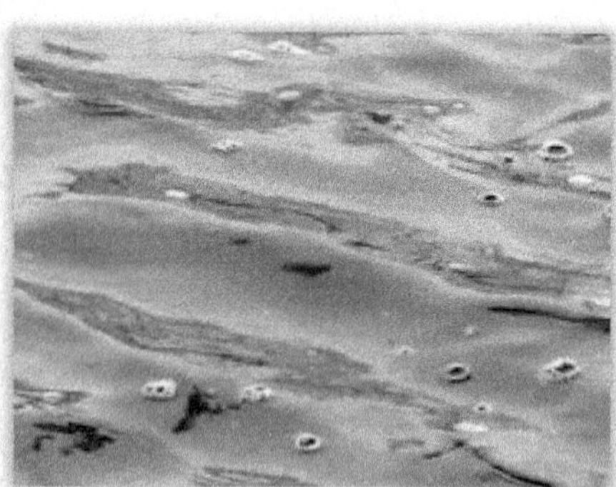

THE MIRACLE OF YESHUA WALKING ON THE WATER

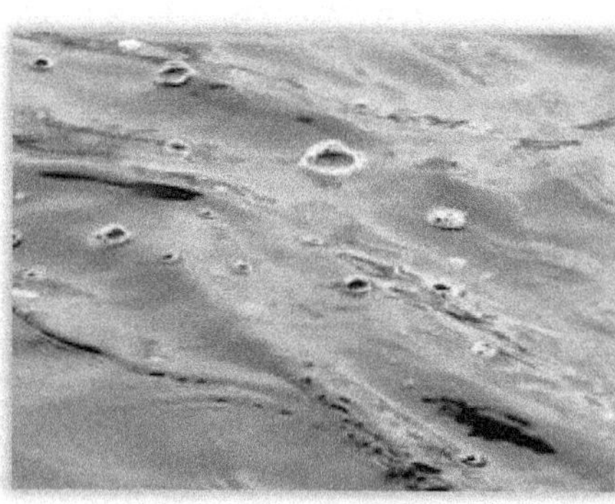

The next exciting miracle happened just after Yeshua miraculously fed the 5,000+ Israelites with the 5 loaves and the 2 fish. He went up alone to the mountain to pray, and the Jewish disciples departed in the ship immediately following this miracle. What happened next was simply astonishing! The Jewish disciples were in the ship and a storm began to toss them about as the wind blew the waves contrary to them. It was the fourth watch of the night and they were in the midst of the sea in the ship. Suddenly, when the Jewish disciples looked up, they saw Yeshua coming towards them in the midst of the sea, walking on the water! This is an

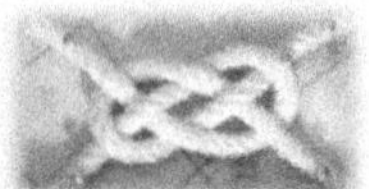

absolutely astounding miracle that has such an incredible deep meaning! What the Holy Spirit revealed to me about this miracle is so thrilling because similar miracles took place with the LORD at the Red Sea crossing, in the wilderness, and at Mount Sinai. By a great and mighty miracle, the Rod of God, full of the power of the Ruach/Holy Spirit, saved them through the midst of the Red Sea at night, and the LORD gave the Israelites the five books of Moses, the five loaves of unleavened bread, the Torah and the two tablets of the Law, the meat. I am so excited about this particular miracle of Yeshua!

In order to fully understand the profound meaning in this miracle, you must start at the very beginning in Genesis! The first chapter of Genesis in the Torah is the key to understanding Yeshua walking on the water on the Sea of Galilee!

3D Hologram of the Shroud of Turin ©2013 Dr Petrus Soons from ©1931 Enrie Photographs
3D Hologram Edited to demonstrate Messiah Yeshua walking on the water on the Sea of Galilee
These are the waves of the Sea of Monterey California Photo ©2013 Kimberly K Ballard All Rights Reserved

Genesis 1:1-5 *In the beginning God created the Heaven and the earth. And the earth was without form, and void; and darkness was upon the face of the deep. And the Spirit of God moved upon the face of the waters. And God said, Let there be light; and there was light. And God saw the light, that it was good; and God divided the light from the darkness. And God called the light day, and the darkness He called night. And the evening and the morning were the first day.*

Reading this text carefully, we are told that *"in the beginning, darkness was over the face of the deep," and "The darkness, the LORD called "night."* So we can see that while it was *"dark and night," the Holy Spirit of God moved upon the face of the waters.* The LORD revealed to me that Messiah Yeshua, the Rod of God, came walking on the face of the waters at night on the Sea of Galilee, because He was full of the Ruach/Holy Spirit of God! So in this miracle, Messiah Yeshua, moved on the face of the waters during the fourth watch of the night. Remember that just as it was in the beginning in Genesis, it was night and darkness was all around the ship as the disciples were rowing. Suddenly the Jewish disciples in the ship in the midst of the Sea looked up, and they saw *the Rod of God, full of the light of the glory of God, coming towards them on the face of the waters!* In this miracle, Yeshua revealed that He existed in the very beginning and that the soul of every living thing was created by Him. Now at the Red Sea crossing, we can see that the LORD saved Israel at night, through the midst of the waters of the Sea. When Moses stretched out his hand, he was lifting up the Almond branch rod over the Sea, at night. The rod, full of the Holy Spirit of God was lifted up and the rod caused the waters to be divided and the Israelites passed through the midst of the Sea at night on dry land. It was the power of the breath of the Ruach/Holy Spirit on the Rod of God that saved Israel. So the crossing of the Red Sea is the same miracle that happened in Genesis, when the Holy Spirit moved on the face of the waters at night, and again, later, it is the same miracle that happened when Yeshua walked on the face of the waters at night. It is incredible to see that all three of these events are the same!

Exodus 15:21-22 *And Moses stretched out his hand over the sea; and the LORD caused the sea to go back by a strong east wind all that night, and made the sea dry land, and the waters were divided. And the children of Israel went into the midst of the sea upon the dry ground; and the waters were a wall unto them on their right hand, and on their left.*

Pacific Ocean Wave Spray Monterey California
Photo ©2014 Kimberly K Ballard All Rights Reserved

Messiah Yeshua performed this miracle on the Sea after feeding the Israelites with the 5 loaves and 2 fish, with the Living Torah! He immediately showed them His power as the Rod of God, full of His Ruach/Holy Spirit, and as the glorious light in the midst of the darkness, and He was the firmament in their midst! We can see the account of this story in the Gospel of Mark. This time, Yeshua sent the disciples away in the ship and He told them to go to *Bethsaida.* The name *"Bethsaida"* means *"House of fishing."* Like Magdala or Migdol, Bethsaida was a fishing village. When Yeshua sent them away in the ship to Bethsaida, Yeshua then came to them walking on the water. This proved the words of Job again that declared, *"The fishes shall declare to you that hand of the LORD hath wrought this."* The word *"wrought" means an "elaborate work"* that was created by the hand of the LORD. So Yeshua not only proved He was the Rod of God in this miracle, but also He proved that He is the Yad, *the right hand of the power of God,* full of the breath of His Ruach/Holy Spirit.

Pacific Ocean Wave crashing on the rocks Monterey California & Nautical Rope Photos

Mark 6:41-54 *And when He had taken the five loaves and the two fishes, He looked up to Heaven, and blessed, and brake the loaves, and gave them to His disciples to set before them; and the two fishes divided He among them all. And they did all eat, and were filled. And they took up twelve baskets of fragments, and of the fishes. And they that did eat of the loaves were about five thousand men. And straightway He constrained his disciples to get into the ship; and to go to the other side before unto Bethsaida, while He sent away the people. And when He had sent them away, He departed to the mountain to pray. And when evening was come, the ship was in the midst of the sea, and He alone on the land. And He saw them toiling in rowing; for the wind was contrary unto them; and about the fourth watch of the night He cometh unto them, walking upon the sea, and would have passed by them. But when they saw Him walking upon the sea, they supposed it had been a spirit and cried out; For they all saw Him, and were troubled. And immediately He talked with them, and saith unto them, Be of good cheer; it is I; be not afraid. And He went up unto them into the ship; and the wind ceased; and they were sore amazed in themselves beyond measure, and wondered. For they considered not the miracle of the loaves; for their heart was hardened. And when they had passed over, they came into the land of Gennesaret, and drew to the shore. And when they were come out of the ship, straightway they knew Him.*

The Jewish disciples were amazed and wondered within their hearts at these astounding miracles. But the verse tells us specifically that *"they considered not, the miracle of the loaves, for their heart was hardened."* In other words, the miracle of the five loaves and the two fish was connected to the following miracle of the Rod of God walking on the surface of the Sea and to *the LORD being between Migdol and the Sea!* When they saw Yeshua walking upon the

Sea, they supposed it had been *a spirit* and they cried out. This is the clue that reveals the Messiah was full of the Holy Spirit of God and they were afraid and cried out! It is interesting that the Jewish disciples used the word *"spirit"* and did not use the word *"ghost"* when they saw Yeshua walking on the face of the waters. I feel this is very important because the definition of a *"spirit"* is an actual reference to *"The Living Holy Spirit."* It is exciting that I also discovered that the word *"spirit"* also means *"the soul or heart, as the seat of feelings or sympathies." The LORD has a heart and His Holy Spirit is the seat of His feelings and sympathies!*

II Chronicles 7:16 *For I have chosen and sanctified this house, that My Name may be there forever; and Mine eyes and Mine heart shall be there perpetually.*

If we grieve the Holy Spirit, then we are actually grieving the LORD'S heart. By contrast, the Jewish disciples did not see a *"ghost"* which by definition is *"the soul of a dead person."* This is why I believe it is wrong to refer to God's Spirit as a holy ghost. He is not the God of the dead, but the God of the Living. So His Spirit is life! What I find absolutely thrilling about this is that the Hebrew term for the Holy Spirit is *"Ruach HaKodesh."* The Hebrew word *"Ruach"* literally means *"Breath" or "Wind."* So remember the words of Job that said, *"In whose hand is the soul of every living thing, and the breath of all mankind?"* Messiah the Yad, the hand of God, full of the Holy Spirit, breathes in our soul, Eternal life. Perhaps the most overlooked part of this miracle is the fact that the wind was contrary to those rowing in the ship, but as soon as Yeshua entered the ship with them, the wind miraculously ceased! What happened at the Red Sea crossing? The LORD caused the Sea to go back by a strong east wind all that night as the power of Holy Spirit on the Rod performed this miracle. The Jewish disciples were all amazed beyond measure that Yeshua could control the elements of the wind and that He caused the Sea and the waves to be calm. They saw firsthand as eyewitnesses that the power of the Holy Spirit was abiding inside Yeshua, and that He is the Rod in the right hand of God. He was the light that came to them in the ship while they were in the midst of the darkness, and the wind ceased at His Word, as *the Living Torah* spoke! It is spectacular! Remember that *the firmament is a support* so that one does not sink, fall or slip!

In the Book of Exodus, the blast of the nostrils of the LORD made the waters to gather and stand up as a heap in the Sea. This was the breath of the Holy Spirit of the LORD, controlling the Sea. He gives life by breathing His breath into all creation. In the following Scripture, *it was the LORD who controlled the wind and the power was in the Rod,* in the right hand of God.

Exodus 15:6-12 *Thy right hand, O LORD, is become glorious in power; Thy right hand, O LORD, hath dashed in pieces the enemy. And in the greatness of Thine Excellency thou hast overthrown them that rose up against Thee; Thou sentest forth Thy wrath, which consumed them as stubble. And with the blast of Thy nostrils the waters were gathered together, the floods stood upright as an heap, and the depths were congealed in the heart of the sea. The enemy said, I will pursue, I will overtake, I will divide the spoil; my lust shall be satisfied upon them; I will draw my sword, my hand shall destroy them. Thou didst blow with Thy wind, the sea covered them; they sank as lead in the mighty waters. Who is like unto Thee, O LORD, among the gods? Who is like Thee, glorious in holiness, fearful in praises, doing wonders? Thou stretchedst out Thy right hand, the earth swallowed them.*

So Exodus tells us that *"the right hand of the LORD saves and controls the wind."* Yeshua controlled the wind and it ceased when He spoke *the Word* with His breath. When the Jewish disciples in the ship saw Messiah Yeshua coming toward them on the surface of the waters in the midst of the Sea at night while the darkness was all around, they should have understood immediately that Yeshua was the one who was with the children of Israel walking across the midst of the Red Sea when the rod was lifted up in the hand of Moses. The Rod of

God went before them, as the wind and breath of the Ruach/Holy Spirit made a pathway before them. They believed by faith, and followed after the Rod of salvation, their Messiah!

In another astounding miracle, Yeshua was in the ship with the disciples and Yeshua rebuked the wind and the wind ceased because the Holy Spirit was inside Him! In this situation, the Jewish disciples asked Yeshua *if He cared whether or not they were perishing! So in this situation Yeshua was the Rod and the Living Torah in the Heavenly Ark moving on the surface of the waters that saved them from perishing! The Royal Standard of God was in their midst!*

Mark 4:35-41 *And the same day, when the even was come, He saith unto them, Let us pass over unto the other side. And when they had sent away the multitude, they took Him even as He was in the ship. And there were also with Him other little ships. And there arose a great storm of wind, and the waves beat into the ship, so that it was now full. And He was in the hinder part of the ship, asleep on a pillow; and they awake Him, and say unto Him, Master, carest Thou not that we perish? And He arose, and rebuked the wind, and said unto the sea, Peace, be still. And the wind ceased, and there was a great calm. And He said unto them, Why are ye so fearful? How is it that ye have no faith? And they feared exceedingly, and said one to another, What manner of man is this, that even the wind and the sea obey Him?*

I believe they feared exceedingly because they suddenly understood that *this was the LORD God of Israel* who moved on the face of the waters at night when He said, *"Let there be light!" They questioned one another, asking who this was that could make the wind and the Sea obey Him.* It is the fantastic hidden truth about this miracle!

This miracle explains more about our baptism in Messiah Yeshua. We are baptized in the Living Water and we cast our sins into the sea. We come out of the darkness spiritually and into the light of the LORD and receive His Ruach/Holy Spirit. When we are baptized in the Messiah's baptism, His Ruach/Holy Spirit moves on the Living Waters, as we go down into the darkness of the Sea, and He washes away the darkness that is in our heart. As we come up out of the Living Water, we receive His Ruach/Spirit that breathes the breath of life into our soul and He gives us His life-giving Spirit. Our sins are therefore washed away in the depths of the Sea, and His Ruach/Spirit now lives within our heart and He brings our heart into the LORD'S marvelous light! I feel so blessed that the LORD gave me the understanding to see this truth! Yeshua's miracle as *the Rod of God that moves on the face of the waters at night, as the light of life,* is explained by John the Jewish disciple. Yeshua spoke the Word and the wind ceased!

John 1:1-5 *In the beginning was the Word, and the Word was with God, and the Word was God. The same was in the beginning with God. All things were made by Him; and without Him was not anything made that was made. In Him was life; and the life was the light of men. And the light shineth in darkness; and the darkness comprehended it not.*

Now after having seen this incredible truth, think back to the Jordan River to the time when Yeshua was baptized in the water by John the Baptist. The LORD had told John that he would know who the Messiah was because *"He would see the Ruach/Holy Spirit come down and stay on Him in the waters of the Jordan River and that this is the one who was the anointed of God."* Then John the Baptist declared that Yeshua was the one who baptized with the breath of God *"His Holy Spirit and fire!"* John only came baptizing with *water* to make Messiah Yeshua known to Israel.

John 1:32-33 *And John bare record, saying, I saw the Spirit descending from Heaven like a dove, and it abode upon Him. And I knew Him not; but He that sent me to baptize with water, the same said unto me, Upon whom thou shalt see the Spirit descending, and remaining on Him, the same is He which baptizes with the Holy Spirit.*

The Rod of God baptizes in Living Water with the power of His Ruach/Holy Spirit. He moved on the face of the waters during creation and turned the darkness to light because He is the source of the light. This incredible miracle absolutely revealed that Messiah Yeshua is the LORD God of Israel! *The Jewish disciples in the ship should have comprehended exactly who this was that was dwelling in their midst, and I believe they were beginning to understand when they feared exceedingly! Wow! Messiah Yeshua wanted them to understand in their hearts that He is the LORD God of Israel that fed them in the wilderness with the five loaves, the five books of Moses, the Torah and from the two fish, the two tablets of the Law, the meat and then saved them with the Rod and the Ark on the surface of the sea at night.* They should have known Yeshua from the Torah! Unfortunately they hardened their hearts and could not see what was right in front of their eyes. After they did not understand Him in the first miracle, He performed the second miracle and walked upon the water at night. He is the same Rod that saved Israel lifted up in the right hand of the LORD God! Although they did not recognize Him in His miracles, the miracles themselves prove the Messiah's true identity as the LORD God of Israel, and this is why Yeshua told the Jewish people to at least *believe His works.*

Now there is something else that occurred. Right after they saw Yeshua coming to them in the ship and they thought it was a spirit, Yeshua called out to them and said, *"Do not be afraid it is I!"* By speaking these words, Yeshua was telling them, *"I AM the one you know from long ago children of Israel, so do not be afraid! I AM the one you worship but have never seen!"* Yeshua was saying in essence, *"I AM the loving LORD God of Israel that is dwelling in your midst and I AM here to save you forever!" I AM the Rod of salvation called "Yeshua."* I came here to save you again, just as I did in the past, but they needed to believe this, just as they needed to believe it when Moses lifted up the serpent on a pole in the wilderness.

The Jewish disciple Matthew, who was a Levite, gave us another account of Yeshua walking on the water with Simon Peter. This time, Simon Peter said, *"LORD, if it is You, bid me to come to You on the water and He did!"*

Matthew 14:22-36 *And straightway Yeshua constrained his disciples to get into a ship, and to go before Him unto the other side, while He sent the multitudes away. And when He had sent the multitudes away, He went up into a mountain apart to pray; and when the evening was come, He was there alone. But the ship was now in the midst of the sea, tossed with waves; for the wind was contrary. And in the fourth watch of the night Yeshua went unto them, walking on the sea. And when the disciples saw Him walking on the sea, they were troubled, saying, It is a spirit; and they cried out for fear. But straightway Yeshua spake unto them, saying, Be of good cheer; it is I; be not afraid. And Peter answered Him and said, LORD, if it be Thou, bid me come unto Thee on the water. And He said, Come. And when Peter was come down out of the ship, he walked on the water, to go to Yeshua. But when he saw the wind boisterous, he was afraid; and beginning to sink, he cried, saying, LORD, save me. And immediately Yeshua stretched forth His hand, and caught him, and said unto him, O thou of little faith, wherefore didst thou doubt? And when they were come into the ship, the wind ceased. Then they that were in the ship came and worshipped Him, saying, Of a truth thou art the Son of God. And when they were gone over, they came into the land of Gennesaret. And when the men of that place had knowledge of Him, they sent out into all that country round about, and brought unto Him all that were diseased; And besought Him that they might only touch the hem of His garment; and as many as touched were made perfectly whole.*

All Yeshua said was the Word, "Come." So at His Word, Simon Bar Jonah was able to walk toward Yeshua on the surface of the waters. When Simon Peter saw that the wind was boisterous, fear fell upon him and he forgot that Yeshua had the power to calm the wind and the Sea and the power to save him. When Simon doubted that Yeshua was in control, Simon began to sink and of course he reached out for Yeshua's hand and cried saying, *"LORD save me!"* At this point, *the Rod of God* stretched forth His hand/Yad and caught Simon Bar Jonah so he would not sink, fall, or slip. Simon was saved by the LORD, by the Living Ark of Heaven.

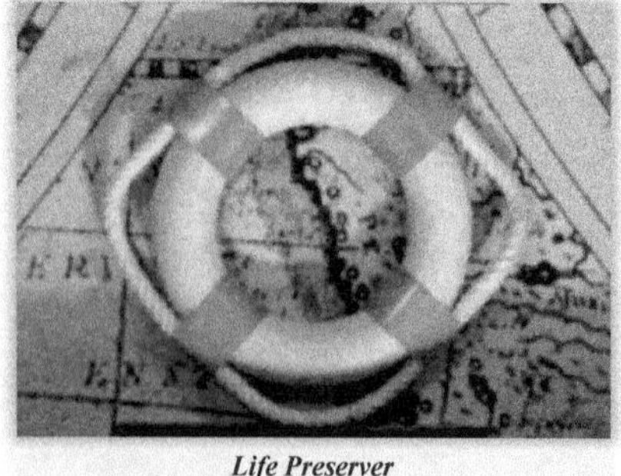

Life Preserver
Photo ©2014 Kimberly K Ballard

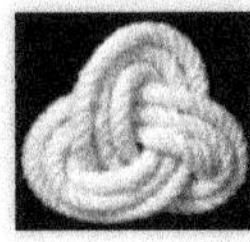

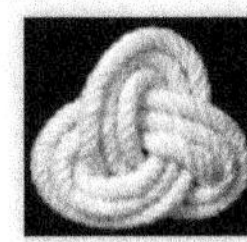

Yeshua was once again the firmament in the midst of the waters at night in the darkness as He walked on the surface of the waters, coming to him as the light of God, full of the power of God's Ruach/Holy Spirit. The firmament was the support that kept Simon from sinking!

Pacific Ocean Wave with Spray Mist Monterey California Photo ©2013 Kimberly K Ballard All Rights Reserved

After this miracle happened, Yeshua got into the ship and they came into *"the land of Gennesaret" which means "Garden of Riches." The Messiah had just revealed Himself as the LORD God of Israel and Yeshua brought them to "the Garden of Riches!" This foreshadowed the LORD bringing His people into His Eternal Garden of Riches, the Eternal Promised Land.*

Then Yeshua immediately began to heal many who were diseased in the Land of Israel. He restored them completely and it was like being with the LORD in the Garden of Eden. By touching the hem of Yeshua's garment, they were touching the hem of the High Priest of Heaven. It was so obvious that the Israelites were being cleansed and healed by the power of the Ruach/Holy Spirit that was abiding upon *the Rod of God,* as they touched Yeshua's garment. This was their Eternal High Priest who was there to make atonement for their sins.

Perhaps the greatest sign of Job that declared, *"The fishes shall declare unto thee that the hand of the LORD hath wrought this,"* is the sign of Jonah. In Jonah's story, *the hand of the LORD appointed a great fish* to swallow Jonah. This was an elaborate work of the hand of

the LORD God. *Yeshua performed the miracles of the multitude of fishes, before Simon Bar Jonah who was the "Son of Jonah."* It was *Simon Bar Jonah* that walked on the surface of the waters while the Rod and Heavenly Ark, full of the Holy Spirit was in his midst. Yeshua sat in Simon Bar Jonah's ship, when He taught the people who were on dry land the *Living Torah* and in the miracle, when He took them out to Sea for a draught. After Yeshua miraculously multiplied *the fishes* and they were gathered in the net, Simon Bar Jonah hoisted the net into his ship. The story of Jonah is parallel to the story of Yeshua in the ship and on the Sea. *So Yeshua gave the sign of Jonah at the Synagogue of Magdala and ironically this Synagogue was unearthed just after the LORD showed this to me and I had written it! Miraculous!*

Official Photograph taken December 2009, "The Magdala Synagogue," Photograph ©2009 Magdala Center Excavations Israel All Rights Reserved

Matthew 12:38-40 *Then some of the Scribes and Pharisees answered Him, saying, Teacher, we want to see a sign from you. But He answered and said to them, An evil and adulterous generation craves for a sign; and yet no sign shall be given to it but the sign of Jonah the Prophet; for just as Jonah was three days and three nights in the whale's belly, so shall the Son of Man be three days and three nights in the heart of the earth.*

Just as John the Baptist was sent by the LORD to preach repentance, Jonah was sent by the LORD to preach repentance to the city of Nineveh. If the people repented, God said that He would spare Nineveh, but if they would not repent, they would certainly be destroyed. So John was sent by the LORD to preach repentance to Israel, but many people would not repent before the coming of Messiah the LORD, and so destruction came upon them. When the two witnesses, Moses and Elijah, come in the future, they will also be preparing the people of Israel for repentance during the great tribulation. Yeshua told the Jewish authorities the following words.

Luke 11:30 *For just as Jonah became a sign to the Ninevites, so shall the Son of Man be to this generation.*

In the story of Jonah, the wind and the waves were fierce upon the Sea as they were floating in the ship because the LORD made the storm come against them. The LORD made their rowing contrary with the storm in the story of Jonah. This, of course, is parallel to the disciples of Yeshua who were rowing contrary to the waves and the wind in the storm before Yeshua came walking to them upon the Sea. Yeshua made the waves contrary to the disciples in the ship, so that when He calmed the Sea by His Word, they would understand that *He was the Rod of God, speaking the Living Torah.* When the men threw Jonah into the Sea, the Sea stopped raging because Jonah was full of the Ruach/Holy Spirit! This is parallel to Yeshua walking on the Sea and calming the wind and waves since He was full of His Ruach/Spirit. In Jonah's story, *the Word of the LORD came to Jonah.* The Word is Messiah, the Rod of God!

Jonah 1:1-17 *The Word of the LORD came to Jonah the son of Amittai saying; Arise, go to Nineveh the great city, and cry against it, for their wickedness has come up before Me. But Jonah rose up to flee to Tarshish from the Presence of the LORD. So he went down to Joppa, found a ship which was going to Tarshish, paid the fare, and*

went down into it to go with them to Tarshish from the Presence of the LORD. And the LORD hurled a great wind on the sea and there was a great storm on the sea so that the ship was about to break up. Then the sailors became afraid, and every man cried to his god, and they threw the cargo which was in the ship into the sea to lighten it for them. But Jonah had gone below into the hold of the ship, lain down, and fallen sound asleep. So the captain approached him and said, How is it that you are sleeping? Get up, call on your God. Perhaps your God will be concerned about us so that we will not perish. And each man said to his mate, Come, let us cast lots so we may learn on whose account this calamity has struck us. So they cast lots and the lot fell on Jonah. Then they said to him, Tell us, now! On whose account has this calamity struck us? What is your occupation? And where do you come from? What is your country? From what people are you? And he said to them, I am a Hebrew, and I fear the LORD God of Heaven who made the sea and the dry land. Then the men became extremely frightened and they said to him, How could you do this? For the men knew that he was fleeing from the presence of the LORD, because he had told them. So they said to him, What should we do to you that the sea may become calm for us? For the sea was becoming increasingly stormy. And he said to them, Pick me up and throw me into the sea. Then the sea will become calm for you, for I know that on account of me this great storm has come upon you. However, the men rowed desperately to return to land but they could not, for the sea was becoming even stormier against them. Then they called on the LORD and said, We earnestly pray, O LORD, do not let us perish on account of this man's life and do not put innocent blood on us; for Thou, O LORD, hast done as Thou hast pleased. So they picked up Jonah, threw him into the sea, and the sea stopped its raging. Then the men feared the LORD greatly, and they offered a sacrifice to the LORD and made vows. And the LORD appointed a great fish to swallow Jonah, and Jonah was in the stomach of the fish three days and three nights.

Jonah 2:1-9 *Then Jonah prayed to the LORD his God from the stomach of the fish, and he said, I called out of my distress to the LORD, And He answered me. I cried for help from the depth of Sheol; Thou didst hear my voice. For Thou hast cast me into the deep, Into the heart of the seas, And the current engulfed me. All Thy breakers and billows passed over me. So I said, I have been expelled from Thy sight. Nevertheless I will look again toward Thy Holy Temple. Water encompassed me to the point of death. The great deep engulfed me, weeds were wrapped around my head. I descended to the roots of the mountains, The earth with its bars was around me forever, But Thou hast brought up my life from the pit, O LORD my God. While I was fainting away, I remembered the LORD; And my prayer came to Thee, into Thy Holy Temple. Those who regard vain idols forsake their faithfulness, But I will sacrifice to Thee With the voice of thanksgiving. That which I have vowed I will pay.* ***.*** *Salvation is from the LORD.*

Jonah knew that the Sea would be calm for those in the storm tossed ship, if they threw him overboard into the waters. Jonah knew that the Holy Spirit moved on the surface of the waters and He knew that at the Word of God, the wind and the waves would be stilled, and he had come with the Word of God in the power of the Holy Spirit. So the moment that Jonah's body fell onto the surface of the waters of the Sea, the storm was calmed. Jonah was fleeing from the Presence of the LORD, but the LORD had given Jonah *His Word* to go to Nineveh. Then the hand of the LORD did a great work and *appointed a great fish* to swallow Jonah in the depths of the darkness of the Sea. *This particular fish, probably a whale shark, was the work that the hand of the LORD hath wrought once more!* Jonah was baptized in the midst of the Sea and as He repented with his heart, His sins were washed away in the great depths of the Living Waters and He came to life in the Holy Spirit. Now after three days and three nights, Jonah was miraculously saved and brought forth alive from the belly of the great fish and went to preach the Word of God and repentance to Nineveh. Jonah was asleep in the ship just like Yeshua was asleep in the ship. Both were awakened when the storm came up and was tossing the ship about. The men on the ship, who went into the hold to awaken Jonah as he slept, told him *to call upon his God, so that perhaps his God would be concerned about them in the ship and that perhaps they would not perish.* When the stormy winds tossed Yeshua's ship about, the Jewish disciples went to awaken Yeshua as He slept in the hold and instead of asking Yeshua to call upon His God to save them from perishing, *Yeshua spoke the Word* and the Sea, the waves and the wind were calmed and stilled. *Yeshua did not need to call upon His God because He is the LORD God of Israel and He cared about them in the ship. He performed this mighty work to show them His true identity.* Yeshua the Rod of salvation came to their rescue, and He kept them from perishing. *The LORD was again the Living Ark of salvation floating on*

the surface of the Sea, and *He saved them* when they said, *"Master, carest Thou not that we perish?" The Living Torah* calmed the storm, and the wind fulfilled His Word after He walked on the surface of the water full of His Ruach/Holy Spirit, just as Jonah previously did when He was tossed onto the surface of the Sea.

Psalm 148:7-9 *Praise the LORD from the earth, sea monsters and all deeps; Fire and hail, snow and clouds; Stormy wind, fulfilling His Word; Mountains and all hills; Fruit trees and all cedars.*

Sea of Monterey California Photo ©2013 Kimberly K Ballard All Rights Reserved

After Yeshua gave the sign of Jonah to His generation, He proved by His Words and miracles that He is the Messiah of Israel and yet they still would not believe it. So Yeshua declared that judgment would come to His generation for their disbelief and for their lack of repentance.

Matthew 12:41-42 *The Men of Nineveh shall rise in judgment with this generation, and shall condemn it; because they repented at the preaching of Jonah; and, Behold, a Greater than Jonah is here. The queen of the south shall rise up in the judgment with this generation, and shall condemn it; for she came from the uttermost parts of the earth to hear the Wisdom of Solomon; and, behold, a Greater than Solomon is here.*

The one who was dwelling among us, that was greater than King Solomon and Jonah, *was Messiah Yeshua, the LORD God of Israel! They were so blind to His identity!*

There was another sign of *the fishes* hidden within the sign of Jonah, and it reveals the day of Yeshua's second coming and His return at the end of the age. By using Simon Bar Jonah the fisherman, the LORD signaled that His return would be at the great harvest to come and this was the sign that Yeshua gave to the Pharisees and Sadducees in the Synagogue of Magdala or Migdol, after arriving there in the ship on the Sea. This would involve the turning of many hearts from all the Nations unto the LORD KING, just as the catch of the multitude of fishes in Simon Peter's net had foreshadowed. Yom Kippur, the Holiest Day of the LORD, will be the day of Yeshua's second coming and return for Israel because it is on Yom Kippur that the Jewish people read and study the entire book of Jonah. Yeshua hid this truth within the one sign that He gave to His people, Israel. They will be reading about the great fish that the LORD appointed when Yeshua descends from Heaven! Of course, it is at the second coming that the hand of God will do an elaborate work and the Rod of God will save Israel once again. There is more to this that I will discuss in the last chapter. Yeshua spoke the following Words, revealing that He is the LORD of the Sabbath day. He is greater than the earthly Temple. He is the Heavenly Temple!

Matthew 12:6-8 *But I say to you, That in this place is one greater than the Temple. But if ye had known what this means, I will have mercy, and not sacrifice, ye would not have condemned the guiltless. For the Son of man is LORD even of the Sabbath.*

If we know that Messiah Yeshua calmed the Sea and the LORD of Hosts calmed the Sea, then we can conclude that Messiah is the Rod of God because only the Creator of the universe has the power to control His creation. The *voice* of the LORD caused the turbulent waters to be calmed, and this is what Yeshua did on the Sea of Galilee when He spoke to the waters and they obeyed Him. Psalm 107 clearly reveals Yeshua and His works on the Sea of Galilee, *as the Living Torah.*

Psalm 107:25-30 *For He commandeth, and raiseth the stormy wind, which lifteth up the waves thereof. They mount up to the Heaven, they go down again to the depths; their soul is melted because of trouble. They reel to and fro, and stagger like a drunken man, and are at their wit's end. Then they cry unto the LORD in their trouble, and He bringeth them out of their distresses. He maketh the storm a calm, so that the waves thereof are still. Then are they glad because they are quiet; so He bringeth them unto their desired haven.*

The next miracle happened when Yeshua entered the ship. The ship containing His Jewish disciples *arrived instantly at the shore. So the Jewish disciples were immediately brought to their "haven" after Yeshua saved them speaking the Living Torah.* The word *"haven"* means *"a place of shelter, a port, a place of safety or rest."* The LORD showed me that their sudden arrival at their destination revealed that Yeshua was the *"Deliverer"* of Israel. By definition a *"Deliverer"* is one who *"brings you to, or transports you to the proper place!"* This event not only revealed that Yeshua is the LORD God of Israel who is our Deliverer, but it also reveals that Yeshua is the one who instantly transports us to His Heavenly place of rest and shelter in the Heavenly Kingdom of God, which is the true *"Garden of riches!"* This is what will happen in the rapture because Yeshua *"delivers us from the wrath to come."* In other words, *Yeshua will transport us instantly to our haven in Heaven,* to our place of rest with Him, thereby saving us from the wrath to come because He is the Rod and the Ark of Heaven that saves us and this is what Yeshua demonstrated on the Sea of Galilee. It is such a blessing to discover this truth!

I Thessalonians 1:9-10 *For they themselves shew of us what manner of entering in we had unto you, and how ye turned to God from idols to serve the living and true God; And to wait for His Son from Heaven, whom He raised from the dead, even Yeshua, which delivered us from the wrath to come.*

In Psalm 89, the LORD of Hosts rules the Sea and calms the waves with His strong arm, the Rod of God.

Psalm 89:8-9 *O LORD God of Hosts, who is a strong LORD like unto Thee? Or to Thy faithfulness round about Thee? Thou rulest the raging of the sea; when the waves thereof arise, Thou stillest them. Thou hast broken Rahab in pieces, as one that is slain; Thou hast scattered Thine enemies with Thy strong arm.*

Psalm 65:5-7 *By terrible things in righteousness wilt thou answer us, O God of our salvation; who art the confidence of all the ends of the earth, and of them that are afar off upon the sea; Which by His strength setteth fast the mountains; being girded with power; Which stilleth the noise of the seas, the noise of their waves, and the tumult of the people.*

The Jewish disciples were astonished that Yeshua spoke with His voice and the waves of the Sea were calmed and the wind ceased. Remember that Yeshua was asleep in the hold of the ship and the disciples awaked Him and they asked Him to save them. Of course Yeshua's sole mission as the Rod lifted up was to save the world from the curse of the Garden of Eden. Before the children of Israel crossed the Red Sea, the waves roared, just as they were roaring on the Sea of Galilee as Yeshua walked toward them on the surface of the water. At the Red Sea crossing, the LORD also calmed the waves and saved Israel through the midst of turbulent waters by making the waters to stand up in a heap, on the right side and on the left side. The Rod of God carved a pathway through the midst of the Living Waters with Yeshua, the Rod and Ark of Heaven, leading them across to the other side upon dry land.

Remember that I said previously that when Yeshua, *the Living Torah* sat in the ship floating on the surface of the water, which is a type of Ark, the people of Israel stood upon dry ground as they listened to *the Words of the Living Torah* coming out of Yeshua's mouth and they were blessed as He spoke to them in parables about sowing the seed of *the Living Torah!*

"The Jesus Boat" an Original Artistic Rendering Photo ©2013 by Kimberly K Ballard All Rights Reserved

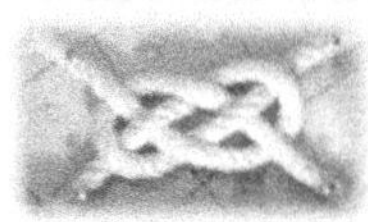

Matthew 13:1-2 *The same day went Yeshua out of the house, and sat by the sea side. And great multitudes were gathered together unto him, so that He went into a ship, and sat; and the whole multitude stood on the shore. And He spake many things unto them in parables, saying, Behold, a sower went forth to sow...*

Isaiah 51:15 *But I AM the LORD thy God, that divided the sea, whose waves roared; The LORD of Hosts is His Name.*

Now in every one of Yeshua's miracles we are told that *"immediately"* the disabled person received their sight or *"immediately"* they could hear. The leprosy *"immediately"* left them. When the LORD speaks His Word, the results are absolutely *immediate* and this is the reason why the ship full of Yeshua's disciples suddenly and *immediately* arrived at their destination after Yeshua revealed He was the Rod. Yeshua would stretch out His right hand and touch a person, and at once, the person was made completely well. This is exactly what happened when the LORD spoke the creation into existence by the Word of His voice. When Yeshua spoke the Word, the lame, blind, and sick were *immediately* healed by the power of His voice filled with His Ruach/Holy Spirit speaking Hebrew. Now all this was accomplished *to make His mighty power known to all people, not only to those who were eye witnesses.*

Psalms 106:4-10 *Remember me, O LORD, with the favour that Thou bearest unto Thy people; O visit me with Thy salvation; That I may see the good of Thy chosen, that I may rejoice in the gladness of Thy Nation, that I may glory with Thine inheritance. We have sinned with our fathers, we have committed iniquity, we have done wickedly. Our fathers understood not Thy wonders in Egypt; they remembered not the multitude of Thy mercies; but provoked Him at the sea, even at the Red Sea. Nevertheless He saved them for His Name's sake, that He might make His Mighty power to be known. He rebuked the Red Sea also, and it was dried up; so He led them through the depths, as through the wilderness. And He saved them from the hand of him that hated them, and redeemed them from the hand of the enemy.*

The Prophet Isaiah wrote that the LORD spoke His Word and the land was dried up, so the children of Israel were redeemed. It is the hand that redeems. Messiah Yeshua is called *"the Redeemer."* This verse in Isaiah reveals the Messiah's miracles!

Isaiah 50:2 *Wherefore, when I came, was there no man? When I called, was there none to answer? Is My hand shortened at all, that it cannot redeem? Or have I no power to deliver? Behold, at My rebuke I dry up the sea, I make the rivers a wilderness; their fish stinketh, because there is no water, and dieth for thirst.*

In Proverbs, the Rod of God instructs us with *"the Words of knowledge"* that come from Messiah, *the Living Torah.* Messiah, the Rod of the LORD, is our correction and instruction, and *He delivers* our soul from hell and gives us Eternal Life.

Proverbs 23:12-14 *Apply thine heart unto instruction, and thine ears to the Words of knowledge. Withhold not correction from the child; for if thou beatest him with the rod, he shall not die. Thou shalt beat him with the rod, and shalt deliver his soul from hell.*

The moral of this Proverb is really that we are not to be beaten with a stick called a *"rod,"* but we are, instead, to be corrected *by the Word of God,* by *the Living Torah.* It is so amazing how this all comes together. The Word of God, which is *the Word of knowledge,* is to be used to guide us and our children throughout our lives, but if you keep your children from the correction of *the Rod of God, from the Living Torah,* then He is telling us that you do not love them because His Words give us the key to Eternal life! When you give your children this Eternal hope they will be blessed. By God's *Royal Standard,* the Rod of correction is the Lawgiver, and, as I said, this is not in reference to beating us with a stick or a switch as a punishment, but it means that the Word of God alone changes our hearts to love, as the Good Shepherd guides us in His love with His Living Torah Covenant of the heart.

Proverbs 13:24 *He that spareth his rod hateth his son; but he that loveth him chasteneth him betimes.*

Romans 8:32-34 *He that spared not His own Son, but delivered Him up for us all, how shall He not with Him also freely give us all things? Who shall lay anything to the charge of God's elect? It is God that justifieth. Who is he that condemneth? It is Messiah that died, yea rather, that is risen again, who is even at the right hand of God, who also maketh intercession for us.*

Hebrews 12:1-11 *Wherefore seeing we also are compassed about with so great a cloud of witnesses, let us lay aside every weight, and the sin which doth so easily beset us, and let us run with patience the race that is set before us, Looking unto Yeshua the author and finisher of our faith; who for the joy that was set before Him endured the cross, despising the shame, and is set down at the right hand of the throne of God. For consider Him that endured such contradiction of sinners against Himself, lest ye be wearied and faint in your minds. Ye have not yet resisted unto blood, striving against sin. And ye have forgotten the exhortation which speaketh unto you as children, My son, despise not thou the chastening of the LORD, nor faint when thou art rebuked of Him. For whom the LORD loveth He chasteneth, and scourgeth every son whom He receiveth. If ye endure chastening, God dealeth with you as with sons; for what son is he whom the father chasteneth not? But if ye be without chastisement, whereof all are partakers, then are ye bastards, and not sons. Furthermore we have had fathers of our flesh which corrected us, and we gave them reverence; shall we not much rather be in subjection unto the Father of Spirits, and live? For they verily for a few days chastened us after their own pleasure; but He for our profit, that we might be partakers of His Holiness. Now no chastening for the present seemeth to be joyous, but grievous; nevertheless afterward, it yieldeth the peaceable fruit of righteousness unto them which are exercised thereby.*

John 3:14-22 *And as Moses lifted up the serpent in the wilderness, even so must the Son of man be lifted up; That whosoever believeth in Him should not perish, but have eternal life. For God so loved the world, that He gave His only begotten Son, that whosoever believeth in Him should not perish, but have everlasting life. For God sent not His Son into the world to condemn the world; but that the world through Him might be saved. He that believeth on Him is not condemned; but he that believeth not is condemned already, because he hath not believed in the Name of the only begotten Son of God. And this is the condemnation, that light is come into the world, and men loved darkness rather than light, because their deeds were evil. For everyone that doeth evil hateth the light, neither cometh to the light, lest his deeds should be reproved. But he that doeth truth cometh to the light, that his deeds may be made manifest, that they are wrought in God. After these things came Yeshua and His disciples into the land of Judaea; and there He tarried with them, and baptized.*

Now, if all the miraculous works of Yeshua were not enough to convince you that He is *the Living Torah,* then you will be thrilled to see the next exciting detail. As I said previously, Yeshua the Word of God is the Unleavened Bread from Heaven. So I suddenly realized that when Yeshua was walking on the Sea of Galilee He was *"the Bread that was cast upon the surface of the waters," as it states in Ecclesiastes.* The Bible tells us that *Israel will find this Bread after many days* and two thousand years have passed since Yeshua was here! *Messiah Yeshua is the Heavenly Bread that was walking on the surface of the waters that Israel will find after many days!* It is written that we do not know the activity of God who makes all things, and surely they did not see this back then, but they will very soon and it will be thrilling!

Ecclesiastes 11:1-7 *Cast your bread upon the surface of the waters, for you will find it after many days. Divide your portion to seven, or even to eight, for you do not know what misfortune may occur on the earth. If the clouds are full, they pour rain upon the earth; and whether a tree falls toward the south or toward the north, wherever the tree falls, there it lies. He who watches the wind will not sow and he who looks at the clouds will not reap. Just as you do not know the path of the wind and how bones are formed in the womb of the pregnant woman, so you do not know the activity of God who makes all things. Sow your seed in the morning and do not be idle in the evening, for you do not know whether both of them alike will be good. The light is pleasant, and it is good for the eyes to see the sun.*

So the miracles of Yeshua proclaim that He fed the Israelites with the true Bread, the true meat and the Living Water and then He went and healed many diseases of His people who had been suffering for such a long time. This was the power of God.

Exodus 23:25 *And ye shall serve the LORD your God, and He shall bless thy bread, and thy water; and I will take sickness away from the midst of thee.*

After studying all of this at length, I discovered that there is another deeper meaning in the miracle of the 5 loaves and 2 fish. The five loaves, the five books of Moses, *the Torah,* and the two fish, *the two tablets of the Law,* the meat, not only revealed that *Yeshua is the Living Torah,* the Unleavened Bread from Heaven and the pure meat of the Lamb, the Word of God, but the two fish can also represent the two witnesses, Moses and Elijah. They are the two olive trees that stand on either side of the LORD, the Lamp stand of the whole earth! They were the two eyewitnesses of Yeshua's glory when He was transfigured on the Holy Mountain. Moses and Elijah already knew Yeshua the LORD, and they spoke with Him in the glory cloud and He told them everything that He was about to fulfill with His Living Testimony of the Heavenly Ark, as the budded Almond Rod, before the events ever came to pass. *So Moses also represents the 5 loaves and the two fish, the bread and the meat, because he was given the earthly copy of the Heavenly Torah and tablets of the Law of God. Elijah represents the Law, the two fish, the meat and the Prophets, who wrote down the Word of God, which is the bread from Heaven.* Yeshua was in the glory cloud on the Holy Mountain, just as the LORD God was in the glory cloud on Mount Sinai, the Holy Mountain. The three Jewish disciples saw the glory of the LORD, as Yeshua was glistening in pure white garments and His countenance was changed into its full glory. It is interesting that the three Jewish disciples were on the ground with their faces to the earth, when this miracle transpired. I will speak more about this later.

Moses and Elijah were, therefore, the two witnesses that are required by Jewish law that witnessed the glory of the LORD in Messiah Yeshua's transfiguration. The Jewish disciples were not to tell anyone what they saw on the Holy Mountain until after Yeshua was raised from the dead, as the First Fruits of Eternal life. During the time of Jacob's trouble, Moses and Elijah will be the two witnesses that come to prepare the way of the LORD before the Messiah comes to reign. *The two witnesses will turn the hearts of the children of Israel back to the LORD, just before He comes back from Heaven in the glory cloud. Moses and Elijah will preach the Living Testimony of Messiah and this will prepare Israel to meet the LORD face to face!* Simon Bar Jonah, the Jewish disciple and the Jewish Torah Scholar named *"Saul"* who was *"Paul"* also could be called *"two fish"* because they took the Word of God, the 5 loaves and the two fish, the Heavenly Living Torah to the world. Saul was from the tribe of Benjamin and he was a Hebrew of Hebrews. He was a very learned Torah Scholar, under Rabbi Gamaliel. These two men, Simon Bar Jonah and Paul, represent two witnesses who were founders of the LORD'S Church that includes millions of Jews and people from all Nations of the earth. They took the Living Testimony of the LORD Messiah to the Jew first and then to the Gentiles. Through the Messiah, the Gentiles could now be saved through the Rod of God. Paul declared that the LORD allowed Israel to not believe in Messiah Yeshua for a time, so that the righteous Gentiles could be brought to the knowledge of the LORD. After the LORD gathers a remnant of the righteous Gentiles for salvation, the LORD will reveal to Israel that He is their Messiah. The Rod, the Messiah, will come to save them! He will graft in His original branches of Israel to the Almond Tree of Life. Nothing is impossible with God!

Romans 11:11-21 *I say then, Have they stumbled that they should fall? God forbid; but rather through their fall salvation is come unto the Gentiles, for to provoke them to jealousy. Now if the fall of them be the riches of the world, and the diminishing of them the riches of the Gentiles; how much more their fullness? For I speak to you Gentiles, inasmuch as I am the Apostle of the Gentiles, I magnify mine office; If by any means I may provoke to emulation them which are my flesh, and might save some of them. For if the casting away of them be the reconciling of the world, what shall the receiving of them be, but life from the dead? For if the first fruit be holy, the lump is also holy; and if the root be holy, so are the branches. And if some of the branches be broken off, and thou being a wild olive tree, wert grafted in among them, and with them partakest of the root and fatness of the olive tree; Boast not against the branches. But if thou boast, thou bearest not the root, but the root thee. Thou wilt say then, branches were broken off, that I might be grafted in. Well; because of unbelief they were broken off, and thou standest by faith. Be not high minded, but fear; For if God spared not the natural branches, take heed lest He also spare not thee.*

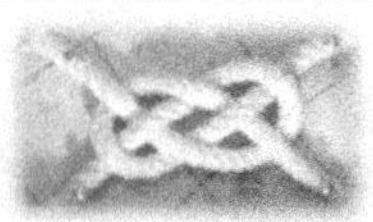

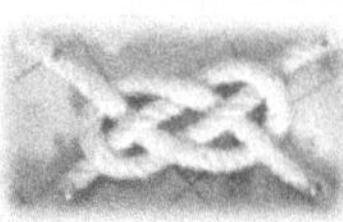

The five loaves and two fish reveal that *Yeshua is the Living Torah,* and then He proved it when He stilled the wind and the waves of the Sea with His voice, which came off the mercy seat of the Living Ark of God, when He walked at night on the surface the Sea. Yeshua's miracles prove that He is the arm of the LORD revealed and He said that one day we would all know the LORD, as the waters cover the Sea!

Isaiah 11:9-10 *They shall not hurt nor destroy in all My Holy Mountain; for the earth shall be full of the knowledge of the LORD, as the waters cover the sea. And in that day there shall be a root of Jesse, which shall stand for an ensign of the people; to it shall the Gentiles seek; and His rest shall be glorious.*

Five Loaves & Two Fish = The Living Torah
Photo ©2013 Kimberly K Ballard
All Rights Reserved

Seashells, Nautical Ropes & Ship
Photos ©2014
Kimberly K Ballard
All Rights Reserved

Pacific Ocean spray on the rocks Monterey California Photo ©2014 Kimberly K Ballard All Rights Reserved

THE MIRACLE OF HEALING THE CRIPPLED MAN AT THE POOL OF BETHESDA

The fantastic miracle of Yeshua healing the crippled man at the Pool of Bethesda is not exactly what it appears to be! I was again absolutely astonished when the Holy Spirit opened my mind and heart to understand what was happening in the miracle at the Pool of Bethesda between the crippled man and Messiah Yeshua. For centuries, the common teaching and preaching of the meaning of this miracle has been that it refers to having enough faith and belief that God will heal you. They say *"If you do not have enough faith or you do not believe in your heart that the LORD will actually heal you,"* then according to this traditional viewpoint, *"You will not be healed by Him."* It was due to this teaching and long held belief that I thought this was the true meaning of this miracle. I am now writing, though, that there is something that I have seen within this miracle that is far more spectacular! For this reason, I am excited to say that I believe that the traditional teaching is incorrect! I think you will get the chills when you see this new truth that I am about to present. As I pondered it another great shiver ran through me. The following Scripture is the account of this miracle that took place at the Pool of Bethesda. It is written in the Gospel of John.

John 5:1-9 *After this there was a great Feast of the Jews; and Yeshua went up to Jerusalem. Now there is at Jerusalem by the sheep market a pool, which is called in the Hebrew tongue Bethesda, having five porches. In these lay a great multitude of impotent folk, of blind, halt, withered, waiting for the moving of the water. For an angel went down at a certain season into the pool, and troubled the water; whosoever then first after the troubling of the water stepped in was made whole of whatsoever disease he had. And a certain man was there, which had an infirmity thirty and eight years. When Yeshua saw him lie, and knew that he had been now a long time in that case, He saith unto him, Wilt thou be made whole? The impotent man answered Him, Sir, I have no man, when the water is troubled, to put me into the pool; but while I am coming, another steppeth down before me. Yeshua saith unto him, Rise, take up thy bed, and walk. And immediately the man was made whole, and took up his bed, and walked; and on the same day was the Sabbath.*

The name of the Pool called *"Bethesda"* means *"House of Mercy."* The five porches represent the Living Torah! Now here is what the LORD showed me about this miracle! First, notice that the crippled man was healed immediately! This is the sign of the power of the Rod of God! As I was pondering this in my heart, the LORD brought into my mind the part of the story where the angel of the LORD came down and stirred up the water. Whoever got into the pool first was healed. This is just incredible! I suddenly realized that when the angel of the LORD came down and stirred up the water, the angel of the LORD was turning the water into *"LIVING WATER"* and this explains why those who got into the water first were healed! The Holy Spirit of God was moving on the surface of the waters through the agitation of the angel of the LORD. This unusual phenomenon occurred once a year and it took place during one of the special Feast days of the LORD. I believe that this miracle likely occurred on Pentecost, which is Shavuot. This would make it the same Feast that the Holy Spirit came down from Heaven in flaming tongues of fire upon the Jewish disciples and they suddenly had the power from the LORD to accomplish great miracles in His Name. So Yeshua went up to this crippled man and He asked him if he wanted to get well. The crippled man told Yeshua that he could not get into the water fast enough when the water was stirred up and that everyone got into the water first before him. So what happened next? Yeshua looked squarely into the eyes of the crippled man and He said, *"Rise, take up thy bed and walk!"* So what is the astounding truth in this miracle? It is the greatest punch line that was ever written! You are about to see the astonishing hidden truth in this miracle!

The crippled man did not need to get into the Pool to be healed because The "Living Water" was speaking to him!

This was hidden all this time within this miracle. The LORD revealed it to me by the mighty power of His Holy Spirit and it is breathtaking! So when the LIVING WATER spoke the Word, the crippled man was immediately healed! So what is the amazing moral of this story? *Who needs to get into a pool of living water when the LORD, the true LIVING WATER, is standing there speaking to you?* This is so fantastic that this hidden meaning was in Yeshua's miracle! Once again, the mighty Rod of God, full of the Holy Spirit, spoke the Word and the crippled man instantly got up and took up his bed and walked for the first time in thirty eight years. Honestly, this miracle makes me cry because no one has ever seen the truth of *the great power within Yeshua's miracle before*. I also can say that I am so thrilled that this miracle is not at all a matter of the man having enough faith or not. *This miracle was to reveal that Messiah Yeshua is the LORD God of Israel!* It just gives me the chills! This miracle is another example of the Holy Spirit on the Rod of God, performing the works of God. In the beginning, the Word of God, the LIVING WATER spoke and He created the universe and His Holy Spirit moved on the surface of the waters, and this is exactly how the crippled man was healed!

It is amazing that just before this miracle took place at the Pool of Bethesda, Yeshua was at Jacob's well, and it was here that Yeshua sat down at Jacob's well and revealed to the Samaritan woman that He is the Messiah of Israel. *Yeshua had just told the woman at Jacob's well that He is "The LIVING WATER" and He offered to give her this "Life-giving Water."* Then immediately after Yeshua had this conversation with the woman who was drawing water out of Jacob's well, Yeshua went to the Pool of Bethesda and He asked the crippled man if he wanted to get well. In this miracle, Yeshua proved through His works what He had just told the woman at Jacob's well! *Yeshua is the well of salvation!*

It is also interesting that Yeshua healed the crippled man by speaking with His voice because the LORD'S voice is like the sound of many waters. The Word is *the LIVING WATER* that gives us life! It is also written in the Psalms that the voice of the LORD is upon the waters. Yeshua spoke the Word as He walked upon the surface of the waters on the Sea of Galilee! So *Yeshua's voice was the LIVING WATER* and His Word calmed the storm! It is absolutely thrilling to see this!

Psalm 29:3 *The voice of the LORD is upon the waters; the God of glory thundereth; the LORD is upon many waters.*

Ezekiel 43:2 *And, behold, the glory of the God of Israel came from the way of the east; and His voice was like noise of many waters; and the earth shined with His glory.*

Revelation 1:15 *And His feet like unto fine brass, as if they burned in a furnace; and His voice as the sound of many waters.*

Revelation 19:6 *And I heard as it were the voice of a great multitude, and as the voice of many waters, and as the voice of mighty thunderings saying, Allelulia; for the LORD God omnipotent reigneth*

To hear this passage preached all your life by thousands of people about the crippled man at the pool of Bethesda and whether or not he had enough faith to believe that he would be healed is unbelievable to me because this story is profoundly deeper than that. If the power of the Holy Spirit had not revealed this to me, I never would have seen it in Yeshua's miracle at the Pool of Bethesda, and I shed tears over it in humility because He allowed me to see it. Thinking back to Yeshua's baptism, remember that Yeshua was standing in the midst of the waters in the Jordan River when Heaven opened and the Holy Spirit descended from Heaven like a dove and abode upon Yeshua, *the Ark of Heaven.* At this exact moment when Yeshua was standing in the midst of the waters of the Jordan River, *a voice was heard saying, "This is My beloved Son, in Whom I AM well pleased," and the Divine Presence at that moment was standing in the midst of the waters.* This is exactly what happened when Joshua was crossing the Jordan River with the Ark. The Divine Presence was abiding upon the Ark that stood in the midst of the waters of the Jordan River with the Holy Spirit of God resting upon it. So Messiah Yeshua, the Word of God, was standing in the Jordan River as the *Spiritual LIVING WATER* of Heaven. The Second Adam was cut off just like the waters of Jordan were cut off, near the city of Adam! *The LORD'S voice was upon the waters, as Yeshua stood in the midst of the River.* The incredible truth is that in the beginning, when the Holy Spirit of the LORD God moved on the surface of the waters, He turned the waters into *"LIVING WATERS"* and everything came to life at that moment, at His Word. This is essentially how the crippled man at the Pool of Bethesda was healed when Yeshua spoke to him. The man was immediately restored to abundant life without the affliction of disease. *The miracle was not at all about the crippled man and what he could or could not do by his weak faith. It was all about the LORD and His power on the Rod.* Therefore, by submerging ourselves into *the LIVING WATER* of the LORD, we die to our sins. The LORD Messiah, the true LIVING WATER and the Holy Spirit stirs up the waters, in the midst of the waters. We are raised up out of the midst of the waters at that moment and the Divine Presence of the Holy Spirit seals us for Eternal life, as He rests within our purified hearts. This is the circumcision of the heart, the Eternal Covenant of the heart of the LORD. In the incredible miracle at the Pool of Bethesda, the fountain of *LIVING WATER* instantly healed the man. During the Feast of Tabernacles, Yeshua stood in the Holy Temple in Jerusalem and He declared that if we believe on Him, then rivers of *Living Water* will flow out of us and He spoke this about His Holy Spirit.

Tropical Pool of living water with Flora Photo ©2013 Kimberly K Ballard All Rights Reserved

Revelation 7:17 *For the Lamb which is in the midst of the throne shall feed them, and shall lead them unto Living fountains of Waters; and God shall wipe away all tears from their eyes.*

Jeremiah 17:13 *O LORD, the hope of Israel, all that forsake Thee shall be ashamed, and they that depart from Me shall be written in the earth, because they have forsaken the LORD, the fountain of Living Waters.*

***John 7:37-39** In the last day, that great day of the Feast, Yeshua stood and cried, saying, If any man thirst, let him come unto Me, and drink. He that believeth on Me, as the Scripture hath said, out of his belly shall flow rivers of Living Water. But this spake He of the Spirit, which they that believe on Him should receive; for the Holy Spirit was not yet given; because that Yeshua was not yet glorified.*

Butterfly Photo ©2014 Kimberly K Ballard All Rights Reserved

One of the greatest works of the LORD, that demonstrates Messiah's baptism in *the LIVING WATER*, is the great flood of Noah. If you think about it, the flood of the living rushing water cleansed the earth by washing away the sinful wickedness of mankind. It was through *the flood of LIVING WATER* that all things were given new life in the LORD, who saved the righteous in the Ark. This year is the first year that rain has fallen in Colorado, as I was editing this book, after many years of drought. I began to wonder if the rains are returning because Messiah *"The LIVING WATER"* is very close to taking us to the Heavenly Kingdom in the rapture. Then suddenly as I prayed for rain, while lifting up an Almond rod in Yeshua's Name, a very rare flood came and in seven days the waters ended the extreme drought and broke the unbearable heat wave! In Eden everything was beautiful when the LORD was dwelling in our midst because a mist came up from the ground and watered the surface of the land. The LORD'S Divine Presence abiding in our midst was the reason for this extreme beauty. We have been deprived of this *LIVING WATER* for so long! When Yeshua returns from Heaven to restore the earth, He will wipe every tear from our eyes because we have endured the curse for so long, without His refreshing pools of *LIVING WATER.*

***Isaiah 41:17-20** When the poor and needy seek water; and there is none, and their tongue faileth for thirst, I the LORD will hear them, I the God of Israel will not forsake them. I will open rivers in high places, and fountains in the midst of the valleys; I will make the wilderness a pool of water, and the dry land springs of water. I will plant in the wilderness the cedar, the shittah tree, and the myrtle, and the oil tree; I will set in the desert the fir tree, and the pine, and the box tree together; that they may see, and know, and consider, and understand together, that the hand of the LORD hath done this, and the Holy One of Israel hath created it.*

***Psalm 107:35-37** He turneth the wilderness into a standing water, and dry ground into watersprings. And there He maketh the hungry to dwell, that they may prepare a city for habitation; And sow the fields, and plant vineyards, which may yield fruits of increase.*

The day that the LORD opened my eyes to understand the miracle at the Pool of Bethesda, I was shocked when I understood the inspiring mighty power of Almighty God, in Yeshua's great works. *By healing the crippled man in this way, Yeshua revealed that He is, the great KING Messiah of Israel.* He is indeed verified again to be the Rod of God, full of the Holy Spirit of God, who moved on the face of the waters in the beginning. He is the same one that healed the crippled man, who did not need to get into the Pool while the water was stirred up because the *"LIVING WATER"* was standing in their midst speaking to him! This is absolutely fantastic!

Tropical Pool of living water with Flora & Butterfly Photo ©2013 Kimberly K Ballard All Rights Reserved

THE KINGDOM OF HEAVEN IS LIKE A MUSTARD SEED!

When the LORD inspired me to write about the mustard plant, I had no idea that within the mustard plant, there are numerous botanical elements that are quite stunning. Yeshua told the parable of the mustard seed, to the people who followed Him in Israel and it was recorded in the Gospel of Mark, in Chapter 4. A few of the facts regarding the mustard seed include the following details. *"The mustard plant has many healing properties and it is considered to be antibacterial and is said to naturally relieve arthritis and it heals many other ailments. Mustard that comes from the crushed seed is a natural preservative that will not mold or grow bacteria, so it is beneficial as a food preservative. Mustard was used by the Romans and it was combined with vinegar."* **(Source: Mustard Plant Cruciferae Facts ©2011 Encyclopaedia Britannica Inc.).**

These elements reveal that Yeshua was crushed like a mustard seed and He was given vinegar to drink for our transgressions. He was bruised for our iniquities. Messiah Yeshua is *"the preservative agent"* that preserves us for Eternal life, as the children of God. Since Yeshua's body did not see decay, it was preserved like the mustard seed.

Mark 4:26-33 *And He said, So is the Kingdom of God, as if a man should cast seed into the ground; And should sleep, and rise night and day, and the seed should spring and grow up, he knoweth not how. For the earth bringeth forth fruit of herself; first the blade, then the ear, after that the full corn in the ear. But when the fruit is brought forth, immediately he putteth in the sickle, because the harvest is come. And He said, Whereunto shall we liken the Kingdom of God? Or with what comparison shall we compare it? It is like a grain of mustard seed, which, when it is sown in the earth, is less than all the seeds that be in the earth; But when it is sown, it groweth up, and becometh greater than all herbs, and shooteth out great branches; so that the fowls of the air may lodge under the shadow of it. And with many such parables spake He the Word unto them, as they were able to hear it.*

As I asked the LORD to reveal more of Himself to me, I was impressed with the thought that Yeshua was revealing hidden truths about the LORD that are not visible in the mustard seed, unless you search for the meaning within them. One of the most astonishing features that is hidden within this parable is the fact that the mustard plant itself is a member of the *"cruciferae family" or "crucifer"* family and the blossom is shaped like a cross or like two staves of wood crossing each other. The Mustard plant is considered to be in the *cruciferae family* because all *crucifer plants* have four petals and it is the signature mark of this species of the plant family. The four petals of the blossoms on the mustard plant shaped like a cross represent the same shape of the ancient Hebrew letter *"Tav."* The ancient Hebrew letter *"Tav"* means *"Covenant of Truth." As the Living Torah Covenant, Yeshua declared, "I AM the way, the truth and the life!*" In this parable, Yeshua was foreshadowing exactly how He was going to die, by declaring it before it came to pass. The Scripture tells us specifically that the Messiah had to be cut off in this way because He was sent to become the cut off Branch and the Rod lifted up for the salvation and for *the preservation* of Israel and the world!

Regarding the origins of the Hebrew letter *"Tav,"* we find that in very ancient times this letter was a very simple cross mark that was used as a signature, to sign important documents. It was this ancient form of the Hebrew letter *"Tav"* that is written in Ezekiel's vision in Chapter 9. Apparently, the LORD used the mark of the *Tav,* shaped like the upright cross, to save the LORD'S people when He sent forth an angel to place this mark on those who cried out against the abominations that were going on within His Holy Land. The LORD sealed His servants with this mark and with the life blood of the Lamb to separate the LORD'S people called the wheat from the chaff. In other words, the LORD made them cleft, so the light and the darkness could not abide together, as it was in the beginning of creation. This was the LORD'S signature again! Those who were not given the *Tav* mark by the angel were considered to be the chaff. The LORD then sent forth an angel to destroy the chaff and this included all the people, that not only committed abominations in the Land, but it also included those that did not believe the LORD or put their lives and trust in Him, by keeping His Laws, Commandments, and Testimonies.

Ezekiel 9:3-4 *And the glory of the God of Israel was gone up from the cherub, whereupon He was, to the threshold of the House, And He called to the man clothed with linen, which had the writer's inkhorn by his side; And the LORD said unto him, Go through the midst of the city, through the midst of Jerusalem, and set a mark upon the foreheads of the men that sigh and that cry for all the abominations that be done in the midst thereof. And to the others he said in mine hearing, Go ye after him through the city, and smite; let not your eye spare, neither have ye pity; Slay utterly old and young, both maids, and little children, and women; but come not near any man upon whom is the mark; and begin at My Sanctuary. Then they began at the ancient men which were before the House. And He said unto them, Defile the House, and fill the courts with the slain; go ye forth. And they went forth, and slew in the city. And it came to pass, while they were slaying them, and I was left, that I fell upon my face, and cried, and said, Ah LORD GOD! Wilt Thou destroy all the residue of Israel in Thy pouring out of Thy fury upon Jerusalem?*

All of this is quite fascinating because during the time of the tribulation, we see, in the book of Revelation, the same events take place. The LORD sends forth His angel to mark His people or His servants on their foreheads with His own mark. Those who are not sealed by the LORD'S angel will be considered the chaff. So the Hebrew letter *"Tav"* was originally the shape of the cross, the shape of the mustard blossom. I believe that the Tav or the cross of Messiah's Eternal Testimony is the mark that the LORD will once again place upon His servants to protect them as it symbolizes the LORD'S life blood of the Lamb that causes death to Passover us, but it is *not* the upside down cross, rather the lifted upright cross. The LORD'S people will be sealed only by the LORD'S Royal Seal for Eternal life and for total protection during the great tribulation and the LORD'S Name will be upon His Royal seal. The seal of the LORD is His signature, as the Royal Sovereign KING, full of all power and authority. This seal is on the KING'S signet ring. Yeshua declared that all power and authority has been given to Him in Heaven and on earth. So the seal, in essence, is the protection of *the Royal Standard of God.* Yeshua's mark of the cruciferae mustard plant, *"The Tav,"* is the sign of the Eternal Covenant of Truth, and, as I said before, it is the preservative! In Revelation, we see that it is only after the LORD'S servants are sealed with His Royal seal mark by the angel that those without it are consumed in the LORD'S fury. He will pour forth His wrath upon those that take the mark of the beast, 666, the abominable unbelieving world and upon those who defile His Holy Land and His Holy Mount Moriah called *"The Temple Mount."* Anyone that sadly turns their back to the LORD'S Holy of Holies will be considered chaff. Exactly as it happened in Ezekiel, the LORD will cut off the evil doers and those who do abominable things against the LORD God of Hosts. It makes perfect sense that those who have the light of Messiah will be separated and made cleft at this time from those who do not have the light of Messiah. This is also the difference between Heaven and Hell. To be in Heaven is to be with the light of the LORD in the Almond Tree Menorah of Life. To be in Hell is to be cut off from the LORD and to be separated from the light which is to be left in the total darkness of death forever. It is a chilling thought just imagining it. The LORD is so beautiful, though, that no one should ever want to be without Him! The servants of the LORD that are sealed by the LORD'S angel will be preserved like *the mustard seed, the preservative,* because they have the sign of the

Covenant in truth, containing the life blood of the Lamb of God, placed upon them. Messiah takes away the sins of the world. His life blood is on the door leading into Heaven, which is the only blood that can give us Eternal life. This explains why the sacrificial blood of animals is not good enough to give us Eternal life, as we see in the following Scriptures.

Hebrews 9:11-14 *But Messiah being come an High Priest of good things to come, by a greater and more perfect Tabernacle, not made with hands, that is to say, not of this building; Neither by the blood of goats and calves, but by His own blood entered in once into the Holy Place, having obtained eternal redemption for us. For if the blood of bulls and of goats, and the ashes of an heifer sprinkling the unclean, sanctifieth to the purifying of the flesh; How much more shall the blood of Messiah, who through the eternal Spirit offered Himself without spot to God, purge your conscience from dead works to serve the Living God?*

Hebrews 10:4-22 *For it is not possible that the blood of bulls and of goats should take away sins. Wherefore when He cometh into the world, He saith, Sacrifice and offering thou wouldest not, but a body hast Thou prepared me; In burnt offerings and sacrifices for sin Thou hast had no pleasure. Then said I, Lo, I come (in the volume of the book it is written of Me,) to do Thy will, O God. Above when He said, Sacrifice and offering and burnt offering for sin Thou wouldest not, neither hadst pleasure therein; which are offered by the Law; Then said He, Lo, I come to do Thy will, O God, He taketh away the first, that He may establish the second. By the which will we are sanctified through the offering of the body of Yeshua Messiah once for all. And every Priest standeth daily ministering and offering oftentimes the same sacrifices, which can never take away sins; But this man, after He had offered one sacrifice for sins forever, sat down on the right hand of God; From henceforth expecting till His enemies be made His footstool. Whereof the Holy Spirit also is a witness to us; for after that He had said before, This is the Covenant that I will make with them after those days, saith the LORD, I will put My Laws into their hearts, and in their minds will I write them; And their sins and iniquities will I remember no more. Now where remission of these is, there is no more offering for sin. Having therefore, brethren, boldness to enter into the Holiest by the blood of Yeshua, By a new and living way, which He hath consecrated for us, through the veil, that is to say, His flesh; And having an High Priest over the House of God; Let us draw near with a true heart in full assurance of faith, having our hearts sprinkled from an evil conscience, and our bodies washed with pure water.*

It is now easy to understand that the opposite or opposing mark of the LORD is called *"the mark of the beast or the Anti-Christ."* This is Satan who opposes the LORD God of Israel and Yeshua in every way possible. So the evil mark of the beast originates from ancient pagan cultures like ancient Babylon, and the Bible warned us that it is the name of a false god and his false prophet. So this should give us a clue, never to take any mark that comes from any of these ancient pagan cultures because there is only one true Living loving God that created the universe with His Rod and His Holy city is Jerusalem forever! The LORD warned us that we should never take the mark of the sun or the moon, nor worship any manmade gods from these ancient pagan cultures, or have their names written on us in any way, because the LORD God directly commanded us not to worship these things, *"Lest we be defiled and corrupted by them,"* as it is written in the book of Deuteronomy.

Deuteronomy 4:15-20 *Take ye therefore good heed unto yourselves; for ye saw no manner of similitude on the day that the LORD spake unto you in Horeb out of the midst of the fire; Lest ye corrupt yourselves, and make you a graven image, the similitude of any figure, the likeness of male or female, The likeness of any beast that is on the earth, the likeness of any winged fowl that flieth in the air, The likeness of anything that creepeth on the ground, the likeness of any fish that is in the waters beneath the earth; And lest thou lift up thine eyes unto Heaven, and when thou seest the sun, and the moon, and the stars, even all the host of Heaven, shouldest be driven to worship them, which the LORD thy God hath divided unto all nations under the whole Heaven. But the LORD hath taken you, and brought you forth out of the iron furnace, even out of Egypt, to be unto Him a people of inheritance, as ye are this day.*

On the other hand, the Holy Almond Tree Menorah of the LORD God of Israel is the true sign of Israel because it represents the LORD'S Living Testimony. The account in Revelation of the sealing of the LORD'S servants with His *Royal mark* occurs in Chapter 7 and it is only *later* that we see that the mark of the beast comes upon the earth, in Revelation

Chapter 13. It is interesting that the name *"Anti-Christ" or "Anti-messiah" does* actually mean *"One who opposes the LORD God of Israel and Messiah Yeshua."*

The LORD is faithful, however, to seal His servants well before the mark of the beast comes to mark the world. The LORD will pour out His fury upon those who have taken the mark of the beast which is put on all those who are perishing. It is a covenant of death, while the LORD has the Covenant of Eternal life! Satan is death, the LORD is life! In the following Scripture, we see that the LORD seals His servants first for protection.

Revelation 7:2-4 *And I saw another angel ascending from the east, having the seal of the Living God; and he cried with a loud voice to the four angels, to whom it was given to hurt the earth and the sea, Saying, Hurt not the earth, neither the sea, nor the trees, till we have sealed the servants of our God in their foreheads, and I heard the number of them which were sealed; and there were sealed an hundred and forty and four thousand of all the tribes of Israel.*

Revelation 13:16-18 *And he causeth all, both small and great, rich and poor, free and bond, to receive a mark in their right hand, or in their foreheads; And that no man might buy or sell, save he that had the mark, or the name of the beast, or the number of his name. Here is wisdom. Let him that hath understanding count the number of the beast; for it is the number of a man; and his number is Six hundred three-score and six.*

Now it is interesting that the flower blossom of the *cruciferae plant,* that is shaped like the ancient Hebrew letter *"Tav,"* points to all four directions of the earth. Yeshua told us that *"the Gospel, the Living Torah, would be preached in all the world and then the end would come."* So when the LORD'S crop is ready to be harvested because it has become fully ripe and ready fruit, then the LORD will come to remove the chaff.

Now in the parable of *the mustard seed,* we see that the seed becomes a tree that spreads out like a canopy with its branches as a covering, and the birds of the air come to rest under the shadow of the tree. Yeshua was crushed as the mustard seed and came to life as the Living Branch of the Tree of Life. When His Kingdom comes, we will dwell in the Divine Presence of the Almighty under the branches of the LORD, since He is the Tree of Life. Remember in Psalm 84:3 that the sparrow built her house at the Temple of the LORD. So the birds in the parable are abiding under the covering of the Tree of Life in Heaven, in the LORD'S Holy Temple!

The method of treading the mustard seed is exactly the same method that is used to tread the wheat grain on the threshing floor that I discussed before. In ancient times, when the mustard seed was threshed, the oxen tread it down in a circle and left the halo pattern on the threshing floor, as they tread the grain. Messiah was the mustard seed, threshed and crucified, just as He foreshadowed it in the parable of the mustard seed. *It is interesting that after the mustard seed is threshed and crushed, it is then mixed with vinegar and water.* So Yeshua was literally offered vinegar mixed with gall, while He was lifted up as the Rod of God upon the cross. The Messiah's crucifixion is written in Psalm 69, within the following Words and fulfilled by Yeshua in the Gospel of Matthew.

Psalms 69:21 *They gave Me also gall for My meat; and in My thirst they gave Me vinegar to drink.*

Matthew 27:34-35 *They gave Him vinegar to drink mingled with gall; and when He had tasted thereof, He would not drink. And they crucified Him, and parted His garments, casting lots; that it might be fulfilled which was spoken by the Prophet, They parted My garments among them, And upon My vesture did they cast lots.*

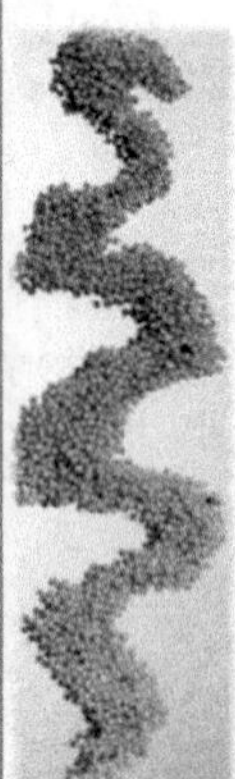

The Hebrew letter *Tav,* the cross, is the 22nd letter of the Hebrew alphabet and the Scripture regarding the crucifixion and casting of lots for Messiah's clothing is in Psalms 22!

Psalm 22:16-18 *For dogs have compassed Me; the assembly of the wicked have inclosed Me; They pierced My hands and My feet. I may tell all My bones; they look and stare upon Me, They part My garments among them, and cast lots upon My vesture.*

The Roman soldiers offered the vinegar and gall to Yeshua on a hyssop stalk. The hyssop was used as a means of purification to make one white as snow.

John 19:28-30 *After this, Yeshua knowing that all things were now accomplished, that the Scripture might be fulfilled, saith, I thirst. Now there was set a vessel full of vinegar; and they filled a sponge with vinegar, and put it upon hyssop, and put it to His mouth. When Yeshua therefore had received the vinegar, He said, It is finished; and He bowed His head, and gave up the Spirit.*

When you take a Nazarite vow *you do not drink vinegar or wine vinegar or grapes.* They truly represent Yeshua the Nazarite, bearing the bitterness of the curse for us. When Yeshua tasted the vinegar mixed with gall on the hyssop stalk, He was purifying us on the cross from our sins and after He tasted it He said, *"It is finished!"* King David asked the LORD to purify him with hyssop to make him white as snow.

Psalms 51:7 *Purge me with hyssop, and I shall be clean; wash me, and I shall be whiter than snow.*

Isaiah 1:18 *Come now, and let us reason together, saith the LORD; though your sins be as scarlet, they shall be as white as snow; though they be red like crimson, they shall be as wool.*

Psalms 147:16 *He giveth snow like wool; he scattereth the hoarfrost like ashes.*

Isaiah 55:10 *For as the rain cometh down, and the snow from Heaven, and returneth not thither, but watereth the earth, and maketh it bring forth and bud, that it may give seed to the sower, and bread to the eater.*

We know Daniel the Prophet saw the LORD, the Ancient of Days, and he described Him as having a garment that is as white as snow and His hair was like the pure wool.

Daniel 7:9-10 *I beheld till the thrones were cast down, and the Ancient of days did sit, whose garment was white as snow, and the hair of His head like the pure wool; His throne was like the fiery flame, and his wheels as burning fire. A fiery stream issued and came forth from before Him; thousand thousands ministered unto Him, and ten thousand times ten thousand stood before Him: the judgment was set, and the books were opened.*

Yeshua was purified with the hyssop, making His hair in Heaven white as the pure wool, like snow, and His garment is pure white linen like snow because He has purified us from our sins, and now what once was scarlet has been made white as snow by the High Priest of Heaven after the Order of Melchizedek. On the Day of Atonement, Aaron confessed the sins of the sons of Israel onto the head of the scapegoat and a red ribbon was tied to it. Then it was sent into the wilderness. If God forgave their sins, the ribbon would turn pure white. *Messiah Yeshua became the scapegoat, sent by the Spirit into the wilderness, eventually bearing the sins of many.*

This leads me to something interesting that happened to me one day when I was sitting outside on my porch in the lawn rocking chair, reading part of this text that I had printed off. To describe the scene, there were two wind chimes hanging from ceiling hooks. One set of chimes was to my left and it was a set of very long metal tubes forming a circle. The other set, to my right, was much smaller set, but it also formed a circle of rather small metal tubes. There was no wind and not even a breeze was stirring the air. I was sitting on the edge of the rocking chair and reading aloud, but very softly, so that my words were almost inaudible. When I got to the words describing Messiah Yeshua in Heaven, I read the words, *"His eyes were like a flame of fire and His feet were like burnished bronze. His head and His hair were white like snow, like the pure wool."* Suddenly with no wind or even the slightest breeze blowing, I had to stop reading and look up because I felt the Presence of the LORD and both chimes were moving in a circle, so that every single tube was being struck at the same time! I was so shocked that I stopped reading and just watched them both going around, astonished that there was not even a breeze. Once again, that feeling of electricity was in the air that I felt before when my Almond Tree revelation was given to me. I thought it was stunning. So when the chimes stopped moving, I thought I would read those words again to see if the chimes would make the melody again. To my surprise they both began moving again, so that every single chime was struck. The strange thing is that if there is wind that moves the chimes, it usually blows the chimes from one side and not every tube is struck evenly and they never ring and move in a circle at the same time! These were visibly moving in a circle making the most beautiful melody together! I believe the LORD was with me in Spirit as I read His description softly into the air! Incredible! It is astonishing then, as I mentioned previously in another place, that a recent documentary said that Yeshua's hair on His burial Shroud appears to be white hair, although He was not old enough to have white hair. Yeshua did not have white hair while He was here on the earth, but His hair is white like snow, like the pure wool in His glorified state in Heaven. So the white hair on the image of Yeshua, on His burial Shroud, must reveal the exact moment of His glory, the instant of His resurrection!

Revelation 1:13-14 *And in the midst of the seven candlesticks one like unto the Son of man, clothed with a garment down to the foot, and girt about the paps with a golden girdle. His head and His hairs were white like wool, as white as snow; and His eyes were as a flame of fire.*

Official Shroud Face
Photograph ©1978 Barrie M. Schwortz Collection,
STERA Inc., All Rights Reserved

In the wilderness, all the people were sprinkled with the blood, water, scarlet wool and hyssop, and without His blood there is no remission of our sins. Yeshua has cleansed us and tasted the bitter vinegar on the hyssop stalk for us, to purify us forever, as our Heavenly Jewish High Priest.

Hebrews 9:19-28 *For when Moses had spoken every precept to all the people according to the Law, he took the blood of calves and of goats, with water, and scarlet wool, and hyssop, and sprinkled both the book, and all the people, Saying, This is the blood of the Testament which God hath enjoined unto you. Moreover he sprinkled with blood both the Tabernacle, and all the vessels of the ministry. And almost all things are by the Law purged with blood; and without shedding of blood is no remission. It was therefore necessary that the patterns of things in the Heavens should be purified with these; but the Heavenly things themselves with better sacrifices than these. For Messiah is not entered into the Holy Places made with hands, which are the figures of the true; but into Heaven itself, now to appear in the Presence of God for us; Nor yet that He should offer Himself often, as the High Priest entereth into the Holy Place every year with blood of others; For then must He often have suffered since the foundation of the world; but now once in the end of the world hath He appeared to put away sin by the sacrifice of Himself. And as it is appointed unto men once to die, but after this the judgment; So Messiah was once offered to bear the sins of many; and unto them that look for Him shall He appear the second time without sin unto salvation.*

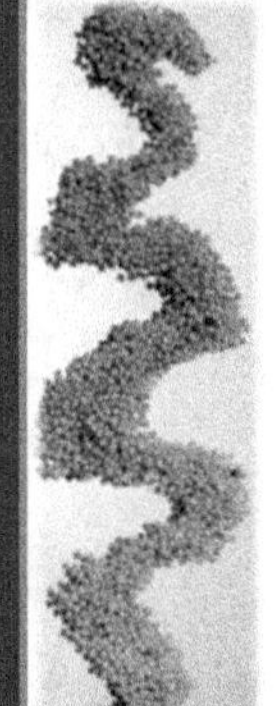

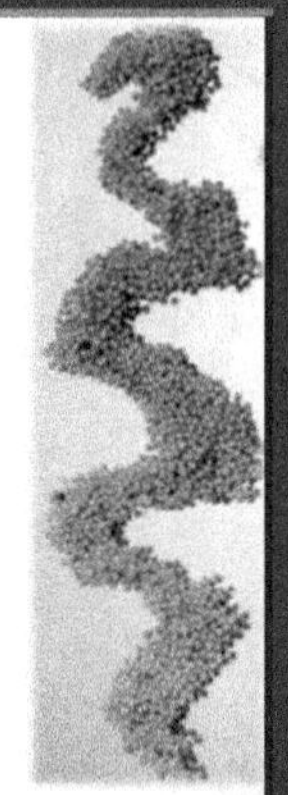

The mustard seed is ground to make a fine powder and it is very soothing to put it in bath water for various ailments. It has been used since ancient times for arthritic conditions. Yeshua heals our ailments by restoring and regenerating our bodies. Messiah Yeshua is the mustard seed preservative, so He told us that the Kingdom of Heaven was like the mustard seed that had branched out like a tree and all that believe by faith shall forever sit under the shelter of this Eternal Living tree!

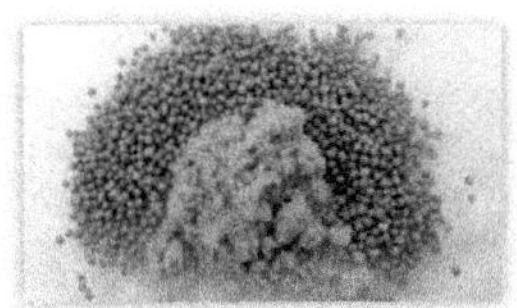

Mustard seed & powder
Photo ©2014 Kimberly K Ballard
All Rights Reserved

MESSIAH IS REVEALED IN THE ATTRIBUTES OF THE 12 TRIBES OF ISRAEL MOURNING SEVENTY TIMES SEVEN

Lion of Judah Jerusalem Emblem
Photos ©2013 Kimberly K Ballard All Rights Reserved

After I wrote that Messiah Yeshua was the cut off Fruitful Branch from the Almond Tree, my eyes were opened to see something else that was profoundly exciting and it is that Yeshua was encoded and revealed within the special attributes that Jacob gave to his sons, the twelve tribes of Israel. Each tribe had its own emblem and symbol. Jacob gave special blessings to each of his 12 sons. The blessings pinpointed their personal attributes, as individual tribes. So this morning, as I was studying Genesis 49:22-24, I saw this connection to the Messiah. I have written the Scripture below from Genesis, containing all of Jacob's attributes in detail as they were given to each one of his sons.

Genesis 49:1-28 *And Jacob called unto his sons, and said, Gather yourselves together, that I may tell you that which shall befall you in the last days. Gather yourselves together and hear, ye sons of Jacob; and hearken unto Israel your father. Reuben, thou art my first-born son, my might, and the first fruits of my strength, the excellency of dignity, and the excellency of power; Unstable as water, thou shalt not excel; because thou wentest up to thy father's bed; then defilest thou it; he went up to my couch. Simeon and Levi are brethren; instruments of cruelty are in their habitations. O my soul, come not thou into their secret; unto their assembly, mine honour, be not thou united; for in their anger they slew a man, and in their self-will they digged down a wall. Cursed be their anger, for it was fierce; and their wrath, for it was cruel; I will divide them in Jacob, and scatter them in Israel. Judah, thou art he whom thy brethren shall praise; thy hand shall be in the neck of thine enemies; thy father's children shall bow down before thee. Judah is a lion's whelp; from the prey, my son, thou art gone up; he stooped down, he couched as a lion, and as an old lion; who shall rouse him up? The sceptre shall not depart from Judah, nor a lawgiver from between his feet, until Shiloh come; and unto him shall the gathering of the people be. Binding his foal unto the vine, and his ass's colt unto the choice vine; he washed his garments in wine, and his clothes in the blood of grapes; His eyes shall be red with wine, and his teeth white with milk. Zebulon shall dwell in at the haven of the sea; and he shall be for an haven of ships; and his border shall be unto Zidon. Issachar is a strong ass couching down between two burdens; And he saw that rest was good, and the land that it was pleasant; and bowed his shoulder to bear, and became a servant unto tribute. Dan shall judge his people, as one of the tribes of Israel. Dan shall be a serpent by the way, an adder in the path, that biteth the horse heels, so that his rider shall fall backward. I have waited for Thy salvation, O LORD. Gad, a troop shall overcome him; but he shall overcome at the last. Out of Asher his bread shall be fat, and he shall yield royal dainties. Naphtali is a hind let loose; he giveth goodly words. Joseph is a fruitful bough, even a fruitful bough by a well; whose branches run over the wall; The archers have sorely grieved*

him, and shot at him, and hated him; But his bow abode in strength, and the arms of his hands were made strong by the hands of the Mighty God of Jacob; From thence is the shepherd, the stone of Israel; Even by the God of thy father, who shall help thee; and by the Almighty , who shall bless thee with blessings of the deep that lieth under, blessings of the breasts, and of the womb; The blessings of thy father have prevailed above the blessings of my progenitors unto the utmost bound of the everlasting hills; they shall be on the head of Joseph, and on the crown of the head of him that was separate from his brethren. Benjamin shall ravin as a wolf; in the morning he shall devour the prey, and at night he shall divide the spoil. All these are the twelve tribes of Israel; and this is it that their father spake unto them, and blessed them; everyone according to his blessing he blessed them.

Now below, I have extracted each element of the 12 tribes of Israel to show how they all apply to the Messiah of Israel.

Messiah Yeshua is revealed in these specific attributes:

1. Reuben-You are my first-born, my might and first fruit of my strength. The excellency of dignity and the excellency of power. Water

1. Messiah Yeshua- Is the First born son of Mary and the only begotten Son of God the Father. Messiah is the First Fruits of Salvation and has the Excellency of dignity and the Excellency of power, as the Rod of God. He is the Living Water.

2. Simeon- Cursed Anger so fierce, wrath

2. Messiah Yeshua- Bore the Curse of death from Eden and pours out the wrath of God's fierce anger at the end of days.

3. Levi- Cursed Anger so fierce, wrath

3. Messiah Yeshua- Bore the Curse of death from the Garden of Eden and unleashes the fierce anger of the LORD'S wrath at the end of days.

4. Judah- Thou art he whom thy brethren shall praise; thy hand shall be in the neck of thine enemies; thy father's children shall bow down before thee. Judah is a lion's whelp; from the prey, my son, thou art gone up; he stooped down, he couched as a lion, and as an old lion; who shall rouse him up? The sceptre shall not depart from Judah, nor a lawgiver from between his feet, until Shiloh come; and unto him shall the gathering of the people be. Binding his foal unto the vine, and his ass's colt unto the choice vine; he washed his garments in wine, and his clothes in the blood of grapes; His eyes shall be red with wine, and his teeth white with milk.

4. Messiah Yeshua- Thou art He whom Thy brethren shall praise. The Yad or hand of God, from the tribe of Judah, will destroy all His enemies. All Thy Father's children shall bow down before Thee. Yeshua is the Lion of the tribe of Judah, the Son, who will be roused to stand in Heaven to return to slay the wicked on the earth. Yeshua is the Royal Sceptre that shall not depart from Judah, because He is the Rod of God that rests between the feet of the KING and this Sceptre is the Lawgiver of the Eternal Living Torah Covenant. He is the Messiah who will come again and unto Him shall the gathering of the people be. He rode into Jerusalem on a foal and an ass's colt, because He is the choice vine. He has a robe dipped in blood, represented by wine. His eyes are a flame of fire and He is pure white, as He speaks the pure Word of God with His mouth.

5. Zebulon- He shall be a haven of the sea.

5. Messiah Yeshua- Is a haven of rest for all people that put their trust in Him. Remember that Yeshua instantly brought the Jewish disciples in the ship to their haven called *"the Garden of Riches."* As the Living Water, He is *"the Great Sea"* of the Heavenly Temple who purifies us and who takes us to our haven, into the Eternal Kingdom of Heaven.

6. Issachar- Strong, Among the sheepfolds. He saw that rest was good and the land that was pleasant. He bowed his shoulder to bear, and became a servant unto tribute.

6. Messiah Yeshua- Is the Strong Rod, the Good Shepherd of the sheepfold and He has chosen the pleasant Land as His Eternal abode. Though He was the KING, He became a suffering servant called Mashiach Ben Joseph, Messiah the Son of Joseph, and paid the tribute to the Roman Caesar.

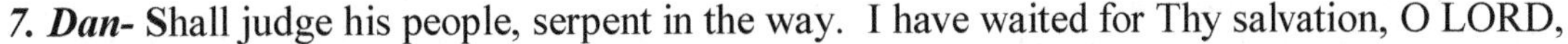

*7. **Dan-*** Shall judge his people, serpent in the way. I have waited for Thy salvation, O LORD,
*7. **Messiah Yeshua-*** Shall judge His people. Destroys the Serpent, Satan. Messiah has crushed the head of the Serpent who bruised His heels. Yeshua is our Salvation, as the LORD.
*8. **Gad-*** A troop shall overcome him; but he shall overcome at the last.
*8. **Messiah Yeshua-*** The Roman troops overcame Him; but He has overcome to reveal His greatest victory at last, when He returns as the KING from Heaven with a shout.
*9. **Asher-*** His bread shall be fat, and he shall yield royal dainties.
*9. **Messiah Yeshua-*** Is the Unleavened Bread from Heaven that makes us fat in *the Living Torah.* He yields His Royal dainties to us, which are His exquisite Royal Words of love as a crown of righteousness.
*10. **Naphtali-*** Is a hind let loose. He giveth goodly words.
*10. **Messiah Yeshua-*** Sets our feet like a hind on high places. He giveth the goodly Word of God, *the Living Torah* of Eternal life.
*11. **Joseph-*** Is a fruitful bough, even a fruitful bough by a well; whose branches run over the wall; The archers have sorely grieved him, and shot at him, and hated him; But his bow abode in strength, and the arms of his hands were made strong by the hands of the Mighty God of Jacob; From thence is the shepherd, the stone of Israel; Even by the God of thy father, who shall help thee; and by the Almighty , who shall bless thee with blessings of the deep that lieth under, blessings of the breasts, and of the womb; The blessings of thy father have prevailed above the blessings of my progenitors unto the utmost bound of the everlasting hills; they shall be on the head of Joseph, and on the crown of the head of him that was separate from his brethren. His Arms were made firm by the hands of the Mighty one of Jacob, there the Shepherd, the Rock of Israel, the God of your father who helps you. Shaddai who blesses you with blessings of Heaven above. Blessings of the deep, blessings of the breast and womb. Eternal
*11. **Messiah Yeshua-*** Is the Fruitful bough, even a Fruitful bough by a well. He is the Branch that runs over the wall. His enemies have sorely grieved Him, wounded Him and hated Him, but He is the Rod abiding in strength, as the arm of the LORD revealed. He is the Yad, the hand made strong as the Mighty God of Jacob. He is the Good Shepherd, the Stone and the Rock of Israel, even by His Father who helps Him. The Crown shall be upon Yeshua's head, on the head of Yeshua of Nazareth, who separated Himself from His brethren. He is the firm outstretched arm of God. The Rock of Israel, Yeshua, is the God of your father who helps you. Yeshua blesses you with all the blessings of Heaven above. *The Living Torah* blesses us with the deep blessings because He is our Spiritual food and the source of Eternal Life.
*12. **Benjamin-*** In the morning he shall devour the prey, and at night he shall divide the spoil.
*12. **Messiah Yeshua-*** In the morning, the Rod devours the prey and He comes as a thief in the night, to divide the spoil.

Stone Wall Photo ©2014 Kimberly K Ballard

When Yeshua fed the 5,000 +, He told the children of Israel that He will gather all the pieces that were lost, that represented the twelve tribes of Israel, in the twelve baskets. Though they were scattered, Yeshua indicated that not one of them will be lost. This is why the LORD impressed me to write twelve chapters for this book, after the twelve tribes of Israel and twelve disciples! So the Messiah is coming just as Jacob prophesied through the blessings that he spoke over his twelve sons, who were the heads of the twelve tribes of Israel. *The words of Jacob proclaimed what would happen to them in the last days and I believe the words actually pertain to the revelation of the Messiah.*

Now within the story of Jacob's son, *Joseph,* there came a time when all was restored, but this only happened after Joseph was first hated, rejected, and sold by his own brothers, as a servant. Joseph's brothers could not see that the ruler Joseph was their own brother, who had been separated from them. Then the time came when Joseph revealed his identity to them, after having been betrayed by them. So Joseph saved his brothers by giving them grain to make bread, so they would not die. What the brothers meant for evil was turned to good to save many alive. Now with Messiah Yeshua, a time is coming when all will be restored, but this would only happen after Yeshua was first hated, rejected, and betrayed by His own brethren to the Gentiles. Messiah Yeshua came as a servant. Yeshua's people Israel could not see that the ruler KING stood in their midst as their own brother, who was the Branch cut off and made cleft from Israel, to be separated from them. The Messiah was a Nazarite who was *separated, "Kadesh,"* as the Rod of God. A time is coming, though, when Yeshua will reveal His true identity to Israel. So Yeshua saved Israel and the world by becoming the grain that was threshed, as the Unleavened Bread from Heaven, which is the Staff of Eternal Life. Yeshua saved us by destroying the curse, so we would no longer die. What His generation did and meant for evil, was turned to good to save many people alive. This was *"Mashiach Ben Joseph,"* but Yeshua returns from Heaven the victorious ruling and reigning KING, *"Mashiach Ben David,"* Messiah the Son of David. This is when Yeshua will unveil His identity to His own brethren and they will weep bitterly for Him, as one weeps for an only Son, just as Joseph's brothers wept on his shoulder for him like a lost son, after their eyes were opened to recognize Him the second time they saw him. Messiah is the Spirit of grace and supplications. The grace of Messiah refers to *"Mercy and Pardon, unmerited Divine assistance, given to humans for their regeneration or sanctification. It is an act of kindness that comes from God." The Supplications of Messiah refer to "Humble earnest prayers and petitions to God."* Yeshua is humble and He intercedes in prayer for us with groaning in His heart by His Holy Spirit. He is the Living Water that is poured out, full of the Holy Spirit, upon the inhabitants of Jerusalem. Remember the LORD says, *"They shall look upon Me who they pierced and they shall mourn for Him, as an only Son."* This is a future event!

Stone Wall Tower Photo ©2013 Kimberly K Ballard All Rights Reserved

Perhaps the LORD will use this book full of Divine revelations to be a final witness before He returns to reign in Jerusalem!

Zechariah 12:9-10 *And it shall come to pass in that day, that I will seek to destroy all the Nations that come against Jerusalem. And I will pour upon the House of David, and upon the inhabitants of Jerusalem, the Spirit of Grace and of supplications; and they shall look upon Me whom they have pierced, and they shall mourn for Him, as one mourneth for his only son, and shall be in bitterness for Him, as one that is in bitterness for his firstborn.*

When Yeshua returns to gather all His brethren together, He will give them the good grain, *the Living Torah,* the Unleavened Bread from Heaven. *All Israel will be saved, as it is written in the book of Romans, when He comes on the Day of Atonement.* This event will come at the time of the end of the transgression, when Yeshua brings in everlasting righteousness and the final restoration to Israel.

Now the next thing that I have to show you is so remarkable because the LORD revealed to me that *"the mourning period" of Israel's children after Jacob died is the exact same amount of time of mourning that Israel's children will mourn for the Messiah, from the time that He is cut off as "The Branch" to the time that He returns to rule over them forever, as the Eternal KING OF KINGS!*

If this does not boggle your mind, I do not know what will! As we can see in the following Scripture, Jacob died and he was gathered unto his fathers. Then they mourned for him for a specific amount of time.

Stone Wall Photo ©2013 Kimberly K Ballard All Rights Reserved

Genesis 50:1-20 *And Joseph fell upon his father's face, and wept upon him, and kissed him. And Joseph commanded his servants the physicians to embalm his father. And the physicians embalmed Israel. And forty days were fulfilled for him; for so are fulfilled the days of embalming. And the Egyptians wept for him threescore and ten days. And when the days of weeping for him were past, Joseph spoke unto the house of Pharaoh, saying; If now I have found favour in your eyes, speak, I pray you, in the ears of Pharaoh, saying; My father made me swear, saying; Lo, I die in my grave which I have digged for me in the land of Canaan, there shalt thou bury me. Now therefore let me go up, I pray thee, and bury my father and I will come back. And Pharaoh said; Go up, and bury thy father, according as he made thee swear. And Joseph went up to bury his father; and with him went up all the servants of Pharaoh, the elders of his house, and all the elders of the land of Egypt, and all the house of Joseph, and his brethren, and his father's house; only their little ones, and their flocks, and their herds, they left in the land of Goshen. And there went up with him both chariots and horsemen; and it was a very great company. And they came to the threshing floor of Atad, which is beyond the Jordan, and there they wailed with a very great and sore wailing; and he made a mourning for his father seven days And when the inhabitants of the land, the Canaanites, saw the mourning in the floor of Atad, they said; This is a grievous mourning to the Egyptians. Wherefore the name of it was called Abel-mizraim, which is beyond the Jordan. And his sons did unto him according as he commanded them. For his sons carried him into the land of Canaan, and buried him in the cave of the field of Machpelah, which Abraham bought with the field, for a possession of a burying place, of Ephron the Hittite, in front of Mamre. And Joseph returned into Egypt, he, and his brethren, and all that went up with him to bury his father, after he had buried his father. And when Joseph's brethren saw that their father was dead, they said; It may be that Joseph will hate us, and will fully requite us all the evil which we did unto him. And they sent a message unto Joseph, saying; Thy father did command before he died, saying; So shall ye say unto Joseph; Forgive, I pray thee now, the transgression of thy brethren, and their sin, for that they did unto thee evil. And now, we pray thee, forgive the transgression for the servants of the God of their father. And Joseph wept when they spoke unto him. And his brethren also went and fell down before his face; and they said; Behold, we are they bondsmen. And Joseph said unto them; Fear not; for am I in the place of God? And as for you, you meant evil against me; but God meant it for good, to bring to pass, as it is this day, to save much people alive.*

What the LORD showed me is that when Jacob died this was a great time of mourning for Israel, and for the Egyptians that knew him. Jacob, who was renamed *"Israel,"* had been cut off from the land of the living. *Forty days* were fulfilled for him to be embalmed. Then there was a defined mourning period where they wept for Jacob for a total of *threescore and ten days,* which is equal to *70 days* of mourning. Then when Joseph went into Canaan at the threshing floor at Atad, they wailed and grieved for a total of *7 days.* So the designated *time of mourning or weeping for Jacob* was actually *70 and 7 days* (plus *forty days* for his embalming). Therefore, I realized that the same amount of time that they mourned for Jacob is exactly parallel to and is the exact same amount of time, that the children of Israel have been in mourning, from the time that Messiah Yeshua was cut off from the land of the living in His death, until the time of the end of Daniel's prophecy of the *70 x 7* is fulfilled. Yeshua died and was resurrected, and He was seen *forty days (Acts 1:3).* Then He ascended into Heaven. So what remains until He returns to usher in the Kingdom of God is the entire mourning period of *70 x 7.* This last *7* is actually called *"The time of Jacob's trouble"* at the end of days! *It is the last 7 years to mourn for Messiah, to raise up Israel.* Isaiah wrote that Yeshua would be cut off out of the land of the living for His people Israel.

Isaiah 53:8 *He was taken from prison and from judgment; and who shall declare His generation? For He was cut off out of the land of the living; for the transgression of My people was He stricken.*

When the 70 x 7 is fulfilled and only the 7 still remains today, then Messiah Yeshua will return from Heaven, bringing an end of sin and He will put an end to the transgression and restore all things! This is an astonishing revelation! Therefore, Israel will stop mourning, weeping at *the Western wall in Jerusalem* (which also weeps water), when the Good Shepherd comes back to reveal His face to them as the LORD God of Israel, showing them that He is alive forevermore and that this was done *"to save many people alive."* They will see this, at the end of the 70 x 7 when their time of mourning for Him as an only Son is fulfilled!

The End of Israel's Mourning for the Messiah = 70x7 The Wall is still weeping Photo ©2013 Kimberly K Ballard All Rights Reserved

70 X 7 THE RETURN OF MESSIAH YESHUA ON A WHITE HORSE

MESSIAH YESHUA RETURNS AT THE END OF 70 X 7!

MESSIAH YESHUA RETURNS AT THE END OF 70 X 7!

The Heavenly White Horse of Messiah Yeshua
Photo ©2013 Kimberly K Ballard All Rights Reserved

Now if we compare the prophecy of Daniel Chapter 9 to the time of Joseph's mourning for his father Israel or Jacob that was 70 and 7 *(plus forty days),* then we can see that Messiah *the Branch* was cut off before the fulfillment of the 70 x 7 of Daniel's prophecy was completed. Yeshua was resurrected, and appeared to them for *forty days* speaking to them of *the things pertaining to the Kingdom of God!* The prophecy of the Messiah is written in the following Scripture, revealing the 70 x 7 time frame. Notice that *the end of the transgression* brings in everlasting righteousness!

Daniel 9:24-27 *Seventy weeks are determined upon Thy people and upon Thy holy city, to finish the transgression, and to make an end of sins, and to make reconciliation for iniquity, and to bring in everlasting righteousness, and to seal up the vision and Prophecy, and to anoint the Most Holy. Know therefore and understand, that from the going forth of the commandment to restore and build Jerusalem unto the Messiah the Prince shall be seven weeks, and threescore and two weeks; the street shall be built again, and the wall, even in troublous times. And after threescore and two weeks shall Messiah be cut off, but not for Himself; and the people of the prince that shall come shall destroy the city and the sanctuary; and the end thereof shall be with a flood, and unto the end of the war desolations are determined. And he shall confirm the covenant with many for one week; and in the midst of the week he shall cause the sacrifice and the oblation to cease, and for the overspreading of abominations he shall make it desolate, even until the consummation, and that determined shall be poured upon the desolate.*

At this point, there is something remarkable that I must now show you, regarding the time frame of the Messiah in the 70 x 7. When the LORD showed this to me, I was stunned. I suddenly understood that Yeshua's own Words revealed that He is the one fulfilling this Divine prophecy. Yeshua's Words are said to mean one specific thing, but for some reason, the Holy Spirit showed me another very different and quite astonishing perspective on the very same passage of Scripture. I am now referring to the Scripture that pertains to *Simon Peter who was asking Messiah Yeshua how many times that his brother should sin against him and that he should forgive him.*

Matthew 18:21-22 *Then came Peter to Him, and said, LORD, how often shall my brother sin against me, and I forgive him? Till seven times? Yeshua said unto him, I say not unto thee, until seven times, but until seventy times seven.*

The traditional teaching of the meaning of this answer from Yeshua is *that you should keep on forgiving your brother again and again no matter how many times he sins against you, and even up to 70 times if necessary.* I believe now that this is not what Yeshua meant! I suddenly realized that Messiah Yeshua was actually revealing precisely and accurately when He will return at the end of the age for Israel's restoration at the time of her redemption! Yeshua told Simon Peter that you should forgive your brother until *"seventy times seven."* Yeshua was saying in essence that when He returns as the victorious KING Messiah, the Son of

David, it will be *at the end of the last 7 weeks of the 70x7 of Daniel's Prophecy.* It suddenly came to me, and I was truly astonished that at that time when the Messiah comes, *there will no longer be any sin! So therefore, because sin will no longer exist, then of course there will no longer be any need to forgive your brother! When Messiah returns from Heaven this is the end of the transgression, and sin, so there is no need to forgive your brother anymore because he will no longer be sinning against you ever again!* Yeshua was revealing to Simon Peter that when 70 x 7 is completed, *He will return from Heaven.* He will have made an end of sin and transgression, and will forgive iniquity at that time with the land of Israel. The Rod of God, the KING Messiah, restores everything in everlasting righteousness in a jubilee year at the end of this time frame of 70 x 7. So when Yeshua told Simon Peter to forgive his brother *until "Seventy times seven,"* Yeshua was revealing the exact time of His arrival at the end of days.

The word *"transgression"* pertains to *"a violation of the law, command, or duty."* As I thought about the meaning of this word, I remembered that the LORD had allowed His Holy Land to become desolate during the Babylonian fall of Jerusalem for *three score and ten years* (II Chronicles 36:21). The LORD said in this verse that He allowed the desolation of the land, *"To fulfill the Word of the LORD by the mouth of Jeremiah, until the land had enjoyed her Sabbaths: for as long as she lay desolate she kept Sabbath, <u>to fulfill three score and ten years</u>."* Of course *three score and ten years* equals the *seventy years* that the land of Israel was not cultivated because the people were taken away captive to Babylon for transgressing God's laws. In the Torah, in Leviticus 25, the LORD said that He intended for the land or soil of Israel to have His Sabbath rest. In Hebrew it is referred to as the *"shmittah"* or *"shmita"* year and it means *"release."* It is the seventh year of the seven year agricultural cycle. It is a time for the people to take their hands off the land from plowing and cultivating so they can acknowledge that the land and everything on the earth belongs to the LORD God. Psalm 24:1 states, *"The earth is the LORD'S, and the fullness thereof; the world, and they that dwell therein."* The Shmittah is explained here in the following passage along with the jubilee pertaining to sets of years.

Leviticus 25:1-10 *And the LORD spake unto Moses in mount Sinai, saying, Speak unto the children of Israel, and say unto them, When ye come into the land which I give you, then shall the land keep a Sabbath unto the LORD. Six years thou shalt sow thy field, and six years thou shalt prune thy vineyard, and gather in the fruit thereof: But in the seventh year shall be a Sabbath of rest unto the land, a Sabbath for the LORD: thou shalt neither sow thy field, nor prune thy vineyard. That which groweth of its own accord of thy harvest thou shalt not reap, neither gather the grapes of thy vine undressed: for it is a year of rest unto the land. And the Sabbath of the land shall be meat for you; for thee, and for thy servant, and for thy maid, and for thy hired servant, and for thy stranger that so-journeth with thee, And for thy cattle, and for the beast that are in thy land, shall all the increase thereof be meat. <u>And thou shalt number seven Sabbaths of years unto thee, seven times seven years; and the space of the seven Sabbaths of years shall be unto thee forty and nine years. Then shalt thou cause the trumpet of the jubilee to sound on the tenth day of the seventh month, in the Day of Atonement shall ye make the trumpet sound throughout all your land</u>. And ye shall hallow the fiftieth year, and proclaim liberty throughout all the land unto all the inhabitants thereof: it shall be a jubilee unto you; and ye shall return every man unto his possession, and ye shall return every man unto his family.*

The first Holy Temple was destroyed, and the land had its Sabbath rests. Centuries later the second Holy Temple was built by Herod. It was destroyed forty years after Messiah Yeshua was cut off through crucifixion. The land of Israel once again became desolate, and she enjoyed centuries of her Sabbaths to the LORD. When Messiah Yeshua was descending from the Mount of Olives He wept over Jerusalem because He prophesied that the land was about to become desolate again, and the people of Israel were going to be dispersed into all the nations of the earth for transgressions.

Luke 19:41-44 *And when He was come near, He beheld the city, and wept over it. Saying, If thou hadst known, even thou, at least in this thy day, the things which belong unto thy peace! But now they are hid from thine eyes. For the*

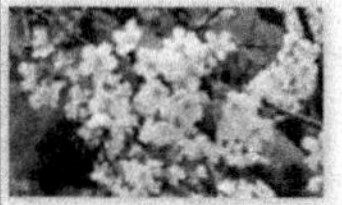

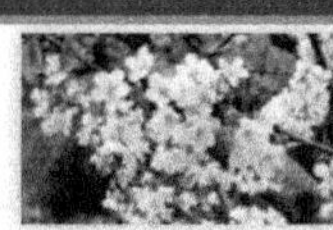

days shall come upon thee, that thine enemies shall cast a trench about thee, and compass thee round, and keep thee in on every side, And shall lay thee even with the ground, and thy children within thee; and they shall not leave in thee one stone upon another; because thou knewest not the time of thy visitation.

The land was about to experience more than *three score and ten days* of Sabbaths, and more than its share of years until the Messianic jubilee. It would endure centuries of Sabbath rests because the Holy Temple was going to be burned to the ground, and Jerusalem was going to be made desolate for two thousand years.

Isaiah 64:10-11 *Thy holy cities are a wilderness, Zion is a wilderness, Jerusalem a desolation. Our holy and our beautiful house, where our fathers praised Thee, is burned up with fire: and all our pleasant things are laid waste.*

Joel 2:3 *A fire devoureth before them; and behind them a flame burneth: the land is as the garden of Eden before them, and behind them a desolate wilderness; yea, and nothing shall escape them.*

The writer Mark Twain wrote about his travels to the land of Israel in the late 1800's. It had been renamed *"Palestine"* by the Roman Emperor Hadrian because the Philistines were Israel's ancient enemy, and he removed the Jews off their land. It is interesting that Mark Twain wrote in his book *"The Innocents Abroad"* that the land was desolate. He said, *"We never saw a human being on the whole route....There was hardly a tree or a shrub anywhere. Even the olive and the cactus, those fast friends of the worthless soil, had almost deserted the country."* ***(Quote; 1867 printed in London England 1881) - (Source; jewishvirtuallibrary.org/jsource/Quote/TwainJews.html).***

So Israel was a desolation, and now it is coming to life because the Messiah is about to return bringing an end to Israel's time of mourning. The desert is blossoming because Israel has been restored to her promised land.

Isaiah 51:3 *For the LORD shall comfort Zion: He will comfort all her waste places; and He will make her wilderness like Eden, and her desert like the garden of the LORD; joy and gladness shall be found therein, thanksgiving, and the voice of melody.*

Ezekiel 36:34-35 *And the desolate land shall be tilled, whereas it lay desolate in the sight of all that passed by. And they shall say, This land that was desolate is become like the garden of Eden; and the waste and desolate and ruined cities are become fenced, and are inhabited.*

What I find interesting in Leviticus 25:9 is *the blowing of the trumpet on the tenth day of the seventh month* after the land has the Sabbath rest during the jubilee. The trumpet blast of the LORD Messiah will occur in the fall of the year, in the seventh month! The seventh month is the beginning of the High Holy Days! Rosh HaShanah is the first of these special Holy appointments of the LORD also called *"the Feast of Trumpets."* It proclaims the LORD God is KING over Israel.

Astonishingly, I realized that it is when the transgression is over that Yeshua will also forgive His brothers, and reveal His face to them! As I said before, the purpose of this blinding of the eyes of Joseph's brothers regarding his identity was for the purpose of saving many people alive. After Joseph had said this to his brother's he said, *"I will sustain you and your little ones. Then he comforted them and spoke kindly to them."* The Last KING of Judah will open the eyes of the blind and they will see that Messiah is the LORD God of Israel. When He forgives His brothers there is no more sin, just everlasting beauty in the garden paradise of God! He returns riding upon a white horse! This is the truth about the 70 x 7 of Messiah and it is absolutely glorious!

Revelation 19:11 *And I saw heaven opened, and behold a white horse; and He that sat upon him was called Faithful and True, and in righteousness He doth judge and make war.*

Official Shroud Face Photograph

Messiah Yeshua bearing the curse of the Fig Tree of the Knowledge of Good and Evil from the Garden of Eden

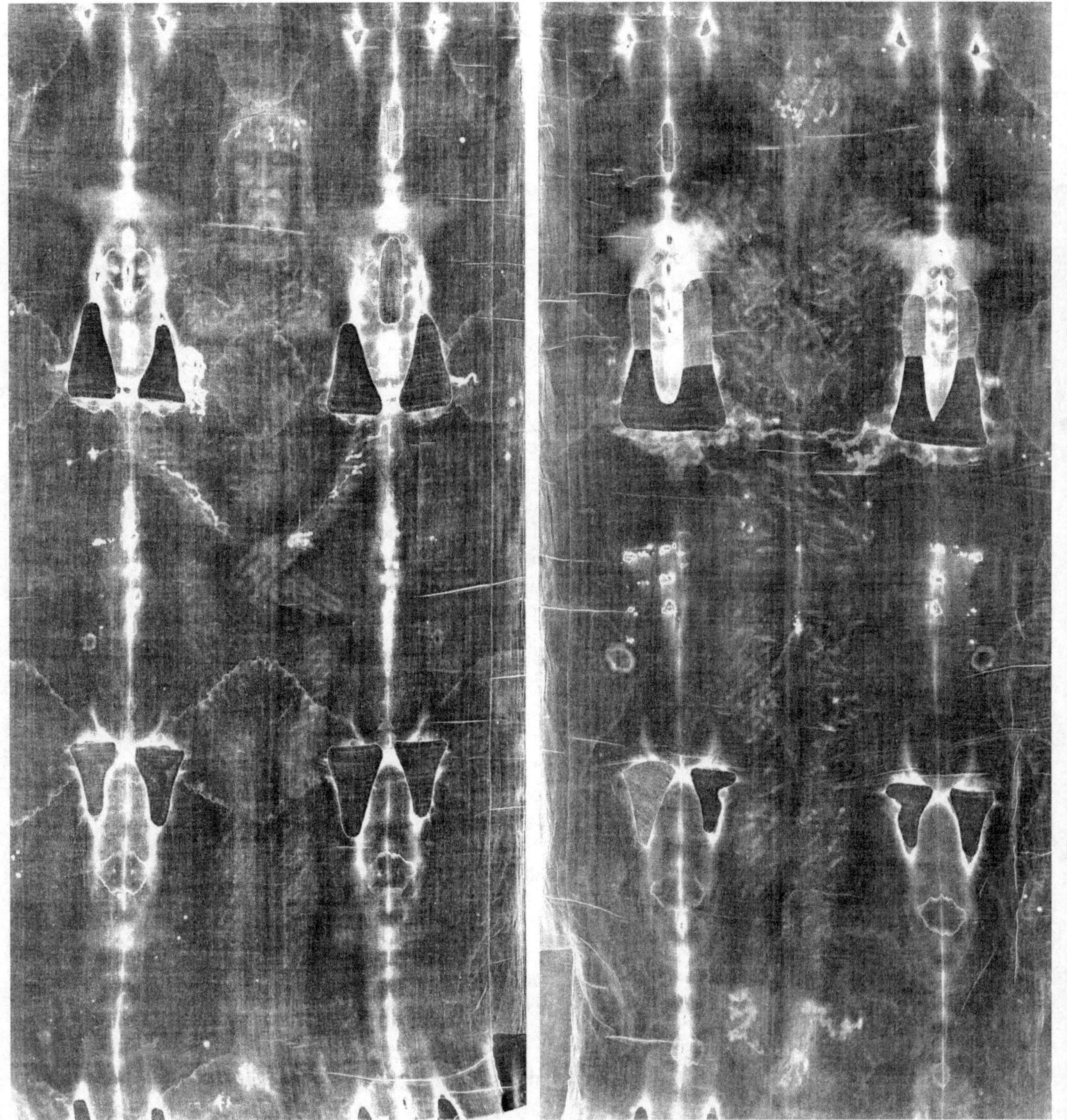

Ficus carica Fig Tree
Photograph ©2013 A. Danin, Jerusalem, Israel All Rights Reserved

THE FIG TREE OF KNOWLEDGE OF GOOD & EVIL

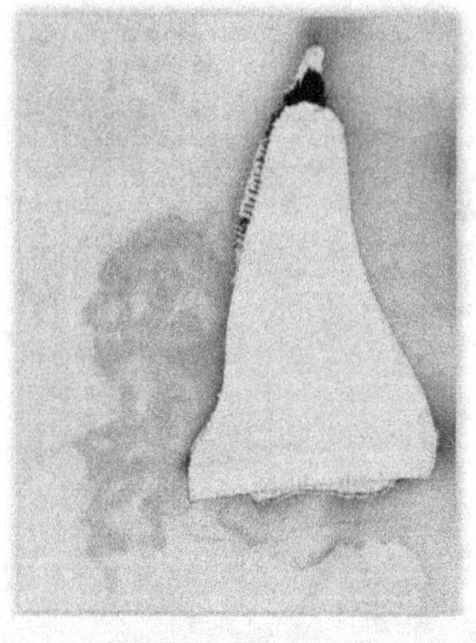

Official Shroud Sword Wound
Photo ©1978 Barrie M. Schwortz Collection, STERA Inc., All Rights Reserved

After my miracle of the Almond Tree occurred in 2007, the LORD inspired me to write about the Fig Tree, after He opened my eyes to see a very profound revelation of the Messiah in it. The Sycamore fig tree is a member of the Ficus family. I was fascinated and astonished when I also discovered by another Divine revelation that the Sycamore fig tree also bears a fantastic part of the Testimony of Messiah Yeshua.

Now Yeshua, who came as the second Adam, bore the curse of Eden, so He could redeem us back to Eternal life, so we could enter the Garden of God called *"Heaven"* and live with the LORD forever, as it was in the beginning before the curse. The Sycamore fig tree is said to have originated in Egypt and it was called *"the fig tree of Pharaoh."* According to the Word of the LORD and as I discussed previously, Pharaoh the great dragon was cursed and he descended into Sheol with all of his army, along with the trees of Eden that were already there. If the fig tree in the Garden of Eden was, in fact, the tree of the curse of sin and death, then it is interesting to note that figs and fig trees are sadly worshipped by some pagan cultures, probably because they also originated from the tree of the original curse.

In another miracle of Messiah Yeshua, He cursed the fig tree and made it wither. *So I believe that Yeshua was revealing that the Sycamore fig tree was the tree of the knowledge of good and evil that was once in the Garden of Eden.* The fig fruit of this tree was therefore the forbidden fruit. The curse of sin, death, and suffering came upon the whole earth when Adam and Eve turned away from the Word of God and began to eat the fruit that God had commanded them not to eat. Messiah Yeshua is *the Word of reconciliation, as the Living Torah.*

Ficus carica Fig Tree
Photo ©2013 A. Danin, Jerusalem Israel All Rights Reserved

As I studied the details in the Sycamore fig tree, *I suddenly noticed a connection between the fig tree and the death of Messiah Yeshua.* This means that He bore the curse in the place of the LORD'S Holy Mount Moriah in Jerusalem and this was, in fact, *the true location of the Garden of Eden.* To understand what I mean by this, we must look at all the

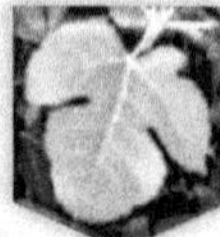

Botanical elements of the fig tree itself and the Ficus carica variety that produces the better fruit. The first thing we have to remember is that Yeshua bore the curse of the Garden of Eden, in order to redeem us from the curse of death, giving us Eternal life at the gate of Heaven. The purpose of this act was to reconcile us back to the Kingdom of the LORD God. *God was in Messiah, reconciling the world unto Himself.*

II Corinthians 5:17- 19 *Therefore if any man be in Messiah, he is a new creature; old things are passed away; behold, all things are become new. And all things are of God, who hath reconciled us to Himself by Yeshua Messiah, and hath given to us the ministry of reconciliation; To wit, that God was in Messiah, reconciling the world unto Himself, not imputing their trespasses unto them; and hath committed unto us the Word of reconciliation. Now then we are ambassadors of Messiah, as though God did beseech you by us; we pray you in Messiah's stead, be ye reconciled to God. For He hath made Him to be sin for us, who knew no sin; that we might be made the righteousness of God in Him.*

Galatians 3:13 *Messiah hath redeemed us from the curse of the Law, being made a curse for us; for it is written, Cursed is everyone that hangeth on a tree; That the blessing of Abraham might come on the Gentiles through Messiah Yeshua that we might receive the promise of the Spirit through faith.*

Romans 6:20-23 *For when ye were the servants of sin, ye were free from righteousness. What fruit had ye then in those things whereof ye are now ashamed? For the end of those things is death. But now being made free from sin, and become servants to God, ye have your fruit unto holiness, and the end everlasting life. For the wages of sin is death; but the gift of God is eternal life through Yeshua Messiah our LORD.*

The following astonishing facts that I discovered reveal Messiah's Testimony. *"The fig flowers are pollinated by a certain wasp known as the "fig wasp." This wasp is essential in the development of the fig fruit. In order to accomplish the task of pollination, the female fig wasp must enter into the green receptacle, which is a hollow that appears to be a fig fruit from the outside, but what looks like a fig from the outside is actually called a "Syconium." Inside the hollow of this fruit there are three types of flowers."* According to scientific facts, *"The female fig wasp can only lay her eggs in the short flowers that are sheltered inside of the Syconium. This is where the fleshy fig fruit later develops."* ***(Sources: Fig Tree Facts ©2010-2011 en.wikipedia.org/wiki/Fig_trees © simple.wikipedia.org/wiki/Fig and Fig Wasp and Syconium). (Fig Fruit; ©2010 March 5 waynesword.palomar.edu/pljune99.htm by W.P. Armstrong) AND (Dr. Avinoam Danin, Professor Emeritus of Botany from The Hebrew University of Jerusalem Israel, Fig photographs ©2013 from www.flora.huji.ac.il).***

Now it is said that in ancient times, a fig dresser would tend to the figs on the fig tree. It was his or her responsibility to climb up into the fig tree at the time of the first fruit, to pierce the fruit with an awl or he would gash it with a knife, while the fruit was hanging on the tree. In the Bible, the Prophet Amos mentions that he was a gatherer of figs and it is likely that he was also a fig dresser, as mentioned in Amos 7:14. It was very important for the fig dresser to pierce the fruit at the apex, before the wasp larvae could grow inside the hollow and develop to maturity. *Piercing the fruit, would allow the fig wasps to escape through the tiny portal that was created by the awl or the knife gash.* A truly fascinating aspect of this is the fact that after the fig dresser pierced the fruit, it took only 3 days for the fruit to quickly develop into the finest and the highest quality fruit before any damage could be done to the fruit by the wasps. The fig tree in Israel is said to produce at least two crops of figs in a year.

The more I began delving into this study, after my Almond Tree miracle, through the Divine guidance of the LORD, the more profound it became. When Yeshua bore the curse of the fig tree of death, at the place of the Garden of Eden, Yeshua was pierced and gashed with a knife while He was hanging upon the tree. The awl of the fig dresser came in the form of the Roman iron spikes or nails that were used to pierce Yeshua's hands and feet. The knife gash in Yeshua's side came in the form of a Roman lance wielding a sharp knife blade on the end of its shaft. This was the lance that pierced Yeshua's side and it was plunged into the cavity of His heart. As the Rod of God suffered this wound in the heart, blood and water gushed forth from the side injury. After Yeshua was pierced like the fig fruit, it only took 3 days before Yeshua quickly bore the best quality fruit, as the First Fruit on the Feast of First Fruits on Nisan 17, which was 3 days after Passover.

As you know by now, this First Fruit was from the Almond Tree of Life, parallel to Aaron's rod that budded. Yeshua's flesh never saw corruption, just like the fig fruit flesh never saw corruption, because it was gashed and pierced at the right time by the fig dresser. Now this brings us to something that is quite unexpected! In the beginning, when God created a Bride for Adam, God caused a deep sleep to fall upon him. As Adam slept, the LORD took one of the ribs from Adams side and He closed up the flesh. From this rib in Adams side, the LORD created a woman for Adam and the LORD brought her to the man. Since Adam was the Bridegroom and Eve was the Bride, they were to become one flesh. As I was studying this scenario, miraculously something came up that revealed to me, actually from the Jewish movie, *"Yentl,"* that the original Hebrew word for *"rib"* actually meant *"side."* *(Movie references – Yentl ©1983 MGM Metro-Goldwyn-Mayer Studios Inc. TM).* Now when I researched this further, I discovered that it is the Hebrew word *"Tsela,"* meaning *"side."* So Adam's Bride, the woman, was taken out of Adam's side, *"Tsela,"* from the rib that protected his heart. The LORD then showed me something so outstanding, that I cried when I saw it. When *Messiah Yeshua* came as the second Adam, He took for Himself a Bride and He sealed His Eternal Covenant or Testimony with His life blood and Living Water of the heart. This came gushing forth out of Yeshua's side, *"Tsela,"* through His ribs and from His heart, as the Roman lance pierced His heart. To my complete and utter astonishment I realized, *Yeshua was gashed with the Roman lance between the fifth and the sixth rib. It is written that in the beginning, God created Adam and Eve between sundown of the end of the fifth day and before sundown, of the end of the sixth day.* The evidence of this is found on the Shroud of Yeshua, called the Shroud of Turin.

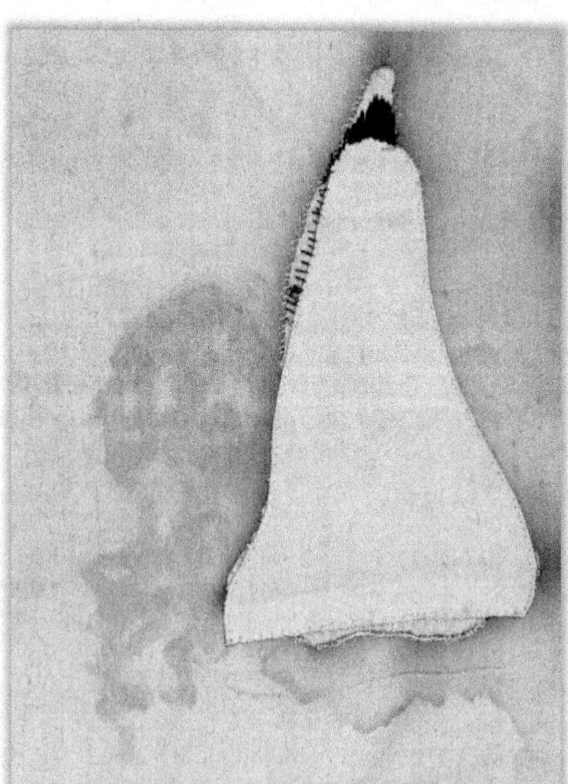

Official Shroud Sword Wound
Photograph ©1978 Barrie M. Schwortz Collection, STERA Inc., All Rights Reserved

What I realized next, was even more exciting. Remember that I said that the fig must be *pierced or gashed in the apex* of the fruit while it is hanging upon the tree? As I studied a diagram of the heart, instantly it came into my mind that the heart also has an apex like the fig fruit. As I was pensively pondering the Roman lance, I tried to visualize it entering between the fifth and sixth rib of Yeshua, *the second Adam.* Then I gasped in wonder because at that moment *I saw that for the lance to gash between the fifth and sixth rib, it had to have entered the part of the heart called "the apex!"* The moment the LORD revealed this to me, it was truly miraculous to say the least! I knew for certain that Yeshua took the full curse of Eden upon Himself, while hanging upon the tree. Just like the gashing of the fig, it then only took 3 days for Yeshua to quickly bear the best and finest Fruit of Eternal life, on the third day! What shocks

me the most about the word *"Tsela" or "Side"* is that it is from *an unused Hebrew word.* The Hebrew word *"Tsela"* is actually pronounced *"Tsay-law."* When I said the word phonetically to myself, my eyes were opened to see that this word is pronounced exactly like the mystery word in King David's Psalms that is written as *"Selah."* This is a very great discovery if the words *"Tsela" and "Selah"* mean the same thing. No one has known for certain what the true meaning of the word *"Selah"* means, as it appears within the Psalms of King David. So now I believe that this word actually refers to Israel as the Bride of the LORD. This would mean that Messiah as the second Adam sealed His Eternal Covenant of the heart with His Bride with His own life blood and Living Water that gushed forth out of His side, *"Tsela," from the apex of His own heart, between the fifth and sixth rib!* Perhaps it could also refer to the bitterness of the curse of the Garden of Eden on the one hand and then to the sweetness of salvation, in the Garden of God, through Messiah our First Fruits of Eternal life on the other hand, because as believers, we are His Bride. The fig tree testifies that only the LORD could restore us to His Garden called *"Heaven."* So I want to thank you Barrie M. Schwortz my friend, the distinguished Shroud photographer, for providing the Roman lance wound image of Messiah Yeshua for my book! Yeshua created all things. His Living Testimony is encoded not only in the fig tree, but also in the Almond Tree of Life. I find this parallel of Yeshua bearing the curse of the fig tree to be quite breathtaking!

Without a doubt, I do believe with certainty, that the fig was the fruit of the tree of Knowledge of good and evil that mankind was instructed not to eat and when they disobeyed God and ate it, the curse of death came upon the earth and this curse is removed by the Almond Tree of Life. This makes sense because the Scriptures tell us *"Cursed is the man who hangs upon a tree."* Messiah Yeshua bore *the curse* in the flesh for us in the Garden of God to reverse the curse of death, to take us as His Eternal Bride. Little by little, the fig tree unveiled itself to me, like a tantalizing puzzle.

The next incredible feature of the fig tree that was directly connected to Messiah Yeshua, was the Botanical part of the tree called the *"gall."* The first thing I should mention here is the fact that in the first century, when Yeshua lived on the earth, it was possible to make wine out of figs. The Romans not only made wine out of fig fruit, but they also made vinegar out of the fig fruit. Some facts about this are: *"The fig tree itself is susceptible to vinegar or gall flies and they can carry bacteria and fungus into the fruit. If this happens, the fruit becomes sour. The fig wasps that pollinate the fruit also have the potential to carry bacteria and fungus into the fruit, while they are pollinating it. This will again cause the figs to be sour."* ***(Sources: Fig Tree Facts ©2010-2011 en.wikipedia.org/wiki/Fig_trees © simple.wikipedia.org/wiki/Fig and Fig Wasp and Syconium). (Fig Fruit; ©2010 March 5 waynesword.palomar.edu/pljune99.htm by W.P. Armstrong) AND (Dr. Avinoam Danin, Professor Emeritus of Botany from The Hebrew University of Jerusalem Israel, Fig photographs ©2013 from www.flora.huji.ac.il).***

This is all very interesting because during the crucifixion, Yeshua was offered *the vinegar mingled with gall.* This mixture is often referred to as *"sour wine."* Now I could clearly picture in my mind that the *sour wine* during the crucifixion was completely symbolic of the curse of death from *the fig tree* in the Garden of Eden. Yeshua was hanging on the tree, bearing the curse, when He was given the vinegar mingled with gall on the hyssop stalk. I believe this was actually *the sour fig wine mingled with gall* that was placed to Yeshua's mouth during the crucifixion. The hyssop stalk was the sign of purification that we looked at before. I mentioned this in the parable of the mustard seed about vinegar being made from the mustard seed, but this particular mixture of vinegar and gall was known specifically as *"sour wine," which indicates that it was made from the sour fruit of the fig tree.* It was *very bitter,* just like the curse of Eden was *very bitter.* This is written in the following Scripture.

Matthew 27:33-34 *And when they were come unto a place called Golgotha, that is to say, a place of a skull, They gave Him vinegar to drink mingled with gall; and when He had tasted thereof, He would not drink. And they*

crucified Him, and parted His garments, casting lots; that it might be fulfilled which was spoken by the Prophet, They parted My garments among them, and upon My vesture did they cast lots. And sitting down they watched Him there; And set up over His head His accusation written, THIS IS YESHUA THE KING OF THE JEWS.

The moment that Yeshua was offered the vinegar mingled with gall, it was the fulfillment of Psalm 69:21. Just as the Prophet foretold, *Yeshua was given gall for His meat, and for His thirst, they gave Him vinegar to drink. It is all symbolic of the Messiah bearing the curse of the fig tree in the place of the former Garden of Eden, in Jerusalem.*

Psalm 69:21 *They gave Me also gall for My meat; and in My thirst they gave Me vinegar to drink.*

The *gall* that is associated with *the fig tree* is therefore associated with *the bitterness of the curse.* This is written in Deuteronomy. The word *"bitter"* is another name for *"wormwood."* Believe it or not, there is a plant that goes by the name *"wormwood."* I think it is no coincidence that the wormwood plant itself is said to be poisonous and that it is known for being extremely bitter. In Deuteronomy, when it speaks of Sodom and Gomorrah, it speaks of *the gall that is bitter, which is the wine of dragons.* The dragon is the Serpent from Eden who brought forth this curse of death. The victory that Yeshua obtained on the cross was to ultimately defeat the serpent dragon forever so we could live forever. So the *wormwood and the gall* certainly bring misery, as it is written.

Deuteronomy 32:31-33 *For their rock is not as our Rock, even our enemies themselves being judges. For their vine is of the vine of Sodom and of the fields of Gomorrah; their grapes are grapes of gall, their clusters are bitter; Their wine is the poison of dragons, and the cruel venom of asps. Is not this laid up in store with me, and sealed up among my treasures?*

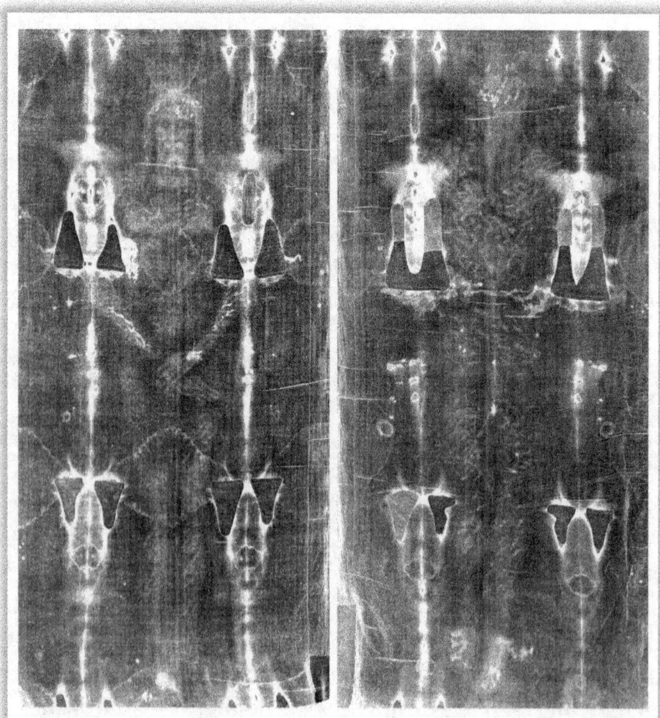

Official Shroud Pair Photograph ©1978 Barrie M. Schwortz Collection, STERA Inc., All Rights Reserved

Lamentations 3:15-19 *He hath filled me with bitterness, he hath made me drunken with wormwood. He hath also broken my teeth with gravel stones; he hath covered me with ashes. And thou hast removed my soul far off from peace; I forgat prosperity. And I said, My strength and my hope is perished from the LORD; Remembering mine affliction and my misery, the wormwood and the gall.*

This now brings us to another interesting feature that appears on a fig tree. *The "gall" that appears on a fig tree is "an abnormal tissue swelling, caused by damage or from wounds that have been inflicted upon the tree."* The clear evidence that we can still see today on Yeshua's burial Shroud testifies to the fact that He suffered *abnormal tissue swelling* due to the damage and wounds inflicted upon Him through the great brutality of the Roman Soldiers. Yeshua's wounds have been thoroughly investigated on the Shroud by many top forensic Pathologists.

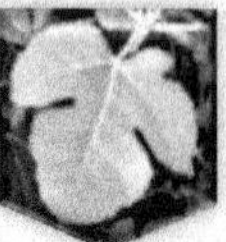

The analysis of their findings prove *"Yeshua's tissues were severely swollen from the many contusions, abrasions, piercing wounds, bruises, lacerations, as well as a knee cap injury and broken nose cartilage that He suffered."* **(Source: Forensic Pathologist reports ©2010 Shroud.com – Barrie M. Schwortz, STERA, Inc. All Rights Reserved).**

All these terrible wounds were inflicted upon Yeshua as He was severely brutalized. Let us not forget, too, that His head and scalp were also pierced with a Crown of Thorns. *"Crown Galls"* are actually *"swollen tissues on the trunk and branches of the fig tree!"* Therefore, Messiah Yeshua the Branch wore the *"Crown gall"* in the form of the Crown of Thorns while suffering *the bitterness of the curse* of *the fig tree*, and I have written exclusively about the Crown of Thorns in another place, but He is the main trunk of the Living Almond Tree of the Holy Menorah. Let us not forget that part of the curse of Eden was that the ground was now cursed, and, from that time forward, it would only produce thorns and thistles while we toiled for our bread. The good news, however, is that Yeshua came to take away the thorns and thistles as *He suffered from the gall in the tissues of His flesh.* With His stripes we are healed.

Yeshua came to bring us the true Living Bread from Heaven, so that we would not have to toil anymore for our bread. This was *the Living Torah,* the Everlasting Word of God, that would restore us to His Garden like Eden called *"Heaven."* Yeshua declared it before it came to pass.

Matthew 20:17 *And Yeshua going up to Jerusalem took the twelve disciples apart in the way, and said unto them, Behold, we go up to Jerusalem; and the Son of man shall be betrayed unto the Chief Priests and unto the Scribes, and they shall condemn Him to death, And shall deliver Him to the Gentiles to mock, and to scourge, and to crucify Him; and the third day He shall rise again.*

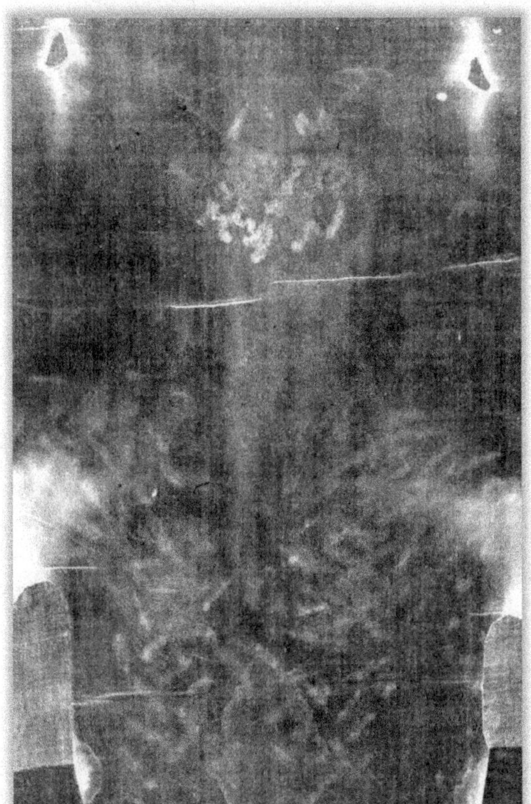

Shroud Scourge Marks & Crown of Thorns Wounds
Official Shroud Photograph
©1978 Barrie M. Schwortz Collection, STERA Inc., All Rights Reserved

Definition:
Gall- *a sore on the skin, vexation, a spot worn bare. To hurt or break, as the skin, by rubbing or chafing. To injure, to harass, A Tumor on plant tissue caused by irritation due to fungi, insects, bacteria. Anything bitter, rancor, malignity, bitterness of mind.*

The instrument of torture that was used to scourge Yeshua was a weapon called *"the Roman flagrum."* It contained sharp shards of bone or metal attached to the end of three leather thongs that were mounted upon a wooden handle. The Shroud evidence shows that Messiah Yeshua was whipped by two different Roman Soldiers. As one Soldier scourged Yeshua from the right side and the other soldier scourged Him from the left side, *the Rod of God was in the middle!* As Yeshua was scourged, the flagrum ripped and perforated Yeshua's flesh. This created long stripes of severely bloodied, pulsating muscle, tissue, and skin all over His entire body and *the Living Water and life blood came out of the Rod of God from the Branch of the Tree of Life and dripped onto the ground.* When Yeshua

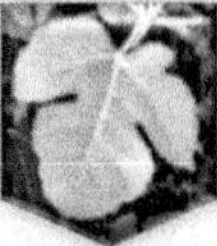

was hanging upon the cross, the back of His shoulders, bearing the painful stripes, continually rubbed back and forth against the rough wood of the crossbeam. The wounds in Yeshua's flesh, therefore, are profoundly defined in the word *"gall." Yeshua's flesh did break.* Remember that Yeshua told us to remember Him in the Passover Seder in the *"breaking"* of the unleavened bread, the Matzah! When Yeshua took the bread, He broke it and said, *"This is My body which is broken for you. Do this in remembrance of Me."* This again is LORD'S signature on all His works. Isaiah wrote in chapter 53, *"By Messiah stripes, we are healed."* When the LORD laid out His rules in Deuteronomy, He explained that *the curse is a vexation.* Part of the curse comes from forsaking God. Because Adam and Eve forsook God their KING, the curse came upon them and all their descendants in this very place.

Deuteronomy 28:15 *But it shall come to pass, if thou wilt not hearken unto the voice of the LORD thy God, to observe to do all His commandments and His statutes which I command thee this day; that all these curses shall come upon thee; Cursed shalt thou be in the city, and cursed shalt thou be in field. Cursed shall be thy basket and thy store. Cursed shall be the fruit of thy body, and the fruit of thy land, the increase of thy kine, and the flocks of thy sheep. Cursed shalt thou be when thou comest in, and cursed shalt thou be when thou goest out. The LORD shall send vexation, and rebuke, in all that thou settest thine hand for to do, until thou be destroyed, and until thou perish quickly; because of the wickedness of thy doings, whereby thou hast forsaken Me.*

If Yeshua came to bear the entire curse, then it included being *forsaken.* So it came to pass that *as the Rod of God was lifted up upon the cross,* Yeshua uttered the following Words that were already written about Him in Psalm 22.

Mark 15:34 *And at the ninth hour Yeshua cried with a loud voice, saying, Eloi, Eloi, lama sa-bach-tha-ni? Which is, My God, My God, why hast Thou forsaken Me?*

Psalm 22:1 *My God, My God, why hast Thou forsaken Me? Why art Thou so far from helping Me, and from the Words of my roaring?*

Now there is something else about the Messiah that is so profound that my eyes filled with tears when the LORD revealed it to me on top of everything else! There are some exotic fruits, such as bananas and the fig from the fig tree that are sometimes known as *"Accessory fruit, spurious fruit, pseudofruit, false fruit, or pseudocarp."* This simply refers to *"a fruit in which some of the flesh is derived not from the ovary but from some adjacent tissue exterior to the carpel."* **(Source: *Accessory fruit* – *en.wikipedia.org/wiki/Accessory_fruit*).** *In other words, this fruit does not derive from inside the ovules of the flower, but instead, they are derived, exterior to the carpel of the flower and usually from some outside nearby tissue. The word "carpel" is intriguing!*

Now this is fantastic because the word *"carpel"* in Latin is *"carpellum,"* but the Greek form of the word *"carpel"* is the word *"Karpos"* which means *"fruit or the fruit of trees."* The definition of the Greek word *"Karpos"* is extremely significant to Yeshua as our Passover!

Ficus carica Fig Tree
Photo ©2013 A. Danin, Jerusalem Israel

Definition:
Karpos
1. Fruit
2. The fruit of trees
3. To gather Fruit into Eternal life

The Greek word *"karpos"* is incredibly the same word as the Hebrew word *"karpas."* It has two distinctly significant meanings, *"fine linen and fruit."* The Greek word *"karpasos"* refers *to flax*

or linen. How remarkable it is, then, that Yeshua was buried in a fine linen burial Shroud after He bore the curse, and after He was gashed in the apex of the heart, He quickly bore the finest Fruit, as the Branch of the Almond Tree of Life, in three days. This is unbelievable! During the Passover Seder *"the karpas" is the first element that begins the Haggadah.* The karpas is usually parsley that is dipped in salt water and it represents *the tears* of the Israelites from the bondage of their suffering in Egypt. Sometimes the karpas is dipped in red wine vinegar, to represent blood. The famous Rabbi, named *"Rashi,"* apparently associated the *striped* garment of Joseph, that was dipped in blood by his brothers, with the word *"karpas,"* and it is said that the tragedy began *"when Joseph's brother's sold Joseph into slavery. The brother's later lied about it to their father and they told Jacob, that Joseph had been killed by wild animals. They had even dipped Joseph's striped garment in animal blood, to cover their sin. The Karpas is therefore, a remembrance of the beginning of this tragedy that eventually led the Israelites to become slaves in Egypt, for about 400 years."* So dipping the karpas into a blood substitute is the first element of the Passover Seder. Even though Joseph's brothers had dipped Joseph's striped garment in blood to cover their sin, the LORD redeemed the Israelites out of their bondage and He brought them into the glorious liberty of their freedom and into the LORD'S marvelous light.

The Passover Seder is called *"the LORD'S Passover."* So the first element down to the last element of the Passover is about the LORD'S own Testimony as Messiah Yeshua. *This means that the karpas is now all about the Messiah. His flesh as the clean Lamb is the garment of flesh that bore the stripes and the blood that covered all our sins, as He bore the gall of the bitterness of the bondage of death from Eden. The Messiah brought us out of the bondage of death into the glorious liberty of Eternal life, after being wrapped in the fine linen of His burial Shroud.* In the book of Revelation, we see that Messiah Yeshua returns from Heaven, wearing a robe dipped in blood, and His Name is called *"THE WORD OF GOD."* Truly, as the Prophet Isaiah's words declared, *"By the Messiah's stripes we are healed."* So Yeshua brought Israel the ultimate redemption from the captivity of the bondage of corruption in the flesh and He brings them into the glorious liberty of the children of God. *Messiah the LORD is the ultimate redemption that is far superior to the Exodus!*

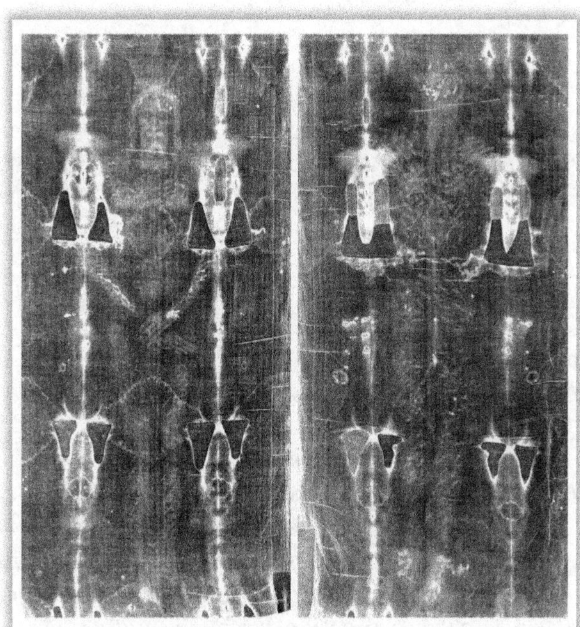

Official Shroud Pair
Photograph ©1978 Barrie M. Schwortz Collection, STERA Inc., All Rights Reserved

Hebrews 2:14-18 *Forasmuch then as the children are partakers of flesh and blood, He also Himself likewise took part of the same; that through death He might destroy Him that had the power of death, that is, the devil; And deliver them who through fear of death were all their lifetime subject to bondage, For verily He took not on Him the nature of angels; but He took on Him the seed of Abraham. Wherefore in all things it behoved Him to be made like unto His brethren, that He might be a merciful and faithful High Priest in things pertaining to God, to make reconciliation for the sins of the people. For in that He Himself hath suffered being tempted, He is able to succor them that are tempted.*

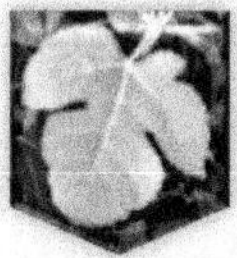

Psalm 130:7-8 *Let Israel hope in the LORD; for with the LORD there is mercy, and with Him there is plenteous redemption. And He shall redeem Israel from all his iniquities.*

In Psalm 49, after it says, *"God will redeem my soul from the grave,"* it uses the word *"Selah."* I believe that this is an indication that the word *"Selah"* as it is used within this passage, is the same as *"Tsela."* So this means that the following Scripture is also referring to us as the LORD'S Bride and that we will be *"married"* to the Bridegroom, *the KING Messiah,* after the resurrection from the grave and after Israel's redemption is complete. In other words, He shall receive me as His Bride, *"Selah" or "Tsela!"*

Psalm 49:15 *But God will redeem my soul from the grave; for He shall receive me. Selah.*

Zacharias was John the Baptist's father, the High Priest who offered incense in the Holy Temple in Jerusalem, and he was filled with the Holy Spirit of God. As he Prophesied, he spoke the following words.

Luke 1:68-75 *Blessed be the LORD God of Israel; for He hath visited and redeemed His people, And hath raised up an horn of salvation for us in the House of His servant David; As He spake by the mouth of His Holy Prophets, which have been since the world began. That we should be saved from our enemies, and from the hand of all that hate us; To perform the mercy promised to our fathers, and to remember His Holy Covenant; The oath which He sware to our father Abraham, That He would grant unto us, that we being delivered out of the hand of our enemies might serve Him, all the days of our life.*

"Karpos," as it appears in the Greek, is found once in the Talmud. Here it refers to *"fine white wool."* This brings one Scripture to my mind. Once the curse of death was removed by Messiah the LORD, the sins of Israel and the world will be made like pure white wool, and remember this was the fulfillment of the scapegoat.

Isaiah 1:18 *Come now, and let us reason together, saith the LORD; though your sins be as scarlet, they shall be as white as snow; though they be red like crimson, they shall be as wool.*

Now in reference to the fig fruit, I discovered something else that is absolutely astonishing! The word *"parthenocarpy"* is the combination of the Greek word *"parthenos"* meaning *"virgin,"* and the Greek word *"karpos,"* meaning *"fruit."* The two words together form the word *"parthenocarpy,"* meaning *"virgin fruit."* In literal terms, *"parthenocarpy is the development of a ripe fruit without the fertilization of the ovules in the fruit."* As I pondered this, I began to search for the Greek word that was used to describe Yeshua's mother Mary, to see if the Greek word that was used for *"virgin"* was by any chance the word *"parthenos."* Now I was floored! I discovered much to my amazement that *"parthenos"* is, in fact, *the very word* that is used as *"virgin"* in every single instance in both the Old Testament and in the New Testament. So I discovered that Yeshua's mother Mary, *"the virgin,"* was written as the Greek word *"parthenos"* in many places. Do you know what this means? Yeshua was the *"virgin fruit!"* ***(Sources: "Parthenocarpy," Greek Karpos Facts: Lewis, Helen. Mastering Horticulture (Parthenocarpy Greek word meaning Parthenos & karpos virgin fruit Copyright 2010). AND (©2010 en.wikipedia.org/wiki/Parthenocarpy) AND (The Free Encyclopedia ©2010-2011 thefreedictionary.com/parthenocarpy) AND (Dr. Avinoam Danin, Professor Emeritus of Botany from the Hebrew University of Jerusalem Israel, Fig photographs ©2013 from www.flora.huji.ac.il).***

Ficus carica Fig Tree Photograph ©2013 A. Danin, Jerusalem Israel All Rights Reserved

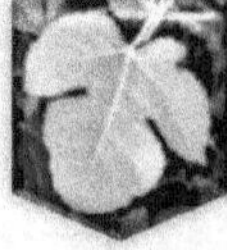

Matthew 1:23 *Behold, a virgin shall be with child, and shall bring forth a Son, and they shall call His Name Emmanuel, which being interpreted is, God with us.*

"Parthenos" is also the word that is used for *"virgin"* in Isaiah 7:14. *"Parthenos"* is used for *"virgin"* in many other Scriptures, including the following passage in Genesis. In this passage, a woman at the well became the Bride *"Tsela,"* and Yeshua revealed that He was the Bridegroom of Israel as He sat at Jacob's well! ***(Source: Parthenocarpy – Greek Karpos Facts ©2010 en.wikipedia.org/wiki/Parthenocarpy - The Free Encyclopedia© thefreedictionary.com/parthenocarpy).***

Isaiah 7:14 *Therefore the LORD Himself shall give you a sign; Behold, a virgin shall conceive, and bear a Son, and shall call His Name Emmanuel.*

Genesis 24:43-44 *Behold, I stand by the well of water; and it shall come to pass, that when the virgin cometh forth to draw water, and I say to her, Give me, I pray thee, a little water of thy pitcher to drink; And she say to me, both drink thou, and I will also draw for thy camels; let the same be the woman whom the LORD hath appointed out for my master's son.*

So Messiah Yeshua was born of *"a virgin,"* named Mary. When Mary's cousin, Elisabeth, first heard Mary's voice, not only did the baby, the messenger named John the Baptist, leap in her womb, but Elisabeth, who was filled with the Holy Spirit, declared in a loud voice to Mary, *"Blessed is the Fruit of thy womb." By definition "fruit" is "The ripened ovary or ovaries of a seed bearing plant." The fruit contains seeds to disperse and the flesh of the fruit is eaten. This is why we are to eat the First fruit of Yeshua, called His flesh.*

So it is fantastic that the word *"parthenocarpy"* literally means *"virgin fruit!"* This process is *"the natural or artificial production of the fig fruit, without the fertilization of the ovules." "This is the part of the plant that contains the embryonic sac."* Of course the word *"ovule"* means *"small egg."* So it contains the female cells of the flower and if it is fertilized, it produces a seed of the plant. I could not believe that this connection was so parallel to Yeshua's miraculous conception. *Messiah Yeshua was conceived when the Holy Spirit of the LORD God "overshadowed" the Virgin Mary.* To *"overshadow"* literally means to *"becloud."* To *"becloud"* is *"to cover or obscure with a cloud, a mist or to eclipse, as one celestial divine body obscures another."* This was a promise to Israel that the LORD God swore to David that of *the fruit* of his body, the Messiah would sit upon His throne forever.

Psalm 132:11-12 *The LORD hath sworn in truth unto David; He will not turn from it; Of the fruit of thy body will I set upon thy throne. If thy children will keep My Covenant and My Testimony that I shall teach them, their children shall also sit upon thy throne forevermore.*

Fruiting Fig Tree
Photo ©2013 Mary & Maurice Carroll - Texas, USA All Rights Reserved

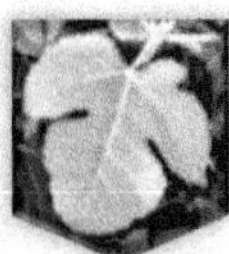

The account of the *"virgin fruit"* of Mary is written in Matthew and Luke. *The Messiah was*

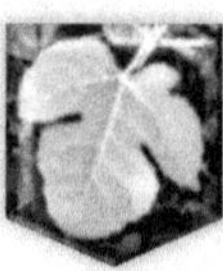

conceived only when the Holy Spirit of God overshadowed Mary, thus bringing forth this life of the second Adam and not through the human process of fertilization. The Messiah was not formed by mankind but by the hand of God and He dwelt with us!

Remember that with *the Accessory fruit, the fruit does not derive from inside the ovules of the flower, but instead they are derived exterior to carpel of the flower, and usually from some outside nearby tissue. The Accessory fruit which used to be referred to in Botany as a "false fruit" does not mean "deceptive" or "fake." It literally means that it is "derived from the outside" which is "out of the ordinary." Messiah Yeshua is extremely out of the ordinary because He was "derived exterior to the carpel of the flower Mary" from an "outside" source of life known as the Ruach/Holy Spirit who formed man in the beginning from the dust of the ground, and not through a woman or a man's natural fertilization process! Yeshua is our karpas our true fruit!* In the beginning, the Holy Spirit moved on the surface of the waters turning it to *"Living Water." So Yeshua, the Living Water, was inside Mary's womb by the power of the Highest as His Holy Spirit overshadowed her. He was the all powerful Rod of God who creates life and forms the body of every living thing! God created a body to dwell in as a temporary sukkah as the "Fruitful Branch!" Nothing is impossible with God! Remember that! I never dreamed the LORD would explain the virgin birth to me, but miraculously He showed me all these details in the fig tree fruit! It is stunning!*

Fruiting Fig Tree
Photo ©2013 Mary & Maurice Carroll – Texas USA

Matthew 1:20-25 *But while he thought on these things, behold, the angel of the LORD appeared unto him in a dream, saying, Joseph, thou son of David, fear not to take unto thee Mary thy wife; for that which is conceived in her is of the Holy Spirit. And she shall bring forth a Son, and thou shalt call His Name Yeshua; for He shall save His people from their sins. Now all this was done, that it might be fulfilled which was spoken of the LORD by the Prophet, saying, Behold, a virgin shall be with child, and shall bring forth a Son, and they shall call His Name Emmanuel, which being interpreted is, God with us. Then Joseph being raised from sleep did as the angel of the LORD had bidden him, and took unto him his wife; And knew her not till she had brought forth her firstborn Son; and he called His Name Yeshua.*

Luke 1:27-38 *And in the sixth month the angel Gabriel was sent from God unto a city of Galilee, named Nazareth, To a virgin espoused to a man whose name was Joseph, of the House of David; and the virgins name was Mary. And the angel came in unto her, and said, Hail, thou that art highly favoured, the LORD is with thee; blessed art thou among women. And when she saw him, she was troubled at his saying, and cast in her mind what manner of salutation this should be. And the angel said unto her, Fear not, Mary; for thou hast found favour with God. And, behold, thou shalt conceive in thy womb, and bring forth a Son, and shalt call His Name Yeshua. He shall be great, and shall be called the Son of the Highest; and the LORD God shall give unto Him the throne of His father David; And He shall reign over the House of Jacob forever; and of His Kingdom there shall be no end. Then said Mary unto the angel, How shall this be, seeing I know not a man? And the angel answered and said unto her, The Holy Spirit shall come upon thee, and the power of the Highest shall overshadow thee; therefore also that Holy thing which shall be born of thee shall be called the Son of God. And, behold, thy cousin Elisabeth, she hath also conceived a son in her old age; and this the sixth month with her, who was called barren. For with God nothing shall be impossible. And Mary said, Behold, the handmaid of the LORD; be it unto me according to thy Word. And the angel departed from her.*

I might mention here that the angel Gabriel made this announcement to Mary in the sixth month. Yeshua came as the second Adam and Adam was created during the sixth day of creation. Elisabeth, who was suddenly filled with the Holy Spirit, spoke in a loud voice, declaring that the fruit of Mary's womb was blessed and she called Mary, *"The mother of my LORD."* Of course God has no beginning and no end, so Yeshua always existed, but God was manifested in the flesh as His Ruach/Holy Spirit gave this seed a body, just as He wished, through a process like *"parthenocarpy." If the "Power of the Highest overshadowed Mary," then you must remember that the power is in the Rod of God, and this Rod had the ability to create flesh from nothing and the ability to restore flesh from decay. Remember that He is the seed and the Spirit of life is inside Him!* The Rod also had the ability to turn water to blood and the reverse, blood into water. The seed of the woman, by the power of the Highest which is the seed of life, brought forth life inside Mary *without the process of fertilization. Adam was also created by the LORD, without the fertilization process.* Yeshua was the second perfect Adam, who came in the flesh, to destroy the curse of death in the flesh. The LORD therefore created the natural process of *parthenocarpy*. He proved through His Divine Testimony that His Word is true. He has verified the *"virgin birth"* through the details within His own marvelous creation so that we could understand it, and believe that it is true!

All flesh had corrupted itself unto death and this is why it had to be the LORD God that manifested Himself in the flesh to purify us and to give our flesh new life through His Holy Spirit and reverse the curse from the Garden of Eden. As God's Spirit overshadowed Mary He brought forth life inside her womb. The human body is made from a very high percentage of living water! The LORD is the giver of life who created all flesh. He prepared a body, a vessel to dwell in, so that by the stripes in His flesh as the perfect Lamb, we would be sprinkled with His life blood and be healed, and restored to God.

I Timothy 3:16 *And without controversy great is the mystery of godliness; God was manifest in the flesh, justified in the Spirit, seen of angels, preached unto the Gentiles, believed on in the world, received up into glory.*

I John 4:2-3 *Hereby know ye the Spirit of God; Every spirit that confesseth that Yeshua Messiah is come in the flesh is of God; And every spirit that confesseth not that Yeshua Messiah is come in the flesh is not of God; and this is that spirit of anti-messiah, whereof ye have heard that it should come; and even now is it in the world.*

Yeshua was born of the Spirit. Yeshua told us that He had the power over all flesh. He was going to restore our corrupted flesh and give us a life that was not perishable. Yeshua said that we must worship God in Spirit and in truth. He is truth and all flesh would see the *Yeshua of God* as it is written!

Luke 3:6 *And all flesh shall see the salvation of God.*

The *"Son of God"* is therefore *"Yeshua ha-Ben"* the vessel of perfect flesh, without spot or blemish, that was the temporary dwelling of God in our midst upon the earth.

John 17:1-6 *These Words spake Yeshua, and lifted up His eyes to Heaven, and said, Father, the hour is come; glorify Thy Son, that Thy Son also may glorify Thee; As Thou hast given Him power over all flesh, that He should give eternal life to as many as Thou hast given Him. And this is life eternal, that they might know Thee on the earth; I have finished the work which Thou gavest Me to do. And now, O Father, glorify Thou Me with Thine own self with the glory which I had with Thee before the world was. I have manifested Thy Name unto the men which Thou gavest Me out of the world; Thine they were, and Thou gavest them Me; and they have kept Thy Word.*

By definition *"meat"* is flesh. Yeshua said that unless we eat His flesh as the pure Lamb of the Holy Passover Seder, *the Living Torah,* then we would not have life inside us, as His Spirit gives us life and in Him alone can we have Eternal life.

Romans 8:1-11 *There is therefore now no condemnation to them which are in Messiah Yeshua, who walk not after the flesh, but after the Spirit. For the law of the Spirit of life in Messiah Yeshua hath made me free from the law of sin and death. For what the law could not do, in that it was weak through the flesh, God sending His own Son in the likeness of sinful flesh, and for sin, condemned sin in the flesh; That the righteousness of the law might be fulfilled in us, who walk not after the flesh, but after the Spirit; For they that are after the flesh do mind the things of the flesh; but they that are after the Spirit the things of the Spirit. For to be carnally minded is death; but to be spiritually minded is life and peace. Because the carnal mind is enmity against God; for it is not subject to the law of God, neither indeed can be. So then they that are in the flesh cannot please God. But ye are not in the flesh, but in the Spirit, if so be that the Spirit of God dwell in you. Now if any man have not the Spirit of Messiah, he is none of His. And if Messiah be in you, the body is dead because of sin; but the Spirit is life because of righteousness. But the Spirit of Him that raised up Yeshua from the dead dwell in you, He that raised up Messiah from the dead shall also quicken your mortal bodies by His Spirit that dwelleth in you.*

Mary declared that *"her soul does magnify the LORD and that her Spirit rejoiced in God her Saviour."*

Luke 1:39- 47 *And Mary arose in those days, and went into the hill country with haste, into a city of Judah; And entered into the house of Zacharias, and saluted Elisabeth. And it came to pass, that, when Elisabeth heard the salutation of Mary, the babe leaped in her womb; and Elisabeth was filled with the Holy Spirit; And she spake out with a loud voice, and said, Blessed art thou among woman, and blessed is the fruit of thy womb. And whence is this to me, that the mother of my LORD should come to me? For lo, as soon as the voice of thy salutation sounded in mine ears, the babe leaped in my womb for joy. And blessed is she that believed; for there shall be a performance of those things which were told her from the LORD. And Mary said, My soul doth magnify the LORD, And my Spirit hath rejoiced in God my Saviour.*

The Rod of God was about to *"perform"* this mighty work of God! If we go back to Deuteronomy, we will see that when there is blessing and not the curse, then *the fruit of the body will increase and be blessed.* So it is written that Yeshua, *the virgin Fruit,* bore the finest Fruit of Eternal life and in this, *we are blessed* because the curse is removed from us through the Fruitful Rod of God.

Deuteronomy 28:1-4 *And it shall come to pass, if thou shalt hearken diligently unto the voice of the LORD thy God, to observe and to do all His commandments which I command thee this day, that the LORD thy God will set thee on high above all nations of the earth; And all these blessings shall come on thee, and overtake thee, if thou shalt hearken unto the voice of the LORD thy God. Blessed shalt thou be in the city, and blessed shalt thou be in the field. Blessed shalt be the fruit of thy body, and the fruit of thy ground, and the fruit of thy cattle, the increase of thy kine, and the flocks of thy sheep. Blessed shall be thy basket and thy store. Blessed shalt thou be when thou comest in, and blessed shalt thou be when thou goest out.*

Zacchaeus climbed into a Sycamore Fig tree, so he could see Messiah Yeshua as He was walking by. The name *"Zacchaeus"* is a Greek name that means *"innocent."* When Yeshua came upon the Sycamore fig tree, He stopped walking and He told Zacchaeus to come down from the fig tree, so He could have dinner with him. This makes me so excited! This story is another testimony proving that Messiah Yeshua invites us to come eat with Him at the marriage supper of the Lamb in the Kingdom of Heaven. This story reveals that through Messiah the LORD, we are made *"innocent"* like the pure wool of the sheep. Zacchaeus essentially came down out of the symbolically cursed Sycamore fig tree to dine at the table with the LORD, *with the Living Torah,* the Branch from the Almond Tree of Life! Miraculously, in this story, Yeshua was entering and passing through Jericho when He stopped by the Sycamore fig tree. This is so fantastic because Jericho is the exact place where Joshua led the Israelites when they came out of their bondage from Egypt as they crossed over into the Promised Land, and Messiah Yeshua, as I have said before, is the second *"Joshua,"* leading Israel and all of us out of our bondage of death and *out of the curse of the fig tree from the Garden of Eden* and into the Heavenly Promised Land! Remember that the LORD came to seek and save that which was lost. Zacchaeus was a sinner who had the curse of Adam upon him,

but the Messiah was going to reverse the curse and joyfully bring him the blessing of Eternal life, in the Kingdom of Heaven. As you will notice, the last words of this passage indicate that when the people saw these things transpire, they thought *that the Kingdom of God should immediately appear* and now we know exactly why they thought this!

Luke 19:1-11 *And Yeshua entered and passed through Jericho, And behold, there was a man named Zacchaeus, which was the chief among the publicans, and he was rich. And he sought to see Yeshua who He was; and could not for the press, because he was little of stature. And he ran before, and climbed into a Sycamore tree to see Him; for he was to pass that way. And when Yeshua came to the place, He looked up, and saw him, and said unto him, Zacchaeus, make haste, and come down; for today I must abide in thy house. And he made haste, and came down, and received Him joyfully. And when they saw it, they all murmured, saying, That he was gone to be guest with a man that is a sinner. And Zacchaeus stood, and said unto the LORD; Behold, LORD, the half of my goods I give to the poor; and if I have taken anything from any man by false accusation, I restore him fourfold. And Yeshua said unto him, This day is salvation come to this house, forsomuch as he also is a son of Abraham. For the Son of man is come to seek and to save that which was lost. And as they heard these things, He added and spake a parable, because He was nigh to Jerusalem, and because they thought that the Kingdom of God should immediately appear.*

The Word of Yeshua that He spoke about planting the Sycamore tree in the sea also has profound meaning. Here, Yeshua is telling us that when we are washed in Him as the Living Water by the power of His Holy Spirit, our sins, including those that brought forth the curse of sin and death from the fig tree in Eden, are planted in the Sea, and He remembers our sins no more. The LORD has made us innocent and He casts our sins into depths of the Sea. This is why Yeshua said *that we might say to the Sycamore tree, Be thou planted in the Sea and it should obey you.*

Luke 17:6 *And the LORD said, If ye had faith as a grain of mustard seed, ye might say unto this Sycamore tree, Be thou planted in the Sea; and it should obey you.*

In the miracle of the withered fig tree, Yeshua spoke to the fig tree with the breath of His mouth and He made the fig tree wither and die. *It was symbolic of the curse of death of the fig tree in the Garden of Eden.* When the Jewish disciples saw this miracle, they were amazed. I believe the reason why they were amazed was because they knew that the LORD God of Israel had said that He makes things wither by the breath of His mouth. Isaiah wrote about this and the Jewish disciples were already well acquainted with the Holy Scriptures and with the Word of God through the Prophets of Israel. So the Scripture that Isaiah wrote is the key to understanding Yeshua's miracle of making the fig tree wither.

Isaiah 40:21-25 *Have ye not known? Have ye not heard? Hath it not been told you from the beginning? Have ye not understood from the foundations of the earth? It is He that sitteth upon the circle of the earth, and the inhabitants thereof are as grasshoppers; that stretcheth out the Heavens as a curtain, and spreadeth them out as a tent to dwell in; That bringeth the princes to nothing; He maketh the judges of the earth as vanity. Yea, they shall not be planted; yea they shall not be sown; yea, their stock shall not take root in the earth; and He shall also blow upon them, and they shall wither, and the whirlwind shall take them away as stubble. To whom then will ye liken Me, or shall I be equal? Saith the Holy One.*

 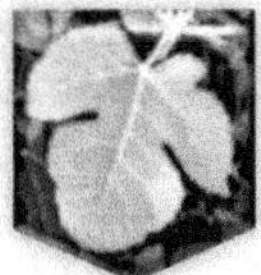 

THE GREEN FIG LEAF OF SHAME

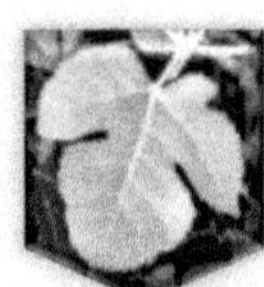 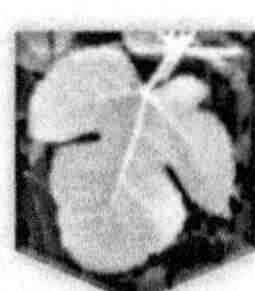 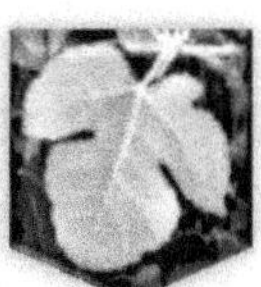

In the miracle of the withered fig tree, there was no fruit found on the fig tree that Yeshua cursed. There were only green leaves upon it. *Yeshua was hungry, but the fig tree was fruitless. Right after this occurred Yeshua was given gall for His meat and vinegar for His*

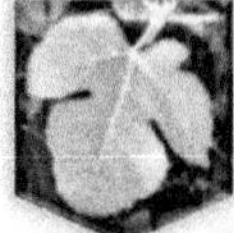

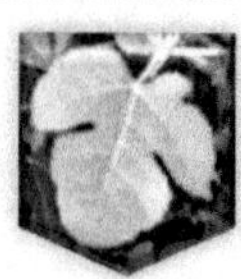

thirst as He bore the curse, so no one would ever eat of this fruit again! Ironically, the fig leaves in the Garden of Eden covered the shame of Adam and Eve, after the curse of death came upon them from disobeying the LORD and eating the fruit of this tree. Some fig leaves are shaped with five distinct sections. This reminds me of the five books of Moses and it reminds me of Yeshua, *the Living Torah.* In some cases, the fig leaf is shaped like a hand and Yeshua is the right hand, the Yad of the LORD God. By disobeying God, Adam and Eve essentially rejected God as their KING. All curses came upon them as they turned away from His Holy Spirit that gave them life. *They covered their spiritual nakedness with fig leaves from the tree of knowledge of good and evil. So the green fig leaf became the green fig leaf of shame!* In the following story and miracle, we see that Yeshua entered Jerusalem riding upon the colt of a donkey and the people shouted for joy as they immediately wanted to make Yeshua their KING, as He entered the Holy Temple. Immediately after this, Yeshua went to *"Bethany."* If you can believe another astonishing detail *"Bethany" means "House of Figs!"* On the morrow, when Yeshua was hungry, *He came upon the fig tree bearing only the green leaves and no fruit,* so He spoke the Word and cursed the fig tree because *the time of figs* was not yet. This is a very significant phrase, as we will see. When Yeshua returns from Heaven and restores all things, *the curses of the fig tree of Eden will be cast off like untimely figs* and it will no longer be bearing the curse of Eden. So the time of figs to bud and fruit again without the curse will be at hand when Messiah the LORD is about to appear on the earth! Yeshua said that when we see the fig tree bud, the Kingdom of God is nigh at hand!

Mark 11:1-22 *And when they came nigh to Jerusalem, unto Bethphage and Bethany, at the Mount of Olives, He sendeth forth two of His disciples, And saith unto them, Go your way into the village over against you; and as soon as ye be entered into it, ye shall find a colt tied, whereon never man sat; loose him, and bring him. And if any man say unto you, Why do ye this? Say ye that the LORD hath need of him; and straightway he will send him hither. And they went their way, and found the colt tied by the door without in a place where two ways met; and they loose him. And certain of them that stood there said unto them, What do ye, loosing the colt? And they said unto them even as Yeshua had commanded; and they let them go. And they brought the colt to Yeshua, and cast their garments on him; and He sat upon him. And many spread their garments in the way; and others cut down branches off the trees, and strawed them in the way. And they that went before, and they that followed, cried, saying, Hosanna; Blessed is He that cometh in the Name of the LORD; Blessed be the kingdom of our father David, that cometh in the Name of the LORD; Hosanna in the Highest. And Yeshua entered into Jerusalem, and into the Temple; and when He had looked round about upon all things, and now the eventide was come, He went out unto Bethany with the twelve. And on the morrow, when they were come from Bethany, He was hungry; And seeing a fig tree afar off having leaves, He came, if haply He might find anything thereon; and when He came to it, He found nothing but leaves; for the time of figs was not yet. And Yeshua answered and said unto it, No man eat fruit of Thee hereafter forever. And His disciples heard it. And they come to Jerusalem; and Yeshua went into the Temple, and began to cast out them that sold and bought in the Temple, and overthrew the tables of the moneychangers, and the seats of them that sold doves; And would not suffer that any man should carry any vessel through the Temple. And He taught, saying unto them, Is it not written, My House shall be called of all nations the House of prayer? But ye have made it a den of thieves. And the Scribes and Chief Priests heard it, and sought how they might destroy Him; for they feared Him, because all the people was astonished at His doctrine. And when even was come, He went out of the city. And in the morning, as they passed by, they saw the fig tree dried up from the roots. And Peter calling to remembrance saith unto Him, Master, behold, the fig tree which thou cursedst is withered away. And Yeshua answering saith unto them, Have faith in God.*

Remember that God was the Master in His Garden. The fig leaves covered the shame of Adam and Eve after they ate the fruit from this tree. *So Yeshua's fig tree in Bethany was only bearing leaves and no fruit was on it because Adam and Eve symbolically had already eaten the fruit from it!* So now Yeshua the LORD made the leaves and tree to wither to its roots, so it would never bear fruit again! Yeshua said, *"No man eat fruit of thee hereafter forever!"* He was here to remove the curse, once and for all, from them eating *the forbidden fruit from the fig tree of the knowledge of good and evil.* It is interesting that when Yeshua cursed the fig tree, *His disciples heard it.*

Then right after Yeshua made the fig tree wither, Yeshua rode into Jerusalem on a donkey and He entered through *"The gate of Mercy." Immediately, the Living Branch from the Almond Tree of Life* went into the courtyard of the Holy Temple that was standing on the same piece of ground where the LORD'S original Garden of Eden was located on Holy Mount Moriah and Yeshua overturned the tables of the money changers. *Yeshua removed the leaven from the House and Garden of the LORD God at Passover!* He was getting the leaven out of His House! Every Jewish family searches their house for leaven at Passover. If they find any in the house, they gather it up and they take it outside to burn it as the chaff, and I previously professed that fire is one of the methods that the LORD uses to cleanse and purify. Yeshua was zealous for the Holiness of His House. The fig tree that brought us the bitterness of death is the opposite of the sweet Living Almond Tree of life. The fig was cursed and it died when Yeshua spoke His Words with the breath of His mouth, full of His Ruach/Holy Spirit, but it had been a living tree. In this miracle, Yeshua demonstrated His power *as the Rod of God,* to either make things wither and die or through the breath of His mouth, through His Ruach/Holy Spirit, to resurrect things to life. Those who do not abide in KING Yeshua, *the Living Branch,* are therefore like the dried up fig tree that bore no fruit because the curse still abides on those who do not eat the Fruit from the Almond Tree of Life.

Another aspect of this is that the branches withered because they did not drink the Living Water that the LORD KING supplied so they might have life abiding in them. The fig tree looked good on the outside because it was full of green leaves, but it soon withered and died. If we are not careful, we can also appear good on the outside, but if we do not have His Holy Spirit dwelling in us, then the Living Water is not in us to produce the best fruit. If the breath of life, His Ruach, is not in us, then we will wither and die like the fig tree in its shame because we are still living in the sin of the curse of the Garden of Eden. As Yeshua cursed the green leafy fig tree in the place called *"House of Figs,"* He professed He was here to destroy the curse of death.

The Almond Tree of Life not only brought Eternal salvation to us, but the leaves from the LORD are the pages of *the Living Torah.* They are for the healing of the nations because the LORD bore the curse of Eden in His flesh for us! The green leaves from the Tree of Life will regenerate all things to the LORD'S righteousness and remove the curse. In the future, everything will once again be like it was in the beginning in God's new Garden called *"Heaven," which is the "New Jerusalem!"* In Israel, there is a celebration of the New Year of Trees and I have written about it in more detail in the last chapter, but I briefly want to mention it here. This holiday is known as *"Tu B' Shevat"* and it marks *the beginning of life or death for the trees.* When my miracle of the Almond Tree revelation occurred, without my knowledge, the celebration of *"Tu B' Shevat"* had just occurred in Israel on *the third day* of February that year in 2007 and on the 16th my Israeli friend, by a miracle of God, walked past that Almond Tree and took the picture *the third time* that she passed by that tree.

Is it any wonder then that the Messiah, who breathes new life into us, is represented in the Almond Tree of Life that is celebrated on Tu B' Shevat and is depicted on the Holy Almond Tree Menorah? Yeshua was here to take away sin and particularly the sin of the Garden of Eden! In the future, those who do not get the leaven out of their house and who do not abide in the LORD, but choose to live in sin will be as the chaff. The sin in Jerusalem at the time of Messiah Yeshua, had reached unto Heaven and because of this sin, the LORD was going to destroy the Temple and burn Jerusalem with fire, to get the leaven out. It was burned up and the Land made desolate through the Diaspora for almost 2,000 years. They rejected their KING! The LORD gave His generation forty years to repent, but they would not and so these events truly happened in the historical record of Jerusalem. The Roman occupation led to much sin, as the LORD'S people participated in the defilement and they were bowing to

Caesar, instead of bowing only to the LORD God of Israel. Also, they did not pay attention to the time of the Messiah's arrival and visitation. In essence, they became like the fig tree that withered because they did not bear the righteous fruit of the LORD in that generation. The LORD expected Israel to bear the life giving fruit, just as Psalm 1 states, but they became corrupted like the fig tree when they were controlled by Rome and they began profiting by the Roman authority, instead of trusting in the authority of God and bearing the fruit of the LORD. This is interesting because just after Yeshua overturned the tables of the moneychangers, the Chief Priests and Scribes asked Yeshua by what authority that He did these things! He did them by His own authority which is the *Royal power and authority* of the Rod of God. The sign of the withered fig tree was a sign to show them that unless they brought forth good fruit, their generation would wither like this cursed fig tree, and He illustrated it by causing this particular fig tree to wither from the curse of the Garden of Eden. This withering happened to Yeshua's generation because they were not abiding in the LORD of life and they continued to live in sin, disregarding the Testimony of the reversal of this curse by the LORD KING Messiah Yeshua. Abiding in Messiah the LORD makes us like a green tree with green branches, planted by streams of *Living Water* and we prosper with fruitful branches. We grow only because we are grafted into the Living Branch of the Almond Tree of Life, into Messiah Yeshua. The withered fig tree only represents the curse and those who are not bearing good fruit, who do not have the life of the LORD inside of them. When one is not eating the Fruit from the Living Branch of the Almond Tree of Life, the curse still abides upon them. Yeshua was speaking to those at the Temple and He told them that if they did not believe Him, *they would remain in their sins* and this meant that the curse of Eden would still abide upon them. In order to have life, they had to eat the good Fruit of the Branch that was sent to them from Heaven, from the Almond Tree of Life, and they were to be baptized in His Name by the power of His Holy Spirit, so they might have life in their Eternal KING!

John 8:23-24 *And He said unto them, Ye are from beneath; I AM from above; ye are of this world; I AM not of this world. I said therefore unto you, that ye shall die in your sins; for if ye believe not that I AM He, ye shall die in your sins.*

Now the Law, in and of itself, is not a curse; it is perfect. So, if one fails in one tiny area to completely and utterly obey God's Law, who fails to measure up to the whole Law of the LORD God, the curse abides upon them. Since it was impossible for mankind to attain this level of perfection, because of the fall of mankind, the LORD sent Himself as the perfect sinless Lamb sacrifice, the perfect flesh of Messiah as the second Adam, to bear the curse that came upon us by failing to keep the whole Law of God. So the LORD sent us a Branch from the Almond Tree of Life. By doing this, the LORD removed the curse of the Law off His people because they had failed to completely obey all of God's Law's to perfection. *The Diaspora verifies this truth. Only the Living Torah of the Heavenly Ark of God could fulfill the Law of the Eternal Covenant to perfection. So Yeshua's Living Testimony, as the budded Almond Rod of God, is a perfect and complete number seven in the Heavenly Ark.*

Galatians 3:13 *Messiah hath redeemed us from the curse of the Law, being made a curse for us; for it is written, Cursed is every one that hangeth on a tree.*

The LORD gives us all a choice to choose the blessing or the curse and to have *life in Him Eternally* or to be separated from Him in death! He told us to choose life, so we may cleave unto Him and love the LORD God and obey His voice with all our heart. I just love the LORD so much for showing all of this to me! Yeshua's Living Testimony of the Heavenly Ark leads Israel to dwell in the Promised Land forever. The LORD said He would bring others who were not of this sheep fold! The Gospel has spread throughout the earth to bring us Eternal life.

Deuteronomy 30:19-20 *I call Heaven and earth to record this day against you, that I have set before you life and death, blessing and cursing; therefore choose life, that both thou and thy seed may live. That thou mayest love the LORD thy God, and that thou mayest obey His voice, and that thou mayest cleave unto Him; for He is thy life, and the length of thy days; that thou mayest dwell in the Land which the LORD sware unto thy father's, to Abraham, to Isaac, and to Jacob, to give them.*

One more thing I should mention is that the miracle of the withered fig tree took place just before the last Passover Seder when Yeshua sealed the New Covenant with His Bride, as the Bridegroom of Israel, and then He budded to life after bearing *the curse* on His Holy Mountain. The Chief Priests were astonished at the miracles that Yeshua was performing and they questioned Him about it. They wanted to know how it was that He could perform all these miracles. I believe they questioned this because they knew that only the LORD God of Israel could perform the miracles that they were witnessing with their own eyes. Yeshua would not tell them by what authority He did these things. They seemed unable to figure out that Yeshua was Emmanuel, *"God with us,"* who was showing all the signs of the power of the Rod of God, full of His Holy Spirit. Believe it or not, Yeshua's power and authority came from the very one that they claimed to worship! The Chief Priests were afraid to answer the question regarding where John the Baptist received his authority because they knew that everyone in Jerusalem and in the surrounding territories believed that John was a Prophet sent by God. So if they believed that John was a true Prophet of God, then they should have believed that John was telling them the truth when he told them that *"Yeshua is the Lamb of God, who takes away the sins of the world."* John told them that He was preparing them to go before the face of the LORD, by preparing the way of the LORD to travel. So the LORD is Messiah. They realized that in answering the question as to whether John's baptism was of Heaven or not, if they said it was of Heaven, then Yeshua would say to them, *"Then why do you not believe that I AM your Messiah, the LORD?"* Israel is very beloved by the LORD and His Covenant is with them forever. The LORD who has no limits at all said that if branches were broken off the tree, He is able to graft those branches back into the original tree. This is exactly what He plans to do in the future. This is exactly how the LORD God of Israel would cause the best and most abundant fruit to be produced for His Kingdom of Heaven. Remember that when you prune a tree and cut off some of the branches, the tree flourishes and bears only the best fruit! So He said He would give the vineyard to one who was not seeking Him. So when the Good News Gospel message of Messiah Yeshua's Living Testimony of *the Living Torah* has been preached to the entire world, the Messiah will return and fulfill the promises that He made to Israel.

Yeshua is betrothed to Israel as a Bridegroom is betrothed to His Bride. His love for His people *"Israel"* stands forever. Even though His generation corrupted the Holy Temple of God, the LORD said that He would graft these branches back into the original tree that had been broken off. The LORD said that He is able to take a withered dead branch and bring it back to life and He demonstrated it with Messiah the Living Branch! He promised to keep an everlasting Covenant with Israel for the sake of their forefathers. The withering of the fig tree happened for a period of time for the purpose of allowing the Gentiles from all the nations to come and know the LORD God of Israel. Those who were considered unclean could be purified in Him and have Eternal life through Him.

The Scripture also states that Israel in part has temporarily had their eyes blinded from seeing His face until the fullness of the Gentiles comes in. At this time and for two thousand years, the LORD has been gathering a remnant of righteous Gentiles through Messiah Yeshua until the time when the age of grace ends. Those who refuse the Living Branch of the Almond Tree of Life will wither and die in their sins, just like the fig tree of Eden. The LORD KING is a God of great mercy and love. He does not wish for any to perish, but to have Eternal life in Him. The Jewish Apostle Paul, from the tribe of Benjamin, verified this truth.

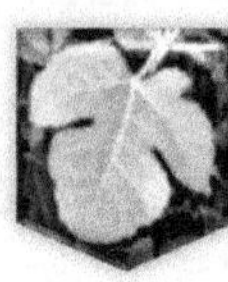

Romans 11:1-32 *I say then, Hath God cast away His people? God forbid. For I also am an Israelite, of the seed of Abraham, of the tribe of Benjamin. God hath not cast away His people which He foreknew. Wot ye not what the Scripture saith of Elias? How he maketh intercession to God against Israel, saying, LORD, they have killed Thy Prophets, and digged down Thine altars; and I am left alone, and they seek my life. But what saith the answer of God unto him? I have reserved to Myself seven thousand men, who have not bowed the knee to the image of Baal. Even so then at this present time also there is a remnant according to the election of grace. And if by grace, then is it no more of works; otherwise grace is no more grace. But if it be of works, then is it no more grace; otherwise work is no more work. What then? Israel hath not obtained that which he seeketh for; but the election hath obtained it, and the rest were blinded, According as it is written, God hath given them the spirit of slumber, eyes that they should not see, and ears that they should not hear; unto this day. And David saith, Let their table be made a snare, and a trap, and a stumbling block, and a recompense unto them; Let their eyes be darkened, that they may not see, and bow down their back always. I say then, Have they stumbled that they should fall? God forbid; but rather through their fall salvation is come unto the Gentiles, for to provoke them to jealousy. Now if the fall of them be the riches of the world, and the diminishing of them the riches of the Gentiles; how much more their fullness? For I speak to you Gentiles, inasmuch as I am the Apostle of the Gentiles, I magnify mine office; If by any means I may provoke to emulation them which are my flesh, and might save some of them. For if the casting away of them be the reconciling of the world, what shall the receiving of them be, but life from the dead? For if the First Fruit be Holy, the lump is also Holy; and if the root be Holy, so are the branches. And if some of the branches be broken off, and thou, being a wild olive tree, wert grafted in among them, and with them partakest of the root and fatness of the olive tree; Boast not against the branches. But if thou boast, thou bearest not the root, but the root thee. Thou wilt say then, the branches were broken off, and that I might be grafted in. Well; because of unbelief they were broken off, and thou standest by faith. Be not high minded, but fear, for if God spared not the natural branches, take heed lest he also spare not thee. Behold therefore the goodness and severity of God; on them which fell, severity; but toward thee, goodness, if thou continue in His goodness; otherwise thou also shalt be cut off. And they also, if they abide not still in unbelief, shall be grafted in; for God is able to graft them in again. For if thou wert cut out of the olive tree which is wild by nature, and wert grafted contrary to nature into a good olive tree; how much more shall these, which be the natural branches, be grafted into their own olive tree? For I would not, brethren, that ye should be ignorant of this mystery, lest ye should be wise in your own conceits; that blindness in part is happened to Israel, until the fullness of the Gentiles be come in. And so all Israel shall be saved; as it is written, there shall come out of Zion the Deliverer, and shall turn away ungodliness from Jacob; For this is My Covenant unto them, when I shall take away their sins. As concerning the Gospel, they are enemies for your sakes; but as touching the election, they are beloved for the fathers' sakes. For the gifts and calling of God are without repentance. For as ye in times past have not believed God, yet have now obtained mercy through their unbelief; Even so have these also now not believed, that through your mercy they also may obtain mercy. For God hath concluded them all in unbelief, that He might have mercy upon all.*

Ficus carica Fig Tree Photo 2013
A. Danin, Jerusalem Israel

The sudden return of Yeshua from Heaven, causes *the curse to be off the fig tree of Eden once and for all and it will bud with new life, and produce good fruit forever.* In the next section, we will see that this event will fulfill the prophecy that says, *"When Messiah comes, every man will sit under his vine and under his fig tree."* When they see the Son of man coming in a cloud with power and great glory, this is the time of Israel's final redemption, and Yeshua then spoke the parable of the fig tree budding with new life! This tells us that when we see this happen, then the Kingdom of God is at hand and the reign of Messiah will begin in Jerusalem. When all these things begin to come to pass, Yeshua said, *"Look up and lift up your heads!"* We will no longer hang our heads under the green fig leaf of shame! Messiah Yeshua's Testimony of bearing the curse of the fig tree of Eden is absolutely stunning!

Luke 21:27-31 *And then shall they see the Son of man coming in a cloud with power and great glory. And when these things begin to come to pass, then look up, and lift up your heads; for your redemption draweth nigh. And He spake to them a parable; Behold the fig tree, and all the trees; When they now shoot forth, ye see and know of your own selves that summer is now nigh at hand. So likewise ye, when ye see these things come to pass, know ye that the Kingdom of God is nigh at hand.*

THE VINE AND THE FIG TREE

In the beginning, the LORD planted a vineyard and He sent His servants out into His vineyard to produce the fruit of it. Yeshua described Himself as *"the True Vine"* and His Father as *"the Vinedresser."* The Father and the Word are one. The LORD'S vineyard was on Mount Moriah, but this place of the Garden of Eden became the Garden of thorns and desolation, as well as *"the place of the skull"* and death. Yeshua spoke about this vineyard in His parable, just after He cursed the fig tree.

John 15:1-9 *I AM the true vine, and My Father is the husbandmen. Every branch in Me that beareth not fruit he taketh away; and every branch that beareth fruit, He purgeth it, that it may bring forth more fruit. Now ye are clean through the Word which I have spoken unto you. Abide in Me, and I in you. As the branch cannot bear fruit of itself, except it abide in the vine; no more can ye, except ye abide in Me. I AM the vine, ye are the branches; He that abideth in Me, and I in Him, the same bringeth forth much fruit; for without Me ye can do nothing. If a man abide not in Me, he is cast forth as a branch, and is withered; and men gather them, and cast them into the fire, and they are burned. If ye abide in Me, and My Words abide in you, ye shall ask what ye will, and it shall be done unto you. Herein is My Father glorified, that ye bear much fruit; so shall ye be My disciples. As the Father hath loved Me, so have I loved you; continue ye in My love.*

Vines trail and grow long tendrils that climb upward or spread outward until they cover a vast area with lush green living foliage. Sometimes vines cover castle walls or climb up steep rugged hills and over tall fortified fences. *Vines flourish in the sun and in the shade,* just as we do when we abide in the LORD who sustains our lives. The ants and insects eat the sap of the vine for nourishment.

Yeshua's Living Testimony as *"the True Vine"* has spread throughout the earth into all nations as a witness. It has prevailed through every type of adversity, reaching every impossible, formidable place. At times, it has traveled down into the lowest valleys, into the darkest places. This was especially true during the *"Dark Ages"* when the people were prevented from having or reading the Bible, so they did not have the light of the LORD. Wherever the green leaves flourished on the Living Vine, the landscape was carpeted in rich, vibrant foliage. As the LORD'S branches, we grow on the same Vine that He established and the LORD feeds us His *"life-giving sap."* Our Living Water is full of vital nutrients and as He flows through us, He gives us Eternal life. Now if you really want your leaves to shine, you need to polish them with the oil of His Holy Spirit. As we absorb this oil, we shine beautifully and reflect His light. If one turns away from the LORD and does not abide in the Vine, he also becomes a dried up dead branch. If the life-giving sap was never allowed to flow into the branch to begin with, it quickly dies and withers like the cursed fig tree. We must have the vital sap of the LORD in order to have life inside of us. After this parable, Yeshua said, *"The Kingdom of Heaven is like a landowner, who went out early in the morning to hire laborers for His vineyard."*

Matthew 20:1-16 *For the Kingdom of Heaven is like unto a man that is an householder, which went out early in the morning to hire labourers into His vineyard. And when He had agreed with the labourers for a penny a day, He sent them into His vineyard. And he went out about the third hour, and saw others standing idle in the marketplace, And*

said unto them; Go ye also into the vineyard, and whatsoever is right I will give you. And they went their way. Again He went out about the sixth and ninth hour, and did likewise. And about the eleventh hour he went out, and found others standing idle, and saith unto them, Why stand ye here all the day idle? They say unto Him, Because no man hath hired us. He saith unto them, Go ye also into the vineyard; and whatsoever is right, that shall ye receive. So when even was come, the LORD of the vineyard saith unto His steward, Call the labourers, and give them their hire, beginning from the last unto the first. And when they came that were hired about the eleventh hour, they received every man a penny. But when the first came they supposed that they should have received more; and they likewise received every man a penny. And when they had received it, they murmured against the good man of the house, Saying, These last have wrought but one hour, and Thou hast made them equal unto us, which have borne the burden and heat of the day. But He answered one of them, and said, Friend, I do thee no wrong; didst not thou agree with me for a penny? Take that thine is, and go thy way; I will give unto this last, even as unto thee. Is it not lawful for Me to do what I will with mine own? Is thine eye evil, because I AM good? So the last shall be first, and the first last; for many are called, but few chosen.

So in this parable, the vinedresser and landowner or the householder is the LORD. He hires laborers to tend His vines full of branches, so they will bear fruit for Him. The LORD sent the laborers known as *"Israel"* out into His vineyard to bear this fruit first. The LORD came to Israel first with His Word, *His Torah*, and He expected them to work His vineyard to produce a good crop for the harvest. Lastly, the LORD came to the Gentiles and He gave them His Word Messiah, *the Living Torah,* so they would tend the vines and produce a good crop of fruit for His Eternal Kingdom. The labourers that bore the scorching heat in the parable, worked longer and suffered in the vineyard, and this refers to Israel. The two groups of labourers did not work the same length of time. However, the labourers that came last were also blessed with the same reward as the labourers who came to work the vineyard first. He proclaimed that they both belonged to Him.

At the end of the parable, Yeshua said, *"Thus the last shall be first, and the first last."* This is a profound statement. I believe that the LORD showed me something incredible about it. *"The last that shall be first" are the Gentiles and the "first that shall be last" refers to Israel.* Now this is very interesting because I believe this pertains to the promise that the LORD made to the righteous Gentile believers who will be raptured first into Heaven in the glory cloud with the LORD. Thus, this event will bring forth the end of the Church age. Immediately after this happens, it will usher in Israel's final redemption and eternal restoration. The Messiah will come for them *"last"* at the end of the 7 year time of Jacob's trouble, after the mourning time of Messiah is fulfilled. The righteous Gentile believers worked the vineyard *"last"* because they were given the Word of God *"last."* Israel was given the Word of God *"first"* at Mount Sinai, so their redemption, at the end of the 7 years will bring about the completion and perfection that ushers in the Kingdom of God. In essence, this is why Israel must come *"last"* because they came *"first."* They are like the bookends of the history of the world. Thus, Yeshua's Words revealed that *"the last shall be first, and the first last."* When the rapture occurs, this will trigger the so called *"Time of Jacob's Trouble,"* and the last 7 years of the 70 x 7 Prophecy will be fulfilled. The LORD will work for *"Rachel" (Israel),* during the 7 years and He will marry her last! The LORD will have already taken *"Leah"* the righteous remnant of the Gentile believers to be married to Him first. The Gentiles are like Leah, in the sense that she was *the unloved* who became *the first Bride of Jacob.* The LORD started with Israel and He will finish the redemption with Israel, just like Jacob received his Bride Rachel last after working for her for 7 years! The timing of the marriage and wedding of the LORD to Rachel/Israel was revealed within Yeshua's miracle of the Wedding in Cana of Galilee that took place on the third day. The Gentiles were allowed to come to Him during the time of the age of grace. The LORD comes at the end of the 7 years to fight as He did in the day of battle. He will come and restore Israel and renew the earth forever. All the children of God will be with Him forever and the LORD will come down from Heaven, as the Eternal Holy Temple of the LORD. When the LORD brought forth His judgment, it was because His vine was not

producing the fruit that He expected it to. The Holy Temple on the earth was destroyed because of this great sin, but the Messiah became the Fruitful Branch in His very Fruitful hill called *"Holy Mount Moriah!" This was the LORD'S vineyard in His Garden and the place of His winepress and tower where Yeshua bore the best fruit of His resurrection!*

Isaiah 5:1-7 *Now will I sing to my well-beloved a song of my beloved touching His vineyard. My well-beloved hath a vineyard in a very fruitful hill; And He fenced it, and gathered out the stones thereof, and planted it with the choicest vine, and built a tower in the midst of it, and also made a winepress therein; and He looked that it should bring forth grapes, and it brought forth wild grapes. And now, O inhabitants of Jerusalem, and men of Judah, judge, I pray you, betwixt Me and My vineyard. What could have been done more to My vineyard, that I have not done in it? Wherefore, when I looked that it should bring forth grapes, brought it forth wild grapes? And now go to; I will tell you what I will do to My vineyard; I will take away the hedge there of, and it shall be eaten up; and break down the wall thereof, and it shall be trodden down; And I will lay it waste; it shall not be pruned, nor digged; but there shall come up briers and thorns; I will also command the clouds that they rain no rain upon it. For the vineyard of the LORD of Hosts is the House of Israel, and the men of Judah His pleasant plant; and He looked for judgment, but behold oppression; for righteousness, but behold a cry.*

The Scripture goes on to say that they considered not the work of the LORD'S hands. *The moral of the story is that the LORD'S Garden was in Eden, in Mount Moriah, where He planted His vineyard and built His winepress.* His vine only flourished when it was abiding in the LORD in this place in Jerusalem and because of the curse of Eden, the LORD'S Garden was trodden down and laid waste. This is why the LORD was always calling people back to Jerusalem Israel, to His Holy Mount Moriah. The Messiah bore the curse of the briers and thorns of His Garden and vineyard near His winepress, as He redeemed us and delivered us from the bondage of death. It was here that He showed us the way back to His Eternal Heavenly Garden. We must stay close to the LORD and we must consider the work of His hands because in His hand, He holds the Rod of salvation. This is how it was in the beginning and this is why the Holy Temple was built in this location. The LORD formed the earth from water and by water and His Spirit brought it to life. So the truth is that we must have this special Spirit stirred Water inside our soul to have Eternal life and, as I have said so many times, we receive it through Messiah's baptism. Now the LORD revealed the following astonishing details to me about *the fig tree and the vineyard. When Yeshua spoke His Word to Nathaniel, who was a righteous Jew, Yeshua revealed to Nathaniel exactly when He plans to marry Israel in the future.*

Ficus carica Fig Tree
Photo ©2013 A. Danin,
Jerusalem Israel
All Rights Reserved

John 1:45-51 *Philip findeth Nathaniel, and saith unto him, We have found Him, of whom Moses in the Law, and the Prophets, did write, Yeshua of Nazareth, the son of Joseph. Nathaniel said unto him, Can there any good thing come out of Nazareth? Philip saith unto him, Come and see. Yeshua saw Nathaniel coming to Him, and saith of him, Behold an Israelite indeed, in whom is no guile! Nathaniel saith unto Him, Whence knowest thou me? Yeshua answered and said unto him, Before that Philip called thee, when thou wast under the fig tree, I saw thee. Nathaniel answered and saith unto Him, Rabbi, Thou are the Son of God; Thou art the KING of Israel. Yeshua answered and said unto him, Because I said unto thee, I saw thee under the fig tree, believest thou? Thou shalt see greater things than these. And He saith unto him, Verily, verily, I say unto you, Hereafter ye shall see Heaven open, and the angels of God ascending and descending upon the Son of man.*

The wedding in Cana is *"the first"* miracle that Yeshua performed. The wedding occurred on *"the third day,"* and it was the event that took place *immediately* after Yeshua met Nathaniel. Yeshua told Nathaniel, *that He saw him, sitting under the fig tree, before He met him.* This is extremely important! Yeshua was revealing the exact time of His marriage to Israel, as He spoke to Nathaniel. Now when Yeshua saw Nathaniel

coming to Him, Yeshua said to him, *"Here is a true Israelite indeed and in Him, there is nothing false."* Nathaniel said to Yeshua, *"How do you know me?"* Yeshua said, *"I saw you when you were sitting under the fig tree."* Nathaniel realized at once that this statement was extremely profound pertaining to his future because Nathaniel knew this ancient prophecy from Micah 4:4, and Zechariah 3:10 that says *that when the Messiah would come and restore Israel that "every man would sit under his vine and under his fig tree."* This is what Yeshua revealed to Nathaniel. Suddenly realizing this was the LORD, Nathaniel instantly proclaimed, *"Rabbi, you are the Messiah, the KING of Israel!" As I pondered this event, I suddenly realized that Messiah the LORD, "the True Vine," was standing there speaking to Nathaniel and He revealed to righteous Nathaniel that He saw Him sitting under the fig tree!* This is very chilling and prophetic because it means that the wedding in Cana took place *"the third day"* immediately after Yeshua said that *He saw the righteous Israelite sitting under the fig tree as "the True Vine"* was standing in his midst speaking to him! *So the Living Torah, the Ark of Heaven, was standing in His midst. "Nathaniel"* literally means *"Gift of God."* Yeshua knew that Nathaniel was a righteous Jew before He met Him that day, and only *the righteous* ever enter the Kingdom of Heaven. Yeshua was actually revealing that He saw Nathaniel as he appeared in the Kingdom of Heaven, in the future redemption, when he was sitting under the fig tree because it was no longer cursed at the arrival of KING Messiah, *"the True Vine!"* This is how Yeshua already knew Nathaniel who realized that Yeshua was the Messiah and proclaimed at once *"Rabbi, you are the Messiah, the KING of Israel!" Yeshua was revealing a future event to Nathaniel.* Now this means that Nathaniel was not just sitting outside under a fig tree, just before he came inside and met Yeshua. Messiah Yeshua was revealing *the final redemption* to this righteous Jew named *"Nathaniel!"* After this happened, it was *the third day* when the wedding took place in Cana when Yeshua revealed that He was *the Bridegroom of Israel, the Rod of God,* who turned the water into the best wine! Remember that at the wedding, Yeshua saved *"the best wine for last."* When the LORD Messiah marries His Bride Rachel/Israel, it will be *the last* thing that happens because this was *the first* miracle that Yeshua performed and Yeshua said that *the first shall be last*. This will occur on *the third day,* fulfilling the prophecy in Hosea that declares that *"on the third day, the LORD will raise Israel up."* Their redemption occurs at the end of the last 7 years, at the end of the time of Jacob's trouble and after the LORD Yeshua works for 7 years, as the Rod, to obtain His beloved Israel/Rachel! Immediately after proclaiming His Words to Nathaniel, Yeshua went forth to the wedding in Cana and proved beyond a shadow of a doubt that He is the Bridegroom that will marry His Bride Israel the third day. This is absolutely stunning! At the time that this ancient prophecy comes to pass in the future, *we will dwell in the Presence of the LORD and the curse will finally be removed from the fig tree of Eden* because the Messiah has taken it away in His vineyard! The fig tree will bud as a sign of Yeshua's return and mankind will sit under the fig tree and under *"the True Vine," forever,* because the LORD has been revealed as the Almond Tree of Life, the Word of God and *The Living Torah. (I must come back to add here that in 2013 as I was doing my final editing, another miracle happened when it was revealed to me that Jim & Penny Caldwell actually discovered a fig tree bearing figs on the real Mount Sinai! This was absolutely stunning to me, because I had written all of this already about the fig tree by Divine Providence and guidance and now the LORD was providing the stunning proof!)*

Micah 4:2-4 *And many nations shall come, and say, Come, and let us go up to the Mountain of the LORD, and to the House of the God of Jacob; and He will teach us of His ways, and we will walk in His paths; for the Law shall go forth of Zion, and the Word of the LORD from Jerusalem. And He shall judge among many people, and rebuke strong nations afar off; and they shall beat their swords into plowshares, and their spears into pruning hooks; nation shall not lift up a sword against nation, neither shall they learn war any more. But they shall sit every man under his vine and under his fig tree; and none shall make them afraid; for the mouth of the LORD of Hosts hath spoken it.*

It is amazing when you realize that the events took place in this exact order. Now in the beginning in the Garden of Eden, the LORD God, the KING, was dwelling in the midst of the man and woman that He had created. At that time, they were *under a fig tree and under "the True Vine,"* just before the curse happened. So Yeshua actually saw Nathaniel in the Garden in Heaven before it came to pass because Yeshua was there with Him in Heaven, as the KING of Israel, the Rabbi of Righteousness! When the Messiah comes down from Heaven, to bring the everlasting Kingdom of God to earth again as it was in the beginning, then every man and woman will again *sit under the fig tree and under "the True Vine."* The curse will be gone and the redemption will be complete. If you recall, in the beginning, *as they ate the fruit of the fig tree, the curse came upon them,* and they sewed the fig leaves together to hide their shame.

Vine (clematis)
Photo ©2013 Kimberly K Ballard
All Rights Reserved

***Genesis 3:6-8** And when the woman saw that the tree was good for food, and that it was pleasant to the eyes, and a tree to be desired to make one wise, she took of the fruit thereof, and did eat, and gave also unto her husband with her; and he did eat. And the eyes of them both were opened, and they knew that they were naked; and they sewed fig leaves together, and made themselves aprons. And they heard the voice of the LORD God walking in the Garden in the cool of the day; and Adam and his wife hid themselves from the Presence of the LORD God amongst the trees of the Garden.*

So what Nathaniel must have recognized is the fact that the fig tree was there at the beginning of creation *(at first)* and it will be there in the end *(at last)*. Therefore, Yeshua was also revealing to Nathaniel that He is *"The First and the Last."* This is so exciting! Remember that Yeshua made the fig tree wither because of the curse! Then Yeshua gave the parable of the fig tree budding, as the sign when He will gather His elect. This is recorded in Matthew, Mark, and Luke. The fig tree will no longer be withered, but it will bloom and bud and produce fruit at the arrival of KING Messiah from Heaven! So Yeshua said that He would return *soon after we see the fig tree bud* and we will know that summer is near. The budding of the fig tree occurs at the second coming of the Messiah. This is the very moment of Israel's final redemption at the end of the 7 years, and the LORD takes Israel for His Bride on the third day.

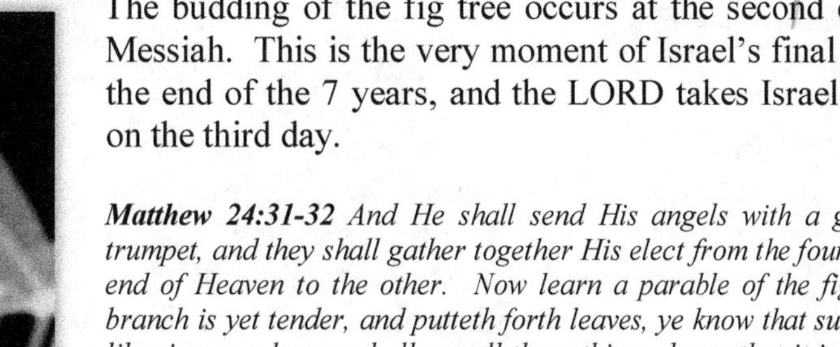

***Matthew 24:31-32** And He shall send His angels with a great sound of a trumpet, and they shall gather together His elect from the four winds, from one end of Heaven to the other. Now learn a parable of the fig tree; When his branch is yet tender, and putteth forth leaves, ye know that summer is nigh; So likewise ye, when ye shall see all these things, know that it is near, even at the doors. Verily I say unto you, This generation shall not pass, till all these things be fulfilled.*

Ficus carica Fig Tree
Photo ©2013 A. Danin
Jerusalem, Israel All Rights Reserved

In the Gospel of Luke, the redemption of Israel takes place *"when the fig tree begins to shoot forth with new life!"* Yeshua said in Luke's Gospel that *"they would see Him coming in a cloud with great glory."* When this happens they are to *"look up, because their redemption draws nigh."* Israel is to behold the fig tree and all trees bearing the curse of Eden and watch for them to bud to life. Yeshua said that when they bud forth and you see these things coming to pass, *"You will know that the Kingdom of God is at hand!"* This tells us plainly that the Kingdom of God is in our midst, the moment the fig tree buds without the curse!

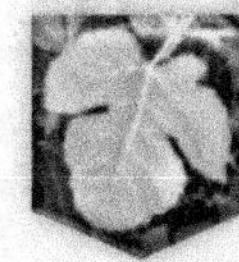

Luke 21:27-31 *And then shall they see the Son of man coming in a cloud with power and great glory. And when these things begin to come to pass, then look up, and lift up your heads; for your redemption draweth nigh. And He spake to them a parable; Behold the fig tree, and all the trees; When they now shoot forth, ye see and know of your own selves that summer is now nigh at hand. So likewise ye, when ye see these things come to pass, know ye that the Kingdom of God is nigh at hand.*

Fig Tree
Photo ©2013 A. Danin,
Jerusalem, Israel All Rights Reserved

Yeshua of Nazareth gave us all the clues, miracles, signs and wonders that prove that He is Israel's true KING Messiah. Only the LORD could have known that this would happen in another 2,000 years, in the future with Israel. All I can say is how astounding it is to see this, even before it comes to pass! Now, I have to say that something remarkable just happened to me right after I finished editing this section! Yeshua gave a list of signs that would signal His return back to earth.

Matthew 24:3 *And as He sat upon the Mount of Olives, the disciples came unto Him privately, saying, Tell us, when shall these things be? And what shall be the sign of Thy coming, and of the end of the world?*

Of course the budding of the fig tree without the curse was one sign, but another thrilling sign is that the earth will be *"as it was in the days of Noah, before the flood came and took them all away,"* which refers to the wicked who were not in the Ark.

Matthew 24:37-39 *But as the days of Noah were, so shall also the coming of the Son of man be. For as in the days that were before the flood they were eating and drinking, marrying and giving in marriage, until the day that Noah entered into the Ark, And knew not until the flood came, and took them all away; so shall also the coming of the Son of man be.*

The day I finished this section there was a story on the internet that showed that a 30,000 year old seed, and its fruit buried by a squirrel from a plant that was frozen in permafrost in Siberia, just sprouted to life! *This plant existed before Noah's flood!* I have already declared that the fig tree that existed before the flood of Noah, in the Garden of Eden, will sprout to life and produce fruit without the curse just before the coming of Messiah Yeshua from Heaven. The rare Siberian plant, ironically has pure snow white flowers, each bearing five petals with heart shaped tips on the end of its petals. This reminds me that the LORD makes us pure like snow because He is *the Living Torah* and the Eternal Covenant of the heart. *This plant is a great sign, as well as Jim & Penny Caldwell's miraculous fruiting fig tree on Mount Sinai, proclaiming that the Kingdom of Heaven is drawing near to us, through this book of revelation!* We need to repent and get right with the LORD God, so we can enter the Ark of our salvation. *The astounding fact that the seed of this beautiful little plant was alive and developing before the flood of Noah and was frozen in permafrost for centuries and that it just came to life and blossomed from a fruit as I was writing this is so shocking!* I believe the LORD is giving us a signal, that His arrival is about to take place. What is His message? We must believe in KING Messiah Yeshua now because He is coming very soon for those who love Him and I know for certain that I want to dwell under *"the True Vine"* forever! At the end of this book you will see that another miraculous tree came to life!

THE MIRACLE OF THE WEDDING IN CANA

The Wedding scene in Cana amphora, house & pitchers & California Palm tree

Now realizing that the first miracle that Messiah Yeshua performed after speaking to Nathaniel took place in Cana of Galilee, Yeshua appeared to have made a rather strange statement during the wedding feast to His Mother. Now Mary, Yeshua's earthly Mother, was from the Royal lineage of King David through Nathan, a son of King David. The Bride at the wedding feast is clearly *Israel* because in the book of Isaiah, the LORD actually *"called to Israel as a woman"* and this is what Yeshua revealed at the wedding feast! She told Yeshua that they were out of wine. Yeshua replied to her, *"Woman, what have I to do with thee? Mine hour is not yet come."* Now I always thought that this was such an odd statement, but I figured out that when He called her *"woman"* Yeshua the LORD was actually revealing that He was about to perform the miracle about His Bride. In Genesis, remember that the *"woman"* was made for the man, so she represented the Bride of Adam. Yeshua, the second Adam, revealed that He will not be drinking the wine yet with His Bride because His time has not yet come to marry her, for she was like a *"woman"* forsaken.

John 2:1-11 *And the third day there was a marriage in Cana of Galilee; and the mother of Yeshua was there; And both Yeshua was called, and his disciples, to the marriage. And when they wanted wine, the mother of Yeshua saith unto Him, They have no wine. Yeshua saith unto her, Woman, what have I to do with thee? Mine hour is not yet come. His mother saith unto the servants, Whatsoever He saith unto you, do it. And there were set there six water pots of stone, after the manner of the purifying of the Jews, containing two or three firkins apiece. Yeshua saith unto them. Fill the water pots with water. And they filled them up to the brim. And He saith unto them, Draw out now, and bear unto the governor of the feast. And they bare it. When the ruler of the feast had tasted the water that was made wine, and knew not whence it was; but the servants which drew the water knew; the governor of the Feast called the Bridegroom, And saith unto him, Every man at the beginning doth set forth good wine; and when men have well drunk, then that which is worse; but thou hast kept the good wine until now. This beginning of miracles did Yeshua in Cana of Galilee, and manifested forth His glory; and His disciples believed on Him.*

Now I was so astonished when I discovered that the LORD said *"The hiding of His face from Israel was like the waters of Noah to Him,"* but when He reveals His face to Israel, as KING Messiah Yeshua, near the time of His return from Heaven, He says that *He will have everlasting kindness and mercy upon Israel.* It was for this profound reason that Yeshua revealed that *"His return from Heaven would be like the days of Noah!" He meant that His Bride will suddenly see His face as the LORD God of Israel and this is about to take place before our eyes! Chilling!*

Isaiah 54:5-14 *For thy Maker is thine husband; the LORD of Hosts is His Name; and thy Redeemer the Holy One of Israel; The God of the whole earth shall He be called. For the LORD hath called thee as a woman forsaken and grieved in spirit, and a wife of youth, when thou wast refused, saith thy God. For a small moment have I forsaken thee; but with great mercies will I gather thee. In a little wrath I hid my face from thee for a moment; but with everlasting kindness will I have mercy on thee, saith the LORD thy Redeemer. <u>For this is as the waters of Noah unto Me;</u> for as I have sworn that the waters of Noah should no more go over the earth; so have I sworn that I would not be wroth with thee, nor rebuke thee. For the mountains shall depart, and the hills be removed; but My kindness shall not depart from thee, neither shall the Covenant of My Peace be removed, saith the LORD that hath mercy on thee. O thou afflicted, tossed with tempest, and not comforted, behold, I will lay thy stones with fair colours, and lay thy foundations with sapphires. And I will make thy windows of agates, and thy gates of carbuncles, and all thy borders of pleasant stones. And all thy children shall be taught of the LORD; and great shall be the peace of thy*

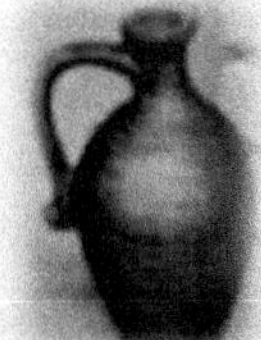
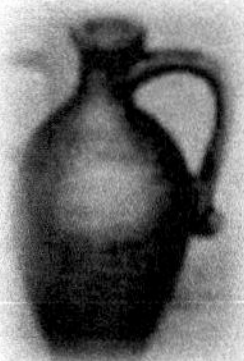

children. In righteousness shalt thou be established; thou shalt be far from oppression; for thou shalt not fear; and from terror; for it shall not come near thee.

Yeshua also said that at His return *"they will be eating, drinking, marrying and being given in marriage."* They will see that Yeshua is the LORD God of Israel! After Noah entered the Ark, he was saved and then the flood came and the earth was cleansed and all things were made new. So this means that Israel will not only see that *the face of Messiah is the LORD'S face,* but they will enter the Ark of His Eternal Covenant and the final judgment will come upon the wicked. Yeshua then ushers in the Kingdom of Heaven and makes all things new, as it was in the days of Noah!

Luke 17:26-27 *And as it was in the days of Noah, so shall it be also in the days of the Son of man. They did eat, they drank, they married wives, they were given in marriage, until the day that Noah entered into the Ark, and the flood came, and destroyed them all.*

Isaiah also recorded here that *"the LORD laid the foundation stones and the gates."* Remember that I said that these are *the Living foundation stones* of the Jewish disciples of Messiah Yeshua that He chose after His feet stood in the Jordan River as the Ark of the Eternal Covenant and as the second Joshua, who was leading Israel into the Eternal Promised Land, and remember that *the gates are the twelve tribes of Israel!*

In the miracle of the wedding in Cana, remember there were six stone water jars filled with kosher purified water and I said that the LORD Yeshua is the *seventh complete and perfect vessel of Living Water* who will marry His Bride on the seventh day Sabbath of the LORD. When *the Deliverer* takes them to their *haven,* they will enter His rest and they will celebrate *the Feast of Tabernacles,* which is the time that the water libation of *"Living Water"* is poured out upon the altar of the LORD. The life blood is also upon this altar, so it represents the Rod of God that became the Lamb. For seven days, the Priest would take the jar of water that was drawn from the Pool of Shiloach/Siloam the previous evening, where the Priests washed in the Living Water, and they would take it up to the altar where they would pour this Living Water into a bowl that drained onto the altar. In 2014 during Sukkot, for the first time in 2,000 years, they did this! Remember that Yeshua walked upon the water, full of His Holy Spirit, in the evening and was later poured out upon the altar. The Pool of Siloam contained water that flowed into it from the Gihon Spring. *This water was the living water that was used specifically to anoint all the King's that came from the line of King David and the Holy Spirit moved upon the waters in this Pool and turned them into living water.* All of the elements in this ceremony reveal the Bridegroom, Messiah Yeshua, and that He is the well of salvation. According to Jewish tradition, it was a jubilant ceremony with musicians playing and dancing. It is written in the Jewish writings that *"they would light three very tall candlesticks in the Temple court and that the Priest would blow the shofar three times. They performed this ceremony in jubilance, with the words of Isaiah."* Remember that it was during this ceremony that Yeshua stood in the Holy Temple and told the Jewish people, *"Let all who thirst come to Me."* The number three of the shofar blasts and candlesticks is pictured here again as part of Yeshua's Eternal resurrection Testimony as the Almond Rod that budded the third day.

Isaiah 12:3-6 *Therefore with joy shall ye draw water out of the wells of salvation. And in that day shall ye say, Praise the LORD, call upon His Name, declare His doings among the people, make mention that His Name is exalted. Sing unto the LORD; for He hath done excellent things; this is known in all the earth. Cry out and shout, thou inhabitant of Zion; for great is the Holy One of Israel in the midst of thee.*

Now I understand from *the Torah* that Yeshua's first miracle was proclaiming, *"In this thou shalt know that I AM the LORD" who plans to marry Israel!*

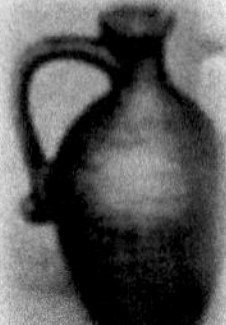

In Exodus, the last of the three signs that the LORD told Moses to perform with the Rod, in case they refused to believe the first two signs, was the miracle of the LORD turning the water into blood and Yeshua turned the water into the best wine that represented the life blood of His Eternal Covenant with mankind. So the miracle of the wedding in Cana took place on the third day, and Yeshua the Bridegroom will return the second time on the third day to raise Israel to her Eternal glory and to marry her. Of course the Bridegroom was also resurrected the third day.

Yeshua stood before the wedding guests as the Heavenly Bridegroom. In that day, when the Lamb Messiah attends His marriage supper, I believe that it will be right after He ushers in the Kingdom of Heaven in Jerusalem when He will finally drink the *best wine that He has saved for last.* Yeshua and the Jewish disciples were singing about the Lamb sacrifice in the Hallel after they drank the cup of redemption in the Last Passover Seder as they went to the Mount of Olives, and Yeshua was about to pay the Bride's price! So this is one more final miracle that we find in the wedding of Cana that is marvelous! It was Yeshua's *"First"* miracle and He has saved the best wine for *"Last!"* He is indeed *"the First and the Last,"* who sealed us in His heart forever with His love. He will drink this cup from His vineyard again at His future wedding.

Isaiah 62:3-5 *Thou shalt no more be termed Forsaken; neither shall thy Land anymore be termed Desolate; but thou shalt be called Hephzibah, and thy Land Beulah; for the LORD delighteth in thee, and thy Land shall be married. For as a young man marrieth a virgin, so shall thy sons marry thee; and as the Bridegroom rejoiceth over the Bride, so shall thy God rejoice over thee.*

Revelation 19:7-9 *Let us be glad and rejoice, and give honour to Him; for the marriage of the Lamb is come, and His wife hath made herself ready. And to her was granted that she should be arrayed in fine linen, clean and white; for the fine linen is the righteousness of Saints. And He saith unto me, Write, Blessed are they which are called unto the marriage supper of the Lamb. And He saith unto me, These are the true sayings of God.*

Yeshua revealed that His Jewish disciples were betrothed to Him as a Bride. What was the Word that Yeshua used when He beckoned to Simon Peter as He walked on the water? He simply said, *"Come." He calls you to, "Come!" He wants you to be at the wedding of the KING of glory! The Bridegroom is the one who brings the earth back to an Eden-like state. We have absolute certainty in Him that He is faithful to share His Paradise with us forever.*

Matthew 14:28-29 *And Peter answered Him and said, LORD, if it be Thou, bid me come unto Thee on the water. And He said, Come. And when Peter was come down out of the ship, he walked on the water, to go to Yeshua.*

Revelation 22:16-17 *I Yeshua have sent Mine angel to testify unto you these things in the churches. I AM the root and the offspring of David, and the bright morning star. And the Spirit and the Bride say, Come. And let him that heareth say, Come. And whosoever will, let him take the water of life freely.*

Now I realized this was like Yeshua's parable of the prodigal son and *Israel* is the lost son in this parable that returns to love the father. Israel will realize Messiah Yeshua is the Saviour of Israel, and they will return to love Him. The LORD will give a joyful Feast!

Luke 15:29-32 *And he answering said to his father, Lo, these many years do I serve thee, neither transgressed I at any time thy commandment; and yet thou never gavest me a kid, that I might make merry with my friends; But as soon as this thy son was come, which hath devoured thy living with harlots, thou hast killed for him the fatted calf. And he said unto him, Son, thou art ever with me, and all that I have is thine. It was meet that we should make merry, and be glad; for this thy brother was dead, and is alive again; and was lost, and is found.*

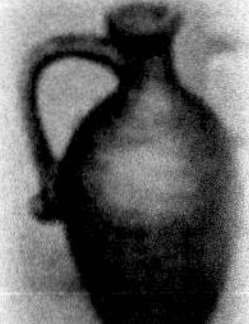

Jeremiah 31:3-4 *The LORD hath appeared of old unto me, saying, Yea, I have loved thee with an everlasting love; Therefore with loving kindness have I drawn thee. Again I will build thee, and thou shalt be built O virgin of Israel; thou shalt again be adorned with thy tabrets, and shalt go forth in the dances of them that make merry.*

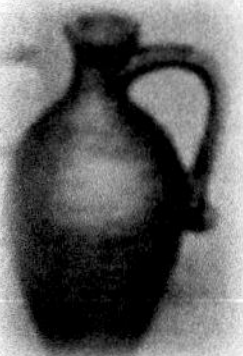

Matthew 9:15-17 *And Yeshua said unto them, Can the children of the bride-chamber mourn, as long as the Bridegroom is with them? But the days will come, when the Bridegroom shall be taken from them, and then shall they fast. No man putteth a piece of new cloth unto an old garment, for that which is put in to fill it up taketh from the garment, and the rent is made worse. Neither do men put new wine into old bottles; else the bottles break, and the wine runneth out, and the bottles perish; but they put new wine into new bottles, and both are preserved.*

Palm trees & Cana house ©2013 Kimberly K Ballard All Rights Reserved

RESTORATION OF FLESH HEALING THE WITHERED HAND YESHUA RAISES THE DEAD AND HEALS LEPROSY

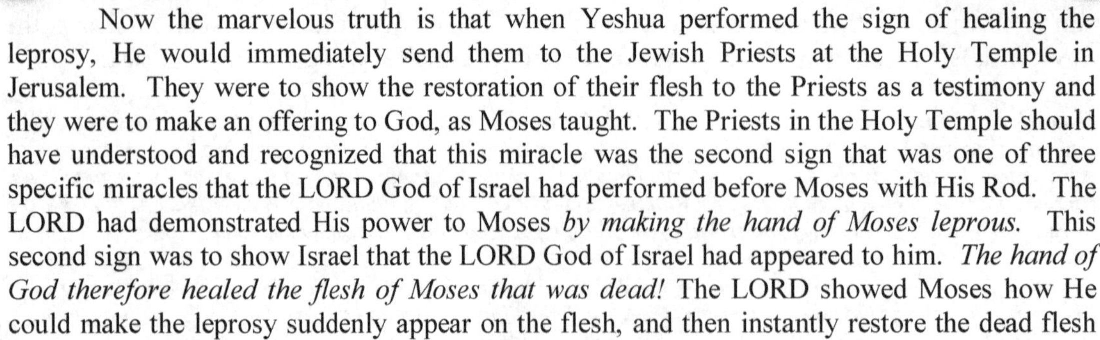

Jasmine lying on a chair & last paw prints, miracle whiskers & a piece of his fur
I believe the LORD will restore everything in Heaven including the animals
Photos ©2013 Kimberly K Ballard All Rights Reserved

Now the marvelous truth is that when Yeshua performed the sign of healing the leprosy, He would immediately send them to the Jewish Priests at the Holy Temple in Jerusalem. They were to show the restoration of their flesh to the Priests as a testimony and they were to make an offering to God, as Moses taught. The Priests in the Holy Temple should have understood and recognized that this miracle was the second sign that was one of three specific miracles that the LORD God of Israel had performed before Moses with His Rod. The LORD had demonstrated His power to Moses *by making the hand of Moses leprous.* This second sign was to show Israel that the LORD God of Israel had appeared to him. *The hand of God therefore healed the flesh of Moses that was dead!* The LORD showed Moses how He could make the leprosy suddenly appear on the flesh, and then instantly restore the dead flesh

and give it life again. Now again, the LORD God of Israel performed the sign of healing the leprosy with Miriam! When the LORD departed in anger, Miriam's flesh became leprous, and this happened because the LORD'S protection had departed from her. Miriam was not healed of the leprosy until they called upon the LORD in repentance. As soon as they admitted their sin and repented, the LORD returned and healed her flesh! Aaron prayed and cried out to the LORD and pleaded with the LORD *"not to make Miriam as one who is dead and whose flesh is half consumed."* In this story, the LORD departed in the cloud exactly as Yeshua departed in the cloud!

Numbers 12:9-13 *And the anger of the LORD was kindled against them; and he departed. And the cloud departed from off the Tabernacle; and, behold, Miriam became leprous, white as snow; and Aaron looked upon Miriam, and, behold, she was leprous. And Aaron said unto Moses, Alas, my LORD, I beseech Thee, lay not the sin upon us, wherein we have done foolishly, and wherein we have sinned. Let her not be as one dead, of whom the flesh is half consumed when he cometh out of his mother's womb. And Moses cried unto the LORD, saying, Heal her now, O God, I beseech thee.*

Now in the following Scriptures, Messiah Yeshua healed the leprosy. The Priests should have made the connection *to the LORD God of Israel and His works,* but they did not seem to understand that *"this was God visiting His people"* and that Yeshua was showing them the same signs that He had previously shown to Moses and Miriam. The Testimony that Yeshua was referring to in this miracle was to show that His Living Covenant will take away our corrupted flesh and give us Eternal life because we have repented for our sins.

Matthew 8:1-4 *When He was come down from the mountain, great multitudes followed Him. And, behold, there came a leper and worshipped him, saying, LORD, if Thou wilt thou canst make me clean. And Yeshua put forth His hand, and touched him, saying I will; be thou clean. And immediately his leprosy was cleansed. And Yeshua saith unto him, See thou tell no man; but go thy way, shew thyself to the Priest, and offer the gift that Moses commanded, for a Testimony unto them.*

The mere fact that the leper was worshipping Yeshua and calling Him *"LORD"* testifies that *Yeshua is the Rod of God.* Now as soon as Yeshua spoke *the Word* and proclaimed, *"I will,"* suddenly the leprosy left him and he was cleansed. It was the will of the LORD to heal this man and restore life to him. The human body is made of flesh and blood, containing a very high percentage of water and we need vast amounts of water to live and to thrive. So when *the Living Water* was speaking to the leper by *His Word* through His Holy Spirit, the flesh was resurrected to life. Once again, *the Living Torah spoke* and instantly the leper was healed.

Mark 1:39-45 *And He preached in their Synagogues throughout all Galilee, and cast out devils. And there came a leper to Him, beseeching Him, and kneeling down to Him, and saying unto Him, If thou wilt, thou canst make me clean, And Yeshua, moved with compassion, put forth His hand, and touched him, and saith unto him, I will; be thou clean. And as soon as He had spoken, immediately the leprosy departed from him, and he was cleansed. And He straitly charged him, and forthwith sent him away; And saith unto him, See thou say nothing to any man; but go thy way, shew thyself to the Priest, and offer for thy cleansing those things which Moses commanded, for a Testimony unto them. But he went out, and began to publish it much, and to blaze abroad the matter, insomuch that Yeshua could no more openly enter into the city, but was without in desert places; and they came to Him from every quarter.*

Yeshua also raised the dead man in Nain Israel who was the only son of a widow. As the dead man sat up and began to speak at Yeshua's Word, *"Young man, I say to thee, Arise," then the people glorified God.* Most of the city witnessed this great miracle and they boldly proclaimed, *"God hath visited His people!"* They were right because *the Living Torah* had the resurrection power to raise the dead man to life.

Acts 26:8 *Why should it be thought a thing incredible with you, that God should raise the dead?*

Luke 7:12-23 *Now when He came nigh to the gate of the city, behold, there was a dead man carried out, the only son of his mother, and she was a widow; and much people of the city was with her. And when the LORD saw her, He had compassion on her, and said unto her, Weep not. And He came and touched the bier; and they that bare him stood still. And He said, Young man, I say unto thee, Arise, And he that was dead sat up, and began to speak. And He delivered him to his mother. And there came a fear on all; and they glorified God, saying, That a great Prophet is risen up among us; and, That God hath visited His people. And this rumour of Him went forth throughout all Judaea, and throughout all the region round about. And the disciples of John shewed him of all these things. And John calling unto him two of his disciples sent them to Yeshua, saying, Art Thou He that should come? Or look we for another? When the men were come unto Him, they said, John Baptist hath sent us unto Thee, saying, Art thou He that should come? Or look we for another? And in that same hour He cured many of their infirmities and plagues, and of evil spirits; and unto many that were blind He gave sight. Then Yeshua answering said unto them, Go your way, and tell John what things ye have seen and heard; how that the blind see, the lame walk, the lepers are cleansed, the deaf hear, the dead are raised, to the poor the Gospel is preached. And blessed is he, whosoever shall not be offended in Me.*

On another occasion, Yeshua raised a young dead girl to life. Messiah Yeshua performed this miracle before the ruler of the Synagogue. Yeshua took the hand of the little girl and He spoke *the Word* of God to her from His mouth and the girl came to life. *The Living Torah* was speaking to her and her flesh was restored!

Mark 5:35-43 *While He yet spake, there came from the ruler of the Synagogue's house certain which said, Thy daughter is dead; why troublest thou the Master any further? As soon as Yeshua heard the word that was spoken, He saith unto the ruler of the Synagogue, Be not afraid, only believe. And He suffered no man to follow Him, save Peter, and James, and John the brother of James. And He cometh to the house of the ruler of the Synagogue, and seeth the tumult, and them that wept and wailed greatly. And when He was come in, He saith unto them, Why make ye this ado, and weep? The damsel is not dead, but sleepeth. And they laughed Him to scorn. But when He had put them all out, He taketh the father and the mother of the damsel, and them that were with Him, and entereth in where the damsel was lying. And He took the damsel by the hand, and said unto her, Talitha cumi; which is, being interpreted, Damsel, I say unto thee arise. And straightway the damsel arose, and walked; for she was of the age of twelve years. And they were astonished with a great astonishment. And He charged them straitly that no man should know it; and commanded that something should be given her to eat.*

II Corinthians 1:9-11 *But we had the sentence of death in ourselves, that we should not trust in ourselves, but in God which raiseth the dead; Who delivered us from so great a death, and doth deliver; in whom we trust that He will yet deliver us; Yes also helping together by prayer for us, that for the gift bestowed upon us by the means of many persons thanks may be given by many on our behalf.*

Of course the most famous resurrection of the dead that Yeshua performed was the resurrection of Lazarus who was the brother of Mary and Martha. This particular resurrection of the dead is so significant that I have written about it exclusively in the next chapter because it pertains to the next subject. Yeshua also raised *Tabitha or Dorcas*, which I wrote about exclusively in the following chapter. Yeshua performed this miracle to show that in the future, He will raise the dead and restore the flesh of those who come out of their graves at the resurrection of the dead when He descends from Heaven with a shout, with the voice of the Archangel and with the *"Last Trump"* of God. The dead will hear the voice of *the Living Torah* and they will come forth out of their graves to Eternal life!

There were other miraculous signs that Yeshua performed. Messiah Yeshua healed the man with the withered hand and this miracle just happens to be the same miracle that the LORD God of Israel performed in the book of I Kings. Those who witnessed Yeshua restoring the withered right hand were shocked. They definitely should have recognized that this was a sign that was given by the LORD God when He made the hand of Jeroboam, the King of Judah, to wither and then He restored it to life again. Of course Messiah Yeshua, the LORD, *the Word,* inherits Judah as His portion because He came in the lineage of King David.

In this miracle the King of Judah was to intreat *"the face" of the LORD God* to restore his hand! It was miraculously restored when he was seeking the LORD.

I Kings 13:1-10 *AND, behold, there came a man of God out of Judah by the Word of the LORD unto Bethel; and Jeroboam stood by the altar to burn incense. And he cried against the altar in the Word of the LORD, and said, O altar, thus saith the LORD; Behold, a child shall be born unto the house of David, Josiah by name; and upon thee shall he offer the Priests of the high places that burn incense upon thee, and men's bones shall be burnt upon thee. And he gave a sign the same day, saying, This is the sign which the LORD hath spoken; Behold, the altar shall be rent, and the ashes that are upon it shall be poured out. And it came to pass, when King Jeroboam heard the saying of the man of God, which had cried against the altar in Bethel, that he put forth his hand from the altar, saying, Lay hold on him. And his hand, which he put forth against him, dried up, so that he could not pull it in again to him. The altar also was rent, and the ashes poured out from the altar, according to the sign which the man of God had given by the Word of the LORD. And the King answered and said unto the man of God, Intreat now the face of the LORD thy God, and pray for me, that my hand may be restored me again. And the man of God besought the LORD, and the King's hand was restored him again, and became as it was before. And the man of God said unto the King, If thou wilt give me half thine house, I will not go in with thee, neither will I eat bread or drink water in this place; For so was it charged me by the Word of the LORD, saying, Eat no bread, nor drink water, nor turn again by the same way that thou camest. So he went another way, and returned not by the way that he came to Bethel.*

When the man of God came with *the Word* of God, the hand of the man withered and it was restored by God. The man of God was instructed by God not to eat bread or drink water. This sign also proved that *the Word of God* is the Living Bread and the Living Water. The man of God prayed to *"the face"* of God, for the hand to be restored and after he prayed, the hand was completely brought back to life, and this was to be *a sign* to them. Remember that John the Baptist was also sent to go before *"the face"* of the LORD God, just before Yeshua arrived at the Jordan River to be baptized in the place where the Ark of the Covenant of the LORD once stood with Joshua and the Priests. *Yeshua performed the same miracle on a man whose right hand was withered, and notice that the Scribes and Pharisees were watching Him closely!* This miracle shows us that the right hand of God restores our flesh to life.

Luke 6:6-11 *And it came about on another Sabbath, that He entered the Synagogue and was teaching; and there was a man there whose right hand was withered. And the Scribes and the Pharisees were watching Him closely, to see if He healed on the Sabbath, in order that they might find reason to accuse Him. But He knew what they were thinking, and He said to the man with the withered hand, Rise and come forward! And he rose and came forward. And Yeshua said to them, I ask you, is it lawful on the Sabbath to do good, or to do harm, to save a life, or destroy it? And after looking around at them all, He said to him, Stretch out your hand! And he did so; and his hand was restored. But they themselves were filled with rage, and discussed together what they might do to Yeshua.*

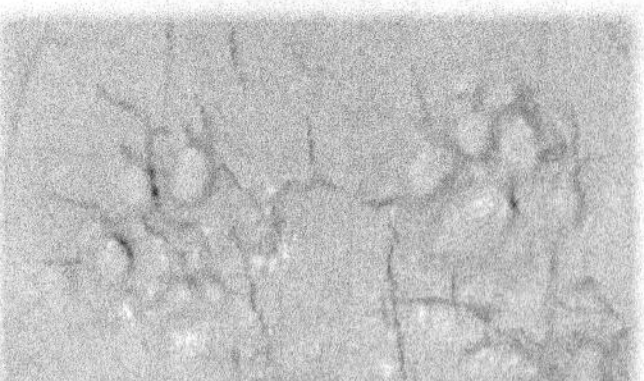

The LORD will restore all flesh - Jasmine's last paw prints Photo ©2013 Kimberly K Ballard All Rights Reserved

Yeshua specifically said to the man with the withered right hand, *"Rise and come forward!"* In this miracle, Yeshua revealed that *He would become the withered hand of God* and that He would die as the cut off Branch. Then by the power of God's Ruach/Holy Spirit dwelling inside Him, He would be completely restored to life again and He would *"rise and come forward"* out of the grave. Just as Yeshua always healed on the 7th day Sabbath, Yeshua was restored to life as the Living Rod before the 7th day Sabbath of the LORD ended.

Isaiah specifically wrote that *"God will come and save you. He will make the blind eyes to be opened and the deaf ears to be unstopped."* So remember, Yeshua came and He put His fingers into the ears of one who could not hear. Suddenly the ears were unstopped and the hearing was completely restored *by the finger of God.*

Mark 7:33-37 *And He took him aside from the multitude, and put His fingers into his ears, and He spit, and touched his tongue; And looking up to Heaven, He sighed, and saith unto him, Ephphatha, that is, Be opened. And*

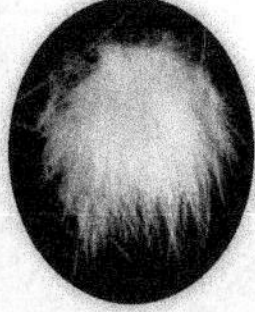

straightway his ears were opened, and the string of his tongue was loosed, and he spake plain. And He charged them that they should tell no man; but the more He charged them so much the more a great deal they published it; And were beyond measure astonished, saying, He hath done all things well; He maketh both the deaf to hear, and the dumb to speak.

Isaiah wrote of these specific miracles of God in the following verse.

Isaiah 35:4-6 *Say to them that are of a fearful heart, Be strong, fear not; Behold, your God will come with vengeance, even God with a recompense; He will come and save you. Then the eyes of the blind shall be opened, and the ears of the deaf shall be unstopped. Then shall the lame man leap as an hart, and the tongue of the dumb sing; for in the wilderness shall waters break out, and streams in the desert.*

Psalm 103:1-5 *Bless the LORD, O my soul; and all that is within me, bless His Holy Name. Bless the LORD, O my soul, and forget not all His benefits; Who forgiveth all thine iniquities; who healeth all thy diseases; Who redeemth thy life from destruction; who crowneth thee with loving-kindness and tender mercies; Who satisfieth thy mouth with good things; so that thy youth is renewed like the eagle's.*

Psalm 146:8-9 *The LORD openeth the eyes of the blind; the LORD raiseth them that are bowed down; the LORD loveth the righteous; The LORD preserveth the strangers; he relieveth the fatherless and widow; but the way of the wicked He turneth upside down.*

When Yeshua touched the eyes of a blind man and healed him, something interesting happened. When the man looked up he said, *"I see men as trees walking." Standing before this blind man was the Almond Tree of Life, who restores the Davidic Dynasty.* Then Yeshua touched his eyes again and he could see every man. After this, Yeshua revealed He is *"I AM."*

Mark 8:22-27 *And He cometh to Bethsaida; and they bring a blind man unto Him, and besought Him to touch him. And He took the blind man by the hand, and led him out of the town; and when He had spit on his eyes, and put His hands upon him, He asked him if he saw ought. And he looked up, and said, I see men as trees, walking. After that He put His hands again upon his eyes, and made him look up; and he was restored, and saw every man clearly. And He sent him away to his house, saying Neither go into the town, nor tell it to any in the town, And Yeshua went out, and His disciples into the towns, of Caesarea Philippi; and by the way He asked His disciples, saying unto them, Whom do men say that I AM?*

THE PARABLE OF THE TALENTS THE DOVE OF PEACE

My Doves of Peace & Dove Feather

The Parable of the Talents has a remarkable hidden meaning and I was only able to discern it after the Holy Spirit revealed to me the secret of the miracle of the five loaves and two fish. Yeshua said, *"The Kingdom of Heaven is as a man travelling into a far country."* He was referring to Himself as the LORD, who travelled from Heaven to earth. He called to His servants and delivered to them His goods and they were to use His goods wisely for the Kingdom of Heaven. The LORD God speaks in parables in order to proclaim the hidden things that have been kept secret from the foundation of the world. Those who diligently seek Him will begin to understand that the parables reveal the full glory of His Majesty because all the parables were spoken by the Word of God, *the Living Torah.*

Psalm 78:1-2 *Give ear, O My people, to My Law; incline your ears to the Words of My mouth. I will open My mouth in a parable; I will utter dark sayings of old; Which we have heard and known, and our fathers have told us.*

Matthew 13:34-35 *All these things spake Yeshua unto the multitude in parables; And without a parable spake He not unto them; That it might be fulfilled which was spoken by the Prophet, saying, I will open My mouth in parables; I will utter things which have been kept secret from the foundation of the world.*

So Yeshua's Words as *the Living Torah* uncover the secrets of God and He made them discernible to us in His parables. When I pensively studied His parable of the talents, the LORD opened my mind to comprehend the Spiritual meaning behind it.

Matthew 25:14-34 *For the Kingdom of Heaven is as a man travelling into a far country, who called His servants, and delivered unto them His goods. And unto one He gave five talents, to another two, and to another one; to every man according to his several ability; and straightway took his journey. Then he that had received the five talents went and traded with the same, and made them other five talents. And likewise he that had received two he also gained other two. But he that had received one went and digged in the earth, and hid his LORD'S money. After a long time the LORD of those servants cometh, and reckoneth with them. And so he that had received the five talents came and brought other five talents, saying, LORD, Thou deliveredst unto me five talents; behold, I have gained beside them five talents more. His LORD said unto him, Well done thou good and faithful servant; thou hast been faithful over a few things, I will make thee ruler over many things; enter thou into the joy of thy LORD. He also that had received two talents came and said, LORD, Thou deliveredst unto me two talents; behold, I have gained two other talents beside them. His LORD said unto him, Well done, good and faithful servant; thou hast been faithful over a few things, I will make thee ruler over many things; enter thou into the joy of thy LORD. Then he which had received the one talent came and said, LORD, I knew Thee that Thou art an hard man, reaping where thou hast not sown, and gathering where thou hast not strawed; And I was afraid, and went and hid Thy talent in the earth; lo, there Thou hast that is Thine. His LORD answered and said unto him, Thou wicked and slothful servant, thou knewest that I reap where I sowed not, and gather where I have not strawed; Thou oughtest therefore to have put My money to the exchangers, and then at My coming I should have received Mine own with usury. Take therefore the talent from him, and give it unto him which hath ten talents. For unto every one that hath shall be given, and he shall have abundance; but from him that hath not shall be taken away even that which he hath. And cast ye the unprofitable servant into outer darkness; there shall be weeping and gnashing of teeth. When the Son of man shall come in His glory, and all the Holy angels with Him, then shall He sit upon the Throne of His glory; And before Him shall be gathered all Nations; and He shall separate them one from another, as a Shepherd divideth His sheep from the goats; And He shall set the sheep on His right hand, but the goats on the left. Then shall the KING say unto them on His Right Hand, come ye blessed of My Father, inherit the Kingdom prepared for you from the foundation of the world.*

Now that you have read the parable, I want to share what Messiah Yeshua revealed within this story. I believe that *"the five talents"* in the parable refer to *the five books of Moses, "The Torah."* It was to be taken as a Testimony to the entire world to proclaim the glory of God in all the places where the LORD did not sow this seed. *The Torah, the Word of God, is the seed of life.* The two talents that were given to His servant secretly refers to *"the two tablets of the Law,"* containing the Ten Commandments of God. *The two talents represent the Covenant of the Torah* and the LORD sealed this Covenant with Israel and Moses. Finally in the parable, we come to the most astonishing and prized talent of all the talents. *The one talent* that the LORD gave to His servants last was Himself as Messiah Yeshua, *"The Living Torah."* The Word of God became flesh and dwelt among us!

This one talent was the most important talent of all of them because it was the *Living Heavenly* fulfillment of all the talents combined into one and this is why it was not supposed to be buried in the ground by His servants. *This one talent was, however, buried in Holy Mount Moriah by His servants! The one talent is the final complete Living Heavenly Ark of the Covenant, but Moses and the Israelites had the earthly pattern of it containing the five talents and the two talents.* This is why Yeshua said that after He was lifted up, He would draw all people unto Himself. It is this one Living Testimony of Yeshua that glorified the LORD God because the Living Almond Rod of God revealed the resurrection power of God, and it was obvious that this work was wrought by the hand of God. This was the work that was made without hands because this workmanship came from God, like His image on His burial Shroud was not made by the hands of men. The seed of life was inside Messiah Yeshua *the Living Torah* and this seed came to life in Holy Mount Moriah! Yeshua was lifted up in mercy and He was held out to us like an olive branch of peace, in order to give us life. Therefore, the Messiah came to reconcile mankind to God and to make peace between us.

We will come back to the parable of the talents, but first I want to talk about the dove again. It was this revelation that allowed me to comprehend that this was another reason why the Holy Spirit of God descended in bodily form as a dove from Heaven and abode upon Messiah Yeshua as He stood in the Jordan River! As I said earlier, I realized that the dove of His Holy Spirit was sent out of the Ark of God in Heaven and it came down and returned to the Living Ark, Messiah the LORD, who was now standing on the earth in the Jordan River, and it alighted upon the hand of God and was drawn back inside the Ark! So it is interesting that in the beginning, *"The Divine Presence of God"* in Jewish theology *was represented as a dove, as His Spirit moved on the surface of the waters.* ***(Ben Zoma interpretation c. 100), (Hag. 15a), (Talmud, Berachot 3a), (Shab. 31a; Sanh.96a), (jewishencyclopedia.com/articles/7833-holy-spirit) AND (jewishencyclopedia.com/articles/13537-shekinah).*** *So Messiah Yeshua was indeed the Divine Presence of God standing in the Jordan River, as the Heavenly Ark of the Covenant, and the dove abode upon Him as His feet stood in the midst of the Living Waters.* The dove that Noah sent out of the Ark returned to him in the Ark and she rested upon Noah's hand and was drawn back into the Ark when she found that there was no place to rest the sole of her foot. Now if you think about it, Noah sent the dove out of the Ark and she flew out to see if the waters were abated from off the face of the ground. Remember that the Holy Spirit moved on the face of the waters in the beginning and later, Messiah Yeshua moved on the face of the waters on the Sea of Galilee because He is the LORD God who is full of His Holy Spirit.

Genesis 8:8-12 *Also he sent forth a dove from him, to see if the waters were abated from off the face of the ground; But the dove found no rest for the sole of her foot, and she returned unto him into the Ark, for the waters were on the face of the whole earth; then he put forth his hand, and took her, and pulled her in unto him into the Ark. And the dove came in to him in the evening; and, lo, in her mouth was an olive leaf plucked off; so Noah knew that the waters were abated from off the earth. And he stayed yet other seven days; and sent forth the dove; which returned not again unto him anymore.*

The dove of Noah had no place to rest her foot and interestingly enough, Yeshua had no place to rest His head. The dove of the Holy Spirit reveals that the Messiah is *the First and the Last.* I say this because the dove, who was sent out from Noah's Ark, brought back the olive leaf in her mouth as *a sign of life, after the death* of all the people in the flood waters that were now abated from off the face of the earth. In Noah's case, the flood was a judgment upon the wicked. However, the LORD preserved Noah in the Ark and the dove came to him there in the Ark, holding the olive leaf in her mouth that *symbolized new life.* So when the Holy Spirit in the form of the dove alighted upon Yeshua in the Jordan River, He was the Ark of God's Living Testimony. He breathed the Word of peace or Shalom through the dove of His Ruach/Holy Spirit, as *the Living Torah* from His Divine Presence came out of His mouth.

Loving Cuddling Doves
Photo ©2013 Kimberly K Ballard
All Rights Reserved

Luke 3:21-22 *Now when all the people were baptized, it came to pass, that Yeshua also being baptized, and praying, the Heaven was opened, And the Holy Spirit descended in a bodily shape like a dove upon Him, and a voice came from Heaven, which said, Thou art My beloved Son; in Thee I AM well pleased.*

Messiah Yeshua, the resurrected Almond Branch, anointed with the pure Olive Oil of the Holy Spirit, is *the symbol of new life* that abides in the Living Ark in Heaven. He takes away the curse of death from Eden. *The Living Branch Messiah is our dove of peace.* Yeshua said that *The Word that comes out of His mouth gives us life!* It is *the Living Torah, the Living Water, and the well of salvation!*

Matthew 4:4 *But He answered and said, It is written, Man shall not live by bread alone, but by every Word that proceedeth out of the mouth of God.*

Yeshua quoted the following verse when Satan tempted Him in the wilderness, but Yeshua did not need bread and water there since *He is the Living Torah, the Word of God.*

Deuteronomy 8:3 *And He humbled thee, and suffered thee to hunger, and fed thee with manna, which thou knewest not, neither did thy fathers know that man doth not live by bread only, but by every Word that proceedeth out of the mouth of the LORD doth man live.*

Romans 10:5-13 *For Moses describeth the righteousness which is of the Law, That the man which doeth those things shall live by them. But the righteousness which is of faith speaketh on this wise, Say not in thine heart, Who shall ascend into Heaven? (that is, to bring Messiah down from above;) Or, Who shall descend into the deep? (that is, to bring up Messiah again from the dead.) But what saith it? The Word is nigh thee, even in thy mouth, and in thy heart; that is, the Word of faith, which we preach; That if thou shalt confess with thy mouth the LORD Yeshua, and shalt believe in thine heart that God hath raised Him from the dead, thou shalt be saved. For with the heart man believeth unto righteousness; and with the mouth confession is made unto salvation. For the Scripture saith, Whosoever believeth on Him shall not be ashamed. For there is no difference between the Jew and the Greek; for the same LORD over all is rich unto all that call upon Him. For whosoever shall call upon the Name of the LORD shall be saved.*

Remember that when Yeshua healed the blind man who had been born blind, Yeshua mixed the *Living Water* from His mouth, that had *the dove of His Spirit of the Divine Presence resting upon it,* and He mixed it with the dirt in His hand. Then He put the mixture upon the eyes of the blind man and sent him to wash in the Pool of Living Water, the Pool of Siloam. Miraculously, the man could see with new eyes that were given *new life by the one who restores the Davidic Dynasty!* Just as the olive branch of the dove was *the sign of life, Yeshua is the Branch full of the Holy Spirit in bodily form as a dove that came to us to give us life.* The dove that had no place to rest her foot with Noah came back into the Ark and landed on his hand. Likewise the Holy Spirit, as a dove, came and rested upon Yeshua, the Yad or hand of God, and He had no place to rest His head! When Yeshua ascended up to Heaven, He went to sit upon the Ark of the LORD with the dove of His Spirit abiding there.

Whispering Doves Photo ©2013 KK Ballard All Rights Reserved

Luke 9:57-58 *And it came to pass, that, as they went in the way, a certain man said unto Him, LORD, I will follow Thee whithersoever Thou goest. And Yeshua said unto him, Foxes have holes, and birds of the air have nests; but the Son of man hath not where to lay His head.*

All things will continue as they are until Messiah, who is the head of all things, makes His enemies His footstool. We see this clearly in the book of Ephesians. Yeshua is the head, the authority over His Bride, but His enemies will be under His feet. So Yeshua is represented in the head and feet, in the dove of the Heavenly Ark.

Ephesians 1:19-23 *And what is the exceeding greatness of His power to us-ward who believe, according to the working of His mighty power, Which He wrought in Messiah, when He raised Him from the dead, and set Him at His* *own right hand in the Heavenly places, Far above all principality, and power, and might, and dominion, and every Name that is named, not only in this world, but also in that which is to come; And hath put all things under His feet, and gave Him to be the head over all things to the Church, Which is His body, the fullness of Him that filleth all in all.*

Noah's dove came first as the sign of new life, and Messiah's dove, the Divine Presence of His Holy Spirit, came to us last, as the sign of new life. This is the one talent that the LORD gave to His servants last! Yeshua is therefore the olive leaf of life and *"the Branch"* held out to us in peace and reconciliation to God. Yeshua sprouted to life because the Holy Spirit in bodily form as a dove was still abiding in Him, and now we can live because of Him. He is the beginning and the end, the First and the Last. The five talents and the two talents were given to the LORD'S servants first and then finally *The Living Torah, the one talent,* was given to His servants last, as a fulfillment of all things. All in all, the LORD is our Messiah and His Testimony abides in the Eternal Ark of the Covenant, as the First and the Last. Messiah Yeshua spoke about the peace that He provides through His Spirit in John's Gospel. Yeshua said that if we love Him and keep His Word, He will send the dove of His Holy Spirit, *the Comforter of His Eternal peace,* to make His abode with us. Yeshua is our Peace, *"the Sar Shalom,"* which in English is *"the Prince of Peace."* His peace is perfect peace. As our dove of peace, *the Sar Shalom,* the Rod of God, brings us comfort through His Living Testimony. All things are restored to the Heavenly Kingdom of God through Him as the Living Rod of God who is our Heavenly Divine Temple!

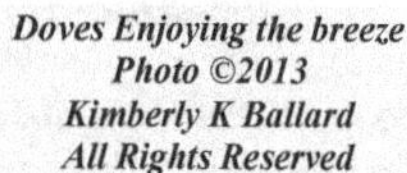

Doves Enjoying the breeze
Photo ©2013
Kimberly K Ballard
All Rights Reserved

Ephesians 2:13-22 *But now in Messiah Yeshua ye who sometimes were far off are made nigh by the blood of Messiah. For He is our Peace, who hath made both one, and hath broken down the middle wall of partition between us; Having abolished in His flesh the enmity, even the Law of Commandments contained in ordinances; for to make in Himself of twain one new man, so making peace; And that He might reconcile both unto God in one body by the cross, having slain the enmity thereby; And came and preached peace to you which were afar off, and to them that were nigh. For through Him we both have access by one Spirit unto the Father. Now therefore ye are no more strangers and foreigners, but fellow citizens with the Saints, and of the Household of God; And are built upon the Foundation of the Apostles and Prophets, Yeshua Messiah Himself being the Chief Corner stone; In whom all the building fitly framed together groweth unto an Holy Temple in the LORD; In whom ye also are builded together for an habitation of God through the Spirit.*

John 14:23-27 *Yeshua answered and said unto him, If a man love Me, he will keep My Words; and My Father will love him, and we will come to him, and make our abode with him. He that loveth me not keepeth not My sayings; and the Word which ye hear is not mine, but the Father's which sent me. These things have I spoken unto you, being yet present with you. But the Comforter, which is the Holy Spirit, whom the Father will send in My Name, He shall teach you all things, and bring all things to your remembrance, whatsoever I have said unto you. Peace I leave with you, My peace I give unto you; not as the world giveth, give I unto you. Let not your heart be troubled, neither let it be afraid.*

The Sar Shalom, the Prince of Peace, was a fulfillment of Isaiah's prophecy regarding Messiah and the Scripture says that the zeal of the LORD of Hosts will *perform* this! *This means that He has a tireless diligence to perform this Testimony!*

Isaiah 9:6-7 *For unto us a child is born, unto us a Son is given; and the government shall be upon His shoulder; and His Name shall be called, Wonderful, Counsellor, The Mighty God, The everlasting Father, The Prince of Peace. Of the increase of His government and peace there shall be no end, upon the throne of David, and upon His Kingdom, to order it, and to establish it with judgment and with justice from henceforth even forever. The zeal of the LORD of Hosts will perform this.*

It is also interesting that after *seven days, Noah sent the dove out of the Ark a second time* and in the evening, the dove returned to Noah and this is when she was holding the freshly plucked olive leaf in her mouth. *Just like the dove was sent out from the Ark a second time, Yeshua with the dove of the Divine Presence of His Holy Spirit of peace, the Living Branch, will return to us again a second time out of the Ark of Heaven.* This will happen after the *seven year* tribulation. He will come to abide with us forever to usher in the Eternal Kingdom of His peace. *The second time* that the dove of His peace returns to us will mark the reconciliation of all things to God through the Rod that budded to life. Then we will be given *new life forever* through the Spirit-filled Branch of the Almond Tree of Life.

Loving Kissing Doves
Photo ©2013
Kimberly K Ballard All Rights Reserved

Hebrews 9:28 *So Messiah was once offered to bear the sins of many; and unto them that look for Him shall He appear the second time without sin unto salvation.*

Isaiah 11:11-12 *And it shall come to pass in that day, that the LORD shall set His hand again the second time to recover the remnant of His people, which shall be left, from Assyria, and from Egypt, and from Pathros, and from Cush, and from Elam, and from Shinar, and from Hammath, and from the islands of the sea. And He shall set up an ensign for the Nations, and shall assemble the outcasts of Israel, and gather together the dispersed of Judah from the four corners of the earth.*

The Word of God came a second time to Solomon, Jeremiah, Simon Peter, Abraham, and Haggai. So the Word of God will come to us a second time. As I was pondering the fact that the dove of Noah was sent out from the Ark after *seven days,* I soon realized that this was also connected to the events that transpired on Shavuot or Pentecost. After Yeshua ascended to Heaven, the Holy Spirit went with Him into the Ark of Heaven and abode there. Now remember that Yeshua told the Jewish disciples *"to tarry in Jerusalem until they were endued with power from on high."* Then exactly *seven weeks after Passover,* Yeshua sent the dove of His Holy Spirit from the Ark of Heaven and it descended upon the Jewish disciples on Shavuot in flaming tongues of fire. Ironically, this is exactly the same time-frame that *the Torah* was originally given to the people of Israel on Mount Sinai! Remember it is *the voice* of the LORD that divides the flame of fire. So when the Holy Spirit descended in a mighty rushing wind and it rested upon the Jewish disciples in flaming tongues of fire, they were endued with *the power of the Living Torah* and the dove of Eternal peace was sent from the *Sar Shalom* abiding on the Ark of Heaven. It was *the olive Branch of peace* from the LORD God Himself and this Branch of Eternal life, the Messiah's Testimony, was to be taken to the entire world as *"the one last talent." It was the hope of everlasting life.* So all the miracles of the Jewish disciples proclaimed *the Living Torah Testimony of the LORD,* demonstrating the glory of God and the reconciliation that Yeshua brought us in the Garden of God on Holy Mount Moriah, and this is where His Name dwells forever in Jerusalem! *The beloved Jewish disciples took the one talent to the world!*

Courtship Doves Photo ©2013
Kimberly K Ballard
All Rights Reserved

When *Yeshua appeared in the evening* and stood in the midst of His disciples after His resurrection, He said to them, *"Peace be unto you."* Remember that in Genesis it said, *"And the dove came in to him in the evening; and, lo, in her mouth was an olive leaf plucked off." Remember it was the sign of life. So Yeshua brought the dove of Peace in the evening!* The LORD had shut the door of the Ark and Noah was shut inside. After His resurrection, Yeshua

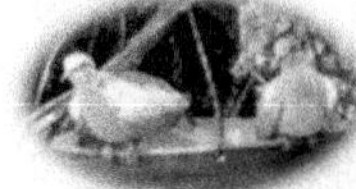

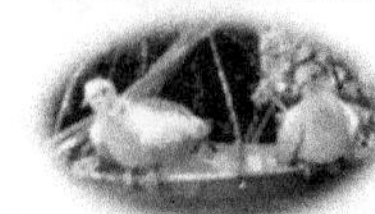

the Ark of Heaven appeared alive, showing the Jewish disciples the sign of life *when the doors were shut* and with His Divine Presence, He brought the dove of His Peace to give to His Jewish disciples and He breathed the dove of His Holy Spirit of life into them as the firmament in their midst!

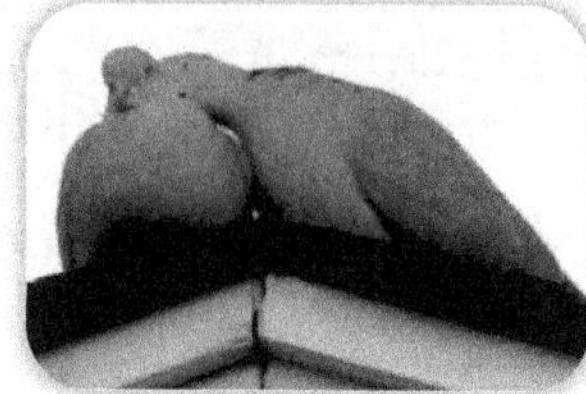

Dove Love Photo ©2013 Kimberly K Ballard All Rights Reserved

John 20:19-21 *Then the same day at evening, being the first day of the week, when the doors were shut where the disciples were assembled for fear of the Jews, came Yeshua and stood in the midst, and saith unto them, Peace be unto you. And when He had so said, He shewed unto them His hands and His side. Then were the disciples glad, when they saw the LORD. Then said Yeshua to them again, Peace be unto you; as My father hath sent Me, even so send I you. And when He had said this, He breathed on them, and saith unto them, Receive ye the Holy Spirit.*

Romans 15:20 *Now the God of Peace be with you all. Amen.*

Romans 16:20 *And the God of Peace shall bruise Satan under your feet shortly. The grace of our LORD Yeshua Messiah be with you. Amen.*

I find that the dove detail is so fabulous in the fact that the earth was cut down in the flood like an olive tree, but when the dove of Noah brought back the freshly plucked olive leaf and gave it to Noah, it was symbolic of the fact that the LORD was going to raise all things in the earth from death to life again. The olive leaf of the dove truly became the *symbol of life after death* in the flood. In essence, the flood was a prototype or early model of the death, burial, and resurrection of Messiah who gives us life! The LORD gave us a picture that clearly details that He is able to resurrect the dead and restore life again. Yeshua's Eternal Living Testimony is therefore visible in the flood story of Noah and in the living olive leaf that the dove brought back in her mouth into the Ark. Yeshua was crushed like the olives in the olive press and although all life perished in the flood, the LORD restored life to the earth again!

Gazing Doves Photo ©2013 Kimberly K Ballard All Rights Reserved

Now this is also a prototype of the destruction of the Holy Temple and the city of Jerusalem in 70AD. Although the city and the Temple were destroyed and cut down like an olive tree, after Messiah Yeshua ascended into Heaven, He would raise Jerusalem from death to life and glory again just like He did *"the Jesus Boat," and "Magdala Synagogue"* after 2,000 years! He will set His Heavenly Temple on His Holy Mountain forever and bring the dove of His Eternal Peace and the rejuvenation of life to this Eternal city again. In this place He will return to dwell in our midst and reign forever as the everlasting KING of glory upon the throne of His Ark of the Eternal Covenant with all mankind.

Now it is obvious that we need to take hold of the olive leaf of new life that He held out to us as the Living Fruitful Branch to have the most Holy First Fruit from the Almond Tree of Life. This is such a beautiful part of the LORD'S Divine Covenant of everlasting life! My olive leaves from the Mount of Olives reveal the new life I have!

Happily ever after Doves Photo ©2013 Kimberly K Ballard All Rights Reserved

The two Cherubim angels that stood guarding the Testimony of the Ark of the LORD in the Holy Temple were made from *olive wood.* The two *olive wood Cherubim angels are two witnesses* that testify of the LORD'S Living Testimony on the Ark. The *two witnesses* in the book of Revelation are therefore called *"The two olive trees that stand before the LORD of the earth."* I will talk more about them later.

I Kings 6:23 *And within the oracle he made two Cherubim's of olive tree, each ten cubits high.*

Revelation 11:3-4 *And I will give power unto My two witnesses, and they shall prophesy a thousand two hundred and threescore days, clothed in sackcloth. These are the two olive trees, and the two candlesticks standing before the God of the earth.*

The Branch of Peace abode with His disciples on *the Mount of Olives*, and taught them *the Living Torah in the Temple.*

John 8:1-2 *Yeshua went unto the Mount of Olives. And early in the morning He came again into the Temple, and all the people came unto Him; and He sat down, and taught them.*

Mark 13:1-4 *And as He went out of the Temple, one of His disciples saith unto Him, Master, see what manner of stones and what buildings are here! And Yeshua answering said unto him, Seest thou these great buildings? There shall not be left one stone upon another, that shall not be thrown down. And as He sat upon the Mount of Olives over against the Temple, Peter and James and John and Andrew asked Him privately, Tell us, when shall these things be? And what shall be the sign when all these things shall be fulfilled?*

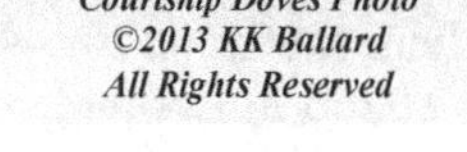

Courtship Doves Photo
©2013 KK Ballard
All Rights Reserved

Now in the Parable of the Talents, we finally see that at the time of the LORD'S return, He goes to His servants to see what they have done with His goods and His servants are rewarded according to what they have done with the talents that He gave to them. The parable tells us that the servant that was given the five talents gained five more. The five talents again represent the LORD as the Bread of life. *This means that the one with the Torah of Moses went and proclaimed it to the servants who did not have it. This servant was faithful and he doubled his five original talents into ten. The number ten is the fulfillment of the Law of the Covenant of the Torah.* Then the servant with the two talents had the Commandments of the Law of God written in stone. These were given to Moses and they were placed inside the Ark. They represent the meat that the LORD provided for His servants. *So this servant took the two talents, the Law of God, to those who did not have it and he doubled it from two to four. The number four is representative of the Torah and the Law going out to the four corners of the earth as a Testimony of the one true God.* This reminds me of the four sets of poker holes that appear on the Shroud of *the Living Torah* because Yeshua's Living resurrection Testimony was to go out proclaiming Eternal life to the four corners of the earth. *Finally, the one glorious talent that was given to the LORD'S servant last was the LORD dwelling in our midst in the flesh as the Rod of our salvation, as Messiah Yeshua. The Messiah is the fulfillment of the complete and perfect Torah and Law of God. The Living Torah, therefore, was sent from Heaven to His servant last as the final Living Testimony of Eternal life. This is the reason that the one talent was the most crucial of all the talents in the parable.* However, the servant who had the one talent went and buried it in the ground. He was afraid to do anything with it, from the time of his Master's departure until the time of His return.

He said that he knew that *"his LORD was a hard man, reaping where the LORD had not sown and that He gathers where He had not scattered this seed."* So the servant hid this precious talent in the earth and because he was afraid, he did not boldly proclaim *the glorious*

Living Testimony of God to the world. Because of his pathetic and fearful attitude, the most valuable and precious talent of all was not taken by this servant to the four corners of the earth to reach those who did not have God's seed of truth and life. The servant with the one talent actually returned it to the LORD and said, *"Here is what is Yours."* At this point, the LORD became furious. The LORD called this servant *"a wicked and slothful servant, who knew that his Master would gather where He had not sown seed."* This message was to go out to the heathen who did not know God, but some of His servants refused to take it to the dying world. The LORD then cast this servant into the outer darkness and he literally was separated from God's Presence and from the light of His glory because he hid the Testimony of life and received death as a reward. *In the one talent, the one true God of Israel conquered death and redeemed us back to Heaven after He was buried in the earth.* This is the glorious Eternal Gospel of His love toward us. The Messiah is the total of all the talents combined into *the one final talent* because it contains the five talents, the two talents, and this equals a perfect and complete number seven in the Living Testimony of the LORD. So finally, the LORD takes away from this servant the *one precious talent* that was faithfully given to Him by His Master and the LORD gives His Living Testimony of Eternal life to those who doubled the LORD'S goods before. In the end, the LORD was going to reap through the Messiah, where He had not previously sown His Word before. *The Living Torah* would go to the entire world as a final Testimony. The ten northern tribes of Israel that were lost needed the shepherds of Israel to bring them the Good News of the LORD'S Living Covenant, but many of their leaders failed to do it. They are the lost son in the prodigal story. Through the one talent that came last, the LORD in His mercy sent His Living Branch, full of the dove of His Divine Presence, the Spirit of Peace, to the Gentiles of the nations and to the Israelites who were lost. Now everyone in the world who turned to the God of Israel could obtain Eternal life. Again, the LORD'S goods went *first* to Israel and to the Gentiles *last,* because *He is the First and the Last.* In the end, the LORD would draw all mankind back to His Garden to dwell with Him forever.

When we share Yeshua, the Living Torah with people, we are giving them the true Spiritual Bread and meat from Heaven and His seed sprouts new life inside of them as His Holy Spirit comes to dwell within their heart. In this good work and by His power, we gain more servants for the Kingdom of God. The Parable of the Talents reveals that Yeshua is the Rod and Staff of the Good Shepherd who comforts us with this hope. When He comes, He will gather His beloved children to Himself. Those who have the Testimony of *the Living Torah and the oil of His Holy Spirit* burning in their lamps will be called His *"sheep."* Those without either of these things will be called *"the goats."* The sheep are taken into the LORD'S Kingdom, but the goats are thrown into the outer darkness away from His Divine Presence.

Now if we compare the Parable of the Sower to the Parable of the Talents, it tells us again that *"the seed is the Word of God."* When the sower went forth to sow the seed, it landed in various places and did not always prosper or come to life where it fell, based upon how it was received. The seed only produced fruit when it fell upon good ground. Of course, the Messiah was the seed of life that was placed in the good ground in Holy Mount Moriah in God's Garden, so that when He sprouted to life, He dispersed the seed of life, *the Living Torah,* throughout the earth for the glory of the LORD God. The Parable of the Sower reveals that these hidden secrets of God that are contained within Yeshua's parables are *the mysteries of the Kingdom of Heaven.*

Matthew 13:1-9 *The same day went Yeshua out of the house, and sat by the sea side. And great multitudes were gathered together unto Him, so that He went into a ship, and sat; and the whole multitude stood on the shore. And He spake many things unto them in parables, saying Behold, a sower went forth to sow; And when He sowed, some seeds fell by the way side, and the fowls came and devoured them up; Some fell up upon stony places, where they had not much earth; and forthwith they sprung up, because they had no deepness of earth; And when the sun was up, they were scorched; and because they had no root, they withered away. And some fell among thorns; and the thorns*

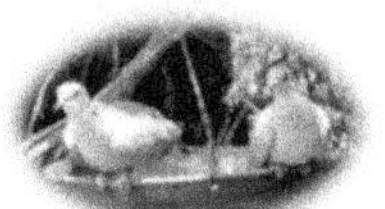

sprung up, and choked them; But other fell into good ground, and brought forth fruit, some an hundredfold, some sixtyfold, some thirtyfold. He who hath ears to hear, let him hear. And the disciples came, and said unto Him, Why speakest Thou in parables? He answered and said unto them, because it is given unto you to know the mysteries of the Kingdom of Heaven, but to them it is not given.

The Jewish Scriptures are composed of *three* groups of books called *"the Torah, the Nevi'im, and the Ketuvim."* These three groups of books make up the entire Jewish Bible known as *"the Old Testament."* The three books are bound together into one book. The three bound together make up *the one talent* or the fullness of the Living Testimony of Messiah Yeshua, *the Living Torah,* who came to life the third day. In another parable, Yeshua spoke about the Kingdom of Heaven. He said that the Kingdom of Heaven is like unto leaven which a woman took and hid in three measures of meal until it all was leavened.

Matthew 13:33 *Another parable spake He unto them; The Kingdom of Heaven is like unto leaven, which a woman took and hid in three measures of meal, till the whole was leavened.*

Messiah Yeshua is telling us that the Kingdom of Heaven is all about the three measures of meal, which I believe are *"The Torah, Nevi'im, and Ketuvim."* When the woman hid the leaven within it, the whole was leavened. Since the leaven makes the bread rise and spread, this means that the Word of God, the Messiah, the Bread from Heaven, did rise in three days and spread to the whole earth. As *the Living Torah,* the LORD Yeshua is the embodiment of the three books in one as *"the one perfect talent."* His Testimony for 2,000 years has been spread throughout the entire world and this will continue until everyone has heard it. Now it is interesting that the seed of Messiah would not take in certain areas where it was heard or sown. Remember, it would only grow where it fell upon good ground. The Testimony of Yeshua has spread the Jewish Bible like nothing else ever has in the history of the world, just like the leaven that was hidden in the three measures of meal until the whole was leavened. Remember that Messiah Yeshua told the Jewish people when He was in their midst *that the Kingdom of Heaven was suddenly upon them!* If the First Fruit is Holy, so is the lump, its root, and its branches.

Romans 11:16 *For if the First Fruit be Holy, the lump is also Holy; and if the root be Holy, so are the branches.*

Loving cuddling Doves
Photo ©2013 KK Ballard
All Rights Reserved

Psalm 68:13 Though ye have lien among the pots, yet shall ye be as the wings of a dove covered with silver, and her feathers with yellow gold.

I guess you could say that the moral of the Parable of the Talents is to be bold and tell everyone the glorious truth about the LORD'S Eternal Living Testimony, so that all who hear it will be able to enter the everlasting Kingdom of Heaven. After the Word of God is spread around the world, the end will come and each person will have to give an account to the LORD for what they have done with His Good News, *"the one perfect talent."* With that I say *"Blessed are you, LORD our God, KING of the Universe, who gave to us the way of salvation through Messiah Yeshua our First Fruits and the Living Bread from Heaven, who gives us His dove of peace!*

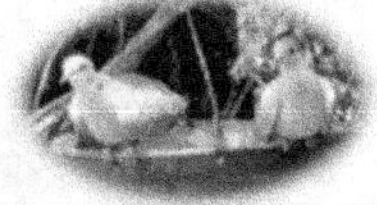

MESSIAH YESHUA BREATHED THE SPIRIT OF LIFE

Menorah Candles blowing in the Snow
Photo ©2013 Kimberly K Ballard All Rights Reserved

As Yeshua was about to send His Jewish disciples out into the world as His witnesses with the message of His Testimony, Yeshua did something unique that we just looked at in the last section. Yeshua breathed on the Jewish disciples and He said, *"Receive ye the Holy Spirit."* Just before Yeshua said these words He said, *"Peace be unto you."* So now we can see that this was the dove of Peace sent to the Jewish disciples in the Holy Spirit that I was talking about! I had never quite understood exactly why Yeshua did this until now. This was written in the same verses where Yeshua came and stood in their midst in the evening on the first day of the week as they sat in the room with the door shut, *but now there was more to the story!*

John 20:18-22 *Mary Magdalene came and told the disciples that she had seen the LORD, and that He had spoken these things unto her. Then the same day at evening, being the first day of the week, when the doors were shut where the disciples were assembled for fear of the Jews, came Yeshua and stood in the midst, and saith unto them, Peace be unto you. And when He had so said, He shewed unto them His hands and His side. Then were the disciples glad, when they saw the LORD. Then said Yeshua to them again, Peace be unto you; as my Father hath sent Me, even so send I you. And when He had said this, He breathed on them, and said unto them, Receive ye the Holy Spirit.*

The Jews would often read and study the Torah behind locked doors and as we know the disciples were behind locked doors when Yeshua came and stood in their midst and gave them peace! So the rest of this verse is quite intriguing and we must go back to Genesis again to the very beginning, to understand what Yeshua was doing as He breathed on them. If any event revealed Yeshua as the Messiah to Israel, this was truly the one event that revealed His identity. The key to understanding it is written in Genesis and in Job.

Job 33:4 *The Spirit of God hath made me, and the breath of the Almighty hath given me life.*

Genesis 2:7 *And the LORD God formed man of the dust of the ground, and breathed into his nostrils the breath of life; and man became a living soul.*

Job 34:12-16 *Yea, surely God will not do wickedly, neither will the Almighty pervert judgment. Who hath given him a charge over the earth? Or who hath disposed the whole world? If He set His heart upon man, if He gather unto Himself His Spirit and His breath; All flesh shall perish together, and man shall turn again unto dust. If now thou hast understanding, hear this; hearken to the voice of My Words.*

It was the LORD God who breathed the breath of life upon mankind and man became a living soul! So we know that the Holy Spirit of God is upon His Rod. As Yeshua, *the Rod of God, full of the Holy Spirit,* breathed upon the Jewish disciples, they received the breath of life and they became living souls for the Eternal Kingdom of God. It was this breath of Messiah Yeshua that enabled the disciples to go and be His witnesses throughout the world, *to take the Living Torah* to the people that did not have it yet. They were endued with power from on

High so they could take the LORD'S Living Ark of the Eternal Testimony to as many people as possible before the Messiah returned from Heaven. In this situation, the LORD was dwelling in their midst and He was breathing the breath of Eternal life into His Jewish disciples, so their souls could live Spiritually with Him forever. This is exactly how the Rod of God, full of the Holy Spirit, will give life to the dead who are in their graves. When He breathes the Word of God upon them, they will be resurrected from death to Eternal life and become living souls.

Ezekiel 37:9-14 *Then said He unto me, Prophesy unto the wind, Prophesy, son of man, and say to the wind, Thus saith the LORD God; Come from the four winds, O breath, and breathe upon these slain, that they may live. So I Prophesied as He commanded me, and the breath came into them, and they lived, and stood up upon their feet, an exceeding great army. Then he said unto me, Son of man, these bones are the whole House of Israel; behold they say, Our bones are dried, and our hope is lost; we are cut off for our parts. Therefore Prophesy and say unto them; Thus saith the LORD God; Behold, O My people, I will open your graves, and cause you to come up out of your graves, and bring you into the Land of Israel. And ye shall know that I AM the LORD, when I have opened your graves, O My people, and brought you up out of your graves. And shall put My Spirit in you, and ye shall live, and I shall place you in your own Land; then shall ye know that I the LORD have spoken it, and performed it, saith the LORD.*

Then Job tells us that *"the soul of every living thing and the breath of all mankind is in the hand of the LORD."* Of course, Yeshua, *the hand of God,* was the one breathing the breath of life into His Jewish disciples when He told them to receive the Ruach/Holy Spirit. Now if Yeshua's actions, in this case, are recorded in Genesis during the creation, then He is the Almond Tree of Life containing the oil of the Holy Spirit of life. He is proven to be the Branch and the lifted up arm of the LORD revealed from the Living Almond Tree Menorah.

Job 12:9-10 *Who knoweth not in all these that the hand of the LORD hath wrought this? In whose hand is the soul of every living thing, and the breath of all mankind.*

Yeshua revealed how He would fulfill His Divine Testimony before it came to pass. The New Covenant that He made with mankind was one of the new things He declared before He fulfilled it before their eyes!

Isaiah 42:5-10 *Thus saith God the LORD, He that created the Heavens, and stretched them out; He that spread forth the earth, and that which cometh out of it; He that giveth breath unto the people upon it, and Spirit to them that walk therein; I the LORD have called thee in righteousness, and will hold thine hand, and will keep thee, and give thee for a Covenant of the people, for a light to the Gentiles; To open the blind eyes, to bring out the prisoners from the prison, and them that sit in darkness out of the prison house. I AM the LORD; that is My Name and My glory will I not give to another, neither My praise to graven images. Behold, the former things are come to pass, and new things do I declare; before they spring forth I tell you of them. Sing to the LORD a new song, and His praise from the end of the earth, ye that do down to the sea, and all that is therein; the isles, and the inhabitants thereof.*

Aaron's rod, the cut off dead branch of the Almond Tree, came to life by the power of God's Holy Spirit that was on it, and Yeshua, the dead Rod, the Almond Branch, came to life by the power of His Holy Spirit that was inside Him. So shall it be when the resurrection of the dead occurs in the future as the Messiah breathes the Spirit of life within those who have already died in Him because they have been sealed by His Spirit for Eternal life. The dead will come up out of their graves like Lazarus did when Yeshua spoke the Word through the breath of His mouth and Lazarus came forth alive! The God of the Living is the power of God Almighty!

Mark 12:23-37 *In the resurrection therefore, when they shall rise, whose wife shall she be of them? For the seven had her to wife. And Yeshua answering said unto them, Do ye not therefore err, because ye know not the Scriptures, neither the power of God? For when they shall rise from the dead, they neither marry, nor are given in marriage; but are as the angels which are in Heaven. And as touching the dead, that they rise; have ye not read in the book of*

Moses, how in the bush God spake unto him, saying, I AM the God of Abraham, and the God of Isaac, and the God of Jacob? He is not the God of the dead, but the God of the Living; ye therefore do greatly err.

Yeshua spoke about the resurrection of the dead in John's Gospel.

John 5:24-29 *Verily, verily, I say unto you, He that heareth My Word, and believeth on Him that sent Me, hath everlasting life, and shall not come into condemnation; but is passed from death unto life. Verily, verily, I say unto you, The hour is coming, and now is, when the dead shall hear the voice of the Son of God; and they that hear shall live. For as the Father hath life in Himself; so hath He given to the Son to have life in Himself; And hath given Him authority to execute judgment also, because he is the Son of man. Marvel not at this; for the hour is coming, in the which all that are in the graves shall hear His voice, And shall come forth; they that have done good, unto the resurrection of life; and they that have done evil, unto the resurrection of damnation.*

The devastating aspect of the death of a loved one is the seemingly never ending separation. The heart feels crushed and empty as our souls are parted from one another. Can we hold on to our faith and trust God that He will resurrect the dead at the sound of His voice? Although it may feel hopeless right now as your heart grieves the loss, we have an Almighty KING who changes this separation and He has the power to resurrect them to life! The KING is coming! Yeshua said that the dead that are in their graves will hear the voice of the Son of God and they that hear shall live. The breath of the Spirit of life out of Yeshua's mouth is one incredible revelation from the LORD!

Wind blowing flames in the Snow Photo ©2013 Kimberly K Ballard All Rights Reserved

My Beautiful Doves of Peace in the Snow, "The Girls!"

Shaked! Watch!

The Lamb's Ear Maror

The Rock Quarry & Meleke Limestone

The Abu Badd Great Rolling Stone

The Rooster

Simon's Rock Samples

Simon's friend Peter in the Garden Tomb

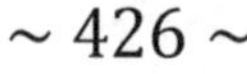

Chapter 9

ALMOND IS "SHAKED" "WATCH" "A HASTY AWAKENING"

A Peach tree on top & an Almond tree on the bottom, Almonds in bowl & Snow
Photos ©2013 Kimberly K Ballard All Rights Reserved

Many people would be surprised to know that the marvelous Almond Tree is a member of the peach tree family. Enclosed within the Almond Tree's small fuzzy fruit is the Almond seed. From all outward appearances, the Almond fruit perfectly resembles a peach fruit as it grows, but as the Almond seed ripens and matures, an amazing thing occurs that is parallel to the resurrection of Messiah Yeshua. In *the third year* of its growth, the Almond tree produces its first crop of fruit! So in parallel, *on the third day,* the Almond Branch Yeshua came to life and produced the First Fruit on the LORD'S Feast of First Fruits. Near harvest time, *the outward fuzzy husk of the Almond splits open to reveal the hard shell pit containing the living Almond seed.* After the *exterior fuzzy fruit splits opened,* the pit inside it eventually dries out and *then it splits open* on the seam of its hardened shell. After this occurs, the living Almond seed comes out of its darkened chamber and it is ready to be eaten. By pure definition *"a nut or Almond, enclosed in a hard shell, is a dry fruit that consists of an edible meat."* Of course the Almond is a one-seeded fruit. So Yeshua is the parallel one-seeded First Fruit and meat of Heaven as *the Living Torah.* In the resurrection of Messiah Yeshua, *the rocks were split opened or rent the third day* and the Branch bearing the Living Almond seed, the Spiritual meat of the Almond Tree of Life, came forth out of the darkened chamber and out of His husk in the form of His burial Shroud, revealing the Testimony of the light of *the Living Torah,* just as the Almond splits opened to reveal its seed.

A Peach tree at the top & an Almond tree on the bottom Photo ©2013 Kimberly K Ballard All Rights Reserved

After this happened on *the third day,* the First Fruit from Messiah was *ready to be eaten* from the Branch of the Almond Tree of Life! Even the Almond Blossoms bear witness of Messiah Yeshua's Testimony because five petals make up each Almond flower on the Branch. When fully opened, the five petals of each Almond blossom testify that Yeshua is *the Living Torah* and the glory of God. This is another reason *the Testimony* of Messiah Yeshua is eternally depicted on the Divinely designed, Holy Almond Tree Menorah made of solid pure gold. So the *opened Almond blossom cups* on the Almond Tree Menorah and *the branches or arms bearing ripe Almonds* proclaim the majesty and glory of the mighty works of the KING OF KINGS!

I am reminded in these details, the importance of my original miracle and recall that when my Almond Tree revelation went to Jerusalem, on February 16th

2007, that specific Almond Tree was just beginning to flower, opening its blossoms. My Israeli friend said she photographed the Almond Tree *"the third time,"* that she passed by it and it was *"the first Almond Tree that she saw beginning to flower in the Old City of Jerusalem on Holy Mount Moriah* in the place where God said His Name would be forever*!"* When our miracle took place in Jerusalem, she did not know all these other details yet that transpired later. *The hand of God* was the only one that could bring all these miracles together, announcing that His glory is forever discovered within His Divine creation. We were eyewitnesses of this glory!

A year after I sent the letter to Jerusalem, my friend in Israel wrote another letter to me in 2008 and she told me that *"Shaked"* is the Hebrew word for *"Almond!"* At first, I thought this was just a nice little Hebrew word, so I did not think too much about it. However, I soon discovered that my miracle of the Almond Tree went far beyond anything I could imagine. The LORD began to show me that there is an exceedingly great significance to the definition of the word *"Shaked" or "Almond."* I have to say that I was absolutely stunned when I discovered that the word *"Shaked"* actually means *"Watch" or "Hasty Awakening!"* I was able to discern this by the power of the Holy Spirit and it was shocking to me. The light went on in my mind and I suddenly remembered that Yeshua spoke of *His return* using these exact Words! I immediately remembered that Yeshua said that we should *"Watch"* for His return and not only that, but Yeshua said that we should stay *"Awake, Watching for Him!"* Wow! I knew the minute I made this connection that this was one more Divine miracle from the LORD proving that Messiah Yeshua is indeed *the Almond Rod of God* that gives us Eternal life! Yeshua is indeed the Messiah, the everlasting KING of Israel from the tribe of Judah!

A Peach tree on the left & an Almond tree on the right
Photo ©2013 Kimberly K Ballard

Now if you think about Messiah Yeshua's Words regarding His return at the end of the age, Yeshua said that the resurrection of the dead would occur *"in the twinkling of an eye, at the Last Trump."* Those who are alive and remain will be caught up in the cloud to meet the LORD in the air with those who have just been resurrected from the dead. So not only did Yeshua use the word *"Watch"* in this circumstance, but when Yeshua spoke of the resurrection of the dead, Yeshua always used the term *"Awaken"* because it will be a *"Hasty Awakening,"* when those who have been dead for so long suddenly arise to life! The significance of this exciting discovery means that *the Branch of the Almond Tree of Life told of His return and about the resurrection of the dead* within the Hebrew word for *"Almond"* which is *"Shaked!"* Now I just mentioned that the trumpet blast called *"the Last Trump"* is the day of the resurrection of the dead, and this blast occurs *only* during the LORD'S Holy Convocation known as *"Rosh HaShanah, The Feast of Trumpets, or Yom Teruah."* If you are not absolutely astonished already, then what I have to say next will absolutely thrill you! It just so happens that Rosh HaShanah is known by another name and they call it *"the Day of the Awakening Blast!"* So the *"Awakening Blast"* is the *"Almond"* or the *"Shaked"* because Yeshua is *the Almond Rod of God* who descends from Heaven with a shout and with the Trump of God to resurrect the dead and to take us into His glory cloud in the rapture to be with Him forever! *This is the day of the resurrection of the dead* and the rapture of believers in the Living Almond Branch, our Messiah Yeshua. Rosh HaShanah always occurs in the fall of the year. It occurs in early to late September or early October. The Hebrew Biblical calendar moves around a bit.

The following Scripture is also a direct reference to the rapture and the resurrection of the dead at *"the Last Trump." It can only take place on the Feast of Trumpets, Rosh HaShanah, or Yom Teruah.*

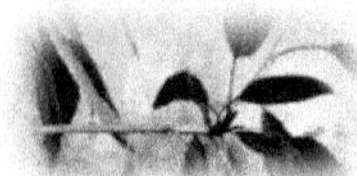

I Corinthians 15:51-52 *Behold, I shew you a mystery; We shall not all sleep, but we shall all be changed, In a moment, in the twinkling of an eye, at the Last Trump; for the trumpet shall sound, and the dead shall be raised in corruptible, and we shall be changed.*

The *Jewish people* have always believed and taught that *the resurrection of the dead would, in fact, occur during Rosh HaShanah* which is one of the seven Holy Festivals of the LORD. The seven Festivals are *the LORD'S appointed times* and when the Messiah was sent to us, He fulfilled all of them and said *"It is finished." The Last Trump is only blown during the Feast of Trumpets, on the Day of the Awakening Blast!* When Yeshua said, *"No one knows the day or the hour" that He would come,* He was specifically revealing, to those who understood it, that Rosh HaShanah or the Feast of Trumpets is the exact time frame of the resurrection of the dead and the rapture of the believers in the Messiah. There are two reasons why this particular phrase that was spoken by Yeshua pertains specifically to Rosh HaShanah. The first reason is because it moves around on the Hebrew Biblical calendar. This Holy Convocation *absolutely cannot and does not begin until the witnesses,* who happen to be diligently *"Watching,"* can verify that they have seen the sliver of the *new moon* in the sky. It is only at the point when the *new moon* is first sighted that the Feast of Trumpets can begin from that point on, and then it continues for two days. So the saying, *"No one knows the day or hour, when it will begin,"* is a common saying that refers specifically *to the Feast of Trumpets, Yom Teruah, or Rosh HaShanah* because Yeshua could return anytime within the two days, but only after the *new moon* is sighted or discovered in the sky. Therefore, because *no one knows which day or hour* that the *new moon* sighting will occur, we have the phrase, *"No one knows the day or the hour!" This is often misinterpreted by those not familiar with this holy day as meaning we will be clueless.*

He is coming in the cloud Photo ©2013 Kimberly K Ballard All Rights Reserved

Mark 13:32-33 *But of that day and that hour knoweth no man, no, not the angels which are in Heaven, neither the Son, but the Father. Take ye heed, watch and pray; for ye known not when the time is.*

In Yeshua's phrase, He is of course speaking as a Jewish Bridegroom who returns for His Bride at a time when she is not expecting Him to return. Only the Father knows when He will send His Son to go and get His Bride. *Sometimes there is a delay in the timing of Rosh HaShanah if no one can see or find the new moon in the sky. Then Rosh HaShanah cannot begin yet and the Holy Convocation is delayed.* It is extremely important to realize also that *this particular phrase* of Messiah Yeshua only pertains to *Rosh HaShanah, the Feast of Trumpets.* Interestingly enough, *Yeshua indicated that there could be a delay in His coming!*

Matthew 24:48-51 *But and if that evil servant shall say in his heart, My LORD delayeth His coming; And shall begin to smite his fellow servants, and to eat and drink with the drunken; The LORD of that servant shall come in a day when he looketh not for Him, and in an hour that he is not aware of, And shall cut him asunder, and appoint him his portion with the hypocrites; there shall be weeping and gnashing of teeth.*

Hebrews 10:37 *For yet a little while, and He that shall come will come, and not tarry.*

Luke 12:40 *Be ye therefore ready also; for the Son of man cometh at an hour when ye think not.*

Another exciting factor to the resurrection of the dead and the rapture of believers on *Rosh HaShanah* is the fact that *the Jewish people teach that the door of Heaven is opened during the High Holy Days* beginning with the start of the Feast of Trumpets! ***(Source: Hebraic Heritage Ministries International ©2010-2014 Rosh HaShanah by Eddie Chumney Chapter 7 - mayimhayim.org/Festivals/Feast7.htm).*** This is exciting because if you remember the Jewish disciple John, in the book of Revelation in chapter three, *saw a door opened in Heaven and He went up! Yeshua is the door and Heaven is opened on Rosh HaShanah!*

The next fascinating aspect of The Feast of Trumpets or Rosh HaShanah is the fact that it is known as *"Coronation Day"* for the LORD God Almighty as the KING of Israel. Only on Rosh HaShanah is the special Challah bread shaped into a crown to honour the LORD God on His Coronation Day as the KING OF KINGS! Rosh HaShanah is also the time when Adam was created and it is known as *"the birthday of mankind."* Yeshua came to earth as the second Adam. So all these factors put together give us great insight into the time-frame that we need to *"Watch"* for Yeshua's arrival. This is the time when we need to be *"Awake"* and prepare ourselves in advance *before* the Feast of Trumpets arrives.

Ironically, the whole month before Rosh HaShanah arrives is a time for introspection. This is the time when we are to examine our lives and to get right with God through repentance before that day arrives. We are to prepare ourselves before the High Holy Days begin, and we are not to be taken unaware and snared by the coming tribulation. Yeshua admonished the Jews 2,000 years ago for not knowing and seeing the time of their visitation. So we are to be aware of His coming even though we will never know the exact hour or time until it happens, but Messiah Yeshua did give us some great clues that reveal exactly when to *watch* for His return. He did not leave us in ignorance about this because *He told us specifically to "Watch!"* Rosh HaShanah continues for two days beginning at sundown, the moment that *the witnesses testify* to the first sighting of the new moon. *The two witnesses in Revelation are also resurrected from death, probably on another Rosh HaShanah, as they hear a voice from Heaven and ascend up in the glory cloud!* Yeshua told His Jewish disciples something profound when he said, that those who live and believe in Him will never die. The following Scripture refers to the dead who will be resurrected, and it says *"Those who are alive will never die."* They are taken up in the glory cloud with Him in the rapture. He is the resurrection and the life! Yeshua reveals the rapture and resurrection of the dead within the following Words.

Cloud portal ©2014 Kimberly K Ballard All Rights Reserved

John 11:25-27 *Yeshua said unto her, I AM the resurrection, and the life; he that believeth in Me, though he were dead, yet shall he live; And whosoever liveth and believeth in Me shall never die, Believest thou this? She saith unto Him, Yea, LORD; I believe that Thou art the Messiah, the Son of God, which should come into the world.*

I Thessalonians 5:14-18 *For if we believe that Yeshua died and rose again, even so them also which sleep in Yeshua will God bring with Him. For this we say unto you by the Word of the LORD, that we which are alive and remain unto the coming of the LORD shall not prevent them which are asleep. For the LORD Himself shall descend from Heaven with a shout, with the voice of the archangel, and with the Trump of God; and the dead in Messiah shall rise first; Then we which are alive and remain shall be caught up together with them in the clouds, to meet the LORD in the air; and so shall we ever be with the LORD. Wherefore comfort one another with these Words.*

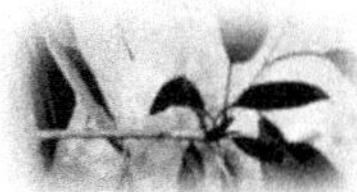

At the sound of *"the Last Trump,"* the dead in Messiah will rise first. When He speaks *the Word, the breath of life* will come into the dead and they will be resurrected to life. Then we who remain, who are still alive, will be caught up together with them in the clouds and we are changed into our glorious Eternal bodies. Thus, we shall always be with the LORD.

The *shofar or the ram's horn* is, therefore, sometimes engraved upon the headstones of Jewish graves because the Jewish Prophets said that *the resurrection of the dead* would occur during the Feast of Trumpets. Although no one knows exactly the year when Messiah the LORD will come, we are told that we are not to be taken unaware so that the day of the LORD comes upon us as *a thief in the night. Rosh HaShanah is a very important appointed time of the LORD on His Biblical calendar.* Jews were required to *go up to the Temple! In the rapture we go up to the Heavenly Temple, the LORD!*

Shofar Photo ©2014
Kimberly K Ballard All Rights Reserved

When Yeshua declared, *"No one knows the day or the hour, but My Father only,"* this phrase is spoken by a Jewish Bridegroom after His betrothal to His Bride. Many people know this already that He goes away to His Father's House to build a place for her. He will return to get her, to take her there. He is not sure when the Father will send Him to go get His Bride to take her away to the Father's House. The moment that the Father tells the Bridegroom to go and get His Bride, there is no more delay. The Bridegroom will not tarry. He comes at once to get her and He takes her to live in the place that He has prepared for her. Now she will dwell with Him in the gorgeous House that He built for her. In Messiah Yeshua's case, Yeshua will rapture His Bride and take her to the Heavenly Temple of the LORD, into His Divine Presence!

In the Jewish tradition, the Bridegroom usually returned for His Bride at midnight, but there is one fascinating aspect of this that I would like to mention here! *The cloud that hid the LORD was always seen in the very early morning hours or in the daytime.* Twilight is the earliest part of the morning between dawn and sunrise. Twilight also occurs in the evening between dusk and sunset. A Biblical day begins in the evening at the time of twilight. If He is coming then, we should get ready for Rosh HaShanah and prepare ourselves to meet the LORD in the air! Can you imagine being raptured alive in the glory cloud and never having to die?

John 14:1-3 *Let not your heart be troubled; ye believe in God, believe also in Me. In My Father's House are many mansions; if it were not so, I would have told you. I go to prepare a place for you. And if I go and prepare a place for you, I will come again, and receive you unto Myself; that where I AM, there ye may be also.*

This is the greatest promise that the LORD gave us! Yeshua, *the Jewish Bridegroom,* ascended in the glory cloud. He went into Heaven to prepare a place for His Bride. Of course, as I mentioned in a previous chapter, Yeshua revealed that He was the Jewish Bridegroom during the miracle at the wedding in Cana of Galilee when He turned the water into wine and saved the best wine for last! He will drink this cup with His Bride during His marriage supper in the Eternal Kingdom. The cup that Yeshua offered to us was *the cup of salvation, the opened Almond blossom of the Holy Menorah,* and He asked that this cup be removed from Him, so that the will of the Father would prevail. So *the Rod of God* gave us *the cup of salvation, which is the cup of redemption!* Remember, that *the Rod of God* did not come to take the cup of salvation for Himself! The Rod came to be lifted up, to save us forever!

Psalm 116:12-15 *What shall I render unto the LORD for all His benefits toward me? I will take the cup of salvation, and call upon the Name of the LORD. I will pay my vows unto the LORD now in the presence of all His people. Precious in the sight of the LORD is the death of His Saints.*

Apparently, *Rosh HaShanah is also the day when all men will pass under the Rod!* Now considering that Messiah Yeshua is *the Rod of God,* this is quite appropriate. On Rosh HaShanah, one is either *written in the book of life, given death, or is somewhere in between.* One has ten days to repent before Yom Kippur arrives, and if one fails to repent, their fate is sealed. The judgment comes immediately following the end of Rosh HaShanah. Once the book is shut, the judgment comes. *"The Last Trump" does not refer to any of the trumpets in the book of Revelation.* It is not one of the trumpets blown during the time that the wrath of God is poured out upon the earth. *"The Last Trump"* is specific to the Feast of Trumpets and it has always been called by this name. *It does not at all refer to the last of the seven trumpet judgments.* During Rosh HaShanah, the shofar or ram's horn is blown at least 100 times all over the world and in thousands of Synagogues and Messianic Churches. It is the time for us to *"Awaken from our sleep!"* Some Churches that observe the seven Feast Days of the LORD also blow the shofar during Rosh HaShanah. When we do this, *we shout a proclamation to KING Messiah Yeshua, as we blow the shofar,* so that He knows for certain we are diligently *watching* and *waiting* for His arrival. *The one final, very long wailing blast of the shofar that is blown on the Feast of Trumpets at the end is the blast known as "The Last Trump."*

Now, there is a very profound bit of information that I will share with you. As I mentioned earlier, I was blessed to have found online, Rabbi Simcha Pearlmutter of blessed memory. Before his passing, Rabbi Pearlmutter proclaimed the reasons for his belief in Yeshua as the Jewish Messiah. He did not believe in converting himself to Christianity. He was truly a righteous Jewish Rabbi who found the truth in the Jewish books about his Messiah! I will now refer to one of his discoveries pertaining to Rosh HaShanah that he said is found in a very kosher prayer book called *"Machzor Rabbah."* Rabbi Simcha Pearlmutter said the following important words about *the fact that the Jews speak the Name of Yeshua in this prayer on Rosh HaShanah between the first and second set of soundings of the shofar. Quote: "Now there comes a time during Rosh HaShanah that we blow the shofar the ram's horn. Many of you know it. Many of you may even have heart it. I happen to blow it here, and it's something that one will never forget once he experiences that. But during the time of the blowing of the ram's horn there is a little prayer that we say in between the various sets of soundings. The first set of sounds of the shofar is called "Tashrat."* (There is more to the quote, and then the Rabbi says the following words). *"The prayer that we say between the first set of soundings and the second set of soundings, which you see here, is this prayer. And I am going to read it to you as I point to it."* (Now the Rabbi gives the prayer in Hebrew providing an English translation for the reader and when he gets to the part of Elijah this is what he says comes after that). *"Notice this very clearly and carefully, vi' Yeshua, "and Yeshua." Yeshua. Here is the name that I spoke of, the name which you have received, Yeshua. We give him a title, and right after that, the title is called Sar Ha-Panim, "the Prince, the Minister of the Face," meaning the face of Hashem. In other words, this one called Yeshua, is no less given the title of the very reflection of the insides, the panim, the face, panim, of G-d. And we utter his name between the first and second soundings of the shofar, called the ram's horn.* (Rabbi Pearlmutter finishes the prayer). *V'Sar Metatron, "and also the minister, Metatron." That, by the way, is sometimes used as another name for the name Yeshua. It means, The Guide of the Way, Metatron. U'timalei aleinu, "and fill us up," b'rachamim, "with Your mercies." Barukh atah, "Blessed are you, Ba'al Harachamim, "He who possesses all mercies." "All Right, We have now uttered the name during the time of the sounding of the shofar. But we have one final prayer that we must say, which relates to that prayer I've just read to you. And after we have sounded the final set of sounding in this portion of the service, we then refer to the final little prayer and it say's this:* (I cut to the middle of the prayer here). *"the three soundings, the three sets of soundings, lifnei khisei chevodekha, remember the name that we called out that it should go "before Your throne of glory," vayamlitzu, "and that" in our behalf," l'khapeir, in order to atone," al kol chatoteinu, in order to atone "for all our sins." So the last prayer says that we call upon the name of*

Yeshua that it may atone for all our sins. Now I want you to understand very clearly that I did not write this prayer, and I did not publish this book, and I did not write this book. This book was written by Rabbis long ago, and this prayer cannot be taken out of this prayer book, not by me, and not by any other Rabbi." ***(Source: Part Six of Nine from Rabbi Simcha Pearlmutter, Rabbi testimony of Jesus, Yeshua, Messiah - Full text available from: jerusalemcalling.org/Rabbi_Simcha_Pearlmutter.htm).***

Yeshua's Name goes before the throne of glory! The rapture is clear in *(I Thessalonians 4:16-18)*, and *(I Thessalonians 5:9-11)*. The wrath of God is clear in *(Romans 1:18-19)*.

Thanks to Rabbi Simcha Pearlmutter from Israel, we know that *when we blow the shofar during the Feast of Trumpets, we also call Yeshua's Name and wait for Him to arrive!* I believe that He will hear us and come take us in the rapture when the gate of Heaven is open!

"WATCH"

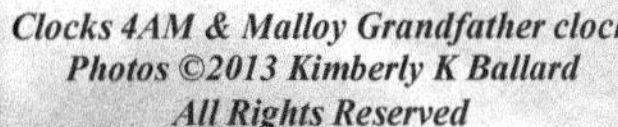

Clocks 4AM & Malloy Grandfather clock
Photos ©2013 Kimberly K Ballard

In the garden of Gethsemane, Yeshua kept telling His Jewish disciples to stay *"awake and watch"* but they kept falling asleep. I truly believe that He was revealing that they would die or be asleep and would therefore be *"Hastily Awakened"* at His return in the future because they would die before His return. Remember when Yeshua told the Jewish disciples that He would go and *"Awaken"* Lazarus? They thought that Yeshua meant that Lazarus was only *asleep,* but Yeshua said that Lazarus was *dead.* This was the same term that Yeshua used in the Garden of Gethsemane with the sleeping Jewish disciples. He said they were *asleep,* but He was giving a sign that they would be *dead* and resurrected at the sound of *the awakening blast* in the future when He returns. Yeshua went to them *three times* and told the Jewish disciples to *"watch and stay awake with Him."* They could not stay awake and Yeshua finally said to them, *"Sleep on now and take your rest!"* We already know from Hosea's prophecy that Messiah Yeshua will return to usher in the everlasting Kingdom and bring with Him the Heavenly Holy Temple to Jerusalem on *the third day.* So *the third time,* Yeshua told them to *sleep on.* This indicates that they will be dead and resurrected the third day, just as He came alive the third day, because they were Jewish children of Israel. The Bible tells us that one day to us is like a thousand years to the LORD. This means that 2 days or 2,000 years have almost past since Yeshua ascended into Heaven and this means that the third day of His arrival is about to come. Remember that I told you that the fruit bearing trees came to life in Genesis on the third day during creation? I explained that this is the reason why Messiah Yeshua was raised to life as the Living Fruitful Almond Branch bearing the First Fruits of Almonds on the third day because He is the LORD who created everything. So, *in the Garden of Gethsemane,* when Yeshua spoke to the Jewish disciples, He actually used the word *"Watch"* or *"Shaked."* He used the word *"Almond"* because the Almond Branch is the giver of Eternal life. At that moment, Yeshua was actually revealing that He would bear the fruit of Almonds on the third day and this would be *a sign* that they would be *awakened from death to life* on the third day at His return.

Mark 14:37-41 *And He cometh, and findeth them sleeping, and saith unto Peter, Simon, sleepest thou? Couldest not thou watch one hour? Watch ye and pray, lest ye enter into temptation. The spirit truly is ready, but the flesh is weak. And again He went away, and prayed, and spake the same Words. And when He returned, He found them asleep again, for their eyes were heavy, neither wist they what to answer Him. And He cometh the third time, and saith unto them, Sleep on now, and take your rest; it is enough, the hour is come; behold, the Son of man is betrayed into the hands of sinners.*

I want to mention that Yeshua specifically told His Jewish disciples that those who are *"Watching"* for His return will be *blessed.* By definition, *"blessed"* refers to *"eternal bliss."* Blissfulness refers to *"ecstasy."* I believe that the reason why they will be *blessed* is because those who are diligently *watching* for His return will see the signs approaching that warn ahead of time that His arrival is near. Since they stayed *awake and watched* for Him, they prepared themselves *to meet Him face to face* before His arrival. At the sound of His Last Trump, they entered into the Kingdom of Heaven and they went through the door of the Ark of Heaven and *the LORD shut them in.* The door was then closed by the LORD and everyone else was shut outside the door. Therefore, those that went into the Ark of salvation were *blessed,* but those who did not pay attention to His prophecies or to the times and seasons of His coming were not prepared to meet Him. So they were left outside the door after He shut it. Remember that with Noah, those who were left outside the door of the Ark perished and were not *blessed* with the salvation that came to those who were safe inside the Ark. *A blessing comes upon those watching. They are suddenly standing in the ecstasy and bliss of the LORD'S Divine Presence, and meeting the LORD face to face in the glory cloud!*

Noah walked with God, so he was ready to enter the Ark. After he went into the Ark the LORD shut him in, and closed the door so that no one else could get in. Right now, we can clearly see that many of the signs of His return are being fulfilled right before our eyes. I believe that He is even at the door right now and that He is ready to come and take the believers to be with Him in the cloud. Those who make themselves ready will be taken to His Father's House in Heaven. The Gospel of Luke speaks of the LORD coming and the door being opened. *He clearly says that those who are watching will sit down to meat.* This means that we will eat the Heavenly meat with Messiah the LORD because He is the Almond seed, *the meat of the Living Torah!* He said that He could come in the second or third watch!

Luke 12:35-46 *Let your loins be girded about, and your lights burning; And ye yourselves like unto men that wait for their LORD, when He will return from the wedding; that when He cometh and knocketh, they may open unto Him immediately. Blessed are those servants, whom the LORD when He cometh shall find watching; verily I say unto you, that he shall gird himself, and make them to sit down to meat, and will come forth and serve them. And if He shall come in the second watch, or come in the third watch, and find them so, blessed are those servants. And this know, that if the good man of the house had known what hour the thief would come, he would have watched, and not have suffered his house to be broken through. Be ye therefore ready also; for the Son of man cometh at an hour when ye think not. Then Peter said unto Him, LORD, speakest thou this parable unto us, or even to all? And the LORD said, Who then is that faithful and wise steward, whom his LORD shall make ruler over His Household, to give them their portion of meat in due season? Blessed is that servant, whom his LORD when He cometh shall find so doing. Of a truth I say unto you, that he will make him ruler over all that he hath. But and if that servant say in his heart, My LORD delayeth His coming; and shall begin to beat the men servants and maidens, and to eat and drink, and to be drunken; The LORD of that servant will come in a day when he looketh not for Him, and at an hour when he is not aware, and will cut him in sunder, and will appoint him his portion with the unbelievers.*

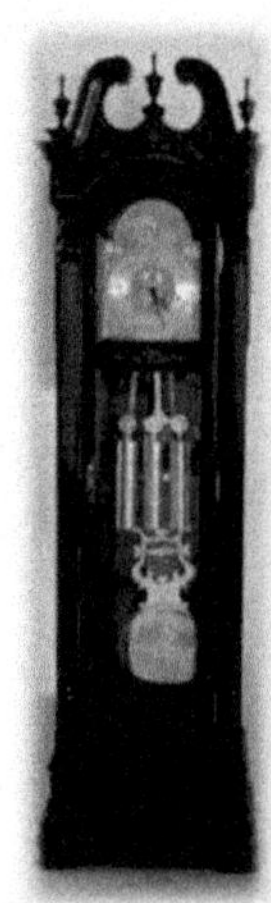

The point here is that we are not to be taken off guard by the return of Messiah Yeshua when He comes to rapture the believers. On numerous occasions, Yeshua said that if we are *not watching* for Him, then He will come at *an hour that we are not aware of,* and He said that He will appoint those who are *not watching* as unbelievers, destined to destruction. So one of the ways to make sure that we are *watching* and are ready for Him is to learn about and understand the LORD'S times and seasons that He appointed for Messiah's return. The key to

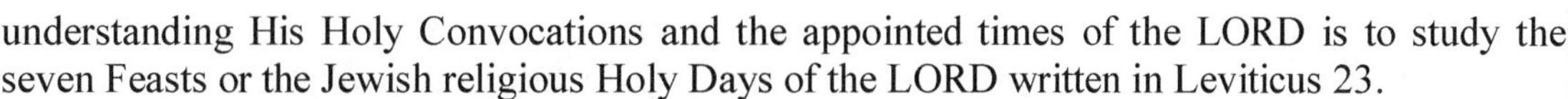
understanding His Holy Convocations and the appointed times of the LORD is to study the seven Feasts or the Jewish religious Holy Days of the LORD written in Leviticus 23.

A special blessing is also given to those who read and hear the Words of the Prophecy of the book of Revelation. To be *shut outside the door of the Ark* means that you will not escape the time of the wrath of God after Yeshua closes the door of the Heavenly Ark. Yeshua clearly warned us to be alert! *I want you to be there with me, so please get ready!*

In the following passage, Yeshua told them to *"Watch"* and this occurred *as they listened to His voice early in the morning at the Temple.* This is quite possibly another indication that His voice will shout from Heaven very early in the morning (at twilight). The time of His judgment and wrath will come as *a snare* to all the people on the earth who are not aware of the times and seasons of His arrival. By definition, a *"snare" is "a trap or a gin and an ambush!"* Interestingly enough, "*ambush"* refers to *"a military tactic of lying concealed or hidden, where the element of a surprise attack is implemented," and "a trap suddenly springs shut without warning." Satan is the thief that sets this trap to implement his evil end time plans. He steals, kills, and destroys. He has already secretly and blatantly placed his Babylonian tower at ground zero in New York City, where he eventually plans to use the new spire as a broadcast tower to offer up pagan prayers. He has already signed it with a blasphemous phrase from ancient Babylon that goes against God!*

Luke 21:35-36 *For as a snare shall it come on all them that dwell on the face of the whole earth. Watch ye therefore, and pray always, that ye may be accounted worthy to escape all these things that shall come to pass, and to stand before the Son of man. And in the day time He was teaching in the Temple; and at night He went out, and abode in the Mount that is called the Mount of Olives. <u>And all the people came early in the morning to Him</u> in the Temple, for to hear Him.*

Mystery Babylon is *a thief in the night, a snare or trap* to those *not watching* for Messiah Yeshua. *He told us to hold fast to His Testimony, and repent. Rosh HaShanah is the time to repent* before the final judgment comes! He gave us many warnings!

I Peter 4:7 *But the end of all things is at hand; be ye therefore sober, and watch unto prayer.*

Revelation 16:15 *Behold, I come as a thief. Blessed is he that watcheth, and keepeth his garments, lest he walk naked, and they see his shame.*

Revelation 3:2-3 *Be watchful, and strengthen the things which remain, that are ready to die; for I have not found thy works perfect before God. Remember therefore how thou hast received and heard, and hold fast, and repent. If therefore thou shalt not watch, I will come on thee as a thief, and thou shalt not know what hour I will come upon thee.*

The Jewish disciples who were well versed in the meanings and traditions of the Holy religious Convocations or the seven Feasts of the LORD did not need to have *the times and seasons* explained to them. They understood that *"the Day of the LORD,"* which is the time of the wrath of God poured out on the earth, would come on one of the LORD'S specific seven appointed times, and they also knew that *Messiah Yeshua would return* on one of the LORD'S Holy Feasts or appointed times. The reason why many Churches do not understand *the times and seasons* of the LORD is because the Jewish meaning has been lost to the Churches and many of us have never learned about the Jewish Biblical Feasts of the LORD. For this reason, it is widely spread within many of the Churches *"that He can come for us at anytime whatsoever,"* but this is not correct. He will come at *an hour* that no one is sure of, but He told us we are not to be taken off guard and unaware of the *times and seasons* of His coming. *The LORD did not leave us without a single clue as to when to watch for His arrival.* Yeshua actually gave some *very specific clues that point to one specific appointed time of the LORD*, and prepares us for the advent of His arrival. *The season of His coming in the cloud at the rapture is during the Feast of Trumpets on Rosh HaShanah.* The appointed time He

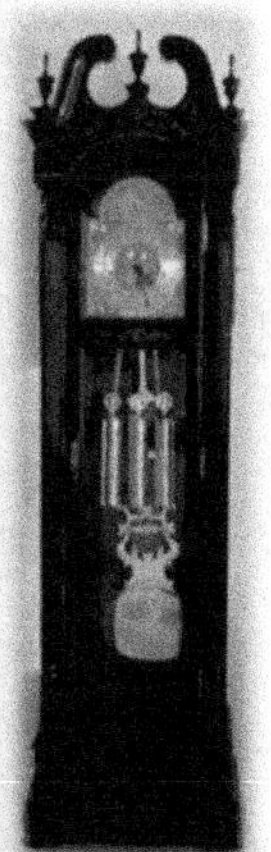
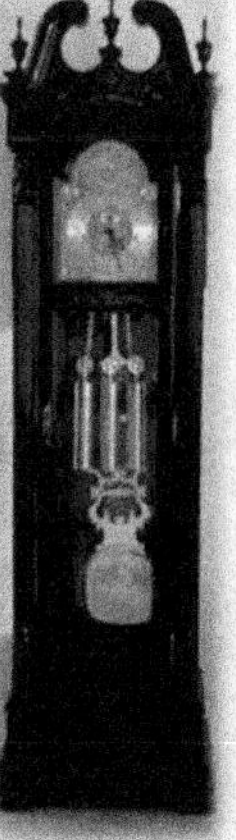

foreshadowed for the rapture of believers is clearly at the blowing of *"the Last Trump"* blown exclusively on the Feast of Trumpets, on Rosh HaShanah in the Hebrew month of Tishrei. It is not blown at any other time of the year. Also, the Ark of the Covenant was *"taken up"* in the seventh month of Tishrei and Messiah Yeshua is the Heavenly Ark that *takes us up!*

I Thessalonians 5:1-11 *But of the times and the seasons, brethren, ye have no need that I write unto you. For yourselves know perfectly that the Day of the LORD so cometh as a thief in the night. For when they shall say, Peace and safety; then sudden destruction cometh upon them, as travail upon a woman with child; and they shall not escape. But ye, brethren, are not in darkness, that that day should overtake you as a thief. Ye are all the children of light, and the children of the day; we are not of the night, nor of darkness. Therefore let us not sleep, as do others; but let us watch and be sober. For they that sleep, sleep in the night; and they that be drunken are drunken in the night. But let us, who are of the day, be sober, putting on the breastplate of faith and love; and for an helmet, the hope of salvation. For God hath not appointed us to wrath, but to obtain salvation by our LORD Yeshua Messiah, Who died for us, that, whether we wake or sleep, we should live together with Him. Wherefore comfort yourselves together, and edify one another, even as also we do.*

Colossians 4:2-5 *Continue in prayer, and watch in the same with thanksgiving; Withal praying also for us, that God would open unto us a door of utterance, to speak the mystery of Messiah, for which I am also in bonds; That I may make it manifest, as I ought to speak. Walk in wisdom toward them that are without, redeeming the time.*

Messiah Yeshua gave us *the signs of His coming* in the following verse and He used the word *"Watch"* or *"Shaked."* Yeshua's *Parable of the Fig Tree and all the trees* came just before He said to *"Watch!"* Yeshua returns at the time the curse is removed from the earth. *In the Parable of the Fig Tree, Yeshua said four times to "Watch!" It is likely at the fourth Watch!*

Mark 13:28-37 *Now learn a parable of the fig tree; When her branch is yet tender, and putteth forth leaves, ye know that summer is near; So ye in like manner, when ye shall see these things come to pass, know that it is nigh, even at the doors. Verily I say unto you, that this generation shall not pass, till all these things be done. Heaven and earth shall pass away; but My Words shall not pass away. But of that day and that hour knoweth no man, no, not the angels which are in heaven, neither the Son, but the Father. Take ye heed, watch and pray; for ye know not when the time is. For the Son of man is as a man taking a far journey, who left His House, and gave authority to his servants, and to every man his work, and commanded the porter to watch. Watch ye therefore; for ye know not when the Master of the House cometh, at even, or at midnight, or at the cockcrowing, or in the morning; Lest coming suddenly he find you sleeping. And what I say unto you I say unto all, Watch.*

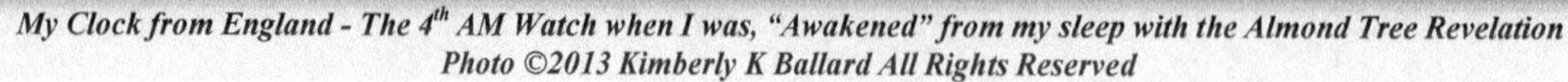
My Clock from England - The 4th AM Watch when I was, "Awakened" from my sleep with the Almond Tree Revelation

Rooster Photos ©2014 DeRieux family
Edited by KK Ballard All Rights Reserved

Almond Is "Shaked" "Watch" "A Hasty Awakening"

THE ROOSTER

Rooster Photos ©2014 DeRieux family
Edited by KK Ballard All Rights Reserved

The LORD put it in my heart that the rooster crowing might have something to do with His arrival in the rapture, and I pondered this and asked the LORD to show me what the rooster meant. Of course, I knew that three times Simon Peter denied Yeshua and the rooster crowed before he denied Him three times. *Yeshua specifically mentioned the cockcrowing as one of the times that He could return in the rapture.* He instructed us to be *watching* for His arrival then or *during one of the military time intervals* called *"watches."* I want to mention this specifically because the LORD put this in my heart about the rooster crowing. So I stopped writing and researched this and I was absolutely shocked at what I discovered about the rooster! I found out that the rooster has an extremely significant meaning in regards to the LORD God of Israel! Of course, the rooster was used as a natural alarm clock in ancient times, before the clock was invented. When I studied the rooster, I was simply astonished at what the Holy Spirit showed me. Every detail seemed to fall right into place when I studied this!

As it turns out, I discovered that, in Judaism, the rooster crowing precisely meant *"The heralding of the morning arrival of the LORD God, known as the Master!"* The crowing of the rooster, therefore, would usher in *the morning service* of the LORD and it spoke specifically of *His arrival!* Now with this information in mind, read Mark 13 and look at the specific Words that Yeshua used when He spoke about the time to *"Watch"* for His arrival! *Incredibly, He referred to the arrival of the Master!* Wow fantastic and exciting!

Mark 13:35-37 *Watch ye therefore; for ye know not when the Master of the House cometh, at even, or at midnight, or at the cockcrowing, or in the morning; Lest coming suddenly He find you sleeping. And what I say unto you I say unto all, watch.*

The Jewish blessing pertaining to the rooster says this, *"Blessed are you, LORD our God, KING of the universe, who gave the rooster understanding to distinguish between day and night."* This *morning or dawn blessing* called *"Birchot HaShachar"* is fascinating because the word *"rooster"* is sometimes replaced with the word *"heart"* since both the rooster and the heart were given wisdom by God to distinguish between day and night *(the wording is from Job 38:36)*. ***(Source: The Jewish Chronicle Online or thejc.com "Thanking the Rooster" by Rabbi Julian Sinclair, ©2014 June 1) – (Source 2: hebrew4christians.com/Blessings/Synagogue_Blessings/Birchot_HaShachar/bir chot_hashachar.html).*** As we know already Messiah Yeshua's Covenant is the Testimony of the heart. This was of course verified when the Living Water and life blood of the LORD came out of His heart as He was pierced with the Roman lance. Now this was not all that I discovered that was so fantastic! The same *Jewish prayer or blessing about the rooster* gives us another tantalizing clue that the crowing of the rooster could actually be the very time when the Messiah will come in the rapture. *This prayer clearly defines for us, that the moment that the rooster crows is the exact same moment of time that divides the light from the darkness and day from night!* The rooster was believed to have been blessed with a God-given intelligence because it could discern *the*

separation of the day from the night and the light from the darkness! So when Yeshua mentioned that we did not know *when the Master of the House would come and that it could be at the rooster crowing,* then perhaps He was giving us some type of Spiritual discernment that reveals the exact moment when He will come to *separate the light from the darkness* before the tribulation begins! If you go back to the Scripture in I Thessalonians that I mentioned in the last section, you will see that this same verse verifies what I am saying about *the separation of the light and the darkness at the time of the rapture* when the wrath of God comes only upon those who are in *the darkness.* Look at this passage and see it in a whole new light in regards to the rooster crowing. When *the rooster crows,* He has God's discernment and He signals the separation of the darkness of the night from the light of the new day.

I Thessalonians 5:1-11 *But of the times and seasons, brethren, ye have no need that I write unto you. For yourselves know perfectly that the Day of the LORD so cometh as a thief in the night. For when they shall say, Peace and safety; then sudden destruction cometh upon them, as travail upon a woman with child; and they shall not escape. But ye, brethren, are not in darkness, that that day should overtake you as a thief. Ye are all children of the light, and the children of the day; we are not of the night, nor of the darkness. Therefore let us not sleep, as do others; but let us watch and be sober. For they that sleep sleep in the night; and they that be drunken are drunken in the night. But let us, who are of the day, be sober, putting on the breastplate of faith and love; and for an helmet, the hope of salvation. For God hath not appointed us to wrath, but to obtain salvation by our LORD Yeshua Messiah, Who died for us, that, whether we wake or sleep, we should live together with Him. Wherefore comfort yourselves together, and edify one another, even as also ye do.*

I already discussed before that the tribulation itself is *the separation of the light,* represented by the believers who have the LORD, *from the darkness* that represents the unbelievers who do not have the light of the LORD, but live in darkness. Yeshua told us that *"the Day of the LORD is a day of great darkness that has no light in it!"* In fact, remember, that He said *"It is utter darkness and that there is no light in it at all."* So this means that at the moment of the rapture, the two are not abiding together anymore, but the light and the darkness are made cleft and separated from one another as it was in the beginning during creation when the LORD separated the light and the darkness. At *the crowing of the rooster,* the light of the day is separated from the darkness of the night *by the Rod of God* and those who have the light will go to be with the source of the light. Those who are left in the darkness of the night experience the wrath of God because they do not have the source of the light. Of course, the thief comes in the night to steal when they are not aware of it. I believe that this is when the Anti-Christ who is empowered by Satan comes in the tribulation. It is truly remarkable to see this! Before the LORD urged me to ponder *the rooster,* I had not yet connected *the rooster crowing* to the exact moment that the separation of the light of the believers will occur and separate them from the darkness that is left behind when only the unbelievers and the wicked are left behind after the rapture!

Now that I have spoken about the significance of the rooster in the Jewish blessing, I have to show you something else about this profound little bird!

In Christian tradition, the crowing of the rooster is symbolic of *"the victory of light over the darkness and the triumph of good over evil,"* and *"It is also the emblem of the Christian's attitude of watchfulness and readiness for the sudden return of Christ, the resurrection of the dead, and the final judgment of humankind."* ***(Source: en.wikipedia.org/wiki/Gallic_rooster).*** This is fantastic! When Yeshua raptures the living believers, this will happen just a split second after the resurrection of the dead. So the moment of *the separation of the light from the darkness of death, as the rooster crows,* will be a great victory not only over death, but also it will be the greatest triumph of the goodness of the LORD God over the evil workings of Satan in history. Therefore, we find that the rooster crowing is extremely significant, to both Judaism and Christianity.

Now I truly believe in my heart that Yeshua was telling us specifically that *the crowing of the rooster* would indeed *herald the time of His arrival as our Master!* To me, this was

absolutely chilling! The LORD then showed me a few more exciting details about the rooster! I should mention that *the rooster* itself is ironically symbolic of *"watching and preparing oneself to be ready for the arrival of the Messiah!"* Incredibly, I found out that in ancient times, *the rooster did symbolize that the resurrection of the dead would occur at the Messiah's arrival! For this reason, the rooster was painted on some early ancient tombs of the martyrs of Messiah Yeshua!* It served as a reminder of the promise that the dead would *"awaken"* out of sleep the moment that the resurrection of the dead occurs at the sound of the *"Last Trump"* when Messiah descends from Heaven with *a shout.* The rooster tells us specifically when to *watch* to be ready for Yeshua's arrival! We will be raptured in the light of the LORD, and separated from the wicked living in darkness because they have rejected the LORD. We are not of the night, but of the day, and *the rooster has discernment to tell us exactly what time that separation takes place!* The rooster is an amazing little piece of the LORD'S puzzle.

Incredibly, in 2014, when my book was at my publisher in NY, I was listening to Anne Graham Lotz. She was standing on the Mount of Olives in 2012 in a video *(I wrote this about the rooster way before 2012).* Ann was saying we need to *"watch,"* that Jesus was coming soon! She had no idea of this connection, *and that a rooster was repeatedly crowing behind her in Jerusalem* when she said the word *"watch!"* It was so chilling, and when I showed my publisher she was stunned and said *"No way!" She knew this was in my book about the rooster!*

Now, when Simon Peter denied Yeshua three times, in the Gospel of John in Chapter thirteen, we find something else that is incredible that is hidden within His Words!

John 13:36-38 *Simon Peter said unto Him, LORD, whither goest Thou? Yeshua answered him, Whither I go, thou canst not follow Me now; but thou shalt follow Me afterwards. Peter said unto him, LORD, why cannot I follow Thee now? I will lay down my life for Thy sake. Yeshua answered him, Wilt thou lay down thy life for My sake? Verily, verily, I say unto thee, The cock shall not crow, till thou hast denied me thrice.*

Interestingly enough at the Democratic Convention in 2012, the delegates denied God three times as they waved their arm's and wagged their fingers shouting, *"No!"* They were indicating that they did not want God associated with their platform. They wanted God removed from their party platform and this event took place about a week before Rosh HaShanah! They also denied that Jerusalem is the Eternal Capital of Israel, but then later reinstated it! *It is written by God that Jerusalem is His Eternal Capital*! So getting back to this Scripture, Simon Peter is asking Yeshua where it is that He is going. He wants to follow the Messiah immediately to the place where Yeshua is going, which is Heaven. Then immediately, we see that Yeshua mentions *the rooster crowing* in connection to this previous question. *The rooster shall not crow* until he has denied Him three times. The LORD is returning the third day for Israel and Israel will be denying Yeshua until He comes for them, on the third day. Yeshua was not only referring to the events preceding the crucifixion because Simon Peter would literally deny Him three times, but His Words also tell quite a prophetic detail and picture about the future resurrection of the dead at the crowing of the rooster! After Yeshua said these things, He spoke the Words of a Jewish Bridegroom who comes to get His Bride and takes her to His Father's House to the place that He has prepared for her, and they go into the *"Chuppah,"* which is the Jewish wedding canopy to be married. This is basically a white sheet suspended by four poles and it forms a square shaped gazebo. This white sheet reminds me of Simon Peter's vision, which I discuss in a later chapter in great detail. Sometimes they use a Tallit. ***(Source: en.wikipedia.org/wiki/Chuppah).*** If the Bridegroom is *the Living Torah,* then the *Chuppah* is even more significant. The *Chuppah* is placed outside. There should be *"open sky" directly above the Chuppah. Now Yeshua said that the dead would rise first and then the living believers would be "caught up" with them to meet the LORD "in the air."* Remember that Heaven is opened during Rosh HaShanah and *we are meeting Him outside in the air!* I believe Yeshua was actually revealing that the Bride would go to Heaven on Rosh HaShanah when

Heaven is opened. If the *Chuppah* is opened to the sky and we are looking up, *watching* for the Bridegroom, then His cloud will descend in the *open sky* above the *Chuppah.* Those who love Him will be caught up in the air to be His Bride and we will be taken into His Bridal chamber! Even though the Jewish Bridegroom often would return for His Bride at midnight, *she could never be certain when He would actually come for her,* and remember that Yeshua said that He was coming at an hour that no one expects Him to arrive! The betrothed Bride had to wait patiently for Him while she prepared herself to meet Him. The truth is that He could return for her at any hour and take her to His Father's House. What I find interesting though is that the first thing Yeshua said, after He mentioned *the rooster crowing,* was not to be troubled because He was going to His Father's House to prepare a place for them in Heaven! Immediately after saying this Yeshua told them that if He goes to prepare this place for them in Heaven, He will *come again and take them to be with Him in the place that He has prepared. Yeshua told Simon Peter that he could not go to this place now, but he would follow the Messiah there later. The rooster crowing is mentioned just before he says this part about taking them to be in the place that He has prepared!* I think this is absolutely magnificent! I realized that if the crowing of the rooster signifies *the triumph of good over evil* and *the separation of the light from the darkness*, the believers must be removed and taken away from the ungodly before the tribulation, before the wrath of God is poured out on the unbelieving world. There is no light at all in the tribulation period, so the believers simply cannot be here at that time.

John 14:1-7 *Let not your heart be troubled; ye believe in God, believe also in Me. In My Father's House are many mansions; if it were not so, I would have told you. I go to prepare a place for you. And if I go and prepare a place for you, I will come again, and receive you unto Myself; that where I AM, there ye may be also. And whither I go ye know, and the way ye know. Thomas saith unto Him, LORD, we know not whither thou goest; and how can we know the way? Yeshua saith unto him, I AM the way, the truth, and the life; no man cometh unto the Father, but by Me. If ye had known Me, ye should have known my Father also; and from henceforth ye know Him, and have seen Him.*

Hen DeRieux Photo
©2014 DeRieux
All Rights Reserved

Now our little friend the rooster behaves like *"a watchman on the wall"* because He sits up high on a perch overlooking his territory and he guards all *the hens* below him. If any predators come near his territory, *the rooster sounds an alarm,* to guard and protect his flock of hens. *The hens remind me of the Bride and the rooster as the Bridegroom!* Yeshua said that He longed to gather Israel as a Hen that gathers her chicks, but she would not! Was the LORD giving us a clue by revealing when to expect *the alarm* that will come at *the rooster crowing* at the *awakening blast of "the Last Trump?"* Can we learn something else reading the passage in Isaiah about *the watchman on the wall?*

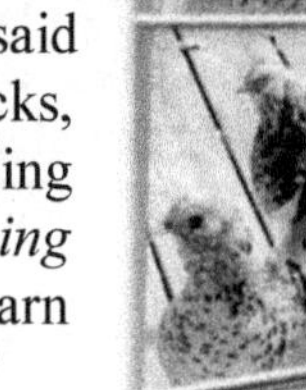

Hens DeRieux
Photos ©2014
All Rights Reserved

Isaiah 21:5-12 *Prepare the table, watch in the watchtower, eat, drink; arise, ye princes, and anoint the shield. For thus hath the LORD said unto me, Go, set a watchman, let him declare what he seeth. And he saw a chariot with a couple of horsemen, a chariot of asses, and a chariot of camels; and he harkened diligently with much heed; And he cried, A lion; My lord, I stand continually upon the watchtower in the daytime, and I am set in my ward whole nights; And, behold here cometh a chariot of men, with a couple of horsemen, And he answered and said, Babylon is fallen, is fallen; and all the graven images of her gods he hath broken to the ground. O my threshing, and the corn of my floor; that which I have heard of the LORD of Hosts, the God of Israel, have I declared unto you. The burden of Dumah, He calleth to me out of Seir, Watchman, what of the night? Watchman, what of the night? The Watchman said, The morning cometh, and also the night; if ye will enquire, enquire ye, return, come.*

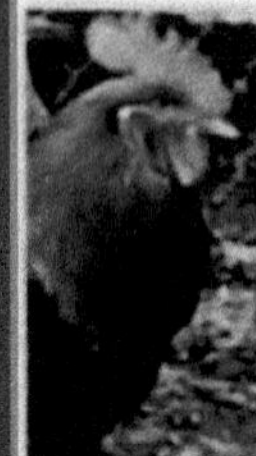

The watchman actually said, *"The morning cometh and also the night."* He also said, *"Return, come," and Yeshua is returning and coming!* So when the watchman saw that the night was ending and he saw the first light of the dawn of the new morning (twilight), he said

these words! This is how it will be at the rapture when the very first light dawns. The rooster crows and *sounds the alarm* that signals the end of night. It is the time of the separation of the light from the darkness. He mentions His threshing floor and we know that the good wheat is separated from the chaff. The good wheat is taken and held in the LORD'S *"barn,"* while the chaff is removed from off His threshing floor during the tribulation. In this Scripture, He also says, *"Babylon is fallen, is fallen."* Babylon is the great mother of harlots and full of abominations. This passage in Isaiah is significant to the time of the tribulation because we actually see the fulfillment of this condemnation in the book of Revelation. The condemnation of Babylon the great and all things associated with her takes place during the tribulation. The destruction happens only after the Messiah has taken His Bride, whom He loves, into His Heavenly Ark for protection. At this time, the LORD will shatter the kingdoms that were depicted on the statue in Nebuchadnezzar's dream in Babylon. In Revelation, we see that it is during the time of great darkness that the angel is declaring, *"Babylon is fallen, is fallen, that great city, because she made all nations drink the wine of the wrath of her fornication."*

Revelation 14:6-12 *And I saw another angel fly in the midst of Heaven, having the everlasting Gospel to preach unto them that dwell on the earth, and to every nation, and kindred, and tongue, and people, Saying with a loud voice, Fear God, and give glory to Him; for the hour of His judgment is come; and worship Him that made Heaven, and earth, and the sea, and the fountains of waters. And there followed another angel, saying, Babylon is fallen, is fallen, that great city, because she made all nations drink the wine of the wrath of her fornication. And the third angel followed them, saying with a loud voice, If any man worship the beast and his image, and receive his mark in his forehead, or in his hand, The same shall drink of the wine of the wrath of God, which is poured out without mixture into the cup of His indignation; and he shall be tormented with fire and brimstone in the presence of the Holy angels, and in the Presence of the Lamb; And the smoke of their torment ascendeth up forever and ever; and they have no rest day or night, who worship the beast and his image, and whosoever receiveth the mark of his name. Here is the patience of the Saints; here are they that keep the Commandments of God, and the faith of Yeshua.*

The judgment that can only begin *after the rooster or the watchman sounds the alarm* pertains to the darkness and condemnation on all the evils that are associated with ancient Babylon. This is also mentioned in Revelation 18. It says the LORD will consume all things connected to her wickedness because she birthed all false gods. *The judgment comes because people are worshipping her false gods, her false prophets, false messiahs, and her tall insulting towers that can never ever reach God! The colors of the horses of apocalypse match her flags.*

Revelation 18:1-5 *And there came one of the seven angels which had the seven vials, and talked with me, saying unto me, Come hither; I will shew unto thee the judgment of the great whore that sitteth upon many waters; With whom the kings of the earth have committed fornication, and the inhabitants of the earth have been made drunk with the wine of her fornication. So he carried me away in the Spirit into the wilderness; and I saw a woman sit upon a scarlet coloured beast, full of names of blasphemy, having seven heads and ten horns. And the woman was arrayed in purple and scarlet colour, and decked with gold and precious stones and pearls, having a golden cup in her hand full of abominations and filthiness of her fornication; And upon her head was a name written, MYSTERY, BABYLON THE GREAT, THE MOTHER OF HARLOTS AND ABOMINATIONS OF THE EARTH.*

The fourth *"watch"* of the night that I mentioned above is the last portion of the night just before the dawn of the first light comes when we *"Awaken"* from our sleep. This is the moment when the rooster crows. If the LORD suddenly descended from Heaven with a shout and with the blast of the shofar, we would truly have *"a Hasty Awakening."*

The fourth watch of the night is interesting because Yeshua came to the Jewish disciples in the ship, walking on the water, in the fourth watch of the night, and He saved the disciples from perishing in the ship that was in the storm of the wind tossed Sea. In this situation, you could say that the ship represented an Ark and Messiah Yeshua came to them on the surface of the water as the Ark of Heaven and saved them from perishing. At the time of the rapture, when He takes us into the Ark of Heaven, He will be saving us from perishing in

the dark storm of the great tribulation. If *the rooster* is the watchman that *sounds the alarm,* then the words in the book of Joel come to mind about *"the Day of the LORD!"*

Joel 2:1-2 *Blow ye the trumpet in Zion, and sound an alarm in My Holy Mountain; let all the inhabitants of the Land tremble; for the Day of the LORD cometh, for it is nigh at hand; A day of darkness and of gloominess, a day of clouds and of thick darkness, as the morning spread upon the mountains; a great people and a strong; there hath not been ever the like, neither shall be any more after it, even to the years of many generations.*

As soon as the trumpet is blown, *the alarm is sounded* and after these two things take place then comes *"The Day of the LORD."* This is a Day of great darkness and gloominess. There has never been anything like it before and there will never be anything like it again. Yeshua said the same Words in Matthew 24 and you can see that He is talking about the great tribulation, which is the Day of darkness and gloominess, *but the trumpet and the alarm sounded before the Day of darkness came!*

Matthew 24:21 *For then shall be great tribulation, such as was not since the beginning of the world to this time, no, nor ever shall be.*

Ezekiel 33:1-7 *Again the Word of the LORD came unto me, saying, Son of man, speak to the children of the people, and say unto them, When I bring the sword upon a land, if the people of the land take a man of their coasts, and set him for their watchman; If when he seeth the sword come upon the land, he blow the trumpet, and warn the people; Then whosoever heareth the sound of the trumpet, and taketh not warning; if the sword come, and take him away, his blood shall be upon his own head. He heard the sound of the trumpet, and took not warning; his blood shall be upon him. But he that taketh warning shall deliver his soul. But if the watchman see the sword come, and blow not the trumpet, and the people be not warned; if the sword come, and take any person from among them, he is taken away in his iniquity; but his blood will I require at the watchman's hand. So thou, O Son of man, I have set thee a watchman unto the House of Israel; therefore thou shalt hear the Word at My mouth, and warn them from Me.*

When Jeremiah was shown *"the rod of an Almond Tree,"* the LORD was telling Jeremiah to go *"sound the alarm" and warn the people of Israel that the judgment was coming.* It would only come to them if they refused to turn back to God and repent before Him. Jeremiah shattered a clay jar to symbolize the destruction of Jerusalem. What fascinates me so much in this story is that Jeremiah saw *"the Rod of an Almond Tree" just before the tribulation and destruction of Jerusalem by the Babylonians.* During *the destruction of the tribulation,* the feet of Nebuchadnezzar's statue are made of *iron mingled with clay* and Yeshua comes from Heaven to shatter it!

Jeremiah 1:11-12 *Moreover the Word of YHVH came unto me, saying, Jeremiah, what seest thou? And I said, I see a rod of an Almond Tree. Then said YHVH unto me, Thou hast well seen; for I watch over My Word to perform it.*

Notice that the LORD says to Jeremiah, *"I watch over My Word to perform it." The LORD was literally saying to Jeremiah the word for "Almond" in Hebrew, "Shaked" meaning "Watch."* When Jeremiah saw *"the Rod of the Almond Tree,"* he heard *"the Word of the LORD"* who told him to *"sound the alarm"* and He would *"watch"* over His Word to perform it. This proves that Yeshua is the Rod of the Almond Tree and the Word that performs the works of the LORD God. I truly believe now that Jeremiah actually saw *"the Rod of God!"* Jeremiah saw *the Messiah* who was bringing the wrath and judgment against His people who were worshipping the idols that originated in Babylon! *In this situation, the Word of God with the Rod of the Almond Tree appears and the alarm is sounded just before the judgment and tribulation comes.* When I saw this for the first time, I found it to be so astonishing because the LORD showed me His end time Testimony in *"the Rod of an Almond Tree,"* and He gave me *the Rod of a living Almond Tree just before the judgment and tribulation comes!* Here we are near the time of Yeshua's arrival and *I have seen the Rod of an Almond Tree*, and I too, have

heard the Word of the LORD and because of this miracle, I accomplished everything that I could for the glory of the LORD and *I come to you as a watchman on the wall, sounding the alarm. Incredibly, Anne Graham Lotz was sounding the alarm on the Mount of Olives in 2012!* I believe that the LORD is sending out His final message to repent before the final tribulation and judgment that is coming upon all the people that are worshipping the false religious idols of Babylon. I never expected such a coincidence to occur with me and the Prophet Jeremiah!

The word *"Shaked"* is verifying that we need to repent and *"Watch"* because the Messiah is close at hand. When I sent the Almond Tree revelation to Jerusalem and my Almond Tree was just starting to bud and blossom on the LORD'S Holy Mountain called *"Holy Mount Moriah,"* this was more than an incredible miracle, it was absolutely a sign, signaling that we must *"get ready and watch"* because *"THE KING IS IN THE FIELD,"* which is a Jewish phrase leading up to Rosh HaShanah and the High Holy Days in the fall. He is coming! Hallelujah!

"HASTY AWAKENING"

Sunrise after twilight at Boulder Creek CO & Shofar Photo ©2013 Kimberly K Ballard All Rights Reserved

I want to share more about the term *"Hasty Awakening"* that I discovered in the meaning of *"Shaked" or "Almond."* It also pertains to the resurrection of the dead. The LORD used the words *"Awaken, Awake, or Awakening," in reference to this event.* It will occur on *"the Day of the Awakening Blast."* We anticipate it and listen for Him!

Rabbi Simcha Pearlmutter told this story about an event that transpired in Spain during the terrible inquisitions. The Jews were forbidden to worship, but they managed to blow their shofar on Rosh HaShanah even though no Papal Roman Christian understood what was happening. In his own words Rabbi Pearlmutter said the following about it. *Quote: "And all the Jews in the hall knew what was happening. And every heart beat faster. Every ear and every eye watched for and listened for the Mashiach. They knew it, they felt it, they could see Him coming, they could hear Him coming and not a single Christian knew what was happening. Not a single Christian realized that every Jew in that hall was calling upon the name of Yeshua and not upon the name that they had accepted via the Christians under forced conversion, that they were listening to the sound of the shofar and that they were uplifting the name of Yeshua, which had they been discovered, they would have met with a terrible death at the stake."* ***(Source: Rabbi Simcha Pearlmutter, Rabbi testimony of Jesus, Yeshua, Messiah. Full text: jerusalemcalling.org/Rabbi_Simcha_Pearlmutter.htm).*** *The Jews calling Yeshua at Rosh HaShanah is profound!*

It is interesting that Isaiah wrote that *"the dead will rise out of their graves and they will "awake and sing."* After the dead *"awake,"* he said that *"they go into their chambers and they shut their doors."* Now I could clearly discern that Isaiah's text was literally proclaiming

that the resurrected *"awakened" Saints* in this verse are singing praises to the LORD because *He has just resurrected their dead bodies from the grave* and *they came to life to live forever!* I figured out that they are all rejoicing, singing, and *shouting praises* to the Great KING because they were dead, but the LORD just fulfilled His promise to them of everlasting life. So you can imagine how I felt when I realized another name for Rosh HaShanah is *"the Day of Shouting!"* I knew this text in Isaiah was referring to the time of the rapture and resurrection because they are all *singing and shouting* praises to the LORD because death no longer has the victory over them. Messiah Yeshua, who *awakens* them with a shout and with the blast of the Last Trump of God, has just given them the greatest victory over death! The fact that the *awakened Saints* in this text went into their chambers and shut the door behind them provokes a picture of the parable of the virgins. Those *watching* for the Bridegroom were ready to go in through the door when Yeshua opened it.

Isaiah wrote that after they go into their chambers and the doors are shut they are *"hidden away for a little moment until the indignation be overpass."* Rosh HaShanah is incredibly also called *"the hidden day or in Hebrew Yom HaKeseh!"* In Isaiah's text, we see that the LORD then comes to punish the inhabitants of the earth, but the resurrection of the dead has already occurred before the indignation or the righteous anger of the LORD is poured out. The dead that are *awakened from their graves* go into Heaven with Messiah Yeshua and the door is shut until the tribulation is past.

Isaiah 26:19-21 *Thy dead men shall live, together with my dead body shall they arise. Awake and sing, ye that dwell in dust; for thy dew is as the dew of herbs, and the earth shall cast out the dead. Come, My people, enter thou into thy chambers, and shut thy doors about thee; hide thyself as it were for a little moment, until the indignation be overpass. For, behold, the LORD cometh out of his place to punish the inhabitants of the earth for their iniquity; the earth also shall disclose her blood, and shall no more cover her slain.*

As I further pondered Isaiah's text, I was fascinated by his words indicating that those who came out of their graves were resurrected to life and they were hidden in *"chambers"* with their doors shut until the time that *"the indignation be overpass."*

The most exciting thing happened when I looked up the word *"chambers."* I was truly astonished to discover that the *"chambers" are actually connected to the House of the LORD!* I could not believe it! By definition a *"chamber"* is *"a room in a House where a person of authority or rank receives visitors!"* This explained everything to me! Messiah Yeshua is the *Royal Authority* that takes us up in the rapture and resurrection *as His visitors* to dwell in the Father's House in Heaven. Wow, this is so thrilling!

Now Yeshua used the word *"mansions"* in John 14. By definition the term *"mansions"* refers to *"separate dwellings enclosed within a very large, stately House!"* So this new information shows us that when we are raptured to be with the LORD forever, *we will dwell as invited guests in the stately Royal House of God in Heaven.* I already feel like shouting Hallelujah! Yeshua said that *"He was going to prepare a place for us in the mansions that are in the House of God!"* He said He would come back and take us there! This is absolutely the rapture without a doubt!

John 14:2-3 *In My Father's House are many mansions; if it were not so, I would have told you. I go to prepare a place for you. And if I go and prepare a place for you, I will come again, and receive you unto Myself; that where I AM, there ye may be also.*

Notice in the following Psalm that *those who are dwelling in the House of God are blessed,* and they are *"still praising the LORD."* Why are they *"still,"* praising Him, you ask? Because of the fact that death could not keep them in the grave and those who are still living who are *"caught up to meet the LORD in the glory cloud in the air"* went up alive to meet the

LORD Yeshua, so they never experienced the curse of death! They are now dwelling in the LORD'S House *in the mansions, in the chambers,* and they are *"still praising Him"* for His mighty victory of Eternal life over death and of the triumph of good over evil. The word *"Selah" or "Tsela"* here, I believe again, refers to the Bride of Messiah.

Psalm 84:4 *Blessed are they that dwell in Thy House; they will be still praising Thee. Selah.*

Now, the *High Palaces of His Sanctuary* that He built specifically reveals that *His House with many mansions is the official Royal Residence of the KING!*

Psalm 78:69 *And He built His Sanctuary like High Palaces, like the earth which He hath established forever.*

A Palace by definition is *"a large stately mansion of the Royal Sovereign."* Therefore, the Palace of the KING OF KINGS is a very fine, rich, elegant residence. This Royal Palace Residence often has a lovely view, especially when it is built on a hill like the High Palaces of the LORD. Without hesitation, I can say that the gardens and grounds of the Royal Palace are exquisite. Joyful birds come to sing and dwell in the branches of the pristine gardens that are full of hundreds of colorful, vivid, blossoming trees, flowers, and shrubs. Birds and animals are drawn to the Palace grounds because they love to rest in the midst of the pleasant trees in the soft vivid green grass. This is where they feel comfortable, secure, and at peace in the Presence of the Prince of Peace. They also delight as they roam about the Palace grounds, quenching their thirst in the refreshing fountains of Living Water! Does this sound anything like the Palace of the Great KING? It is such a heartwarming thought! The Official Royal Palace Residence with its Heavenly Sanctuary is, without a doubt, so magnificent that the visitors who come to enter into their chambers, that are enclosed within the Royal Palace and House of God, lift up their heads in praise and wonder as they are escorted into this enchanting Heavenly realm. They shut their doors behind them in their chambers because they have entered the Heavenly Ark of salvation. So much creative design and detail has gone into the artistic landscape and buildings of the KING'S Royal Palace Residence, with all of its mansions. The Gardens that are full of lush foliage gently sway in peaceful and serene harmony and the musical sound of rejoicing is blended with the sound of refreshing bubbling springs of Living Water. The Sanctuary of this Royal Palace Residence is by definition *"the Holy Temple of the Great KING."* The Holy of Holies dwells within it and the throne of the Ark of His Royal Majesty, THE KING OF KINGS AND LORD OF LORDS, displays His Eternal Living Covenant and Testimony in this place. The Sanctuary of the Great KING is a sacred and Holy place of worship. Everyone that enters into it will praise the KING forever. He alone is worthy to be praised, so all the Saints are still praising Him, even now!

Baby Rabbit on Palace the grounds!
Photo ©2013 Kimberly K Ballard
All Rights Reserved

Baby Rabbit on the Palace grounds!
Photo ©2013 Kimberly K Ballard
All Rights Reserved

Now I was curious to know the exact meaning of *"indignation" and "overpass."* As I thought about this, I wondered if the definitions within these two words could shed any light on what was truly happening within Isaiah's text. In some Bible translations the word *"overpass"* is written as *"overpast,"* but they have the same meaning. Therefore, I did a little research on these two words. The word *"indignation"* is *"extreme anger that is mingled with disgust, contempt, or abhorrence. It is anger brought*

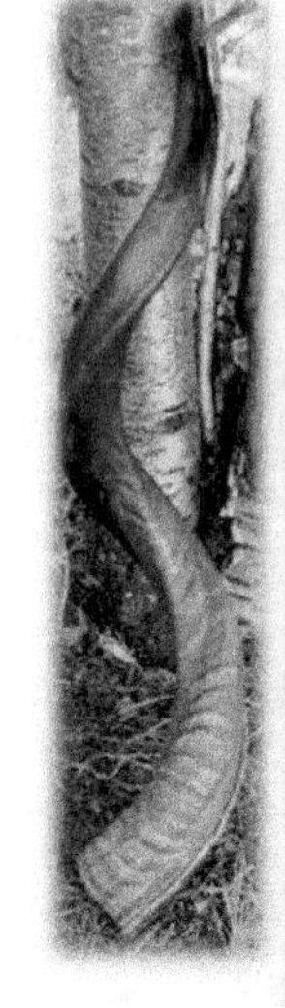

about by something unjust, mean, or unworthy." If you speak of *"righteous indignation"* this refers to *"a reactive emotion of anger of perceived mistreatment or insult, as a result of a sense of injustice."* So this indicates that the tribulation will begin when the LORD arises from His place from the Royal Palace Residence of Heaven. He will certainly have *righteous indignation* during the tribulation when His wrath is poured out because He has been provoked to extreme anger. The Holy Land of Israel, the Temple Mount, and Mount Moriah all belong to the Great KING OF KINGS AND LORD OF LORDS, but the wicked one will try to be elevated in that place instead and he will divide God's Holy Land for selfish gain out of the evil in his own heart. When the Land is divided against His approval, you will see the wrath of God poured out on all who do such evil against the LORD God of Israel. This is also the time when His people are being insulted and mistreated with great injustice as all the enemies of God continue to try and steal what belongs to the LORD God of Israel. When the enemies of the Great KING set up an abhorrence, which is the abomination of desolation, on His Holy Mountain, this will spark the fury of the LORD in *righteous indignation.* Believe me you do not want to insult the KING of Glory! These events will bring about the judgment and tribulation of the last days. The wicked will not get away with their evil plot against the Living God. It is written and it is already determined that vengeance belongs to the LORD of Hosts.

Psalm 7:6 *Arise, O LORD, in Thine anger, lift up Thyself because of the rage of mine enemies; and awake for me to the judgment that Thou hast commanded.*

Now the most exciting and thrilling part of the rapture is something that I found within the definition of the word *"overpass" or "overpast."* I was absolutely astonished and thrilled to discover that within the word *"overpass"* there is a true description of the rapture and meeting the LORD up in the air. I truly had the chills when I saw this for the first time! So, as you read the following definitions of the word *"overpass"* think about what Yeshua said about the *"catching up"* of believers in the rapture! During the resurrection and the rapture, we know that the dead will be raised first and those alive remaining over will be *caught up* together with them in the cloud to meet the LORD in the air and thus we shall always be with the LORD. Think of us *going up into Heaven* in the glory cloud and think of those that are left behind *as remaining on the same level on the earth* where they already are, as they are left in the darkness of the tribulation in judgment. *During the rapture, we are on two different levels when this happens! We are given a passage into Heaven as we rise above what is happening below us,* the moment that the LORD separates the light of the believers from the darkness of the wicked at the sound of *"the Last Trump." Those remaining on the lower level on the earth will actually be the spectators on the ground that will see our low level flight in the upper level above them!* Think of the disciples gazing up as the cloud received Yeshua into Heaven. The disciples were left as spectators on the ground on the earth as they were looking up at Yeshua who was ascending into Heaven in the glory cloud! They were on two different levels! This is an overpass! This is so astonishing!

Definitions of Overpass or Overpast;

1. A bridge formed by the upper level of a crossing of two highways at different levels.
2. A flyover, a fly-past.
3. In Civil Engineering an overpass is a grade separation in which the higher level is raised and traffic at the lower level moves at approximately its original level.
The upper level of such a grade separation.
4. To go over a limit or boundary.
5. Crossing over some barrier.
6. A passage, roadway or bridge that crosses above another roadway.
7. To overpass limits.

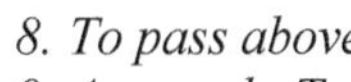

8. To pass above.
9. As a verb; To pass over or traverse a region or space.
10. To pass beyond specified limits or bounds.
11. To pass over, or beyond, across, away or off, to cross.
12. To go over or beyond; to overpass a river, to overpass limits.
13. A low altitude flight usually of military aircraft over spectators on the ground.

Yeshua is coming in *the glory cloud.* One definition of the word *"cloud"* means *"a visible mass of water or ice particles suspended at a considerable altitude."* As the LORD, the Living Water, comes for us in the glory cloud, He is suspended with us in the air! Yeshua is our *passage* into Heaven. He is our *"Passover"* or our *"overpass."* As we cross over from this life into Eternal life, we are changed as we enter the cloud to meet the LORD in the air and we now are *without limits and boundaries!* When this happens suddenly, in the twinkling of an eye, we will have a *low altitude flight over the spectators on the ground!* We will take *the passage or the roadway* leading into Heaven that the LORD has set before us, just like in the Exodus! We will cross over from this life which is limited to Eternal life which is unlimited, and we will go away with the LORD who is going before us *as the Ark of Heaven,* just like Joshua crossed over Jordan with the LORD going before him into the Promised Land. We will be on the *upper level* of the atmosphere, overlooking those who are left at the *lower level* on the earth. Literally, we will be on the *"overpass"* into Heaven as we *"Passover"* to the other side of everlasting life from this life on the earth. This instantaneous flash or *"twinkling of an eye"* that Rabbi Saul spoke about in the rapture is the separation of the light from the darkness at twilight (at morning or night). Just as it is in Civil engineering, *"It is a grade separation, in which the higher level is raised and traffic at the lower level moves at approximately its original level."* Life on the lower level will be going on as usual, moving at the same pace. When we go to be with the LORD, we have no limits because limits only exist in this world, but the LORD has no limits or boundaries in Heaven. The rapture is therefore literally, *"A flyover!" This flyover or flight takes place in the upper atmosphere as the glory cloud overshadows us to be in the Presence of the LORD.* It is written in the ancient Jewish texts, as recorded by the Jewish Historian Flavious Josephus, that Moses prayed the following words to God at the Red Sea. They were trapped between the turbulent waters and the insurmountable mountains. They only had *one way of escape* and it was through the Divine salvation of the LORD. I discovered this thrilling passage about what Moses said! Here is a small portion of it.

Twilight in the morning while the Blood Moon was setting over the west on October 8th 2014 in a rare event called a selenelion Photo ©2014 Kimberly K Ballard All Rights Reserved

Quote from "Antiquities of the Jews by Flavious Josephus" Book 2, Chapter 16 Section 12.16.1

"We despair of any other assistance or contrivance, and have recourse only to that hope we have in Thee; and if there be any method that can promise us an escape by Thy providence, we look up to Thee for it. And let it come quickly, and manifest Thy power to us; and do Thou raise up this people unto good courage and hope of deliverance, who are deeply sunk into a disconsolate state of mind. We are in a helpless place, but still it is a place that Thou possesseth; still the sea is Thine, the mountains also that enclose us are Thine; so that these mountains will open themselves if Thou commandest them, and the sea also, if Thou commandest it, will become dry land. <u>Nay, we might escape by a flight through the air, if Thou shouldst determine we should have that way of salvation.</u> When Moses had thus addressed himself to God, he smote the sea with his rod, which parted asunder at the stroke, and receiving those waters into itself, left the ground dry, <u>as a road and a place of flight</u> for the Hebrews.

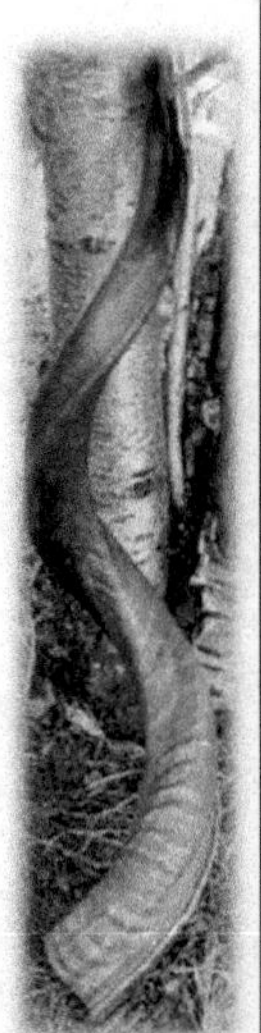

Moses believed that the LORD could provide an escape through the air, if it was His will! After the rapture in the air, the indignation comes upon the earth from the LORD as He separates the

righteous and the wicked. Some are awakened and are raised up from death to life and are taken to *the higher level* as they rise to meet the LORD in the glory cloud in the air, with the living believers, but the wicked shall *remain and are left on the earth at the same level* where they were before. *Messiah is, therefore, "the Passover, the way of salvation, to cross over into Heaven as our roadway or affording passage!"* Remember that the lamb's blood on the doorposts, during the original Passover, did not allow them to experience the judgment of death, but they were given salvation and life! I was so astonished at the depth of meaning that I found within the word *"overpass!"* So this shows us that the rapture and resurrection of the dead was hidden within Isaiah's text and in the prayer of Moses centuries ago. This realization sent a shiver and a chill right through me because it is so astonishing!

In each of the following passages, the LORD speaks of the *"awakening"* that takes place at the resurrection of the dead! *The Shaked, the Almond seed of the Living Torah,* Messiah Yeshua will shout and suddenly the dead will arise out of their graves and experience their great *"Hasty Awakening"* from death to life.

Daniel 12:2 *And many of them that sleep in the dust of the earth shall awake, some to everlasting life, and some to shame and everlasting contempt.*

In the book of Ephesians, we see that when the dead are *"awakened"* in the resurrection, they have Messiah, the light. Notice that this means that they are not in the darkness of the tribulation judgment. They have *awakened from death* and they are now standing in the Divine Presence of Messiah's light in the glory cloud. This is the *overpass* that takes them to the Royal Palace Residence, the Stately House of His Royal Highness, THE KING OF KINGS AND LORD OF LORDS! Then in the following Ephesians passage, we are told that the believers that have the light are not of the darkness, and then it says, *"Awake thou that sleepest, and arise from the dead and Messiah shall give thee light."* Before you get to verse 14, notice that the text clearly says that the wrath of God does not come upon those who have the light of Messiah Yeshua. The wrath of God in the tribulation judgment comes only upon those that are in the darkness of disobedience. The last verse that we come to again, as you will see below, is verse 14 and Messiah *awakens the dead in the resurrection* and they are now in the Divine Presence of the light of Messiah the LORD in the glory cloud in the rapture of believers that have His light, having *no fellowship* with evil.

Ephesians 5:6-14 *Let no man deceive you with vain words; for because of these things cometh the wrath of God upon the children of disobedience. Be not ye therefore partakers with them. For ye were sometimes darkness, but now are ye light in the LORD; walk as children of light; For the Fruit of the Spirit is in all goodness and righteousness and truth; Proving what is acceptable unto the LORD. And have no fellowship with the unfruitful works of darkness, but rather reprove them. For it is a shame even to speak of those things which are done in secret. But all things that are reproved are made manifest by the light; for whatsoever doth make manifest is light. Wherefore He saith, Awake thou that sleepest, and arise from the dead, and Messiah shall give thee light.*

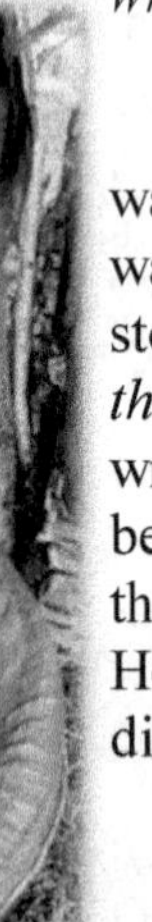

When Jacob *"awakened"* out of his sleep in Bethel, in Israel, He said that the LORD was in this place. Jacob was asleep and was not dead. So it is interesting that as soon as he was *"awakened"* which is *"Shaked"* he immediately saw the LORD before Him. I believe this story reveals that Jacob saw the LORD as the *"Shaked," the Living Almond Rod that Awakens the dead that are asleep.* I wanted to briefly mention this story about Jacob, even though I have written more about him within the last chapter. This story shows us that there is a connection between the *"awakening"* of those who are asleep or dead and those that suddenly find themselves standing in the Divine Presence of Messiah the LORD, instantly recognizing that He is the Almond Tree of Life. Jacob actually saw the Living Testimony of the Messiah and he did not know the LORD was in this place!

Genesis 28:16 *And Jacob awaked out of his sleep, and he said, Surely the LORD is in this place; and I knew it not.*

Isaiah used the word *"Awake"* in connection with *the arm of the LORD* who performs all the works of the LORD. The arm held out holds the Rod of God, the Messiah. It is interesting to note that the arm of the LORD fights the battles of the LORD with *righteous indignation* in Isaiah's Biblical text. This means the arm of the LORD, the Rod, is associated with the *"Awakening"* in the resurrection of the dead, and He comes to destroy Satan.

Isaiah 51:9 *Awake, awake, put on strength, O arm of the LORD; awake, as in the ancient days, in the generations of old. Art thou not it that hath cut Rahab, and wounded the dragon?*

The LORD *"Awakened"* His beloved underneath *"the Fruitful Tree."* This is written in the Biblical text of the Song of Solomon. When Yeshua, the arm of the LORD, *awakens the dead,* they will sit underneath the Almond Tree of Life. Remember that the Holy Spirit of His Eternal Covenant, *the dove of His Peace,* is the seal of life that is sealed upon our hearts and breathes the breath of life into the dead, so they may live again forever. As soon as the resurrection takes place and we are abiding under the Fruitful Tree, the flaming fire of His judgment comes upon the earth at once with no way of escape, just as the Egyptians had no way of escape at the Red Sea crossing after God's people were given *"Yeshua"* by the LORD!

Song of Solomon 8:5-6 *Who is this that cometh up from the wilderness, leaning upon her beloved? Under the apple-tree I awakened thee; there thy mother was in travail with thee; there was she in travail and brought thee forth. Set me as a seal upon thy heart, as a seal upon thine arm; for love is strong as death, jealousy is cruel as the grave; the flashes thereof are flashes of fire, a very flame of the LORD.*

Finally *"the Shaked,"* the Almond Rod, Messiah Yeshua the Branch, was buried in the Garden tomb in the Holy Mountain of God. In this place, on the same mountain where my Almond Tree budded, Yeshua was *"Awakened"* from His sleep, and here He bore the best Fruit of the resurrection of the dead because He grafted Himself back into the Almond Tree of Life in His Garden in Jerusalem. He is very much alive right now showing us His majestic glory!

MESSIAH "AWAKENS" LAZARUS

Glory through the Flowering Tree
Photo ©2013 Kimberly K Ballard
All Rights Reserved

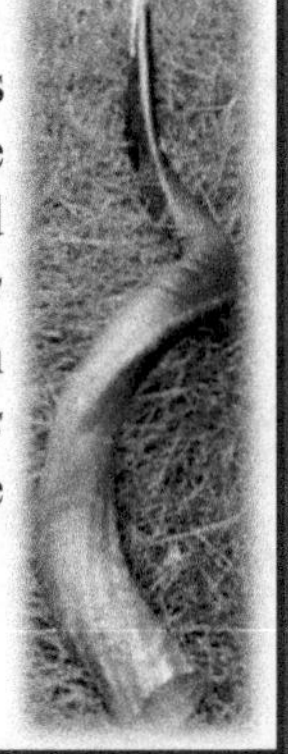

When Yeshua told His Jewish disciples that He was going to Bethany to see Lazarus who had already died, He told them that He was going to go *"Awaken"* him! By saying this, He was testifying that He is the one coming in the future, before the judgment, to raise the dead with the sound of His voice and with the trump of God. *Yeshua demonstrated one of the signs that the LORD showed to Moses, so the people would believe that He is the LORD of Hosts.* In this particular miracle, while raising Lazarus from death to life, Yeshua demonstrated that *He is the Rod of God.* So it was *at the sound of His Master's voice* that Lazarus came forth out of the

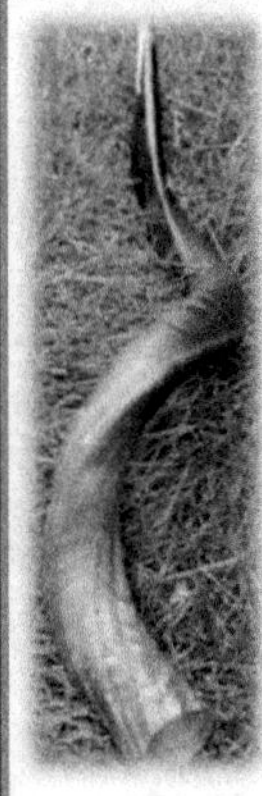

grave where his body had already been corrupted by decay after laying there for four days in the grave. *The Rod of God* was the only one who could restore the decayed flesh and bring this man out of the grave. In the case of Lazarus, when Yeshua said that He would go *"Awake him out of sleep,"* Lazarus was already dead, but Yeshua used the word for Almond, *"Shaked,"* in the *"Awakening"* of the dead. It was Yeshua who spoke with a loud voice and told Lazarus to come forth. Lazarus not only came back to life, but his flesh was completely restored and he walked out of the tomb and stood before his relatives and Jewish friends who stood by *watching!* Notice that the people were, *"watching"* when Yeshua gave the *"shout,"* and then suddenly Lazarus was given a *"Hasty Awakening" at the sound of the Word of God* that came out of Yeshua's mouth, and Lazarus came out of the grave and was resurrected to life! This is the exact order of the resurrection of the dead and the future rapture of living believers that takes place with Messiah Yeshua!

John 11:11-14 *These things said He; and after that He saith unto them, Our friend Lazarus sleepeth; but I go, that I may awake him out of sleep. Then said His disciples, LORD, if he sleep, he shall do well. Howbeit Yeshua spake of his death; but they thought that he had spoken of taking of rest in sleep. Then said Yeshua unto them plainly, Lazarus is dead.*

John 11:39-45 *Yeshua said, Take ye away the stone. Martha, the sister of him that was dead, saith unto Him, LORD, by this time he stinketh; for he hath been dead four days. Yeshua saith unto her, Said I not unto thee, that if thou wouldest believe, thou shouldest see the glory of God? Then they took away the stone from the place where the dead was laid. And Yeshua lifted up His eyes, and said, Father, I thank Thee that thou hast heard Me. And I knew that Thou hearest Me always; but because of the people which standby I said it, that they may believe that Thou hast sent Me. And when He thus had spoken, He cried with a loud voice, Lazarus, come forth. And he that was dead came forth, bound hand and foot with grave clothes; and His face was bound about with a napkin. Yeshua saith unto them, Loose him, and let him go. Then many of the Jews which came to Mary, and had seen the things which Yeshua did, believed on Him.*

Yeshua said that they would see *"the glory of God"* in this miracle. He lifted His eyes, which means that Yeshua was looking up, when He did these things, so they would believe. *The Rod lifted up His eyes and spoke the Word, the Living Torah and Lazarus came forth alive.* Yeshua was performing the signs, miracles, and wonders of the LORD God of Israel. Notice also, that Yeshua spoke in a loud voice. This is exactly what happened to Elisabeth when Mary came to her pregnant with the Messiah and she was *full of the Holy Spirit.* She cried in a loud voice saying, *"Blessed art thou among women and blessed is the Fruit of thy womb."* This also revealed Yeshua as the First Fruit of the Almond Tree of Life. So when Yeshua spoke *the Word of God* in a loud voice, this demonstrated that *He was full of His Ruach/Holy Spirit. He was breathing the breath of life in His Word to Lazarus.* This is exactly what will take place in the future resurrection of the dead. First we were instructed to *"Watch"* for Yeshua's return, and He will give a *"Shout"* at the Last Trump and *those who hear His voice, the Word of God* from the power of the Rod, will come forth out of their graves to their *"Hasty Awakening."*

John 5:25 *Verily, verily, I say unto you, The hour is coming, and now is, when the dead shall hear the voice of the Son of God; and they that hear shall live.*

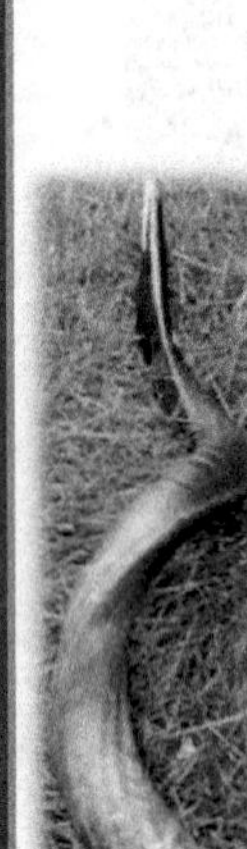

John 5:28 *Marvel not at this; for the hour is coming, in the which all that are in the graves shall hear His voice, And shall come forth; they that have done good, unto the resurrection of life; and they that have done evil, unto the resurrection of damnation.*

I Thessalonians 4:16 *For the LORD Himself shall descend from Heaven with a shout, with the voice of the archangel, and with the trump of God; and the dead in Messiah shall rise first.*

In the first chapter of the book of Revelation, the Jewish disciple, *"John,"* was in Spirit on the LORD'S Day. This is said not to be a reference to the Sabbath day. It is the Hebrew

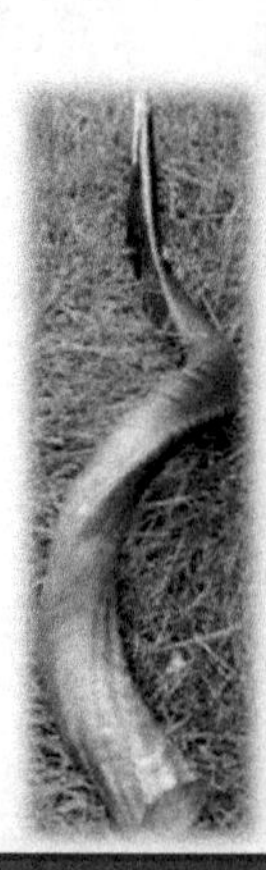

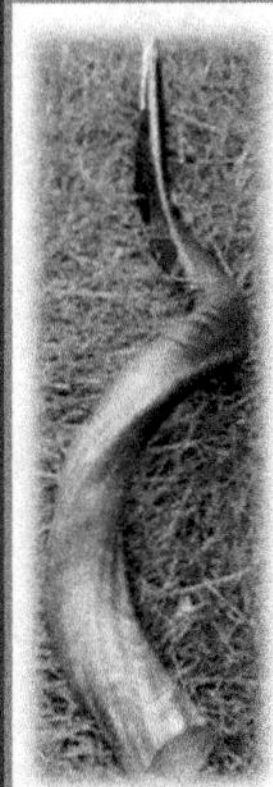

equivalent of saying, *"The Day of the LORD."* With this in mind, take notice that John heard a loud voice speaking to him as a trumpet. This would coincide with the fact that on Rosh HaShanah when the LORD descends from Heaven with a shout and with the trump of God, then the breath of the Spirit of Life revives the dead at Yeshua's Word and the dead will come up out of their graves.

Revelation 1:10 *I was in the Spirit on the LORD'S Day, and heard behind me a great voice, as of a trumpet.*

John turned *"To see the voice that was speaking to him."* After this, John experienced all the events pertaining to Rosh HaShanah, the Feast of Trumpets. First, John saw *a door opened in Heaven.* Then John *heard the voice that sounded like the trumpet.* After this, *the voice* told John to, *"Come up hither."* John was *going up to the place where the voice was speaking to him.* The loud voice came from a level above John, as in the *"overpass,"* and John was down on the earth on the lower level. The definition of the term *"hither"* means *"to go toward the place and to come nearer."* This event took place immediately when John ascended up and he was in Spirit. Instantly, John found himself before the Divine Presence of His Royal Highness, His Majesty the KING OF KINGS in Heaven. John then saw the LORD Yeshua sitting upon His Royal throne, which is the Eternal Ark of His Living Testimony in Heaven!

Revelation 4:1-2 *After this, I looked, and behold, a door was opened in Heaven; and the first voice which I heard was as it were of a trumpet talking with me; which said, Come up hither, and I will shew thee things which must be hereafter. And immediately I was in the Spirit; and, behold, a throne was set in Heaven, and one sat on the throne.*

In the miracles of Yeshua, when He healed the people the change was sudden and it was immediate. As the voice told John to come up to Heaven, he was *immediately* with the LORD and he was standing in His Divine Presence. He had to be changed in order to see the LORD on His throne! This event with John is precisely how the rapture will unfold. We must be changed in the rapture before seeing the LORD! Heaven will be opened on the Feast of Trumpets and the dead will hear His voice. They will rise out of their graves like Lazarus and the living believers will never die. Those who hear *"the Last Trump"* of the LORD will instantly ascend up and find that they are standing in the Divine Presence of the LORD Messiah. The Biblical name *"Lazarus"* is derived from the Hebrew name *"El'azar or Eleazar."* The *"El"* in his name means *"God, might and power."* Yeshua revealed He is God with His might and power, as the Rod of God, when He performed this miracle. It is no coincidence that *"Lazarus" means "God has helped."* Messiah, the Almond Rod went to *"awaken"* Lazarus from death to life. The Rod of God raises the dead and restores the dead flesh back to life again. Yeshua demonstrated this when He healed the lepers and raised others that were dead throughout the Holy Land of Israel.

In the book of Isaiah, the LORD told Israel to *"Awake."* The LORD spoke to them saying, *"My people shall know in that day that I AM He that doeth speak and behold, "It is I."* Yeshua proclaimed the same Words to His Jewish disciples when He approached them walking on the water as *the Rod of God, full of His Holy Spirit.* Yeshua called out to His Jewish disciples in the ship and He said to them, *"Do not be afraid, "It is I."* Yeshua is the same one who declared this same phrase in Isaiah. This is the one who publishes Peace, the *"Sar Shalom, the Prince of Peace."* Messiah publishes peace with His New Covenant of Eternal life.

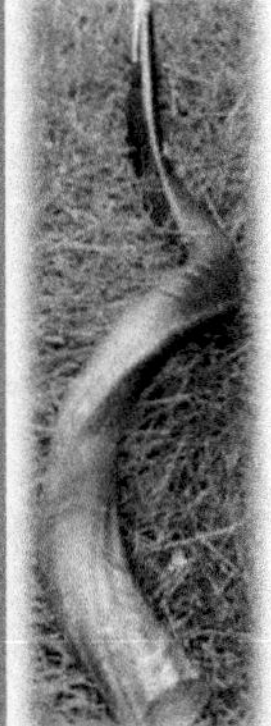

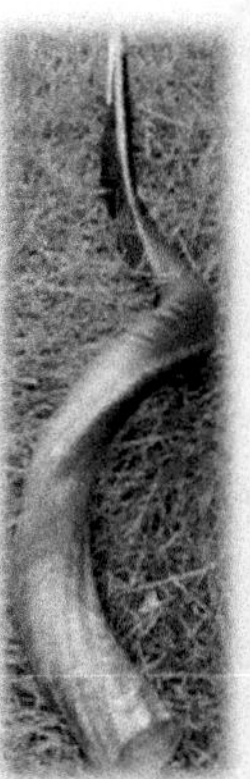

Isaiah 52:1-15 *Awake, awake; put on thy strength, O Zion; put on thy beautiful garments, O Jerusalem, the Holy City; For henceforth there shall no more come into thee the uncircumcised and the unclean. Shake thyself from the dust; arise, and sit down, O Jerusalem; loose thyself from the bands of thy neck, O captive daughter of Zion. For thus saith the LORD, Ye have sold yourselves for nought; and ye shall be redeemed without money. For thus saith the LORD God, My people went down aforetime into Egypt to sojourn there; and the Assyrian oppressed them without cause. Now therefore, what have I here, saith the LORD, that my people is taken away for nought? They*

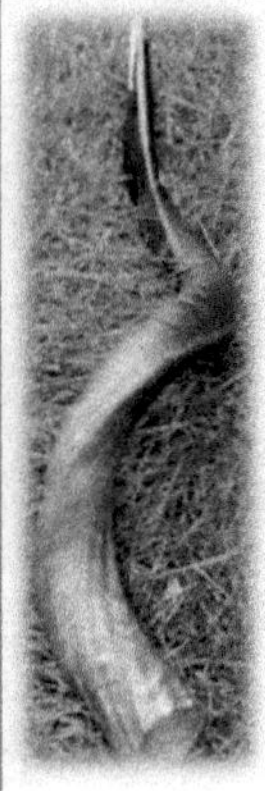

that rule over them make them to howl, saith the LORD; and My Name continually every day is blasphemed. Therefore my people shall know My Name; therefore they shall know in that day that I AM He that doth speak; behold, it is I. How beautiful upon the mountains are the feet of Him that bringeth good tidings, that publisheth peace; that bringeth good tidings of good, that publisheth salvation; that saith unto Zion, Thy God reigneth! Thy watchmen shall lift up the voice; with the voice together shall they sing: for they shall see eye to eye, when the LORD shall bring again Zion. Break forth into joy, sing together, ye waste places of Jerusalem; for the LORD hath comforted His people, He hath redeemed Jerusalem. The LORD hath made bare His Holy Arm in the eyes of all the Nations; and all the ends of the earth shall see the salvation of our God. Depart ye, depart ye, go ye out from thence, touch no unclean thing; go ye out of the midst of her; be ye clean, that bear the vessels of the LORD. For ye shall not go out with haste, nor go by flight; for the LORD will go before you; and the God of Israel will be your reward. Behold, my servant shall deal prudently, he shall be exalted and extolled, and be very High. As many were astonied at Thee; His visage was so marred more than any man, and His form more than the sons of men; So shall He sprinkle many Nations; the kings shall shut their mouths at Him; for that which had not been told them shall they see; and that which they had not heard shall they consider.

Romans 13:11 *And that, knowing the time, that now it is high time to awake out of sleep; for now is our salvation nearer than when we believed.*

The Jewish belief has always been that the soul would leave the body after three days. This is why Yeshua was in the tomb for three days. Yeshua demonstrated with Lazarus, *"the future resurrection of the dead, by the Living Almond Branch."* The entire creation, including the animals and birds, will have the curse of death removed from them in the future redemption. The Bible states in Genesis that there are 4 kinds of flesh. There is one flesh of man, one flesh of birds, one flesh of beasts of the field and one flesh of fish. God made His Covenant with Noah and *all His creation* and His redemption includes them! As I was writing this part of the story, suddenly the interior of the window and the sky outside became a strange shade of orange. This prompted me to get up and go downstairs, so I could figure out exactly what was causing the strange coloration in my window. When I looked outside the door, it was raining. It basically never rains here, so this was a rare moment indeed. The refreshing rain was wonderful and the strange orange glow prompted me to go outside into the yard. When I looked up, I was astonished to see a beautiful full rainbow going completely over my house from one end to the other. I ran inside again to get the camera, to take pictures of this miracle.

This was quite astonishing because for four years in a row now, the same thing has happened during the same week. I talk about this in the last chapter too, but for two years in a row, there was a double rainbow going directly over my house, and then again last year, there was a single rainbow going directly over my house. The rainbow that was outside this time was a single rainbow and this one came a week earlier than usual. This rainbow appeared exactly seven days before the anniversary of the death of my beloved cat who passed away in 2004! Of course, I was just writing about the Hebrew meaning of Lazarus, the one that God helped. I was just getting to the paragraph about all the animals coming to life in the redemption and as I was about to edit that paragraph, I looked over at the picture of my cat on the desk and I said, *"I love you honey and I miss you!"* All of a sudden the window began to glow the strange orange color. This was enough to get my attention to investigate it. I

Jasmine's kitten picture 1986
Photo ©2013 Kimberly K Ballard
All Rights Reserved

The Double Rainbow on August 27th 2014
Photo ©2014 Kimberly K Ballard All Rights Reserved

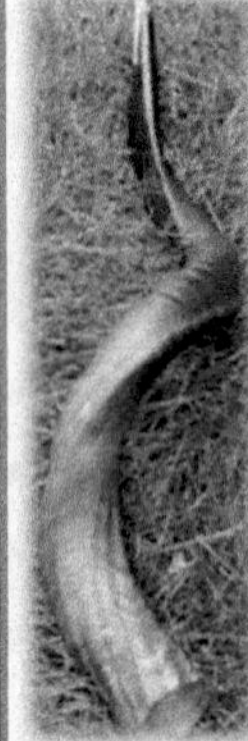

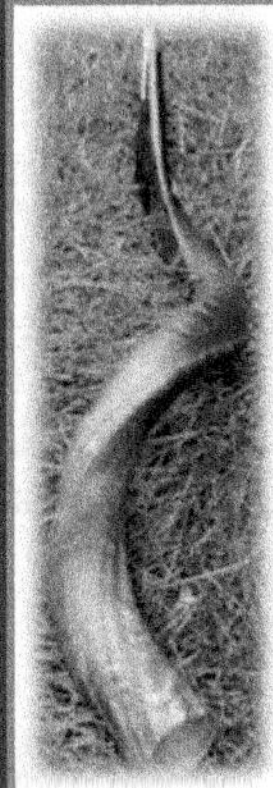

looked at the time and I was shocked to see that the rainbow with the vivid sky appeared at 8PM. This is an extremely unusual time to find a rainbow arching over your house from one end to the other! Noah's rainbow was a Covenant with all the living creatures that God saved in the Ark. What a beautiful gift from the LORD! I also must mention that as I was doing the very final editing, I was searching for my source for the *"Jesus Boat."* Remember that rainbow that appeared over the *"Jesus Boat" as they excavated it from the Sea of Galilee?* I put my *"Jesus Boat"* DVD down because the sky was dark outside on one side, and light on the other. I knew a rainbow was coming with rain! I went outside to find another double rainbow going over my house on July 23, 2014! When I went back upstairs I saw that the paragraph I was working on was about the *"Jesus Boat"* rainbow! It was beautiful! Then a few weeks later when I was reducing the fonts and again I reached the part of my book that had the photos of the *"Jesus Boat"* in it, another double rainbow appeared outside on August 27th, 2014, and it was quite spectacular and stayed for a very long time! It is vivid even in black and white!

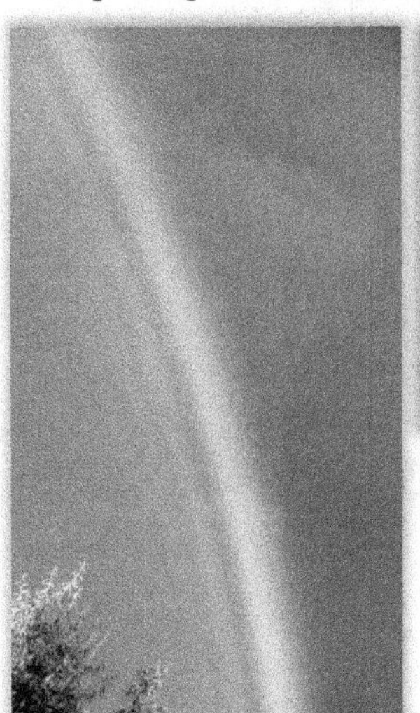

Double Rainbow over the house on August 27th 2014
Photos ©2014 Kimberly K Ballard All Rights Reserved

While I was still thinking about the resurrection of the dead I wanted to bring up a great discovery in Israel that included Lazarus, and now I mention it in reference to Mary and Martha, the close friends of Messiah Yeshua. On November 13, 1873 a great archaeological discovery was made near Jerusalem. A cave was discovered near Bethany by Charles Claremont-Gannueau, who was a French Christian Archaeologist. Within this cave near Bethany, he found a group of first century Jewish ossuaries. The ossuaries contained the names of Mary, Martha, and Eleazar or Lazarus. The ossuaries, although Jewish, bore the inscription of the cross along with the Name *"Yeshua."* These were among the first Jewish Christians who lived at the time of Yeshua, the Messiah. Later in 1873, a man was constructing his house on the eastern slope of the Mount of Olives and he came across the same cave. The bone boxes were all inscribed with the Jewish names of many of the New Testament believers. The most astonishing find of all was the ossuary of Simon Bar Jonah or the disciple Simon Peter whose bone box not only differed in shape, but it also bore a large cross that was etched beneath his name and it was dated to the first century. This incredible Biblical archaeological evidence was hushed up by those that did not want it known that Simon Peter or Simon Bar Jonah was not buried in Rome. He was buried on the eastern slope of the Mount of Olives near Bethany and his bone box was discovered within a short distance of the burial place of Mary, Martha, and Lazarus, along with Salome. This miraculous discovery sadly never received any attention in the media. The ossuary bearing the name *"Salome"* was important to me because I knew that *"Salome"* came to the Garden tomb with Mary Magdalene and Mary to anoint Messiah Yeshua for His burial, but she is often overlooked.

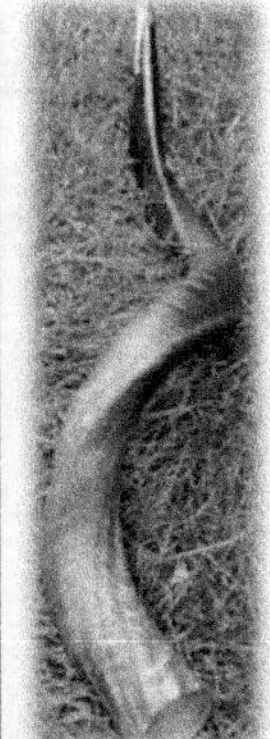

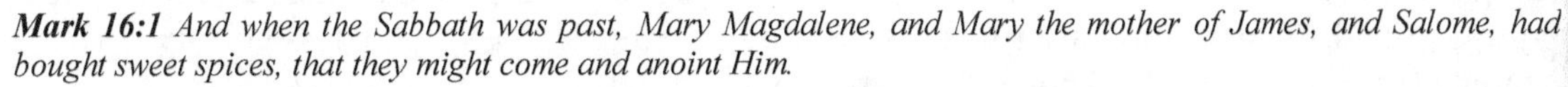

Mark 16:1 *And when the Sabbath was past, Mary Magdalene, and Mary the mother of James, and Salome, had bought sweet spices, that they might come and anoint Him.*

Mark 15:40-41 *There were also women looking on afar off; among whom was Mary Magdalene, and Mary the mother of James the less and of Joses, and Salome; Who also, when He was in Galilee, followed Him, and ministered unto Him; and many other women which came up with Him unto Jerusalem.*

Salome was also one of the loyal women to Messiah Yeshua who witnessed the crucifixion as she watched from afar. Salome followed Yeshua from Galilee with the other women. I believe that her husband's ossuary was also buried in this place and it was inscribed with the name *"Judah,"* indicating that he was from the tribe of Judah, like Yeshua. The most astonishing detail about Salome, though, is the fact that she was considered to be the mother of the son's of Zebedee! So Salome was the mother of the brothers, James and John, the Jewish fishermen, who were disciples of Messiah Yeshua and they were business partners with Simon Peter or Simon Bar Jonah and his brother Andrew Bar Jonah. They owned the ships that Yeshua sat in when He preached *the Living Torah* to the Jewish people. When Yeshua performed the miracle of the fishes, it was Simon's ship that was filled up and James and John came to help with their ship to get the rest of the fish! For this reason I do believe that *"The Jesus Boat"* that was excavated that I showed you earlier in photographs was this very ship!

Matthew 27:55-56 *And many women were there beholding afar off, which followed Yeshua from Galilee, ministering unto him; Among which was Mary Magdalene, and Mary the mother of James and Joses, and the mother of Zebedee's children.*

Double Rainbow over my house August 27th 2014
Photo ©2014 Kimberly K Ballard All Rights Reserved

If Judah was Salome's husband, then his full name was *"Judah Zebedee."* When the Zebedee brothers went to follow the Messiah, *the Heavenly Ark,* they left their father, *"Zebedee,"* in the ship and they followed the Heavenly Father!

Mark 1:19-20 *And when He had gone a little farther thence, He saw James the son of Zebedee, and John his brother, who also were in the ship mending their nets. And straightway He called them; and they left their father Zebedee in the ship with the hired servants, and went after Him.*

Also there was found in the same burial cave, an ossuary of a man who was called *"Simeon the Priest, who served in the Holy Temple." I believe without a shadow of doubt that this "Simeon, the Priest" was likely the same Simeon who dedicated the baby Messiah Yeshua in the Holy Temple just before he died in peace, knowing that he had lived to see the Saviour Messiah, the KING of Israel. One thing is for certain, these faithful loyal followers of Messiah Yeshua will one day come out of their graves in the resurrection to a "hasty awakening."* ***(Source: Pubblicazioni Dello Studium Biblicum Franciscanum N. 13 "GLI SCAVI DEL "DOMINUS FLEVIT" Parte I LA Necropoli Del Periodo Romano & P. B. Bagatti & J. T. MILIK ©1958 source; jamestabor.com).***

As I studied the truth about Mary Magdalene, I realized that she was the most beautiful faithful follower of the LORD, Yeshua. Mary was given the great blessing of being the first one to witness the resurrection of the LORD in Mount Moriah, the Holy Mountain and Garden of God. Mary was faithful to the LORD at the crucifixion and she was present at His burial. She faithfully honored the LORD. I want to set the record straight! *Mary Magdalene was a righteous Holy Jewish woman and she was never a prostitute or harlot.* She has been falsely portrayed and slandered by unscrupulous people for centuries that wanted to portray her in a degraded manner for evil purposes. Far from being a harlot, *Mary of Magdala was the most wonderful, loving, kind, and compassionate Jewish woman who loved the LORD with all her heart and she followed the Lamb wherever He went!* After the LORD revealed so much to me

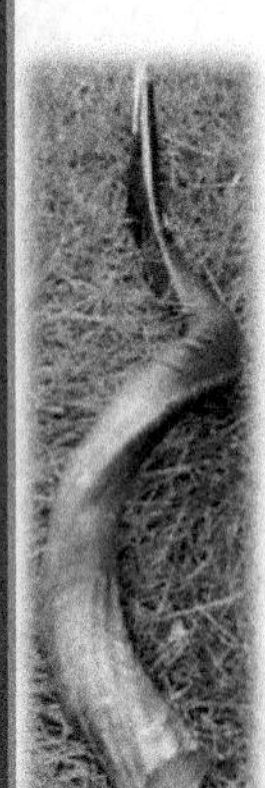

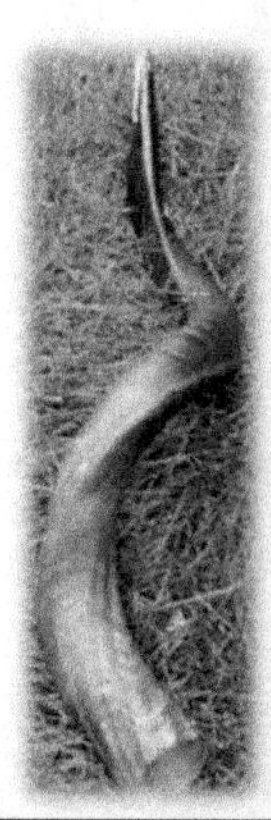

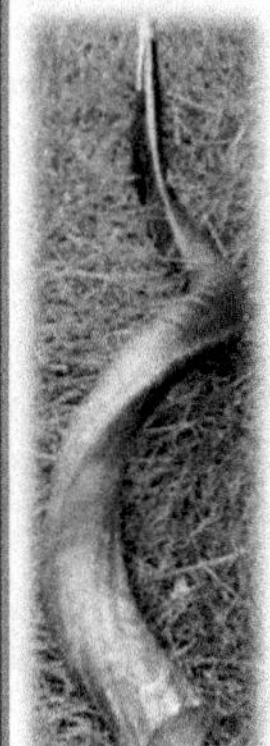

about Mary Magdalene, I truly began to understand what an important role she played in the final redemption and I just discovered the most fantastic part of her story!

As usual, the women back then barely received the credit that they were due and deserved and Mary is no exception. When all the other disciples abandoned Messiah Yeshua, Mary remained loyal and extremely faithful to God. I believe that she was humble and pure in heart. Can you imagine how incredible Mary's *awakening* will be when she hears the sound of His voice and the trumpet call of Yeshua, the LORD?

All of these other Jewish believers, including Mary, Martha, Lazarus, Simeon the Priest, Salome and Judah will *"awaken"* from their graves and they will rise up in the glory cloud to meet the LORD in the air at the resurrection of the dead because they loved Yeshua, and they had the privilege of living in His Divine Presence and they knew Him personally. They believed by faith in the resurrection of the dead and they will not be disappointed!

This brings to mind another exciting archaeological discovery. In the year 1990, the ossuary of Caiaphas the High Priest was unearthed in a tomb in Jerusalem and it contained human remains! It was featured in archaeological magazines, such as the *"BAR," Sept/Oct. 1992 article.*

Double Rainbow when I worked on the section about the "Jesus Boat"

Now it seems so incredible to me that they actually removed the ossuary of Caiaphas from its original burial location and they reburied it upon the Mount of Olives. This gave me a shiver when I suddenly realized that when the resurrection of the dead occurs, Caiaphas will rise up and come face to face with the one that he condemned 2,000 years ago. He will be trembling! So Caiaphas will see Yeshua come down from Heaven and set His feet upon the Mount of Olives and the land will be made cleft before Him. It is chilling to think about. If the remains of Caiaphas had not been reburied in this new location on the Mount of Olives, then he would not be front and center to see Messiah Yeshua, the KING of Israel in all His glory, when He returns from Heaven. Caiaphas will come face to face with Yeshua who is indeed THE KING OF KINGS AND LORD OF LORDS. He will be shocked!

When these people come out of their graves they will experience the most glorious *"Hasty Awakening"* to Eternal life. Yeshua is our *Passover and our overpass* to cross over into the Eternal Promised Land called *"Heaven." For behold! I have seen the Rod of an Almond Tree! He is the voice of our "Hasty Awakening" and He is our reason to "Watch!"*

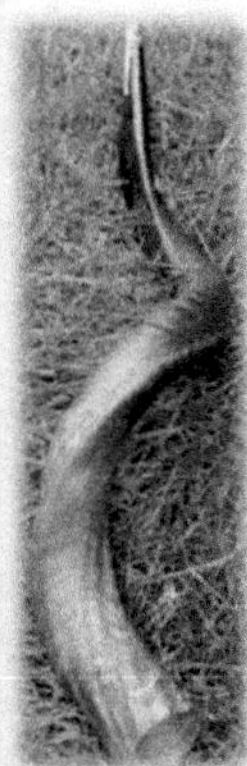

The LORD is coming in the cloud WATCH!

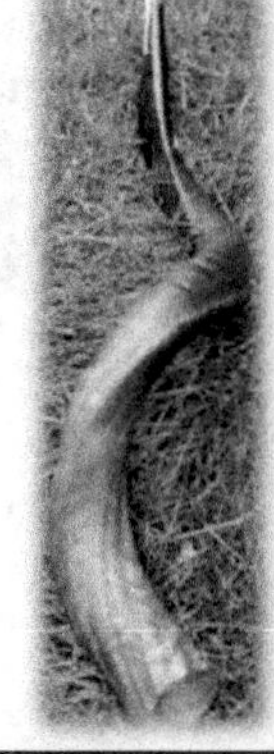

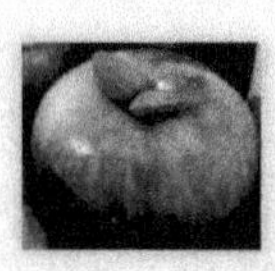

THE LIVING BRANCH PRODUCED BITTER AND SWEET ALMONDS

Almond Tree Menorah made of Almonds & Snow & Almonds on an Apple

The next portion of my Almond Tree miracle is extremely stunning! I can hardly wait to show it to you! There are two types of Almonds. There are *bitter* Almonds and there are *sweet* Almonds. In traditional Judaism, Aaron's rod not only came to life, budded and bore the fruit of Almonds, *but one side of his living branch bore bitter Almonds and the other side of his living branch bore sweet Almonds.* It is said that in ancient times, the LORD told Israel that if they obeyed Him, they would receive the *sweet Almonds,* but if they did not hearken unto His voice and obey His Commandments, they would receive the *bitter Almonds.* The fabulous part of this miracle, though, is not merely in the fact that Aaron's rod bore both *bitter and sweet Almonds,* but in the fact that Messiah Yeshua, as the Living Branch from the Almond Tree of Life, *also bore both the bitter and the sweet Almonds! This morning, I woke up startled with the most incredible truth that came into my mind about the bitter and sweet Almonds that were on Aaron's rod that budded to life. The LORD showed my heart this morning that this has everything to do with the Garden of Eden and the Garden tomb of Yeshua.* This Garden is of course in Holy Mount Moriah, the same Mountain where the LORD placed His Name forever and it is the same place where Abraham was told to take Isaac to offer him to the LORD God. It came to me at about 6AM this morning that after the resurrection occured, Messiah Yeshua was standing alive in the Garden next to the tomb that was hewn out of the rock in the Mountain of God, and this brings to mind a Scripture that is written in Isaiah.

Isaiah 51:1-6 *Hearken to Me, ye that follow after righteousness, ye that seek the LORD; look unto the rock whence ye are hewn, and to the hole of the pit whence ye are digged. Look unto Abraham your father, and unto Sarah that bare you; for I called him alone, and blessed him, and increased him. For the LORD shall comfort Zion; He will comfort all her waste places; and He will make her wilderness like Eden, and her desert like the Garden of the LORD; joy and gladness shall be found therein, thanksgiving, and the voice of melody. Hearken unto Me, My people; and give ear unto Me, O My nation; for a Law shall proceed from Me, and I will make My judgment to rest for a light of the people. My righteousness is near; My salvation is gone forth, and Mine arms shall judge the people; and the isles shall wait upon Me, and on Mine arm shall they trust. Lift up your eyes to the Heavens, and look upon the earth beneath; for the Heavens shall vanish away like smoke, and the earth shall wax old like a garment, and they that dwell therein shall die in like manner; but My salvation shall be forever, and My righteousness shall not be abolished.*

Grapevine Photo ©2014 Kimberly K Ballard All Rights Reserved

Mount Moriah contains the grotto of Jeremiah and it was used as a rock quarry. It was indeed *"a hole with a pit,"* just as the LORD declared it, and the tomb of Yeshua was not a cave, it was literally hand hewn in the side of Mount Moriah from this same rock! When the LORD said, *"Look to the rock out of which you were hewn,"* this was the place that Adam was created out of this same rock! This is when I first realized, by the power of the Holy Spirit, *that this was the location of the Garden of Eden and the place where the LORD planted a Garden with His Royal vineyard!* Yes I did mention before that one of the largest wine presses ever found in Israel is located in this area of the Garden tomb in the Holy Mountain of God and the experts do believe that it was a vineyard! *It was the vineyard that the LORD planted in the beginning!*

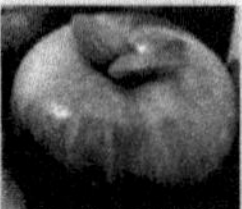

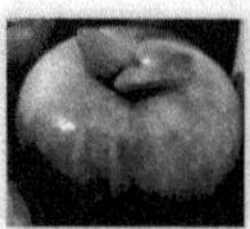

Rock samples from the Garden Tomb

MELEKE LIMESTONE AND THE SERPENTINE

My Meleke Limestone from Israel on snow

Simon's friend Peter in the Garden Tomb

Now, before I go on with the story about the *bitter and sweet Almonds,* something came up about this hewn rock that I felt that I should include here. I had already said that Adam was created out of this rock on Holy Mount Moriah and the Garden tomb is part of this rock. On February 3rd 2012, I asked Simon Brown in England if he had tested his rock samples from the Mount Nebo Rolling Stone and from inside the Garden tomb to see what type of rock they were. In my mind, I was thinking that if he found out that his samples contained travertine aragonite, this could connect his samples to the Shroud of Turin because the Shroud of Yeshua bears small traces of travertine aragonite from Jerusalem. I wrote several emails to him and I finally asked him point blank if his rock samples were determined to be *"Limestone."* He finally wrote back to me and said, "*Yes, I believe that is what the Scientist told me, it is Limestone.*" Then he told me, *"The rock sample from the Rolling Stone on Mount Nebo was found to be identical to the rock sample from the Garden tomb."* Then Simon Brown added, *"No doubt whatsoever, the Scientist told me."* So right after he verified that it was *Limestone,* the LORD opened another insight to me that was simply fantastic!

Simon's rock samples from the Garden Tomb (left)
And from The Mount Nebo Great Rolling Stone (right)

There are three basic types of *Limestone* in Jerusalem. The one that really stood out to me was called *"Meleke Limestone"* because I had already studied the archaeological excavations of Sir Charles Warren at the Holy Temple Mount in Jerusalem from the late 1800's. So I knew that the Hebrew word *"Melech"* was discovered in some of the artifacts from the South East angle and that this word meant *"King." I was therefore absolutely speechless when I realized that this Limestone at the Garden tomb could in fact be Meleke Limestone or "The King's Limestone."* Simon was told that his rock samples were just common rock, so this is what he told me, but he was about to get a very big surprise! I wrote the results of my investigation in the following brief letter to him because I was so excited and astonished!

Letter I Sent to Simon Brown in England; Friday, February 3, 2012 3:50 PM:

Ha, Ha! Praise God I am jumping up and down but you can't see me over there in England! No, there is something very special about this Rock! Yes it is common as you say, but it was used for *someone extremely special.* The LORD just showed me something, and my eyes filled with tears. I am about to *"rock"* your world! This Limestone, I believe the LORD just showed me is *"Meleke Limestone"* from Jerusalem. Do you know what that means? No? It means, *"KINGLY STONE, ROYAL STONE!" THIS WAS THE TOMB OF THE GREAT KING!* You have a treasure in your hands! A great treasure! If there is travertine aragonite in the stone that would likely connect it to the Shroud of Turin. *(End of my letter to England).*

The name Meleke Limestone means *"Kingly Stone" and "Royal Stone."* Most impressive of all though is the fact that it is called *"THE ROYAL STONE OF KING'S."* Wow! This was fantastic! *So if this was in fact "Meleke Limestone" then Yeshua, the KING of the Jews, the KING OF ISRAEL, was proven to be buried with the rich, exactly as the Scriptures in Isaiah foretold and this was God's Holy Mountain.* The round style of Rolling Stone, like the one used to seal Yeshua's sepulchre, was used only for the wealthy. Remember that Joseph of Arimathaea, who buried Yeshua in his own hewn tomb, was a rich man, *so he would have chosen the place with the finest Royal Stone in the quarry for the greatest KING of glory!*

Isaiah 53:8-9 *He was taken from prison and from judgment; and who shall declare His generation? For He was cut off out of the land of the living; for the transgression of My people was He stricken. And He made His grave with the wicked, and with the rich in His death; because He had done no violence, neither was any deceit in His mouth.*

There was no deceit in Messiah Yeshua's mouth because He speaks *the Living Torah*, the Word of God. This is why He confounded the Jewish Torah Scholars in the Holy Temple at age 12! They were all astonished at His understanding of the meaning within *the Torah* and He was teaching them as *"the Rabbi of Righteousness!"* They did not understand that the LORD was dwelling in their midst and He was teaching them astonishing truths about His Word!

Now there was something else that was quite profound about the *Meleke Limestone.* I discovered that this rock is said to be fairly soft when it is first quarried. It is said that *"it is soft enough to cut with a knife when first quarried, but this stone later hardens into very strong solid Limestone and it is extremely erosion resistant."* This is the reason why Golgotha has remained very much the same over 2,000 years and has not eroded away in Holy Mount Moriah! These special qualities made the *Meleke Limestone* the perfect choice for constructing the fabulous stone buildings in and around Jerusalem. It was this particular stone that was used and quarried by King Solomon to build the First Holy Temple. For the first time in my life, I could now understand how Joseph of Arimathaea could have fairly easily cut the rock for his own hand hewn tomb in Holy Mount Moriah that later hardened. ***(Sources: Soft when quarried and hardens; (thefullwiki.org/Meleke), Jerusalem stone at the Garden tomb Meleke; (en.wikipedia.org/wiki/Jerusalem_stone).***

Another detail about this *Kingly Royal Stone* that I just find to be so remarkable is the fact that Yeshua's body did not see decay and corruption, just like the *Royal Kingly rock* that He was laid upon in the Garden tomb that was also erosion resistant. The LORD made sure that His permanent memorial would last for more than 2,000 years. *The KING OF KINGS was therefore laid upon only the finest Royal Stone of KING'S within this quarry in the Holy Mountain of God.* The corner photos on this page are my own samples from this quarry.

How could all of these facts come together like this and why did I suddenly decide to ask what type of rock Simon Brown's samples were? I had forgotten, though, until the LORD reminded me, that a couple of years earlier before meeting Simon online, I had ironically been given my own rock samples from this quarry that had never been tested! These unexpected discoveries, I believe, came at such a time as this to show that Messiah Yeshua's Testimony is perfect and I humble myself in awe of His glorious power, for He has performed mighty deeds!

On Sunday February 5th 2012, just after the Holy Spirit showed me the connection of Yeshua to the *Meleke Limestone,* Simon emailed a photograph to me. It was a picture of his friend Peter squatting down inside the burial niche of Yeshua in the Garden tomb in the hewn out rock of Mount Moriah. It was quite ironic that here I was receiving a letter from *"Simon"* who was sending me a photograph of his friend *"Peter"* who was standing in Yeshua's sepulchre! *"Simon Peter"* was, of course, one of the disciples who ran to Yeshua's tomb, and when he went inside, he found Yeshua's burial Shroud and head linen lying there.

As I studied the photograph, I was looking at Peter squatting down in the niche in the place where the body of Yeshua would have rested 2,000 years ago and I noticed something unusual about the wall behind him. I noticed that there was a change in the color of the stone in the niche at the level where Peter was squatting down. I could see this strange green line that appeared to be running straight across in a level line from a certain point, going downward in the sepulchre. From that green line and downward, in his color photo, the stone appeared to be a mottled green color, but above the green line, the rock was a sandy color. So I wrote to Simon and asked him if he had seen this green color before in the stone. I said the following to him in my email.

Garden Tomb Sepulchre in Jerusalem & Simon's friend "Peter" squatting down
My arrows are pointing to the line that I saw on the wall behind Peter
Original Photograph ©2011 Simon Brown England
All Rights Reserved – Photo Edited by Kimberly K Ballard

"You know Simon, I just noticed something interesting where Peter is squatting down. I noticed that there is a distinct line that starts part way down the wall and it is a different color, almost green in the stone. It's almost as if that part of the stone, in the lower half of the niche, was covered for a long time and then opened. Hmmm, I will have to ponder that and see if the Holy Spirit will reveal anything about it to me. Do you see what I mean? The line goes from just where Peter's pants start at the end of his white shirt and it comes toward you in a perfect straight line. There must be something that caused this green line and the color difference." Blessings, Kimberly

After I noticed the green coloration in the lower half of the rock, I proceeded to wait and see if the Holy Spirit would reveal anything about it to me. If there was anything to be discovered in the green color, I knew that the LORD would reveal it to me, since He had brought it to my attention for some reason, but I did not know why yet. I probably only noticed this green line in the stone because for years I kept a fish aquarium. The algae in the tank would grow and leave a green line straight across the glass from a certain point and downward. Below this green line, the green algae clung to the glass, but above the green line, the glass was crystal clear. For this reason, I suspected that perhaps the green coloration in the Garden tomb niche was some type of mineral or moisture marking in the stone. Before I did much searching though, the LORD miraculously gave me the answer! This discovery not only completely shocked me, but it verified my entire book! First of all Yeshua was the LORD, the Living Water and His body had rested in this stone. The LORD then showed me that it was indeed a green mineral and the name of the mineral that was causing the green coloration in the *Meleke Limestone* was unbelievably called *"Serpentine."* The Serpentine green is said *"to occur in Limestone that bears a high ratio of magnesium silicate."*

After I discovered this green mineral was likely the culprit in the Garden tomb, I found a statement that was written in the 1911 Classic Encyclopedia about Serpentine and I have to say, I was floored by it! The Holy Spirit gave me this answer!

SERPENTINE "A mineral which, in a massive and impure form, occurs on a large scale as a rock, and being commonly of variegated colour, is often cut and polished, like marble, for use as a decorative stone. It is generally held that the name was suggested by the fancied resemblance of the dark mottled green stone to the skin of a serpent, but it may possibly refer to some reputed virtue of the stone as a cure for snake-bite. Although popularly called a "Marble," serpentine is essentially different from any kind of limestone, in that it is a magnesium silicate, associated however, with more or less ferrous silicate. (Continued) The purest kind of serpentine, known as "noble serpentine," is generally of pale greenish or yellow colour, slightly translucent, and breaking with a rather bright conchoidal fracture. It occurs chiefly in granular limestone, and is often accompanied by forsterite, olivine or chondrodite." ***(Source: Encyclopedia Britannica, Classic ©1911 11th Edition).***

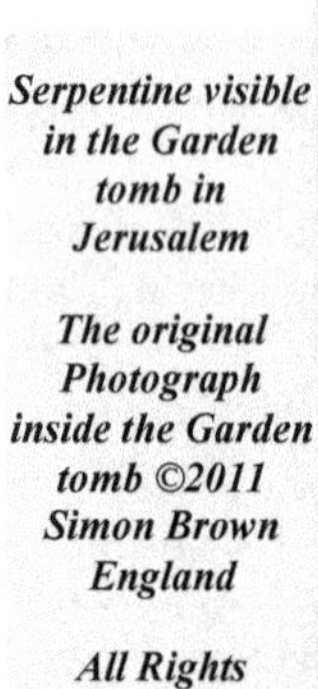

Serpentine visible in the Garden tomb in Jerusalem

The original Photograph inside the Garden tomb ©2011 Simon Brown England

The stunning connection between the green mottled stone in the sepulchre of Yeshua drove home the fact that Yeshua's Words came true! I instantly saw, within this description, one of the greatest final pieces of the puzzle of the Messiah. This took me back to the beginning to what had originally started my journey in writing this book in the first place. Remember that my miracle had all started when I questioned the meaning of Yeshua's statement to Nicodemus when He said, *"As Moses lifted up the serpent on a pole in the wilderness, so too must the Son of man be lifted up, so that all who believe in Him would not perish, but have everlasting life." Here* in the Garden of God, *where Yeshua the Rod of God had rested,* was the mottled green stone referring to *"the virtue of the stone, as a cure for the snake-bite!"* I think I just about fell over in total astonishment! Whoa! What this revealed was marvelous! In the place where Yeshua came to life as the Living Almond Branch, the Rod of God, He swallowed up the curse of death from Satan, *"the serpent,"* and this green coloration just happened to be in the Garden tomb where *"the serpent"* thought that he had won! Instead of the serpent having the victory over us with the curse of death, however, Yeshua came to life from being the cut off dead Branch, *and unbelievably, He is the Rock from God's quarry that became the cure for the snake bite in the Garden of God in the place of the Garden of Eden, as the Rod was lifted up alive in this same place!*

3D Hologram of Yeshua's face on His burial Shroud
Upper right & left Photographs ©2013 Dr. Petrus Soons
From Enrie Photographs ©1931 All Rights Reserved

THE ROCK QUARRY

My small cut rock samples from this quarry in Jerusalem Israel (To the right & left of the title) Cut, Finished & polished Jerusalem Stone from Israel (background tile) & a large local white stone (center) Photos ©2013 Kimberly K Ballard All Rights Reserved

Now, as I said before, the area of Golgotha is an ancient rock quarry and for centuries it has been known as *"Solomon's Quarries."* It was from this quarry that the ancient stones were chiseled and removed out of the rock and they were taken to be used in the construction of Solomon's Holy Temple and to build the city of Jerusalem! My photos above show the cut stone from this quarry from 2010! Now after having written that the LORD said, *"Look to the rock out of which you were hewn,"* there was something deeper within this detail that was stunning. So now, Yeshua as the second Adam bore the curse of death from *"the serpent"* in the Garden of Eden and *Yeshua was laid in the very same rock out of which Adam was brought forth to life from the foundation stone in the beginning in Holy Mount Moriah! So when Yeshua came to life, He reversed the curse that originated here in the Garden of God!* Yeshua's Testimony reveals *He is the Alpha and Omega, the Beginning and the End, the First and the Last!* Ironically, these titles are written inside Yeshua's Garden sepulchre above the place where His body was resurrected from death to life, thereby defeating the serpent! He first appeared to Mary Magdalene here and she went to get the men to witness this Testimony.

The LORD of Hosts said that He is this *"Rock of offense and Stone of stumbling!"* The LORD said, *"Whoever believeth on Him shall not be ashamed!"* This is the LORD'S Testimony of the Living Torah that He faithfully sealed among His disciples! Through the centuries many would stumble because of this Jewish Messiah.

Isaiah 8:13-16 *Sanctify the LORD of Hosts Himself; and let Him be your fear, and let Him be your dread. And He shall be for a Sanctuary; but for a Stone of stumbling and for a Rock of offense to both the Houses of Israel, for a gin and for a snare to the inhabitants of Jerusalem. And many among them shall stumble, and fall, and be broken, and be snared, and taken. Bind up the Testimony, seal the Law among My disciples.*

***Romans 9:31-33** But Israel, which followed after the Law of righteousness, hath not attained to the Law of righteousness. Wherefore? Because they sought it not by faith, but as it were by the works of the Law. For they stumbled at that stumbling Stone; As it is written, Behold, I lay in Zion a stumbling Stone and Rock of offense; and whosoever believeth on Him shall not be ashamed.*

The story is about to get even more exciting because my heart knew that Yeshua the LORD was indeed *"The Rock"* that was quarried and removed out of God's Holy Mountain. It was out of *this Rock* that we were hewn! Adam was created out of this Rock and he was made in the image of God! *Probably the most astonishing thing that I just realized about this is the fact that when a rock is quarried out of a Mountain, the removed rock leaves behind a reverse impression of itself in the place where it once stood!* Wow! Do you see how profound this is? *Yeshua is "The Rock" that was quarried out of God's Holy Mount Moriah in the location of the Garden of Eden as the perfect second Adam without the curse of death. This means that when the true Rock came out of the quarry of God's Holy Mountain, as the Living Almond Branch, Yeshua left behind a negative impression of Himself upon His linen burial Shroud. He came out of the rock quarry that contained the Royal Stone of KING'S! So if this "Rock" left an "impression" where He was quarried out of God's Holy Mountain, then we should find a reverse impression of Yeshua inside the Garden sepulchre in Solomon's rock quarry.* The reverse or negative impression of Yeshua would then be found in the place where His body was resting upon the *Royal Kingly stone,* in the rock hewn sepulchre of Mount Moriah. We should therefore find more details about the Messiah's resurrection in the definition of the word *"impression."*

3D Hologram of Yeshua's face Shroud Photographs ©2013 Dr. Petrus Soons from Enrie Photos ©1931 All Rights Reserved

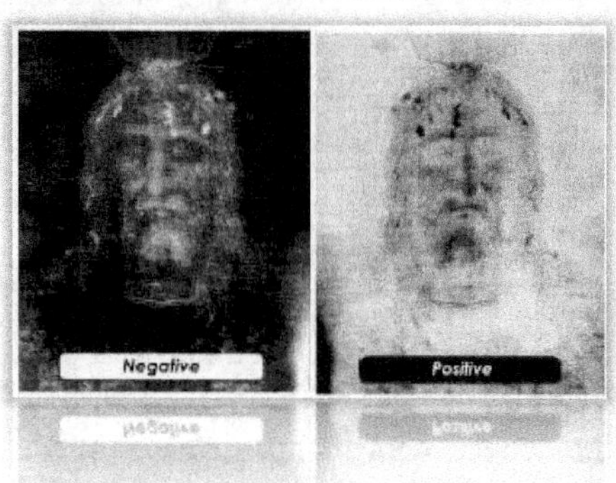

Impression;

1. The process of printing, from type or plates.
2. A printed copy from type or a plate, an engraved block.
3. A portion of a dye having in reverse the intended form of an object to be forged.
4. An image in the mind caused by something external.
5. An imitation of recognizable traits of famous persons.
6. An image retained as a consequence of experience.
7. A mold for making plastic models
8. An impression of a Notary's seal
9. A gold ingot of a refiner's stamp

This definition is so incredible! From all the descriptions that we see within the word *"impression,"* it is clear that *Yeshua, "The Rock," left His reverse image behind on the burial Shroud in the Royal quarry of God's Holy Mount Moriah in the place of the Garden of God.* Now, if we apply the definitions of the word *"impression"* to Yeshua, who was quarried out of the rock, we can clearly see the following truths.

1. Yeshua's burial Shroud image was first viewed as a positive image after it was taken from *the photographic plates of Secondo Pia and as a printed copy of the Shroud.*

2. The Shroud image itself *is the reverse of the intended form* that would one day be discovered *through the invention of photography.*

3. *The image of the consequence of Yeshua's crucifixion have been retained on the image, so we can still see His recognizable traits. We feel His experience from it.*

4. The Shroud has been used *as a mold for making models* of the man on the Shroud.

5. Yeshua as the Royal KING OF KINGS is the Highest ranking official witness of His Eternal Testimony and Covenant, who has given us *His Notary seal and signature,* His Spirit of Life.

6. The word *"impression"* also refers to *"gold refining and the use of the refiner's stamp, to place a seal upon the gold ingots." The LORD Yeshua is the refiner and He seals us with His stamp of Eternal life after He purifies us as the gold and silver ingots.*

In the book of Malachi, John the Baptist was the prophesied messenger that was going to be sent before Messiah Yeshua, to declare these things to us!

Malachi 3:1-4 *Behold, I will send My messenger, and he shall prepare the way before Me; and the LORD, whom ye seek, shall suddenly come to His Temple, even the messenger of the Covenant, whom ye shall delight in; behold, He shall come, saith the LORD of Hosts. But who may abide the day of His coming? And who shall stand when He appeareth? For He is like a refiner's fire, and like fuller's soap; And He shall sit as a refiner and purifier of silver; and He shall purify the sons of Levi, and purge them as gold and silver, that they may offer unto the LORD an offering in righteousness. Then shall the offering of Judah and Jerusalem be pleasant unto the LORD, as in the days of old, and as in the former years.*

All I could think about was the LORD telling Israel to *"Look to the Rock, out of which you were hewn."* It is this Rock Messiah Yeshua, the Rock of offense and Stone of stumbling that was quarried out of Mount Moriah and used as the Chief Cornerstone in the Eternal Holy Temple in Heaven. Everyone who believes is sealed by the KING, *by the refiner's stamp* and they are living stones that are built upon this sure Foundation Stone that I spoke about earlier.

To summarize this, *Yeshua left behind a negative impression of Himself, in the rock quarry of God's Holy Mount Moriah.* This all testifies to His Eternal glory because *Adam was created in the image of the God in this quarry from the Foundation Stone!* As the Almond Rod of God budded to life in this place, Yeshua *the Rock,* the second Adam, became the cure for the snake bite of Satan's curse of death and the evidence was left on *the negative impression* or image that Yeshua the LORD left in the hewn rock on His linen burial Shroud. Finding the *"Serpentine"* in the rock inside the Garden sepulchre of God's Garden was so fantastic and unexpected! I was floored when the Holy Spirit revealed this to me because in a million years, you could never make all of these details fall into place like they do. Only the LORD God could have orchestrated these precise details in the place where His Name dwells forever. Yeshua is the Living Water, who left behind the green line and coloration in the stone where His body once rested in the burial niche. Messiah Yeshua is not only *the Rock* and the Chief Cornerstone that the Heavenly Temple is built upon, but it is interesting that the LORD Yeshua came to earth as the son of a carpenter, which was *a stone mason!*

Now just for a moment, ponder the fact that the place where the LORD was quarried out of the Royal Stone of KING'S in Holy Mount Moriah is the gate of Heaven and it is the place where the LORD will reign forever! The Chief Cornerstone of the Heavenly Temple was therefore quarried out of THE FOUNDATION ROCK out of the Royal Stone of KING'S in God's Garden from the place that was once the Garden of Eden, and the LORD left His photographic negative image in the Rock quarry, in the place where Adam was hewn out of the rock and created in the image of God in the beginning! Therefore, the powerful Rod of God left His negative impression in the rock quarry on His linen burial Shroud exhibiting the evidence that He bore the curse of Eden in God's Garden by swallowing up death forever. Then He came to life as the Living Branch from the Almond Tree of Life, the parallel of Aaron's rod that budded. It is absolutely fantastic and stunningly brilliant! After these thrilling details developed unexpectedly through the Holy Spirit, by Divine Providence, I had to tell this part of the story in this location before going on about the bitter and sweet Almonds of the Messiah. Professor Avinoam Danin, Professor Emeritus of Botany at The Hebrew University of Jerusalem, found many nut images on the Shroud. I believe that they could be Almonds!

Now I left off talking about things that were revealed to me when I woke up at 6AM and they were very startling revelations that were just verified by the above facts. So now I

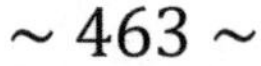

will continue telling you about the *bitter and sweet Almonds!* When I woke up at 6AM, the morning I wrote this, it suddenly came to me that Mary Magdalene was the first to see Yeshua, the Living Almond Branch, after He was raised to life and she said that she thought Yeshua was *"the Gardener."* Mary came to the Garden very early in the morning, which is in the cool part of the day, and she stood near the hewn rock tomb and the vineyard. In the beginning in Genesis, the LORD walked in the cool of the day in the Garden of Eden where He planted His vineyard! Mary then called Yeshua, *"Rabboni,"* which is to say, *"Master."* In the Garden of Eden, the LORD God was indeed *"the Master Gardener."* This was the Garden of the LORD God of Israel and this was the place where He walked and dwelt in the midst of the presence of Adam and Eve before the curse! Yeshua, *the Living Rod of God,* stood in the midst and presence of Mary, resurrected to life as *the Living Almond Branch* after the removal of the curse of the serpent in the same Garden!

As history will recall, Adam and Eve sinned against the LORD and so, essentially, they were the first to reject God as their KING. Due to the sin of disobeying the KING and eating from *the Tree of Knowledge of good and evil (the fig tree)* which the LORD had commanded them not to eat, they went against the KING'S commandment and they ate the fruit of that fig tree in the Garden of God. Therefore, the LORD evicted them from the Garden *before they could eat of the Tree of Life (the Almond Tree) and live forever.* So the curse of death was upon all their descendants. The serpent Satan did an evil work in this Garden. He caused the first rebellion against God and so the curse of death was pronounced here in this place! The curse came not only upon Adam and Eve, but upon every living thing that dwells upon the face of the earth. The pronouncement of the curse meant that life would become very *bitter and it became "the Place of the Skull!"*

Now there are some more amazing things that the Holy Spirit revealed to me! In the Garden of Eden, it was the woman Eve (Chavah in Hebrew) who was the first to eat the fruit from the tree that she was commanded not to eat, which was the *Fig Tree of Knowledge of Good and Evil.* I want to mention that Messiah Yeshua spent much of His time in the Garden on the Mount of Olives and on Holy Mount Moriah. We must remember that God was dwelling with us as *"Emmanuel"* when He stood in the same Garden, appearing alive as *the Branch, as Messiah Yeshua, from the Almond Tree of Life.* The Mount of Olives means *anointed* because of the sweet olive oil that was produced from the fruit of the olive trees in the Garden of Gethsemane. The word *"Messiah" means "anointed"* and Yeshua was God's anointed one. So the other important tree that stood in the Garden of God was called *"the Tree of Life."* What I am about to say is so astonishing because I never saw this until this morning! It came to me through the Holy Spirit that when Yeshua was resurrected, He was standing in the same Garden when He revealed Himself to Mary Magdalene. She was *the first woman* to see Him alive in the Garden after the crucifixion and she was standing in the Garden, with Him in her midst, in the cool of the day.

Mark 16:9-10 *Now when Yeshua was risen early the first day of the week, He appeared first to Mary Magdalene, out of whom he had cast seven devils. And she went and told them that had been with Him, as they mourned and wept.*

The disciple John gave us a very good description of the events of Yeshua's resurrection, as we can see in the following account.

John 20:1-18 *The first day of the week cometh Mary Magdalene early, when it was yet dark, unto the sepulchre, and seeth the stone taken away from the sepulchre. Then she runneth, and cometh to Simon Peter, and to the other disciple, whom Yeshua loved, and saith unto them, They have taken away the LORD out of the sepulchre, and we know not where they have laid Him. Peter therefore went forth, and that other disciple, and came to the sepulchre. So they ran both together; and the other disciple did out-run Peter, and came first to the sepulchre. And he stooping down, and looking in, saw the linen clothes lying; yet went he not in. Then cometh Simon Peter following him, and*

went into the sepulchre, and seeth the linen clothes lie, And the napkin, that was about His head, not lying with the linen clothes, but wrapped together in a place by itself. Then went in also that other disciple, which came first to the sepulchre, and he saw, and believed. For as yet they knew not the Scripture, that He must rise again from the dead. Then the disciples went away again unto their own home. But Mary stood without at the sepulchre weeping; and as she wept, she stooped down, and looked into the sepulchre, And seeth two angels in white sitting, the one at the head, and the other at the feet where the body of Yeshua had lain. And they say unto her, Woman, why weepest thou? She saith unto them, Because they have taken away my LORD, and I know not where they have laid Him. And when she had thus said, she turned herself back, and saw Yeshua standing, and knew not that it was Yeshua. Yeshua saith unto her, Woman, why weepest thou? Whom seekest thou? She, supposing him to be the Gardener saith unto him, Sir, if thou have borne him hence, tell me where thou hast laid him, and I will take him away. Yeshua saith unto her, Mary. She turned herself, and saith unto him, Rabboni; which is to say, Master. Yeshua saith unto her, Touch me not; for I am not yet ascended to my Father; but go to my brethren, and say unto them, I ascend unto my Father, and your Father; and to My God, and your God. Mary Magdalene came and told the disciples that she had seen the LORD, and that He had spoken these things unto her.

So I realized that Yeshua bore both the *bitter and the sweet Almonds* in the location of God's Garden! Yeshua first bore the *bitter* Almonds on the cross, as the Rod lifted up, in the place called *"Golgotha," the place of a skull, on Holy Mount Moriah.* It was here in the Garden where the curse originally transpired that He removed our *bitterness* of the curse of death from the serpent forever. Then when Yeshua came to life, bearing the *sweet Almonds,* as the Living Almond Branch on the Feast of First Fruits, He was resurrected in the same Garden where Eden was originally located on Holy Mount Moriah in Jerusalem Israel. It was in this Garden that Messiah Yeshua the LORD came to life, the parallel of Aaron's rod that budded.

Now as an amazing side note, because they were evicted from the Garden of God in the beginning, the LORD came to us as *the Living Branch* because we were drowning in our sins. This is exactly what you do when a person is drowning. When a person falls into water and cannot escape, you hold out a Branch to them. As they grab hold of *the Branch,* they are saved and they escape death! This is how the LORD saved us! The Holy Menorah with its budding Almond Branches, bearing fruit of Almonds is the Eternal Living Testimony of Messiah the LORD from the Garden of God. The Almond Tree of Life held out His Living Branch to us to save us forever. We could not save ourselves! *The fruit is on the Branch of the Almond Tree of Life!*

John 19:41-42 *Now in the place where He was crucified there was a Garden; and in the Garden a new sepulchre, wherein was never man yet laid. There laid they Yeshua therefore because of the Jews' preparation day; for the sepulchre was nigh at hand.*

I Corinthians 15:20 *But now is Messiah risen from the dead, and become the First Fruits of them that slept.*

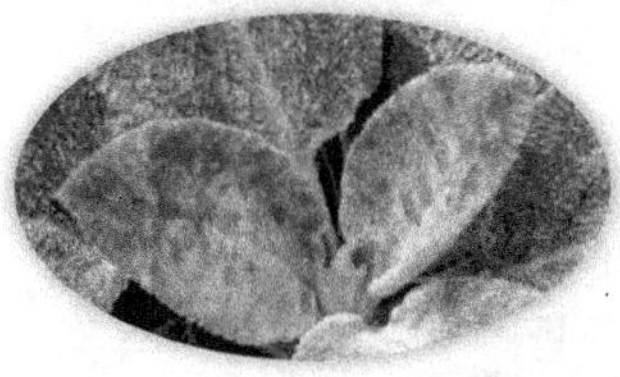

"MAROR" = "BITTER"

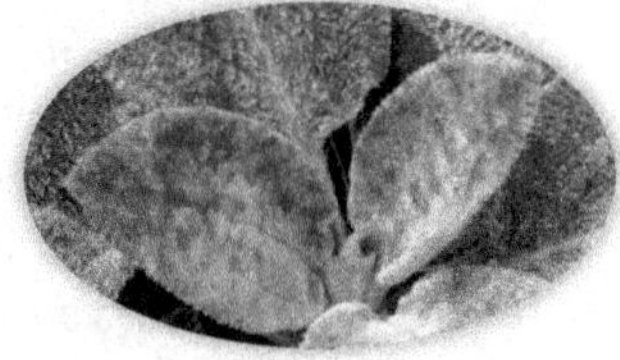

Lamb's Ear Plant Photos ©2014 KK Ballard All Rights Reserved

Now back to the *bitter and sweet* Almonds story. One day, when I traveled out of town on a brief vacation, I went into a gift shop where they sold name cards that were printed with first names, their meanings, and origins. As I was flipping through the *"M's,"* looking for my sister's names, I happened to run across the name, *"Marion."* At this point, I pulled out the card and I read that the name, *"Marion,"* is a derivative of the name, *"Mary"* and they both mean *"bitter."* It also said, *"You have turned my mourning into joy,"* which was a verse from Psalms. It touched me deeply because, as I briefly mentioned earlier, my life had become *bitter* from the very sudden unexpected betrayal of my very beloved, trusted precious close friend,

and music mentor Marion. I never understood why this heartbreaking turn of events happened to me because I was always a very kind, hard working, and extremely loving person. This one event changed my life forever, and there was nothing I could do about it. I cried many tears for years because this unexpected change severely altered my life. This devastating loss was my main reason for leaving college at first, and I began my spiral downward. I had lost my father at age 5 or 6 on Christmas day through parental divorce, and had not heard from him in 17 years. After this event, while I was still working in college on my percussion degree, I lost this important friendship with my favorite person Marion who was like family to me. I was crushed emotionally, and in my soul I could not recover from this loss. Soon after this happened, I lost my step-father through a terrible divorce at age 26, and strangely wound up not hearing from him for 17+ years too. All of these major events were more than I could take in my heart. At that time I had no college funding. I then lost my long time job, and I moved home to help my devastated Mother for years. My degree was left behind. I had worked so hard in college. I had just passed my percussion Sophomore jury that advanced me to a higher musical level. After a few of years of deep struggle trying to pick up the pieces I went to find my mentor to make amends to restore things but it only became worse for me. I never expected to experience such deep pain from someone I loved and trusted. I never felt so terrible in my entire life. Sometimes I only found comfort knowing that Yeshua had gone through deep pain like this before. He had been rejected in the worst way possible. I had great sympathy for the LORD.

As the next events began to unfold within my story, I suddenly knew the LORD had been preparing me through my years of anguish and sorrow in the wilderness, losing everything that I had worked so hard to achieve, to unveil this incredible Testimony to me. *Yeshua the Almond Branch turned my mourning, (the bitter) into sweet joy!* The realization of this was so overwhelming and for the first time, *I knew that it had all happened to me for a much higher purpose.* Then Yeshua's love for me became so apparently beautiful, so glorious and faithful.

I purchased the name card Marion and kept it inside my Bible. So this morning when the LORD revealed the details to me about Mary at the Garden tomb with Messiah Yeshua, I instantly remembered that *"Mary" and "Marion" mean "bitter."* I have to say honestly, I never knew the LORD was going to use this truth in my life years later in such a profound way as you are about to see for yourself! It was this knowledge that opened my understanding to see the hidden details about Yeshua's resurrection in the Garden tomb. Now it was also due to *Marion's name* that I instantly remembered that the Hebrew name *"Miriam"* is also a derivative of *"Mary."* The names all come from the Hebrew root word *"Mar" meaning "bitter."* The same root of the word *"Mar"* is also in the word *"Maror."* The *Maror* are actually the *bitter herbs* that are eaten during the Passover Seder by the children of Israel. When Yeshua sealed His Covenant with us on Passover in the Seder, the *Maror* was present on the Seder plate. Messiah Yeshua died on Passover as the Lamb of God, and it was during Passover that He bore *the bitterness* of the curse of the Garden of Eden for our sins. He came to life in the same Garden to bring us back to the Garden of God, through the removal of the curse. So the truth is Messiah Yeshua bore *the bitter* Almonds on the Branch first, in order to eternally take away *the bitterness* of death from us. Then in His resurrection to life, as *the Rod of God,* He bore *the sweet* Almonds, as the First Fruit from the Eternal Almond Tree of Life. *This means that the LORD bore the bitter and the sweet for us in the same location of His original Garden.* This was fantastic! Not only was the woman, Mary Magdalene, the first to see Yeshua alive at the rock hewn tomb in the Holy Mountain of God, but Yeshua was the first born son of another Mary and this also presents something incredible. Eve, or *"Chavah"* in Hebrew, was *the first woman* of all mankind. *She was the woman who was the first to eat the fruit from the Fig Tree of Knowledge of good and evil and then she gave this fruit to Adam and he ate it.* It was this sin that caused Adam and Eve to be driven out of the Garden and away from the Divine Presence of God. Every evil thing that has befallen mankind since the curse is

due to Satan's rebellion against the LORD. For this reason, we all bear *the bitterness* of the curse of Eden because it was appointed once for man to die. For this reason, at the end of the age, Satan will try to set himself up to be worshipped as god/the Anti-Christ in this place on the LORD'S Holy Mountain, as the final act of rebellion against God.

The LORD had a plan though! He would draw all people back to Jerusalem to His Holy Mountain, to Mount Moriah and to His Garden, through His Living Testimony as our Saviour Messiah and as the Living Almond Branch from the Ark of Heaven. After the curse happened in the Garden of Eden, the glory of the LORD departed and He was no longer dwelling on the earth or in our midst. *So not only was this curse heartbreaking, it was very bitter.* I was suddenly given the revelation that this is why the LORD called Abraham back to Jerusalem to Mount Moriah. This is why King David purchased this Holy Mountain to prepare a House for God *in the place of the Garden of Eden.* Adam set up the first altar here and Noah came to make offerings here after leaving the Ark. The earthly Ark was brought to this place, so that the Divine Presence of the LORD God could return to us, as He descended upon the throne of His Ark, within the Holy of Holies. I suddenly visualized in my mind that the main goal of the LORD for all these centuries has been to draw us all back to His Garden to His Holy Mount Moriah where His Name dwells forever. *The fact that this was the Garden of Eden explains the constant fighting over Jerusalem and particularly over Mount Moriah and the Holy Temple Mount.* I now understand that this is the reason that God brought Israel out of Egypt, out of bondage with His Rod of salvation, and brought them back into the Promised Land. The LORD brought them out of their *"bitterness"* and back into *"the sweetness"* of His Holy Land because His Garden was in this place and *The Living Torah* abides here forever! The Messiah was also taken away to Egypt and then brought out of Egypt and back into the Promised Land to live in Nazareth as *"the Branch."* In essence, we were sent out of this Garden to be scattered throughout the entire earth and into every nation. I realized this morning that Mystery Babylon in the book of Revelation is a beast that spreads violence and terror wherever it goes. This began as the people were all *scattered away* from God's Garden in Jerusalem because of Satan's curse of death. *Through the Messiah's Testimony, God was calling us back to Jerusalem to the true place of worshipping the one true Living God.* Yeshua is *the Rock* from His quarry on Holy Mount Moriah that will come from Heaven in the last days to smash these earthly corrupted kingdoms from this corrupt system of Ancient Babylon, whose false system will be destroyed forever. Ancient Babylon continues to spread her wickedness throughout the earth *with an agenda to rule the world,* and to force conversions with *a badge of servitude* to Satan's allegiance. So when the fullness of the scattering is complete, the LORD will draw His remnant back to His Garden in Jerusalem. *Therefore, it is only the Living Rod of God that could deliver us out of our bondage of the curse of death to give us the sweetness of Eternal life.* The LORD would draw us back to His Garden on Mount Moriah through His Living Testimony because *Yeshua bore the bitter and the sweet in the same place.* The whole idea all along was to bring us all back to *the Garden of God* through the resurrected Messiah. In the last days, when He draws us all back to Jerusalem to His Garden, He will return from Heaven to once again dwell in our midst as it was in the beginning without the curse. This is the redemption of mankind! Adam was, in fact, created from the dust of Mount Moriah. It was out of this rock that we were hewn. It all suddenly became perfectly clear to me that the LORD was going to redeem all mankind in His Garden in Jerusalem. *Yeshua is therefore leading everyone out of the wilderness and back into the Eternal Promised Land and back across the Jordan River, just like Joshua!* It was therefore necessary for Yeshua to accomplish all things, according to all that the Prophets of Israel wrote about Him. Yeshua removed our *bitterness* our, *"Maror,"* of the bondage of death as our Passover Lamb. His life blood is on the door of Heaven. The Messiah is therefore, of course, the only door that we can go through to enter His Eternal Garden called *"Heaven."* His life blood upon the door to Heaven opens the door to us

and causes death to Passover us, so we have Eternal life. Then He will reign as our Almighty KING. This is exactly what He wanted in the beginning but He was rejected in the Garden of Eden as our KING. This also happened when the people of Israel asked for an earthly King, instead of the LORD as their KING. Then the LORD gave them King Saul. The LORD was again rejected as the KING and He sent Israel into captivity into Babylon because they were worshipping all the false gods of Babylon instead of the LORD. Another time, the LORD was rejected as the KING when He was dwelling in the midst of Israel as the Messiah. So then Israel was scattered into all nations in the Diaspora. Now we must tell the LORD God Almighty to please come back to us immediately and to reign and dwell in our midst forever in His Eternal Garden in Jerusalem because He is our KING OF KINGS AND LORD OF LORDS! We must repent and tell Him how much we love Him and desire to see His beautiful face! *We must forgive those that have broken our innocent hearts, wounding our spirit!*

Now, in the beginning, the LORD cast Adam and Eve out of His Garden. He did this in order to prevent them from taking and eating *the fruit from the Tree of Life* lest they live forever in the state of the curse of death. They rebelled and disobeyed the KING of glory by eating the fruit from the Fig Tree of Knowledge of good and evil. It was in this Garden that the woman, *"Eve or Chavah,"* became *bitter* through the curse of death because *she was the first woman to eat the forbidden fig fruit. Secondly, she went to get Adam and he ate the fig fruit after her in this same Garden. The KING of glory knew that things were about to drastically change for them.*

Genesis 3:2-6 *And the woman said unto the serpent, We may eat of the fruit of the Trees of the Garden; But of the fruit of the Tree which is in the midst of the Garden, God hath said, Ye shall not eat of it, neither shall ye touch it, lest ye die. And the serpent said unto the woman, Ye shall not surely die; For God doth know that in the day ye eat thereof, then your eyes shall be opened, and ye shall be as gods, knowing good and evil. And when the woman saw that the Tree was good for food, and that it was pleasant to the eyes, and a Tree to be desired to make one wise, she took of the fruit thereof, and did eat, and gave also unto her husband with her; and he did eat.*

Now remember, that as they were cast out of the Paradise Garden, their lives became *very bitter!* The woman was particularly *bitter* from having eaten the *"first fruit"* from the Tree of Knowledge of Good and Evil and then she invited *"the man"* to eat the fruit after her. So now I want to share the astounding truth that I realized by the power of the Holy Spirit when I woke up at 6AM about *Mary of Magdala* who came to the Garden tomb first! The LORD put this thrilling revelation in my heart about it. At the rock hewn Garden tomb in Holy Mount Moriah, the woman, *"Mary,"* meaning, *"bitter,"* was the first person that Yeshua appeared to in the Garden after He was resurrected to life as the Living Branch. So what did the first woman, *"Mary,"* do after she saw that Yeshua was resurrected to life and was standing before her eyes in the Garden? I was absolutely shocked when the LORD revealed this to me! *Mary whose name means, "bitter," was the first woman to come to the Garden tomb and she was the first woman to see the LORD standing in her midst and she took hold and ate "The First Fruit from the Almond Tree of Life!"* She was accompanied by another Mary, whose name also means *"bitter,"* and she became one of two witnesses of Yeshua's first appearance in the Garden in the place where the LORD said, that His Name would dwell forever. A woman came to the tomb first and not a man because the woman *Eve was the first woman to eat the forbidden fruit* in the Garden of Eden and now Yeshua, *the Rod that budded,* was reversing the curse from death to life, thereby *taking away the bitterness and replacing it with the sweetness of Eternal life! Mary, "bitter,"* has therefore now taken hold of Messiah, our First Fruit from the Almond Tree of Life, because He is *The Living Torah* and our Holy Almond Tree Menorah. I believe that this Divine Testimony is therefore depicted on *"the Magdala stone"* that I showed earlier that was discovered in the Ancient Synagogue of Mary Magdalene. I believe there are two trees of the Garden of Eden depicted on the stone.

So now, because Mary has taken and eaten *the First Fruit from the Branch of the Almond Tree of Life,* the curse of the *bitterness* of the Garden of Eden has been reversed. *As Mary takes hold of the First Fruit of salvation in the Garden of God, the bitter curse is removed and the sweetness of Eternal life has been restored to mankind through the LORD'S Living Testimony!* Yeshua had to bear *both the bitter and the sweet Almonds in the same place of the Garden of God and of course the seed of life in Him is the Living Torah. The LORD is also the Almond Tree Menorah of Eternal life, as depicted on the Magdala stone!* For this reason, it was not possible for death to hold Him in the grave because He is the resurrection and the life. Remember that *He is not the god of death; He is the God of the Living!* This is the power of the Rod of God that gives us Eternal life!

Official Photograph taken in October 2009 of "THE MAGDALA STONE," Photograph ©2009 Magdala Center Excavations Israel All Rights Reserved

"The Magdala Stone," that was recently discovered in excavations in the Ancient Synagogue of Magdala, on the shore of the Sea of Galilee in Israel in 2009, is etched with the Holy Almond Tree Menorah, The two trees from the Garden of Eden and Yeshua's Eternal Covenant of the heart. Also etched on this stone are the Living Water jars, The emblems of the Bread of Heaven and cup of wine, signifying Yeshua's Marriage betrothal. It was all discovered in Mary Magdalene's Synagogue! Mary Magdalene was the first woman to eat the sweet First Fruit from the Almond Tree of Eternal life in God's Garden On Holy Mount Moriah! Eve was the first woman to eat the first bitter fruit from this Garden from the Fig Tree. Now remember what I said on page 331? The LORD showed me that Hezekiah's pool on Holy Mount Moriah, was also known as the "Amygdalon pool" which is Greek for "Almond Tree" and means "Magdala or Migdol! So Mary Magdalene, who saw the budded Almond Tree of Life first at the Garden tomb, is also miraculously connected to the Almond Tree in this way!

Matthew 22:29-32 *Yeshua answered and said unto them, Ye do err, not knowing the Scriptures, nor the power of God. For in the resurrection they neither marry, nor are given in marriage, but are as the angels of God in Heaven. But as touching the resurrection of the dead, have ye not read that which was spoken unto you by God, saying, I AM the God of Abraham, and the God of Isaac, and the God of Jacob? God is not the God of the dead, but of the living. And when the multitude heard this, they were astonished at His doctrine.*

Now I am so excited to tell you that there is more that was transpiring with Mary Magdalene at the Garden tomb! Mary not only referred to Yeshua as *"Master,"* but she also turned around and thought that Yeshua was *"the Gardener."* Within Mary's own words, it is shockingly clear that she revealed that Messiah Yeshua, who was standing alive in His Garden, was indeed *"the Master Gardener!" Yeshua died and came to life in the place of the Garden of Eden.* So it was here that He lovingly removed the curse, the bondage of death, as our Passover into Heaven and gave us life in Himself. In the beginning, He was *The Master Gardener in this Garden! After Mary took hold of the First Fruit from the Almond Tree of Life, by holding onto Yeshua, He told her that He had not yet ascended up to Heaven. He told her that she should go and tell His disciples, otherwise known as "the men," that He has been resurrected from death to life. Mary then ran out of the Garden and she ran to tell the men!* Do you see how exciting this is? Then the two men, who are also two witnesses as required by Jewish Law, ran to the Garden and they saw and believed because they saw the Shroud bearing the LORD'S impression, and His face cloth by itself. Yeshua's impression was left behind in the LORD'S

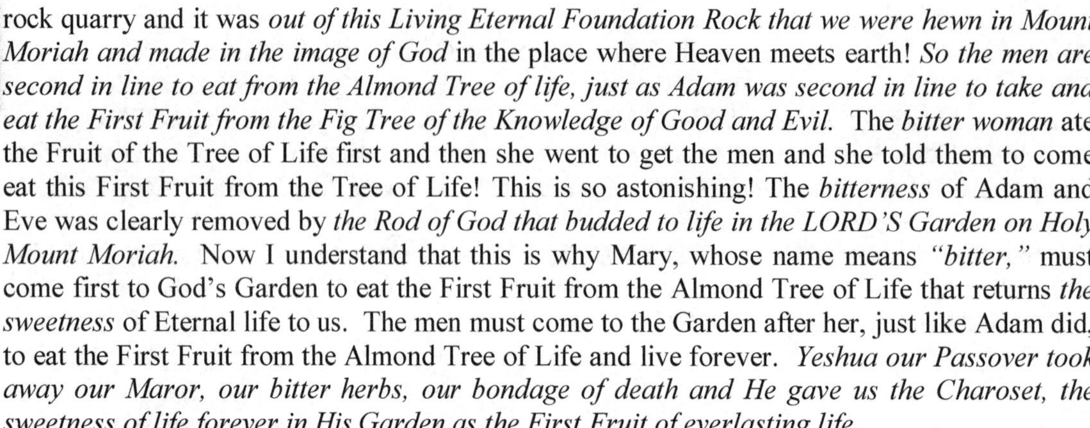

rock quarry and it was *out of this Living Eternal Foundation Rock that we were hewn in Mount Moriah and made in the image of God* in the place where Heaven meets earth! *So the men are second in line to eat from the Almond Tree of life, just as Adam was second in line to take and eat the First Fruit from the Fig Tree of the Knowledge of Good and Evil.* The *bitter woman* ate the Fruit of the Tree of Life first and then she went to get the men and she told them to come eat this First Fruit from the Tree of Life! This is so astonishing! The *bitterness* of Adam and Eve was clearly removed by *the Rod of God that budded to life in the LORD'S Garden on Holy Mount Moriah.* Now I understand that this is why Mary, whose name means *"bitter,"* must come first to God's Garden to eat the First Fruit from the Almond Tree of Life that returns *the sweetness* of Eternal life to us. The men must come to the Garden after her, just like Adam did, to eat the First Fruit from the Almond Tree of Life and live forever. *Yeshua our Passover took away our Maror, our bitter herbs, our bondage of death and He gave us the Charoset, the sweetness of life forever in His Garden as the First Fruit of everlasting life.*

Mary's surname, *"Magdalene,"* is a variant spelling of "*Migdalia*" or *"Migdol."* In ancient times it was quite common for a person to take a surname from the name of their village or town of residence. This would allow them to be identified as having come from a certain place. So now these brand new excavations are the ruins of the ancient village and Synagogue of Magdala or Migdol excavated by the shore of the Sea of Galilee. So Mary's surname reflects the fact that *"Magdala"* was her town of origin. *Migdol* is the modern name of the ancient village of *Magdala.* This fact led me to another unexpected surprise. The name, *"Migdol,"* that I have discussed earlier in depth actually means *"Tower of God" and "Fortress of God."* Now I was pondering this in my heart and I wondered why the LORD would appear first to Mary, who had the *surname* meaning *"Tower or Fortress of God."* Suddenly it came to me! When Mary Magdalene became the first woman to see Yeshua alive at the Garden tomb in Mount Moriah in the place of the Holy Mountain of God, *Yeshua was revealing that this rock at the Garden tomb is the place of His eternal abode in the former Garden of Eden. Holy Mount Moriah is the place where He will set His Towering Temple Fortress in the future.* It is *the place* at the gate of Heaven where the Eternal House of God will rest when the LORD returns to dwell with us forever as our KING. *This is the place where Heaven meets earth and it is the place where His Towering Temple Fortress will rest for eternity. It was here that He saved us, and this is where He calls us home to dwell within His House that Towers above it all! The LORD is our High Tower and He is the Rock out of which we have been hewn from His rock quarry from THIS FOUNDATION STONE!*

The Excavation site of Mary Magdalene's Synagogue
Official Photograph taken in December 2009
Photograph ©2009 Magdala Center Excavations Israel All Rights Reserved

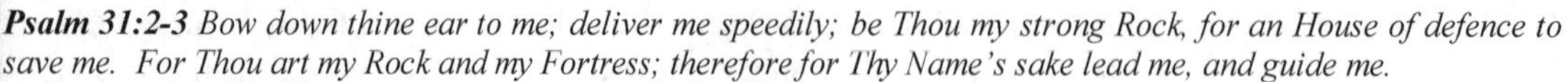

Psalm 31:2-3 *Bow down thine ear to me; deliver me speedily; be Thou my strong Rock, for an House of defence to save me. For Thou art my Rock and my Fortress; therefore for Thy Name's sake lead me, and guide me.*

Psalm 61:1-4 *Hear my cry, O God; attend unto my prayer, From the end of the earth will I cry unto thee, when my heart is overwhelmed; lead me to the Rock that higher than I. For Thou hast been a shelter for me, and a strong Tower from the enemy. I will abide in Thy Tabernacle forever; I will trust in the covert of Thy wings. Se'lah.*

II Samuel 22:2-3 *And he said, the LORD is my Rock, and my fortress, and my deliverer; The God of my Rock; in Him will I trust; He is my shield, and the horn of my salvation, my High Tower, and my refuge, my Saviour; Thou savest me from violence.*

Remember that we were driven out of the LORD'S Garden in Jerusalem! The Garden of God was eastward in the east and this was the place of His threshing floor. So Holy Mount Moriah is the place in the east from where all the people were scattered and driven out of the Garden of Eden. *So it was in this Garden that "Eve or Chavah"* was bearing the curse of *travailing in birth pains in childbirth until the time of the redemption of mankind* because she is the Mother of all the living. She was the first to give birth to *a man child,* but God formed the very first man, *"Adam,"* out of the dust of the ground from the hewn rock in the LORD'S quarry in Holy Mount Moriah where Yeshua came to life and came out of the same quarry!

Genesis 2:8 *And the LORD God planted a Garden eastward in Eden and there he put the man whom He had formed.*

Genesis 3:22-24 *And the LORD God said, Behold, the man is become as one of us, to know good and evil; and now, lest he put forth his hand, and take also of the Tree of Life, and eat, and live forever; Therefore the LORD God sent him forth from the Garden of Eden, to till the ground from whence he was taken. So He drove out the man; and He placed at the east of the Garden of Eden Cherubim's, and a flaming sword which turned every way, to keep the way of the Tree of Life.*

So we cry aloud because our KING is not with us! He remains in Heaven until the time that the end of days is fulfilled and He rescues us out of the false system of Babylon, whose *rebellious spire and false tower to heaven* will soon crumble into dust!

Micah 4:6-12 *In that day, saith the LORD, will I assemble her that halteth, and I will gather her that is driven out, and her that I have afflicted; And I will make her that halted remnant, and her that was cast far off a strong nation; and the LORD shall reign over them in Mount Zion from henceforth, even forever. And Thou, O Tower of the flock, the Strong Hold of the daughter of Zion, unto thee shall it come, even the first dominion; the Kingdom shall come to the daughter of Jerusalem. Now why dost thou cry out aloud? Is there no King in thee? Is thy counselor perished? For pangs have taken thee as a woman in travail. Be in pain, and labour to bring forth, O daughter of Zion, like a woman in travail; for now shalt thou go forth out of the city, and thou shalt dwell in the field, and thou shalt go even unto Babylon; there shalt thou be delivered; there the LORD shall redeem thee from the hand of thine enemies. Now also many nations are gathered against thee, that say, Let her be defiled, and let our eye look upon Zion. But they know not the thoughts of the LORD, neither understand they His counsel; for He shall gather them as the sheaves into the floor.*

So now Eve, the Mother of all living was travailing in birth pangs because of the curse.

Genesis 3:16-17 *Unto the woman He said, I will greatly multiply thy sorrow and thy conception; in sorrow thou shalt bring forth children; and thy desire shall be to thy husband, and he shall rule over thee. And unto Adam He said, Because thou hast hearkened unto the voice of thy wife, and hast eaten of the tree, saying, Thou shalt not eat of it; cursed is the ground for thy sake; in sorrow shalt thou eat of it all the days of thy life; Thorns and thistles shall it being forth to thee; and thou shalt eat the herb of the field; In the sweat of thy face shalt thou eat bread, till thou return unto the ground; for out of it wast thou taken; for dust thou art, and unto dust shalt thou return. And Adam called his wife's name Eve; because she was the mother of all living.*

So I began to realize that at the time of the final redemption, in the book of Revelation, the woman is still travailing in pain trying to give birth because the whole creation is groaning from the curse of the Garden of Eden until the time that the LORD returns to dwell in our midst as it was in the beginning. *This is the first woman who gave birth to the man child in the Garden on Holy Mount Moriah, which is Eve or Chavah.*

***Genesis 4:1** And Adam knew Eve his wife; and she conceived and bare Cain, and said, I have gotten a man from the LORD.*

Notice in the following Scripture *that part of the curse was for the man to start ruling over the woman.* This was not God's idea, *as men and women were created equal in the image of God,* as it is written in Genesis, and this is why Messiah Yeshua spoke openly to women and taught them *"The Living Torah"* when it was frowned upon to teach them *"Torah"* by the male dominated religious establishment! *The LORD KING Yeshua did not discriminate as He spoke the Word to them!* The long suffering and often vile, brutal persecution of women has gone on for so many centuries. The truth is that men have ruled over women in all things *because of the curse.* Sometimes women have been treated inferior to men and they have been abused and belittled, often kept from using their God given talents. The truth is, however, women are as precious to God as men are because they both were created in the image of God.

***Genesis 1:27** So God created man in His own image, in the image of God created He Him; male and female created He them.*

It is therefore no surprise that in the book of Revelation, we find that the woman who gave birth to *"the man child"* is travailing in pain right up to the time that Messiah Yeshua returns from Heaven in the final redemption. As Messiah's arrival comes closer to being fulfilled, the birth pangs of the woman get worse until the birth of our final redemption is complete and this brings about Eternal life with the LORD. The LORD God does not treat people with certain prejudices. We are all one in Him, through His Ruach/Holy Spirit and by faith in Messiah, but He expects us to worship Him alone because He is the One that created all of us and the entire universe.

***Galatians 3:26-29** For ye are all children of God by faith in Messiah Yeshua. For as many of you as have been baptized into Messiah have put on Messiah. There is neither Jew nor Greek, there is neither bond nor free, there is neither male nor female; for ye are all one in Messiah Yeshua. And if ye be Messiah's, then are ye Abraham's seed, and heirs according to the promise.*

Now the woman in the book of Revelation, who is travailing in pain, is trying to give birth and she is the woman who gave birth to the man child and it is through this line that the Messiah would come. So Satan was trying to kill off this righteous line, so the Messiah could not come to redeem us. As we can clearly see in the following Scripture, the dragon, the serpent or Satan, tried to destroy her seed, but God preserved her seed and saved them from the flood. He saved the remnant who kept the Testimony of Yeshua the Messiah. People wonder why there is so much violence and hatred on this earth and the answer is that throughout the centuries, Satan has ruled this earth through *the curse* and he has been trying to destroy those that belong to God and destroy those who keep God's Living Testimony. In the end they overcome the serpent and his terrors on the earth by the blood of the Lamb, the LORD'S Covenant of life, through the saving Ark of Messiah Yeshua the LORD, the powerful Rod of God. Satan was cast down to the earth where he roams about seeking to kill, steal, and destroy. He has tried to destroy the man child that was made in the image of God, in as many ways as possible, from the days of the Garden of Eden, trying to prevent the Messiah from coming to fulfill His Divine Testimony of the Heavenly Ark. He does not want us to return to the restored Garden of Eden called *Heaven* to worship the one true Living God of Israel.

***Revelation 12:2-16** And she being with child cried, travailing in birth, and pained to be delivered. And there appeared another wonder in Heaven; and behold a great red dragon, having seven heads and ten horns, and seven crowns upon his heads. And his tail drew the third part of the stars of Heaven, and did cast them to the earth; and the dragon stood before the woman which was ready to be delivered, for to devour her child as soon as it was born.*

And she brought forth a man child, who was to rule all nations with a rod of iron; and her child was caught up unto God, and to His throne. And the woman fled into the wilderness, where she hath a place prepared of God, that they should feed her there a thousand two hundred and threescore days. And there was war in Heaven; Michael and his angels fought against the dragon; and the dragon fought and his angels, And prevailed not; neither was their place found any more in Heaven. And the great dragon was cast out, that old serpent, called the Devil, and Satan, which deceiveth the whole world; he was cast out into the earth, and his angels were cast out with him. And I heard a loud voice saying in Heaven, Now is come salvation, and strength, and the power of His Messiah; for the accuser of our brethren is cast down, which accused them before our God day and night. And they overcame him by the blood of the Lamb, and by the Word of their Testimony; and they loved not their lives unto death. Therefore rejoice, ye Heavens, and ye that dwell in them, Woe to the inhabiters of the earth and of the sea! For the devil is come down unto you, having great wrath, because he knoweth that he hath but a short time. And when the dragon saw that he was cast unto the earth, he persecuted the woman, which brought forth the man child. And to the woman were given two wings of a great eagle, that she might fly into the wilderness, into her place, where she is nourished for a time, and times, and half a time, from the face of the serpent. And the serpent cast out of his mouth water as a flood after the woman, that he might cause her to be carried away of the flood. And the earth helped the woman, and the earth opened her mouth, and swallowed up the flood which the dragon cast out of his mouth. And the dragon was wroth with the woman, and went to make war with the remnant of her seed, which keep the Commandments of God, and have the Testimony of Yeshua Messiah.

Satan corrupted the earth with death, brutality, chaos, and violence. Therefore, mankind was nearly destroyed by the great flood, by holocausts, and other diabolical deeds, but the LORD had already saved a righteous remnant of the woman's seed in Noah's Ark.

Micah also prophesied about the travailing of the woman. All of this refers to *the redemption* because it is obvious that the woman will be travailing until the time of the arrival of the Messiah and until the ushering in of the Kingdom of God. This is when the curse will be removed from the woman and her seed and the curse is removed from off the earth forever.

Micah 5:2-3 *But thou, Bethlehem Ephratah, though thou be little among the thousands of Judah, yet out of thee shall come forth unto me that is to be ruler in Israel; whose goings forth have been from of old, from everlasting. Therefore will He give them up, until the time that she which travaileth hath brought forth; then the remnant of his brethren shall return unto the children of Israel.*

The book of Romans indicates that the whole creation is groaning and travailing, waiting for the LORD to come in the final redemption.

Romans 8:22-23 *For we know that the whole creation groaneth and travaileth in pain together until now. And not only they, but ourselves also, which have the First Fruits of the Spirit, even we ourselves groan within ourselves, waiting for the adoption, to wit, the redemption of our body.*

Since the Scriptures tell us that Yeshua came to destroy the workings of Satan, *our redemption is the removal of the curse of death from our body,* so we might live forever with the LORD. It is all about the return of Messiah Yeshua to reign as the KING of glory on the Ark of His Testimony in Jerusalem Israel. We are saved by the Heavenly Ark of God. Satan has for centuries spread evil through killing, trying to prevent our final redemption with the LORD. He likes us to feel worthless. He steals our dreams that God put into our hearts, and he takes father's away from their children. As part of the curse, we were scattered abroad, being driven out of God's Garden in the east out of Jerusalem. Some of the descendants went and settled in Shinar *away from the one true God of Israel.* It was here in Babylon that the people began to defy God. The people set up a false place and system of worship in Babylon and *they tried to build a prayer Tower that reached unto Heaven.* So Babylon became the Mother of harlots of all false religions. It was in Shinar that the people began to worship every abominable thing that offends the one true Living God that created the universe. In Shinar the people created *The Tower of Babel in defiance* of the one true Living God, *whose true Holy abode and Royal Temple Fortress Tower is forever set in the Holy city of Jerusalem where*

Heaven meets earth. Now I understand the great significance of the LORD God bringing Mary Magdalene, whose surname means *"Tower of God or Fortress of God,"* first to the Garden tomb in Holy Mount Moriah. My name, *"Kimberly,"* ironically means *"From the Royal meadow Fortress."* Yeshua was revealing in the Garden tomb on Mount Moriah that this was the place where He will dwell forever in Jerusalem with the Ark of His Testimony and He was bringing us out from all the scattered places and out of the pagan system of Babylon back to the one true Holy city, which is the Garden of the Eternal dwelling of the one true Living God, the KING Messiah Yeshua. The evil corrupted *god of death and war* with his worldly system known as *"Babylon"* spreads its abominations everywhere. The LORD warns us to come out of this false pagan system of Babylon, in the book of Revelation, and *He tells us to remain separate from her,* so that we will not be partakers of her plagues during the tribulation. *Since they are bloodthirsty the LORD will turn their water into blood to drink by the rod of one of the two witnesses!* In Ancient Babylon, *men tried to make a name for themselves* instead of praising and honoring the one true God who created Heaven and earth. In total arrogance and pride, the people proclaimed they would build a prayer Tower unto Heaven in a place that was not holy. *By definition, "this Tower had a spire that was a lighthouse with a temple at the top where prayer was broadcast to false gods," but this man-made Tower can never reach unto God!* No one could enter the Garden of God in Jerusalem until the Messiah made *the way* back to the LORD'S Garden. In the book of Isaiah, we see that the false gods that came out of Babylon *have had dominion in the earth,* but those who know the LORD God of Israel know that He is the one true God who created all things. He is our Saviour, Redeemer, and the Messiah. All these centuries the LORD has been calling us back to Jerusalem!

So Isaiah tells us that we are as a woman with child, travailing in pain, until the time of our delivery into the Heavenly Kingdom of God. This is the same Scripture that goes on to mention God's people *"hiding themselves behind closed doors until the indignation be overpast,"* pertaining to the rapture of the believer's in Messiah Yeshua. In the book of Isaiah, we can see that after we are *hidden in the Heavenly Ark,* the LORD comes forth out of His place to punish the inhabitants of the earth who are holding onto the false religions and worldly systems that originated in pagan Babylon. It will be a just punishment when the plagues come upon the bloodthirsty. They will have no water! God will make them drink blood as payment for their evil. *Then after the indignation is overpast, the LORD returns from Heaven and sets up His everlasting Kingdom in the original place of the Garden of Eden in Mount Moriah, where His Towering Temple Fortress reaches from Heaven to earth in Jerusalem Israel.* This Mount includes the Garden tomb area where Yeshua came to life as the second perfect Adam, fashioned as a vessel by the LORD Himself. In Isaiah notice that these other lords have had dominion over the people, but they are dead because they are not the true God of the Living! Yeshua visited us and destroyed the power of this system of Satan. Notice also that he says that *we have been like a woman with child that cries out in pangs near the time of her delivery.*

Isaiah 26:13-21 *O LORD our God, other lords beside Thee have had dominion over us; but by Thee only will we make mention of Thy Name. They are dead, they shall not live; they are deceased, they shall not rise; therefore hast Thou visited and destroyed them, and made all their memory to perish. Thou hast increased the nation; Thou art glorified; Thou hadst removed it far unto all the ends of the earth. LORD, in trouble have they visited Thee, they poured out a prayer when Thy chastening was upon them. Like as a woman with child, that draweth near the time of her delivery, is in pain, and crieth out in her pangs; so have we been in Thy sight, O LORD. We have been with child, as it were brought forth wind; we have not wrought any deliverance in the earth; neither have the inhabitants of the world fallen. Come, My people, enter thou into thy chambers, and shut thy doors about thee; hide thyself as it were for a little moment, until the indignation be overpast. For, behold, the LORD cometh out of His place to punish the inhabitants of the earth for their iniquity; the earth also shall disclose her blood, and shall no more cover her slain.*

Mystery Babylon makes war against Messiah Yeshua, and His righteous heavenly army.

Revelation 17:1-18 *And there came one of the seven angels which had the seven vials, and talked with me, saying unto me, Come hither; I will shew unto thee the judgment of the great whore that sitteth upon many waters; With whom the kings of the earth have committed fornication, and the inhabitants of the earth have been made drunk with the wine of her fornication. So he carried me away in the spirit into the wilderness; and I saw a woman sit upon a scarlet coloured beast, full of names of blasphemy, having seven heads and ten horns. And the woman was arrayed in purple and scarlet colour, and decked with gold and precious stones and pearls, having a golden cup in her hand full of abominations and filthiness of her fornication; And upon her forehead was a name written, MYSTERY, BABYLON THE GREAT. THE MOTHER OF HARLOTS AND ABOMINATIONS OF THE EARTH. And I saw the woman drunken with the blood of the Saints, and with the blood of the martyrs of Yeshua; and when I saw her, I wondered with great admiration. And the angel said unto me, Wherefore didst thou marvel? I will tell thee the mystery of the woman, and of the beast that carrieth her, which hath the seven heads and ten horns. The beast that thou sawest was, and is not; and shall ascend out of the bottomless pit, and go into perdition; and they that dwell on the earth shall wonder, whose names were not written in the book of life from the foundation of the world, when they behold the beast that was, and is not, and yet is. And here is the mind which hath wisdom. The seven heads are the seven mountains, on which the woman sitteth. And there are seven kings; five are fallen, and one is, and the other is not yet come; and when he cometh, he must continue a short space. And the beast that was, and is not, even he is the eighth, and is of the seven, and goeth into perdition. And the ten horns which thou sawest are ten kings, which have received no kingdom as yet; but receive power as kings one hour with the beast. These have one mind, and shall give their power and strength unto the beast. These shall make war with the Lamb, and the Lamb shall overcome them; for He is Lord of lords, and King of kings: and they that are with Him are called, and chosen, and faithful. And he saith unto me, The waters which thou sawest, where the whore sitteth, are peoples, and multitudes, and nations, and tongues. And the ten horns which thou sawest upon the beast, these shall hate the whore, and shall make her desolate and naked, and shall eat her flesh, and burn her with fire. For God hath put in their hearts to fulfill His will, and to agree, and give their kingdom unto the beast, unto the Words of God shall be fulfilled. And the woman which thou sawest is that great city, which reigneth over the kings of the earth.*

In the book of Jeremiah it is written that the LORD was going to draw the Gentiles out of the false pagan system of Babylon and bring a righteous remnant back to His Garden in Jerusalem, through the Messiah, through the mighty hand of God. Through the LORD'S Living Testimony as the Saviour, all the people of the earth would be blessed as they would know that He is the Royal Sovereign, the KING of glory, who reigns forever in Jerusalem.

Jeremiah 16:19-21 *O LORD, my strength, and my fortress, and my refuge in the day of affliction, the Gentiles shall come unto Thee from the ends of the earth, and shall say, Surely our fathers have inherited lies, vanity, and things wherein there is no profit. Shall a man make gods unto himself, and they are no gods? Therefore, behold, I will this once cause them to know, I will cause them to know My hand and My might; and they shall know that My Name is The LORD.*

God *is love and in Him there is no darkness at all.* He does not approve of the murder of His Saints and those who hold the Testimony of Messiah Yeshua/Jesus. In fact, Yeshua said in Matthew 5:22 *"you have heard it said you shall not murder!"* Then He said that whoever says to his brother *"Raka"* (now revealed as bowing to a crescent moon god in prayer, which is the same as *Raqqah* the stronghold) shall be subject to the judgment and hell fire. Mystery Babylon is now revealed as those worshipping *the Dog Star "Sirius!"* In Revelation 22:15 it is clear *dogs* do not enter paradise! In the last days God's House shall be established in Jerusalem in the top of His Holy Mountain, *His Holy Temple Mount. Jerusalem is the true "Gate of Heaven or Gate of God"* but pagan *"Babylon" (the counterfeit) also means "Gate of heaven or gate of god.* ***(Source: en.wikipedia.org/wiki/Babylon).*** The LORD raised Himself up in His Holy Mountain in His Garden in Jerusalem Israel. He calls us from all nations, tribes and tongues to come to Him so He can return to dwell with us forever in Jerusalem Israel, the true Garden of Eden.

Isaiah 2:1-3 *The Word that Isaiah the son of Amoz saw concerning Judah and Jerusalem. And it shall come to pass in the last days, that the Mountain of the LORD'S House shall be established in the top of the Mountains, and shall be exalted above the hills; and all nations shall flow unto it. And many people shall go and say, Come ye, and let us go up to the Mountain of the LORD, to the House of God of Jacob; and He will teach us of His ways, and we will walk in His paths; for out of Zion shall go forth the Law, and the Word of the LORD from Jerusalem.*

Zechariah 2:10-13 *Sing and rejoice, O daughter of Zion; for, lo, I come, and I will dwell in the midst of thee, saith the LORD. And many nations shall be joined to the LORD in that day, and shall be My people; and I will dwell in the midst of thee, and thou shalt know that the LORD of Hosts has sent Me unto thee. And the LORD shall inherit Judah His portion in the Holy Land, and shall choose Jerusalem again. Be silent, O all flesh, before the LORD; for He is raised up out of His Holy habitation.*

Jeremiah 51:60-62 *So Jeremiah wrote in a book all the evil that should come upon Babylon, even all these words that are written against Babylon. And Jeremiah said to Seraiah, When thou comest to Babylon, and shalt see, and shalt read all these words; Then shalt thou say, O LORD, Thou hast spoken against this place, to cut it off, that none shall remain in it, neither man nor beast, but that it shall be desolate forever.*

After I saw all these remarkable things, I then understood something else that was quite spectacular. Remember that after Yeshua ascended into the glory cloud into Heaven, He sent His Holy Spirit from Heaven seven weeks after Passover, and the Holy Spirit descended upon His Jewish disciples in flaming tongues of fire as they tarried in Jerusalem on Shavuot on Pentecost. They were waiting to be endued with power from on High. *I suddenly realized that the LORD, who had confused the languages in Shinar at the Tower of Babel, known as "the tower of tongues" where the false god system was established, was now, through His Ruach/Holy Spirit, restoring the languages in Jerusalem, so that everyone heard the disciples speaking clearly about the mighty works of the one true Living God and about His mighty Testimony as the Living Branch of the Almond Tree of Life in the city where He dwells forever!*

The Holy Temple Mount in Jerusalem Israel Original Photograph ©2011 Simon Brown England
All Rights Reserved – Photo Edited by Kimberly K Ballard

This was further proof that the only Towering Fortress that will ever reach unto Heaven is the Eternal Temple of God that will rest forever in Holy Mount Moriah in Jerusalem Israel. So the giving of the Holy Spirit from Heaven in Jerusalem upon the Jewish disciples brought forth the ability for everyone to understand in their own language. *God confused the languages at the Tower of Babel at the false place of worship, but He allowed everyone to hear the Word in their own languages in Jerusalem in the true place of worship as the disciples of Yeshua went about preaching the good news of Eternal Life, in the place where the one true Living God resides forever and sets His Towering Temple Fortress that reaches from Heaven to earth!* This alone proves again that God was drawing all men and women, back to His Garden in the east where Heaven truly meets the earth in Jerusalem! *As I proclaimed before, this was the location of the Garden of Eden in the beginning where Yeshua came to life.* It is truly remarkable! In the reading of Genesis 11:1-9, we can compare this Scripture with Acts 2:1-24 and you can clearly see that the languages were confused by the LORD God. The people could not understand each other's languages and this caused them to be scattered throughout the earth and abroad. I suddenly grasped the fact that the LORD was reversing this action on Pentecost, on Shavuot, when He sent His Holy Spirit to abide upon the Jewish disciples. Now, through the one true Living God and through His Ruach/Holy Spirit that was abiding upon the LORD'S Jewish disciples *in Jerusalem,* the people of many countries understood each other, even as they spoke in different languages and they wondered what this meant! I know what it means! It means that the LORD was drawing us out of Babylon, where we had been scattered away from Eden and into all nations, and He was drawing us away from the false system. The LORD through Messiah was drawing us back to the place in Jerusalem, where His Royal Towering Fortress will be set in our midst forever as He returns to dwell among us, in His Eternal Royal Garden, in the final redemption! As you will see in the following Scriptures, *"They understood as they heard them speak in their own tongues about the wonderful works of God!"* This was a restoration that would come about through Messiah dwelling among us. *He sent the Holy Spirit to dwell within our hearts to guide us back to the right place where He will always reign in His Heavenly Garden.* This explains perfectly why Babylon the Great and its corrupted system are absolutely destroyed in the book of Revelation. After it is destroyed, the LORD returns to dwell in our midst and He is Coronated as our Eternal Royal Sovereign KING. The people, who were once scattered by the LORD, were now being gathered back to the LORD out of the system of Babylon and into the Eternal system of the one true Living God of Israel. Notice in the following Scripture that the people journeyed from the east and they went out and found a plain in Shinar where they set up camp.

Genesis 11:1-9 *And the whole earth was of one language, and of one speech. And it came to pass, as they journeyed from the east, that they found a plain in the land of Shinar; and they dwelt there. And they said one to another, Go to, let us make brick, and burn them thoroughly. And they had brick for stone, and slime had they for mortar. And they said, Go to, let us build us a city and a tower, whose top may reach unto Heaven; and let us make us a name, lest we be scattered abroad upon the face of the whole earth. And the LORD came down to see the city and the tower, which the children of men builded. And the LORD said, Behold, the people is one, and they have all one language; and this they begin to do; and now nothing will be restrained from them, which they have imagined to do. Go to, let us go down, and there confound their language, that they may not understand one another's speech. So the LORD scattered them abroad from thence upon the face of all the earth; and they left off to build the city. Therefore is the name of it called Babel; because the LORD did there confound the language of all the earth; and from thence did the LORD scatter them abroad upon the face of all the earth.*

Now compare what happened in Genesis in Shinar to what happened later as the LORD began to draw all men and women back to the true place of worship in Jerusalem. Notice here that it says, *"They were all with one accord in one place!"* Dwelling in Jerusalem, there were not only Jews, but devout men out of every nation under Heaven, and they all heard about the Glory of God in their own languages, through the Holy Spirit of God that was dwelling in them.

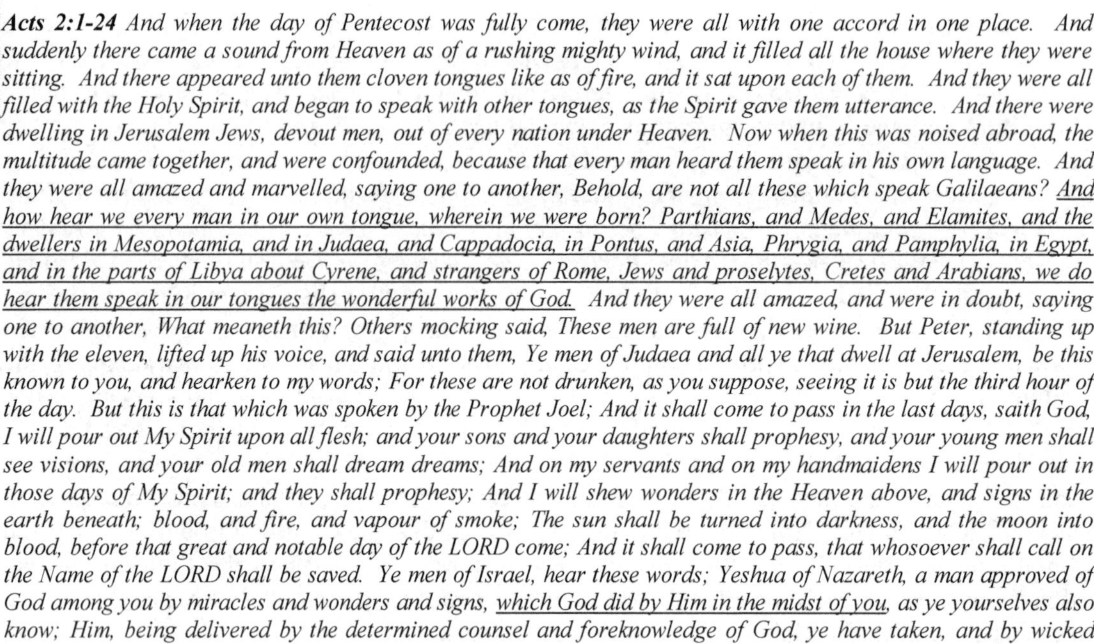

Acts 2:1-24 *And when the day of Pentecost was fully come, they were all with one accord in one place. And suddenly there came a sound from Heaven as of a rushing mighty wind, and it filled all the house where they were sitting. And there appeared unto them cloven tongues like as of fire, and it sat upon each of them. And they were all filled with the Holy Spirit, and began to speak with other tongues, as the Spirit gave them utterance. And there were dwelling in Jerusalem Jews, devout men, out of every nation under Heaven. Now when this was noised abroad, the multitude came together, and were confounded, because that every man heard them speak in his own language. And they were all amazed and marvelled, saying one to another, Behold, are not all these which speak Galilaeans? And how hear we every man in our own tongue, wherein we were born? Parthians, and Medes, and Elamites, and the dwellers in Mesopotamia, and in Judaea, and Cappadocia, in Pontus, and Asia, Phrygia, and Pamphylia, in Egypt, and in the parts of Libya about Cyrene, and strangers of Rome, Jews and proselytes, Cretes and Arabians, we do hear them speak in our tongues the wonderful works of God. And they were all amazed, and were in doubt, saying one to another, What meaneth this? Others mocking said, These men are full of new wine. But Peter, standing up with the eleven, lifted up his voice, and said unto them, Ye men of Judaea and all ye that dwell at Jerusalem, be this known to you, and hearken to my words; For these are not drunken, as you suppose, seeing it is but the third hour of the day. But this is that which was spoken by the Prophet Joel; And it shall come to pass in the last days, saith God, I will pour out My Spirit upon all flesh; and your sons and your daughters shall prophesy, and your young men shall see visions, and your old men shall dream dreams; And on my servants and on my handmaidens I will pour out in those days of My Spirit; and they shall prophesy; And I will shew wonders in the Heaven above, and signs in the earth beneath; blood, and fire, and vapour of smoke; The sun shall be turned into darkness, and the moon into blood, before that great and notable day of the LORD come; And it shall come to pass, that whosoever shall call on the Name of the LORD shall be saved. Ye men of Israel, hear these words; Yeshua of Nazareth, a man approved of God among you by miracles and wonders and signs, which God did by Him in the midst of you, as ye yourselves also know; Him, being delivered by the determined counsel and foreknowledge of God, ye have taken, and by wicked hands have crucified and slain; Whom God raised up, having loosed the pains of death; because it was not possible that He should be holden of it.*

So the LORD restored the languages in Jerusalem, so that everyone understood in their own language, instead of the confusion in Babylon that caused everyone to be scattered! *Now everyone would return to the former Garden of Eden in Jerusalem and we would all be united as one here through the LORD, but not under a man-made one-world global system of corrupted Babylon!* This is such a revelation from the Holy Spirit! By the way, *the tower of tongues* in Babylon brought forth incoherent babblings or speaking in tongues that made no sense, and the Jews knew that anyone who did this was a pagan. Rabbi Maimonides states in his code of laws and ethics, Mishneh Torah, that *"A charmer who is one that utters words that are not part of any spoken language and are meaningless, foolishly fancying that these words are helpful. The charmers go so far as to say that if one utters certain words over a snake or scorpion, it will become harmless…All these strange and uncouth sounds and names have no power to do good, even though they do no harm…These practices are all false and deceptive; they were employed by ancient idolaters to deceive the peoples of the world and induce them to become their followers. It is improper for Jews, who are highly intelligent, to be deluded by such absurdities, or to imagine that they are of any consequence…Sensible people, who possess sound mental faculties, know by clear proofs that all these practices which the Torah prohibits have no scientific basis…only those who are deficient in knowledge are attracted by these follies…" (Yad, Avodah Zarah).* ***(Source: A Book of Jewish Concepts by Philip Birnbaum (Pg 295) Revised Edition, ©1964, 1975 Hebrew Publishing CO, New York).***

From the same source where I found the quote from Maimonides, it is written about the history of the Tower of Babel quote; *"Modern scholars generally assume that the reference is to a Babylonian temple tower, a step-temple or ziggurat. An ancient ziggurat in Babylon existed already in the second millennium before the common era. It had eight stories, and was referred to as the "house of the foundation stone of heaven and earth." It was a step-pyramid, about three hundred feet high above the foundation. The top was reached by a stairway leading from terrace to terrace. It was begun by Hammurabi and developed by a number of other kings; Nebuchadnezzar completed it in the sixth century before the common era. The tower-temple has been regarded by architects as a stage in the development of minaret and spire."* ***(Source: A Book of Jewish Concepts by Philip Birnbaum (Pg 322) Revised Edition, ©1964, 1975 Hebrew Publishing CO, New York).***

Now I want to return to discussing the *Maror* in the Passover Seder. The *Maror* are, of course, the *bitter* herbs that represent the *bitterness* that the Israelites suffered in Egypt as the slaves of Pharaoh. The Israelites were instructed to eat the Passover meal with *the bitter herbs* as commanded by the LORD. They were to eat *the bitter herbs* on Nisan 14 of the Biblical calendar and Yeshua experienced *the bitterness of the curse of death* on Nisan 14. So the third cup of wine in the Passover Seder called *"the cup of redemption"* represents Yeshua's cup of *bitterness* that became *the sweet fruit* in the cup of redemption.

Numbers 9:11 *The fourteenth day of the second month at even they shall keep it, and eat it with unleavened bread and bitter herbs.*

There is one more ironic coincidence that I want to mention. Nisan 14 is the day that Messiah Yeshua bore the curse. So just out of curiosity, I calculated by adding the numbers of the day years ago that the *bitterness* came upon my life through my close friend whose name means, *"bitter,"* and it was February 2nd of the year 1984. Adding the number 2 of February to the year, 8+4, equals 14! February was the month that the LORD allowed *the bitterness* to come into my life in 1984 and February was the month in 2007, twenty three years later, that He restored me with *the sweetness* of His Living Almond Tree revelation. It was also February when I sent the astounding message from the LORD to Jerusalem! It was *February* when my Israeli friend sent me the photograph of the first budding Almond Tree, in the Old City of Jerusalem because the LORD directed her to take the photograph without having seen my email yet! In the same month, the LORD had turned my *bitter to sweet* through the revelation that He is the Living Branch from the Almond Tree of Life! He turned my mourning into joy!

This is why I know for certain that the LORD is the one who took my Israeli friend by the arm, as *"the Invisible Assistant,"* to photograph an Almond Tree that was budding and flowering at the exact moment that I sent her my Almond Tree revelation. This is why I knew for certain that God was allowing me to understand His Eternal Living Testimony through my own time of suffering *the bitterness.* You have to recall that at the time it was the dead of winter where I live in Colorado when my Almond Tree miracle happened, but the Almond Tree was budding and coming to life in Jerusalem on Holy Mount Moriah without my knowledge on the very day that God gave me the revelation and I emailed it to Jerusalem! In this astounding miracle, we both witnessed the Testimony of the resurrection of Messiah Yeshua in our precious Jerusalem Almond Tree and it came to life before our eyes after it had been resting dormant all winter.

"CHAROSET" = "SWEET"

During the Passover Seder, *the Charoset is the sweet mixture* that represents the mortar that the Israelites used to make bricks for Pharaoh. The *"sweetness,"* of this mixture, that consists of fruit of apples, cinnamon, nuts (almonds), wine or honey represents *the sweetness* of God's deliverance and redemption from *the bitterness* of being slaves under Pharaoh. So Messiah Yeshua is, *"The sweetness,"* of the First Fruit of Almonds, representing God's deliverance and redemption from *the bitterness* of Eden's curse. We can eat this Fruit from the Tree of Life and live forever. He is the Unleavened Bread from Heaven and the honey that is *the Living Torah,* the hidden manna, because it is sweet to our mouth like food from Heaven. Remember in the wilderness, the manna tasted like wafers and honey! As believers, we are the

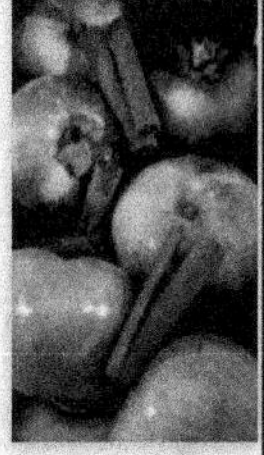

bricks that make up His Eternal House! The *Maror,* the *bitter* herbs, are dipped in *the Charoset, the sweet mixture*, and they are both eaten with unleavened bread. The Branch that bore both the *bitter and sweet* Almonds is Messiah. After having suffered *the bitterness* of the crucifixion, Yeshua was placed in the rock hewn Garden tomb in Mount Moriah on the Feast of Unleavened Bread. It was here that He gave us *the sweetness* of Eternal life. You could say that eating *the Charoset* represents the fact that even though life has its *bitterness,* the *Maror,* this is taken away by *the sweetness of the Charoset,* containing the fruit mixed with almonds, honey, and sweet spices! As I thought pensively about this, I began to make another remarkable connection. I was thinking about the *cinnamon and spices* within *the sweet mixture of the Charoset* and I remembered that the LORD'S anointed, *the right Sceptre,* wears garments that smell of *cinnamon* also known as, *"cassia."* The Rod is the Sceptre of the Great KING!

Psalm 45:6-8 *Thy throne, O God, is forever and ever; the Sceptre of Thy Kingdom is a Right Sceptre. Thou lovest righteousness, and hatest wickedness; therefore God, thy God, hath anointed thee with the oil of gladness above thy fellows. All thy garments smell of myrrh, and aloes, and cassia, out of the ivory palaces, whereby they have made thee glad.*

Incredibly, we see in the Gospel of John that *Yeshua, after bearing the bitterness of the curse, was buried on the Feast of Unleavened Bread with the myrrh, aloes, and spices that included the sweet spices of cinnamon or cassia. So the LORD brought it to mind that Yeshua's body came to life, smelling of the sweetness of the Charoset mixture, as the Fruitful Living Almond Branch!* Out of His mouth, came the sweetness of honey, *the Living Torah,* the Unleavened Bread from Heaven.

Cinnamon or Cassia Spice & Apples & Honey corner
Photos ©2014 Kimberly K Ballard All Rights Reserved

John 20:39-41 *And there came also Nicodemus, which at the first came to Yeshua by night, and brought a mixture of myrrh and aloes, about an hundred pound weight. Then took they the body of Yeshua, and wound it in linen clothes with the spices, as the manner of the Jews is to bury. Now in the place where He was crucified there was a Garden; and in the Garden a new Sepulchre, wherein was never man yet laid.*

The Royal Sceptre of God was buried with myrrh, aloes, and spices including cinnamon, in the rock hewn sepulchre in the Garden and rock quarry of Holy Mount Moriah! Messiah Yeshua became the fulfillment of every single detail in the Passover Seder. *When I suddenly realized that Yeshua was buried with the sweet spices and that He was the parallel of the Almond rod of Aaron, I knew in my heart that this was the reason that His garments in Heaven have the fragrance of the sweet spices of His burial and resurrection!* The *sweet mixture of the Charoset* is therefore very clearly representative of Messiah Yeshua and all the fine details are part of His wonderful Living Testimony as the Fruitful Branch from the Almond Tree of Life. The Almond Branch bore *the bitterness* of the bondage of death to give us *the sweetness* of Eternal Life! Now believe it or not, there is even more to this story! When Judas betrayed Yeshua, he betrayed Him during the Last Passover Seder, during the Feast of Unleavened Bread. During this last Passover Seder, sitting on the table was the *Maror, the*

bitter herbs, and *the Charoset, the sweet fruit, nut, and cinnamon mixture with honey or wine.* All the Jewish disciples sat at this meal with Yeshua. He had told them in advance exactly what was about to take place before it came to pass.

John 13:18-32 *I speak not of you all; I know whom I have chosen; but that the Scripture may be fulfilled, He that eateth bread with Me hath lifted up his heel against Me. Now I tell you before it come, that, when it is come to pass, ye may believe that I AM He. Verily, verily, I say unto you, He that receiveth whomsoever I send receiveth Me; and He that receiveth Me receiveth Him that sent Me. When Yeshua had thus said, He was troubled in Spirit, and testified, and said, Verily, verily, I say unto you, that one of you shall betray Me. Then the disciples looked one on another doubting of whom He spake. Now there was one leaning on Yeshua's bosom one of his disciples, whom Yeshua loved. Simon Peter therefore beckoned to him, that he should ask who it should be of whom He spake. He then lying on Yeshua's breast saith unto Him, LORD, who is it? Yeshua answered, He it is, to whom I shall give a sop, when I have dipped it. And when He had dipped the sop, He gave it to Judas Iscariot, the son of Simon. And after the sop Satan entered unto him. Then said Yeshua unto him, That thou doest do quickly. Now no man at the table knew for what intent He spake this unto him. For some of them thought, because Judas had the bag, that Yeshua had said unto him, Buy those things that we have need of against the Feast; or, that he should give something to the poor. He then having received the sop went immediately out; and it was night. Therefore, when he was gone out, Yeshua said, Now is the Son of man glorified, and God is glorified in Him. If God be glorified in Him, God shall also glorify Him in Himself, and shall straightway glorify Him.*

What exactly happened during this betrayal of Messiah the LORD by Judas Iscariot? I believe that Judas dipped the Unleavened Bread, the Matzah, into the *Maror, into the bitter herbs, at the same time as Yeshua.* The moment that *Judas accepted the bitterness of the curse, Messiah was the sweetness* of the Almond Branch who was about to take away our bondage from the curse of death from the Garden of Eden. The very moment that Judas dipped in the *Maror,* the Scripture says that Satan entered him. Judas accepted *the bitterness* of his destruction and the betrayal of the LORD. After Judas left the table, he went out to betray the LORD (Yeshua ha-Ben) for the redeeming price of thirty pieces of silver. This fulfilled the Scriptures that declared that Messiah the anointed Branch would be cut off. This event also fulfilled the Scripture that said that *"thirty pieces of silver was the price that the LORD was valued of by them,"* as it is written in Zechariah 11:13. Messiah then by Divine Providence became *the Branch cut off from Israel,* exactly as Daniel had prophesied in Daniel 9:26. So when the Branch, the Rod of God, was lifted up on the cross, *bearing the bitterness of the curse,* the Rod fulfilled the work of God, bringing glory to Himself, and He would be brought to life again *because the seed of life of the Living Torah was inside Himself.* So He bore the First Fruit on the third day, after sprouting to life as the Fruitful Almond Branch from the Almond Tree of Life. So in order for us to live forever, we must eat the First Fruit from the Almond Tree of Life, the First Fruit of salvation, which is the LORD Messiah, *the Living Torah.* This is why there is only one way into Heaven that God provided for us to enter into His Eternal Kingdom and it is through His Rod of salvation, *"Yeshua" who redeemed us!*

Now when I said earlier that I believed that the three niches in the exterior rock face of the Garden tomb in Holy Mount Moriah held the elements of Yeshua's Living Testimony and that I believe there was a Mezuzah set in the rock face of the exterior wall, remember that this also verifies that this Garden is the true *"Gate of Heaven,"* and we can only enter Heaven through this gate in Jerusalem by the Living Testimony of Messiah Yeshua, the Rod of God. This place is where the letters *Alpha and Omega* are to be found in the signet shaped object *where the LORD produced the First Fruit from His Almond Tree of Life. If we eat the First Fruit from the Living Almond Rod or Branch, like Mary Magdalene and the other Mary, as well as the other Jewish disciples of the LORD, then we can enter Heaven through the gate, which is Messiah the LORD, from Holy Mount Moriah where He comes to us as our Deliverer to take us to our haven of Heaven!* This was a fantastic verification that the whole process over the centuries, since the fall of mankind and through countless wars and invasions, has been the work of the LORD, drawing us all back to Jerusalem to His Garden, on Holy Mount Moriah.

THE LAMB'S EAR MAROR

Lamb's Ear Plant
Photos ©2013 Kimberly K Ballard

At times, I have felt so strongly that the LORD was watching over my work as I proceeded in writing this book for His glory. I have always felt that His Divine Presence was with me every time that some completely unexpected topic would come forth and present itself to my heart. This happened to me again in this section on the Maror. I came back to investigate the Maror a little bit more because I wanted to see if I could determine the original herb that was used in the ancient Passover Seder. The Jewish Virtual Library was, of course, one of my first sources for finding the details of the description of the plant that was used in the Seder for this bitter herb. Although it is true that certain bitter vegetables have been used for the Divine service, the identification of the correct plant of the Maror has been difficult to determine. When a plant is hard to determine, substitutes are often used instead of the original plant source.

According to the Jewish Virtual Library *"The Rabbis profess that this plant had to possess certain common characteristics. The plant first of all, had to be bitter and it had to contain a sap with a grayish appearance, (Pes. 39a). The description goes on to say that this meant wild or cultivated vegetables, with leaves of a silvery-grayish-green color that have a milk-like sap and leaves with a bitter taste. This definition applies to a number of plants, particularly some of those belonging to the family, "Compositae." The plant was said to be recommended, "As a remedy for various ailments."* ***(Source: Maror Copyright ©2010 The Jewish Virtual Library).***

As I read the text about the Maror and the description presented by the Rabbi's, there was one plant that instantly came into my mind that fit this exact description! When I read that the leaves were a silvery-grayish-green color, the thought immediately came to me that this was the plant known as *"Lamb's Ear!"* At one time, I worked in a Greenhouse and I loved this fuzzy perennial plant. Why the Lamb's Ear came into my mind is a curious thing, but the description of the silvery-grayish-green leaves is what sounded so familiar to me. So, I decided to type the Lamb's Ear plant in the search box just to see what would come up for this lovely little fuzzy plant. I had no idea at that moment that this search was about to lead somewhere that was completely unexpected and what I discovered next shocked me. I could hardly believe it when I saw that this Lamb's Ear plant was called by another name. Why was this other name shocking to me? Well, I had already written about this man in my book who was one of the Seventy Apostles specifically appointed by Messiah Yeshua to go forth from Jerusalem and to go before His face into all the cities where He would travel to proclaim the glory of God. The Lamb's Ear plant, much to my surprise, just happened to be called by this man's name and he was recorded in the Gospel of Luke and in the book of Romans! The strange thing about suddenly making this connection to the Lamb's Ear with the Maror is the fact that not only did this man have a very unusual name, but I was shocked by the fact that I had written about his historical connection to the Messiah in my text from my research several months ago when I was trying to figure out exactly how the Great Rolling Stone came to be standing upon Mount Nebo. It was during the time that I researched this that I came up with the name of one of the *Seventy Apostles* who was appointed directly by Messiah Yeshua in Jerusalem to preach that the Kingdom of God had come. I discovered that *the Seventy* were likely an important part of

how the Great Rolling Stone was saved, and probably how it eventually wound up in a Byzantine monastery near Mount Nebo where it was discovered. Centuries later, when it was unearthed, they stood it upright on Mount Nebo. Now I discovered by Divine Providence that this plant was named after one of the Messiah's followers! This was fantastic! It was a man named *"Stachys the Apostle."* As you will read later I found information that *"Stachys"* was a great friend and assistant to the Apostle Andrew, who was Simon Peter's brother. I found out in the historical record that *Stachys* was a friend of Yeshua and they knew each other quite well. This is all recorded in Luke Chapter 10. Now as I said in my other text, the Apostle Andrew, is said to have appointed *Stachys* as the First Bishop of Byzantium, in the year 38AD! This means that he became the Bishop of Byzantium only five years after the death and resurrection of Yeshua. There is absolutely no doubt in my mind that if Stachys was so close to the original twelve Jewish disciples and also lived among them, even following the Jewish Messiah, this means that without a doubt that Stachys participated in the original Jewish Passover Seder! This means that Stachys had to have eaten *the original ancient Maror* with the other Jewish followers of Yeshua and perhaps even with Yeshua Himself. So why is this all so important? The truth is that when the Holy Spirit brought the Lamb's Ear plant into my mind, simply because I knew that it matched the Rabbi's description of the Maror perfectly, I decided to look up some details about this particular plant. It is surprising to discover that the Lamb's Ear herb is *"a member of the Mint family"* and of course it is very wooly, soft and tender, just like a lamb's ear. Instead of being a member of the Compositae family, *"The Lamb's Ear is a member of the "Lamiaceae" plant family. This plant family ironically includes many of the culinary herbs such as, Basil, Oregano, Catnip or Catmint, Sage, Spearmint, Lavender, and Peppermint."* ***(Source: Lamb's Ear facts ©2011 Wikipedia, the free encyclopedia).***

I believe that the Holy Spirit brought the Lamb's Ear plant into my mind in regards to *the Maror* because much to my astonishment, the Lamb's Ear is coincidentally called *"Stachys Byzantina."* This was an unbelievable connection! Yeshua the Messiah our Passover *"Lamb,"* is the *"Lamb"* of God, and *Stachys,* the first Bishop of Byzantium is a follower of the Jewish Messiah. The Rabbis had stated that *the Maror* had the benefits of healing various ailments and this is true of the Lamb's Ear herb. In fact, I was completely astonished when I discovered that the Lamb's Ear herb was said to have been particularly useful in *"binding up wounds!"* The moment that those words rang in my ears, my heart was deeply touched because the LORD Yeshua is the Lamb of God who binds up our wounds!

The Stachys Byzantina, Lamb's Ear that I planted in my garden after this discovery!
Photo ©2014 Kimberly K Ballard All Rights Reserved

Jeremiah 30:17 *For I will restore health unto thee, and I will heal thee of thy wounds, saith the LORD; because they called thee an Outcast, saying, This is Zion, whom no man seeketh after.*

Hosea 6:1-2 *Come, and let us return unto the LORD; for He hath torn, and He will heal us; He hath smitten, and He will bind us up. After two days will He revive us; in the third day He will raise us up, and we shall live in His sight.*

I have written further about the binding of the Messiah in a coming chapter, but this was such an unexpected turn of events that I wanted to write it as this miracle occurred. Messiah is the LORD who would *bind up the wounds of the brokenhearted!* Messiah Yeshua is the Lamb of God who ate the Passover Seder with His followers. They endured many hardships for following after the LORD of glory.

Isaiah 53:7 *He was oppressed, and He was afflicted, yet He opened not His mouth; He is brought as a Lamb to the slaughter, and as a sheep before her shearers is dumb, so He opened not His mouth.*

John 1:29 *The next day John seeth Yeshua coming unto him, and saith, Behold the Lamb of God, which taketh away the sin of the world.*

Perhaps the next piece of evidence is even more convincing that Lamb's Ear may have been the original herb for the Maror. I was shocked again when I happened to find a book that was written in the 1800's. In this book, the Lamb's Ear plant was called *"Saviour's Blanket."* ***(Source: Woundwort ©1897 William Thomas Fernie UK).*** This was even more evidence that the Lamb's Ear was not only connected to one of *the Seventy Apostles* that Yeshua sent out from Jerusalem, but now this title connected the Lamb's Ear to the Saviour Himself, to our LORD. The term *"Saviour's Blanket"* was so profound because *"Saviour"* is a title of God, the Messiah. By definition, He is the one who rescues and saves us. By definition the word *"Blanket" means to "cover."* A Blanket is a covering that is all-encompassing. This term is also associated with the words *"bury, conceal, hide, cloud, eclipse, and crown."* These are the same words that also describe being *"overshadowed"* by the Holy Spirit. All of the details within the meaning of the term *"Saviour's Blanket"* reveal so many of the astounding truths about the Messiah's identity. The LORD God of Israel hid His face and concealed it in His glory cloud. He was *buried* as part of His Testimony after an *eclipse* and He will wear the *Crown* of the KING OF KINGS. His *covering* is over the Tabernacle and over the Ark of His Living Testimony.

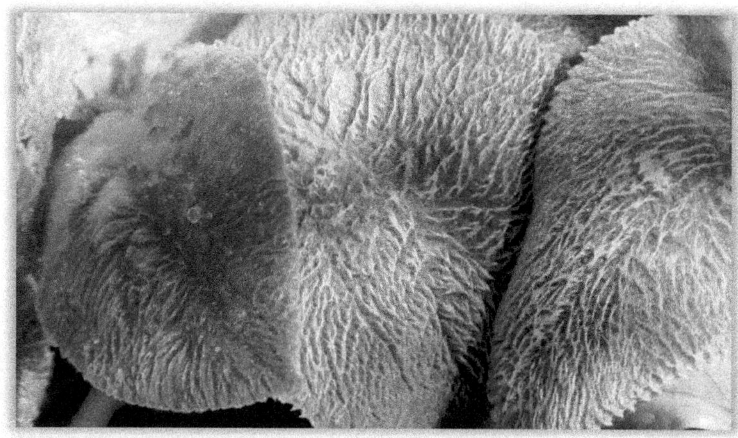

Stachys Byzantina, Lamb's Ear Plant Photo ©2014 Kimberly K Ballard All Rights Reserved

Stachys Byzantina Lamb's Ear Photo ©2013 Kimberly K Ballard All Rights Reserved

Psalm 105:39 *He spread a cloud for <u>a covering</u>; and fire to give light in the night.*

Job 22:13-14 *And thou sayest, How doth God know? Can He judge through the dark cloud? Thick clouds are <u>a covering</u> to Him, that He seeth not; and He walketh in the circuit of Heaven.*

Exodus 40:19-21 *And he spread abroad the tent over the Tabernacle, and put the covering of the tent above upon it; as the LORD commanded Moses. And he took and put the Testimony into the Ark, and set the staves on the Ark, and put the Mercy Seat above upon the Ark; And he brought the Ark into the Tabernacle, and set up the veil of <u>the covering</u>, and covered the Ark of the Testimony; as the LORD commanded Moses.*

The Scriptures testify to the fact that the *LORD Messiah is our covering* because *His Testimony is the Living Ark of Heaven.* After these things were shown to me by the LORD, I went back to read Luke 10 about *the Seventy Apostles* of the Messiah.

Luke 10:1 *After these things the LORD appointed other Seventy also, and sent them two and two before His face into every city and place, whither He Himself would come.*

Notice that the Scripture says that *Yeshua sent them "before His face," two by two.* Remember that when the LORD drew the animals and birds to the Ark of Noah *to be saved, they were sent to the Ark two by two! In this case, the LORD was drawing us back to Himself, as the Ark of Heaven.* We would be brought into the Ark to be saved through Messiah's Living Testimony. It was to be proclaimed by *the Seventy,* who were sent out from Jerusalem *two by two* by the Messiah. Eventually, the LORD would draw us back to the Garden of God by drawing us into the Ark of His salvation. The *Seventy* went forth preaching the Kingdom of God. In these things, we can see that His face is no longer hidden or concealed from us *as with a covering,* but His face is revealed to us in the face of Messiah, the *Sar HaPanim "the Prince of the face of the LORD God."* As I continued reading in Luke, I was thinking about Stachys and the Lamb's Ear. At once, I got tears in my eyes as I read Yeshua's words to the *Seventy.*

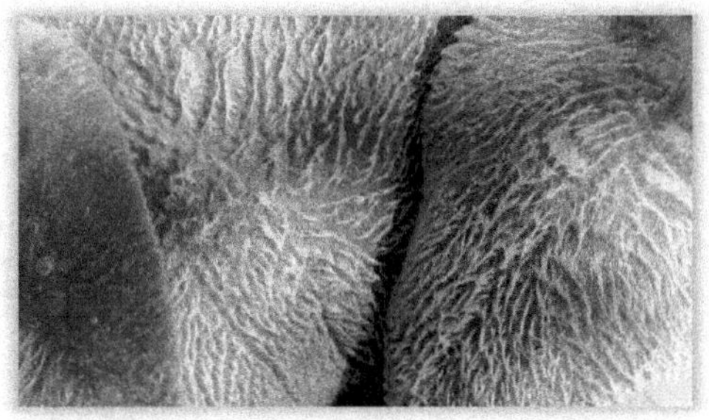

Stachys Byzantina
Photo ©2014 Kimberly K Ballard All Rights Reserved

Luke 10:2-3 *Therefore said He unto them, The harvest truly is great, but the labourers are few; pray ye therefore the LORD of the harvest, that He would send forth labourers into His harvest. Go your ways; behold, I send you forth as lambs among wolves.*

Yeshua called Stachys one of His lambs! The Scripture goes on to say that *the Seventy* came back to Yeshua to proclaim the following to Him.

Luke 10:17-20 *And the Seventy returned again with joy, saying, LORD, even the devils are subjected to us through Thy Name. And He said unto them, I beheld Satan as lightening fall from Heaven. Behold, I give unto you power to tread on serpents and scorpions, and over all the power of the enemy; and nothing shall by any means hurt you. Notwithstanding in this rejoice not, that the spirits are subject unto you; but rather rejoice, because your names are written in Heaven.*

Within this text was the proof that *Stachys was called "a lamb" sent out among wolves, by Messiah Yeshua Himself.* Therefore, the plant called *"Lamb's Ear Plant,"* that I now believe is the original Maror, was at some point given this name, *"Stachys Byzantina."* He was one of *the lambs* of God sent forth to proclaim the Kingdom of God by declaring the Living Testimony of Messiah, who is the Passover Lamb of God. The mere fact that Yeshua sent them forth as lambs directly connects the Lamb's Ear plant to Stachys, the first Bishop of Byzantium. Stachys is later mentioned by name in the greetings of the Apostle Paul in the book of Romans.

Romans 16:9 *Salute Urbane, our helper in Messiah, and Stachys my beloved.*

When Yeshua bore *the bitterness of the curse* and sealed His Living Testimony in the Passover Seder with *the Maror,* does it not stand to reason that *the Maror itself would also reflect the element of the true Lamb, the Saviour God, in every single way*? All of the remarkable connections that I found to the Lamb's Ear plant proved that it was far too significant to ignore because it had a direct connection to the LORD and to His Living Testimony as the Lamb of God, who takes away the sins of the world. I believe the LORD was showing this to me for a reason. I truly felt that He was showing me that *the Lamb's Ear* was

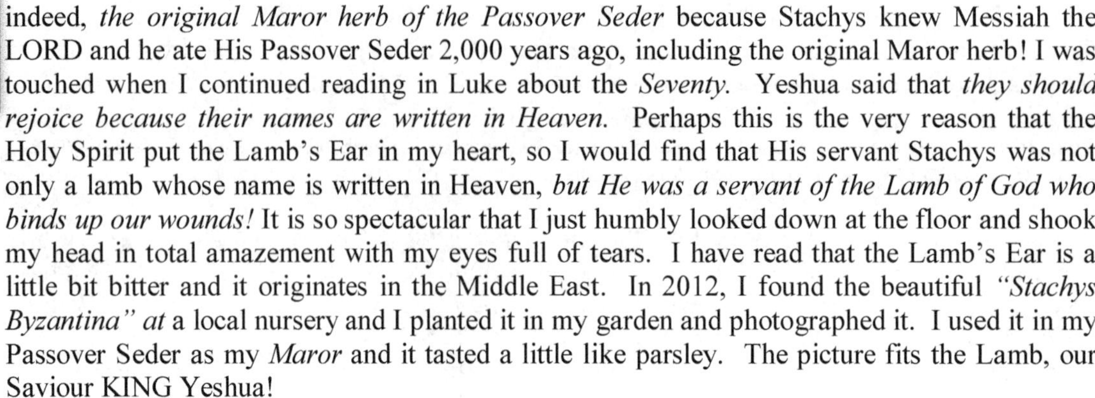

indeed, *the original Maror herb of the Passover Seder* because Stachys knew Messiah the LORD and he ate His Passover Seder 2,000 years ago, including the original Maror herb! I was touched when I continued reading in Luke about the *Seventy.* Yeshua said that *they should rejoice because their names are written in Heaven.* Perhaps this is the very reason that the Holy Spirit put the Lamb's Ear in my heart, so I would find that His servant Stachys was not only a lamb whose name is written in Heaven, *but He was a servant of the Lamb of God who binds up our wounds!* It is so spectacular that I just humbly looked down at the floor and shook my head in total amazement with my eyes full of tears. I have read that the Lamb's Ear is a little bit bitter and it originates in the Middle East. In 2012, I found the beautiful *"Stachys Byzantina" at* a local nursery and I planted it in my garden and photographed it. I used it in my Passover Seder as my *Maror* and it tasted a little like parsley. The picture fits the Lamb, our Saviour KING Yeshua!

THE TREE THAT TURNED BITTER TO SWEET, PASSOVER AND THE MARAH, THE SWEET LIVING WATER, THE SWEET CHAROSET

Moses was in the wilderness with the children of Israel and they could not drink the waters of Marah for they were *bitter.* So what happened? The LORD showed Moses a tree and when this tree was cast into the waters, the waters that were *bitter* became *sweet.* They were *three days* into the wilderness without water when this happened!

When Yeshua, the Branch of the Almond Tree of life, was raised to life on the third day in God's Garden in Holy Mount Moriah, He turned *the bitter to sweet,* thus proving that He is the source of the sweet Living Water and that He was with the children of Israel in the wilderness with Moses centuries before this event. This is why the miracle at the Pool of Bethesda is so fantastic. *Remember that in that miracle the bitterness of the suffering crippled man was suddenly turned into the sweetness of restoration when the Living Water and the Tree of Life spoke to him and told him to get up and walk, just like the tree made the bitter waters of Marah sweet.* All along, the LORD was revealing to the children of Israel in the wilderness that He is their Saviour, the Rod Messiah. He is their Yeshua! The LORD hid these truths throughout His Torah. These mighty works are like a treasure hidden in a field, waiting for us to diligently dig for them and search until we find them. When we do find them, we become rich with the wisdom and knowledge of the LORD God, and only the Ruach/Holy Spirit reveals them to us!

Exodus 15:22-27 *So Moses brought Israel from the Red sea, and they went out into the wilderness of Shur; and they went three days in the wilderness, and found no water. And when they came to Marah, they could not drink of the waters of Marah, for they were bitter; therefore the name of it was called Marah. And the people murmured against Moses, saying, What shall we drink? And he cried unto the LORD; and the LORD shewed him a tree, which when he*

had cast into the waters, the waters were made sweet; there he made for them a statute and an ordinance, and there he proved them, And said, If thou wilt diligently hearken to the voice of the LORD thy God, and wilt do that which is right in his sight, and wilt give ear to his commandments, and keep all his statutes, I will put none of these diseases upon thee, which I have brought upon the Egyptians; for I AM the LORD that healeth thee. And they came to Elim, where were twelve wells of water, and threescore and ten palm trees: and they encamped there by the waters.

The Scriptures tell us that *the bitter is the curse and the sweet is the removal of the curse.* The LORD Messiah had to fulfill His Eternal Testimony by *bearing both the bitter and the sweet Almonds* in the same place on Holy Mount Moriah. Golgotha, *the place of the skull,* was the place of *death and bitterness.* The LORD'S vineyard was the place of *sweetness,* as the resurrection took place here in His Garden.

James 3:11 *Doth a fountain send forth at the same place sweet water and bitter?*

Now, the following verses that speak of the word *"bitter"* all pertain to *"the curse."*

Revelation 8:10-11 *And the third angel sounded and there fell a great star from heaven, burning as it were a lamp, and it fell upon the third part of the rivers, and upon the fountains of waters; And the name of the star is called Wormwood; and the third part of the waters became wormwood; and many men died of the waters, because they were bitter.*

Proverbs 5:3-4 *For the lips of a strange woman drop as an honeycomb, and her mouth is smoother than oil; But her end is bitter as wormwood, sharp as a two edged sword.*

Numbers 5:23-24 *And the priest shall write these curses in a book, and he shall blot them out with the bitter water; And he shall cause the woman to drink the bitter water that causeth the curse; and the water that causeth the curse shall enter into her, and become bitter.*

Since we now understand that *Yeshua is the sweet Charoset of Passover that took away our bitter Maror,* then we can understand why the LORD said the following Words in the book of Isaiah about the *bitter and the sweet.*

Isaiah 5:20-21 *Woe unto them that call evil good, and good evil; that put darkness for light, and light for darkness; that put bitter for sweet, and sweet for bitter! Woe unto them that are wise in their own eyes, and prudent in their own sight!*

The truth about this verse is that when the LORD came from Heaven to save us as our Branch Yeshua, *He became the sweet that took away the bitter,* but some have traded the marvelous works of His Living Testimony in the Heavenly Ark for the *bitterness* of remaining in the curse of death by saying evil things about Messiah Yeshua. Thus, they have put *bitter for sweet and sweet for bitter.* Therefore, if people do not believe that the LORD is good and instead they call Him evil, in reverse of the truth, and if they deny that the Messiah Yeshua has *taken away the bitterness of the curse of death* for us, giving us the *sweetness of Eternal life,* then those who trade His *sweet for bitter* are still living under *a curse.* Those who say such things are actually bringing condemnation upon themselves, along with many *curses.* Again, we can see in the verse that when they take the Word of God, Yeshua, *the Living Torah,* which is *the light that came out of the darkness* of the sepulchre during His Divine resurrection *as evening was becoming morning of the first day of the week in Holy Mount Moriah,* and they do not believe it, then they are trading God's Living Testimony for the darkness of false religions and doctrines, putting darkness for light. A Satanic god of death brings *bitterness,* and they celebrate their ungodly killing of God's Saints by eating *sweets* in the streets, but the LORD says, *"Woe unto those who do this!"* They have done what is evil or *bitter* and called it *sweet!* When the LORD has stretched out His mighty hand with the Rod of salvation in it and brought forth the *sweet* good news of everlasting life by the grace of God, which is a *New and Living*

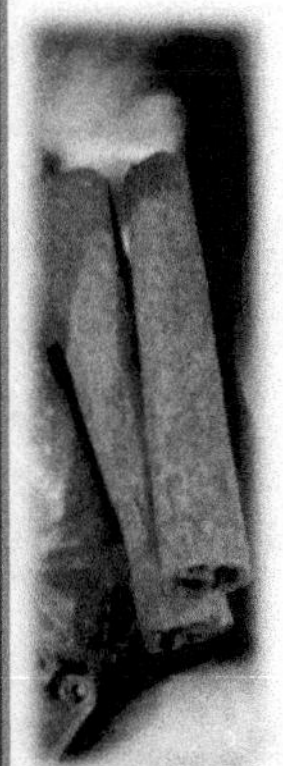

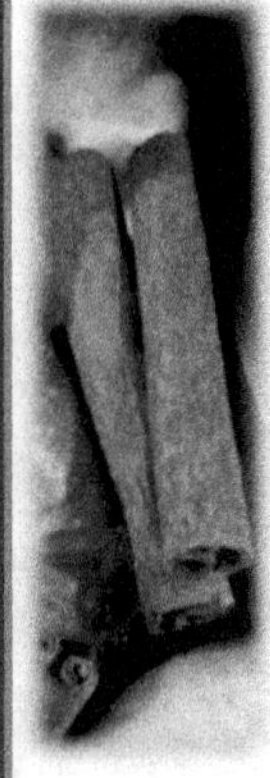
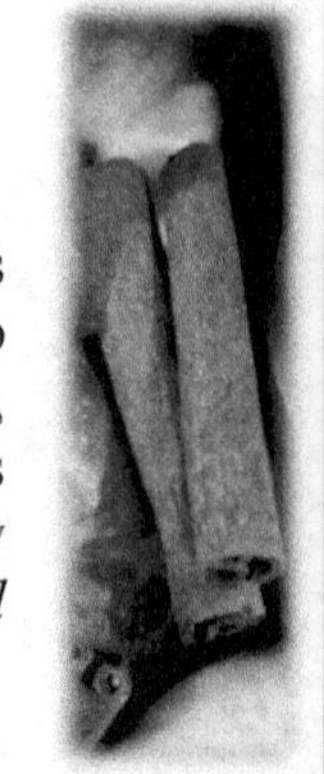

Eternal Covenant He made with us, and they still do not believe that the LORD performed this mighty work, then they have put *bitter for sweet and sweet for bitter* because they refused to *validate the KING* and believe Him. If people do not believe God, that He is Messiah Yeshua, the Branch who came to life, the exact parallel of Aaron's rod that budded because the life is inside Him and that this budded Almond Rod, *is the Living Rod in the Heavenly Ark,* then they have traded *the sweetness of Eternal life for the bitterness of the curse of death and they will die in their sins under the curse.* Yeshua said this to those who refused to believe His Word.

John 8:20-24 *These words spake Yeshua in the treasury, as He taught in the Temple; and no man laid hands on Him; for His hour was not yet come. Then said Yeshua again unto them, I go My way, and ye shall seek Me, and shall die in your sins; whither I go, ye cannot come. Then said the Jews, Will He kill Himself? Because He saith, Whither I go, ye cannot come. And He said unto them, Ye are from beneath; I AM from above; ye are of this world; I AM not of this world. I said therefore unto you, that ye shall die in your sins; for if ye believe not that I AM HE, ye shall die in your sins.*

Now we can understand how Yeshua, *the sweet Living Water,* instantly healed thousands of people in the Holy Land. *The Branch from the Almond Tree of Life turned our bitter to sweet, so we could drink this sweet Living Water and live forever in God's Garden.* These were the very works of Messiah Yeshua at Jacob's well. This Living Water, if we drink it, shall be in us *a well of water springing up to Eternal life.* Remember that wherever abundant water is found, life thrives there! This is why there is abundant life in the Divine Presence of the LORD God of Israel.

John 4:13-14 *Yeshua answered and said unto her, Whosoever drinketh of this water shall thirst again; But whosoever drinketh of the water that I shall give him shall never thirst; but the water that I shall give him shall be in him a well of water springing up into everlasting life.*

In the book of Ruth, we see that Naomi went back to Bethlehem, which later became the place of Yeshua's birth. When the people saw her, she told them not to call her Naomi, but to call her *"Mara"* because the LORD had dealt *very bitterly* with her. The LORD restored her and took away her *bitterness* when she returned to Bethlehem.

Ruth 1:19-22 *So they two went until they came to Bethlehem. And it came to pass, when they were come to Bethlehem, that all the city was moved about them, and they said, Is this Naomi? And she said unto them, Call me not Naomi, call me Mara; for the Almighty hath dealt very bitterly with me. I went out full, and the LORD hath brought me home again empty; why then call ye me Naomi, seeing the LORD hath testified against me, and the Almighty hath afflicted me? So Naomi returned, and Ruth the Moabitess, her daughter in law, with her, which returned out of the country of Moab; and they came to Bethlehem in the beginning of barley harvest.*

Messiah the Living Branch was born in Bethlehem because He came to restore His people as the Living Water and the Almond Tree of Life! It is also remarkable that when Naomi and Ruth came to Bethlehem and the LORD took away her *bitterness,* it was the beginning of the barley harvest in Israel. The barley harvest is called *"the Feast of First Fruits."* Passover is the 14th of Nisan. The Feast of Unleavened Bread begins on Nisan 15th and the waving of the omer of the barley harvest is from Nisan 16 through Nisan 17. *The barley harvest happens on the third day of Passover week on the same day that Yeshua was raised to life as the Almond bearing Branch that turned the bitter Almonds into the sweet Almonds, and He restored us to Eternal life by offering us the First Fruit from the Almond Tree of Life on this particular third day.* Remember that Yeshua fed the 5,000+ with five loaves of *barley bread* and two small fish because *He is the Living Torah!* When Naomi went back to Bethlehem, it was *"the Feast of First Fruits,"* and they were giving a thanksgiving celebration to the LORD for the barley harvest. It was to thank the LORD for *the first grain* of the season. Therefore, Yeshua was

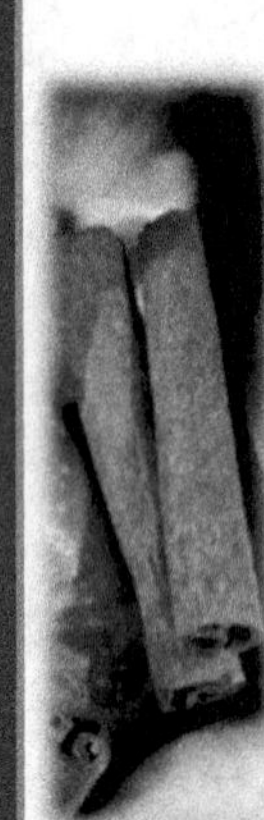
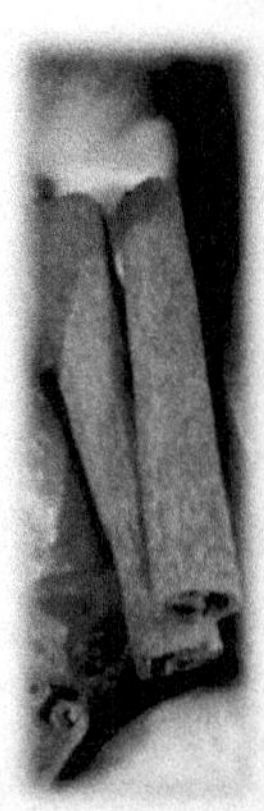

raised to life on the third day on the Feast of First Fruits at the very same time that Israel was thanking the LORD for *the first grain* of the harvest. So Yeshua was indeed the seed that was placed in the earth on Nisan 14 and He sprouted to life on this very day, on Nisan 17, and became *the first grain* of the harvest of the LORD. It is interesting too that *Stachys,* who is named for the Lamb's Ear Maror, has this unusual name that means *"an ear of grain"* and He followed Yeshua the Messiah, the hidden manna of Heaven!

King Solomon built a huge aqueduct system. Water came from the mountains of Hebron, to Bethlehem. From Bethlehem it flowed into the Holy Temple that King Solomon built. It provided fresh *living water* for the offerings of the LORD. ***(Sources: bible.ca/archeology/bible-archeaology-jerusalem-temple-mount-threshing-floor-aqueduct.htm) AND (en.wikipedia.org/wiki/Solomon's_Pools).*** *Messiah Yeshua came into this world in the little town of Bethlehem, the House of Bread, as the Living Water that will flow out from the Heavenly Holy Temple when He returns from Heaven.* I mentioned before in *(chapter 1 and chapter 4)* this not the Third Temple (which is really the sixth Temple), it is the seventh Temple, the Heavenly Temple that is the body of Messiah. God is everything! We will live in His Presence as He reigns forever in Jerusalem Israel.

Now remember, *the sweetness of the LORD, our Passover Charoset,* is in the fragrance of His garments. In King Solomon's Song of Songs, the LORD is in His Garden and says, *'Awake,' O north wind come and come thou south; blow upon My Garden."* He is saying, *"Shaked!"* The spices that I talked about before are once again mentioned here in this Scripture, along with the myrrh, aloes, and spices. *Everything that the Messiah was buried with is found in this Garden.* Now the spice called *"Spikenard"* is also mentioned this time as one of the spices, and Mary anointed Yeshua's feet for His burial with the *Spikenard. Yeshua was indeed the life giving fountain and well of Living Water as He was sealed in the tomb in the Garden of God.* He is the pleasant fruit in the Garden. We are His Bride, bought with a price.

Song of Songs 4:12-16 *A garden inclosed is my sister, my spouse; a spring shut up, a fountain sealed. Thy plants are an orchard of pomegranates, with pleasant fruits; camphire, with spikenard, Spikenard and saffron; calamus and cinnamon, with all trees of frankincense; myrrh and aloes, with all the chief spices; A fountain of gardens, a well of living waters, and streams from Lebanon. Awake, O north wind; and come, thou south; blow upon my garden, that the spices thereof may flow out. Let my beloved come into his garden, and eat his pleasant fruits.*

After Yeshua was laid in the Garden of Holy Mount Moriah as the Living Water, and sealed in the tomb, He would *"Awaken," "Shaked" or "Almond,"* and come to life. *As the resurrected sweet Charoset of the Passover Seder, His garments would be fragrant from all the spices that He was buried with at the resurrection of the First Fruit of salvation.* So not only was Yeshua buried with the myrrh, aloes, and spices of cinnamon, but Mary previously anointed Yeshua with the *Spikenard* before His crucifixion and burial. His Word is *the honey* that binds the sweet spices together with the First Fruit and nuts of Almonds from His Living Branch Testimony of the LORD! Remember that Yeshua stated that she did this for His burial!

John 12:3 *Then took Mary a pound of ointment of spikenard, very costly, and anointed the feet of Yeshua, and wiped His feet with her hair; and the house was filled with the odour of the ointment.*

John 12:7-8 *Then said Yeshua, Let her alone; against the day of My burying hath she kept this. For the poor always ye have with you; but Me ye have not always.*

In the Song of Songs, the Song of Solomon, we see that the KING, the LORD, is sitting at His table with the scent of Spikenard in the air. The KING is Yeshua the LORD who has the fragrance of the Spikenard because He was anointed and buried with the Spikenard in His Royal KINGLY Garden in Holy Mount Moriah in Jerusalem!

Song of Songs 1:12 *While the King sitteth at His table, my spikenard sendeth forth the smell thereof.*

Yeshua was not only anointed on His feet with the *Spikenard,* He also had the *Spikenard* poured upon His head. *The KING was sitting at a table! So He was their Saviour! The Angel of His Divine Presence saved them!*

Mark 14:1-3 *After two days was the Feast of the Passover, and of Unleavened bread; and the Chief Priests and the Scribes sought how they might take Him by craft, and put Him to death. But they said, Not on the Feast day, lest there be an uproar of the people. And being in Bethany in the house of Simon the leper, as He sat at meat, there came a woman having an alabaster box of ointment of spikenard very precious; and she brake the box, and poured it on His head.*

Isaiah 63:8-14 *For He said, Surely they are My people, children that will not lie; so He was their Saviour. In all their affliction He was afflicted, and the angel of His Presence saved them; in His love and in His pity He redeemed them; and He bare them, and carried them all the days of old. But they rebelled, and vexed His Holy Spirit; therefore He was turned to be their enemy, and He fought against them. Then He remembered the days of old, Moses, and his people, saying, Where is He that brought them up out of the sea with the Shepherd of His flock? Where is He that put His Holy Spirit within him? That led them by the right hand of Moses with His glorious arm, dividing the water before them, to make Himself an everlasting Name? That led them through the deep, as an horse in the wilderness, that they should not stumble? As a beast goeth down into the valley, the Spirit of the LORD caused him to rest; so didst Thou lead Thy people, to make Thyself a glorious Name.*

Hosea 14:5-9 *I will be as the dew unto Israel; He shall grow as the lily, and cast forth His roots as Lebanon. His branches shall spread, and His beauty shall be as the olive tree, and His smell as Lebanon. They that dwell under His shadow shall return; they shall revive as the corn, and grow as the vine; the scent thereof shall be as the wine of Lebanon. Ephraim shall say, What have I to do any more with idols? I have heard Him, and observed Him; I AM like a green fir tree. From Me is thy Fruit found. Who is wise, and he shall understand these things? Prudent, and he shall know them? For the ways of the LORD are right, and the just shall walk in them; but the transgressors shall fall therein.*

Cinnamon & Spices

The secrets of Messiah Yeshua that are hidden within the bitter Maror and the sweet Charoset of the Passover Seder of the LORD unveil the face of the Living God. These truths testify of the LORD'S mighty works that are hidden within the finest details of His glorious Living Testimony as *our freedom from bondage forever.*

Now I can reveal that the last King of Judah was Zedekiah after King Jeconiah was deposed *(dethroned)* as King. Zedekiah, the uncle of Jeconiah was put on the throne instead by Nebuchadnezzar. This last King of Judah was blinded by Nebuchadnezzar. *The Prophet Jeremiah cursed Jeconiah saying that none of his descendants would ever sit upon the throne of Israel (Jeremiah 22:28-30). Jeconiah was in Joseph's genealogical line (Matthew 1:11). This was the line of King David. Now the bitter curse placed upon Jeconiah, and his descendants was taken away by the sweet Fruitful Branch Yeshua, of the tribe of Judah. The Messiah has restored the tribe of Judah thus establishing forever the Eternal Davidic Dynasty through Messiah the LORD!* The sweet Fruit of everlasting life comes from the KING in His Garden and we will sit and dine at the KINGS table in His Divine Presence!

THE FRUITFUL BOUGH BY JACOB'S WELL

Joseph was given a coat of many colors by His father Jacob. With this gift came a special blessing and a Divine attribute that was spoken over him by the mouth of his father. I discussed how *the Messiah was evident in the attributes of each of the twelve tribes of Israel,* however, the blessing and attribute that pertains to Joseph had a very special meaning because, hundreds of years later, Messiah Yeshua would come and sit down at Jacobs well. This well belonged to Jacob and it was mentioned in the blessing that was given to Joseph by his father. Now, hundreds of years later, a descendant of the Patriarch Jacob was also named *"Joseph!"* This descendant, *"Joseph,"* was the son of another Jacob in the same family line. This Joseph was betrothed to a young Jewish maiden and virgin named *"Mary!"* So to be clear, *Messiah Yeshua's earthly father was Joseph and His earthly grandfather was Jacob* and they were both descendants of Jacob, the Patriarch, called *"Israel."* You should keep this in mind when I show you what Messiah Yeshua revealed about Himself in the encounter with the Samaritan woman as He sat down at Jacob's well. This encounter is said to mean one thing, but there was a far deeper meaning to it that I will share with you in a moment! The actual blessing that *Jacob, "Israel," prayed over Joseph* is written in the following passage in Genesis.

The Living Bough of an Almond Tree like a right arm!
Photo ©2014 Kimberly K Ballard All Rights Reserved

Genesis 49:22-24 *Joseph is a fruitful bough, even a fruitful bough by a well; whose branches run over the wall; The archers have sorely grieved him, and shot at him, and hated him; But his bow abode in strength, and the arms of his hands were made strong by the hands of the mighty God of Jacob; From thence is the shepherd, the stone of Israel.*

I must say, this was absolutely stunning! Now I understood exactly what was happening hundreds of years later when Yeshua came and sat down at Jacobs well in the place where Jacob had fed his flocks, and the flocks all drank the water from this well. Jacob, *"Israel,"* and his entire family also drank the water from this well. The well was in the parcel of ground that this Jacob gave to his son Joseph!

YESHUA THE MESSIAH AT JACOB'S WELL

What I have to say next is so fantastic that I am thrilled to write it! The LORD showed me the hidden things about this event and it was the key to understanding what Yeshua was revealing about Himself as the Messiah as He sat down at Jacob's well.

John 4:3-21 *He left Judea, and departed again into Galilee. And He must needs go through Samaria. Then cometh He to a city of Samaria, which is called Sychar, near to the parcel of ground that Jacob gave to his son Joseph. Now Jacob's well was there. Yeshua therefore, being wearied with His journey, sat thus on the well; and it was about the sixth hour. There cometh a woman of Samaria to draw water; Yeshua saith unto her, Give me to drink. For his disciples were gone away unto the city to buy meat. Then saith the woman of Samaria unto Him, How is it that thou, being a Jew, askest drink of me, which am a woman of Samaria? For the Jews have no dealings with the Samaritans. Yeshua answered and said unto her, If thou knewest the gift of God, and who it is that saith to thee, Give me to drink; thou wouldest have asked of Him, and He would have given thee Living Water. The woman saith unto Him, Sir, thou hast nothing to draw with, and the well is deep; From whence then hast thou that Living Water? Art thou greater than our father Jacob, which gave us the well, and drank thereof himself, and his children, and his cattle? Yeshua answered and said unto her, Whosoever drinketh of this water shall thirst again; But whosoever drinketh of the water that I shall give him shall never thirst; but the water that I shall give him shall be in him a well of water springing up into everlasting life. The woman saith unto Him, Sir, give me this water, that I thirst not, neither come hither to draw. Yeshua saith unto her, Go, call thy husband, and come hither. The woman answered and said, I have no husband. Yeshua said unto her, Thou hast well said, I have no husband; For thou hast had five husbands; and he whom thou now hast is not thy husband; in that saidst thou truly. The woman saith unto Him, Sir, I perceive that thou art a Prophet. Our fathers worshipped in this mountain; and ye say, that in Jerusalem is the place where men ought to worship. Yeshua saith unto her, Woman, believe me, the hour cometh, when ye shall neither in this mountain, nor yet at Jerusalem, worship the Father. Ye worship ye know not what; We know what we worship; for salvation is of the Jews. But the hour cometh, and now is, when the true worshippers shall worship the Father in Spirit and in truth; for the Father seeketh such to worship him. God is a Spirit; and they that worship Him must worship him in spirit and in truth. The woman saith unto Him, I know that Messiah cometh, which is called Christ; when He is come, He will tell us all things. Yeshua saith unto her, I that speak unto thee am He. And upon this came His disciples, and marveled that He talked with the woman; yet no man said, What seekest thou? Or, Why talkest thou with her? The woman then left her water pot, and went her way into the city, and saith to the men, Come, see a man, which told me all things that ever I did; is not this the Messiah?*

The Holy Spirit showed me that when Yeshua sat down at the well of Jacob, He was revealing that He is Messiah, *"The Fruitful bough, even a Fruitful bough by a well, whose branches run over the wall!"* Yeshua was not only revealing that *He is the Branch that would bear Fruit, but He was sitting on the well, revealing to the Samaritan woman that He is the well of salvation!* The third largest water cistern in Israel is located near the Garden tomb, along

with the KINGS vineyard, where the Fruitful Branch came to life. *So Yeshua the Living Almond Branch that bore the Eternal Fruit sat down at the well of Jacob!* Because of the fact that Yeshua was the *son of Joseph and the grandson of Jacob* and they were descendants of the Patriarch Jacob, known as *"Israel,"* the Messiah fulfilled this blessing of Joseph at Jacob's well. *Jacob gave the blessing and said, "The arms of his hands were made strong by the hands of the mighty God of Jacob; From thence is the shepherd, the stone of Israel." This is describing the arm of the LORD revealed, the hand of God and the Rod of the Good Shepherd, who feeds His flock from the well of Living Water forever. He is the Stone of Israel that is quarried out of God's Holy Mount Moriah.* The Messiah would, therefore, come to this place at the well and sit down as the Rod held out by the arm and hand of the LORD by the mighty God of Jacob. Then Yeshua was cut off and He died and He was hated by His brothers, just like Joseph.

When 17 inches of flood waters fell in September 2013 It created a deep well of water
Photo ©2013 Kimberly K Ballard All Rights Reserved

As Yeshua sat down at Jacob's well, He revealed that *He is the Stone* that the builders rejected from the Holy Heavenly Temple. Yeshua specifically told the Samaritan woman that *He was the Messiah of Israel, the Living Water.* He offered her the Eternal source of life when He told her that she could drink from this fountain and well of Living Water. She then said to Yeshua that she would no longer have to come to the well to draw water if He would give her this life-giving Living Water. Messiah will feed His flock, and the entire nation of Israel and everyone else that comes to Him will drink this Living Water of life that comes from the Fruitful Bough sitting by Jacob's well!

John 4:14 *But whosoever drinketh of the Water that I shall give him shall never thirst; but the Water that I shall give him shall be in him a well of water springing up into everlasting life.*

Now I discovered by Divine revelation that there are more exciting elements within this story. The encounter at Jacob's well occurred when Yeshua sat down about *the sixth hour* at Jacob's well. The *sixth hour* was the time of *"the Mussaf prayers"* that are spoken on Rosh HaShanah in the Synagogues. Now this is very exciting because of what took place after the First Fruit of salvation sat down at Jacob's well. The Mussaf prayer of Rosh HaShanah includes Kingship, shofar blasts, and the following English version of the prayer called *"Zichronot" or "Remembrances." Quote: "We recognize that HaShem is above time, and the idea of forgetting does not apply to Him, nor is He limited in understanding the inner thoughts of His creatures. Nevertheless, we ask that He remember only the good in our behalf when He Judges us. For all of humanity, for the whole world is judged today. We ask that He remember the faith of Noah who endured taunts and threats for 120 years while he built the Ark, and tried to explain its purpose to his wayward generation. For the Jewish People in particular, we ask that He remember the early loyalty of our people, who followed Him as a bride, as He said, "I remember your youthful devotion, the love of your bridal days, how you followed Me through the desert, in a barren land" (Jeremiah 2:2) and later as a precious child." Is it because Ephraim is my favorite son, my beloved child? As often as I speak of him, I remember him fondly. My heart yearns for him, I will have pity on him, says the LORD." (Jeremiah 31:19) Most of all, we ask that He remember the supreme act of devotion performed by our fathers Abraham and Isaac, where Abraham suppressed his natural feelings of mercy towards his son, and was prepared to sacrifice him at the command of God. And Isaac was prepared to be sacrificed, thereby suppressing his natural feelings of self-preservation, in fulfillment of God's command. So should HaShem suppress, so to speak, His Midat HaDin, His Attribute of Strict Justice, which would require that we be punished for our misdeeds, in favor of His Midat HaRachamim, His Attribute of Mercy."* ***(Sources: netglimpse.com/holidays/rosh_hashanah/rosh_hashanah_prayers_-_prayers,_mussaf_prayer_of_rosh_hashanah_in_english.) AND (the holidayspot.com/rosh_hashana/prayer.htm), (en.wikipedia.org/wiki/Mussaf).***

So when Yeshua sat at the well of Jacob at *the sixth hour,* which translates to the time that the Mussaf prayers are recited, Yeshua was revealing that He is the Bridegroom of Israel and the one true husband who has remembered His promises to the early followers of the LORD, and He has come as the Living Ark of the Testimony to save them! The Mussaf *refers to an "additional" prayer service that is recited on Festival days that takes the place of additional sacrifices that were once made in the Holy Temple on Rosh Chodesh. In the Mussaf prayer, Israel asks the LORD God to renew this month for them, for good, for pardon of sin and forgiveness of iniquity.* **(Source: ualberta.ca/~yreshef/Shabbat/roshprayers.html).**

Now the LORD God was dwelling in their midst as the Messiah, and He was sitting on the well at *the sixth hour,* revealing that He had come to pardon Israel's sins and to forgive them for their iniquity! He is the Ark of the Testimony of God that makes their sins purified white like snow, and during this time of the High Holy days, the curtain on the Ark of God containing the Torah is changed in the Synagogue to a white one, symbolizing exactly what Yeshua fulfilled *as the Living Torah!* As Yeshua sat at Jacob's well, the KING of Israel was revealing that He is the life-giving Water. Ironically, the name, *"Mussaf,"* is related to the Hebrew name, *"Yosef,"* which is *"Joseph,"* and Yeshua, the son of Joseph and the grandson of Jacob, was sitting on the well that Jacob gave to his son Joseph! The shofar or ram's horn is traditionally blown during Mussaf. During this prayer service, there is a reading from the Biblical book of Numbers *regarding the sacrifices* that were performed at the Holy Temple in Jerusalem. *Yeshua became our sacrificial Lamb* in order to take away our sins. During leap years, it is said *"that a prayer verse is also inserted for the atonement of willful sin."* There are also three middle blessings that pertain to *the LORD'S Kingship,* Remembrance, and Shofar blowing. *The three middle blessings remind me that Yeshua was resurrected on the third day as the Fruitful Bough who was sitting at Jacob's well.* The Messiah was revealing some incredible things at this well!

Now there was something else that was spectacular that the LORD revealed to me about this event that I want to share next. The Jewish disciples had left to go into the city to buy *"meat."* So as the story begins, *Yeshua is revealed as the Bridegroom of Israel* and the Word of God, *the Living Torah,* which is the true *"meat"* from Heaven. Remember that the Word of God is the Almond meat from the Living Branch who was raised to life on *the third day.* I already discussed exactly why Yeshua, the Fruitful Branch, came to life on the third day to be our spiritual meat, based upon the following verse in Genesis from the Torah of God! I found it completely staggering to have this revealed to me.

Genesis 1:29 *And God said, Behold, I have given you every herb bearing seed, which is upon the face of all the earth, and every tree, in the which is the fruit of a tree yielding seed; to you it shall be for meat.*

What I find fascinating about the term *"meat"* here is the fact that in the book of Hebrews the *"strong meat"* is said *"to belong to those who are full of age and even to those who by reason of use, have their senses exercised to discern both good and evil."* This was the other Tree in the Garden of Eden from which Adam and Eve took the forbidden fruit and ate thereof! This fig fruit came from the Tree of Knowledge of good and evil, and when they ate it, they could *discern between good and evil! This special knowledge is tied to "the oracles of God!"*

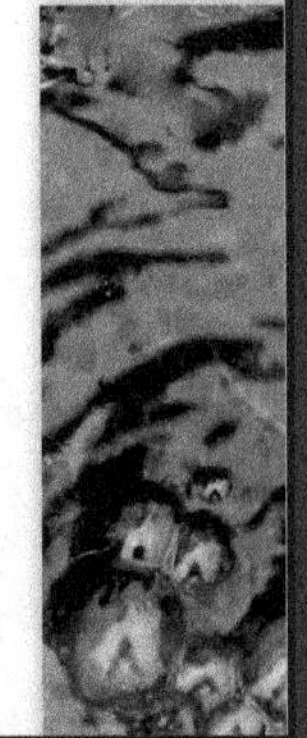

Hebrews 5:9-14 *And being made perfect, He became the author of eternal salvation unto all them that obey Him; Called of God an High Priest after the Order of Melchizedek. Of whom we have many things to say, and hard to be uttered, seeing you are dull of hearing. For when for the time ye ought to be teachers, ye have need that one teach you again which be the first principles of the oracles of God; and are become such as have need of milk, and not of strong meat. For every one that useth milk is unskilled in the Word of righteousness; for he is a babe. But strong meat belongeth to them that are of full age, even those who by reason of use have their senses exercised to discern both good and evil.*

So the first principles of *"the oracles of God"* are the *"strong meat"* that allows one to be full of age and to discern both good and evil. *The oracles of God must be the Fig Tree of Knowledge of good and evil that was in the Garden of Eden and the Almond Tree of Life seen on the Magdala Stone!* The Hebrew word *"debir"* means *"oracle"* and it first appears in I Kings 6:5 in the description of Solomon's Temple. This word was also translated as *"dabar"* in Hebrew and it means *"Word."* It is found in II Samuel 16:23. This actually refers to *the Holy of Holies* or to *"the Place"* of the Ark of His Covenant where He spoke from His throne. This is where He gave the people the Word of God and the place where the Almond Branch that budded to life dwells *with His secret knowledge of the Living Torah.*

So in the oracles, we have a direct connection to The Word of God, The Living Torah, The Holy of Holies, and The Ark of His Covenant. All of these elements describe Yeshua, the Messiah. *As Yeshua sat down at Jacob's well, He was revealing that He is The Word of God, The Living Torah, which is the pure meat of Heaven. This means that the Word of God, the oracle of God, came down in the flesh to dwell with us to reveal this secret knowledge of God (John 1:14, Luke 8:11, Matthew 24:45)!*

Now the LORD showed me something else! *Yeshua asked the Samaritan woman to go call her husband and she said that she had no husband.* Yeshua then told her that she was right when she said that *she had no husband,* but the truth is, Yeshua was revealing Himself as the Jewish Bridegroom and as the Messiah of Israel while sitting at Jacob's well. So Yeshua was agreeing with her that she did not have a husband, since she was a Samaritan and not a Jew, and, therefore, she did not have a husband. The LORD revealed to me that *Yeshua was revealing things to this woman in spiritual Heavenly terms and not in earthly marriage terms!* After stating these things to her, *Yeshua then said that she has had five husbands and "the one that you now have is not your husband."* When Yeshua said these words, the woman immediately thought Yeshua was *a Prophet,* which proves that *Yeshua was speaking spiritually about the husbands in this context.* Then Yeshua told her, *"You Samaritans worship what you do not know but we worship what we do know, for salvation is from the Jews."* What does this mean? Well, the LORD revealed to me that *this Samaritan woman had heard the Word of God from the Samaritan Torah* as it had been read to her *by five Rabbi men in her town,* which is not the same as the Jewish Torah. One of the differences is that the Samaritan Torah has a commandment to build the Temple on Mount Gerizim near Nablus instead of in Jerusalem because the Samaritans claimed to be descendants of the two sons of Joseph. So there was indeed a Temple built there that resembled the Holy Temple in Jerusalem. The LORD revealed to me that *the five husbands that she has had are the five books of Moses read from the Samaritan Torah. This means that each one of the five books of Moses was read out loud by five different Rabbis in her village, and each one of the five was like a husband to her because only the husband of the family or the men were allowed to read from the Torah, so the women could hear it.* She was *hearing the Word of God* from a Samaritan viewpoint, but the Samaritans were worshipping what they did not know. She had a form of the ritual worship that was done in Jerusalem, but her people performed these rituals in Samaria and not in Jerusalem. This is why she was questioning Him about where to worship God. *Hence it is true that the five husbands that she has had are the five books of Moses from the Samaritan Torah, but Yeshua said that she did not know what she was worshipping because she was not Jewish.* She did not have the true Jewish Torah! Yeshua also said unto her, *"Thou hast well said, I have no husband; For thou hast had five husbands; and He whom thou now hast is not thy husband; in that saidst thou truly."* Messiah Yeshua, *the Living Torah* who just offered her the Living Water was sitting on Jacob's well speaking to her as the Bridegroom of Israel! I suddenly comprehended with astonishment that <u>*He is the one husband*</u> *that she has now that is not her husband!" Remember that this woman already told Yeshua that she had no husband, and He agreed saying that the one husband that she has now is not her husband! He was talking about*

Himself as the true husband and Bridegroom of Israel and as the true Living Torah from Jerusalem where God will dwell forever! This story is so marvelous because it shows that *Yeshua spoke the Living Torah to a woman! He offered it to her!* Rabbi Yeshua proved through His kind action that women are not to be discriminated against in the study of God's Word! Yeshua offered her the free gift of Living Water of Eternal salvation at Jacob's well, even though He was the Jewish Messiah, and the Jewish Bridegroom who was to become the husband of Israel, and she accepted His offer when she said, *"Sir, give me this water and I will never have to come draw water from this well again."* How fantastic! *The LORD Messiah of Israel is the husband that she has now and she accepted the Living Water from the well of salvation!*

If you ever watch the movie, *"Yentl,"* that I mentioned before, you will see that the main character, a woman, disguises herself as a man *(Anshel),* so she can go to school to study the Torah and Talmud. Women were forbidden to study the Torah and they were never allowed to read it for themselves. Only the men were allowed to read sacred texts *(the Torah)* and study them! ***(Source: The Movie "Yentl," references ©1983 MGM Metro-Goldwyn-Mayer Studios Inc. TM).***

So when Messiah Yeshua came and sat next to the woman at Jacob's well, the Living Torah was speaking to a woman! This is fantastic news! This was unheard of in ancient times! Remember that Yeshua the Fruitful Branch took away *the curse* of Eden which included men ruling over women! After Yeshua was alone speaking to her, the Scripture goes on to say, *"And upon this came His disciples, and marveled that He talked with the woman; yet no man said, What seekest thou? Or, Why talkest thou with her?"* Now I could clearly see that this is why *the Jewish disciples, upon returning to Jacob's well, marveled that Yeshua was talking to a woman!* They were marveling at the fact that the Greatest Rabbi who ever lived, the Messiah, *the Living Torah,* was lovingly speaking to a woman openly. He was offering her the life-giving water from the well of salvation and the men did not question Him about it because they knew that He was the LORD God of Israel! *The Fruitful bough was sitting by a well.* Wow! This is so fantastic! The Jewish Messiah offered this Samaritan woman His Covenant that was a marriage proposal to her and she accepted it. She told Yeshua that she would like to have a drink of this life-giving Water. When she said that she believed in her heart that the Messiah would come and tell her everything, Yeshua said, *"I that speak unto thee am He."* She was so excited He offered the Living Water to her she ran off, leaving her water jar at the well! She hurriedly ran into town and specifically told *"the men"* to *"Come and see a man which told me all things that I ever did; is not this the Messiah?" Yeshua was telling her all things she ever did in regards to her worship of Torah!* Then she confronted *the Rabbi men* in her town, *who had read the Samaritan Torah to her, "the five husbands that she has had, which are the five books of Moses,"* and she was telling the Rabbis what she had just heard from *the Messiah,* who was just speaking *the Living Torah to her!* He was the completeness of the whole Torah in One! The Greatest Rabbi in the history of the world had just told a woman everything she had done in regards to her worship and about her past with the Torah and her future marriage to Him! *Her husband is now the LORD! Jacob's well was a blessing to her!*

Now Jacob the Patriarch told his son Joseph he would wear the crown. Joseph wore the crown after being cut off from his brothers. Messiah Yeshua, the Fruitful Branch was cut off, but He wears the Eternal crown as the KING of Israel. He was sitting in the place where Jacob gave *this blessing* to Joseph, *as it pertained to the end of days!* Yeshua told the Samaritan woman that a day was coming when everyone would worship God in Spirit and in Truth. *Yeshua is the Living Torah full of His Holy Spirit of Truth* now revealed at the end of days!

Genesis 49:26 *The blessings of Thy father have prevailed above the blessings of my progenitors unto the utmost bound of the everlasting hills; they shall be on the head of Joseph, and on the crown of the head of him that was separate from his brethren.*

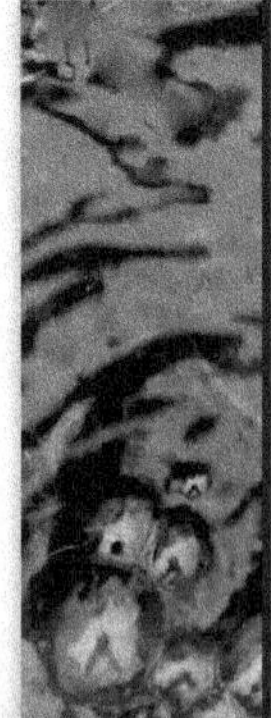

I would now like to share another piece of Rabbi Simcha Pearlmutters testimony pertaining to the *Mussaf prayers!* In part eight of the nine it says, *Quote:* "And I am going to give you now the next thing which is what we say on Yom Kippur, ten days after Rosh HaShanah. After we have just said the name of Yeshua during the time of the blowing of the shofar or the ram's horn, we then come ten days later to Yom Kippur, and on Yom Kippur we come to the high point of the service which is called "Mussaf," the additional service. And at the Mussaf of Yom Kippur we have another aspect of the service called the Kedushah. And in the Kedushah we interrupt that holy point, that high point of the service to say what we call a "Piyut." A piyut is like a poem. It is really more than a poem, but I don't have a better word for it. And we read these words: Notice, *Pinah menu Mashiach Tzidkeinu,* "Torn away from us is Messiah our Righteousness." Someone tore him away from us. Someone ripped him away from us. *Pulatznu v'ein mi l'tzadkeinu.* "We are in a state of collapse, for we have no one to justify us." *Avonoteinu v'ol p'sha'einu omeis,* that "our transgressions and our cryings are burdened upon him." *V'hu m'cholal,* "And he has become desecrated." He—he has become, that one that we have seen as Yeshua—has become desecrated. *Mipe 'sha 'einu,* "from our cryings." *Soveil al shechem chatoteinu,* "he suffers from the shoulder, the brunt of, our sins," *Slichah m'tzo la'avonoteinu,* "he finds forgiveness for our transgressions." *Nirpah lanu b' chaburato,* "though we are healed by his wounds, by his stripes." *Netzach briah chadashah et livroto,* "that he is eternally recreated anew." *Mei'chug ha'aleihu,* "from the circle of the Gentiles, raise him up, cause him to ascend." Let's get him back, let's bring him home. *Mi'Seir,* Seir means Mt. Seir. By the way, here we're sitting just a few kilometers to the east of us, where Mt. Seir is. Mt Seir is another word for the mountain of Edom. Edom is another word for Rome. Rome is another word for, in Jewish eschatology, for the Christian religion under the Roman Kingdom. And it says, "from Seir," or from the Christian faith, *hadleihu,* "Bail him out!" Bail him out. And by the way, we have this in our notes, our explanations. I'm not giving you something original, I am giving you something that has been given to you by the tradition of the wise men of blessed memory, *"Chazal,"* our Rabbis before us. *L'hashmi'einu b'Har Ha'Levanon,* "That he may be heard on the Mount of Lebanon," which is called the mountain of the L-rds House, it was called Lebanon because the House of Hashem was made by the cedars of Lebanon. *Sheinit,* that we will hear it, "for a second time," *b'yad Yinon,* "by the hand of Yinon." And Yinon is another name that we use in gematria to stand for the same name that we read during Rosh HaShanah, Yeshua. Yinon is another one of those secret names. So you see with all that, we talk about the same thing, a Mashiach who has been forcibly taken away and bound in chains and kept in chains by the non-Jewish world for all these years while they have upheld, not him, but someone who is not really a defender of Israel as Moses was to be, and as the one who would be like Moses was to be, the accuser of Israel. And so, we are to rescue him. We Jews are to redeem the Mashiach, can you imagine that? We Jews have a job of redeeming the Mashiach! Yes, in good Jewish eschatology in midrashim written by our Rabbis, we are told that the Mashiach has been sitting in the exile together with us and suffering every death that we have suffered because Isaiah 53 talks about, *b'motav,* "in his many deaths." And he has suffered over and over again, especially in our generation…"
(Source: Rabbi Simcha Pearlmutter, Rabbi testimony of Jesus, Yeshua Messiah Full Text: jerusalemcalling.org/Rabbi_Simcha_Pearlmutter.htm).

When Yeshua sat at Jacob's well He revealed He would be the suffering Jewish Messiah in this Mussaf prayer. Rabbi Pearlmutters stunning testimony continues after this section. I encourage everyone to read the full text of it. This portion of it was to show that Yeshua removes the bitterness of death! He bore the curse of Eden on His shoulders to break it.

Freely we can come, like the Samaritan woman, to drink from the well of salvation through the *Fruitful bough by a well!* The *"city of Ephratah"* meaning *"Fruitful" is the birth place of Yeshua.* Naomi returned to this city and was restored. *Her bitterness was replaced with sweetness.* The mighty men of valour took water from the well here for David to drink. The Fruitful city of *"Ephratah"* changed its name to *"Bethlehem"* or *"House of Bread,"* and Yeshua is the *Staff of Life.* The Living Water came from this city and flowed into the Holy Temple of the LORD on Holy Mount Moriah. The LORD fine-tuned these details. KING Yeshua is the Messiah of Israel. In Jacob's prophesy, He told his sons what would befall them in the end of days referring to the mighty Testimony of Messiah Yeshua. *Now every single woman in the world can freely hear and read the Living Torah from the GREAT MESSIAH KING OF ISRAEL without any discrimination! How fantastic! This is absolutely thrilling!*
(I dedicate this revelation to Barbra Streisand for Yentl!)

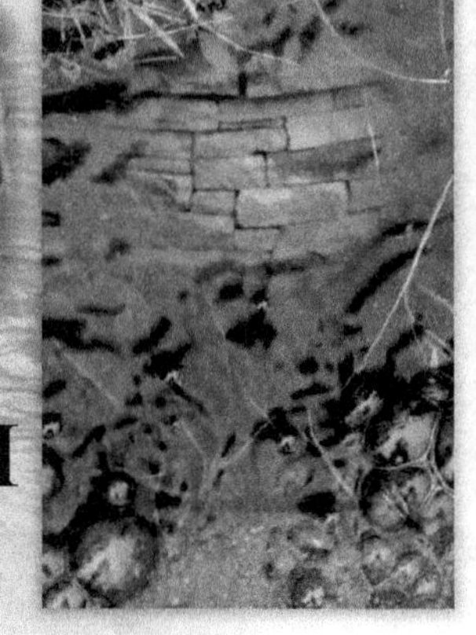

THE HISTORY OF JACOB AT THE WELL IN HARAN AND HIS WELL IN SHECHEM

In the story of Jacob's life that is written in Genesis 29, they gathered the flocks and watered the flocks from a well in Haran where he met Rachel *(his future bride)*. A few chapters later in Genesis 33:18-20 it is written *"when Jacob returned to Shechem from Paddan Aram, he camped 'before' the city and bought the land on which he pitched his tent. Biblical scholars contend that the plot of land is the same one upon which Jacob's well was constructed."* **(Source: en.wikipedia.org/wiki/Jacob's_Well) AND (Shechem - bible-history.com/links.php?cat=40&sub=680).**

In his plot of land in Shechem which is also called *"Sichem, Sychem, and Sychar," Jacob dug a well.* It was here that Messiah Yeshua sat down hundreds of years later to reveal His identity as the Bridegroom of Israel. First Jacob is at the well in Haran, and later he goes to Shechem. Read this Scripture in Genesis and then I will show you, the most outstanding secret of God that is hidden within this astonishing story.

Genesis 29:1-35 *Then Jacob went on his journey, and came into the land of the people of the east. And he looked, and behold a well in the field, and, lo, there were three flocks of sheep lying by it; for out of that well they watered the flocks; and a great stone was upon the well's mouth. And thither were all the flocks gathered; and they rolled the stone from the well's mouth, and watered the sheep, and put the stone again upon the well's mouth in his place. And Jacob said unto them, My brethren, whence be ye? And they said, Of Haran are we. And he said unto them, Know ye Laban the son of Nahor? And they said, We know him. And he said unto them, Is he well? And they said, He is well; and, behold, Rachel his daughter cometh with the sheep. And he said, Lo, it is yet high day, neither is it time that the cattle should be gathered together; water ye the sheep, and go and feed them. And they said, We cannot, until all the flocks be gathered together, and till they roll the stone from the well's mouth; then we water the sheep. And while he yet spake with them, Rachel came with her father's sheep; for she kept them. And it came to pass, when Jacob saw Rachel the daughter of Laban his mother's brother, and the sheep of Laban his mother's brother, that Jacob went near, and rolled the stone from the well's mouth, and watered the flock of Laban his mother's brother. And Jacob kissed Rachel, and lifted up his voice, and wept. And Jacob told Rachel that he was her father's brother, and that he was Rebekah's son; and she ran and told her father. And it came to pass, when Laban heard the tidings of Jacob his sister's son, that he ran to meet him, and embraced him, and kissed him, and brought him to his house. And he told Laban all these things. And Laban said to him, Surely thou art my bone and my flesh. And he abode with him the space of a month. And Laban said unto Jacob, Because thou art my brother, shouldest thou therefore serve me for nought? Tell me, what shall thy wages be? And Laban had two daughters; the name of the elder was Leah, and the name of the younger was Rachel. Leah was tender eyed; but Rachel was beautiful and well favoured. And Jacob loved Rachel; and said, I will serve thee seven years for Rachel thy younger daughter. And Laban said, It is better that I give her to thee, than that I should give her to another man; abide with me. And Jacob served seven years for Rachel; and they seemed unto him but a few days, for the love he had to her. And Jacob said unto Laban, Give me my wife, for my days are fulfilled, that I may go in unto her. And Laban gathered together all the men of the place, and made a feast. And it came to pass in the evening, that he took Leah his daughter, and brought her to him; and he went in unto her. And Laban gave unto his daughter Leah Zilpah his maid for an handmaid. And it came to pass, that in the morning, behold, it was Leah; and he said to Laban, What is this thou hast done unto me? Did not I serve with thee for Rachel? Wherefore then hast thou beguiled me? And Laban said, It must not be so done in our country, to give the younger before the firstborn. Fulfill her week, and we will give thee this also for the service which thou shalt serve with me yet seven other years. And Jacob did so, and fulfilled her week; and he gave him Rachel his daughter to wife also. And Laban gave to Rachel his daughter Bilhah his handmaid to be her maid. And he went in also unto Rachel, and he loved also Rachel more than Leah, and served with him yet seven other years.*

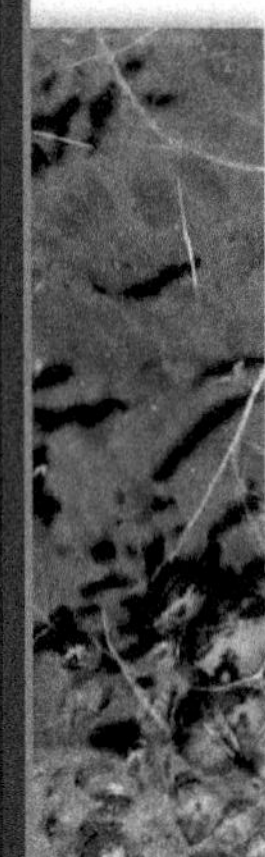

And when the LORD saw that Leah was hated, he opened her womb; but Rachel was barren. And Leah conceived, and bare a son, and she called his name Reuben; for she said, Surely the LORD hath looked upon my affliction; now therefore my husband will love me. And she conceived again, and bare a son; and said, Because the LORD hath heard that I was hated, He hath therefore given me this son also; and she called his name Simeon. And she conceived again, and bare a son; and said, Now this time will my husband be joined unto me, because I have born him three sons; therefore was his name called Levi. And she conceived again, and bare a son; and she said, Now will I praise the LORD; therefore she called his name Judah; and left bearing.

As I was reading this story, suddenly the Holy Spirit opened my understanding and I was again absolutely astonished! The first thing I noticed in the story, is the fact that there were three flocks of sheep sitting by Jacob's well. The text says, *"For out of that well they watered the flocks."* Now on the mouth of the well, there was a great stone and all the flocks were gathered to drink from Jacob's well, to quench their thirst, but the most important part of this text regarding the Messiah is found in the following portion of the whole story.

Genesis 29:2-3 *And he looked, and behold a well in the field, and, lo, there were three flocks of sheep lying by it; for out of that well they watered the flocks; and a great stone was upon the well's mouth. And thither were all the flocks gathered; and they rolled the stone from the well's mouth, and watered the sheep, and put the stone again upon the well's mouth in his place*

Now skip to the next three verses and specifically notice the words, *"They could not water the sheep until all the flocks were gathered and until they rolled the great stone from the mouth of the well."*

Genesis 29:7-9 *And he said, Lo, it is yet high day, neither is it time that the cattle should be gathered together; water ye the sheep, and go and feed them. And they said, We cannot, until all the flocks be gathered together, and till they roll the stone from the well's mouth; then we water the sheep. And while he yet spake with them, Rachel came with her father's sheep; for she kept them.*

Now remember that Messiah Yeshua sat down at Jacob's well in Sychar (a city in Samaria), and He revealed to the Samaritan woman He is the Living Water and the well of salvation, springing up to everlasting life, and He proved it in His miracle at the Pool of Bethesda. The Holy Spirit revealed the most astonishing hidden Messianic prophecy written within this text that I believe has been kept secret from the foundation of the world! If what I am about to tell you, does not give you the chills and shivers of a lifetime, I do not know what else will! Remember these words; *In order for all of the flocks of Israel to drink from the well of salvation and drink the water from the well, all the sheep must first be gathered together and the great stone rolled away from the mouth of the well!* I marveled at these incredible words! I suddenly fell back in my chair in complete wonder and astonishment when I realized what this meant! The look of awe was on my face!

It suddenly came to me that when the Living Water, the Messiah, the well of salvation, was sealed in the rock hewn tomb in God's Garden in Holy Mount Moriah, the angel of the LORD descended from Heaven and rolled "the Great Stone away" from the mouth of the well of salvation! This is the greatest secret of God that may have never been seen or understood before this moment in history! *Therefore, the LORD literally brought forth Living Water from the Rock of God and now, because the angel of the LORD rolled the Great Stone from the mouth of the well of salvation in God's Garden after Yeshua's miraculous resurrection to life, the LORD'S sheep will all be gathered together out of all the places in the world where they were scattered. The LORD'S entire flock could now drink freely from the life-giving Living Water from the well of salvation forever in the Heavenly Jerusalem! The Living Water literally sprang to life, flowing out of this Rock of the LORD in the Garden of God and the angel rolled away the Great Stone, so that now His sheep would be gathered here to drink from His well forever in Jerusalem Israel at THE FOUNDATION STONE where Adam and Eve were*

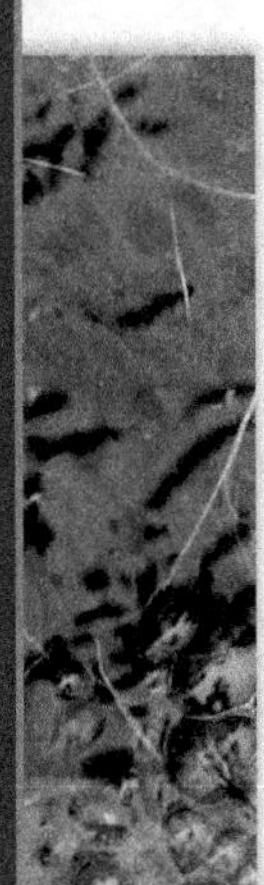

created! Remember that Yeshua said that the water that He would give is the Eternal life-giving Water! In the story of Jacob at the well in Haran with Rachel in Genesis, we see that it is only after the great stone is rolled away from the mouth of the well and after all the flocks are gathered together, that the sheep can drink from the one who sat down at Jacob's well. So the truth is, the LORD has been in the process of gathering His entire flock of sheep out of all the places where they were scattered for about two thousand years, and through Messiah, they will come back to Jerusalem where it all began in Genesis! After He has gathered all His flock, the LORD will return to feed them forever from His fountain of refreshing. He then ushers in the Messianic Kingdom of God, restoring the earth like Eden. The Great Rolling Stone at the tomb of the Messiah has the greatest significance for our time in history and this message has been hidden all of these centuries until today! It is an astonishing message of hope for all God's people. His sheep hear His voice and they will come to Him!

Perhaps the most remarkable thing is that during Hanukkah, the Festival of Lights, there is a Hebrew song called *"the Ma'oz Tzur"* and it is sung every night after the lighting of the Festival lights. This hymn is very significant, not only for the fact that Yeshua is encoded in the Holy Menorah as the Living Almond Rod or Branch and that He was conceived during Hanukkah, but also for the fact that He is mentioned within the words of this Jewish liturgical poem that is set to music. The first lines of the song include the words, *"The Mighty Rock of my Salvation."* The Hebrew for the term, *"My Salvation,"* written within this song is the word *"Yeshu'ati"* which literally means *"My Yeshua!"* This hymn includes the words, *"Make bare Thy Holy Arm, and bring near the final Salvation." Of course the Rod of God is the Holy Arm of the LORD revealed to us as "Yeshu'ati!"* It is so incredible that this same word is also found in Isaiah 12 in the most significant way. It also relates to what the LORD revealed to me about the Great Rolling Stone being rolled away from Mount Moriah, so that the flocks of Israel could drink from the well of salvation in this place forever.

Isaiah 12:1-6 *And in that day thou shalt say, O LORD, I will praise Thee; though Thou wast angry with me, Thine anger is turned away, and Thou comfortedst me. Behold, God is my Salvation; I will trust, and not be afraid; For the LORD YHVH is my strength and my song; He also is become my Salvation. Therefore with joy shall ye draw Water out of the wells of Salvation. And in that day shall ye say, Praise the LORD, call upon His Name, declare His doings among the people, make mention that His Name is exalted. Sing unto the LORD for He hath done excellent things; this is known in all the earth. Cry out and shout, thou inhabitant of Zion; for great is the Holy One of Israel in the midst of thee.*

Now imagine how I felt after the LORD showed this true revelation to me? This was truly breathtaking! The significance of the Great Rolling Stone of Yeshua's Garden tomb was so astonishing now, especially in context to the Messiah sitting at Jacob's well, revealing His true identity. So when I later discovered the Jewish Priestly Angel at the Garden tomb, by Divine Providence as I wrote this, I just knew how significant it was to the glory of the LORD God! So I kept it in my file for an entire year!

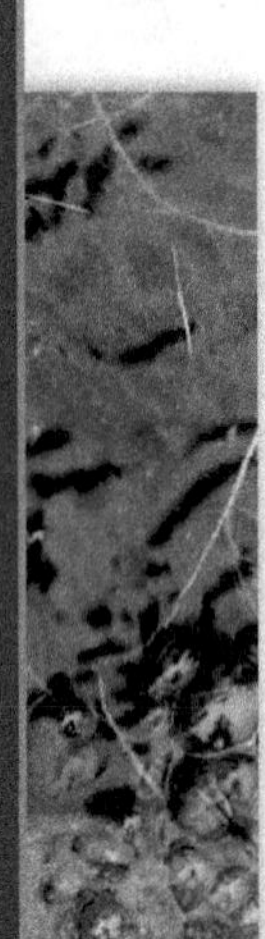

Now here is where I have to come back to tell you what happened. I had to add here while editing that about a year after this Divine revelation was given to me about the significance of the Great Rolling Stone of Yeshua's tomb, by Divine Providence, the LORD connected me to Simon Brown of England, and brought to my attention that the Great Rolling Stone from Yeshua's tomb was not only in existence, but was just verified by him to be standing upon Mount Nebo. As I showed you earlier in the book, Simon had traveled to Mount Nebo in 2011 and measured the stone and the Garden tomb, to see if his speculation was correct. It all matched up perfectly. This is exactly how the LORD works! This is why I felt the LORD had connected us in such a miraculous way. The LORD was at this point clearly adding this verification of what I had written through the Holy Spirit. Here was the Great Rolling Stone of such great significance standing upon Mount Nebo. This was such an incredible miracle! Now

you can understand why I went back into my text while editing, to add the stone earlier in the book that Simon measured on Mount Nebo that fit perfectly under my angel at the Garden tomb. Even though I had saved that angel for a year, as soon the Rolling Stone was measured in 2011, the Great Rolling Stone could be proven true with my angel (on Shavuot/Pentecost)! I was connected to Simon in 2011! I wrote the above revelations before knowing the whereabouts or existence of this stone today. So this is exactly why I told Simon that the Great Rolling Stone was acting like a compass on Mount Nebo and was overlooking the Promised Land, guiding the LORD'S sheep in the right direction. This is what prompted me to contact Simon Brown to tell him that I believed he was right that this was indeed the Great Rolling Stone that has such great significance! This miracle alone was more than magnificent! Most astonishing, however, was the fact that I knew because of what was in my book that the Great Rolling Stone was actually facing the Garden of God where Eden had been. This is the place where the Living Water came out of the Rock! Yeshua is the well of salvation and when the Great Stone was rolled away from the mouth of sepulchre in Holy Mount Moriah, the Living Water came out of the Rock and now the LORD'S sheep would be gathered to this place to drink forever in the Eternal Promised Land! When this astounding miracle of Biblical proportions happened I was further convinced, not only that the LORD was putting together one of the final pieces of His incredible Testimony, but I also knew for certain that the LORD was up to something spectacular in the last days! The LORD is a deep well!

The Great Rolling Stone on Mount Nebo
Photo ©2011 Simon Brown England

After He revealed His identity at Jacob's well, Yeshua immediately went to the Pool of Bethesda and healed the crippled man by *speaking to him!* It all came together!

John 4:11-15 *The woman saith unto Him, Sir, Thou hast nothing to draw with, and the well is deep; from whence then hast Thou that Living Water? Art Thou greater than our father Jacob, which gave us the well, and drank thereof himself, and his children, and his cattle? Yeshua answered and said unto her, Whosoever drinketh of this water shall thirst again; But whosoever drinketh of the water that I shall give him shall never thirst; but the water that I shall give him shall be in him a well of water springing up into everlasting life. The woman saith unto Him, Sir, give me this Water, that I thirst not, neither come hither to draw.*

Zechariah 13:1 *In that day there shall be a Fountain opened to the House of David and to the inhabitants of Jerusalem for sin and for uncleanness.*

Jeremiah 2:13 *For My people have committed two evils; they have forsaken Me the Fountain of Living Waters, and hewed them out cisterns, broken cisterns, that can hold no water.*

Jeremiah 17:13 *O LORD, the hope of Israel, all that forsake Thee shall be ashamed, and they that depart from Me shall be written in the earth, because they have forsaken the LORD, the Fountain of Living Waters.*

Romans 9:33 *As it is written, Behold, I lay in Zion a stumbling stone and Rock of offense; and whosoever believeth on Him shall not be ashamed.*

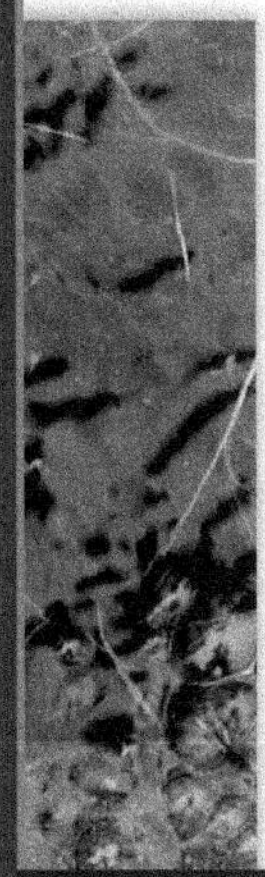

As I mentioned before, Jeremiah was thrown into the pit in Holy Mount Moriah, in the same rock quarry where Yeshua was quarried as *"The Rock." Adam was created from this same Foundation Stone in Jerusalem Israel!*

Isaiah 51:1 *Hearken to Me, ye that follow after righteousness, ye that seek the LORD; look unto the Rock whence ye are hewn, and to the hole of the pit whence ye are digged.*

Matthew 27:59-66 *And when Joseph had taken the body, he wrapped it in a clean linen cloth. And laid it in his own new tomb, which he had hewn out in the rock; and he rolled a great stone to the door of the sepulchre, and departed. And there was Mary Magdalene, and the other Mary, sitting over against the sepulchre. Now the next day, that followed the day of the preparation, the Chief Priests and Pharisees came together unto Pilate, Saying, Sir, we remember that that deceiver said, while He was yet alive, After three days I will rise again. Command therefore that the sepulchre be made sure until the third day, lest His disciples come by night, and steal Him away, and say unto the people, He is risen from the dead; So the last error shall be worse than the first. Pilate said unto them, Ye have a watch; go your way, make it as sure as ye can. So they went, and made the sepulchre sure, sealing the stone, and setting a watch.*

Remember that Messiah Yeshua said at Jacob's well that He would give the life-giving Water. On the third day, on Nisan 17, *as evening was becoming morning on the first day of the week,* the angel of the LORD appeared *and rolled away the Great Stone from the mouth of the well of Salvation in Holy Mount Moriah!* The good news of Messiah Yeshua's resurrection into glory was then taken to the whole world. Through His Living Testimony, the LORD began to gather His flocks of sheep back to His original Garden in Jerusalem, on His Holy Mountain. *The Great Rolling Stone was actually rolled away from the well of Salvation at the end of the seventh day Sabbath of the LORD and now we can enter His rest in His Heavenly Kingdom!*

Matthew 28:1-5 *In the end of the Sabbath, as it began to dawn toward the first day of the week, came Mary Magdalene and the other Mary to see the sepulchre. And, behold, there was a great earthquake; for the angel of the LORD descended from Heaven, and came and rolled back the stone from the door, and sat upon it. His countenance was like lightning, and his raiment white as snow; And for fear of him the keepers did shake, and became as dead men. And the angel answered and said unto the women, Fear not ye; for I know that ye seek Yeshua, which was crucified. He is not here; for He is risen, as He said, Come, see the place where the LORD lay. And go quickly, and tell His disciples that He is risen from the dead; and, behold, He goeth before you into Galilee; there shall ye see Him; Lo, I have told you. And they departed quickly from the sepulchre with fear and great joy; and did run to bring His disciples word.*

In the miracle of Yeshua feeding the 5,000+, I said that the twelve baskets represented the twelve tribes of Israel and they would be gathered by the Messiah and not one of them will be lost. This represents the whole flock of the House of Israel that Messiah Yeshua will gather. They were scattered into many nations. It just so happens that the time called *"Jacob's trouble"* lasts for 7 years. Remember Jacob had to work 7 years to obtain His beloved Rachel after having married Leah who was unloved. So again, I believe this is the reason why Yeshua will come to rapture the Gentile remnant of righteous believers, represented by unloved Leah, and then *He will work the 7 years of Jacob's trouble for Israel to obtain the Bride that He is in love with, represented by Rachel.* In the story of Jacob, it is very interesting to note that Rachel comes with the sheep! Rachel is the Matriarch of Israel! So Messiah Yeshua comes for His beloved Bride Rachel after working the 7 years time of Jacob's trouble for her, as the Living Ark removes His enemies, preparing to enter the Eternal Promised Land! The Living Rod of God is the Heavenly Holy Temple that comes down from Heaven and descends to the earth, setting Himself forever in the midst of Holy Mount Moriah in Jerusalem Israel. The flocks of the LORD will then forever drink from the Fountain of Living Waters

Gethsemane Church of All Nations Jerusalem Israel
The original Photograph ©2011 Simon Brown England
All Rights Reserved – Photo Edited by Kimberly K Ballard

from this Heavenly Garden of God. The LORD Yeshua will fight the final battle of Armageddon (a seven stage battle), and take Rachel *(Israel)* as His beloved Bride.

Zechariah 14:3 *Then shall the LORD go forth, and fight against those nations, as when He fought in the day of battle. And His feet shall stand in that day upon the Mount of Olives, which is before Jerusalem on the east, and the Mount of Olives shall cleave in the midst thereof toward the east and toward the west, and there shall be a very great valley; and half of the mountain shall remove toward the north, and half of it toward the south. And ye shall flee to the valley of the mountains; for the valley of the mountains shall reach unto Azal; yea, ye shall flee, like as ye fled from before the earthquake in the days of Uzziah king of Judah; and the LORD my God shall come, and all the Saints with Thee. And it shall come to pass in that day, that the light shall not be clear, nor dark; But it shall be one day which shall be known to the LORD, not day, nor night; but it shall come to pass, that at evening time it shall be light. And it shall be in that day, that living waters shall go out from Jerusalem; half of them toward the former sea, and half of them toward the hinder sea; in summer and in winter shall it be. And the LORD shall be KING over all the earth; in that day shall there be one LORD, and His Name one.*

Matthew 24:31 *And He shall send His angels with a great trumpet, and they shall gather together His elect from the four winds, and from one end of Heaven to the other.*

From the four winds Yeshua will gather His elect, and will water them from *the Rock* that rests forever at the Holy Temple Mount in Jerusalem Israel. This is truly fantastic!

MOSES' WELL

Well Water Photo ©2013
Kimberly K Ballard All Rights Reserved

In the Book of Exodus, there is a foreshadowing of Messiah Yeshua that I discovered in the actions of Moses. Moses also married a woman who came to the well and Messiah will marry those who come to the well of Salvation!

Exodus 2:15-21 *Now when Pharaoh heard this thing, he sought to slay Moses. But Moses fled from the face of Pharaoh, and dwelt in the land of Midian; and he sat down by a well. Now the priest of Midian had seven daughters; and they came and drew water, and filled the troughs to water their father's flock. And the shepherds came and drove them away; but Moses stood up and helped them, and watered their flock. And when they came to Reuel their father, he said, How is it that ye are come so soon today? And they said, An Egyptian delivered us out of the hand of the shepherds, and also drew water enough for us, and watered the flock. And he said unto his daughters, And where is he? Why is it that ye have left the man? Call him, that he may eat bread. And Moses was content to dwell with the man; and he gave Moses Zipporah his daughter.*

Messiah Yeshua delivered Israel from the hand of the bad shepherds who did not care for the flock of the LORD. He helps them and He draws the water for His flocks to drink, just like Moses did at the well. In this Scripture, the father Reuel asks, *"Where is he? Why is it ye have left the man? Call him that He may eat bread!"* As they ate the bread, Moses was content to dwell with them in that place. The Good Shepherd gives us the Bread from Heaven, so *the Living Staff of life,* is content to dwell with us, as His Bride! Moses took his wife from the women that came to the well and Yeshua revealed this about Himself to the woman at Jacob's well. *By partaking of His Living Covenant of the heart, we are betrothed to the LORD.*

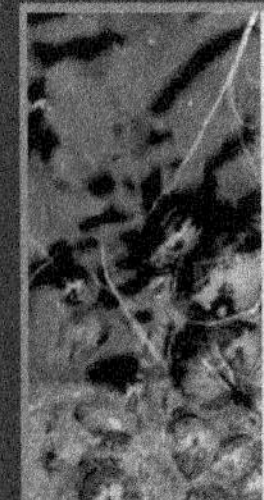

Moses was a prophet, a lawgiver, a liberator, and a leader who brought the scattered people of Israel together. Moses was said to be "the human instrument in the creation of the nation of Israel." Messiah is the human instrument, a prophet, the lawgiver, a liberator, and the leader who brings all the scattered people of God from all the nations together to Israel!

The Holy Temple Mount in Jerusalem Israel - The original Photograph ©2011 Simon Brown England All Rights Reserved
Photo Edited by Kimberly K Ballard

The Holy Temple Mount of the LORD God of Israel in Jerusalem Israel - Original Photograph ©2011 Simon Brown England All Rights Reserved
Photo Edited by Kimberly K Ballard

The Golden Gate, The Gate of Mercy on the Holy Temple Mount Jerusalem Israel - Original Photograph ©2011 Simon Brown England
All Rights Reserved – Photo Edited by Kimberly K Ballard

The Abu Badd Rolling Stone
Photo ©2011 Simon Brown England
All Rights Reserved

FINDING THE MEANING IN THE ABU BADD ROLLING STONE

The Abu Badd Rolling Stone
Photo ©2011 Simon Brown England
All Rights Reserved

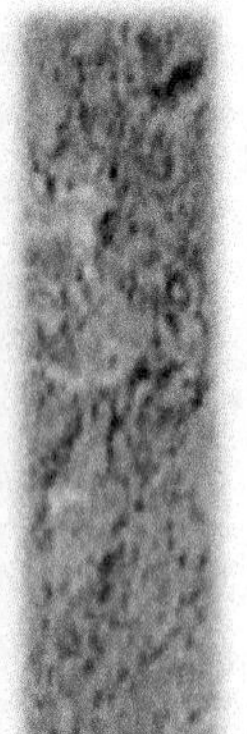

I knew that the LORD was going to bring all of this truth together into one incredible Testimony for His glory, so that it would be shown in the last days and now I believe that another final piece of the puzzle has been solved! *I found that in 1881, the Rolling Stone was not at the Garden tomb during the very first excavations. It was missing!* The Great Rolling Stone that stands facing the Promised Land like a compass on Mount Nebo is called *"The Abu Badd."* I automatically assumed that this name came from the ancient Monastery where the Great Rolling Stone was said to be discovered among the ruins near Mount Nebo, according to Simon Brown of England.

I never actually thought about researching the meaning of the name, *"Abu Badd."* This Great Rolling Stone was rumored to be an ancient door that stood in the Sanctuary of an ancient Byzantine Monastery in this location. The truth is, however, that the stone is far too heavy and large to be used on a daily basis as a door. There is only one purpose for a Great Rolling Stone of this size and that is to seal the door of an ancient tomb. Most of the ancient tombs in Israel were sealed with square sealing stones and *the round rolling stones were not as common because they were only used for the rich. This one was exceedingly large because it was used to seal the tomb of the KING OF KINGS!* Once it was rolled into place, no one really needed to roll it opened again, except to prepare the body with spices. Miraculously, though, this Great Stone was rolled open by the Angel of the LORD who sat upon it while glistening in his pure white garments! This particular Rolling Stone is, therefore, an extremely significant part of the Living Testimony of the LORD, *so they preserved it.* The fact that this huge Rolling Stone was standing in a Sanctuary at all indicates that it was very special and significant and that it was put there to be preserved. I believe that it was either taken to the mountains of Israel for protection, or it was taken away to the city of Constantinople where it was preserved in the Pharos Chapel when the Roman's invaded Jerusalem near the end of the first century. It also may have been kept in the so-called *"Temple of Peace"* in Rome at some point and perhaps later returned by the Romans to a Byzantine Church near Mount Nebo or kept for centuries in the Vatican, perhaps as a trophy or spoil of war as the Romans kept many large stone trophy's. Based upon the facts within the historical record, the Byzantine era believers in Yeshua must have protected this relic from destruction by placing it in the Sanctuary of one of their Monasteries, perhaps near the vicinity of Mount Nebo, or it was taken with the other relics to the Pharos Chapel in Constantinople and later was taken to Rome. Some of the Apostles went to Antioch because it was a major city of early Christianity. It had a very large Jewish population and the Jewish disciples, Simon Peter and later Barnabas and Paul, came to this city to preach Messiah's Living Torah Testimony to the Jews who were living in this place. Yeshua had already prophesied that the destruction of Jerusalem was near and He had already warned His disciples to flee into the mountains when they saw that Jerusalem about to be surrounded by Roman armies.

The mountains where they fled, were always part of the Land of Israel because, back then, there was no border or barrier that divided God's Land. Today, however, there is a land border and barrier and the mountains of Israel where they fled are now in the land that is called *"Jordan."* This is the mountainous area and some of them, especially *the Seventy* of Messiah, fled to this place from the siege and from the destruction of Jerusalem and the Second Temple. Any treasure that pertained to the resurrection of the Messiah was preserved as part of His Living Testimony. I believe, therefore, that the Great Rolling Stone was no exception and that it was also preserved for its extreme significance in the future and because the Angel of the LORD had miraculously rolled it away. At first, I did not think that the words *"Abu Badd"* actually meant something extraordinary, pertaining to the LORD God of Israel. It was incredible that just as I was editing this final Testimony of Messiah Yeshua, the LORD decided to show me the meaning of this phrase *"Abu Badd."* What I found in my research is such an important message for the nation of Israel in this critical moment of her history.

On September 14th 2011, I was doing some reading about the Hebrew month of Av. Before I go on with the story, I must mention that the Hebrew month of Av is quite significant on the Jewish calendar. On this day in history, Solomon's Temple was destroyed and hundreds of years later on the ninth of Av on the same day Herod's Temple was destroyed. In the year 1492 on this date, the Jewish people were expelled from Spain. Near the beginning of WWII, on the ninth of Av, the night known as *"krystallnacht"* occurred in Germany. WWI started on this day. All of this destruction occurred on the same day, but years and even centuries apart. The LORD told Israel, however, that one day He would turn their mourning on the ninth of Av into dancing and it would no longer be a time for them to mourn. To my astonishment, as I was reading about the Hebrew month of Av, I found the word *"Abu"* was written near the word *"Av."* It was such an uncommon word in the west that I never expected to run into it while I was reading about a completely different topic. So I believe that the LORD put it before me at that moment to show me the meaning of the name of the Great Rolling Stone. Astonishingly, it reveals the LORD as the Messiah! I already knew that the word, *"Av"* means *"Father"* in Hebrew, but I had no idea that the word *"Abu"* from another ancient Semitic language also means *"Father."* To be specific, it said that the word *"Abu"* refers *"to a Father who has living children.* **(Source: Ab, Av, Abu, en.wikipedia.org/wiki/Ab_Semitic).** *In this case, the name of the Great Rolling Stone standing on Mount Nebo is referring to the Father of many children, including the children of Israel."* It is therefore, referring to the LORD! This was so exciting! So the name of the stone that is facing the Promised Land like a compass has the name *"Father"* on it. The word *"Abu"* is like a prefix and it precedes another word, which in our case is the word *"Badd"* to complete the full name, *"Abu Badd."* So in order to discern the identity of the *"Father"* of the children of Israel, we must look at both words, *"Abu and then Badd."* The truth is that *"Abu"* also means *"a Holy man."* It is true that Messiah Yeshua is a Holy man! This is further proof that this Rolling Stone was from Yeshua's tomb, but it was now standing like an ensign on Mount Nebo. At this point, the LORD opened my eyes to understand the deeper meaning within these words.

I then decided to research the second part of the name which is the word *"Badd."* At first I had a very difficult time finding the word *"Badd"* in any context but later discovered that this word is of Semitic origin: *"Semitic etymology query Number: 1746 Proto-Semitic word: bad (d) - Meaning: 'pole, stick, beam.' Hebrew: bad– Aramaic: badd- Arabic: badd-)."* **(Source: starling.rinet.ru/cgi-bin/response.cgi?root=config&morpho=0&basename=/data/semham/semet&first=1741).** Incredibly, the earliest history of this word means *"pole" and "pole" is defined as "staff" or "rod!" So with this definition we can see that the Rolling Stone itself verifies that Yeshua is the Rod of God!*

Now I found another reference to the word *"Badd"* in Israel, in the title of a Museum called *"The Badd Giacaman Museum"* where they demonstrate Olive Oil Production. It is located near the Church of the Nativity in Bethlehem where Messiah Yeshua was born! The word *"Badd"* was now in connection with the *"Staff"* in Semitic Etymology, and to the Museum of the *"Olive Press!"* The Olive is a picture of perfection and completion due to it going through *seven stages of maturity* until it becomes a fully ripe Olive! *So it is fantastic that "Abu Badd" pertains to the Father God, and the anointed Messiah who's Living Testimony is perfection, and completion.* Yeshua wept in the Garden of Gethsemane when He was on the Mount of *anointing* in the midst of the Olive trees! He departed from the *Mount of Olives* after He fulfilled His Living Testimony. The word *"Gethsemane"* means *"oil press."* It refers to the Olives grown in this particular Garden, across from the Holy Temple. The Olives from this Garden fell from the trees and they were bruised, crushed, and pressed into oil. It was used in the seven lamps of the Holy Almond Tree Menorah in the Holy Temple! *I must come*

Olives growing on an Olive Tree
Photo ©2014 Kimberly K Ballard All Rights Reserved

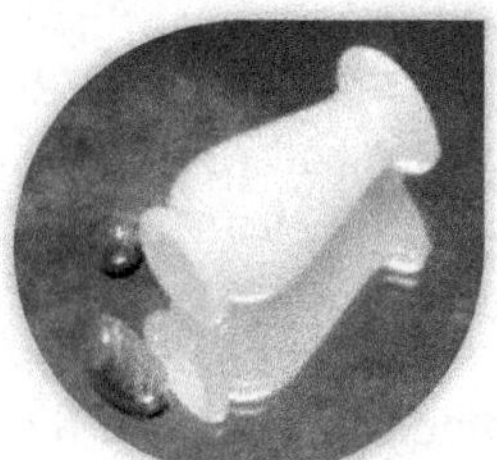

Olive oil with Alabaster flask
Photo ©2013 KK Ballard
All Rights Reserved

back and add here that in 2013, the LORD appointed this book to be published by "Olive Press Publisher!" Remember that *the two witnesses* are the *two Olive Trees!* Like the Olive, Yeshua was bruised and crushed for our transgressions, just as Isaiah foretold about the Messiah.

Isaiah 53:5 *But He was wounded for our transgressions, He was bruised for our iniquities; the chastisement of our peace was upon Him, and with His stripes we are healed.*

After the LORD revealed this to me, I happened to be looking up something else completely unrelated in the Strong's Concordance and I suddenly ran across the Hebrew word *"Bad."* The definition was so astonishing because it verified my book and it verified the completed Testimony of the LORD for the last days!

Now I read that if a Hebrew word has a *"dagesh"* within a letter, then you double the letter. So in our case, if you take this Hebrew word *"Bad"* and place a dagesh within the letter *"d"* the word becomes *"Badd."* Therefore, the extra letter *"d"* gives the completed word emphasis! The letter *"d"* is the Hebrew letter *"dalet"* and when it is doubled, it becomes a *"double dalet."* I can imagine that anything pertaining to the LORD'S incredible Living Testimony would indeed be emphasized with boldness! The most astonishing truth, however, is that the Hebrew letter *"dalet"* actually means *"door." So the "door" in this case has been emphasized and Messiah Yeshua is the door to Heaven!* The truly remarkable miracle in this fact is that the *"double dalet"* is actually the special knot on the *Tefillin, "Shel Rosh,"* or the *"Head Tefillin."* The double dalet knot is placed on the back of the head, so that it is not seen! I believe that this is a great miracle because the Messiah is the one building the Eternal Temple and this knot is in the shape of a square, like the blueprint of the Holy Temple. The Messiah is not seen yet by some of the Jewish people, but He is the *"door"* that is opened and is leading the sheep of the House of Israel into the Heavenly Promised Land!

So how amazing it is then that the Great Rolling Stone of Yeshua's tomb that is on Mount Nebo stands facing the LORD'S Garden on Mount Moriah where Eden was located and testifies that what He said was true, that Messiah Yeshua is the *"door"* of Heaven and that we must enter the Eternal Kingdom of God through the *"Gate of Heaven,"* the Rod of the Good Shepherd! This is why it is mind boggling to go back and look at the Scriptures and read what Yeshua declared about Himself in the Gospel of John, in chapter 10. Remember Yeshua said, *"I AM the door"* meaning that He leads the children of Israel to Eternal life. So the Great Rolling Stone *"door"* from Yeshua's Garden tomb *that is emphasized* because it was *"extremely vehement"* was rolled away by the Angel of the LORD, so His flocks would be gathered to drink forever on Holy Mount Moriah in Jerusalem Israel. The word *"vehement"* is interesting here. It is defined as *"powerful, intensity of conviction, intensely emotional, and marked by forceful energy."* Thinking upon these definitions it is clearly evident that when the Angel of the LORD rolled away this stone, it was *powerful, and it was intensely emotional* that Yeshua who had died such a brutal death that they believed was Israel's Messiah, was suddenly resurrected to life. The women that came to the tomb first revealed the LORD'S Living Testimony with *intensity of conviction* because there was *a forceful energy* present at the Garden tomb revealing this marvelous Testimony in the sepulchre inside Holy Mount Moriah. Miraculously, today, this *"extremely vehement stone"* is facing Jerusalem and *the Garden of God* from the top of Mount Nebo! *Of course this coincides with the fact that Messiah Yeshua is the Living Ark that is going before Israel across the Jordan River into the Eternal Promised Land in the final redemption that is soon to transpire!* Yeshua is the second Joshua, the second Moses, and the second Adam. Remember that as Yeshua stood in the Jordan River, *Heaven was parted by the hand of God*, so we may follow Him through this door by His power!

Habakkuk 3:4 *And His brightness was as the light; he had horns coming out of his hand; and there was the hiding of his power.*

John 10:9-18 *I AM the door; by Me if any man enter in, he shall be saved, and shall go in and out, and find pasture. The thief cometh not, but for to steal, and to kill, and to destroy; I AM come that they might have life, and that they might have it more abundantly. I AM the Good Shepherd; the Good Shepherd giveth His life for the sheep. But he that is a hireling, and not the Shepherd, whose own the sheep are not, seeth the wolf coming, and leaveth the sheep, and fleeth; and the wolf catcheth them, and scattereth the sheep. The hireling fleeth, because he is a hireling, and careth not for the sheep. I AM the Good Shepherd, and know My sheep, and am known of Mine. As the Father knoweth Me, even so know I the Father; and I lay down My life for the sheep. And other sheep I have, which are not of this fold; them also I must bring, and they shall hear My voice; and there shall be one fold, and one Shepherd. Therefore doth My Father love Me, because I lay down My life, that I might take it again. No man taketh it from Me, but I lay it down of Myself. I have power to lay it down, and I have power to take it again. This Commandment have I received of My Father.*

You can see why all the flocks of Israel could all drink from the well of Living Water forever since Yeshua accomplished destroying the curse of Eden and *the Great Stone was rolled away from the mouth of the gate of Heaven, inviting us back to His Garden* to drink from the Living Water that came forth out of *the Rock!* This is why the Great Rolling Stone is so incredibly important to all the sheep of the House of Israel today, and to everyone that believes in Him all over the world! Today this stone truly stands like an ensign on Mount Nebo by Divine Providence! This makes me weep great tears of joy because the LORD has performed the most magnificent work of our time. I feel so humbled that He loved me enough to show me His deep secrets and that while I was writing this Testimony, the LORD sent Simon Brown to measure the Rolling Stone on Mount Nebo and the Garden Tomb in Jerusalem, so at just the right time it would testify to this story that I have written! The LORD touches my heart deeply.

Now within the Hebrew word *"Bad"* in the Strong's Exhaustive Concordance, miraculously I found Yeshua, *the Branch from the Tree of Life and the Staff of Life!*

#905 ***Bad****, bad from 909; prop. Separation; by impl. A part of the body, branch of a tree, bar for carrying; fig. Chief of a City; espec. (With prep. Pref.) As adv., aparat, only, besides—alone, apart, bar, besides, branch, by self, of each alike, except, only part, staff, and strength.* **(Source: ©1995 Strong's concordance).**

All the following details about Yeshua are found in this definition of the Hebrew word *"Bad."* Yeshua is a Nazarite and a Nazarite *separates* Himself and dedicates Himself to God's service. Yeshua is *the Branch of the Almond Tree of Life.* Messiah Yeshua is the KING OF KINGS and the *Chief of the Eternal City* of God in the New Jerusalem. Yeshua was left *alone,* when He was taken to be tried. Yeshua, the Branch, is the *Staff* of Life of the Good Shepherd and the Unleavened Heavenly Bread of Life, which is our *strength and Israel's strength* to endure this sin cursed world. Remember what I said earlier about the Nativity story and Yeshua's conception at Hanukkah on the Festival of Lights? I said that during Hanukkah, a special Menorah called a *"Hanukkiyah"* is used and it has a total of nine branches. One of the branches called the *"servant" or "shamash"* candle is elevated or lifted up above all the others. From this shamash candle all the other candles are lit. Occasionally, this one that is *set apart* is set lower than the others. This teaches us that although the Great KING was among us and He was lifted up for us on the cross, He came to the earth as a humble servant, making Himself lower than His usual *KINGLY* position for our sakes out of the love of His heart! The Hebrew word *"Bad"* implies being *"set apart,"* just like the Shamash candle that lights all the other candles on the hanukkiyah and *it depicts the Rod and Staff of God being lifted up* to give us the Eternal light of His Majestic glory! Yeshua is the light that fills us with the Eternal oil of His Ruach/Holy Spirit. The LORD said that Messiah is the horn that He will make to bud. The Messiah is *set apart* as the Nazarite and the Holy Almond Branch lifted up.

The primary Root word of *"Bad"* has the following description that testifies of Yeshua dividing and making things cleft. The shoot of Jesse was solitary or alone when He prayed.

#909 Badad, baw-dad; <u>shoots, to divide</u>, i.e. (reflex.) be solitary—alone." **(Source: ©1995 Strong's concordance).**

The astonishing final piece of the puzzle is that the word *"Bad"* ironically refers to linen! The fine Linen burial Shroud of Messiah Yeshua bears His image and the Testimony of His death, burial, and resurrection that took place in God's Garden in Holy Mount Moriah.

#906 ***Bad,*** *bad; from #909 (in the senses of divided fibres); flaxen thread or yarn; hence a linen garment—linen."* ***(Source: ©1995 Strong's concordance).***

The miraculous negative image on the linen burial Shroud is a significant piece of the Testimony of the LORD, proving that He is the Rock quarried out of God's Mountain, leaving a reverse impression of Himself in the quarry of His Garden, showing us that we were indeed made in His image from *the original FOUNDATION STONE* on Holy Mount Moriah! As the High Priest of Heaven, after the order of Melchizedek, Yeshua wears a pure white *linen* garment in the Heavenly Kingdom of God. *So the name, "The Abu Badd," means linen with extra emphasis!* When the disciples saw the *linens,* they believed! This *linen* proclaims *(with extra emphasis)* the glory of the Living Branch of God! Every one of the descriptive words has extra emphasis in the double dalet or double letter *"d"* because we are talking about the LORD God of Israel! We are talking about the Majesty of the KING of Heaven!

The Hebrew letter *"a"* which is *"aleph"* is in the center of the word *"Badd"* and it represents the LORD as the first and the beginning. Aleph is the *first or beginning* letter of the Hebrew alphabet. The *aleph* represents the LORD, who created the universe in *the beginning.* The LORD declared that *He is the First and the Last, the Beginning and the End.* So remarkably, we also find this meaning in the name of the Great Rolling Stone that is facing the Promised Land. The Hebrew letter *"b"* which is *"bet"* means *"a dwelling, tent, or house,"* and the Great stone faces the place where *God's House* is established forever in Jerusalem Israel. This is so significant since the LORD God of Israel came down to *dwell* in our midst, to Tabernacle with us in a *temporary dwelling* of flesh as the Messiah of Israel. The Living Sukkah is His temporary *tent!* The Testimony of the LORD is a miracle of Biblical proportions! I wept again after the LORD showed this to me because I knew the Great Rolling Stone of Yeshua's tomb was now miraculously verifying again for me that He is the Branch from the Almond Tree of Life, and that as the door to Heaven this Joshua/Yeshua leads Israel into the Eternal Promised Land. The Great Rolling Stone faces the view that Moses saw before He entered into Heaven. Yeshua said that He has other sheep that are not of this fold that He would also gather from all nations. They would also be His people and believe His Eternal Testimony so they may enter His Garden, to go into the Heavenly Promised Land.

By Divine appointment, *"The Abu Badd, the Great Rolling Stone"* is now standing on Mount Nebo facing what God Promised to Israel forever! One Joshua took Israel into the earthly Promised Land with the LORD leading the way, abiding on His Ark, and Messiah Yeshua takes Israel into the Eternal Promised Land leading the way, as the Ark of the LORD'S Living Testimony. I remain forever stunned by His magnificent Testimony that has now been revealed by the power of His Holy Spirit, and the Third Temple is about to rebuilt for the first time in 2000 years, preparing the way for the return of the Great KING!

Deuteronomy 32:3-4 *Because I will publish the Name of the LORD; ascribe ye greatness unto our God. He is the Rock, His work is perfect; for all His ways are judgment; a God of truth and without iniquity, just and right is He.*

The Abu Badd on Mount Nebo is therefore, actually facing *"The Rock"* that formed us in His image on Mount Moriah where Yeshua was resurrected in the rock quarry, leaving His image behind on linen as an everlasting Testimony with *extra emphasis!*

Deuteronomy 32:18 *Of the Rock that begat thee thou art unmindful, and hast forgotten God that formed thee.*

Deuteronomy 29:29 *The secret things belong unto the LORD our God; but those things which are revealed belong to us and to our children forever, that we may do all the Words of this Law.*

Simon Brown of England on Mount Nebo
Standing in front of The Abu Badd Rolling Stone the day that he measured it!
(The "V" shaped notch above his head matches
the "V" at the Garden Tomb window)

The crevice markings above (starting under the large niche) match each other, going toward and under the Mantle of the Angel across the stone from left to right

These pictures show the Rolling Stone face down over a photo of the Garden tomb on a light table
I am showing congruent lines & markings when the stone is facing the Garden Tomb

Horizontal "V" shaped notch on the rolling stone lines up with the "V" shaped notch on the right corner of the window of the Garden tomb

The Great Rolling Stone
As viewed on a light table
Overlaid on the Garden Tomb
By Kimberly K Ballard

Now I wanted to add here that in the Hebrew month of Shevat, in January 2013, as I carefully studied an enlarged picture of the Abu Badd Rolling Stone on a light table, the LORD brought to mind, and I was able to determine, that *the smooth side of this stone had to have been the part of the stone that was on the ground because it rolled inside the trench thereby making it smooth while the upper portion of the stone that is not as smooth that appears to be rougher was towards the top,* touching the upper portion of the Garden tomb near the face of the Angel. When I placed this picture of the Garden tomb on a light table facing me or facing upward and then placed a picture of the Great Rolling Stone that I had turned, so that the picture of the Rolling Stone was face down on top of it, as if it was resting on the front of the Garden tomb with the stone facing the tomb, I was stunned by what I saw! There is a large mark on the Rolling Stone that is notched out, shaped like a letter *"V."* I discovered that if you turn this mark sideways like this, "<," with the point aimed towards the left, it perfectly lines up with the lower right corner of the window of the Garden tomb in Mount Moriah. Another mark corresponds to the left corner of the window. Then I believe that I noticed *a line on the Rolling Stone that corresponds with the curve of the Angel wing at the Garden tomb, just above the window.* So perhaps the rolling stone was sitting farther to the right than we first thought. After I saw these corresponding marks, I noticed that the rather *large gaping crevice that comes down from the mantle of the Angel like a zigzag and continues straight across towards the left of the exterior wall* of the Garden tomb and goes underneath the niches at the tomb, and matches up perfectly with zigzag crevice markings that are on the Great Rolling Stone. I believe I can see a faint flower shape on the Rolling Stone on the far upper left side where the signet was once resting against it and there are *marks corresponding to the finger and hand of the Angel* on the Rolling Stone, as well as *marks of the two letters of the signet.* Now they bricked up the center of the tomb with Jerusalem stone where the rock had fallen out in the earthquake and the *lower right corner of this bricked up wall corresponds to a large crevice mark in the lower right side of the Rolling Stone.* One photo was placed over the other with light going through them. *So the window and the bricked stone perfectly line up with these markings.* I actually believe now that when the Angel descended to roll away the stone, the Rolling stone was rolled backward and this rubbed the stone upon stone, *leaving long white streak marks on the Rolling Stone* and the earthquake caused this part of the tomb to collapse. The rubble fell out of this part of the tomb, so it had to be bricked up with Jerusalem stone. At the top of the Rolling Stone and at the top of the Garden tomb, there are *square line markings* that match up. In the place of the entry of the tomb and going downward to the lower left and at the very bottom of the Rolling Stone, *there are coloration patterns that appear be stain marks where plant growth was once attached to it, as well as dirt*. There are a few important smaller gouge markings that correspond between the Great Rolling Stone on Mount Nebo and the markings on the Garden tomb of Mount Moriah. I only noticed this in January of 2013, when I felt that the LORD was prompting me to put the pictures together on a light table. The greatest evidence of all is *the huge crevice that lines up coming down from the Angel's mantle in a zigzag pattern* that goes across the width of the stone with the "<" notch set at the lower right corner of the window. When you line up that mark on the Rolling Stone and place it at the lower right corner of the window in the Garden tomb, then everything else appears to line up. It is so remarkable and I have yet to show this stunning piece of evidence to Simon Brown in England, but I think he will be thrilled by it!

This overlay technique was first used on the Shroud of Turin by Dr. Alan Whanger, so that the congruent markings could be matched up, and I found that the same technique could be used on the Great Rolling Stone to demonstrate that the congruent markings on it could be matched up to the Garden tomb of Yeshua in Mount Moriah. I am not certain, but I now believe that it is possible that the Rolling Stone may have covered the wing of the Angel, leaving only his face and head visible and exposed. In my research by the grace of God, in

The Garden Tomb, Great Rolling Stone & my Angel Photo ©2011 Simon Brown England All Rights Reserved

January 2013, I was able to find a historical document that referred to the earliest Garden tomb excavations. In this document from 1878, I found that the excavators had written about the existence of two stopper stones for the rolling stone in the place of the rolling track in front of the Garden tomb in Jerusalem. What fascinated me the most, though, is that they said *that this proves there was at one time a Rolling Stone rolled in this track.* This tells me that they never saw or found the Great Rolling Stone there, which means that it was indeed gone from the tomb well before the earliest excavations! The doorway was broken and there was a huge hole four feet wide! *In 1878 Captain Conder wrote in his book, "Tent Work in Palestine," that the Garden tomb was the true tomb of Yeshua.* Captain Conder wrote; *"The whole is very rudely cut in the rock, which is of inferior quality. The doorway is much broken, and there is a loophole or window, four feet wide, on either side of the door. The outer court, cut in the rock, is seven feet square; and two stones are so placed in this as to give the idea that they may have held in place a rolling-stone before the door."* ***(Source: ©1881 "Survey of Western Palestine," Jerusalem volume, p. 432 (Source; Jerusalem, Bethany, and Bethlehem, p.166).***

My Olive Branch with five Olives & three rocks from the Mount of Olives Photos ©2013 Kimberly K Ballard All Rights Reserved

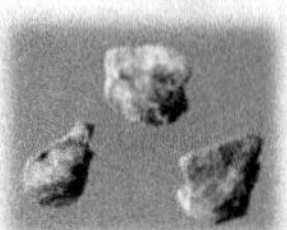

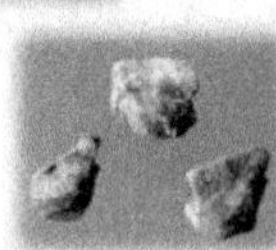

The Promised Land of Israel
The Great Rolling Stone on Mount Nebo & the Holy Temple Mount
Original Photos ©2011 Simon Brown England

both Edited to a scene on the snow with tropical landscape by KKB

Majestic Cloud & Half Rainbow from the peak of my roof into a Cloud Portal

Chapter 10

THE LORD IS COMING IN THE CLOUD OF HEAVEN

Behold He is coming in the clouds with great power and glory and every eye shall see Him! It's time to *"Watch," "Shaked!"* The time is near! It is time to *"Awaken"* because the KING is at the door! I was so thrilled when I began to realize that the one who left in the glory cloud is the same one that will return in the glory cloud from Heaven!

Daniel 7:13 *I saw in the night visions, and, behold, one like the Son of man came with the clouds of Heaven, and came to the Ancient of days, and they brought Him near before Him.*

Revelation 1:5-8 *And from Yeshua Messiah, who is the faithful witness, and the first begotten of the dead, and the Prince of the kings of the earth. Unto Him that loved us, and washed us from our sins in His own blood, And hath made us kings and priests unto God and his Father; to Him be glory and dominion forever and ever. Amen. Behold, He cometh with clouds; and every eye shall see Him, and they also which pierced Him; and all kindred's of the earth shall wail because of Him. Even so, Amen. I am Alpha and Omega, the beginning and the ending, saith the LORD, which is, and which was, and which is to come, the Almighty.*

In the historical record of Moses, it is quite evident, that wherever the LORD was…

THE LORD APPEARED "IN" THE CLOUD.

The LORD was not *"the cloud,"* rather the LORD was always *"IN"* the cloud. It is written in I King's 8:12 that *"the cloud of the LORD was a dark cloud that filled the House of the LORD!"* The cloud is a shield that hides His full glory from the sight of men. One day He will return in the cloud and reveal His full glory to us. Then we will see Him as He is, face to face, when He comes to earth at the time of His glorious appearing. What a sight it will be as the sound of His trumpet blast echoes throughout the whole earth!

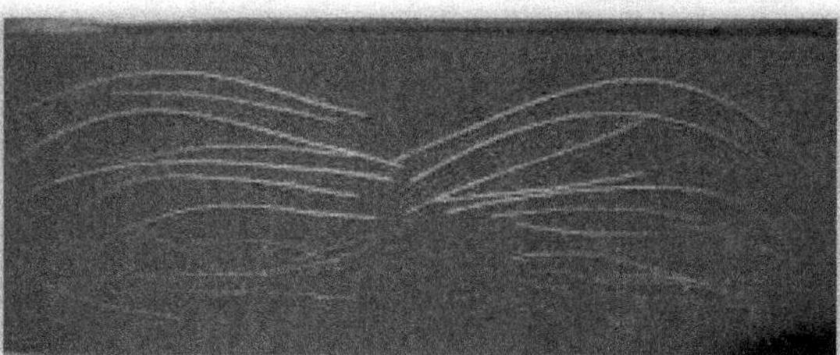

Miracle whiskers! Jasmine died July 22nd 2004. I would cry missing him & suddenly I would find a whisker from his face. The LORD comforted me & it continued until I had several little boxes of them! Based on Genesis I know Jasmine is in Heaven. The Bible indicates that all creatures will be delivered from the bondage of death.

THE SHECHINAH GLORY AND SAUL MOUNT SINAI AND THE TRANSFIGURATION

Fire & Smoke on the Mountain & Cloud
Photos ©2013 Kimberly K Ballard All Rights Reserved

The Rabbi Saul, known as the Apostle Paul, studied Torah under Rabbi Gamaliel**,** who was a leader of the Sanhedrin in Jerusalem. Saul/Paul was blinded by the Shechinah glory light on the road to Damascus and he heard Yeshua speaking to him from the midst of the light, saying in Hebrew, *"I AM Yeshua, whom you are persecuting."* This is one more clue to solving the mystery of Messiah Yeshua! As I read more about Saul's encounter with Yeshua in my Bible, something came across my path that was profoundly exciting. Paul said that after this Heavenly encounter happened to him on the road to Damascus, he did not go to Jerusalem. Instead, Paul went to Arabia! I was astonished to read this in Galatians and I had the chills when I suddenly realized that Paul went to Arabia, so he could go up to Mount Sinai after His encounter with Yeshua the LORD!

Galatians 1:15-18 *But when it pleased God, who separated me from my mother's womb, and called me by His grace, To reveal His Son in me, that I might preach Him among the heathen; immediately I conferred not with flesh and blood; Neither went I up to Jerusalem to them which were Apostles before me; but I went into Arabia, and returned again unto Damascus. Then after three years I went up to Jerusalem to see Peter, and abode with him fifteen days.*

So Paul did not confer with Rabbi's in Jerusalem, instead, he immediately went into Arabia and it has never been known why Paul went into Arabia, but because of what the LORD showed me, I now believe that he went to Mount Sinai to confer with the LORD. Perhaps he spent three years there and then returned to Damascus to show that he was not appointed by man, but by God! The three years correspond to the resurrection Testimony of the Messiah on the third day and you will begin to understand why I say that Paul went to Mount Sinai, as you read all the follow chapters. *After Paul went to Mount Sinai, Paul wrote about the meaning of the Law of God and how it was fulfilled in the Messiah. He talks about how the Law was our schoolmaster to bring us to Messiah that we might be justified by faith.* Immediately after discussing this truth about *the Law of God,* Paul goes on to say the following about Mount Sinai in Arabia, and he said it because he had been there himself to confer with the LORD about his mission to take *"The Living Torah" that abides in the Heavenly Ark to the heathen Gentiles, who did not have God. This is why he did not go to Jerusalem to confer with the Rabbi's, but went to Arabia to confer with God!* Paul *the Torah Scholar* was now appointed to take *"The Living Torah, the LORD Messiah, who was the total fulfillment of the Law, to the Gentiles!"* Remember that Paul was from the tribe of Benjamin and as a Jewish Torah Scholar, Mount Sinai had great significance to him as part of the LORD'S Eternal Testimony. In the following Scripture, Paul said that Mount Sinai was *"the bondage of the Law"* and that Jerusalem in his day was still living under this same bondage. Paul then said that *Messiah the LORD, who is the Testimony of the Heavenly Ark of God, brings us freedom from this bondage because His Kingdom is in the Jerusalem of Heaven above that is free!* The LORD God is of course the Law and Covenant of perfection! So this is the Covenant that blesses us forever.

A Burnt Peak Photo ©2013

Galatians 4:19-26 *My little children, of whom I travail in birth again until Messiah be formed in you, I desire to be present with you now, and to change my voice; for I stand in doubt of you. Tell me, ye that desire to be under the law, do ye not hear the law? For it is written, that Abraham had two sons, the one by a bondmaid, the other by a freewoman. But he who was of the bondwoman was born after the flesh; but he of the freewoman was by the promise. Which things are an allegory, for these are the two Covenants; the one from the Mount Sinai, which gendereth to bondage, which is Agar. For this Agar is Mount Sinai in Arabia, and answereth to Jerusalem which now is, and is in bondage with her children. But the Jerusalem which is above is free, which is the mother of us all.*

Moses and Elijah, at different times, stood upon Mount Sinai. The LORD was on top of the high Mountain of Sinai when He appeared in a cloud to Moses. Elijah also went up at the command of the LORD because the people of Israel had broken God's Covenant. Moses and Elijah happen to be *the two witnesses* that appeared with Messiah Yeshua in the glory cloud at the transfiguration upon the high Mountain. Yeshua took the three Jewish disciples apart to be alone with Him on this high Mountain. No one seems to know exactly which high Mountain it was where Yeshua took the three disciples to be alone with Him. Through Divine revelation, though, I now believe with all my heart that Yeshua the LORD took His Jewish disciples to the destination of Mount Sinai because it was known as a high Mountain and guess who appeared in the glory cloud with Yeshua on this high Mountain, but Moses and Elijah who had both stood before the LORD in this place before. Yeshua was talking with them on the high Mountain in the glory cloud in His glorified state and they knew Him. *Yeshua spoke to Moses and Elijah about fulfilling His Eternal Living Covenant of the Heavenly Ark that was about to come to pass.* Now remember Paul was in Arabia and then he went to Damascus. Elijah went to Arabia and he was instructed by the LORD to come up to the top of Mount Sinai or Mount Horeb. On his way to the Holy Mount, Elijah survived 40 days and 40 nights on the bread and water that the Angel of the LORD provided for him, to strengthen him. Elijah heard the voice *and the Word of the LORD came to him there.* The LORD then instructed Elijah to return to Damascus and this is exactly what Paul did! They both went into Arabia to Mount Sinai and returned to Damascus! Here is Elijah's encounter with the LORD on top of Mount Sinai in I Kings. The Word of the LORD came to Elijah there in the cave!

I Kings 19:5-15 *And as he lay and slept under a juniper tree, behold, then an angel touched him, and said unto him, Arise and eat. And he looked, and, behold, there was a cake baked on the coals, and a cruse of water at his head. And he did eat and drink, and laid him down again. And the angel of the LORD came again the second time, and touched him, and said, Arise, and eat; because the journey is too great for thee. And he arose, and did eat and drink, and went in the strength of that meat forty days and forty nights unto Horeb the Mount of God. And he came thither unto a cave, and lodged there; and, behold, the Word of the LORD came to him, and He said unto him, What doest thou here, Elijah? And he said, I have been very jealous for the LORD God of Hosts; for the children of Israel have forsaken Thy Covenant, thrown down Thine altars, and slain Thy Prophets with the sword; and I, even I only, am left; and they seek my life, to take it away. And He said, Go forth, and stand upon the Mount before the LORD. And, behold, the LORD passed by, and a great and strong wind rent the Mountains, and brake in pieces the rocks before the LORD; but the LORD was not in the wind; and after the wind an earthquake; but the LORD was not in the earthquake; And after the earthquake a fire; but the LORD was not in the fire; and after the fire a still small voice. And it was so, when Elijah heard it, that he wrapped his face in his mantle, and went out, and stood in the entering in of the cave. And, behold, there came a voice unto him, and said, What doest thou here, Elijah? And he said, I have been very jealous for the LORD God of Hosts; because the children of Israel have forsaken Thy Covenant, thrown down Thine altars, and slain Thy Prophets with the sword; and I, even I only, am left; and they seek my life, to take it away. And the LORD said unto him, Go, return on thy way to the wilderness of Damascus; and when thou comest, anoint Hazael to be king over Syria.*

Now the question is, how did Yeshua get to Mount Sinai? Yeshua was in Caesarea Philippi about 8 days before the transfiguration. Damascus is only 50 miles from Caesarea Philippi and perhaps Yeshua traveled to Mount Sinai, like any normal person would have traveled there, and then He returned to Galilee, but I think that something more spectacular happened that was truly breathtaking! Consider the fact that when Yeshua walked on the water and got into the ship with His Jewish disciples, *suddenly the ship was at its destination!* A similar event happened when the disciple Philip baptized the Ethiopian eunuch. When they came up out of the water, the Spirit of the LORD *caught away* Philip, so that the eunuch saw him no more. Then Philip was found at Azotus, which is Ashdod. So I believe that Yeshua took the three Jewish disciples instantly to Mount Sinai, their destination where the disciple proclaimed with excitement, *"LORD, it is good for us to be here!"* Remember that by definition, *the Deliverer* takes us *instantly* to our haven!

Yeshua the LORD, who is the Living Torah, was standing in their midst. His Heavenly pure white garments were brilliantly shining and Yeshua was revealing His final Eternal Living Testimony that would soon be fulfilled in Jerusalem Israel, as the Branch from the Almond Tree of Life. The Covenant at Mount Sinai was the Covenant of bondage and the New Living Eternal Heavenly Covenant of Messiah Yeshua the LORD was freedom from this bondage forever, to everlasting life with the LORD God of Israel in the Eternal Promised Land.

When they came down from the high Mountain, Yeshua instructed them that they should tell no man what things they had seen in *"the vision"* until the Messiah was raised from the dead. *They questioned what rising from the dead meant!* They did not understand completely the concept of Yeshua, as the Almond Rod of God that must be cut off, die, and come to life, bearing the First Fruit from the Almond Tree of Life on the third day, as part of the Living Testimony of the Ark of Heaven, as the parallel of Aaron's Rod that budded!

Then the Jewish disciples asked Yeshua if Elijah must come first. Yeshua told them that Elijah does come first to restore all things. *The fact is that Elijah did come!* Elijah was standing on Mount Sinai with Moses as one of *the two witnesses* and Yeshua, who was suddenly in His glorified state as the LORD God of Israel, stood before them in His Divine Royal Majesty! So the Jewish disciples were given *a vision revelation on top of Mount Sinai* of Messiah Yeshua's true identity as the LORD God of Israel! By definition a *"vision" is defined as "something seen in a dream, trance or ecstasy; especially a supernatural appearance that conveys a revelation. A vision is a direct mystical awareness of the supernatural, usually in visible form."* So this was a supernatural revelation that showed them the mystery of Messiah the LORD God of Israel on His Holy Mount!

Matthew 17:9 *And as they came down from the Mountain, Yeshua charged them, saying, Tell the vision to no man, until the Son of man be risen from the dead.*

The disciples fulfilled the LORD'S request. They kept silent about it. Not a soul heard about *"the vision"* until Yeshua had fulfilled His Living Testimony in Jerusalem at the Garden tomb. First, God's Almond Rod had to bud inside Holy Mount Moriah. This was the Eternal Living Covenant inside the former Garden of Eden. There can be no doubt this *vision did* occur on top of Mount Sinai in the wilderness. They were eyewitnesses of the unveiling of the glory of the LORD Yeshua standing in the midst of the glory cloud on top of Mount Sinai, speaking with Moses and Elijah.

Remember that Moses was to make a copy of this Heavenly Ark, but now Messiah the LORD was in the glory cloud in His Majesty, *revealing that He is the Ark of Heaven that Moses replicated!* The Rod became our Yeshua! It is interesting that soon after this event transpired with Moses and Elijah standing on either side of Yeshua, *the Living Ark on Mount Sinai,* there was an incident when the mother of James and John actually requested that the

LORD allow her two sons to sit on either side of Him in Heaven and the people who heard it quickly reprimanded her! I think they understood this was a very profound statement!

Matthew 20:21 *And He said unto her, What wilt thou? She saith unto Him, Grant that these my two sons may sit, the one on Thy right hand, and the other on the left in Thy Kingdom.*

Official Photograph of Mount Sinai in Arabia
The burnt peak of Mount Sinai is to the left of center and was discovered by Jim & Penny Caldwell of splitrockresearch.org

The *vision* was, indeed, *a revelation of the identity of the Messiah* and of His final Eternal Testimony. On Mount Sinai, the cloud hid the Presence of the LORD and Moses went into the cloud to meet with the LORD and to speak with Him. First, Moses read the Covenant to the people and when they agreed to the Covenant, Moses took the blood of the Covenant and dashed the blood upon the people. The first element shows us why the blood of Messiah Yeshua must be dashed upon us. Yeshua offered the Eternal Covenant to us. When we accept His offer, Yeshua's life blood of the Mercy Seat of the Heavenly Ark is dashed upon us and we are purified by it and we know that just before His crucifixion, Yeshua sealed the Eternal Covenant in His life blood, represented in that third cup of wine, during His Last Passover Seder. Messiah Yeshua's life blood was placed upon the Mercy Seat and upon the altar of the LORD, as our final sin atonement. This is the sign of the Covenant that seals us with the breath of His Ruach/Holy Spirit for Eternal life. The life blood of the LORD is a key element of the Heavenly Ark of God and without it, we could not live forever!

Another astonishing thing that I discovered about this is in the Exodus account. *With Moses, the cloud hid the Presence of the LORD for six days and it was on the seventh day Sabbath that the LORD called to Moses out of the midst of the glory cloud.* On the seventh day, the Presence of the LORD appeared in a consuming fire on top of the Mountain and Moses spoke with the LORD. The LORD provided water and manna and meat to the full to the children of Israel. Hundreds of years later, Messiah Yeshua met with His sheep Israel and He fed them water and manna and gave them meat to the full. After six days, Messiah Yeshua went up to the high Mountain and He was transfigured before the three Jewish disciples, Peter, James, and John. *This means that Yeshua was transfigured out of the midst of the cloud on the seventh day Sabbath of the LORD!*

Moses had remained on the Mountain for forty days and forty nights. Yeshua was baptized and led by the Holy Spirit to the wilderness for forty days and nights. Elijah was given bread and water by the LORD because He is the Living Water and the Unleavened Bread of Heaven and he was strengthened by this *"meat" for forty days and nights.*

It was on Mount Sinai that *the LORD revealed the Holy design for the Ark of the Covenant* that contained His Eternal Testimony. So *the Jewish disciples* were eyewitnesses of *the Living Heavenly Ark of the LORD God* that was revealed with Yeshua in His glorified state. Moses was to place the Testimony inside the Ark, and the Testimony was inside Yeshua!

What is also interesting about this event is the fact that the LORD revealed to me that right before the transfiguration a few things transpired first, before *the vision.* When you read to the end of this book you will then understand why I believe that they were on Mount Sinai, although it might not be as clear right now in this chapter. First, Yeshua asked His Jewish disciples *who they thought that He was,* and Simon Peter proclaimed that Yeshua was the Messiah, the Son of the Living God. Then Yeshua said *that flesh and blood had not revealed this to Simon, but the Ruach/Holy Spirit had revealed it to him.* Then, just before going to the high Mountain *(Mount Sinai),* Yeshua said that He would give them *"The keys of the Kingdom of Heaven." The Messiah was about to reveal in a vision, in a revelation on Mount Sinai, the things that had not been seen or known since the foundation of the world.* He was about to show them that He fulfills every detail of *His Law and Living Torah Covenant of the Heavenly Ark of God,* from the beginning of time. Yeshua was about to give them the keys that unlocked the great mystery of the Messiah. When they saw His Majesty transfigured upon Mount Sinai, they understood that *Messiah Yeshua was the LORD God of Israel. After they were shown the keys to the Kingdom by Yeshua there, His Jewish disciples kept the miraculous things that they had witnessed on Mount Sinai secret, until Yeshua fulfilled His Divine Testimony, as the budded Rod of God. He had to bud to life the third day, but they did not understand it yet until after it took place inside Holy Mount Moriah in Jerusalem Israel.*

Matthew 16:19-21 *And I will give unto thee the keys of the Kingdom of Heaven; and whatsoever shall be bound in Heaven; and whatsoever thou shalt bind on earth shall be bound in Heaven;and whatsoever thou shalt loose on earth shall be loosed in Heaven. Then charged He His disciples that they should tell no man that He was Yeshua the Messiah. From that time forth began Yeshua to shew unto His disciples, how that He must go unto Jerusalem and suffer many things of the Elders and Chief Priests and Scribes, and be killed, and be raised again the third day.*

Simon Peter later wrote about *Yeshua's Majesty, as he had witnessed it,* during Yeshua's transfiguration on the Holy Mount (Mount Sinai), but he only wrote about it *after Yeshua was resurrected* inside Holy Mount Moriah in Jerusalem Israel! When Simon Peter wrote about it he made it clear that this Testimony was not a cunningly devised fable!

II Peter 1:16-18 *For we have not followed cunningly devised fables, when we made known unto you the power and coming of our LORD Yeshua Messiah, but were eyewitnesses of His Majesty. For He received from God the Father honour and glory, when there came such a voice to Him from the excellent glory, This is My beloved Son, in whom I AM well pleased. And this voice which came from Heaven we heard, when we were with Him in the Holy Mount.*

Now it is fascinating that Simon Peter said that He saw Messiah's Majesty, *"the glory of the LORD," on the "Holy Mount"* because Moses had set boundaries around Mount Sinai to sanctify it and make it *holy*. It is a fact that Mount Sinai was called the *"Holy Mount!"* This is a major clue, testifying to the location of Yeshua's transfiguration.

Exodus 19:23-24 *And Moses said unto the LORD, The people cannot come up to Mount Sinai; for Thou chargedst us, saying, Set bounds about the mount, and sanctify it. And the LORD said unto him, Away, get thee down, and thou shalt come up, thou, and Aaron with thee; but let not the Priests and the people break through to come up unto the LORD, lest he break forth upon them.*

The Hebrew word for sanctify is *"Kadesh, also spelled Kadash and Kiddush."* Kadesh is mentioned at Passover. It refers to *"Separating a person, place or thing and setting it apart and devoting it to the LORD, for Holy or Divine purposes."* So Mount Sinai was *"Holy"* and so were Moses and Aaron. In Psalm 68:17, the LORD is among His chariots as *in Sinai, in the holy place. So they were the only ones that were made separate or "Kadesh" from the rest of the people and the Priests, who were not allowed to come up to the Holy Mount.* Now incredibly, the Holy Spirit revealed to me that Yeshua's account verifies the *"Kadesh"* even before going up to Holy Mount Sinai! *The three Jewish disciples were "set apart by themselves" as "Kadesh" and they were the only disciples chosen to go up onto the Holy Mount with Messiah Yeshua to witness His Majestic glory in the thick cloud, just as Moses and Aaron did! The rest of the disciples did not go up onto Holy Mount Sinai!*

Cloud Photo ©2013 Kimberly K Ballard All Rights Reserved

Mark 9:2 *And after six days Yeshua taketh with Him Peter, and James, and John, and leadeth them up into an High Mountain apart by themselves; and He was transfigured before them.*

Moses wrote that there was one coming in the future of Israel, who was like unto himself. Moses told Israel that they were *"to listen to Him."* So it is interesting that when Yeshua was standing on top of Mount Sinai with the three Jewish disciples and Moses and Elijah, a voice came out of the cloud that was overshadowing them and said, *"This is My beloved Son, Hear Him."* Israel was *to listen* to Messiah Yeshua!

Another astonishing detail came to light, as I was writing this down and it gave me the chills when I saw it! Just before Moses and Elijah appeared on the high Mountain of Mount Sinai with Yeshua, He said, *"There are some standing here that will not taste of death until they see the Son of man coming in His Kingdom."* I believe that *Yeshua was talking about Moses and Elijah, who were standing next to Him on Mount Sinai, just after Yeshua declared these prophetic Words.* They are *the two witnesses* who will come to Jerusalem to preach the LORD'S Eternal Covenant of *the Living Torah* during the great tribulation, just before Messiah Yeshua returns from Heaven to dwell in our midst forever. By the mouth of *the two witnesses,* every Word of God shall be established (*II Corinthians 13:1)*! On Mount Sinai, Yeshua took three witnesses with Him and the other *two witnesses* were Moses and Elijah. This adds up to five, the number of the books of the Torah! Moses and Elijah represent the Law and Prophets, which equals a perfect number seven and they represent Yeshua, the number 7 of the *Living Torah* Covenant of the Heavenly Ark. When they arrive, it will be their last Testimony that prepares Israel for the arrival of their Eternal KING OF KINGS AND LORD OF LORDS. When Joshua crossed over the Jordan River, he was only foreshadowing the Ark of Heaven. Therefore, Messiah Yeshua leads all believers into *the Eternal Heavenly Promised Land,* but we must follow behind *the Living Ark!*

The two witnesses come just after the Third Holy Temple is built in Jerusalem! They have power to shut up the Heavens so it does not rain. Fire comes out of their mouths, and they will produce plagues. King Solomon mentioned *the lack of rain and plagues* in his Temple dedication prayer in I King's 8:35-40, *but it is interesting to note that they were mentioned only after the Ark was taken up (I Kings 8:1)! Perhaps we are taken up in the rapture before the two witnesses produce these two things!* If the people turn back to God, they will be stopped!

Revelation 11:1-4 *And there was given me a reed like unto a rod; and the angel stood, saying, Rise, and measure the Temple of God, and the altar, and them that worship therein. But the court which is without the Temple leave out, and measure it not; for it is given unto the Gentiles; and the Holy City shall they tread under foot forty and two months. And I will give power unto My two witnesses, and they shall prophesy a thousand two hundred and threescore days, clothed in sackcloth. These are the two olive trees, and the two candlesticks standing before the God of the earth.*

Moses and Elijah were standing before the God of the earth when they stood before Yeshua on Mount Sinai. They are definitely revealed as *the two witnesses* who taste death during the great tribulation. *It was the seventh day Sabbath of the LORD when Yeshua went to Mount Sinai.* As the bright Shechinah glory cloud overshadowed them, *and His countenance was changed before them, they fell on their faces and they were sore afraid at the sight of His shining raiment and Majestic glory.* This is exactly what happened at Yeshua's birth with the Star of Bethlehem. The people who witnessed it were also sore afraid!

When Saul had his Divine encounter with Messiah Yeshua in the Shechinah glory, on the way to Damascus, he remained blind for three days. Suddenly, when Ananias came to lay hands on him, the scales fell from Saul's eyes and his spiritual blindness was taken away. Saul, the Hebrew Torah Scholar, the student of Rabbi Gameliel, *could now see who the LORD was from the Torah of Moses.* Saul was forever changed. Paul, the Hebrew Torah Scholar was given a mission by the LORD God. He was to take the *Living Torah* to the Gentiles. This was also the Divine will for Simon Peter, James, and John who were sent to proclaim the *Living Torah* to both Jews and Gentiles, starting in Jerusalem! *Paul returned from His visit with Yeshua on Mount Sinai, to reason with the Jewish people in the Synagogues from the Torah Scroll, showing them that the LORD God of Israel is KING Messiah Yeshua, the Living Torah and Heavenly Ark!* Paul was not reasoning with them from the New Testament. It was not written yet! *Paul revealed it to them from the Torah of Moses,* showing them that *the Heavenly Ark is the Living Testimony of Messiah, the LORD God of Israel, and He is the fulfillment of the entire Law and the Prophets!* Paul maintained his strength through severe tribulations by knowing this hidden knowledge of the mystery of the Messiah.

Acts 17:1-3 *Now when they had traveled through Amphipolis and Apollonia, they came to Thessalonica, where there was a Synagogue of the Jews, And according to Paul's custom, he went to them, and for three Sabbaths reasoned with them from the Scriptures, explaining and giving evidence that the Messiah had to suffer and rise again from the dead, and saying, This is Yeshua whom I am proclaiming to you is the Messiah.*

YESHUA APPEARS IN GLORY IN THE CLOUD

Glory Cloud & Glory light

The next detail that I want to write about is the *"glory cloud"* of the LORD. Yeshua went up on Mount Sinai and a cloud appeared. The cloud overshadowed Yeshua, as he stood before Simon Peter, James, and John. At that moment on the Mountain, Yeshua was changed before their eyes and they saw Him glowing with a radiance of light. His garments were shining brilliantly, like pure white snow. They could suddenly see Him in His full glory, *but only as they entered into the cloud with Him.* They saw Messiah Yeshua in His Divine Majesty and power, in a glorified state, as He was changed in outward appearance before their eyes, but they were face down on the ground. As they entered the cloud that overshadowed them, they saw the LORD face to face! In the rapture, the LORD will come in the cloud and this cloud will overshadow us. We will be changed in a moment, in the twinkling of an eye, at the Last Trump at twilight, as we are transformed, just as Yeshua was transfigured in the cloud! What also makes this very interesting, remember, is the fact that during Rosh HaShanah, which is the beginning of the High Holy Days, *the curtain on the Ark is changed into a white one.* I mentioned before that this symbolizes that our sins are made white as snow. This was the appearance of Yeshua's garments, as He was transformed in the cloud. *He was changed into a bright glistering snow white appearance.* I believe this transfiguration of Yeshua, *as the Eternal Ark of God,* was an example of what will occur during the future rapture and resurrection of believers. When we enter the cloud with Him at the Last Trump on Rosh HaShanah, we will be transformed and we will also wear the white garments that are pure like snow. The transfiguration of Yeshua is recorded within the Gospel of *(Mark 9:1-16), (Matthew 17:1-9), and (Luke 9:26:36)*. I will show you the accounts in Mark and Luke.

Mark 9:1-16 *And He said unto them, Verily I say unto you, That there be some of them that stand here, which shall not taste of death, till they have seen the Kingdom of God come with power. And after six days Yeshua taketh with him Peter, and James, and John, and leadeth them up into a high Mountain apart by themselves; and He was transfigured before them. And His raiment became shining, exceeding white as snow; so as no fuller on earth can white them. And there appeared unto them Elijah with Moses; and they were talking with Yeshua. And Peter answered and said to Yeshua, Master; it is good for us to be here; and let us make three tabernacles; one for Thee, and one for Moses, and one for Elijah. For he wist not what to say; for they were sore afraid. And there was a cloud that overshadowed them; and a voice came out of the cloud, saying, This is my beloved Son; hear Him. And suddenly, when they had looked round about, they saw no man any more, save Yeshua only with themselves. And as they came down from the Mountain, He charged them that they should tell no man what things they had seen, till the Son of man were risen from the dead. And they kept that saying with themselves, questioning one with another what the rising from the dead should mean. And they asked Him, saying, Why say the Scribes that Elijah must first come? And He answered and told them, Elijah verily cometh first, and restoreth all things; and how it is written of the Son of man, that He must suffer many things, and be set at nought. But I say unto you, That Elijah is indeed come, and they have done unto him whatsoever they listed, as it is written of him. And when He came to His disciples, He saw a great multitude about them, and the Scribes questioning with them. And straightway all the people, when they beheld Him, were greatly amazed, and running to Him saluted him. And He asked the Scribes, What question ye with them?*

Luke 9:26-36 *For whosoever shall be ashamed of Me and of My Words, of him shall the Son of man be ashamed, when He shall come in His own glory, and in his Father's, and of the Holy angels. But I tell you of a truth, there be some standing here, which shall not taste of death, till they see the Kingdom of God. And it came to pass about eight days after these sayings, He took Peter and John and James, and went up into a Mountain to pray. And as He prayed, the fashion of His countenance was altered, and His raiment was white and glistering. And, behold, there* *talked with Him two men, which were Moses and Elijah; Who appeared in glory, and spake of His decease which He should accomplish at Jerusalem. But Peter and they that were with Him were heavy with sleep; and when they were awake, they saw His glory, and the two men that stood with Him. And it came to pass, as they departed from him, Peter said unto Yeshua, Master, it is good for us to be here; and let us make three tabernacles; one for Thee, and one for Moses, and one for Elijah; not knowing what He said. While He thus spake, there came a cloud, and overshadowed them: and they feared as they entered into the cloud. And there came a voice out of the cloud, saying, This is my beloved Son; hear Him. And when the voice was past, Yeshua was found alone. And they kept it close, and told no man in those days any of those things which they had seen.*

Rays of Glory Photo ©2013 Kimberly K Ballard All Rights Reserved

This event reveals that we are to *"Awaken"* from sleep to our *"Shaked," our "Hasty Awakening."* We must be ready for the coming of Messiah, the Branch of the Almond Tree of life. *The Jewish disciples were heavy with sleep,* but when they were *"Awake,"* the cloud overshadowed them. This is a pattern! Sometimes Yeshua spoke of death as *sleep* and in the case of the resurrection of Lazarus, remember that Yeshua went to *awaken him out of his sleep,* even though Lazarus was already dead. This is another indication of the rapture and resurrection in the Shechinah glory cloud with Yeshua, the LORD. Even though Moses and Elijah had been gone from the earth for centuries, *these two men that appeared in their glory (honor & distinction)* suddenly appeared in the glory cloud of the LORD, alive with Yeshua.

Exodus 24:15-18 *And Moses went up into the Mount, and a cloud covered the Mount. And the glory of the LORD abode upon the Mount of Sinai, and the cloud covered it six days; and the seventh day He called unto Moses out of the midst of the cloud. And the sight of the glory of the LORD was like a devouring fire on the top of the Mountain in the eyes of the children of Israel. And Moses went into the midst of the cloud, and gat him up into the Mount; and Moses was in the Mount forty days and forty nights.*

When Moses went up on the mountain, the glory of the LORD abode upon it and the cloud covered the mountain for six days. The LORD spoke to Moses out of the midst of the cloud on the seventh day. Likewise, it was after six days that Yeshua took Peter, James, and John up into a high Mountain that was Mount Sinai. When the glory of the LORD appeared and the cloud overshadowed them, the LORD spoke out of the midst of the cloud on the seventh day and He was speaking with Moses! Yeshua was not only speaking with Moses in the cloud of glory, He was also speaking with Elijah because Elijah prepares the way for Messiah, the LORD, the Heavenly Ark of God! When I saw this parallel, I knew for certain that the glory cloud of the LORD at Mount Sinai was actually the same glory cloud on the Mountain with Messiah Yeshua! Then I knew that this was *the same cloud* that received Yeshua out of their sight, as He ascended back into Heaven after His resurrection. It is therefore *the same cloud of glory* that will appear with Messiah Yeshua at the resurrection of the dead and the rapture of the living believers! Think of it! Yeshua will descend from Heaven in the Shechinah glory cloud and there will be a shout with the voice of the Archangel at the Last Trump and this will occur sometime during Rosh HaShanah. The dead will rise first at the sound of the *"Awakening blast"* and the living believers will simply be caught up in the glory cloud to meet the LORD in the air and thus we shall always be with the LORD. *So we are going to enter the same cloud that Moses and the disciples entered when the LORD revealed His glory to them! It makes me shiver!*

One of the descriptive words used to describe the Messiah's appearance is the word, *"Glistering."* This word is the same as *"glistening or glisten."* The word *"Glistering,"* means *"to shine brilliantly, to glitter or sparkle."* One of the most exciting definitions within this word is the detail that says, *"To shine by reflection of light or to sparkle with a soft twinkling or shimmering light!"* Remember the phrase that Paul used in reference to Yeshua's return when he said it would be *"in the twinkling of an eye?"* This is clear evidence that the Rod of God, Messiah Yeshua, is reflective and He refracts light from Himself. *So the Rod reflects like a mirror and it is therefore revealing the face of the one who is holding the Rod!* The reason that I mention this is because, by sheer coincidence, my eyes landed on the Hebrew word for *"Glisten"* in the Strong's Concordance. This word is revealing about the Messiah as the light!

Glisten; #6671 Tsahar – glisten -to press out oil – make oil. (see root #3323)
#3323 Yitshar – oil (as producing light) fig. anointing + anointing oil. ***(Source: ©1995 Strong's Concordance).***

Glistering Glory Rays Photo ©2014 Kimberly K Ballard All Rights Reserved

It was a miracle that the page landed open for me by itself on the Hebrew word for *"Glisten"* because I never would have thought it was a Hebrew word! So again we see that Yeshua the LORD, who had the appearance of *"glistening,"* is the anointed one who burns the light from the oil of His Holy Spirit, as depicted on the Holy Almond Tree Menorah.

In the book of Chronicles, the stones that were gathered for building Solomon's Temple out of the rock quarry, were called *"glistering stones."* So it is fascinating that Yeshua is the Chief Cornerstone of the Heavenly Temple. He is, therefore a *"Glistering Living Stone"* and *the Rock* that was quarried out of Solomon's quarry in Holy Mount Moriah for the building of the Living Heavenly Temple. It is when our garments become white as snow during our *Eternal transformation with the LORD in the glory cloud* that we will also become pure white, glistering, living stones that make up the Heavenly Temple of the LORD built upon this sure foundation. This is the Eternal Spiritual House of God that is made by the hand of God, not by the hands of mankind. Just like Yeshua's Shroud image is made without hands!

I Chronicles 29:2 *Now I have prepared with all my might for the House of my God the gold for things to be made of gold, and the silver for things of silver, and the brass for things of brass, the iron for things of iron, and the wood for things of wood; onyx stones, and stones to be set, glistering stones, and of divers colours, and all manner of precious stones, and marble stones in abundance*

Moses went into the midst of the cloud to converse with God. Now I said that when the Jewish disciples went into the midst of the cloud to converse with God, Yeshua was standing in the glory cloud conversing with Moses and Elijah. According to Luke, this event took place on *the eighth day* after Yeshua had told the Jewish disciples *that there are some standing here that would not taste death until they had seen the Kingdom of Heaven come.* The *eighth day* of the Feast of Tabernacles is a High Holy Day. The words of the Jewish disciples in the glory cloud actually reveal that this event of the transfiguration, took place at the time of the Feast of Tabernacles which is also called *"Sukkot."* This is when the Jewish disciples asked Yeshua if they should build three sukkahs. A sukkah, of course, is only built for *the Feast of Tabernacles* and everyone will be required to keep this Feast when Yeshua comes back to reign on the earth. *Since the sukkah represented the Israelites wandering in the wilderness, dwelling in these temporary shelters around Mount Sinai,* this part of the story verifies that the Jewish disciples who were set apart as, *"Kadesh"* were specifically taken up on Mount Sinai by Yeshua, *to be shown the Divine Revelation. It was here they became eyewitnesses that Yeshua is the LORD God of Israel.* Pondering that He had been here centuries before with Moses and Elijah is absolutely mind boggling!

This event foreshadowed the return of the Messiah at the end of the tribulation when He comes in great power and glory. It is a reflection of the time in the future, when we will go to Jerusalem to honor and worship the KING OF KINGS AND LORD OF LORDS on the Feast of Tabernacles and to remember the splendid works that the LORD performed in this place on Mount Sinai. Since the Messiah will dwell in the midst of His people, as the Living Testimony of the Fruitful Bough by a well that gave us *the sweetness* over our *bitterness,* everyone will come to Jerusalem to honour the KING OF KINGS on the Feast of Tabernacles. Every living thing will be vibrant in splendor and beauty because of His Royal Divine Majesty. He gives us the thrilling promise of a glorious resurrected Heavenly body that will never die.

Now miraculously, the LORD began to show me more fantastic things! The Jewish historian Flavious Josephus gave us a *very detailed description* of *"the glory cloud of the LORD,"* and this leads us to many intriguing surprises and outstanding details about the Eternal KING of glory!

"Antiquities of the Jews," by Flavious Josephus - Book VIII, Chapter 4 Section 2

"Now as soon as the Priests had put all things in order about the Ark, and were gone out, there came down a thick cloud, and stood there, and spread itself after a gentle manner, into the Temple; such a cloud it was as was diffused and temperate, not such a rough one as we see full of rain in the winter season. This cloud so darkened the place, that one Priest could not discern another, but it afforded to the minds of all a visible image and glorious appearance of God's having descended into this Temple, and of His having gladly pitched His Tabernacle therein. So these men were intent upon this thought."

So *the same cloud* also appeared over the Ark of the Covenant when the Divine Presence abode upon it. The LORD spoke to Moses and the children of Israel from inside the cloud. If the cloud covers His glory so we cannot behold Him until we enter the cloud, then this event of entering the cloud is called the *"glorious appearing."* The rapture *in the cloud of glory* is the blessed hope of the Saints. When He descends from Heaven with a shout, all that are diligently *"watching"* for His *glorious appearing* will be blessed. They will enter the Eternal Kingdom to stand before the Divine Presence of the LORD in His abode, which is the Ark of His Testimony in Heaven. He redeemed us by giving Himself to us as the Bridegroom!

Titus 2:11-13 *For the grace of God that bringeth salvation hath appeared to all men, Teaching us that, denying ungodliness and worldly lusts, we should live soberly, righteously, and godly, in this present world; Looking for that blessed hope, and the glorious appearing of the great God and our Saviour Yeshua Messiah; Who gave Himself for us, that He might redeem us from all iniquity, and purify unto Himself a peculiar people, zealous for good works.*

II Timothy 4:1 *I charge thee therefore before God, and the LORD Yeshua Messiah, who shall judge the quick and the dead at His appearing and His Kingdom.*

In this passage of Scripture, it is interesting to note the term *"quick and the dead"* because the word *"quick"* means *"alive or living."* It means *"a quick succession of events and hastiness of action."* So this verifies what I wrote earlier that the living and the dead will quickly be given a *"Hasty Awakening"* in the rapture, as the judgment comes to those left upon the earth when the final events of history begin to unfold *in rapid succession* at the LORD'S *sudden glorious appearing.*

II Timothy 4:8 *Henceforth there is laid up for me a crown of righteousness, which the LORD, the righteous judge, shall give me at that day; and not to me only, but unto all them also that love His appearing.*

Titus 3:4-5 *But after that the kindness and love of God our Saviour toward man appeared. Not by works of righteousness which we have done, but according to His mercy He saved us, by the washing of regeneration, and renewing of the Holy Spirit; Which He shed on us abundantly through Yeshua Messiah our Saviour; That being justified by His grace, we should be made heirs according to the hope of eternal life.*

The following Scripture says that there is *an inheritance* in Heaven waiting for those who have this blessed hope. *It includes property rights*! This redemption is what creation has been waiting for since the beginning after the expulsion from the Garden of Eden! This is ready to be revealed in the last time *and that time is right now!* We are part of the Biblical story!

I Peter 1:3-8 *Blessed be the God and Father of our LORD Yeshua Messiah, which according to His abundant mercy hath begotten us again unto a lively hope by the resurrection of Yeshua Messiah from the dead. To an inheritance incorruptible, and undefiled, and that fadeth not away, reserved in Heaven for you, Who are kept by the power of God through faith unto salvation ready to be revealed in the last time. Wherein ye greatly rejoice though now for a season, if need be, ye are in heaviness through manifold temptations; That the trial of your faith, being much more precious than of gold that perisheth, though it be tried with fire, might be found unto praise and honour, and glory at the appearing of Yeshua Messiah. Whom having not seen, ye love; in whom though now ye see Him not, yet believing, ye rejoice with joy unspeakable and full of glory.*

I Timothy 6:13-16 *I give thee charge in the sight of God, who quickeneth all things, and before Messiah Yeshua, who before Pontius Pilate witnessed a good confession; That thou keep this commandment without spot, unrebukable, until the appearing of our LORD Yeshua Messiah; Which in His times He shall shew, who is the blessed and only Potentate, The KING OF KINGS, AND LORD OF LORDS; Who only hath immortality, dwelling in the light which no man can approach unto; whom no man hath seen, nor can see; to whom be honour and power everlasting. Amen.*

Exodus 16:10 *And it came to pass, as Aaron spake unto the whole congregation of the children of Israel, that they looked toward the wilderness, and, behold, the glory of the LORD appeared in the cloud.*

THE ASCENSION AND THE RAPTURE

Rapture Cloud
Photo ©2013 Kimberly K Ballard

As I further studied the rapture of the believers, I began to see that the rapture really takes place in *the glory cloud* of the LORD and not in the regular clouds of the sky! The LORD descends in the cloud that abides on His Ark of the Testimony in Heaven, which is His throne. Josephus left us such an incredible description of the glory cloud of the LORD that we do not have to think about flying upward into the sky, as is often depicted when one speaks of the rapture. The following Scripture details the rapture as *"the catching away"* of believers in the cloud.

I Thessalonians 4:13-18 *But I would not have you to be ignorant, brethren, concerning them which are asleep, that ye sorrow not, even as other which have no hope. For if we believe that Yeshua died and rose again, even so them also which sleep in Yeshua will God bring with Him. For this we say unto you by the Word of the LORD, that we which are alive and remain unto the coming of the LORD shall not prevent them which are asleep. For the LORD Himself shall descend from Heaven with a shout, with the voice of the archangel, and with the trump of God; and the dead in Messiah shall rise first; Then we which are alive and remain shall be caught up together with them in the clouds, to meet the LORD in the air; and so shall we ever be with the LORD. Wherefore comfort one another with these words.*

I can visualize, based upon Josephus' description of the glory cloud, that the cloud will descend and Yeshua will be in the midst of the cloud. The cloud will spread itself in a gentle manner, overshadowing us, and we will simply go into the cloud, just like the disciples did, to meet the LORD in the air with the resurrected dead that have come out of their graves at *"the awakening blast during Rosh HaShanah."* Notice that the LORD is always in the cloud and the voice is heard. This is the same voice that told the Jewish disciples that Yeshua is the beloved Son and to listen to Him on Mount Sinai. The original Greek translation for the words *"caught up"* come from the Greek word *"harpazo"* which was translated into Latin as *"rapturo,"* and then this was translated into the English word *"rapture."* This term literally means *"to seize or to suddenly catch away or carry away."* It will happen so quickly, *in the twinkling* of an eye, that we must be ready before hand, watching for His glorious appearing. Now we know that the word *"glistening"* in reference to the LORD'S appearance actually refers to *"twinkling."* The glorious appearing occurs the moment that we enter the cloud after the LORD descends in it. *Yeshua's sudden Presence in the cloud is the twinkling or glistering of His shining garments and countenance.* After we enter the cloud like Moses and the disciples did, we will behold His Royal Divine Majesty. We can only see Him in His full glory if we enter the cloud and are transformed into our joyous Heavenly bodies. The cloud of glory is a veil. When the Scripture says that the veil is taken away in Messiah, this is quite literal. The next Scripture is the one that reveals that the rapture will occur sometime at the Last Trump on Rosh HaShanah. *Notice that as we are changed, the twinkling occurs.* We have been transformed into glory, like the Messiah whose garments are *glistering and pure white like snow and twinkling the moment that we see Him face to face in the glory cloud.*

I Corinthians 15:51-52 *Behold, I shew you a mystery; We shall not all sleep, but we shall all be changed, In a moment, in the twinkling of an eye, at the Last Trump; for the trumpet shall sound, and the dead shall be raised incorruptible, and we shall be changed.*

Rosh HaShanah is *"the Day of Shouting"* and *"the Awakening Blast."* The passage in I Thessalonians said that the LORD will descend from Heaven with a *"Shout."* The *Shout and the Last Trump* that are mentioned together in this Scripture give us absolute proof that the *Messiah does come in the cloud* during Rosh HaShanah on the Jewish Biblical New Year celebration on the Biblical calendar. Yeshua gave us these signs to signal approximately when to be watching for His *glistening* appearing *in the cloud* with His Heavenly *musical instrument.*

Glistering & Twinkling light & Heavenly Musical Instruments Photos ©2013 Kimberly K Ballard All Rights Reserved
My Heavenly Drums, Cymbals, Congas & Heavenly Stringed Instruments Photos ©2013 Kimberly K Ballard All Rights Reserved

Behold! He is coming in the cloud with exceeding great glory!
Majestic Glory Cloud, Glistering & Twinkling, Votive, Silver Decoration & Joy of Rapture

Majestic Cloud Photo ©2013 Kimberly K Ballard All Rights Reserved

Yeshua departed into Heaven *in the glory cloud* from the Mount of Olives. In Acts 1:10 the *two men that were dressed in white apparel* said to His Jewish disciples, *"Ye men of Galilee, why do you stand here gazing up into Heaven? This same Yeshua will come in like manner as you have seen Him go."*

Acts 1:9-12 *And when He had spoken these things, while they beheld, He was taken up; and a cloud received Him out of their sight. And while they looked stedfastly toward Heaven as He went up, behold, two men stood by them in white apparel; Which also said, Ye men of Galilee, why stand ye gazing up into Heaven? This same Yeshua, which is taken up from you into Heaven, shall so come in like manner as ye have seen him go into Heaven. Then returned they unto Jerusalem from the Mount called Olivet, which is from Jerusalem a Sabbath day's journey.*

Moses knew Yeshua and he spoke to Him as one speaks to a friend! Moses and Elijah were *the two eyewitnesses* as required by Jewish Law who saw Yeshua's Divine glory as He was transformed *in the glory cloud.* This leaves us with an interesting thought. The *two witnesses* that appear before the second coming of the Messiah will be Moses and Elijah. Perhaps they are sent *in the glory cloud* at the time of the rapture when Yeshua takes the believers up in the cloud with Him.

Moses and Elijah will stand in Jerusalem prophesying and preaching this Living Torah Testimony of Messiah, the LORD God of Israel. It is this Living Testimony of the Heavenly Ark of God that will *turn the hearts of the children of Israel to their God and Saviour Yeshua* who is the KING of glory. Now it is also fascinating to realize that after the *two witnesses* appear during the tribulation and have finished prophesying in Jerusalem, they are killed and then resurrected after three and a half days. The *two witnesses* are then taken up *in the glory cloud* to be with the LORD! They are given the mighty power of *the Almond Rod of God* to testify of the LORD'S Living Testimony and to perform His Divine miracles!

Revelation 11:1-12 *And there was given me a reed like unto a rod; and the angel stood, saying, Rise, and measure the Temple of God, and the altar, and them that worship therein. But the court which is without the Temple leave out, and measure it not; for it is given unto the Gentiles; and the Holy City shall they tread under foot forty and two months. <u>And I will give power unto My two witnesses</u>, and they shall prophesy a thousand two hundred and threescore days, clothed in sackcloth. These are the two olive trees, and the two candlesticks standing before the God of the earth. And if any man will hurt them, fire proceedeth out of their mouth, and devoureth their enemies; and if any man will hurt them, he must in this manner be killed. These have the power to shut Heaven, that it rain not in the days of their prophecy; and have power over waters to turn them to blood, and to smite the earth with all plagues, as often as they will. And when they shall have finished their Testimony, the beast that ascendeth out of the bottomless pit shall make war against them, and shall overcome them, and kill them. And their dead bodies shall lie in the street of the Great City, which spiritually is called Sodom and Egypt, where also our LORD was crucified. And they of the people and kindred's and tongues and nations shall see their dead bodies three days and an half, and shall not suffer their dead bodies to be put in graves. And they that dwell upon the earth shall rejoice over them, and make merry, and shall send gifts one to another; because these two Prophets tormented them that dwelt on the earth. And after three days and an half the Spirit of life from God entered into them, and they stood upon their feet; and great fear fell upon them that saw them. And they heard a great voice from Heaven saying unto them, Come up hither. And they ascended up to Heaven <u>in a cloud</u>; and their enemies beheld them.*

Let me explain why I know for certain that the *two witnesses* who declare *this Testimony of the Messiah* in the last days are indeed Moses and Elijah. First, they are called the two Olive trees and the two candlesticks standing before the God of the earth. This means they are filled with the LORD'S Holy Spirit and anointing oil and have the power through Him to perform His miraculous signs. *Some of these signs were also performed with the Rod.* So the power of Yeshua, *the Almond Rod of God,* is upon them. Moses and Elijah performed some of the same miracles before as a witness and to testify of the LORD'S glory, showing that His power is in His Rod. The *two witnesses* were standing before Yeshua, full of the Holy Spirit at the transfiguration on Mount Sinai *in the glory cloud,* when the Jewish disciples saw His Royal Majesty. Moses had the rod that was given to him by the LORD God that turned the water into blood and he brought forth the plagues with it. This is exactly what we see happening in Revelation in the tribulation. Elijah, full of the Holy Spirit, had the power that could shut up the Heavens, so it did not rain. So the elements that Moses and Elijah already performed when they were here the first time that revealed the LORD'S power, will be the same miracles that they perform the second time in the tribulation in the book of Revelation. Moses was *in the cloud* on Mount Sinai with the LORD in the beginning and He was with the LORD Messiah *in the cloud* on Mount Sinai at the transfiguration of His glory. *The two witnesses have the fire of the Ruach/Holy Spirit in their mouths to prophesy about the Living Torah.* Interestingly, by definition, *to prophecy,* can mean their Testimony could come as an *inspired message in writing!* The Jewish disciples had the flaming tongues of fire descend upon them and the Word of God came out of their mouths and in writing! At the end of this chapter I will show you why I believe that Moses perhaps did not die, even though it was recorded in the Bible that he did. *It is written in the Bible that he died because he was too humble to say that God took him! Moses ascended up in the cloud,* based upon an account that I discovered that was recorded by Josephus *(I will show you my source there). Elijah also ascended up into Heaven in the chariot of Israel. He did not die.* I believe that *Moses and Elijah did not taste death, but in the great tribulation, they will taste death.* On the third day, they will be resurrected to life before their enemies, who will flee for fear and they will ascend into Heaven in the glory cloud! These two will be resurrected from the dead just like Yeshua was resurrected from the dead, because His power is abiding in them. Just like John was preparing the heart of Israel in repentance through the living water baptism in the Jordan River, *so will the two witnesses who stand before God, be preparing the way for the Ark of the Testimony of Heaven to descend to the earth with the LORD enthroned upon it!* Now that is a truly remarkable visual picture! They will come to Jerusalem *with a Divine message,* preparing Israel in repentance, just as it happened before, and they will be getting Israel ready to receive their KING OF KINGS AND LORD OF LORDS. Again, Rosh HaShanah is Coronation Day of the Great KING.

After they are resurrected, the *two witnesses* hear a great voice from Heaven saying, *"Come up hither"* and they ascend up into Heaven *in a cloud!* Yeshua ascended into Heaven *in a cloud* and He returns the same way *in the glory cloud with the two representatives of the Living Torah and the Prophets!* As believers, we are raptured into this very same cloud! This is very exciting! After the *two witnesses* prepare the way for the Heavenly Ark, for Messiah the LORD, Yeshua will descend from Heaven in blazing glory. The earth will behold His radiant Majesty as He comes to usher in the Heavenly Kingdom on earth. He will reign forever! I believe this clears up misunderstandings people have that they will fly upward like a rocket to meet the LORD in the clouds of the sky in the rapture! Frankly, the thought of flying outside a plane at 33,000 feet is a bit frightening, but the truth is the LORD will simply spread His cloud over us and we will enter into it to see His glorious face with His Divine Presence forever! This is such a wonderful picture of the magnificent rapture revealing the brilliance of His Majesty! Remember, the same type of event happened to the Apostle John, early in the book of Revelation. *The event with John when he heard the voice like a trumpet from Heaven beckoning for him to "Come up hither" into Heaven, takes place before the two witnesses come to the earth to prophesy regarding the Living Testimony of Messiah Yeshua.* The LORD blows the trumpet on the Feast of Trumpets or Rosh HaShanah. The ascension of John into Heaven occurs at the end of the Church age just before the tribulation begins! This, in my opinion, has to be John's resurrection from the dead and the time of the rapture of believers into Heaven in the glory cloud when the LORD descends from Heaven with a shout, with the voice of an Archangel. *After John is taken up to see the LORD in His glory on His throne, then he is shown the horrible events that will occur after these things, during the tribulation.*

Revelation 4:1-2 *After this I looked, and, behold, a door was opened in Heaven; and the first voice which I heard was as it were of a trumpet talking with me; which said, Come up hither, and I will shew thee things which must be hereafter. And immediately I was in the spirit; and, behold, a throne was set in Heaven, and one sat on the throne.*

John was *looking and "watching"* and he saw a door opened in Heaven and the door of Heaven is opened only during the High Holy Days, beginning with Rosh HaShanah and ending with Yom Kippur which includes the 10 days of awe. We know that Yeshua is the door and we must enter into Heaven by Him.

The sound of the Heavenly shofar blast by the LORD at Rosh HaShanah is also a time of *the gathering of believers in an assembly* into the cloud of glory. The Jewish disciple is in spirit and he is taken up through the door of Heaven after he hears that voice sounding like a trumpet. John is *changed at that moment* and he can suddenly see the LORD face to face and John sees the LORD sitting upon His throne, upon the Ark of His Testimony in Heaven. Then the one on the throne proceeds to tell John of the things to come in the future. John is speaking to Messiah Yeshua the LORD and He is the only one on the throne in Heaven. At the moment of the rapture, we enter into His cloud of glory after we hear *the shout and the sound of the voice of His trumpet and we are gathered together in a great assembly!* We are *changed* and after our transformation in Spirit, we see the LORD face to face, sitting upon His throne in Heaven, exactly as John did. We will be with the LORD and descend with Him when He returns at the end of the seven year tribulation that occurs on the earth, but believers will be in Heaven those seven years abiding with the LORD. Another truly interesting thing about the rapture occurring during Rosh HaShanah in the month of Tishrei is the fact that as I was researching Adam, I ran across an incredible statement about *"the shortening of the days after Tishrei."* This statement is prophetic, I believe, because in the twinkling of an eye, the rapture will occur and the split second after that happens, the judgment and wrath of God will suddenly fall upon the earth. What I discovered is the fact that the LORD apparently *"shortened the days after Tishrei and Adam saw this as a sign of God's wrath!"* ***(Source: jewishencyclopedia.com/articles/758-adam).*** Based upon this statement, I could now completely understand Yeshua's Words regarding the great tribulation. Yeshua actually said *"Unless those days be shortened, no flesh would be* *saved."* In my opinion, I believe this is one more sign that the wrath of God will be poured out instantaneously after the rapture on Rosh HaShanah, *during the days after Tishrei.* Rosh HaShanah lands on *Tishrei 1* of God's Hebrew Biblical calendar. This would mean the tribulation begins immediately after this rapture event on Tishrei 1. It is a time of great darkness with no light in it at all. The light of the world is removed. Therefore, the LORD *shortened the days* otherwise no flesh would be saved!

I believe the following Scriptures prove the believers in Messiah will not be on earth during the great tribulation because they have been given the *"Passover or overpass"* into their Eternal glory and this has *prolonged their days in an Eternal state in Heaven,* while the days and years of the wicked that are on the earth *are shortened. Again, Rosh HaShanah is "Yom Hakeseh" the "Day of Hiding" or the "hidden day."* ***(Source: mayimhayim.org/Festivals/Feast7.htm).***

Matthew 24:21-22 *For then shall be great tribulation, such as was not since the beginning of the world to this time, no, nor ever shall be. And except those days should be shortened, there should no flesh be saved; but for the elect's sake those days shall be shortened.*

Proverbs 10:27 *The fear of the LORD prolongeth days; but the years of the wicked shall be shortened.*

I Thessalonians 5:1-11 *But of the times and the seasons, brethren, ye have no need that I write unto you. For yourselves know perfectly that the Day of the LORD so cometh as a thief in the night. For when they shall say, Peace and safety; then sudden destruction cometh upon them, as travail upon a woman with child; and they shall not escape. But ye, brethren, are not in darkness, that that day should overtake you as a thief. Ye are all the children of light, and the children of the day; we are not of the night, nor of darkness. Therefore let us not sleep, as do others; but let us watch and be sober. For they that sleep sleep in the night; and they that be drunken are drunken in the night. But let us, who are of the day, be sober, putting on the breastplate of faith and love; and for an helmet, the hope of salvation. For God hath not appointed us to wrath, but to obtain salvation by our LORD Yeshua Messiah, Who died for us, that, whether we wake or sleep, we should live together with Him. Wherefore comfort yourselves together, and edify one another, even as also ye do.*

Those who have the light will go to be with the source of the light, leaving the wicked in utter darkness upon the earth. Their days will indeed be *shortened after Tishrei 1.* It will be an ominous time! *The outstanding truth is that Rosh HaShanah is specifically known for "the gathering of an assembly & for hiding us!" So away we go in the glory cloud!*

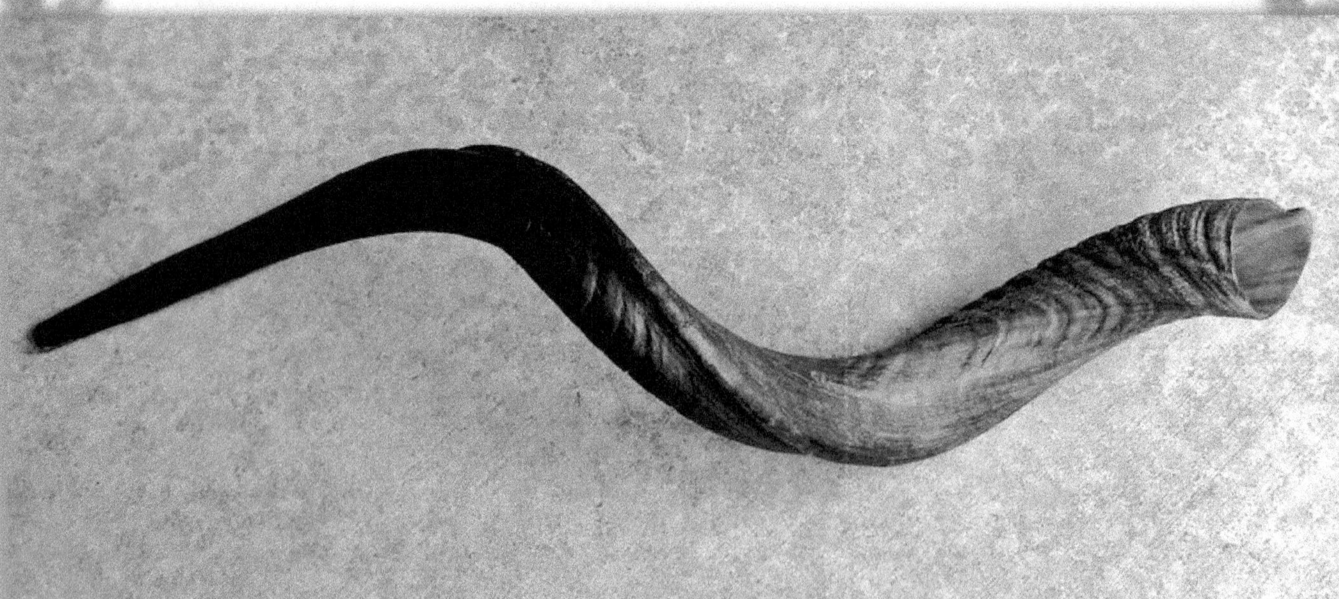

The Last Trump of God is at Rosh HaShanah on Tishrei 1 - Shofar Photo ©2013 Kimberly K Ballard All Rights Reserved

THE PROPERTIES OF PHYSICS WITHIN THE CLOUD OF THE LORD

Majestic Cloud Photo ©2013 Kimberly K Ballard All Rights Reserved

Josephus wrote *"the LORD came in the cloud and the cloud stood in the Holy place."* It must have been quite an unimaginable experience. He described the glory cloud of the LORD as *"a thick cloud that stood there. It spread itself after a gentle manner into the Temple; such a cloud it was as was diffused and temperate, not such a rough one as we see full of rain in the winter season."* The cloud of the LORD is so gentle, that the disciples walked right into the bright cloud on Mount Sinai at the transfiguration. They were a bit afraid as they entered into the cloud. The disciples did not fly up into the clouds of the sky and see the glory of the LORD. They entered into the glory cloud of the LORD as the cloud *"overshadowed"* them in a gentle manner. The word *"overshadowed"* is significant because it is defined in several ways. This word means to *"shelter or protect."* The Cherubim Angels that *"overshadow"* the Ark of the Covenant are there to *"shelter and protect it."* When one enters the cloud of the LORD as it *"overshadows"* them, they can see the Ark of His throne. I find this truth to be absolutely fascinating because the purpose of *the rapture* in the cloud is to be *"sheltered, hidden, and protected"* by the LORD, as He saves us from the wrath to come. So in essence we are *"sheltered and protected"* in the Ark of Heaven where the LORD resides.

Cloud Portal Photo ©2013 Kimberly K Ballard All Rights Reserved

The angel Gabriel appeared to Yeshua's Mother Mary and he declared special tidings to her.

Luke 1:35 *And the angel answered and said unto her, The Holy Spirit shall come upon thee, and the power of the Highest shall overshadow thee; therefore also that Holy thing which shall be born of thee shall be called the Son of God.*

Remember that during Yeshua's birth in Bethlehem, the door of Heaven was opened. A multitude of Heavenly Hosts appeared in the glory of the LORD and a star came and stood over the place where the baby was lying in a manger. In the case of Mary, the power of the LORD *overshadowed* her and He gave Mary *"shelter and protection."* The LORD'S Divine Ruach/Holy Spirit was upon Mary, who was a descendant of King David. The Holy Spirit abides upon whatever is pure and Mary the Jewish virgin maiden was pure and righteous, having found favor with God. More definitions of the word *"overshadow,"* include the words *"eclipse, mist, and cloud."* In Genesis, a *mist* watered the earth.

Genesis 2:6 *But there went up a mist from the earth, and watered the whole face of the ground.*

These are significant words, pertaining to the LORD'S Testimony. The LORD, the Living Water was in the Garden in the beginning, and this *mist* came from Him, watering the whole ground. After the curse, when mankind was removed from the Divine Presence of the LORD, the earth was no longer watered with this *mist.* The LORD was no longer dwelling with us. Remember some of the same words that are used in the definition of *"overshadow"* are found in the word *"impression"* in reference to *the image of Yeshua on the Shroud of Turin.* Each one of these words is a descriptive detail that uncovers the LORD'S identity.

Another meaning of the word *"overshadow"* is *"to be greater in significance than others."* The LORD is greater than us, *so He overshadows us!* Now I completely understand John the Baptist, who proclaimed in effect the LORD *overshadows* him.

John 3:30 *He must increase, but I must decrease.*

Rainforest mist Butterfly Pavilion Photo ©2013 Kimberly K Ballard All Rights Reserved

Josephus described *the glory cloud of the LORD* as *"temperate."* This means that it is not extreme, but rather moderate. There are rainforests that are called *"temperate."* This gives us a vision in our minds of the appearance of the glorious Garden of God. A temperate rainforest is usually along a coastline. Israel is along a coastline and the LORD said that His Name would dwell there forever. In the beginning, the LORD was in the Garden as the Living Water and His cloud of glory was *"temperate,"* like a rainforest! If you can imagine a beautiful temperate rainforest with a mist, then you can imagine the Garden of Eden. This is the Garden that the LORD planted where He was abiding with us on Mount Moriah in Jerusalem. A temperate rainforest is humid full of tropical mist, and it receives a high percentage of rainfall. This abundance of living water produces a deep green, lush, broadleaf forest. The rainforest thrives with an exuberant amount of plant life, including ferns, trees, foliage, flowers, moss, and all kinds of animals, birds and moving creatures, that dwell in the midst of it and drink from the living waters that rush there. I think of the Cedars of the LORD that grew in the Garden of Eden in this beautiful rainforest.

Rainforest mist Butterfly Pavilion Photo ©2013 Kimberly K Ballard All Rights Reserved

So this all reveals that the LORD is in the *temperate cloud* because He is the early and latter rain! He produces the refreshing rain as the Living Water of Life with a mist! When the Kingdom of the LORD comes to the earth from Heaven and the curse is finally removed from the earth, then the LORD will restore the earth like a Paradise Garden. It will be rejuvenated to a *temperate rainforest.* The Living Water will be dwelling in our midst, refreshing the earth with His Divine Presence. He will make the environment perfect, just as He did in the beginning before the curse transpired. The earth can only be restored to this state when the Living Water comes back to us to dwell in our midst. Every living thing in the LORD'S Kingdom will thrive in that day and now I know why the Scriptures tell us that *"the trees clap their hands!"* We have no concept of the beauty of this restored Royal Palace Garden. The earth will be like *a well-watered Garden of God and as temperate as a rainforest* when He quenches our thirst forever and gives perfect life to everything. *I remember how the waters sway in the ocean with a rhythm of life. It is a very soothing peaceful existence.*

Me holding a starfish that has a face in Monterey California at the Pacific Ocean in 1994
Photo ©2013 Kimberly K Ballard
All Rights Reserved

In Isaiah 55, the LORD proclaims that the seed and the bread is the Word of God that goes forth out of His mouth. Notice that the restored, well-watered Garden occurs and the trees clap their hands when the curse is gone. The rains come with the LORD after there are no more thorns and briers of the curse upon the earth. His voice of *the Living Torah* is like the sound of many waters.

Isaiah 55:10-13 *For as the rain cometh down, and the snow from Heaven, and returneth not thither, but watereth the earth, and maketh it bring forth and bud, that it may give seed to the sower, and bread to the eater; So shall My Word be that goeth forth out of My mouth; it shall not return unto Me void, but it shall accomplish that which I please, and it shall prosper in the thing whereto I sent it. For ye shall go out with joy, and be led forth with peace; the mountains and the hills shall break forth before you into singing, <u>and all the trees of the field shall clap their hands</u>. Instead of the thorn shall come up the fir tree, and instead of the brier shall come up the myrtle tree; and it shall be to the LORD for a name, for an everlasting sign that shall not be cut off.*

Turtle in the Tropical Pool
Photo ©2013 Kimberly K Ballard All Rights Reserved

The glory cloud of the LORD is described as being *"diffused."* This means *"spreading or widely spread."* The glory cloud *overshadowed* them as it *spread widely* over them and they walked into the cloud and saw the LORD. It is interesting that *"light"* is often called *"diffused light."* The LORD is the light. So the term *"diffused light"* presents some rather startling information about the LORD that I now want to discuss. This takes us to a whole new level!

Diffused Light*;* A light ray that is reflected from a surface and broken up and scattered into different directions. The reflection of light from a surface, reflecting a ray at numerous angles. Light rays subjected to scattering by reflection. Lighting that is diffused provides even illumination without shadows or glare. ***(Source: Definition from the Random House College Dictionary First Edition, the Unabridged Edition, Copyright © 1975 by Random House, Inc.).***

When I saw this definition of the glory cloud, I instantly remembered that the Jewish disciple James wrote *"The Father of lights has no variableness, neither shadow of turning." Diffused light is illumination without shadows or glare!*

James 1:17 *Every good gift and every perfect gift is from above, and cometh down from the Father of lights, with whom is no variableness, neither shadow of turning.*

Now this miraculously pertains to the Shroud of Yeshua. The image of Yeshua on the Shroud of Turin is rare because the image has no shadows! When a person's face is photographed, light reflects or bounces off the subject, leaving at least a few shadows on the face area in the resulting image. Strangely, this is not the case with the burial Shroud image of Messiah Yeshua. Part of the great mystery that has confounded the experts, who have tried to solve the mystery as to how the image of Yeshua was formed on the linen burial cloth has to do with this image having no shadows. *As we can see in the above Scripture, the Father of lights does not change or have variables and He has no shadows!* For shadows to be completely absent on the Shroud image, the source of the light had to have come from inside Yeshua. *The light inside Yeshua, which is the Ruach/Holy Spirit of life, reflected the light in a diffused manner at angles and it radiated outward and onto the fine linen cloth.* There are no images of Yeshua's sides on the cloth. The Bible says that our days are like a shadow and I understand now that we have shadows because we will die, but notice in Psalm 23 that King David wrote, *"Yea, though I walk through the valley of the shadow of death, I will fear no evil; for Thou art with me; Thy Rod and Thy Staff they comfort me."* I just realized that *when the Rod and Staff, the Messiah, is with us, there is no shadow of death* because when we are in His Divine Presence, there are no shadows, there is only the glory of His light of Eternal life. This is our comfort of the Living Rod of God who is our Staff of Life! The Hebrew word *"Ma' ohr"* appears in Genesis 1:14 and it means *"the source of the light"* and *"diffused light."* This is the exact type of light that is coming out of *the glory cloud of the LORD.* It is a *diffused light.* In the beginning, in Genesis, the LORD is described as being *the source* of this *diffused light.*

Light in the Firmament
Photo ©2013 Kimberly K Ballard All Rights Reserved

Genesis 1:14 *And God said, Let there be lights in the firmament of the Heaven to divide the day from the night; and let them be for signs, and for seasons, and for days and years.*

The Hebrew word *"Ma'or"* and another form of the word *"Ma'ohr"* incredibly means *"Star"* and it is significant to the Prophecy of the coming Jewish Messiah as it is written in the book of Numbers in the Torah of Moses!

Numbers 24:16-17 *He hath said, which heard the Words of God, and knew the knowledge of the Most High, which saw the vision of the Almighty, falling into a trance, but having his eyes open; I shall see Him, but not now; I shall behold Him, but not nigh; there shall come a Star out of Jacob, and a Sceptre shall rise out of Israel, and shall smite the corners of Moab, and destroy all the children of Sheth.*

The exciting fact is that this *"Star"* appeared in *"the light"* of the glory of the LORD when Messiah Yeshua was born in Bethlehem or Ephrathah.

Luke 2:9 *And lo, the angel of the LORD came upon them, and the glory of the LORD shone round about them; and they were sore afraid.*

The Shechinah glory of the LORD *"is the radiance in which God's Majestic Presence is visibly manifested in the midst of His people."* This manifestation of the Shechinah occurs *"when the LORD has descended to dwell among men."* So the Shechinah comes from the Hebrew word *"Shakhan"* meaning *"to dwell."* The Divine Presence of God was in the Shechinah that settled on the Ark of the Covenant with the glory cloud of the LORD hovering over it. The *Shechinah* actually means *"Light or radiance"* by definition. The *"Star"* of Bethlehem is the *"Ma'ohr"* the light of the LORD that is found in Genesis and it came and stood, *hovering over the place of Yeshua's birth, just like it hovered over the Ark of the*

Covenant. This is exactly what the shepherds witnessed at the birth of Messiah Yeshua. The LORD was manifested in the flesh as the Messiah and He was coming to dwell in our midst as the source of the light of our salvation, known in Hebrew as *"Yeshua."* The Host of Heavenly angels appeared in the glorious radiant Shechinah light. This was *"the Star"* that led them to the place and it came and stood and was hovering over Him. Remember that Yeshua is the Living Ark of the Living Testimony of the LORD God!

Matthew 2:9 *When they had heard the king, they departed; and, lo, the star, which they saw in the east, went before them, till it came and stood over where the young child was. When they saw the star, they rejoiced with exceeding great joy.*

Now the deeper meaning of the word *"diffused"* pertains *to the laws of physics* and it means *"To spread by diffusion."* The word *"diffusion,"* as it applies to physics, is defined in the following manner.

Diffusion; 1. An intermingling of molecules, ions, etc., resulting from random thermal agitation, as in the dispersion of a vapor in the air. 2. A reflection or refraction of light or other electromagnetic radiation from and irregular surface or an erratic dispersion through a surface; scattering. ***(Source: Definition from the Random House College Dictionary First Edition, The Unabridged Edition, Copyright ©1975 By Random House, Inc.).***

There are two very interesting facts within this description of the word *"diffusion."* By definition *"diffusion" is "a reflection or refraction of light or other electromagnetic radiation."* Please remember that diffusion also pertains to *"thermal agitation."* Both of these parameters I believe pertain to the burial Shroud of Yeshua. I believe that both of these remarkable aspects of physics indicate how the image was formed on the fine linen burial cloth. Now this topic can become quite complex in the science of physics, but I am going to show the basics of my own findings, based upon the truths hidden in the Holy Bible. The LORD revealed the following details to me that I believe are extremely significant. I realized that within these word definitions, there are the true realities and proofs that the LORD made the universe. This means that the LORD encoded Himself in all aspects of His creation. He encoded Himself in physics, science, mathematics, art, music and the list goes on. I therefore did not approach this information from anything that I previously read or heard scientifically. I only came to these conclusions based upon the account of Josephus and through his own descriptive words, detailing *the glory cloud* of the LORD.

It soon became quite obvious that *the laws of physics,* within the word definitions, describe every element that pertains to the LORD and to His Living Testimony. Josephus left us such a great description of the glory cloud of the LORD that these elements of physics were *encoded in his words* about the LORD and I was pursuing and researching them. So I do believe this is Divine proof that *"diffusion"* reveals the code to the formation of the image of Yeshua, on His burial Shroud.

If we take a look at *"electromagnetic radiation,"* its various elements *"pertain to waves, frequencies and to the electromagnetic light spectrum. From this light spectrum, comes an entire array of all the frequencies of electromagnetic radiation. A rainbow is visible within a certain range of the light spectrum, but not all the colors of the light spectrum are humanly visible."* ***(Source: Light Spectrum ©2011 Encyclopaedia Britannica Inc.) AND (Electromagnetic Radiation and Spectrum ©1975 by Random House Inc. The Random House College Dictionary).***

So the LORD'S Shechinah glory shines with *a full range of the entire light spectrum* and this causes *the refraction of light* that creates the rainbow over His throne and over the Ark of His Testimony in Heaven. A funny way to say this would be to say that on the earth, we only have a small crayon box with the minimal amount of the colors of the light spectrum in it. However, the Heavenly crayon box is like the big box of crayons that you always dreamed of having as a child. The Heavenly crayon box contains colors that our eyes have never seen because the light spectrum is not limited in Heaven. So, when we go from the earthly light spectrum and enter into the Heavenly light spectrum, there are colors that exist beyond our comprehension. Likewise, the sound waves and music frequencies that we hear and use on the earth have a very limited range. However, in the LORD'S Kingdom, the sound waves and frequencies and the scales for music will extend tremendously beyond what we hear on the earth. Therefore, the musical scales on earth are very limited to only a small number of notes that we can hear. In Heaven, the musical scales and ranges will be profoundly expanded, giving us a much wider and unlimited range of new sound waves and frequencies that are unlike any that we have ever heard before. The music of Heaven will not be limited to simply a few keys, scales, and notes. There are many musical notes within the sound frequency that do exist in the physics of sound waves and in acoustics, but we do not hear them on the earth and so these notes are not included when we play an instrument or compose a piece of music. The earth is limited, but Heaven is not limited. When we enter the Kingdom of Heaven, I think that we will be astonished to hear the incredible frequencies of sound that will come into our ears.

The beautiful sounds will be overwhelming to us! I just try to imagine what our eyes will see in Heaven with this extended range of colors of the light spectrum, and I imagine the sound of the music in Heaven and ponder it. It is not possible to know how beautiful it will be there. This makes Heaven an incredible place that is truly beyond our most vivid imaginations! I do not think that we can even begin to visualize how spectacular Heaven will be with the Divine Presence of the LORD in our midst! This actually reminds me of two Scriptures that pertain to this thought. Do we have the proof of this in the Bible? Yes! The following Scripture in Isaiah proves that what I have just said is absolutely true.

Isaiah 64:4 *For since the beginning of the world men have not heard, nor perceived by the ear, neither hath the eye seen, O God, beside Thee, what He hath prepared for him that waiteth for Him.*

Again, it is written in I Corinthians! These are the deep things of God!

I Corinthians 2:9-10 *But as it is written, Eye hath not seen, nor ear heard, neither have entered into the heart of man, the things which God hath prepared for them that love Him. But God hath revealed them unto us by His Spirit; for the Spirit searcheth all things, yea, the deep things of God.*

Now the reason that I said to remember the words *"electromagnetic radiation"* as well as the term *"thermal agitation"* is because I had already written this down by the guidance of the Holy Spirit and almost a year later I was sent the most recent speculation by some scientists who have studied the Shroud image formation. The experts studying the Shroud of Turin suddenly began saying that the image on the Shroud *may have been formed by some type of radiation!* Then just this week, as I came back to this section to edit it, I received a Shroud letter and I was just floored because it said that some scientists were speculating now that the image on the Shroud was likely formed by *electromagnetic radiation.* I was totally floored by this timely coincidence! When this news came forward, it was after I had written the same thing down by a revelation of the LORD'S Holy Spirit. I never at any time approached this writing from a scientific study or from their point of view, which at the time was not released yet, because I am not a scientist! This again, proves that the LORD is involved in my work on this book for His glory! The term *"thermal agitation"* in the description of the word *"diffusion"* and the glory cloud of the LORD has to do *"with the electric charge in conductors."* ***(Source: Electrical Conductor ©2011 en.wikipedia.org/wiki-Wikipedia, the free encyclopedia).***

From what I understand, within these conductors, *"there is a spontaneous voltage that occurs, thus creating an electric discharge."* ***(Source: Electromagnetic Radiation and Spectrum ©1975 by Random House Inc. The Random House College Dictionary) AND (Source: Corona discharge ©2011 en.wikipedia.org/wiki/Corona_discharge- From Wikipedia, the free encyclopedia).*** This is what I believe happened at the moment of Yeshua's resurrection. The spontaneous voltage discharge, which was the spark of life by the power of the Holy Spirit of the LORD, occurred within Yeshua, the Rod of God, and the Heavenly Ark. The light source that is *the Ma' ohr* came from within because the seed of life was inside Yeshua as *the Living Torah.* Remember that I told you that His resurrection on the third day, as the Fruitful Branch, had the seed of life within it and this explains why there are absolutely no shadows on the Shroud image because *the light source* came from inside the Messiah. *The Ruach/Holy Spirit residing within Yeshua in this case is "the conductor" the spark of life that caused the Rod of God to bud and bear the First Fruit of Eternal life!*

Now remember, I have discussed within this book that a *Corona discharge that creates a spontaneous high voltage charge, also having to do with conductors,* may be the very thing that created the image on the Shroud of Turin. If you recall, a *Corona discharge* has photographic properties and it is used to make an image in a copy machine. Remember that when I asked Barrie Schwortz, the distinguished Shroud photographer, if the *Corona discharge* was the possible cause for the formation of Yeshua's image on the Shroud, he told me it was possible, but *"it would take an extremely high voltage!"* As I previously discussed, *the Corona discharge* is one of the elements that is hidden in the Holy Almond Tree Menorah of the LORD. *The elements of radiation appear to be contained within the very words that were used to describe the glory cloud of the LORD.* So I thought there must be more to this than meets the eye because Yeshua ascended back to Heaven in this same cloud. This makes it highly likely that one of these elements, either a *Corona discharge of high voltage or the electromagnetic radiation,* is what caused the image of Yeshua of Nazareth on His burial Shroud. *By definition the word "conductor" has several meanings, but, in regards to the resurrection of Yeshua, there is one that particularly stands out.* ***Conductor;*** *A substance or device that readily conducts heat, electricity, sound etc.* ***(Source: Conductor ©1975 by Random House Inc. The Random House College Dictionary).***

Lightning from the West over the Rocky Mountains
Photograph ©2013 Kimberly K Ballard All Rights Reserved

Now in talking about the *"thermal agitation"* having to do with *the electric charge in conductors,* this brings up another incredible factor that we must approach now. If we apply the fact that *"a conductor produces electricity"* then we will see something else that is quite shocking and astounding! By definition *"electricity"* is defined as; *a fundamental physical agency caused by the presence and motion of electrons, protons, and other charged particles, manifesting itself as attraction, repulsion, magnetic, luminous and heating effects, and the like. Electrical current.* ***(Source: Electricity ©1975 by Random House Inc. The Random House College Dictionary).***

When I was thinking of Yeshua as *"The Rod of God,"* it suddenly occurred to me that a *"lightning rod"* is actually *"a rod-like conductor!"*

Lightning is *"a discharge of electricity in the atmosphere that produces static electricity."* Yeshua is the Rod! Now think about this while reading this Scripture in Matthew!

Matthew 24:27 *For as the lightning cometh out of the east, and shineth even unto the west; so shall also the coming of the Son of man be.*

So if a *"lightning rod is a rod like conductor that diverts lightning away from a structure,"* then this explains how lightning proceeds out of the throne of the Ark of God, as the Rod, Messiah, sits on the throne in the hand of the LORD God. *He is a reflection of Himself in His Rod, refracting the light outward creating static electricity!* ***(Source: Lightning Rod or Rod like Conductors ©1975 By Random House Inc. The Random House College Dictionary Revised Edition & Static Electricity) AND (Electrostatic Discharge ©2011 en.wikipedia.org/wiki/Static_electricity).***

In the Book of Revelation, we see that lightning and thunder comes out of the throne of God. *Yeshua is the Rod-like conductor, full of the Holy Spirit, diverting the lightning out and away from the throne from the Ark of His Eternal Testimony.* I have to tell you that I was so astonished and excited to make this profound connection by Divine Providence! In the following Scriptures of the Bible, we see that the LORD sits with His *Rod-like conductor* in His right hand on the throne. *Lightning and thunder comes out and diverts or deflects out of the Ark* of the throne of the LORD God, along with the voice that we hear in the glory cloud! ***Lightning comes out of Him, the Living Heavenly Ark and Rod!***

Revelation 11:19 *And the Temple of God was opened in Heaven, and there was seen in His Temple the Ark of His Testament; and there were lightnings, and voices, and thunderings, and an earthquake, and great hail.*

Revelation 4:5 *And out of the throne proceeded lightning and thundering and voices; and there were seven lamps of fire burning before the throne.*

Revelation 17:17-18 *And the seventh angel poured out his vial into the air; and there came a great voice out of the Temple of Heaven, from the throne, saying, It is done. And there were voices, and thunders, and lightnings; and there was a great earthquake, such as was not since men were upon the face of the earth, so mighty an earthquake, and so great.*

When the Angel of the LORD descended from Heaven and rolled away the Great Stone from the Garden tomb of Yeshua, it is written that the Angel's countenance was like *lightning!* Now Daniel also had a very profound experience when he had a vision, and I believe that He saw Yeshua, the Word of God, whose face had the appearance of *lightning.* Daniel heard the voice of *The Living Torah* speaking to him, and he was on his face on the ground, trembling! Remember that Yeshua repeatedly said that He was *"sent!"* The voices come out of the Ark of Heaven and so does *the lightning, the very high voltage!*

Daniel 10:5-12 *Then I lifted up mine eyes, and looked, and behold a certain man clothed in linen, whose loins were girded with fine gold of Uphaz; His body also was like the beryl, and His face as the appearance of lightning, and His eyes as lamps of fire, and His arms and His feet like in colour to polished brass, and the voice of a multitude. And I Daniel alone saw the vision; for the men that were with me saw not the vision; but a great quaking fell upon them, so that they fled to hide themselves. Therefore I was left alone, and saw this great vision, and there remained no strength in me; for my comeliness was turned in me into corruption, and I retained no strength. Yet I heard the voice of His Words; and when I heard the voice of His Words, then was I in a deep sleep on my face, and my face toward the ground. And, behold, an hand touched me, which set me upon my knees and upon the palms of my hands. And He said unto me, O Daniel, a man greatly beloved, understand the Words that I speak unto thee, and stand upright; for unto thee am I now sent. And when He had spoken this Word unto me, I stood trembling. Then said He unto me, Fear not, Daniel; for from the first day that thou didst set thine heart to understand, and to chasten thyself before thy God, thy words were heard, and I AM come for thy words.*

Daniel saw Messiah Yeshua whose face was like *lightning.* Remember this was a vision, but when Daniel heard His Words, the hand or Yad touched him and He told Daniel to stand upright. In the book of Revelation, they are fleeing into the rocks and the mountains and they are not able to stand because they are hiding themselves from the *"face"* of the LORD Messiah Yeshua, who sits on His throne! It is Yeshua, whose face is like *lightning,* who's Word and voice causes the quaking!

Revelation 6:15-17 *And the kings of the earth, and the great men, and the rich men, and the chief captains, and the mighty men, and every bondman, and every free man, hid themselves in the dens and in the rocks of the mountains; And said to the mountains and rocks, Fall on us, and hide us from the face of Him that sitteth on the throne, and from the wrath of the Lamb; For the great day of His wrath is come; and who shall be able to stand?*

In the book of Exodus, in the Torah, the LORD came down in the cloud and He descended upon Mount Sinai. There was *lightning and thunder and a thick cloud* on the top of the Mountain. It was the third day when this took place and the Messiah descends the third day in the glory cloud to usher in the Kingdom of Heaven in Jerusalem Israel. The rocks quaked at the Garden tomb as Yeshua was resurrected by *the spark of life* on the third day. As the passage in Matthew said, *"The coming of the Messiah will be as the lightning coming out of the east and shining even unto the west!" Yeshua is the lightning producing high voltage, Rod-like Conductor!*

Exodus 19:16 *And it came to pass on the third day in the morning, that there were thunders and lightnings, and a thick cloud upon the Mount, and the voice of the trumpet exceeding loud; so that all the people that was in the camp trembled.*

Now *lightning* is *"a buildup of static electricity within the clouds."* It occurs *"between the earth and the clouds."* From what I understand, "the static electricity of the lightning discharges after it builds to a certain point, and this is the electrostatic discharge. The negative charge goes down from the lightning rod towards the earth, while the positive charge goes up into the clouds into the atmosphere. The negative charge at that moment, hits an object on earth and it returns up into the clouds in the atmosphere. It then reconnects to the positive charge that is still residing in the upper clouds." ***(Source: Static Electricity - Electrostatic Discharge ©2011 en.wikipedia.org/wiki/Static_electricity).***

So *the lightning rod* makes the two poles, the positive and negative, as though they are cleft at the moment of the *electrostatic Corona discharge* and this is when the spark happens! This phenomenon of being made cleft is the signature of God on the resurrection of Yeshua, the Rod of God! It is absolutely astonishing! What astonishes me the most is the fact *"that static electricity is the buildup of an electric charge on the surface of an object!" By some Divine profound miracle, this electrostatic discharge of lightning, proceeding outward from the Rod of God, would explain the reason why the image of Yeshua is only on the very surface of the fibers of His linen burial Shroud!* When the electrostatic discharge or Corona occurs, *"the charge is then neutralized as it sparks and fires off." So at the moment of the resurrection, an electrostatic buildup between the lightning Rod of God and the fine linen Shroud discharged and it left a negative image on the earth, while the positive charge went up into the clouds into the Heavens.* The signature of God was on the resurrection of the Messiah as the positive and negative charges were made cleft in that instant. *Incredibly, the image of Yeshua on the Shroud is indeed a negative image that was left on the earth as His Spirit went up into the upper atmosphere!* Of course Yeshua made the unleavened bread cleft and He sealed His Covenant with this sign and He split the rock in Horeb like a *lightning bolt! If Yeshua is the lightning Rod or the Rod-like conductor,* then it is probable that when the high voltage spark of life occurred as *lightning* from within Him, then the negative charge went down toward the earth and grounded, while the positive charge went up through the linen Shroud and into the atmosphere as the power radiated out of the Rod. *The body of Yeshua was therefore "electrically charged and an excess of electrons created a negative charge." This would mean that an "electrostatic field" existed or was created between the body and the linen burial Shroud, as the high voltage charge was generated from within and radiated outward like a diffused light source from the center of Yeshua's body.*

Now if you think about it, as the negative charge returned toward His body that was now in its glorified state as *"burnished bronze" or "molten brass," it's very top surface was charged with an electrostatic build up and this created a "photoelectric effect" like an interface.* Photoelectric refers to *"electric effects produced by light." Yeshua is the source of the light.* Therefore the Shroud was attracted to the body as a magnet and *the positively charged surface* of the linen Shroud was drawn towards the body through an electrostatic field. Although Yeshua's image is definitely a photographic image and not a painting, I found that a similar *electrostatic effect* occurs in *"Electrostatic painting."* From the online source, *"ehow,"* this method of painting is achieved when "there is a chemical catalyst that is mixed with paint and it is given a positive charge. A metal object that is going to be painted is grounded with a negative charge. Therefore, the paint and the metal object are oppositely charged and now the paint will be attracted to the metal object as if it were a magnet." According to the process as it is described, "As the positively charged paint is sprayed toward the negatively charged metal object, the paint is drawn toward its surface. This attraction is so strong that if an object is only sprayed from one side, the charge will actually pull the paint around so that it covers the entire metal surface." ***(Source: Electrostatic Painting Facts ©2012 ehow.com/how-does_5565360_electrostatic-painting-works.html).***

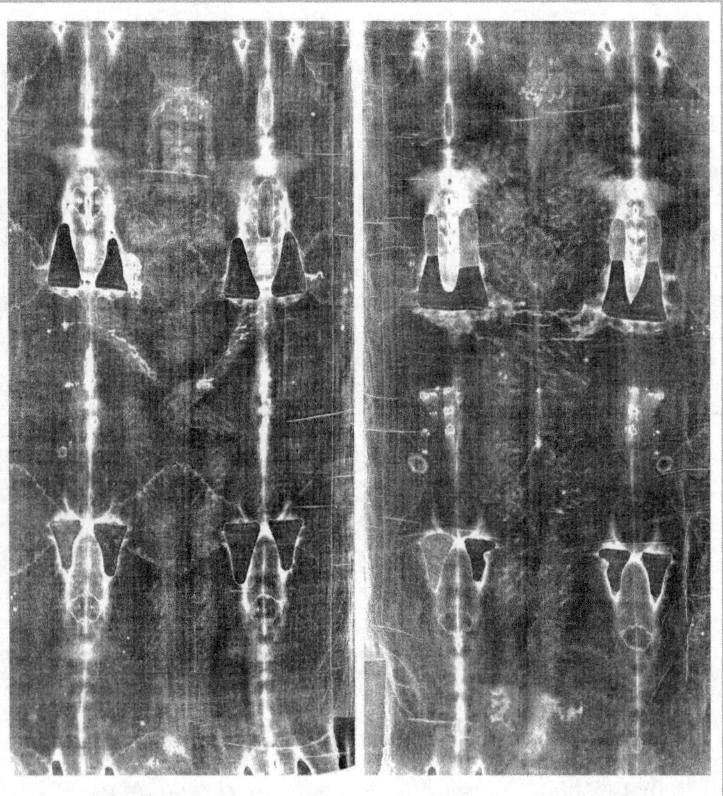

Official Shroud Pair Photograph ©1978 Barrie M. Schwortz Collection, STERA Inc., All Rights Reserved

I only used this reference to show how I believe that the *"electrostatic negative and positive charges"* played a role in the resurrection of Messiah, the LORD God of Israel, *whose glorified body is like molten metal, thus making it the conductor. The Shroud image is a photographic negative that is only on the very surface of the linen because there was an electrostatic field between the body and the linen. Perhaps the aloes and spices that Yeshua was buried with created some type of chemical catalyst that reacted with the conductor.*

Anyway, in order to achieve this same kind of static electricity on the very surface of a balloon, "you rub it against something and this gives its surface a negative charge due to more electrons that are created. Now because the top surface is negatively charged, it will stick to the positive or neutralized object."

So I believe that *the lightning flashed within Yeshua* as *the Rod of God* came to life and this fired off a high voltage charge that radiated outward and this created an electrostatic field. His image in the form of a photographic negative was then imprinted through the *Corona* that sparked and was imprinted only on the *very surface* of the linen that was highly charged with electrons. *Electromagnetic radiation* also played a role in the creation of the image and I will discuss this outstanding revelation in the last chapter. Now, as I said before, these are the elements that the LORD revealed to me that I studied and I based this on the fact that *Yeshua is the Rod-like conductor and lightning flashes out of the Ark of God. So lightning flashes out of Yeshua and I believe this happened when He came to life!*

Remember that after Yeshua was resurrected He *"materialized"* through the door when it was shut and He appeared alive to the Jewish disciples in the midst of the room. This means that He also had to *"materialize"* through the linen burial Shroud. If you look at the definition of the word *"materialize"* you find a rather curious description! *Materialize means "to make physically perceptible, to cause a Spirit or the like to appear in bodily form."* Yeshua was in *bodily form* when He appeared to the Jewish disciples after the resurrection because He told them to touch the wounds in His hands or wrists and in His side. *So the Rod of God, full of the Holy Spirit of God, is the conductor of lightning called "The LORD'S arrow"* and this brings up another aspect of the Messiah that we have not looked at yet. The arrow is like a flint, which is like the rock at Horeb!

Zechariah 9:14 *And the LORD shall be seen over them, and His arrow shall go forth as the lightning; and the LORD God shall blow the trumpet, and shall go with whirlwinds of the south.*

If we study the arrow, we see that an arrow has a shaft or *a rod* with a weapon at one end of it. Yeshua is the shaft of the arrow, the Rod. At one end of this Rod is His weapon of battle. This weapon is the Word of God, *the Living Torah*, that He speaks out of His mouth, which is at one end of the Rod. He battles against the enemies of God with His arrow that shoots forth as *lightning.*

Psalm 64:7 *But God shall shoot at them with an arrow; suddenly shall they be wounded.*

The Prophet Jeremiah wrote about the anger of the LORD and he talked about the Rod of the LORD'S wrath and the arrow from His quiver.

Arrow Photo ©2014 Kimberly K Ballard

Lamentations 3:1 *I am the man that hath seen affliction by the Rod of His wrath.*

Lamentations 3:12-13 *He hath bent His bow, and set me as a mark for the arrow. He hath caused the arrows of His quiver to enter into my reins.*

I must tell you something incredible. It has been blazing hot for weeks on end without any rain here. As I was just writing about the arrow and *the lightning Rod of the LORD,* a sudden burst of heavy rain began to fall outside the window. At once, the rain was fiercely beating upon the window pane and *lightning* flashed very close to the house! I was really shocked because the *lightning* flashed just as I opened the window to smell the fresh rain falling. I then went outside to the porch to watch the huge unexpected downpour. After it subsided just a little, I went out with the umbrella and I saw a gorgeous double rainbow going over my house! I ran to get the camera and I took some pictures of it. This is the fourth year in a row in this specific week that we have had the double rainbows going over our house from one side to the other side as I worked on my book for the glory of the LORD! Incredibly, there have been three rainbows this past week and the first one happened seven days ago. As it began to fade out, the sky became darker and suddenly a second rainbow formed. What a gift and a blessing from the LORD and perhaps *a verification* of all that I have written about Him through His Divine revelation! *I was thanking the LORD for this beautiful miracle, as I wrote about the lightning Rod of God as the Rod-like conductor!* Lightning is *very rarely* ever flashing just outside my window! The LORD never disappoints me at all with His love. So I had to include this sweet miracle in my story as I remembered that He refreshes us like the rain!

The LORD, who uses His Rod as His weapon, explains the phenomenon that happened with Moses. Remember when Moses lifted up the rod, the Israelites were saved, but when he lowered the rod, representing the power of the Word of God, then the enemy prevailed to win. Yeshua could not come down from the cross because if He had, the enemy would have prevailed. This battle was between God and Satan. God won this battle with His Rod Messiah Yeshua was lifted up to save Israel and the world forever! Since the Rod is the arrow of the LORD that wins battles over His enemies, this explains why Yeshua is coming to fight in the future against those who hate the LORD and do not obey His Word. Yeshua will return in the cloud of the Shechinah glory *"as the lightning" the Rod-like conductor!* This is written again in Luke 17:24.

Luke 17:24 *For as the lightning, that lighteth out of the one part under Heaven, shineth unto the other part under Heaven; so shall also the Son of man be in His day.*

I must come back to add something exciting here! I just got my book back from my publisher with the final small edit errors to fix. Incredibly, on July 1 2014, an article appeared online that verified everything I had written about this through the revelation of the Holy Spirit! This was fantastic timing! An article appeared in Mad Science titled; *"The Engineer Who Said The Ark Of The Covenant Was A Giant Capacitor."* You will not believe what it said! In 1933, an engineering professor theorized that the real cause of death for Uzzah who laid his hands upon the Ark of the Covenant, was 10,000 volts of static electricity! The article stated: "According to an article that appeared in the March 5th, 1933 edition of the Chicago Daily Tribune, Frederick Rogers, the Dean of the Department of Engineering at the Lewis Institute of Technology, conducted a careful study of the construction of the Ark as described in the Bible, and concluded that its design matched a perfectly constructed simple electric condenser: The scientific interest in the construction pointed out by Prof. Rogers was that the acacia wood box—about 40 inches long and slightly less than 30 inches in width and in depth—not only was lined with gold teal on the inside but overlaid with the same metal without. This according to Prof. Rogers, is the first step that any modern boy with a flare [sic] for electrical experimentation will take to create a Leyden jar, except that in a Leyden jar, a glass receptacle is coated on the inside and outside with tin foil instead of gold. Then, with the aid of a rod with a small knob at the top and short chain at the bottom which is inserted through the cork so that the chain can make contact with the bottom of the jar, the young experimenter is ready to collect small charges of bottled lightning. But the Ark of the Covenant was a much larger condenser…The divine directions called for the creation of two cherubim of pure gold to be placed on a gold slab or "mercy seat" overtop the Ark. These cherubim, Prof. Rogers explained, made up what he believes to have been the positive pole of the circuit. He explained…that it is known among physicists that a "difference of potential" exists between the earth and the air which may be collected in electrical charges under certain favorable conditions…It was explained that even slight movements of heat rising in smoke—such as from burning sacrifices or even incense—would distribute lesser charges of electricity…This, Prof. Rogers explained, may have accounted for the collecting of bolts powerful enough to cause death." ***(Source: Article filed to Mad Science July 1st 2014, by Mark Strauss: io9.com/the-engineer-who-said-the-ark-of-the-covenant-was-a-gia-1598583115).***

Clearly it is evident from this article that *a rod* is involved in producing electricity! By definition, *"A Capacitor in a radio set, is an instrument for storing electrical energy in electrostatic form (see Electricity). It ordinarily consists of two conducting surfaces, approximately parallel, separated by an insulator or dielectric material. It is also called a condenser (Electrical).* ***(Source: Encyclopedia Britannica, Inc. ©1960 William Benton, Publisher Chicago: London: Toronto).***

Now if we take this knowledge, that *Messiah Yeshua is the Rod-like conductor,* that diverts and deflects *lightning* out of the throne of the Ark of His Testimony in Heaven, then we discover a fantastic new bit of information. *To deflect the lightning, means to bend it.* This truth opens the door to an astonishing new speculation regarding the formation of the image of Yeshua on the Shroud of Turin, and to His stunning quality of *invisibility!*

THE TELESCOPE AND THE IMAGE

Zoom Lens
Photos ©2013 Kimberly K Ballard All Rights Reserved

If we go back to investigate the term *"electromagnetic radiation"* we find that these are types of particles that are gathered onto the lens of a telescope. The telescope is used, of course, to study the universe. Now through my research I found that there are different types of telescopes, but the main object is to magnify an image as one looks through the lens. The ancient telescope lenses were apparently made of glass. I found the following explanation. "One lens was convex and the other lens was concave and the rays of light that fall on the front lens, cause electromagnetic radiation particles to be collected on it. The rays of light are bent and concentrated into a beam to a focal point and an image can be seen. As the telescope developed over time, it became possible to place a photographic plate where the eye piece was on the telescope. This enabled a person to take a photograph of the image that they saw through the lens and they could later study the image from the photograph that was taken." *(Source: Telescope Facts ©2011-12 amazing-space.stsci.edu/resources/explorations/groundup/lesson/eras/early-refractors/page2.php).*

This is exactly what we do with the Shroud of Turin. The image was first photographed by supernatural means and it has been studied later. So this image on the Shroud is an exact photographic negative of Messiah Yeshua, *the Rod who reflects the light rays of glory from His throne as lightning* and from Himself. *He is a reflective and refractive light and He is the conductor of the spark of life.* Now it is said *"that when white light separates and bends, we see the colors of the light spectrum. This is why we see colors of the light in a prism and in a rainbow." (Source: Light Spectrum ©2011 Encyclopaedia Britannica Inc.).*

Of course, we are talking about very scientific topics here that could go on forever into different scientific fields of study with many experts involved. It is clear to me, however, that the LORD has revealed, through physics, all the elements of nature that are needed to understand how the image of Yeshua was created, at the moment of His resurrection.

Zoom Lens Photo ©2013 Kimberly K Ballard All Rights Reserved

There are two types of telescopes that I want to briefly discuss first that I studied. There is the *"reflective telescope and the refractor telescope."* I soon realized that Yeshua *the Rod* is revealed in both types of telescopes. *Yeshua is reflective like the lens and He refracts the light from Himself. This means that He not only reflects the light like a reflective telescope, but* ***He also bends the light like a refractor telescope.*** Therefore, *"electromagnetic radiation"* would be collected on the reflective part of Him and I suspect that this would be on the outer surface of His being, since His face is radiant with light shining from it. Remember that when Moses met with the LORD on Mount Sinai, his own face was glowing from having seen this *reflective quality* of the LORD'S light. So it is highly probable that *electromagnetic radiation* was involved during the imprinting of the photographic image of Yeshua on His linen burial Shroud. The image itself is truly a photographic negative of the Messiah. *To sum it up, Yeshua the Rod of God, is both* *reflective and refractive.* Although the first telescope lenses were clear glass, it is said that *"the telescope developed into a more precise instrument when a thin layer of silver was added to the lens. This silver layer turned the lens into a reflective mirror. With this type of reflective telescope, it was now possible to see much sharper images as compared to the earlier refractor type of lens. The images taken from the silver lined lenses also had a deeper clarity. It was now possible to obtain more detail in a higher quality image."* ***(Source: Telescope ©2011-12 amazing-space.stsci.edu/resources/explorations/groundup/lesson/eras/early-refractors/page2.php).***

Lens Photo ©2013 Kimberly K Ballard

This is what I felt was important as I studied this topic, since the Shroud image of Yeshua is so clear and detailed. We now have the recent evidence within the last few years that Yeshua's image on the Shroud is encoded with amazing 3-D qualities. It was discovered, some time ago, that the image of Yeshua on the Shroud does not perform the same way that a typical two dimensional photograph performs under the same scientific tests. Of course, *the third day* was so significant to Yeshua's resurrection and it is interesting that His image is encoded in 3-D! From this Divine revelation, *I soon began to realize that the Rod of God, the Messiah, is projecting a mirror image of the face of the one that is holding this reflective Rod in His hand. The God of Israel is one LORD God, who is holding a Rod in His right hand that reflects His own face like a mirror. This is why Yeshua is reflecting and refracting the light as the Rod of God.* Remember that I said before that Yeshua is called *"The Prince of the face of the LORD God,"* which is to say the *"Sar HaPanim,"* in Hebrew. He is *the face of HaShem* that Rabbi Simcha Pearlmutter mentioned on page 432.

Official 3D Hologram Shroud face Photograph ©2013 Dr. Petrus Soons, taken from Enrie Photographs ©1931

Suddenly, as if by Divine Providence, the LORD showed me stunning proof that what I was saying was correct. In my research, I discovered that there were some Rabbis, who actually wrote that *"the Divine Presence of God was compared to a mirror!"* This truth was discovered by the Rabbis, within the book of Numbers, in the following verses of the Torah. The Hebrew word used for *"vision"* here is the word #4758 *"bam-mar'ah" or "Mar'eh."* It literally means *"glass, a mirror, a looking glass, a vision."* ***(Source: ©2010 Strong's Concordance).*** The word *"U-mar'eh"* refers to *"Countenance"* which is the LORD'S face.

Numbers 12:5-6 *And the LORD came down in the pillar of cloud, and stood in the door of the Tabernacle, and called Aaron and Miriam; and they both came forth. And He said, Hear now My Words; If there be a Prophet among you, I the LORD will make Myself known unto him in a vision, and will speak unto him in a dream.*

In medical terms the word *"vision"* is *"the sense by which objects in the external environment are perceived, by means of the light they give off or reflect."* **(Source: Vision ©2010 thefreedictionary.com).** The Rabbis stated that the word *"vision"* in this Scripture in Numbers, in the Torah, also means *"mirror!"* The Jewish Rabbis said that within this statement, *The LORD is actually saying, "In a vision (in a mirror), I make Myself known to him."* ***(Source: ©1997-2012 by Yeshivat Har Etzion, The Israel Koschitzsky Virtual Beit Midrash, From; "Reading Midrash Aggada," By Dr. Moshe Simon-Shoshan, Shiur #12; Mirror Images Vayikra Rabba 1:14-15 onlne source found at; vbm-torah.org/archive/midrash69/12midrash.htm).***

Mirror reflecting the sky
Photo ©2014 Kimberly K Ballard All Rights Reserved &
3D Shroud Hologram ©2013 Dr Petrus Soons from Enrie Photos ©1931 All Rights Reserved
(Edited to be on mirror by KKB)

In this passage, the LORD is speaking about revealing Himself to the Prophet who is among them. *This is just incredible because this verifies what I have been saying that the Rod of God, the Messiah, is a mirror reflection of the LORD God of Israel who is absolutely making Himself known to us in a reflective mirror as our Messiah Yeshua!* In this state we can see Him and live. This means that the image on the burial Shroud of Yeshua is also a mirror image of Messiah the Rod, who is a mirror reflection of the LORD God of Israel, who holds this Rod in His hand and *refracts the light from Himself like a telescope lens.* This is exactly the reason why *Messiah Yeshua said, "If you have seen Me, you have seen the Father!" Adam and Eve were made in His image from the rock quarry in Jerusalem in the Mountain of God.*

The technique of taking a photograph that is *a reflection* with a telescope is called *"Astrophotography."* There is a phenomenon that occurs in *Astrophotography* known as *"mach banding."* This refers to *"Horizontal and vertical black and white banding that occurs in connection with the sharpening of the image. When a digital image is sharpened, you can see halos around it and this occurs with the lens of our eyes. It creates an illusion of mach bands."* ***(Astrophotography ©2010-2011 en.wikipedia.org/wiki/Astrophotography All Rights Reserved).*** Why is this fascinating? As it turns out, the Shroud of Turin has *both horizontal and vertical mach banding* that appears when the image is photographed by a photographer, but these lines are barely visible to the naked eye. So the photographic images that are taken with a telescope have this effect of mach banding. *Heavy mach banding can occur when attempting to photograph a planet that is far from the earth with a telescope. Of course, Yeshua resides in Heaven!* In my mind, this is thrilling proof that the Shroud image that was left inside Holy Mount Moriah with the mach banding on it, is a mirror image of Messiah Yeshua, who ascended into Heaven. Just as we use the telescope images to study the universe that the LORD made, *we have been given a mirror image of the creator of the universe, so that we could study it!* This is a true miracle that was only made possible by the mighty hand of the LORD God. Another Scripture from the Bible proves this without a doubt! The Gospel proclaims *the Living Torah,* revealing the LORD'S Eternal Testimony. It reveals the glory of the Divine resurrection of the KING in His Garden in Jerusalem. His resurrection glory reveals His face as it appears on His linen burial Shroud.

II Corinthians 4:3-4 *But if our Gospel be hid, it is hid to them that are lost; In whom the god of this world hath blinded the minds of them which believe not, lest the light of the glorious Gospel of Messiah, who is the image of God, should shine unto them.*

The LORD said that He would reveal Himself in a mirror to a Prophet. So this tells us that *"to see a vision (a mirror) of the LORD, is to behold Him, to look upon Him and to see His face."* The Hebrew words *"Chazah and chazown"* reveal this to us. #2372 **Chazah;** meaning to gaze at; to perceive, contemplate; spec. to have a vision of behold, look, prophesy, provide, to see. # 2377 Chazown; a sight, a dream, revelation, or oracle – vision. ***(Source: ©2010 Strong's Concordance).***

Remember that the oracles of God were to be revealed in the Fig tree of the knowledge of good and evil and the Almond Tree of Life. We gaze upon the Shroud image of Yeshua and contemplate and behold His Divine Testimony in them!

Some of the latest technology using advanced telescopes involves the use of *"molten mirrors."* A molten mirror is literally *"a reflective pool of liquid molten silver and salt. This type of reflective molten mirror is much more precise in capturing a pure image."* ***(Source: Liquid molten mirror telescopes ©2010-2011 en.wikipedia.org/wiki/Liquid-mirror_telescope).***

The LORD spread out the sky as a *molten mirror!* This Scripture is found in Job. Although the Scripture uses the word *"glass,"* in the Hebrew it is supposed to be the word *"mirror."* So this verse should read *"as a molten mirror."* I find it to be truly astonishing that the advanced and more precise molten mirror telescope was mentioned centuries ago in the book of Job! The molten mirror telescope is an advanced technology that was not known or used in ancient times, except for the Great Sea in the Holy Temple in Jerusalem and it was a *liquid molten mirror!*

It was the creative Divine design of the LORD God of Israel and now you must read the last chapter of this book about the Great Sea in the Holy Temple and see what I wrote about *the reflective LORD God, the KING Messiah!*

Job 37:18 *Hast thou with Him spread out the sky, which is strong, and as a molten looking glass?*

When Yeshua appears in Heaven, in the book of Revelation, His feet have the appearance of *"molten brass."* The sapphire sky of the earth is the floor of His throne where His feet rest. The ancient mirrors were made from polished brass and bronze! The LORD'S laver was made from these mirrors that reflected the sky. It contained liquid living water and the sky appeared to float on its surface, like a molten mirror. There is much more to discover about the universe and the LORD and the Great Sea! As the LORD showed these facts to me, I knew they were all important details of His Testimony. It is chilling to have discovered that not only do the *laws of physics* reveal the LORD in the description of the glory cloud, but also in the elements of the resurrection and in the formation of the image of the LORD on His burial Shroud, as the Messiah of Israel. The LORD is the greatest source of light, so His light has these *reflective and refractive* qualities to it. This demonstrates how the image came to be on the Shroud and this reveals why the Scriptures tell us that *"we see the image of God, in the face of Messiah."* So the light of Messiah, who is the image of God, shines upon us and reflects from us, just as it did on the face of Moses. This is evident in the Torah in the Aaronic Blessing that puts His Holy Name upon you!

Mirror reflecting the sky
Photo ©2014 Kimberly K Ballard All Rights Reserved & 3D Shroud Hologram ©2013 Dr Petrus Soons from Enrie Photos ©1931 All Rights Reserved (Edited to be on mirror by KKB)

Numbers 6:22-27 *And the LORD spake unto Moses, saying, Speak unto Aaron and unto his sons, saying, On this wise ye shall bless the children of Israel, saying unto them, The LORD bless thee, and keep thee; The LORD make His face shine upon thee, and be gracious unto thee; The LORD lift up His countenance upon thee, and give thee peace. And they shall put My Name upon the children of Israel; and I will bless them.*

The Aaronic Blessing says, *"The LORD lift up His countenance upon thee."* So the word *"countenance"* means *"the expression of His face!"*

Psalm 67:1 *GOD be merciful unto us, and bless us; and cause His face to shine upon us; Selah.*

Psalm 119:135 *Make Thy face to shine upon thy servant; and teach me Thy statutes.*

This means that when we look upon Yeshua, we are looking upon *the light of the KINGS countenance* and He is the Rod that gives us life! When the veil is taken away in Messiah, we can now see that we are looking upon the face of the LORD God of Israel. He is the Living Water of the cloud of glory and He is our latter rain.

Proverbs 16:15 *In the light of the King's countenance is life; and His favour is as a cloud of the latter rain.*

In the same way, His exact image was imprinted on the burial Shroud, the instant He was raised to life as the Living Almond Branch. *The spark of light, the lightning or high voltage was coming from His interior and it was radiating outward.* I believe that the LORD left this photographic image in His rock hewn Garden tomb inside Holy Mount Moriah, so we could study it as soon as we developed the technologies to study the universe with the telescope and through *Astrophotography.* This means that the LORD'S power and His advanced knowledge was evident on the Shroud centuries before we developed the technologies that could unravel the marvelous mysteries of God. Remember that Moses face was radiant as he talked with the LORD and Moses put the veil over his face when he later spoke with the Israelites. Perhaps *the electromagnetic radiation* had something to do with not being able to see the LORD'S full glory and live which is why we are only allowed to see His *reflection.*

Exodus 34:29-30 *And it came to pass, when Moses came down from Mount Sinai with the two tablets of the Testimony in Moses hand, when he came down from the Mount, that Moses wist not that the skin of his face shone while he talked with Him. And when Aaron and all the children of Israel saw Moses, behold, the skin of his face shone; and they were afraid to come nigh him.*

Moses face was radiant and the Angel of the LORD had a countenance that was radiant. The word *"radiant"* refers specifically to *"radiating rays or reflecting beams of light."* It also refers to *"emitting light as radiation."* To be radiant is to be *"marked with an expression of love."* The LORD loves us and His *countenance* is an expression of love towards us. There is also *"Radiant Energy"* and it refers to *"Energy that is emitted as electromagnetic wave motion." Wave motion and electromagnetic radiation* are possible factors in the image formation on the Shroud. The wave fringes in the Radiant Energy take us into the deeper realm of 3-D imaging or Holographic imaging. It is no wonder then that only very recently the Shroud image of Yeshua was turned into a Hologram, due to its 3-D properties because it contained these wave fringes! Dr. Petrus Soons, who is a Holographic expert, worked with the Shroud of Yeshua and he discovered letters under the neck on the Shroud of Turin that are Aramaic. He produced the Hologram 3-D images of Yeshua from photographic information. Dr. Soons discovered that the letters under Yeshua's neck in Aramaic spelled, *"The Lamb!"* ***(Source: 3D Imaging Shroud Wave Fringes Dr. Petrus Soons ©2010 shroud3d.com/).*** This reminds me of the Lamb's Ear plant for the Maror in the Passover Seder! In 2013, I contacted Dr. Soons and Barrie Schwortz to tell them *I saw letters in Hebrew* under Yeshua's neck that appeared to say, *"Yeshua."* If we look upon the Shroud image of Yeshua, we are fulfilling the Scripture in Zechariah!

Zechariah 12:10 *And I will pour upon the House of David, and upon the inhabitants of Jerusalem, the Spirit of grace and of supplications; and they shall look upon Me whom they have pierced, and they shall mourn for Him, as one mourneth for his only Son, and shall be in bitterness for Him, as one that is in bitterness for his firstborn.*

BENDING THE LIGHT THE INVISIBILITY CLOAK

Mirror reflecting sky & Glory light

The *bending of light* that I mentioned with the telescopes presents another startling aspect of the LORD as *the Invisible Assistant.* The LORD is said to be *"omnipresent"* or everywhere at the same time, yet He is not visible.

Psalm 139:7-10 *Whither shall I go from thy spirit? Or whither shall I flee from thy presence? If I ascend up into heaven, thou art there: If I make my bed in hell, behold, thou art there. If I take the wings of the morning, and dwell in the utter-most parts of the sea; Even there shall thy hand lead me, and thy right hand shall hold me.*

Since the LORD is the source of the light *"Ma'Ohr,"* then all the LORD has to do to be invisible to us, is to *bend the laws of light* so we cannot see Him. In essence the LORD, who is wrapped in a robe of light, *bends the light by refraction* into an *"invisibility cloak!"* With this thought in mind it is not hard to comprehend how Yeshua twice appeared in the room with His Jewish disciples when the door was shut after His resurrection *(John 20:19; John 20:26).* It is important to understand that the Creator of the laws of light uses His own physics of the laws of light to appear to us. He can be present, *refract the light,* and not be seen.

Recent technology reveals the stunning affects of this phenomenon called the *"invisibility cloak."* In a recent article in the *©2014 August 10, Volume XV Issue II of "Illumin, A review of engineering in everyday life,"* we find the following facts about *"The Prospects of Invisibility Cloaks: Bending the Laws of Light." In this article, Emily Sylvester wrote: "Current research and experimentation with metamaterials have led to advancements in the development of invisibility. Metamaterials can be used to make objects appear invisible by bending light around those objects though refraction instead of away from those objects by reflection. Though no natural material exhibits this behavior, engineers are working to design cloaking devices with metamaterials that will refract light around an object and towards the viewer in the same path as if the object were not present. The engineering breakthrough of manipulating the properties of light to create the appearance of invisibility may ultimately have significant future applications." (She goes on to say): "Engineers are synthesizing materials that can bend light around whatever object they encompass, creating the illusion that the object is not actually there, thereby making it seem invisible."* ***(Source: ©2014 August 10, Volume XV Issue II of "Illumin," A review of engineering in everyday life – The Prospects of Invisibility Cloaks: Bending the Laws of Light – by Emily Sylvester-illumin.usc.edu/printer/211/the-prospects-of-invisibility-cloaks-bending-the-laws-of-light/).***

As I thought pensively about this, I began to see that *the LORD'S qualities of refracting and reflecting light,* also give Him the ability *to stand in our presence, while His very nature equips Him with the ability to cloak Himself in invisibility.* This is how He can be everywhere and we do not see Him. I remember that once while writing this book I mentioned that I felt the LORD'S Presence. He was *invisible* but I felt Him there like an energy field. The article by Emily Sylvester goes on to explain *"How Light Bends." She said: "The nature of light has always been a puzzling concept for physicists. Light exhibits the properties of both waves and particles. It travels in straight lines, like an unaccelerated particle; yet, it exhibits diffraction patterns as do water and sound waves. This dichotomy is called the wave-particle duality. It is the wave properties of light that make cloaking possible. When light interacts with an object (a wall, mirror, or even air), it reflects and refracts. Light reflects from a mirror like a ball bouncing off a wall: the incident and reflected rays make equal angles with the normal line (perpendicular line) to the reflecting surface. We can use this understanding to direct light along precise paths. Lasers and holograms make use of this simple law of reflection. It is the more complicated law of refraction, however, that describes the bending of light."* ***(Source: ©2014 August 10, Volume XV Issue II of "Illumin," A review of engineering in everyday life by Emily Sylvester-illumin.usc.edu/printer/211/the-prospects-of-invisibility-cloaks-bending-the-laws-of-light/).***

If the law of reflection pertains to Holograms, and the Shroud image has been made into a Hologram, then understanding the *"more complicated law of refraction," I believe, will reveal more scientific aspects of the* LORD that will solve the mystery of the Shroud image.

Another article I found in the *"MIT Technology Review, Emerging Technology From the arXiv ©2013 June 6"* article states the following: *"Human-Scale Invisibility Cloak Unveiled."* It says *"the first is the idea of 'transformation optics' – the ability to bend light around a region of space to make it look as if it weren't there."* In this application they were able to make an invisibility cloak with the use of lenses and mirrors. ***(Source: ©2013 June 6 - www.technologyreview.com/view/515776/human-scale-invisibility-cloak-unveiled/).***

It is apparent that the LORD who reveals Himself in a *mirror,* who exhibits these *qualities of refraction, reflection,* and like the lens of a telescope can also *bend the light rays, causes His own invisible quality.* The LORD wears light as a garment or cloak. This is the radiance that surrounds His Shechinah glory. Although the power of the LORD is supernatural it is also explained by the very nature of His creation, and this includes *the physics of our KING as an invisible but very present force.* Therefore, He assists us like He assisted King David in battle without being seen. We find then that the LORD is truly *the Invisible Assistant* as we see in Hebrews 11:27; Colossians 1:15-16; Romans 1:20; I Timothy 1:17; and Hebrews 11:3. Another passage that I have spoken about before in another section also reveals *the LORD'S invisibility cloak.* He is not far away like we assume Him to be but He is close to us, *even in the room without our knowledge!* In Psalm 104:1-2 we find the following words.

Mirror Photo ©2014 Kimberly K Ballard

Psalm 104:1-6 *Bless the LORD, O my soul, O LORD my God, thou art very great; thou art clothed with honour and majesty. Who coverest thyself with light as with a garment: who stretchest out the heavens like a curtain: Who layeth the beams of his chambers in the waters: who maketh the clouds his chariot: who walketh upon the wings of the wind: Who maketh his angels spirits; his ministers a flaming fire: Who laid the foundations of the earth, that it should not be removed for ever. Thou coveredst it with the deep as with a garment: the waters stood above the mountains.*

Hebrews 11:24-27 *By faith Moses, when he was come to years, refused to be called the son of Pharaoh's daughter; Choosing rather to suffer affliction with the people of God, than to enjoy the pleasures of sin for a season; Esteeming the reproach of Christ greater riches than the treasures in Egypt: for he had respect unto the recompense of the reward. By faith he forsook Egypt, not fearing the wrath of the king: for he endured, as seeing Him who is invisible.*

Colossians 1:12-17 *Giving thanks unto the Father, which hath made us meet to be partakers of the inheritance of the saints in light: Who hath delivered us from the power of darkness, and hath translated us into the kingdom of His dear Son: In whom we have redemption through His blood, even the forgiveness of sins: Who is the image of the invisible God, the firstborn of every creature: For by Him were all things created, that are in heaven, and that are in earth, visible and invisible, whether they be thrones, or dominions, or principalities, or powers: all things were created by Him, and for Him: And He is before all things, and by Him all things consist.*

PILLAR OF CLOUD BY DAY PILLAR OF FIRE BY NIGHT

Pillar of cloud & Pillar of fire
Photos ©2013 Kimberly K Ballard

The LORD spread His cloud as a covering. This statement was written in the Psalms and clearly Josephus declared this in his book when he said that *the cloud of the LORD was diffused.* The cloud of the LORD would descend from Heaven and *spread out with a diffused light.* It covered the entire area and the Shechinah glory cloud of the LORD is also spread out in a gentle manner upon His throne, the Ark of His Covenant. His pillar of fire gave light in the night to the Hebrews.

Job 26:8-9 *He bindeth up the waters in His thick clouds; and the cloud is not rent under them. He holdeth back the face of His throne, and spreadeth His cloud upon it.*

Psalm 105:39 *He spread a cloud for a covering; and fire to give light in the night.*

In each instance, we have seen that *the light* of the LORD is in the glory cloud. When Moses or the disciples of Yeshua entered the cloud, they entered into the LORD'S Divine Presence where *the light* of His Majestic glory was revealed.

Job 37:15-16 *Dost thou know when God disposed them, and caused the light of His cloud to shine? Dost thou know the balancing of the clouds, the wondrous works of Him which is perfect in knowledge?*

The LORD was leading Israel as He went before them in a pillar of cloud by day and in a pillar of fire by night. His path eventually took them to the Promised Land. The spies were sent into the land to scope it out for 40 days and only two came back with a good report. The LORD was angry with the others for not accepting what the LORD had promised them and they wanted to appoint a captain to return to Egypt! Because of this sin, only Joshua and Caleb pleased God and did what He asked and trusted that the LORD was giving them only the best. The LORD was provoked because He had performed so many miraculous signs before the people, yet they still did not believe. This is exactly what happened when Yeshua arrived in Jerusalem. Although He showed all the signs of *the Rod of the LORD God of Israel,* Yeshua was still rejected and only a few were left to follow the Messiah into the Eternal Promised Land. The LORD had the following reaction in Numbers 14. *The LORD'S cloud stood over the people and they saw the LORD face to face in the radiant Shechinah glory cloud!*

***Numbers 14:11-14** And the LORD said unto Moses, How long will this people provoke Me? And how long will it be ere they believe Me, for all the signs which I have shewed among them? I will smite them with the pestilence, and disinherit them, and will make of thee a greater nation and mightier than they. And Moses said unto the LORD, Then the Egyptians shall hear it, for Thou broughtest up this people in Thy might from among them; And they will tell it to the inhabitants of this land; for they have heard that Thou LORD art among this people, that Thou LORD art seen face to face, and that Thy cloud standeth over them, and that Thou goest before them, by day time in a pillar of a cloud, and in a pillar of fire by night.*

***Exodus 13:21** And the LORD went before them by day in a pillar of a cloud, to lead them the way; and by night in a pillar of fire, to give them light; to go by day and night:*

So again, the LORD was *in the cloud,* marching before the children of Israel, and Messiah is coming *in the cloud* to lead the children of Israel into the Eternal Promised Land. When the cloud would rest, the people would also rest. When the cloud would pick up and move, the Israelites would march forward. They would march in the direction that the LORD was leading them as He covered and spread out His cloud over them and this is His cloud of protection. The cloud covered the Testimony!

***Numbers 9:15-23** And on the day that the Tabernacle was reared up the cloud covered the Tabernacle, namely, the tent of the Testimony; and at even there was upon the Tabernacle, as it were the appearance of fire, until the morning. So it was always, the cloud covered it by day, and the appearance of fire by night. And when the cloud was taken up from the Tabernacle, then after that the children of Israel journeyed; and in the place where the cloud abode, there the children of Israel pitched their tents. At the commandment of the LORD the children of Israel journeyed, and at the commandment of the LORD they pitched; as long as the cloud abode upon the Tabernacle they rested in their tents. And when the cloud tarried long upon the Tabernacle many days, then the children of Israel kept the charge of the LORD, and journeyed not. And so it was, when the cloud was a few days upon the Tabernacle; according to the commandment of the LORD they abode in their tents, and according to the commandment of the LORD they journeyed. And so it was, when the cloud abode from even unto the morning, and that the cloud was taken up in the morning, then they journeyed; whether it was by day or by night that the cloud was taken up, they journeyed. Or whether it were two days, or a month, or a year, that the cloud tarried upon the Tabernacle, remaining thereon, the children of Israel abode in their tents, and journeyed not; but when it was taken up, they journeyed. At the commandment of the LORD they rested in the tents, and at the commandment of the LORD they journeyed; they kept the charge of the LORD, at the commandment of the LORD by the hand of Moses.*

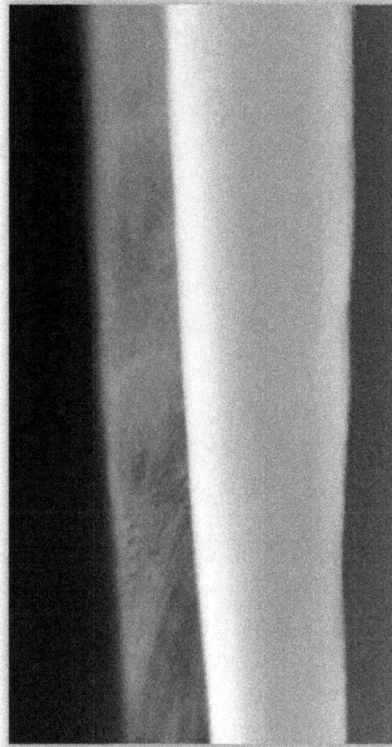

Pillar of Cloud - Roll Cloud Photo ©2013 Kimberly K Ballard All Rights reserved

Now again, when I think about the rapture of believers, I think about the above passage because it is quite clear *that the cloud abode from evening unto morning* and as I explained earlier, the new day begins at sundown, according to the Biblical calendar. *The cloud was then taken up in the morning and the people journeyed.* So this is like the Israelites who crossed the Red Sea *"from evening until morning"* toward the land of promise, and when they got to the other side, they journeyed with the LORD, *with the Rod of God,* who was leading them *in the pillar of cloud.* This makes me believe even further that when the rapture occurs, the cloud will descend from Heaven and *the cloud will also be taken up in the morning.* The people, who have entered the cloud, will be taken up *to journey* into the Heavenly Kingdom of God into the Eternal Promised Land. The LORD will be leading the way before us *in the glory cloud,* as *the Rod* goes before us! In Exodus, the Angel of the LORD went before the camp of Israel and the Pillar of cloud was there with them. At the same time that the Angel of the LORD moved from before the camp and went behind them, so did the Pillar of cloud move from in front of them and then it stood behind them. What this reveals to me is that the LORD was leading them with His Rod that was going in front of them and when the Rod moved behind them, the cloud also moved behind them because the LORD was *"in"* the cloud. This cloud gave light to them by night.

Now it is interesting that there are two types of nerve cells in the human eye called the *"rods and cones."* They both help the eye to adapt to light. From what I understand, *the cones are sensitive to bright light and the rods function in the dim or darker light,"* helping us to see properly when it is dark. So the Rod of God performs like the rods that are in our eyes. Yeshua is, therefore, the light in the darkness as the Pillar of cloud!

Pillar of cloud Photo ©2013 Kimberly K Ballard All Rights Reserved

Exodus 14:19-21 *And the Angel of God which went before the camp of Israel removed and went behind them; and the Pillar of the Cloud went from before their face, and stood behind them; And it came between the camp of the Egyptians and the camp of Israel; and it was a cloud and darkness to them, but it gave light by night to these; so that the one came not near the other all the night.*

Nehemiah 9:12 *Moreover thou leddest them in the day by a cloudy pillar; and in the night by a pillar of fire, to give them light in the way wherein they should go.*

Nehemiah 9:19 *Yet thou in thy manifold mercies forsookest them not in the wilderness; the pillar of the cloud departed not from them by day, to lead them in the way; neither the pillar of fire by night, to shew them light, and the way wherein they should go.*

By night the LORD also led the children of Israel in a pillar of fire. The cleft tongues of fire upon Yeshua's disciples in Jerusalem gave them the mighty power of His Rod.

Acts 2:1-5 *And when the day of Pentecost was fully come, they were all with one accord in one place. And suddenly there came a sound from Heaven as of a rushing mighty wind, and it filled all the house where they were sitting. And there appeared unto them cloven tongues like as of fire, and* ***it*** *sat upon each of them. And they were all filled with the Holy Spirit, and began to speak with other tongues, as the Spirit gave them utterance. And there were dwelling at Jerusalem Jews, devout men, out of every Nation under Heaven.*

Fire Photo ©2014 KK Ballard All Rights Reserved

The account of the disciples, who received the Holy Spirit of the LORD, also occurred another time in the book of Numbers. Again, the Spirit rested upon *the Seventy* just as the LORD sent forth His Spirit in *tongues of fire* and it rested upon each one of His Jewish disciples. Remember that Yeshua also appointed *the Seventy* to go before His face! In the story in the book of Numbers, *the Seventy* began prophesying without ceasing after this encounter happened to them. The same LORD who sent His Spirit down from Heaven to rest upon *the Seventy with Moses* is the same God who sent His Spirit to speak His Word through the mouths of the Jewish disciples of Yeshua and *the Seventy, chosen directly by Messiah Yeshua who is indeed the LORD God of Israel.*

Numbers 11:24-25 *And Moses went out and told the people the Words of the LORD, and gathered the seventy men of the elders of the people, and set them round about the Tabernacle. And the LORD came down in a cloud, and spake unto him, and took of the Spirit that was upon him, and gave it unto the seventy elders; and it came to pass, that when the Spirit rested upon them, they prophesied, and did not cease.*

Luke 10:1 *After these things the LORD appointed other seventy also, and sent them two and two before His face into every city and place, whiter He Himself would come.*

There is a fascinating Scripture that says, *"The LORD descended in the cloud and stood next to Moses and declared the Name of the LORD."*

Exodus 34:5 *And the LORD descended in the cloud, and stood with him there, and proclaimed the Name of the LORD.*

I could now understand this Scripture because if the LORD came and stood and then proclaimed the Name of the LORD, this has to be *the Rod Messiah* who is speaking as *the reflection* of the LORD God of Israel. *This is one God!* The Rod declares the Word of God, *the Living Torah*, and He proclaims His own Name, which is seen in *the reflection of His Rod.* The LORD'S Divine Presence descended *in the cloud* from Heaven to dwell upon the Ark of His throne and upon His Seat of Mercy.

Pillar of cloud (roll cloud)

Leviticus 16:2 *And the LORD said unto Moses, Speak unto Aaron thy brother, that he come not at all times into the Holy Place within the veil before the Mercy Seat, which is upon the Ark; that he die not; for I will appear in the cloud upon the Mercy Seat.*

The cloud of the LORD always settled over the tent of the Testimony. Yeshua returns in the cloud because He is the LORD'S own Testimony and the Heavenly Ark.

Ezekiel 10:4-5 *Then the glory of the LORD went up from the cherub, and stood over the threshold of the House; and the House was filled with the cloud, and the court was full of the brightness of the LORD'S glory. And the sound of the Cherubim's wings was heard even to the outer court, as the voice of the Almighty God when He speaketh.*

Exodus 19:9 *And the LORD said unto Moses, Lo, I come unto thee in a thick cloud, that the people may hear when I speak with thee, and believe thee forever. And Moses told the words of the people unto the LORD.*

Israel was to always trust in the LORD'S *salvation, "Yeshua,"* and to follow in *the way* that He would lead, as the Rod of the Good Shepherd gave them meat to eat.

Psalm 78:22-23 *Because they believed not in God, and trusted not in His salvation; Though He had commanded the clouds from above, and opened the doors of Heaven. And had rained down manna upon them to eat, and had given them of the corn of Heaven. Man did eat Angel's food; He sent them meat to the full.*

The LORD looked through the cloud and through the pillar of fire at Pharaoh and the Egyptians and He troubled them. In the book of Revelation, Yeshua's eyes are *like a flame of fire.* So He was in the wilderness, protecting the children of Israel in the pillar of fire and His eyes looked through the cloud troubling the enemies of God.

Exodus 14:24 *And it came to pass, that in the morning watch the LORD looked unto the host of the Egyptians through the pillar of fire and of the cloud, and troubled the host of the Egyptians.*

Revelation 2:14 *His head and His hairs were white like wool, as white as snow; and His eyes were as a flame of fire.*

In Exodus 24 it says that, *"The sight of the glory of the LORD was like devouring fire and Moses went into the cloud!"*

Exodus 24:17-18 *And the sight of the glory of the LORD was like devouring fire on top of the mount in the eyes of the children of Israel. And Moses went into the midst of the cloud, and gat him up into the mount; and Moses was in the mount forty days and forty nights.*

The flaming fire also appeared in the burning bush and the Angel of the LORD spoke with Moses out of the bush that was on fire, but was not consumed.

Acts 7:30 *And when forty years were expired; there appeared to him in the wilderness of Mount Sinai an Angel of the LORD in a flame of fire in a bush.*

The Hebrew word for fire is, *"Esh."* There are a couple of interesting ways to make fire and ironically they both include, *"The use of a Rod!"* One method of making fire is to use a *Rod* of ferrocerium, which is a metal alloy. When *the Rod* is struck by a short piece of steel, sparks descend from it and thus it creates a fire. Another method of making fire is by spinning a short *Rod* with a bow drill. The friction creates sparks. The sparks are then set upon material that will ignite to create a fire. As soon as the spark ignites, you must breathe upon the spark, until it comes to life and grows into a larger fire. As I pondered this in my heart, I began to see that the LORD starts a fire within us with the use of His Rod, by using these exact same methods. After Yeshua the Rod was struck, the spark of life came out of Him. The Holy Spirit breathed upon Him and He came to life, full of the fire of the Holy Spirit that was dwelling inside Him. As believers, we now have the Rod that was struck in Messiah Yeshua. *We represent the material that accepts the spark of life from the Rod of God.* When His Holy Spirit breathes upon us, after the Rod creates the spark in us, His breath ignites *the fire* of the Holy Spirit within us and this fire grows, as He breathes the breath of life into us. Our souls become living souls due to His Holy Spirit that is now residing within us *because of the actions of the spark of the Rod! The Rod of ferrocerium that starts the fire is also called a, "flint."* It just so happens that in the wilderness the rock was struck with the Rod and the Living Water came forth out of this *flinty rock.* All of this was due to the actions of the Rod! ***(Source: Ferrocerium ©2010 en.wikipedia.org/wiki/Ferrocerium, From Wikipedia, the free encyclopedia).***

Psalm 114:7-8 *Tremble, thou earth, at the Presence of the LORD, at the Presence of the God of Jacob; Which turned the rock into standing water, and the flint into a fountain of waters.*

The Hebrews hardened their hearts like a *flint, but the Spirit of the LORD softened it.*

Zechariah 7:12 *Yea, they made their hearts as an adamant stone, lest they should hear the law, and the words which the LORD of Hosts hath sent in His Spirit by the former prophets; therefore came a great wrath from the LORD of Hosts. Therefore it is come to pass, that as He cried, and they would not hear, saith the LORD, so they cried, and I would not hear, saith the LORD of Hosts; But I scattered them with a whirlwind among all nations whom they know not. Thus the land was desolate after them, that no man passed through nor returned; for they laid the pleasant land desolate*

John 11:35-36 *Yeshua wept. Then said the Jews, Behold how He loved him!*

The LORD wept and they would not hear Him, so He scattered them into all nations!

THE LORD IS COMING AGAIN IN THE CLOUD FROM HEAVEN

The glory cloud of the LORD went up from the city of Jerusalem and stood upon the *Mount of Olives* and His glory departed from this place. Yeshua stayed many times in the same place, in the Garden on the *Mount of Olives,* and Yeshua departed in the glory cloud and ascended into Heaven from the *Mount of Olives*. The *Mount of Olives* is considered to be *"east of the city"* because it sits east of the Holy Temple Mount of LORD God of Israel.

Ezekiel 11:23 *And the glory of the LORD went up from the midst of the city, and stood upon the mountain which is on the east side of the city.*

Acts 1:9-12 *And when He had spoken these things, while they beheld, He was taken up; and a cloud received Him out of their sight. And while they looked stedfastly toward Heaven as He went up, behold, two men stood by them in white apparel; Which also said, Ye men of Galilee, why stand ye gazing up into Heaven? This same Yeshua, which is taken up from you into Heaven, shall so come in like manner as ye have seen Him go into Heaven. Then returned they unto Jerusalem from the Mount called Olivet, which is from Jerusalem a Sabbath day's journey.*

Yeshua returns the triumphant *KING OF KINGS* and will set His feet on the very same place on the *Mount of Olives* where His glory departed and He is coming in the cloud again with great blazing glory the next time! The earth will shine brilliantly with His glory.

Mark 14:62 *And Yeshua said, I AM; and ye shall see the Son of man sitting on the right hand of power, and coming in the clouds of Heaven.*

Mark 13:26 *And then shall they see the Son of man coming in the clouds with great power and glory.*

Ezekiel 43:1-7 *Afterward he brought me to the gate, even the gate that looketh toward the east; And, behold, the glory of the God of Israel came from the way of the east; and His voice was like a noise of many waters; <u>and the earth shined with His glory</u>. And it was according to the appearance of the vision which I saw, even according to the vision that I saw when I came to destroy the City; and the visions were like the vision that I saw by the river Chebar; and I fell upon my face. And the glory of the LORD came into the House by the way of the gate whose prospect is toward the east. So the Spirit took me up, and brought me into the inner court; and, behold, the glory of the LORD filled the House. And I heard Him speaking unto me out of the House; and the man stood by me. And He said unto me, Son of man, the place of My throne, and the place of the soles of My feet, where I will dwell in the midst of the children of Israel forever, and My Holy Name, shall the House of Israel no more defile, neither they, nor their kings, by their whoredom, nor by the carcasses of their kings in their high places.*

When Yeshua descends from Heaven *in the cloud,* we will hear the voice and the trumpet call of God. Ezekiel described the God of Israel in the exact same words that also describe Messiah Yeshua. The whole purpose of the prophecy of the book of Revelation is to declare and reveal that Messiah Yeshua is the LORD God of Israel. The word *Apocalypse* means: *"a disclosure of knowledge, a lifting of the veil, or revelation."* When the seventh angel sounds the mystery of God is finished. It is the unveiling of His Divine mysteries. The Second coming of Messiah in the cloud will be a spectacular event that will prove once and for all that Yeshua is the one true Living God of Israel. *The Testimony* was in the tent of meeting with Moses, but *the Living Testimony* of the LORD is the fulfillment of everything!

Luke 2:27-28 *And then shall they see the Son of man coming in a cloud with power and great glory. And when these things begin to come to pass, then look up, and lift up your heads; for your redemption draweth nigh.*

Matthew 26:64 *Yeshua saith unto him, Thou hast said; nevertheless I say unto you, Hereafter shall ye see the Son of man sitting on the right hand of power, and coming in the clouds of Heaven.*

Psalm 57:10 *For Thy mercy is great unto the Heavens, and Thy truth unto the clouds.*

Psalm 99:7 *He spake unto them in the cloudy pillar; they kept His Testimonies, and the ordinance that He gave them.*

Daniel 7:13 *I saw in the night visions, and, behold, one like the Son of man came with the clouds of Heaven, and came to the Ancient of days, and they brought him near before him.*

Revelation 1:5-8 *And from Yeshua Messiah, who is the faithful witness, and the first begotten of the dead, and the Prince of the kings of the earth. Unto Him that loved us, and washed us from our sins in His own blood, And hath made us kings and priests unto God and his Father; to Him be glory and dominion forever and ever. Amen. Behold, He cometh with clouds; and every eye shall see Him, and they also which pierced Him; and all kindred's of the earth shall wail because of Him. Even so, Amen. I AM Alpha and Omega, the beginning and the ending, saith the LORD, which is, and which was, and which is to come, the Almighty.*

MOSES TAKEN UP IN THE CLOUD?

Vortex Cloud, roll cloud & glory clouds with sun

After I wrote this section about the LORD in the glory cloud, to my astonishment, I found an incredible excerpt about Moses that I had never seen before. I became so excited by this excerpt verifying that Messiah Yeshua will rapture the believers in the same glory cloud of the LORD that led Moses and the children of Israel and not in the regular clouds of the sky! As I stated before, when His glory cloud descends from Heaven it will spread out over us and we will simply walk into the cloud and see Him face to face in His glory, at the Last Trump, and take a journey into Heaven!

Even though the Bible records that Moses died, there is another incredible account of what became of Moses, and it was *taken from ancient records obtained by Flavious Josephus*, the first century Jewish Historian. He said in his book that it was written that *"Moses did not die, rather, Moses was taken up in the glory cloud of the LORD into Heaven!"* This would explain why Moses appeared in the glory cloud with Yeshua and Elijah on Mount Sinai when the Messiah was dwelling with us! Josephus wrote, *"It was only out of fear that it was written that Moses died, and because of his virtue he went to God." Incredibly I discovered that "virtue" can mean an order of angels!* In the following account, Moses is telling His beloved friends goodbye and all of a sudden... *The cloud appeared and stood over Moses!*

"Antiquities of the Jews" by Flavious Josephus Book IV, Chapter 8 Section 48

"Now as he went thence to the place where he was to vanish out of their sight, they all followed after him weeping; but Moses beckoned with his hand to those that were remote from him, and bade them stay behind in quiet, while he exhorted those that were near to him that they would not render his departure so lamentable. Whereupon they thought they ought to grant him that favor, to let him depart according as he himself desired; so they restrained themselves, though weeping still towards one another. All those who accompanied him were the senate, and Eleazar the High Priest, and Joshua their commander. Now as soon as they were come to the mountain called Abarim, (which is a very high mountain, situate over against Jericho, and one that affords, to such as are upon it, a prospect of the greatest part of the excellent land of Canaan), he dismissed the senate; and as he was going to embrace Eleazar and Joshua, and was still discoursing with them, a cloud stood over him on the sudden, and he disappeared in a certain valley, although he wrote in the Holy Books that he died, which was done out of fear, lest they should venture to say that, because of his extraordinary virtue, he went to God." ***(Source: © From William Whiston, Translator 1737).***

Wow! If this is true, it would mean that *the cloud of the LORD appeared suddenly and stood over Moses and he disappeared in the cloud!* I love this passage! Yeshua ascended into Heaven the same way. The cloud appeared suddenly and He disappeared in the cloud out of their sight. The rapture will occur exactly the same way! Remember Yeshua's Words about watching and about coming *suddenly?*

Mark 13:32-37 *But of that day and that hour knoweth no man, no, not the angels which are in Heaven, neither the Son, but the Father. Take ye heed, watch and pray; for ye know not when the time is. For the Son of man is as a man taking a far journey, who left His House, and gave authority to His servants, and to every man His work, and commanded the porter to watch. Watch ye therefore; for ye know not when the Master of the House cometh, at even, or at midnight, or at the cockcrowing, or in the morning; Lest coming suddenly He find you sleeping. And what I say unto you I say unto all, Watch.*

When the Heavenly Hosts appeared during Yeshua's birth, they *appeared suddenly* from Heaven and the glory of the LORD shone round about them!

Luke 2:13-14 *And suddenly there was with the angel a multitude of the Heavenly Host praising God, and saying, Glory to God in the highest, and on earth peace, good will toward men.*

This creates such an exciting clear picture of the rapture of the believers in Messiah! When Saul had His Divine encounter with Yeshua on the road to Damascus, it also *happened suddenly!* Saul saw a great light shining round about him from Heaven at about noon, and he heard a voice from Heaven, speaking in Hebrew saying, *"I AM Yeshua of Nazareth, whom thou persecutest."* Saul then goes on to tell us, *"I could not see for the glory of that light!"* This is evidence that Saul saw *the Shechinah glory light of the LORD and Yeshua spoke to him out of the midst of the light.* This event was similar to Daniel's vision of Yeshua, because the people that were with Saul also saw the light and they were afraid, but they did not hear Yeshua's voice. Saul also fell to the ground like Daniel did on his face. Saul, the learned Torah Scholar, immediately said, *"Who art Thou LORD?"* The reply came back, *"I AM Yeshua of Nazareth."* Remember that the voice comes off the Ark of Heaven.

Acts 22:6-11 *And it came to pass, that, as I made my journey, and was come nigh unto Damascus about noon, suddenly there shone from Heaven a great light round about me. And I fell unto the ground, and heard a voice saying unto me, Saul, Saul, why persecutes thou Me? And I answered, Who art Thou, LORD? And He said unto me, I AM Yeshua of Nazareth, whom thou persecutest. And they that were with me saw indeed the light, and were afraid; but they heard not the voice of Him that spake to me. And I said, What shall I do, LORD? And the LORD said into me, Arise, and go into Damascus; and there it shall be told thee of all things which are appointed for thee to do. And when I could not see for the glory of that light, being led by the hand of them that were with me, I came into Damascus.*

In another instance remember, Philip was caught away by the Spirit of the LORD and the Ethiopian eunuch saw him no more! Philip was raptured *suddenly!*

Acts 8:39 *And when they were come up out of the water, the Spirit of the LORD caught away Philip, that the eunuch saw him no more; and he went on his way rejoicing.*

Elijah was taken up alive, without ever dying, in the glory cloud with the chariots of Heaven! Enoch was also taken up to Heaven by faith alive without ever dying. Enoch was not found and neither was the sepulchre of Moses! *Only the LORD knew where He had taken Moses!*

Hebrews 11:5 *By faith Enoch was translated that he should not see death; and was not found, because God had translated him; for before his translation he had this testimony, that he pleased God.*

Now the LORD allowed the eyes of Moses to see the earthly Promised Land from Mount Nebo, but the LORD told Moses in Deuteronomy 34:5-6, *"I have caused thee to see it with thine eyes, but thou shalt not go over thither."* Then the Scripture tells us *"Moses the servant of the LORD died there in the land of Moab, according to the Word of the LORD. And He buried him in a valley in the land of Moab, over against Beth-pe'or; but no man knoweth of his sepulchre unto this day."* So Moses did not get to cross over into the earthly Promised Land. *Instead, Moses suddenly crossed over into the Eternal Promised Land by the Word of the LORD, from the Living Heavenly Ark, who instantly gave Moses Eternal Life and in his glorified body, Moses became like an Angel in Heaven.* So it is interesting to consider what Jude wrote about the body of Moses. First Jude said, *"The Angels did not keep their first estate."* Lucifer had been a covering Angel of the LORD, but he lost his position when he elevated himself above the LORD on God's Holy Mountain.

Ezekiel 28:16 *By the multitude of thy merchandise they have filled the midst of thee with violence, and thou hast sinned; therefore I will cast thee as profane out of the Mountain of God; and I will destroy thee, O covering cherub, from the midst of the stones of fire.*

Jude 6 *And the Angels which kept not their first estate, but left their own habitation, he hath reserved in everlasting chains under darkness unto the judgment of the Great Day.*

Jude 9 and 10 *Yet Michael the archangel, when contending with the devil he disputed about the body of Moses, durst not bring against him a railing accusation, but said, The LORD rebuke thee. But these speak evil of those things which they know not; but what they know naturally, as brute beasts, in those things they corrupt themselves.*

The word *"contending"* in this context means *"To strive or vie in contest or rivalry and to contend with the enemy for control or to argue and strive in opposition against."* So Lucifer or Satan, the fallen covering Cherub, was in rivalry against the body of Moses. *This means that Satan was in competition over Moses! This was a struggle for victory and superiority of a position!* So I now believe that when the LORD took Moses into the Eternal Promised Land into Heaven, Moses was allowed to stand beside the LORD on one side of Yeshua as a *Living Cherubim Angel*, and Moses in his new glorified state may have obtained the former position that was once held by Lucifer before he fell into *"sin,"* and thus the devil was contending over Moses body in rivalry. Remember that *"Sin"* is the name of the moon-god! ***(Source: en.wikipedia.org/wiki/Sin_(mythology)).*** The *"man of sin" (II Thessalonians 2:3),* is now revealed! In Ezekiel 28:2 the LORD called Satan, *"a man"* who was attempting to elevate himself as a god by saying he is greater. Later in Ezekiel 28:14, the LORD said that Lucifer was a covering anointed Cherub who was in Eden on the Mountain of God. It is truly an incredible thought! I say this because Moses appeared standing in his glorified state beside Yeshua on one side during His transfiguration on Mount Sinai and Elijah was standing in his glorified state on the other side of the LORD, as another *Living Cherubim Angel.* Consider Yeshua's Words *"Those who go to Heaven are like the Angels of God in Heaven." Moses represents the Law and Elijah represents the Prophets,* and Yeshua said that on these *"Two Commandments" hang all the Law and the Prophets,* because they stand on either side of the LORD as *two Living Cherubim Angels* who are guardians of the Living Testimony of the LORD. As I was editing this I discovered that *virtue* means *an order of angels*. Moses had extraordinary virtue! By definition *extraordinary* means *"employed for special service."* This is miraculously revealed now as a *"Celestial Hierarchy"* which by definition includes nine orders of angels ranked from lowest to highest and it includes *Cherubim!* ***(Source: Virtue - see Celestial Hierarchy: www.merriam-webster.com/dictionary/).***

Matthew 22:29-33 *Yeshua answered and said unto them, Ye do err, not knowing the Scriptures, nor the power of God. For in the resurrection they neither marry, nor are given in marriage, but are as the Angels of God in Heaven. But as touching the resurrection of the dead, have ye not read that which was spoken unto you by God, saying, I AM the God of Abraham, and the God of Isaac, and the God of Jacob? God is not the God of the dead, but of the living. And when the multitude heard this, they were astonished at his doctrine. But when the Pharisees had heard that He had put the Sadducees to silence, they were gathered together. Then one of them asked Him a question, tempting Him, and saying, Master, which is the greatest Commandment in the Law? Yeshua said unto him, Thou shalt love the LORD thy God with all thy heart, and with all they soul, and with all thy mind. This is the first and great Commandment. And the second is like unto it, Thou shalt love thy neighbour as thyself. On these two Commandments hang all the Law and the Prophets.*

It was not meant to be that Moses should take the people of Israel into the Promised Land, *but it was meant to be that Joshua would accomplish this* because Joshua was the parallel of Messiah Yeshua the LORD, the commander of God's Army, who would take Israel into the Eternal Promised Land in the future! When I found the account of Moses in Josephus and I saw that he went to be with the LORD *in the glory cloud as it overshadowed him,* this gave me such great hope! A new excitement filled my heart with the revelation of *extraordinary virtue!* Moses only wrote in the Torah that he died because he was too humble to say that the LORD raptured him and this is what happened to Elijah! This is why I am certain that Moses and Elijah will come in the cloud as *the two witnesses of the Law and the Prophets* to prepare the way for the arrival of Messiah Yeshua from Heaven and to usher in the Kingdom of God. Now the thought of the rapture in the glory cloud was so much more thrilling to me! Rosh HaShanah is the gathering of people into an assembly, while shouting praises to the KING OF KINGS because we are suddenly standing in His Divine Presence, in the Eternal Promised Land!

I Thessalonians 4:16-18 *For the LORD Himself shall descend from Heaven with a shout, with the voice of the archangel, and with the Trump of God; and the dead in Messiah shall rise first; Then we which are alive and remain shall be caught up together with them in the clouds, to meet the LORD in the air; and so shall we ever be with the LORD. Wherefore comfort one another with these words.*

The truth is that we will go into the glory cloud as it overshadows us. Moses and Elijah will already be standing on either side of the LORD Yeshua, just as they did at the transfiguration on Mount Sinai, and they spoke with the LORD face to face! Now speaking of Yeshua's face, when I obtained permission from Dr. Petrus Soons in 2013 to use his 3-D face image of Messiah Yeshua from the Shroud in my book, I put an effect on the picture of an outer glow line to see what would happen. At that moment I was shocked because it appeared to me that large blue pupils of the eye appeared in the hollow of the eye sockets! The blood appeared red and the outline of His face was in white. Blood was on the end of His nose and the blue color was on the pupils of His eyes! The ancient Sanhedrin records that were said to be kept in the Vatican for several centuries and translated into the book called *"The Archko Volume"* that I read years ago, reported that eyewitnesses 2,000 years ago stated that Yeshua had rather large heavy blue eyes. I promptly sent the photo to Dr. Petrus Soons to show it to him and he gave me his kind permission to include this photo inside my book, which is a black & white version of the picture. I also believe that the Name *"Yeshua"* is written in Hebrew on His neck on the Shroud which I show on the next page. When I put a warm filter on the 3D Shroud photo the face became so real. See the two 3D photos below with warm filter and the glow line and outline photos on the next page. Incredibly, as you know, the LORD also showed me at that time what I showed you in a previous chapter that the large number 3 with the line coming down from it on Yeshua's forehead in blood is an ancient form of the Hebrew letter *"Shin."* This is the Hebrew letter that just so happens to be mounted *on the forehead,* on the shel Rosh or Jewish Tefillin and it is on *Yeshua's forehead* in blood on His burial Shroud, and it has to do with the Name of God, *"Shaddai!"* It is said that the modern shape of the letter *"Shin"* is like a human heart! I mentioned earlier that I made an astonishing connection of this letter to the ancient Hebrew picture language, and this letter on Yeshua's forehead incredibly means *"Pierced, thorn, shepherd who protects His sheep as a shield (see page 165)."* ***(Source: Meaning of the Ancient Hebrew letter Shin - Ancient Hebrew Research Center ©1999-2013 Jeff A. Benner - ancient-hebrew.org/3_sin.html).***

Believe me when I say that the KING is coming in a cloud with exceeding great glory, and we will rejoice singing praises in unison forever in Heaven!

3D Original Hologram Photograph
©2013 Dr. Petrus Soons
from ©1931 Enrie photographs
All Rights Reserved
Edited in Photoshop with a warm filter
by Kimberly K Ballard to show the real face of KING MessiahYeshua! Dedicated to all the Shroud Photographers!

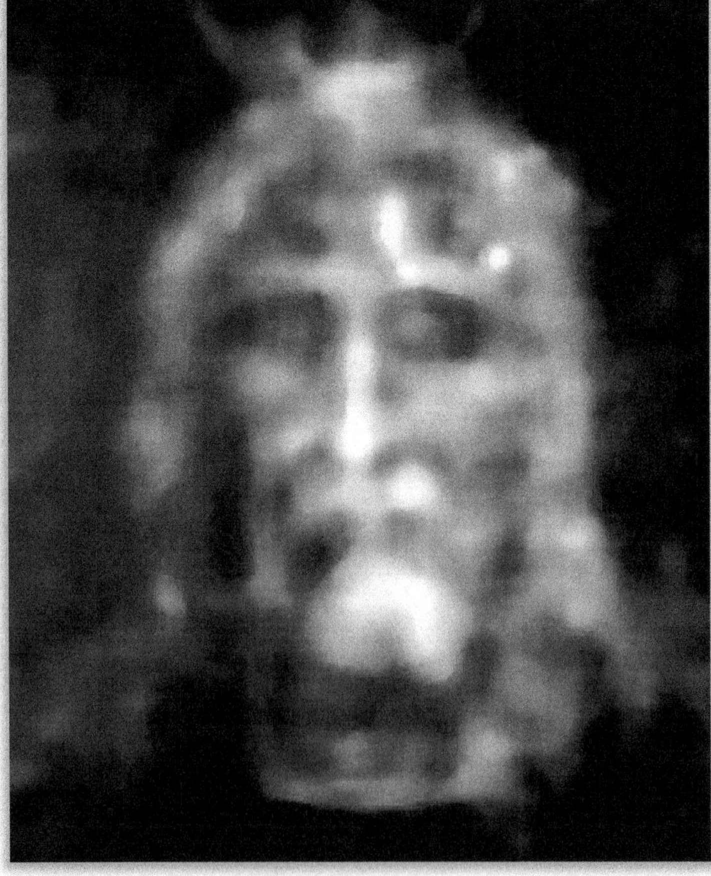

Dr Petrus Soons 3D Hologram of the Shroud face I made the edges glow on his photograph, which I believe miraculously revealed the large pupils of the eyes within the hollow sockets on the Shroud. The left eye is damaged. It was revealed to me at the time of Pentecost or Shavuot 2013. I now believe that the Hebrew word, "Yeshua," is on the neck reading from right to left and is worn at the bottom of the letters. The ancient "Shin" shaped like a number 3 with a line coming down from it, is on Yeshua's forehead in blood! This letter, "Shin" that is also in the Shema prayer, reveals God's heart for us, as the Shepherd of Israel. The, "Shin," reveals that the hand of God is the High Priest of Heaven. The Messiah of Israel is now revealed to the world in a brand new way! The name Yeshua is visible but also has a dot above the Shin and to the left of the Vav letter which I outlined in the above photo

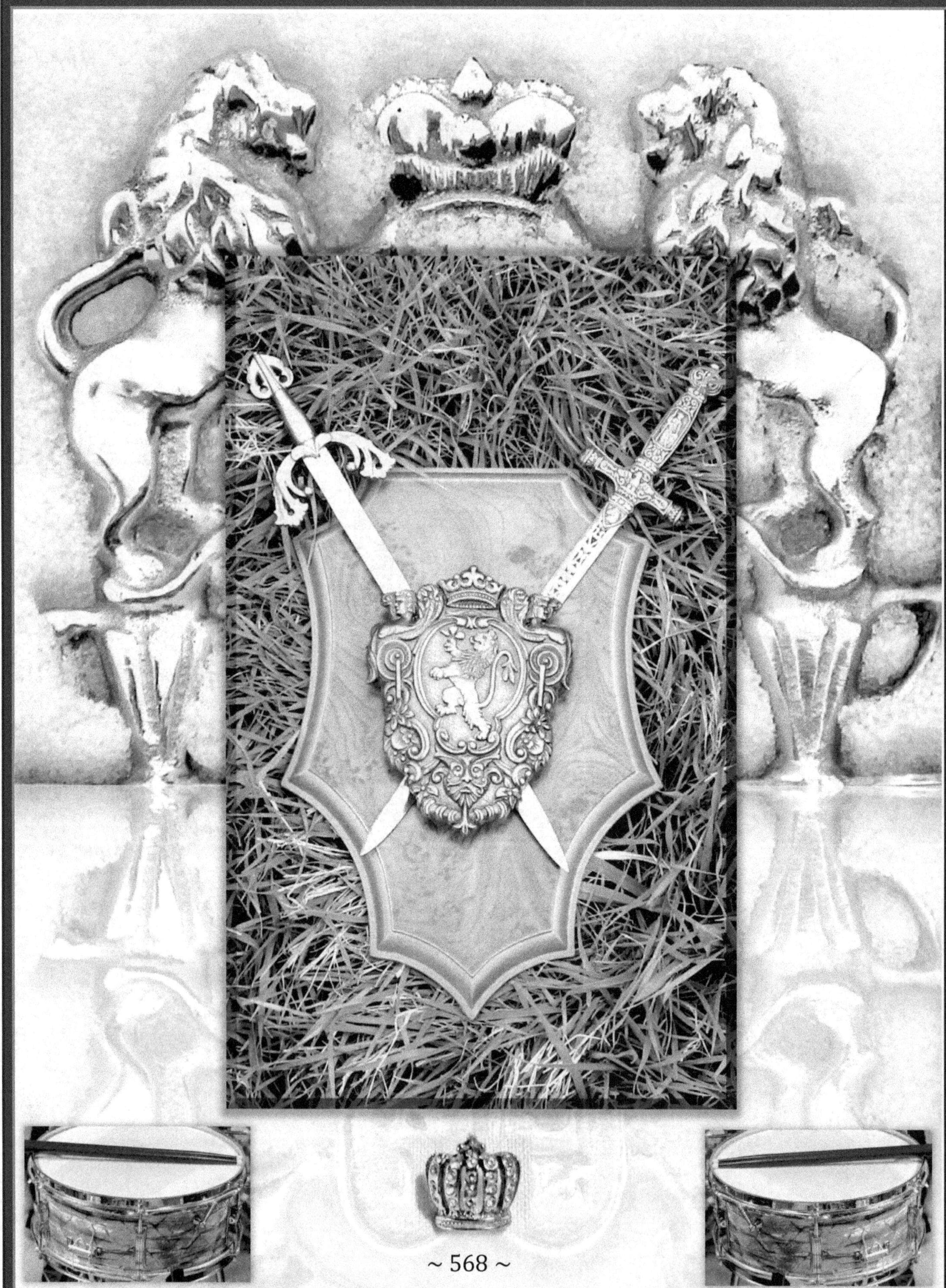

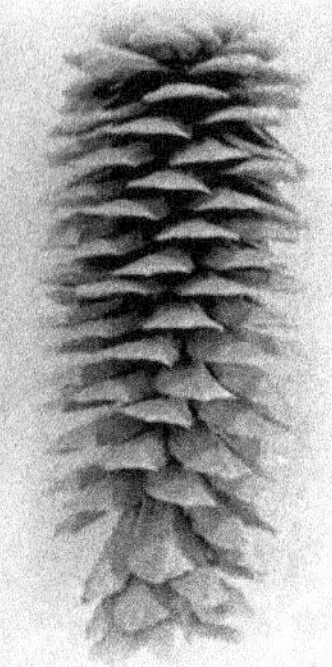
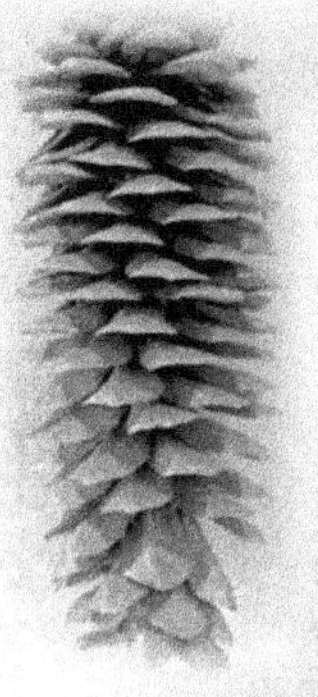

Chapter 11

THE ROYAL SCEPTRE IS THE ROD QUEEN ESTHER REVEALS THE PLAN OF THE KING!

Shield & Swords, Lions, Snare Drum, Snow & Crown Photos ©2013 Kimberly K Ballard All Rights Reserved

How are we to understand the power bestowed upon the Messiah or His authority? From the beautiful book of Esther came the latest revelation to my heart from the Holy Spirit on April 7th and 8th in 2008. Ironically it was shown to me just after the celebration of the holiday of Purim that commemorates Queen Esther. Her real name in Hebrew is *"Hadassah"* which means *"Myrtle Tree."* It is also just before the new month of Nisan when Israel celebrates the Passover. It is often said, that the book of Esther is the only book in the Old Testament that does not mention the LORD God at all. After my revelation of the Almond Tree, the Holy Spirit began to show me that the LORD is indeed written in the book of Esther, but you have to look for Him! It had never occurred to me before, but when I began studying the story carefully, I noticed that the LORD actually hid Himself within the text of the story of Esther. So not only is Esther's life a true historical record of actual events, but I was given the most profound revelation that the LORD used her life *to tell a parable about Himself!* This is the greatest blessing that is now discovered within Esther's story because her life is really *"a parable"* that unveils the salvation plan of the KING OF KINGS, through His Royal Sceptre! Esther's amazing story sheds the greatest light on the reversal of the death decree from Satan in the Garden of Eden. The LORD God is the KING and His reflective Rod, that reveals His KINGLY face, is the Royal Sceptre in His right hand, known as Messiah Yeshua.

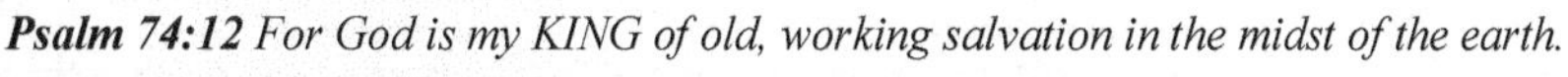

Psalm 74:12 *For God is my KING of old, working salvation in the midst of the earth.*

Psalm 10:16 *The LORD is KING forever and ever; the heathen are perished out of His Land.*

Psalm 47:2 *For the LORD Most High is terrible; He is a Great KING over all the earth.*

Large Sugar-Pinecones & Bristle Cone Pinecone Photos ©2013 Kimberly K Ballard All Rights Reserved

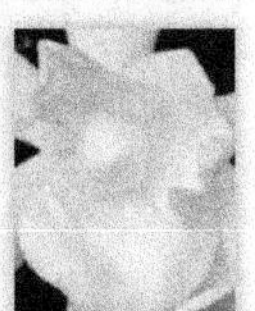

Now as we open the book and begin to read, we find that the KING is holding a Royal Sceptre in His right hand! The Royal Sceptre represents the Rod of God, the Branch that budded from the Almond Tree of Life. It is the Royal Sceptre that reflects the face of the

LORD God of Israel, the KING OF KINGS, who sits on the Ark of His throne of glory. The Royal Sceptre is the *"Sar HaPanim," the Prince of the face of the LORD God!* Through the Heavenly Royal Sceptre that sits on the Ark of His throne, all things are accomplished. Messiah Yeshua is therefore mentioned in the following Messianic prophecy in Genesis. When Yeshua was sent to the earth, He came into the Royal line of King David of the tribe of Judah, and *"Shiloh"* is a direct reference to the Messiah. So the Messiah is the Royal Sceptre of Judah, who gathers His flocks back to Holy Mount Moriah to the well of Salvation.

Genesis 49:10 *The Sceptre shall not depart from Judah, nor a lawgiver from between His feet, until Shiloh come; and unto Him shall the gathering of the people be.*

The design of the Majestic Royal Sceptre was fashioned as a long Rod. The Rod of the Royal Monarch was literally placed on the floor with the tip or point of the Royal Sceptre between the King's feet, and as he held it, he angled it outward toward the right side, as he sat upon his throne. The KING could see His own face in the reflection of His Rod, and this is why the Messiah reveals the face of the LORD God of Israel! Historically, the Royal Sceptre was always held in the right hand of the Sovereign.

Yeshua ascended into Heaven and He is seated as the Royal Sceptre of the KING at the right hand of the Majesty on High, and He will come to rule and reign as the righteous arm of the LORD revealed. Since the Rod of God, the Messiah, is *the Living Torah,* He is the Royal Sceptre that is *"the Lawgiver" between* the KING'S feet. The Royal Sceptre will never depart from Judah because the LORD inherits Judah as His portion and He will make His enemies as His footstool under His feet!

Zechariah 2:11-13 *And many nations shall be joined to the LORD in that day, and shall be My people; and I will dwell in the midst of thee, and thou shalt know that the LORD of Hosts hath sent Me unto thee. And the LORD shall inherit Judah His portion in the Holy Land, and shall choose Jerusalem again. Be silent, O all flesh, before the LORD; for He is raised up out of His Holy habitation.*

In the book of Esther, we see something interesting. When the King in his favor holds out his golden Sceptre to Esther, she is given life and not death! Later in the story, the King stretches out his arm, holding his golden Sceptre in his right hand, in favor again to Esther. Now the Royal Sceptre is made of pure gold *and it is reflective like a mirror, so the King can see the reflection of His own face in His Rod!* The parable reveals that when the King stretches out his arm with the Royal Sceptre in his right hand, he extends the Royal Sceptre to her. In that moment, the King reverses the evil decree of death with his Royal Sceptre that Haman put upon the Jewish people. In this parable, Haman wants to destroy Esther's people, Israel. So the amazing truth is that Haman actually represents Satan *(Sin)* in the Garden of Eden, *who plotted and imposed a death decree upon all mankind and upon every living thing!* Through the centuries, Satan *(Sin)* has tried to blot out Israel because he has been trying to prevent the Messiah, the Royal Sceptre of the Great KING of Judah, from coming to save us and *from reversing the death decree that was placed upon the earth in the beginning!* As Yeshua said in John 4:22 to the Samaritan woman, *"Ye worship ye know not what; we know what we worship; for salvation is of the Jews."* In other words, the Messiah would come in the Royal line of Judah of Israel. So Satan came to make war with the seed of Israel in a grand attempt to stop the redemption of the world. However, the exciting truth is that the Royal Sceptre would be held out and lifted up in the right hand of the KING OF KINGS to reverse the death decree, in the same manner that the King in Esther's story reversed the decree of death that Haman placed

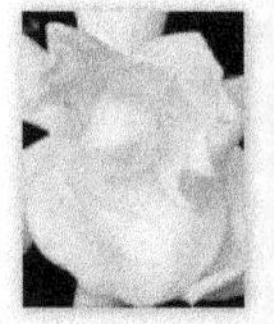

upon Esther and her people, Israel. This is why Messiah Yeshua absolutely had to be lifted up on the cross by the mighty KING Himself because the Royal Majestic Rod of Judah is the Rod of Salvation to Eternal life. Just like Esther's King, the LORD God held out His Royal Sceptre in favor to us and His Rod budded to life because it was the seed, *the Living Torah,* which is *the Lawgiver between the KING'S feet.* This is exactly the reason why Yeshua would not come down from the cross because He did not come to save Himself. The Messiah came to save us and therefore it had to happen this way! The KING'S Royal Sceptre had to be lifted up and stretched out in the right hand of the LORD God to save us from Satan's diabolical plot! Haman, who also hatched a diabolical plot, thought that if he destroyed all the Jews, this would prevent the Messiah of Israel from coming in the future through an unknown Jewish woman.

One of the first instances of this type of plot from Satan occurred when the male Jewish babies were killed by Pharaoh in the Nile River. This was an attempt to prevent the birth of Moses because Moses was a type of Redeemer. Moses was a model, depicting the Messiah who was to come, to take His people into the Eternal Promised Land. The same plot occurred at the birth of Messiah Yeshua. Herod ordered all the male Jewish babies to be slain in Bethlehem and in all the surrounding areas, who were just born and up to two years old. The plot of Satan, once again, was to try to destroy the Redeemer at His arrival, so that He could not fulfill the LORD'S Eternal Living Testimony for Israel and for the whole earth. Satan used the wicked Roman Soldiers to try to prevent the Messiah's plan at the cross, but the LORD had a superior plan that far exceeded the evil plotters. The LORD bore the curse, as our KING, to save us forever! Remember that it is written that Caiaphas, who was the High Priest, even prophesied when he said the following words.

John 11:49-53 *And one of them, named Caiaphas, being the High Priest that same year, said unto them, Ye know nothing at all, Nor consider that it is expedient for us, that one man should die for the people, and that the whole Nation perish not. And this spake he not of himself; but being High Priest that year, he prophesied that Yeshua should die for that Nation; And not for that Nation only, but that also He should gather together in one the children of God that were scattered abroad. Then from that day forth they took counsel together for to put Him to death.*

The LORD caused His people to fulfill His destiny, as He determined it. At this point, *Messiah the Branch was cut off from Israel by the hand of God* and through His servants they knowingly fulfilled the Divine plan of God. The plan of the Great KING was to *lift up His Royal Sceptre* to bear the bitterness of the curse of death, *in the place of the original curse,* in order to bring us the sweetness of the Almond Tree of Eternal life in His Garden on Mount Moriah, as our Passover. In this way, the Great KING OF KINGS saved Israel forever, and the Messiah could gather all of us out of many nations together to be His people! We belong to the LORD! The High Priest Caiaphas prophesied not of himself, but by the Spirit of God that was upon him! *This was the plan of God, the KING, and therefore they took counsel to put the Messiah to death immediately, so that He could save us and give us Eternal life forever.* The Rod of Salvation always must be lifted up to save Israel. So the LORD God made sure that *"Yeshua,"* the Royal Sceptre, was lifted up like the serpent on a pole in the wilderness, so that Satan *(Sin)* would no longer be able to give us his death decree.

It was at this point that it suddenly dawned upon me that *the life blood* of *Yeshua, the Lamb of God,* was supposed to be upon Israel and her children because *the life blood of the LORD would save them forever,* just as Moses put the Lamb's blood on God's people. Remember that *the LORD God also commanded Israel to put the Lamb's blood on the doorposts of their houses, so that death would Passover them.* So now I could comprehend that this Scripture was definitely not offensive at all! It was remarkable! It was fantastic and it was a blessing! *Yeshua's life blood seals us with His new Living Covenant of Eternal life, so death will Passover us.* Now if you read the controversial Scripture in light of what I have just said, you will be blessed when you realize just how magnificently the LORD orchestrated it all because, by Divine Providence, the multitude in Jerusalem asked for Yeshua's blood to be upon

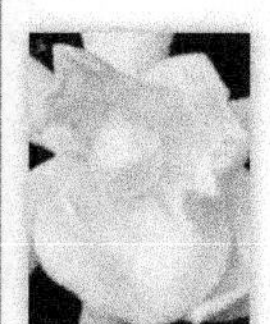

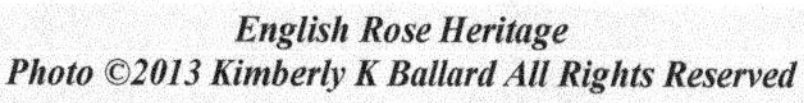

them and their children and this is what saved them eternally! It is fantastic! Pilate, however, washed his hands of the LORD'S life blood and therefore he did not have the Messiah's life blood saving him! You must have the life blood of the Messiah, the Heavenly Lamb of God, upon the doorposts of your heart to have life and not death!

Matthew 27:24-25 *When Pilate saw that he could prevail nothing, but that rather a tumult was made, he took water, and washed his hands before the multitude, saying, I am innocent of the blood of this just person; see ye to it. Then answered all the people, and said, His blood be on us, and our children.*

Now we can clearly understand that having the blood of Messiah the Lamb on Israel and her children is the most excellent thing, and therefore it could never ever be a bad thing. The Lamb of God takes away the sins of the world, and now, by Divine Providence, they have asked for Yeshua's blood to be upon them and their children, just like Israel was commanded by the LORD to put the life blood upon their houses, so that death would Passover them! When these Israelites had the life blood of Messiah, then all Israel would be saved by the Divine will of God, as it written in Romans chapter 11! *We are told not to be ignorant of this mystery!* According to the Word of the LORD, Israel will not see this truth until the times of the Gentiles is fulfilled and then they will understand and see the truth of what it really means for them! Praise God for the great things He has done! Israel has been saved by the blood of the Lamb and this is His Eternal Covenant with them, when He took away their sins!

Romans 11:25-27 *For I would not, brethren, that ye should be ignorant of this mystery, lest ye should be wise in your own conceits; that blindness in part is happened to Israel, until the fullness of the Gentiles be come in. And so all Israel shall be saved; as it is written, There shall come out of Zion the Deliverer, and shall turn away ungodliness from Jacob; For this is My Covenant unto them, when I shall take away their sins.*

The Lamb's life blood is a blessing and not an offense, just as Yeshua proclaimed it!

Matthew 11:6 *And blessed is he, whosoever shall not be offended in Me.*

The LORD raised His Living Branch from the grave by the breath of His own mouth, and, at that moment, the Rod came from death to life *and the curse was reversed by the Royal Sceptre of the KING OF KINGS* in the Garden of God on Holy Mount Moriah. The LORD controlled every circumstance by His own power throughout history and therefore Satan failed and has been defeated by Messiah Yeshua! The Royal Sceptre was victorious in saving Israel and the world from the evil death decree of Satan, in the original place of the Garden of God in Jerusalem. During the tribulation, the time of Jacob's trouble, it is written that Satan will be plotting evil destruction against Israel. It is written that Satan will try to prevent the Messiah of Israel from returning to reign over Jerusalem forever, but there is nothing Satan can do now because the Messiah, the KING of Israel, has already won the victory over him!

Haman, who hatched the plot of destruction in Esther's story, wound up being the one who was destroyed through his own wicked schemes. In the same way, Satan who has plotted and schemed over the centuries, creating chaos, terror, and destruction in people's lives, in the end will meet his own fate of destruction through his own evil works and deeds. The love of God is not in him at all. There is nothing but hatred in the heart of Satan *(Sin)* for all of us. He wants our destruction desperately. He will not prevail. He stole years of my life and my percussion degree, but I am not destroyed!

Remember that Messiah Yeshua the Rod is the one who swallowed up death from the Garden of Eden, just like Aaron's rod swallowed up the serpents of Pharaoh to prove that the powerful Rod of God is the God of Israel who created the universe. *Yeshua reversed the death decree on Holy Mount Moriah in His Garden that had been the Garden of Eden.* This is why

Gardenia Blossom

there is only one way into Heaven. We must come to the LORD through His Rod of Salvation because this is the plan of the Great KING!

In Esther's story, the one law of the King is that *"Anyone who comes to the King in the inner court without being summoned by the King will be put to death, unless the King holds out his golden Sceptre, so that he may live."* Likewise, we have been summoned by the Great KING to come into His inner court because He has held out Messiah, His Royal Sceptre, to us in favor, so that we may also live. The Ark of the Testimony, the LORD KING'S throne, rests in the inner court of His Holy Temple in the Holy of Holies. *Because we have been summoned by the KING OF KINGS, we will enter into His Heavenly Temple to see Him face to face because we have been saved by the Royal Sceptre!* In the following Scripture, we find the account of the Royal Sceptre that gives life in the inner court. In the story, the King must hold out the Sceptre so the person may live and not die and enter His inner court.

Esther 4:11 *All the king's servants and the people of the king's provinces know that for any man or woman who comes to the king to the inner court who is not summoned, he has but one law, that he be put to death, unless the king holds out to him the golden Sceptre so that he may live. And I have not been summoned to come to the king for these thirty days.*

As we look further at Esther's text, there is another astounding parallel to the Messiah, the Royal Sceptre of Judah, in the parable of the King. It was *the third day* when Esther went before the King, obtained his favor, and the King extended the golden Sceptre in his hand to give Esther life and not death!

Esther 5:1-2 *Now it came about on the third day that Esther put on her royal robes and stood in the inner court of the king's palace in front of the king's rooms, and the king was sitting on his Royal throne in the throne room, opposite the entrance to the palace. And it happened when the king saw Esther the queen standing in the court, she obtained favor in his sight; and the king extended to Esther the golden Sceptre which was in his hand. So Esther came near and touched the top of the Sceptre.*

Just like Queen Esther we have been given favor with the KING OF KINGS and have not been condemned to die. *The Royal Sceptre of the LORD God came to life the third day and offered the Eternal First Fruit to all who would eat the Fruit from the Almond Tree of Life. Yeshua appeared alive on the third day and Mary was the first to touch the KING'S Royal Sceptre of Judah for life in the KING'S Garden on Holy Mount Moriah!" When she obtained the KING'S favor, life became sweet.* It is only the LORD God that could encode Himself like this, within the true life parable of Esther! How did Esther obtain the King's favor? She humbled herself before her King by expressing a meek, opened heart full of love towards her King. By doing so, Esther received the King's favor for life instead of for death. This is how we must also come before the KING OF KINGS, into the inner court of His Heavenly Temple to obtain His favor of life through His Royal Sceptre.

Hummingbird & Blush Rose Photos ©2013 Kimberly K Ballard All Rights Reserved

Remember also that when the Rod was lifted up, the veil leading into the inner court of the Holy of Holies was made cleft and now we could come to the KING and enter into His inner Heavenly court, if we humbled ourselves in repentance, showing meekness of heart, in love. *When we have accepted the KING'S Royal Sceptre of favor that has been held out to us for life and not for death, then we can boldly enter into the inner court in Heaven to meet the KING OF KINGS face to face, just like Esther boldly entered into the King's inner court and met him face to face.* Esther did this through bold faith, and so do we, with an expectation of love from the KING. The Great KING is in the Holiest Place,

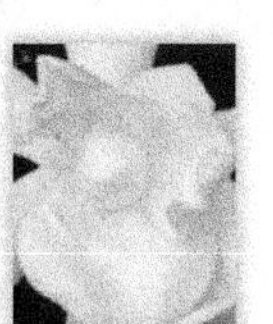

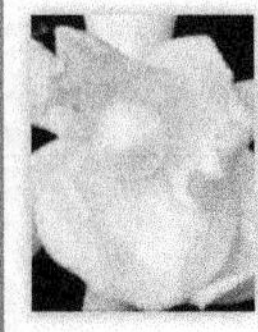

seated between the two Cherubims of His throne. We should come before the KING with holiness, reverence, and with a heart that understands the magnitude of the KING'S Royal position. We must honour His Royal authority.

Hebrews 10:12-22 *But this man, after He had offered one sacrifice for sins forever, sat down on the right hand of God; From henceforth expecting till His enemies be made His footstool. For by one offering He hath perfected forever them that are sanctified. Whereof the Holy Spirit also is a witness to us; for after that He had said before, This is the Covenant that I will make with them after those days, saith the LORD, I will put My Laws into their hearts, and in their minds will I write them; And their sins and iniquities will I remember no more, Now where remission of these is, there is no more offering for sin. Having therefore, brethren, boldness to enter into the Holiest by the blood of Yeshua, By a new and living way, which He hath consecrated for us, through the veil, that is to say, His flesh. And having an High Priest over the House of God; Let us draw near with a true heart in full assurance of faith, having our hearts sprinkled from an evil conscience, and our bodies washed with pure water.*

In the next part of the story of Esther, *the death decree is reversed by the King* and this occurred in the *third* month! It is an interesting historical fact that the evil Haman's father's name was *"Hammedatha" meaning "given by the moon."*

Esther 8:1-8 *On that day did the King Ahasuerus give the house of Haman the Jews enemy unto Esther the Queen, And Mordecai came before the King; for Esther had told what he was unto her. And the King took off his ring, which he had taken from Haman, and gave it unto Mordecai. And Esther set Mordecai over the house of Haman. And Esther spake yet again before the King, and fell down at his feet, and besought him with tears to put away the mischief of Haman the Agagite, and his device that he had devised against the Jews. Then the King held out the golden sceptre toward Esther. So Esther arose, and stood before the King, And said, If it please the King, and if I have found favour in his sight, and the thing seem right before the King, and I be pleasing in his eyes, let it be written to reverse the letters devised by Haman the son of Hammedatha the Agagite, which he wrote to destroy the Jews which are in all the King's provinces; For how can I endure to see the evil that shall come unto my people? Of how can I endure to see the destruction of my kindred? Then the King Ahasuerus said unto Esther the Queen and to Mordecai the Jew, Behold, I have given Esther the house of Haman, and him they have hanged upon the gallows, because he laid his hand upon the Jews. Write ye also for the Jews, as it liketh you, in the King's name, and seal it with the King's ring; for the writing which is written in the King's name, and sealed with the King's ring, may no man reverse.*

The King reversed the curse of death by a decree and the King then sealed it with his signet ring. Once the King sealed the decree for life with his signet ring, the decree could not ever be reversed! So wherever this decree went, there was light, gladness, and joy for the Jewish people because they had the hope of life. This was the King's decree for life. So profoundly enough, the LORD KING also reversed the decree of death from Satan and He sealed it with His signet for life, in the place of His Garden in Holy Mount Moriah where Yeshua was resurrected to life. Now God's decree for Eternal life can never be reversed.

The signet ring is on the KING'S third finger of the right hand! *Now what is remarkable is that the LORD just showed me the signet shaped object at the Garden tomb in Holy Mount Moriah.* Remember that Yeshua is the Yad, the right hand of God and life was sealed by the KING on the third day. When Yeshua came to life the third day, reversing the death decree, *He sealed it with the KING'S signet in the Royal stone of King's, in Holy Mount Moriah.* I believe that this signet is the object that the Jewish Priestly Angel is pointing to with his index finger at the Garden tomb. This is why I believe that *the Angel* is trying to get our attention as *a messenger,* by pointing to the Living Testimony of the KING OF KINGS that I believe was once displayed at the Garden tomb in the niches at *the gate of Heaven.* It is so profound that the LORD brought all this together for such a time as this! This is the signet shaped object that appears to be inscribed with the letters *"Alpha and Omega."* The King's signet had his initials inscribed upon it and our KING is the *"Alpha and Omega."* When the LORD revealed this to me, I knew that this object was extremely significant, for Israel in particular, at the Garden tomb. It is a promise for all who take and eat the First Fruit from the

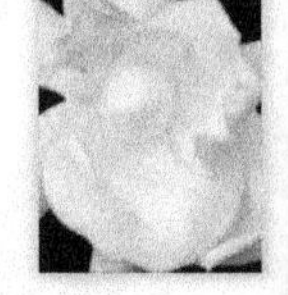

Tree of Life in God's Garden, which is the Word of God, *the Living Torah,* the Lawgiver from the Rod of God, from the KING. This *signet* is a sign of *the seal of the Great KING* that proves that *the reversal of the curse of death took place the third day in God's Garden in Jerusalem.* The King's ring has more significance and I will share this later.

If you do not accept the KING'S Royal Sceptre, as it is lovingly and mercifully held out in favor to you, then what would be the result? Since it is true, that only the Royal Sceptre of the Great KING gives life, then, in essence, you would be rejecting the KING'S mercy, and death would be the only other option for you. This is why Yeshua stated that whoever has Him also has the Father, and whoever has the Father also has the Messiah. *You cannot have the KING without His Royal Sceptre of life, the Rod of Salvation.* The KING rules with His Royal Sceptre in his right hand. We must go through the Royal Sceptre to have life, as we can clearly see in the Gospel of John.

John 14:6 *Yeshua saith unto him, I AM the way, the truth, and the life; no man cometh unto the Father but by Me.*

John 16:28 *I came forth from the Father, and am come into the world; again I leave the world, and go to the Father.*

Remember that Yeshua told us that when we have seen Him, we have seen the one who sent Him!

John 13:45 *And he that seeth Me seeth Him that sent Me.*

I mentioned before *that the Rod reflects and refracts light, which is a mirror or prism of light. He is the molten looking glass! The face of the KING OF KINGS is seen in the reflection of His Royal Sceptre!* If this is truly the case, then Yeshua was telling us the truth when He told us that to see Him is to see the Father. Therefore it is true that when we look upon Yeshua, we have indeed seen the one who sent Him! This means that the image that was left on the Shroud of Yeshua is an exact photographic negative image that becomes a positive image of the face of the KING OF KINGS in His Royal Garden! This explains how the veil is taken away in Messiah. When the veil is taken away, we can see the face of the LORD God of Israel and enter into the KING'S inner court in Heaven. Because the Rod Messiah is a mirror and He reflects the face of the one Sovereign KING who is holding the Royal Sceptre in His hand, Yeshua shows us the face of the one who is looking into it! This is how Moses could speak to the LORD as one speaks to a friend and live and yet at the same time, Moses could not look at God and live! Moses was speaking to the Royal Sceptre, to the reflection Messiah, as the LORD held up His hand or Yad, and Moses wrote about Yeshua! This is why Yeshua said, *"Moses wrote of Me" and He said, "I and the Father are One."* The KING had one plan. That plan was to lift up His Royal Sceptre to save us, just as He did at the Red Sea crossing and just as He did with Queen Esther.

John 5:46-47 *For had ye believed Moses, ye would have believed Me; for he wrote of Me. But if ye believe not his writings, how shall ye believe My Words?*

At first, I thought that maybe this was the end of this story and perhaps there were not anymore hidden things that were contained within Esther's story, but the LORD continued to reveal things to me and it astonished me so much! Now it happened that King Ahasuerus summoned all the virgins to his palace. The King in Esther's story is the Bridegroom! All the virgins who were brought to the King's Royal Palace were to prepare to meet the King because He was looking for a Bride! Now this part of the story is a mirror image of the Great KING who is also the Bridegroom. He is preparing and gathering those who are like the virgins in Esther's story. He is calling those virgins who are pure, holy, and humble of heart. The KING

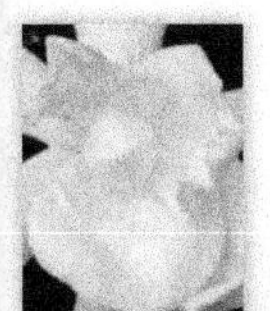

Peony Flower

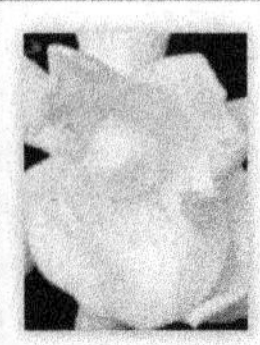

is preparing His future Bride now, so He can take her into the inner chamber of His court, into the Eternal Kingdom of Heaven to be His Eternal Bride. We must be pure, especially in heart, and we must prepare ourselves before we go to meet the KING, just like Esther did! He will come like a thief in the night to steal away His Bride. In the parable of the ten virgins that I mentioned on page 123 the five foolish virgins look like the five wise virgins on the outside but inside they are the parallel opposite of the five wise virgins. The foolish virgins are in the dark. Wheat and tares look alike but the Anti-Christ is their Messiah. The lamps of the five wise virgins have the oil of His Living Spirit lighting them. They are the good wheat and they are ruled by Christ, the Jewish Messiah. The KING will not allow the foolish virgins to enter the KING'S inner chamber to meet Him. They will be cast out to face the judgment. Esther is the Bride in the parable who is taken from among the other virgins, and she was taken into the Bridal chamber and betrothed to the King because she was ready to meet Him! The rest of the virgins never made it into the inner chamber of the King. This part of Esther's story is miraculously parallel to those who prepare themselves to meet the Eternal KING OF KINGS. Esther spent time in prayer and fasting. Remember that the five wise virgins have *the Living Torah,* represented in the number five, and they are betrothed to Messiah Yeshua, the Jewish Bridegroom. By having the Bridegroom, the KING Messiah, we have everything that we need. *We are made ready in His righteousness* to meet the KING face to face. God is our Saviour. When the five wise virgins were summoned by the KING, they went in through the door into His inner chamber and met Him, just like Esther who prepared herself before she was summoned by the King. She only went in to meet the King when he summoned her, which reminds me of the LORD giving us a shout in the rapture. *To be summoned is to have your presence requested before Him.* Esther represents the chosen Bride, like believers are the chosen Bride of Messiah. The third day Esther entered into the inner court and faced the King.

This reminds us that the Sceptre of Judah will return for His Bride Israel on *the third day.* We clearly see that this is true in the passage where Yeshua told the Jews in the Holy Temple to tear down this Temple and He would build it again in three days. The prophecy in Hosea tells us, that in two days the LORD would revive Israel and in *the third day* He would raise her up. The LORD KING will return on the third day and bring the Kingdom of Heaven down to earth and the Bridegroom will marry His Bride in His inner chamber! On the third day, when Yeshua returns, Israel will stand in the inner court and face their KING! Sitting on the KING'S throne will be the Royal Sceptre in His right hand. This is the Royal Sceptre that shall not depart from Judah until Shiloh comes. Then we will look at our KING, knowing that He held out His Royal Sceptre in favor to us, so we could have Eternal life through the love inside His heart. If we think about the Ark, the throne of God, as being set in the inner Holy of Holies with the veil covering the Ark, we can understand that the inner court of the King in Esther's story actually represents the Holy of Holies. So the KING sits upon His Royal throne, in His inner court, *holding His gold reflective and refractive* Royal Sceptre in His right hand, which is *"the Testimony of life"* that was offered to us. We will live by His Royal Standard!

Exodus 40:3 *And thou shalt put therein the Ark of the Testimony, and cover the Ark with the veil.*

Hebrews 6:19-20 *Which hope we have as an anchor of the soul, both sure and stedfast, and which entereth into that within the veil; Whither the forerunner is for us entered, even Yeshua, made an High Priest forever after the order of Melchizedek.*

Exodus 40:20-21 *And he took and put the Testimony into the Ark, and set the staves on the Ark, and put the Mercy Seat above upon the Ark; And he brought the Ark into the Tabernacle, and set up the veil of the covering, and covered the Ark of the Testimony; as the LORD commanded Moses.*

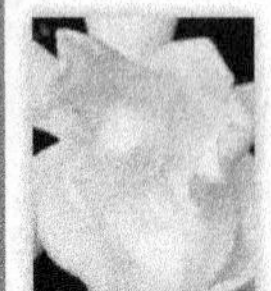

Remember that when Moses spoke with the LORD, his face was shining from *"the reflection"* of the LORD'S glory upon it. Moses then put a veil over his face to speak to the

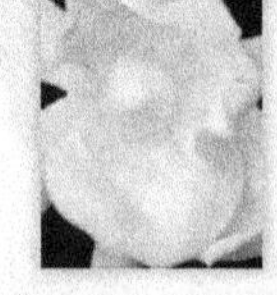

Gardenia Blossom

people, but he removed the veil when speaking with the LORD. *Yeshua removes the veil that allows us to stand before Him to see that He is the KING of glory, and now because this veil is removed in Messiah, we can meet the KING face to face. When the veil is taken away, we can speak to Him in the inner Holy of Holies in His Heavenly Temple.* Moses stood in the inner court of the earthly Tabernacle and he saw the glory of God face to face. Moses, therefore, saw the Heavenly Ark of the Testimony which is the Living Testimony of Messiah Yeshua. The veil is taken away between mankind and the inner court of the KING *through His Royal Sceptre.*

King Ahasuerus had asked Vashti his Queen to come before him, but she would not listen to the King and this enraged him. He cast her out of the kingdom and chose, from amongst the virgins, a Bride who would listen to him. The King wanted a Bride who would love him with all her heart. The LORD has always wanted to become Israel's KING, but instead they asked for an earthly King and they were given King Saul. So the LORD was rejected by His Queen, just like King Ahasuerus was rejected by his Queen. Esther is symbolic of Israel, who the LORD was preparing as His Bride from amongst the virgins. The LORD summoned for them to come and meet their KING and to find His favour, but many of them in that generation would not come and they refused to listen to the KING when He summoned them. Vashti did not listen to the King and she did not come when she was summoned. So it was in Yeshua's generation. At the transfiguration, the voice in the cloud said, *"This is my beloved Son, HEAR HIM."* The KING wants us to hear Him and to listen to Him! Moses told us that when the Messiah would come, we were to *"listen to Him."*

Esther's story is definitely like a parable that Yeshua taught that reveals that He is Israel's KING who has summoned for His Bride, but she would not listen to Him in His generation. The current generation that has been brought back from the nations now has the opportunity to listen to the KING, but will they accept Him and prepare themselves to meet Him? In Yeshua's parable, the KING was enraged because those who were invited to the wedding feast were unwilling to come when He called. *Yeshua is the KING and the Son in His parable who summoned His Bride.*

Matthew 22:1-14 *And Yeshua answered and spake unto them again by parables, and said, The Kingdom of Heaven is like unto a certain KING, which made a marriage for His Son, and sent forth His servants to call them that were bidden to the wedding; and they would not come. Again, He sent forth other servants, saying Tell them which are bidden, Behold, I have prepared My dinner; My oxen and My fatlings are killed, and all things are ready; come unto the marriage. But they made light of it, and went their ways, one to his farm, another to his merchandise; And the remnant took His servants, and entreated them spitefully, and slew them. But when the KING heard thereof, He was wroth; and He sent forth His armies, and destroyed those murderers, and burned up their city. Then saith He to His servants, The wedding is ready, but they which were bidden were not worthy. Go ye therefore into the highways, and as many as ye shall find, bid to the marriage. So those servants went out into the highways, and gathered together all as many as they found, both bad and good; and the wedding was furnished with guests. And when the KING came in to see the guests, He saw there a man which had not on a wedding garment; And He saith unto him, Friend, how camest thou in hither not having a wedding garment? And he was speechless. Then said the KING to the servants, Bind him hand and foot, and take him away, and cast him into outer darkness; there shall be weeping and gnashing of teeth. For many are called, but few are chosen.*

When KING Messiah Yeshua came into Jerusalem in His generation, many did not prepare themselves in John's baptism of living water. John was sent as the messenger to make the Messiah known to Israel and to prepare the way of the Heavenly Living Ark of the Testimony that stood in the Jordan River, but some absolutely refused to listen to their KING! The Pharisees and lawyers rejected the counsel of God in this matter!

Luke 7:29-30 *And all the people that heard him, and the publicans, justified God, being baptized with the baptism of John. But the Pharisees and lawyers rejected the counsel of God against themselves, being not baptized of him.*

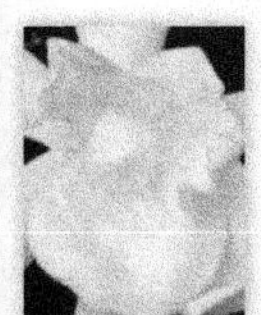

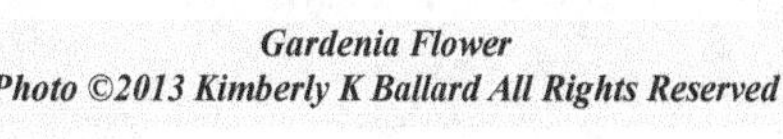
Gardenia Flower

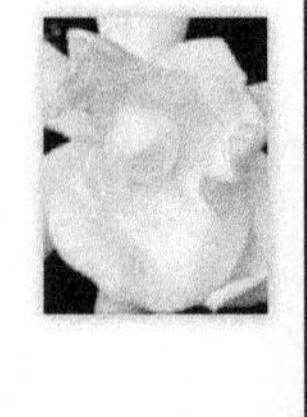

The KING sent His Son to call those who were chosen to Himself. This is the King in Esther's story with His Royal Sceptre, calling for Vashti the Queen. The Messiah's generation did not listen to Him and they went their own way. In the parable, it says that the KING was enraged and He sent his armies to destroy those murderers and set their city on fire. The LORD is obviously talking about the siege and burning of the city of Jerusalem, along with the Second Holy Temple, because His generation refused to come when the KING summoned them. They did not hear when the KING wept. So the KING in His mercy invited others to the wedding feast. In the parable, the KING sent out His servants to gather others unto Himself who would listen to Him and who would love Him with all their heart. These are the virgins who are willing to prepare themselves to meet the KING and to come into His wedding feast that was prepared. They first had to wash in the Living Water to be purified, so they had on a white wedding garment. Anyone that was willing to come when the KING summoned, even if they were not originally invited, could now be part of the Royal Wedding Party. So every person now must get ready, just as a Bride gets ready for her wedding day, to meet the Bridegroom when He summons for her. It does not matter whether they are Jewish or Gentile, but if we refuse to listen to the KING, then, like Vashti, we will be cast out of the Wedding Feast, out of the Wedding Party, and out of the Kingdom, just like those in Yeshua's generation who refused to come when the KING summoned for them because the Kingdom of Heaven was truly at hand.

What will this generation do? Will they be any different? Will Israel open her heart and come when the KING summons her into His inner court? I believe in my heart that this time it will happen! This time it will be different! The LORD God said that He will be KING over Israel forever and that their eyes have been veiled for a time, but this veil is taken away in Messiah. I truly believe with all my heart that this generation will prepare their hearts to meet the KING OF KINGS in the inner court of His Holy Temple, in the Heavenly Kingdom of God. Not only does Israel need to prepare her heart today to meet the KING, but He will have mercy on everyone that comes to Him and prepares before hand to meet Him face to face. Remember that the LORD uses His Rod to chasten everyone that He loves! He has used His Rod, the Messiah Yeshua, to chasten Israel, because He loves her with His whole heart!

I John 4:7-16 *Beloved, let us love one another; for love is of God; and every one that loveth is born of God, and knoweth God. He that loveth not knoweth not God; for God is love. In this was manifested the love of God toward us, because God sent His only begotten Son into the world, that we might live through Him. Herein is love, not that we loved God, but that He loved us, and sent His Son to be the propitiation for our sins. Beloved, if God so loved us, we ought also to love one another. No man hath seen God at any time. If we love one another, God dwelleth in us, and His love is perfected in us. Hereby know we that we dwell in Him, and He in us, because He hath given us of His Spirit. And we have seen and do testify that the Father sent the Son to be the Saviour of the world. Whosoever shall confess that Yeshua is the Son of God, God dwelleth in him, and he in God. And we have known and believed the love that God hath to us. God is love; and he that dwelleth in love dwelleth in God, and God in him.*

Matthew 23:36-46 *Master, which is the great Commandment in the Law? Yeshua said unto him, Thou shalt love the LORD thy God with all thy heart, and with all thy soul, and with all thy mind. This is the first and great Commandment. And the second is like unto it, Thou shalt love thy neighbour as thyself. On these two Commandments hang all the Law and the Prophets. While the Pharisees were gathered together, Yeshua asked them, Saying, What think ye of Messiah? Whose Son is He? They say unto Him, The Son of David. He saith unto them, How then doth David in Spirit call Him LORD, saying, The LORD said unto my LORD, Sit Thou on My right hand, till I make Thine enemies Thy footstool? If David then call Him LORD, how is He His Son? And no man was able to answer Him a word, neither durst any man from that day forth ask Him anymore questions.*

Jude 1:21 *Keep yourselves in the love of God, looking for the mercy of our LORD Yeshua Messiah unto eternal life.*

The answer is simple. The Royal Sceptre of the KING is the Messiah. *He is the image of the face of KING OF KINGS AND LORD OF LORDS,* but this KING has more *Royal Regalia* besides His Royal Sceptre!

Gardenia Flower
Photo ©2013 Kimberly K Ballard

A KING'S REGALIA

A King's Regalia include all the emblems or ensigns of His Royalty. These include, *"the Sceptre, the Sword, the Crown, and the King's engraved Signet Ring."* Each one of these emblems reveals a certain aspect of the King's power and authority. In this chapter, I will be unveiling how each one of these emblems reveals that the Messiah is the right hand of the Majesty on High.

The LORD of Hosts is the KING who rules with His Righteous right hand. The Royal emblems that are called *"ensigns"* of the KING'S Royal Regalia are used in very specific ways. I want to share what the Royal Regalia reveals about the Messiah. Yeshua is the Royal Sceptre of Judah and *He is the Royal Ensign or Emblem of the Royal Sovereign,* the KING OF KINGS in Heaven. Yeshua is the root of Jesse and *the ensign* that was spoken about in the book of Isaiah.

Isaiah 11:10 *And in that day there shall be a root of Jesse, which shall stand for an ensign of the people; to it shall the Gentiles seek; and His rest shall be glorious.*

Now I talked earlier about this passage that tells us that this root of Jesse would stand for an ensign and that the Gentiles would seek it. *The Royal Sceptre of the KING is the Royal Rod of God.* This is the Monarch's Royal ensign. The Gentiles have been seeking Yeshua for two thousand years. Those who believe in the Messiah of Israel will be given His rest at His glorious appearing. *A Royal ensign of the Royal Regalia is the symbol of the Royal Office of His Majesty, the Supreme Monarch.*

Now I discovered more proof that *Yeshua is the Royal ensign of the KING.* There was a time when the anger of the LORD was kindled against His people and the LORD said that *He would lift up an ensign to the nations from afar and He would bring invaders into His land.* They would cleanse the land of those doing wicked deeds. The LORD said that none of the people would stumble in this endeavor and *"not even the latchet of their shoes would be broken or loosed."*

Isaiah 5:26 *And He will lift up an ensign to the nations from far, and will hiss unto them from the end of the earth; and, behold, they shall come with speed swiftly; None shall be weary nor stumble among them; neither shall the girdle of their loins be loosed, nor the latchet of their shoes be broken; Whose arrows are sharp, and all their bows bent, their horses' hoofs shall be counted like flint, and their wheels like a whirlwind.*

So John the Baptist actually revealed that Messiah Yeshua was *the Royal ensign of the House of David, the KING of Glory,* when he said the following words to the Soldiers who came to question him about whether or not he was the Messiah. John said that one was coming who was *"Mightier than I."* Then John said, *"The latchet of whose shoes I am not worthy to unloose."* With this statement, John revealed that Messiah, *the Royal ensign of the Sovereign KING,* was coming soon and this Royal ensign, the Rod of God, would be lifted up, so that all nations would be drawn to come into His land. This would only happen after Messiah Yeshua, *the Royal ensign of the Great KING, was lifted up on display* and this would draw all men and

women to the LORD, to the Holy city of Jerusalem in the Holy Land of Israel! Then in the year 70AD, forty years after Yeshua ascended up into Heaven, the Romans flooded the city of Jerusalem and burned the Holy Temple to the ground and from that time forward, thousands upon thousands of foreign invaders came into the Holy Land of Israel!

Matthew 24:1-2 *And Yeshua went out, and departed from the Temple; and His disciples came to Him for to shew Him the buildings of the Temple. And Yeshua said unto them, See ye not all these things? Verily I say unto you, There shall not be left here one stone upon another, that shall not be thrown down.*

Nothing could prevent all the different nations from coming to Jerusalem after the Royal ensign of the KING OF GLORY was lifted up on His Holy Mount Moriah in the place of the former Garden of Eden! Now everyone would believe the LORD'S Living Testimony and all people, tribes, and tongues would return to God *through the way of righteousness, which is the Living Torah,* to the Great KING OF KINGS. Only through His righteousness would they be able to enter the Heavenly Kingdom of God and the new Heavenly Garden of the New Jerusalem. So the LORD put it within the heart of all the people of the earth to come to Israel!

Luke 3:14-18 *And the soldiers likewise demanded of him, saying, And what shall we do? And he said unto them, Do violence to no man, neither accuse any falsely; and be content with your wages. And as the people were in expectation, and all men mused in their hearts of John, whether he were the Messiah, or not; John answered, saying unto them all, I indeed baptize you with water; but one mightier than I cometh, the latchet of whose shoes I am not worthy to unloose; He shall baptize you with the Holy Spirit and with fire; Whose fan is in His hand, and He will thoroughly purge His floor, and will gather the wheat into His garner; but the chaff He will burn with fire unquenchable. And many other things in his exhortation preached he unto the people.*

THE ROYAL SCEPTRE THE EMBLEM OF A KING THAT GIVES HIM ALL POWER AND AUTHORITY!

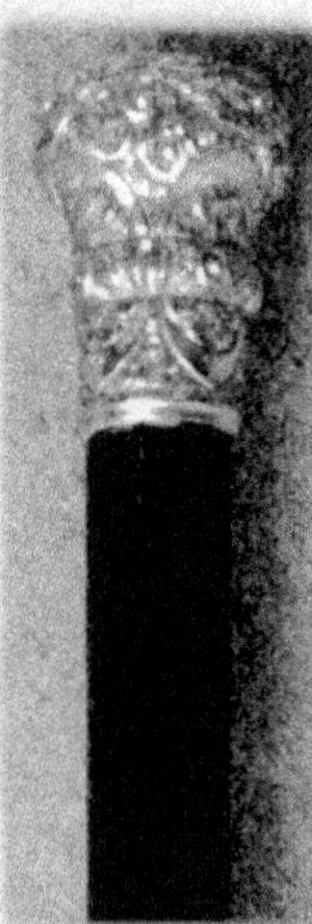

The first emblem or ensign of the Royal KING that I want to discuss is of course the Royal Sceptre. Now I first proposed the question, *"How are we to understand that Yeshua has all power and authority?"* The answer is simple! When a King or Sovereign holds the Royal Sceptre in His right hand, *the Royal Sceptre itself is the sign of all power and authority of the KING that he uses to rule His Kingdom!* The Living Rod is therefore *"the Royal Sceptre"* in the right hand of the KING, full of all power and authority. This is why Yeshua is seated at the right hand of the Majesty on High in the Heavenly Kingdom. Yeshua spoke to the Elders, to the Chief Priests, and to the Scribes at the Holy Temple and He revealed to them that He is the Eternal Royal Sceptre of Judah of the Davidic Dynasty.

Luke 22:67-69 *Art thou the Messiah? Tell us, And He said unto them, If I tell you, ye will not believe; And if I also ask you, ye will not answer Me, nor let Me go. Hereafter shall the Son of man sit on the right hand of the power of God.*

On Coronation Day, the Monarch, whether a Queen or a King, *holds the Royal Sceptre in their right hand during the Coronation Ceremony.* The Coronation Day of the KING OF KINGS is during Rosh HaShanah. Special prayers are spoken by Israel on Rosh HaShanah to Coronate God as their KING and the heralding trumpet is blown. Usually there are many heralding trumpets sounding a fanfare. This KING holds a Royal Sceptre in His right hand called *"the Rod of Salvation."* This is the precise reason that Yeshua told the Jews in Jerusalem, *"All power and authority has been given to Me."* The Words of the Messiah of Israel declare boldly *that He is the Royal Sceptre that saves and brings justice to the earth!*

Matthew 28:18 *And Yeshua came and spake unto them, saying, All power is given unto Me in Heaven and in earth.*

Hebrews 1:1-3 *GOD, who at sundry times and in divers manners spake in time past unto the fathers by the Prophets, Hath in these last days spoken unto us by His Son, whom He hath appointed heir of all things, by whom also He made the worlds; Who being the brightness of His glory, and the express image of His person, and upholding all things by the Word of His power, when He had by Himself purged our sins, sat down on the right hand of the Majesty on High.*

Now it is very interesting to see the definitions contained within the word *"Sceptre."* Clearly the Sceptre by definition reveals that *this Rod is the symbol of all power and authority* of the KING, but is known also as the King's *"staff."* It literally means *"to clothe with Authority."* The Sceptre is defined as *"the Royal emblem of the Sovereign Office of the Royal KING and it is the sign of His power."*

Definition of Sceptre (British version) or Scepter (American English version);

1. A rod or wand borne in the hand as an emblem of regal or imperial power.
2. royal or imperial power or authority; sovereignty.
3. to give a sceptre to; invest with royal authority ***(Source: Definition of Scepter from the Random House College Dictionary revised edition, ©1975 by Random House, Inc.).***

A Sceptre is held in the right hand. In Greek the word *"Sceptre"* is *"skeptrom"* which means *"Staff or Stick."* This is why David wrote, *"Thy Rod and Thy Staff, they comfort me." King David knew this Royal protocol.* The Royal Rod gives Messiah the Priesthood and because He is the Royal Sceptre of the Sovereign, this means that He is the KING who is gloriously invested with all power and authority in His Imperial Kingdom! Remember that Yeshua purchased us with a price. So the KING purchased us as His Bride, *"as the profitable returns for His Eternal Kingdom of Heaven."*

To Invest with Authority; Invest;

1 To put to use by purchase or expenditure, in something offering profitable returns.
4 To furnish with power, authority, rank, etc.
9 To install in an office or position
10 To clothe ***(Source: Definition from the Random House College Dictionary revised edition, ©1975 by Random House, Inc.).***

Isaiah 61:10-11 *I will greatly rejoice in the LORD, my soul shall be joyful in my God; for He hath clothed Me with the garments of Salvation, He hath covered me with the robe of righteousness, as a Bridegroom decketh Himself with ornaments, and as a Bride adorneth herself with her jewels. For as the earth bringeth forth her bud, and as the Garden causeth the things that are sown in it to spring forth; so the LORD God will cause righteousness and praise to spring forth before all the nations.*

It was only when I understood that *a King's Sceptre was the sign of all power and authority,* that I finally understood Yeshua's Words when He made the statement that all power and authority has been given to Him. Yeshua was telling the absolute truth when He said these Words. The Jews in Jerusalem also said this about Yeshua! *The Jews said that Yeshua, "Spoke as one having Authority and not like the Scribes!"* This is because *He is the Living Torah* and they were astonished at His doctrine!

Mark 1:22 *And they were astonished at His doctrine; for He taught them as one that had Authority, and not as the Scribes.*

Matthew 7:29 *For He taught them as one having Authority, and not as the Scribes.*

John 5:25-27 *Verily, verily, I say unto you, The hour is coming, and now is, when the dead shall hear the voice of the Son of God; and they that hear shall live. For as the Father hath life in Himself; so hath He given to the Son to have life in Himself; And hath given Him Authority to execute judgment also, because He is the Son of man.*

This passage that says that Yeshua has been given *"Authority to execute judgment"* is provable. This brings us back to my chapter on *the Roman Military Standards* that were a type of mockery of *God's Royal Standards* and to the fact that a Royal emblem or ensign of the Sovereign King can be used as *"His Standard." God's Standard is the Living Ark and the lifted up budded Almond Rod of God, the Living Torah, bearing His own image as the Commander of His Heavenly Army!* Isaiah also spoke about *"The Standard"* for the people. Then in the following verse after Isaiah mentions *"The Standard,"* he said that the LORD hath proclaimed unto the end of the world and to the daughters of Zion the Words, *"Behold Thy Salvation cometh; and behold His reward is with Him."* So the Salvation that cometh is the Royal Sceptre of the LORD who is, *"The Standard of the Royal Regalia of the Royal Sovereign, The KING OF KINGS."* We see that this is true in the following Scripture, written in Isaiah 63.

Isaiah 63:10-11 *Go through, go through the gates; prepare ye the way of the people; cast up, cast up the highway; gather out the stones; lift up a Standard for the people. Behold, the LORD hath proclaimed unto the end of the world, Say ye to the daughters of Zion, Behold, thy Salvation cometh; behold, His reward is with Him, and His work before Him.*

It is interesting that by definition the word *"Standard"* actually does contain elements pertaining to the Messiah of Israel!

Definition of "Standard"
2. Anything, as a rule or principle, that is used as a basis for judgment.
4. Standards, morals, ethics, habits, etc., established by authority, custom, or an individual acceptance.
10. A flag indicating the presence of a Sovereign or public official.
11. A flag, emblematic figure, or other object used as the emblem of an army.
12. Something that stands or is placed upright.
14. Hort., a plant trained or grafted to have a single, erect, treelike stem.
2. *gauge, basis, pattern, guide, STANDARD, criterion refers to the basis for making a judgment.*
A Standard is an authoritative principle or rule that usually implies a model or pattern for guidance, by comparison with which the quantity, excellence, correctness, etc., of other things may be determined. ***(Source: Definition from the Random House College Dictionary revised edition, ©1975 by Random House, Inc.).***

Now if the *Standard* of the LORD is *the measure of His Rod,* then all His *morals, rules, and principles* are determined as the measure of His judgment. In other words, the LORD Messiah, *The Living Torah,* is the model or pattern of the earthly Torah that is used for our guidance, excellence, and correctness. What I find interesting about this is that, in the passage that speaks about the future Temple, it is *measured by a Rod.* The Messiah is building this Heavenly Temple with Living Stones because He is *"The Standard"* of its measure and whenever you see this *Standard,* it indicates *"The Divine Presence,"* of His Royal Highness and Majesty, the KING OF KINGS. This is apparent in the pattern of the Royal protocol of Her Royal Highness and Majesty, Queen Elizabeth II of England UK. Whenever the *Standard* of Her Royal Highness and Majesty the Queen, is raised up on the Rod, this means that she is in residence and that her presence is there in her castle. So when His Royal Highness and Majesty, the KING OF KINGS AND LORD OF LORDS, raised up His Royal Standard on the Rod, this also indicated that *the KING'S Divine Presence was in residence* and that His Presence was in His castle, which in Messiah Yeshua's case would be the Holy Temple in Jerusalem! This is the Royal residence of His Royal Highness and Majesty, the KING OF KINGS AND LORD OF LORDS! The KING was dwelling in our midst, *raising His Standard, the Living Torah,* so the entire world would return to *the ensign* of the KING'S *Royal Standard.* Yeshua is the *"stem of Jesse from the Almond Tree of Life,"* and this is one of the definitions of a *Standard, "A Treelike Stem!"* The Messiah is consequently *Israel's Standard* or *Emblematic figure of the Army of God.* So the Rod, *"The Standard,"* is lifted up to perform the battle maneuvers of the KING. In the following Scripture in Isaiah, the LORD God spoke these Words, saying that He would *"lift up His hand to the Gentiles and set up His Standard to the people."* So the *Standard* in the hand of the KING is the Rod lifted up in His hand.

Isaiah 49:22-23 *Thus saith the LORD God, Behold, I will lift up mine hand to the Gentiles, and set up My Standard to the people; and they shall bring thy sons in their arms, and thy daughters shall be carried upon their shoulders. And Kings shall be they nursing fathers, and their Queens thy nursing mothers; they shall bow down to thee with their face toward the earth, and lick up the dust of thy feet; and thou shalt know that I AM the LORD; for they shall not be ashamed that wait for Me.*

God's *Standards* are therefore measured by His Royal Sceptre, by the Rod in His right hand. Messiah Yeshua is this Royal Sceptre of Judah, as the head of God's Army. He is *"the Standard by which the Armies in Heaven follow behind Him on pure white horses."* Their collars say *"Holiness to the LORD!"* We find this in the book of Revelation. As the Royal Sceptre is *the Living Torah,* He is called *"the Right Sceptre,"* mentioned in the Psalms.

Psalm 45:6 *Thy throne, O God, is forever and ever; the Sceptre of Thy Kingdom is a right Sceptre.*

When the LORD'S Sceptre comes in the future judgment, it will be based upon the LORD'S *Standards, rules, and principles* that He instructed us to obey. He will rule with a *"Rod of iron."* The term, *"Rod of iron,"* is interesting because the majority of the earth's inner and outer core is made of iron. So this means that the Royal Sceptre, the Rod of God, is going to rule the entire earth that is made of iron and He will rule the entire universe.

Revelation 19:10-16 *And I fell at his feet to worship him. And he said unto me, See thou do it not; I am thy fellow servant, and of thy brethren that have the Testimony of Yeshua; worship God; for the Testimony of Yeshua is the Spirit of Prophecy. And I saw Heaven opened, and behold a white horse; and He that sat upon him was called Faithful and True, and in righteousness He doth judge and make war. His eyes were as a flame of fire, and on His head were many crowns; and He had a Name written, that no man knew, but He Himself. And He was clothed with a vesture dipped in blood; and His Name is called The Word of God. And the armies which were in Heaven followed Him upon white horses, clothed in fine linen, white and clean. And out of His mouth goeth a sharp sword, that with it He should smite the Nations; and He shall rule them with a Rod of iron; and He treadeth the winepress of the fierceness and wrath of Almighty God. And He hath on His vesture and on His thigh a Name written, KING OF KINGS, AND LORD OF LORDS.*

"The vesture" that the Messiah is wearing that is dipped in blood means that He is *"Clothed with Authority"* because the life blood of the Lamb purifies us from our sins. The Official Royal Title that is written on the KING'S vesture and on His thigh is *"KING OF KINGS AND LORD OF LORDS."* The white horses and the Armies of Messiah Yeshua that are dressed in white linen, indicate the purity of *"The Standard"* of the LORD God. So *The Royal Standard of God* is found within the pattern of Aaron's rod that budded to life and so this

pattern is the criterion for making judgment. In the book of Joel, the LORD speaks *"The Word"* to execute His judgment. This all verifies that the Word of God is *the Living Torah* and the Living Branch that was *"The Standard of the Royal Sceptre of righteous judgment that was lifted up for our salvation!"*

Joel 2:10-11 *The earth shall quake before them; the Heavens shall tremble; the sun and the moon shall be dark, and the stars shall withdraw their shining; And the LORD shall utter His voice before His Army; for His camp is very great; for He is strong that executeth His Word; for the day of the LORD is great and very terrible; and who can abide it?*

For this reason, *the power and authority of the Royal Rod of God,* who speaks His Word, performs all the miracles of the Great KING.

Luke 4:36 *And they were all amazed, and spake among themselves, saying, What a Word is this! For with Authority and Power He commandeth the unclean spirits, and they come out.*

In this next Scripture, the Centurion asked Yeshua to simply speak *"the Word"* to heal his servant. So this Centurion realized that *Yeshua was the Royal Sceptre of God, who had the power and authority just by speaking with His voice, to perform the miracles of God.* He must have known that Yeshua was *"the Standard of the Heavenly Army"* because he said *that he too was a man of Authority, having soldiers under him!* The Centurion also called Yeshua, *"LORD!" When we put on the full armour of God we are His soldiers who stand faithful to our KING!*

Luke 7:2-9 *And a certain Centurion's servant, who was dear unto him, was sick, and ready to die. And when he heard of Yeshua, he sent unto Him the elders of the Jews, beseeching Him that He would come and heal his servant. And when they came to Yeshua, they besought Him instantly, saying, That he was worthy for whom He should do this; For he loveth our nation, and he hath built us a Synagogue. Then Yeshua went with them. And when He was now not far from the house, the Centurion sent friends to Him, saying unto Him, LORD, trouble not Thyself; for I am not worthy that thou shouldest enter under my roof; Wherefore neither thought I myself worthy to come unto Thee; but say in a Word, and my servant shall be healed. For I also am a man set under Authority, having under me soldiers, and I say unto one, Go, and he goeth; and to another, Come, and he cometh; and to my servant, Do this, and he doeth it. When Yeshua heard these things, He marveled at him, and turned him about, and said unto the people that followed Him, I say unto you, I have not found so great faith, no, not in Israel.*

Yeshua marveled at this Centurion because even this Gentile was able to understand that the Messiah had the Authority to simply speak a Word and his servant would be healed. The leaders in the Holy Temple were always questioning and asking who gave Yeshua His Authority! He has all Power and Authority as the Royal Sceptre of Judah. *The Living Torah* is the source of Yeshua's Authority.

Mark 11:27-33 *And they come again to Jerusalem; and as He was walking in the Temple, there come to Him the Chief Priests, and the Scribes, and the Elders, And say unto Him, By what Authority doest thou these things? And who gave thee this Authority to do these things? And Yeshua answered and said unto them, I will also ask of you one question, and answer me, and I will tell you by what Authority I do these things. The baptism of John, was it from Heaven, or of men? Answer me. And they reasoned with themselves, saying, If we shall say, From Heaven; He will say, Why then did ye not believe Him? But if we shall say, of men; they feared the people; for all men counted John, that he was a Prophet indeed. And they answered and said unto Yeshua, We cannot tell. And Yeshua answering saith unto them, neither do I tell you by what Authority I do these things.*

Royal Sovereigns are not the only officials that hold Sceptres. The Sceptre is also an emblem of those within the High Order of the Priesthood! Yeshua is God's Sceptre, then, because He is the High Priest of Heaven, after the Order of Melchizedek. Since *the Living Torah* is pure righteousness, the LORD reigns forever as High Priest and KING, holding His Royal Sceptre in His right hand as He is seating upon His Heavenly throne.

***Hebrews 7:1-3** For this Melchizedek, King of Salem, Priest of the Most High God, who met Abraham returning from the slaughter of the Kings, and blessed him; To whom also Abraham gave a tenth part of all; first being by interpretation King of righteousness, and after that also King of Salem, which is, King of peace; Without father, without mother, without descent, having neither beginning of days, nor end of life; but made like unto the Son of God; abideth a Priest continually.*

***Hebrews 5:8-11** Though He were a Son, yet learned He obedience by the things which He suffered; And being made perfect, He became the author of eternal Salvation unto all them that obey Him; Called of God an High Priest after the Order of Melchizedek. Of whom we have many things to say, and hard to be uttered, seeing ye are dull of hearing.*

Again, they were dull of hearing and did not listen to the KING! It is incredible to me, how the LORD has woven His Testimony into every *Royal* detail! In my research, I found that all Royal Sovereigns hold their Royal Sceptre in their right hand and through the centuries, the Royal Sceptre has always *symbolized* their *"Power and Authority."* Some of the ancient Royal Sceptres are composed of a Rod with a hand at one end of the Rod. This reminds me so much of the Yad or the Torah pointer. This, if you will recall, is the Rod with the right hand attached to one end of it with the index finger extended and pointing from the hand. The finger of God is pointing to *"the Word of God."* This explains why Messiah Yeshua is not only the Rod, the hand and the finger of God, but it explains why He is also the Word of God, as the Royal Sceptre of the KING. Remember that I said that the Romans had a mockery version of this hand on their *Military Standard.* The Angel at the Garden tomb is pointing to the Word of God, the Living Torah and to His Eternal Living Testimony in God's Garden. God is a God of justice and the hand that is on top of the Royal Sceptre is actually called *"the hand of justice!"* So the Messiah comes to *restore justice* upon the earth. This is why *"Truth, the Living Torah goes before His face,"* and in the former Garden of Eden, this KING brought us mercy with His hand.

***Psalm 89:13-14** Thou hast a mighty arm; strong is Thy hand, and High is Thy right hand. Justice and judgment are the habitation of Thy throne; mercy and truth shall go before Thy face.*

There is a very fine example of a beautiful Royal Sceptre that I can relate to you, that I observed. At the Louvre Museum in Paris, one can view the Royal Sceptre of Charles V of France. When I saw a photograph of this Royal Sceptre, I understood how it is that Messiah is the Royal Sceptre of Heaven in the right hand of the KING, sitting upon His throne. I will try to describe it for you. By observing the details of this particular Royal Sceptre, one can first see the Rod, or the portion that the Sovereign holds in his right hand. The Rod has a globe on top of it and above this, there is a lily blossom. Above the lily blossom is the KING, seated on His throne. So his feet are on the floor of his throne which sits upon the globe, underneath the blossom. The globe represents the earth because the KING is seated above it. It is easy to see, from this model, exactly how the earth is the LORD'S footstool. The Sceptre is ornamented with blossoms and precious gemstones. There is no doubt in my mind that the Royal Sceptre of the LORD of Hosts is ornamented with Almond Blossoms, as His Testimony bears witness of the Almond Tree of Life! Seeing a representation of this Sceptre helps to clarify how the LORD sits on a throne with Messiah, His Royal Sceptre. ***(Source: The Royal Sceptre of Charles V ©2007 en.wikipedia.org/wiki/Crown_Jewels_of_France).***

Now, it is also true that some Royal Sceptres have a dove on one end of the Rod. Of course, this instantly brought to mind that the Holy Spirit descended in the form of a dove and stayed upon Yeshua, the Yad of God in the Jordan River! I therefore believe with all my heart that the dove was descending from Heaven and was resting on the end of the Rod of God in the Jordan River, and this dove of the Royal Regalia symbolizes Mercy! Thus, we can now understand how Yeshua is the Royal Sceptre of Mercy. The KING gave us His Mercy when

He sent His Rod, filled with the dove of His Holy Spirit, to save us. This is of course the dove of peace that I discussed before. It is therefore the KING'S *"Sceptre of Mercy"* that has reversed the death decree in the Garden of God on Holy Mount Moriah, as the Living Ark of the Testimony. Having described various types of Royal Sceptres, we can understand the following words in Psalms. It becomes perfectly clear! The LORD who says to my LORD, *"Sit at my right hand until I make Thine enemies Thy footstool"* is referring to the LORD KING, who is looking at His own reflection in His Royal Sceptre and declaring Himself as the LORD Messiah who will fight against the enemies of God as their *Royal Standard* and He will save His people with justice! Messiah is the Rod of the KING'S strength! *The ways of the Royal Sovereign KING are always the way of Truth, Justice, Righteousness, and Mercy!*

Psalm 110:1-7 *The LORD said unto my LORD, Sit Thou at My right hand, until I make Thine enemies Thy footstool. The LORD shall send the Rod of thy strength out of Zion; rule Thou in the midst of Thine enemies. Thy people shall be willing in the day of Thy power, in the beauties of holiness from the womb of the morning; thou hast the dew of thy youth. The LORD hath sworn, and will not repent, Thou art a Priest forever after the Order of Melchizedek. The LORD at Thy right hand shall strike through kings in the day of His wrath. He shall judge among the heathen, He shall fill the places with the dead bodies; He shall wound the heads over many countries. He shall drink of the brook in the way; therefore shall He lift up the head.*

In the book of Numbers, we see that the *Sceptre* was prophesied to rise out of Israel. When Yeshua came out of *"the Royal Stone of Kings in God's Garden,"* the Sceptre did rise out of Israel! The two men in shining garments declared, *"He is not here, He is risen!"*

Numbers 24:17-18 *I shall see Him, but not now; I shall behold Him, but not nigh; there shall come a Star out of Jacob, and a Sceptre shall rise out of Israel, and shall smite the corners of Moab, and destroy all the children of Sheth.*

Luke 24:4-8 *And it came to pass, as they were much perplexed there-about, behold, two men stood by them in shining garments; And as they were afraid, and bowed down their faces to the earth, they said unto them, Why seek ye the living among the dead? He is not here, but is risen; remember how He spake unto you when He was yet in Galilee, Saying, The Son of man must be delivered into the hands of sinful men, and be crucified, and the third day rise again. And they remembered His Words.*

Notice that the two men in shining garments bowed their faces to the earth! The angels on the Ark of the Covenant bow their faces towards God's throne! Yeshua the Yad of God points us to *the Living Torah.* The KING, the God of the living, had no place to rest His head.

Isaiah 66:1-2 *Thus saith the LORD, The Heaven is My throne, and the earth is My footstool; where is the House that ye build unto Me? And where is the place of My rest? For all those things hath Mine hand made, and all those things have been, saith the LORD; but to this man will I look, even to him that is poor and of a contrite spirit, and trembleth at My Word.*

The Horticulture definition of the word *"Standard"* is in association with *"a plant that is trained or grafted to have a single, upright, 'tree-like' stem."* It is, a Rod from a Tree! This, *"Standard,"* is the Almond Tree of Life, the pure gold Holy Almond Tree Menorah, bearing the Living Branch Testimony of Messiah Yeshua, the Almond Rod of God that budded to life. The central rod, the solid gold shaft that is made from one piece of gold on the Menorah, bears the LORD'S Living Testimony. We are said to be *"grafted into this original Tree, as believers."* The Majestic Royal Sovereign KING of Heaven holds His Royal Sceptre on His throne as *"The Tree-like Standard!"* His Royal Highness, Messiah Yeshua, is the emblem or ensign of this tree, the giver of Eternal life! The KINGS image bearing the wounds He suffered is visible on His burial Shroud and this was left inside Holy Mount Moriah in the Garden of God as *the Royal Standard of God's Army* after He was lifted up! The *Military Standards* always had the image of the Emperor on the Rod and his soldiers would look to him!

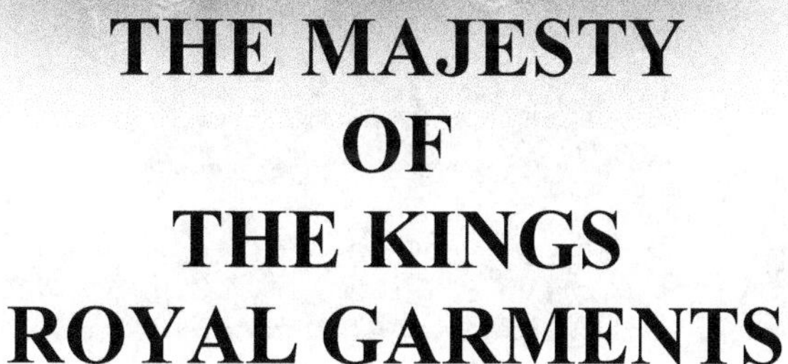

THE MAJESTY OF THE KINGS ROYAL GARMENTS

A KING is clothed in Royal Majesty! The LORD of Hosts is Regal in His Sovereignty. When an earthly King wears a cloak, robe, or mantle, it is a sign of His *power and authority.* When Elijah was taken up in the chariot of Heaven, His mantle fell off and the *power and authority* of the LORD was upon the mantle. Elisha then took this mantle and parted the waters of the Jordan with it and crossed over the River. Elisha was able to perform the sign of the Rod of God by making the waters of the Jordan River cleft again as He touched the mantle to the water. Elisha had asked for a double portion of Elijah's power. Since the mantle, the cloak, and the Royal Garments of the Great KING and High Priest of Israel are a sign of *the KING'S power and authority,* Elijah's mantle represented the mighty power of God Almighty.

Psalm 104:1 *Bless the LORD, O my soul. O LORD my God, Thou art very great; Thou art clothed with Honour and Majesty.*

Job 40:9-10 *Hast thou an arm like God? Or canst thou thunder with a voice like Him? Deck thyself now with Majesty and Excellency; and array thyself with glory and beauty.*

II Peter 1:16 *For we have not followed cunningly devised fables, when we made known unto you the power and coming of our LORD Yeshua Messiah, but were eyewitnesses of His Majesty.*

In the Psalms passage in Chapter 104, it tells us that the LORD *"Covers Himself with light, like a cloak."* The *light* of His Shechinah glory is *His garment or mantle. He is literally wrapped in a robe of radiant light, emitting His Divine glory.*

Psalm 104:1-2 *Bless the LORD, O my soul! O LORD my God, Thou art very great; Thou art clothed with Splendor and Majesty, Covering Thyself with light as with a cloak, Stretching out Heaven like a tent curtain.*

Psalm 145:1-21 *I will extol Thee, my God, O KING; and I will bless Thy Name forever and ever. Every day will I bless Thee; and I will praise Thy Name forever and ever. Great is the LORD, and greatly to be praised; and His greatness is unsearchable. One generation shall praise Thy works to another, and shall declare Thy mighty acts. I will speak of the glorious Honour of Thy Majesty, and of Thy wondrous works. And men shall speak of the might of Thy terrible acts; and I will declare Thy greatness. They shall abundantly utter the memory of Thy great goodness, and shall sing of Thy righteousness. The LORD is gracious, and full of compassion; slow to anger, and of great Mercy. The LORD is good to all; and His tender Mercies are over all His works. All thy works shall praise thee, O LORD; and Thy Saints shall bless Thee. They shall speak of the glory of Thy Kingdom, and talk of Thy power; To make known to the sons of men His mighty acts, and the glorious Majesty of His Kingdom. Thy Kingdom is an everlasting Kingdom, and Thy dominion endureth throughout all generations.*

I Chronicles 29:11-13 *Thine, O LORD, is the Greatness, and the power, and the glory, and the victory, and the Majesty; for all that is in the Heaven and in the earth is Thine; Thine is the Kingdom, O LORD, and Thou art exalted as head above all. Both riches and Honour come of Thee, and thou reignest over all; and in Thine hand is power and might; and in Thine hand it is to make great, and to give strength unto all. Now therefore, our God, we thank Thee, and praise Thy glorious Name.*

When Yeshua guided the Jewish disciples to pray the LORD'S prayer, He revealed to them within the prayer that He is *the Royal Sceptre* that forgives our sins, *the Staff* that gives us our Living Bread from Heaven and that He is *the Royal Rod full of power and authority* that delivers us from evil. Also, He revealed that His Kingdom that is coming from Heaven will last forever! The word *"hallowed"* that Yeshua used in this prayer actually means to *"set apart as Holy or consecrated."* Remember that a Nazarite is *set apart and consecrated* unto God. It also means to *"honour as Holy."* When you say, *"hallowed ground,"* this refers to ground that is blessed. So Messiah Yeshua is *"the Blessed Hope."* The LORD has many Testimonies to pay attention to and all of them declare His glorious Majesty and magnificent, unlimited power.

Matthew 6:9-13 *After this manner therefore pray ye; Our Father which art in Heaven, Hallowed be Thy Name. Thy Kingdom come, Thy will be done in earth, as it is in Heaven. Give us this day our daily Bread. And forgive us our debts, as we forgive our debtors. And lead us not into temptation, but deliver us from evil; For Thine is the Kingdom and the power, and the glory, forever. A'men.*

Psalm 93:1-5 *The LORD reigns, He is clothed with Majesty; The LORD has clothed and girded Himself with strength; Indeed, the world is firmly established, it will not be moved. Thy throne is established from of old; Thou art from everlasting. The floods have lifted up, O LORD, The floods have lifted up their voice; the floods lift up their pounding waves. More than the sounds of many waters, than the mighty breakers of the sea, The LORD on High is Mighty. Thy Testimonies are fully confirmed; Holiness befits Thy House, O LORD, forevermore.*

The cloak of the LORD'S light envelopes us and wraps us into His glorious rapture!

CONSIDER THE LILIES OF THE FIELD

Lilies Photo ©2013
Kimberly K Ballard All Rights Reserved

A statement that was made by the Jewish Historian Josephus, regarding the Tabernacle of Moses, specifies that *the colors* that were used for dying the Jewish Priestly garments came from various types of *flowers.* Even the purple color came from a *flower!* Royal Purple was the Regal color of the KING and of all other Royal Monarchs. The Royal purple and Priestly Tekhelet blue dye came from the murex snail known as *"Bolinus Brandaris."* It is also called *"the purple dye murex."* Today in Israel, they have rediscovered the spectacular colors for the dye in the ocean snail known as the *"Murex Trunculus."* Josephus wrote his information *based upon ancient records that the purple dye in the Tabernacle of Moses came from a flower.* After seeing this excerpt, written by Josephus, I suddenly had a vivid picture in my mind to understand Yeshua's Words *"Consider the lilies of the field."* The various parts of the flowers

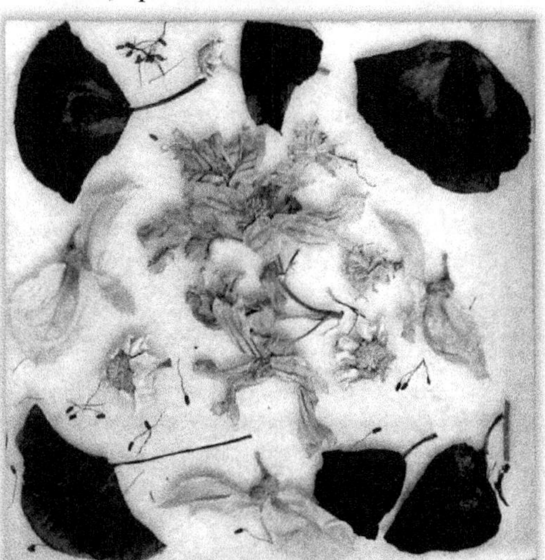

Flowers from the Holy Temple Mount in Jerusalem Israel
A gift to me from LV my Israeli friend
Photo ©2013 Kimberly K Ballard All Rights Reserved

were used to make special colors of dyes. The Stigmas of the Crocus and the Stamens of the Lilies were just two of the sources for making dye from the flowers.

Lily of the Valley
Photo ©2013 Kimberly K Ballard
All Rights Reserved

"Antiquities of the Jews," by Flavious Josephus, Book 3 Chapter 6 Section 1

1. HEREUPON the Israelites rejoiced at what they had seen and heard of their conductor, and were not wanting in diligence according to their ability; for they brought silver, and gold, and brass, and of the best sorts of wood, and such as would not at all decay by putrefaction; camels hair also, and sheep-skins, some of them dyed of a blue color, and some of a scarlet; some brought the flower for the purple color, and others for white, with wool dyed by the flowers aforementioned; and fine linen and precious stones, which those that use costly ornaments set in ouches of gold; They brought also a great quantity of spices; for of these materials did Moses build the Tabernacle, which did not at all differ from a movable and ambulatory Temple.

An "ouch" of gold (mentioned by Josephus) is the setting of a precious stone, a clasp, buckle, or brooch, especially one worn for ornament. ***(Source: The Random House College Dictionary revised edition, ©1975 Random House, Inc).***

Yeshua said that not even King Solomon in all his splendor was dressed like *one of the lilies of the field* that the Heavenly Father hath made. I believe that Yeshua was saying that King Solomon's Royal garments that were *dyed from the flowers* that the LORD made on the earth, do not compare to how the LORD will clothe us in Heaven. These Heavenly garments are pure in color, having more beauty, splendor and perfection, than all the garments that the Great King Solomon wore, to display his own Majesty on the earth. Of course, flowers are designed, created, and brought to life by the LORD'S own hand. They blossom to display great beauty and fragrance, but they thrive with life under the power of the LORD'S hand.

Purple Crocus
Photo ©2013 Kimberly K Ballard
All Rights Reserved

Luke 12:27-31 *Consider the lilies how they grow; they toil not, they spin not; and yet I say unto you, that Solomon in all his glory was not arrayed like one of these. If then God so clothe the grass, which is to day in the field, and tomorrow is cast into the oven; how much more will he clothe you, O ye of little faith? And seek not ye what ye shall eat, or what ye shall drink, neither be ye of doubtful mind. For all these things do the nations of the world seek after; and your Father knoweth that ye have need of these things. But rather seek ye the Kingdom of God; and all these things shall be added unto you.*

The *KING'S garment* that symbolizes His *power and authority* under Heaven and earth, has the *power of God* upon it for healing. This was demonstrated when Yeshua healed a woman, as she touched the hem of His garment. Yeshua was wearing a Jewish Tallit with the tzitzit tassels on its four corners.

Matthew 9:20-22 *And, behold, a woman, which was diseased with an issue of blood twelve years, came behind Him, and touched the hem of His garment; For she said within herself, if I may but touch His garment, I shall be whole. But Yeshua turned Him about, and when He saw her, He said, Daughter, be of good comfort; thy faith hath made thee whole. And the woman was made whole from that hour.*

So the fact is that all one had to do was to touch *the hem of the garment of the High Priest or the tzitzit of the Royal Sovereign KING of Heaven,* and they were completely and instantly healed of all their diseases! Remember that I said that *the Rod of God* stopped her plague of blood from flowing from the curse of disease, just like *the Rod of God* stopped the plague of blood from flowing in Egypt from the curse!

Matthew 14:35-36 *And when the men of that place had knowledge of Him, they sent out into all that country round about, and brought unto Him all that were diseased; And besought Him that they might only touch the hem of His garment; and as many as touched were made perfectly whole.*

In the Song of Solomon, we find prophetic words about the KING, the lilies, and His banner of love that brings us to His Royal Stately House to His banqueting table! This song foreshadows KING Messiah who was revealed in all these attributes through the miracles that Simon Peter performed in Acts 5:15.

Song of Solomon 2:1-4 *I AM the rose of Sharon, and the lily of the valleys. As the lily among thorns, so is my love among the daughters. As the apple tree among the trees of the wood, so is my beloved among the sons. I sat down under his shadow with great delight, and his fruit was sweet to my taste. He brought me to the banqueting house, and his banner over me was love.*

When the Royal power and authority of *KING Messiah, the Royal Sovereign of Heaven, came upon His disciples on* the day of Pentecost or Shavuot, the people hoped they would be in the place where *Simon Peter's shadow* would *overshadow* them as he passed by. As he did, *KING Yeshua's Spirit healed them,* revealing He was the fruit that was sweet to their taste and that He is the banner, *the Standard of love!* The Jewish Simon Peter was, in essence, wrapped in this robe of light that revealed God's glory.

Acts 5:15 *Insomuch that they brought forth the sick into the streets, and laid them on beds and couches, that at the least the shadow of Peter passing by might overshadow some of them.*

In Yeshua's description, as He is standing in the Temple in Heaven, among the seven candlesticks, we see that *He is wearing a garment that goes down to His feet, which is the High Priestly garment of the Jewish Temple.* However, He is also wearing a *Regal Royal golden girdle, which is the gold sash or belt that goes around the chest* that I discussed earlier as the *"curious golden girdle."* The Regal nature of His clothing defines Him as the KING OF KINGS over the entire universe.

Yellow Crocus
Photo ©2013 Kimberly K Ballard
All Rights Reserved

Definition of Regal*;*

1. Of or pertaining to a King; Royal.
2. Befitting or resembling a King.
3. Stately; splendid.
(Source: Definitions from the Random House College Dictionary revised edition, ©1975 by Random House, Inc.).

This Regal description of Yeshua, as He is standing in the Heavenly Temple, is written in the book of Revelation, where He is unveiled as *"The LORD God of Israel."* We can see that this description of *Yeshua clothed in His Majestic, Royal garments* in Revelation matches the description of the person that Daniel called *"LORD"* in Daniel Chapter 10. Daniel's vision of *the man clothed in linen* resembles *"the First and the Last"* who is mentioned in the following passage of Revelation.

Sunflower Photo ©2013

***Revelation 2:13-19** And in the midst of the seven candlesticks one like unto the Son of man, clothed with a garment down to the floor, and girt about the paps with a golden girdle. His head and His hairs were white like wool, as white as snow; and His eyes were as a flame of fire; And His feet like unto fine brass, as if they burned in a furnace; and His voice as the sound of many waters. And He had in His right hand seven stars; and out of His mouth went a sharp two edged sword; and His countenance was as the sun shineth in His strength. And when I saw Him, I fell at His feet as dead. And He laid His right hand upon me, saying unto me, Fear not; I AM the First and the Last; I AM He that liveth, and was dead; and, behold, I AM alive forevermore, Amen; and have the keys of hell and of death.*

The one like *the Son of man* is *"the First and the Last"* and He is called *"I AM."* Messiah Yeshua is the one in Daniel's vision that Daniel saw *dressed in fine linen.* This was *the voice of the Living Torah* and His face appeared as lightning while His eyes were like lamps of fire!

***Daniel 10:5-7** Then I lifted up mine eyes, and looked, and behold a certain man clothed in linen, whose loins were girded with fine gold of Uphaz; His body also was like the beryl, and His face as the appearance of lightning, and His eyes as lamps of fire, and His arms and His feet like in colour to polished brass, and the voice of His Words like the voice of a multitude. And I Daniel alone saw the vision; for the men that were with me saw not the vision; but a great quaking fell upon them, so that they fled to hide themselves.*

When Daniel had no strength remaining in him and when there was no breath left in him, then *the one who had the appearance of a man* came and strengthened him and *put breath in him.* This is the Rod of God, the Messiah, the LORD that came to the earth to dwell in the body of a man. So this is the one who touched him, who breathed the Holy Spirit of life into him, to strengthen him.

French Lilac Photo ©2013 Kimberly K Ballard

***Daniel 10:17-18** For how can the servant of this my Lord talk with this my Lord? For as for me, straightway there remained no strength in me, neither is there breath left in me, then there came again and touched me one like the appearance of a man, and He strengthened me.*

The one *appearing like a man,* that was speaking with Daniel, was full of *power and authority* because the men that were with him, although they did not see the vision, they quickly fled to hide themselves. *This is definitely the Rod of God, having all power and authority under Heaven.* The same thing happened when Saul had his encounter with Yeshua on the road to Damascus that I discussed earlier. Remember that the bright light was shining around him and it blinded him and the voice from Heaven proclaimed that this was Yeshua, who Saul was persecuting. When Saul saw *the bright light,* he immediately said, *"Who art Thou LORD?"* The others who were with Saul, although they saw *the bright light,* they did not hear the voice, just as the men with Daniel did not see the vision, but fled to hide themselves from *the Great power and authority of the KING that was coming from the Rod of God.* Now if we look ahead to verse 21, we see that the one who is speaking with Daniel tells him, *"There is none that holdeth with Me in these things, but Michael your Prince."*

Daniel 10:21 *But I will shew thee that which is noted in the Scripture of truth; and there is none that holdeth with Me in these things, but Michael your Prince.*

Clearly, the LORD appeared to Daniel in his vision. *The power of the Rod of God made the other men flee. The Royal Sceptre of the Great KING, the Messiah, was speaking to Daniel as the leader of His Heavenly Army when He said, "There is none that holdeth with Me in these things, but Michael your Prince."* So clearly this was not Michael who was dressed like this in Daniel's description in his vision! *This was the Rod of God, Messiah Yeshua, appearing as a man. This was the LORD and the commander of the Armies of Heaven, who was leading the Heavenly Armies to fight in battle against the enemies of God. Michael the Archangel, who was a high ranking member of the LORD'S Heavenly Army, was standing with the LORD in battle to help Daniel.* The word *"holdeth"* means *"to support or to keep in one's grasp, or to keep them from falling."* Michael the Archangel is assigned to watch over Israel, but *he is underneath the KING'S power and authority, under the Rod of God,* which is to say that *Michael was following under the Royal Standard of this Saintly Heavenly Army!* Nevertheless, the splendid garments of the KING that Daniel saw in his vision are Majestic and they are emblematic of His glorious brilliant *Sovereignty, power, and authority.* These Royal garments were exclusively dyed with very expensive dyes that were hard to extract from their sources and from them, they obtained the Royal purple, Royal blue, and Scarlet colors for the Monarchs. The colors were quite expensive to produce, since they were hard to extract. So the common citizens did not wear the vivid colors of Royalty. ***(Source: Historical Dye sources Facts © 2009 en.wikipedia.org/wiki/Natural_dye).***

Fragrant Cloud Rose in my garden Photo ©2013 Kimberly K Ballard All Rights Reserved

Royal Purple fabric in B& W with Royal Lions of Judah lifting up the crown of KING Yeshua and the Ten Commandments Photo ©2013 Kimberly K Ballard All Rights Reserved

Now the fabric that was used for the clothing was made of fine linen thread. Linen is made from the fibers of the flax plant. Ironically, my second and third Great Grandfathers were fine linen weavers in Ireland! Below you can see two photographs of fine linen samples of their work from the early to mid 1800's. The flax was grown, harvested, and woven into fine linen thread by my ancestors in County Cork Ireland! I have now written some facts about flax and linen in Ireland, and I relate how it connects to the Royal Holy Temple in Jerusalem and connects to the burial Shroud of Yeshua. *Quote: "In the ancient Egyptian and Israelite cultures, a hand loom or small spindle was the method of spinning flax. The fine pure white linen was made through a special process that started with growing the flax in the fields. The flax was harvested when its blue blossoms flowered. The stalks of flax were then gathered in bundles. Then they were soaked in water, usually in a river or stream for several weeks, to soften the outer coating of the stalks. The outer coating of the flax had to first be removed from the inner flax fibers. After this process was completed, the flax was laid out in the sun to dry for several weeks. In Ireland, in the nineteenth century, they called these fields for flax, "bleaching greens." The fibers were then beaten and combed, to smooth out the fibers. Usually the fibers were spun into thread, either with a hand loom, or with a small hand spindle. After this was accomplished, the linen thread was used to weave the fine linen clothing and to make fabric. Linen naturally has a brownish tint to it and so it was whitened by soaking it in buttermilk or in chlorine. The linen was only referred to as "fine linen" after it became white through this soaking method. The fine linen that was made in Egypt was very high quality fabric and it was used by Nobles and Royals for dress and also for burial. Through the centuries and even now, the linen from these places is still considered*

Genuine 19th Century Fine Irish Linen grown, handspun, and woven in County Cork Ireland in the early to mid 1800's by my Great, Great, Great Grandfather & his Son William & James Irvin

Genuine 19th Century Fine Irish Linen Grown, handspun, and woven in County Cork Ireland in the early to mid 1800's by my Great Great Great Grandfather and his Son William & James Irvin

to be very fine quality. The fabric of linen, was cool in the summer and warm to wear in the winter." **(Source: Irish Flax Growing Facts ©2010 irishlinenmills.com/History/history.htm).**

The LORD used this fabric so the Priests who were officiating in His Holy Temple would not sweat and stain the garments. This allowed the Priestly garments to remain clean, pure, and white. The Priests could then perform their sacred duties before the LORD in the Holy Temple in Jerusalem Israel. The fine linen thread had certain requirements the weavers were to follow as they made the Priestly garments. *"The Priestly garments of the Holy Temple required each thread to be a six-ply thread of fine twined linen."* **(Source: ©2007 The Temple Institute in Jerusalem Israel All Rights Reserved).**

One of the best places in Israel to grow the linen flax in ancient times was in the Galilee region. Now there is something fascinating about this linen that I will pause to mention here. There is a Scripture that speaks about *Aholiab of the tribe of Dan* that is found in the book of Exodus. *He was an embroiderer in the Royal colors and he was a worker of fine linen.* So he made these specific items for the Tabernacle.

Exodus 38:22-23 *And Bezaleel the son of Uri, the son of Hur, of the tribe of Judah, made all that the LORD commanded Moses. And with him was Aholiab, son of Ahisamach, of the tribe of Dan, an engraver, and a cunning workman, and an embroiderer in blue, and in purple, and in scarlet, and fine linen.*

Exodus 36:35 *And he made a veil of blue, and purple, and scarlet, and fine twined linen; with Cherubim's made he it of cunning work.*

Tapestry detail Photo ©2013 Kimberly K Ballard All Rights Reserved

In the book of Chronicles, *the workers of fine linen were from "the House of Ashbea," and they were descendants of "Shelah the son of Judah."* It says that *they wrought fine linen.* The word *"wrought"* actually means *"to work, embellish or elaborate."*

I Chronicles 4:21 *The sons of Shelah the son of Judah were, Er the father of Lecah, and Laadah the father of Mareshah, and the families of the house of them that wrought fine linen, of the House of Ashbea.*

This means that *the workers of fine linen* were also *embroiderers of linen* and perhaps they are the workers that worked the *fine linen* veil that hung in the Temple of King Solomon. This veil was embroidered with beautiful elaborate Cherubim Angels and with a lovely flower blossom design that was very detailed. It took the skill of an artist to accomplish it. In fact, if we look at the true definition of the words *"Elaborate" and "Embellish,"* we can see that the workers of *fine linen* from the tribe of Judah were quite talented and skilled in executing all the complicated and minute detail in their artistic inventions and fine works of craftsmanship.

Elaborate;*1. Worked out with great care and nicety of detail, executed with great minuteness. 2. Marked by intricate and often excessive detail; complicated.* **Embellish;***1. To beautify by or as ornamentation; ornament or adorn with decoration.* **(Source: Random House College Dictionary revised edition, ©1975 by Random House, Inc.).**

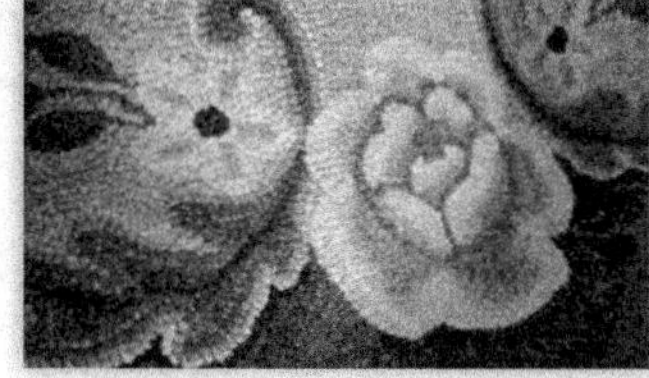

Design detail of a hand woven rug Made by my Great Grandmother Irvin Photo ©2014 KK Ballard All Rights Reserved

So the *fine linen weavers* of Ashbea, of the House of Judah, that were living in the Galilee region were experts in their field! They could execute *design detail* with the greatest minuteness and they could create or embellish the fabric with beautiful, complicated works of art. *The veil that was in the Holy Temple and in the Tabernacle of the LORD was embroidered in the Royal colors of blue, purple, and scarlet, with the flower and Cherubim Angel designs.* This veil was not only elaborate it was beautifully embellished and adorned with fabulous artistic designs, that were delicately and tediously worked upon it by hand. The Scriptures tell us that the LORD filled the heart of certain people with this ability and skill to perform the fine design detail.

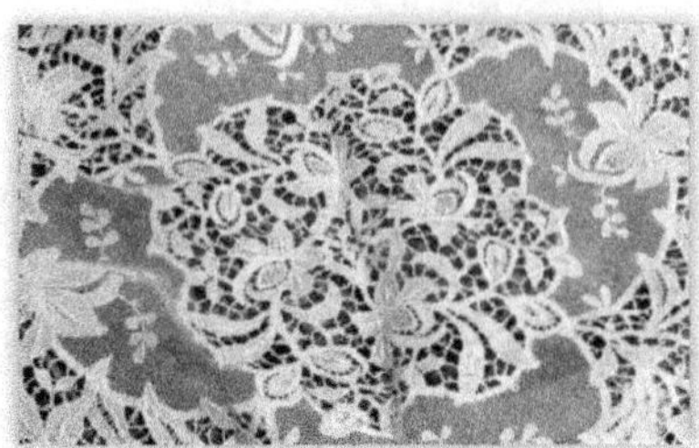

Design detail old lace Photo ©2014 Kimberly K Ballard All Rights Reserved

Exodus 35:35 *Then hath He filled with wisdom of heart, to work all manner of work, of the engraver, and of the cunning workman, and of the embroider, in blue, and in purple, in scarlet, and in fine linen, and of the weaver, even of them that do any work, and of those that devise cunning work.*

The sons of "Shelah, the son of Judah" are mentioned in the Scripture as being connected with *the workers of fine linen.* Now the reason why I say this is because the name *"Shelah"* is the same name as the word *"Shelach."* In Strong's Concordance, the word *"Shelach"* is #7974. Now the word *"Shelach"* is the same as the word *"Shiloach"* which is #7975. Shiloach is a passive form of *"Shiloah."* This happens to be the name of the Pool where Yeshua sent the blind man to be healed. The Shiloach or Siloam Pool is the Pool where the Priests took a Mikveh ritual bath in the living water before going up to minister in the Holy Temple in Jerusalem. The word as it is written in the New Testament means *"sent."* What is interesting about this connection is the fact that the word *"Shelach"* has an incredible meaning that pertains to Messiah Yeshua the Branch from the tribe of Judah. *Messiah Yeshua was positively and absolutely a descendant of the very highly skilled artistic tribe that embroidered the fine linen garments from the House of Ashbea!* So I discovered that the definitions that are within this word *"Shelach"* incredibly describe the Messiah.

Design detail on fabric Photo ©2014 Kimberly K Ballard All Rights Reserved

Water from the 2004 excavated Pool of Shiloach/Siloam in Israel Photo ©2013 Kimberly K Ballard All Rights Reserved

Shelach- *sheh-lakh; from #7971; a missile of attack, i.e. spear; Also (fig.) a shoot of growth; i.e. Branch- dart, plant, x put off, sword, weapon.* **(Source: Strong's Concordance ©1995).**

When Yeshua sent the blind man to wash in the *Shiloach Pool,* which is written in Greek as *"the Pool of Siloam," He actually was revealing that He is the Branch, the shoot of Jesse, as well as the Rod and Sword of God.* This Pool had also been called *"the Pool of Shelah or Shelach." So the Messiah was a descendant of Judah and He was from the very same family line that produced the Priestly garments of fine twined linen and produced the veil in the Holy Temple of King Solomon! These were the highly skill workers of embroidery! So the connection that the High Priest of Heaven has to the Priestly garments that were wrought in Israel is just incredible to me.* The Pool of Shiloach or Siloam is supposed to be in the very center of the Holy Land. If *"Selah"* that is written in the Psalms refers to the Bride of Messiah as I believe it does, I have also become convinced that it pertains to *the pure white, fine linen garment that the Bride of Messiah wears.* This is a remarkable connection I discovered through the LORD'S guidance. There was a conduit that led to the Pool of Shiloach. *(Source: jewishencyclopedia.com/articles/13578-shiloah).* It is said that *a perennial source of water that has streamed through a tunnel cut through a rock from this conduit into the Pool of Shiloach actually comes from a spring called "the Fountain of Mary" or "fountain of the Virgin" or "Virgin's spring" which is also referred to as "Ain Sitti Maryam."* Yeshua's Mother Mary was said to have visited her cousin Elisabeth at this spring. Mary frequented the spring and drank from its water when she visited Elisabeth in Ein Karem. *(Source: tiuli.com/track_info.asp?lng=eng&track_id=91). Mary is said to have washed Yeshua's swaddling cloth in this spring or fountain. (Source: (en.wikipedia.org/wiki/Fountain_of_the_Virgin).* I will speak about this swaddling cloth later, but miraculously it showed up in this section on the Pool of Shiloach, after I had written about it already in another place and, believe me, it is one of the most profound things I have written about in this book! This spring of Mary is *regarded as the upper water course of Gihon which also flows into the Pool of Shiloach.* It is very clear water. *(Source: classic.net.bible.org/dictionary.php?word=GIHON).* It is said that *"the only natural spring of water in or near Jerusalem is the "Fountain of the Virgin" (q.v.), which rises outside the city walls on the west bank of the Kidron valley." (Source: Easton's Bible Dictionary 1897 Public Domain from biblestudytools.com/dictionary/gihon/).* The spring has been a main source of water over the centuries for Jerusalem. The Shiloach Pool itself may have originally been called *"Gihon."* The *"Virgins Fount"* is also called *"ancient Gihon." (Source: bibleapps.com/s/shiloah.htm).* The waters of the Gihon spring also flow into the Pool. The Gihon was one of the rivers coming out of Eden when God was dwelling with mankind. The true Pool of Shiloach was discovered in 2004. The Messiah whose Name is *"The Branch,"* comes from Nazareth meaning *"branch."* Then the word *"Shelach"* which is the same as *"Shiloah," and "Shiloach"* also means *"a shoot of growth or a branch."* This is no coincidence! Within the finest details, the LORD has proven His identity as the Messiah of Israel and this is final proof for the entire world. Yeshua sent the blind man to wash in the very waters of the Pool of Shiloach or Siloam and when the blind man washed, he had eyes to see! *So now I believe that this was the source of water that rushed out of the Garden of God, in Eden, where mankind was created out of the dust of the ground!* When Yeshua made mud from His spit and put it on the eyes of the blind man, He sent the man to wash in this Pool of living water. The LORD, *the Living Water* was dwelling in our midst, and the man was given eyes to see from the LORD, *who mixed His spit with the dirt in this place that was formerly the Garden of Eden!* Messiah Yeshua restores our flesh. This is the same fountain that has been the source of *living water* for the Pool of Shiloach, for the Priests of the Holy Temple to wash in for thousands of years, before ministering in the Temple of the LORD! After the Priests would wash in this Pool, they put on their garments and walked up the stair stepped pathway that led from the Pool in the City of David, and they would go up the stairs and into the Holy Temple to minister to the LORD. So the garments that the Priests wore were made by *Bezaleel of Judah and by Aholiah of Dan.* They were responsible for making all these fine linen garments and embellishing any linen fabric that needed to be worked. They just found one of the gold High Priestly bells from one of the High Priestly garments in an archaeological site in Israel near the Temple Mount and you can listen to it ringing on the internet! *(Source: Sound of Jerusalem Bell from Second Temple Period – youtube.com/watch?v=xjx9tP3yTRI).*

Water from the 2004 excavated Pool of Shiloach/Siloam in Israel Photo ©2013 Kimberly K Ballard All Rights Reserved

Exodus 39:24-31 *And they made upon the hems of the robe pomegranates of blue, and purple, and scarlet, and twined linen. And they made bells of pure gold, and put the bells between the pomegranates upon the hem of the robe, round about between the pomegranates; A bell and a pomegranate, round about the hem of the robe to* *minister in; as the LORD commanded Moses. And they made coats of fine linen of woven work for Aaron, and for his sons, And a mitre of fine linen, and goodly bonnets of fine linen, and linen breeches of fine twined linen, And a girdle of fine twined linen, and blue, and purple, and scarlet, of needlework; as the LORD commanded Moses. And they made the plate of the Holy Crown of pure gold, and wrote upon it a writing, like to the engravings of a signet, HOLINESS TO THE LORD. And they tied unto it a lace of blue, to fasten it on high upon the Mitre; as the LORD commanded Moses.*

Wool was also dyed into many colors for the Royal garments and for the Priests. The Royal colors that were used before the Roman period and known in the ancient world included all the following colors and sources of dyes. The scarlet color for dying the wool has been rediscovered within the last few years and it has been harvested for the first time in 2,000 years by the Temple Institute in Jerusalem Israel. According to the Temple Institute, This scarlet dye comes from the crimson worm known in Hebrew as, the tola'at shani, from the cochineal insect, and it is apparently found, on cactus plants in South America and in places around Jerusalem, as well as in other parts of Israel. They also state that, another source for this crimson color, is the Kermes insect and it is crushed to produce the dye. ***(Source: ©2007 The Temple Institute, Jerusalem Israel All Rights Reserved).***

I have written a few facts about the Royal colored dyes for making the garments of the ancient King's, Nobles and Priests. The plants for these dyes include*, "The evergreen plant, madder root."* The roots were used to make another crimson dye that was not as expensive to produce. The blue dye known as, *"Indigo,"* was obtained from the leaves of the *"woad plant."* Carmine is another red that was used later in the Royal historical records. Brazilwood was used heavily in the Middle Ages to obtain the red color for Royal garments and it was known as *"Brazilin."* Tyrian purple can be produced in various shades of red-purple dye and it was developed from the *"Bolinus Brandaris Murex."* The Roman Emperors actually used this color, but the method of obtaining this purple dye goes way back to a much earlier date before the Roman period. It was used in very ancient times. The gland of the *"Bolinus Brandaris Murex"* was used to create the *"Imperial or Royal Purple"* for the Monarch's Royal garments. Since it took so many Murex snails to make only one purple garment, the purple dye was quite expensive and valuable, making it the Royal purple worn only by the Royal Sovereigns, Nobles, and Priests. ***(Source: Historical Dye sources Facts ©2009 en.wikipedia.org/wiki/Natural_dye).***

It is so fascinating that within the last twenty years or so, the researchers working with the Temple Institute in Jerusalem, *"Discovered that if the purple color, obtained from the 'Brandaris Murex' was left out in the sunlight for some length of time, it would become the long sought after Priestly blue color known as Tekhelet blue."* This Tekhelet blue is the color that the Priests wore on the tassels *(tzitzit)* of the four corners of their Tallit prayer shawls and they still wear this color today on the tzitzit. This very special blue dye was recreated by the Temple Institute in Jerusalem, for the coming Third Temple service. ***(Source: ©2007 The Temple Institute, Jerusalem Israel, All Rights Reserved).***

It is very exciting indeed that all of the color dyes for the exclusive Royal garments are being rediscovered and made in our generation. The recent rediscoveries of the ancient dying methods for the Fine Royal Garments are preparing the way for the *Grand Royal Coronation Day of the KING OF KINGS AND LORD OF LORDS!*

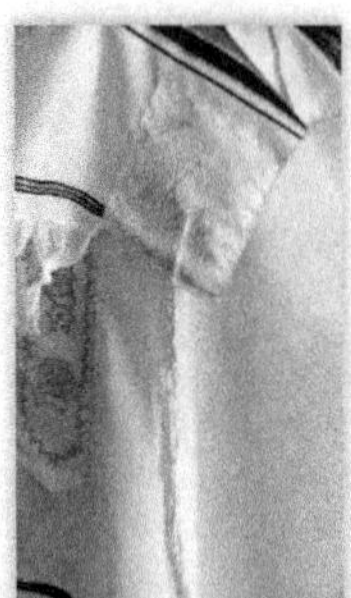

Tallit Photo ©2013 KK Ballard All Rights Reserved

It is hard to imagine that nearly 2,000 years have elapsed from the time of the Second Temple period. I have personally seen some of the blueprints for the coming Third Temple with my own eyes, in January 2011. I talk exclusively about this in the last chapter!

I should not fail to mention also, in reference to the Royal garments, that pure solid gold was often beaten into thin strips or spun into thread and it was incorporated into very intricately woven and embellished Royal garments for the Kings and Queens. They were then encrusted with rare Jewels and this accentuated the exquisite splendor and illustriousness of their Royal Majesty!

THE KING'S SIGNET RING A PROMISE TO MARRY THE LAND

Sterling Silver Signet Ring fashioned by & Rose Photos ©2013 Kimberly K Ballard

Throughout history, a Royal King would wear an engraved signet ring on his third finger. This engraved signet ring is considered to be part of *"the Royal garment of the Royal Regalia."* The signet ring is placed upon the hand of the Royal Sovereign during His Coronation Ceremony. *The Royal Signet is "a sign" that the King is now considered to be "married" to the land that He is to rule!* So *the land* becomes like a *"Bride"* to the King and it is the King's responsibility to care for His Bride, *which is the entire land that He rules.* The LORD'S signet ring would be on the right hand, as part of the Messiah's Testimony, as the KING of Israel.

The signet of the KING OF KINGS is therefore *"the Official Royal seal of His promise to marry the Land of Israel!* This is the main reason that I was simply astonished when the LORD later showed me the signet shaped object etched in the Royal Stone of Kings at the Garden tomb with the letters, *"Alpha and Omega!"* This was especially exciting because the Jewish Priestly Angel was pointing directly to this signet shaped object, and I knew that this was a miracle and that this was very significant for the Land of Israel in our generation! *The signet shaped object is engraved in Holy Mount Moriah in the Garden of God where His Name is written forever, and remember this was to be "a sign and a promise, sealed by the KING!" Once the KING seals the decree for Eternal life with His signet, thereby reversing the decree of death in His Garden, no one can ever reverse it!* The Bible says that the Jews always ask for *"a sign,"* and the LORD left one through one of his Holy Spirit filled disciples written in His Holy Mount Moriah in Jerusalem! So you can imagine how I felt after I had already written about the signet ring of the KING and then later the Angel was revealed to me at the Garden tomb and he was pointing to this *signet* shaped object that I believe was etched in Greek with the lowercase letters, *"Alpha and Omega."*

As if this miracle was not enough, the *signet* shaped object happens to be carved in *"The Royal Stone of Kings in God's Garden!"* This was the Meleke Limestone! *Therefore, this would mean that Messiah Yeshua, the KING of Israel, sealed His promise to marry the Land of Israel in God's Garden on the third day!* The letters, *"Alpha and Omega,"* are not only written inside this tomb in Greek, but I showed you how I believe they are carved in the raised oval stone that is shaped like an opened flower, above the niches. *This is the reason I believe that the niches at the Garden tomb once held the elements of the Living Testimony of Messiah Yeshua, including the Shroud bearing His image, the Sudarium, and the Mezuzah that declares that the LORD our God is one like in the Shema blessing!* This is one Royal KING of glory! The Jewish Priestly Angel that the LORD revealed to me in the rock formation is pointing to this object with his index finger. This means that the Angel is trying to get our attention! Angels are, after all, messengers that come to deliver and herald specific messages and tidings from the LORD, our KING! Since the King wears the ring on the third finger, the Messiah, who is *the finger of God,* was resurrected *the third day, leaving a promise of His future marriage to Israel in His Royal Garden.* So the Royal signet that is engraved at the Garden tomb in Holy Mount Moriah is therefore *a promise* that Yeshua is going to return for His Bride,

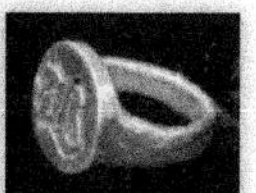

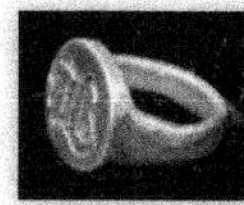

and He will care for *the Land of Israel* for Eternity. He will raise her up the third day, just as He was raised to life the third day, and He will give His Bride Eternal life. It is extraordinary! The LORD will make Jerusalem *"a praise"* when He rules as KING OF KINGS AND LORD OF LORDS.

The term *"Hephazibah"* in the following Scripture means *"My delight is in her."* The Hebrew term *"Beulah"* refers to a young virgin or maiden who is engaged to be a Bride. This was the state of Mary, the Mother of Yeshua, when the Angel Gabriel appeared to her telling her that she was chosen to give birth to the Messiah of Israel.

It is written in Isaiah *that the Land of Israel will be married to the LORD, the Great KING!* The fact that it tells us that *"they will be a crown of glory and a Royal diadem in the hand of the KING"* is remarkable since *Yeshua is the right hand, as the Rod of God. This means that the promise and the sign at the Garden tomb proclaim that the Jewish Messiah, KING Yeshua, will marry the Land of Israel at His return. He is in love!*

Isaiah 62:2-7 *And the Gentiles shall see thy righteousness, and all Kings thy glory; and thou shalt be called by a new name, which the mouth of the LORD shall name. Thou shalt also be a crown of glory in the hand of the LORD, and a royal diadem in the hand of thy God. Thou shalt no more be termed Forsaken; neither shall thy land anymore be termed Desolate; but thou shalt be called Hephazibah, and thy land Beulah; for the LORD delighteth in thee, and thy land shall be married. For as a young man marrieth a virgin, so shall thy sons marry thee; and as the bridegroom rejoiceth over the bride, so shall thy God rejoice over thee. I have set watchmen upon thy walls, O Jerusalem, which shall never hold their peace day or night; ye that make mention of the LORD, keep not silence, And give Him no rest, till He establish and till He make Jerusalem a praise in the earth.*

Remember that in Esther's story, the King was the Bridegroom who *ruled the land* with His Sceptre from his throne. *The Sceptre is just one emblem of the King and the Royal signet ring is on the same hand, that marries the land that the King rules!* When Yeshua went to the wedding in Cana and performed the miracle of the LORD, by turning the water into wine, He was indeed signifying to all the attending Jewish guests, that *He is the Bridegroom that will marry the Land of Israel.* There is a prophecy and the LORD said that He will make Zerubbabel *"as a signet."* Yeshua is a direct descendant of Zerubbabel who rebuilt the Holy Temple. So again, we see that the Messiah will be the one to fulfill this prophecy that was given to Yeshua's ancestor *regarding the Royal Signet ring.* It is the seal of the LORD God. The Messiah would therefore come from the chosen line of Zerubbabel who rebuilt the Holy Temple after the Jewish people returned from their 70 year Babylonian captivity. The Messiah is the one who is building the Eternal Holy Temple that will be set up for His Coronation Day after the 2,000 years of Israel's Diaspora.

Haggai 2:23 *In that day, saith the LORD of Hosts, will I take thee, O Zerubbabel, my servant, the son of Shealtiel, saith the LORD, and will make thee as a signet; for I have chosen thee, saith the LORD of Hosts.*

The Royal Signet ring of the KING comes with the Staff or the Royal Sceptre as part of the Royal Regalia. Messiah Yeshua is returning for His Bride! *The Coronation of the KING includes the wearing of two bracelets.* The two bracelets in the British Royal Regalia are called *"Armills."* These two bracelets are worn on the wrists of the Royal Sovereign as part of the garments of the Royal Regalia. Now the *two bracelets* in the British Royal Coronation of the Monarch are today called *"the Bracelets of Sincerity and Wisdom."* This information is found on the British Royal Household website of HRH Queen Elizabeth II. ***(Source: The British Royal Monarchy of HRH Queen Elizabeth II - The Royal Household ©2011 Crown Copyright www.royal.gov.uk/MonarchUK/Symbols/TheCrownJewels.aspx).***

What I find so interesting in this emblem of the Royal Regalia is the fact, that I discovered in my studies, that Judah, who was the forerunner of King David, *carried the Staff, the two bracelets, and the signet ring of the Royal Regalia! Therefore, what Judah had in his possession were all the emblems of the Royal Regalia of the Royal line of Judah.* In the

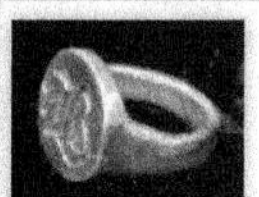

Biblical story, Judah gave these specific emblems of the Royal Regalia to Tamar when she asked Judah to give them to her. *They included Judah's Staff that was in his hand, along with the signet ring and the two bracelets.* Tamar was very intelligent because she was secretly taking these from Judah for a future purpose. She would soon reveal, by having these *Royal items of Regalia in her possession,* that Judah was the father of her baby. Tamar knew for a fact that when she returned *the emblems of the Royal Regalia to Judah* and revealed that he was the father of her child, *it would mean that Tamar's baby was now in the Royal bloodline of the King's of Israel and she had the proof!*

Genesis 38:18 *And he said, What pledge shall I give thee? And she said, Thy signet, and thy bracelets, and thy staff that is in thine hand. And he gave it her, and came in unto her, and she conceived by him.*

Genesis 38:25 *When she was brought forth, she sent to her father in law, saying, By the man, whose these are, am I with child; and she said, Discern, I pray thee, whose are these, the signet, and bracelets, and staff. And Judah acknowledged them, and said, She hath been more righteous than I; because that I gave her not to Shelah my son. And he knew her again no more.*

Remember what I said about the word *"Shelah?"* This was the name of Judah's son and it is a derivative of the name of *"the Pool Shiloach"* where the Priests would wash before going to the Holy Temple to perform the Divine service of the LORD, and it was from this Pool that Messiah Yeshua healed the blind man. This form of the word *"Shelah"* has a root that indicates *the Branch or shoot of Jesse. Of course Yeshua is the Branch, the shoot of Jesse, the Staff of life, the Living Water and He is the KING of Judah who wears the signet ring and the two bracelets of Sincerity and Wisdom!* The Royal lineage of Judah, who gave *his emblems of the Royal Regalia* to Tamar, would become very important in the future because Messiah Yeshua would also come directly through Judah's Royal family line. Tamar had the King's Signet! She would one day be an ancestor to Messiah Yeshua, and Yeshua left His Royal signet in the LORD'S Garden, etched in the Royal Stone of King's in Holy Mount Moriah, proving that He is the Staff of the KING of Judah who is betrothed to the Land of Israel. Forever, He wears the Royal signet and the two bracelets of *"Sincerity and Wisdom!"*

Now the *two bracelets* of the KING present another fantastic detail that I discovered by Divine Providence. In the book of Corinthians, it is written that Messiah Yeshua is our Passover Lamb who has been sacrificed for us and that we should keep the Feast! How are we to keep the Feast? *With the Unleavened Bread of "Sincerity and Truth!" Of course, "Truth" is the Living Torah and this is wisdom!* So Messiah Yeshua is the Unleavened Bread of Heaven, which is the Staff of life, the Living Torah. *Therefore, Yeshua is the Eternal KING of Judah, the Rod of God, who also wears the two bracelets of "Sincerity and Wisdom." When He speaks the Living Torah to us with all power and authority in Truth and Sincerity, this teaches us His wisdom, and remember, He sat in "the Jesus Boat," a type of Ark, to preach it to Israel!*

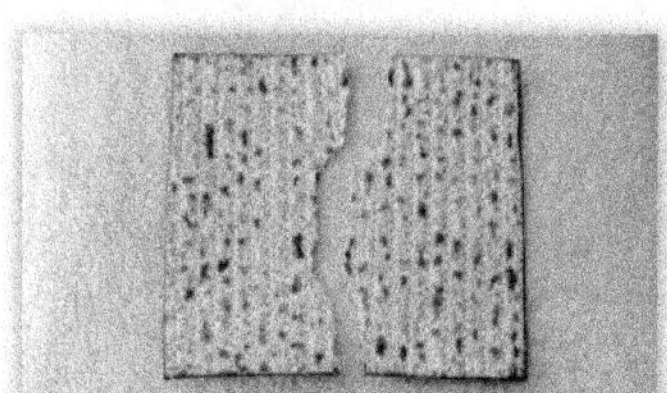

Unleavened bread Photo ©2013 Kimberly K Ballard All Rights Reserved

I Corinthians 5:7-8 *Purge out therefore the old leaven, that ye may be a new lump, as ye are unleavened. For even Messiah our Passover is sacrificed for us; Therefore let us keep the Feast, not with old leaven of malice and wickedness; but with the unleavened bread of Sincerity and Truth.*

John 8:31-32 *Then said Yeshua to those Jews which believed on Him, If ye continue in My Word, then are ye My disciples indeed; And ye shall know the truth, and the truth shall make you free.*

Joshua told the Israelites that they were to serve the LORD *"in Sincerity and Truth."*

Joshua 24:14 *Now therefore fear the LORD, and serve Him in Sincerity and in Truth; and put away the gods which your fathers served on the other side of the flood, and in Egypt; and serve ye the LORD.*

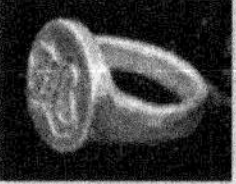

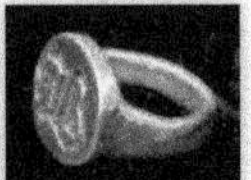

It is interesting that when Yeshua was standing before Pontius Pilate, he asked Yeshua, *"Are you a KING then?"* Yeshua told Pilate that this was the reason that He came into the world, *that He should bear witness of the Truth and that everyone who hears His voice is of the Truth.* Then Pilate said, *"What is Truth?"* Pilate said that he found no fault in Yeshua and it was because *He is the Living Torah of Truth!*

John 18:38-39 *Pilate saith unto Him, What is Truth? And when he had said this, he went out again unto the Jews, and saith unto them, I find in Him no fault at all. But ye have a custom, that I should release unto you one at the Passover; will ye therefore that I release unto you the KING of the Jews?*

Official Shroud Face Photograph
©1978 Barrie M. Schwortz Collection, STERA Inc.,
All Rights Reserved

KING Messiah Yeshua sealed the Living Covenant of the Living Torah of Truth in our hearts, to give us His Royal Eternal wisdom in Sincerity!

Psalm 51:6 *Behold, thou desirest Truth in the inward parts; and in the hidden part Thou shalt make me to know wisdom.*

Another fascinating truth is the fact that the King's Royal signet ring usually bore "the image" of the King! The King's name was engraved upon the signet as a sign of His Royal power. This ring was the official seal of the King. When the ring was pressed into hot wax, *the image of the King* and His name was visible in the wax seal that was impressed upon the Royal documents. The documents were declared *"Official"* by *Royal decree*, and no one could open the seal to read the documents, except the person for whom the Royal documents were intended. The King's signet did not necessarily have to have *His image* engraved in it. It was also sometimes engraved with His Royal Family Crest or with His emblem of Heraldry. So think about how significant the signet shaped object with the letters *"Alpha and Omega"* are at the Garden tomb, where the Angel is pointing with his *"Yad or Torah pointer!"* The Angel is pointing to *the Living Torah and to the Living Testimony of the Messiah,* which ironically I believe, *contained Yeshua's burial Shroud that bore the KING'S image upon it!* Fantastic! *This would mean that the Eternal KING of Judah, who restores forever the Royal Davidic Dynasty, left His image and His signet that is bearing His Name, engraved in God's Garden, in the Royal Stone of King's, in His Holy Mount Moriah in Jerusalem Israel!* This is so spectacular! It is truly astonishing!

Then in the book of Revelation, there is another verification that we must not overlook. In Heaven there was a book and no one could open it because it was sealed with seven seals! Who is the *only one* that was able to break the seal and open the book to read it? Of course it was *"The Lion of the Tribe of Judah, the Root of David who hath prevailed to open the book and to loose the seven seals thereof!"* Did I mention that this book was in the right hand of the one sitting on the throne? The right hand holds *the Staff* of the KING, which is His Royal Sceptre, bearing the sign of having all *power and authority!*

Revelation 5:1-5 *And I saw in the right hand of Him that sat on the throne a book written within and on the backside, sealed with seven seals. And I saw a strong Angel proclaiming with a loud voice, Who is worthy to open the book, and to loose the seals thereof? And no man in Heaven, nor in earth, neither under the earth, was able to open the book, neither to look thereon. And I wept much, because no man was found worthy to open and to read the book, neither to look thereon. And one of the Elders saith unto me, Weep not; behold, the Lion of the Tribe of Judah, the Root of David, hath prevailed to open the book, and to loose the seven seals thereof.*

Only the one who has sealed the documents with His signet can open it! Messiah Yeshua is the only one who was found worthy to open the seals, not only because He was the perfect and complete Passover Lamb sacrifice in the number seven, but He is the Lion of the Tribe of Judah, the Rod of God, the KING OF KINGS who gave us Eternal life and reversed the death decree, showing that He has all *power and authority* with His *Royal Sceptre or Staff* and *He wears the bracelets of Sincerity and Wisdom! The KING Messiah sealed the Royal decree of Eternal life in His Garden that can never be reversed!* So He was resurrected to life as the Living Almond Branch, in the KING'S Royal Garden in Jerusalem, in the Royal Stone of Kings. *This is where the Great KING, left His image and His signet of promise to marry the Land of Israel forever!* This is so stunning that it proclaims God's exalted glory! Remember that the Ten Commandments, the Law of God, was written with the finger of God and was etched in stone, on the front and backside, just like the book in Heaven that is sealed with the seven seals is written within and on the backside. *It is written within because the Laws of God are kept inside the Ark of the Testimony of the KING'S Royal throne.* So, the perfect and complete Testimony of the KING is sealed with seven seals in Heaven. The Messiah, as the High Priest of Heaven, would wear the twelve stones, representing the 12 tribes of Israel, mounted upon His breastplate. He would wear them over His heart. These stones are engraved as a signet ring is engraved, just as the LORD commanded Moses. It is a promise to the Bride. Yeshua's Living Testimony as *the Living Torah* is the LORD'S life blood of the Covenant of the heart through the love of God. *Therefore, remarkably, I discovered the Hebrew letter "Shin" on KING Yeshua's forehead in His life blood on His burial Shroud image!*

Exodus 28:11 *With the work of an engraver in stone, like the engravings of a signet, shalt thou engrave the two stones with the names of the children of Israel; thou shalt make them to be set in ouches of gold.*

Exodus 28:21 *And the stones shall be with the names of the children of Israel, twelve, according to their names, like the engravings of a signet; every one with his name shall they be according to the twelve tribes.*

Joseph was given Pharaoh's *signet ring* as a sign of the power of the Kingdom and it was placed upon his hand. Pharaoh gave Joseph the name Zaphnath-Paaneah when he raised Joseph's rank to the highest position of *Grand Vizier or Prime Minister* of Egypt (Genesis 41:42-45). He would have acted as Pharaoh's *seal bearer,* meaning that he would have used Pharaoh's Royal signet ring to impress his name into clay or hot wax, sealing everything from Royal documents to Royal tombs, and if the seal was broken there was punishment. Something happened as I was editing this and I wanted to add this news. Recently, on July 9, 2014, an article appeared in the news saying: *"Archaeologists uncovered a Bronze Age ceramic coffin and a golden scarab in Israel's Jezreel Valley, the Israel Antiquities Authority (IAA) announced Wednesday."* ***(Source: foxnews.com/science/2014/04/09/israeli-archaeologists-uncover-3300-year-old-coffin-gold-signet/).*** There was a perfectly preserved face on the lid of this Egyptian sarcophagus that was found in Israel. There were several items found inside the sarcophagus with the bones of the deceased male. There were two men and two women found buried near the site. Now this is interesting because in the following Bible passage in Genesis it says that Abraham & Sarah, and Isaac & Rebekah were buried near Joseph. It mentions that Abraham purchased *the field* along with a cave, and clearly in one photo of the news article that I sent to my friend in Israel showing the excavation site, it was clear that this sarcophagus was found *in a field* in the Valley of Jezreel.

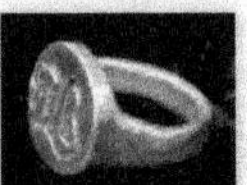

Genesis 24:17-18 *And the field of Ephron, which was in Machpelah, which was before Mamre, the field, and the cave which was therein, and all the trees that were in the field, that were in all the borders round about, were made sure Unto Abraham for a possession in the presence of the children of Heth, before all that went in at the gate of his city.*

Genesis 49:30-31 *In the cave that is in the field of Machpelah, which is before Mamre, in the land of Canaan, which Abraham bought with the field of Ephron the Hittite for a possession of a burying place. There they buried Abraham and Sarah his wife and Rebekah his wife: and there I buried Leah.*

Now this Egyptian Sarcophagus contained the gold Egyptian *signet ring* of Pharaoh Seti I of Egypt from the nineteenth dynasty. Seti I has the most preserved mummy of any of the rulers of ancient Egypt. It is interesting that Genesis 47 mentions Joseph collecting money in Egypt and *in Canaan* for the corn they sold there to the starving people. Joseph probably would have used *the signet ring* during these sales in the land of Canaan, where he was eventually buried.

Genesis 47:14 *And Joseph gathered up all the money that was found in the land of Egypt, and in the land of Canaan, for the corn which they bought: and Joseph brought the money into Pharaoh's house.*

I was looking at an ancient map of Israel trying to determine where the Jezreel Valley was located exactly, and guess what I discovered, much to my excitement? Joseph's older son Manasseh owned the territory that is the Jezreel Valley, or the Plain of Jezreel, and Jezreel is pronounced *"Yizre'al"* in Hebrew. Joseph's father Jacob was Yizre'al/Israel! *Manasseh* asked Joshua for this territory, and to drive out the Canaanites in the Valley of Jezreel. This is ironically, the exact area where they found the Egyptian Sarcophagus that I believe could be Biblical Joseph! In Joshua 17 it states clearly that Joseph's son *Manasseh* asked Joshua for this territory as a possession because they were not given enough land for the amount of children they had. The Valley of Jezreel is known for its very rich fertile soil for growing crops. Seti I was said to have conquered this area and Egypt ruled over it. So several other coffins similar to this one (without the Royal signet of Seti I) have already been found in the valley.

Joshua 17:14-18 *And the children of Joseph spake unto Joshua, saying, Why hast thou given me but one lot and one portion to inherit, seeing I am a great people, forasmuch as the LORD hath blessed me hitherto? And Joshua answered them, If thou be a great people, then get thee up to the wood country, and cut down for thyself there in the land of the Perizzites and of the giants, if mount Ephraim be too narrow for thee. And the children of Joseph said, The hill is not enough for us: and all the Canaanites that dwell in the land of the valley have chariots of iron, both they who are of Bethshean and her towns, and they who are of the valley of Jezreel. And Joshua spake unto the house of Joseph, even to Ephraim and to Manasseh, saying, Thou are a great people, and hast great power: thou shalt not have one lot only: But the mountain shall be thine; for it is a wood, and thou shalt cut it down: and the out-goings of it shall be thine: for thou shalt drive out the Canaanites, though they have iron chariots, and though they be strong.*

Now, incredibly, I had already written about Joseph wearing Pharaoh's *signet ring,* so it is a miracle that the *pure gold signet ring* of Pharaoh Seti I was found in this sarcophagus. But what is really stunning, is the fact that they said there was a *"dagger"* in the sarcophagus. Now because I had written about the *signet ring* of the King, I knew that *the Royal Sceptre always goes with the Royal ring.* Then I knew that *the Egyptian Royal Sceptre* was most likely this so-called *"dagger"* that was an artifact found in the sarcophagus. I compared this artifact to the tip of the well-preserved Egyptian Royal Sceptre of King Tut, and they appear to be similar in size, if you hold the shaft of the *"dagger,"* and hold it upright in your hand. I also believe you can see a faint lotus flower at the end of the Sceptre near the base of its shaft. ***(Source: eyeconart.net/history/ancient/egypt/tut.htm).*** This artifact was found on *the right side* of the sarcophagus, which is interesting because *the Sceptre is held in the right hand.* Honestly, I believe that they may have just unearthed Joseph's sarcophagus without knowing it, and I hope they will research this! The so-called *"dagger"* would be the Egyptian *"Sekhem."* The *same*

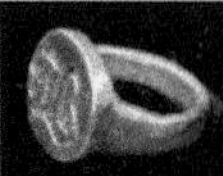
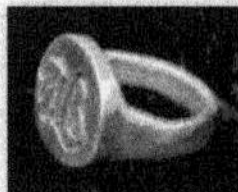

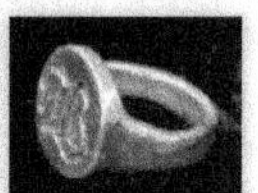

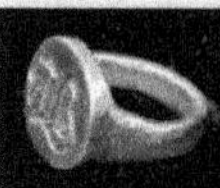

day that this news article was released, there was another article showing that a 4,000 year old limestone statue, thirty inches high, was set to be auctioned at Christie's in New York. Joseph actually lived approximately 4,000 years ago. The statue depicted an official named *"Sekhema"* with his wife, and it is believed to have come from the Royal Cemeteries at Saqqara, south of Giza. ***(Source: news.yahoo.com/egypt-challenges-sale-valuable-ancient-statue-104733054.html#).*** *Sekhem* appears to me to be another spelling of *"Shechem," or "Sikima"* which is the place where they took the bones of Joseph to bury him in the parcel of land in Israel that belonged to his ancestors. From the Encyclopedia, I found the following: SHECHEM she'-kem (shekhem, "shoulder"; Suchem, he Sikima, ta Sikima, etc.; the King James Version gives "Sichem" in Genesis 12:6; and "Sychem" in Acts 7:16): To the rich pasture land near Shechem Joseph came to seek his brethren (Genesis 37:12). It is mentioned as lying to the West of Michmethath (el-Makhneh) on the boundary of Manasseh (Joshua 17:7). (***Source: bibleatlas.org/shechem.htm).***

Joshua 24:25 *And the people said unto Joshua, The LORD our God will we served, and his voice will we obey. So Joshua made a covenant with the people that day, and set them a statute and an ordinance in Shechem.*

Joshua 24:32 *And the bones of Joseph, which the children of Israel brought up out of Egypt, buried they in Shechem, in a parcel of ground which Jacob bought of the sons of Hamor the father of Shechem for an hundred pieces of silver: and it became the inheritance of the children of Joseph.*

When the *signet ring* was *given to another person,* it came with special privileges. All the *powers and authorities of the King* were invested with *the King's ring,* so that whoever was *given the ring* by the King's authority controlled at least part of the Kingdom. Joseph wore Pharaoh's signet showing his authority to control at least part of the Kingdom of Pharaoh.

Genesis 41:42-43 *And Pharaoh took off his ring from his hand, and put it upon Joseph's hand, and arrayed him in vestures of fine linen, and put a gold chain about his neck; And he made him to ride in the second chariot which he had; and they cried before him, Bow the knee; and he made him ruler over all the land of Egypt.*

If this Egyptian sarcophagus proves to be Biblical Joseph, then it is astounding that this ancient find was made during the time I had so much written about the Royal Sceptre, as well as the Royal signet ring of the KING! There is no doubt that this person was of the highest rank!

Now after adding this news here I will carry on with what I wrote already about the Royal signet ring of the Royal Sovereign. Isaiah wrote the following Words of the LORD.

Isaiah 60:12-16 *For the nation and kingdom that will not serve Thee shall perish; yea, those nations shall be utterly wasted. The glory of Lebanon shall come unto Thee, the fir tree, the pine tree, and the box together, to beautify the place of My Sanctuary; and I will make the place of My feet glorious. The sons also of them that afflicted Thee shall come bending unto Thee; and all they that despised Thee shall bow themselves down at the soles of Thy feet; and they shall call Thee, The City of the LORD, The Zion of the Holy One of Israel. Whereas thou hast been forsaken and hated, so that no man went through thee, I will make thee and eternal excellency, a joy of many generations. Thou shalt also suck the milk of the Gentiles, and shalt suck the breast of kings; and thou shalt know that I the LORD am thy Saviour and thy Redeemer, the mighty One of Jacob.*

The place of His feet is *the resting place of the Royal Sceptre* in the KINGS hand. Israel will become *"An Excellency"* by the Divine Presence of His Royal Majesty, the mighty KING. Often the Royal Monarch was called, *"You're Excellency."* The word *"Excellency"* refers to having *"Virtue"* and this pertains ironically to, *"A Standard of Right."* So the Royal Sceptre, the Messiah, is without a doubt *"the Standard of Right and Morality,"* as the Living Torah. Just as it happened with Joseph, the Messiah will have His enemies bow the knee before Him as their KING. *Virtue* also reveals *"the KINGS strength, courage, valour, power, and capability to act, as well as being Potent."* The word *"Potent"* actually refers to *"the KING'S Force or power to achieve a particular result."* This was evident when Yeshua was raised from death to life as the First Fruits from the Almond Tree of Life. The KING achieved

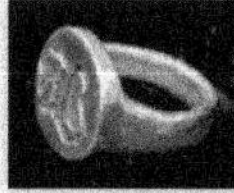

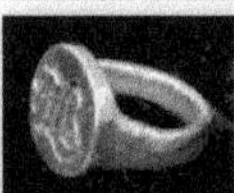

the everlasting result of the LORD'S Living Testimony in order that we might be saved, so we could once again dwell in His Divine Presence in His Garden, as it was before the curse of the Garden of Eden. The word *"Potent"* is evidence that the KING is the *"Potentate."* This means that He is the ruler or Sovereign who wields great power. *Yeshua is actually called the blessed and only "Potentate," the KING OF KINGS AND LORD OF LORDS in I Timothy.*

I Timothy 6:13-16 *I give thee charge in the sight of God, who quickeneth all things, and before Messiah Yeshua, who before Pontius Pilate witnessed a good confession; That thou keep this Commandment without spot, unrebukable, until the appearing of our LORD Yeshua Messiah; Which in His times He shall shew, who is the blessed and only Potentate, the KING OF KINGS, and LORD OF LORDS; Who only hath immortality, dwelling in the light which no man can approach unto; whom no man hath seen, nor can see; to whom be Honour and Power everlasting. Amen.*

In the future Kingdom of the LORD God, all things are engraved with the KING'S Name upon them, like a Royal signet. *So it makes perfect sense that the KING left His seal, bearing His image and His Name, engraved in the Royal Stone of King's, at His Garden tomb. The Messiah left the evidence of the KING'S image on His linen burial Shroud, pointing to His Living Testimony, showing us we were made in His image from this Foundation Stone!* All The Holy vessels and even the horse's bridals will of course be engraved with the saying, *"Holiness to the LORD."* This is engraved like a *signet* upon the Crown of the High Priest.

Exodus 39:30 *And they made the plate of the Holy Crown of pure gold, and wrote upon it a writing, like to the engravings of a signet, HOLINESS TO THE LORD.*

Exodus 28:36 *And thou shalt make a plate of pure gold, and grave upon it, like the engravings of a signet, HOLINESS TO THE LORD.*

Royal crown seal Photo ©2014 Kimberly K Ballard All Rights Reserved

The Royal Signet ring of this KING is now revealed as the *LORD'S promise to marry the Land of Israel* because Jerusalem is the city of God forever, and although many have tried to steal *His Land,* they will not succeed in their evil plot. All things have the seal of the KING OF KINGS AND LORD OF LORDS engraved upon them. Even *the Living Stones* of the Heavenly Temple bear the seal of the Great KING. The incredible truth that I have to proclaim in summary is that when the KING seals a Royal decree with His Royal signet, no one can ever reverse the decree but the KING himself. So when Yeshua destroyed the workings of Satan and reversed the curse, by *the power and authority of the Royal Sceptre* of the KING OF KINGS, *in the place that was the Garden of Eden,* this signified that Satan can never reverse the decree of Eternal life that the LORD Messiah sealed with mankind in His Eternal Garden in Jerusalem Israel! This is the Good News, this is the Gospel! The Life-giving Testimony and Covenant of Messiah Yeshua is now forever sealed by the KING'S signet ring and no one can ever undo this *decree of Eternal life* because the KING OF KINGS has placed *His seal of His Royal signet* in His Holy Garden. *The LORD showed it to me and it is written in the Royal Stone of King's, at the Garden tomb in Jerusalem, in Holy Mount Moriah.* The Scripture that really shocks me is the following verse in Daniel.

Garden Tomb with Rolling Stone Photo ©2011 Simon Brown England All Rights Reserved

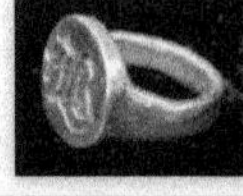

Daniel 6:17 *And a stone was brought and laid upon the mouth of the den; and the King sealed it with his own signet, and with the signet of his lords; that the purpose might not be changed concerning Daniel.*

Wow! *"A stone was brought and laid upon the mouth of the den and the KING sealed it with His own signet so it might not be changed?"* This is exactly what happened at the Garden tomb! A stone was rolled upon the mouth of the rock hewn tomb *in the Garden in Mount Moriah and the KING OF KINGS sealed it with His own signet here so that the purpose might not be changed forever concerning us!* This is absolutely chilling and it is profoundly exciting and Eternally stunning! Thank you LORD!

The Garden Tomb Angel is pointing to the KINGS Royal Signet, the Alpha & Omega
Original Photo of the Garden Tomb ©2011 Simon Brown England All Rights Reserved
Edited by Kimberly K Ballard
Jeremiah 3:14 Turn, O backsliding children, saith the LORD; for I am married unto you: and I will take you one of a city, and two of a family, and I will bring you to Zion.

Mark 15:46 *And he bought fine linen, and took Him down, and wrapped Him in the linen, and laid Him in a sepulchre which was hewn out of a rock, and rolled a stone unto the door of the sepulchre.*

Matthew 27:59-60 *And when Joseph had taken the body, he wrapped it in a clean linen cloth, And laid it in his own new tomb, which he had hewn out in the rock; and he rolled a great stone to the door of the sepulchre, and departed.*

Whatever is sealed with the KING'S signet no man can reverse, just as it is also written in Queen Esther's story!

Esther 8:8 *Write ye also for the Jews, as it liketh you, in the King's name, and seal it with the King's ring; for the writing which is written in the King's name, and sealed with the King's ring, may no man reverse.*

When Messiah Yeshua reversed the curse of Satan's death decree at the Garden tomb, *in the place of the Garden of Eden,* by coming to life as *the Living Almond Branch,* we could now be given Eternal life as *a permanent state of being* through Messiah Yeshua. *The Great KING will never allow anyone to reverse the Living Testimony of the Royal Sceptre of the Tribe of Judah from the Eternal Davidic Dynasty!*

The Kings Royal signet seal Photo ©2014 Kimberly K Ballard All Rights Reserved

II Timothy 2:19 *Nevertheless the foundation of God standeth sure, having this seal, The LORD knoweth them that are His. And, Let everyone that Nameth the Name of Messiah depart from iniquity.*

Only Messiah the LORD, the Royal KING from the Tribe of Judah, could open the seal of His Royal signet ring and look at the contents of the book that was written in Heaven. I believe that the book that He is holding, that is sealed with the seven seals, reveals His mighty glorious reversal of the death decree through His perfect Testimony *and it reveals His Eternal inheritance of the restored earth!* Worthy is the Lamb to open the seals thereof! This is why they were told not to weep because *"The Lion of the Tribe of Judah hath prevailed!* Hallelujah and glory to God in the highest! The LORD KING has performed marvelous things!

The Kings Royal signet seal Photo ©2014 Kimberly K Ballard All Rights Reserved

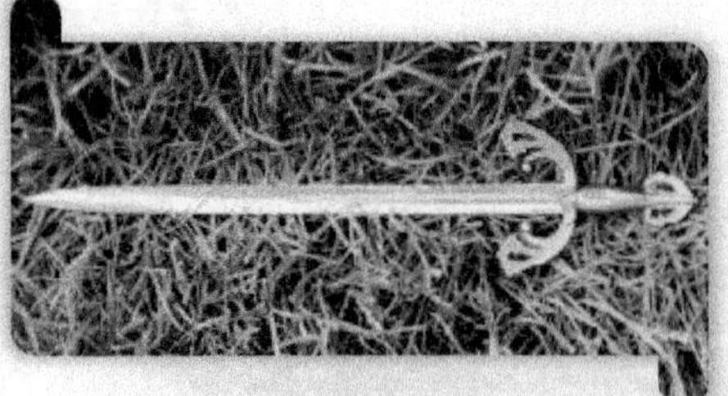

† THE SWORD †

Sword & Irvin Sword Photos ©2013
Kimberly K Ballard All Rights Reserved

We move now to another important emblem of the Royal Regalia, which is the Sword of the King. *"The Sword of Justice and the Sword of Mercy"* are presented at the Coronation Ceremony. The King is to rule by these truths and to be fair minded in *Justice and in Mercy.* The LORD our KING fits this description as a *just and merciful* KING. The Sword is another emblem that represents *"the power of the King."*

In ancient times in Scotland, a King was crowned while seated upon a Coronation stone to symbolize the King becoming united to His people and to His land, and this is how it will be when Messiah Yeshua returns from Heaven. He will be treated to a lavish Royal ceremony to be Coronated KING. He will reign as the Royal Sceptre and Sovereign of the universe and He will be united to His Land and to His people Israel. His throne, the place where He sits to reign, is *the Foundation Stone* of the Heavenly Temple and He will be Coronated upon this stone because He is the Chief Cornerstone. Then with Royal fanfare and the sound of heralding trumpets, our Sovereign KING of Righteousness, Messiah Yeshua, wields the two-edged Sword. This flaming two-edged Sword is the Holy Spirit and the Word of God, *the Living Torah* that comes out of the mouth of the Messiah. When He speaks, *justice* comes upon the earth. The LORD used His *Sword of Justice and Mercy* to save us Eternally so that judgment would no longer abide on us. We are *pardoned* by the KING, through His Mercy, with His own shed life blood upon the Ark of His Living Testimony and, because we have faith in Him, His wrath does not abide on us.

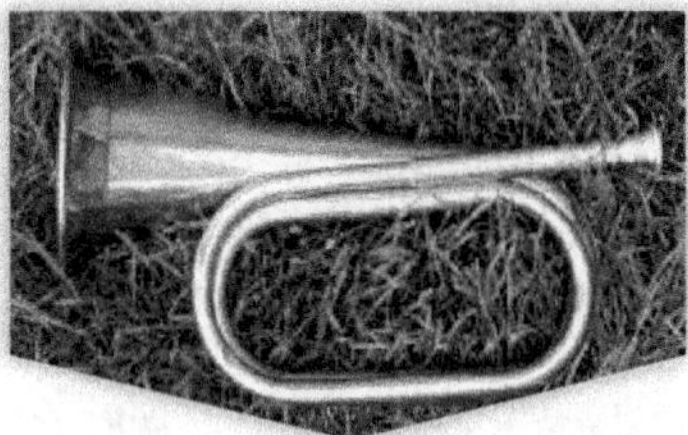

Bugle Photo ©2014 Kimberly K Ballard
All Rights Reserved

In the Garden of Eden, God placed the flaming Sword that turned every way between the two Cherubim Angels.

Genesis 3:24 *So He drove out the man; and He placed at the east of the Garden of Eden Cherubim's, and a flaming Sword which turned every way, to keep the way of the Tree of Life.*

The flaming Sword was placed at the east entrance of the Garden of Eden and this flaming Sword protected *"the way"* to the Tree of Life, so that no one could take the fruit from this tree and live forever and *this Sword was Yeshua,* breathing *the Living Torah.*

Ephesians 6:17-20 *And take the helmet of Salvation, and the Sword of the Spirit, which is the Word of God; Praying always with all prayer and supplication in the Spirit, and watching thereunto with all perseverance and supplication for all Saints; And for me, that utterance may be given unto me, that I may open my mouth boldly, to make known the mystery of the Gospel, For which I am an ambassador in bonds; that therein I may speak boldly as I ought to speak.*

Yeshua made *"the way"* back to the Tree of Life through the two Living Cherubim Angels and into the Eternal Garden of God on Holy Mount Moriah. This is one more reason why the Great Rolling Stone is standing upon Mount Nebo, facing Jerusalem and Mount Moriah, and this proves to me, without a doubt, that Yeshua is pointing *the way* to His Eternal Garden. It is so spectacular! The only way that one could get to the Tree of Life and eat its fruit and live forever was by going back through the two Cherubim Angels, *past the Sword of the Spirit,* and into the Garden to dwell with the LORD forever. This makes it clear that

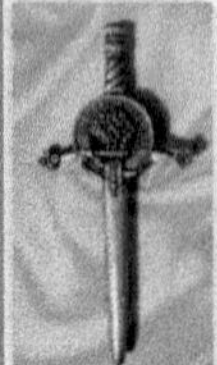

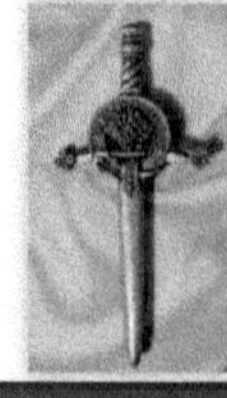

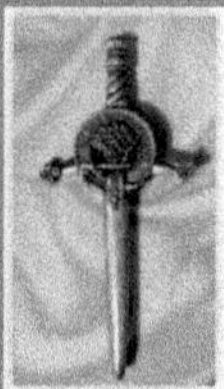

Messiah Yeshua is the only way to get into Heaven. There is only one way back to Heaven and *the way* is through the *two Cherubim Angels,* through the *flaming Sword,* to the Tree of Life. We must come through *the Sword of the Living Torah,* the Rod of God, who gives us His Holy Spirit. This *flaming Sword* is the same *Royal Sword that wields justice* when the LORD Messiah comes to judge the earth in the future. After what I already wrote about *lightning* during Yeshua's resurrection and the Shroud bearing His image, it is interesting that it is written that *"the sword of the KING is polished like lightning!"*

Ezekiel 21:9-10 *Son of man, Prophesy and say, Thus says the LORD, Say, A Sword, a Sword sharpened, and also polished! Sharpened to make a slaughter, Polished to flash like lightning! Or shall we rejoice, the rod of My son despising every tree?*

"The Rod of My Son" is *Yeshua ha-Ben* who wields *the Regal Sword of the Royal KING.* The Gentiles have been given to the Messiah for an inheritance and the uttermost parts of the earth are His possession by Royal decree, as it is written in the Psalms.

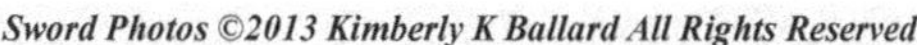

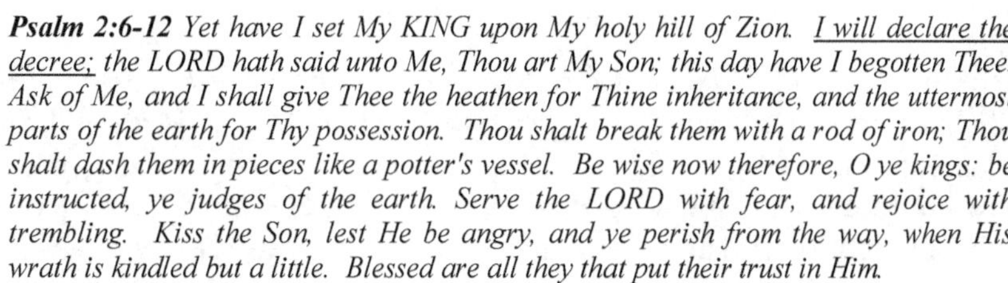

Psalm 2:6-12 *Yet have I set My KING upon My holy hill of Zion. <u>I will declare the decree;</u> the LORD hath said unto Me, Thou art My Son; this day have I begotten Thee. Ask of Me, and I shall give Thee the heathen for Thine inheritance, and the uttermost parts of the earth for Thy possession. Thou shalt break them with a rod of iron; Thou shalt dash them in pieces like a potter's vessel. Be wise now therefore, O ye kings: be instructed, ye judges of the earth. Serve the LORD with fear, and rejoice with trembling. Kiss the Son, lest He be angry, and ye perish from the way, when His wrath is kindled but a little. Blessed are all they that put their trust in Him.*

Messiah Yeshua is *the Son* in this Psalm who comes to fight His enemies with *His Royal Sword,* the Word of His mouth.

Isaiah 66:15-16 *For, behold, the LORD will come with fire, and with His chariots like a whirlwind, to render His anger with fury, and His rebuke with flames of fire. For by fire and by His Sword will the LORD plead with all flesh; and the slain of the LORD shall be many.*

His Word itself is called *"the Sword of Truth, Justice and Mercy."* Everyone that trusts in this KING, that is the Son and the Rod that rules will be called *"blessed."* The reason that we will be *blessed* is because His mercy brings us back to the Tree of Life to eat His Fruit forever. Once we eat this Fruit from the Almond Tree of Life, from The Branch Messiah, we will live forever because of the fact that KING Yeshua reversed the death decree in the Holy Mountain of God. The following description of Yeshua reveals *His Sword* and this description matches Psalm 2.

Revelation 19:15-16 *And out of His mouth goeth a sharp Sword, that with it He should smite the nations; and He shall rule them with a Rod of iron; and He treadeth the winepress of the fierceness and wrath of Almighty God. And He hath on His vesture and on His thigh a Name written, KING OF KINGS, AND LORD OF LORDS.*

The Scriptures tell us, *"There is none righteous, no not one."* Many of the Jewish Rabbi's throughout history have been considered righteous, but they have made mistakes, especially in regards to the identity of the Messiah. Now because the LORD KING is the only truly Righteous Rabbi, the Living Torah, then clearly the LORD God

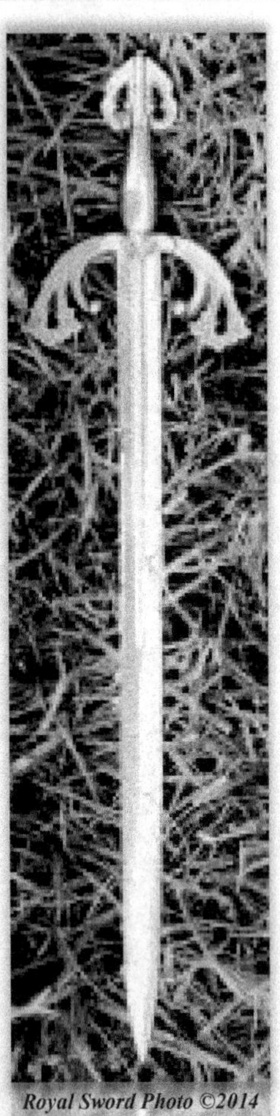
Royal Sword Photo ©2014 Kimberly K Ballard

of Israel has to be the Messiah. *The Messiah is the only one worthy and Righteous enough to reign forever as the KING of the universe.* So we must receive His Righteousness *because His Righteousness as the Word of God, the Living Torah, is the only Righteousness that exceeds the Scribes and the Pharisees!* Yeshua said in Matthew 5:20 that *unless our righteousness exceeds the Scribes and the Pharisees,* we will never enter the Kingdom of Heaven. It is only possible through Him, as our Rabbi of Righteousness. The Messiah, who is called *"The First and the Last," who was dead and is alive,"* is the one who has *the sharp two-edged Sword* coming out of His mouth. *Yeshua is the Sword of the LORD.*

Revelation 1:16-20 *And in His right hand He held seven stars; and out of His mouth came a sharp two-edged Sword; and His face was like the sun shining in its strength. And when I saw Him, I fell at His feet as a dead man. And He laid His right hand upon me, saying, Do not be afraid, I AM the First and the Last, and the Living One; and I was dead, and behold, I am alive forevermore, and I have the keys of death and of Hades.*

Matthew 10:34 *Do not think that I came to bring peace on the earth; I did not come to bring peace, but a Sword.*

In Psalm 45, *The Royal KING who has the Sword is the LORD, and His Bride wears clothing wrought of pure gold.* The KING'S Bride is brought before Him and she is wearing raiment of needlework. It is interesting that the virgins follow her to enter the KING'S Palace! This is the Heavenly Temple of the LORD. It refers to the virgins that prepare themselves to meet the Bridegroom having the oil of the Spirit burning in their lamps. They come behind the Bride into the city of God. This is a Messianic Prophecy about the Royal Sceptre of Judah, the Bridegroom.

Psalm 45:3-15 *Gird thy Sword upon thy thigh, O most Mighty, with Thy Glory and Thy Majesty. And in Thy Majesty ride prosperously because of Truth and Meekness and Righteousness; and Thy right hand shall teach Thee terrible things. Thine arrows are sharp in the heart of the King's enemies; whereby the people fall under thee. Thy throne, O God, is forever and ever; the Sceptre of Thy Kingdom is a Right Sceptre. Thou lovest Righteousness, and hatest wickedness; therefore God, thy God, hath anointed thee with the oil of gladness above thy fellows. All thy garments smell of myrrh, and aloes, and cassia, out of the ivory palaces, whereby they have made thee glad. King's daughters were among thy honourable women; upon Thy right hand did stand the queen in gold of Ophir. Hearken, O daughter, and consider, and incline thine ear; forget also thine own people, and thy father's house; So shall the KING greatly desire thy beauty; for He is thy LORD; and worship thou Him. And the daughter of Tyre shall be there with a gift; even the rich among the people shall intreat thy favour. The King's daughter is all glorious within; her clothing is of wrought gold. She shall be brought unto the KING in raiment of needlework; the virgins her companions that follow her shall be brought unto Thee. With gladness and rejoicing shall they be brought; they shall enter into the KING'S Palace.*

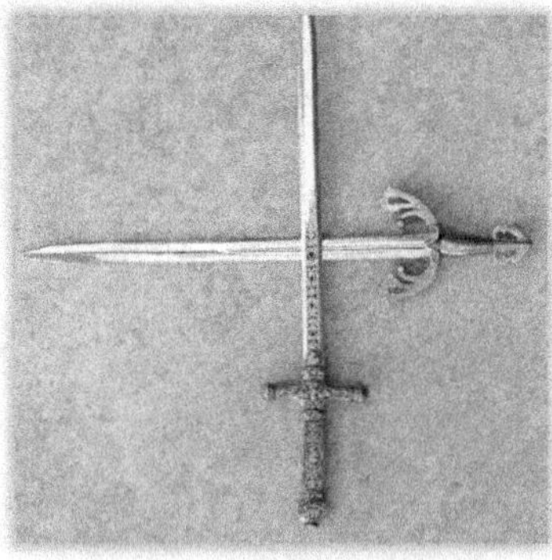
Crossed Swords
Photo ©2014 Kimberly K Ballard

A KING of true greatness possesses all the qualities of *"Compassion, grace, and mercy,"* and His Highness, the LORD KING Messiah, is full of *Justice, Mercy, Grace, and Truth.* The Living Torah is therefore, the KING'S Royal Sword. *The Sword of the LORD has the sharpness of His keen intellect to reveal the Eternal wisdom of His power by His Holy Spirit.* The sword is emblematic of military honour and power and is worn ceremonially for various occasions. The double edged sword of the LORD is the great Royal force of the Great KING OF KINGS, used to keep us out of the Garden of Eden, until the earth is restored!

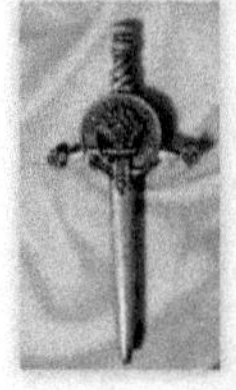

THE CROWN

The Royal diadem or crown is *"the Royal emblem of the power, honour, and authority of the Royal Sovereign."* The Coronation crown is fashioned of pure gold of the highest caliber and is encrusted with diamonds and many rare precious jewels. The crown jewels are often gifts that have been presented to the Royal Sovereign from nations around the world. This crown is placed upon the head of the King, or Sovereign, during the Royal Coronation Ceremony. However, the Sovereign usually has more than one crown and different crowns are used for a variety of other purposes on other Royal occasions. The British Royal Monarch HRH Queen Elizabeth II uses among her crowns *"a State crown that is ceremonial in nature, as well as the Coronation crown on Coronation Day."* ***(Source: The British Royal Monarchy of HRH Queen Elizabeth II - From The Royal Household © Crown Copyright 2013 & 2014 www.royal.gov.uk/MonarchUK/Symbols/TheCrownJewels.aspx).***

When Yeshua, the LORD KING comes, to His Coronation Ceremony in Jerusalem Israel, He will specifically wear the *Coronation crown.* He has another *official elegant crown* that He will wear to perform the duties of the office of the High Priest of Heaven after the Order of Melchizedek. Like any true Royal, the KING OF KINGS wears a variety of crowns and Royal diadems of majesty, and honour, exhibiting with great splendor that He alone is the all powerful Divine Sovereign authority ruling over the universe that He created.

Revelation 19:12 *His eyes were as a flame of fire, and on His head were many crowns; and He had a Name written, that no man knew, but He Himself.*

The LORD God gave the instructions to Moses for fashioning the solid gold Priestly crown or tzitz. It incorporated the Hebrew mitre with the *special blue colored lace* that affixed the pure gold crown upon the mitre of the High Priest. *"The Temple Institute has completed the recreation of this pure solid gold crown of the High Priest for the Third Temple in Jerusalem. It is fashioned in pure gold and is embossed with the Hebrew words, "HOLINESS TO THE LORD"* or *"Holy to God."* ***(Source: ©2007 The Temple Institute, Jerusalem Israel All Rights Reserved).***

This is the crown or mitre that I discovered by Divine Providence that is hidden within the fine details on the Holy Almond Tree Menorah. As I told you in chapter seven regarding the detail of the Holy Menorah, the LORD showed me that within the *"Calyx"* next to the Almond blossom we find the *"Corona," which is veiled inside the Calyx.* Inside the meaning of the definitions of the *"Corona" is the mitre or headdress of the Jewish High Priest.* So Messiah Yeshua wears this sacred and holy Jewish Priestly gold mitre in the Holy Temple and He wears the pure solid gold crown encrusted with precious diamonds and rare jewels for His Coronation Ceremony on Tishrei 1. This Jewish Crown of the Priest is engraved like a signet.

Exodus 39:30-31 *And they made the plate of the Holy Crown of pure gold, and wrote upon it a writing, like to the engravings of a signet, HOLINESS TO THE LORD. And they tied unto it a lace of blue, to fasten it on high upon the mitre; as the LORD commanded Moses.*

It is quite interesting that crowns are also placed on the top of the Torah scroll, because *KING Yeshua is the Living Torah,* so He wears these crowns!

Revelation 14:14 *And I looked, and behold a white cloud, and upon the cloud one sat like unto the Son of man, having on His head a golden crown, and in His hand a sharp sickle.*

Isaiah 28:5 *In that day shall the LORD of Hosts be for a crown of glory, and for a diadem of beauty, unto the residue of his people.*

Over the centuries, representatives of ancient kingdoms willingly presented *gifts of rare precious jewels* from their native lands to Royal Monarchs. They were decoratively mounted in the crowns and sceptres of Royalty. When KING Yeshua comes to reign over all the kingdoms of the earth it will be the desire of the people to bring Him their finest gifts! This is what happened when KING Yeshua was born! The King's brought their finest gifts of gold, frankincense, and myrrh to present before the Heavenly KING. Although these precious jewels of the highest caliber, with the rarest beauty on the earth already belong to one who created them, we will be giving them to Him in love, to honour and exalt Him in glory and majesty.

Psalm 68:29 *Because of thy temple at Jerusalem shall kings bring presents unto thee.*

Revelation 21:24-26 *And the nations of them which are saved shall walk in the light of it; and the kings of the earth do bring their glory and honour into it. And the gates of it shall not be shut at all by day; for there shall be no night there. And they shall bring the glory and honour of the nations into it.*

Every excellent Royal gift will be fit for the KING OF KINGS. It is stunning to think of all the *crown jewels* of all the Monarchs of the earth that will be presented on Coronation Day to honour the Most Sovereign KING of the universe. If the Kings and Queens of the earth bring their glory and honour into the Kingdom of God, then some of the grandest Royal jewels will be used to fashion a Regal Royal Crown for our glorious KING. Only the finest diamonds, amethysts, rubies, emeralds, sapphires, gold, and pure silver, and many other gemstones, will be encrusted upon the KING'S Royal Coronation Crown. From all over the world, in the near future, people will come to Jerusalem bringing their gifts to present before Him with great admiration and love! What a glorious and magnificent *Coronation Day* it will be for KING Yeshua. I mentioned several times that the Jewish New Year *"Rosh HaShanah"* is Coronation Day for the KING OF KINGS AND LORD OF LORDS. On this day, even the Challah bread is shaped into a Crown that is adorned with edible jewels to honor God as the KING. The KING who wears this crown is ironically called *"the Bread from Heaven!"* On this appointed Feast Day, sometime soon, the LORD KING will be Coronated and He will rule with majesty and spread His glory and Heavenly light throughout the entire earth. When that time comes, the love of our KING will radiate His glory forever upon us, and we will see Him face to face. Our hearts will be bursting with love for Him! It is written in the book of Zechariah exactly what I have stated. *All nations will come up to Jerusalem to honour the KING and to keep, The Feast of Tabernacles or Sukkot,* which comes after Rosh HaShanah and Yom Kippur.

Zechariah 14:16-17 *And it shall come to pass, that everyone that is left of all the nations which came against Jerusalem shall even go up from year to year to worship the KING, the LORD of Hosts, and to keep the Feast of Tabernacles. And it shall be, that whoso will not come up of all the families of the earth unto Jerusalem to worship the KING, the LORD of Hosts, even upon them shall be no rain.*

The Feast of Tabernacles is a time to dwell with the KING in our midst, to dine with Him at His supremely Royal banquet table. It is most Holy to the LORD. As we dine in His Royal Palace Pavilion, *the Living Torah* will give us the best to eat. *The crown made from Challah bread reminds us that the Bread of Life rises up into a majestic crown of glory for KING Yeshua.* His joy and Righteousness is exceedingly great. His Royal Majesty sent His Right Sceptre to us, who is the exact image of the invisible God. We can all honour the KING. *His Royal Majestic Coronation Crown proclaims He will begin to reign on the earth forever!*

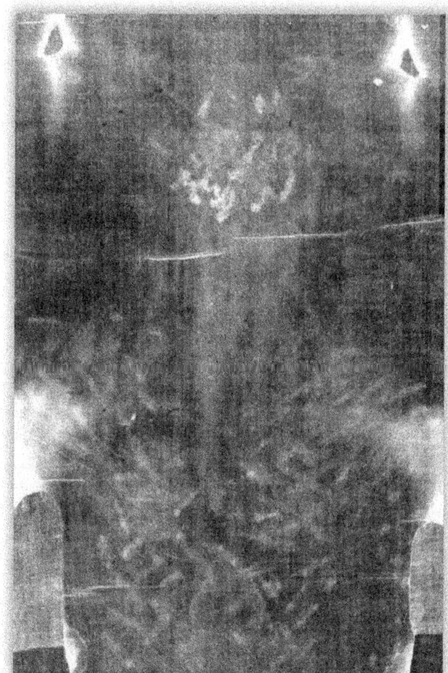

Official Shroud Photograph
Head & Back wounds of Messiah Yeshua

©2014 A. Danin Jerusalem Israel

THE CROWN OF THORNS THE ACACIA TORTILIS TREE

©2014 A. Danin Jerusalem Israel

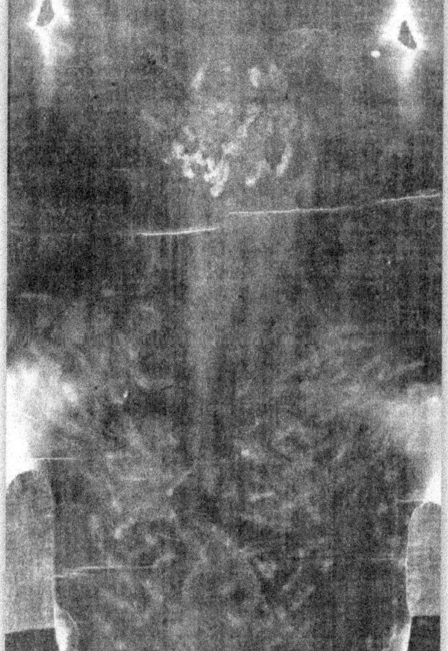

Official Shroud Photograph
Head & Back wounds of Messiah Yeshua

3 Acacia tortilis thorn Photos ©2014 A. Danin Jerusalem Israel

The Crown of Thorns was one of the most important Crowns of the KING OF KINGS. The LORD told Moses to make the Ark of the Covenant from *Shittim wood.* The Shittim wood tree is the *"Acacia Tortilis tree."* The wood was taken from the Acacia Tortilis tree to build the Ark of the Testimony. Earlier in this book, I described how the Holy Spirit came and stayed upon Yeshua in the Jordan River, in the same place where Joshua crossed into the Promised Land with the Ark. This is when I had the Divine revelation that Yeshua is the second Joshua, who leads Israel across the Jordan River into the Eternal Promised Land because *His Testimony is the Heavenly Ark* that goes before them.

So, I began to study the Acacia Tortilis tree that is also known as the *"Umbrella Thorn Acacia"* because the Ark was built from the wood of this tree by the Divine instruction of the LORD. This tree is from the *"Mimosa family"* and this is a very special tree! This species of Acacia tree is said to be easily identified because the Acacia Tortilis tree grows two types of thorns out of its branches. The thorns are thick and woody. On the very same branches, grow very straight long thorns as well as very short curved or hooked thorns and this is very unusual. The long straight thorns stick straight out from the branches like spikes, but up near the bark on each branch, there are shorter hooked thorns that look a bit like a cat's claw.

Now there are some incredible facts regarding this tree. When the LORD showed me these things, I felt certain that the *"Acacia Tortilis tree"* was, in fact, the source of material that was used by the Roman Soldiers to make the Crown of Thorns that was forced down upon Yeshua's head just before His crucifixion. Since Messiah Yeshua is the Living Testimony of the LORD God of Israel and His Testimony abides in the Heavenly Ark, *we must look at the wood of the Ark of the Covenant* to find out how it pertains to Messiah Yeshua!

Next I have written a few known facts about the Acacia Tortilis tree that I believe are extremely relevant to this revealing study. The Acacia tree grows in the Judean Desert and it begins flowering in April. Passover occurs on Nisan 14th around April, the very time that Yeshua was crucified.

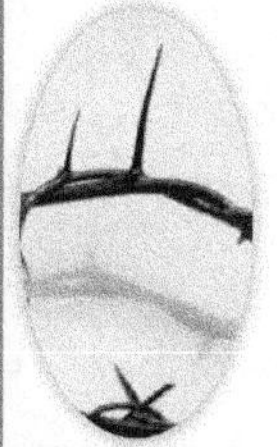

ACACIA TORTILIS TREE FACTS; Quote from "Flowers In Israel."

"This Acacia grows in Israel in hot areas of the Judean Desert. The Acacia Tortilis flowers in the months from April through December. The spines are in pairs some short and hooked up to

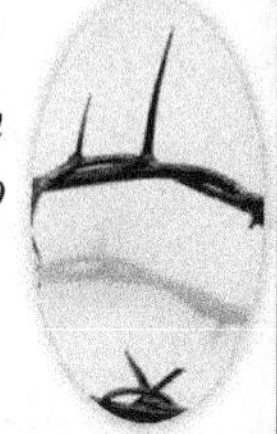

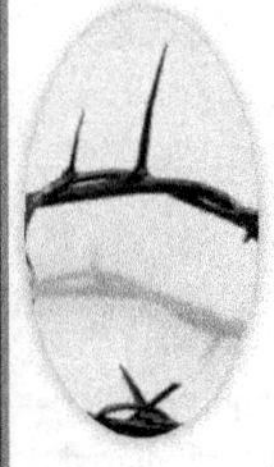

5mm long mixed with long straight spines. The presence of these two types of thorns distinguishes the Umbrella Thorn Acacia from other Acacias. ***"Acacia"*** *is from the Greek word, "akis," meaning a point or a barb. "Tortilis" means "twisted" and refers to the pod structure. "The Acacia has a Crown that spreads out like an umbrella."* ***(Source: "Flowers In Israel" - Acacia Tortilis page ©2005-2011 Martha Modzelevich Israel).***

"ACACIA" The Jewish Encyclopedia of Rabbinical Literature states;
See Tan. l.c.: "Of all these the Shittim-wood alone was selected in order to atone for the sin that Israel was to commit in Shittim [Num. xxv. 1 et seq.]" ***(Source: ©2002 The Jewish Encyclopedia).***

Notice first, that the statement above says that the Acacia Tortilis tree has *"a crown that spreads out like an umbrella."* When I saw this description, it reminded me of the umbrella shaped Crown of Thorns that appears in evidence on the Shroud of Turin, the burial Shroud of Yeshua of Nazareth. Now if it is true, as the Jewish Encyclopedia states that *the Acacia Tortilis wood is the only wood selected by the LORD God to atone for the sins of Israel,* then the Acacia Tortilis tree branches were likely the source of the wood for the Crown of Thorns for the Jewish Messiah, who atoned for the sins of the world! Furthermore, Yeshua was being mocked as *the Jewish KING!* Yeshua did atone for the sins of Israel, as their Great High Priest and KING, and He is found in every element of the Testimony of the Heavenly Ark. Therefore, I absolutely believe and I am convinced, after what I have discovered that this Acacia tree was the source of the wood for KING Yeshua's Crown *when He bore the curse of Eden to atone for our sins as the following Scriptures testify!*

Romans 11:26-27 *And so all Israel shall be saved; as it is written, There shall come out of Zion the Deliverer, and shall turn away ungodliness from Jacob; For this is My Covenant unto them, when I shall take away their sins.*

Isaiah 53:8 *He was taken from prison and from judgment; and who shall declare His generation? For He was cut off out of the land of the living; for the transgression of My people was He stricken.*

Matthew 26:28 *For this is My blood of the New Testament, which is shed for many for the remission of sins.*

Hebrews 9:28 *So Messiah was once offered to bear the sins of many; and unto them that look for Him shall He appear the second time without sin unto salvation.*

I Peter 2:21-25 *For even hereunto were ye called; because Messiah also suffered for us, leaving us, an example, that ye should follow His steps; Who did no sin, neither was guile found in His mouth; Who, when He was reviled, reviled not again; when He suffered, He threatened not; but committed Himself to Him that judgeth righteously; Who His own self bare our sins in His own body on the Tree, that we, being dead to sins, should live unto righteousness; by whose stripes ye were healed. For ye were as sheep going astray; but are now returned unto the Shepherd and Bishop of your souls.*

The Crown of Thorns represented *the atonement* of God, as He reversed the curse of death from the Garden of Eden, because the curse had only given us *"thorns and thistles, as we worked the ground for our bread."*

The Messiah came to bear the curse in order to give us the Bread of Life, the Living Torah or Bread from Heaven, so that we would no longer have to toil the cursed ground for our bread. With the Crown of Thorns, the KING not only atoned for our sins, but He also took away our bondage on Passover and death passed over us because His life blood, the blood of the Lamb, was now upon us and our children! So Yeshua bore *the bitterness* of the curse with a Crown of Thorns and then He was resurrected to life to wear the *sweet Crown of the victorious Eternal Living Majestic KING!* It states above, that the Greek word for Acacia is *"Akis"* meaning *"point or barb."* This is obviously referring to the very sharp thorns that grow on this tree that are said *"to be as long as 5mm."* The Thorns of the Acacia not only pierced Yeshua's head, but the smaller curved thorns hooked into His head. The two types of thorns on this Crown definitely held the Crown firmly in place in Yeshua's skull. *Therefore, you could say*

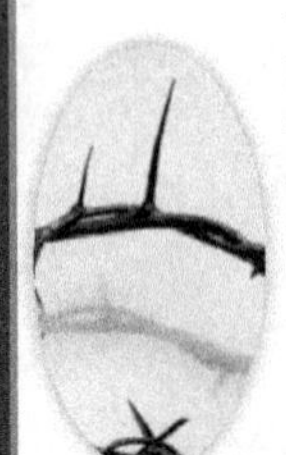

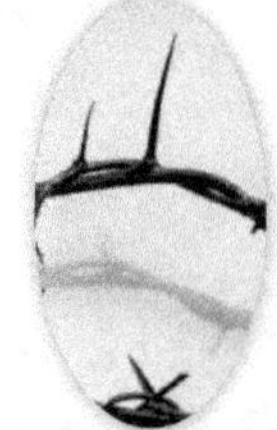

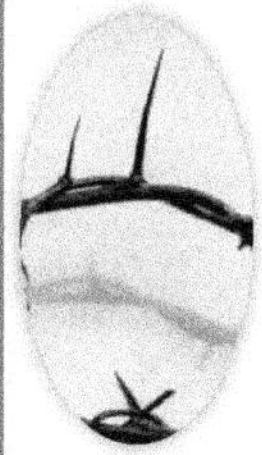

that the Greatest Jewish Rabbi KING Messiah wore the Crown of Thorns that was a "skull cap!" Astonishingly, another *point* to make is that the very word *"Tortilis" already means "twisted."* I believe now that it is very possible that the Gospel accounts reveal the type of wood of the Crown of Thorns because it is written that the Roman Soldiers *"plaited or twisted"* a Crown of Thorns. If the very word *"Akis or Acacia"* means *"point or barb"* and *"Tortilis"* means *"twisted"* (referring to the pod structure), then the only thing that the Roman Soldiers would have to do is cut a few short branches from this Acacia Tree to form it into a cap like wreath and force the Acacia Tortilis branches down upon His head, like an umbrella shaped Crown. The Acacia Tortilis tree is already known as having twisted pods, and for having an umbrella shaped Crown! Remember that the Roman Soldiers were deliberately *mocking Yeshua as the Jewish KING!*

So I believe that the Romans already knew the value of *this special atoning wood of the Ark of the Covenant for the Jewish people* because they were controlling the Jewish Temple at that time! I believe that the Soldiers knew that the Acacia Tortilis was the only wood to atone for Israel's sins! Therefore, the Romans deliberately used the most significant wood from the Acacia Tortilis to mock the KING of Israel and they bowed the knee to Yeshua. The Roman Soldiers pushed the Crown of Thorns down into Yeshua's skull as a *skull cap* and they hit Him repeatedly with blows on the head, on the thorny Crown, with the reeds that were in their hands because they meant this as an insult and as a curse to the KING of the Jews. You must remember what I told you in my chapter on the Holy Almond Tree Menorah. I said that I discovered, much to my astonishment, that the Divine design of the Holy Almond Tree Menorah hides *"a Crown that is given by the Romans for a great military victory."* It is this Crown of the Roman mockery that is hidden in the design detail on the Holy Almond Tree Menorah *within the "Corona" and inside the "Calyx."* This is why they were mocking Yeshua! The Roman Soldiers knew that the Jews were expecting a great military leader to come defeat them and He was to be *"The KING Messiah of Israel."* Yet the Messiah was not fighting back. Instead, by the Divine will of God, Yeshua, the Rod of God, was lifted up on the cross to accomplish the reversal of the curse of Eden that produced the thorns and thistles and to destroy the workings of Satan forever. What they did not understand is the fact that the KING came humbly upon the colt of a foal the first time, but He will return as the victorious glorious KING OF KINGS riding upon a white horse. He will destroy the enemies of God and restore Israel in the last days. Right now He is busy gathering as many people into His camp as possible before the wrath is poured out. The Roman Soldiers also mocked Yeshua as the Royal Sceptre in the right hand of the KING by putting a reed in His right hand!

Matthew 27:29 *And when they had platted a Crown of Thorns, they put it upon His head, and a reed in His right hand; and they bowed the knee before Him, and mocked Him, saying, Hail, KING of the Jews!*

Mark 15:17-18 *And they clothed Him with purple, and platted a Crown of Thorns, and put it about His head, And began to salute Him, Hail, KING of the Jews!*

John 19:1-5 *Then Pilate therefore took Yeshua and scourged Him, And the Soldiers platted a Crown of Thorns, and put it on His head, and they put on Him a purple robe, And said, Hail, King of the Jews! And they smote Him with their hands. Pilate therefore went forth again, and saith unto them, Behold, I bring Him forth to you, that ye may know that I find no fault in Him. Then came Yeshua forth, wearing the Crown of Thorns, and the purple robe. And Pilate saith unto them, Behold the man!*

The term *"platted"* that is used here in connection with the Crown of Thorns actually means *"plaited, twisted, or braided."* Now, notice the words that the Roman Soldiers shouted jeeringly at Yeshua just after they forced their Crown of Thorns upon Yeshua's head *while crowning Him for a great Roman military victory in total mockery.* The words of the Roman Soldiers tell us everything! They immediately began saluting Yeshua and saying, *"Hail, KING OF THE JEWS!"* Their words reveal to us that the Roman Soldiers knew exactly what they

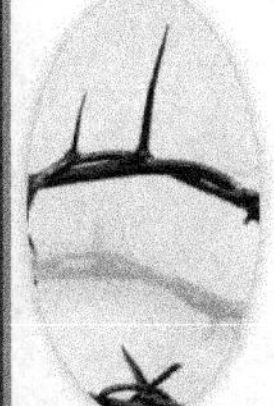

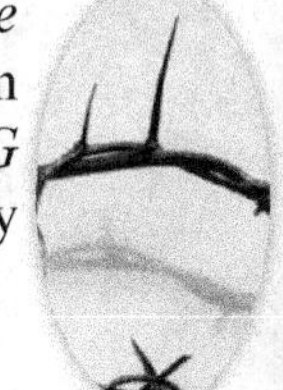

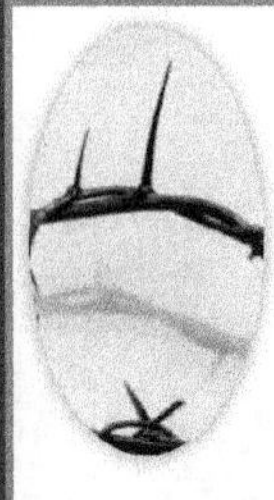

were doing against the Jews. They were using the very symbols or emblems of *the Royal Regalia* and of the Jewish religion to mock *Yeshua, the Jewish KING.* As I said, they knew that the Jews were anticipating a Messiah who would lead them into a great military victory over Rome. So when the Roman Soldiers could see that Yeshua was not going to fight back or win, according to their interpretation of things, *they turned Him into a mockery, as if He was a great KING, winning a great military victory.* The truth is, however, that *Yeshua is the Great KING* and He did win the greatest victory over Satan forever because He fulfilled the Living Testimony of God that abides upon the Heavenly Ark, and so He was Crowned with *Acacia Tortilis thorns!* They slapped Yeshua and spit in His face. They struck Him with the reeds on the head on top of the Crown of Tortilis Acacia thorns. This KING did bring the atonement for the children of Israel, but not in the way that they were expecting Him to accomplish it! He was meek, gentle, and humble of heart. *They did not know that this Crown was only one of the many Crowns that this Great KING will wear.* This time, however, He rode into Jerusalem on a donkey and He came as the suffering servant to fulfill the Word of God and to complete the Living Testimony of the LORD, *as the Heavenly Ark.* The Roman Soldiers also mocked Yeshua with *the purple Royal Garment of the Royal Regalia for the Highest Royal Sovereign!* Because the Acacia Tortilis tree is the only source of wood that is acceptable to God for the atonement of the sins of Israel, it is the only wood that could be used to build the LORD'S Ark of the Covenant. Yeshua stood in the Jordan River as the Living Ark of the Testimony of Heaven and the dove rested upon Him. Therefore, each element of the Holy Ark absolutely pertains to Yeshua's Eternal Testimony. So it is very significant that Yeshua wore this Crown made of the special wood for the sin atonement of Israel, as the Passover Lamb on Nisan 14.

Because of the fact that *the Acacia Tortilis tree grows in the Judean desert and it blooms at the very time of Passover when Yeshua was crucified,* the Roman Soldiers definitely had access to this specific tree because it grows right there in Jerusalem. So it is astonishing to realize that *"the Lion of the Tribe of Judah," the KING,* actually wore *"a Judean desert Crown"* during the crucifixion, and the LORD will inherit Judah as His portion! It is quite astounding to me that this tree fits so much of the description of the Crown of Thorns. Every aspect of this tree is representative of the Ark and when you read the rest of this chapter, you will understand exactly why I am certain that this was the wood source for Yeshua's Crown of Thorns. The fact that the Crown of Thorns fit like an *umbrella* upon Yeshua's head, and *the Acacia Tortilis is also called "The Umbrella Thorn Acacia"* is truly remarkable. As I pondered this, it suddenly occurred to me that an umbrella covers all who are underneath it. *So Yeshua covered all our sins like an umbrella when He wore the Crown of Thorns*, and remember that I discovered that the Lamb's Ear Maror was called *"Saviour's blanket because He covered all our sins!"* After I wrote all of this down, there was something that surprised me that I found in my study and it is also quite astonishing. In Jerusalem, they discovered one crucifixion victim whose bones were still in an ossuary box and it was dated to the same century as Yeshua of Nazareth. The bones belonged to a young man named *"Yohanan."* It is a fact and, believe me, it is no coincidence that between his ankle bone and the iron nail, they found traces of *Acacia wood!* Perhaps he was crucified beside Yeshua! This is unbelievable to say the least and shows proof that *the Acacia* was used during crucifixion. So Yeshua bore the curse of death of the thorns and thistles of Eden and then He came to life to restore us to His Eternal Garden in Jerusalem without the curse, so we could have the Bread from Heaven and the First Fruit from the Almond Tree of Life. The KING has sealed the decree of Eternal life with His Royal signet in His Garden where Yeshua came to life. No one can reverse what Yeshua has accomplished with the atoning wood of the Ark of His Testimony. When He returns from Heaven to gather His elect, He will wear the Royal Coronation Crown of the KING of Glory. He will return to Jerusalem victorious over death! Although the Romans believed in their wickedness that they had achieved a great military victory over *the Jewish KING,* they had no idea how wrong they

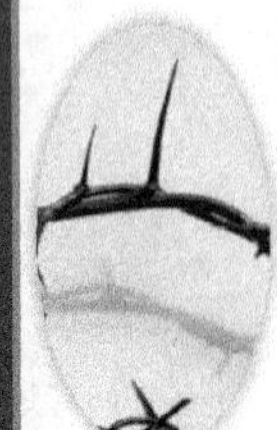

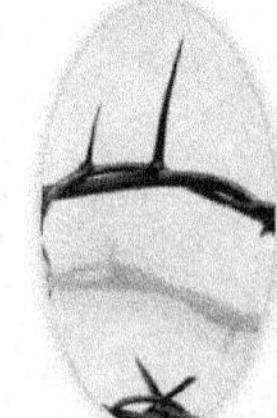

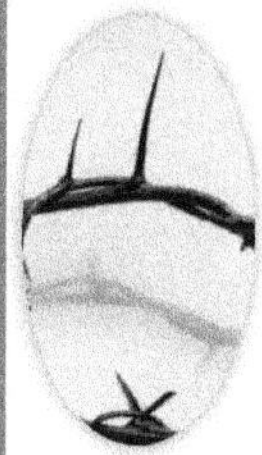
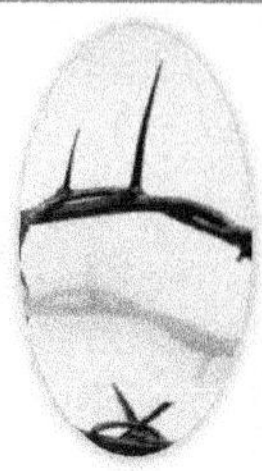

were. What they meant for evil against *the Jewish KING* turned out to be the greatest victory in human history. It was absolutely impossible for them to destroy the LORD God of Israel. They could not defeat this Royal Sovereign, *THE KING OF KINGS.*

As I was about to complete this topic on the Crown of Thorns, I just knew in my heart that there was more to this part of the story. So I asked the LORD to show me something else about this Crown and then it happened! I woke up thinking of the *Kippah* that is also known as the Jewish *Yarmulke.* I knew the LORD was directing me to look at this aspect of the Crown and I believe that this led me to more fantastic details about Yeshua's Crown of Thorns. You must continue to keep in mind that the Romans were *deliberately mocking the Jewish KING.* The first thing that came to me that was so fantastic is the fact that the Yarmulke is indeed called *"a skull cap." This means that Yeshua bore the curse and wore the Jewish Kippah of Thorns in the place of the Skull, which is Golgotha on Holy Mount Moriah! The Crown of Thorns was therefore clearly "a skull cap" that was worn on the head of the Jewish KING!* As I thought more about the Crown of Thorns, I wondered in my heart if there was a Kippah or Yarmulke that fit the whole head with the front of it coming down to the middle of the forehead just like the Crown of Thorns comes to the middle of Yeshua's forehead, on the Shroud of Turin. Sure enough, I found the Yarmulke that was almost precisely the size of the Crown of Thorns and it was called a *"Frik Kippah."* Not only did it fit just like the Crown of Thorns, it fit the whole head, even going down to the middle of the forehead on the front. On the back of the head, it fit down below the middle of the head and this is exactly how it appears on the Shroud of Turin. The modern Frik Kippah comes in sizes 7 to 10 inches in diameter. Although I have seen Kippahs many times, I was only familiar with the smaller round type that sits on the crown of the head, but I was not familiar with the kind that covers the whole head like a ski cap. The Frik Kippah covers the whole head, exactly like the Crown of Thorns. As I researched, I found a woman who demonstrated different styles of Kippahs and I saw the Frik Kippah as it was displayed on the head of a mannequin. When I saw this image, it looked just like the Crown of Thorns appears to fit on the Shroud image of Yeshua and the same as it appears in films about Yeshua's crucifixion. Now I mentioned that I believe that this Crown was made from the Umbrella Thorn Acacia and I was telling you that Yeshua covered all our sins like an umbrella. So the LORD gave me verification of this in the Yarmulke! The Kippah is actually called *"a covering"* on the head. Usually it is worn by a Jewish male, as the Jewish women do not need to wear a Kippah. *So Yeshua, the Ark of Heaven, wore a covering of Acacia Tortilis wood!* The Yarmulke or Kippah exhibits *"the sign of humility."* The man who wears a *"skull cap"* is considered to be constantly focused and *aware of the Divine Presence of the LORD* that is always above him. Without this covering, one is considered to be in a state of *"nakedness"* and the Scriptures speak of His people not being found in this state of *"nakedness."* I believe Adam and Eve experienced being found in this state of *"nakedness"* after they disobeyed their KING! The Yarmulke is worn when one wants to honour God's Name or to mention His Divine Name. So the truth is that because Yeshua came as the humble suffering servant, *He showed the utmost humility to atone for our sins* because He was really the KING of glory, but He humbled Himself for our benefit as a suffering servant. When the Rod was lifted up on the cross, He was constantly focused and aware that He was sent for this purpose to fulfill the everlasting Testimony of the Heavenly Ark. God has highly exalted His powerful Rod and under His Name, *"Yeshua,"* every knee shall bow and every tongue shall confess that Yeshua the Messiah is LORD, to the glory of God the Father. The works of the exalted Rod brings the ultimate glory to the KING OF KINGS, who is holding His reflective mirrored Royal Sceptre in His hand.

Philippians 2:5-11 *Let this mind be in you, which was also in Messiah Yeshua; Who, being in the form of God, thought it not robbery to be equal with God; But made Himself of no reputation, and took upon Him the form of a servant, and was made in the likeness of men; And being found in fashion as a man, He humbled Himself, and*

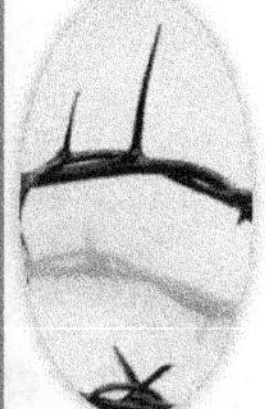
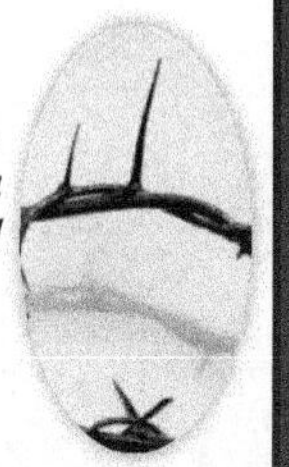

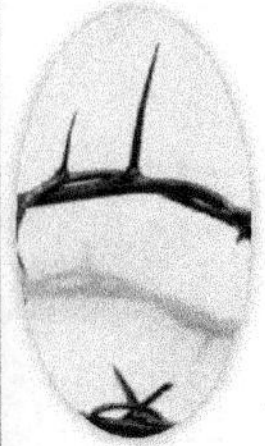
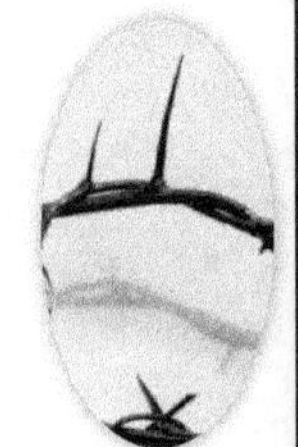

became obedient unto death, even the death of the cross. Wherefore God also hath highly exalted Him, and given Him a Name which is above every Name; that at the Name of Yeshua every knee should bow, of things in Heaven, and things in earth, and things under the earth; And that every tongue should confess that Yeshua Messiah is LORD, to the glory of God the Father.

Now I found the most profound statement in the words of *Rabbi Ronen Levi Yitzchak Segal z"l, (z"l stands for zichrona livracha in Hebrew. It is placed behind the name of a Jewish person who has died, and it means of blessed memory).* **(Source: en.wikipedia.org/wiki/Z"l).** May God bless his soul in Heaven! Although he is now departed from this world and has gone to be with the LORD, he left some very profound words behind *about the Kippah* that I was thrilled to find.

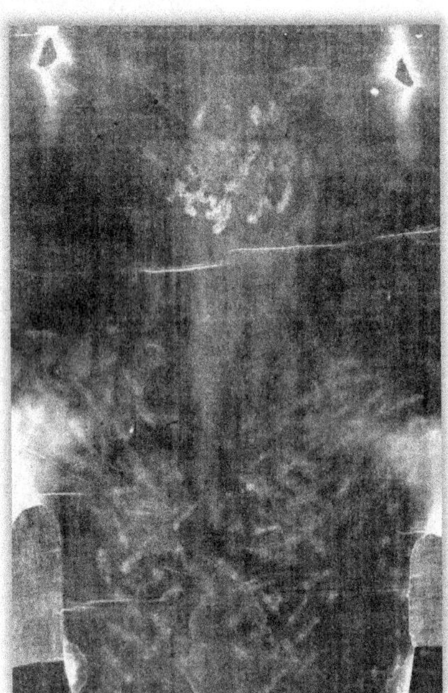

Official Shroud Photograph Back of Head
©1978 Barrie M. Schwortz Collection, STERA Inc., All Rights Reserved

Ronen said, *"It's to remind you that there's a God above you and that He see's everything that you do and this way you will always be fearful of Him."* Then Ronen said, *"What is more respectful to the KING? To have your head covered to show your humility to the KING or to not have the head covering to show that you completely nullified the KINGS Presence!"* So Ronen was basically saying that the Yarmulke was a covering to show your humility before the KING OF KINGS and before His Divine Presence! When Yeshua wore the Crown of Thorns in humility, the KINGS Divine Presence was with us! The KING was in our midst! Now Ronen mentioned something else that was potentially very profound. He said *"Sometimes the Jewish man wears two coverings on his head"* and again, I quote his words while speaking of the Kippah. Rabbi Ronen said, *"It adds to your fear of God or when honoring God's Name or mentioning God's Name in prayer and the like, you should have a covering and then a covering on top of that. That is just the custom of the pious."* ***(Source: Rabbinical Quotes from; Rabbi Ronen Levi Yitzchak Segal z"l © ronennachman770).*** Without knowing this, the words that Rabbi Ronen left on a video before he died, that I happened to run across at this time, were potentially extremely profound. The Bible indicates that there was only one Crown of Thorns forced upon Yeshua's head, but it is interesting to note that, in March 2003, Professor Alan D. Whanger MD, who is the head of *"The Council For Study of The Shroud of Turin,"* claimed to have discovered *"Two Crowns of Thorns"* on the Shroud image of Yeshua, but it was never understood why this would be the case. As I thought about the Yarmulke and the *"two coverings" of the extremely humble and pious Jewish Orthodox men who wear a smaller Kippah on the back crown of the head with a hat over it,* then it occurred to me that when the Romans mocked the Jewish KING, they may have placed two Crowns upon Yeshua in mockery, but it appeared as though it was one large thorny Crown or skull cap. The Jewish men clip the small round disc to the back of their skull and then they wear a hat over the top of it and the hat covers the head down to the middle of the forehead in the front and down to the lower portion of the head in the back, just like the Frik Kippah. Yeshua was a Jewish male who was *the KING of Israel* and He was not only extremely pious and humble, He was also very Torah observant, as the Living Torah! This would mean that Yeshua's Crown of Thorns was *the sign of ultimate humility* because He was extremely pious, just as the Kippah with *"two coverings"* is the sign of ultimate humility! It is a constant reminder of the Divine Presence of God that was dwelling with us! *So Yeshua, the Bread of Heaven, wore the "skull cap" of Acacia wood and reversed the curse that brought forth the*

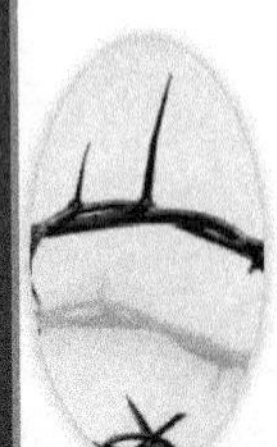
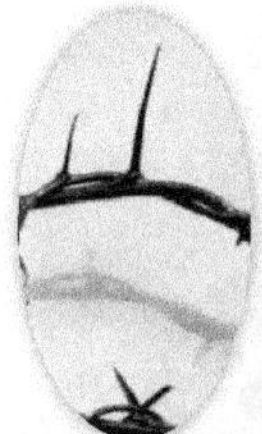

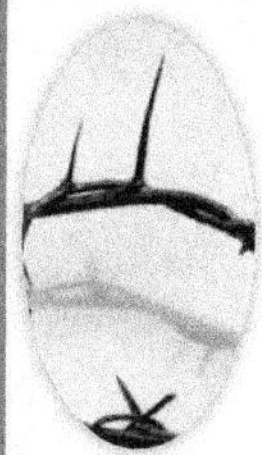

thorns and thistles in the cursed place, "the place of the skull," on Holy Mount Moriah, in the place where death originated that had been the Garden of Eden! Therefore, it was with this Crown of Acacia thorns that *the KING OF KINGS atoned for our sins in extreme humility,* so we would no longer have to toil under the curse for our bread! It is fantastic! In this place, after He reversed the curse, He came to life and offered us the First Fruit from the Almond Tree of Life and showed us the way back through the two Cherubims, to enter the Eternal Promised Land called *"Heaven."* If two coverings were used to mock the Jewish KING, then it would explain why Professor Alan D. Whanger MD found the two Crowns on the Shroud image. My personal view point has always been based upon the Gospel account that seems to mention a single Crown, but you must remember that we were not present to see or witness this mockery of the Great Jewish KING by the Romans for a mocked Roman military victory and remember that a Royal Sovereign KING wears more than just one Crown. Messiah Yeshua was extremely humble and pious as an observant Torah Rabbi. Messiah Yeshua was our covering. The LORD God of Israel bore the curse for our sins and He covered us with His atoning life blood with the sacred Acacia wood, as the Eternal Covenant of the heart!

I later found another amazing connection to the two Crowns that I had not considered yet. I discovered that there are *two Crowns* in the sacred Hebrew spelling of the Name, *"Yeshua."* In Hebrew letters, *"Yeshua" is written as "Yod, Shin, Vav, Ayin."* In sacred Torah script however, *the first Crown is placed over the letter "Shin," and a second Crown is placed over the letter "Ayin."* These Crowns are often referred to as *"Crownlets or Tagin."* On each *"Crown or Crownlet,"* there are three flourishes. The three flourishes correspond to Yeshua's resurrection on the third day as the KING of glory. These decorative crowned letters are only used in the sacred Torah Scrolls. Only eight Hebrew letters have Crowns above them and Yeshua's Name just happens to have two of the crowned letters. Therefore, Yeshua has two Crowns just like a Torah Scroll!

Another interesting detail about the Acacia Tortilis tree is the fact that the inner part of the bark of this tree is used to make rope. While reading Professor Whanger's research about the discovery of the two Crowns on the Shroud, I read that he believes that he also discovered rope on the Shroud image! All of these factors combined together are quite amazing to say the least. Two coverings or Crowns would definitely indicate that the man on the Shroud was not only very humble and Jewish, but it also reveals that the Messiah was Yeshua and that *He was the Divine Presence of God that was dwelling with us! "The head of Messiah is God,"* as it is written in the New Testament of the New Covenant. During Pentecost 2013, I wrote in here that the LORD just showed me that the blood stain on Yeshua's forehead on the Shroud that looks like a large number 3 with a line coming down from it is a form of the ancient Hebrew letter *"shin,"* and according to the ancient Hebrew picture language from *"The Ancient Hebrew Research Center,"* it means *"thorn, pierce, sharp."* The large Hebrew letter shin in blood on Yeshua's forehead on the Shroud is the same letter that is put on the forehead *Tefillin,* the shel Rosh that reminds us to keep the Word of God in our minds. *Shin is put on the door on the mezuzah, revealing that God, our crucified Messiah, is the door to Heaven.* As I said earlier, The Ancient Hebrew Research Center says that this letter *"shin"* also *"has the meaning of a shield, as thorn bushes were used by the shepherd to build a wall or shield, made to enclose his flock during the night to protect them from predators, and another meaning is to grab hold, as a thorn is a seed that clings to hair and clothing."* ***(Source: ©2013 Ancient Hebrew Research Center).*** The Acacia is a thorn bush and a tree! Yeshua was the seed, the Living Torah, and this Good Shepherd became our shield from Satan by wearing the Acacia thorns on His forehead to enclose and encompass His flock. Fantastic! If the *head of Messiah is God* (I Corinthians 11:3), then *the Living Torah* wore the Crowns of *ultimate humility* to rescue us from the curse of death. Our KING of glory will reign forever from the Ark of His Living Covenant. It is absolutely breathtaking, astonishing, and stunning! I love Yeshua my precious KING of Glory!

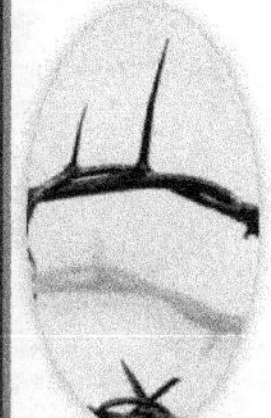

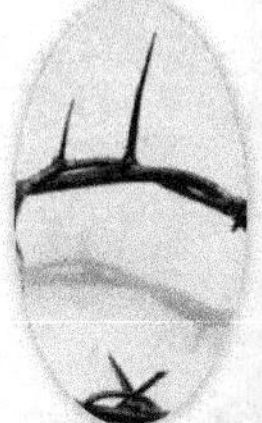

Ocean Waves & Sheepskin

After writing about the Acacia Tortilis tree, I found two other varieties of Acacia trees that are said to be *the Biblical Shittah tree.* We should therefore consider them as possible candidates as the source of wood for the Crown of Thorns. They also have the cat's claw hooked thorns and the woody spiked thorns. The Acacia Seyal has also been considered as the wood source for building the Ark of the Covenant, but it only grows into a small or medium sized tree, having a smaller diameter trunk and branches. Another possibility is the *"Acacia Albida Delile"* also called *"The Shittah tree"* mentioned in the Bible. Ironically, I found a reference to this particular type of Acacia. According to the Jewish Virtual Library, *"The Acacia Albida is written in "Exodus 26:15 and in Isaiah 41:19."* ***(Source: Encyclopedia Judaica © 2008 The Gale Group, Copyright 2012 The American-Israel Cooperative Enterprise, The JewishVirtualLibrary.com).***

Exodus 26:15-16 *And thou shalt make boards for the Tabernacle of Shittim wood standing up. Ten cubits shall be the length of a board, and a cubit and a half shall be the breadth of one board.*

When the measurements of the boards of Shittah wood in this context are converted from cubits to feet, we find that the boards had to be approximately 14.7 feet long and 2 ½ feet wide or more, depending on how you convert the cubit. So it is interesting that the Shroud of Turin measures 14.3 feet x 3.7 feet wide. As I began to research this further, I soon discovered, well after writing about the Acacia Tortilis tree, that Acacia Albida pollen grains were indeed discovered on the Shroud of Turin! I had no knowledge of this at all when the LORD revealed the Acacia Tortilis to me, as the source of wood for Yeshua's Crown of Thorns.

Now I was absolutely thrilled! It is interesting that in the second Scripture mentioned above, the *"Acacia Albida tree" is called "the Shittah tree that the LORD planted" and He said that it will cause us to see, know, consider, and understand together that the hand of the LORD hath done this!* Messiah Yeshua is clearly the Rod in the hand of God who did this marvelous work.

Isaiah 41:19-20 *I will plant in the wilderness the cedar, the Shittah tree, and the myrtle, and the oil tree; I will set in the desert the fir tree, and the pine, and the box tree together; That they may see, and know, and consider, and understand together, that the hand of the LORD hath done this, and the Holy One of Israel hath created it.*

What I find fascinating about this particular species is the fact that the lumber that is acquired from this tree is considered to be very valuable. Since many of the Acacia varieties are small to medium size trees, I have often wondered how Noah could build the Ark from such small trees. The *"Acacia Albida tree"* was the first Acacia that ever stood out in my mind as a possible candidate because it possesses enough wood to build Noah's Ark. According to

various sources, this tree is known as the *"Apple-ring Acacia" and also known as the "Winter Thorn Acacia"* and *"it thrives in dried up river beds. It is the largest tree of the Acacia family and it is said to grow to be 80 feet high."* This fact alone makes it an excellent source of lumber. The most exciting detail though that I discovered in this particular Acacia Tree that I feel connects it to Noah's Ark is the fact that the wood from this particular Acacia Albida is considered *"to be excellent for building canoes."* When this presented itself to me and it was only mentioned with this specific Acacia tree, I felt that it was more than likely the type of Acacia that Noah used for the lumber boards of the Ark. The wood is a very densely grained, beautiful bright red Mahogany color, and its durability made it useful for building ancient Egyptian coffins. This tree also grows very fast. Noah needed access to fast growing Acacia trees in order to have enough Acacia lumber for building the Ark. Since it took Noah around 120 years to build the Ark, perhaps part of this time was spent waiting for more Acacia trees to grow while Noah harvested the mature trees. The Albida variety, like the Acacia Tortilis, *"is thorny, having woody spikes and has similar twisted seed pods, filled with legumes that are high in protein. The flowers, leaves, and pods are edible, so this Acacia tree provides plenty of food for animals, birds, and people."* When the Acacia tree blossoms *it puts forth a beautiful profusion of bright yellow globes, or round powder puff flowers attached to single stems.* According to many sources, *the tree also has excellent medicinal benefits.* The most unusual detail written about the Acacia Albida is the fact that *"it sprouts leaves in the winter in the dry season, and it sheds its leaves in the summer in the rainy season and, therefore, it provides shade and shelter for many birds and animals."* This amazing tree *"helps the desert soil and turns it into fertile nitrogen rich soil, which of course benefits all the other crops around it."* *(Source: Acacia Albida ©2012 Encyclopedia Britannica).* So the Acacia Albida may be the wood known in the Bible as *"Gopher wood,"* in reference to Noah's Ark. It is also possible that *the burning bush* was some type of Acacia tree because the LORD spoke out of the thorn bush and the LORD also spoke out of the Ark that was made of Acacia wood. It is true that *"some Acacia species are more like a bush than a tree."*

Acacia Wood
Photo ©2013 Kimberly K Ballard

It is also said that "a large quantity of tannin is extracted from the bark of the Acacia Albida tree. This source of dye is bottled and sold for tanning leather." As I thought about this little detail, I began to realize that there was something more profound about Simon Peter going to stay at Simon the Tanner's house in Joppa! *I now began to wonder in my heart if Simon the Tanner was using the tannin from the same type of Acacia tree that Noah had used to build the Ark and from the same type of Acacia tree that was used to build the Ark of the Covenant when Simon Peter came to stay at his house.* Simon Peter was in Lydda performing miracles and then he came to Joppa by the sea. I noticed on the Bible map that the city of Arimathaea is near this place and is only a short distance north east of Lydda. It appears to be a shorter distance from Lydda to Arimathaea, than it is from Lydda to Joppa. So Arimathaea is only 7-8 miles from Lydda, while Joppa is 11 miles west of Lydda. Joseph of Arimathaea supplied the fine linen burial Shroud for Messiah Yeshua. While he was in Joppa, Simon Peter raised the devout Jewish disciple named *"Tabitha or Dorcas,"* who was a woman of good works or *"Mitzvot"* in Hebrew. She gave alms to the poor, performing charitable deeds, and she was a believer in Messiah Yeshua. The names *"Tabitha" and "Dorcas" both mean "Gazelle."* I was quite shocked to discover that there is actually a gorgeous Gazelle named the *"Dorcas Gazelle!"* It is amazing that it is also called the *"Ariel Gazelle."* I already knew that the name *"Ariel"* was a very ancient name for Jerusalem and it means *"Lion of God"* in reference to the Tribe of Judah. When all these things came together, I thought it was really exciting because Dorcas was a believer in *"The Lion of the Tribe of Judah named, Yeshua Ha Mashiach!"* She came to life through His Name! Another astonishing fact about the Dorcas Gazelle is that it ironically *"feeds upon Acacia trees!"* It is a gorgeous animal that loves *"To eat the leaves, legume pods, and the flowers of this particular type of tree!"* Gazelles are said *"to go without water for very long periods of time."* ***(Source: Dorcas Gazelle ©2012 Wikipedia, the free encyclopedia).*** This made me think of another interesting connection because I knew that the Biblical shofar or ram's horn could be obtained from the ram, from antelope horns, or from gazelle horns! All these facts spoke volumes to me that there was something profoundly Godly about *"Tabitha" or "Dorcas."* So the LORD put it in my heart to go back and carefully ponder this woman. Then I suddenly noticed a much overlooked passage of Scripture and I was astonished to discover that Tabitha or Dorcas was the maker of Holy Jewish Priestly garments and tunics, translated as coats!

Acts 9:39 *Then Peter arose and went with them. When he was come, they brought him into the upper chamber; and all the widows stood by him weeping, and showing the coats and garments which Dorcas made, while she was with them.*

In this translation, the word *"coats"* is specifically the word *"tunics."* I discovered that it is rendered as *"Kethoneth"* in Hebrew. This garment is therefore considered to be the same type of tunic as Joseph's coat of many colors. The coats and garments made by Dorcas or Tabitha were therefore very specifically referring to the *fine linen tunic undergarments of the High Priest of the LORD.* The Greek translation is written in the Bible as *"Chiton"* or *"Chitonas."* The Greek translation of the word *"garments"* in this same Scripture is rendered as *"Himatia."* It specifically refers to *"the outer garments"* of the High Priest. It is a rectangular shaped garment worn on the outside of the clothing. It can be fastened at the shoulders in some fashion. This would definitely describe the Ephod on the outside of the High Priestly garment, as well as the Ephod Robe that goes under it and over the white linen tunic. The Ephod has mounted engraved onyx stones fastened to each shoulder of the outer garment, bearing the names of the 12 tribes of Israel. So now I realized that this woman Dorcas was obviously very busy creating the garments and tunics of the High Priest for the Holy Temple because she was devoted to the LORD. The city where she lived was located in a place called *"Shephelah"* which was the place known as *"the Valley of Craftsmen" or "ge ha-charashim."* Perhaps she was from the tribe of Judah because the linen weavers were all sons of Judah. As I said earlier, I happened to notice that the city of Arimathaea was very close to Joppa and that it was even closer to Lydda where Simon Peter traveled. As I thought about this, I began to wonder if Joseph of Arimathaea purchased the fine linen burial Shroud for Messiah Yeshua in Joppa. Perhaps it was even woven by Tabitha or Dorcas herself, who obviously was a linen textile expert! Yeshua's burial Shroud has been called *"a very precious piece of fine woven linen"* by the Swiss textile Historian, *Mechthild Flury-Lemberg.* The garments of Aaron were of fine linen woven work, just like the burial Shroud of Messiah Yeshua. Again the word *"coat"* is the word *"tunic"* in the original Hebrew translation, as we see in the following Scriptures.

Leviticus 16:4 *He shall put on the Holy linen coat, and he shall have the linen breeches upon his flesh, and shall be girded with a linen girdle, and with the linen mitre shall he be attired; these are Holy garments; therefore shall he wash his flesh in water, and so put them on.*

Exodus 28:39-40 *And thou shalt embroider the coat of fine linen, and thou shalt make the mitre of fine linen, and thou shalt make the girdle of needlework. And for Aaron's sons thou shalt make coats, and thou shalt make for them girdles, and bonnets shalt thou make for them, for glory and for beauty.*

Exodus 39:27 *And they made coats of fine linen of woven work for Aaron, and for his sons.*

Not only did the High Priest wear the white linen tunic, but the ordinary Priests also wore white linen garments. The tunic may indeed also refer to the rectangular linen garment known as the *"Tallit."* I have spoken about the Tallit before which has the tzitzit or tassels on its four corners. *Messiah Yeshua, the High Priest of Heaven, was likely buried in a Priestly Tallit that was His burial Shroud.*

As I researched the relics of Yeshua, I discovered a statement verifying my hypothesis, much to my delight! It was titled, *"THE SHROUD SENT TO LOUIS IX OF FRANCE BY BALDWIN II, THE LATIN EMPEROR AT CONSTANTINOPLE."* It stated the following, *"We do not know when the missing rectangles from the Shroud of Turin's corners were cut off. It is just as possible that they were cut before 1238 as more recently."* ***(Source: ©2011 shroud.com/pdfs/n56part5.pdf).***

This statement was proof to me that *Yeshua's Shroud was probably a Priestly Tallit* because the corners were cut off! Now according to Jewish custom, I have read that one of the corners of the Tallit is cut off when the man's funeral takes place. So perhaps it was cut off when Yeshua was wrapped in His Tallit just before burial. I ran across a second statement in another place that verifies that the Shroud had corners that were cut off and that were missing! The second statement said, *"Two pieces of cloth from the corners of the Shroud of Turin are missing. Very often the piece of funeral cloth obtained by Louis IX has been thought to belong to the Shroud today, kept in Turin as one of its missing corners."* ***(Source: © December 30, 2011 A.A.M. van der Hoeven, JesusKing.info).***

When I was observing the so called *"Cluny Medallion"* that commemorated the exhibition of the Shroud of Turin in the year 1356, I noticed two interesting objects on the Medallion. At first I thought that they were two Roman flagrums, but as I considered the fact that *Yeshua's burial Shroud was a Tallit for the High Priest,* it suddenly occurred to me that these two identical objects are similar in appearance to the special knotted fringes called *"Tzitzit."* The two objects appear to have knots in them and at the top there is an opened loop. There are several tassels hanging downward below the knotted section on the two objects. On the Medallion, the cross is encircled by a Crown of Thorns and it is rising up out of the empty tomb. This design is on top of a large round circular object in the middle of the Medallion and this design appears to me to be the Great Rolling Stone of Yeshua's tomb. The two tzitzit objects are on either side of the large round stone. God's Name is incorporated in the specially knotted fringes of the tzitzit with the dyed Tekhelet blue strands. The word *"Tallit" means "Sheet" or "cloak."* The *"Sindone"* is the Greek name of the Shroud of Turin, which means *"burial Sheet." Do we have verification that the ancient Jewish Tallit was used as a burial Shroud?* Yes we do!

In the following statement, I found verification that Yeshua was indeed buried in a Jewish Tallit or Prayer shawl. Regarding the ancient Tallit it is stated, *"Originally it was a large white rectangular garment with tzitzit in the four corners and it was used as a garment, a bed sheet and as a burial Shroud."* A second statement about the history of the Tallit said, *"Its design began to change during the second half of the 1st century CE/AD and began to take on the forms known today, beginning around 1000 CE/AD, when the Tallit was modified."* ***(Source ©2010 The Ancient Jewish Shroud At Turin, by John N. Lupia, Regina Caeli Press).***

Now right after Simon Peter raised Dorcas back to life again, if you will recall, the angel of God appeared to Cornelius, who was staying in Caesarea Philippi, and he told him to send men to Joppa. The angel told him to call for one, *"Simon Peter,"* who was lodging with Simon the Tanner by the sea. As I thought about this connection, I was so excited because I realized that it was during Simon Peter's stay at the house of Simon the Tanner that Simon Peter had the vision of the Great Sheet containing all the animals. Simon Peter, the Jewish disciple of Yeshua, had a profound vision from the LORD, and it is recorded in Acts 11.

Acts 11:1-10 *And the Apostles and brethren that were in Judea heard that the Gentiles had also received the Word of God. And when Peter was come up to Jerusalem, they that were of the circumcision contended with him, Saying, Thou wentest in to men uncircumcised, and didst eat with them. But Peter rehearsed the matter from the beginning, and expounded it by order unto them, saying, I was in the city of Joppa praying; and in a trance I saw a vision, A certain vessel descend, as it had been a Great Sheet, let down from Heaven by four corners; and it came even to me; Upon the which when I had fastened mine eyes, I considered, and saw four-footed beasts of the earth, and wild beasts, and creeping things, and fowls of the air. And I heard a voice saying unto me, Arise, Peter; slay and eat. But I said, Not so, LORD; for nothing unclean hath at any time entered into my mouth. But the voice answered me again from Heaven, What God hath cleansed, that call not thou common. And this was done three times; and all were drawn up again into Heaven.*

As I was pondering this vision, I asked the LORD to show me what *"The Great Sheet"* was that appeared to Simon Peter from Heaven. Within moments of pondering this and praying about it, I turned my radio on only to hear a woman Bible counselor, *June Hunt,* giving her advice to a person that had called in to her radio program. It was not a Jewish program, so she had never mentioned the Bible in Jewish terms before by using the word *"Torah."* I was floored, though, when she suddenly went off the main subject. The next words that came out of her mouth over the airwaves, suddenly struck me. It was like the LORD was speaking through her, giving me the answer to my question about Simon Peter's vision. Keep in mind that she was not talking about Simon Peter at all! She was not speaking of his vision at all. For some strange reason, she momentarily spoke out of context and the LORD used her words to spark my memory about something that I already knew. She said, *"The Torah was made out of sheepskin and it was scraped and made clean and white before the writing went on it, so that it became like a sheet of paper."* ***(Source: Statement ©2010 June Hunt, Hope for the Heart Ministries, Dallas Texas).***

Wow! That's it! I could not believe it! The LORD knew that the instant that I heard her say the word *"Sheet,"* that I would understand the vision. Ahhhh! Now I've got it my friend! I was so excited and amazed! After she spoke one sentence about *the Torah,* she went on talking about her previous subject. It was fantastic! Now we know that the Torah is composed of the five books of Moses and that it is stored in the Ark of the Testimony, so it was like a light went on inside my head and my heart! That dear friends is the Holy Spirit! I gasped in a little bit of air in excitement the instant that those words clicked in my mind and I knew that this was the Great Sheet that Simon Peter saw that was coming down from Heaven! I suddenly understood that the *"certain vessel"* that Simon Peter mentioned in his vision was *The Ark from Heaven containing the Living Torah!* Now this was astonishing! I suddenly remembered that the Ark of Noah contained both the clean and the unclean animals, birds, and living things. The LORD was revealing to me the true meaning of the vision. This was so thrilling! Simon Peter had been battling with the issue of the clean and the unclean, which referred to the Jews and the Gentiles. I then wrote down the verse from the Torah that pertains to Noah's Ark, from Genesis 7, that contained the clean and the unclean living things.

Genesis 7:1-3 *And the LORD said unto Noah, Come thou and all thy house into the Ark; for thee have I seen righteous before me in this generation. Of every clean beast thou shalt take to thee by sevens, the male and his female; and of beasts that are not clean by two, the male and his female. Of fowls also of the air by sevens, the male and the female; to keep seed alive upon the face of all the earth.*

The Jews were of course considered clean in the circumcision of the flesh because they knew God and they were given the earthly Torah. The Gentiles were considered unclean because they were uncircumcised and did not know God, but the Gentiles were going to be given the circumcision of the heart *through the Living Torah, through Messiah Yeshua.* So when the LORD lowered the Great Sheet that was full of both clean and unclean creatures in Simon Peter's vision, He told Simon Peter to take and eat of anything in the Great Sheet. Simon Peter declared that nothing unclean had at any time entered into his mouth. Simon Peter was revealing that he had only *spoken the pure Torah from His mouth* and only taught the Laws and Commandments of God to the Jews who were clean. As a Torah observant Jew, he had not eaten any unclean thing, and he did not eat with the Gentiles who were considered unclean because they were not circumcised and did not have God. *In this vision, the LORD was revealing to Simon Peter that he was not to discriminate against the Gentiles because of their uncleanness in not having the Word of God yet, which is the earthly Torah. Simon Peter was now being given Divine direction and instruction to take the Living Torah, the Messiah, to the Gentiles and they would be made clean through the LORD because He is the Great Sheet, who sits on the Ark of His Living Testimony!* I suddenly understood that the meaning of the vision of the Great Sheet means that the LORD intended to save both the clean and the unclean, both Jews and Gentiles, in the Ark of His Testimony in Heaven, through Messiah, the Living Torah, *and He is the Great Sheet in Simon Peter's vision!* The LORD had saved both the clean and the unclean in Noah's Ark before the flood came. So the LORD was going to cleanse us both in *the Living Torah,* in the Great Sheet, and bring us into His Ark to be saved, before the wrath of God is poured out in flaming fire upon the earth.

The Great Sheet in Simon Peter's vision was held by the four corners. The LORD showed me that this represents the fact that *the Living Torah of* Messiah's Gospel was going out to the four corners of the earth to save millions of clean and unclean people from all nations, tribes, and tongues. Then the Messiah, *the Great Sheet and Heavenly Ark,* will gather us up into Heaven to live forever in His Divine Presence. The Great Sheet ascended and descended three times. Of course the number three is the number of the resurrection of the Living Almond Rod which is part of Messiah's Testimony inside the Eternal Ark, and Yeshua descends from Heaven to earth to usher in the Kingdom of God on the third day in the future. Like the Great Sheet, Yeshua descended from Heaven and ascended back into Heaven. Remember that the LORD instructed the people at Mount Sinai to get ready and to prepare to meet Him on the third day? They were instructed to wash their garments ahead of time, so they would be white and clean before meeting the LORD. As I pondered this truth, there was something else that came to mind about this vision that was so fantastic! John wrote the following words about Yeshua.

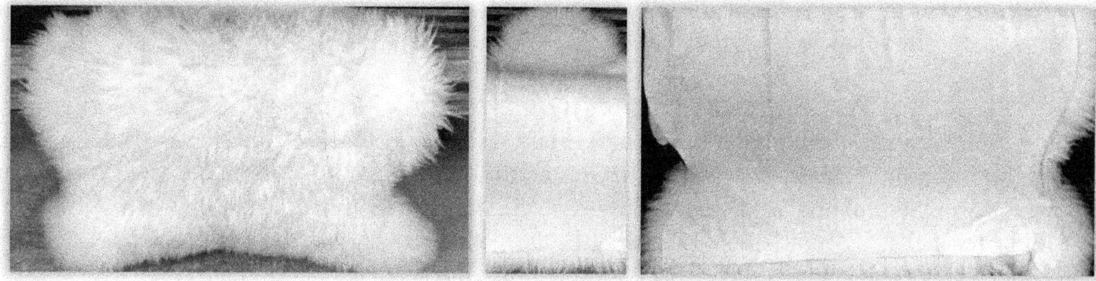

John 1:1 *In the beginning was the Word, and the Word was with God, and the Word was God.*

John 1:14 *And the Word was made flesh, and dwelt among us, and we beheld His glory, the glory as of the only begotten of the Father, full of grace and truth.*

So now a profound truth about the LORD suddenly entered my heart and mind, and at once, I finally understood the reason why the LORD came to us as *"The Lamb of God!" Messiah Yeshua is the Living Torah, so He is the pure white sheepskin that the Eternal Word of God is written upon. In other words, God, the Living Torah, came to dwell with us in the flesh as the pure Lamb of God. This verifies that Yeshua is the Great Sheet of the Heavenly Ark! Therefore, when Yeshua bore the stripes in His flesh as the Lamb of God, we were healed, purified, and cleansed by this Great Sheet!* This, of course, is the Living Heavenly Ark that saves both the clean and the unclean, that gathers us into Heaven!

Now another exciting truth is the fact that I remembered that we are also called *"the sheep of the LORD'S flock."* So I realized that before the LORD writes His Word or Living Torah upon our hearts forever and before we can enter the Ark of Heaven to dwell forever, we must first be cleansed or, in essence, scraped clean and made pure and white by Messiah, exactly like the sheep skin is purified and prepared to have the Word of God written upon it, so it can be preserved inside the Ark forever! The Living Torah is the Covenant of the heart, so it removes the hardness of our hearts and circumcises our hearts in love towards God.

Remember, our garments are purified and cleansed in the Living Water of the Messiah's baptism and in the fire of His Holy Spirit, and this preparation ahead of time makes us ready to meet the LORD face to face! Like the LORD Messiah, we are also like the sheep skin and His Word is written upon us, after He has purified us, because He has saved us forever in the Ark of His Eternal Testimony! He wrote His Eternal Testimony on the two tablets of our heart because His life blood and Living Water is what breathes His breath of Eternal life into us! In Heaven, Yeshua wears the pure white linen garments that are as white as snow, whiter than any fuller can make them. *This is proof that He is the Great Sheet and the Ark that saves us!* After the LORD told Simon Peter not to call common what He has cleansed, then three men appeared in the story and they came to Simon Peter to be saved and to be baptized in *the Living Torah,* in Messiah. It is the LORD who makes our robes white as He writes His Living Torah upon our hearts forever!

Daniel 12:10 *Many shall be purified, and made white, and tried; but the wicked shall do wickedly; and none of the wicked shall understand; but the wise shall understand.*

Revelation 3:5 *He that overcometh, the same shall be clothed in white raiment; and I will not blot out his name out of the book of life, but I will confess his name before My Father, and before his angels.*

Revelation 7:9 *After this I beheld, and, lo, a great multitude, which no man could number, of all nations, and kindred's, and people, and tongues, stood before the throne, and before the Lamb, clothed with white robes, and palms in their hands.*

Revelation 7:14 *And I said unto him, Sir, thou knowest. And he said to me, These are they which came out of great tribulation, and have washed their robes, and made them white in the blood of the Lamb.*

The white garments that have been *scraped clean and washed by the Great Sea of Living Water* are the wedding clothes that Yeshua referred to in the parable of the KING who invited the wedding guests, but then no one came to the wedding. So the KING sent forth His servants to gather anyone who was willing to come to the wedding. Then one came into the wedding feast that did not have on a wedding garment and he was cast outside into the outer darkness. This conjures up a picture of Noah entering the Ark.

As I said in another place, those who were not prepared ahead of time and those who were not wearing the garments of righteousness were left outside the Ark and cast into the outer darkness of the raging flood. The truth is that the Messiah has prepared us ahead of time by giving us the white garments that we must have in order to enter through the door of His Ark, before He closes the door and the raging fire of God's wrath comes upon the earth in the final judgment of the Great Tribulation. The pure white garments are our wedding clothes and they prepare us as a Bride for Messiah. We are ready to meet Him when we are clothed in white through His Righteousness. Then He will come to gather us together to take us home to His Father's House. *So we are truly His sheep when He has inscribed His Living Torah upon our hearts!*

Snow heart Photo ©2014

Psalm 100:3 *Know ye that the LORD He is God; it is He that hath made us, and not we ourselves; we are His people, and the sheep of His pasture.*

John 10:11 *I AM the Good Shepherd; the Good Shepherd giveth His life for the sheep.*

I John 2:5 *But whoso keepeth His Word, in him verily is the love of God perfected; hereby know we that we are in Him.*

Because Heaven was opened when Simon Peter saw the vision, it made me wonder if the vision occurred on Rosh HaShanah. The exciting truth is that the Great Sheet was gathered up into Heaven, carrying a multitude of clean and unclean living beings in it because they had all been cleansed in *the Living Torah and the Great Sea of Living Water* and they were taken up in the Ark of Messiah's Living Testimony! We also find that the Great Sheet in Simon Peter's vision was knit at the four corners. This brings up another very interesting point since the Jewish Priestly prayer shawl has four corners.

Acts 10:10-12 *And he became very hungry, and would have eaten; but while they made ready, he fell into a trance, And saw Heaven opened, and a certain vessel descending upon him, as it had been a Great Sheet knit at the four corners, and let down to the earth; Wherein were all manner of four-footed beasts of the earth, and wild beasts, and creeping things, and fowls of the air.*

As the High Priest of Heaven, Yeshua is, again, represented in the Great Sheet that Simon Peter saw in the vision that was knit at the four corners. The four corners of Simon Peter's Great Sheet were knit together and this signifies that we will be gathered together from the four corners of the earth, purified by the LORD, whether Jew or Gentile, clean or unclean, and saved in the LORD'S Ark as one new man, having our souls knit together and lifted up into Heaven. It is truly the rapture! Simon Peter's vision of the Great Sheet was clearly a picture of Noah's Ark. In the book of Judges, all the men of Israel were knit together as one man. Being knit together is *a sign of love* between those who have the LORD, just as Jonathan and David's souls were knit together as one man because they both loved the LORD.

Judges 20:11 *So all the men of Israel were gathered against the city, knit together as one man.*

Samuel 18:1 *And it came to pass, when he had made an end of speaking unto Saul, that the soul of Jonathan was knit with the soul of David, and Jonathan loved him as his own soul.*

So in the Great Sheet knit at the four corners, we become one loving, living soul, saved together in the pure Ark of Yeshua's Living Testimony, just as it is recorded in the book of the Ephesians.

Ephesians 2:11-22 *Wherefore remember, that ye being in time past Gentiles in the flesh, who are called uncircumcision by that which is called circumcision in the flesh made by hands; That at that time ye were without Messiah, being aliens from the commonwealth of Israel, and strangers from the Covenants of promise, having no hope, and without God in the world; But now in Messiah Yeshua ye who sometimes were far off are made nigh by the blood of Messiah. For He is our peace, who hath made both one, and hath broken down the middle wall of partition between us; Having abolished in His flesh the enmity, even the Law of Commandments contained in ordinances; for to make in Himself of twain one new man, so making peace; And that He might reconcile both unto God in one body by the cross, having slain the enmity thereby; And came and preached peace to you which were afar off, and to them that were nigh. For through Him we both have access by one Spirit unto the Father. Now therefore ye are no more strangers and foreigners, but fellow citizens with the Saints, and of the household of God; And are built upon the foundation of the Apostles and Prophets, Yeshua Messiah Himself being the Chief Cornerstone; In whom all the building fitly framed together groweth unto an Holy Temple in the LORD; In whom ye also are builded together for an habitation of God through the Spirit.*

The LORD Messiah is the only one that could *prepare His sheep to meet Him* face to face. Yeshua spoke the following words. The pure in heart that are *blessed* are those who now have the circumcision of the heart through the LORD, the Living Torah. *When we are clean sheep, He writes His Word upon our hearts and we will see His face.* This is the blessing! Yeshua said this in His Sermon on the Mount.

Matthew 5:8
Blessed are the pure in heart; for they shall see God.

The Great Sheet - The pure sheepskin of the Lamb – The Living Torah
Photo ©2013 KK Ballard
All Rights Reserved

Acacia tree & Acacia branch bearing twisted pods & blossoms with thorns
©2014 Avinoam Danin
Jerusalem Israel All Rights Reserved

Now putting all of this together with the Acacia Albida tree, I figured out that Simon the Tanner was not only preparing the animals skins by stretching them out to dry, after scrapping them clean by the sea, but he was probably supplying the sheep skins for the Torah scrolls to have the Word of God written upon them! The LORD showed this to me later and it proved that what I had written by the power of the Holy Spirit was true about Simon Peter's vision! *Simon the Tanner was preparing Torah Sheets! Simon the Tanner, was also using the tannin from the same type of Acacia Tree that Noah had used hundreds of years earlier to build the Ark!* This is why Simon Peter had the vision of the Great Sheet that was *the Ark and the Living Torah,* while staying at the home of Simon the Tanner! This home was on a tiny peninsula, overlooking the Great Sea and this symbolizes the Ark on the flood waters and that the LORD is the basin called *"the Great Sea of Living Water"* in His Heavenly Temple, which I will discuss thoroughly in chapter twelve. In Exodus 25:5, *tanned ram skins* were mentioned with the Shittah or Acacia wood for the use in the Sanctuary of the LORD. Another type of Acacia is the *"Acacia Seyal Tree."* It is considered by some to be the source of wood for Noah's Ark and for the Ark of the Covenant. It is very similar to the Acacia Tortilis tree in the fact that it produces the straight spiked thorns, as well as the shorter *"cat's claw"* thorns, but this variety of Acacia only grows as a small to medium sized tree. It also has very unusual colorful bark that is said *"to produce at least 18% tannin, for dying leather."* Tanners would always scrape the skins clean by the sea near a prolific water source. ***(Sources: Acacia Seyal and Delile Facts ©1983 James A. Duke, Handbook of Energy Crops. Unpublished From; hort.purdue.edu/newcrop/duke_energy/Acacia_seyal.html). AND (Acacia Seyal Facts ©2007 Acacia Plant All Rights Reserved).***

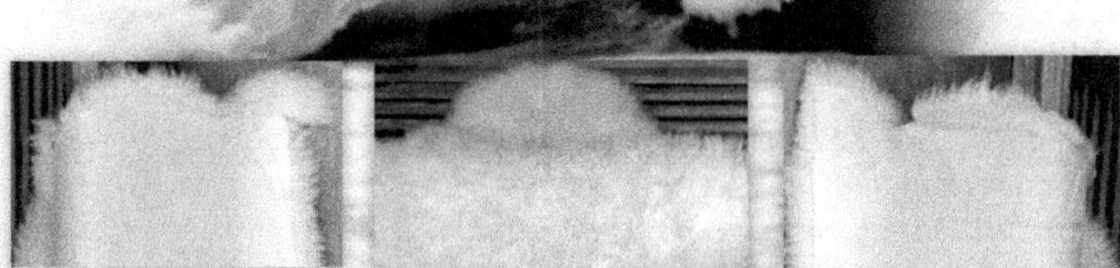

Acts 10:6 *He lodgeth with one Simon a Tanner; whose house is by the sea side; he shall tell thee what thou oughtest to do.*

Acts 9:43 *And it came to pass, that he tarried many days in Joppa with one Simon a Tanner.*

The Sea and the pure Torah Sheepskin
Photos ©2013
Kimberly K Ballard
All Rights Reserved

Now, because *the Acacia is the only wood to atone for the sins of Israel,* the LORD instructed that this *"Shittah or Shittim"* wood must be used for building the items in the Tabernacle of the LORD. The Acacia is, therefore, the so called *"Gopher wood"* of Noah's Ark, covered with pitch. I found that the word that is translated as *"Gopher"* in the Bible is actually written in Hebrew as *"Kopher."* It refers not only to pitch, but it also refers *"to a redemption price or ransom."*

The LORD gave *redemption* to Noah and his family as they abode in the Ark of Acacia wood that was covered in Kopher. The word *"Kopher"* comes from the root *"Kaphar"* and it means *"to cover specifically with bitumen."* It is very important to realize that it also refers to *"cleansing, forgiving, mercy, pardon, and reconciliation."* These elements connect the deep meaning of Noah's Ark to the earthly copy of the LORD'S Ark of the Covenant. Both of these Arks were copies of the Heavenly Ark, which is the Living Testimony of the LORD our KING in Heaven. This reveals that Messiah Yeshua wore the Acacia wood that was the *"Crown" of the redemption price* of the Bride because Yeshua *the firstborn son* of God *(Yeshua ha-Ben)* ransomed us from Satan's grasp. *The Bridegroom of Israel wore the Crown of reconciliation, mercy, pardon, forgiveness, and cleansing in order to save us in His Eternal Ark of the Living Covenant.*

#3724 ***Kopher****, from #3722; prop, a cover, i.e. (lit.) a village (as covered in); (spec.) bitumen (as used for coating), and the henna plant (as used for dyeing); fig. a redemption price; camphire, pitch, ransom, satisfaction, sum of money, village.* **(Source: ©1995 Strong's Concordance).**

#3722 ***Kaphar****, a prim. Root; to cover (spec. with bitumen); fig. to expiate or condone, to placate or cancel; appease, make (an atonement, cleanse, disannul, forgive, be merciful, pacify, pardon, to pitch, purge (away), put off. (Make) reconcile (reconciliation).* **(Source: ©1995 Strong's Concordance).**

What is interesting about these two words that deal with the Ark is the fact that the Hebrew word *"Kippur"* as in *"Yom Kippur, the Day of Atonement"* is connected to *"Kaphar"* and also to *"Kopher"* in connection to Noah's Ark and the Ark of the Covenant. Yom Kippur, as I wrote in this book, is of course connected to the sign of Jonah because Messiah will come the second time for Israel on Yom Kippur, on the Day of Atonement in the future, during the time when they are reading the entire book of Jonah. It is therefore interesting that Jonah left from the sea port at Joppa, from the same area where Simon Peter was dwelling with Simon the Tanner. Jonah was sent by the LORD God to preach repentance to the pagan unclean, non-Jewish moon-god worshipping civilization of Nineveh. They were saved when they believed the Word of God and repented. Hundreds of years later, Simon Bar Jonah was in Joppa by the sea port, receiving the vision of the Great Sheet that revealed that he was to preach God's Word to the clean and unclean Jews and Gentiles, so they would repent and be forgiven. They would also be saved if they repented and believed God's Word, which is *Messiah Yeshua, the Living Torah.* The Messiah is the Ark that will save Israel on the Day of Atonement. The Hebrew word *"Kapporeth,"* referring to the cover of the Holy Ark, pertains to the Mercy Seat. The LORD covered Noah and his family with mercy in the Ark made of Kopher wood.

Genesis 6:14 *Make thee an Ark of gopher wood; rooms shalt thou make in the Ark, and shalt pitch it within and without with pitch.*

Of course Kopher wood is strictly the Acacia wood because, again, it is the only wood that atones for the sins of Israel. This is why the Messiah's Crown of Thorns that covered Yeshua's head was from the Acacia tree. *The head of Messiah is God! So God covered our sins when He wore this Crown!* Now it is even more interesting that I found that the Kopher not only refers to pitch, but it also refers to dyeing, the tannin that is obtained from the Acacia tree!

As I thought more about the term *"pitch,"* I made the connection to the Gum Arabic that exudes out of this species of Acacia Tree. The gum is a resin and it is used as a binding agent. In art, a gum resin mixture is indeed called *"pitch,"* and Noah coated the Ark in pitch, which is the same as *"bitumen."* The Acacia tree is without a doubt, the Shittah or Shittim wood that was used to build the Holy Tabernacle of the LORD, as we see in the following Scriptures.

Exodus 37:28 *And he made the staves of Shittim wood, and overlaid them with gold.*

Exodus 38:1 *And he made the altar of burnt offering of Shittim wood; five cubits was the length thereof, and five cubits the breadth thereof; it was foursquare; and three cubits the height thereof.*

Exodus 30:1 *And thou shalt make an altar to burn incense upon; of Shittim wood shalt thou make it.*

Exodus 36:36 *And he made thereunto four pillars of Shittim wood, and overlaid them with gold; their hooks were of gold; and he cast for them four sockets of silver.*

Exodus 37:1-2 *And Bezaleel made the Ark of Shittim wood; two cubits and a half was the length of it, and a cubit and a half the breadth of it, and a cubit and a half the height of it; And he overlaid it with pure gold within and without, and made a crown of gold to it round about.*

One of the interesting features that I have talked about on the Acacia tree is the smaller curved thorns that are shaped like a cat's claw. Why is this interesting? Well, as I was reading about the incense for the Holy Temple, there was one spice or resin that has not been clearly identified yet and it is called *"onycha"* in the Greek language and it ironically means *"claw."* The original Hebrew word is *"Shecheleth"* and it means *"to roar like a Lion."* So I began to wonder if perhaps the gum resin that exudes in massive amounts from the Acacia tree is the element that we have here that was used as part of the LORD'S incense mixture, called in Hebrew the *"Ketoret."* Remember that the Messiah wore the Acacia Crown of Thorns with the cat's claw shaped thorns as well as the long spiked thorns, and *He is the Lion of Judah that roars out of Zion!* This resin is mentioned in the following Scripture as *"onycha."* There are other gum resins to the Ketoret mixture, such as *"Galbanum and Frankincense."* It was all put before the Testimony in the Tabernacle. It is most Holy because it pertains to the LORD'S Living Testimony as our Messiah!

Lion Photo ©2014 Kimberly K Ballard

Exodus 30:34-38 *And the LORD said unto Moses, Take unto thee sweet spices, stacte, and onycha, and galbanum; these sweet spices with pure frankincense; of each shall there be a like weight; And thou shalt make it a perfume, a confection after the art of the apothecary, tempered together, pure and holy; And thou shalt beat some it very small, and put of it before the Testimony in the Tabernacle of the congregation, where I will meet with thee; it shall be unto you most holy. And as for the perfume which thou shalt make, ye shall not make to yourselves according to the composition thereof; it shall be unto thee holy for the LORD. Whosoever shall make like unto that, to smell thereto, shall even be cut off from his people.*

Hosea 11:10 *They shall walk after the LORD; He shall roar like a lion; when He shall roar, then the children shall tremble from the west.*

Amos 1:2 *And he said, The LORD will roar from Zion, and utter His voice from Jerusalem; and the habitations of the shepherds shall mourn, and the top of Carmel shall wither.*

Amos 3:7-8 *Surely the LORD God will do nothing, but He revealeth His secret unto His servants the prophets. The lion hath roared, who will not fear? The LORD GOD hath spoken, who can but prophecy?*

Revelation 5:5 *And one of the elders saith unto me, Weep not; behold, the Lion of the tribe of Judah, the Root of David, hath prevailed to open the book, and to loose the seven seals thereof.*

The Lion is Messiah the LORD and His Holy incense could very well incorporate the gum resin from the Acacia tree on the incense altar of Acacia wood. The claw like thorns on Yeshua's Crown of Thorns testify that Messiah is the LORD and the Lion, who atoned for our sins, with the only wood that God said would atone for the sins of Israel. This incense was not to be manufactured and used by anyone else because it was a special blend that was considered to be *"HOLY TO THE LORD."* It is interesting that the bright yellow globe shaped Acacia flowers scent the air with a *sweet perfume*. So I believe that the resin of the Acacia was more than likely burned upon the altar of the LORD God. Remember that when we pray, our prayers go up to Heaven to the LORD like incense and like a *sweet smelling perfume*. Our prayers are often full of tears and they are represented in the drops of Acacia resin. When our tears are sent up to Heaven on the LORD'S incense altar in the Holy Temple, this is most Holy to the LORD. I have cried oceans of tears and this is very comforting to me!

Now the LORD revealed that the earthly Ark of the Covenant will no longer be remembered, and the reason why He said this is because *He is the Heavenly Ark of the Covenant*. When the LORD returns to dwell in our midst, there is no need for the earthly Ark because the LORD, the Messiah, rules from the throne of His Eternal Ark that contains His Living Testimony in Jerusalem Israel!

Psalm 99:1 *The LORD reigneth; let the people tremble; He sitteth between the Cherubim's; let the earth be moved.*

When KING Messiah Yeshua the LORD returns from Heaven as the Heavenly Ark of God, He will place this Ark on Holy Mount Moriah, and they will call Jerusalem His throne forever, as it was written by the Prophet Jeremiah!

Jeremiah 3:16-17 *And it shall come to pass, when ye be multiplied and increased in the land, in those days, saith the LORD, they shall say no more, The Ark of the Covenant of the LORD; neither shall it come to mind; neither shall they remember it; neither shall they visit it; neither shall that be done anymore. At that time they shall call Jerusalem the throne of the LORD; and all the nations shall be gathered unto it, to the Name of the LORD, to Jerusalem; neither shall they walk anymore after the imagination of their evil heart.*

Notice in the book of Revelation, it specifically says that in the Temple of God in Heaven there is seen *"THE ARK OF HIS TESTAMENT!"* This is Yeshua's Living Testament!

Revelation 11:19 *And the Temple of God was opened in Heaven, and there was seen in His Temple the Ark of His Testament; and there were lightning, and voices, and thunderings, and an earthquake, and great hail.*

Thorn Photo ©2013 Kimberly K Ballard All Rights Reserved

Every detail of this Testimony that was revealed to me through His Holy Spirit was so thrilling and astonishing. Then as I came to the end of this section, I just ran across a Roman source that verified what I have just said about there being two types of thorns on Yeshua's Crown of Thorns. The Roman statement said, *"The Holy Shroud of Turin shows 13 major blood outlets caused by the thicker thorns and about 60 minor points, caused by smaller thorns."* ***(Source: Roman Religious Source; ©2010 perpetuacatholic.info/index.php?p=1.17).***

Yeshua's Crown of Thorns was indeed the Acacia Tortilis, the Acacia Albida, or Seyal, and when all of this spectacular revelation came together, the hand of the LORD God was upon it, revealing the KING'S Majestic works and the Living Divine Testimony of the Heavenly Ark of God, which is the Great Sheet! This is so beautiful!

THE PURPLE ROBE THE MANTLE AND BREASTPLATE

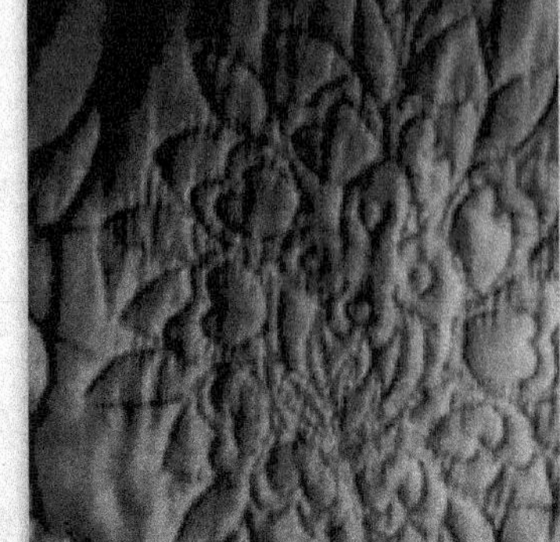

Royal Purple Robe & Gemstones

A Torah scroll is placed inside a decorative upright box, known as an *"Ark."* Obviously there was Noah's Ark, Moses Ark, the Ark of the Covenant, the Ark of the LORD, bearing the Testimony of Messiah Yeshua in Heaven, and the Ark of the Torah scroll. Before a Torah scroll or *"The Word of God"* is placed inside the Ark for storage, it is dressed or clothed in a Mantle that is usually purple in color. It does not have to be purple, but it is the most popular color to use for a Torah scroll because purple is the Royal color that represents God as the KING. Remember that Elijah wore the Mantle and when his Mantle fell off, as he ascended in the chariot of fire to Heaven, Elisha picked up the Mantle and he parted the waters with it because he asked for a double portion of the Spirit of the LORD that was upon Elijah. The *"Mantle"* is also an article of clothing that is worn by a Royal Sovereign, in a King's Royal Coronation Ceremony. The Royal Mantle is usually embroidered with gold thread and when it is worn by the KING on Coronation Day, he wears it like a cape over his shoulders. I discussed a little bit about this before, but since it also pertains to this section about the Royal Regalia, there was more to say about it now. When Elijah's Mantle fell off, the power of the Holy Spirit of the LORD was upon it because the Mantle was an emblem of *the Royal Regalia of the KING OF KINGS.* Elisha, who picked up the Mantle that fell off Elijah, was then able to perform the *miracles of the Rod of God* by parting the waters of the Jordan River. This sign of the power of the Rod of God was also present when the Rod parted the Red Sea for the Israelites to cross over. The power of the LORD is on the Mantle as the Royal Sovereign KING. During the Coronation Ceremony, the Royal Mantle is also a Royal symbol of the KING'S *power and authority.* Now we can see the most incredible hidden truth in the Mantle of the Torah scroll! Think about this! Yeshua is *"The Word of God," the "Living Torah."* So I suddenly realized that KING Yeshua was clothed with a gorgeous purple robe, in a Royal purple *"Mantle,"* before being put away! Then He was placed inside the Royal Stone of Kings in God's Garden in Holy Mount Moriah! As a Torah scroll is sealed inside the Ark, it is dark inside the box, just like it was dark inside Yeshua's tomb after He was put away. When the Ark is opened, *the Torah scroll is brought out into the light,* just like Yeshua's sepulchre was opened and the Living Torah Scroll shined the light of life out of the darkness of the sepulchre of death in the Garden in Mount Moriah, in the place of the former Garden of Eden. The *power and authority* of the Rod raised the KING to life again and this Testimony is the Heavenly Ark of the victorious KING. After the Living Torah was put away in God's Garden, He came to life *as evening was becoming morning the first day of the week and as evening was becoming morning the third day after Passover, as the Fruitful Almond Branch from the Almond Tree of Life, and He went before the people, shining the light of Eternal life through the Living Torah to all the people.* Then He ascended up to His Royal throne in Heaven to sit on this Ark at the right hand as the Royal Sceptre of Judah and the Eternal KING of Glory! A Torah Mantle is made out of gorgeous fabric. It is usually made from luxurious purple velvet, although the fabric does not necessarily have to be velvet either. The Torah Mantle may also be embroidered with the Ten Commandments of the LORD. This is interesting because some of the purple Mantles that are used for wrapping the Torah scroll are embroidered with *the Lion of the Tribe of Judah* upon the Mantle. There are two Lion's embroidered on it and a Lion is on either side of the two stone tablets of the Law of God. In this case, the Lion of the tribe of Judah is lifting up the tablets of the Law of God, displaying them, as you can see on the spine of my book and in this photograph. At the top, above the Lion of Judah who is lifting up the Law of God, there is an embroidered Crown and this Royal purple Mantle is wrapped around the Torah scroll. So now think about this chilling fact! The Royal purple Mantle was wrapped around KING Messiah Yeshua who is the Lion of the Tribe of Judah, and He was lifted up so that everyone could see *the Living Torah displayed* and then He was put away in the Ark of Heaven! He is the KING and the Living Torah Scroll who wears the Royal Crown and the Royal purple Mantle! The Lion of the Tribe of Judah was lifted up on the cross and He was wearing the desert Crown of Judah! Just before that happened, the KING was clothed with Majesty, as they put the Royal purple Mantle on Yeshua!

Lion of Judah Hanukkiah
Photo ©2013
Kimberly K Ballard
All Rights Reserved

Mark 15:17-18 *And they clothed Him with purple, and platted a Crown of Thorns, and put it about His head, And began to salute Him, hail, King of the Jews!*

Luke 23:11 *And Herod with his men of war set him at nought, and mocked Him, and arrayed Him in a gorgeous robe, and sent Him again to Pilate.*

For a moment I just want to look at the word *"mocked"* as it applies to this Scripture because it means *"imitating in derision, or mimicking with contempt or ridicule."* The word *"Mimic"* literally means *"to copy in action or to imitate closely."* So the definitions reveal that Herod and his men were mocking the Jewish KING by imitating or copying the true KING, through ridicule, contempt, and heckling. The fact that they were copying Yeshua in derision *proves that Yeshua really is the KING of Israel and the Lion of Judah that will roar out of Zion.*

In the Gospel of Luke, we find that this purple robe was gorgeous which makes me think of an elaborate embroidered cloth. *A little while after the Living Torah Scroll was wrapped in this Royal purple Mantle, this Living Testimony was put away inside the Ark in Heaven, containing the Bread from Heaven, the Almond Rod that budded, the Word of God written in this Living Stone, the Rock that was quarried out of God's Holy Mountain from the Foundation Stone and the Word written upon the pure sheepskin of the Lamb of God!* So The Lion of the Tribe of Judah was lifting up the Word of God on the cross after wearing the Royal purple Torah Mantle of the KING, and then, as I said, He was put away in God's Garden inside Holy Mount Moriah. Yeshua revealed His true Royal identity as *the Sceptre that shall not depart from Judah until Shiloh comes* and the Royal Sceptre of the KING holds *all power and authority* forever to give Eternal life to all that call upon His Name.

The purple robe or Mantle had another great significance. On the Jewish High Priestly garment, this purple color represented *"the reconciliation between God and man."* When Messiah Yeshua, the High Priest of Heaven, wore the Royal purple robe or Mantle just before His crucifixion, it signified He was bringing *"the reconciliation between God and man" in the place of the former Garden of Eden.* This gorgeous Royal purple Mantle is part of the *Royal Regalia* of the Sovereign KING of Israel, *the Living Torah Scroll* that shines His light upon the earth as the budded Almond Tree Menorah. *This Living Torah Scroll was put away at the gate of Heaven, in the place of the Royal Eternal Residence of God.*

Another piece of the Torah Scroll is called the *"Breastplate."* The Breastplate is put over the Torah Scroll, just after the Royal purple Mantle is wrapped around it. The High Priest also wears a similar Breastplate. The twelve mounted gemstones of this Breastplate are engraved with the names of the twelve tribes of Israel. The twelve stones are set in order. Yeshua wears this Breastplate of the High Priest, but His engraved gemstones actually make up the Foundation stones of the Heavenly Temple because He chose the twelve Living Stones that are His twelve Jewish disciples.

The LORD has graven the names of the twelve tribes of Israel upon the palm of His hand, which is to say, upon Messiah, the Yad of God.

Isaiah 49:16 *Behold, I have graven thee upon the palms of My hands; thy walls are continually before Me.*

Yeshua reconciled us to Himself, as the LORD God of Israel. His Breastplate is the shield over His heart, so it goes over the Torah Scroll last because His Living Testimony is the Eternal Covenant of the heart through His life blood and Living Water, and these are the secret oracles of God.

Exodus 28:30 *And thou shalt put in the Breastplate of judgment the Urim and the Thummim; and they shall be upon Aaron's heart, when he goeth in before the LORD; and Aaron shall bear the judgment of the children of Israel upon his heart before the LORD continually.*

Messiah Yeshua bore the judgment of the children of Israel upon His heart, as it was pierced with the Roman lance and His Life blood and Living Water flowed out and fell to the ground on Holy Mount Moriah when He sealed His Covenant with them for Eternal life! The KING'S powerful Royal Mantle was revealed through Elijah and Elisha. His Royal Highness and Majesty, Yeshua the KING, is wrapped in the Royal Purple Mantle that reveals His mighty power as the Royal Rod, the Sceptre of God!

TWO STAVES OF WOOD LIFTED UP

Two Staves of wood lifted up in the clouds & Lifted up Living Almond Rod Photos ©2013 Kimberly K Ballard All Rights Reserved

The Ark of the Covenant was lifted up by two wooden staves. They were never to be removed from the Ark because they are part of the Eternal Testimony of the LORD Messiah. The Ark contained the Word of God written in stone, the Rod that budded from a dead cut off Almond Branch, and the golden jar of manna, the bread from Heaven. The Ark of God is lifted up on two wooden staves so it is raised up into the air and held aloft, while it is being carried.

Exodus 25:13-16 *And thou shalt make staves of shittim wood, and overlay them with gold. And thou shalt put the staves into the rings by the sides of the Ark, that the Ark may be borne with them. The staves shall be in the rings of the Ark; they shall not be taken from it. And thou shalt put into the Ark of the Testimony which I shall give thee.*

A Torah scroll in the Synagogue, which is the Word of God, is also lifted up by two wooden staves. In Jewish terms, the two staves are known as *"the Trees of Life."* In the Synagogue, as the Torah scroll is lifted up for public display, the Rabbi completely stretches out his arms almost full length while lifting up the wooden rods in his hands holding *"the Trees of Life."* He lifts the Word of God into the air to display the Torah aloft where everyone can see it. This is called *"Hagbaha"* which means *"to lift or raise up the Torah Scroll!"* So now, incredibly, when Yeshua, the Living Torah and Ark of the LORD'S Living Testimony were lifted up on two wooden staves of the cross for public display, His arms were almost completely outstretched. The Tree of Life at that moment was lifted up in God's hands, as the Rabbi of Righteousness, and later the Living Torah was *"raised up!"* So Yeshua, the Branch from *the Almond Tree of Life,* took away the curse of *the Fig Tree of knowledge of good and evil* in God's Garden on Holy Mount Moriah. Yeshua is again revealed within every little detail of the Ark of Heaven!

John 3:13-17 *And no man hath ascended up to Heaven, but He that came down from Heaven, even the Son of man which is in Heaven. And as Moses lifted up the serpent in the wilderness, even so must the Son of man be lifted up; That whosoever believeth in Him should not perish, but have eternal life. For God so loved the world, that He gave His only begotten Son, that whosoever believeth in Him should not perish, but have everlasting life. For God sent not His Son into the world to condemn the world; but that the world through Him might be saved.*

After the LORD Yeshua, the Heavenly Ark was lifted up and held aloft on two wooden staves, He revealed the secret knowledge and wisdom of God. The glory of the LORD was manifested as the Holy Almond Tree of Life which is the light of the world. For centuries, those who looked upon the Testimony of the Rod lifted up have been drawn to *the Word of God, to the Living Torah*, and drawn back to Jerusalem, to Israel. Yeshua said that when He was lifted up, He would draw all mankind to Himself.

John 12:32-41 *And I, if I be lifted up from the earth, will draw all men unto Me. This He said, signifying what death He should die. The people answered Him, We have heard out of the Law that Messiah abideth forever; and how sayest thou, The Son of man must be lifted up? Who is this Son of man? Then Yeshua said unto them, Yet a little while is the light with you. Walk while ye have the light, lest darkness come upon you; for he that walketh in darkness knoweth not wither he goeth. While ye have light, believe in the light, that ye may be the children of light. These things spake Yeshua, and departed, and did hide Himself from them, But though He had done so many miracles before them, yet they believed not on Him; That the saying of Esaias the prophet might be fulfilled, which he spake, LORD, who hath believed our report? And to whom hath the arm of the LORD been revealed? Therefore they could not believe, because that Esaias said again, He hath blinded their eyes, and hardened their heart; that they should not see with their eyes, nor understand with their heart, and be converted, and I should heal them. These things said Esaias, when he saw His glory, and spake of Him.*

Isaiah (Esaias), saw Messiah Yeshua in His glory, lifted up and he spoke of Him in this prophecy! This is fantastic! Isaiah had the promise that the LORD would bring the Eternal Living Torah to all mankind and spread it throughout the world, by lifting up the Living Torah on two wooden staves, as the Almond Tree of Life. He would lift up His own Royal Sceptre of the tribe of Judah to save us, as the Living Ark of God. In His Gospel account, John wrote the following profound words of Yeshua.

John 8:28-32 *Then said Yeshua unto them, When ye have lifted up the Son of man, then shall ye know that I AM He, and that I do nothing of Myself; but as My Father hath taught Me, I speak these things. And He that sent Me is with Me; the Father hath not left Me alone; for I do always those things that please Him. As He spake these Words, many believed on Him. Then said Yeshua to those Jews which believed on Him, If ye continue in My Word, then are ye My disciples indeed; And ye shall know the truth, and the truth shall make you free.*

Remember that Yeshua said, *"Before Abraham was born, "I AM."* This means that Yeshua was from the Ancient of Days. The ancient Hebrew letter *"Tav"* that I discussed in another chapter, also had the meaning *"The Kingdom of the Ancient of Days."* The Tav is the Hebrew letter that was originally shaped like two wooden staves of Yeshua's cross lifted up.

Now the Torah scroll is actually wound on the two wooden rods or staves. At the upper end of the staves or wooden rods, there are finials. The finials are called *"Rimonim" which means "Pomegranate"* in Hebrew. King Solomon is said to have designed his Royal Crown after the shape of the *calyx* of the Pomegranate. The finials are therefore called *"Rimonim"* because they originally resembled this fruit and they are the crowns of the Torah scroll. Messiah Yeshua was raised to life as the First Fruit from the Tree of Life after he was lifted up on the two wooden staves and, as the Living Torah, He wears the crowns of the KING.

This brings up another profound truth from the Holy Spirit. The Torah scroll, the Word of God, *is kissed* just before it is put away inside the Ark. Judas betrayed *the Word of God, the Living Torah, with a kiss,* just before Yeshua was put away in Holy Mount Moriah, in the Garden of God, as the Ark of the Heavenly Testimony! It is absolutely stunning!

Mark 14:44 *And he that betrayed Him had given them a token, saying, Whomsoever I shall kiss, that same is He; take Him, and lead Him away safely. And as soon as he was come, he goeth straightway to Him, and saith, Master, Master; and kissed Him.*

Matthew 26:47-50 *And while he yet spake, lo, Judas, one of the twelve, came, and with him a great multitude with swords and staves, from the Chief Priests and Elders of the people. Now he that betrayed Him gave them a sign, saying, Whomsoever I shall kiss, that same is He; hold Him fast. And forthwith he came to Yeshua, and said, Hail, Master; and kissed Him. And Yeshua said unto him, Friend, wherefore art thou come? Then came they, and laid hands on Yeshua, and took Him.*

Luke 22:47-48 *And while He yet spake, behold a multitude, and he that was called Judas, one of the twelve, went before them, and drew near unto Yeshua to kiss Him. But Yeshua said unto him, Judas, betrayest thou the Son of man with a kiss?*

In the Psalms, it is written to *"Kiss the Son, lest you perish from "the Way!"*
Psalm 2:12 *Kiss the Son, lest He be angry, and ye perish from the way, when His wrath is kindled but a little. Blessed are all they that put their trust in Him.*

It is interesting that the woman who anointed Messiah Yeshua before He was lifted up on the two wooden staves *kissed His feet and when she did this, she was kissing the Tree of Life and the Living Torah Scroll! Then* right after she kissed and anointed Yeshua, *the Word of God,* He went into every place teaching the glad tidings of the Kingdom of God. They sat with Him at meat, but they were dining with the Heavenly meat of *the Living Torah!* Notice also, that because she understood and *kept kissing the Living Torah,* her sins were forgiven and she was purified in the Great Sheet of the Ark of Heaven! She was saved by the Rod of God, who was about to be lifted up! Humbly she anointed His feet for burial to fulfill His Divine Testimony.

Luke 7:45-47 *Thou gavest Me no kiss; but this woman since the time I came in hath not ceased to kiss My feet. My head with oil thou didst not anoint; but this woman hath anointed My feet with ointment. Wherefore, I say unto thee, Her sins, which are many, are forgiven; for she loved much; but to whom little is forgiven, the same loveth little.*

In the Book of Samuel, a similar event took place.
I Samuel 10:1 *Then Samuel took a vial of oil, and poured it upon his head, and kissed him, and said, Is it not because the LORD hath anointed thee to be Prince over His inheritance?*

Yeshua is the anointed Prince of the inheritance who was *kissed as "the Sar Shalom, the Prince of Peace."* Judas betrayed *the Living Torah with a kiss,* just before *the Living Torah was lifted up on two wooden staves* and put away in the Heavenly Ark of the Eternal Covenant!

THE SAVIOR KING THE BIRTH OF MESSIAH YESHUA ON ROSH HASHANAH

Shofar, New Moon, Crown, Challah Bread
Photos ©2013 Kimberly K Ballard All Rights Reserved

One day I was talking to my Jerusalem friend about the birth of Messiah Yeshua. I told her that I believed that the LORD had just revealed to me from the Holy Scriptures that Messiah Yeshua was born on Rosh HaShanah!

I believe Yeshua was likely conceived at Hanukkah during the Festival of Lights in December, which is the Biblical month of Kislev. Hanukkah begins on the 25th day of Kislev. I truly believe that Messiah Yeshua was not born on December 25th. Yeshua was born on Rosh HaShanah and specifically on *"Tishrei 1"* which occurs in late September. Rosh HaShanah is the head of the New Year and something new was coming! *It was a Jewish KING, who was the Messiah of Israel and He was bringing a New Covenant of the heart to Israel!* I have to tell you that as I read the Scriptures carefully, the LORD began unraveling the incredible truth to me about Yeshua's Nativity story. When you begin to understand some of the facts about the Jewish celebration of Rosh HaShanah, then the Nativity story of Messiah Yeshua's birth falls right into place and it is stunning!

Now the first astonishing point that I want to make (remember), is the fact that on Rosh HaShanah, Jewish tradition proclaims that the door of Heaven is opened. This is an interesting detail because the LORD showed me that the so-called *"Star of Bethlehem"* that was present at Yeshua's birth was in fact *"The Shechinah glory light of God"* that was shining down through the open door of Heaven. The glory of the LORD guided the shepherds to the place where the Jewish KING was found lying in a manger. *The Star came and stood over the place where the Messiah was born!*

Now, at first, I was speculating whether or not it was the Shechinah. Since I wanted to make sure that I spelled the word *"Shechinah"* properly, I looked it up in the Jewish Encyclopedia. Then I discovered that the page regarding the *"Shechinah,"* that is also spelled there as *"Shekinah,"* revealed some very profound statements that happened to prove my speculation! Then I knew without a doubt that *"the Star of Bethlehem"* was in fact *"the Shechinah glory of God that shone round about them and they were sore afraid!"* The Star of Bethlehem was not the alignment of planets, but it was the powerful Shechinah glory light of the LORD God Almighty! This was stunning!

The first definition I will show you is a shocker. It explains exactly what was transpiring at Messiah Yeshua birth. To me, this was proof that when the Star of Bethlehem appeared, the LORD God of Israel manifested Himself in the flesh as the Messiah. This was proof that He descended from Heaven to dwell among us as *"Immanuel,"* or *"God with us."*

The JewishEncyclopedia.com stated the following;
1. ***Shekinah****; "The Majestic Presence or the Manifestation of God which has descended to "dwell" among men."*
In The New Testament;
2. "Since the Shekinah is light, those passages of the Apocrypha and New Testament which mention radiance, and in which the Greek text reads δόξα, refer to the Shekinah, there being no other Greek equivalent for the word. Thus, according to Luke ii. 9, "the glory of the Lord [δόξα Κυρίου] shone round about them" (comp. II Peter i. 17; Eph. i. 6; II Cor. iv. 6); and it is supposed that in John i.14 and Rev. xxi. 3 the words σκηνοῦν and σκηνή were expressly selected as implying the Shekinah. The idea that God dwells in man and that man is His temple (e.g., Col. ii. 9; II Cor. vi. 16; John xiv. 23) is merely a more realistic conception of the resting of the Shekinah on man." ***(Source: JewishEncyclopedia.com ©2002 "Shekinah" by Kaufmann Kohler & Ludwig Blau).***

In the second statement, it specifically says *"that because there is no Greek equivalent for the word "Shekinah or Shechinah," they translated this word into the phrase, "the glory of the LORD shown round about them."* I was so thrilled when the LORD verified this to me. This proves without a doubt that this passage about the Nativity of Messiah Yeshua was specifically referring to *"the radiance of the Shechinah glory of the LORD"* in the New Testament. This was the first detail and fact that verified that Yeshua was born on Rosh HaShanah, when the door of Heaven was opened! Now my second point is that Rosh HaShanah is also known as *"the Feast of Trumpets"* which is *"Yom Teruah"* in Hebrew and remember that it is literally *"Coronation Day for God, as the KING of Israel and the universe."*

So the astonishing truth is that the Jewish KING Messiah, the LORD God, was manifested in the flesh in the Shechinah glory light and He came to dwell with us on the very day that was known as Coronation Day of the Great KING OF KINGS! Do you remember when the Jewish disciples entered the Shechinah glory cloud of the LORD at Yeshua's transfiguration on Mount Sinai? They were afraid when they entered the cloud! This is because they were eyewitnesses of the Divine Presence of the LORD and they saw His face shining in its radiance in His complete Majestic glory.

The same thing happened at the birth of Messiah Yeshua. When they saw the Shechinah glory of the LORD shining down from Heaven and round about them, they were *"sore afraid."* The word *"sore,"* incredibly, comes from the Anglo Saxon word *"Sar"* which means *"affliction."* The word *"Sar"* is also the Hebrew word that means *"Prince or Master."* This is remarkable because the ten days of repentance that begin with the first two days of Rosh HaShanah is the time to *"afflict"* your soul in repentance to the LORD and *this is when God was manifested in the flesh* as the Shechinah glory light shone round about them from Heaven. KING Messiah Yeshua came to dwell with us on Rosh HaShanah and He would also become *"The Bread of affliction."* I have written about this topic further in the final chapter. So the end of this period of repentance ends with Yom Kippur. It is on Yom Kippur that Israel was instructed by the LORD *"to afflict their souls,"* as it is written in Leviticus 23:27. So it is clear that when Messiah Yeshua arrived, who is called the *"Sar HaPanim,"* which is *"The Prince of the face of the LORD God,"* then it was time for Israel's repentance by *afflicting their souls.* The word *"Sar"* also means *"distressing, painful, grievous, and bodily pain."* Of course the Messiah came to die for our sins, to reverse the curse of death, and *He endured the distressing, painful, grievous bodily pain* that would come from the cross and from His scourging. Actually, I found that the English word *"sorry"* originated from the word *"Sar."* So the time of Yeshua's birth was the time of repenting and casting your sins away in the Living Water to show the LORD that you were *"sorry"* for your sins. This is a very profound discovery that was only made known to me by the power of the Holy Spirit. So all these truths are clearly verifying that the Messiah's birth was during the time of the beginning of the High Holy Days.

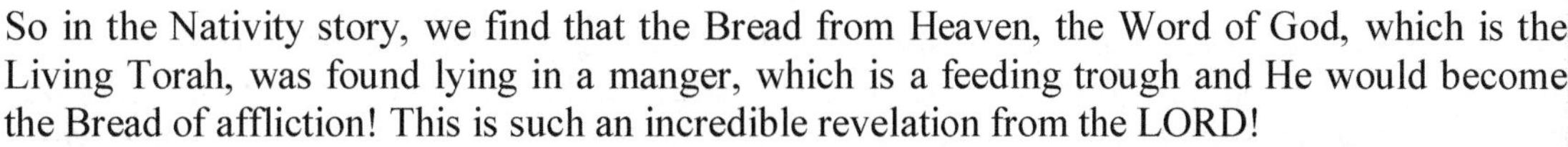

So in the Nativity story, we find that the Bread from Heaven, the Word of God, which is the Living Torah, was found lying in a manger, which is a feeding trough and He would become the Bread of affliction! This is such an incredible revelation from the LORD!

Now, in essence, the Shechinah glory is the light of the LORD. In chapter ten, I discussed the fact that the meaning of the Hebrew word *"ohr"* is *"light,"* and *"Ma'ohr"* means *"the source of the light."* I wanted to add here again in this part of the story that it also means *"Star!"* I was waiting to show this thrilling piece of Yeshua's Testimony to you in the Nativity story! Therefore the *"Star"* of Bethlehem that guided the shepherds to the place where the Messiah was found lying in the manger was indeed *"the Shechinah glory light of the LORD and this light involved the manifestation of God in the flesh, which descended through the open door of Heaven and down to the earth to dwell among men!"* So at the birth of Messiah Yeshua, *the Divine Presence* and the Royal Majesty of the glory light of the LORD God was present and *the Living Torah* was lying in the feeding trough! Rosh HaShanah is the head of the New Year on the Biblical calendar and God is celebrated as Israel's KING on the very day that Yeshua arrived! Therefore, the KING OF KINGS had come to dwell with us to fulfill the Living Testimony of the LORD God of Israel as the Rod lifted up, so He could reverse the curse of death in the flesh and became the Almond Rod that budded.

The statement from the Jewish Encyclopedia that said, *"God dwells in man and that man is His Temple,"* proves that Yeshua's words are true, that the believers are indeed *the living stones* that make up the Eternal Heavenly Temple. Through Yeshua's baptism in the Living Water, we receive His Holy Spirit and now the Divine Presence that dwells within us makes us *the living stones* or building stones of the Heavenly Temple. It was such a Divine blessing to find this Jewish definition of the word *"Shechinah!"*

Now I want to share the account of the birth of Messiah Yeshua from Scripture. Picture this! Heaven is opened and the Shechinah glory of the LORD, *"The Star,"* the source of *the Eternal light,* is shining down from Heaven, guiding the people to the place where Messiah the KING has come to dwell in our midst as *"God with us!"*

Angel & lights
Photo ©2013 Kimberly K Ballard

Luke 2:9-11 *And, lo, the angel of the LORD came upon them, and the glory of the LORD shone round about them; and they were sore afraid. And the angel said unto them, Fear not; for, behold, I bring you good tidings of great joy, which shall be to all people. For unto you is born this day in the City of David a Saviour, which is Messiah the LORD.*

The angel of the LORD proclaimed that the Saviour was none other than *the LORD God,* who was called the *"Messiah!"*

When they saw the *"Star,"* they rejoiced with exceeding great joy, and the *"Star"* that went before them came and stood over the place where Yeshua was resting!

Matthew 2:9-10 *When they had heard the King, they departed; and, lo, the star, which they saw in the east, went before them, till it came <u>and stood</u> over where the young child was. When they saw the star, they rejoiced with exceeding great joy.*

Now remember that the LORD came down before and *"stood"* in the pillar of cloud, in the book of Exodus.

Exodus 33:9 *And it came to pass, as Moses entered in to the Tabernacle, the cloudy pillar descended, <u>and stood</u> at the door of the Tabernacle, and the LORD talked with Moses.*

Exodus 14:19 *And the angel of God, which went before the camp of Israel, removed and went behind them; and the pillar of the cloud went from before their face, <u>and stood</u> behind them.*

When the LORD came down with the Shechinah glory cloud, it stood over the place where He descended. So the *Star* of Bethlehem, the Shechinah glory light, came and *stood* over the place where the Messiah was found lying in a manger because this is the place where the LORD God descended when Heaven was open! Then the angel of the LORD appeared and proclaimed *the great salutation* about the birth of Messiah Yeshua and proclaimed that this was *"Messiah, the LORD."* Every detail within the story of Yeshua's birth fell right into place when I looked at it from the date of Rosh HaShanah and from a Jewish perspective and mindset. The story just came alive when these things came to light for the first time in many centuries. The Messiah is the Jewish KING and this made perfect sense! Ah, now I get it! Thank you LORD!

Now this explained to me in vivid detail why King Herod felt so threatened that *a Jewish KING had been born!* Herod knew that this Jewish baby was born on Rosh HaShanah and that He had just fulfilled the ancient Jewish prophecy of the coming Jewish KING Messiah! So a Great KING was indeed born on Coronation Day and He was Messiah Yeshua, the LORD! This KING, however, was going to eventually rule Israel forever! This KING was far superior and far greater than King Herod, who had the title, *"The King of the Jews!"* This KING was the everlasting KING OF KINGS, who has all *power and authority* over Herod forever! The Scriptures tell us that Herod and all the people in Jerusalem were wondering about the birth of this Messiah, who had just come into the world! Now it all made perfect sense that Herod thought that he was about to be usurped by this Jewish KING! Can you imagine that King Herod felt so threatened by a Jewish baby? Now I completely understand *that the reason why Herod felt so threatened by this particular Jewish baby was because of the fact that Yeshua was born on Rosh HaShanah, on Israel's Coronation Day, to honor the LORD God as their KING.* Yeshua had just fulfilled the ancient prophecy of the coming Messiah because the name *"Yeshua"* is the Hebrew word for salvation! Herod was already well informed that the Jewish people were anticipating the arrival of their KING Messiah. This miraculous birth was such a threat that Herod sent his soldiers to kill all the babies in Bethlehem and in all the surrounding areas from the age of 2 and under. Herod clearly did not want this Jewish KING Messiah to come and fulfill the prophecy! As usual, Satan tried to prevent Yeshua from fulfilling the prophecy and from reversing the death decree that was upon all mankind from the Garden of Eden. However, the KING had already sealed the decree of life for us with His Royal Signet Ring through His Living Branch from the Almond Tree of Life. Remember that once a KING has sealed His decree of life, it can never be reversed again! Satan, through Herod, was trying to prevent it from being reversed and therefore, he continued to try to destroy Yeshua at His arrival, but it was impossible for Herod to interfere with God's decree of Eternal life. It is during Rosh HaShanah, that the texts regarding *the Kingship of God* are read by the Hebrew people. One of the texts actually says, *"So you shall proclaim Me KING over you!"* Israel was to proclaim this by blowing the shofar! Remember that Rabbi Simcha Pearlmutter said that they proclaim the name Yeshua between the first and second set of shofar blasts and this was Messiah Yeshua's birthday! Fantastic! On Rosh HaShanah you are *inscribed in the book of life* and on Yom Kippur your fate is sealed. A person is to be prepared by *"awakening"* their minds from Spiritual slumber. This is the *"Shaked"* before *the Almond Branch* arrived to dwell with us.

Another incredible fact about Rosh HaShanah is that it commemorates the giving of the Torah on Mount Sinai. *At the birth of Messiah Yeshua, we were given "The Living Torah, the Word of God," from Heaven.* This is the light of the Heavenly Menorah, full of Almond blossoms and fruit and the oil and fire of His Holy Spirit. Yeshua was wrapped in swaddling clothes and He was lying in a *manger* in a feeding trough for grain and water and these are the two elements that we use to make our Matzah, the Unleavened bread! I was so astounded when the Holy Spirit opened my eyes to see this truth. *The Living Torah* was therefore found resting in a type of Ark and the angel said that *"the Saviour born this day was Messiah the LORD!"* So it is clear that if we eat this Living Bread from Heaven and drink this Living Water, then we will live forever and the seed grain of the Word of life was inside Him. So the giving of *"the Living Torah"* on Rosh HaShanah, which is *the LORD God of Israel* manifested in the flesh as our pure Torah Lamb sheepskin and our KING Messiah, makes this story extremely thrilling and absolutely stunning! I already said before that Messiah Yeshua wore the Crown of Thorns to reverse the curse, so we would no longer have to toil the earth for our bread among the thorns and thistles!

Another incredible coincidence is that Rosh HaShanah is also the time that a blessing is recited called *"The She'Hecheyanu Blessing."* This blessing is to thank God for giving us life! This is the reason that the Messiah came to us on the earth *to give us Eternal life* as He was born KING on Rosh HaShanah! It is fantastic because when the Rapture happens on Rosh HaShanah, this is when we receive our glorified bodies on the birthday of mankind! The shofar that is blown on Rosh HaShanah will be heard when the Messiah returns from Heaven and clearly this has to be the time of the rapture of believers, who have already accepted God's Heavenly Ark of salvation.

This brings me to my next point. Thousands of Hebrews made the annual pilgrimage to Jerusalem for the celebrations and Holy convocations during the High Holy Days that begin with Rosh HaShanah. The festivities could not begin for Rosh HaShanah until the sliver of new moon was sighted in the early evening sky by two witnesses. This celebration continued for two days from the moment that the first sliver of the moon sighting was verified by the Sanhedrin. After the celebration of Rosh HaShanah, the ten days of repentance known as *"The days of awe"* begin and they continue up to Yom Kippur. The High Holy Days, therefore, all run together like one very long appointed time of God.

The New Moon of Rosh HaShanah 2014
Photo ©2014 Kimberly K Ballard
All Rights Reserved

The LORD had declared that Israel should keep the Feasts forever in Jerusalem. So it became clear to me that if the cities surrounding Jerusalem were packed with thousands of pilgrims who had arrived for the celebrations during the High Holy Days beginning with Rosh HaShanah, then this would explain why *"there was no room at the Inn"* when Mary and Joseph arrived in Bethlehem, which is approximately 5 miles south to southwest of Jerusalem. All the rooms were occupied for this extremely special and most Holy time of the year which takes place in the fall. *There was no vacancy!* This part of the historical record of Yeshua's birth, once again, verified that this event occurred at the beginning of the High Holy Days, during the start of Rosh HaShanah!

Luke 2:7 *And she brought forth her firstborn son, and wrapped Him in swaddling clothes, and laid Him in a manger; because there was no room for them in the Inn.*

The moment that the wise men came into the city looking for the baby who was *born "KING of the Jews,"* Herod realized that someone very powerful had just been born! This brings up another fact that proves Yeshua was born on Rosh HaShanah. Yeshua is referred to as the *"Second Adam."* Now it is a well known Jewish fact that Adam was created on Rosh HaShanah and this celebration is the birthday of mankind! *So Messiah Yeshua was born as the Second Adam on the same day that Adam was created, and probably the very moment they blew the shofar in the Holy Temple and called the name Yeshua!* Since the Messiah is the LORD He is without sin. He was coming into the world on the birthday of mankind to remove the curse of death that was upon Adam and Eve and their descendants, in order to restore us to life again on this special day of the giving of the glad tiding that says, *"May you be inscribed in the Book of Life!"* It is even written in the book of I Corinthians that the first man Adam was of the earth, but the *"second man"* was *"The LORD from Heaven."*

I Corinthians 15:47 *The first man is of the earth, earthy; the second man is the LORD from Heaven.*

I Corinthians 15:22 *For as in Adam all die, even so in Messiah shall all be made alive.*

Now at this point, I actually did not think that I would be able to find any more connections to Rosh HaShanah and Yeshua's birth. To my amazement, however, the LORD directed me to a certain Scripture that contained an important conversation between Yeshua and Pontius Pilate, and this revealed the exciting truth! I could not believe it! The truth of Yeshua's birthday is actually found within this conversation!

John 18:37 *Pilate therefore said unto Him, Art Thou a KING then? Yeshua answered, Thou sayest that I AM a KING. To this end was I born, and for this cause came I into the world, that I should bear witness unto the truth. Every one that is of the truth heareth My voice.*

Wow that is a powerful statement! This is an extremely overlooked passage of Scripture! I suddenly realized that when Pontius Pilate asked Yeshua, *"Are you a KING then?"* Yeshua actually said, *"Thou sayest, I AM a KING, To this end was I born!"* Yeshua reveals that He was *"born a KING,"* and, therefore, Yeshua verified in His own Words that He came into the world and *was born KING on Rosh HaShanah, on the LORD'S Coronation Day!*

Yeshua said that everyone that is of the truth hears His voice and the truth that He was referring to was the Word of God that comes out of His mouth as the Living Torah!

I Thessalonians 2:13 *For this cause also thank we God without ceasing, because, when ye received the Word of God which ye heard of us, ye received it not as the Word of men, but as it is in truth, the Word of God, which effectually worketh also in you that believe.*

Remember when Pilate said to Yeshua, *"What is truth?"* I realized that because *the Living Torah* was standing before Him, the truth was looking him in the eyes! It was for this cause that He came into the world to reverse the death decree from the Garden of Eden, so we could again dwell in His Divine Presence forever. It is incredible that all these centuries, this was written right in the text in front of our eyes and no one has ever seen it! Now I wondered why the Romans altered Yeshua's true birthday and put it on one of their pagan Roman festival days instead of acknowledging the truth! It is because of this alteration of the truth that the whole world has been celebrating the birth of Messiah Yeshua on a day that was not His true birthday.

However, I do believe that the Angel Gabriel came to Mary at *"Hanukkah"* and announced to her, in the month of Kislev or December, that she was going to have Yeshua because He is the Holy Almond Tree Menorah and the light of the world, full of the Eternal oil of the Holy Spirit! Hanukkah commemorates the miracle of the oil for the Holy Almond Tree Menorah. The Holy Temple was rededicated on December 25th by the Maccabee's, and Messiah builds the permanent Heavenly Temple. So the celebration of lights in December at Hanukkah is a great reminder of the glory of the Messiah, the light of the world that came to dwell in our midst, who will one day rededicate the Holy Temple by setting the permanent Heavenly Temple in our midst in Jerusalem. He sealed His Eternal Covenant at Passover and three days later proved He was the Heavenly Almond Tree Menorah and the light of life. Yeshua was resurrected to life on the LORD'S *"Feast of First Fruits"* and not on a Roman pagan day from Babylon known as *"Easter." Mary is not the abomination "queen of heaven."*

The wise men from the east also revealed that Messiah's birth took place on Rosh HaShanah! The wise men actually came to Jerusalem looking for *"The one born KING of the Jews!"* They asked, *"Where is He who has been born KING of the Jews?"* The wise men traveled from afar and they brought with them *"gifts fit for a Jewish KING!"* The wise men knew exactly when they should travel to the Holy Land and they knew exactly when to expect

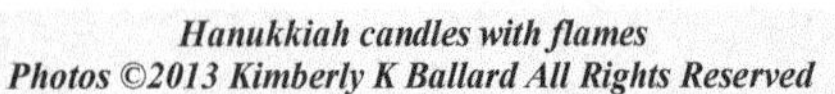
Hanukkiah candles with flames

their KING Messiah because they had calculated it from the Hebrew prophecy! They knew for certain that the KING of Israel would be born on Rosh HaShanah, on the Feast of Trumpets! After all they were *"wise,"* remember? Now we should read the story of the birth of Yeshua again, in light of this new Jewish truth! Why would they bring gifts fit for a Jewish KING, unless it was Rosh HaShanah, which is the LORD'S Coronation Day as Israel's KING? One day, I heard a prominent Jewish Rabbi speaking in Jerusalem and when he spoke about the Prophets of Israel as *"the wise men,"* I was so shocked! This jumped out at me, as I suddenly made the connection to the Nativity story of Yeshua! Wow, this explained everything! The Jewish Prophets of the Bible, the so-called *"Sages of Israel"* are still called *"the wise men"* even to this day! So, *"the wise men"* in Yeshua's Nativity story were Jewish Prophets who knew the Scriptures in their hearts. They were learned Torah Scholars! This explains why *"The wise men"* in Yeshua's Nativity story knew exactly when to expect the arrival of the Jewish KING Messiah! The wise men knew the Messianic prophecies that were written hundreds of years before this event occurred. This explains to me why *"the wise men"* traveled from afar to be in Jerusalem for the birth of the Jewish KING Messiah. They wanted to be in Jerusalem, not only because it was Rosh HaShanah and the start of the High Holy Days and because the KING was coming, but also because of the fact that the prophetic amount of time of 483 years had elapsed, and it was time for the Messiah to arrive! The wise men understood this from Daniel's prophetic timetable. So they wanted to be present when the KING Messiah arrived, so they could offer Him gifts that were fit for a Royal Sovereign KING. *Then what happened when they saw the KING on Coronation Day?* They fell down and worshipped Him and presented their gifts! They were worshipping the LORD, who was manifested in the Shechinah glory of God, in the flesh.

Herod then made an inquiry of all the Chief Priests and the Scribes in the Holy Temple, asking them where the Messiah was to be born. They told Herod that the Messiah was to be born *"in Bethlehem of Judaea,"* as the Prophets foretold! Here is the account, as it is written! Remember that His *"Star"* is the Shechinah light of the LORD'S glory and the wise men came to worship Him! Notice here that Messiah Yeshua was born *"in the Land of Israel,"* and His parents returned later to *"the Land of Israel,"* as it is written in this historical record!

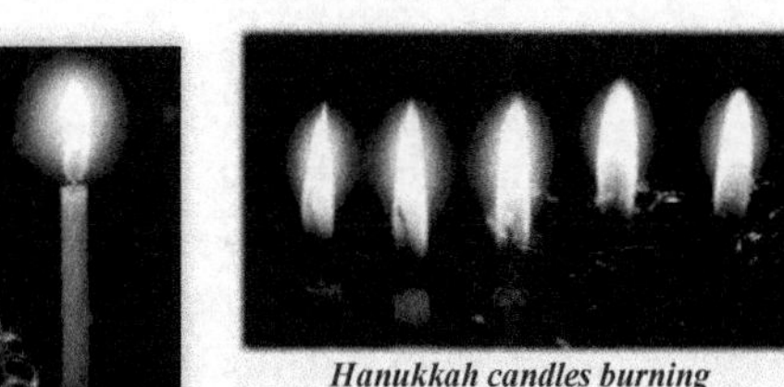

Hanukkah candles burning
Photo ©2013 Kimberly K Ballard

Matthew 2:1-23 *Now when Yeshua was born in Bethlehem of Judea in the days of Herod the King, behold, wise men from the East came to Jerusalem, saying, Where is He who has been born KING of the Jews? For we have seen His star in the East, and have come to worship Him. When Herod the King heard this, he was troubled, and all Jerusalem with him; and assembling all the Chief Priests and Scribes of the people, he inquired of them where the Messiah was to be born. They told him, In Bethlehem of Judea; for so it is written by the Prophet; And you, O Bethlehem, in the land of Judah, are by no means least among the rulers of Judah; for from you shall come a ruler who will govern my people Israel. Then Herod summoned the wise men secretly and ascertained from them what time the star appeared; and he sent them to Bethlehem, saying, Go and search diligently for the child, and when you have found Him bring me word, that I too may come and worship Him. When they had heard the King they went their way; and lo, the star which they had seen in the East went before them, till it came to rest over the place where the child was. When they saw the star, they rejoiced exceedingly with great joy; and going into the house they saw the child with Mary His mother, and they fell down and worshiped Him. Then, opening their treasures, they offered Him gifts, gold and frankincense and myrrh. And being warned in a dream not to return to Herod, they departed to their own country by another way. Now when they had departed, behold, an angel of the Lord appeared to Joseph in a dream and said, Rise, take the child and his mother, and flee to Egypt, and remain there till I tell you; for Herod is about to search for the child, to destroy him. And he rose and took the child and his mother by night, and departed to Egypt, and remained there until the death of Herod. This was to fulfill what the LORD had spoken by the Prophet, Out of Egypt have I called My Son. Then Herod, when he saw that he had been tricked by the wise men, was in a furious rage, and he sent and killed all the male children in Bethlehem and in all that region who were two years old or under, according to the time which he had ascertained from the wise men. Then was fulfilled what was spoken by the Prophet Jeremiah, A voice was heard in Ramah, wailing and loud lamentation, Rachel weeping for her children; she refused to be consoled, because they were no more. But when Herod died, behold, an angel of the LORD appeared* *in a dream to Joseph in Egypt, saying, Rise, take the child and his mother, and go to the Land of Israel, for those who sought the child's life are dead. And he rose and took the child and his mother, and went to the Land of Israel. But when he heard that Archelaus reigned over Judea in place of his father Herod, he was afraid to go there, and being warned in a dream he withdrew to the district of Galilee. And he went and dwelt in a city called Nazareth, that what was spoken by the Prophets might be fulfilled, He shall be called a Nazarene.*

In this account, Herod summoned *"the wise men" secretly* to find out *"what time the Star appeared!"* Still, we find more exciting clues that this was indeed Rosh HaShanah through the words of King Herod. The LORD revealed this to me, so I had the chills when I saw it for the first time! The Biblical calendar is a lunar calendar. The days begin at sundown and they go through to the next sundown of the following day. Rosh HaShanah is the only Holy Day that could not begin until the sliver of the new moon was sighted. They would post messengers throughout the Land of Israel and light torches to get the message out *the exact moment* that the very first faint, slight sliver of the new moon was sighted. As I recall, the first messenger actually stood on the Mount of Olives across from the Holy Temple and he lit the first torch. The sliver of the new moon had to be sighted by two witnesses and verified through the Sanhedrin. As soon as word of the first sighting came, the messengers lit their torches to spread the word as quickly as possible that the New Year was to begin. So Rosh HaShanah could not begin until they knew *"what time they had seen the sliver of the new moon."* So the sighting time was the critical factor for Rosh HaShanah. Everyone was looking to be the first to discover when it would first appear and be visible in the sky, so they could get the word out quickly that the Holy Convocation of the LORD could begin. It was an exciting event and everyone was full of anticipation as they prepared to see it first! What I have to say next is absolutely astonishing and it was also revealed to me by the Holy Spirit!

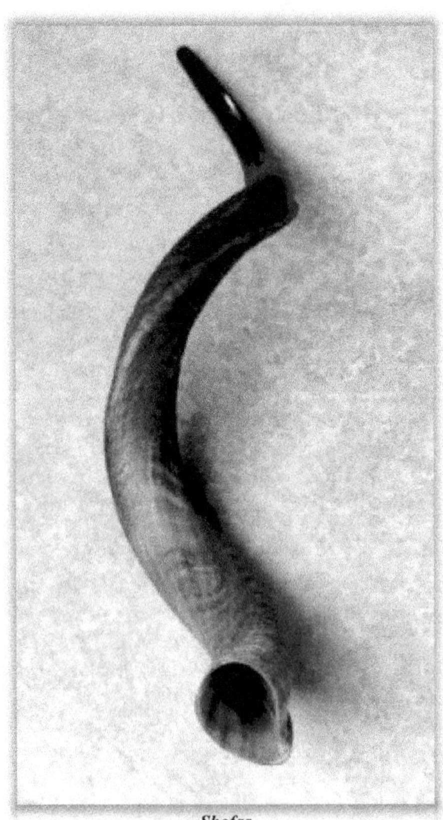

Shofar

Herod questioned the Chief Priests and the Scribes and he asked them where the Messiah was prophesied to be born *and they are the members of the Sanhedrin, who verify the timing of Rosh HaShanah!* Now this explained why Herod summoned *"the wise men" secretly to find out what time the Star appeared!* The wise men knew all about the timing of Rosh HaShanah! In this case, when the *Star* appeared that meant that the Jewish KING had arrived! Remember that the word *"Star" is "Ma'ohr or light"* and it is the Shechinah glory of the LORD that shone round about them and they were sore afraid! This *Star* was the light of the glory of God that came and stood over the place where Messiah the KING was lying in the manger, just like it stood over the Ark of the Covenant *because Yeshua's Testimony is the Heavenly Ark of God!* I believe, therefore, that Herod was speaking of the sighting of the New moon of Rosh HaShanah and *this is why Herod summoned the Prophets of Israel, "the wise men," who could determine it! The Jewish "wise men" therefore knew exactly "what time the Star had appeared!" So the Star of the Shechinah glory appeared at the time of the sighting of the New Moon, on Tishrei 1, which is the beginning of Rosh HaShanah on the LORD'S Feast of Trumpets.* It is incredible, just astonishing to see this truth for the first time! The Jewish wise men had traveled from afar to Jerusalem to be there at the right time for the arrival of the KING Messiah and they saw *the Star appear at a certain time in the sky* and this was absolutely critical to Herod, who realized that there was nothing he could do to stop it from happening! Herod therefore panicked! The *"Star"* went before *"the wise men,"* and it came to rest over the place where the child was lying in a manger in Bethlehem. *The LORD always descended over the Ark of the Covenant and came to rest there!*

Herod became furious when he discovered that the wise men had tricked him! They were called *"wise men"* for a reason! They knew that Herod wanted to destroy their Jewish KING! So Herod flew into a rage and destroyed all the potential candidates that had been born in Bethlehem and in all the surrounding areas. Herod actually provided the most exciting clues to the timing of Yeshua's birth in his summoning of the wise men and the Priests and Scribes of the Sanhedrin!

Now the Hebrew word for *"Star"* is the word *"Kokhav."* Therefore, Yeshua is the fulfillment of the prophecy that is found in Numbers 24 that states, *"A Star shall come out of Jacob and a Sceptre shall rise out of Israel!"*

Numbers 24:17 *I shall see Him, but not now; I shall behold Him, but not nigh; There shall come a Star out of Jacob, and a Sceptre shall rise out of Israel, and shall smite the corners of Moab, and destroy all the children of Sheth.*

The New Moon of Rosh HaShanah
Taken September 26th 2014
Photo ©2014
Kimberly K Ballard All Right Reserved

Another important account of the Nativity story of Messiah Yeshua is written in the Gospel of Luke.

Luke 2:1-20 *And it came to pass in those days, that there went out a decree from Caesar Augustus, that all the world should be taxed. And this taxing was first made when Cyrenius was governor of Syria. And all went to be taxed, every one into his own city. And Joseph also went up from Galilee, out of the city of Nazareth, into Judaea, unto the city of David, which is called Bethlehem; because he was of the House and lineage of David; To be taxed with Mary his espoused wife, being great with child. And so it was, that, while they were there, the days were accomplished that she should be delivered. And she brought forth her firstborn son, and wrapped Him in swaddling clothes and laid Him in a manger; because there was no room for them in the Inn. And there were in the same country shepherds abiding in the field, keeping watch over their flock by night. And, lo, the angel of the LORD came upon them, and the glory of the LORD shone round about them; and they were sore afraid. And the angel said unto them, Fear not; for, behold, I bring you good tidings of great joy, which shall be to all people. For unto you is born this day in the city of David a Saviour, which is Messiah the LORD. And this shall be a sign unto you; Ye shall find the babe wrapped in swaddling clothes, lying in a manger. And suddenly there was with the angel a multitude of the Heavenly Host praising God, and saying, Glory to God in the highest, and on earth peace, good will toward men. And it came to pass, as the angels were gone away from them into Heaven, the shepherds said one to another, Let us now go even unto Bethlehem, and see this thing which is come to pass, which the LORD hath made known unto us. And they came with haste, and found Mary, and Joseph, and the babe lying in a manger. And when they had seen it, they made known abroad the saying which was told them concerning this child. And all they that heard it wondered at those things which were told them by the shepherds.*

But Mary kept all these things, and pondered them in her heart. And the shepherds returned, glorifying and praising God for all the things that they had heard and seen, as it was told unto them.

Could there be another hidden truth in this account that reveals that the Nativity story took place on Rosh HaShanah? The text says *"There were shepherds abiding in the field, keeping watch over their flock* ***by night.****"* When the angel of the LORD came as the messenger to herald the good tidings, the angel actually said, *"For unto you* ***is born this day,*** *in the city of David, a Saviour who is Messiah the LORD."* So what we have here is fascinating indeed!

One of the major Rabbis known as *"Perush ha' Rambam to Rosh HaShanah"* verified and declared that *"It is possible for the moon to be seen at both sunrise and sunset of the same day for Rosh HaShanah."* I quote from another source that says, *"It is written in the Mishnah in Rosh HaShanah 25, that there was a case where the witnesses said that they saw the moon in the morning in the east and in the evening in the west. The president of the Sanhedrin at the time was Rabban Gamaliel and he verified this event."* The time that the new moon is *"born"* is called *"Molad." This is all ironically linked to the return of the Davidic Dynasty!* Now one of these references was from the famous Rabbi Rashi who said that *"in the Mishnah, in verse Tehilim 89:37, it compares the Davidic Dynasty to the moon."* ***(Source; ©2010-2011 dafyomi.co.il/rhashanah/insites/rh-dt-025.htm).***

The New Moon of Rosh HaShanah 2014
Photo ©2014
Kimberly K Ballard
All Rights Reserved

The following information is very important because it is also connected to the new moon of Rosh HaShanah *and the return of the Davidic Dynasty.* When I saw the following statements by the Rabbis after what I had already written, it was simply breathtaking!

From the same source that I just quoted above, apparently at the time of the destruction of Solomon's Temple, it was written that, *"The Davidic Dynasty ended when the eyes of Zedekiah were blinded, (the last King of Judah) and this was compared to the loss of the light of the moon."* However, it also stated and again I quote *"The return of the moon's light after the Molad is a sign that the Davidic Dynasty of David Ha'Melech will return to its former glory. It was therefore, common practice to announce the new month with the phrase, "David Melech Yisrael."* ***(Source: ©2010-2012 dafyomi.co.il/rhashanah/insites/rh-dt-025.htm).***

If the Davidic Dynasty ended with the blinding of the eyes of King Zedekiah, the last King of Judah, and the return of the moon's light after the Molad was a sign that the Davidic Dynasty would return to its former glory, then I understood what was truly going on when Messiah Yeshua confronted the leaders in the Holy Temple after He healed the blind man, and this sent a shiver right through me! *Standing before them was the Eternal KING Messiah of the Davidic Dynasty who came into the world on Rosh HaShanah, at the time of the birth of the new moon! This was the restoration of the Eternal King of Judah through King David's line!* Yeshua showed them many signs that He is the one who will restore the Davidic Dynasty to its former glory, but they could not see it because they were blind to it! After the blind man was miraculously healed by Messiah Yeshua, *"The Son of David,"* the man was questioned by the Pharisees, who kept on pondering how this man had received his sight. The Pharisees refused to see that the return of the Davidic Dynasty was fulfilled in KING Messiah Yeshua, who was now standing before them. So Yeshua said that their sin remained because they claimed that they could see, yet they were completely blind to His identity! So they cast the former blind man, who could now see, out of the Holy Temple, while their own eyes were spiritually blinded. Yeshua then revealed His identity as the LORD to the man who had formerly been born blind, while Yeshua blinded the eyes of those that claimed that they could see! The former blind man worshipped the LORD God, the Eternal KING of Judah, who had just healed him!

John 9:35-41 *Yeshua heard that they had cast him out; and when He had found him, He said unto him, Dost thou believe on the Son of God? He answered and said, Who is He LORD, that I might believe on Him? And Yeshua said unto him, Thou hast both seen Him, and it is He that talketh with thee. And he said, LORD, I believe. And he worshipped Him. And Yeshua said, for judgment I AM come into this world, that they which see not might see; and that they which see might be made blind. And some of the Pharisees which were with Him heard these words, and said unto Him, Are we blind also? Yeshua said unto them, If ye were blind, ye should have no sin; but now ye say, We see; therefore your sin remaineth.*

In the book of Isaiah, the LORD said the following words about His servants!

Isaiah 42:18-20 *Hear, ye deaf; and look, ye blind, that ye may see. Who is blind, but My servant? Or deaf, as My messenger that I sent? Who is blind as the LORD'S servant? Seeing many things, but thou observes not; opening the ears, but he heareth not.*

Now in the following miracle, we know for certain that Messiah Yeshua was born on Rosh HaShanah and that He will restore the Davidic Dynasty because another blind man fervently and unrelentingly called out to Yeshua as *"the Son of David."* He pleaded with Yeshua that He might have mercy on him and restore his sight! As the blind man said the words, *"Son of David,"* Yeshua stood still as the Heavenly Ark because He is the *Davidic KING that will restore the Eternal Davidic Dynasty*! The people charged the man to keep it quiet, but the man called out to Him even louder with this salutation. Immediately the blind man received his sight from the power of the Royal Sceptre of the Great Eternal KING of Judah!

Mark 10:46-52 *And they came to Jericho; and as He went out of Jericho with His disciples and a great number of people, blind Bartimaeus, the son of Timaeus, sat by the highway side begging. And when he heard that it was Yeshua of Nazareth, he began to cry out, and say, Yeshua, Thou Son of David, have mercy on me. And many charged him that he should hold his peace; but he cried the more a great deal, Thou Son of David, have mercy on me. And Yeshua stood still, and commanded him to be called. And they call the blind man, saying unto him, Be of good comfort, rise; He calleth thee. And he, casting away his garment, rose, and came to Yeshua. And Yeshua answered and said unto him, What wilt thou that I should do unto thee? The blind man said unto Him, LORD, that I might receive my sight. And Yeshua said unto him, Go thy way; thy faith hath made thee whole. And immediately he received his sight, and followed Yeshua in the way.*

After this man received his sight, he immediately followed behind Yeshua, the Heavenly Ark in *"the way"* to Heaven! *KING Messiah Yeshua, who restores the Eternal Davidic Dynasty, was born in the City of David on Rosh HaShanah and even though it was night, the angel declared that the Saviour that was born this day was "Messiah the LORD."*

Luke 2:11 *For unto you <u>is born this day</u> in the City of David a Saviour, which is Messiah the LORD.*

The Shechinah glory light of the LORD was shining all around them at the time of the sighting of the new moon of Rosh HaShanah, and this reminds me of a prophecy in Zechariah that foreshadows the unusual cosmic disturbances and events in the Heavens that will transpire at the LORD'S return as Messiah.

Zechariah 14:6-7 *And it shall come to pass in that day, that the light shall not be clear, nor dark; But it shall be one day which shall be known to the LORD, not day, nor night; but it shall come to pass, that at evening time it shall be light.*

Now all of these truths about Yeshua's birth on Rosh HaShanah came to me through the powerful Holy Spirit. I was then able to prove them, not only through the above statements, but also through corresponding Scriptures and from the Rabbis of Israel. *Now I believe that this was a sign from the angel of the LORD that at the time of KING Messiah Yeshua's birth, the Star was seen at both times as evening was becoming morning on the first day of Rosh HaShanah, which is Tishrei 1 and Behold, there was light! Messiah Yeshua's birth was therefore without a doubt, the sign of the return of the former glory of the Eternal Davidic Dynasty! So Yeshua was born as the evening of the sixth day was becoming the morning of the seventh day Sabbath of the LORD!* Adam was created on the sixth day of the week and then God rested on the seventh day. So Messiah Yeshua was born the same day that Adam was created. He came as the perfect Second Adam and Messiah came in the flesh as the perfect Lamb that the Word of God is written upon forever, as the Living Torah Scroll. *The KING Messiah from the Eternal Davidic Dynasty therefore arrived as the evening was becoming morning on the seventh day.* So by the time that KING Yeshua was born, *it became the seventh day Sabbath of the LORD* and guess what? Yeshua, the LORD God of Israel, the KING of Glory, *the Living Torah,* was found *resting* in the manger, in a type of Ark, as the Shechinah glory stood over Him! *So on the seventh day Sabbath, the LORD KING rested in the Ark, as our Living Bread and Living Water from Heaven!* I am thrilled to see how this all comes together so accurately. Yeshua's birth was written in such a miraculous way, so the timing of His true birth date could finally be discerned for the Jewish people! Praise God for this story! Rosh HaShanah is also called *"Yom Teruah"* and Israel was commanded by the LORD *"to keep the First day of the Seventh month." The KING Messiah would therefore, have been born on the First day of the Seventh month! "Yom Teruah" means "Day of Shouting."* Yom Teruah pertains to a large gathering of people shouting in unison together or making a loud joyful noise while shouting praises to God, and I already mentioned this in regards to the rapture! Now this is extremely important because guess what happened at the birth of KING Yeshua on *"Yom Teruah?"* There appeared from Heaven *"a multitude of Heavenly Hosts of angels in the Shechinah glory light, praising God and shouting in unison saying, "Glory to God in the Highest and on earth, peace and good will toward men!"* This exciting and extraordinary part of Yeshua's Nativity story is written in the Gospel of Luke and I was so thrilled and chilled to see this connection to Rosh HaShanah, through the power of the Holy Spirit!

Luke 2:13-14 *And suddenly there was with the angel a multitude of the Heavenly Host praising God, and saying, Glory to God in the Highest, and on earth peace, good will toward men.*

So the Heavenly Hosts were praising God in a large gathering while shouting in unison the joyful tidings of the birth of the Saviour, the LORD Messiah KING Yeshua! This makes it clear that Yeshua's birth was definitely on *"Yom Teruah" on "the Day of Shouting!" This was indeed Coronation Day of the LORD God as KING!* After this happened with the multitude of Heavenly Hosts of angels, we find that *all the shepherds were also in unison, shouting praises and glorifying God!*

Luke 2:20 *And the shepherds returned, glorifying and praising God for all the things that they had heard and seen, as it was told unto them.*

New Moon of Yom Teruah 2014 Photo ©2014 Kimberly K Ballard All Rights Reserved

All of these voices in unison were joyfully praising God together, declaring that the KING of Heaven had arrived and that the Saviour was with us, as the KING Messiah of Israel! On Rosh HaShanah, the sound of the shofar or ram's horn is supposed to *"awaken"* us to the fact that *the LORD God is the KING of the Universe!* So the Almond Branch, KING Yeshua, arrived as Heaven was opened as the Heavenly Hosts, and shepherds were shouting, declaring His glory! The shofar was blowing! It was time to *"awaken, Shaked." The Branch* from the Almond Tree of Life was here!

On Rosh HaShanah, it is customary to eat *"fruit."* This is usually apples dipped in sweet honey. A Hebrew declaration is spoken on Rosh HaShanah in the words, *"Shana tovah u'metuka,"* which means *"Wishing you a good Sweet New Year!"* Joseph, who was Yeshua's chosen earthly father, and Mary, his chosen mother, went out from the city of Nazareth, or the place called the, *"Branch,"* and they went into the city of Bethlehem, the *"House of Bread"* and *"Ephratah"* which of course means *"Fruitful."* Bethlehem was a territory in Judah or Judaea. This is where the Lambs of Passover were kept until they were taken to the Holy Temple to be offered to God, as a perfect atonement for our sins. The LORD KING Messiah of the Davidic Dynasty of the Tribe of Judah, the Fruitful Branch, the Almond Rod of God, the Living Torah was resting in the manger, the Ark, on the seventh day Sabbath of the LORD and now, through this Divine miracle, we could all eat the First Fruit from the Almond Tree of Life with this sweet honey and live forever! So this means that KING Messiah's birth would bring us *"a Sweet New Year" on Rosh HaShanah* and through Him, we could be inscribed in the Lamb's book of Life forever. Of course, the Lamb's book of life contains all the names of believers in the Living Torah Covenant of the Heavenly Ark of God. Rosh HaShanah occurs on the seventh month of the Biblical calendar. The Nativity story was, therefore, a picture of perfection and completion in the number seven! So this proclamation proves that KING Messiah Yeshua is the Living Almond Branch that bore the sweet First Fruit, as our perfect Torah Passover Lamb. Israel's KING is the *"Sweet Branch"* of Rosh HaShanah that took away our *"bitterness"* of the curse of death from the Garden of Eden. Learning the earthly Torah of Moses is therefore like milk, but as soon we come to understand that the LORD God of Israel is the fullness of it all, as our KING Messiah Yeshua, we now have the Heavenly Living Torah, which is the First Fruit, dipped in sweet honey, mixed with spices of cinnamon! The Eternal Promised Land or Heaven is a land flowing with milk and honey because the LORD is in that place! No one could have written such an incredible story, but the LORD Himself!

Hebrews 5:13-14 *For every one that useth milk is unskilled in the Word of righteousness; for he is a babe. But strong meat belongeth to them that are full of age, even those who by reason of use have their senses exercised to discern both good and evil.*

Challah Bread Crown for Rosh HaShanah to honour the KING, made by Kimberly K Ballard

Now I mentioned already that on Rosh HaShanah, special Challah bread is made into the shape of a crown to symbolize God as KING and *the Bread from Heaven was the KING, the Rod and Staff that feeds us forever.* The mystery is solved why they continually asked Yeshua, just before His crucifixion, if He was a KING! They even placed the Name of His tribe on His rod of wood and the Name that they identified with Yeshua was *"THE KING OF THE JEWS."* The LORD inherits Judah as His portion! I believe that they were asking this question of Yeshua because they knew that *He had been born KING on the Feast of Trumpets, on Rosh HaShanah.* The Jewish Messianic prophecy was fulfilled when Yeshua was born KING and they knew it! The Roman soldiers even mocked Yeshua as the Jewish KING. Remember He came to save Israel and the world, not Himself. The Rod of God could not be lowered from the cross, so Israel and the world could be saved by the KING, who succeeded in this Eternal victory. As we know, Yeshua had to be lifted up to save us and this is why Yeshua did not come down from the cross when the people scoffed at Him.

Luke 23:35-38 *And the people stood beholding. And the rulers also with them derided Him, saying, He saved others; let Him save Himself, if He be Messiah, the chosen of God. And the soldiers also mocked Him, coming to Him, and offering Him vinegar, And saying, If Thou be the KING of the Jews, save Thyself. And a superscription also was written over Him in letters of Greek, and Latin, and Hebrew, THIS IS THE KING OF THE JEWS.*

Mark 15:26 *And the superscription of His accusation was written over, THE KING OF THE JEWS.*

Pontius Pilate specifically asked Yeshua if He was a KING. Then Yeshua spoke the startling truth when He said that *"His Kingdom is not of this world!"* In this way, the Messiah revealed that *He is the KING from Heaven and that He is "THE ETERNAL DAVIDIC KING OF ISRAEL!"* The Messiah was delivered by the Jews by Divine Providence to fulfill the Eternal Covenant of God!

John 18:36 *Yeshua answered, My Kingdom is not of this world; if My Kingdom were of this world, then would My servants fight, that I should not be delivered to the Jews; but now is My Kingdom not from hence.*

Now it is interesting that *Yeshua was so named* of the angel Gabriel *before He was even conceived in the womb.* The angel told Mary, *"For with God, nothing shall be impossible."* This Name *Yeshua* was always the Name of the Rod of God who brings forth *life* by His power!

Luke 1:37 *For with God nothing shall be impossible.*

Luke 2:21 *And when eight days were accomplished for the circumcising of the child, His name was called Yeshua, which was so named of the angel before He was conceived in the womb.*

In the Gospel of Luke, the angel Gabriel proclaimed *that God shall give unto Yeshua the throne of His father David and that He shall reign forever in a Kingdom that shall never end. Yeshua's birth is verified in this verse to be the return of the Eternal Davidic Dynasty.*

Luke 1:30-33 *And the angel said unto her, Fear not, Mary; for thou hast found favour with God. And, behold, thou shalt conceive in thy womb, and bring forth a son, and shalt call His name Yeshua. He shall be great, and shall be called the Son of the Highest; and the LORD God shall give unto Him the throne of His father David; And He shall reign over the house of Jacob forever; and of His kingdom there shall be no end.*

Now in Matthew 2, it is written that the angel of the LORD appeared to Joseph, the son of David, in a dream and told him to flee to Egypt with the baby Messiah Yeshua. So he fled to Egypt as he was instructed to by the angel Gabriel.

Matthew 2:13-15 *And when they were departed, behold, the angel of the LORD appeareth to Joseph in a dream, saying, Arise, and take the young child and his mother, and flee into Egypt, and be thou there until I bring thee word; for Herod will seek the young child to destroy Him. When he arose, he took the young child and his mother by night, and departed into Egypt; And was there until the death of Herod; that it might be fulfilled which was spoken of the LORD by the prophet, saying, Out of Egypt have I called My Son.*

In verses 19-20 the angel appeared to Joseph again and told him to leave Egypt for Israel and *they came into the Land of Israel. Yeshua was coming out of the wilderness and into the Promised Land of Israel!* So with this defining truth, look at what God said in the book of Hosea about Himself coming out of Egypt as their Saviour!

Hosea 13:4-11 *Yet I AM the LORD thy God from the land of Egypt, and thou shalt know no god but Me; for there is no Saviour beside Me. I did know thee in the wilderness, in the land of great drought. According to their pasture, so were they filled; they were filled, and their heart was exalted; therefore have they forgotten Me. Therefore I will be unto them as a lion; as a leopard by the way will I observe them; I will meet them as a bear that is bereaved of her whelps, and will rend the caul of their heart, and there will I devour them like a lion; the wild beast shall tear them. O Israel, thou hast destroyed thyself; but in Me is thine help. I will be thy KING; where is any other that may save* *thee in all thy cities? And thy judges of whom thou saidst, Give me a king and princes? I gave thee a King in Mine anger, and took him away in My wrath.*

In Hosea the LORD God said that *He would come to them as the lion, the leopard, the bear, and wild beast,* if His servants rejected Him as their KING and hardened their hearts toward Him. Just as those who remained in disbelief in the wilderness did not enter into His rest in the Promised land but died in the wilderness, so will we if we hearken not unto His voice as our Eternal KING of glory. It is interesting that in Revelation 13, we find judgment again with *the lion, the leopard, the bear, and the beast and it says "who can make war with him?"* In Lamentations, Jeremiah said he saw the wrath of *the Rod of God* and later he said that *the LORD was unto him as a bear and a lion.*

Lamentation 2:1 *I AM the man that hath seen affliction by the rod of His wrath.*

Lamentation 3:10 *He was unto me as a bear lying in wait, and as a lion in secret places.*

On Rosh HaShanah, *"the Feast of Trumpets,"* the shofar or ram's horn is blown at least 100 times during the two day Feast. *The exciting news is that the birth date of KING Yeshua is the time of the Rapture!* When the KING blows *"the Awakening Blast"* at the Last Trump on Rosh HaShanah, the dead who are *"asleep"* will rise from their graves to Eternal life. The *"awakening blast"* of Rosh HaShanah that brings the dead to life will take place a split second before the rapture of the believers in Messiah who have accepted the salvation of the Rod of God. The LORD descends from Heaven with a *"Shout" on "the Day of Shouting!"* This refers not only to *the shout of the voice of the LORD,* but it is a reference to *His trumpet blast on the Feast of Trumpets that is meant to awaken the dead.* Now the most exciting detail is that *when the rapture happens on Rosh HaShanah, at the Last Trump, it will involve the gathering of a multitude who will all be shouting joyful praises in unison to the LORD KING who has just transformed us in the rapture* into our Eternal bodies when He has just fulfilled His promise of Eternal life to us through His Rod of salvation *on Yeshua's birthday which is the new birth of mankind!* This is so incredible and it gives me such joy to see it! At this point, death has no victory over us anymore because *the Rod of God came to give us life on Rosh HaShanah!* Those who are gathered up in the rapture, into the glory cloud at the Last Trump are called *"the first fruits of Messiah."*

James 1:18 *Of His own will begat He us with the Word of Truth, that we should be a kind of first fruits of His creatures.*

The blast of *the LORD'S shofar on Rosh HaShanah* is to remind us to wake up from Spiritual slumber, so we can welcome *the KING of the universe, and every year we blow the shofar to remind Him! At Yeshua's birth, Israel was to wake up from Spiritual slumber and welcome the Divine Presence of God, as Messiah, their KING!*

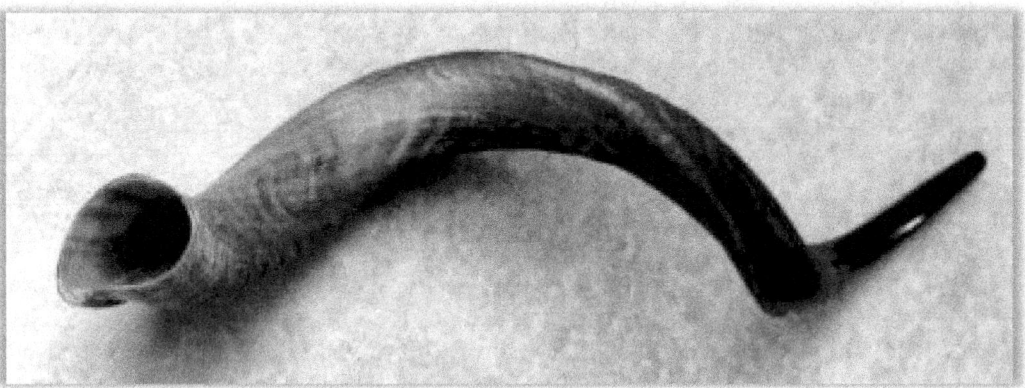

Shofar Photo ©2013 Kimberly K Ballard All Rights Reserved

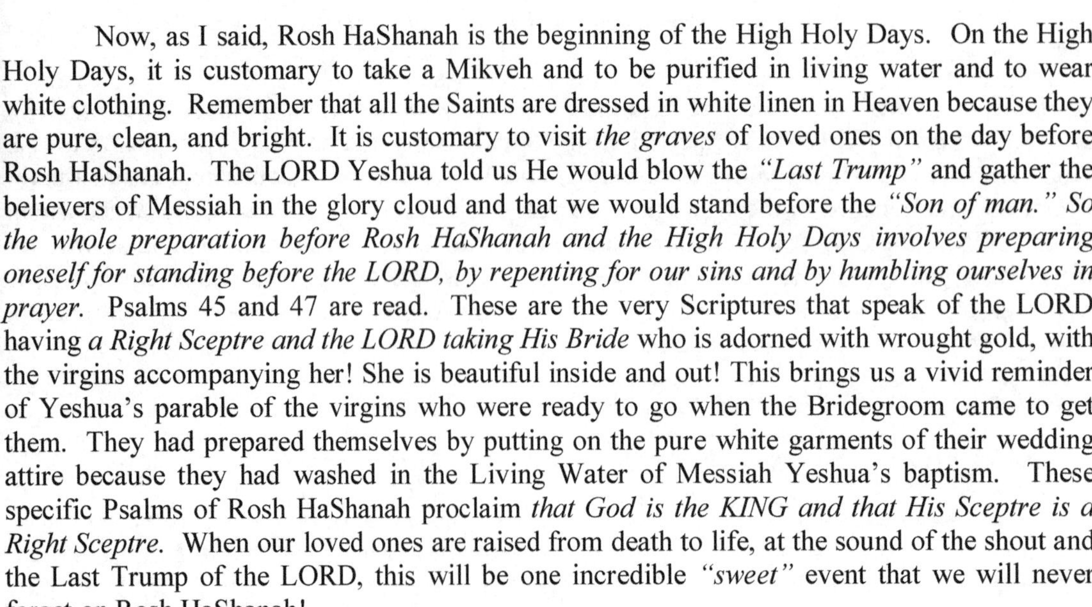

Now, as I said, Rosh HaShanah is the beginning of the High Holy Days. On the High Holy Days, it is customary to take a Mikveh and to be purified in living water and to wear white clothing. Remember that all the Saints are dressed in white linen in Heaven because they are pure, clean, and bright. It is customary to visit *the graves* of loved ones on the day before Rosh HaShanah. The LORD Yeshua told us He would blow the *"Last Trump"* and gather the believers of Messiah in the glory cloud and that we would stand before the *"Son of man." So the whole preparation before Rosh HaShanah and the High Holy Days involves preparing oneself for standing before the LORD, by repenting for our sins and by humbling ourselves in prayer.* Psalms 45 and 47 are read. These are the very Scriptures that speak of the LORD having *a Right Sceptre and the LORD taking His Bride* who is adorned with wrought gold, with the virgins accompanying her! She is beautiful inside and out! This brings us a vivid reminder of Yeshua's parable of the virgins who were ready to go when the Bridegroom came to get them. They had prepared themselves by putting on the pure white garments of their wedding attire because they had washed in the Living Water of Messiah Yeshua's baptism. These specific Psalms of Rosh HaShanah proclaim *that God is the KING and that His Sceptre is a Right Sceptre.* When our loved ones are raised from death to life, at the sound of the shout and the Last Trump of the LORD, this will be one incredible *"sweet"* event that we will never forget on Rosh HaShanah!

I Corinthians 15:20-23 *But now is Messiah risen from the dead, and become the First Fruits of them that slept. For since by man came death, by man came also the resurrection of the dead. For as in Adam all die, even so in Messiah shall all be made alive. But every man in his own order; Messiah the First Fruits; afterward they that are Messiahs at His coming.*

Now there are some technical aspects of the Nativity story that are important, involving Yeshua's birth at Rosh HaShanah. The facts are determined by the time of the conception and birth of John the Baptist. His mother Elisabeth was a daughter of Aaron's Priestly line, making John a direct descendant of Aaron, God's High Priest. John's father Zacharias, also a Priest, was ministering in the Holy Temple in Jerusalem during the Priestly course of *Abijah.* The Priestly course of *Abijah* occurred in the spring time at the end of the Biblical month of Iyar which is between the middle of April and the middle of May. The Priestly courses were based upon a system of rotation and they would serve for one week, twice during a year. So the course of *Abijah* occurred a second time in the fall between the middle of October and the middle of November in the Biblical month of Cheshvan. The lot of the Jewish Priest Zacharias was to burn incense in the Temple of the LORD. The angel of the LORD appeared to Zacharias as he was burning the incense, and the angel was standing at the right side of the incense altar when he declared the Heavenly message from the LORD. I just realized that there is a connection to the incense in the Holy Temple, that represents the prayers and tears of the Saints, to Zacharias, who was offering up his prayers and tears for a son as he made the incense offering! So the first thing that the angel of the LORD said to Zacharias was that his prayers had been heard in Heaven! At the same time that this was happening to Zacharias, there were multitudes of Jewish believers who were also praying outside the Holy Temple at the time of the incense offering, while Zacharias was inside the Temple, offering incense to the LORD. They were all praying together in unison as the prayer of Zacharias was heard by the LORD!

Luke 1:13 *But the angel said unto him, Fear not, Zacharias; for thy prayer is heard; and thy wife Elisabeth shall bear thee a son, and thou shalt call his name John.*

King David set up the 24 Priestly courses for the Divine service in the Holy Temple. The Priestly course of *Abijah,* that Zacharias was appointed to minister, was the 8th course. So Zacharias would have completed his Priestly course by the end of May and returned home.

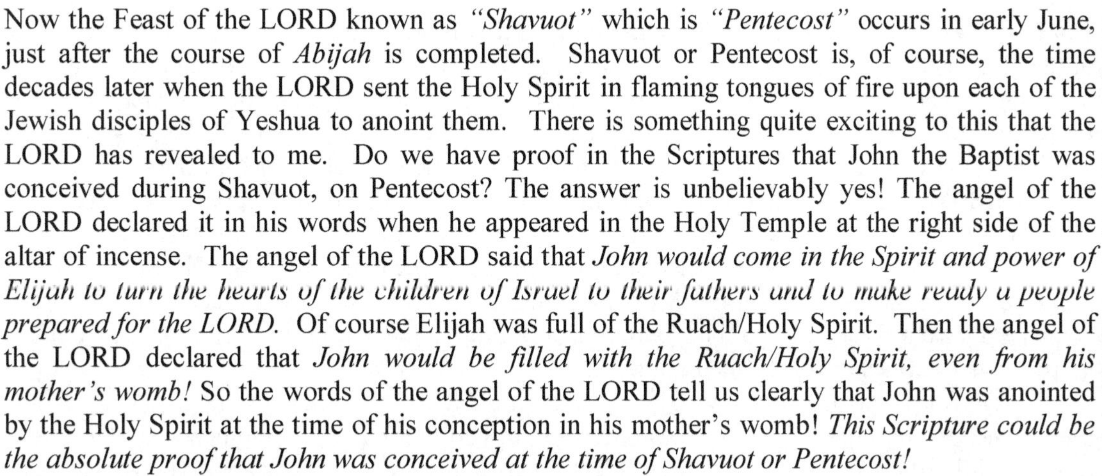

Now the Feast of the LORD known as *"Shavuot"* which is *"Pentecost"* occurs in early June, just after the course of *Abijah* is completed. Shavuot or Pentecost is, of course, the time decades later when the LORD sent the Holy Spirit in flaming tongues of fire upon each of the Jewish disciples of Yeshua to anoint them. There is something quite exciting to this that the LORD has revealed to me. Do we have proof in the Scriptures that John the Baptist was conceived during Shavuot, on Pentecost? The answer is unbelievably yes! The angel of the LORD declared it in his words when he appeared in the Holy Temple at the right side of the altar of incense. The angel of the LORD said that *John would come in the Spirit and power of Elijah to turn the hearts of the children of Israel to their fathers and to make ready a people prepared for the LORD.* Of course Elijah was full of the Ruach/Holy Spirit. Then the angel of the LORD declared that *John would be filled with the Ruach/Holy Spirit, even from his mother's womb!* So the words of the angel of the LORD tell us clearly that John was anointed by the Holy Spirit at the time of his conception in his mother's womb! *This Scripture could be the absolute proof that John was conceived at the time of Shavuot or Pentecost!*

Luke 1:15 *For he shall be great in the sight of the LORD, and shall drink neither wine nor strong drink; and he shall be filled with the Holy Spirit, even from his mother's womb.*

Pregnancy is divided into 3 trimesters, each being 3 months long. We know how significant the number three is to the LORD, since the Living Branch of the Almond Tree of Life came to life on the third day as it was in the beginning!

Now if we read further in the Scripture, we see that after the time that Zacharias fulfilled his ministration in the Holy Temple, he returned home and his wife conceived. His ministration ended at the end of May and John was conceived in Elisabeth's womb shortly after this time, in early June!

Luke 1:23-24 *And it came to pass, that, as soon as the days of his ministration were accomplished, he departed to his own house. And after those days his wife Elisabeth conceived and hid herself five months.*

Elisabeth conceived and hid herself for five months. If you count five month from Shavuot or Pentecost, you come to approximately the Hebrew month of Cheshvan and specifically the 17th on the Biblical calendar. This is when Elisabeth came out of her five months of hiding. Cheshvan 17 commemorates *the day that the rain started falling in the flood* as Noah was safe in the Ark. Noah was hid in the Ark for five months until the rains abated from off the earth. In the sixth month, the angel Gabriel appeared unto Mary in Nazareth and he gave her the glad tidings that she was to conceive and bear a son and call Him *"Yeshua," who was so named of the angel Gabriel before He was conceived in the womb."*

Luke 1:26 *And in the sixth month the angel Gabriel was sent from God unto a city of Galilee named Nazareth.*

The angel Gabriel declared the following message, one month after Elisabeth came out of her five months of hiding.

Luke 1:31 *And behold, thou shalt conceive in thy womb, and bring forth a son, and shalt call His Name Yeshua.*

The approximate time on the Biblical calendar when the angel appeared to Mary would have been in the Hebrew month of Kislev. This would have occurred in December. *So I believe Yeshua was conceived at the time of Hanukkah, during the Festival of Lights. If Yeshua was conceived in the month of Kislev, this is profound because His Living Testimony is the Almond Tree Menorah and He is of course called the light of the world, full of the anointing oil of the Holy Spirit.* Yeshua fulfilled the prophecy that says *"A light hath shined, in the Land of Zebulon and the Land of Naphtali, in Galilee of the Nations."* The date of Kislev 25, in the year

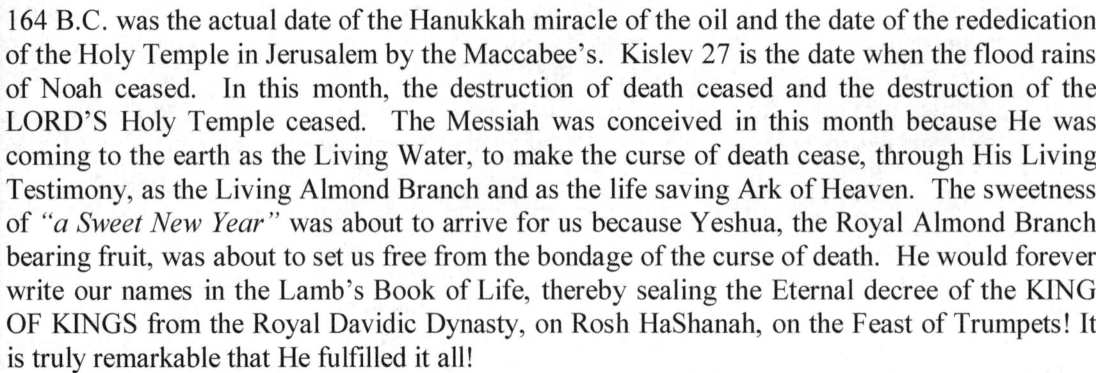

164 B.C. was the actual date of the Hanukkah miracle of the oil and the date of the rededication of the Holy Temple in Jerusalem by the Maccabee's. Kislev 27 is the date when the flood rains of Noah ceased. In this month, the destruction of death ceased and the destruction of the LORD'S Holy Temple ceased. The Messiah was conceived in this month because He was coming to the earth as the Living Water, to make the curse of death cease, through His Living Testimony, as the Living Almond Branch and as the life saving Ark of Heaven. The sweetness of *"a Sweet New Year"* was about to arrive for us because Yeshua, the Royal Almond Branch bearing fruit, was about to set us free from the bondage of the curse of death. He would forever write our names in the Lamb's Book of Life, thereby sealing the Eternal decree of the KING OF KINGS from the Royal Davidic Dynasty, on Rosh HaShanah, on the Feast of Trumpets! It is truly remarkable that He fulfilled it all!

During Hanukkah, the special Menorah called a *"hanukkiyah"* is lit. It has a total of nine branches. I thought it was important to remind you that one of the branches is elevated or raised and lifted up above all the others. Occasionally this one that is set apart is set lower than the others. Remember that Yeshua came as a lowly humble suffering servant, but He was lifted up and elevated as the Nazarite, as the set apart *Kadesh* righteous Branch that gives us the Eternal light of the salvation of His glory. Kislev is the ninth month on the ecclesiastical or religious calendar, but it is *the third month* on the civil calendar. It is from this single Shamash candle that is lifted up above the others that all the other candles are lit on the hanukkiyah. This reminds me so much that when we have the anointing of the Holy Spirit, through the purification of Messiah's baptism, our light is lit by the one who was lifted up and who is set apart from all others. His Eternal light shines through us because He is the source of the light within us.

Now in the Nativity story, if you account for the fact that the average length of the gestation period for the birth of a human baby is about 41 weeks or between 37-42 weeks, then we can calculate the time when John was born and consequently discern the time when Messiah Yeshua was born. John was sent as the messenger to prepare the way for the LORD to travel and to prepare the LORD'S people Israel for the arrival of their KING. It is therefore incredible that the name *"Abijah,"* that was Zacharias Priestly course, actually means in Hebrew *"My Father is YHVH!"* It can also mean *"My Father is the Sea!"* Messiah Yeshua declared that His Father was YHVH and that He is the Living Water, which is *the Great Sea of the Holy Temple that washes and purifies us.*

Shavuot, the day of the conception of John the Baptist, is also the time that signifies the arrival of the first fruits of the wheat harvest. The wheat in Israel needs *the latter rain* to fully develop. From this, you can calculate the 9 months to John's birth. *John the Baptist was born in the spring at Passover,* which on the Biblical Calendar would be in March-April. If this is true, which I believe that it is, then Yeshua was born 6 months after John, which on the Biblical calendar falls in late September to early October. *On the Biblical calendar, Yeshua's birth falls right into place exactly on Tishrei 1 of Rosh HaShanah, on the Feast of Trumpets, on the 1st day of the seventh Hebrew month exactly when the Jews are proclaiming the name Yeshua!*

Now the truth is that the shepherds only have their flocks out in the fields in Israel from about Passover in March-April, until October-November on the Jewish Biblical calendar. As soon as *the first rain* comes in Israel, the sheep are no longer kept in the fields. This means that there are no sheep out in the fields in December, as other people have suggested, and we know that when the angel of the LORD appeared to the shepherds, they were abiding in the fields with their flocks at night, during the birth of Yeshua in Bethlehem. What is remarkable about *the first rain* is that it usually begins in Israel sometime within the time frame of the High Holy Days, which begins at the time of Rosh HaShanah and onward. The last rain or latter rain usually comes right at Passover near the Seder. This is absolutely incredible. *This pinpoints the birth of Messiah Yeshua precisely!* If the sheep were out in the pastures at the birth of

Messiah Yeshua, then this means that His birth occurred at Rosh HaShanah and not any later than the High Holy Days in the fall. Think of what this means!

MESSIAH YESHUA THE LORD, IS THE EARLY AND THE LATTER RAIN!

If KING Messiah was born on Rosh HaShanah near the early rain and died at the time of the latter rain, then He is the fulfillment of the early and the latter rain! Messiah Yeshua is absolutely the LORD God of Israel. Incredibly this is found in the book of James, where he talks about the coming of the LORD!

The latter Rain Photo ©2014 Kimberly K Ballard All Rights Reserved

James 5:7-8 *Be patient therefore, brethren, unto the coming of the LORD. Behold, the husbandman waiteth for the precious fruit of the earth, and hath long patience for it, until He receive the early and latter rain. Be ye also patient; stablish your hearts; for the coming of the LORD draweth nigh.*

Deuteronomy 11:13-14 *And it shall come to pass, if ye shall hearken diligently unto My Commandments which I command you this day, to love the LORD your God, and to serve Him with all your heart and with all your soul, That I will give you the rain of your land in his due season, the first rain and the latter rain, that thou mayest gather in thy corn, and they wine, thine oil.*

The fact that the first rain comes sometime within the High Holy Days means that the time of Yeshua's birth is absolutely pinpointed to be at the time of *Rosh HaShanah* before the rains begin to fall and before the sheep are kept in until spring. Job was filled with the Holy Spirit of the LORD and he spoke of the secrets of God. When he spoke of the early and the latter rain, He revealed the secret of the Messiah, who is the LORD God of Israel, coming to gather His first fruits of the harvest for salvation. Now it is also interesting that Job gave a parable when he spoke about the LORD in Chapter 29. In the parable he says, *"The LORD'S candle shined upon my head, and when by His light I walked."* This is the secret of God that Messiah is the LORD and He is the candle that shined upon Job's head. The secret is that Messiah is the Living Branch of the Holy Almond Tree Menorah. Yeshua is the light of our salvation! The other secret that came out of Job's mouth tells us a prophetic word about the LORD. Job said *"And they waited for Me as for the rain; and they opened their mouth wide as for the latter rain."* The secret of God is that the LORD God of Israel is Messiah Yeshua and He is indeed *the early and the latter rain! So Yeshua descended to earth at the time of the early rain and He ascended back into Heaven at the time of the latter rain.* This makes the LORD God our Saviour both the early and latter rain that causes the fruit to be in abundance for the coming harvest. If Yeshua descended from Heaven at the time of the early rain, when Heaven was opened, then we can expectantly wait for Him to arrive again in the rapture during the time of Rosh HaShanah, at the beginning of the High Holy Days on Tishrei 1 when Heaven will again be open!

Joel 2:23 *Be glad then, ye children of Zion, and rejoice in the LORD your God; for He hath given you the former rain moderately, and He will cause to come down for you the rain, the former rain, and the latter rain in the first month.*

The latter rain is in the first month of Nisan on the Biblical calendar, and Passover comes on Nisan 14. *Yeshua died and came to life as the First Fruits of salvation during the time of the latter rain!* Most telling of all, though, is a verse that is found in Hosea, which says about the LORD God that, *"He shall come unto us as the rain, as the latter and former rain unto the earth!"*

Hosea 6:1-3 *Come, and let us return unto the LORD; for He hath torn, and He will heal us; He hath smitten, and He will bind us up. After two days will He revive us; and in the third day He will raise us up, and we shall live in His sight. Then shall we know, if we follow on to know the LORD; His going forth is prepared as the morning; and He shall come unto us as the rain, as the latter and former rain unto the earth.*

Wow! This was the Scripture that Yeshua was referring to when He said in three days He would build the Temple and restore Jerusalem! *He said He would come unto us as the latter rain and the former rain unto the earth and He did exactly that!* We now have Scriptural proof that Messiah Yeshua did come to the earth at His birth at the time of the former rain at Rosh HaShanah, and He left during the latter rain at Passover with His death, resurrection, and ascension into Heaven! The Living Branch that produces the fruit of the harvest yet to come is Messiah Yeshua! The believers in Yeshua that are raptured in the glory cloud will therefore become the first fruits of His harvest!

Now the LORD declared in the book of Deuteronomy, in the Torah that *"The Words of My mouth, My doctrine shall drop as the rain."*

Deuteronomy 32:1-4 *Give ear, O ye Heavens, and I will speak; and hear, O earth, the Words of My mouth. My doctrine shall drop as the rain, My speech shall distil as the dew, as the small rain upon the tender herb, and as the showers upon the grass; Because I will publish the Name of the LORD; ascribe ye greatness unto our God. He is the Rock, His work is perfect; for all His ways are judgment; a God of truth and without iniquity, just and right is He.*

So when KING Yeshua, *the Living Torah,* of the Davidic Dynasty was born on Rosh HaShanah at the time of the early rain, He came from Heaven *dropping His doctrine as the rain upon the earth.* He published the Name of the LORD in His Gospel of Eternal life for all mankind. Now do we have proof that Yeshua's Words were the doctrine of the LORD that fell as rain? Incredibly, the answer is yes!

Luke 4:32 *And they were astonished at His doctrine; for His Word was with power.*

Matthew 7:27-28 *And the rain descended, and the floods came, and the winds blew, and beat upon that house; and it fell; and great was the fall of it. And it came to pass, when Yeshua had ended these sayings the people were astonished at His doctrine; For He taught them as one having Authority, and not as the Scribes.*

Mark 1:27 *And they were all amazed insomuch that they questioned among themselves, saying, What thing is this? What new doctrine is this? For with Authority commandeth He even the unclean spirits, and they do obey Him.*

When Yeshua told the Jews that the rain descended, *He is referring to Himself as the early and the latter rain, and in this verse,* we see that Messiah Yeshua is the Royal Sceptre who has all *power and authority* of the KING OF KINGS. The Scriptures declare Messiah Yeshua did come to us on Rosh HaShanah as the early rain and left at Passover as the latter rain, dropping His Words and doctrine as the dew upon the earth, as *the Living Torah*, and they were all astonished at His doctrine! It is absolutely astonishing. As He spoke His doctrine, He healed and astonished all who heard it, and He raised the dead to life again, revealing His true identity as the LORD God of Israel!

We can only conclude that the LORD came to us in the flesh as the second perfect Adam, as the Messiah on Rosh HaShanah because He is *"THE KING OF KINGS AND LORD*

OF LORDS." The LORD God truly came to us in the flesh on the birthday of mankind. The Feast of Trumpets is Yeshua's true birthday, and you can imagine Royal heralding trumpets with a blazing fanfare! The Living Water of the Great Sea came to cleanse us from all our sins and to wash our garments pure, clean, and white, as a Bride prepared for her husband.

When the rains fall abundantly from Heaven, life thrives and every beautiful thing grows vigorously. The LORD Messiah is our refreshing, as the rain refreshes the earth. When the LORD returns from Heaven, the earth will once again be refreshed by His glorious Divine Presence. One week after Tishrei 1 in 2013 seventeen inches of heavy rain fell here!

Rare Rain Flood Waters of September 12th 2013 on my Street one week after Rosh HaShanah!
Photo ©2013 Kimberly K Ballard All Rights Reserved

Now I can say, let us honour the true birth of Yeshua our Saviour on Rosh HaShanah on Tishrei 1! Let us lift up our voices in unison with a shout and blow a shofar on the Feast of Trumpets, to proclaim that the LORD *Yeshua* is KING over us forever and let the Heavenly Hosts praise Him and glorify His Holy Name! Hallelujah! HE IS THE KING!

GIFTS FOR A JEWISH KING THE JUBILEE YEAR OF MESSIAH

Shofar on Tallit, Honor tassels & Snow
Photos ©2013 Kimberly K Ballard All Rights Reserved

It was *Tishrei 1* on the Biblical calendar when *"the wise men"* presented their gifts to Yeshua the KING and they fell down and worshipped Him because He is the LORD. The LORD has set His Jewish KING on Mount Zion which is KING Yeshua!

Matthew 2:11 *And when they were come into the house, they saw the young child with Mary His mother, and fell down, and worshipped Him; and when they had opened their treasures, they presented unto Him gifts; gold, and frankincense, and myrrh.*

The LORD'S resurrection in three days, as the Living Branch from the Tree of Life, is again symbolized in the three gifts that were given to the Jewish KING at His birth. The gold represents the KING'S Crown, but it also represents the gold Menorah that is made out of one solid piece of pure gold, bearing Almond Blossoms and Almonds, with the central Rod in the middle, symbolizing Messiah the Branch. The gold Crown is another Crown of His Royal Regalia for His Coronation Ceremony. Gold is also symbolic of the pureness of the KING OF KINGS, who is the pure, shining, and Eternal light of Heaven. When gold is very pure, it becomes almost translucent, and this is what we see in the halo of those who have the light of the LORD abiding in them. The streets of gold in the Heavenly Kingdom of God also have this appearance. This precious metal that was given to the Royal KING contains many healing properties. ***(Source: Gold, Myrrh & Frankincense ©2011 en.wikipedia.org/wiki/Myrrh, From Wikipedia, the free encyclopedia).*** Yeshua demonstrated the healing power of the LORD, as the Rod of God. The Frankincense and Myrrh are two of the spices that are used upon the Altar of Incense inside the Holy Temple of the LORD. The spice mixture containing Myrrh, Frankincense, and the other spices that I spoke about before are called the *"Ketoret."* The Myrrh was used at the crucifixion of Yeshua and as one of the spices for His burial in the linen Shroud. As I mentioned before, the KING Messiah's garments are said to smell of Frankincense and cinnamon. Myrrh is often used as an antiseptic to treat skin ailments and to treat illnesses and infections. I have shared how the Messiah bore the bitter and the sweet at the place of Golgotha, on Mount Moriah, so the interesting connection to Myrrh and the Messiah is profound. The word *"Myrrh"* actually derives from the Aramaic word *"murr,"* meaning *"bitter."* So the Messiah was offered Myrrh on the cross as part of the *bitterness* of bearing the curse in the flesh for us. Myrrh is also a resin and when it is harvested, the tree is said to be *"Wounded to bleed out the resin."* As the Messiah, the Tree of Life was wounded, drops of blood came out and hardened like resin, which took away the sins of our flesh and our bitterness. Frankincense

Myrrh Photo ©2013 Kimberly K Ballard All Rights Reserved

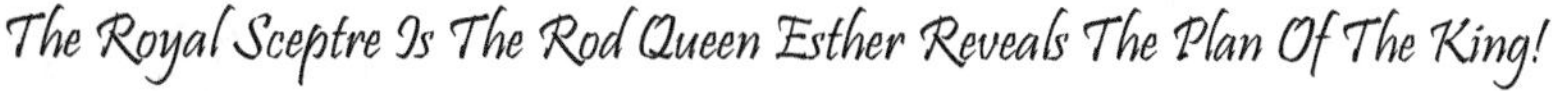

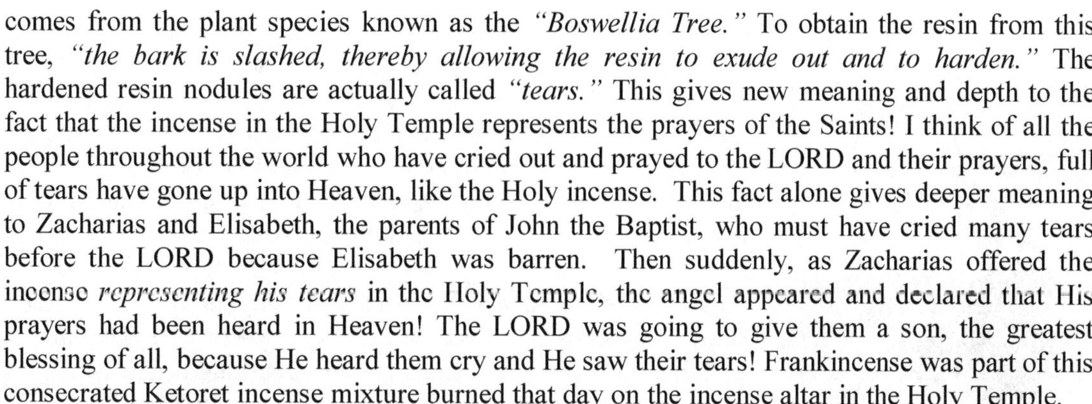

comes from the plant species known as the *"Boswellia Tree."* To obtain the resin from this tree, *"the bark is slashed, thereby allowing the resin to exude out and to harden."* The hardened resin nodules are actually called *"tears."* This gives new meaning and depth to the fact that the incense in the Holy Temple represents the prayers of the Saints! I think of all the people throughout the world who have cried out and prayed to the LORD and their prayers, full of tears have gone up into Heaven, like the Holy incense. This fact alone gives deeper meaning to Zacharias and Elisabeth, the parents of John the Baptist, who must have cried many tears before the LORD because Elisabeth was barren. Then suddenly, as Zacharias offered the incense *representing his tears* in the Holy Temple, the angel appeared and declared that His prayers had been heard in Heaven! The LORD was going to give them a son, the greatest blessing of all, because He heard them cry and He saw their tears! Frankincense was part of this consecrated Ketoret incense mixture burned that day on the incense altar in the Holy Temple.

The Myrrh and the Frankincense that were given to Yeshua at His birth, truly *symbolized the tears that the KING would cry and the wounds that He would suffer* because of His rejection. Yeshua was slashed with the Roman spear in His heart. In Yeshua's case the resin called *"tears"* represented the *bitterness* of bearing the curse of death in the flesh, so we could be reconciled to God forever, through His Eternal Covenant of the heart! The Frankincense also symbolizes the tears and the *bitterness* of the Saints throughout the ages, who have cried out to God since the being of time because of the separation from the LORD'S Divine Presence, in the Garden of Eden, and from the absence of Yeshua's Presence for nearly two thousand years. Since that time, we have cried out to Him for justice. We long to be restored to the *sweetness* of dwelling in His Divine Presence again and we miss our loved ones who have died! Messiah Yeshua made the way back to the Garden, so we could dwell in His Presence forever and this is the *sweetness* of Eternal life. *This is why His birth on Rosh HaShanah is so profound, because Rosh HaShanah is symbolic of the LORD giving us life, and the aroma of the Holy incense actually represents life.* Frankincense is sometimes mixed with oil to anoint a person as they begin living a new life in the LORD. So the incense represents our new Spiritual life in Messiah Yeshua, in *the Living Torah.* Just like *the Living Torah* heals us, the pure gold, the Myrrh, and the Frankincense also have healing properties. The LORD came to heal the broken hearted and to dry every tear from our eyes. He came healing our diseases and conquering death, to remove this bondage from us forever that was far greater than the bondage of Pharaoh in Egypt. He was a superior Exodus and Passover for the entire world!

I was astonished when the LORD showed me that the Feast of Trumpets was the key to the whole Nativity story of Yeshua! *If Yeshua had not been a born a Jewish KING, then the wise men would not have traveled from afar, bringing the special gifts with them for the KING OF KINGS on His Coronation day and they knew what time the star appeared!*

At age thirty, Messiah Yeshua stood in the Synagogue, proclaiming the Jubilee year. He told them that Isaiah 61 was fulfilled in their hearing as He read from the scroll. This event transpired after His baptism and after His 40 days in the wilderness. As He spoke this gracious proclamation to the Jews in Israel, they were all amazed at His Words!

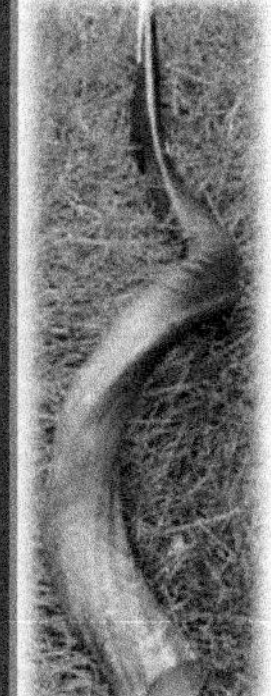

Luke 4:14-22 *And Yeshua returned in the Power of the Spirit into Galilee; and there went out a fame of Him through all the region round about. And He taught in their Synagogues, being glorified of all. And He came to Nazareth, where He had been brought up; and, as His custom was, He went into the Synagogue on the Sabbath day, and stood up for to read. And there was delivered unto Him the book of the Prophet Esaias. And when He had opened the book, He found the place where it is written, The Spirit of the LORD is upon Me, because He hath anointed Me to preach the Gospel to the poor; He hath sent Me to heal the brokenhearted, to preach deliverance to the captives, and recovering of sight to the blind, to set at liberty them that are bruised, To preach the acceptable year of the LORD. And He closed the book, and He gave it again to the minister, and sat down. And the eyes of all them that were in the Synagogue were fastened on Him. And He began to say unto them, This day is this Scripture fulfilled in your ears. And all bare Him witness, and wondered at the gracious Words which proceeded out of His mouth. And they said, Is not this Joseph's son?*

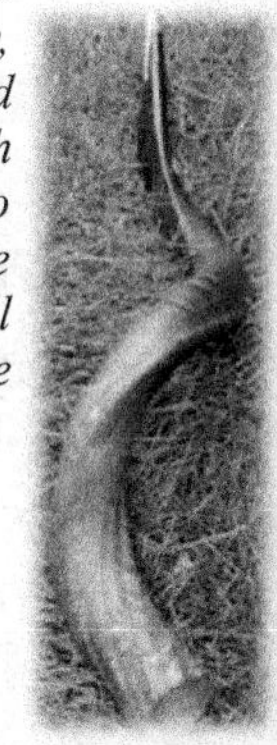

The Jubilee year was announced with the blowing of the shofar at the end of the Day of Atonement or Yom Kippur. The word *"Jubilee"* means, *"Shout for joy with the blowing of the ram's horn."* This is a victory cry that Yeshua declared as He began preaching the Good News, the Living Torah Covenant that would set us free forever. I believe this Great trumpet will be blown at His second coming on Yom Kippur to proclaim freedom and the restoration of His Land forever! It is recorded in some of the historical records *"that the thirtieth Jubilee occurred in the thirtieth year of our LORD."* ***(Source: ©2003 Larry & Marion Pierce; The Annals of the World USSHER).*** This means that this Jubilee was the starting point, marking the preaching of the Gospel, *the Eternal Living Torah Testimony* of the KING OF KINGS AND LORD OF LORDS.

Shofar
Photo ©2014 Kimberly K Ballard

Yeshua was proclaiming that He would be the one to heal the brokenhearted and set all things in their right order, to restore us forever to His Eternal Kingdom of the Davidic Dynasty. *Israel will have her Jubilee in 2017, marking 70 years since becoming a state!* The four blood moons and other heavenly signs are occurring on all the Jewish Feast days from 2014 through 2017. So the time is getting near for the Messiah's return! The declaration of the KING on this day is that He will forever take away the captivity of Israel. He will restore us and give us the First Fruit from the Almond Tree of Life. He declared this on the seventh day Sabbath of the LORD. Now we know the truth that Messiah Yeshua was born KING on The Feast of Trumpets and there was a *great Heavenly fanfare!* He came to give liberty to the captives, and to proclaim the LORD'S Jubilee! I believe something profound is about to take place because the signs in the heaven's declare that the KING is coming!

THE TASHLIKH CEREMONY AND MESSIAH YESHUA THE LORD

River & Apples & Honey
Photos ©2014 Kimberly K Ballard All Rights Reserved

I happened to be proof reading this part of the book in the week leading up to Rosh HaShanah 2010 when the LORD blessed me again, revealing Himself in another astonishing miracle for Rosh HaShanah.

The Messiah, who was raised to life on the third day, caused me to finish the initial writing of this book on the third day before Rosh HaShanah. So I immediately had to write to Jerusalem to my beautiful Israeli friend because of this outstanding revelation that the LORD just gave to me. I just emailed the following letter to her. Ironically, I also just noticed that today is the third day of September! In my letter, I wrote the Hebrew phrase, *"May you be*

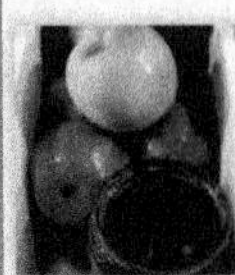

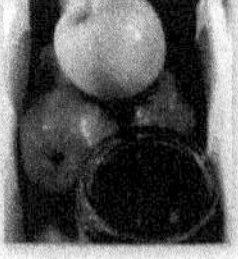

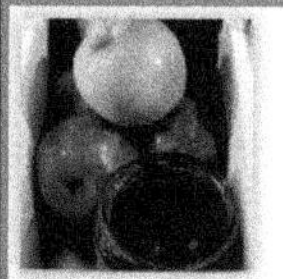

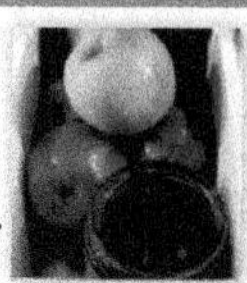

inscribed in the Book of Life for "A Sweet New Year!" This revelation is truly the final piece of evidence that the Jewish KING Messiah Yeshua was born on Rosh HaShanah.

Email to Jerusalem September 3rd 2010;

L' Shanah Tovah Tikatevu Friend!!! Blessings and greetings, beloved of the LORD! I have an incredible Rosh HaShanah message for you from the LORD. God is the Redeemer, the Saviour. THE KING came into the world as the second Adam on Rosh HaShanah and became our (use the Hebrew word for Salvation), Yeshua! I have been writing that all the customs for Rosh HaShanah speak of this KING! Let me show you what the LORD showed me just moments ago and this is a gift for you, just in time for Rosh HaShanah!

THE ROSH HASHANAH CUSTOMS INCLUDE THE FOLLOWING THINGS;

1. The Candle Lighting represents that He is the light of the world.
2. Apples dipped in Honey represents that He was raised to life as the First Fruit of Eternal salvation. He is the Branch bearing the sweet Fruit, who takes away the bitterness of death. There are sweet and bitter Almonds that are the Shaked on this Branch. He is the Living Torah, the sweetness of honey!
3. The Awakening Blast of Rosh HaShanah represents that He is awakening the dead, and the *"Hasty Awakening"* is the meaning of Shaked or Almond.

The Round Challah loaves are shaped like a Crown for the KINGSHIP of God. This also reminds us that if we follow Him and persevere, we also will receive a Crown. Rosh HaShanah is the Day to Coronate God as the KING OF KINGS and this is why Messiah, the Saviour God, came to dwell with us on this day! And most chilling of all, I have to tell you the following.

4. In the Tashlikh ceremony on Tishri 1, when Messiah Yeshua was born, the Jewish people perform the ritual of Tashlikh or the casting off of sins ceremony. On the first day of Rosh HaShanah before sunset, as you know, Jews go to a body of water, usually a river or stream of running water, and preferably one with fish in it. They symbolically cast their sins into this body of water by emptying their pockets of bread crumbs containing leaven which represents the casting off of their sins into the water, and they are washed away. This one will astound you my friend!

Now I have to remind you of these two things first. *Messiah Yeshua revealed Himself as the Living Water while sitting at Jacob's well. Later He proved this at the Pool of Bethesda when the crippled man was trying to get in the pool because the angels came down once a year and stirred up the water and whoever got in the water first was healed. The LORD showed me that this stirring up of the water made the water to become "LIVING WATER." So when Yeshua asked the man, "Do you want to get well?" The man said to Him, "Sir, I can't get into the pool in time while the water is stirred up." The Messiah simply said to Him, "Pick up your mat and walk." The man got up and walked and he was healed! The curse of sin was taken away from him, because He later saw Yeshua in the Temple and the LORD told him not to sin anymore or something worse might happen to him. The moment that I saw this, the lights went on and I suddenly realized that the man was instantly healed because "The Living Water was speaking to him!" Therefore, the man did not need to get into the pool of living water to be healed!* I had to remind you of this part of the story again because something else was just revealed to me about this truth, by the LORD. This is astonishing and it has to do with the ceremony that is performed on Rosh HaShanah! The LORD just showed me that this pertains to the Tashlikh ceremony in the following way. *At the Tashlikh ceremony, on the first day of Rosh HaShanah, on Yeshua's birthday before sunset, we take our sins to the river and cast them into the water, but I realized that the water that we go to in order to perform this ceremony is actually called "a body of LIVING WATER!" Then it hit me! The LORD God manifested Himself in a body. So Messiah Yeshua is therefore a "BODY OF LIVING WATER" that believers have cast our sins into!* We have always cast our sins upon Messiah Yeshua and have been baptized in His baptism of the Holy Spirit, in the living water that is representative

of Him as the LORD, the true Living Water! *However, we never knew or understood this link of Messiah the LORD to the Tashlikh ceremony of Rosh HaShanah!* This explains everything about Messiah Yeshua and why He came to save us from our sins, through His symbolic baptism in the living water of a river! The LORD has washed our sins away, as far as the east is from the west. Then I remembered that the human *"body"* is composed mostly of water. This means that Messiah the LORD came into *"A body of flesh, as the Living Water,"* because this was the body that was prepared for Him, so He could dwell on earth with us as the KING of the Jews. The Living Water, of course, is a sign of the creation of life and so Yeshua, who came to dwell with us on Rosh HaShanah, on the KING'S Coronation day, is symbolic of the LORD washing our sins away, into the Great Sea of the Holy Temple and giving us Eternal life. So we dip fruit in honey because this is one *sweet* day! *He bore our sins in His own body, the true "Body of Living Water" and this body came to dwell with us on Rosh HaShanah, as the second perfect Adam. The LORD KING Messiah is, therefore, the true Tashlikh ceremony of Rosh HaShanah!* After we come up out of the living water of His baptism we are given new life!

I Peter 2:24 *Who His own self bare our sins in His own body on the tree, that we, being dead to sins, should live unto righteousness; by whose stripes ye were healed. For ye were as sheep going astray; but are now returned unto the Shepherd and Bishop of your souls.*

Isaiah 53:6 *All we like sheep have gone astray; we have turned everyone to his own way; and the LORD hath laid on Him the iniquity of us all.*

Yeshua revealed that He is the unleavened Bread from Heaven when He miraculously walked upon the surface of the water because He was full of the Holy Spirit. The Holy Spirit moved on the surface of the waters in Genesis and turned the water into *"Living Waters." So when we cast our bread crumbs into the Living Water of the LORD, the Messiah, He washes our sins away, just like in the Tashlikh ceremony and, of course, He is our Bread upon the water that we shall find after many days because He has given us the true Bread from Heaven in place of the leavened bread of sin!*

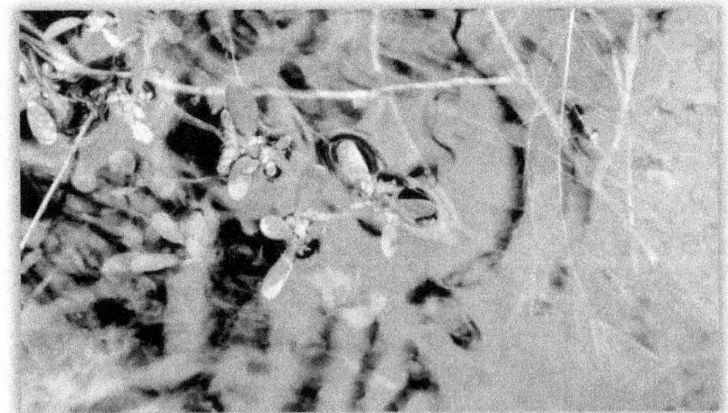

Body of living water Photo ©2013 Kimberly K Ballard All Rights Reserved

Ecclesiastes 11:1 *Cast thy bread upon the waters; for thou shalt find it after many days.*

Now the Rabbis prefer a body of water with fish in it for performing the Tashlikh ceremony! So I instantly knew that this is what Yeshua was revealing in the catching of fish as *"fishers of men,"* like it says about the LORD in Habakkuk 1:14, *"And makest men as the fishes of the sea."* The fish are found swimming in the Living Water! When Yeshua had the disciples cast their nets into the water and a multitude of fish came up on the right side of the boat, this represented the people that *"Messiah, the Living Water, would catch!" It all has to do with the Jewish KING of Judah, who was born on Rosh HaShanah, when this ceremony is performed in Israel!* Yeshua said the following Words!

John 7:38 *He that believeth on Me, as the Scriptures hath said, out of his belly shall flow rivers of LIVING WATER.*

I Corinthians 6:11 *And such were some of you; but ye are washed, but ye are sanctified, but ye are justified in the Name of the LORD Yeshua, and by the Spirit of our God.*

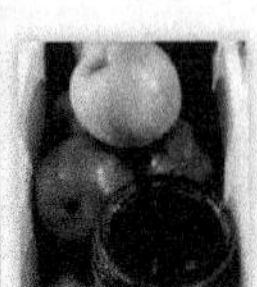

Hebrews 10:22 *Let us draw near with a true heart in full assurance of faith, having our hearts sprinkled from an evil conscience, and our bodies washed with pure water.*

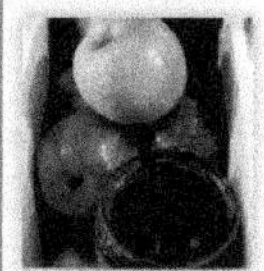

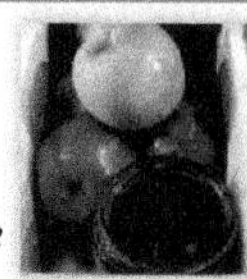

Revelation 1:5 *And from Yeshua Messiah who is the faithful witness, and the first begotten of the dead, and the Prince of the Kings of the earth, Unto Him that loved us, and washed us from our sins in His own blood.*

The fish represent men, so we are the LORD'S catch, in the true LIVING WATER. This is exactly what Yeshua was revealing in the Gospels of Luke and John.

Luke 5:5-10 *And Simon answering said unto Him, Master, we have toiled all the night, and have taken nothing; nevertheless at Thy Word I will let down the net. And when they had this done, they inclosed a great multitude of fishes; and their net brake. And they beckoned unto their partners, which were in the other ship, that they should come and help them. And they came, and filled both the ships, so that they began to sink. When Simon Peter saw it, he fell down at Yeshua's knees, saying, Depart from me; for I am a sinful man, O LORD. For he was astonished, and all that were with him, at the draught of the fishes which they had taken; And so was also James, and John, the sons of Zebedee, which were partners with Simon. And Yeshua said unto Simon, Fear not; from henceforth thou shalt catch men.*

In John 21, it was the third time after His resurrection that Yeshua appeared to the disciples. This is when He told them to cast their net on the right side of the boat. When they did this, they filled the net with so many fish and that is when they realized that it was the LORD! *These fish were swimming in the LIVING WATER* and Messiah revealed that His catch would come on the third day, when He returns to gather them. One more incredible fact is that on the first day of Rosh HaShanah, the Torah portion that is read, is about the birth of Isaac. The second day of Rosh HaShanah, the Torah portion that is read, is about the binding of Isaac. In Genesis 22:8 Abraham said, *"My son, God will provide Himself a Lamb for a burnt offering; so they both went together."* The LORD said that He would provide, *"Himself a Lamb!" Messiah the LORD is the Lamb, the sheepskin of the Living Torah, who washed away our sins in His body of Living Water.* I pray this blesses your heart more than anything.

Happy Rosh HaShanah! The KING is coming at the Last Trump, perhaps this Rosh HaShanah! *"Watch! Shaked! The Almond Tree of Life has come!"*
THE END OF MY LETTER TO JERUSALEM, for Rosh HaShanah 2010.

Body of Living Water, The Flooded River of the Tashlikh ceremony - Flood of September 12th Photo ©2013 Kimberly K Ballard All Rights Reserved

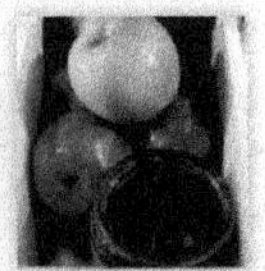
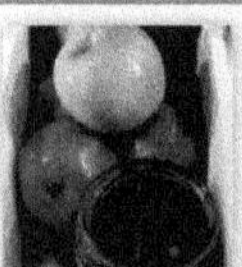

The Jewish disciple Simon Peter wrote later that Yeshua the LORD, the mighty hand of God, is the one on whom we are to *cast* our sins and our cares. The word *"casting"* reveals more about the Messiah in the Tashlikh ceremony in I Peter.

I Peter 5:6-7 *Humble yourselves therefore under the mighty hand of God, that He may exalt you in due time; Casting all your care upon Him; for He careth for you.*

A fisherman *casts* a fishing line out over the water by means of *his rod and reel* to catch fish. So in this case, *The Rod of God was catching us!* By definition a *"reel" will pull and draw in by winding a line on a reel. The Rod of God draws us to Himself!*

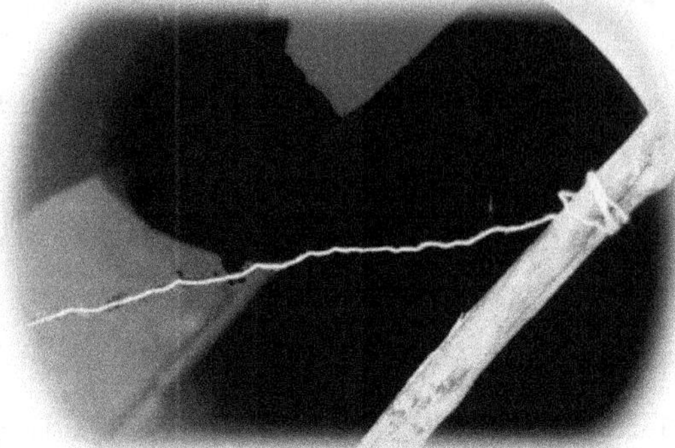

Fishing Photo ©2014 Kimberly K Ballard

Jeremiah 16:14-16 *Therefore, behold, the days come, saith the LORD, that it shall no more be said, The LORD liveth, that brought up the children of Israel out of the land of Egypt; But, The LORD liveth, that brought up the children of Israel from the land of the north, and from all the lands whither He had driven them; and I will bring them again into their land that I gave unto their fathers. Behold, I will send for many fishers, saith the LORD, and they shall fish them; and after will I send for many hunters, and they shall hunt them from every mountain, and from every hill, and out of the holes of the rocks.*

John 6:44 *No man can come to me, except the Father which hath sent Me draw him; and I will raise him up at the last day.*

Fishing Photo ©2014 Kimberly K Ballard

The fishes of a great multitude from His catch will live in His Living Water forever!

There is another definition of the word *"manger"* besides the feeding trough which is *"a space across the deck of a ship within the hawse holes where the cables go separated from the after part of the deck to prevent the water which enters the hawse holes from running over the deck."* This definition reminds me of another verse in Isaiah about the LORD. *He will not allow the waters to overflow us.*

Isaiah 43:2 *When thou passest through the waters, I will be with thee; and through the rivers, they shall not overflow thee; when thou walkest through the fire, thou shalt not be burned; neither shall the flame kindle upon thee.*

Messiah Yeshua is the Eternal Tashlikh ceremony of Rosh HaShanah. Tishri 1 is the KING'S birthday and the birthday of mankind to Eternal life, through the second perfect Adam. So the Living Water came to wash away our sins, and this is why John came baptizing in *living water* to make the Messiah known to Israel!

The Garden Tomb with Great Rolling Stone
Photo ©2011 Simon Brown England
All Rights Reserved

YHVH YIREH
YHVH RA'AH

The Garden Tomb with Great Rolling Stone
Photo ©2011 Simon Brown England
All Rights Reserved

The reading about Isaac on Rosh HaShanah led to another discovery about Messiah the LORD. There is something special about Holy Mount Moriah where the Great Stone was rolled away from Yeshua's sepulchre, and I could not believe how incredible it was when the Holy Spirit showed this to me on top of everything else! *This is the place where the Testimony of Yeshua was once displayed to be seen in the Holy Mountain of God.* There was an astonishing addition to this that came to me, after I had written my article about the Jewish Priestly Angel at the Garden tomb and I added it here because I thought that it was so profound!

If you recall, the LORD showed me the signet shaped object that I believe is inscribed in the Royal Stone of Kings with the letters *"Alpha and Omega"* in the rock at the Garden tomb, with the Name *"Yeshua."* Then I told you that I believe that one tiny niche held the Mezuzah because Yeshua is the door of Heaven. This is the gate of Heaven and this tiny niche is to the right side of the niches that held the two articles of His Living Testimony, as the Branch that came to life from the Almond Tree of Life. The LORD showed me that the linen burial Shroud of Yeshua and His Sudarium were placed in earthen jars and displayed as the LORD'S Testimony in the cut out niches of the Royal rock hewn tomb, but this was not just any Mountain! *The Testimony of Messiah, the Living Almond Branch, was placed in the Mountain where the LORD sent Abraham to offer up his son Isaac.* Centuries before Yeshua's Testimony was fulfilled at this same Holy Mountain, this is where Abraham went up on the third day to offer Isaac. Then Abraham declared and spoke some mighty prophetic words.

What I was shown next by the LORD both excited me and astonished me. After Isaac was spared by the LORD, Abraham actually named the place of Mount Moriah, *"YHVH Yireh."* The Hebrew word origin is *"YHVH and Ra'ah." I had declared already in my article about the Jewish Priestly Angel that the LORD had revealed to me that His Testimony was kept in the niches in the Royal Kingly Stone of this Holy Mountain.* I only saw this, though, when the LORD showed me the Jewish Priestly Angel who was pointing to it with his index finger. This is, of course, when the LORD reminded me that Angels are messengers that declare a Divine truth about the LORD. So I knew immediately that the LORD was revealing something incredible about this Jewish Priestly Angel. The messenger was proclaiming and pointing with his finger like a Torah pointer to the place in the Garden of the Holy Mountain of the LORD where the elements of Yeshua's Living Testimony had been kept on display in the Royal Stone of Kings. I knew that the Angel was pointing to *the Divine Testimony of the Living Torah!* So, what Abraham called this place is profoundly stunning and significant. This is perhaps the greatest evidence that everything the LORD revealed to me is true. I believe that this was shown to me to testify about it in the last days, to turn the hearts of the world to the LORD.

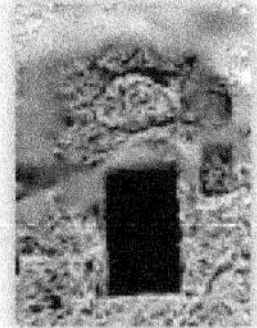

Genesis 22:14 *And Abraham called the name of that place YHVH Yireh; as it is said to this day, In the Mount of the LORD it shall be seen.*

Within Abraham's words He declared, *"In the Mount of the LORD it shall be seen!"* I suddenly understood that Abraham was revealing that the Testimony of the resurrected Messiah, the true Lamb of God, would be seen in this Holy Mount in the future! God did not spare His own Son, but He lifted Himself up as the Rod of God and it was here that God provided Himself the Lamb, the pure Torah sheepskin of flesh! I had just been writing about how the Testimony of the Messiah was seen in Holy Mount Moriah and that it was out of this Royal Foundation rock that Adam was hewn. It was this same Royal rock that Yeshua's tomb was hewn and He is, of course, the second Adam and *the Rock* quarried out of God's Holy Mountain. When we look at the definitions within the Hebrew word *"Ra' ah,"* it reveals Messiah Yeshua and the Garden Tomb with the Jewish Angel pointing like a Torah pointer to the Testimony of the LORD KING *that was once displayed and exhibited here.* This is the place in Mount Moriah where we *"ponder and discern the resurrection of the LORD."* The Hebrew word *"Ra'ah"* means many things, but I have written a few of them here.

Ra'ah*;* To see, to look at, learn about, inspect, perceive, consider, give attention to, discern. To be seen, to be visible. To cause to look intently at, to behold, cause to gaze at, to cause to be exhibited, to be shown. Become visible, become aware, think, view, and make me see.

This is exactly what we have been doing in God's Holy Mountain in the place of Messiah's resurrection! When I said that I believe that the Messiah left the elements of His Living Testimony at the Garden tomb and we look intently at the tomb and consider what happened here, this definition was just icing on the cake! We gaze at the Holy Mountain of God and consider His resurrection to life in the very Mount that His Divine Testimony was once *"exhibited and shown"* and is still viewed today by many visitors in the place where God provided Himself *"The Lamb!"* The Angel is still sending us a message from the LORD! It was written in the Royal Stone of Kings, where people from all over the world come to *"inspect, perceive, look intently at and behold this place!"* Remember, that the Angel is trying to get our attention to discern this message from the LORD in the place where He said that His Name would be written forever and this is where the signet shaped object is engraved with the letters, *"Alpha and Omega!" The Alpha and Omega letters are also written inside* the Royal Stone of the Garden tomb in the hewn rock with Yeshua's Name! Yeshua's resurrection in the Garden of God causes us *"to behold, think, visibly discern, and inspect it, so we can perceive and consider" the marvelous works of the LORD that He accomplished here in His Royal Holy Mount Moriah, as the Ark of the Living Testimony of Messiah the LORD! The Angel is still pointing to the Living Torah after almost two thousand years and Yeshua is the way back to the Garden of the LORD, in Jerusalem!* It is absolutely stunning! The LORD is called my *"Rock"* in Psalm 18:2. This refers to the LORD as *"Adonai Sal'i"* which means *"a crag in a cliff or a hiding place."* The Royal rock hewn sepulchre of Yeshua is indeed *a crag in a cliff,* in the LORD'S Holy Mount Moriah. This tomb was hidden for 1900 years and it was buried under mounds of dirt since the time of the last Jewish revolt against the Romans and because it was covered up with so much dirt (I believe by Roman Emperor Hadrian) no one saw it again until the late 19th century when it was unearthed for the first time.

The LORD, the *"body of Living Water"* was placed in this *crag in the cliff* of Holy Mount Moriah, in the tomb that became a hiding place, and one day we would gaze and behold His glory here where the great stone was rolled from the mouth of the well of salvation! Abraham was called by the LORD to this place. Adam was hewn from this rock. The second perfect Adam, the LORD Messiah, was placed in *"Adonai Sal'i,"* the *crag in a cliff* in the Mount called *"YHVH Ra'ah."* So Abraham's prophetic words have miraculously come true that said, *"In the Mount of the LORD it shall be seen!"* The LORD, *the Rock* brings forth Living Water, from the place we were hewn. The Prophet Jeremiah was cast into the pit here.

Isaiah 51:1 *Hearken to Me, ye that follow after righteousness, ye that seek the LORD; look unto the rock whence ye are hewn, and to the hole of the pit whence ye are digged. Look unto Abraham your father, and unto Sarah that bare you; for I called him alone, and blessed him, and increased him.*

Jeremiah 38:6-9 *Then took they Jeremiah, and cast him into the pit of Malchiah the son of Ham-melech, that was in the court of the prison; and they let down Jeremiah with cords, And in the pit there was no water, but mire; so Jeremiah sunk in the mire. Now when E-bed-melech the Ethiopian, one of the eunuchs which was in the king's house, heard that they had put Jeremiah in the pit; the king then sitting in the gate of Benjamin; E-bed-melech went forth out of the king's house, and spake to the king, saying, My lord the king, these men have done evil in all that they have done to Jeremiah the Prophet, whom they have cast into the pit; and he is like to die in the place where he is because of the famine, for there is no more bread in the city.*

What I find so interesting about Jeremiah being cast into this pit, which is said to be below the rock at Golgotha, is the fact that when Jeremiah was cast into this pit, there was no water there and E-bed-melech feared that Jeremiah would die in this place because there was no more bread in the city. Remember also that this place was the cursed Garden of Eden! So what happened when Yeshua came to life in the rock of this same place? *Messiah Yeshua was the Living Water and the Bread from Heaven that was brought forth out of the Rock that kept us from Eternally dying because He reversed the curse!* Remember in John chapter 2, when Yeshua said to the Jewish leaders in the Temple, *"Tear down this Temple and in three days I will build it again?"* The Scripture goes on to say, *"But the Temple Yeshua was referring to was the Temple of His body."* So the Temple of His body is *the body of Living Water and the Bread of the Living Torah.* Yeshua said that if we eat this Bread that we would never die. So the following statement regarding Adam, who was created from the dust of this place, is so profound. *"An original idea of the Rabbis was that, "Adam was created from the dust of the place where the Sanctuary was to rise for the atonement of all human sin, so that sin should never be a permanent or inherent part of man's nature."* **(Source: ©2002 Jewish Encyclopedia.com By: J. Frederic McCurdy Kaufmann Kohler Richard Gottheil).** Holy Mount Moriah is the place of the Garden of Eden and the place of the dust where Adam was created. *It was therefore in this place that the Eternal Heavenly Temple, the LORD Messiah would rise for the atonement of all human sin! The LORD'S body is the true Heavenly Temple that will descend to dwell in this place forever.* Tradition says that Adam was buried in Holy Mount Moriah at the place of Golgotha. If this is correct, then the second Adam, *the Messiah, did rise from this place in the Garden of the LORD for the atonement of all human sin, so that sin would never be a permanent part of man's nature,* just as it is written! The LORD allowed His Testimony to be shown and displayed in Holy Mount Moriah. It is here that we will always come to view this Living Testimony. It is a permanent memorial to the KING of glory! *This is the same place where Mary Magdalene took hold of the First Fruit of the Living Almond Branch from the Almond Tree of Life, in the Garden of God.*

Now I have to tell you that I remembered the following Scripture, after writing about the Shroud of Yeshua and the Sudarium having been displayed in the niches at the Garden tomb in earthen jars in the Mount called *"YHVH Ra'ah."* In my article, I said that perhaps *the clay jar,* containing the burial Shroud, was made of Jerusalem soil and therefore it contained the travertine aragonite that was discovered on it. Now there is a very curious Scripture that follows and I believe that it may be the key to proving that what the LORD showed me about His Testimony being displayed in the clay earthen jars or vessels was absolutely the truth. Notice in the following Scripture that they are first talking about *"the Gospel being hid to those who are lost."* Then it talks about *"Messiah who is the image of God and that this was the light that shined out of the darkness to give the light of the knowledge of the glory of God in the face of Messiah Yeshua." The light that came out of the darkness of the Garden tomb, as evening was becoming morning on the first day and as evening was becoming morning the third day after Passover, as the Almond Fruit Tree of Life with the seed inside itself, was the glory of the LORD'S resurrection to life and this is the Gospel that is hid to those who are perishing!* Then

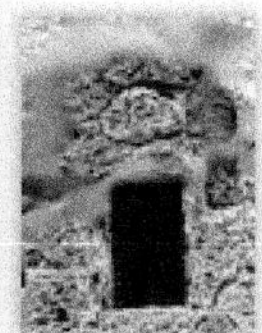

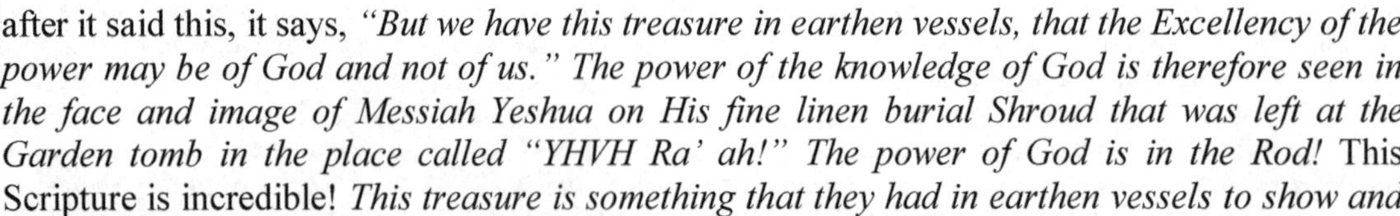

after it said this, it says, *"But we have this treasure in earthen vessels, that the Excellency of the power may be of God and not of us." The power of the knowledge of God is therefore seen in the face and image of Messiah Yeshua on His fine linen burial Shroud that was left at the Garden tomb in the place called "YHVH Ra' ah!" The power of God is in the Rod!* This Scripture is incredible! *This treasure is something that they had in earthen vessels to show and display the Excellency of the power of God in the resurrection, which took away the darkness of death in the sepulchre and forever gave us the glorious light of Eternal life in God!*

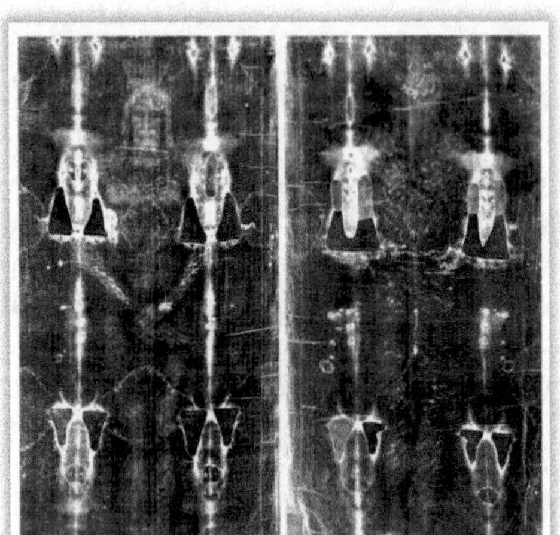

Official Shroud Pair
Photograph ©1978 Barrie M. Schwortz Collection, STERA Inc., All Rights Reserved

II Corinthians 4:3-7 *But if our Gospel be hid, it is hid to them that are lost; In whom the god of this world hath blinded the minds of them which believe not, lest the light of the glorious Gospel of Messiah, who is the image of God, should shine unto them. For we preach not ourselves, but Messiah Yeshua the LORD; and ourselves your servants for Yeshua's sake. For God, who commanded the light to shine out of the darkness, hath shined in our hearts, to give the light of the knowledge of the glory of God in the face of Yeshua Messiah. But we have this treasure in earthen vessels, that the Excellency of the power may be of God, and not of us.*

The Shroud reveals the glory of God in the face of Messiah Yeshua. This Scripture has previously been interpreted as Paul talking about his own body being an earthen vessel containing the Gospel. However, I believe this is incorrect because if you carefully study the words Paul said, *"That the power may be of God and not of us." The power of God is in His Rod!* Then before that statement, Paul was speaking of *"The image and face of God!"* Paul is therefore not speaking of himself as an earthen vessel, as if some glory should come from him. *Instead, I believe that the incredible truth is revealed before our eyes, that God has given us the knowledge of His power in the image of His own face that was left on His fine linen burial Shroud. We were made in His image out of this Foundation Rock in His quarry. So the LORD became the Rock who was quarried out of His Holy Mountain and He left His reverse image behind, revealing His glory. Yeshua's resurrection from the darkness of the tomb into the glorious light of Eternal Life, as the Living Branch from the Almond Tree of Life, obviously bears witness of the knowledge of the glory of God in the face of Messiah Yeshua!* In this way, the *Excellency* of God's power is seen and is testified by those who behold it in the place where Abraham named the Mountain, *"YHVH Ra'ah, In the Mount of the LORD it shall be seen!"* We can see His Divine Testimony to this day as it is written in the Royal Stone of Kings in this very place. One final thing that I have to say about this amazing discovery through Divine Revelation is how the Hebrew word *"Ra'ah"* actually pertains to the investigations that are carried out on the two pieces of linen bearing Yeshua's Testimony. When we look at that image of Yeshua on the Shroud of Turin, do we do any of the following things? The answer is definitely yes! We gaze at the image and we consider it, while looking at it intently and we behold the mighty power of the LORD God! Read the definition of the word *Ra'ah* again, now, to see how it pertains to Yeshua's image that was left behind on His fine linen burial Shroud in Holy Mount Moriah! The Shroud has been *exhibited* for centuries making us think!

Ra'ah; To see, look at, learn about, inspect, perceive, consider, give attention to, discern. To be seen, to be visible. To cause to look intently at, to behold, cause to gaze at, to cause to be exhibited, to be shown. Become visible, become aware, think, view, and make me see.

I am presenting something else that I believe is very profound. Adam, who was created by God in the image of God from the dust of the earth from the Rock on Holy Mount Moriah in Jerusalem, *had no navel* because he was not born of a woman or from the seed of a man. *Therefore Adam had no umbilical cord.* The Scriptures tell us plainly that Messiah Yeshua came as the second Adam in the flesh as the *"seed"* which is the *"Word of life."* He was truly *the Living Torah of life* walking among us. The LORD manifested Himself in the flesh as the Holy Spirit *overshadowed Mary.* The Holy Spirit is the breath of life and Yeshua was given a body of flesh and given life in this earthly body that was prepared for Him through the Holy Spirit. *So in conclusion, if the Shroud of Turin image does not depict Yeshua as having a navel, this could be very significant.* It would show that the Messiah of Israel came as the second perfect man in the flesh in order to reconcile us to Himself by taking away our sins in the flesh through the stripes in His flesh as *the perfect Living Torah Lambskin.* After this occurred to me, I analyzed several photographs of the image of Yeshua on the Shroud of Turin. I studied this image up close for a little while to see if I could see *a navel,* but it did not appear to be in the image as far as I could tell. The truly remarkable aspect of this is the fact that Jerusalem and Holy Mount Moriah, which is the original place of the Garden of Eden, where Yeshua came to life as the second perfect Adam is called, *"The Navel of the World."* It is from this exact point that Heaven meets earth. *The Divine knowledge of the glory of the LORD in Heaven comes down through the Navel of the World in Jerusalem and it is here that all Nations will come to this one central location to return to the one true Living God!* The LORD who has no beginning and no end is our nourishing umbilical cord. I believe that Yeshua had *no navel* because He was the second perfect Adam *made by the power of the Rod of God in the image of God* and the Messiah's image on the Shroud truly appears to have no navel. What I have been longing to explain for some time now pertains to the object that was placed in the middle niche under the signet of the KING, bearing the *Alpha and Omega* at the Garden tomb. The Shroud was in the large niche and the Sudarium, I believe, was placed in an earthen vessel in the other niche under the signet, with the *Alpha and Omega. Now I am going to reveal what the LORD showed me about the Sudarium and its astonishing significance as part of the sign of the Eternal Covenant of the KING OF KINGS that was left in the Garden tomb for Israel.* Abraham was right! In the Mount of the LORD it has been seen and we bear witness of the glory of the LORD KING Messiah in His Garden and we have seen His face!

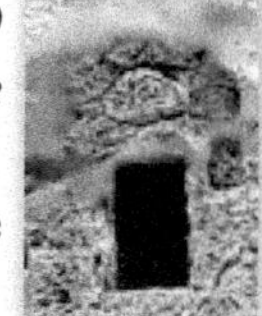

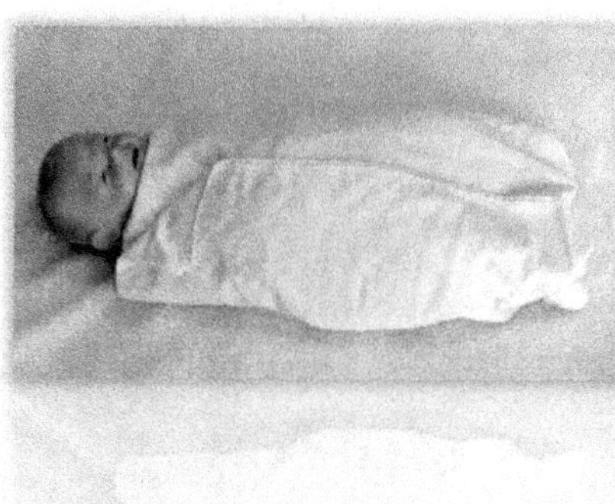

THE SIGN OF THE SWADDLING CLOTH

Baby doll wrapped in Swaddling & Irvin Linen From the 19th century Photos ©2013 & 2014 Kimberly K Ballard All Rights Reserved

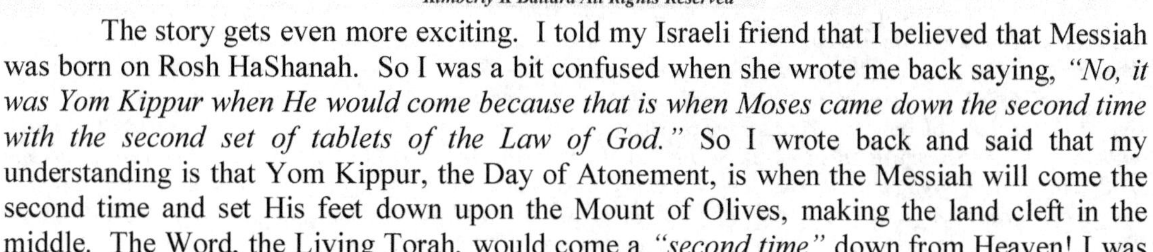

The story gets even more exciting. I told my Israeli friend that I believed that Messiah was born on Rosh HaShanah. So I was a bit confused when she wrote me back saying, *"No, it was Yom Kippur when He would come because that is when Moses came down the second time with the second set of tablets of the Law of God."* So I wrote back and said that my understanding is that Yom Kippur, the Day of Atonement, is when the Messiah will come the second time and set His feet down upon the Mount of Olives, making the land cleft in the middle. The Word, the Living Torah, would come a *"second time"* down from Heaven! I was

trying to figure out her email, because the only thing that she sent in this email was a tiny photograph that was about 1 inch by 1 inch in size, showing some Torah scrolls. I thought to myself, *"What is this little tiny picture that she sent to me?"* The caption read, *"Swaddling Torah scrolls."* The picture was so tiny that I could barely see it, so I had to enlarge it. When I saw the picture up close, I was quite puzzled. Why did she send this picture to me? Then all of a sudden it hit me like a lightning bolt and I wrote back and said, *"Are you telling me that they wrap the swaddling cloth of a Jewish baby boy around Torah scrolls?"* It was astonishingly profound, as I realized what this meant! There was no answer back from her, but I remained stunned in my heart.

At that moment, I realized that I must go back and read the story of the birth of Messiah Yeshua again, while taking in every detail very carefully. I knew that each detail was so important to the story. I remembered the words and the sign from the Angel of the LORD, who appeared to the shepherd's who were abiding in the fields, regarding the birth of Messiah Yeshua. It involved *"a swaddling cloth"* that was wrapped around Messiah Yeshua! The Angel of the LORD had said that this swaddling cloth that was wrapped around the baby Messiah was given as *a sign* to the shepherds who were abiding in the fields! I always just assumed that this statement only meant that you will find this babe wrapped in swaddling clothes, the end of the story, right? Wrong! No, this statement never made much sense to me at all until my friend from Israel showed me the swaddling cloth that was binding the Torah scrolls. What was revealed in this tiny picture was just so incredible! So, I want to establish the full picture of Yeshua's birth from this perspective and show how this swaddling cloth of Messiah Yeshua follows the pattern for a Jewish baby boy at His birth. It is used for the circumcision on the eighth day. It is brought to the Temple in Jerusalem for the dedication when the child is named, and then again at Bar Mitzvah age, it is brought back to the Holy Temple. It is also used later in the life of this child as part of the wedding Chuppah of the Bridegroom when He marries His Bride. Torah Binder examples that you can view can be found on the following websites. ***(Sources: Torah Binders (©2011 en.wikipedia.org/wiki/Wimpel) AND (©2011 brooklynmuseum.org/opencollection/objects/5114/Torah_Binder) AND (©2011 jewishwimpel.com/about_the_wimpel.html).***

So now I want to carefully read again the account of the Messiah's birth in Bethlehem, with this thought in mind, as it was recorded by Luke and Matthew.

Luke 2:1-14 *And it came to pass in those days, that there went out a decree from Caesar Augustus, that all the world should be taxed. And this taxing was first made when Cyrenius was governor of Syria. And all went to be taxed, every one into his own city. And Joseph also went up from Galilee, out of the city of Nazareth, into Judaea, unto the city of David, which is called Bethlehem; because he was of the house and lineage of David; To be taxed with Mary his espoused wife, being great with child. And so it was, that, while they were there, the days were accomplished that she should be delivered. And she brought forth her firstborn son, and wrapped Him in swaddling clothes and laid Him in a manger; because there was no room for them in the Inn. And there were in the same country shepherds abiding in the field, keeping watch over their flock by night. And, lo, the angel of the LORD came upon them, and the glory of the LORD shone round about them; and they were sore afraid. And the angel said unto them, Fear not; for, behold, I bring you good tidings of great joy, which shall be to all people. For unto you is born this day in the city of David a Saviour, which is Messiah the LORD. And this shall be a sign unto you; Ye shall find the babe wrapped in swaddling clothes, lying in a manger. And suddenly there was with the angel a multitude of the heavenly host praising God, and saying, Glory to God in the Highest, and on earth peace, good will toward men.*

Matthew 1:18-25 *Now the birth of Yeshua Messiah was on this wise; When as His mother Mary was espoused to Joseph, before they came together, she was found with child of the Holy Spirit. Then Joseph her husband, being a just man, and not willing to make her a public example, was minded to put her away privily. But while he thought on these things, behold, the angel of the Lord appeared unto him in a dream, saying, Joseph, thou son of David, fear not to take unto thee Mary thy wife; for that which is conceived in her is of the Holy Spirit. And she shall bring forth a son, and thou shalt call his name Yeshua; for He shall save His people from their sins. Now all this was done, that it might be fulfilled which was spoken of the LORD by the Prophet, saying, Behold, a virgin shall be with child, and shall bring forth a Son, and they shall call His name Emmanuel, which being interpreted is, God with us. Then Joseph being raised from sleep did as the angel of the LORD had bidden him, and took unto him his wife; And knew her not till she had brought forth her firstborn son; and he called His Name Yeshua.*

The Angel of the LORD told the shepherds that they would find the babe wrapped in *"swaddling clothes"* lying in a manger and this was to be *"a sign"* to them. So what exactly is *a sign? A sign is a Divine message from God.* As I said before, this struck me like a lightning bolt when my Jerusalem friend showed me the tiny Torah scrolls wrapped in the swaddling clothes of a first born Jewish baby boy. John, the Jewish disciple, as we know, wrote that Messiah Yeshua is *"The Word of God,"* and he said, *"The Word became flesh and dwelt among us, full of grace and truth."* I was simply astounded. *So the fact is that the swaddling cloth was literally used to bind the Word of God and to bind the Torah scroll! Since Messiah Yeshua is the Living Torah, He was wrapped in swaddling clothes, His own Torah binder and was found lying in a manger. This was the sign!* The Living Bread from Heaven and the Living Water was resting in the manger in Bethlehem the *"House of Bread," and* Ephratah *"Fruitful."*

Now Yeshua was *the first born son* of Mary and His swaddling cloth would not only have been used by Mary at His birth, but it was used later as a significant piece of cloth throughout His entire life. The historical account proves this to be the case. The Nativity story of Messiah Yeshua, as I discovered, goes in the exact order of how a swaddling cloth is used in all the important life events of a Jewish baby boy.

Most importantly, this swaddling cloth was used when the baby boy was circumcised on the eighth day and it stood *"as a sign of the Covenant in the life blood!"* The Holy Scriptures verify that Yeshua was circumcised on the eighth day after He was born and, again, He was wrapped during that ceremony in *"the sign" of the swaddling cloth.* This cloth therefore, was extremely significant, because of *the life blood Covenant that is called the "bris."* The swaddling cloth, for this reason, would have been a cherished piece of linen cloth, similar to a family heirloom and it would have been kept by the family. Sometimes the swaddling cloth came from worn-out Priestly garments of white linen that had been used for the Holy Temple service, but were no longer in use and were now used to bind a Torah scroll at the Holy Temple in Jerusalem Israel.

All through His life, this *swaddling cloth* would be presented at special occasions. It was either used at the Holy Temple to bind a Torah scroll or it was used to bind a personal family Torah scroll. It was also used at the Bar Mitzvah ceremony when Yeshua went to the Holy Temple with His family at age 12. This is when He spoke intelligently to the Hebrew Scholars and they were astounded at His knowledge of the Torah! They did not realize that the actual *"Living Torah"* was dwelling in their midst and was astounding them with His Words and Doctrine! No wonder He knew so much! *The swaddling cloth was a sign for Israel and this was a Divine message from God that was declared by the Angel of the LORD.* When the Jewish disciple John wrote that *"The Word was God,"* notice that this verse mentions that *"in Him was life and the life was the light of men."* This goes along with what I said about the earthen vessels containing this Divine Testimony because they reveal *the light of Eternal life, out of the darkness of death in the Garden tomb of Holy Mount Moriah.* Remember Paul's words about the earthen vessels?

II Corinthians 4:6-7 *For God, who commanded the light to shine out of darkness, hath shined in our hearts, to give the light of the knowledge of the glory of God in the face of Yeshua Messiah. But we have this treasure in earthen vessels, that the Excellency of the power may be of God, and not of us.*

John 1:1-7 *In the beginning was the Word, and the Word was with God, and the Word was God. The same was in the beginning with God. All things were made by Him; and without Him was not anything made that was made. In Him was life; and the life was the light of men. And the light shineth in darkness; and the darkness comprehended it not. There was a man sent from God, whose name was John. The same came for a witness, to bear witness of the light, that all men through him might believe.*

Until I saw that tiny photo of *the swaddling cloth binding the Torah scroll,* I did not realize the incredible significance of this *sign* to Israel. *The binding of the Word with the swaddling cloth is the most profound "sign" of the Covenant of God with the LORD'S life blood.* I might also mention that the Jewish men *bind the Word of God to their arm and hand and Messiah is the Word, the arm and hand of God!* Messiah Yeshua's Nativity story is in the correct order for a typical *first born Jewish baby boy's birth,* as it is recorded in the Gospel accounts. The use of Yeshua's swaddling cloth was present in the story at the beginning of His birth and then it goes in order after that through the various stages and circumstances of His life. At His birth, He was swaddled in this cloth. It was tightly bound around Him, just as the cloth is used to bind the Torah scroll. He would have been circumcised using His swaddling cloth on the eighth day after His birth, in *the bris ceremony,* which took place at the Holy Temple in Jerusalem. This is when the baby is given His Name. In the account of the circumcision of Yeshua on the eighth day, Mary named Him *"Yeshua."* This was the Name that was given to Mary by the Angel Gabriel. Then the time of Mary's purification took place. After her time was fulfilled, the family then returned to the Holy Temple in Jerusalem. The Nativity story accurately shows the dedication of the baby in the Holy Temple. *The swaddling cloth and the bris ceremony are a celebration of the life cycle! Yeshua came to give us Eternal Life!* When I saw how everything just fell into the proper order, I realized that when Mary and Joseph arrived with the baby Yeshua at the Holy Temple, after the days of Mary's purification, *Simeon the Priest* was the one who dedicated the baby Messiah Yeshua! The righteous devout Jew, who came into the Holy Temple full of the Holy Spirit of God, was not just any righteous man coming up to say hello. *Simeon was the very one who lifted up the Rod Messiah, the Living Torah scroll that was bound in the swaddling cloth, the sign of the Eternal Covenant, and he said the blessing over Yeshua and dedicated Him to God!* Two turtledoves were made as an offering to the LORD at this time. It was Simeon who gave the prayer and later righteous Anna the Prophetess, came in after the dedication and she also gave a blessing. Simeon the Priest is the one who declared *that His eyes had now seen the Salvation of the LORD,* as He lifted up the Word of God called Yeshua in His hands! *This was the glory of Israel!* I must remind you of something interesting about Simeon! On the Road to Bethany, when they found the burial ossuaries of Mary, Martha and Lazarus and Simon Bar Jonah, they also found the ossuary of *"Simeon the Priest!" This has to be the beloved Simeon who lifted up the Living Torah, the Messiah and dedicated Him on Holy Mount Moriah. Simeon knew that the Rod of God had come to save Israel forever and his comfort was in the Rod and Staff of the LORD.* Now he knew that he could die in peace with the hope of Eternal Life. *Simeon the Priest* served faithfully in the Holy Temple as a righteous Jew who believed without a doubt that Yeshua was the Jewish Messiah! As I wrote earlier, the ossuaries were discovered in a first century Jewish-Christian cemetery. Simon Peter was discovered buried in this same cemetery near Bethany on the Mount of Olives in Jerusalem Israel! The following account reveals the Jewish baby dedication ceremony of the Messiah!

Luke 2:22-33 *And when the days of her purification according to the law of Moses were accomplished, they brought Him to Jerusalem, to present Him to the LORD; As it is written in the law of the LORD, Every male that openeth the womb shall be called Holy to the LORD; And to offer a sacrifice according to that which is said in the law of the LORD, A pair of turtledoves, or two young pigeons. And, behold, there was a man in Jerusalem, whose name was Simeon; and the same man was just and devout, waiting for the consolation of Israel; and the Holy Spirit was upon him. And it was revealed unto him by the Holy Spirit, that he should not see death, before he had seen the LORD'S Messiah. And he came by the Spirit into the Temple; and when the parents brought in the child Yeshua, to do for Him after the custom of the law, Then took he Him up in his arms, and blessed God, and said, LORD, now lettest thou thy servant depart in peace, according to Thy Word; For mine eyes have seen Thy salvation, Which Thou hast prepared before the face of all people; A light to lighten the Gentiles, and the glory of Thy people Israel. And Joseph and His mother marveled at those things which were spoken of Him. And Simeon blessed them, and said unto Mary His Mother, Behold, this child is set for the fall and rising again of many in Israel; and for a sign which shall be spoken against; Yes, a sword shall pierce through thy own heart also, that the thoughts of many hearts may be revealed. And there was one Anna, a Prophetess, the daughter of Phanuel, of the tribe of Asher; she was of a great age, and had lived with an husband seven years from her virginity; And she was a widow of about fourscore* *and four years, which departed not from the Temple, but served God with fastings and prayers night and day. And she coming in that instant gave thanks likewise unto the LORD, and spake of Him to all them that looked for redemption in Jerusalem. And when they had performed all things according to the Law of the LORD, they returned into Galilee, to their own city Nazareth.*

I discovered that the swaddling cloth sometimes had the name of the baby sewn on it with another backing cloth, or sometimes it was just a plain piece of linen, with a bit of sheen to it. Sometimes it contained a brief genealogy of the baby boy, but not always. *The swaddling cloth of a Jewish baby was like a birth certificate in ancient times.* It might tell when He was born and give the date and the names of His parents on the swaddling cloth. Sometimes the name was sewn to the cloth with another little strip of cloth. If Yeshua's *bris cloth,* the sign of the Covenant of the LORD, had His Name on it at one time, it may have faded by now, or perhaps they did not even put His Name on His linen cloth. However, since this was the Messiah of Israel, it seems to me that they would have done something special with His swaddling cloth. Perhaps it had a backing piece at one time, like the Shroud did, that was eventually removed from it or perhaps it was just a simple old linen cloth with no design on it. Perhaps it was a piece of linen from an old Priestly garment from the Holy Temple that was no longer in use. ***(Source: "Wimpeln, or Ashkenazic binders, birth of a male child. Wonderful illuminated letters (painted or embroidered) with animals often described the wish that the boy be raised to a life of Torah, Chuppah (wedding) and good deeds." Copyright ©2011 kolel.org/torahstory/module1/mantles.html).***

Now the Torah scrolls are wrapped with a Torah binder or swaddling cloth from a first born son's circumcision as a sign of the Covenant with God. In the middle ages in Europe, this swaddling cloth became known as a *"wimpel"* which is also spelled *"wimple."* This is also extremely significant for another reason that I will soon discuss! The word *"wimpel"* came from the middle ages in Germany from the word *"bewimfen"* which means to *"cover up" or "conceal."* In ancient times, this piece of linen for the swaddling cloth in Hebrew was known as a *"Mappah"* or by the plural version *"Mappot,"* and it was specifically used as a *Torah binder.* ***(Source: Torah Binders swaddling cloth; The Czech Memorial Scrolls Museum, Archive of the Jewish Museum in Prague; ©2013 Czechmemorialscrollstrust.org/binders.htm).*** The Mappah is part of the Torah Ornaments. *"This binder, called a mappah or wimpel, was fashioned from a piece of square linen cloth which was placed near the infant during the circumcision ceremony."* In Europe, *"The binder is a long narrow strip of cloth with which the Torah is bound, either on top of the wrapper or directly on the parchment."* ***(Source: Torah Ornaments: Encyclopedia Judaica ©2008 The Gale Group All Rights Reserved & ©2013 The American-Israeli Cooperative Enterprise: jewishvirtuallibrary.org/jsource/judaica/ejud_0002_0020_0_19950.html).***

Remember, Mary was said to have washed *Yeshua's swaddling cloth in the Fountain of Mary.* This Fountain or spring is the perennial source of *Living Water* that runs into the Pool of Siloam or the Shiloach Pool connected with Gihon, where the Priests would wash before performing their sacred duties in the Holy Temple. So Yeshua sent the blind man to wash in the *Living Water* of this Pool and the blind man was miraculously healed, *revealing that Yeshua would restore the Davidic Dynasty forever!* The swaddling cloth of Yeshua must have existed because this story is told in Israel at *the Fountain of Mary* near the place where she visited Elisabeth and praised God as her Saviour. At the time of Yeshua's Bar Mitzvah, He and His parents returned to the Holy Temple and they likely had His *swaddling cloth* with them because at age 12 the *swaddling cloth* was often dedicated by the family, and it was left at the Holy Temple *to be ceremoniously used in the binding of a Torah scroll in Jerusalem.* It is so amazing that the Nativity story is found in succession like this in all four Gospel accounts. This is exactly how the swaddling cloth is used by Jewish people today. *The swaddling cloth is so significant because the Covenant in the life blood is Eternal and this is why it is present during all the significant Jewish rites of passage because of the fact that it is symbolic of the life cycle!* After the Jewish boy grew up and became a man of marrying age, his swaddling cloth was used as part of his *wedding Chuppah.* Below is a demonstration I did swaddling a life size baby doll, using the measurements that I will reveal in the next two sections!

ישוע הנצרי ומלך היהודים

A sample swaddling cloth that measures 33" L x 20" W

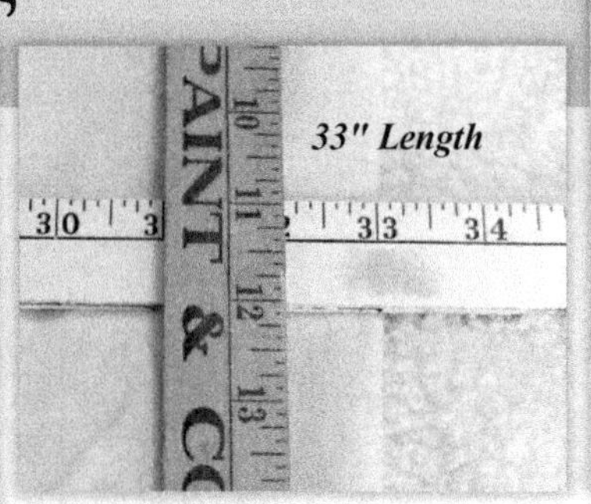

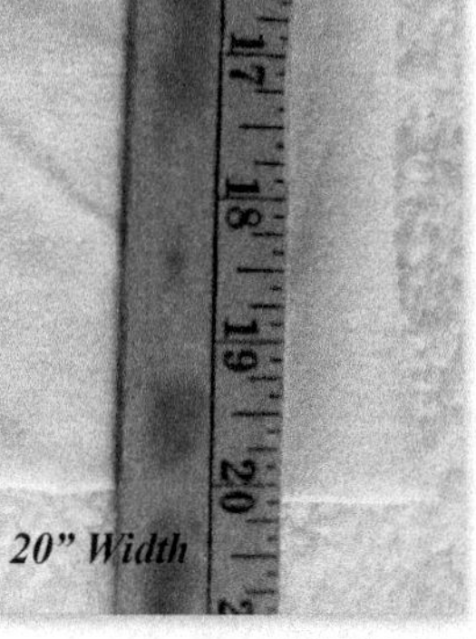

Step 1 Swaddling a baby. The baby is first placed on its back, at the long end of the cloth

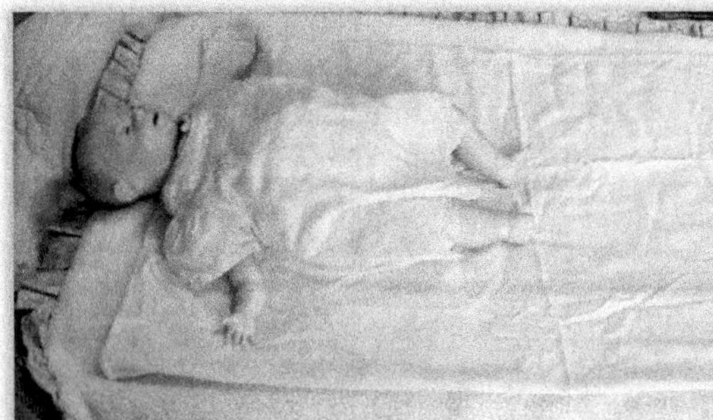

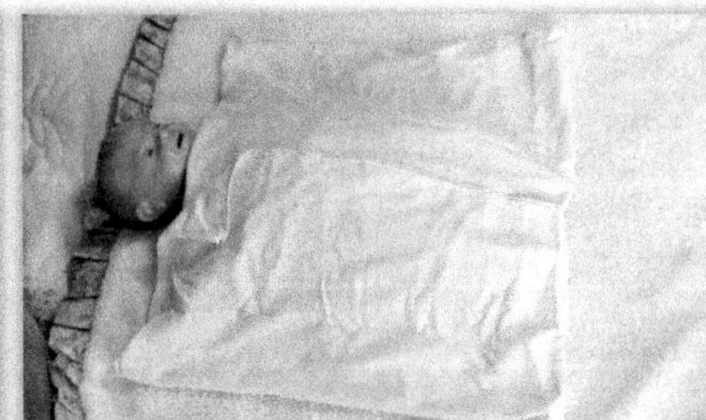

Step 3 The long end is brought up to the chin of the baby and is tucked in so it rests against the chest

Step 2 The cloth is tucked around and underneath both arms of the baby

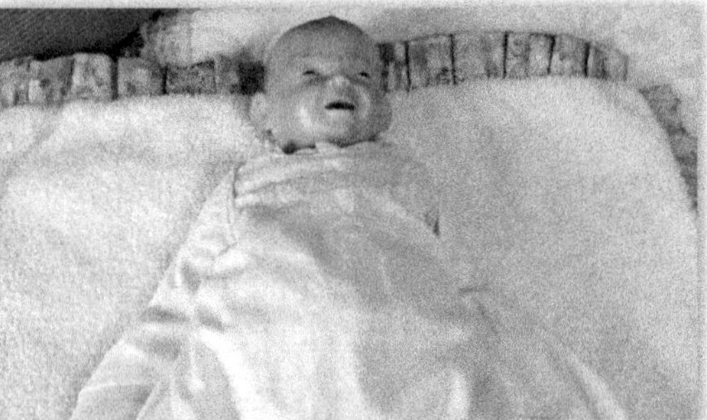

Final Step Both sides of the cloth are tucked underneath the baby and this baby is approx. 20" in length and was swaddled in a 33" x 20" cloth

My demonstration swaddling a baby with a 33" x 20" cloth
Photos ©2013 Kimberly K Ballard All Rights Reserved
This is my Mother's doll from the 1940's

It is interesting to note that the Most Holy Inner Sanctuary of the Holy Temple of King Solomon measured 20 cubits x 20 cubits x 20 cubits & The Holy Temple measured 60 cubits x 30 cubits x 20 cubits

The Sudarium of Oviedo Spain Official Photograph
©2013 El Centro Español de Sindonologia (CES)
All Rights Reserved

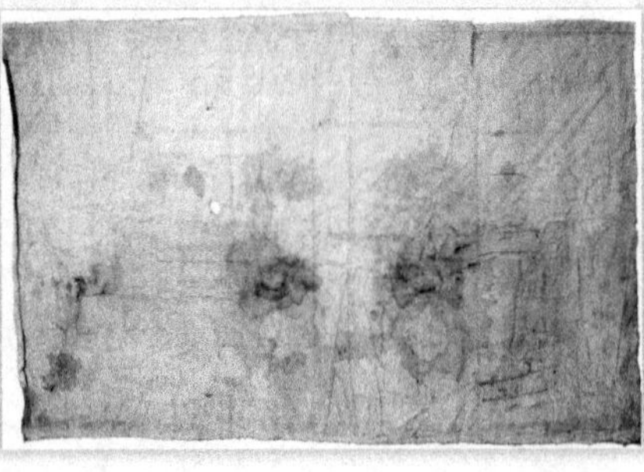

THE SUDARIUM AND THE SWADDLING CLOTH

The Sudarium of Oviedo Spain Official Photograph
©2013 El Centro Español de Sindonologia (CES)
All Rights Reserved

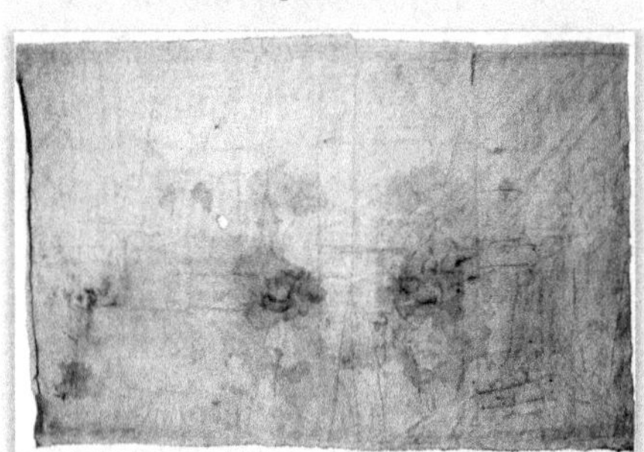

What I am about to say next is truly an earth shattering discovery and it came to me completely by Divine Providence! In Europe in the Middle Ages, a *"wimple"* was also a head covering for the clergy of the Church. The wimple covered the entire head and neck of the devout religious person. The only thing visible was the face while the rest of head was covered and wrapped in fabric. ***(Sources: Wimple;*** *The American Heritage Dictionary of the English Language,* ***Fourth Edition copyright ©2000 by Houghton Mifflin Company. Updated in 2009. Published by Houghton Mifflin Company All rights reserved) AND (©2009 The Free Dictionary.com AND Source; ©2011 en.wikipedia.org/wiki/Wimpel).***

So the small rectangular piece of linen cloth that is known as *"the Sudarium"* was in fact the *"head covering"* that was wrapped around the head of Yeshua during his burial. After His resurrection, it was later taken and stored in a silver Ark. Then it eventually wound up in Oviedo Spain. This cloth has a very significant history. It is known that this linen cloth had been in Jerusalem at one time and it was found in a cave near Jericho, where it had been stored for some time in the silver Ark. Jericho is just opposite from the place where Yeshua was baptized in the Jordan River. This place is quite close to Mount Nebo. This head covering was found by the Jewish disciples, *"John and Simon Peter,"* in the Garden tomb. When they saw the linens lying in the sepulchre, the Bible says that *"they saw and believed."* Yeshua was already alive and He was no longer in the sepulchre. The Gospel accounts tell us that the face cloth was *"rolled, wrapped, or folded and left behind in a separate place by itself."* The linen burial Shroud was found in the place where Yeshua's body had rested, but the head cloth was found in this *separate place by itself.*

Now the head covering that is in Oviedo Spain is stained with blood and other bodily fluids from the man on the Shroud. Due to the fact that the Sudarium was rolled and left in a *separate place* explains why *the fourfold stain* appears on this cloth. It is said that *"the fourfold stain diminishes and gets weaker in intensity on the Sudarium."*

What I discovered in 2008 that is so astonishing is the fact that a *"swaddling cloth" is also called a "wimple."* What I am suggesting, based on the evidence I have been shown by the LORD, is the fact that *"The head covering that was wrapped around Yeshua's head in His burial was indeed the Messiah's swaddling cloth!"* This swaddling cloth or *"bris cloth"* was *"the sign of the Covenant of life and the Angel of the LORD declared that Yeshua's swaddling cloth was to be "a sign" to Israel." I am suggesting that they used Yeshua's swaddling cloth in His burial as one of His Jewish rites of passage from this life to the next.* I definitely believe that they used it at the time of His death because they thought that His life was over. They thought that He would never use it in the future with His Bride under the wedding Chuppah, but they were wrong! *I believe that Yeshua left this swaddling cloth, the head covering, rolled in a separate place as a sign of His life blood Covenant for the future Messianic wedding to the LORD'S beloved Israel! You must remember that this was the Torah binder that had wrapped the Living Torah at birth!* Remember that the swaddling cloth of the first born Jewish baby boy is kept as *a sign of the Eternal Covenant because his life blood is on it.* So when Yeshua was resurrected, He set this linen cloth in a *separate place* inside the tomb as *a sign* of the Eternal life Covenant that He made in *His life blood* as *a sign* of His betrothal to Israel. It was therefore *separated and set apart* as *"Holy" because it had covered and bound the face of the Living Torah!* Remember that I said previously that Yeshua had *separated and set apart* Simon Peter, James, and John as *"Kadesh"* and then He took them up to *Mount Sinai,* the Mountain that was also *"Kadesh"* to reveal the *"Higher purpose of His Covenant?" Yeshua left the swaddling cloth in a separate place as "Kadesh" after He came to life because it was no ordinary cloth. It was considered to be "Consecrated and sacred and set apart for a Higher purpose!"* In my mind I can clearly see that this *sign* signifies that Yeshua is the Bridegroom of Israel, who will one day return and marry His beloved Bride, and the Land of Israel that He is to rule! When the Jewish disciples, *"John and Simon Peter,"* found this cloth in the Garden tomb after the resurrection of Yeshua, they immediately understood what it meant! They must have been so excited by these events. Yeshua therefore sealed *His Living Eternal Covenant of life in His life blood* and *this life blood was on the Sudarium, on His swaddling cloth!* KING Yeshua will be married in the Heavenly Chuppah under this wedding canopy in the Eternal Kingdom. The wedding will take place at Yeshua's return for His Bride in Jerusalem! Earlier as I pondered this, I began to wonder, *"Is it possible that a Jewish swaddling cloth could be used in a Jewish burial?"* So I began researching for any Jewish records about the Jewish swaddling cloth. Then as if by Divine Providence, I discovered an Israeli statement in Israel that said, *"The swaddling cloth can be used in a Jewish burial!"* Wow! I could not believe it! ***(Source: Torah Binders references; "Linen Torah Binders in death;" ©2011 static.skinnerinc.com/rss/sale_2456.xml "Document a boy's life. A man's birth, religious rituals, marriage and death recorded in embroidery by his mother and later his wife.") AND (Source: ©2011 academic.reed.edu/art/faculty/ondrizek/installations/M168/Page9.html).***

This was the Jewish thinking in our generation about the swaddling cloth of a Jewish baby! It was an answer to my prayers! Now if the Angel of the LORD had told you that *the sign* would be to find the Messiah *wrapped in swaddling clothes* and lying in a manger, would you not *keep the swaddling cloth as a very precious sign of the Eternal life Covenant?* After all, Heaven was opened and a multitude of Heavenly Hosts of Angels were praising God and proclaiming that *the Saviour was born who was Messiah the LORD* and this all transpired on *the KING'S Coronation Day on the Feast of Trumpets!* I believe for this reason alone *the swaddling cloth of the Messiah* was very valuable to the family and they would have kept it in their possession to use in binding a Torah scroll, if not in the Holy Temple at least they would have had it wrapped around their own Torah scroll within their own home. It was a tradition that if a family was not wealthy and did not own a Torah scroll, then when their first born son, a baby boy, was dedicated at the Holy Temple the family would leave the swaddling cloth at the Holy Temple, after *the dedication ceremony* of the baby. A Temple Torah scroll was then wrapped in the swaddling cloth and then it was placed and stored inside an Ark within the Holy Temple complex. When the family would visit the Holy Temple in Jerusalem for the important Feast Days of the LORD, the family had access to it again. *This was often done because the Covenant of the circumcision cloth was the Covenant between God and His people, Israel.* Therefore, this linen cloth was wrapped around the Word of God. It was bound to it. As a Torah binder, it was used to bind the two staves (Trees of Life) together before placing *the Word of God inside the Ark* to be kept in the Holy Temple complex. *In Yeshua's case it was also wrapped around the Rod of God, the Tree of Life, as part of the Ark of Heaven.* The swaddling cloth was always present at the dedication ceremony of the Jewish baby boy. So Yeshua's swaddling cloth was bound around the Word of God during His dedication ceremony, as Simeon the Priest gave the dedication. *He lifted Him up to pray a Jewish blessing over the Messiah and over the Living Torah that would save Israel and all of us!*

Now think about the fact that there has to be a reason that the Gospel accounts even mention this face cloth being left in a *separate place* and that it was not lying with the other burial Shroud. If this cloth was only a blood soaked linen cloth, then why would they even bother to write anything about it at all? Why write that it was found rolled together in a *"separate"* place by itself in the Gospel accounts? If someone on the street was bleeding and soaked up their blood with a cloth and threw it down on the sidewalk, do you think that you would write about the blood soaked cloth? Do you think that you would even touch it or keep it? No! You definitely would not write about the bloody cloth that was found in a *separate place, unless it was extremely significant and unless there was more to the story than meets the eye, because it did have a much Higher purpose!"* Another thought that I had about this is in response to the assumption that this cloth was simply tossed aside, just prior to placing Yeshua's body inside the tomb. I believe that this is not correct, because if this was the case, then they never would have mentioned the fact that they found it lying in a *separate place* after the resurrection. They would not have paid any attention to it at all. It therefore would not have been kept, let alone mentioned in the Gospel accounts. *I definitely believe that this cloth was mentioned because it was separated as "Kadesh" as a sign of the Eternal life Covenant because the LORD'S life blood was on it and, therefore as I said, it had a much Higher purpose. The truth is that the Jewish Bridegroom Messiah left it in the rock hewn tomb of God's Garden in Mount Moriah as a sign to His betrothed Bride Israel that He would return to marry the Land and His people forever in the place that was once the former Garden of Eden!* This swaddling cloth was to be *a sign* to the shepherds who were abiding in the fields.

Another exciting piece of evidence that proves to me that this head covering is the *swaddling cloth* of Yeshua is the fact that the Sudarium cloth, has a bit of a taffeta finish to it. A taffeta finish actually refers *"to the piece of linen, having a bit of sheen to the fabric, which indicates that, it is a finer piece of linen."* ***(Source: Taffeta; The American Heritage Dictionary of the English Language, Fourth Edition copyright ©2000 by Houghton Mifflin Company. Updated in 2009. Published by Houghton Mifflin Company. All rights reserved) AND (©2009The Free Dictionary.com).***

Why would anyone use a finer piece of linen to cover the bloody head and neck of a crucifixion victim, unless the cloth was special? Even when my beloved favorite cat Jasmine passed away, I wanted to bury him in his favorite and most cherished *baby blanket,* but this was the KING Messiah of Israel! You have to remember what took place at Messiah's birth. *This swaddling cloth was Yeshua's first baby blanket!* The Angel of the LORD and the Heavenly Hosts were praising God, as the Shechinah glory shone round about them! The fact that traces of flowers and their impressions have been discovered on Yeshua's burial Shroud reveals that they buried Him with love and tenderness and with great lamentation. The answer is clear that this was a very precious piece of linen. It was valued by the family and especially by Yeshua's mother Mary. The cloth that was the sign of the Covenant, that was bound around Yeshua at His birth, I believe, was left with Him in the tomb and was placed around His face, head, and neck because they thought that His life was over. Perhaps Mary placed His *"bris cloth"* over His face herself in tenderness because she loved Him with all her heart, just like I loved my darling cat with all my heart and wrapped him in his finest baby blanket when he died! No one would have cared about leaving an account of this small blood soaked cloth that was *set apart,* if it was not extremely special and significant! The fact remains, though, that they did leave us several accounts about it and that means that it was quite a significant find when they came to the sepulchre and found the two linens of Yeshua's miraculous resurrection. *One cloth bore the image of the LORD Messiah with His life blood on it, and the other cloth was the sign of the Covenant of the life blood of the LORD that saved us.* The Rod of God reversed the curse of death here and put the love of *the Living Torah* into our hearts forever! Thus the Word of the LORD came true, as it was written by the Prophet Jeremiah that said, *"You shall know the LORD, the Bridegroom and no one will ask who He is anymore, when He makes the New Covenant of the heart!"* Now you can understand why it is so significant that the LORD gave me the vision of the niches and the Jewish Priestly Angel at the Garden tomb, pointing to *the Living Testimony of the Living Torah.* If the niches held the Shroud and the Sudarium at one time and the mezuzah was to the right of *the Testimony*, the message is shockingly clear because it says, *"Hear O Israel, the LORD our God, the LORD is one!"* It goes on to say, *"And you shall love the LORD your God with all your heart!"*

Jeremiah 31:31-34 *Behold, the days come, saith the LORD, that I will make a New Covenant with the House of Israel, and with the House of Judah; Not according to the Covenant that I made with their fathers in the day that I took them by the hand to bring them out of Egypt; which My Covenant they brake, although I was an husband unto them, saith the LORD; But this shall be the Covenant that I will make with the House of Israel; After those days, saith the LORD, I will put My Law in their inward parts, and write it in their hearts; and will be their God, and they shall be My people. And they shall teach no more every man his neighbour; and every man his brother, saying, Know the LORD; for they shall all know Me, from the least of them unto the greatest of them, saith the LORD; for I will forgive their iniquity, and I will remember their sin no more.*

Deuteronomy 6:4-9 *Hear, O Israel; The LORD our God is one LORD; And thou shalt love the LORD thy God with all thine heart, and with all they soul, and with all thy might. And these Words, which I command thee this day, shall be in thine heart; And thou shalt teach them diligently unto thy children, and shalt talk of them when thou sittest in thine house, and when thou walkest by the way, and when thou liest down, and when thou risest up. And thou shalt bind them for a sign upon thine hand, and they shall be as frontlets between thine eyes. And thou shalt write them upon the doorposts of thy house, and on thy gates.*

The Jewish Priestly Angel would therefore be pointing to the Living Torah binder and the bris Covenant of the Messiah left as Kadesh in the doorpost or gate of the LORD'S House in Holy Mount Moriah, at the gate of Heaven!

The believers that followed Messiah Yeshua in the Middle Ages had to have known when they began wearing the head covering known as the *"wimple" that Yeshua's head covering was His swaddling cloth of the Covenant of Eternal life.* The cloth was not simply to cover the hair as an act of reverence, but it covered the entire neck, chin, forehead, and sides of the face, as well as the back and top of the head, just as it did in Yeshua's burial, although Yeshua's face was totally covered with the cloth. I believe that this knowledge was eventually lost and therefore the significance of the Sudarium has been greatly overlooked to this day. Another amazing parallel of Yeshua's Sudarium is the fact that *the wimples that were worn in the Middle Ages also had a taffeta finish to them, just like the Sudarium.*

This is why I knew that the Sudarium, the swaddling cloth of the life blood Covenant of the Bridegroom, had to have been placed in a clay jar, just underneath the signet of the KING OF KINGS, in the place that Abraham called *"YHVH Ra'ah,"* where Abraham declared, *"In the Mountain of the LORD it shall be seen!"* This is why the Jewish Priestly Angel is pointing to the signet shaped object inscribed with the *Alpha and Omega* in the Royal KINGLY stone of Holy Mount Moriah at the Garden tomb. The LORD wants us to look at it and perceive it. He wants us to keep His Testimonies in our hearts!

Because of the fact that this New Covenant reverses the curse of death and makes *the way* for us to enter the Eternal Promised Land, we must enter into Heaven through Messiah to have life! This is why I felt certain that the Mezuzah was placed in the tiny niche next to this Testimony of the Covenant of Eternal life and not placed by the door of the tomb. *I believe that when Simon Peter and John saw the swaddling cloth lying in a place by itself as "Kadesh," they knew it was the sign of His marriage Covenant to the Land and people of Israel and it was a sign that God had redeemed all of us in His Garden. It was wonderfully exciting for them then, just as it is for us!* Yeshua was raised to life in the tomb on the seventh day, during the Sabbath of the LORD. I believe He came to life sometime during the fourth watch of the night before morning came. This is the same hour Yeshua came walking on the sea!

John 20:1-31 *The first day of the week cometh Mary Magdalene early, when it was yet dark, unto the sepulchre, and seeth the stone taken away from the sepulchre. Then she runneth, and cometh to Simon Peter, and to the other disciple, whom Yeshua loved, and saith unto them, They have taken away the LORD out of the sepulchre, and we know not where they have laid Him. Peter therefore went forth, and that other disciple, and came to the sepulchre. So they ran both together; and the other disciple did out run Peter, and came first to the sepulchre. And he stooping down, and looking in, saw the linen clothes lying; yet went he not in. Then cometh Simon Peter following him, and went into the sepulchre, and seeth the linen clothes lie, And the napkin, that was about His head, not lying with the linen clothes, but wrapped together in a place by itself. Then went in also that other disciple, which came first to the sepulchre, and he saw, and believed. For as yet they knew not the Scripture, that He must rise again from the dead. Then the disciples went away again unto their own home.*

To reestablish the facts, we can truly say that Messiah died at Passover at the exact moment that the Lamb was slain in the Holy Temple and His blood was sprinkled on the Heavenly Ark of His Living Testimony. His life blood is sprinkled upon all who accept Him as the Rod of God lifted up for Eternal salvation, because He is our High Priest of Heaven. Messiah Yeshua was in the tomb as the Bread of Heaven and the Staff of Life during the Feast of Unleavened Bread. Messiah Yeshua came to life and bore the First Fruit of the Almond Rod on the Feast of First Fruits. Messiah Yeshua, the KING, was born in late September on Rosh HaShanah, on Tishrei 1, the Feast of Trumpets. The dead who believe in Messiah will be raised to life on this same day in the future. John the Baptist came preaching repentance, and I believe that Yom Kippur occurred about this time when Yeshua went out to the wilderness after His baptism in the Jordan River, where He was afflicted or tempted by Satan. Many people are saying that the Messiah only fulfilled the Spring Feasts at His first coming and that He will fulfill the Fall Feasts at His second coming, but I can tell you *Messiah Yeshua fulfilled every single one of the Feast Days of the LORD at His first coming.* The appointed Feasts will always remain special to the LORD because His entire Testimony is based upon all of seven of them. When Yeshua had accomplished His Testimony on the cross He said, *"It is finished."* He was saying that He fulfilled it all. He fulfilled the Fall Feasts beginning with His birth! The Feasts of the LORD have more than one historical fulfillment already in the past. So it stands to reason that in the future, the Messiah will come and fulfill His agenda on the same Feasts Days, just as the LORD did in the past with Israel, before the Messiah came to the earth.

Now, getting back to the details about the Sudarium, the Gospel accounts tell us that Mary, the mother of Yeshua, was indeed present at the sepulchre in the Garden and she was also present during the crucifixion when Yeshua died. Mary could easily have brought with her *the Jewish family heirloom* that was Yeshua's swaddling cloth, His Torah binder. Mary, in a loving gesture, could easily have covered Yeshua's face with dignity with the special cloth that she treasured, just after Yeshua was taken off the cross, especially after He received such brutal treatment. When a loved one dies, it is not unusual to place objects of great meaning with the body of the departed loved one. *People especially want to remember the face of their loved one. They would never see this face again. This was especially true in ancient times, before photography existed. This is why they made death masks or hired artists to paint their portrait in life.* I can imagine that it must have been extremely difficult to bury a loved one back then and *never see their face again* without photographs to remember them by. *Leaving the swaddling cloth in the burial chamber was like leaving Messiah Yeshua's birth certificate with His family's name on it in the tomb for His final burial.*

We can see in the following Scriptures that Mary and the other women were present at the tomb. For some reason, the women are often overlooked which is quite sad because Mary Magdalene was absolutely the most faithful, beautiful follower of Messiah Yeshua. The Scripture clearly tells us that *"the women beheld the sepulchre and how Yeshua's body was laid in the sepulchre."* This means that they gazed upon His body and assisted in his burial. Since the women were preparing the spices to take later to the tomb after the Sabbath rest, we know that the women were definitely going to touch the body of Yeshua. The spices would have been used everywhere on the body, including around Yeshua's head. So the women, including His mother Mary, did have access to putting *the swaddling cloth* of Yeshua over His face and around His head. Flowers and meaningful botanicals were also lovingly placed around the body of the Messiah because He was so precious to them and the world would one day understand the depth of all of it.

Luke 23:50-56 *And, behold, there was a man named Joseph, a counselor; and he was a good man, and a just; The same had not consented to the counsel and deed of them; he was of Arimathaea, a city of the Jews; who also himself waited for the Kingdom of God. This man went unto Pilate, and begged the body of Yeshua. And he took it down, and wrapped it in linen, and laid it in a sepulchre that was hewn in stone, wherein never man before was laid. And that day was the preparation, and the Sabbath drew on. And the women also, which came with him from Galilee, followed after, and beheld the sepulchre, and how His body was laid. And they returned, and prepared spices and ointments; and rested the Sabbath day according to the commandment.*

Matthew 27:55-61 *And many women were there beholding afar off, which followed Yeshua from Galilee, ministering unto Him; Among which was Mary Magdalene, and Mary the Mother of James and Joses, and the Mother of Zebedee's children. When the even was come, there came a rich man of Arimathaea, named Joseph, who also himself was Yeshua's disciple; He went to Pilate, and begged the body of Yeshua. Then Pilate commanded the body to be delivered. And when Joseph had taken the body, he wrapped it in a clean linen cloth, And laid it in his own new tomb, which he had hewn out in the rock; and he rolled a great stone to the door of the sepulchre, and departed. And there was Mary Magdalene, and the other Mary, sitting over against the sepulchre.*

Luke 24:12 *Then arose Peter, and ran unto the sepulchre; and stooping down, he beheld the linen clothes laid by themselves, and departed, wondering in himself at that which was come to pass.*

Mark 15:46-47 *And he bought fine linen, and took Him down, and wrapped Him in the linen, and laid Him in a sepulchre which was hewn out of a rock, and rolled a stone unto the door of the sepulchre. And Mary Magdalene and Mary the mother of Joses beheld where He was laid.*

The Shroud linen was *"a clean linen cloth"* purchased by Joseph of Arimathaea. This Scripture tells us nothing about the linen face cloth that has a slight taffeta finish to it! This statement declares that Joseph wrapped Yeshua's body in a single linen cloth before placing it in the sepulchre. *I believe that Tabitha made it!* However, since we know from Scripture, that Mary and the other women were present at the crucifixion and later present at the tomb, the face cloth could have come from them. So I believe that this cloth likely was brought there by His mother Mary because she loved Him dearly and the *bris circumcision cloth* was so significant to *the life blood Covenant and the life cycle*. Mary definitely had the opportunity to place *the swaddling cloth* from His birth and circumcision over Yeshua's face and upon His head, because she was involved in bringing the spices. Now you also have to think about the fact that Mary went into mourning and lamentation over the loss of her firstborn son, who had been with her from the time of His birth. Yeshua had just been severely and brutally tortured to death by the Roman Soldiers. Soothing Yeshua's face in gentleness would have brought great comfort to Mary. Normally *the family provided the swaddling cloth* that was usually made at home. Some of these *swaddling clothes* were made from plain white linen like the Sudarium, while others were decorated. *I said before that Yeshua's swaddling cloth also may have had a backing that was at some point removed.* A blessing is sometimes embroidered on the *swaddling cloth.* The names of the parents and the date and location of the baby's birth can also be embroidered on the linen, either directly onto the cloth or embroidered on another strip of cloth that is attached to it. If the family was indeed poor, they usually had a very plain simple linen cloth for the *bris* ceremony, just like the Sudarium. Just recently, a new technology was used on the Dead Sea Scrolls by the Leon Levy Dead Sea Scrolls Digital Library in Jerusalem, and I thought this was extremely significant. So I wrote to Barrie M. Schwortz, the official Shroud photographer, and made the suggestion that this new technology might also be useful in reading any ancient text that has become invisible to the naked eye on Yeshua's burial Shroud and Sudarium. Barrie wrote back and said, *"You are correct. These newer technologies could well be applied to the Shroud and Sudarium. Of course, access to the Shroud itself would be necessary for such an undertaking and, as you know, that access has been very limited over the years."* ***(Source: Quote from Barrie M. Schwortz The Official Shroud Photographer).***

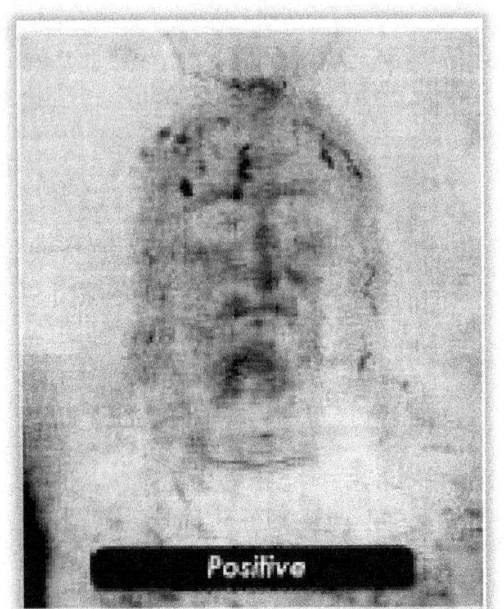

Shroud linen Photo ©2013 Dr Petrus Soons taken from Enrie Photos All Rights Reserved

The Leon Levy Dead Sea Scrolls Digital Library, stated on a video how they used this new technology on the Scroll fragments in the following statement, *"Each fragment was imaged on both sides in twelve different wavelengths, seven in the visible range and five in the near-infrared invisible range, to extract both physical and textual information from each fragment of the parchment. This system allowed them to detect written characters that have become invisible to the naked eye. They could really see into the insides of the parchment and could see much more detail on the images than they could in the past. They could actually see the ink underneath and inside the parchment."* ***(Source: ©2012 transcribed by KKB from a video at: (www.deadseascrolls.org.il/about-the-project/a-note-from-the-iaa-director). Israeli Antiquities Authority.***

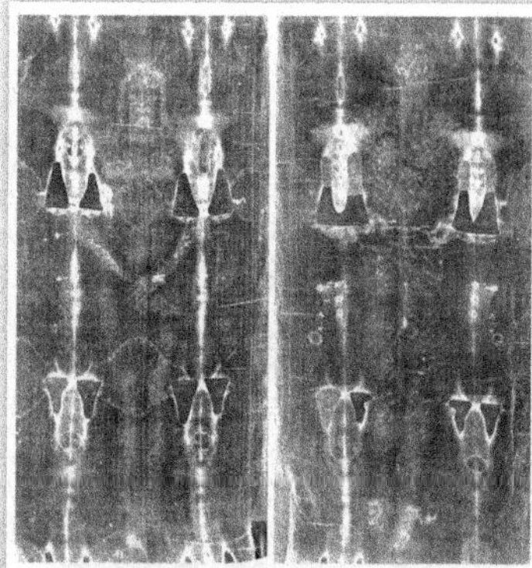

Official Shroud Pair Photograph

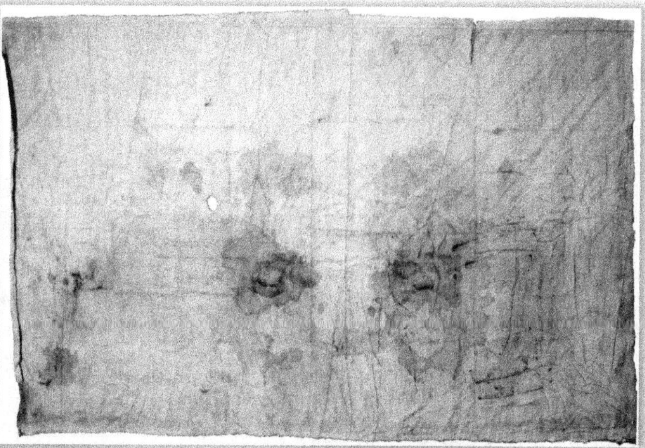

The Sudarium of Oviedo Spain

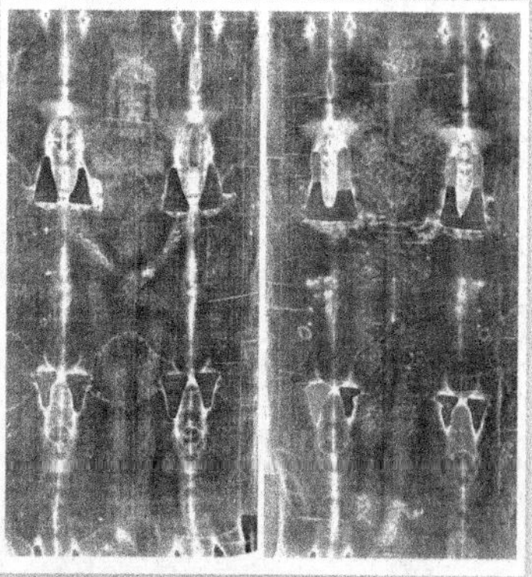

Official Shroud Pair Photograph

PART OF THE BURIAL SHROUD OF MESSIAH

The KINGS Royal seal on Snow & 19th Century Irvin Irish Linen

When this idea first came to me, that *the Sudarium was the swaddling cloth* of Messiah Yeshua in 2008, I began to do some research on the modern swaddling clothes that are made for the Jewish baby boys. I was deep in thought about it, wondering about *the size* of the swaddling cloth, pondering how large it would have to be in order to wrap a baby in it, when I found a wonderful Jewish website in which, lo and behold, this Jewish woman demonstrated how to make a swaddling cloth. She gave several measurements for making one as she showed the step by step instructions. I noticed that there were a few different sizes. So I decided that I would go with the measurement that she gave for the vast majority of the swaddling clothes. Almost all of them were the same size, *33 inches by 17 inches. "Great," I said to myself!* So I wrote down this measurement.

So I began to research the Sudarium, because now I wanted to know what size it was. But of course when I finally located a measurement for it, I found it was measured in centimeters. I seldom have the opportunity to use metric measurements, so the centimeters that were given for the Sudarium did not immediately mean much to me. However, I went ahead and wrote down the measurement of the Sudarium, 84cm x 53cm. Then I began searching for a cm to inches conversion chart. I truly did not expect what happened next! When I typed in the modern measurement for a Jewish baby's swaddling cloth, shock is the only thing that I can say that I felt at that moment! The measurement of the Sudarium from two thousand years ago was almost identical to the measurement of the modern Jewish swaddling cloth! The other swaddling clothes that the woman made were only slightly different from the 33" x 17" measurement. On some of the clothes on her website, the lady added a few inches in the width or she added a couple of inches to the length, depending on the needs of the mother for her new baby. The following measurement conversion shows the result.

The Sudarium measures 84cm x 53cm, which converts to 33.0708 x 20.8661 inches.
The Modern Jewish baby swaddling cloth currently measures 33 x 17 inches.

On page 674 in photographs, I demonstrated swaddling my Mother's childhood life-sized doll from the 1940's, in a cloth that is the exact measurement of the Sudarium and it worked perfectly! Incredibly, the length of *the Sudarium* was exactly and precisely the same length of the modern *Jewish swaddling cloth!* Both were 33 inches! I was floored! I was stunned beyond imagination! The only difference was in the width by a little more than three inches, but this is common, just as I witnessed on the modern Jewish swaddling clothes website. The fact that this Sudarium cloth from almost two thousand years ago is exactly the same size in length and is very close in size to the width of the modern Jewish swaddling cloth is absolutely stunning and I do not think that this is a simple coincidence!

Now the celebration of the *"life cycle"* of the new Jewish baby comes from an ancient Jewish family tradition. Although making a *swaddling cloth* was common in ancient times, it became a tradition that was almost lost. Today, however, I discovered that there are some Jewish women that are attempting to revive this joyful celebration of new life. Is it merely a coincidence, then, that Yeshua gave us *this sign of new life* in God's Royal Garden and left this cloth in the sepulchre after He came to life as a *Kadesh sign* of the Living Almond Branch Covenant of Eternal life and as *a sign* of His future wedding to Israel and the Holy Land?

As with any other family tradition, making a *swaddling cloth* was passed down from generation to generation and from mother to daughter. The community of women gathered together to help the expectant mother, prepare for her firstborn son. They all enjoyed being together, sewing and decorating the *"bris cloth."* Another interesting detail that reveals why linen would be used for wrapping a baby is that linen has the natural ability to absorb water and dries rather quickly. In the days of having no disposable diapers, linen was the perfect cloth for wrapping and swaddling a baby. Linen was, therefore, the perfect fabric for wrapping Yeshua's body that was covered in blood and sweat. *The LORD commanded that the clothing of the High Priest must be woven from fine linen, so Yeshua was wearing it!* The interesting thing that I must mention again here is the fact that *"the Sudarium piece of linen is a smooth, plain woven fabric that has a slight taffeta sheen to it, but the burial Shroud, on the other hand, has a three to one weave and has no sheen or no taffeta finish to it, although it was still considered to be a very fine piece of linen."* Any cloth that was given a taffeta finish was considered a finer piece of cloth. I was absolutely not expecting the Sudarium and the modern Jewish swaddling cloth to be almost an exact match. Nothing has yet been discovered on the Sudarium *"but the massive blood and edema fluid stain and some pin holes with life blood. The cloth had apparently been tied in a knot, due to the creases that still exist on it."* I am saying that the knot could have been put in the cloth after a baby was laid in the center of it, and it was wrapped around the baby and tied in the middle with a knot, or when it was tied as a Torah binder around a Torah scroll, or it may have been tied with a long sash. *Ironically there is a long sash (an extra piece of linen) that was sewn onto the side of Yeshua's burial Shroud, and no one knows what it was for! I made a profound connection of this long sash to the binder of the Scroll of the Law.* **(*Source: See picture- www.jewishencyclopedia.com/articles/13358-scroll-of-the-law*).** The so-called *"pin holes"* on the Sudarium may have been created when the cloth was attached to itself as it held the baby, just like a cloth diaper is pinned to itself. Another possibility is that after the swaddling band was wrapped around the Torah scroll, it was pinned to itself to secure it and to keep it from unraveling. This is something to consider. Perhaps ancient Torah letters rubbed off onto this cloth when it was wrapped around the Torah Scroll two thousand years ago in the Holy Temple! That would be fantastic! The Sudarium needs to be seriously examined again to find any faint images or letters! *"There are a few tiny spots of life blood on the Sudarium, that were shed in life, near some small pin holes."* **(*Source: The Sudarium facts ©2008 El Centro Español de Sindonologia (CES) All Rights Reserved*).** I really do wonder now if the *life blood* stains that are on the Sudarium were shed and preserved at the time of *Yeshua's circumcision on the eighth day* and not later during His crucifixion. If so, this would mean that the *life blood* stains were shed in life, and not after Yeshua's death. The remaining stains on the Sudarium were shed in death. It would also make sense that if this cloth was wrapped around a baby and pinned somehow, perhaps the *life blood* got into the pin holes *at the time of the circumcision. It is fascinating, though, that Yeshua's Covenant is the life blood Covenant and that His life blood is on the Sudarium. It is so significant that the Angel of God appeared from Heaven proclaiming this swaddling cloth was a sign for Israel!*

Remember I said they would write the name of the baby on the linen in Hebrew at the time of the *bris ceremony.* It was sewn onto another cloth and stitched to the main cloth, or it was written directly onto the piece of linen because it was an early type of *birth certificate for the family.* Sometimes decorative ribbon was even stitched onto the main piece of linen with the name of the baby on it. If it did have a backing piece to the cloth, it would have been made like a quilt or pillow case. If the family was not wealthy, however, they would simply use a plain linen cloth without any embroidery on it. Perhaps if there is something written on the Sudarium, it may not be visible to the naked eye and we should use the Leon Levy Technology on it. It very well may have faded over time. I am speculating now, but perhaps this piece was removed and the backing removed and half of it was kept by the mother. Perhaps it never had the name placed upon it, but that would be surprising since this was the KING Messiah of Israel and since the Angel Gabriel told Mary exactly what to name her baby. It is worth investigating this cloth with the new technology to determine if there is anything more to this cloth because it still has not been investigated as much as the Shroud.

I noticed in a photograph that the Sudarium appears to have a small tear in the cloth from the top on the right hand side. A tear in a garment is a Jewish sign of mourning, known as, *"Kriah"* in Hebrew. The tearing or cutting of the garment is a deep outward expression of grief at the loss of a loved one. There are also seven days of mourning in Judaism called *"sitting in Shiva."* Maybe these seven days correspond to the last seven years of mourning for the Messiah until He comes. The last seven years is the time of the great tribulation, the time of Jacob's trouble. We may never know the answer to it, but I wondered in my heart if Yeshua's mother Mary tore the *swaddling cloth* garment in her anguish, as she mourned and grieved her loss, although one usually tears the garment that they are wearing over the heart. *Ironically though, this was God's Eternal Covenant of the heart, through His Living Torah Testimony as our Saviour and Messiah with His Life blood!*

Another fact to consider about the Sudarium and the Shroud containing *Yeshua's life blood* is the simple fact that Jewish Law itself demands that *"the entire body should be buried together, and that they do not embalm because the blood is discarded with embalming." Instead, they are to bury the body with the blood.* So it makes sense that if Yeshua's face cloth was indeed *His Jewish bris swaddling cloth* containing *His life blood* stains on it, then the whole of Yeshua's body was in fact buried together in His sepulchre to fulfill this Jewish Law.

I was able to verify through a source in Israel that the *swaddling cloth* can definitely be used as part of the burial Shroud in a Jewish burial as I said before. It is actually a tradition that some Jewish people say they would like to revive in our generation!

White Bridal flowers Photo ©2013 Kimberly K Ballard All rights Reserved

Now the words of the traditional Jewish blessing that is spoken over *the first born son* as he is dedicated at the Temple are astonishingly profound. The swaddling cloth is always with the baby at this dedication ceremony. When you read this blessing, think of the fact that this *Kadesh* cloth was left in the sepulchre by Messiah Yeshua, *the Living Torah,* after he was raised to life and that it was found wrapped together in a place by itself, I believe, *as a sign that He is the Bridegroom who will marry Israel.* You will be profoundly shocked when you see this blessing!

The Sudarium of Oviedo Spain Official Photograph

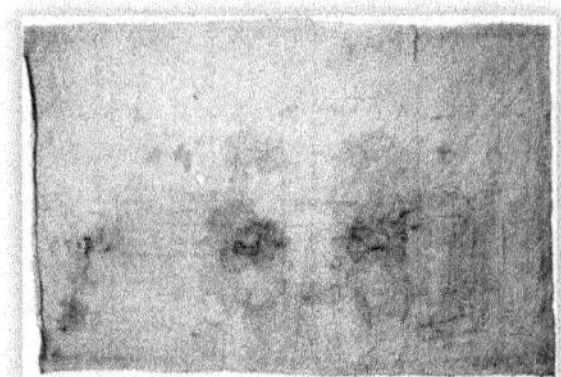

The blessing literally says;

ה' יגדלהו לתורה ולחופה ולמעשים טובים אמן

"May God raise him up to a life of Torah, a successful marriage, and good deeds, Amen."

When I saw this blessing, I was completely shocked and stunned! I will tell you why this Jewish blessing is so incredibly significant, as the baby is dedicated in His *swaddling cloth.* Remember that when the Jewish disciples came to Yeshua's sepulchre, they found the Sudarium that was about His head, not lying with the linen clothes, but wrapped together in a place by itself. When the other disciple entered the tomb it says that *"he saw and believed."* Then it says something that is very exciting in regards to this Jewish blessing, *"For as yet they knew not the Scripture that He must rise again from the dead."* The blessing over the baby in the swaddling cloth says, *"May God raise him up to a life of Torah, a successful marriage and good deeds." Yeshua was raised up to life as the Living Torah, the Bridegroom of Israel, full of good deeds!* I believe that the minute that this Jewish disciple *"saw and believed," it was because he suddenly understood the meaning of the Living Covenant of the Messiah's future marriage to Israel.* You must keep in mind that this cloth had the blessing said over it as it was bound around Yeshua, *the Living Torah,* who was then lifted up and dedicated to God's good deeds during His baby dedication ceremony! *This Jewish disciple must have had the chills, when He suddenly saw the Sudarium set apart as Kadesh, having a Higher sacred purpose. I believe that he suddenly realized that this swaddling cloth was the sign that Yeshua was the Heavenly Ark and the Almond Rod of God that would be raised up to life as the Living Torah. This was a future marriage proposal that was sealed by the KING OF KINGS in His own life blood of the Covenant, in God's Garden in Holy Mount Moriah in Jerusalem! The Sudarium that was Yeshua's swaddling cloth was, therefore, the sign of the LORD'S promise to marry Israel in the future and that is why it was left in a place by itself!* Only the LORD'S *life blood* could atone for our sins! *Remember that Yeshua had previously revealed to these two disciples, John and Simon Peter, the vision of His glory on Mount Sinai and was giving them the keys of the Kingdom of Heaven. They were eyewitnesses of the LORD'S Majesty when He revealed on Mount Sinai that He is the Living Ark of the Heavenly Covenant and everything it contains.* Remember that they were instructed to *"tell no man the vision until Yeshua was raised from the dead." At that time they questioned what "rising from the dead meant!"* The fact is that, even up to the point of entering the empty sepulchre, the Jewish disciples *still* did not understand this saying that, *"He must rise again from the dead," until they saw the Kadesh swaddling cloth and the linen burial Shroud. God had raised Him up, fulfilling the bris blessing as He gave us Eternal life! It is the most stunning piece of the LORD'S Testimony that is now revealed!* ***(Sources: "Wimpeln, or Ashkenazic binders, birth of a male child. Wonderful illuminated letters (painted or embroidered) with animals often described the wish that the boy be raised to a life of Torah, Chuppah (wedding) and good deeds." ©2011 kolel.org/torahstory/module1/mantles.html) AND ("Life-cycle events-whether personal or historical-are always seen as circular in Weisberg's work. Ends engender new beginnings, as with the Torah binder itself, which is made from the fabric, used to swaddle a newborn boy in the circumcision (bris) ceremony and often employed as a funeral shroud at life's end." Excerpt taken from: ©2011 artscenecal.com/Announcements/0407/Skirball0407b.html).***

Mark 9:9-10 *And as they came down from the Mountain, He charged them that they should tell no man what things they had seen, till the Son of man were risen from the dead. And they kept that saying within themselves, questioning one with another the rising from the dead should mean.*

John 20:4-9 *So they ran both together; and the other disciple did outrun Peter, and came first to the sepulchre. And he stooping down, and looking in, saw the linen clothes lying; yet went he not in. Then cometh Simon Peter* *following him, and went into the sepulchre, and seeth the linen clothes lie, And the napkin, that was about His head, not lying with the linen clothes, but wrapped together in a place by itself. Then went in also that other disciple, which came first to the sepulchre, and he saw, and believed. For as yet they knew not the Scripture, that He must rise again from the dead.*

Notice in this Scripture that just after Simon Peter observed *the head covering in a separate place,* the other disciple John came in to look at it and when he saw it, something clicked and they suddenly understood the saying that, *"He must rise again to life!"* This incredible truth has been hidden throughout the centuries! It is astonishing! Yeshua paid the Bride's price at His Last Passover Seder. *He said that this cup of wine, that represented His life blood, was the Covenant that He sealed with His Bride with His loving heart.* Yeshua, *the Living Torah,* also said that He would not drink again of this cup of wine at the Passover Seder until He drinks it again with His Bride in the Eternal Kingdom of God, when Israel says, *"Blessed is He who comes in the Name of the LORD," which in Hebrew is "Baruch Haba B'shem Adonai,"* and they will be singing this in the Passover Hallel!

Luke 5:35 *But the days will come when the Bridegroom will be taken away from them; then they will fast in those days.*

Mark 2:19 *And Yeshua said to them, Can the friends of the Bridegroom fast while the Bridegroom is with them? As long as they have the Bridegroom with them they cannot fast.*

If this Sudarium that was used for the Messiah's burial was just a bloody cloth, it would not have been removed from the Shroud linen and it would not have been put in a *separate* location *by the risen Jewish Saviour, who was about to give us a continuous life cycle!* The linen that was on the face would have remained in the same location with the burial Shroud if it was meaningless. There would be no reason to put it in a place by itself. There would be no reason to write an account that they found it lying by itself and *they suddenly understood what the words meant, "That He must rise from the dead," and that they, "Saw and believed."* The fact is that someone moved it and set it in a place by itself in order for it to be found and observed *because it was the sign of the life Covenant of the Bridegroom of Israel!* I am absolutely convinced of this and you will understand why I can boldly state this as a fact when you read the final segment of this chapter! *The disciples made the connection to what they witnessed on Mount Sinai at Yeshua's transfiguration, that Yeshua was indeed the LORD God of Israel! I thank the LORD for giving me all of these Divine revelations!*

Now as I was stating earlier, in the Middle Ages, the so-called Saints of Messiah Yeshua or Jesus wore a wimple and it covered the head of the pious person. This cloth was usually made of fine linen or silk with a taffeta sheen. I personally believe that they started this tradition from a significant event that had to do with the Messiah of Israel. I believe that only several hundred years after Yeshua's resurrection, they knew that the swaddling cloth was the cloth on the head of the Jewish Messiah and that was found in the sepulchre as *a sign* of the Living Covenant. Yeshua the KING had humbled Himself. I believe this is where the Saints got the idea to wear this cloth over their head in humility and call it a *"wimple,"* which is the same as saying *"a swaddling cloth." In my opinion, the Sudarium was, without a doubt, the swaddling cloth of the Jewish KING Messiah.* Looking at the definition of the word wimple, we see the following facts.

Wimple: *(plural wimples), head covering, a veil, Wimpel.1. A cloth which usually covers the head and is worn around the neck and chin. It was worn by women in medieval Europe and is still worn by nuns in certain orders.*
2. A fold or pleat in cloth.
3. A ripple, as on the surface of water.

4. A curve or bend. ***(Source: The Random House College Dictionary, ©1975 by Random House Inc. United States, NY).***
"A Wimple is a Torah Binder, which is a swaddling cloth that is used for a first born Jewish baby boy and is later used to Bind a Torah Scroll." ***(Source: Torah Binder – ©2013 thejewishmuseum.org/glossary).***

Clearly the wimple was known as a *veil.* We are told in the Gospel accounts that the veil is taken away in Messiah. When we understand the veil and the wimple, then we understand God's Divine plan of Salvation and future marriage! We also explored the fact that the *veil* is a hidden part of the design detail in the Almond Branches of the Holy Menorah for the Holy Temple. *God has been hiding His face until the time of the end. Then Israel will see Him as He is face to face in the face of Messiah! What a great and blessed day this will be, and very soon I hope, because this KING truly loves them forever and ever!*

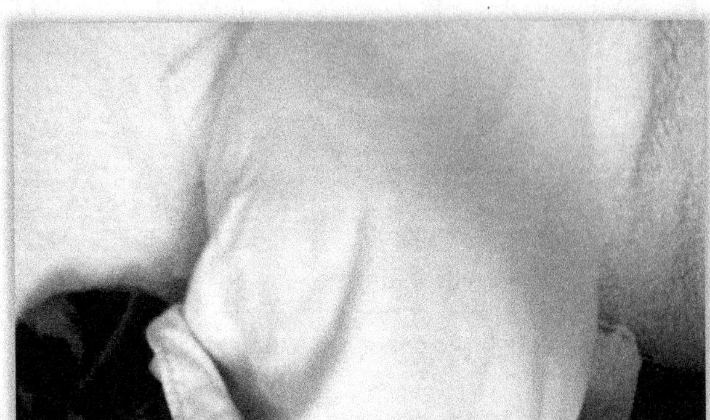

The 33" x 20" swaddling cloth that is the same size as the Sudarium, that was swaddling the life sized baby doll, is now wrapped around my head and face to roughly demonstrate how the Sudarium of Messiah Yeshua, was wrapped around His head in His burial and was Yeshua's infant swaddling cloth, The Jewish Bris Cloth of the circumcision. My nose creates a raised ridge going down toward my neck. As you can see there is plenty of fabric to fit completely around my head.
Demonstration Photo ©2013 Kimberly K Ballard All Rights Reserved

Isaiah 59:2 *But your iniquities have separated you from your God; And your sins have hidden His face from you, so that He will not hear.*

II Corinthians 3:14-16 *But their minds were blinded; for until this day remaineth the same veil untaken away in the reading of the Old Testament; which veil is done away in Messiah. But even unto this day, when Moses is read, the veil is upon their heart. Nevertheless when it shall turn to the LORD, the veil shall be taken away.*

When their hearts turn to the LORD, this veil is taken away to see that He is Messiah Yeshua, the Eternal KING OF KINGS AND LORD OF LORDS!

I was shocked that the word *"wimples"* is actually written in the King James Version of the Bible in Isaiah 3:22.

Isaiah 3:18-23 *In that day the LORD will take away the bravery of their tinkling ornaments about their feet, and their cauls, and their round tires like the moon, The chains, and the bracelets, and the mufflers, The bonnets, and the ornaments of the legs, and the headbands, and the tablets, and the earrings, The rings, and nose jewels, The changeable suits of apparel, and the mantles, and the wimples, and the crisping pins, the glasses, and the fine linen, and the hoods, and the veils.*

The LORD also mentions *the swaddling band* at creation. This is written in the book of Job. Some consider Job to be one of the oldest books in the Bible.

Job 38:9 *When I made the cloud the garment thereof, and thick darkness a swaddling band for it.*

After writing this through God's revelation blessing and Divine Providence, an unbelievable miracle has happened and now I must write this update! I had already written this section a long time ago and I was doing more research as I was editing it. It was at this point that the LORD showed me the Jewish Priestly Angel at the Garden tomb. Then I ran across an ancient letter that was written by *King Philip of the Romans.* He had sealed this letter in the year 1205. *Within this letter, the King had listed the relics that were taken from the LORD'S sepulchre in Jerusalem.* These items had been taken and housed in Constantinople in the Great

Church. The King had listed among the relics from the LORD'S sepulchre, *"The Stone rolled away and the Shroud of Yeshua."* These were both in the Hagia Sophia Church before it was sacked in the year 1204 by the Latin Crusaders. The most astonishing truth, however, was presented to me at this time. You can imagine how I felt when I saw that the King had written in his letter that, *"the swaddling clothes of Messiah Yeshua were also kept inside the huge ancient Church in Constantinople with the Shroud of Yeshua and with His Great Rolling Stone that the Angel of the LORD had rolled away."* Now the stone is facing God's Garden from Mount Nebo like an opened door! Keep in mind that the King said, *"swaddling clothes."* He did not use the word *"Sudarium."* The word *"Sudarium"* is *a Latin word for "napkin,"* and the Latin crusaders are the ones that sacked Constantinople and took the relics in the fourth crusade! So I believe now that they changed the name of the *swaddling clothes* of Messiah Yeshua at this time and began calling this linen cloth *"The Sudarium" as soon as they took it away to Spain, where it remains today in Oviedo. It is still called by this Latin name!* The word *"Sudarium"* in Latin comes from another word *"Sudor," meaning "sweat."* Finding this truth of the existence of the *swaddling cloth* of Yeshua, long after I wrote all of this by the power of the Holy Spirit, was absolutely, unbelievably astonishing! It was again as if the LORD was providing me with the most miraculous verification of everything that He had impressed my heart to write about, concerning His beautiful Living Testimony.

When I found the King's letter that was written in 1205, I knew for certain that the words that the LORD had given my heart to write about *the Sudarium and the swaddling cloth* of Messiah Yeshua were completely and profoundly correct. The *swaddling clothes* of Messiah Yeshua had been kept with the relics from the LORD'S sepulchre in Jerusalem, along with the Shroud bearing His image! *Now we know for certain that the "Sudarium" is, without a doubt, Messiah Yeshua's swaddling cloth, His Jewish bris cloth of the Eternal Jewish life Covenant.* It was taken to Spain in the silver Ark, while the Shroud was taken to Italy by the Romans. ***(Source: Letter from King Philip of the Romans Crusades-Encyclopedia Gunther von Pairis' Historia Constantinopolitana listing the relics stolen by Abbot Martin during the Sack of Constantinople in 1204. Gunther, ch. xxiv, in Riant: Exuviae, Vol. 1, p. 120 ff).***

When Baldwin II, the Latin Emperor at Constantinople, sent 22 relics from Constantinople to his relative Louis IX of France between 1239 and 1242, he sent among these relics *"the Crown of Thorns as the most valuable, a piece of the cross, blood of Messiah, the nappies of the infant Jesus/Yeshua, another piece of the cross, the stone from the tomb and many other relics."* ***(Source: ©2011 Shroud.com).*** This letter referred to the *"nappies"* of the infant Yeshua and I soon discovered that the word *"nappies"* is a French word referring specifically to a *"swaddling cloth!"* The word *"nappies"* is also considered *"to be a reference to a rectangular cloth diaper for an infant."* I believe this term *"nappies"* is also common in England. It is very clear then, that this *Sudarium* was indeed the rectangular linen cloth that once was the Jewish bris cloth of Messiah Yeshua! I thank the LORD God for His goodness in verifying His Eternal Testimony to me!

I was then able to ascertain from Barrie M. Schwortz, the official Shroud Photographer and friend, that the earliest known date for the Shroud of Turin was the year 1349. Barrie stated the following to me in an email about the Shroud, *"The earliest documented date without any interruption in the chain of custody occurs in 1349. See our Shroud History page for details. Of course, this does not take the Hungarian Pray Codex into consideration which is dated circa 1191. Before that, we have to deal with legends and stories about the burial Shroud of Jesus "not made by human hands" that was possibly displayed in Edessa and Constantinople. Unfortunately, we don't have a complete history of the Shroud from the 1st century."* ***(Source: Quote from Barrie M. Schwortz The Official Shroud Photographer & Shroud expert – Shroud.com).***

Now the reason why I asked Barrie Schwortz for this date of the Shroud is because in my own research, I ran across the following translation of a mid-tenth century Byzantine military document that recorded the existence of not only *Yeshua's infant swaddling cloth, but also gave a reference to the existence of the "God-bearing winding sheet" as recorded in the year 958 AD. If the Shroud was Yeshua's death certificate and the Sudarium was Yeshua's ancient birth certificate, then both burial clothes completed the Jewish life cycle of KING Messiah Yeshua, the LORD God of Israel!*

Quote: *"The Byzantine military excerpts of the Dramatic Byzantine victory of Constantine VII, over Saif ad-Dawla at Raban were translated as follows; "Evidently the harangue worked, but to ensure victory, Constantine had sought the prayers of holy men and monks throughout the empire, and dispatched to the army "holy water," which emanated from the most holy relics. The relics from which water was gathered are enumerated, and provide an extremely interesting list of the relics of the Passion gathered in Constantinople. The list begins, as was meet in a Military context, which the true Cross, for it was this relic which supplanted the symbolic cross, as seen by the first Constantine, as the harbinger of Byzantine victory; "Behold that after drawing holy water from the immaculate and most sacred relics of the Passion of Christ our true God – from the precious wooden fragments of the true Cross and the undefiled lance, the precious titulus, the wonder-working reed, the life-giving blood which flowed from His precious rib, the most sacred tunic, the holy swaddling clothes, the God bearing winding sheet, and the other relics of His undefiled Passion – we have sent it to be sprinkled upon you to be anointed by it and to garb yourself with the Divine Power from on High."* ***(Source Quote; Copyright ©2003 December 8 Paul Stephenson homepage.mac.com/paulstephenson/military_texts.html original full translations ©2003 Byzantine Author Eric McGeer; literary activities and preoccupations; texts and translations dedicated to the memory of Nicolas Oikonomides, ed. J. Nesbitt, The Medieval Mediterranean 46 (Leiden, 2003). ©1993 Dennis G., "Religious services in the Byzantine Army," in Eulogema. Studies in Honor of Robert Taft (Rome 1993) = Studia Anselmiana 110 (1993), pp. 107-17, for references to texts and editions).***

This second record, dating to the year 958 AD, verifies that Messiah Yeshua's infant swaddling cloth of the Jewish bris life blood Covenant and the linen burial Shroud *bearing His image as the God of Israel existed even before the year 958AD, because it was housed for almost a thousand years before this date in Constantinople.* This means that it had to have come directly from Jerusalem to this location soon after Yeshua's departure, and was kept there all that time until the crusades! *I believe that now the KING OF KINGS wants the world to know that this Eternal promise is for Israel.* We can all come to the LORD and believe in Him. All of us can come to live with the KING of glory forever in His Garden called *"Heaven!"* This is the greatest blessing that I have ever found in my life! Thank you my glorious KING!

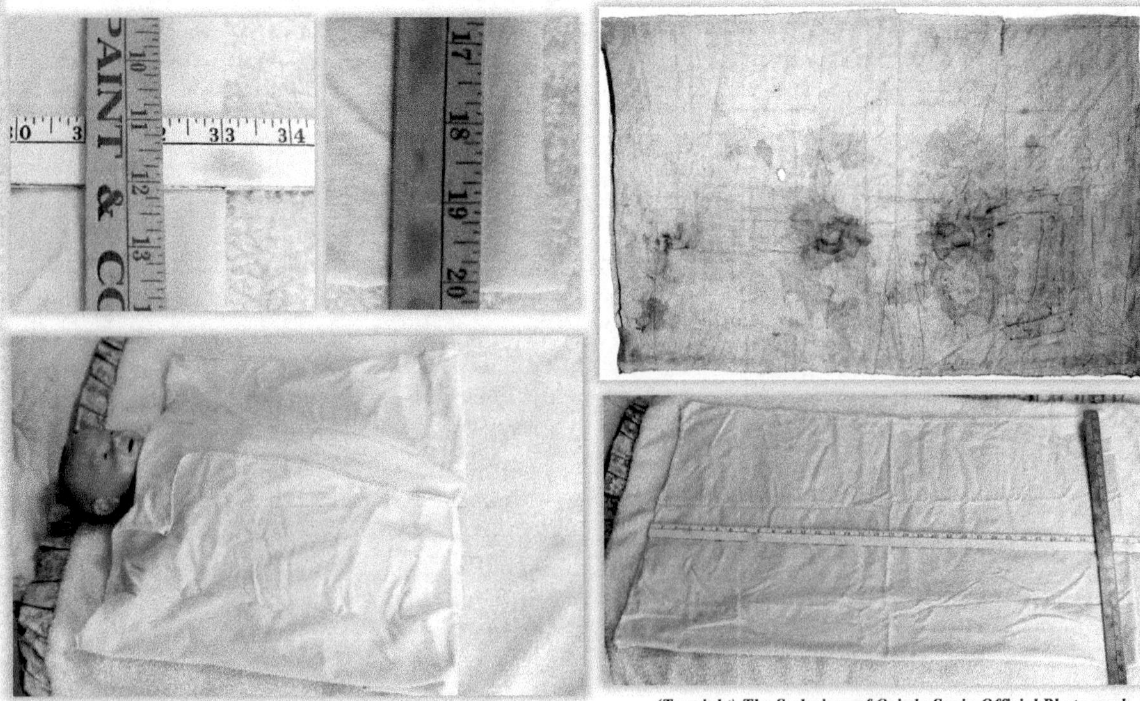

33x20 inches swaddling demonstration same size as the Sudarium And lower right Photos ©2013 Kimberly K Ballard All Rights Reserved

(Top right) The Sudarium of Oviedo Spain Official Photograph ©2013 El Centro Español de Sindonologia (CES) All Rights Reserved

Pistacia lentiscus ©2006+ (Ed) A. Danin Jerusalem Israel All Rights Reserved

PISTACIA lENTISCUS ON YESHUA'S BURIAL SHROUD

Pistacia lentiscus ©2006+ (Ed.) A. Danin Jerusalem Israel All Rights Reserved

Yeshua's linen burial Shroud, not only bears His image, it also bears the faint images of flowers and certain plant species, that bloom only in Jerusalem, around the time of Passover. There was one particular plant that was identified on the Shroud, but the reason why this particular plant was placed upon Messiah Yeshua's Shroud has never been determined. I believe that the Holy Spirit gave me an answer to this mystery, and so I decided to write about it because the topic of my book has to do with Messiah, *"The Branch."* Dr. Avinoam Danin, Professor Emeritus of Botany at the Hebrew University of Jerusalem Israel, discovered images of a plant called *"Pistacia lentiscus"* on the Shroud of Turin. I was not going to write anything about this until I discovered a connection between Messiah Yeshua and this specific plant species. Based upon my own research, I now believe that I know why Dr. Danin found the Pistacia lentiscus on the Shroud of Yeshua and I would like to share it!

Pistacia lentiscus ©2006+ (Ed) A. Danin Jerusalem Israel All Rights Reserved

The first thing that I discovered in my research is the fact that the *Pistacia lentiscus* plant appears to be identified by many Scholars as the *"Baka" or "Bakha,"* that is written in the Bible. So as I studied the Interlinear Hebrew Bible, I found that this plant is mentioned in four places in the Bible. In Hebrew, this word is rendered and written as *"bekhaim"* and as *"habbekaim."* Although the Hebrew Bible connects it to the Balsam Tree, it was translated as the *"Mulberry Tree"* in the English King James Bible. *It has also been translated as the "Pistacia" or "Terebinth tree."* It is interesting, though, that a few Scholars believe it may refer to a species of the Acacia family. The Hebrew *"Bekaim"* is found in the following chapters and verses in the Bible. ***(Source: Baca; ©2010 biblehub.com/topical/b/baca.htm ©International Standard Bible Encyclopedia, Willis J. Beecher Terebinth or Pistacia ©2010 lajupaulk3.blogspot.com).***

Pistacia lentiscus ©2006+ (Ed) A. Danin Jerusalem Israel All Rights Reserved

II Samuel 5:23 "bekaim,"
II Samuel 5:24 "habbekaim,"
I Chronicles 14:14 "habbekaim,"
I Chronicles 14:15 "habbekaim,"

King David was instructed by the LORD go forth into battle only when He heard the sound of marching in the tops of the *"Bekaim trees."* The LORD was leading *the way* before His Heavenly Army. He would go before David into battle as the Royal military Standard, the Rod of God. This connects the *Pistacia* to Messiah Yeshua.

In Strong's Concordance, the *Bekaim* plant is written as, *"Baka."* #1056 **Baka,** weeping, Baca, a valley in Palestine. #1057 the same as 1056. The weeping tree.

(Some gum distilling tree, perhaps the Balsam or Mulberry.) #1058 **Bakah**, a primary root; to weep, general to bemoan, bewail, complain, and make lamentation. x more, mourn, x sore, x with tears, weep. #1059 Bekeh, from 1058, a weeping, x sore. ***(Source: ©1995 Strong's Exhaustive Concordance).***

There are various accounts that record that *"The weeping of the Baka or Bekaim, refers to the tears of pale yellow resin that exude from this so called 'mastic plant' when cuts are made in its branches."* So the Pistacia lentiscus that is identified with the *"Bekhaim"* in the Bible is said to *"make a sad weeping noise when the plant is walked on and its branches are broken. The sad weeping refers to the tears of resin that exude out from a broken branch, after it has been stepped on, cut and crushed under foot."* **(Source: ©2011 en.wikipedia.org/wiki/Pistacia_lentiscus).** This statement is not simply referring to crying. It is specifically referring to beating the breast in extreme lamentation, combined with extreme bitterness, wailing, and moaning. It is severe grief from a deeply wounded broken heart, where the soul is profoundly afflicted. The Prophet Jeremiah lamented the destruction of Jerusalem and the Holy Temple of God. The book of Lamentations is poetic lament over its destruction.

Now I believe from this truth, that the Pistacia lentiscus was laid upon Messiah Yeshua's linen burial Shroud *because Yeshua, "The Branch," was broken and crushed for our transgressions. He was bruised and cut by the Roman flagrum and lance for our iniquities.* Messiah Yeshua was *trampled underfoot* by the Roman Soldiers. So the people in Jerusalem *beat their breasts in extreme lamentation* after His death by crucifixion, and they cried out in pain shedding great tears in mourning because their hearts were very heavy and burdened. This is why I decided to write about the unexpected connection that I found in the Pistacia lentiscus. I believe in my heart this is the precise reason that renown Botany expert Professor Emeritus, Dr. Avinoam Danin in Jerusalem Israel, from the Hebrew University, who was very kind to me and helped me with his photographs and friendship, found the Pistacia lentiscus impressions and images all over Yeshua's linen burial Shroud image. Now I can Biblically prove that the *"Bekhaim"* which is *"The Great Lamentation"* is, in fact, connected to Yeshua's crucifixion because it is written in Luke's Gospel.

Pistacia lentiscus ©2006+ (Ed.) A. Danin, Jerusalem Israel All Rights Reserved

Luke 23:26-27 *And as they led Him away, they laid hold upon one Simon, a Cyrenian, coming out of the country, and on him they laid the cross, that he might bear it after Yeshua. And there followed Him a great company of people, and of women, which also bewailed and lamented Him. But Yeshua turning unto them said, Daughters of Jerusalem, weep not for me, but weep for yourselves, and for your children.*

It is written *that the people smote their breasts* after they beheld the events of Yeshua's crucifixion. They understood that He was Righteous after all! Yeshua had told the daughters of Israel to weep for their children (Luke 23:28). He warned them destruction was soon coming to the Second Holy Temple of God. In forty years it came to pass, and later came the Diaspora.

Luke 23:47-49 *Now when the Centurion saw what was done, he glorified God, saying, Certainly this was a righteous man. And all the people that came together to that sight, beholding the things which were done, smote their breasts, and returned. And all His acquaintance, and the women that followed Him from Galilee, stood afar off, beholding these things.*

Now it is interesting that the Interlinear Bible uses the Greek words *"ekoptonto"* for *"Mourning"* and *"ethrenoun"* for *"Lamentation."* The words are further defined in Strong's Concordance from the primary root words *"kopto" and "threneo."* #2875 **kopto**, a primary verb; "to chop;" specifically to beat the breast in grief; Cut down, lament, mourn, bewail. Comp. the base of #5114. (Tomoteros), comparative of der. Of the primary temno (to cut, more comprehensive or decisive than 2875, as if by a single stroke; whereas that implies repeated blows, like hacking); more keen-sharper. #2354 **threneo** from 2355; to bewail. - lament, mourn. #2355, threnos; from the base of 2360; wailing, lamentation. ***(Source: ©1995 Strong's Exhaustive Concordance).***

From these descriptive words, we have proof that Messiah Yeshua, *"The Branch,"* was *"cut off as by a single stroke!" The Branch was chopped off from the land of the living!* Yeshua sustained *repeated blows* during the entire crucifixion process, especially during His scourging where His flesh was repeated *hacked* by the Roman flagrum. *So the people wailed and beat their breasts in great lamentation shedding tears like the resin that exudes out from the branches of the Pistacia lentiscus when Messiah, the Branch, was crushed underfoot and cut off from Israel.* Through these actions, *the Rod of God, the Branch from the Tree of Life,* dripped His life-giving blood from the cuts in His flesh, and it fell to the ground on Holy Mount Moriah like the latter rain, giving us the Living Water from Heaven. Therefore, we can only conclude, without a doubt, that the *Pistacia lentiscus* has a direct connection to Messiah Yeshua who became *"The Branch cut off"* from the Almond Tree of Life, and the evidence was discovered in the images of *Pistacia lentiscus* found all over the image of the Shroud of Turin by Botany Professor Emeritus from the Hebrew University in Jerusalem, Dr. Avinoam Danin, who I would like to thank for his photographs and friendship! The people continued to mourn, but a miracle happened! The Almond Rod that was cut off suddenly came to life and changed the whole course of history on Nisan 17. The First Fruit from the Almond Tree of Life that was in God's Garden was offered to us on the third day on the LORD'S Feast of First Fruits, so that we could eat this Fruit and live forever! The profound significance of the *Pistacia lentiscus* must not be overlooked. It is now proven to be directly connected to Messiah Yeshua and to lamenting His death in extreme lamentation. Yeshua's burial Shroud also has another detail.

Now I would like to discuss the L shaped or right angle *"poker holes"* that are burned into the linen burial Shroud. On the Shroud of Turin, the LORD showed me that the four L-shaped *"poker holes"* could be the Greek letter *"Gamma."* Much to my astonishment, I found that the same four Gamma letters were discovered on some ancient Jewish linens that were found at Masada and they were dated before 73 AD and before the destruction of Jerusalem and the Holy Temple of the LORD. *I discovered that the four Greek Gamma's or right angles were placed on ancient Jewish clothing for religious purposes.* So the four L-shaped burn holes on Yeshua's burial Shroud could in fact pertain to the four horns of the altar of the LORD, as the LORD God provided Himself *"The Lamb"* which is the Living Torah sheepskin containing the Word of God whose flesh healed us as the Rod of God was lifted up. The Living Torah or Saviour's blanket did bind up our wounds! This is the LORD God, the true Heavenly Ark, that brings us liberty on Holy Mount Moriah! The letter *"Gamma"* is the third letter of the Greek alphabet and it is parallel to the third Hebrew letter *"Gimel,"* and both correspond to the resurrection of Messiah Yeshua on the third day as our First Fruit from the Almond Tree of Life. It is a great discovery that the four letters together actually stood for *"resurrection and for everlasting life,"* and this is what Yeshua accomplished for us! It is also said that the *four*

Gammas spell the Tetragrammaton or the four letters of the sacred Name of God from Mount Sinai and, according to Jewish Pastor Mark Biltz of Bonney Lake Washington, the name of God YHVH, in the ancient Hebrew picture language, reveals *an arm, with two windows and a nail.* Luke 1:68-69 says that *the LORD God of Israel* has visited and redeemed His people and *has raised up a horn of salvation for us in the house of His servant David!* In Habakkuk 3:3-4 it is written that God came and His glory covered the earth. His brightness was as *the light; He had horns coming out of His hand: and there was the hiding of His power*! The *horns* on Yeshua's burial Shroud proclaim He is the *hand* of God resurrected by His *power and light!*

THE EARLIEST HISTORY OF THE SHROUD AND THE SUDARIUM FROM THE GARDEN TOMB

Stacked Library Books Photo ©2013 Kimberly K Ballard All Rights Reserved

The Garden tomb sepulchre was covered over with dirt and debris for about 1900 years before it was unearthed and rediscovered in 1867. This places the tomb in the hands of the original Jewish disciples of Yeshua, up through the three Jewish revolts against the Roman siege of Jerusalem and then it was covered up for centuries. The history is quite complex, so I will try to make this as short as possible and share each detail, as the LORD revealed it to my heart and I have verified it from the historical records.

I wanted to discern exactly why the Garden tomb on Mount Moriah, was determined to be the true location of Yeshua's burial place after His crucifixion. The first thing that happened was that I ran across an old article that said *"There were two graves that were found on the hill right above Yeshua's Garden tomb."* Now these two extremely significant graves were said in this article to be, *"on the plateau above the low cliff and behind the wall, just above the Garden tomb, in an area owned by the St. Stephen's Church that sits among the ruins of earlier structures."* This cemetery was also said to be from the Byzantine era and it is located almost immediately above the Garden tomb of Yeshua. The earlier ruins that were found in this location included the archaeological discovery of this *ancient Jewish cemetery.* After finding this history, I was able to verify by Simon Brown of England UK, who had been to this location in

This photo shows the layout above the Garden Tomb
The fence is on the plateau, the low cliff above Yeshua's sepulchre
And the cemetery is behind the people
Photo provided by ©2011 Simon Brown England
All Rights Reserved

Jerusalem, that there is indeed a very ancient Jewish cemetery just above the Garden Tomb. Now some of the gravestones have been damaged and the writing has been erased from them. So this is either due to extreme age, or it is due to some deliberate destruction that has occurred on top of the hill of Golgotha. The article that I ran across also stated, that one of these graves was inscribed with the words, *"Buried near his LORD."* The other tomb was inscribed with the words, *"Onesimus, Deacon of the Church of the Witnesses of the Resurrection."* ***(Source: Both Quotes ©1983 John A. Tvedtnes, "The Garden Tomb," Ensign, April 1983, 8).***

A cropped close up of the cemetery above the Garden Tomb
Photo provided by ©2011 Simon Brown England
All Rights Reserved & Edited by Kimberly K Ballard

The fact that the graves bearing these inscriptions were directly above and so close to the Garden tomb provided proof that this was definitely the true location of the resurrection of Messiah Yeshua. This person, *"Onesimus," had to be a friend of the eyewitnesses of the resurrection of Messiah Yeshua.* After I found this incredible surprise, this led me to my next discovery.

I soon discovered in my Bible that *Onesimus* was one of the *Seventy* Apostles that were directly appointed by Messiah Yeshua to go before His face, preaching the Good News of the Kingdom of God. *Onesimus did have an important Biblical history.* He was verified to be a servant of Philemon, who was the Bishop of Gaza. So Philemon went to Rome and he visited the Apostle Paul, who was imprisoned at the time. *Onesimus* became a believer in the Jewish Messiah because of the Apostle Paul. The book of Philemon in the New Testament is actually Paul's letter to Philemon, regarding the acceptance and forgiveness of *Onesimus* who had fled from him as his servant, which was like stealing from Philemon, before turning from his sins and becoming a follower of the Jewish Messiah Yeshua. The historical dates for *Onesimus* as a Bishop are written in the annals of history from the year 60-61 AD. *He died in the year 68 AD.* So *Onesimus* is written in the book of Philemon and he is also found in the book of Colossians 4:9 in the New Testament. Yeshua appointed *the Seventy Apostles* in the Gospel of Luke in the following passage. ***(Source: The History of Onesimus ©2011 ec-patr.org/list/index.php?lang=en&id=3) AND (©2011 en.wikipedia.org/wiki/Onesimus) AND (©2011 patriarchate.org/patriarchate/former-patriarchs/Onesimus).***

Luke 10:1 *After these things the LORD appointed other Seventy also, and sent them two and two before His face into every city and place, whither He Himself would come.*

Now the next thing that I should mention is the fact that in the year 66 AD the first Jewish revolt against the Romans took place in Jerusalem. In the year 70 AD the Romans besieged Jerusalem and they burned the Holy Temple to the ground and destroyed Jerusalem. This event, in and of itself, was an incredible story of destruction of the worst kind. Then from the year 81 AD onward, there was great persecution of the Christians in Jerusalem and they were mostly Jewish. At the time of the siege of Jerusalem by the Romans, beginning in the year 66 AD but particularly at the time of the destruction of the Holy Temple in 70 AD, the Jewish believers in the Messiah Yeshua began fleeing Jerusalem. There is a historical account of these events as they unfolded and it was written by *Cornelius Tacitus, who was a historian of the Roman Empire from 56–117 AD.* He wrote a detailed account of the destruction of Jerusalem and the Holy Temple. In his book *"The Works of Cornelius Tacitus," in book 5, on page 515,* Tacitus wrote the following words. *"The Christians who resided in the City of Jerusalem, finding that Titus was approaching at the head of his army, knew their time to depart. They saw according to the warning given to them by Christ Himself, that desolation was nigh and a commanded fled to the mountains. The first impression was made on Salem the lower City on the Northwest side of Jerusalem."* Then on page 519 Tacitus wrote; *"The Temple of Solomon burned in the year of the world 3416, before Christ, 587 Nebuchadnezzar."* ***(Source: ©1864-1877 The Works of Tacitus, translated by Alfred John Church and William Jackson Brodribb).***

So Tacitus tells us that the Jewish believers in Messiah Yeshua that were in Jerusalem did flee to the mountains when they saw that Jerusalem was about to be surrounded by Titus and his Roman legions. As the first Jewish Christians fled Jerusalem, they would have gathered and taken their own personal belongings and, at some point, taken the precious treasures from the LORD'S sepulchre in order to secure and protect them. These were the treasures of the LORD'S Testimony and, because of the great destruction that was about to come upon the city of Jerusalem and the historical Biblical sites, they preserved them. So the question that I was trying to answer was, *"How did the Great Rolling Stone from Yeshua's Garden tomb wind up on the top of Mount Nebo?"* What was the history of it? Mount Nebo is near the place where Joshua crossed into the Promised Land and where John Baptized Yeshua. The Sudarium was said to have been found in a cave near this location near Jericho. So the question is, *"Did they take the Great Rolling Stone from Yeshua's sepulchre somewhere for safe keeping before Jerusalem was completely obliterated?"* The Jewish people, who believed in Yeshua as their Messiah, were dispersed and they went into many surrounding cities. Some left in ships and sailed towards the other surrounding countries. The Gospel was preached outside of Jerusalem as we see in the book of Acts. One of the main areas where they traveled to preach the Gospel was to Asia Minor. *Some of the immediate disciples of Yeshua went to Antioch and spent a great deal of time there.* Other disciples fled to an area that was not yet in the hands of the Romans, but later this territory became one of the central regions of the Eastern Roman Empire.

Now, as it turns out, there was a close connection between the original disciples of Messiah Yeshua to the *Seventy* who were directly appointed by Yeshua. I believe that Simon Peter, who came to the Garden tomb with John, is the one who had the Shroud and the Sudarium in his possession. There was another member of the *Seventy* who was appointed directly by Yeshua and this man's name was *"Stachys."* Several months after I had already written this chapter about *Stachys,* I was writing about the original source of the Passover Maror, and that is when I thought that the Lamb's Ear plant sounded like it fit the description perfectly, according to Rabbinical sources. So when I looked up the Lamb's Ear plant, just to see if its characteristics fit all the requirements for the Passover Maror, by Divine Providence, I discovered that the Lamb's Ear plant has another name which is *"Stachys Byzantina,"* and as you know by now, I had already written about the man, *Stachys.* So I was shocked, because I already knew that he was one of Messiah Yeshua's *Seventy!* This was truly a remarkable miracle! The Lamb's Ear plant had apparently been given the name *"Stachys,"* who was chosen as one of the *Seventy* followers of Messiah Yeshua and he was sent before Yeshua's face to proclaim the LORD'S Testimony, in every city that Yeshua would go throughout the Holy Land. I figured that *Stachys,* who knew the Jewish Messiah personally, had to have eaten the original Maror in the ancient Passover Seder two thousand years ago! The only way this miracle came about was through the Holy Spirit because I could have chosen any plant in the world to look up, but the Lamb's Ear instantly came into my mind because it perfectly fit the Rabbi's description of the Passover Maror. Incredibly, I had already written all of this history about *Stachys* before discovering his connection to the plant that miraculously verified *the*

Passover Lamb of God! Stachys was definitely friends with Messiah Yeshua! Only *five years* after Yeshua was crucified, *Stachys* was made the *Bishop of the city of Byzantium* by the Apostle Andrew. The disciples, Simon Peter and Andrew his brother, were the first ones that had the Shroud and the Sudarium of Yeshua's sepulchre in their possession. At some point, I believe that Andrew took possession of the treasures of the LORD'S sepulchre and took them by ship to Asia Minor because the destruction of Jerusalem was at hand and because he was traveling and sailing into many cities in Asia Minor, preaching the Gospel of Messiah. The history then bears out the truth of what happened next.

One of the most famous cities where Andrew went to preach was to Byzantium on the sea coast. Andrew did not stay very long in this place after he preached there. He appointed one of the Seventy of Messiah Yeshua to carry on the work in the *city of Byzantium,* after he moved on to the other cities in Asia Minor. There were only about two or three that were called *"Bishops"* in this Church that was established by Andrew Bar Jonah, who was the first disciple that was called by the Jewish Messiah Yeshua. ***(Source: Stachys the Apostle; ©2011 patriarchate.org/patriarchate/former-patriarchs/stachys) AND (©2011 en.wikipedia.org/wiki/Stachys_the_Apostle).***

Now, I have always wanted the answer as to how the Shroud and the Sudarium of Messiah Yeshua went from the hands of the original Jewish disciples of the Jewish Messiah into the hands of pagan Rome. So what I discovered is that the *city of Byzantium,* where the Apostle Andrew preached and set up one of the first Churches of Byzantium *that was actually a Synagogue* was a city that was overtaken by Rome when Rome declared that Byzantium was their new Capitol. At this time, it appears that the *city of Byzantium,* as well as the original Jewish Churches or Synagogues that were established there by the Jewish Apostles of Messiah Yeshua, were all overtaken by Rome. The city was then renamed by the Roman Emperor Constantine. This Roman Emperor wanted this city to reflect his own name and so he changed the name of the city to *"Constantinople."* Before this occurred, however, the Jewish Apostles were preaching the true Gospel according to the Jewish Messiah. When the Apostles who were Jews preached Yeshua's original message, they kept to the Torah and told everyone how the Torah was fulfilled by Messiah Yeshua. They preached the original Gospel of repentance, baptism in the living water, and the anointing of the Holy Spirit. The Gospel message of Eternal Life through the Jewish Messiah Yeshua never included converting to a Roman Church, but suddenly Rome began to think they could use the new Jewish Christianity as a tool of control and, because they did not want to give up their pagan Roman rituals and traditions in Rome, they combined the two. This is the actual historical account and not my opinion. At this time, the Romans wanted to break the Jewish connection to Christianity altogether, so they changed the original *Jewish Passover* and moved Yeshua's resurrection day on the calendar to a pagan Babylonian day called *"Easter."* This had nothing to do with *the Jewish Messiah Yeshua who was resurrected on "The Jewish Feast of First Fruits on Nisan 17" that comes three days after Passover.* The Romans created *"Christmas"* which was said to honour the Jewish Messiah, but this was not the day that the Messiah was born! *Remember, that Yeshua was born KING of the Jews on Rosh HaShanah! However, Yeshua was indeed conceived in Kislev/December during the Festival of Lights or Hanukkah, so Christmas is an appropriate celebration.* Rome changed the Jewish dates and times of Messiah Yeshua into something pagan and ever since that time, the Churches, whether Roman or not, were forced to change their worship to the wrong dates and times that had nothing to do with the LORD. If they kept the true Jewish Christian faith of the original disciples of Messiah Yeshua, they were slain by the terrible inquisitions that followed. If you think about it and read the Torah, you will see that the LORD consecrated the seventh day as the Sabbath in the beginning. Sunday was never the Sabbath of the LORD, but Rome appointed Sunday as the day of the Sabbath. *Remember that I clearly showed that Yeshua was resurrected to life on the seventh day Sabbath before the dawn of the first day of the week.* These things are so important to understand so one can discern the times and seasons of the Messiah. It is truly sad that many Churches have no idea when to truly honour the Jewish Messiah because His days were deliberately altered to remove Yeshua's Jewish identity from Him. Instead, tradition has taken place instead of truth. The truth is that the Messiah fulfills all things by the LORD'S calendar on the Seven Biblical Feast Days of the LORD that are listed in Leviticus 23.

Now *Stachys,* one of the very first Bishops of the city of Byzantium, was a close friend of Andrew, the brother of Simon Bar Jonah otherwise known as *"Simon Peter."* The Roman records state that *Stachys* founded the so called *"Roman See"* of Byzantium in the year 38 AD, but *Stachys* was never a Roman. He was originally from Jerusalem and was close to all the Jewish believers. So he really set up a true Jewish Christian Church in this place, but it was overrun and overtaken by the Roman officials in the end. As a matter of history, the house of *Stachys* was burned to the ground by the Romans. Before this happened or around this time frame, many relics of the original Jewish Apostles were collected and kept in the Church in the city of Byzantium, which was really a *Synagogue* called *"The Church of the Apostles."* ***(Source: Stachys the Apostle; ©2011 patriarchate.org/patriarchate/former-patriarchs/stachys) AND (©2011 en.wikipedia.org/wiki/Stachys_the_Apostle).***

Although I am certain that *Stachys* was never called a *"See"* until the Romans gave him that title, in order to claim him as their own. The Romans martyred most of the Jewish Apostles, as well as Yeshua! Our beloved *Stachys* was the Bishop in Byzantium from the year 38 AD to the year 54 AD. When the Romans came into the city of Byzantium and overtook the city, making it their new Capitol and the heartland of the Roman Empire, the Roman Emperor Constantine turned the original *"See"* into something called *"The Patriarchate of Constantinople."* As the records state, the Jewish Apostle Andrew, who was the first called of MessiahYeshua and who was an eyewitness of His Divine Living Testimony, was later known by Rome as *"The Patron Saint and the First Bishop of Constantinople."* The historical record also states that *Stachys* built a Church at Argyropolis which was a historic place in the city of Constantinople. Argyropolis means *"Silver City"* and the name was later changed to *"Tophane."* So it was said that many gathered there to hear *Stachys* preach the original Jewish Gospel message regarding the Jewish Messiah from the Torah. *Stachys* also assisted the Apostle Andrew while he preached in many cities in Asia Minor. They also preached in Scythia along the Black Sea. It is said that the Apostle Paul referred to *Stachys* as *"beloved"* in the Epistle to the Romans, in chapter 16:9. So the historical record states that Andrew *preached as far away as the city of Kiev and the Volga River.* Andrew is also *"The Patron Saint of Russia." Of course Andrew's x-shaped cross is on the national flag of Scotland because Andrew is "The Patron Saint of Scotland." He is associated with the famous city of Saint Andrew's in Scotland, where a University is named after him that is "the third oldest university in the English-speaking world and the oldest in Scotland." The following is said of Saint Andrews: "The name St Andrews derives from the town's claim to be the resting place of bones of the apostle Andrew. According to legend, St Regulus (or Rule) brought the relics to Kilrymont, where a shrine was established for their safekeeping and veneration while Kilrymont was renamed in honour of the saint." Then it is also said: "In the mid-eighth century a monastery was established by the pictish king Oengus I, traditionally associated with the relics of Saint Andrew, a number of bones supposed to be the saints's [sic] arm, knee cap, three fingers and a tooth believed to have been brought to the town by St Regulus.* ***(Source: en.wikipedia.org/wiki/St_Andrews).*** *The Jewish apostle Andrew was crucified in Patras Greece on an x-shaped cross, so his relics are also said to be at the Basilica of St Andrew in Patras Greece. There are also relics of Andrew in Edinburgh Scotland, and in other cathedrals across Europe.*

Now Simon Bar Jonah and the disciple John were the two eyewitnesses that saw the linen Shroud and the head covering lying in a place by itself as they entered the sepulchre, after the resurrection of Messiah Yeshua. So clearly, the relics of the Messiah's Testimony were taken from the tomb in Holy Mount Moriah and were kept, I believe, for a while in the clay jars and remember that I said that this could be how the travertine aragonite came to be on the burial Shroud. Simon Bar Jonah died by crucifixion at the hands of the Romans in approximately the year 67 AD, and his ossuary was found in 1953, buried in the first century Jewish Christian burial cave on the Mount of Olives in Jerusalem near the little town called *"Bethany."* At some point, however, the Shroud and the Sudarium had to have been placed in the hands of Simon's brother Andrew, who was from Bethsaida in Israel and he too, of course, was a son of Jonah. Andrew was also martyred in approximately the year 70 AD. Andrew was led by John the Baptist, until the day that the Messiah appeared, when John declared, *"Behold, the Lamb of God, who takes away the sins of the world."* So Andrew approached Yeshua and he asked Him where He lived and Yeshua told Andrew, *"Come and see!"* After this, Andrew was a faithful follower unto death. So Andrew, who was the first to meet Messiah Yeshua through the declaration of the *Lamb of God,* became the close friend of *Stachys,* whose name was given to the Lamb's Ear plant. This is such a marvelous part of the LORD'S story!

After Yeshua ascended up to Heaven, the Jewish disciples were dispersed and they traveled away from Jerusalem and into many different places to bring the good news of Eternal life to all that would listen to this message and accept the LORD'S free gift of grace and truth, which is *Messiah the LORD, the Living Torah!* Many times they were in serious danger and had to flee. Obviously, they had to take the precious Testimony of the LORD wherever they went for protection from all the persecution in Jerusalem at the hands of the Romans.

The record is clear that Andrew did sail to the *city of Byzantium* and he was the first to preach in that city. He would go to one city and stay for a while preaching and then he would move on to another city and so on. He traveled to many cities abroad and he reached many thousands of people with the joyful message of the Messiah. So when Andrew left the city of Byzantium, this is when he appointed *Stachys* to be the head of this Church in the city of Byzantium. Then Andrew moved on to another city, leaving *Stachys* in Byzantium to preach *the Gospel of the Living Torah.* The records state that, *"the Apostle Andrew was eventually crucified in Patras Greece. Andrew had traveled to Greece and this is where his life ended."* The historical records indicate *"The relics of the Apostle [Andrew] a long time later, during the reign of Constantios, were transferred to Constantinople at the command of the king by the Martyr Artemios and were set with Luke's and Timothy's relics in the temple of the holy Apostles."* ***(Source: Andrew the Apostle; ©2011 patriarchate.org/patriarchate/former-patriarchs/andrew-apostle).***

The Roman Emperor Hadrian, who ruled from 117-138 AD, could be the key to another significant event. The first Jewish Revolt against the Romans occurred from 66-73 AD. Later, when Hadrian came to power, he wanted to eliminate any trace of the Jewish religion and people in Jerusalem and the Land of Israel. So, in approximately 135 AD, Hadrian undertook a massive effort to destroy the Jewish Holy sites. *He used his army to haul in a vast amount of dirt in order to cover a portion of the land around Mount Moriah where the crucifixion had occurred.* From this point onward, the true sepulchre at the Garden tomb and part of Golgotha were covered up with dirt until the year 1867. This means that there were roughly 50 to 60 years or so of exposure to the Garden tomb after Yeshua's resurrection, before it was covered up with dirt and never seen again until it was discovered in 1867. We know that this is a fact because Roman type frescos were etched and painted red in the tomb and they bear the Name *"Alpha and Omega"* with the cross and Messiah Yeshua's Name. After the sepulchre was unearthed, these ancient frescoes, *when exposed to air for the first time* in hundreds of years, began to fade. This is how we know for

On top of Golgotha Photo provided by ©2011 Simon Brown England All Rights Reserved

certain that no air got to them for almost two thousand years until 1867. The Messiah, as the second Adam, had to be buried in Holy Mount Moriah as the Living Testimony of the LORD in the Garden of the KING OF KINGS.

Hadrian visited the ruins of Jerusalem and he renamed the city after himself and after a roman pagan god, and then Jerusalem became *"Aelia Capitolina."* Hadrian did many evil things against the Jews, including expelling them out of the city of Jerusalem. The Jews were not allowed to read the Torah or keep the Biblical calendar. They could no longer keep the religious Holy Days of God. He brutally executed the top Jewish Scholars, including Rabbi Gamaliel *the teacher of the Apostle Paul.* He set up pagan roman god statues in the places of Jewish worship and this includes in the place where the Holy Temple of God once stood, as well as the other *supposed place* of Yeshua's tomb. Perhaps the longest lasting diabolical deed that Hadrian committed, according to the historical record, was his attempt to erase any Jewish history of Judaea and the Holy Land that was once Israel. Hadrian renamed the land after Israel's ancient enemy, the Philistines and he called the Province, *"Syria Palaestina,"* which became the word, *"Palestine."* I believe that in Hadrian's attempt to erase all traces of Jerusalem, as well as the Jewish Messiah, the Garden tomb was buried and was not seen again for centuries. Since the time that the frescos in the Garden tomb were unearthed in 1867, some of the etchings have faded out quite a bit. *So as I said, this means that this tomb was not exposed to the air for approximately 1900 years.* This means that the tomb was untouched from the time of the first century when the original Jewish disciples of Messiah Yeshua lived and basically from the time of the destruction of Jerusalem and the Second Jewish Temple.

Now that we have looked at Simon Peter and his brother Andrew, the other eyewitness that went to the tomb of Yeshua after the resurrection, besides Simon Peter, was the Jewish disciple John. He also saw the linen Shroud and the head covering lying in the sepulchre and *he was an eyewitness to the resurrection miracle.* The historical records regarding John state, *that he had a disciple named, "Polycarp."* It is a fact that between the years 71 AD-89 AD, Polycarp I, John's disciple, became *the successor of Onesimus* who, as we read earlier, was another one of the original *Seventy* like *Stachys,* directly appointed by Yeshua to preach in every city. Polycarp was later appointed, in the year 71 AD, as the Bishop *who succeeded Onesimus* in the *city of Byzantium.* So *Onesimus* was the Bishop of Byzantium after *Stachys.* He remained in this city and held his position for 18 years, according to the historical record, until 89 AD. Polycarp's relics were also buried in a place called *"The Temple of Argyropolis."* His predecessors were said to have also been buried there during the last eight years of his role as Bishop. *However, some of the graves and relics had to have been moved and buried again in Jerusalem near the Garden tomb at a later date, and some of the relics of Yeshua were taken to other places.* The *grave of Onesimus,* one of the original *Seventy* of Messiah Yeshua, was later discovered above the low cliff and behind the wall of the Garden tomb in Jerusalem Israel. *It was the discovery of this particular tomb of Onesimus that helped to verify that the Garden tomb was indeed Messiah Yeshua's burial place in Holy Mount Moriah.* The tomb of *Onesimus* was discovered in the ancient Jewish cemetery just above the Garden tomb on Holy Mount Moriah and, as I stated, it was inscribed with the words, *"Onesimus, Deacon of the Church of the Witnesses of the Resurrection."* ***(Source: Polycarp; ©2011 patriarchate.org/patriarchate/former-patriarchs/Polycarp-i).***

Therefore, those who were eyewitnesses of Yeshua's miraculous resurrection had the relics of the LORD'S Testimony in their possession, immediately following the miracle. I believe that when they later fled Jerusalem and went into Asia Minor, particularly to the *city of Byzantium,* they took the important relics to preserve them from destruction. Of course, when Rome took the *Greek city of Byzantium,* they took control and *they collected all the relics of Yeshua's sepulchre,* as Constantine became Emperor. *This is when the Romans took possession of every important relic of Yeshua, from the first Jewish Apostles.* This happened at the same time that Constantine renamed the city *"Constantinople."* It then became the largest city ruled by the Roman Empire, outside of Rome. The relics of the LORD'S sepulchre, I believe, had to have already been taken to the city. The relics remained housed in *the Great Church of Constantinople* until the Latin Siege of the crusades. Now, going back to the destruction of Jerusalem, this was the major event that occurred when the Roman Emperor Titus besieged Jerusalem in the year 70 AD. Messiah Yeshua had warned the Jewish disciples to flee to the mountains when they saw Jerusalem surrounded by armies. When they saw Titus approaching Jerusalem with the Roman army that was coming to destroy the city, some of the Jews who believed in Messiah Yeshua literally fled to the mountains of Israel. They heeded the warning that Yeshua had given to them previously, when He told them that not one stone would be left upon another that would not be thrown down at the Holy Temple. It was unimaginable what took place on the Temple Mount, as the Holy Temple of the LORD was destroyed and burned to the ground! In *Hugh Smith's History,* the following statement is found: *"Under the reign of Vespasian, Rome declared war against the Jews because of their repeated revolts and General Titus besieged the city of Jerusalem 70 A.D. It is said that one million, one hundred thousand Jews perished in the six month siege, but the church there escaped the horrors of the siege by following the instruction of Messiah in Matthew 24, and fleeing to the mountains beyond the Jordan. This timely retreat was made to the small town of Pella."* ***(Source: © Hugh Smith's History of the destruction of the Second Temple).***

The Jewish Christians, including the *Seventy* appointed by Yeshua, had fled to the mountains of Israel and some of them went to the city of Pella, beyond the Jordan. Could they have taken the Sudarium that was placed inside the silver Ark to hide it in a cave near Jericho at this point? Was the Shroud also once contained in the same Ark? Here they resided for safety. *Pella in the Jordan valley is just north of Mount Nebo.* Some of them later returned to Jerusalem, after going to Pella, when things settled down a bit. Another quote is from *Hurlbut's Story* of the Christian Church: *"In the fall of Jerusalem, few if any Christians perished. From the prophetic utterances of Messiah, the Christians received warning, escaped from the doomed city, and found refuge at Pella, in the Jordan valley."* ***(Source: Quote ©1967 September 10th Jesse L. Hurlbut – The Story of the Christian Church).***

On June 10th 2008, the BBC, as well as other major news agencies, printed news articles about the discovery of *"The oldest Church of the Seventy Apostles of Messiah Yeshua."* This incredible Church was discovered *in a cave in Rihab, in northern Jordan.* This is located north of Ammon Jordan. There were about 30 more of the earliest Churches discovered in this area around Rihab because many Christians who were being persecuted fled there for safety during the time of the Jewish revolts against Rome. The article said that the chapel of this early Church of the *Seventy* dates from 33-70 AD! ***(Source: Quote ©2008 June 10th BBC - The Archaeological discovery of the oldest Church of the 70 in Jordan).***

Now it is important to understand that in the lifetime of Yeshua, the land mass that centuries later became known as the nation of *"Jordan"* was at that time in the first century called *"Perea."* The city that is south of this location is Ammon and this city in 326 AD was called *"Philadelphia." At the time of the Byzantine era, this place was a seat of the Bishops of Christianity and of brotherly love.* There was an inscription discovered in the floor of this ancient Church that the article said referred to *"The Seventy beloved by God."* These were believed to be *the Seventy Apostles of Messiah Yeshua who fled from Jerusalem.* So this information indicates that the first Jewish Christians were, in fact, all over the vicinity of the land mass and nation that is now called *"Jordan,"* and you must cross over the Jordan River to get there, just like you must cross over the Jordan River to get to Mount Nebo. In Yeshua's lifetime, there was no border line of the two nations. There was only Israel. *The mountains of modern Jordan were inside the Holy Land of Israel.* So it is easy to understand how they truly *fled to the mountains of Israel* for safety and now it is easier to understand how the Great Rolling Stone of Yeshua's Garden Tomb sepulchre came to be preserved in this area (approximately 25 miles away), and was eventually, at some point in time, taken to the top of

Mount Nebo where it now stands facing the Promised Land. It is standing there today, showing Israel that Messiah Yeshua is leading them back over the Jordan River from all the nations and into the redemption of the Eternal Promised Land called *"Heaven."* When Saul persecuted the Church, he did this just before his miracle on the road to Damascus. This miracle happened sometime near the year 36 AD. So the persecution of the earliest Jewish Church was already taking place, as it is recorded in the book of Acts. They were all scattered at first to Judaea and Samaria, which has been deliberately renamed *"the West Bank."* The Scripture goes on to say that *"they were scattered abroad and went everywhere."* So as history played out, we know that from the very earliest days after Yeshua's resurrection, the persecution continued.

Acts 8:1-4 *And Saul was consenting unto his death. And at that time there was a great persecution against the church which was at Jerusalem; and they were all scattered abroad throughout the regions of Judaea and Samaria, except the apostles. And devout men carried Stephen to his burial, and made great lamentation over him. As for Saul, he made havoc of the church, entering into every house, and haling men and women committed them to prison. Therefore they that were scattered abroad went everywhere preaching the Word.*

Then in the year 81 AD and onward, there was a very large persecution of the Gentile and Jewish Christians by the Roman Emperor, Domitian. The interesting part of this history is that Domitian was the brother of Titus, who burned down the Holy Temple in Jerusalem and stole all the Holy vessels and treasures of the LORD'S House. Titus carried off all the Jewish relics of the LORD'S House and took them away as spoil to Rome. Perhaps the original Rolling Stone of Yeshua's Garden tomb was taken by the Roman military at that time from Yeshua's sepulchre (rather than originally taken by the Apostles) as another very large stone trophy of the Roman Empire. They often collected these large items as their trophies. After they returned to Rome with the spoils from Jerusalem, Titus led a parade through the city of Rome, arrogantly displaying the spoils that he had stolen from the House and Temple of the LORD God of Israel. Domitian was said to have followed behind the victory parade of the Holy vessels of the LORD, riding upon his white horse. The Roman Coliseum was later built from the melted gold scraped from the burning Holy Temple in Jerusalem!

The Jewish believers fled for their lives to the mountains of Israel, in the area known as *Perea,* where the nation of Jordan is today. Mount Nebo is in the vicinity of *Perea,* and it is likely that some of the relics went with them. As I said, the city of Pella that was in *Perea* was north of Mount Nebo. The *Seventy* Apostles who were scattered abroad not only went into Asia Minor, but some of them went into this mountainous region and now we recently have the outstanding archaeological proof of *the Seventy of Yeshua* having fled to this area. Since Mount Nebo was the place where Moses and Joshua prepared to enter the Promised Land, I believe that the Great Rolling Stone, at some point in time, was taken to this place because Mount Nebo was venerated in the historical record of the Israelites crossing over the Jordan River into the Land that God promised to them. There are several possibilities of how the rolling stone got there. It was taken there either by the Jewish Apostles or by the *Seventy* or by the Romans with the Temple treasures as a stone trophy to the Hagia Sophia Church at Constantinople, or it was taken during the Latin crusades, or later by other later invaders. One record indicates that it was kept near Mount Nebo in a Byzantine Monastery in a Sanctuary and was used as a door. Through my own extensive research, though, we know that it was kept for a very long time in Constantinople because the King of the Romans listed the Great Rolling Stone with the Shroud, the swaddling clothes, and other relics of Messiah Yeshua among the spoils that were taken to Constantinople, but they were originally in the hands of the first Jewish disciples of Messiah Yeshua and in the hands of His earliest followers. It is also possible that the Great Rolling Stone from Yeshua's tomb wound up in Rome inside the huge Basilica and was later commissioned to be taken to Mount Nebo. Maybe one day soon we will have the answer to this question. The Romans kept many other large stone *"Trophies"* as spoils of war. So the Rolling Stone from the Jewish Messiah's sepulchre may well have been considered a *very prized "Trophy"* by the Romans who executed Yeshua. The relics are a very important part of the Testimony of the Jewish KING.

Now I have found very important documents dating to the Middle Ages that were kept in *the Archives,* listing some of the *Holy Temple Treasures of the LORD God of Israel from Jerusalem* that were taken to Rome by Vespasian. The following statement is an important excerpt from this *Archive* that was translated in 1894. *From: "HISTORY OF THE CITY OF ROME THE MIDDLE AGES 213;" "At the same period in the time of Justinian, the Armenian Bishop Zacharias, who compiled a register of the public works in Rome, asserts that five and twenty bronze statues representing Abraham, Sarah, and the Kings of the House of David, which Vespasian had brought with the gates and many other monuments of Jerusalem to Rome, were still preserved in the city, and Roman tradition in the Middle Ages boasted that the Lateran Basilica still preserved the Sacred Ark of the Covenant, the Tables of the Law, the Golden Candlesticks, the Tabernacle and even the Priestly vestments of Aaron. It is possible that on board the same vessel that sailed to Carthage, laden with the spoils of Rome, the Lychnuchus (Seven Branched Menorah) of Solomon and the statue of Capitoline Zs, (the abomination of desolation), symbols of the oldest religions of the East and West, may have rested side by side."* ***(Source: Public Domain; History Of The City of Rome The Middle Ages Ferdinand Gregorovius, Translated from the fourth German Edition Anne Hamilton, London George Bell & Sons 1894- (Archive.org)***

I also read in my research, there were emeralds that belonged to Solomon's Temple that were taken and housed in Rome. Every spoil from Jerusalem was displayed at *"The Temple of Peace."* ***(Source: Procopius with an English translation by H. B. Dewing in seven volumes III History of the Wars, books V and VI London William Heinemann ltd Cambridge, Massachusetts Harvard University Press first printed ©1919 printed in Great Britain gutenberg.org/zipcat2.php/20298/20298-h/20298-h.htm#v_xii_42).***

I also found *a very ancient cypress door,* a bi-folding door, that is carved with a beautiful grapevine pattern. It remains in one of the oldest Basilicas in Rome. It has carved wooden panels depicting ancient Biblical scenes. Many of the oldest panels of the door have been replaced with newer panels. *It is interesting then that King Solomon built a special bi-folding door for the First Holy Temple out of cypress wood!* ***(Source: World's Oldest Cypress Doors ©2012 digital images.net/Gallery/Scenic/Rome/Churches/ Ancient/ancient.html#SanClemente) AND (The Door Panels of Santa Sabina Copyright ©2006-2012 William Storage All Rights Reserved).***

I hope that what I have written and researched helps to solve at least part of the unknown history, revealing how the Shroud and the Sudarium (the swaddling cloth) traveled from Jerusalem in the hands of the original Jewish disciples of Yeshua and went into the hands of the Romans. Some of the relics wound up in various Roman Basilicas within the city of Rome, including the Vatican, and other relics were taken by other invaders during the crusades. I also discovered that five years after Vespasian carried off the Jewish vessels to Rome, in 75 AD, he built the so called *"Temple of Peace"* in Rome, which was also known as *"The Forum of Vespasian." It was not only built to house the precious vessels and items from the Jewish Holy Temple of the LORD that he had carried off as spoil from Jerusalem, but "The Temple of Peace," was built specifically to celebrate his Roman conquest of Jerusalem! The Holy vessels, along with the Jewish Law and the curtains of the Holy of Holies, were kept here in Rome.* As I researched *"The Temple of Peace,"* I noticed that in 2005-2006, they excavated and discovered the *original pink and white marble floor* of this Temple in Rome. ***(Sources; Temple of Peace or Forum of Vespasian - Rome Reborn ©2008 by the Rectors and Visitors of the University of Virginia. All rights reserved. romereborn.frischerconsulting.com/ge/TS-070-PA.html) AND (Temple of Peace Forum of Vespasian - ROMA, CENTRO STORICO â FORI IMPERIALI. Basilica di Massenzio, Tempio della Pace e Fori Imperiali: scavi archeologici per le stazioni della metropolitana C nel Centro Storico (Decr. 16/12/1997 - Roma Capitale 1998, Cod. b4.1) AND (Arch. Giuseppe Morganti (21-07-2004).* flickr.com/photos/imperial_fora_of_rome/sets/72157594587104523/) AND (Temple of Peace Forum of Vespasian - ©2011 en.wikipedia.org/wiki/Temple_of_Peace,_Rome#Temple_of_Peace).*** Immediately I made the connection that this *pink and white marble* was exactly *the same pink and white marble* that is inside the Church of the Holy Sepulchre in Jerusalem that they call the *"unction stone."* Therefore, this *pink and white marble stone slab* came from Rome and likely from *"The Temple of Peace"* and was not a stone that Yeshua's body was laid upon in Jerusalem, after it was taken down from the cross.

The Romans would not have laid Yeshua upon marble after crucifying Him! As the Romans gained control and *established the Roman Church* in the place called the *"Hagia Sophia Church"* in Constantinople, the relics fell into Romans hands. The Holy Roman Empire gathered and took the relics and all the treasures from the original *Jewish Churches or Synagogues that had been established by the Seventy,* who had been appointed as the *"Bishops of Byzantium,"* and the Romans put them into the new Roman Church, where they remained until the Latin Crusades in the fourth century. The City of Constantinople and the Hagia Sophia was sacked and looted of all its rich treasures during the fourth crusade. Some relics were removed to Spain and others went to Venice, to Saint Mark's Basilica. It is said that others were returned to the Vatican in Rome from Saint Mark's. Nevertheless these relics remained mainly in the hands of the Romans. So the Shroud and the Sudarium were once held by Simon Bar Jonah and his family and by John. Then Andrew and the *Seventy* Apostles had them in their possession and that is how they went away from Jerusalem, from the Garden tomb of Messiah Yeshua, to the *city of Byzantium* and from there became the possession of the Romans. It is also very interesting to me, that it was written in the historical records that when the *city of Byzantium* became *"Constantinople,"* the relics from the true cross, the broken pieces of the Rod of Moses, which I presume to be the brass serpent on a pole, and other relics kept there were said to protect the city when it became the new Capitol of Rome. Did Moses serpent Rod still exist in pieces? King Hezekiah, who did that which was right in the sight of God, removed the idols from Israel and he broke Moses brazen serpent into pieces because the people were starting to worship and venerate this object instead of worshipping God, whose power was shown through this relic, but we have no idea if the pieces still existed or not. If they did and were at that time still kept in Jerusalem, they were also confiscated as *"spoils"* from Jerusalem and were taken to the Roman city of *Constantinople.*

II Kings 18:4-5 *He removed the high places, and brake the images, and cut down the groves, and brake in pieces the brazen serpent that Moses had made; for unto those days the children of Israel did burn incense to it; and he called it Nehushtan. He trusted in the LORD God of Israel; so that after him was none like him among all the kings of Judah, nor any that were before him.*

The historically accurate records can be pieced together to explain how the relics of Messiah Yeshua came to be separated from the Jewish disciples and removed from Jerusalem. It took a lot of time, effort, and research to discover the earliest history of the Shroud, the Sudarium (the swaddling cloth), and the Great Rolling Stone. I also found records that indicated that the *original Crown of Thorns* that was sent to France and was housed in *"Saint Chapelle in Paris"* was removed out of its reliquary during the French Revolution and a reed crown was put in its place, but other records indicated that the thorns had been removed from the original Crown and sent to other places. ***(Roman Source; Historical information on the Crown of Thorns at Saint Chapelle; The Mystery of the Crown of Thorns by A Passionist Father Preserving Christian Publications, Inc. Albany, NY ©2011 catholictradition.org/Passion/crown-thorns3.htm).***

I hope that, through God's help, *I have at least revealed how the Sudarium, Yeshua's bris swaddling cloth, came to be in Oviedo Spain, while Yeshua's linen burial Shroud bearing His image, remained in Italy and was eventually taken to Turin.* I also hope I have shown how the Great Rolling Stone from Yeshua's sepulchre was likely taken from Jerusalem to Constantinople and then to Rome and was either kept there for centuries in the Roman Church museum called *"The Vatican,"* or it was later taken back to Israel and placed inside the Byzantine Church near Mount Nebo, in what is now *"Jordan."* We have to remember that there were other barbaric invaders that may have confiscated some of these relics.

I believe and hope that, very soon, the LORD will cause the relics and treasures that belong to Him to be brought back to His Holy city of Jerusalem for His Royal Coronation Ceremony and for His Divine glory, as the Great Royal Sovereign KING of the entire universe!

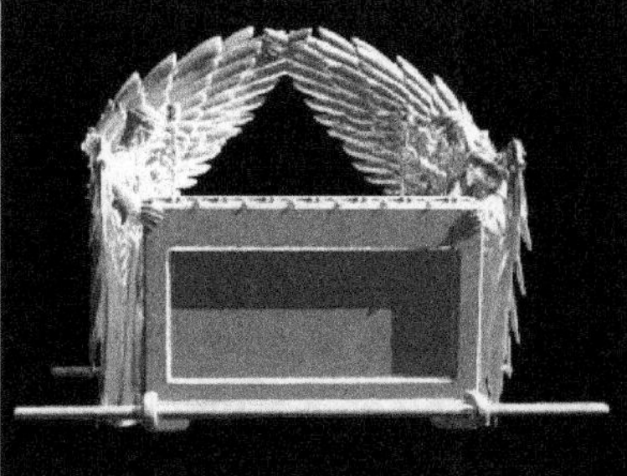

Ark of the Covenant
©2010 Anchor Stone International
All Rights Reserved

TWO ANGEL'S AND TWO CHERUBIM'S!

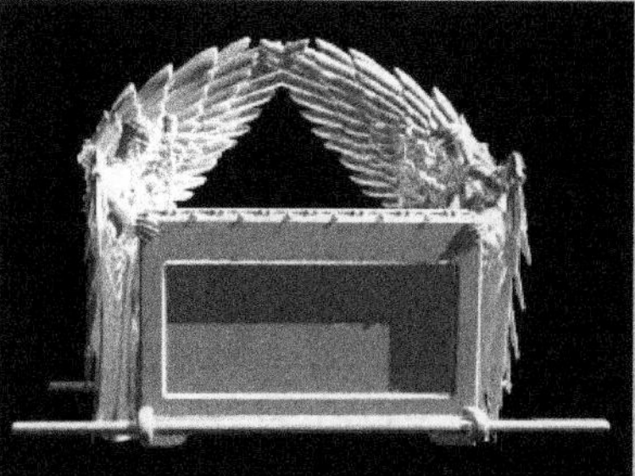

Ark of the Covenant
©2010 Anchor Stone International
All Rights Reserved

The revelations within this book are like the pieces of a Divine puzzle and my Mother always told me that when I was little, I could do very complicated puzzles! Everything I have written by the power of the Holy Spirit must now come together into one picture, revealing the final Testimony of the LORD God of Israel. The following Divine revelation, that I am about to show you, validates the Majesty of the Great KING. It is the fulfillment of the Torah and it is the most astonishing revelation of all!

When I had considered and pondered in my heart and prayed to the LORD, asking Him why two Angels appeared in the Garden tomb, one at the head and the other at the feet after Messiah Yeshua's resurrection, (John 20:12) the stunning answer came to me *when I realized that the linen face cloth was Yeshua's Jewish bris swaddling cloth that was deliberately left by the LORD in a place by itself as "Kadesh," as a sign of His Eternal life blood Covenant with Israel and the world. It was only after I saw this incredible truth that I realized that the "two Living Angels" inside the Garden tomb formed "The Living Heavenly Ark of the Covenant!" This was no longer the earthly copy of the Ark made by human hands from the pattern that Moses replicated! This was the Living model of the Eternal Ark of the Testimony of the LORD God of Israel, made without human hands!* This Ark was *"The LORD God Himself as our Saviour,"* and this one was inside Holy Mount Moriah where God's House will rest forever at the gate of Heaven in the location of the former Garden of Eden! This Living Ark was in *the Rock quarry of "The Foundation Stone!"*

In Exodus 25, the LORD gave the description of the Ark of the Covenant and between the two Cherubim Angels, the LORD placed His pact that He had made. It was from this location that the LORD said, *"I will meet with you and I will impart to you from above the cover from between the two Cherubims,"* and this concerned the Israelites.

The LORD spoke to Moses from the Mercy Seat, from between the two Cherubim Angels that were at either end of the Ark.

Exodus 25:18-22 *And thou shalt make two cherubims of gold, of beaten work shalt thou make them, in the two ends of the Mercy Seat. And make one cherub on the one end, and the other cherub on the other end; even of the Mercy Seat shall ye make the cherubims on the two ends thereof. And the cherubims shall stretch forth their wings on high, covering the Mercy Seat with their wings, and their faces shall look one to another; toward the Mercy Seat shall the faces of the cherubims be. And thou shalt put the Mercy Seat above upon the Ark; and in the Ark thou shalt put the Testimony that I shall give thee. And there I will meet with thee, and I will commune with thee from above the Mercy Seat, from between the two cherubims which are upon the Ark of the Testimony, of all things which I will give thee in commandment unto the children of Israel.*

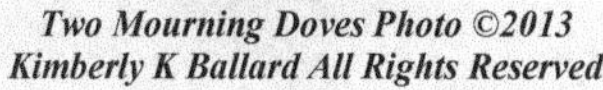

Two Mourning Doves Photo ©2013
Kimberly K Ballard All Rights Reserved

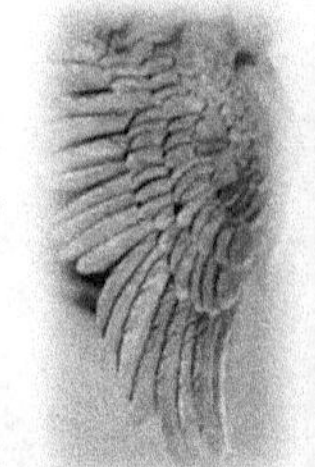

Numbers 7:89 *And when Moses was gone into the Tabernacle of the congregation to speak with him, then he heard the voice of one speaking unto him from off the Mercy seat that was upon the Ark of Testimony, from between the two cherubims; and he spake unto Him.*

So what astonished me as I pondered this is that inside the Garden tomb, one Living Angel appeared at one end where Yeshua's head had rested, and the other Living Angel appeared at the other end where His feet had rested. This meant that after He was raised to life, *"The LORD Yeshua met with us between the two Living Cherubim Angels!"* From the moment that I made this stunning connection, through the power of the Holy Spirit, I realized that between the *two Living Angels (the two men in shining garments),* where Yeshua's body had rested, was *"The Seat of the LORD'S Mercy."* This was the place where God provided Himself *"The Lamb!"* This was the place that Abraham called, *"YHVH Ra'ah,"* which declared, *"In the Mountain of the LORD, it shall be seen!"*

Now because *Messiah the LORD is the Living Ark of Heaven,* this means that the earthly copy of the Ark of Moses will no longer be used and is now obsolete. The earthly Ark is not Eternal, but the LORD God is Eternal. *The Living Ark remains forever incorruptible!* So Yeshua's body did not see decay or corruption! Now the truth is that Messiah Yeshua revealed this truth to His Jewish disciples, Simon Peter, James and John, when He was transfigured before them in the glory cloud on Mount Sinai! This was the key of David that Messiah Yeshua gave to Simon Peter, James, and John on Mount Sinai, when they were set apart as *"Kadesh!" They saw His Shechinah glory and He revealed to them that the earthly Ark of Moses was no longer going to be used because He was the model that Moses replicated on this same Holy Mount.* They saw and believed that the LORD, who was standing before them in His Majesty *between the two men in shining garments, the two Living Cherubim Angels named "Moses and Elijah,"* was the *Living Ark of Heaven* that lasts forever! This Divine knowledge was shown to the Jewish disciples, who were then instructed by Yeshua to take *"The Living Torah from the Heavenly Ark" that saves us to the entire world.* The Jewish disciples were eyewitnesses of these extraordinary events and it changed their lives forever! They died with this knowledge, while taking this glorious Testimony of the LORD to the entire world, so it could shine the light upon everyone! *I believe that this Divine revelation of Yeshua would only be revealed at the end of days and the two witnesses are now revealed, because Moses and Elijah, the two Living Olive Tree Angels that stand on either side of the Heavenly Ark, are coming with this Testimony to show you that they were inside the Garden tomb in Holy Mount Moriah, on either side of Messiah Yeshua, the Heavenly Almond Tree Menorah!* So we are living in the most exciting age! I constantly feel profoundly moved and touched to see that the LORD'S secrets never end, as I am writing this book and He cared enough to reveal these secret details to me.

Hebrews 8:13 *In that He saith, A New Covenant, He hath made the first old. Now that which decayeth and waxeth old is ready to vanish away.*

Hebrews 8:10 *For this is the Covenant that I will make with the House of Israel after those days, saith the LORD; I will put My Laws into their mind, and write them in their hearts; and I will be to them a God, and they shall be to Me a people.*

Hebrews 10:18-22 *Now where remission of these is, there is no more offering for sin. Having therefore, brethren, boldness to enter into the Holiest by the blood of Yeshua, By a New and Living Way, which He hath consecrated for us, through the veil, that is to say, His flesh; And having an High Priest over the House of God; Let us draw near with a true heart in full assurance of faith, having our hearts sprinkled from an evil conscience, and our bodies washed with pure water.*

After the LORD miraculously revealed all of this to me, *I suddenly had the astonishing revelation that also between the two Living Cherubim Angels seated in the Garden tomb, in the hewn Rock sepulchre of Holy Mount Moriah, in the Royal Stone of King's was also placed by*

the LORD God, "The cut off dead Branch that became the Almond Rod of God that budded and bore fruit, which is the rod of His Father's House, bearing His Royal Name, the Unleavened Bread from Heaven, the Rock bearing the Word of God, the Living Torah written on the perfect Lamb of God, and the Well of Living Water of Eternal life." This was *"the pact"* and lying nearby was the head cloth that was *the swaddling cloth of Yeshua's Jewish bris Covenant in Yeshua's life blood* that was found rolled or folded in a place by itself, as the sign! *For the LORD knew that the Jews require a sign and this is it! The seed was raised up "to a life of Torah" on the third day, and Yeshua bore "The First Fruit of the Almond Tree of Life." He sealed His marriage proposal to Israel in the Garden tomb with His bris cloth.*

I Corinthians 1:22 *For the Jews require a sign, and the Greeks seek after wisdom.*

Yeshua's *life blood* rested between the two Living Angels. Now you can understand why the Sudarium, the bris swaddling cloth, and the Shroud bearing the LORD'S image are so significant in this Garden sepulchre! This is *"the life blood Covenant"* of the LORD God of Israel and of course His bris cloth was symbolic of *"the Eternal life cycle."* This cloth was truly *"the Living Torah Binder"* that was wrapped around Yeshua's face because Yeshua speaks *the Living Torah!* It had been wrapped around the face of the *"Sar HaPanim, the Prince of the face of the LORD God."* This forever sealed the final proof for me, that the Sudarium is in fact Yeshua's *bris swaddling cloth* that the Angel declared was to be a sign to Israel! *The KING OF KINGS deliberately left it as a sign of His betrothal to His Holy Land and to His people Israel that He will rule over forever!* The Eternal pact that the KING OF KINGS made with all of us in Jerusalem can never be reversed in His Garden, and now we know for certain, that this *decree for life* was sealed with the KING'S signet in His Garden! The Royal Sceptre of Judah is held out to us in favor, so we can now enter into *"the inner court"* of the KINGS Palace of Glory! We either accept the LORD'S Living Testimony as the Messiah and live forever, or we reject His Testimony of the heart and we die in our sins. *Without the Rod of the Living Torah of life, stretched out and lifted up to us, there is no Eternal life!*

Esther was saved by the outstretched Sceptre of the King. Likewise, we are saved by the outstretched Sceptre of the KING OF KINGS. As soon as the Great Stone was rolled off the mouth of the well of salvation by the angel of the LORD, we could drink forever from the fountain of Living Waters as the LORD'S flock, but first the flocks all had to be gathered out of all the places where they had been scattered on a dark and gloomy day!

When Yeshua told the disciples, *"From now on you know the way."* Thomas said, *"LORD, we do not know where you are going, so how can we know the way?"* Yeshua responded, *"I AM the way the truth and the life, no one comes to the Father but through Me."* Yeshua meant that He was literally *"the Way" back through the two Living Cherubim Angels to the Almond Tree of Life!* This is the Testimony that is written upon the heart of Israel and upon all mankind and upon all creation, forever. There is no other way to be made right with God, but through *the Covenant and the pact that He made with us. This means that the KING OF KINGS literally lifted up His Royal Standard, in the former Garden of Eden, so that we would no longer die, but live forever.* This is the Good News Gospel! It is for this reason that it is astonishing to me that Mary Magdalene or Mary of Magdala was the first woman to eat the first fruit from the Almond Tree of Life in God's Garden. Then when her ancient Synagogue in Magdala was unearthed in 2009, at the same time I was given these revelations. So when they found the Magdala stone, I knew that *Yeshua stood on this stone, speaking as the Living Torah to the Jewish people.* As I said earlier, the Magdala stone depicts Messiah Yeshua's Eternal Covenant of the heart with the Holy Seven Branched Almond Tree Menorah of Life that depicts His Eternal Testimony! This archaeological find is, therefore, even more outstanding than anyone knows yet, but I hope to reveal this very soon! I believe that Yeshua is the opened Almond Blossom on top of the stone! Almond Trees have very slender long narrow leaves.

Almond flowers produce either five or six petals. Now remember that I said miraculously at the beginning of my story, that when the Almond blossom fully opens to our gaze, we will see the identity of the KING of Israel!

Official Photograph taken in October 2009 of "THE MAGDALA STONE," Courtesy and ©2009 Magdala Center Excavations Israel All Rights Reserved

Now if we take this further, another fact about the two Cherubim Angels is that they were embroidered upon the veil of the Holy of Holies in the Tabernacle of Moses, and the same two Cherubim Angels were also embroidered upon the veil in the Holy Temple in Jerusalem. One had to go through the veil that had the two Cherubim Angels embroidered upon it to reach the Ark of the Testimony of the LORD and to meet with the LORD where His pact rested. He appeared between the two Cherubim Angels above the Ark of the Covenant. In the book of Exodus, the LORD gave the description of this veil of great significance that was before the Ark of the LORD.

Exodus 36:35-38 *And he made a veil of blue, and purple, and scarlet, and fine twined linen; with Cherubim's made he it of cunning work. And he made thereunto four pillars of shittim wood, and overlaid them with gold; their hooks were of gold; and he cast for them four sockets of silver. And he made an hanging for the Tabernacle door of blue, and purple, and scarlet, and fine twined linen, of needlework; And the five pillars of it with their hooks; and he overlaid their chapiters and their fillets with gold; but their five sockets were of brass.*

The veil with the two Cherubim Angels kept *"the Way"* to *"The Most Holy Place"* where the LORD spoke from above the Ark *between the two Cherubim Angels* to the High Priest. The scarlet color in the veil represented Adam, meaning *"red,"* because he was formed by God out of the red earth in this place. Messiah Yeshua reconciled us with His *red* life blood in this same place, out of the LORD'S Rock quarry, as the second perfect Adam. The purple color in the veil represented reconciliation between God and mankind through the atonement of the Messiah. So, the purple robe or mantle was wrapped around the Living Torah, the Yad of God, and the Judean desert crown of atoning wood was put upon Yeshua's head before He was put away in the Royal Stone of Kings in the sepulchre that was hewn out of the Rock in God's Garden. The LORD'S body was laid inside His Holy Mountain, Mount Moriah, and He rested in *"the place"* of the Ark of His Living Testimony. As I stated above, Yeshua was the dead Branch, the Rod of His Father's House that was laid before the Testimony, like Aaron's rod. The blue color of the veil represented the earth. The earth is sapphire blue and it is the floor and footstool of the LORD'S throne.

During the crucifixion, the sky became as dark as sackcloth and the veil of the Holy Temple in Jerusalem was torn from top to bottom. The veil was made cleft by the *power of the Rod of God,* as the two staves, *"Trees of Life,"* were literally lifted up into the air, *displaying Messiah Yeshua, the Living Torah,* so the whole world would be drawn to *"the place"* of God's Garden, in Holy Mount Moriah in Jerusalem Israel, over the course of the next two thousand years. This was the signature of the LORD'S Divine work through His Rod. Remember that the Crown of Thorns was the Acacia wood of the atonement of the Ark of the LORD. The fact is that billions of people would come to believe in the LORD God of Israel through the Messiah's Testimony and they would come humbly before Him, accepting His New Living

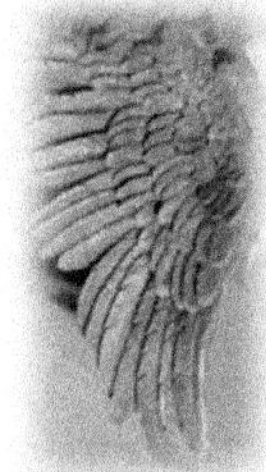

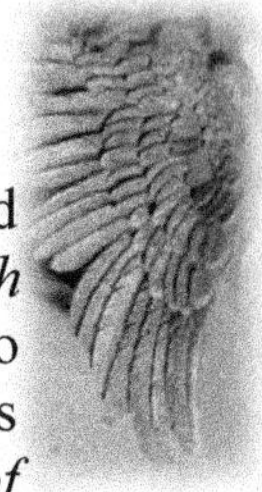

Covenant of the heart that gives them Eternal life! The two staves were never to be removed from the Ark of the LORD'S Testimony! With this event, it is very clear that *KING Messiah Yeshua is the LORD God of Israel.* The veil that was made cleft instantly parted the two Cherubim Angels, and the reconciliation between God and mankind took place in God's Garden on Mount Moriah in Golgotha, *"the place"* of the Rock quarry, where *the curse of death* needed to be reversed, *"in the place of the skull."*

Matthew 27:50-54 *Yeshua, when He had cried again with a loud voice, yielded up the Spirit. And, behold, the veil of the Temple was rent in twain from the top to the bottom; and the earth did quake, and the rocks rent; And the graves were opened; and many bodies of the Saints which slept arose, And came out of the graves after His resurrection, and went into the Holy City, and appeared unto many. Now when the Centurion, and they that were with Him, watching Yeshua, saw the earthquake, and those things that were done, they feared greatly, saying, Truly this was the Son of God.*

John 20:9-18 *For as yet they knew not the Scripture, that He must rise again from the dead. Then the disciples went away again unto their own home. But Mary stood without at the sepulchre weeping; and as she wept, she stooped down, and looked into the sepulchre, And seeth two Angels in white sitting, the one at the head, and the other at the feet, where the body of Yeshua had lain. And they say unto her, Woman, why weepest thou? She saith unto them, because they have taken away my LORD, and I know not where they have laid Him. And when she had thus said, she turned herself back, and saw Yeshua standing, and knew not that it was Yeshua. Yeshua saith unto her, Woman, why weepest thou? Whom seekest thou? She, supposing Him to be the Gardener, saith unto Him, Sir, if thou have borne Him hence, tell me where thou hast laid Him, and I will take Him away. Yeshua saith unto her, Mary, She turned herself, and saith unto Him, Rabboni; which is to say, Master. Yeshua saith unto her, Touch me not; for I am not yet ascended to my Father; but go to my brethren, and say unto them, I ascend unto My Father, and your Father; and to My God, and your God. Mary Magdalene came and told the disciples that she had seen the LORD and that He had spoken these things unto her.*

After Adam and Eve sinned against God in the Garden of Eden, bringing the curse, they hid themselves from the LORD, but now Mary *(bitter)* was seeking Him because Yeshua had just reversed the curse in God's Garden and the LORD appeared to her there and gave her *"The First Fruit from the Almond Tree of life."* The two Cherubim Angels that had been in the Garden of Eden had been guarding *"The Way"* to the Tree of Life, so that no one could eat its fruit and live forever. The flaming sword was placed at *"the entrance"* of the Garden of Eden. *The Living Torah that comes out of Messiah Yeshua's mouth is the flaming sword of the Holy Spirit of God that guards "The Way" to the fruit of the Tree of Life.* So now we can enter Heaven because Yeshua made *"The Way"* in the Garden on Holy Mount Moriah in Jerusalem Israel *through the two Living Cherubim Angels and through the flaming sword,* in the place of the former Garden of Eden. We can therefore only get there through Messiah Yeshua!

Genesis 3:24 *So He drove out the man; and He placed at the east of the Garden of Eden Cherubim's, and a flaming sword which turned every way, to keep the way of the Tree of Life.*

Jeremiah 23:29 *Is not My Word like as a fire? Saith the LORD; and like a hammer that breaketh the rock in pieces?*

Revelation 2:16 *Repent; or else I will come unto thee quickly, and will fight against them with the sword of My mouth.*

So after Yeshua was resurrected, the two Living Cherubim Angels appeared in the Garden and they were showing us that this was *"The Way"* to a new Eden called *"Heaven, The New Jerusalem!"* We must eat the Fruit from the Living Branch, the Rod of God, to live forever. When Yeshua said, *"I AM the door,"* He meant that He was *"the entrance"* going back into the Garden into Heaven. This *"place"* is literally where He budded to life at the gate of Heaven. This is why I believe that the Mezuzah was once mounted in the niche in Mount Moriah to the right of Yeshua's relics, bearing His Living Testimony. I believe that the niches displayed *the Shroud bearing His image, showing us that we were made in His image in His*

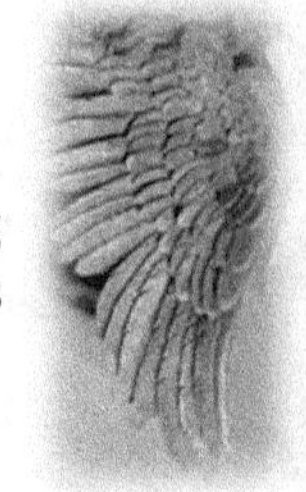

Royal Garden, and the Sudarium, the swaddling cloth from His bris circumcision, both bearing His life blood of the Eternal Covenant upon them. If you read Yeshua's words again in this context, you will see that His Words have a greater depth of meaning.

John 10:9 *I AM the door; by Me if any man enter in, he shall be saved and shall go in and out, and find pasture.*

Now when I looked up the definition of the word *"Way,"* it was very revealing about the Messiah and His Divine plan for us to enter Heaven!

Way*; A road or highway affording passage from one place to another. An opening affording passage; Example; "This door is the only way to the attic."*

In other words, *"This door Yeshua is the only way to Heaven!"* So when I say that Yeshua made *"The Way," I proclaim that He is the "affording passage and the road or highway" that we must take to get from this place on earth to Heaven and we must follow behind the Living Ark to enter into the glorious Eternal Promised Land.* The word *"affording"* in this context by definition means *"bearing the cost or price, to spare or give up and to provide."* So Yeshua *bore the cost of the Bride's price* in this place, leaving His *Kadesh* swaddling cloth as *the sign* of *His betrothal* to Israel. The LORD did not spare His own Son, but He gave Himself to us in the flesh. He was the perfect Torah sheepskin that bore our stripes to heal us. To be in Heaven, then, is to be in the KING'S Divine Presence. *In this Garden, there is an opening affording passage, through the gate of Heaven and the Rod of God is standing at the gate of the sheepfold.* So everyone must pass under the Rod of the Good Shepherd to be saved.

Now, it is profound that Isaiah wrote about *"The Way"* that is *"a highway"* and it is *"our Passover into Heaven!"* The redeemed and ransomed of the LORD shall walk on *this highway!* There will be no more sorrow in Heaven!

Isaiah 35:8-10 *And an highway shall be there, and a way, and it shall be called The way of holiness; the unclean shall not pass over it; but it shall be for those; the wayfaring men, though fools shall not err therein. No lion shall be there, nor any ravenous beast shall go up thereon, it shall not be found there; but the redeemed shall walk there; And the ransomed of the LORD shall return, and come to Zion with songs and everlasting joy upon their heads; they shall obtain joy and gladness, and sorrow and sighing shall flee way.*

Notice that in *"The Way of Holiness,"* the unclean shall not *pass over* it. This is because Messiah Yeshua is our perfect *"Passover."* He purifies us through *His Holiness,* but the unclean do not accept *the Passover* of Yeshua's Eternal Covenant, so they cannot enter through the door or gate into Heaven. *Yeshua the Heavenly Ark of God is going before us on this highway. If we follow behind Him, we will enter into the Heavenly Promised Land and enter the LORD'S Eternal rest.* So the unclean will not be able enter in by *"The Way of Holiness"* through the only door that is available to us on Holy Mount Moriah, through *our Passover.* Remember that I said that there is a connection to the rapture of believers in the word *"Overpass or Overpast,"* and it refers to being on two different levels. *One highway is below, while the other highway is above it.* Some of the people are down below looking up, while those that are taken up in the rapture by the LORD are above them on a higher level on this *"affording passage."* So, *"The Way"* that Messiah Yeshua made between the two Living Cherubim Angels is *"The roadway and the affording passage into Heaven."*

The beloved Jewish disciples were the eyewitnesses of the resurrection and the Living Torah Testimony of the Heavenly Ark and they showed others *"The Way"* of salvation.

Acts 16:17 *The same followed Paul and us, and cried, saying, These men are the servants of the Most High God, which shew unto us the Way of salvation.*

Before he saw *"The Light"* and understood the identity of the LORD God of Israel, Saul of Tarsus persecuted the Jewish believers in Messiah who walked in *"The Way,"* until the LORD Yeshua, spoke to him from Heaven. The Shechinah glory light of the LORD shone around about him and he heard the LORD'S voice. *The voice from Heaven said in Hebrew, "I AM Yeshua of Nazareth, whom you are persecuting!"*

Acts 9:1-2 *And Saul, yet breathing out threatening and slaughter against the disciples of the LORD, went unto the High Priest, And desired of him letters to Damascus to the Synagogues, that if he found any of the way, whether they were men or women, he might bring them bound unto Jerusalem.*

Acts 22:4-11 *And I persecuted the way unto death, binding and delivering into prisons both men and women. As also the High Priest doth bear me witness, and all the estate of the Elders; from whom also I received letters unto the brethren, and went to Damascus, to bring them which were there bound unto Jerusalem, for to be punished. And it came to pass, that, as I made my journey, and was come nigh unto Damascus about noon, suddenly there shone from Heaven a great light round about me. And I fell unto the ground, and heard a voice saying unto me, Saul, Saul, why persecutest thou Me? And I answered, Who art Thou, LORD? And He said unto me, I AM Yeshua of Nazareth, whom thou persecutest. And they that were with me saw indeed the light, and were afraid; but they heard not the voice of Him that spake to me. And I said, What shall I do LORD? And the LORD said unto me, Arise, and go into Damascus; and there it shall be told thee of all things which are appointed for thee to do. And when I could not see for the glory of that light, being led by the hand of them that were with me, I came into Damascus.*

The Way that we are to walk behind Yeshua, *behind the Ark of Heaven is called, "The straight and narrow path."* So Messiah Yeshua, who restores the Eternal Davidic Dynasty, appeared in the Shechinah glory light to Saul on the road to Damascus and Saul was *blinded* by Him! Remember that the blinding of the eyes of the last king of Judah was Zedekiah and when Messiah, the Eternal KING of Judah, came to restore the Davidic Dynasty, they would see *"The light"* of the Rosh HaShanah new moon. So what miraculously happened after Saul was *blinded* by Yeshua? The LORD sent a certain disciple named *"Ananias" to go to "The street called Straight"* because *"Straight is 'The Way' that leads to the Eternal Kingdom of God and to the Living Torah of Life!"* Saul was *three days* without his sight and then Yeshua, the Yad of God, put His Spirit in Ananias so that when he touched Saul with his hand, Saul received his sight, proving that *Yeshua is the Royal Sovereign KING of Heaven.*

Acts 9:8-22 *And Saul arose from the earth; and when his eyes were opened, he saw no man; but they led him by the hand, and brought him into Damascus. And he was three days without sight, and neither did eat nor drink. And there was a certain disciple at Damascus, named Ananias; and to him said the LORD in a vision, Ananias. And he said, Behold, I am here LORD, And the LORD said unto him, Arise, and go into the street which is called Straight, and enquire in the house of Judas for one called Saul, of Tarsus; for, behold, he prayeth, And hath seen in a vision a man named Ananias coming in, and putting his hand on him, that he might receive his sight. Then Ananias answered, LORD, I have heard by many of this man, how much evil he hath done to thy Saints at Jerusalem; And here he hath authority from the Chief Priests to bind all that call on Thy Name. But the LORD said unto him, Go thy way; for he is a chosen vessel unto me, to bear My Name before the Gentiles, and Kings, and the children of Israel; For I will shew him how great things he must suffer for My Name's sake. And Ananias went his way, and entered into the house; and putting his hands on him said, Brother Saul, the LORD even Yeshua, that appeared unto thee in the way as thou camest, hath sent me, that thou mightiest receive thy sight, and be filled with the Holy Spirit. And immediately there fell from his eyes as it had been scales; and he received his sight forthwith, and arose, and was baptized. And when he had received meat, he was strengthened. Then was Saul certain days with the disciples which were at Damascus. And straightway he preached Messiah in the Synagogues, that He is the Son of God. But all that heard him were amazed, and said; Is not this he that destroyed them which called on this Name in Jerusalem, and came hither for that intent, that he might bring them bound unto the Chief Priests? But Saul increased the more in strength, and confounded the Jews which dwelt at Damascus, proving that this is very Messiah.*

Saul was chosen by the LORD and after this miraculous encounter, Saul went to *Mount Sinai to confer with Yeshua!* While he was there on the Holy Mount, the LORD instructed him that he was now to take *"The Living Torah, Yeshua's message of Eternal salvation in the Living Ark, not only to the Gentiles, but also to many Kings and nations and to the children of*

Israel that had been scattered. Saul/Paul then immediately took the message to the Synagogues and confounded the Jewish people, who were completely amazed. Paul was strengthened by the true meat, *by the Living Torah,* proving that this is very much Messiah, KING Yeshua of Israel! *The Heavenly Ark of God leads us to the straight gate behind Him in the narrow pathway that leads us to Eternal life!*

Bridge Photo ©2013 Kimberly K Ballard

Matthew 7:13-14 *Enter ye in at the straight gate; for wide is the gate, and broad is the way, that leadeth to destruction, and many there be which go in thereat; Because straight is the gate, and narrow is the way, which leadeth unto life, and few there be that find it.*

In the story of Balaam and the donkey, the angel of the LORD stood in the very narrow path of the vineyard before Balaam and his donkey. It was here that the angel of the LORD placed himself, so that there was *no passage* for Balaam and his donkey. The *narrow path "was a straight place"* where there was no room to turn around. The LORD was revealing in this story, through force, that *He is the true straight and narrow path that leads to righteousness and Eternal life.* It says, however, that Balaam loved the reward of unrighteousness! It is also written that *"having left the straight way, they have gone astray, having followed the path of Balaam. He loved the reward of unrighteousness."*

Now when John the Baptist prepared *"The Way"* for the arrival of Messiah the LORD, he proclaimed the words, *"The voice of one crying in the wilderness, make ready "The Way" of the LORD, make His paths straight!"* Therefore, when we are walking in *"The Way"* that leads to Heaven, along *His straight and narrow* path that leads to life, *the path of the Living Torah,* ultimately leads to the healing and restoration of the earth! It is *"The Way" everlasting* and we are instructed to walk in it!

Pathway
Photo ©2013 Kimberly K Ballard

Psalm 139:23-24 *Search me, O God, and know my heart; try me, and know my thoughts; And see if there be any wicked way in me, and lead me in the way everlasting.*

Hebrews 12:13 *Make straight the paths for your feet, lest that which is lame be turned out of the way; but let it rather be healed.*

Hebrews 10:19-20 *Having therefore, brethren, boldness to enter into the Holiest by the blood of Yeshua, By a new and living way, which He hath consecrated for us, through the veil, that is to say, His flesh; And having an High Priest over the House of God; Let us draw near with a true heart in full assurance of faith, having our hearts sprinkled from an evil conscience, and our bodies washed with pure water.*

The Messiah, the Living budded Almond Rod and *the Living Torah with the Tree of Life,* was *"raised up"* to sit on His throne between the two Living Cherubim Angels in Heaven, at the gate of Heaven in Mount Moriah, in Jerusalem Israel!

Acts 2:29-30 *Men and brethren, let me freely speak unto you of the patriarch David, that he is both dead and buried, and his sepulchre is with us unto this day. Therefore being a Prophet, and knowing that God had sworn with an oath to him, that of the Fruit of his loins, according to the flesh, He would raise up Messiah to sit on His throne.*

Notice in the following passage that the Cherubim Angels spread their wings *"over the place" of the Ark. In I King's 8:6, "The most Holy place" was considered to be under the wings of the Cherubim Angels!*

II Chronicles 7:8 *For the cherubims spread forth their wings over the place of the Ark, and the cherubims covered the Ark and the staves thereof above.*

Now I believe that we need to look further at this term, *"over the place,"* in respect to the words that were spoken by the *two men in shining garments, the Living Cherubim Angels* in the Garden sepulchre, after Yeshua was raised to life. *This is fantastic because the very words that the two Angels spoke inside the Garden tomb about Yeshua revealed that they were indeed there in "The Holy Place, as the two Living Cherubim Angels of the Heavenly Ark of the Eternal Covenant in Holy Mount Moriah!" I believe and prove they were Moses and Elijah!* This is very exciting because the Holy Place known as *"The Holy of Holies"* is actually called *"The place,"* and this is where the LORD dwells forever between the two Living Cherubim Angels in Holy Mount Moriah, where the Heavenly Temple did rise!

Now it is interesting that Yeshua was raised to life as the First Fruit on the Feast of First Fruits on Nisan 17 because the LORD said in Deuteronomy, *"For Israel to take the First Fruits offering to 'The place' which the LORD God shall choose to place His Name there."*

Deuteronomy 26:2 *That thou shalt take of the first of all the fruit of the earth, which thou shalt bring of thy land that the LORD thy God giveth thee, and shalt put it in a basket, and shalt go unto the place which the LORD thy God shall choose to place His Name there.*

We also find that *"The Lamb"* was to be offered in *"The place."* So Yeshua was *"The Lamb"* killed as the sin offering in *"The place of Holy Mount Moriah."* It is most Holy!

Leviticus 14:13 *And he shall slay the lamb in the place where he shall kill the sin offering and the burnt offering, in the Holy place; for as the sin offering is the Priest's, so is the trespass offering; it is most Holy.*

John 19:41-42 *Now in the place where He was crucified there was a Garden; and in the Garden a new sepulchre, wherein was never man yet laid. There laid they Yeshua therefore because of the Jews preparation day; for the sepulchre was nigh at hand.*

The Passover sacrifice of the Lamb was to be done in *"The place that the LORD was to choose to place His Name there!" In Mount Moriah, the LORD provided the First Fruits offering! He put His Name in the place of the Garden tomb.* I already explained that the *Alpha and Omega* letters are inside and outside the sepulchre of Yeshua in Holy Mount Moriah with the Jewish Priestly Angel pointing to it!

Deuteronomy 16:2 *Thou shalt therefore sacrifice the Passover unto the LORD thy God, of the flock and the herd, in the place which the LORD shall chose to place His Name there.*

The body of the Lamb of God, the Living Torah, was raised to life from "The place" between the two Living Cherubim Angels. The atonement for Israel was always offered in *"The place most Holy."* Yeshua made the sin offering in *"The place most Holy in Mount Moriah."*

I Chronicles 6:49 *But Aaron and his sons offered upon the altar of the burnt offering, and on the altar of incense, and were appointed for all the work of the place most Holy, and to make an atonement for Israel, according to all that Moses the servant of God had commanded.*

Looking back at the story of Esther, the condemnation of Haman, who represents Satan, came just after *"The King came out of the Palace Garden and into "the place" of the banquet of wine."* So Yeshua the KING was resurrected and *He came out of the Palace Garden and into the place of the future banquet of wine in the LORD'S vineyard.* After the KING came out from the Garden and into the place of the banquet of wine, which is Heaven, He condemned Satan forever. Yeshua returns to us as the KING OF KINGS in the banquet of wine at the marriage supper of the Lamb, and He comes to the place where the wine from His vineyard became the Passover cup of our redemption and betrothal.

Esther 7:8 *Then the King returned out of the Palace Garden into the place of the banquet of wine; and Haman was fallen upon the bed whereon Esther was. Then said the King, Will he force the queen also before me in the house? As the word went out of the King's mouth, they covered Haman's face.*

As the Living Torah went out of KING Yeshua's mouth, He covered Satan's face with shame. The two men in shining garments/Living Cherubim Angels were showing Mary Magdalene *"The Seat of Mercy"* in the KING'S Garden. *She was the first to eat the fruit!*

Titus 3:4-7 *But after that the kindness and love of God our Saviour toward man appeared, Not by works of righteousness which we have done, but according to His Mercy He saved us, by the washing of regeneration, and renewing of the Holy Spirit; Which He shed on us abundantly through Yeshua Messiah our Saviour; That being justified by His grace, we should be made heirs according to the hope of Eternal life.*

Luke's Gospel tells us that *"the LORD God of Israel has visited and redeemed His people and that He performed the Mercy that He promised them, giving them "The Way of peace."* The *"raised up horn of salvation"* is the Son of David.

Luke 1:68-79 *Blessed be the LORD God of Israel; for He hath visited and redeemed His people, And hath raised up an horn of salvation for us in the house of His servant David; As He spake by the mouth of His Holy Prophets, which have been since the world began; That we should be saved from our enemies, and from the hand of all that hate us; To perform the Mercy promised to our fathers, and to remember His Holy Covenant; The oath which He sware to our father Abraham, That He would grant unto us, that we being delivered out of the hand of our enemies might serve Him without fear, In holiness and righteousness before Him, all the days of our life. And thou, child, shalt be called the Prophet of the Highest; for thou shalt go before the face of the LORD to prepare His ways; To give knowledge of salvation unto His people by the remission of their sins, Through the tender Mercy of our God; whereby the dayspring from on high hath visited us, To give light to them that sit in darkness and in the shadow of death, to guide our feet into the way of peace.*

The LORD, who meets with us between the Cherubim Angels, was meeting with those who arrived at the Garden tomb, where Yeshua fulfilled the Lamb offering and the First Fruits offering of salvation during Passover, the Feast of Unleavened Bread and the Feast of First Fruits. It was *"The place"* of the condemnation of Satan who's evil curse of death, the *"Baka,"* came to an end forever in *"The place most Holy."* Remember that *"The place"* happens to be by Divine Providence in *"The Royal Stone of Kings"* where I miraculously found the green mineral in the limestone called *"Serpentine!"* The Rock Messiah was quarried out of Mount Moriah, leaving His image behind in the sepulchre, showing us that we were made in His image here, and He became *the cure for the snake bite* of Satan. How incredible is this Testimony? It is *"The place"* where the Royal Sceptre of the Great KING reversed the curse of death forever, giving us His favor and grace. Also, when the two men in shining garments/Living Cherubim Angels told Mary to *"Come and see 'the place' where the LORD lay,"* this was *"The place"* where *"the woman"* was the first to eat the First Fruit from the Almond Tree of Life, taking away her *bitterness* of the curse of death in God's Garden and then she went to tell *"the men"* to come eat this Fruit, so they could live forever with the LORD God of Israel! He who sits between the two Living Cherubim Angels is the Shepherd of Israel and Moses and Elijah in shining garments come to prepare His way as the two witnesses.

Psalm 99:1 *The LORD reigneth; let the people tremble; He sitteth between the cherubims; let the earth be moved.*

Psalm 80:1 *Give ear, O Shepherd of Israel, thou that leadest Joseph like a flock; Thou that dwellest between the cherubims, shine forth.*

Ezekiel 10:1 *Then I looked, and, behold, in the firmament that was above the head of the cherubims there appeared over them as it were a sapphire stone, as the appearance of the likeness of a throne.*

II Kings 19:15 *And Hezekiah prayed before the LORD, and said, O LORD God of Israel, which dwellest between the cherubims, Thou art the God, even Thou alone, of all the kingdoms of the earth; thou hast made Heaven and Earth.*

Remember that I said that the light shined out of the sepulchre at Yeshua's resurrection! The light and the darkness were made cleft, *as evening was becoming morning* on the first day of the week, and *the seed of the fruit tree* came to life *as evening was becoming morning the third day* after Passover.

Now the *two Living Cherubim Angels* appeared again when Messiah Yeshua ascended into Heaven and the Shechinah glory cloud received Him out of their sight. The Jewish disciples were looking toward Heaven, when they saw *"The two men in white apparel," (Moses the Law and Elijah the Prophets)* who proclaimed that Yeshua *(the Living Torah)* would return to the earth *(the Living Ark)* in the same *way* He departed into Heaven in the glory cloud! This is why the *two witnesses* in Revelation arrive shortly before Yeshua returns!

Acts 1:9-11 *And when He had spoken these things, while they beheld, He was taken up; and a cloud received Him out of their sight. And while they looked steadfastly toward Heaven as He went up, behold, two men stood by them in white apparel; Which also said, Ye men of Galilee, why stand ye gazing up into Heaven? This same Yeshua, which is taken up from you into Heaven, shall so come in like manner as ye have seen Him go into Heaven.*

Apparently, Yeshua had been here before and He returns the same way, as we see in the following Scriptures. The Cherubim Angels lifted up their wings and they mounted up from the earth, just like when Yeshua ascended up and the *two men* in white apparel appeared! This Heavenly Ark will return to the earth in Jerusalem Israel in the exact same way!

II Samuel 22:10-11 *He bowed the Heavens also, and came down; and darkness was under His feet. And He rode upon a cherub, and did fly; and He was seen upon the wings of the wind.*

Ezekiel 10:18-19 *Then the glory of the LORD departed from the threshold of the Temple and stood over the Cherubim. And the Cherubim lifted their wings and mounted up from the earth in my sight. When they went out, the wheels were beside them; and they stood at the door of the east gate of the LORD'S House, and the glory of the God of Israel was above them.*

Now there is a very interesting statement about the two Cherubim Angels and the Mercy Seat in the book of Hebrews. This Scripture says *"that they cannot now speak particularly of the Cherubims and the Mercy Seat."* I believe that the reason why they could not speak about them then was because the Heavenly Ark and all it contains is truly *"The mystery of the Messiah of Israel, who is revealed as the LORD God of Israel whose Divine Testimony is the Heavenly Ark of the Eternal Covenant!"* The Testimony of Messiah Yeshua is written into every detail of the Ark of *the LORD* in Heaven and *this has been kept a secret mystery until the time of the end, along with the identity of the two witnesses.* When KING Yeshua returns to earth, He is the Heavenly Ark that descends. He will sit upon His throne of glory between the two men in shining garments/Living Cherubim Angels and rule forever.

Hebrews 9:1-5 *Then verily the first Covenant had also ordinances of Divine service, and a worldly Sanctuary. For there was a Tabernacle made; the first, wherein was the candlestick, and the table, and the shewbread; which is called the Sanctuary. And after the second veil, the Tabernacle which is called the Holiest of all; Which had the*

golden censer, and the Ark of the Covenant overlaid round about with gold, wherein was the golden pot that had manna, and Aaron's rod that budded, and the tables of the Covenant; And over it the Cherubim's of glory shadowing the Mercy seat; of which we cannot now speak particularly.

In this Hebrews passage, *they knew that the earthly Ark was now obsolete, because the LORD was the fulfillment of everything pertaining to the Eternal, Living, and incorruptible Testimony of the Heavenly Ark.* So His Covenant with mankind is forever sealed within this *Living Ark* and it can never be changed or reversed. I believe that Ron Wyatt did find the *earthly Ark* at the crucifixion site complete *(rendering of it is shown on the cover of this book), while inside the Garden tomb was the fulfillment of the Eternal Heavenly Ark of the Covenant that would forever take its place.* Incredibly, I just found out that Ron found two Tiberius coins there at the crucifixion site *(bitter),* one under the cross hole plug and the other inside the cave, and the LORD gave me a Tiberius coin, and this Testimony is at the resurrection site *(sweet)!* Maybe the LORD has been waiting for this to come together to reveal it! *Also, I just noticed that my Jewish Priestly Angel with the mantle at the Garden tomb does appear to resemble one of the Angels on Ron Wyatt's Ark of the Covenant rendering! The moment that Heaven was opened, the Ark of His Living Testament was visible, and it was made without hands!*

Revelation 11:19 *And the Temple of God was opened in Heaven, and there was seen in His Temple the Ark of His Testament; and there were lightnings, and voices, and thunderings, and an earthquake, and great hail.*

Matthew 25:31 *When the Son of man shall come in His glory, and all the Holy angels with Him, then shall He sit upon the throne of His glory.*

Hebrews 9:24 *For Messiah is not entered into the Holy Places made with hands, which are the figures of the true; but into Heaven itself, now to appear in the presence of God for us.*

The Mercy Seat of the Ark of the Covenant is referred to as *"Kaporet"* in Hebrew and was translated into the Greek word *"hilasterion,"* which was translated into the word *"propitiation."* The Mercy Seat itself is therefore referred to as *"The propitiation."* This is *"The place"* where the body of Messiah Yeshua was resting between the two Living Cherubim Angels. Now the Mercy Seat was not only *the atonement piece* of the Ark, but *"The Mercy Seat"* actually refers *"To cleansing or taking away sins by the grace of God."* Yeshua was called *"The propitiation"* in the New Testament and grace and truth came by Him. The two men in shining garments/Angels were pointing to *"The place"* of the taking away of our sins by the *life blood atonement* of the LORD turning them white as snow. The LORD God sprinkled His life blood on the Mercy Seat in *"The place"* between the two Living Angels, who verified that Yeshua had become *"The propitiation"* of the LORD God of Israel.

Romans 3:23-25 *For all have sinned, and come short of the glory of God; Being justified freely by His grace through the redemption that is in Messiah Yeshua; Whom God hath set forth to be a propitiation through faith in His blood, to declare His righteousness for the remission of sins that are past, through the forbearance of God.*

I John 2:1-2 *My little children, these things write I unto you, that ye sin not. And if any man sin, we have an advocate with the Father, Yeshua Messiah the righteous; And He is the propitiation for our sins; and not for ours only but also for the sins of the whole world.*

I John 4:9-10 *In this was manifested the love of God toward us, because that God sent His only begotten Son into the world, that we might live through Him. Herein is love, not that we loved God, but that He loved us, and sent His Son to be the propitiation for our sins.*

Strange occurrences transpired in the Holy Temple in Jerusalem before it was destroyed in 70 AD, in the forty years after the resurrection and ascension of Messiah Yeshua. The Jewish sages recorded the details of the peculiar happenings that were most unusual.

I believe they detail that Messiah Yeshua precisely fulfilled the Testimony of the LORD. *Rabbi Jonathan Cahn from "Hope of the World Ministries," who has spoken of these strange occurrences said; Quote; "Talmud Bavli Yoma 39b states the following." "The Rabbis taught that forty years before the Temple was destroyed, the lot never came into the right hand, the red wool did not become white, the western light did not burn, and the gates of the Temple opened of themselves, till the time that R. Johanan b. Zakkai rebuked them, saying: "Hekel, Hekel, why alarmest thou us? We know that thou art destined to be destroyed. For of thee hath prophesied Zechariah ben Iddo [Zech. xi. 1]: "Open thy doors, O Lebanon, and the fire shall eat thy cedars."* " The LORD revealed the following understanding of the strange events to me.

1. The red wool did not become white on earth because Messiah Yeshua had become *"The propitiation."* In Heaven, as it is written in the book of Revelation, it tells us that Yeshua's head and hair are white like wool, white as snow. We only wear the shining white garments when we are transformed into our glorious Eternal state through Messiah, the Bridegroom of Israel.

2. The lot never came into *the right hand* because Messiah is the Rod, *the Royal Sceptre in the right hand of God, the Great KING.* He is *the Yad* who came to save us from our sins.

3. The light would not burn on the Holy Menorah because *Yeshua is the light of the world* and He had left the building! *The light of the Living Almond Tree Menorah had departed from us and He had ascended back into Heaven.*

4. The gates of the Heavenly Temple were opened on their own accord because *Yeshua made "The Way" through the two Living Cherubim Angels, so we could enter through His gates into the Eternal Temple in Heaven.* (Rabbi Cahn verified this one too with the torn veil!) The earthly Temple was destroyed, but the Messiah builds the Spiritual Eternal Temple of Heaven that will eventually dwell in our midst at His return from Heaven.

Matthew 12:6-8 *But I say unto you, that in this place is one greater than the Temple. But if ye had known what this meaneth, I will have Mercy, and not sacrifice, ye would not have condemned the guiltless. For the Son of man is LORD even of the Sabbath day.*

Jude 21 *Keep yourselves in the love of God, looking for the Mercy of our LORD Yeshua Messiah unto Eternal life.*

In Psalm 136, it is written *26 times* that *"The LORD'S Mercy endures forever!"* The Jewish disciple Simon Peter wrote that this is the *Mercy that Messiah would bring us* when the LORD became *"The propitiation,"* by God's grace in *"The place"* where the Majestic KING inscribed His Name forever in Jerusalem on His Holy Mount Moriah. We must enter Heaven at this gate because this is where His throne will be established forever. This is ready to be revealed in the last time!

I Peter 1:2-5 *Elect according to the foreknowledge of God the Father, through sanctification of the Spirit, unto obedience and sprinkling of the blood of Yeshua Messiah; Grace unto you, and peace, be multiplied. Blessed be the God and Father of our LORD Yeshua Messiah which according to His abundant Mercy hath begotten us again unto a lively hope by the resurrection of Yeshua Messiah from the dead. To an inheritance incorruptible, and undefiled, and that fadeth not away, reserved in Heaven for you, Who are kept by the Power of God through faith unto salvation ready to be revealed in the last time.*

Matthew 7:13-14 *Enter ye in at the strait gate; for wide is the gate, and broad is the way, that leadeth to destruction, and many there be which go in there at; Because strait is the gate, and narrow is the way, which leadeth unto life, and few there be that find it.*

John 14:19-21 *Yet a little while, and the world seeth Me no more; but ye see Me; because I live, ye shall live also. At that day ye shall know that I AM in My Father, and ye in Me, and I in you. He that hath My Commandments, and keepeth them, he it is that loveth Me; and he that loveth Me shall be loved of My Father, and I will love him, and will manifest Myself to him.*

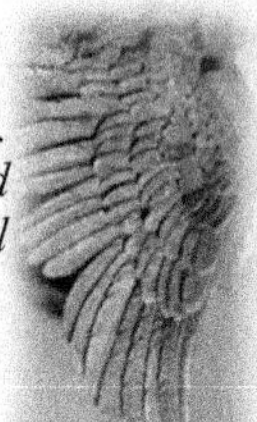

Yeshua said, *"Yet a little while and the world will see Me no more,"* but we see Him and we are part of His Eternal Covenant of life and yet a little while the wicked shall be no more because the Royal Divine KING has prevailed!

Psalm 37:10 *For yet a little while, and the wicked shall not be; yea, thou shalt diligently consider his place, and it shall not be.*

The mystery of Messiah Yeshua is ready to be revealed because it is the last time and the last hour. We are very near to His return from Heaven. I have shown by many true inspiring and profound Divine revelations that the Messiah is the KING OF KINGS AND LORD OF LORDS. Messiah Yeshua holds all power and authority to rule the universe forever.

The details of the Royal Regalia have given us a Regal, living picture of all the glorious elements involved in the Testimony of the Royal Sovereign and Majestic KING of Glory. The time is soon to come when the LORD will descend from Heaven with a shout and with the trump of God and those who hear His voice will be blessed! The dead will rise first and we that are living and remain over shall be caught away in the glory cloud and thus we shall always be with the LORD forever. What a glorious event this will be and for every single person that puts their trust in the truth of the LORD'S Living Testimony, they will live forever in the Paradise of God. The LORD God of Israel is beautiful and He shines the light of *His Living Torah* in our hearts. *This KING loved us so much that He was willing to die to save us and to resurrect Himself in exalted glory as the glorious Almond Tree of Eternal Life!* Coronation Day for the KING is soon to arrive, as the LORD returns to establish His Holy Kingdom on the earth. Every year at Rosh HaShanah, on the KINGS Coronation Day, Israel celebrates the Coronation of God as their KING and they declare that He will reign over them forever! This is a beautiful change from the days of the rejection of the Great KING.

At the time of the LORD'S investiture, He will be bestowed with the insignia of His Royal authority, holding all the emblems of His Royal Regalia. His Royal Standard, the Rod and the Ark bearing His image, establishes His morals and Laws forever. His Royal Majesty will be stunningly brilliant to behold. As the Trumpeters surround the KING the Living Ark and the singers stand near Him, they will play and sing the sacred ceremonial music of the Heavenly Sovereign, and people from all over the world will rejoice and blow trumpets at the time of His Coronation. In the *Law of the King,* written in *the Temple Scroll,* a Dead Sea Scroll, in Col. 57, it states that on Coronation day, the King will appoint commanders according to their divisions. He shall select from them one thousand men from each of the twelve tribes, to stay with Him. This select group deliberates with him on matters of justice and Law. ***(Source: Wise, Michael, Abegg Jr, Martin & Cook, Edward. The Dead Sea Scrolls: A New Translation. San Francisco: Harper, An Imprint of HarperCollins Publishers, Inc., Copyright 1996 All Rights Reserved).*** So the 144,000 selected from each tribe *(the Jewish males "redeemed" at birth with thirty pieces of silver),* are 12,000 selected from each of the twelve tribes. They will always remain with the KING deliberating Law and justice.

The Majestic Kings and Queens of the earth will also bring their riches into His marvelous Kingdom, bringing Royal gifts of gold emblazoned with His heraldry, presenting precious jewels to adorn the LORD'S Kingdom with splendor. The streets of the Royal Heavenly city of the Great KING are made of gold so pure it is clear as crystal and transparent as glass. His Royal throne is Eternally glorious because He saved us with the Ark of His Testimony and He sealed it forever between His loving heart and our hearts as a Bride. Soon the KING OF KINGS AND LORD OF LORDS will come with His Royal Procession, wearing every emblem of His Royal Regalia, riding upon a pure Holy white horse and all of His Saints will be riding behind Him on white horses into everlasting glory! To that I say, *"LONG LIVE THE KING!" "LONG LIVE THE KING!"* You will reign forever my precious KING!

Jude 1:25 *To the only wise God our Savior, be Glory and Majesty, Dominion and Power, both now and ever. Amen.*

Behold! He is not here, He is Risen!
God has raised up unto King David a qeren (horn) of salvation
that is an Eternal Kingdom with the rays of His glorious light by His power!

The Empty Garden Tomb, "The place" of KING Messiah Yeshua's resurrection Photograph ©2011 Simon Brown England All Rights Reserved

Yeshua sends His Doves of Peace to us from beyond the grave!
Doves Photo ©2013 Kimberly K Ballard All Rights Reserved

The Royal Coronation Anthem is 'Zadok the Priest' which says:
"AND ALL THE PEOPLE REJOICED, REJOICED!"

"Two Living Cherubim Angel's in the Garden Tomb," An Original artistic rendering Photograph ©2013 Kimberly K Ballard
The place of the former Garden of Eden, where nothing died before the curse of death. This is the place of Eternal Life!
The Bris Cloth Torah Binder of Messiah Yeshua set apart as, "Kadesh," as a promise to marry Israel! The Shroud bear's the image of God!

"Two Living Cherubim Angel's in the Rock Garden Tomb of Mount Moriah," Moses & Elijah, the two men in shining garments the two witnesses of the Torah & the Prophets standing on either side of the LORD'S Living Testimony. An Original artistic rendering Photo ©2013 Kimberly K Ballard - Pointing to: "The Eternal place of the Seat of Mercy inside Holy Mount Moriah saying, "Why seek ye the Living among the dead, He is not here, but is risen!"

The Garden Tomb with the Great Rolling Stone and my Angel pointing to the KINGS Signet Alpha & Omega Photo of the Garden Tomb

The two witnesses are coming to reveal this final Testimony during the Great Tribulation! Remember that Moses went into the Tabernacle of witness and he saw the rod of Aaron that had budded, blossomed and bore almonds (Numbers 17:7-8). Moses was the eternal witness of the resurrected Rod of God. So now consider the fact that in Luke 24 when Messiah the LORD budded, blossomed and bore fruit, there were two men in shining garments that appeared to the women in the Garden tomb proclaiming that the Rod of God had budded and was risen. They were the two witnesses of the Living Torah. On the same day after Simon Peter found the Shroud and Sudarium in the tomb, the men walking on the road to Emmaus had the encounter with the resurrected Messiah. Cleopas mentioned to Yeshua that the women saw a vision of angels at the tomb and others among them went there and found it so. They saw the Testimony of the Heavenly Ark inside the Garden tomb of God's Holy Mount Moriah. Yeshua then said that they are slow of heart to believe. At that point Yeshua mentioned the two witnesses when He said to them, Beginning at Moses and all the Prophets all things must be fulfilled which were written in the Law of Moses and in the Prophets (and Psalms) concerning Me. So the very same day that the two men (witnesses) appeared in shining garments in the tomb proclaiming that the Almond Rod of God had budded, twice Yeshua mentioned the Law (Moses) and the Prophets (Elijah) that must be fulfilled. Moses and Elijah are clearly the two men in shining garments (in their glorified state) that are the two witnesses (olive trees) that are symbolic of all the Law on one side, and all the Prophets on the other side of the Living Ark of the Covenant standing before the LORD of all the earth (The Holy Almond Tree Menorah), bearing this Living Testimony of the Heavenly Ark. The two men in shining garments appeared again in Acts 1:10-11 after Yeshua twice mentioned (Moses & the Prophets), and Yeshua (the Heavenly Ark) was taken up into Heaven. The two witnesses that accompany the Living Torah went back into Heaven shortly after the Messiah ascended up after His resurrection as the Living Almond Rod of God. So their witness of this Testimony will arrive shortly before His return to earth to prepare the people for KING Yeshua's arrival. They are anointed to proclaim His mighty power in the near future! The two witnesses (Moses & Elijah) reveal this Testimony of the Rod of God (that is the mystery of God that is finished in Revelation 10:7) to turn the hearts of the children to their fathers in Israel just before KING Yeshua descends from Heaven to reign forever in Jerusalem!

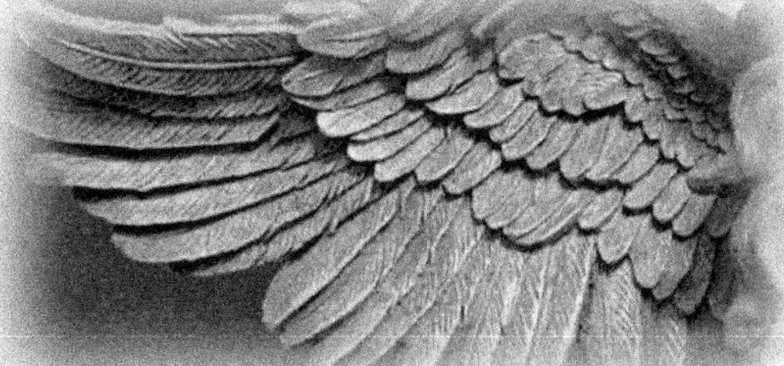

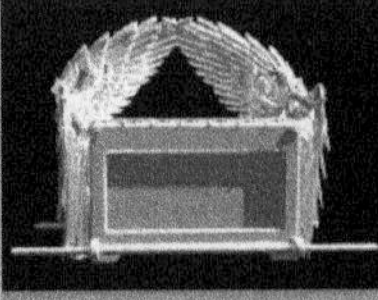

Ark of the Covenant ©2010 Anchor Stone International All Rights Reserved

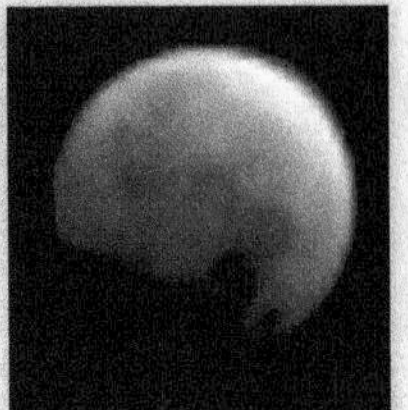

THE SPACE TIME CONTINUUM AND MESSIAH THE ETERNAL ARK

Lunar Eclipse Blood Red Moon October 8th 2014 Photo ©2014 Kimberly K Ballard All Rights Reserved

Lunar Eclipse Blood Red Moon October 8th 2014 Photo ©2014 Kimberly K Ballard All Rights Reserved

As I was writing this down, I had an incredible revelation from the LORD. After the LORD showed me the *two Living Cherubim Angels* in Holy Mount Moriah at the Garden tomb, I miraculously discovered by Divine Providence another fantastic truth, pertaining to the Heavenly Ark and I have to say that I was stunned by it! There is another remarkable connection between Joshua with the earthly Ark and Messiah Yeshua, the Eternal Heavenly Ark. No one has ever understood why there is a gap of two thousand years between the time that Messiah Yeshua was taken up to Heaven until the time that He returns to usher in the Kingdom of Heaven. Now I will use the following Scripture to explain every detail and to demonstrate what the LORD just revealed to me about this that is so astonishing!

Joshua 3:1-7 *AND Joshua rose early in the morning; and they removed from Shittim, and came to Jordan, he and all the children of Israel, and lodged there before they passed over. And it came to pass after three days, that the officers went through the host; And they commanded the people, saying, When ye see the Ark of the Covenant of the LORD your God, and the Priests the Levites bearing it, then ye shall remove from your place, and go after it. Yet there shall be a space between you and it, about two thousand cubits by measure, come not near unto it, that ye may know the way by which ye must go; for ye have not passed this way heretofore. And Joshua said unto the people, Sanctify yourselves; for tomorrow the LORD will do wonders among you. And Joshua spake unto the Priests, saying, Take up the Ark of the Covenant, and pass over before the people. And they took up the Ark of the Covenant, and went before the people. And the LORD said unto Joshua, This day will I begin to magnify thee in the sight of all Israel, that they may know that, as I was with Moses, so I will be with thee.*

Venus Photo ©2013 Kimberly K Ballard All Rights Reserved

Everything on the earth is measured by *"earthly measurements,"* but as you transcend the earth into *Space,* then everything beyond the earth in the universe is measured in *"Space Time."* So I was given the most profound revelation by the LORD. With Joshua, there was to be left a space of 2,000 cubits by earthly measure between the Ark of the Covenant and the people who followed behind it, after it was *taken up*, and they were not to come near the Ark as they prepared to enter the Promised Land. As I thought about Joshua, *three times* the LORD impressed it upon me that with Messiah Yeshua, *"The Space is a Measure of Time!"* I repeated it to myself three times to ponder what it meant. Now I understand what the LORD just revealed to me! Messiah Yeshua said that His Kingdom was not of this world and He ascended into Heaven beyond the earth, somewhere in the *Space* of the universe. *So as I pondered this in my mind and heart, I realized that the Space that was left between Messiah Yeshua, the Heavenly Ark of the Eternal Covenant and the people following after Him, after He was "taken up," who are preparing to enter the Eternal Promised Land is "a Space of 2,000 years as a Measure of Time!"*

This was so astonishing to me because this explained the gap of 2,000 years between the ascension of Messiah Yeshua who was *"taken up"* into Heaven and His return to dwell in our midst forever, completing the redemption process for Israel.

So as soon as I repeated and pondered the LORD'S Words to myself three times that *"the Space is a Measure of Time,"* then I knew that it pertained to physics! The Measure of *"Space Time,"* regarding the LORD Messiah, who created the universe, directly connects Him to the *"Space-Time Continuum,"* and of course this reminds me of Einstein's Theory of Relativity! After three days, Yeshua was resurrected as the Living Almond Rod and later He was *"taken up"* into Heaven, *"leaving the Space of 2,000 years as a Measure of Time between us and the Heavenly Ark." So the Space involving His return pertains to the "Space Time Continuum."*

The Moon lined up with Venus & Jupiter with Stars Photo ©2013 Kimberly K Ballard All Rights Reserved

Of course, the LORD is the source of the light, and light is an additional element of the physics of *Space*. As I pondered this and researched the *Space-Time Continuum,* I found that it is still considered to be a great mystery of the universe. The Scriptures tell us that *"the LORD upholds the universe by the Word of His power."* The Word full of His power is Messiah Yeshua, the Living Torah, the Rod of God. Another interesting thought that I had about this is that the ancient Hebrew system of measure was by weight and usually the weights were small round stones. So the LORD commanded that the Hebrews use a perfect and just measure of weight. This would indicate that when the LORD formed the planets and hung the planets on nothing, which is actually invisible gravity, then the LORD set the planets in the universe as stones bearing a perfect measure of weight and the days that mankind lived were lengthened. Also, we now understand that the LORD Messiah was quarried out of Holy Mount Moriah as the perfect and just Rock that serves as the Chief Cornerstone of the Heavenly Temple.

The Moon Photo ©2013 Kimberly K Ballard All Rights Reserved

Job 26:7 *He stretcheth out the north over the empty place, and hangeth the earth upon nothing.*

Isaiah 28:16 *Therefore thus saith the LORD GOD, Behold, I lay in Zion for a foundation a stone, a tried stone, a precious corner stone, a sure foundation; he that believeth shall not make haste.*

Deuteronomy 25:14-15 *Thou shalt not have in thine house divers measures, a great and a small. But thou shalt have a perfect and just weight, a perfect and just measure shalt thou have; that thy days may be lengthened in the land which the LORD thy God giveth thee.*

The LORD KING Messiah *ascended* far above all Heavens after He was *"taken up,"* and He fills all things.

Ephesians 4:9-10 *Now that He ascended, what is it but that He also descended first into the lower parts of the earth? He that descended is the same also that ascended up far above all Heavens, that He might fill all things.*

If the LORD Messiah is before all things as the Living Ark of the Eternal Covenant, then we must follow behind the Ark of Messiah's Divine Testimony and His Divine Laws of the universe to enter into the Heavenly Dimension, into the Heavenly Eternal Kingdom of God. If it is by Him that all things consist, then this means by definition *"that the universe and everything in it was composed by Him."* In other words, the LORD is *the agent* that holds it all together. He is indeed the *"Invisible Assistant!"*

Colossians 1:16-17 *For by Him were all things created, that are in Heaven, and that are in earth, visible and invisible, whether they be thrones, or dominions, or principalities, or powers; all things were created by Him, and for Him; And He is before all things, and by Him all things consist.*

Now one of the mysteries of *the Space-Time Continuum* is said to be the fact that the universe appears to have one time, but it has three *Space* dimensions. Remember Yeshua said that in three days He would build the Temple and a day with the LORD is like a thousand years. The LORD said that He would complete Israel's redemption on the third day. So for 2,000 years, which is really like two days with the LORD, billions of people all over the world have been gathering and following behind Messiah Yeshua, *the Heavenly Ark of the LORD'S Covenant,* preparing through this *measure of Space of 2,000 years* to enter the Eternal Heavenly Kingdom of God. Yeshua *went before all the people* in Israel and was *taken up* to Heaven. On the third day, Yeshua returns to dwell in our midst forever in Jerusalem, seated upon the Eternal throne of His Heavenly Ark of the Covenant containing His Living Testimony. As I thought about the three *Space* dimensions of *Space Time,* I remembered that the Scriptures indicate that a person was *"caught up to the third Heaven."* Perhaps the *third Heaven* refers to *the third Space dimension?* This place was *Paradise* where this man heard *the Living Torah, the Word of God.* So it is interesting that Yeshua said that *He would return the third day*, and this is of course *after the Space of 2,000 years as a measure of time,* to usher in the Heavenly Kingdom of God when the Heavenly throne and Ark rests in our midst forever in Jerusalem! ***(Source: Spacetime – ©2011 en.wikipedia.org/wiki/Spacetime).***

Super Moon setting over the west Rocky Mountains January 17 2014 Photos ©2014 Kimberly K Ballard All Rights Reserved

II Corinthians 12:2-4 *I knew a man in Messiah above fourteen years ago, (whether in the body, I cannot tell; or whether out of the body, I cannot tell; God knoweth;) such an one caught up to the third Heaven. And I knew such a man, (whether in the body, or out of the body, I cannot tell; God knoweth; How that he was caught up into Paradise, and heard unspeakable Words, which it is not lawful for a man to utter.*

Of course, I have shown in previous chapters that Yeshua's Testimony is the Almond Tree Menorah and that the LORD is the source of the light. So at His command, the light that He appointed lit up the universe with the sun, moon, and stars but we must not worship them.

Blood Red Moon Lunar Eclipse October 8th 2014 Photo ©2014 Kimberly K Ballard All Rights Reserved

Genesis 1:14-15 *And God said, Let there be lights in the firmament of the Heaven to divide the day from the night; and let them be for signs, and for seasons, and for days, and years; And let them be for lights in the firmament of the Heaven to give light upon the earth; and it was so.*

Jeremiah 31:36 *Thus saith the LORD, which giveth the sun for a light by day, and the ordinances of the moon and of the stars for a light by night, which divideth the sea when the waves thereof roar; The LORD of Hosts is His Name; If those ordinances depart from before Me, saith the LORD, then the seed of Israel also shall cease from being a nation before Me forever.*

An ordinance is an authoritative decree or law set forth by a governmental authority. So we know that Yeshua said that all power and authority has been given to Him because, as the Royal Sceptre, *He is the Torah Lawgiver* between the feet of the KING. *This means that the universe is set in order by His Laws, authority, and Royal decree.* At Messiah Yeshua's return from Heaven, He said that there would be signs in the sun, in the

Super Moon May 5th 2012 Photos ©2014 Kimberly K Ballard All Rights Reserved

moon, and in the stars and upon the earth, distress of nations. The sea and the waves will be roaring because the Heavens will be shaken. When these cosmic disturbances occur and the earth is thrown off its axis, shifting the balance of its weight in *Space,* the LORD said that the sun and the moon would be darkened and the stars would fall from the Heavens. During this time, the LORD *shortened* the days, but when everything was in perfect balance and was a just measure of weight, He lengthened the days. When the Heavenly Ark returns to earth from Heaven with KING Messiah Yeshua, the entire universe will react to His Divine Presence. Then the curse that abides upon the earth will finally be removed.

In mathematics I read that a *"bounded set"* is considered to be finite in size, kind of like the universe is finite. The so-called *"Space-Time fabric"* deals with wave motion and gravity, which is an *invisible force*. This is verified by the LORD setting an *invisible bound,* so the oceans or the flood waters of Noah would not pass over this bound. *The LORD, who resides in Heaven in Space, used an invisible Measure of Space and Time to set this bound.*

Psalm 104:9 *Thou hast set a bound that they may not pass over; that they turn not again to cover the earth.*

Blood Red Moon Lunar Eclipse October 8th 2014 Photo ©2014 Kimberly K Ballard All Rights Reserved

Since *the Space-Time Continuum* pertains *"to gravity and wave motion,"* it is also interesting that the Prophet Jeremiah also wrote that the LORD sets boundaries, (through gravity) to prevent the ocean from passing over it. Of course the moon and gravity affect the tides and the ocean waves upon the earth and the LORD put the sand as a bound to prevent the overflow of the ocean waters. It is also written that the LORD did this by *"A perpetual decree"* which by definition means *"that this bound will last for eternity and it is a formal and authoritative order, having the force of Law."*

Jeremiah 5:22 *Fear ye not Me? Saith the LORD; will ye not tremble at My Presence, which have placed the sand for the bound of the sea by a perpetual decree, that it cannot pass it; and though the waves thereof toss themselves, yet can they not prevail; though they roar, yet can they not pass over it?*

Psalm 89:9 *Thou rulest the raging of the sea; when the waves thereof arise, Thou stillest them.*

As I began to research this more, the LORD showed me the precise connections between Messiah Yeshua and Joshua, pertaining to the people following behind the Ark of the Covenant. The first thing that correlated is the phrase *"early in the morning."* Joshua rose, *"early in the morning"* and Mary Magdalene came to the tomb *"early in the morning"* only to find the two men in shining garments/Living Cherubim Angels forming the Heavenly Living Ark in the Garden in Holy Mount Moriah where the LORD Messiah's body came to life as the Almond Rod that budded, bearing the First Fruit from the Almond Tree of Life.

John 20:1 *The first day of the week cometh Mary Magdalene early, when it was yet dark, unto the sepulchre, and seeth the stone taken away from the sepulchre.*

In Joshua's account, it specifically says about the Ark of the Covenant, *"And it came to pass after three days, that the officers went through the host; And they commanded the people, saying, When ye see the Ark of the Covenant of the LORD your God, and the Priests the Levites bearing it, then ye shall remove from your place, and go after it."*

Yeshua told the Jewish disciples, *"After three days I will rise again."* So it happened that, after three days, the people saw Yeshua alive as the Living Ark of the Eternal Covenant of the LORD God of Israel. *So they were to remove from their place and go after Him.*

Matthew 27:62-63 *Now the next day, that followed the day of the preparation, the Chief Priests and Pharisees came together unto Pilate, Saying, Sir, we remember that that deceiver said, while He was yet alive, After three days I will rise again.*

Blood Moon October 8th 2014 Photo ©2014 KK Ballard All Rights Reserved

The Second Temple did not have the earthly Ark of the Covenant in it! The truth is that the Second Temple had the Heavenly Ark dwelling in its midst, but this Ark departed and was *taken up* into Heaven by the High Priest of Heaven with *the two Living Cherubim Angels (I believe Moses and Elijah, the two witnesses)* proclaiming that Yeshua would return the same way that He departed in the Shechinah glory cloud! It was also after three days that Yeshua, *the Living Ark,* was found sitting in the midst of the Rabbinical Scholars in the Holy Temple in Jerusalem and everyone that heard His Word was astonished at His answers, His understanding of the Torah, and His doctrine.

Large Full Moon on January 18 2014 Photo ©2014 Kimberly K Ballard All Rights Reserved

Blood Moon October 8th 2014 Photo ©2014 KK Ballard All Rights Reserved

Luke 2:46-47 *And it came to pass, that after three days they found Him in the Temple, sitting in the midst of the doctors, both hearing them, and asking them questions. And all that heard Him were astonished at His understanding and answers.*

In Joshua's account, Joshua wrote, *"And they took up the Ark of the Covenant, and went before the people."* So as soon as Mary saw the two Living Cherubim Angels in the Garden tomb and saw *"The place"* of the Living Testimony of KING Yeshua's resurrection in Holy Mount Moriah, the Angels proclaimed, *"Behold He goeth before you." As soon as they saw the Ark, they were to remove from their place and go after Him!*

Matthew 28:6-7 *He is not here; for He is risen, as He said. Come, see the place where the LORD lay. And go quickly, and tell His disciples that He is risen from the dead; and, behold, He goeth before you into Galilee; there shall ye see Him; lo I have told you.*

Large Full Moon over Pine Tree January 18 2014 Photo ©2014 Kimberly K Ballard All Rights Reserved

The people were to remove when they saw the Ark of the Covenant and they were to go after it, for the LORD said, *"Yet there shall be a space between you and it, about two thousand cubits by measure, come not near unto it, that ye may know the way by which ye must go; for ye have not passed this way heretofore."* The Scripture indicates that with Joshua, *the space of 2,000 cubits by measure was to be left between the Ark and the people going after it and they were not to come near the Ark.* So Messiah Yeshua told Mary at the Garden tomb, *"Touch Me not; for I AM not yet ascended to My Father."* So with Joshua, the space of 2,000 cubits of measure in length was to show them *"The Way" by which they must go, because they had never been this way before, into the Promised Land!* Messiah Yeshua previously told His Jewish disciples, *"And whither I go ye know, and the way ye know."* Again, I refer to Yeshua speaking of *"The Way"* to enter the Eternal Promised Land after He went before the people, leaving *"a Space of 2,000 years, as a Measure of Time"* between Himself, *the Heavenly Ark, and the people who were to follow after Him.* He left this *Space* so we would know *"The Way" that we must go because we have never been this way before into the Eternal Promised Land of Heaven.* The Eternal Living Torah Testimony of Messiah Yeshua makes Him *"the Way, the Truth and the Life."* This is what Yeshua was telling Thomas!

John 14:3-11 *And if I go and prepare a place for you, I will come again, and receive you unto Myself; that where I AM, there ye may be also. And whither I go ye know, and the way ye know. Thomas saith unto Him, LORD, we know not whither Thou goest; and how can we know the way? Yeshua saith unto him, I AM the way, the truth, and the life; no man cometh unto the Father but by Me. If ye had known Me, ye should have known My Father also; and henceforth ye know Him and have seen Him. Philip saith unto Him, LORD, shew us the Father, and it sufficeth us. Yeshua saith unto him, Have I been so long time with you, and yet hast thou not known Me Philip? He that hath seen Me hath seen the Father; and how sayest thou then, Shew us the Father? Believest thou not that I AM in the Father,*

and the Father in Me? The Words that I speak unto you I speak not of Myself; but the Father that dwelleth in Me, He doeth the works. Believe Me that I AM in the Father, and the Father in Me or else believe Me for the very work's sake.

Moon in the clouds Photo ©2013
Kimberly K Ballard All Rights Reserved

Yeshua breathed the Spirit of Life upon His Jewish disciples and He sent them forth to soon be removed from Jerusalem so *His Living Torah Testimony* would go throughout the entire world by *"a Space of 2,000 years, as a Measure of Time,"* and after this *Space of Time*, the people would enter the Eternal Kingdom of God, as they followed behind the Ark *with Yeshua (Joshua) leading the way!* It is fantastic!

John 20:21-22 *Then said Yeshua to them again, Peace be unto you; as My Father hath sent me, even so send I you. And when He had said this, He breathed on them, and saith unto them, Receive ye the Holy Spirit.*

The Ark was *"taken up"* by the Priests. So Messiah Yeshua, the Living Ark was *"taken up into Heaven"* by the High Priest of Heaven. Joshua wrote, *"And Joshua spake unto the Priests, saying, Take up the Ark of the Covenant, and pass over before the people. And they took up the Ark of the Covenant, and went before the people."* As Messiah Yeshua was *"taken up"* into Heaven, *He passed before the people and then the people removed and went forth to follow in "The Way" after the Heavenly Ark! It is now revealed exactly why KING Yeshua has been in Heaven for two thousand years!* This is so exciting! So clearly I have proven that the *Space between the Ark of Heaven* and the people following after it is a measure of *"Space time" instead of earthly cubits!*

Since the LORD Yeshua left this *Space* of two thousand years between Himself, *(the Heavenly Ark)* and the people who are about to enter His Eternal Promised Land that is a Garden of pure Heaven, *we cannot come near Him until we cross over!*

Super moon Photo ©2013
Kimberly K Ballard All Rights Reserved

Acts 1:6-11 *When they therefore were come together, they asked of Him, saying LORD, will Thou at this time restore again the Kingdom to Israel? And He said unto them, It is not for you to know the times or the seasons, which the Father hath put in His own power. But ye shall receive power, after that the Holy Spirit is come upon you; and ye shall be witnesses unto Me both in Jerusalem, and in all Judaea, and in Samaria, and unto the uttermost part of the earth. And when He had spoken these things, while they beheld, He was taken up; and a cloud received Him out of their sight. And while they looked steadfastly toward Heaven as He went up, behold, two men stood by them in white apparel; Which also said; Ye men of Galilee, why stand ye gazing up into Heaven? This same Yeshua, which is taken up from you into Heaven, shall so come in like manner as ye have seen Him go into Heaven.*

One day soon, *the Heavenly Ark of the Covenant* will return from Heaven and the KING OF KINGS will rest upon His Eternal throne in the New Jerusalem, without the curse of the Garden of Eden. Everyone who sees the Ark and follows after Yeshua/Joshua will enter the Eternal Promised Land, if they have walked in *"the Way,"* that leads to life. Whoever has Messiah Yeshua has *"the Way, the Truth and the Life,"* but whoever does not have Yeshua, *the Living Torah,* cannot have life! We must follow behind the Heavenly Ark of the Eternal Covenant because Yeshua the LORD is leading *"the Way" out of the wilderness of the nations* and He is taking us to *a place that we have never ever been before,* across the Jordan River and into the Heavenly

Jerusalem! Now that the Living Ark has been taken up into Heaven, we must prepare ourselves to enter His Heavenly Garden, the Eternal Promised Land, following behind the *Divine Royal Military Standard* of His Highness and Royal Majesty, the everlasting KING of Glory. Amen! It is thrilling to see this for the first time in history! So I must humbly give special thanks to the LORD KING Messiah for revealing this to my heart so I could share it with the world!

The Sudarium, the Sign from Heaven! The Swaddling Cloth of Messiah Yeshua of Nazareth. The Torah Binder that was bound around the Living Torah lying in the manger, in the feeding trough! Yeshua's "Bris Cloth," the Eternal Life blood Covenant, the symbol of the life cycle and set apart as "Kadesh" in the Garden Tomb, as the sign of the LORD'S future Marriage & Covenant to the Land of Israel! He was raised up to a Life of Living Torah and good deeds! This Torah Binder was over the face of the KING, who speaks the Living Torah!

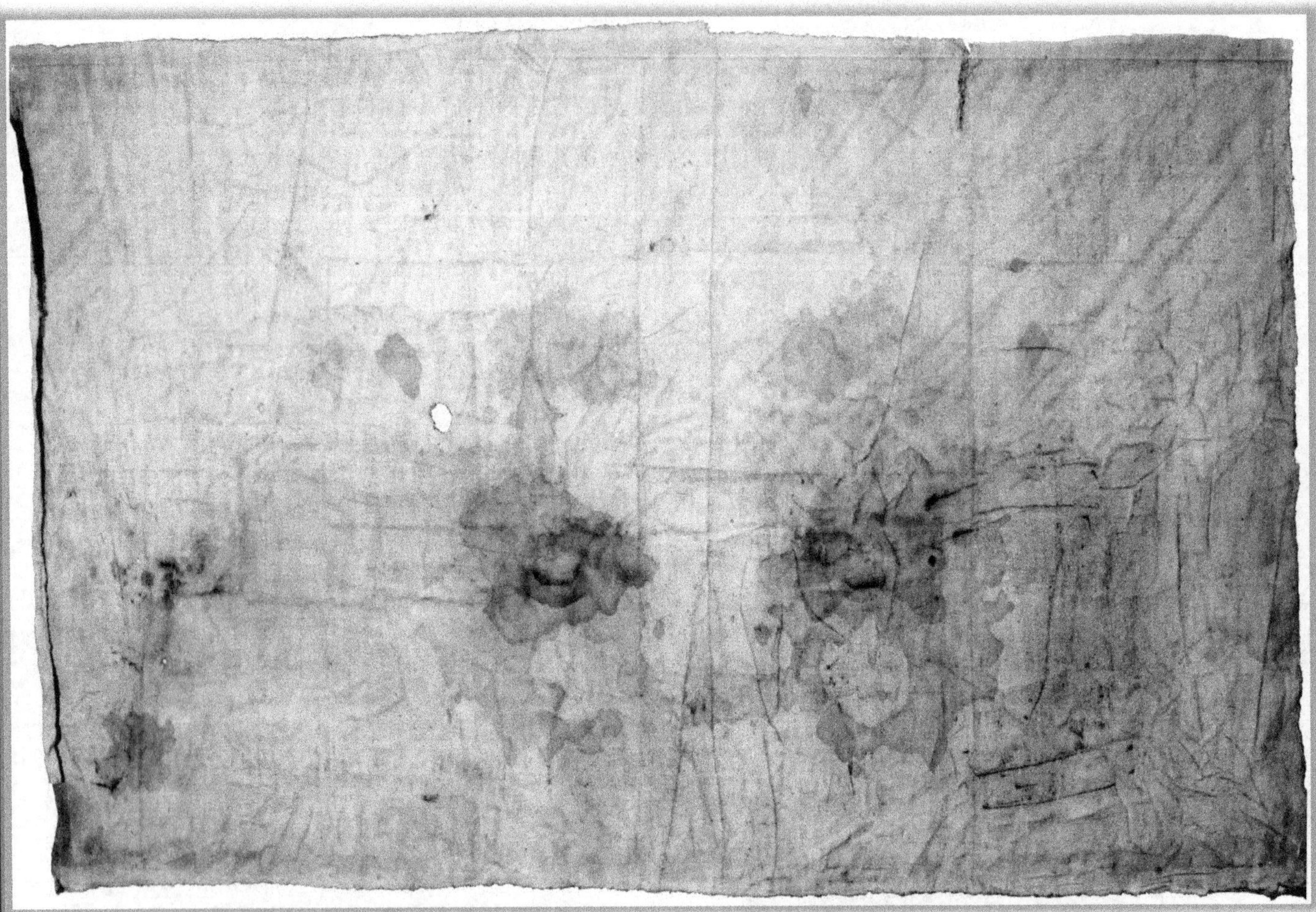

Official Photograph of The Sudarium of Oviedo Spain ©2013 El Centro Español de Sindonologia (CES)
El Centro Español de Sindonologia. Permission to use the Official Photograph of the Sudarium of Oviedo SPAIN, granted on May 8th 2013, By Mark Guscin, LaCoruña, SPAIN and Jorge Manuel Rodriguez, Valencia SPAIN All Rights Reserved

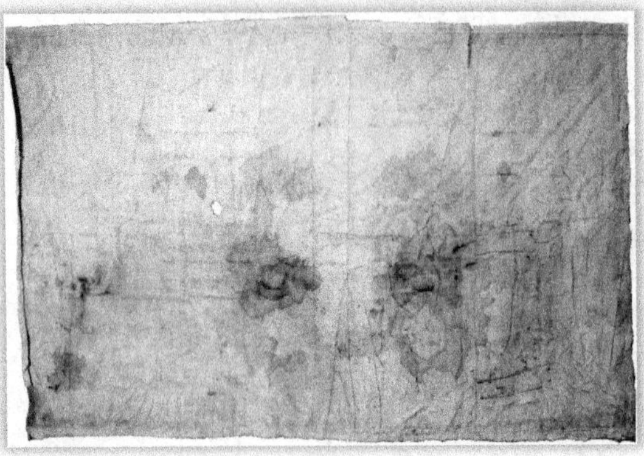

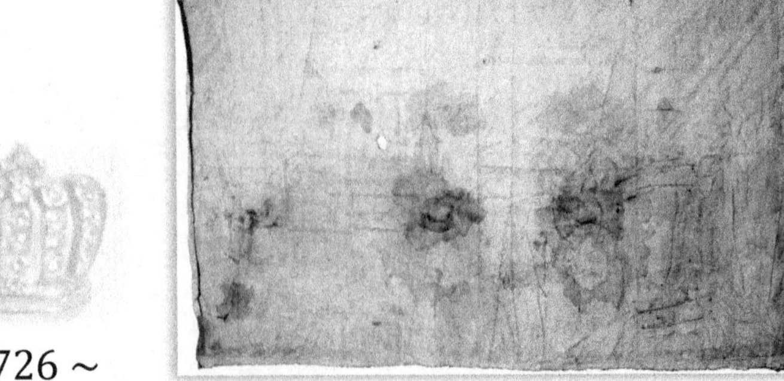

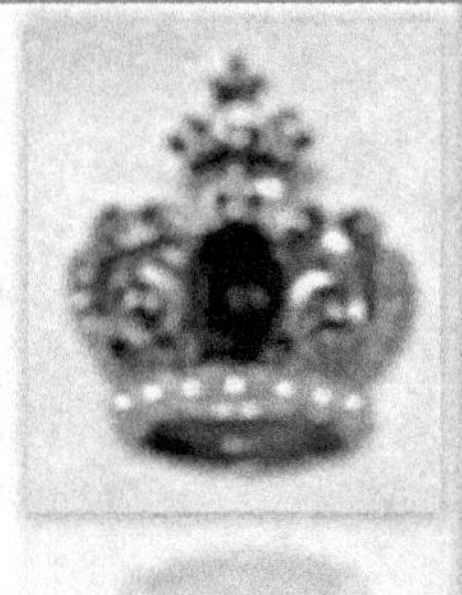

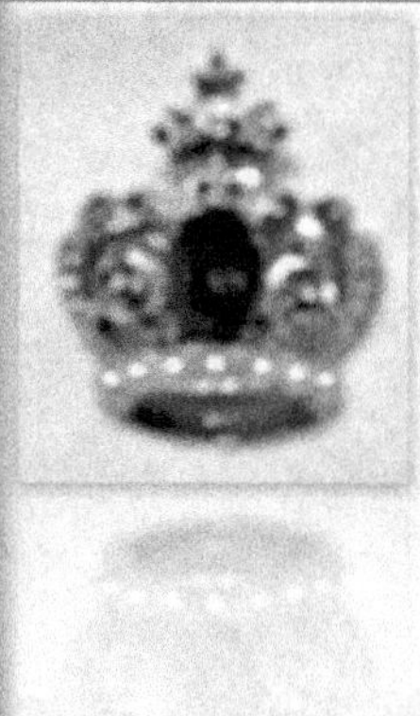

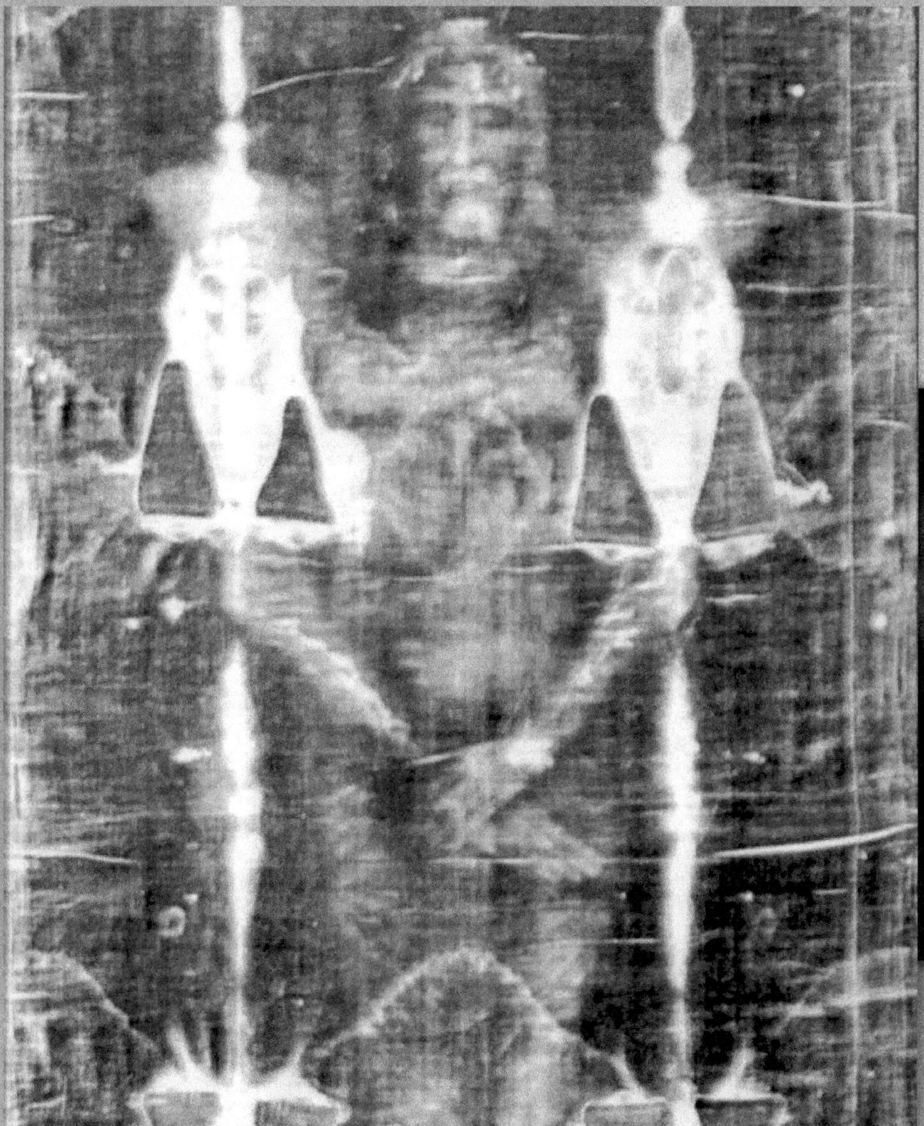

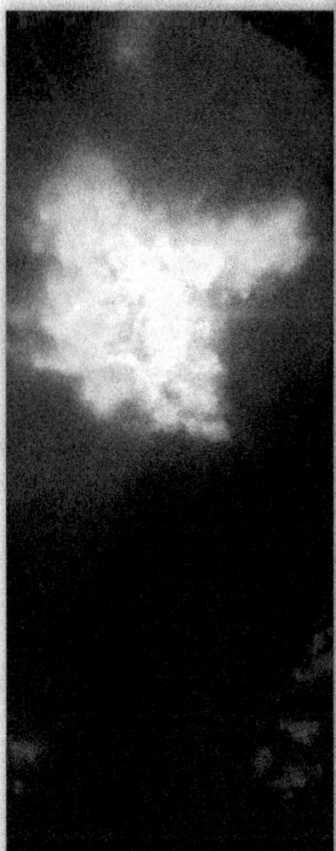

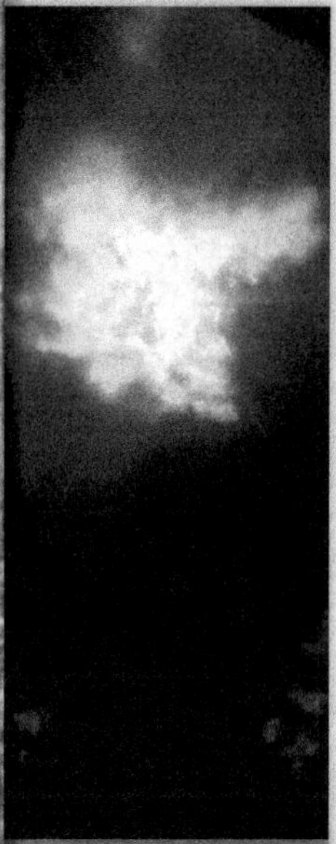

This is the photo I took of a bright figure that appeared in the center of a cloud opening. I thought it looked similar to a Cherubim Angel with two wings! So I put one on either side of this 3D Hologram of Messiah Yeshua's image on His burial Shroud that contains His blood, water and the resurrection power of His Holy Spirit!
& Crown Photo ©2013 Kimberly K Ballard All Rights Reserved

The Heavenly Ark will descend from Heaven in Jerusalem, called His throne in Holy Mount Moriah in the place where He fulfilled the earthly Ark of the Covenant, showing us that He is the Heavenly Ark of the Covenant and all it contains. In that day it is written that they will no longer say "The Ark of the Covenant." For He will be dwelling with us!

John, who was set apart as Kadesh on Mount Sinai was an eyewitness of the majesty of Messiah Yeshua. He saw the Heavenly Ark in His glorified state. He outran Simon Peter and entered the Garden tomb. Earlier, John bore witness nearby at the crucifixion site. When the Almond Rod of God was lifted up, the rocks were cleft in an earthquake along with the Cherubim veil. John saw the blood and water as it gushed from Yeshua's heart. According to Ron Wyatt, it fell through this earthquake crack onto the mercy seat of the earthly Ark (buried at the crucifixion site centuries before). Just before this the people said "Let us see if Elijah will come to save Him!" (Matthew 27:49) Elijah was in the Garden Tomb at the resurrection! In the same place Yeshua fulfilled the Covenant of the Heavenly Ark (sweet), as well as the earthly Ark (bitter)!

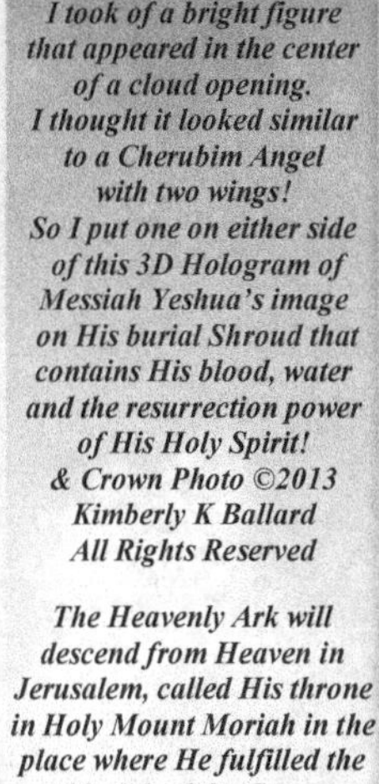

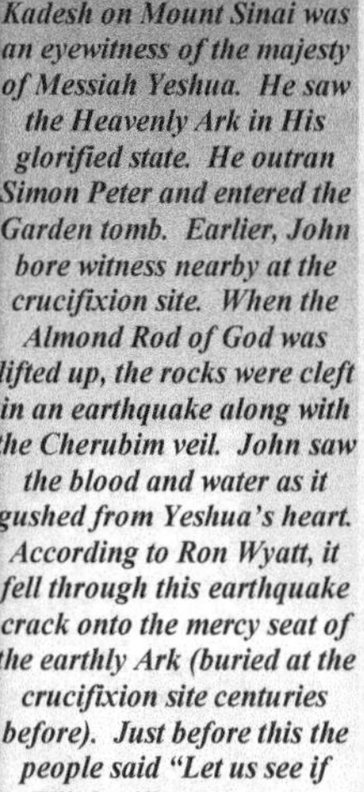

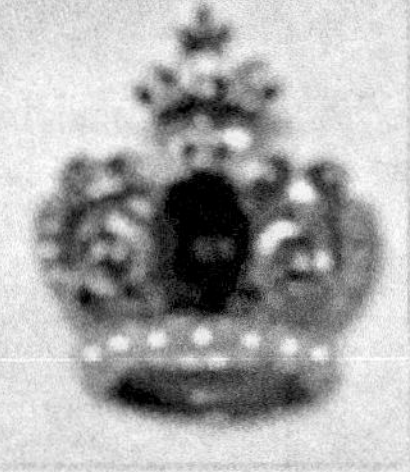

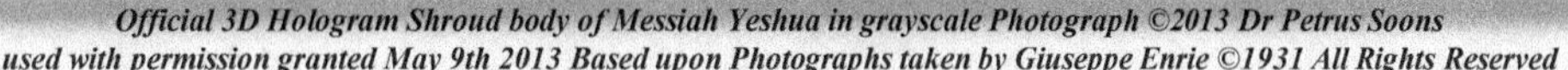

Official 3D Hologram Shroud body of Messiah Yeshua in grayscale Photograph ©2013 Dr Petrus Soons used with permission granted May 9th 2013 Based upon Photographs taken by Giuseppe Enrie ©1931 All Rights Reserved

Official 3D Hologram Shroud face image of Messiah Yeshua in grayscale Photograph ©2013 Dr Petrus Soons used with permission granted May 9th 2013
Based upon Photographs taken by Giuseppe Enrie ©1931 All Rights Reserved

Dedication Farris Memorial
The Stained Glass of Yeshua at Laurel Land Fort Worth, Texas

Dedication 1983 Rose from my friend & mentor Marion

Aleph & Tav & Alpha & Omega Almond Tree in Snow
Photos ©2014 Kimberly K Ballard All Rights Reserved

Chapter 12

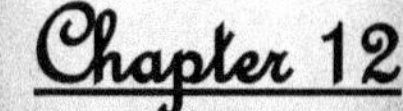

THE ALMOND TREE OF LIFE ALPHA & OMEGA THE FIRST AND THE LAST THE BEGINNING AND THE END

We end this Testimony of the LORD KING by going back to the beginning! After I had emailed my Almond Tree revelation to Jerusalem in 2007, I diligently was researching how the Almond Trees grow in Israel. I was trying to discern if there was anything else that the LORD wanted me to know about Him that was hidden within the Almond Tree. Believe me, it was not a coincidence that the LORD had revealed Himself to me in the Almond Tree at the exact same time that a holiday in Israel, known as *"Tu B' Shevat,"* had just transpired. This holiday is called, *"The New Year of Trees or the Rosh HaShanah of Trees!"* Little did I know *that it is specifically the Almond Tree that comes to life first in Israel, after the winter sap begins to flow through the branches of the Trees on Tu' B Shevat.* The trees literally *"Awaken"* which is *"Shaked"* the word for *Almond!* This is when they *"awaken"* from a type of death or winter rest into a *glorious resurrection* and they spring forth and *bud to life.* I did not know anything about this holiday when the LORD gave me the Almond Tree revelation! I only found out about the holiday and its significance after the fact. When I think about this coincidence, I am overcome with emotion because I know that my miracle from Jerusalem was more of a blessing from the LORD than I ever imagined at first. It was only about a month after my revelation from the LORD that *"Tu B' Shevat"* was brought to my knowledge and attention and I correlated its profound significance to my original miracle!

Remember when the LORD impressed my heart to send that message to Jerusalem, the same day a person who I did not know yet in Israel had photographed the very first Almond Tree that she saw budding and starting to flower in the Old city of Jerusalem on Holy Mount Moriah, just before opening my message. I had no idea that *January-February* in Israel is the time when the sap begins to flow again into the trees, bringing them to *a hasty awakening of life!* Soon the Almond branches would be in full bloom. The flower buds would shoot forth first and then the leaves on each branch, just like the green shoot of Jesse! Without my knowledge, spring was arriving in the Old city of Jerusalem. The Almond Trees were just starting to release their fragrance, filling the air with their sweet delicate perfume. The bees were just beginning to buzz about the flowers in a lively dizzy dance, as they entered the heart of each Almond blossom. They collected the pollen to make honey, *but this sweet honey would*

turn out to be the blessing of the Living Torah from the Almond Branch of the Almond Tree of Eternal Life! At the same time across the ocean, there was a completely different scene. The winter sleep was still abiding on the trees, as their withered branches stood huddled in the stillness of the cold snowy Colorado landscape. I quietly prayed to the LORD, asking Him to show me more about the Almond Tree. Then as He always seemed to hear my prayers, He opened His secrets to my heart again! Then He showed me the final pieces of His Living Testimony and, at the end of this story, His heart was opened to me like the Almond blossom and I could smell the fragrance of Heaven! The glory of the LORD never ends and His miraculous deeds will never be forgotten!

Photos Budding Almond Tree ©2015 All Rights Reserved
Bristle cone pine raindrops, Snow, Crown ©2013 KK Ballard
Alpha & Omega in the Garden Tomb ©2011 Simon Brown England ARR

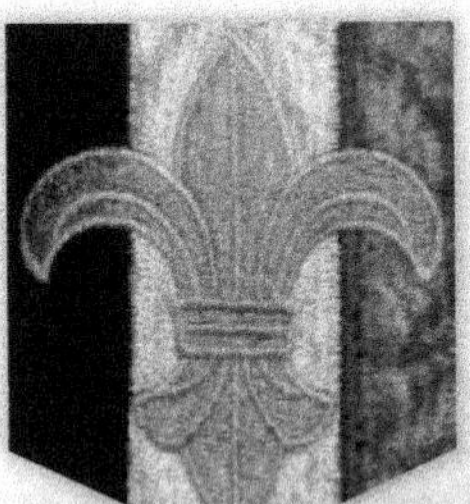

TU B' SHEVAT
THE BUDDING ALMOND

THE NEW YEAR OF TREES
FRANCE

& THE CEDAR OF LEBANON

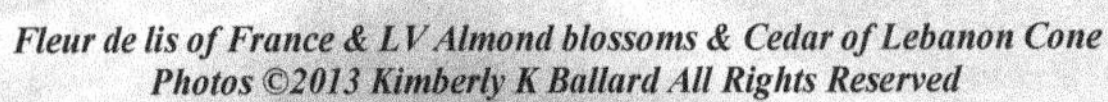

Fleur de lis of France & LV Almond blossoms & Cedar of Lebanon Cone
Photos ©2013 Kimberly K Ballard All Rights Reserved

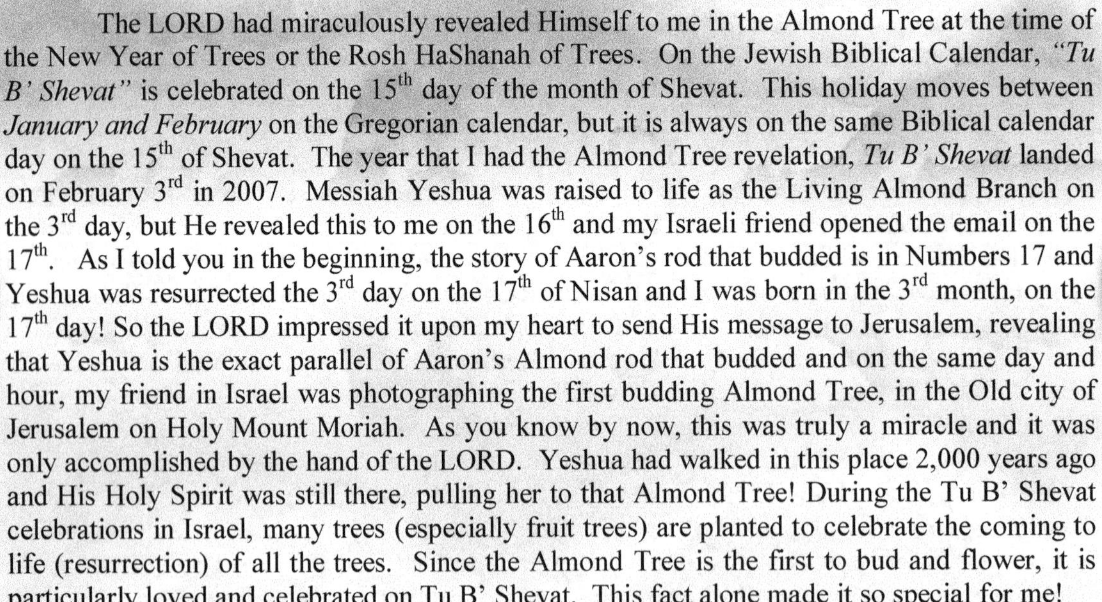

The LORD had miraculously revealed Himself to me in the Almond Tree at the time of the New Year of Trees or the Rosh HaShanah of Trees. On the Jewish Biblical Calendar, *"Tu B' Shevat"* is celebrated on the 15th day of the month of Shevat. This holiday moves between *January and February* on the Gregorian calendar, but it is always on the same Biblical calendar day on the 15th of Shevat. The year that I had the Almond Tree revelation, *Tu B' Shevat* landed on February 3rd in 2007. Messiah Yeshua was raised to life as the Living Almond Branch on the 3rd day, but He revealed this to me on the 16th and my Israeli friend opened the email on the 17th. As I told you in the beginning, the story of Aaron's rod that budded is in Numbers 17 and Yeshua was resurrected the 3rd day on the 17th of Nisan and I was born in the 3rd month, on the 17th day! So the LORD impressed it upon my heart to send His message to Jerusalem, revealing that Yeshua is the exact parallel of Aaron's Almond rod that budded and on the same day and hour, my friend in Israel was photographing the first budding Almond Tree, in the Old city of Jerusalem on Holy Mount Moriah. As you know by now, this was truly a miracle and it was only accomplished by the hand of the LORD. Yeshua had walked in this place 2,000 years ago and His Holy Spirit was still there, pulling her to that Almond Tree! During the Tu B' Shevat celebrations in Israel, many trees (especially fruit trees) are planted to celebrate the coming to life (resurrection) of all the trees. Since the Almond Tree is the first to bud and flower, it is particularly loved and celebrated on Tu B' Shevat. This fact alone made it so special for me!

It is interesting that I have been working on this book since 2007. Now as I write this into my story, it is 2011 during the week of Tu B' Shevat, which occurred from sunset on January 19th through sunset January 20th and by some incredible coincidence, the LORD brought Rabbi Chaim Richman of the Temple Institute from Jerusalem to Colorado. *Even though Tu B' Shevat moved to January, from the month of February this year, the LORD brought this blessing within days of this holiday of the Almond Tree!* Why is this so important

you might ask? Rabbi Richman brought with him *the actual blueprints for the Third Holy Temple in Jerusalem! I saw the Sanhedrin building that will be at the Temple.* He traveled to Colorado on January 25th *during the week that Tu B' Shevat* was celebrated in Israel and I was there in person to see him with his blueprints! For 2,000 years, since the destruction of the Second Temple in the year 70AD, the Temple has not been rebuilt and *no blueprints* have ever been drawn up by an architect. No Rabbi has ever come to visit near my house with *the blueprints* for the Third Temple! Remember the number three is so significant to the LORD!

It is a prophecy in the Bible that the Third Temple will be built in Jerusalem, just before the Messiah returns to the earth. How is it that these two incredible events occurred during Tu B' Shevat in my lifetime? As the Rabbi spoke at the event, he mentioned *"that the time of Tu B' Shevat, is a time of rejuvenation."* He said, *"During this whole month of Shevat, the Divine energy reverberates throughout all creation."* No wonder the LORD chose to reveal Himself to me in the Almond Tree at this special time of the year! *This month is all about renewing our relationship with God. It is a very special Divine time of the year.* As I listened to the Rabbi, I was thinking about how incredible it is that for 2,000 years this Temple has not been rebuilt. Sitting in front of me on the podium, as I listened to him speak, was a complete set of these blueprints of the Third Holy Temple and he lifted them up to view them, and showed a video animation of it. I pondered how many billions of people over the centuries longed for this day to come to pass and here it was before me! It seemed like a regular day, but it was truly the fulfillment of ancient Bible prophecy coming to pass. *This is the Temple that ushers in the Messiah of Israel and the Messiah had just previously manifested Himself to me in the Almond Tree near Tu B' Shevat when the Divine energy reverberates! Incredible!*

Now this reminds me of another miracle that happened to me *during Tu B' Shevat* in 2010. I had been trying to sprout the same type of Cedar trees that King Solomon had used to build the First Holy Temple in Jerusalem. The Cedars from the Forest of the LORD are extremely rare because this Forest in Lebanon is now a protected Forest, so no one can touch it. I relayed the story of this miracle and how it all unfolded in the following letter that I sent to Jerusalem on May 21st 2010 because I thought it was so fabulous! The Altar of the LORD was overlaid with this Cedar wood!

Sent to the Temple Institute in Jerusalem Friday, May 21, 2010 4:07 pm Subject: A Special miracle Cedar Tree once again sprouting to life for the LORD!

Dear Rabbi Yitzchak Reuven,

I have something to share with you that hopefully you will find incredible. In 2005 I had the great honor and privilege to stand beneath a true Cedar of Lebanon Tree, *the Cedrus Libani,* which is the same type of tree that King Solomon used to build the Holy Temple of the LORD that came from the Forest of God in Lebanon. The tree is over 200 years old and was planted in the Gardens of President Madison's home in Montpelier Virginia. Upon my own extensive research, I was able to determine that this Cedar tree was likely from an original Cedar of the Forest of God in Lebanon *that was taken to France to "The Jardin des Plantes"* in the early 1700's. This was the huge beautiful Botanical Gardens in France and this tiny Cedar tree was transplanted from the Forest of God and planted inside the Botanical Gardens in France. Thomas Jefferson, who collected many rare seeds, obtained seeds from this tree when He visited the Botanical Gardens in France and he likely shared the seeds, as he often did, with his friend James Madison. Now the gardener of President Madison was actually from France, so he also may have obtained this tree or a seedling for Madison for his Garden. Nevertheless, this tree was planted by President Madison's gardener over 200 years ago. I knew when I stood underneath this tree in 2005 that the LORD was leading me to begin planting Cedars for His arrival! Within two years I managed to connect to the horticulturist at Montpelier (*Sandra Mudrinich)* at

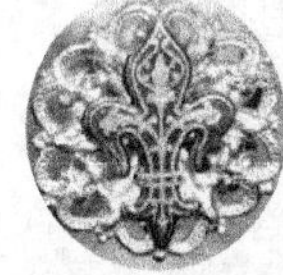

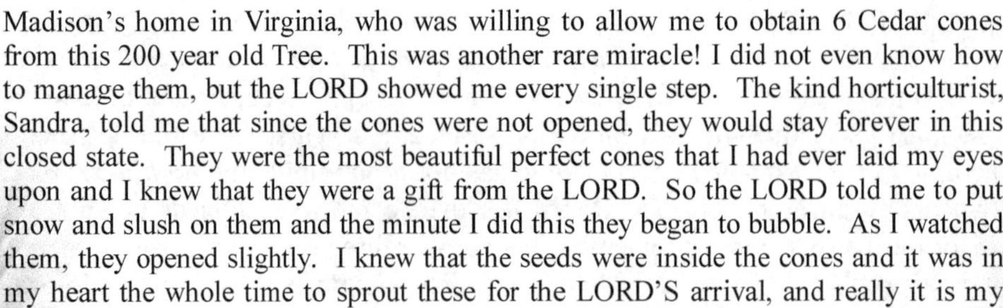

Madison's home in Virginia, who was willing to allow me to obtain 6 Cedar cones from this 200 year old Tree. This was another rare miracle! I did not even know how to manage them, but the LORD showed me every single step. The kind horticulturist, Sandra, told me that since the cones were not opened, they would stay forever in this closed state. They were the most beautiful perfect cones that I had ever laid my eyes upon and I knew that they were a gift from the LORD. So the LORD told me to put snow and slush on them and the minute I did this they began to bubble. As I watched them, they opened slightly. I knew that the seeds were inside the cones and it was in my heart the whole time to sprout these for the LORD'S arrival, and really it is my dream to plant them on the Mount of Olives, since this is the place where the LORD departed from the earth. So for an entire year, I diligently worked with them and had purchased special containers for them to remain clean. I would occasionally put them out in the rain in their special containers. I took them out at one point and tried to pry a seed out, but did not know how they were attached inside the cones. I got one seed out, but, to my surprise, the seed looked shriveled and a strong odor came out from it. I found out later, this is normally how they look.

Cedar Cone Containers
©2013 Kimberly K Ballard
All Rights Reserved

When this happened I began to cry to the LORD, *"Please LORD, You have to open these cones, I have been trying to and cannot do it. I do not want to ruin them! It is up to You to open them!"* I thought that my efforts were gone at that moment, but a miracle took place! So you must understand they were slightly opened for months on end and remained this way. I thought that nothing was going to happen with them. I was just about to give up. Two days after I prayed this, it was the 9th of AV this past summer. I casually went out to open the containers to check on them and to my utter shock, and I mean I was floored because the cones were suddenly opened like huge blossoms on the 9th of AV! I knew it was a miracle of the LORD'S timing.

I had sent in good faith two of these perfect Cedar cones from Montpelier to Israel and had dedicated them to Israel and for the glory of the LORD. After I had sent them there, the person did not follow through and I was deeply saddened by this, but the LORD gave me signs that this was what He wanted me to do anyway, even without that person's help. I had originally received the cones from the horticulturist Sandra in late October and early November of 2008. So I prayed to the LORD, *"LORD, I feel that I cannot get those two rare cones back and they are gone forever, could you please get the horticulturist to send me more cones? A miracle came about a week before Tu B' Shevat.* When I came home this majestic deer was sitting under my tree, the one I build my Sukkah under every year! On my front porch that same day in late January, was the Cedar box and *the deer sitting in the middle of the backyard.* Guess what? There were more cones and this time from the other 100 year old Cedar Tree in Madison's Garden and with it a fresh green sprig as if it was still living and freshly cut from the tree! I was just astounded. I took a picture of the deer sitting under my crabapple tree! I photographed every single step of my Cedar project for the LORD. This time these Cedar cones were already opened and fresh! I am sending photos of the tree as it appeared on Shavuot/Pentecost almost two inches tall and here is how the deer was

Fresh Cedar Bough & Cones as they arrived from Montpelier ©2013 Kimberly K Ballard All Rights Reserved

The Majestic Deer 'Little Prince' resting under my sukkah tree Photo ©2013 Kimberly K Ballard All Rights Reserved

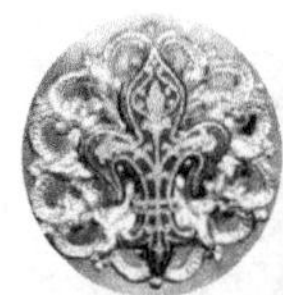

sitting under the tree with the cones and sprig as *it arrived a week before Tu B' Shevat,* the New Year of Trees in Israel. Keep in mind, that the person who sent them (Sandra) was not sending them because of this holiday known as *"Tu B' Shevat!"* She just sent them because she said, *"There was a freak snowstorm and it had broken off a branch"* from this Cedar Tree, and she decided, on her own, to mail me new cones from *"the broken living branch!"* You would not believe that this also goes into another miracle of a tree in Israel that happened to me in 2007. It was a week before Tu B' Shevat when this came to me! Not only that, but Tu B' Shevat this year, landed on the day marking the 5th anniversary of my Dad's passing. So the LORD then provided very special ingredients to sprout these trees. I found the three elements I needed, which was another miracle, in time for the planting on Tu B' Shevat.

So on Tu B' Shevat, January 30th 2010, on Israel's celebration of the Rosh HaShanah or New Year of Trees, I sat outside mixing the soil on a special sheet and gently planted Cedar seeds for the LORD. I read out loud the Scriptures that pertained to the Cedars of the LORD and I sang to them and blessed them with the Hebrew tree blessing, just as it is done in Israel. All the while the deer had moved and was watching me from the edge of the tree line, now resting under the Olive Trees. Every once in a while I would look up, only to see him lying there looking back at me and watching me. After the Cedar seeds were all planted, I went inside the house and I was upstairs. I looked out the window, only to see the deer go around to the left of the house near my garden where it disappeared out of my sight and it did not return until the following summer! I thought that this was so amazing that he disappeared by my garden! It was as if he showed up just for the planting of these special trees on Tu B' Shevat and then he disappeared after I had accomplished it! The LORD'S special gifts to me never seemed to end and I was extremely touched by it all.

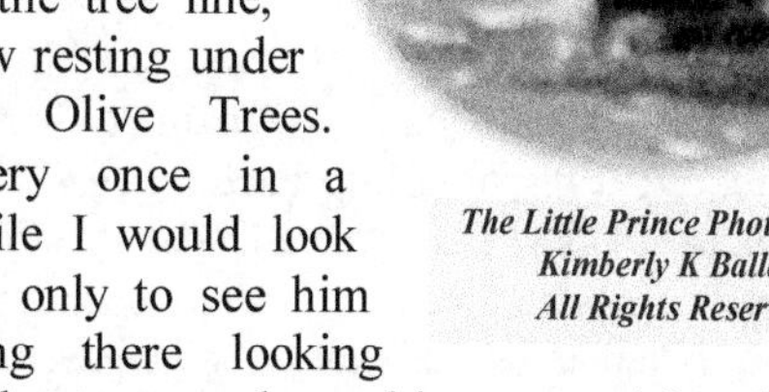

The Little Prince Photo ©2013 Kimberly K Ballard All Rights Reserved

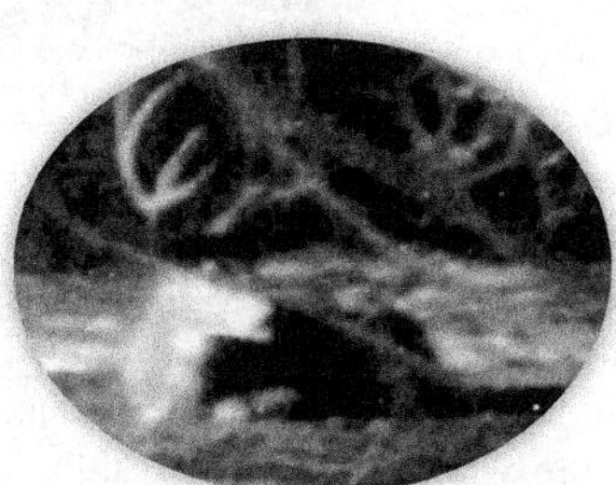

The Little Prince resting under the sukkah tree at evening Photo ©2013 Kimberly K Ballard All Rights Reserved

You must understand that there is something special about this deer. The first time I saw him I was upstairs working on this book. As sunset approached I stopped working on the book, and went downstairs to fix dinner. The first thing I had to do was wash spinach. I was so busy with the spinach, washing each leaf under the faucet, that I did not even look up to glance out the window. At one point I was observing a spinach leaf and I suddenly looked up out the window. To my utter shock this majestic buck deer was across the yard sitting perfectly parallel to me in the kitchen. He was staring directly into my eyes when I looked up. He was gently lying on the ground with his legs curled under him. He had spectacular majestic antlers that took my breath away. I ran to get the camera to take a few pictures quickly before he got up to walk away. *It was extremely rare and unusual for this to happen!* As he looked directly at me it was like he was communicating something through his eyes. He was so friendly. Later I would go outside and he did not run but stood nearby watching me. There was something profound about him. Then the next time I saw

The Majestic deer sitting across from the kitchen window Photo ©2013 Kimberly K Ballard All Rights Reserved

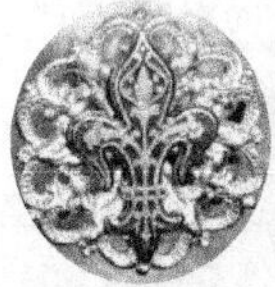

him he came the week of July 22nd the anniversary of the death of my beloved pet cat. The same week for two years in a row now this same deer came and a double rainbow was completely over my house and a very vivid rainbow appeared on the fireplace andiron, out of nowhere. I photographed all of this and this past year on that same week, we also had *a pure snow white dove come* and stay for two days in the yard. I got up close to it and took pictures of it and it even flew up and sat on the pinnacle of my roof. So the fact that this deer showed up *only for Tu B' Shevat and on the same day that I received the Cedar of Lebanon was astonishing to me.* As soon as I accomplished the seed planting on January 30th the deer left and has not returned. So I prayed to the LORD, *"please let these sprout for your glory at Pesach, which is Passover!"* So on the eve of Pesach or Passover this year, miraculously one Cedar Tree came to life! The horticulturist told me not to get my hopes up *because there is only a 1% sprout rate for these Cedars!* Here was a Cedar sprouted on the eve of Passover and ironically my Mother's birthday landed on Passover this year! I have waited and waited for more to sprout. Then a while after this, we were gone for two days during Holocaust Memorial week and I had kept the covers on them. Before this, I made the mistake of touching the seed wing and it messed up the tree that had sprouted on the eve of Passover and it made me heartsick that I ruined it, but on Holocaust Memorial week, a second tree sprouted to life! When I returned from being gone for two days, I opened the lid and a second tree had taken root and the seed was just beginning to lift up off the ground! I know that the roots must have come down on the very day that Israel remembers Holocaust Memorial Day because the trunk came up two days later. This tree is thriving, while I lost the first tree, sadly, due to my hasty actions. I have one tree with needles on it. I am praying for more. I am praying it lives to see the glory of the coming of the LORD!

Pure White Dove on the ground & on the pinnacle of my roof Photos ©2013 Kimberly K Ballard All Rights Reserved

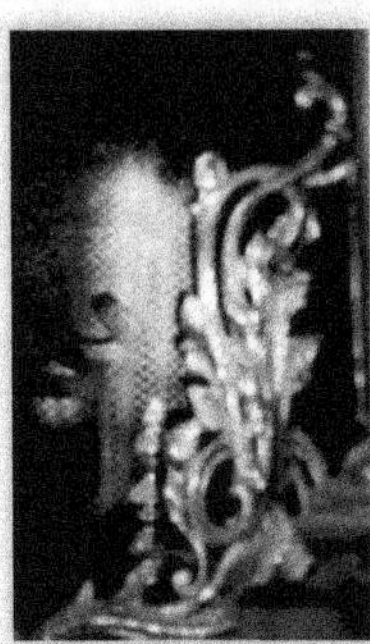

Vivid Rainbow on the fireplace andiron it was even on the chain! in B&W Photo ©2013 Kimberly K Ballard All Rights Reserved

I would love to somehow be able to plant them in Israel for the coming of the KING. I would love for these special trees to be for His glory and honor and planted in a place where He can enjoy them. I was thinking in my heart on the Mount of Olives because that is where He will set His feet. This is an ongoing project which is going to take me a long time, depending on the LORD'S wishes and blessing and I thought it was about time to tell you that the LORD has been doing this miracle behind the scenes. It is no coincidence that all of these events are happening on the special Feast Days of the LORD. *I could not believe that the first Cedar cones opened like a blossom on the 9th of AV this past summer.* What do you think? Sometime, when and if they prosper under the LORD'S hand, perhaps there would be some way to transport them for planting on the Mount of Olives, but time will tell. I will continue with my special project for the LORD God of Israel! If you have thoughts, they would be appreciated! The photos show

Cedar Cones as they looked when they opened on the 9th of Av Photo ©2013 Kimberly K Ballard All Rights Reserved

the deer as I found him sitting underneath my Sukkah tree and the Cedar as it appeared after growing on Shavuot the past two days!

Blessings in the Name of the LORD of Hosts! Kimberly K Ballard

---

So after this miracle happened, I researched and pieced together the following history, showing how President James Madison's Cedar tree was a descendant from the original Cedar Trees in the Forest of God in Lebanon, where King Solomon had obtained the Cedar wood to build the First Holy Temple in Jerusalem. The original tiny seedling was taken by ship to the French Botanical Gardens in 1734 and other Botanists had also collected the rare seeds from the Forest of God during this time period.

The reason why it was such a miracle that the Cedars opened like a huge blossom on the 9th of AV is because this day is the time of Israel's mourning over the loss of the First Holy Temple of Solomon and the Second Temple of King Herod. Both Temples were destroyed on the same day, on the 9th of AV. The LORD had promised Israel, however, that one day He would turn their mourning on the 9th of AV into joy! When my Cedar cones opened and *exposed the seeds* on the 9th of AV and could then be planted, I was so astonished! My Cedars were not only descendants from the same Cedars in the Forest where Solomon obtained the wood for building the Holy Temple of the LORD, but they were now fully opened like huge flower blossoms and the lid was lifting up off the containers on the 9th of AV. It was so incredible and so beautiful! Now I said that I sent two of the original six cones to Israel and I had dedicated them in a special box with a copy of the original letter from Montpelier and they went to the hills of Judea. Although I never knew what happened to them, they were gorgeous cones and I had specifically said that one of the cones was especially meant to remember those who died in the Holocaust. So when one of my own seedlings came up on Holocaust Memorial Day, it was so spectacular!

Cedar of Lebanon Cones as they looked when they opened like a flower on the 9th of Av
Photos ©2013 Kimberly K Ballard
All Rights Reserved

I had researched the archives for any letters or information about how the Cedars from the Forest of the LORD found their way to France. I gathered information indicating that Madison and Jefferson, who were plant enthusiasts and friends, often collected seeds and shared them with other Botanists and botany enthusiasts. Sometimes Jefferson collected plants for the University of Virginia, but often he would share with other professionals that were interested in obtaining rare or unusual seeds or species, for the purpose of growing plants that could be used medicinally or were beneficial to maintaining good health. *I soon discovered that Thomas Jefferson actually wrote to France to inquire about obtaining seeds, specifically from the Cedrus Libani, the Cedar of Lebanon. He was able to get his seeds from "the Jardin des Plantes" in Paris France.* Earlier in the 1600's this botanical Garden was called, *"Jardin du Roi."* It appears on the Monticello website that Jefferson actually went to the Jardin du Roi or Jardin des Plantes and made friends with the Botanists there and brought seeds back with him to America. Now President Madison's own gardener in Montpelier Virginia was a Frenchman named *"Bizet."* I looked up the *Jardin des Plantes* in Paris France and found that they had a huge Cedar of Lebanon Garden and one of the first trees was planted in 1734. Jardin des

Plantes is the main Botanical Garden in Paris France and I believe another Garden with this name is also located in Montpellier France. It is interesting then that President Madison's home was given the name *"Montpelier."* The *Jardin des Plantes* was considered to be a horticulturist's paradise and Botanists came from all over the world to visit it. *So Thomas Jefferson truly did obtain seeds here from the Cedar of Lebanon.* While in France, He also visited many times the beautiful Gardens of Versailles. My understanding from the horticulturist, *Sandra,* at Montpelier, is that it takes at least thirty years before this type of Cedar produces seed cones and for a long time now, it has been impossible to obtain them from the Forest of God in Lebanon, since it is a preserved and protected Forest. So this meant that the Cedar cones that I was given miraculously were an extremely rare and precious gift from the LORD God of Israel!

Cedar of Lebanon Sprouted Tree & seeds Photos ©2013 Kimberly K Ballard All Rights Reserved

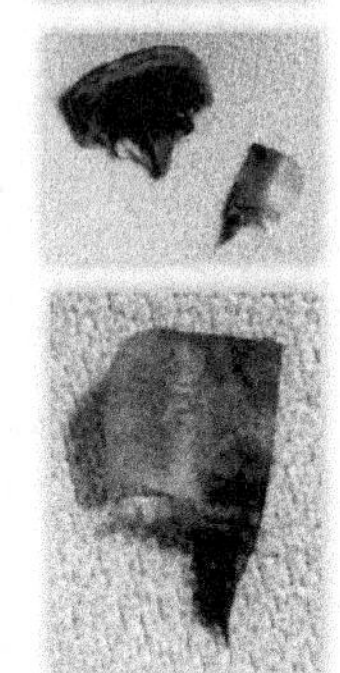

Now there is an interesting story that tells of the introduction of the Cedar of Lebanon from the Forest of God into Europe. The story was apparently an extract from *"Sharpe's London Magazine, London England ©1852-1870" "Many years ago a Frenchman who was traveling in the Holy Land found a little seedling among the Cedars of Lebanon, which he longed to bring away as a memorial of his travels. He took it up tenderly, with all the earth about its little roots, and for a want of a better flowerpot, planted it carefully in his hat, and there he kept it and tended it. The voyage home was rough and tempestuous, and so much longer than usual that the supply of fresh water in the ship fell short, and they were obliged to measure it out most carefully to each person. The captain was allowed two glasses a day; the sailors who had the work of the ship on their hands, one glass each; and the poor passengers, but half a glass of precious water; and so it was, that when the vessel arrived at the port, the traveler had drunk so little water that he was almost dying, and the young Cedar so much that, behold, it was a noble and fresh little tree, six inches high. At Customhouse the officers, who are always suspicious of smuggling, wished to empty the hat, for they would not believe but that something more valuable in their eyes lay hid beneath the moist soil. But our poor traveler implored then so earnestly to spare his tree, and talked to them so eloquently of all that we read in the Bible of the Cedar of Lebanon, telling them of David's House and Solomon's Temple that the men's hearts were softened, and they suffered the young Cedar to remain undisturbed in its strange dwelling. From thence it was carried to Paris, and planted most carefully in the Jardin des Plantes. The Cedar first produced cones in England in the Chelsea Garden about 1766, since which time vast number of trees have been raised both from native, as well as foreign cones."* ***(Source: ©2012 gardenstrust.org.uk/new/archive/cedar.html).***

It is interesting that the article went on to mention that, from this Cedar in the hat of the Frenchman, cones and seeds were later sent to England to the *Chelsea Botanical Gardens* and were planted there in 1766 and some seeds possibly went to Scotland. One of the articles about Thomas Jefferson's Cedars mentioned Edinburgh Scotland and that some Cedars were taken there. Then incredibly, I was able to finally figure out who this Frenchman was that brought the Cedar over from the Holy Land in his hat. It appears as though his brother was a *Professor of Botany at Jardin des Plantes.* I believe his name was *"Bernard de Jussieu."* This gentleman

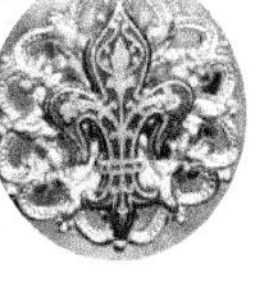

obtained Cedar seeds from his colleague named *"Peter Collinson,"* a Botanist from England, who collected rare seeds and shared them with Americans and others in foreign lands. Peter Collinson specifically made a round trip to Lebanon and apparently *he did go to the Forest of the LORD to obtain the Cedar of Lebanon seeds.* The *Jussieu brothers* at the *Jardin des Plantes apparently were very well known for their vast amount of Botanical work at the French Botanical Gardens.*

So the fact that the LORD gave these rare perfect cones to me during such a special time of the year, that are descendants from the Forest of God in Lebanon, touches my heart so deeply. It is truly another remarkable miracle that came only after I had the Almond Tree revelation and miracle in Jerusalem! Even though I never knew what happened to the two special Cedar cones that I sent as a gift to the Holy Land of Israel, I still continued to work with mine.

Then the second set of Cedars were unbelievably sent to me just in time for Tu B' Shevat in 2010. *The living branch that had broken off in the freak snowstorm* from the younger 100 year old Cedar at Montpelier was still extremely fresh, green and pliable and its fragrance was simply fantastic! The cones were broken opened already, revealing the fresh seeds of the tree! So this time the seeds were ready to plant right out of the box, just in time for Tu B' Shevat, the New Year of Tree! As I took it inside the house, I passed by the picture windows and as I looked out in the backyard, I saw the most incredible sight. The gorgeous buck mule deer with huge Majestic antlers was resting underneath my tree all alone, facing the window. This box had come in the middle of winter and this deer came back the same day and was sitting with his legs folded under him, under the tree. I saw the deer from the kitchen window just that one time but this had never happened before in 30 years of living here! The whole story prompted my close friend, Brenda, to send me a video about the LORD as the majestic deer who would come to visit in the snow. I felt as if I was part of a story book!

Majestic Deer Little Prince Photo ©2013 Kimberly K Ballard
All Rights Reserved

So this year when Rabbi Chaim Richman *(a colleague of Rabbi Yitzchak Reuven who I emailed that letter to)* came from the Temple Institute in Jerusalem, to a small town near my house, after I had specifically prayed for him to come here, I could not believe he came the week of Tu B' Shevat with the blueprints for the Third Temple because He had never before visited Colorado. The last time that he made a trip to the United States, he brought with him the solid gold crown of the High Priest that will be used in the Third Temple. How I wished then that he would come to a place near my house to speak. So I

prayed and asked the LORD if he would get the Rabbi to come to Colorado and not to Denver, which is too far away for me, but to send the Rabbi closer to where I live. Within a couple of months, my direct prayer was answered by the LORD, because the Rabbi on his own added a location on his tour near a place where I live. The Rabbi, completely out of the blue, was suddenly coming here to speak, to reveal these blueprints for the first time in 2,000 years. I wanted some of the Cedar of Lebanon seeds to be planted in Israel! I was also excited that I actually got to touch the case that contained the blueprints, as I walked past it, knowing full well that this was a huge fulfillment of Bible prophecy that was coming to pass right before my eyes. How fantastic it was to have this happen and to be one of very few people to witness this day that thousands had dreamed of over the course of 2,000 years, and here was my little Cedar tree alive, that represented the building of the Holy Temple!

My sprouted Cedar of Lebanon Photo ©2013 Kimberly K Ballard All Rights Reserved

Now after all these things transpired, when I said that the deer came back, what I have not mentioned is that he has come *three years* in a row now, during that specific week in July. As I told the Rabbi, on that same week, for three years in a row, a double rainbow appeared over my house, going from one end of the house to the other end of the house. The pure snow white dove landed in the yard and stayed for two days the same week in 2009. For three years this has occurred to my amazement. The snow white dove only came one year in 2009, a month before my beautiful Aunt passed away, but the double rainbow and the deer came three years in a row in the very same week. So I took pictures of the buck deer, the double rainbows, and the snow white dove, to remember these precious blessings from the LORD. I have to add now that in 2011, this is the fourth year it has occurred.

The left side of the Double Rainbow over my house Photo ©2013 Kimberly K Ballard All Rights Reserved

In July, around the 22nd of 2011, we had a double rainbow and there were a total of three rainbows in one week that went over the house from one end to the other. The summer of 2012, the double rainbow came a month late in August, but this was a season of extreme drought and fires, and not one raindrop fell for four months! For thirty years we never had any doves living in our yard, but suddenly all of these larger Eurasian ring neck doves starting coming into the yard and some of them nested

Majestic Deer Little Prince Photos ©2013 Kimberly K Ballard All Rights Reserved

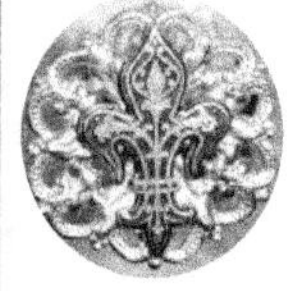

in my grapevine and laid two white eggs. The doves you saw pictured in the section on *the Dove of Peace,* posing for me are these special wild doves that I call *"My girls!"* They are characters and they call out to me in song! We never once had a rainbow going over the house from one end to the other or the Royal buck deer in the yard *until the LORD was revealing so much to my heart.* I felt like the LORD was giving me a special message through all of these beautiful gifts. I was touched to the heart and it showed me that God's heart is so beautiful! I began to see how close the LORD is to us.

Then one day, I was doing genealogical research and I was looking up information on Heraldry that pertains to Royal emblems. I found the meaning of each one of the various symbols in Heraldry and it was quite interesting. On the list of the symbols was the mule deer, *"The Stag,"* like the Majestic deer that was sitting under my tree, the week of Tu B' Shevat when the gift box of the Cedar of Lebanon arrived at my house. So I thought that I would scroll down and read what it said about the mule deer and you are not going to believe what it said! I was so astonished when I saw the connection to the Messiah! *The antlers resemble branches, so the Stag in Heraldry is associated with the "Tree of Life!" The meaning of the mule deer in Heraldry is parallel to my revelation of Messiah as the Branch and the Tree of Life!* I just thought that this was so incredible, because this deer had a huge rack on his head, making him look extremely Majestic. When I saw this, I was astonished and I knew that the LORD had put that Majestic deer under my tree that day as a special gift to my heart, when the fresh Cedar of Lebanon bough box arrived at my door. *The Stag* was also *"a symbol of wisdom," and the LORD is the Living Torah of wisdom.* So the box miraculously arrived just in time for me to plant the seeds for the Rosh HaShanah of Trees on Tu B' Shevat, *at the time of the regeneration of the trees. When the first one sprouted on the eve of Passover, when Yeshua died as the Lamb of God, it was an incredible miracle!* So I named my Majestic deer *"Little Prince"* because he was Royal and *the Branch Messiah came to life in the garden,* and, as I told Rabbi Reuven, my Majestic deer disappeared around the corner by my garden. Without my knowledge at the time, *his antlers represented Messiah the Branch, the Tree of Life, and the life blood.* Remember, the LORD first brought this Majestic deer into my backyard *three* years ago when I saw him lying in the grass, looking directly at me through the kitchen window. It was stunning! This happened right after the LORD had revealed Himself to me as *"The Living Branch from the Almond Tree of Life," and I was writing this book about it!* Incredibly, there was more to the definition of *the Stag* deer in Heraldry. It said that sometimes *"they would put a crucifix between the deer's antlers on the Heraldry, as a sign of the regeneration of life!"* So this meant that the deer was sitting under my Tree during Tu B' Shevat and its antlers had the meaning of *branches of the Tree of Life and the cross of the Messiah, who reversed the curse and brought forth the regeneration of life!* Then when Rabbi

The Majestic Deer Little Prince first came to me with fuzzy antlers & he stood amongst my sunflowers posing for me!
Photo ©2013 Kimberly K Ballard All Rights Reserved

Richman came here on Tu B' Shevat, he made that statement that *"Tu B' Shevat" is "a time of rejuvenation."* There were just too many unbelievable coincidences happening here and I knew that the LORD was behind everything that was happening to me. To this day, I am inspired and astonished to remember these things. Each year the deer's antlers fall away and die and a new set of antlers sprout from his head *and they are full of life blood. This reminded me that Messiah the Branch had to die and sprout to life, in order to save us with His life blood of the Eternal Ark of the Covenant, which is the Covenant of the heart!* I simply could not believe it, because the Rabbi had spoken practically the same words about Tu B' Shevat, but he had no idea at all. *It was definitely a time of rejuvenation and regeneration!* How incredible!

Majestic Deer Little Prince Photo ©2013 Kimberly K Ballard All Rights Reserved

Another interesting part of this story is that when a person used the mule deer or *Stag* on their Heraldry, it was considered to be the enemy of Satan! It said the deer represented the LORD, against Satan who is His enemy! So now it was like the LORD placed the Majestic deer under my tree, representing the LORD, whose revelations I was working on, against Satan the enemy, and Yeshua came here to destroy the workings of Satan. When I think of all these events combined together, I know that the LORD has been showing these things to me in the most profound way. The LORD is *Living* and He does these miraculous things to prove that He is concerned about every detail of our lives. Now what further astounds me about this is that my Majestic deer was not just sitting under any old tree in my yard. This is the very tree that I build my Sukkah or temporary shelter underneath every year, using leafy living branches and fruit for the LORD'S Feast of Tabernacles in the fall. Why the deer chose that tree to sit underneath, I have no idea, because it was out in the open in the middle of the backyard, and he was facing the same direction that I always build the Sukkah, which is facing Jerusalem! I know exactly the direction of Jerusalem because I have a very special compass that came from Israel and it always points toward Jerusalem. So every fall when I build my Sukkah under that tree, so I can sit inside it, I use my Jerusalem compass to line up the door of my temporary Tabernacle, so it is directly facing Jerusalem. How spectacular then, that the deer was facing Jerusalem in the same direction towards the picture windows and that there was such a deep hidden meaning within his *Majestic antlers* and this was exactly how the LORD had revealed Himself to me! This was all simply the Divine plan and Providence of the LORD and I knew that His Presence was very near to me. The deer stayed the entire week until the moment that I had planted the Cedar of Lebanon seeds on Tu B' Shevat. When he disappeared, he did not return until the week in late July when the double rainbow appeared over my house for the third year in a row. I was touched about the rainbow, because it was not only a sign of the LORD'S Covenant with mankind, but it was also a Covenant with all the animals and all living creatures. It was extremely comforting to my heart that the LORD gave the sign of His Covenant over my house

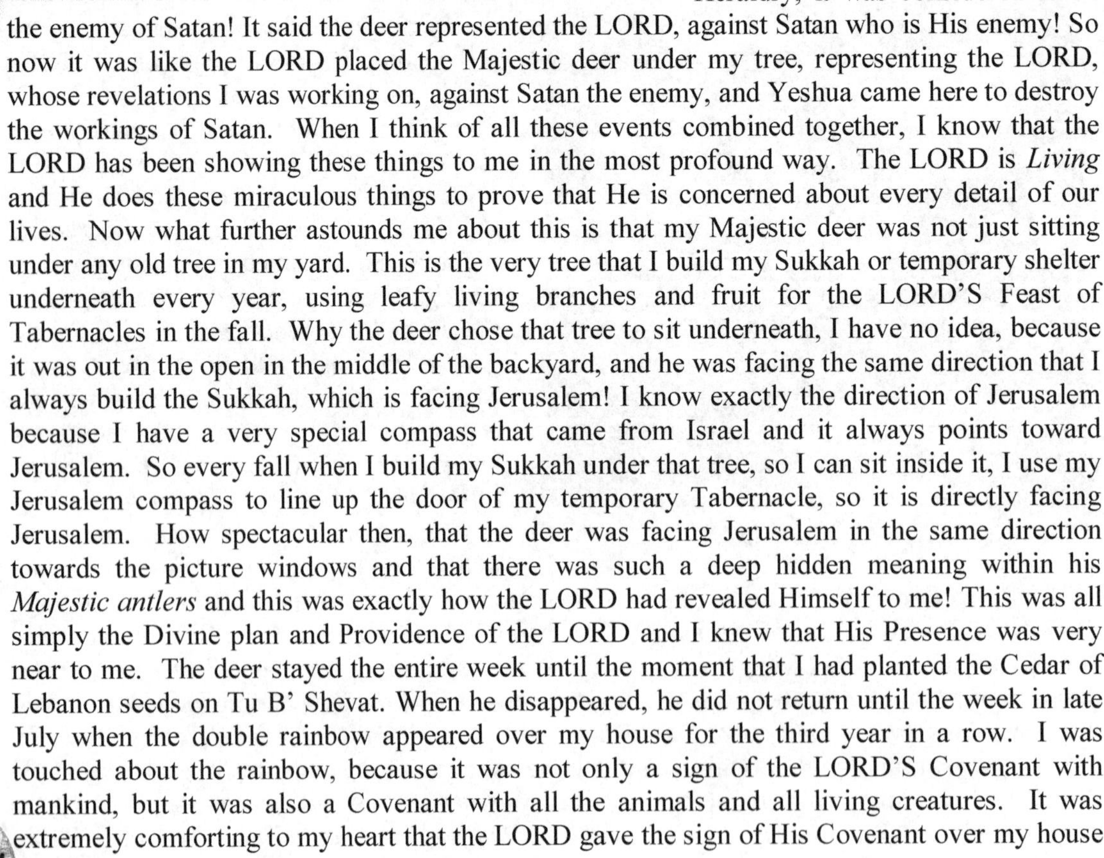

in the sky this particular week because my beloved cat Jasmine, who lived to be 18 years and 4 months old, had died in my arms during this same week in late July, on the 22nd in 2004. It sounds funny, but Jasmine loved to listen to Bible stories as they were preached over the radio, while he sat with his paws folded underneath him. His beautiful blue eyes would remain closed, as his ears were perked upright and twitching, as he was listening to every Word, while he was swaddled in his soft yellow blanket on his fluffy bear bed! He loved Bible stories and if there ever was a *"righteous cat"* for the Kingdom of Heaven, Jasmine was it! He was the most loving and loyal friend that God ever gave to me. After he passed away, these touching events began to happen to me, the week of his passing, with the double rainbow and the deer and they happened like clockwork, for three years in a row and now I can say for a fourth year in a row, in 2011!

Jasmine my beloved kitten & Me
A Siamese Snowshoe with blue eyes
This was his baby picture in 1986!
1986-2004
Photo ©2013
Kimberly K Ballard
All Rights Reserved

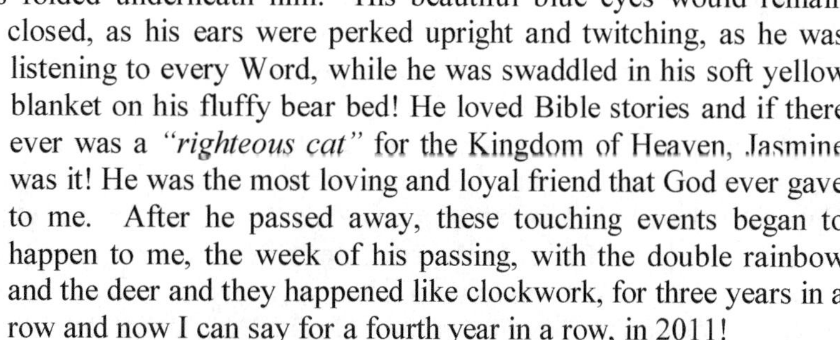

Now getting back to Tu B' Shevat. When the Almond Tree in Israel begins *awakening* to life and starts to bloom, this is part of the excitement of the celebration of *Tu B' Shevat.* Now I mentioned that part of the celebration includes the planting of many trees in Israel. As I said, fruit trees are especially popular to plant during the holiday! Of course, Yeshua's resurrection occurred on the third day, just like the fruit trees in creation came to life on the third day. The year that I had the amazing Almond Tree revelation, *Tu B' Shevat landed on the third day of February.* Many celebrations on this holiday include a special Seder meal. The meal is focused on eating fruits and nuts and this includes Almonds. This is all symbolic of Messiah Yeshua as the Fruitful Branch of the Almond Tree of Life, who was the seed of life and our First Fruit. I was really overwhelmed in my heart to realize just how much the LORD had revealed Himself to me in the Almond Branch at the time of this special holiday that focuses on the Almond Tree and the eating of fruits and nuts! Of course the Almond seed itself is the *"King"* of nuts and the LORD is the KING of Israel, the seed of the Almond Tree of Life! When I read about the traditions of the celebration on Tu B' Shevat, I was shocked to discover that there was something more profound that the LORD was trying to show me about the Almond Tree. As I thought about the Words of Yeshua, it occurred to me that when He referred to *"all the Trees budding,"* in His parable, that He may have been speaking specifically of Tu B' Shevat, the Rosh HaShanah of all the trees.

Luke 22:29-32 *And He spake to them a parable; Behold the fig tree, and all the trees; When they now shoot forth ye see and know of your own selves that summer is now nigh at hand. So likewise ye, when ye see these things come to pass, know ye that the Kingdom of God is nigh at hand. This generation shall not pass away, till all be fulfilled.*

Jasmine & Me in 1986 soon after he was born
Photo ©2013 Kimberly K Ballard
All Rights Reserved

Yeshua said that the generation that sees these things come to pass will be the generation that sees the Kingdom of God come to earth. I believe that because the LORD has revealed Himself to me in the Almond Tree at the time of Tu B' Shevat and brought me these special Cedar trees and revealed Himself to me in the Fig tree, that we are the generation that witnesses the coming of the Kingdom of God! The celebration of Tu B' Shevat is a

way of keeping track of the age of the trees and this is important, because the LORD gave Israel special rules regarding eating the fruit from the fruit trees. The rules are as follows.
1. For the first *three years* of the life of the fruit tree, its fruit should not be eaten.
2. On *the fourth year* of the life of a fruit tree, the fruit is dedicated to the LORD.
3. On *the fifth year* the fruit can be eaten by all.

The LORD said that the fruit should not be eaten the first 3 years. This is symbolic of Yeshua who was in the sepulchre for *three days*. The Fruit that Messiah produced could not be eaten by anyone until He was raised to life as the First Fruit of salvation *on the third day*, which, again, is the same day that the fruit trees were created in the beginning by the LORD. Then Yeshua appeared to Mary *on the fourth day* and He told her not to touch Him yet as He had not yet ascended to the Father in Heaven. Yeshua became the First Fruit from the Almond Tree of Life, dedicated in Heaven to the LORD *on the fourth day. On the fifth day* after the Living Almond Branch came to life and bore Fruit, Yeshua appeared to many people that saw Him alive. All the people could now take and eat the First Fruit of the Tree of Life and live forever, *on the fifth day*. It is so interesting to me that Israel is symbolically celebrating the special New Year of Trees and without their knowledge, some of the final pieces of the mystery of the Messiah are hidden within the celebration of the Almond Tree on Tu B' Shevat. When Israel begins to see this truth about the LORD, they will truly be celebrating it like never before! It is so outstanding! So I am attempting another Cedar of Lebanon and Almond seed planting on Tu B' Shevat 2013!

THE LULAV

Malloy Date Palm (Florida) & Palm fronds & Florida Myrtle Tree Photos ©2013 Kimberly K Ballard All Rights Reserved

The Lulav is made up of the four species and it is waved to the LORD on the Feast of Tabernacles or Sukkot. What is spectacular about the Lulav is that through the Holy Spirit, I have discovered that Yeshua is also hidden in the details of the Lulav. On the first day of this Feast of the LORD, the Jewish people take goodly leafy branches from trees and they bind them together. The Lulav is made up of three species of leafy branches and one perfect fruit. Bound together, they make up *the four species.* Curiously, it is a strict requirement that *"the branch"* of the Lulav has to be very straight, *"like a rod,"* in order to qualify for use in the Divine ceremony. The three species of branches are *"held in the right hand"* in one cluster. The *"rod-like"* date palm goes up the center of the Lulav with the *three myrtle branches* held together in one cluster on the right side of the date palm and the two willow branches held together in one cluster on the left side of the date palm. The *three myrtles* and the *two willows* add up to *five,* which of course symbolizes the Torah or the five Books of Moses. The five branches are brought together toward the single central *"rod"* and they are held together *as one in the right hand.* I believe that the straight, *"perfect Rod" that is central is Messiah the LORD, the Living Torah*, and all the other branches come toward Him *with the one perfect Fruit.* The LORD is to be our central focal point. Held together, the branches of the Lulav form one *"perfect Branch"* full of life. The three species represent the three days that Messiah was in the tomb before He came to life and bore the one *perfect Fruit, the Living Torah,* on the third day. So symbolically, you not only have the requirements for the Fruit Trees in Tu B' Shevat hidden in these details, but you also have *the perfect Rod, the Branch full of life, the one perfect Fruit and the Living Torah* that are the sum of all of the branches that combine into *one central Rod.* Remember also that Messiah is the *central Rod* of the Almond Tree Menorah. All of the branches are held together in the *right hand,* as *the Lulav.* Messiah Yeshua is, of course, the Royal Sceptre, the Rod of the KING OF KINGS in the right hand. This is the fulfillment of the Shema which states, *"The LORD our God is one."* The Fruit, known in Hebrew as the *"etrog,"* is a citrus fruit and it is also called *"The citron."* The perfect Fruit is held in the left hand. *The citron tree bears fruit in all the seasons, just like the Living Torah Messiah bears fruit in all the seasons! The Rod of Living Branches and the perfect Fruit* are brought together in the waving ceremony. The custom is to shake the Lulav, while holding the Rod of branches with one hand, while holding the perfect Fruit in the other hand. The custom is to bring the two hands together, bringing them towards the body first and then away from the body, shaking them in six different directions. The two hands are kind of like *"the two witnesses" that testify of the work of the LORD'S hands!* The six directions of the shaking of *the Rod and the perfect Fruit* are to the right, to the left, up, down, behind you and in front of your body. It is interesting because this shaking is symbolic of the six days of creation and all the work that *the perfect Rod, who bore the perfect Fruit,* accomplished throughout the whole universe with His mighty *right hand* and outstretched arm. Every direction is representative of the whole universe being created by the Royal Sceptre of the LORD KING. It is the LORD who does the true shaking!

Haggai 2:6-7 *For thus saith the LORD of Hosts; Yet once, it is a little while, and I will shake the Heavens, and the earth, and the sea, and the dry land; And I will shake all Nations, and the desire of all Nations shall come; and I will fill this House with glory, saith the LORD of Hosts.*

Everything was made through the Rod of God, through the Living Torah of Life.

John 1:1-5 *In the beginning was the Word, and the Word was with God, and the Word was God. The same was in the beginning with God. All things were made by Him; and without Him was not anything made that was made. In Him was life; and the life was the light of men. And the light shineth in the darkness; and the darkness comprehended it not.*

The custom is to shake the Rod with the Fruit held close to this Branch cluster. *Three times* they pull it toward the body and then away from the body *from the level of the heart.* Remember that my Israeli friend tried to pass that Almond Tree *"three times"* and then she was pulled to the tree by *the Invisible Assistant* to photograph it, which eventually revealed the LORD'S heart! As they wave the Lulav toward the heart and away from the heart three times, this reminds me that Yeshua's resurrection the third day is the Eternal Covenant of the heart. *Three times the LORD tried to show Israel that He was their KING. Three times they pushed Him away from their heart!* The KING was rejected in the Garden of Eden. Then a second time, they asked for an earthly King and Saul became Israel's King. The third time was when the LORD came to them as *"KING Messiah Yeshua,"* and He appeared as the perfect Rod of Salvation. The KING was rejected for the third time. The LORD, however, is always and continually drawing us back with *His own perfect Rod that bore the one perfect fruit,* favoring us with His Royal Sceptre, because His faithful heart is full of love for us.

On the first day of the waving ceremony, the following prayer is spoken, *"Blessed are You, LORD our God, KING of the Universe who has granted us life, sustenance, and permitted us to reach this season."* This prayer reminds me that when *the Living Branch came to life, He offered us the one perfect Fruit from the Tree of Life that is our sustenance.* If you think about it, the entire cluster of branches of the Lulav with the one perfect Fruit add up to *a perfect number 7.* This signifies again that the LORD'S Living Testimony was complete and perfect. It also signifies that Yeshua was raised to life as the Fruitful Rod on the 7th day Sabbath of the LORD. This *one perfect Rod (the Living Torah)* keeps us on the *straight* path to Eternal life. The Lulav is made up of *the two willows, the three myrtles, the perfect Rod of the date palm, and the one Perfect Fruit.* The picture we have is total completeness in Messiah, the KING.

After the total number of days were completed that Daniel had prophesied would occur to the coming of the Messiah, the people in Israel cleared a pathway for Yeshua as He rode into Jerusalem on the foal of the donkey, and they shook the date palm branches toward Him, as they shouted for joy. It was not the Feast day for this ceremony. It was Passover, not, the Feast of Tabernacles, but they wanted to declare that *the perfect Rod of God was the KING* at that moment. *I believe that they were symbolically waving and shaking the date palm branches away from their hearts and toward the one central Rod, who was the Living Torah of perfection, before His time had come to reign!* This was going to be a complete and perfect fulfillment of the LORD'S Divine Testimony, according to the LORD'S time table and according to His own works.

When the KING returns after two thousand years, they will celebrate Sukkot with the LORD, but because of the fact that Messiah was about to be cut off, they were premature in waving the Rod of the Lulav toward KING Yeshua, trying to make Him KING before His time had come! *There was great joy in Israel at that moment, when all the people who were there in Jerusalem with palm branches were symbolically, shaking the central perfect rod of the Lulav away from their hearts and towards the Royal KING of Israel*, and they were shouting, *"Hoshanna to the son of David; blessed is He who comes in the Name of the LORD; Hoshanna in the Highest!"* Then all the city of Jerusalem said, *"Who is this?"* I think they knew in their hearts that this was the LORD God of Israel! Instead of reigning at that point, He first had to die and become the cut off *Branch,* so that He could bear *the one Perfect Fruit.* He had to fulfill His Living Testimony as the Almond Rod of God, in the number seven, because He is the Living Torah, the perfect fruit from the Tree of Life!

Matthew 21:1-13 *And when they drew nigh unto Jerusalem, and were come to Bethphage, unto the Mount of Olives, then sent Yeshua two disciples, Saying unto them, Go into the village over against you, and straightway ye shall find an ass tied, and a colt with her; loose them, and bring them unto Me. And if any man say ought unto you, ye shall say, The LORD hath need of them, and straightway he will send them. All this was done, that it might be fulfilled which was spoken by the Prophet, saying, Tell ye the daughter of Zion, Behold, thy KING cometh unto thee, meek, and sitting upon an ass, and a colt the foal of an ass. And the disciples went, and did as Yeshua commanded them. And brought the ass, and the colt, and put on them their clothes, and they set Him thereon. And a very great multitude spread their garments in the way; others cut down branches from the trees, and strawed them in the way. And the multitude that went before, and that followed, cried, saying, Hosanna to the son of David; Blessed is He that cometh in the Name of the LORD; Hosanna in the Highest. And when He was come into Jerusalem, all the city was moved, saying, Who is this? And the multitude said, This is Yeshua the Prophet of Nazareth of Galilee. And Yeshua went into the Temple of God, and cast out all them that sold and bought in the Temple, and overthrew the tables of the moneychangers, and the seats of them that sold doves. And said unto them, It is written, My House shall be called the House of Prayer; but ye have made it a den of thieves.*

As I thought about *the willow branches* of the Lulav, I considered how they grow along the river banks. So this brought to mind that the river is the body of living water where we symbolically cast our sins during the Tashlikh ceremony of Rosh HaShanah. Messiah is the true *"body of Living Water"* that we have cast our sins into. *I realized then that we are like the willows of the Lulav.* As the LORD provides water for us to drink when we thirst, we are like the willows whose roots constantly drink up the Living Water on the banks of the river. The Living Water of the LORD is an everlasting river and a refreshing rain that quenches our thirst forever.

Flood Raindrops on a Peony Leaf from the flood of September 2013
Photo ©2013 Kimberly K Ballard All Rights Reserved

As I pondered *the three myrtle branches* in the Lulav, the LORD revealed something fantastic to me about it! The myrtle, which is an *"evergreen,"* has leafy branches and the branches were sometimes given to a Jewish Bridegroom before he entered the nuptial chamber after a wedding. The three myrtle branches that are held in one cluster are therefore, *symbolic of Yeshua, the Bridegroom of Israel, who paid the Bride's price with His life, and on the third day became the evergreen Branch. The Messiah is the evergreen or Eternal Bridegroom in the three myrtle branches! Then incredibly, Messiah Yeshua left the sign of the Covenant of marriage to the Land of Israel in the sepulchre with His bris cloth in Holy Mount Moriah. I just simply find this to be so astonishing because the three myrtle branches that are evergreens show us that, in Messiah, we will never die, but have Eternal life, and this KING promised to raise up Israel the third day to Eternal life, as His Bride.* Remember that in the story of Esther, she was the Bride of the King and Esther's name means *"Myrtle Tree."* So perhaps the story of the Bride Esther, marrying the King, was the beginning of this meaningful tradition of giving the three evergreen myrtle branches to a Jewish Bridegroom. Esther fasted and prayed for three days, asking for God the KING to save her people Israel. *This parallels to KING Messiah coming to life the third day as the Living Evergreen Branch to save His people Israel forever and to marry her as His Bride, His wedding nuptials!* The fact that the Living Evergreen Branch made the way in the Garden through the two Living Cherubim Angels to the Heavenly Garden of God to dwell with the KING forever gives the evergreen myrtle a much greater meaning because I found out that, ironically, *"Myrtles were considered to be the scent of the Garden of Eden!"* So the Messiah, the Jewish Bridegroom, is taking us to His Heavenly Garden where we will smell the fragrance of His myrtles!

Now the Fruit of the date palm comes from the Greek word for *"finger,"* and *Messiah the Yad, the finger of God, writes the Living Torah on our hearts!* The entire Lulav is full of Messianic meaning and it reveals the KING OF KINGS! The one perfect Fruit of the Lulav called *"the etrog"* is inspected for absolute perfection, as are the branches that must be straight like *a rod, without blemish.* This reminds me that *Yeshua, the Rod was inspected and found to be without fault or blemish. He is the Fruit of perfection and the Lamb of God without spot or blemish.*

Luke 23:13-15 *And Pilate, when he had called together the Chief Priests and the rulers and the people, Said unto them, Ye have brought this man unto me, as one that perverteth the people; and, behold, I, having examined Him before you, have found no fault in this man touching those things whereof ye accuse Him; No, nor yet Herod; for I sent you to him; and, lo, nothing worthy of death is done unto Him.*

John 19:4-6 *Pilate therefore went forth again, and saith unto them, Behold, I bring Him forth to you, that ye may know that I find no fault in Him. Then came Yeshua forth, wearing the Crown of Thorns, and the Purple Robe. And Pilate saith unto them, Behold the man! When the Chief Priests therefore and officers saw Him, they cried out, saying, Crucify Him, crucify Him. Pilate saith unto them, Take ye Him, and crucify Him; for I find no fault in Him.*

Even Judas came back and said, *"I have sinned in that I have betrayed innocent blood."*

Matthew 27:3-4 *Then Judas, which had betrayed Him, when he saw that He was condemned, repented himself, and brought again the thirty pieces of silver to the Chief Priests and Elders, Saying, I have sinned in that I have betrayed the innocent blood. And they said, What is that to us? See thou to that.*

Deuteronomy 32:4 *He is the Rock, His work is perfect; for all His ways are judgment; a God of truth and without iniquity, just and right is He.*

Matthew 5:48 *Be ye therefore perfect, even as your Father which is in Heaven is perfect.*

Psalm 19:7 *The Law of the LORD is perfect, converting the soul; the Testimony of the LORD is sure, making wise the simple.*

II Samuel 22:31 *As for God, His way is perfect; the Word of the LORD is tried; He is a buckler to all them that trust in Him.*

So the evergreen Rod is sitting at the right hand of the Majesty on High as our First Fruit of the third day without spot or blemish! The term *"Buckler"* in II Samuel 22:31 refers to *a shield that is gripped in the hand or worn on the arm for defense and protection.* So Yeshua is our Buckler. *It was the right hand of the perfect Rod of God that created the universe in six days. So the Lulav represents "The Testimony" of the LORD'S perfect Rod that bore the perfect Fruit!* The *evergreen myrtle* truly represents *the gift of Eternal life* from the Bridegroom of Israel in the Heavenly Garden of God. The *hadas myrtle* of the Lulav has to have *three leaves to a single node* according to the Jewish Virtual Library and *they should resemble a chain.* **(Source: The Jewish Virtual Library - Encyclopedia Judaica ©2008 The Gale Group. All Rights Reserved).** *We are all connected as "one" like a chain, through the Living evergreen Branch!*

Palm Branches like a chain Photos ©2013 Kimberly K Ballard All Rights Reserved

THE LIVING WATER A RIVER OF LIFE FROM THE GARDEN OF GOD

Boulder Falls River & Left hand creek Flood Photos ©2013
Budding Almond Rod & Butterfly Photos ©2015
Kimberly K Ballard All Rights Reserved

Now if we are like *the willows of the Lulav* clinging to the sandy loam along the river banks, drinking the Living Water of the LORD who constantly refreshes us and causes us to thrive, *then we are drinking from the river of life that is coming out of the Garden of God. During the water libation ceremony of Sukkot in Jerusalem in 2014, willows adorned the altar!* In Genesis, there was one river in the Garden of Eden and it was divided into four rivers. The LORD God planted this Garden in the east. *The Rod of the Lulav is first waved toward the east.* The Garden in the Mount of Olives is in the east. The LORD'S glory departed from the Temple and ascended up to Heaven from the Mount of Olives in the east. Yeshua spent quality time in this Garden on the Mount of Olives, and from this same place, Yeshua ascended up to Heaven in the glory cloud. Yeshua proved that He is the Living Water in His miracles.

Genesis 2:10 *Now a river flowed out of Eden to water the Garden; and from there it divided and became four rivers.*

River with Willows and Trees Photo ©2013 Kimberly K Ballard All Rights Reserved

The Almond Tree of Life, the Fig Tree, and all the trees of Eden drank the Living Water of life and the LORD caused them all to grow and thrive. When Yeshua gave us the signs of His return and He referred to *"all the trees budding,"* I realized that this was a reference *"to Him restoring all things like the Garden of Eden in the future"* when He returns to the earth and *Tu B' Shevat is the time when all the trees bud in Israel.* When the LORD returns to dwell in our midst, this will cause all the trees to bud and flourish, as it was in the very beginning. Messiah Yeshua was actually saying in His statement, then, that when we see all the trees bud *(like they did in the Garden of Eden),* we will know *that the Kingdom of God is at hand* because Yeshua made the way back to the Garden through the *two Living* Cherubim Angels. As the Messiah sets His feet on the Mount of Olives in the east and the land is cleft, the Living Water will flow out like rivers from His Eternal Temple *because He has arrived!* It is His sudden Presence that will cause the trees to bud without the curse abiding upon them and when we see this with our own eyes, we will know for certain that the Kingdom of God is at hand. So the budding of the Fig tree of Eden and all the trees is the sign He is near and is coming to usher in His gorgeous Heavenly Garden. It will be the everlasting rejuvenation of life. If you will recall, Rabbi Richman said that this rejuvenation is

something that happens *during the time of Tu B' Shevat* and this is when my Almond Tree miracle and revelation took place, in the month that Tu B' Shevat occurs.

Tropical Leaf Butterfly Photo ©2013 Kimberly K Ballard

Genesis 2:8-10 *And the LORD God planted a Garden toward the east, in Eden; And there He placed the man whom He had formed. And out of the ground the LORD God caused to grow every tree that is pleasing to the sight and good for food; the tree of life also in the midst of the Garden, and the tree of the knowledge of good and evil. Now a river flowed out of Eden to water the Garden; and from there it divided and became four rivers. The first river was called the Pi'son near Havilah where there is gold. The second river is the Gihon which encompassed the whole land of Ethiopia. The third river is Hiddekel which goes toward the east of Assyria. The fourth river is the Euphrates.*

The Presence of the LORD God was among the trees as He walked in His Garden in the cool of the day. When Yeshua told us that we would know that the Kingdom of God was at hand when we saw all the trees bud, *He was actually revealing that He is the KING who walked in His Garden in Eden. He brought forth water like rivers so Adam and Eve were refreshed.*

Genesis 3:8 *And they heard the sound of the LORD God walking in the Garden in the cool of the day, and the man and his wife hid themselves from the Presence of the LORD God among the Trees.*

Melinda's Magnolia Tree seed pod Photo ©2014 DeRieux – Edited B&W by Kimberly K Ballard

When the flood of Noah took place, it altered the landscape and changed the way that the terrain looked. *No one but the Rabbi's have ever really known where Eden was located, but*

it was in Jerusalem which is the center of the earth. Jerusalem is indeed "the Navel of the world." The LORD said that His Name would be in Jerusalem in His Garden forever and it is to this day! So Yeshua was raised to life in this Garden. The KING will return to Jerusalem where He will plant His Garden with all the finest trees. One of the rivers that flowed out of Eden is near the Temple Mount and today it is a spring called *"The Gihon Spring."* Pure crystal clear water still flows out from the Gihon Spring, just opposite from the place in the east where Messiah Yeshua ascended back into Heaven. This spring is coming out from under Holy Mount Moriah. From all the evidence that I have presented in this book, I have verified with absolute certainty *that Jerusalem is the location of the Garden of Eden.* The Garden in Mount Moriah is the Garden that God planted in the beginning. This is why He has been drawing all people back to His Holy Mount, through Messiah. When the LORD said that His Name is *forever* in Jerusalem on Mount Moriah, or Mount Zion, the term *"forever"* includes all the time of the past and all of the time yet to come in Eternity. This tells us that God's Garden was always in this place where Yeshua came to life as the Almond Rod that budded. This is why there is a huge vineyard, water cistern, and winepress in this location. Think about the fact, too, that Jerusalem and the whole Land of Israel became desolate for thousands of years, up to the time of the end. Everyone was driven out and away from God's Garden in the east, but slowly over the centuries, the LORD has been drawing mankind back to His Garden in this place where God's Name is written at the Garden tomb in the Royal Stone of Kings. The twentieth century yielded a great return! At His return, He will reign forever from His Garden that will be perfectly rejuvenated. The Kings of Israel were always anointed at the Gihon!

II Chronicles 33:4 *Also he built altars in the House of the LORD, whereof the LORD had said, In Jerusalem shall My Name be forever.*

After having written so much of what took place in the original Garden of God, I was shocked one day *when Rabbi Richman from the Temple Institute verified that the Temple Mount was in fact the Garden of Eden.* This was a miraculous verification. *The next Scriptures in Ezekiel and in Isaiah indicate that Eden was in the location of the Mountain of God on Mount Moriah where the Holy Temple was built.* This is the location of the Gihon Spring. This is the reason that the LORD called Abraham out of Ur and told him to come out from where he lived to this Mountain. This is why the LORD directed David to prepare and build the Holy Temple of God in this location. This is the reason why Yeshua as a baby was sent to Egypt and then He was called out of Egypt and brought back to Jerusalem. It is the reason that the LORD called Moses to bring His people out of Egypt and into this Promised Land. This is where the condemnation of Satan by the Messiah took place. Remember that Lucifer was in the Garden and he tempted Eve. This is why Yeshua bore the curse of death by crucifixion in this place and why He was resurrected to Eternal Life in God's Garden. This explains why Satan has been trying to steal this place for himself, even to this day! This explains why Satan uses leaders of nations to set up abominations on the Temple Mount and to claim it for other false gods of Babylon. The LORD God of Israel said that this Land belongs to Him and He promised that Israel would inherit this Land forever, but Satan continues to try to hinder this in an attempt to prevent the KING OF KINGS from coming to rule on His Holy Mountain. When all of this came to me, I suddenly understood why this place called *"Jerusalem"* has been the most fought over piece of property from the beginning of time. This was absolutely the location of the Garden of Eden and the people were driven out and the land became a curse. The curse would only be taken away by the Messiah in His Garden where He destroyed the workings of Satan forever, and it will only be restored to the most glorious Eternal Garden of God when the LORD returns to dwell in it. *Ezekiel even tells us that Satan was condemned in this place!* Remember what I said about the Royal Stone of Kings and the Serpentine that I

found in this rock? *Satan was on the Holy Mountain of God in the place of God's Garden. Satan was on the Temple Mount trying to claim it!*

Ezekiel 28:13-14 *Thou hast been in Eden the Garden of God; every precious stone was thy covering, the sardius, topaz, and the diamond, the beryl, the onyx, and the jasper, the sapphire, the emerald, and the carbuncle, and the gold; the workmanship of thy tabrets and of thy pipes was prepared in thee in the day that thou wast created. Thou art the anointed cherub that covereth; and I have set thee so; thou wast upon the Holy Mountain of God; thou hast walked up and down in the midst of the stones of fire. Thou wast perfect in thy ways from the day that thou wast created, till iniquity was found in thee. By the multitude of thy merchandise they have filled the midst of thee with violence, and thou hast sinned; therefore I will cast thee as profane out of the Mountain of God; and I will destroy thee, O covering cherub, from the midst of the stones of fire.*

Tropical Leaf Photo ©2013 Kimberly K Ballard All Rights Reserved

This passage clearly says that in the beginning, the Garden of God or Eden was upon the Holy Mountain of God which is Holy Mount Moriah! When the anointed cherub, Lucifer, was condemned here, the LORD said that He would cast Satan out of the Mountain of God and destroy him. This is why Messiah Yeshua had to bear the curse of death from Eden in this precise location and turn *the bitter to sweet* in the Holy Mountain of God. This is why the Church of the Holy Sepulchre is not the correct location of Yeshua's death, burial, and resurrection because it is not located in the Holy Mountain of God. Only the sepulchre at the Garden Tomb is in the Holy Mountain called *"Moriah." Satan will try to set his "seat" there, to claim it as his throne!*

How ironic then that the Jewish people and the Christians are kept from praying and honoring the LORD, the KING OF KINGS on His Holy Mountain and this is a great sin and *travesty of justice* that has been orchestrated by Satan. The LORD said that iniquity was found in Satan. By definition *"iniquity"* is *"gross injustice or wickedness, a violation of right or duty, immorality, debauchery and depravity." Ezekiel's passage indicates very clearly that Jerusalem and Mount Moriah are the location of the Garden of God.* When Yeshua miraculously came to life in this place, the *two Living Cherubim Angels testified* that He had conquered Satan in this place. They said, *"Why seek ye the Living among the dead?"* The two Angels were pointing to *"the place,"* where Satan was conquered by the light and glory of

Yeshua's miraculous resurrection. As I said before, this location is also called *"Zion"* and Isaiah wrote that God will comfort her and all her waste places. He said that He will *"make her wilderness like Eden and her desert like the Garden of the LORD!"* This further validates that this was *forever* the place where God planted His Garden, where His Almond Rod budded!

Tropical Leaf Photo ©2013 Kimberly K Ballard All Rights Reserved

***Isaiah 51:3** For the LORD shall comfort Zion; He will comfort all her waste places; and He will make her wilderness like Eden, and her desert like the Garden of the LORD; joy and gladness shall be found therein, thanksgiving and voice of melody.*

The KING of righteousness did spring forth from this Garden before all the nations. The Bridegroom of Israel has clothed us with pure garments of salvation, instead of the unclean garments of death and ashes.

Melinda's Magnolia Tree seed pod Photo ©2014 DeRieux Edited to B& W by Kimberly K Ballard All Rights Reserved

***Isaiah 61:10-11** I will greatly rejoice in the LORD, my soul shall be joyful in my God; for He hath clothed me with the garments of salvation, He hath covered me with the robe of righteousness, as a Bridegroom decketh Himself with ornaments, and as a Bride adorneth herself with her jewels. For as the earth bringeth forth her bud, and as the Garden causeth all things that are sown in it to spring forth; so the LORD God will cause righteousness and praise to spring forth before all nations.*

When I finally understood that Satan has been attempting for all these centuries to enthrone himself on God's Holy Temple Mount in Jerusalem and that he will do so again, I knew why the abomination of desolation was set up in this place during the time of the Maccabee's and why this attempt will happen again on Mount Zion. It is because Satan has been attempting to overthrow the one true God and enthrone himself there, but he has already been defeated by the Great and Mighty KING OF KINGS AND LORD OF LORDS! Since the place of Eden had become a curse, the rivers were changed by the LORD and they will not return to their former glory in Jerusalem in His Garden on His Holy Mountain until Messiah Yeshua comes!

Melinda's Fruiting Persimmon Tree Photo ©2014 DeRieux Edited to B& W by KK Ballard All Rights Reserved

***Habakkuk 3:8** Was the LORD displeased against the rivers? Was Thine anger against the rivers? Was Thy wrath against the sea, that Thou didst ride upon Thine horses and Thy chariots of salvation?*

The prophecy also tells us that when the Messiah comes to Israel, the Living Water will go toward *"the former sea."* Half the waters will go to one side and half the waters will go to the other side, like the cleft rivers of Eden. This is the signature of the LORD with His Rod. At least two rivers will come out from each side from one main water source, just like it was in Eden. This means there will be four rivers coming out of one river again in Jerusalem *and the source river is the Divine Presence of the LORD on Holy Mount Moriah in the location of His Heavenly Garden and Eternal Temple.* The LORD is the river of Living Water, and from Him this river divides into four rivers. Thus He waters the entire earth from His Garden in the New Heavenly Jerusalem.

Zechariah 14:8-9 *And it shall be in that day, that Living Waters shall go out from Jerusalem; Half of them toward the former sea, and half of them toward the hinder sea; In summer and in winter shall it be. And the LORD shall be KING over all the earth; in that day shall there be one LORD, and His Name one.*

The Willows clinging to the River bed drinking the Living Water
Photo ©2013 Kimberly K Ballard All Rights Reserved

Now remember that I said that the people were cast out of *God's Garden in Eden* on Holy Mount Moriah in Jerusalem? Then I explained how some of the people, after the grand eviction from God's Garden traveled to Shinar. So in the wrong place, they tried to build a tower to reach unto Heaven and they set up a false system of worshipping other false gods in Babylon, and later Nebuchadnezzar even built the *hanging gardens* there. Now I have the chills again, because it suddenly occurred to me that when the LORD sent the Israelites into exile into Babylon because they had rejected Him in Jerusalem by worshipping the false gods of Babylon, then the people mourned. *They were longing to go back to the Garden of God, where His rivers once flowed without the curse! I suddenly realized that this is why they hung their harps on the willows* by *the rivers of Babylon. This was the Euphrates River that ran past Babylon and had originally flowed out of Jerusalem from the Garden of Eden! The people were the willows that could no longer drink from the rivers in God's Garden on Mount Moriah that had been the former Garden of Eden!* So therefore, when they sat down by the rivers of Babylon they wept as they remembered Zion! Then they declared there that *"if they forgot Jerusalem, to let their tongue cleave to the roof of their mouth!"* I suddenly understood that they thirsted for the one true God whose *Garden of Living Water was in Jerusalem, in the place of Zion or Mount Moriah.* So they wept and therefore, *"How could they sing the songs of Torah or the Psalms of David in a strange land?"* This is incredible, but the LORD just revealed this to me! *King David's Psalm 137 reveals that Jerusalem was the place of the Garden of Eden, where the one true Living God dwells and provides the life-giving Living Water.* Jerusalem Israel, not Babylon, is the place where the LORD caused the rivers to flow from His Garden on Holy Mount Moriah and the Israelites were *the willows* that drank from the rivers of this Holy Mount, but now they could not and their tongues were dried up. So how were they going to worship the LORD there and sing His songs in this foreign land? *Therefore, they did not want to forget Jerusalem where they never had to thirst for the true Living Water from the right hand of God.* Remember that Babylon is where the LORD confused the languages, so all the people would be scattered, but in Jerusalem on Shavuot, the LORD restored the languages through His Jewish disciples. Now all people would be gathered

back to the Garden of God to the true place of worshipping the one true Living God, who rolled the Great stone from the well of Yeshua in Holy Mount Moriah where His flocks would be gathered to drink forever in Jerusalem, His Eternal Holy City in the Land of Israel!

Isaiah 44:1-4 *Yet now hear, O Jacob My servant; and Israel, whom I have chosen; Thus saith the LORD that made thee, and formed thee from the womb, which will help thee; Fear not, O Jacob, My servant; and thou, Jesurun, whom I have chosen. For I will pour water upon him that is thirsty, and floods upon the dry ground; I will pour My Spirit upon thy seed, and My blessing upon thine offspring; And they shall spring up as among the grass, as willows by the water courses.*

Raging River of Living Water (Boulder Creek later damaged by the flood of 2013)
Photo ©2013 Kimberly K Ballard

Jerusalem will be rejuvenated when the KING returns and sets *His towering fortress on Mount Moriah,* and the time of refreshing from the true river of Living Water will return to Jerusalem! Rivers of this Living Water will flow out from the LORD KING to refresh the earth!

Psalm 137:1-6 *By the rivers of Babylon, there we sat down, yea, we wept, when we remembered Zion. We hanged our harps upon the willows in the midst thereof. For there they that carried us away captive required of us a song; and they that wasted us required of us mirth, saying, Sing us one of the songs of Zion. How shall we sing the LORD'S song in a strange land? If I forget thee, O Jerusalem, let my right hand forget her cunning. If I do not remember thee, let my tongue cleave to the roof of my mouth; if I prefer not Jerusalem above my chief joy.*

Isaiah 41:17-18 *When the poor and needy seek water, and there is none, and their tongue faileth for thirst, I the LORD will hear them, I the God of Israel will not forsake them. I will open rivers in high places, and fountains in the midst of the valleys; I will make the wilderness a pool of water, and the dry land springs of water.*

Ezekiel 34:13 *And I will bring them out from the people, and gather them from the countries, and will bring them to their own land, and feed them upon the mountains of Israel by the rivers, and in all the inhabited places of the country.*

It is interesting that it says that while they were captive in Babylon, they required of them mirth. The word *"mirth"* refers to *"laughter and joy, particularly during the special Holy Days"* in *Jerusalem at the Holy Temple of the LORD.* So the Israelites could no longer celebrate the Seven Feasts of the LORD in joy and jubilation until they returned to *the Promised Land, to the original place of God's Eternal Garden where He gave them Living Water for their thirst!*

THE ARC OF THE COVENANT RAINBOW THE BERYL STONE

Imitation Beryl Stone
& the center arch of the intense
Double Rainbows over my house
Photo ©2013 Kimberly K Ballard

As I was pondering all of this about the Living Water in the Garden of Eden, I recalled a photograph that I had seen of the mighty Victoria Falls. In the picture, there was a mighty torrent of rushing living water gushing out over the falls. In the midst of the living water, there appeared a gorgeous double rainbow. When I saw this double rainbow hovering above the rushing living water, it suddenly clicked with me, and I could immediately visualize and understand why there is a rainbow around the throne of God. The LORD, who is the Living Water, sustains all life and He has a rainbow hovering over His throne. The LORD is the only one who could wash away our sins, by casting them upon the *"body"* of Living Water into Messiah the LORD. The rainbow is the LORD'S Covenant, not only with mankind, but with all living creatures.

A powerful image struck my mind when I suddenly made the connection that the rainbow is called an *"Arc,"* and this particular *"Arc of the Covenant"* is hovering over the *"Ark of the Covenant"* in Heaven! How incredible! This touched my heart because as I looked at the rainbow over Victoria Falls, it suddenly came to me that the reason why the *Arc of the rainbow Covenant is over the Ark of His Covenant throne in Heaven is because the LORD KING is the Living Water and He is the Eternal spectrum of light!* The Apostle John wrote about the rainbow in Heaven over the throne of God. Notice that John tells us that one was sitting on the throne!

Revelation 4:2-3 *And immediately I was in the spirit; and, behold, a throne was set in Heaven, and one sat on the throne. And He that sat was to look upon like a jasper and a sardine stone; and there was a rainbow round about the throne, in sight like unto an emerald.*

The Arc of the Covenant rainbow is formed from *a spectrum of light reflecting off water droplets.* I realized that because the LORD shines with the full spectrum of the Shechinah glory light and because He is the Living Water, He is the cause of the rainbow that appears round about His throne. A rainbow is made up of 7 Arcs of color from the light spectrum. The 7 colored Arcs of the rainbow demonstrate again that the LORD'S Covenant is perfect and complete. The Almond Tree of Life, the Holy Menorah of Heaven, has the 7 lamps that burn the oil of the Holy Spirit and this creates light on the 7 branches. The Holy Spirit has 7 attributes, the number of perfection. The LORD is the central light source. So it is intriguing that emerald green is the color in the center of the *"Arc of the Covenant rainbow"* because the emerald green color happens to be the central color around the throne where the KING OF KINGS sits on His throne. Emerald green was the color that John saw in Heaven around the LORD'S throne. Now many people have used green for their own purposes (religious or non-

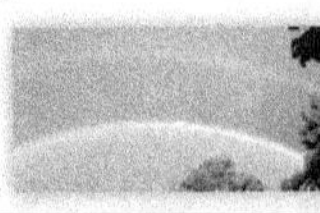

religious), but this emerald green is the color that is associated with *Eternal Life through the LORD God of Israel. He created all the colors of the spectrum!*

Now at this point, I have to tell you the true story of an unusual event that happened to me. This miracle happened the same year that the LORD revealed the Almond Tree to me, in 2007. Ironically, there was a famous diamond designer (Israel Itzkowitz) who had come all the way from Israel to display his work at a fine jewelry store (Snyder Jewelers) near the place where I live. I prayed about this event because I really did want to see some of the precious rare gemstones that he was planning to display. The Israeli designer designed and created the Princess cut diamond, and the gorgeous cut of diamond called *"The Prince cut diamond,"* and it was going to be featured at the show. This diamond design was without a doubt the most spectacular shaped diamond that I have ever laid my eyes on! The Israeli designer gave a special showing of His gemstones from Israel, so I knew that I had to go and see this incredible display and presentation. As I drove into town, I was praying that the LORD would bless this time and allow me to meet the designer from Israel. So I arrived and entered the store. As I was walking around observing the most brilliant gemstones and diamonds that I had ever seen in my life, I was thinking, *"Wow, if this is any indication of how the foundation stones in Heaven appear, it must be stunning up there and far more fabulous than anyone can ever imagine!"* As I was thinking along these lines to myself, I suddenly came upon a glass case that displayed a gemstone whose name I recognized from the Bible mentioned in the book of Revelation. This was my moment to meet the diamond designer! I looked at the stone and asked the *designer, "Is this stone called "Beryl," a stone that is mentioned in the Bible in the book of Revelation about Heaven?"* The owner of the store, Linda, and Israel the designer told me, *"Yes it is one of the stones mentioned in the Bible!"* Actually I was so surprised that they knew the answer to my question. I already knew that it was mentioned in Revelation, I just wanted to see what they would say about it. The Beryl stone that I saw in this case was almost an inch long and approximately half an inch wide. When the light refracted through the Beryl stone, it was fiery brilliant and it gave off a spectacular display of colors that were emanating out of the stone. Words simply cannot describe how beautiful and stunning it appeared with the light shining through it. As I observed this Beryl stone, I knew that I was seeing just a tiny glimpse of Heaven! As I stared down upon this gorgeous gemstone, I could not get over its purity and clarity. It was as clear as crystal, having a slight yellow tint. Now what happened next was really fascinating! Remember that the Holy Spirit had been revealing the Almond Tree Testimony to me around this time, so interesting things kept on happening to me. In order to appreciate this miracle, you have to know that the windows of the store were facing my back and they were far away from the case where I was standing. There was no light shining in from the sun in the area where I was standing, and, therefore, no light from the windows could possibly be shining on the front side of me. As I was seriously staring at this Biblical stone in amazement, thinking of how it would look in Heaven and praising the LORD in my heart about it, all of a sudden the owner and the designer said, *"That is strange, you are illuminated!"* I said, *"What?"* I was really puzzled when they said this to me, and as I looked up from the case to see what they were talking about, they were looking all around me. They were looking up, down, and all around me, trying to figure out where the light source was coming from that apparently was all over me. They both saw it and were baffled by it and, quite frankly, so was I. When I asked where the light was they said, *"All over you!"* They said, *"It's on your face, arms, and body."* Aside from being, *"lit up,"* the owner Linda also said, *"You have rainbows all over you on your face, arms, and on your clothes."* They were seriously checking me out, looking up and down and to my side, and at the front

An imitation Beryl Stone
Photo ©2013 Kimberly K Ballard
All Rights Reserved

windows but no light was emanating from them. As I said, the windows were far away and my back was to them. The light was all over the front of me! They looked up at all the overhead lights that were angled into the display cases and not one of them was shining upon the front of me or on my face. The Beryl stone in the case also was not shining on me. These people, who I did not really know, were a bit baffled and I was sort of shocked too, of course, because I was wondering about this strange occurrence that was happening to me, just after I mentioned the Beryl as one of the foundation stones of Heaven. I knew the Holy Spirit was working in me at this time because the LORD had just given me the revelation of the Almond Tree and the miracle Almond budding in Jerusalem. As I said before, I knew that the LORD had opened the opportunity for me to meet this Israeli artisan diamond cutter and designer. I had told the LORD, as I prayed, that I wanted to see these gemstones because this was an extremely rare opportunity to see diamonds and gemstones of such a high caliber. As I was pondering the Beryl stone and imagining Heaven, suddenly this happened to me, but Linda the owner of the store and Israel the diamond designer were the ones who actually witnessed this strange phenomenon as it was happening to me. I did not see it happening, but they both saw it on me and they told me about it with the look of perplexity on their faces.

They were mystified because they could not seem to find a light source for this phenomenon. This was unusual in the fact that they are experts in dealing with gemstones and they are familiar with setting the lighting in the store so it shines in all the right places! As I looked down on my shirt, I suddenly saw exactly what they were telling me. I was in fact *"lit up,"* as if a soft golden light was shining all over the front of me. There were small rainbows all over my clothes and arms, just as they said and yet no light was coming from the windows, as I stated, nor were any of the small aimed spot lights from over head shining on me or in my direction, to produce the rainbows and the light. There was no prism effect coming from any of the cases either. The LORD knew that I had just mentioned the Bible, as I was silently observing the fantastic refraction of light down inside the case, through that little stone. I was thinking, as I was gazing upon the Beryl, that if this small gemstone was this fantastic, then how fabulous must Heaven appear with all the gemstones of every color in the light spectrum that have the Shechinah glory light of the LORD refracting through them! Linda told me that she had never seen this phenomenon happen in her store before and she has been in business for several generations. She said that she thought it was miraculous.

Since I had prayed in the car, before going to see the exhibit, I already felt an inner glow even before they were telling me about this phenomenon. In my heart, I knew exactly who the light source was that day! She told me that she had only witnessed one other rainbow in her store before. Her father had passed away years ago and she had a large photo of him on the wall by the front windows. She said that a rainbow appeared one day over her father's picture, but she could see the source of the light in that situation. In my situation, however, she said she absolutely could not find the source of the light! As the long time owner of the store, she is extremely familiar with the placement of every single light because the lights must shine properly on the jewelry to produce the greatest lighting effect. This strange occurrence had impressed her so much that she remembered it for a long time. I had only really met her once before in the store. About six months later, I returned to the store and she remembered every detail of this unusual event. She retold the story to my Mother as I was standing there! I thought it was unusual that she remembered the whole story, but it was because she was so impressed by this rare and strange event. It was just incredible to know that I was looking at the fiery spectrums of light coming off these stones down in the case and thinking to myself that if this is what Heaven looks like, then all I can say is a breathtaking, *"Wow, how incredible!"* I know the gemstones in Heaven are huge compared to what I saw that day in the display case. Can you imagine the Shechinah glory of God's Eternal light shining and refracting through these Heavenly foundation stones in the Heavenly Temple? Emanating from

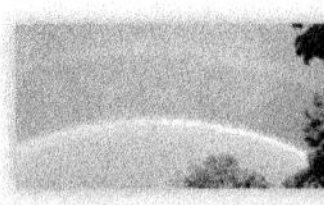

the LORD'S throne is the full light spectrum of His Shechinah glory refracting through Him as the Living Water, and this is why I knew the LORD'S throne, *"The Ark of His Covenant,"* was surrounded by, *"The Arc of His Covenant!"*

After I wrote the details of this story, I ran across a Scripture that just stopped me cold and made me shiver! *I had completely forgotten that the Bible indicates that the body of Messiah Yeshua in Heaven is like the Beryl stone!* So when I asked about the Beryl stone in the store, as I was praying to the LORD in my heart, I later began to wonder, *"Was He standing there beside me, illuminating me?" Was the "Invisible Assistant" watching me? Was it His Invisible Presence that made me glow in His light, with the tiny rainbows all over me? Was it the glory of the LORD?* What a breathtaking thought! It actually brings tears to my eyes.

Daniel 10:6 *His body also was like the Beryl, and His face as the appearance of lightning, and His eyes as lamps of fire, and His arms and His feet like in colour to polished brass, and the voice of His Words like the voice of a multitude.*

It is amazing! Yeshua has the appearance of the Beryl stone! He is described exactly the same way in Revelation 1, where He is called *"The Alpha and Omega."* Now this is a beautiful vision to contemplate when you have lost a loved one who has gone before you into Heaven to be with the LORD. The separation of death is only temporary, but the glory of the LORD is forever. This gives us such a beautiful picture of Heaven and it brings such a sense of peace and comfort to our grieving hearts.

Everything that the LORD created is in some aspect a reflection of His glory and beauty upon the earth. The seven Arcs of the LORD'S Covenant around His throne reveal that He is the rushing mighty Living Water that sustains life forever by reflecting and refracting His glorious Shechinah light as the Heavenly Almond Tree Menorah of life. Just as *the willow* draws water from its roots to drink, we too draw water to quench our thirst from the only source of Eternal Life.

Later, as I thought about the strange event of being *"lit up"* and having small rainbows all over me with no apparent source of light shining upon me, I remembered Moses whose face shone because He had spoken with God!

The right side of the intense Double Rainbow that was over my house B&W Photo ©2013 Kimberly K Ballard All Rights Reserved

Exodus 34:29 *And it came to pass, when Moses came down from Mount Sinai with the two tables of Testimony in Moses hand, when he came down from the Mount, that Moses wist not that the skin of his face shone while he talked with him.*

Moses wist not that the skin of his face shone while he talked with God! The word *"wist"* means *"knew."* So Moses did not know that his face was shining with a glow, while he talked to God just like I did not know that I was *"lit up or illuminated"* as I talked to the Israeli designer and Linda, the owner of the Jewelry store, after talking to God! It is simply a remarkable miracle that I will never forget. Personally, I do not ever claim to be glowing and I say this laughing in humility, but for some reason, they saw the light on me that day! *The Holy Spirit of the LORD abiding on Moses was the source of Moses being lit up!* I think it is fantastic that this happened to me, and two people who I did not know were like *two witnesses* who said that they saw the glow of light upon me, during the time frame that I was given my Almond Tree miracle by the LORD. I never dreamed in a million years that this story would wind up in a book, along with many hidden secrets that the LORD revealed to me, including the fantastic *"Arc of the Covenant."* I felt that when they saw me *"lit up,"* this was an indication that the Holy Spirit

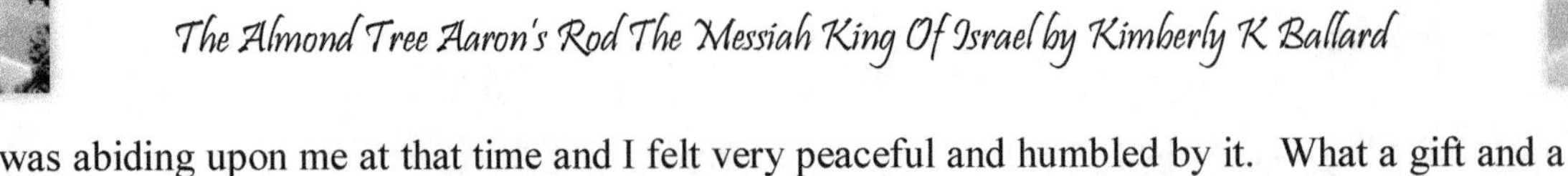

was abiding upon me at that time and I felt very peaceful and humbled by it. What a gift and a blessing that there happened to be these *two witnesses* that saw the light as it illuminated me that day. I did not know what they believed about the LORD, but they saw this miracle anyway. This diffused yellowish glowing light was all over me and I only saw it when I looked down on my shirt and saw it covering me. There are different color shades of Beryl and I found out that it can be a darker golden yellow like amber or a lighter golden yellow, like the stone I viewed in the case that day. What I just discovered though is spectacular, in light of what I already wrote earlier about the Shroud image of Yeshua having been formed by *electromagnetic radiation.* According to information from Cal Tech, Beryl is golden in color or green in color, due to radiation and Gamma rays are used in the lab to transform the color of the crystal into another color! Cal Tech states; *"Much Beryl is heated to remove the golden to green shades that result from radiation in order to turn the crystal into blue aquamarine."* ***(Source: ©2011 minerals.gps.caltech.edu/COLOR_Causes/Radiate/index.html).***

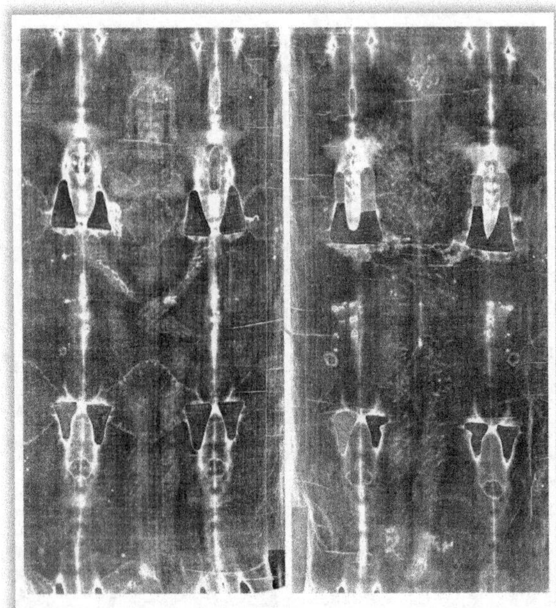
Official Shroud Pair
Photograph ©1978 Barrie M. Schwortz Collection, STERA Inc., All Rights Reserved

Gamma rays have the highest potency of *radiation* and remember that the four sets of poker holes or burn marks of fire in the Shroud of Turin are shaped like the Greek letter *"Gamma,"* the third letter of the alphabet and Yeshua came to life the third day. Recently, I mentioned that I spotted this Gamma design inside the Synagogue of Magdala that was just unearthed. It was the same shape as the L-shaped Gammas on linens found at Masada and on Yeshua's burial Shroud. They represent the Hebrew *"qeren"* or horns of the altar. This word is defined as *"rays of light; power."* It is a stunning connection that Yeshua's appearance in Heaven is like the Beryl that is yellow amber in color. *This further indicates that when Yeshua came to life in the sepulchre, "electromagnetic radiation was present with Gamma rays" because His appearance is like Beryl in Heaven and a fiery light spectrum emanates from Him with green over His throne.* In the book of Ezekiel, we see a description in Heaven of the person sitting on the throne between the two Cherubim Angels. In this Scripture, the rainbow appears with all its radiance surrounding the glory of the Almighty. Ezekiel specifically says that *"the figure of a man"* was sitting on a throne. He was surrounded by the radiance of the rainbow, and this *figure of a man* was Messiah Yeshua, the LORD God of Israel, *and around Him was the color of fiery amber.*

Ezekiel 1:24-28 *And when they went, I heard the noise of their wings, like the noise of great waters, as the voice of the Almighty, the voice of speech, as the noise of an host; when they stood, they let down their wings. And there was a voice from the firmament that was over their heads, when they stood, and had let down their wings. And above the firmament that was over their heads was the likeness of a throne, as the appearance of a sapphire stone; and upon the likeness of the throne was the likeness as the appearance of a man above upon it. And I saw as the colour of amber, as the appearance of fire round about within it, even the appearance of His loins even upward, and from the appearance of His loins even downward, I saw as it were the appearance of fire, and it had the brightness round about. As the appearance of the bow that is in the cloud in the day of rain, so was the appearance of the brightness round about. This was the appearance of the likeness of the glory of the LORD. And when I saw it, I fell upon my face, and I heard a voice of one that spake.*

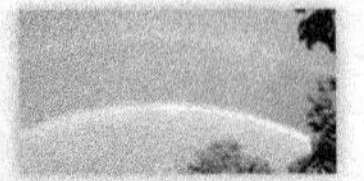

This Scripture is fascinating because it describes a *"fiery radiance"* around the Almighty, whose voice was like the noise of great waters. The word *"radiance"* refers to *"brilliance, brightness, or a glow."* As a synonym, the word *"radiance"* means *"rapture"* and it means *"warmth."* This again explains the rapture in the glory cloud! The rapture, takes us to be with the LORD in the glory cloud and into His Divine *radiance!* So to be *"raptured"* is to be suddenly with Him! The word *"radiance"* can also refer to *fire.* This, of course, reminds me of the LORD appearing in the burning bush in the midst of the fire and in the Pillar of fire. Ezekiel described this *radiance* as the appearance of the likeness of the glory of the LORD. Before the throne, it is like a sea of glass and all this light of His glory is *refracting,* like pure clear crystal and like the fiery brilliant light that I saw shooting forth out of the Beryl stone. The light and the *radiant glory* that is coming from the LORD is beyond our imagination. I saw a tiny glimpse of Heaven and a tiny hint of the glory of the LORD the day that I went to see *"The Prince diamond,"* but these small precious stones were nothing compared to the greatness of God our Saviour and KING! In the next Ezekiel passage, the hand of the LORD GOD appeared with the appearance of fire and He had brightness from His loins upward, *"as the colour of amber and from His loins downward as fire."* This was the vision of God and the Shechinah glory of the God of Israel was present! *This is Yeshua, the Yad or hand glowing with the amber fiery brilliance!* I will never forget my experience with the Beryl stone! I will never forget how the Beryl stone pertains to Yeshua's Shroud!

Imitation Beryl Stone
Photo ©2013
KK Ballard All Rights Reserved

Ezekiel 8:1-4 *And it came to pass in the sixth year, in the sixth month, in the fifth day of the month, as I sat in mine house, and the elders of Judah sat before me, that the hand of the LORD GOD fell there upon me. Then I beheld, and lo a likeness as the appearance of fire; from the appearance of His loins even downward, fire; and from His loins even upward, as the appearance of brightness, as the colour of amber. And He put forth the form of an hand, and took me by a lock of mine head; and the spirit lifted me up between the earth and the Heaven, and brought me in the visions of God to Jerusalem, to the door of the inner gate that looketh toward the north; where was the seat of the image of jealousy, which provoketh to jealousy. And, behold, the glory of the God of Israel was there, according to the vision that I saw in the plain.*

As we stand before the LORD in Heaven and see Him face to face in His *radiance,* we will see *"The Arc of His Covenant"* that is surrounding *"The Ark of His Covenant!"* The Tree of Life is standing in the middle of Heaven. This means that the LORD is the central focal point of Heaven, the central Rod of God, with the emerald green of Eternal Life surrounding His throne, with the fiery Beryl of His glory light *radiating!* The Almond Tree is the LORD and He is everything that we could ever want! He is the Tree of Life that heals the nations!

Revelation 22:1-2 *And he showed me a river of the Water of Life, clear as crystal, coming from the Throne of God and of the Lamb, in the middle of its street and on either side of the river was the Tree of Life, bearing twelve kinds of fruit, yielding its fruit every month; and the leaves of the Tree were for the healing of the nations.*

Revelation 2:7 *He who has an ear, let him hear what the Spirit says to the churches, to him who overcomes, I will grant to eat of the Tree of Life, which is in the Paradise of God.*

The Gamma rays radiate from Him! I am greatly comforted knowing that my beautiful Aunt and Grandparents, my Father and his Brother are in this incredibly spectacular and gorgeous place, shining with the full spectrum of the glory light of the LORD upon them. The KING is sitting on His Ark, refracting every unimaginable color of fiery brilliance, and His *radiance* glows upon my loved ones up there in the Eternal Kingdom of Heaven. Yet a little while and death shall be no more. The brilliance of the LORD'S fiery Shechinah light *raptures* us to Eternal Life and to that I say, *"L' Chaim!"* To Life! Praise the Royal KING of Glory!

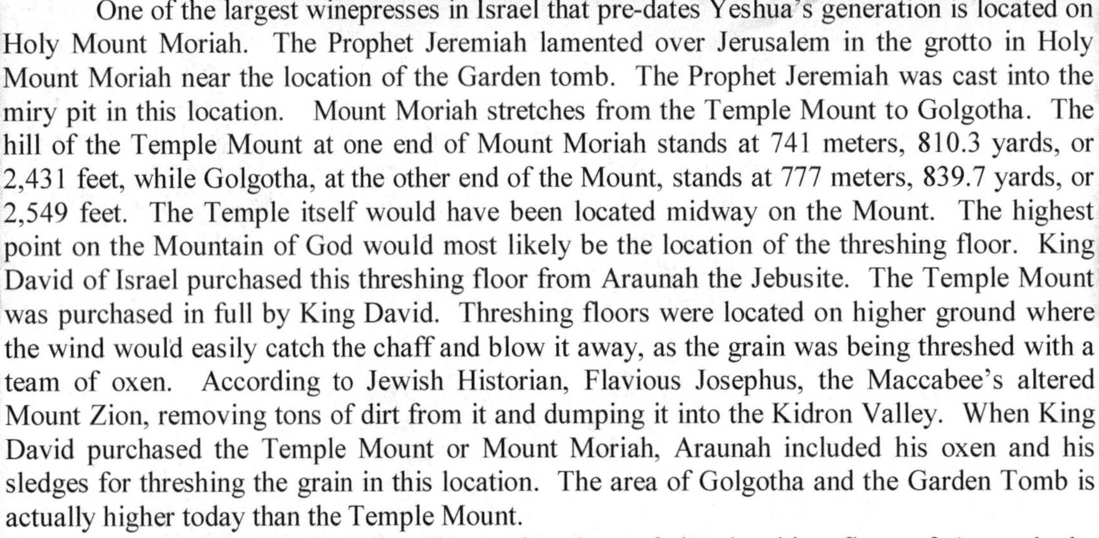

THE WINEPRESS AND WATER CISTERN NEAR THE THRESHING FLOOR THE ROMAN FRESCOES

Wine Bottle in my Grape Vineyard & Stone Pavement

One of the largest winepresses in Israel that pre-dates Yeshua's generation is located on Holy Mount Moriah. The Prophet Jeremiah lamented over Jerusalem in the grotto in Holy Mount Moriah near the location of the Garden tomb. The Prophet Jeremiah was cast into the miry pit in this location. Mount Moriah stretches from the Temple Mount to Golgotha. The hill of the Temple Mount at one end of Mount Moriah stands at 741 meters, 810.3 yards, or 2,431 feet, while Golgotha, at the other end of the Mount, stands at 777 meters, 839.7 yards, or 2,549 feet. The Temple itself would have been located midway on the Mount. The highest point on the Mountain of God would most likely be the location of the threshing floor. King David of Israel purchased this threshing floor from Araunah the Jebusite. The Temple Mount was purchased in full by King David. Threshing floors were located on higher ground where the wind would easily catch the chaff and blow it away, as the grain was being threshed with a team of oxen. According to Jewish Historian, Flavious Josephus, the Maccabee's altered Mount Zion, removing tons of dirt from it and dumping it into the Kidron Valley. When King David purchased the Temple Mount or Mount Moriah, Araunah included his oxen and his sledges for threshing the grain in this location. The area of Golgotha and the Garden Tomb is actually higher today than the Temple Mount.

Yeshua was threshed, literally, at the place of the threshing floor of Araunah the Jebusite on the Holy Mountain of God. It was here that He was beaten by the Roman soldiers and scourged by them and later crucified. We have already seen in a previous chapter how Messiah Yeshua was the wheat seed who was buried in the earth after being threshed and He was raised to life, because the seed of life the breath of the Holy Spirit, was inside Him. We have seen that Messiah was placed inside the tomb in the earth during the Feast of Unleavened Bread as the pure grain, the Bread from Heaven.

In the following Biblical Scriptures, *we can see that the threshing floor was always mentioned in connection with the location of the winepress.* This indicates that wherever a winepress was located, a threshing floor was near it. In the book of Judges, Gideon threshed wheat by the winepress and the angel of the LORD appeared to him there.

Judges 6:11-12 *And there came an angel of the LORD, and sat under an oak, which was in Ophrah, that pertained unto Joash the Abiezrite; and his son Gideon threshed wheat by the winepress, to hide it from the Midianites. And the angel of the LORD appeared unto him, and said unto him, The LORD is with thee thou mighty man of valour.*

The angel of the LORD also appeared near the winepress when he rolled away the Great Stone from Yeshua's sepulchre and the LORD appeared to Mary.

In the following Scriptures, we can see that the location of the winepress seems to be either beside the threshing floor or in very close proximity to the threshing floor.

Nehemiah 13:15 *In those days saw I in Judah some treading wine presses on the Sabbath, and bringing in sheaves, and lading asses; as also wine, grapes, and figs, and all manner of burdens, which they brought into Jerusalem on the Sabbath day; and I testified against them in the day wherein they sold victuals.*

Deuteronomy 16:13 *Celebrate the Feast of Tabernacles for seven days after you have gathered the produce of your threshing floor and your winepress.*

Wine bottle in Grape vineyard Photo ©2014 Kimberly K Ballard All Rights Reserved

Numbers 18:27 *Your offering will be reckoned to you as a grain from the threshing floor or juice from the winepress.*

Deuteronomy 15:14 *Supply Him liberally from your flock, your threshing floor and your winepress. Give to Him as the LORD your God has blessed you.*

Numbers 18:30 *Say to the Levites; when you present the best part, it will be reckoned to you as the product of the threshing floor or the winepress.*

II Kings 6:27 *And he said, if the LORD does not help thee, whence shall I help thee? Out of the barn floor, or out of the winepress?*

The threshing floor is also referred to as *"the barn floor"* and this is where the oxen would tread the grain, leaving the halo circular pattern in the floor as they walked around in a circle. *This is very important because the winepress that was discovered near the Garden tomb is one of the largest winepresses ever found in Israel.* We know that King David built an altar in the threshing floor of Araunah the Jebusite somewhere on Holy Mount Moriah. It was here that King David gave offerings upon the original altar to the LORD. In the same place where King David offered the lambs to the LORD, Messiah Yeshua, *"The Lamb,"* was offered by the LORD to save us from the curse of death from the Garden of Eden. In the Garden where Yeshua came to life, there was *a large vineyard* and, obviously, the grapes were crushed in the winepress next to Yeshua's Garden tomb. The LORD said that the cup of wine in the Passover Seder was to remember Him because He was crushed for our iniquities and bruised for our transgressions. This is symbolic of the grapes that were bruised and crushed underfoot in this place to provide the best wine. Yeshua the KING and High Priest is the anointed of the LORD. As He was crucified He was crushed under the Roman authority like the grapes in the LORD'S vineyard that were put into the winepress. *So out of His threshing floor and out of His winepress, He helped us!*

Isaiah 53:10 *Yet it pleased the LORD to bruise Him; He hath put Him to grief; when Thou shalt make His soul an offering for sin, He shall see His seed, He shall prolong His days, and the pleasure of the LORD shall prosper in His hand.*

Now it is also very intriguing that in the place of the Garden tomb, there is a huge water cistern that is sufficient for watering a vineyard, an orchard, or for watering large grain crops. At the Garden tomb, water troughs were found carved in the pavement in this area, and I believe that they were for the purpose of carrying rain water to the vineyard that once existed near the winepress. The water from this huge cistern supplied the vital minerals to make this Garden vineyard flourish. Some have speculated that these troughs were used to water animals or to baptize believers, but I think this idea is totally incorrect because they are too shallow and they were covered with dirt throughout the Crusades. The troughs are long and narrow, similar to the shape of a rain gutter. It is more likely that the troughs were linked to the cistern, in order to water the vineyard in this huge Garden. I believe that the troughs were used to catch the fresh rain water during strong rainstorms, so it could replenish the supply of water that was stored inside this huge water cistern. The grain that was threshed nearby for centuries was also watered from the huge cistern through these troughs. So, altogether, we have in Holy Mount Moriah, the threshing floor, the winepress, the vineyard, the huge water cistern to water the crops, and the troughs for catching the rain water that was used for watering the vineyard and the grain crops. Ironically, in this same Garden, we have the stone that was rolled away by the

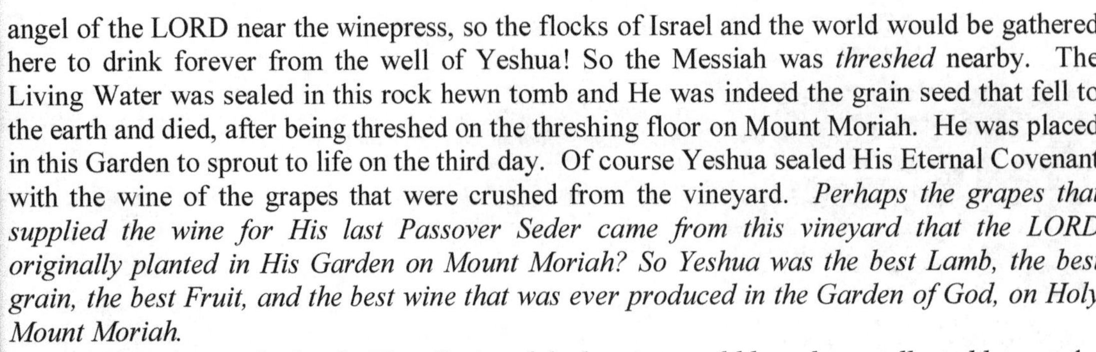

angel of the LORD near the winepress, so the flocks of Israel and the world would be gathered here to drink forever from the well of Yeshua! So the Messiah was *threshed* nearby. The Living Water was sealed in this rock hewn tomb and He was indeed the grain seed that fell to the earth and died, after being threshed on the threshing floor on Mount Moriah. He was placed in this Garden to sprout to life on the third day. Of course Yeshua sealed His Eternal Covenant with the wine of the grapes that were crushed from the vineyard. *Perhaps the grapes that supplied the wine for His last Passover Seder came from this vineyard that the LORD originally planted in His Garden on Mount Moriah? So Yeshua was the best Lamb, the best grain, the best Fruit, and the best wine that was ever produced in the Garden of God, on Holy Mount Moriah.*

Now, interestingly, *the First Fruits of the harvest would have been collected here* at the place of the Garden tomb where the threshing floor and winepress were located. This is the place that the best of the winepress and the best of the grain was gathered and offered to the LORD, as the First Fruits of the harvest. This is why Messiah Yeshua was raised to life here, as the First Fruits of salvation, on the Feast of First Fruits on Nisan 17 and *became the LORD'S First Fruits offering from His own Garden.*

So, one end of Mount Moriah had the winepress with the vineyard and in close proximity to this winepress was the altar that King David built on the threshing floor. The Holy Temple was eventually built on top of this altar and I believe that this was located at the other end of the Mount or in the middle of the Mount. As I studied the Scriptures, I realized that the LORD had originally intended for His altar alone to be set up on the high place in Israel and this is why King David set up the altar on Mount Moriah on the highest place that was the location of the Garden of Eden. So the LORD was drawing people back to His Garden in Jerusalem over the centuries through Messiah Yeshua. I realized this when I read that one of the reasons that the LORD was angry with Israel in ancient times was because they had started building altars on the high places of Israel to all the false gods of Babylon and that is partly why they were sent into captivity to Babylon where they hung their harps on the willows, weeping by the rivers, crying for Jerusalem. So if the high places, where they were building these pagan altars, were on land dedicated to the LORD God of Israel, then this is what truly angered the LORD. It was an abomination to the LORD and the generations who committed this sin paid dearly for their mistakes. This is the very sin that King Solomon committed against the LORD by allowing his pagan foreign wives to lead him into setting up altars to their pagan gods on every high hill in Israel. Even though the LORD had personally appeared at least twice to King Solomon, this did not stop him from setting up pagan altars. The LORD said that the punishment would be that He would divide Solomon's Kingdom after it passed into the hands of his son, Rehoboam, after King Solomon passed away. The Prophet Jeremiah warned the people of Israel to turn from these idols and to turn back to the LORD of Hosts in repentance. In that generation, the failure of Israel to repent led to the destruction of the First Temple that King Solomon built. They were taken into captivity into Babylon for 70 years. The punishment fit the offense. Since they were setting up altars in Israel to the Babylonian false gods on every high place, then the LORD gave them what He thought they wanted. He sent them directly to Babylon where these abominations were being worshipped. While they were stuck there for 70 years, they longed for the days of the Holy Temple and their hearts were turned back to worship the one true God of Israel. The LORD sent them to the place that would be the most difficult for them to worship Him, and so they had to diligently seek the LORD in this place, as they prayed toward Jerusalem toward the Garden of God. He made them desperate for their Holy Temple in Jerusalem, while they were held captive in Babylon for the designated 70 years of punishment. When the 70 years time of their captivity was fulfilled, the LORD allowed them to return to their beloved Jerusalem where they began to rebuild the Holy Temple to the LORD of Hosts. At the time of Zerubbabel, Ezra, and

Nehemiah, the Holy Temple was rebuilt and rededicated solely to the LORD God of Israel. The LORD is loving and patient to all people and He is always willing to forgive them if they humble themselves in repentance with their whole heart. We have proof that the Temple and the altar of the LORD, were set up on the high place, because Moses set up the Tabernacle and the altar in the wilderness in the high place.

I Chronicles 21:29 *For the Tabernacle of the LORD, which Moses made in the wilderness, and the altar of the burnt offering, were at that season in the high place at Gibeon.*

The LORD said that the threshing floor was on the Mountain, so the wind could blow the chaff away and separate it from the grain. The hill was covered in the chaff.

Isaiah 41:14-16 *Fear not, thou worm Jacob, and ye men of Israel; I will help thee, saith the LORD, and thy Redeemer, the Holy One of Israel. Behold, I will make thee a new sharp threshing instrument having teeth; thou shalt thresh the mountains, and beat them small, and shalt make the hills as chaff. Thou shalt fan them, and the wind shall carry them away, and the whirlwind shall scatter them; and thou shalt rejoice in the LORD, and shalt glory in the Holy One of Israel.*

Now remember that I spoke about *"the place,"* in the last chapter, that was between the two Living Cherubim Angels? Yeshua was buried in this place *as the offering in Mount Moriah, in the high place of the LORD'S Holy Mountain.* The LORD had told Abraham to go to this specific Mountain and offer his son Isaac. It was *"the third day"* when Abraham took Isaac his son to become the offering on Mount Moriah in the high place. Yeshua was the sin offering in the high place on Mount Moriah. It was *"the third day"* when Yeshua was raised as the First Fruits of salvation on Mount Moriah in the high place. The wood was cleft by Abraham, the sign that the LORD gave to us that reveals His works. Yeshua was bound to the wood just as Isaac was bound to the wood. The fire of the Holy Spirit was abiding in Him. The Roman lance was the blade that pierced Yeshua's heart, making the blood and water flow out and fall to the ground. These bear witness of the LORD'S work, as the Rod of God. In the place of the crucifixion called *"Golgotha"* on Mount Moriah, there was an earthquake and darkness fell over the land for *"three hours"* and the rocks were rent. As the rocks were made cleft, this was the signature of the work of the LORD God with His Yad and Rod. The LORD offered *"Himself, the Lamb, as the only Son in this same place."* All the natural elements of the LORD'S creation reacted at the time of His crucifixion.

Most people do not know that there are extremely significant words inscribed on the wall inside the Garden tomb where Yeshua came to life. On the wall above *"the place"* where His body rested, there were several red crosses etched. They were painted red, like Roman frescoes. This type of Roman fresco has been found in other places, dating from the First through Second Centuries. This allows us to pinpoint the date of this grave. Frescoes of this type have been found in many of the places where the Jewish Apostle Paul journeyed, including Antioch, Cypress, and Ephesus. Similar frescoes are also found in the Roman catacombs, dating from the First Century to the Second Century. In one of these locations where Paul journeyed, there is an altar with Paul's name inscribed upon it and the cross has a similar shape to the one found on the wall inside the Garden tomb in Jerusalem. If the Garden tomb was covered with dirt and debris from the time of the

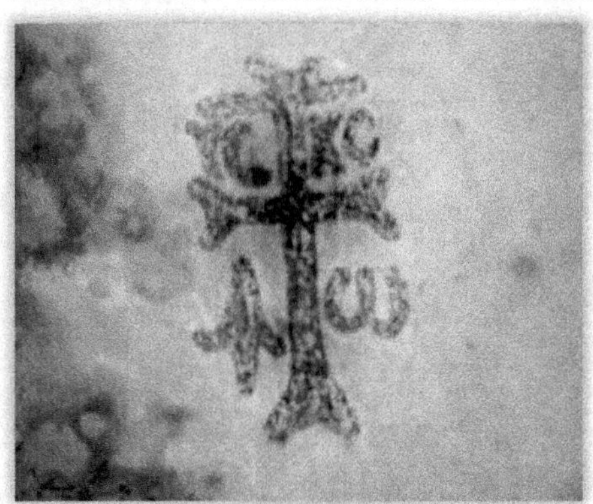

The Garden tomb Fresco with the cross & Alpha & Omega

destruction of Jerusalem, which was approximately 1900 years ago, at the time of the Jewish revolt against Rome, then the crosses and the inscriptions had to have been etched in the wall of the Garden tomb in the earliest part of the Christian era by the earliest Jewish followers of Messiah Yeshua. *These inscriptions, therefore, had to have been placed there possibly even by the Jewish disciples of Yeshua in the First Century shortly after the resurrection took place. The grave of Onesimus proves this.* James was the head of the Jerusalem Church that met in the upper room. In order to make a fresco of this nature, *"One had to etch and paint the artwork on the wall of the tomb, while the plaster was still slightly damp. It was then colored with red pigment, so when it dried, it became a permanent part of the wall."* ***(Source: ©2011 en.wikipedia.org/wiki/Fresco).***

Some of the inscriptions that were discovered when the Garden tomb was first excavated in Mount Moriah have faded considerably since the tomb has been exposed to the outside air. If you think about this objectively and as I mentioned earlier, this is clear evidence that the sepulchre of Yeshua had to have been buried with dirt and debris so that it received absolutely no air exposure, since the time that it was covered with dirt, nearly 1900 years ago. If this was not the case, then the frescoes would have disappeared hundreds of years ago, had they been unearthed at any time prior to the very late 1800's. For this reason, I believe that the frescoes and inscriptions on the wall in the Garden tomb must date to the late First Century Roman period in Jerusalem, during the life of Yeshua's disciples. In the frescoes in the Garden tomb, one can see the true identity of the Messiah of Israel. Inscribed on the rock wall in Mount Moriah where the LORD said that His Name would be inscribed forever is written the Name *"Yeshua"* with the cross and the letters *"Alpha and Omega."*

Revelation 22:13 *I AM the Alpha and the Omega, the First and the Last, the Beginning and the End.*

The LORD preserved these ancient Roman frescoes for our generation, so we could gaze upon His Living Testimony in the Mount that Abraham called *"YHVH Ra'ah"* which again is *"In the Mount of the LORD it shall be seen!"* I mentioned before that the Roman Emperor, Hadrian, hauled in tons of dirt around the Temple Mount area in order to cover up the meaningful Jewish places of worship and this is likely how the true Garden tomb was preserved for centuries. What Hadrian meant for evil, God turned to His glory. So the fact is that from the time of the destruction of Jerusalem, the Garden tomb was completely covered with the dirt and debris. The Garden tomb remained completely covered with dirt through every century until 1867 when it was unearthed for the first time. No one even knew that the Garden tomb was in this location until it was unearthed. No one had access to this sepulchre. No one could have inscribed the phrase *"Alpha and Omega"* with the Name *"Yeshua"* above the place where Yeshua came to life as *"The Living Almond Branch from the Tree of Life,"* except for the very first Jews who believed that Yeshua was the Jewish Messiah. It seems ironic to me that the LORD began to reveal many of the hidden elements of His Divine Testimony, through science and archaeology, around the late 19th century. For example, the British explorer, *"Sir Charles Warren,"* arrived in Jerusalem in February of 1867 to explore the area of the Temple Mount. The Garden tomb was first unearthed in 1867. After this occurred, the very first photograph was taken of the Shroud of Yeshua. The first photographs that were ever taken of the fine linen burial Shroud of Yeshua suddenly revealed the startling image of a crucified man in the positive, as if taken from a negative image. These photographs were taken by Secondo Pia on May 25th and 28th in 1898. The Dead Sea scrolls were then discovered, verifying the Word of God and one complete book of Isaiah was found, prophesying about the coming Messiah! The scrolls were discovered in the Judean wilderness between the years, 1946 to 1956. The directions for building the Third Holy Temple were miraculously discovered among these ancient scrolls! Then incredibly, on May 14th 1948, Israel was restored as a nation after nearly

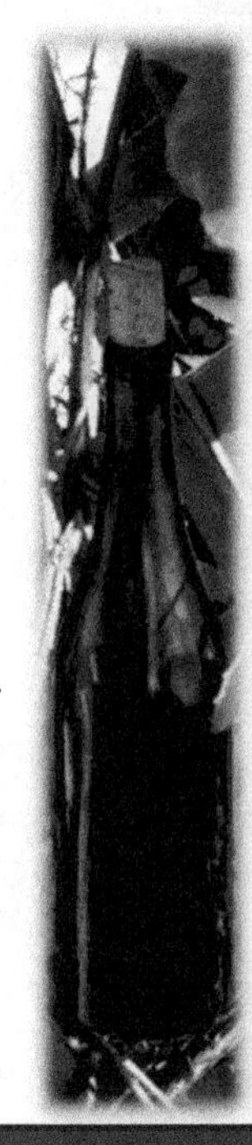

two thousand years of exile. Exactly 100 years from the unearthing of the Garden tomb, there came the liberation of the Holy Temple Mount and Jerusalem by the Jewish soldiers on June 7th 1967. It was all by Divine Providence. The LORD had preserved His Testimony right up to the time when His prophetic clock began to tick for the final stages of the end of days. Piece by piece, the LORD has revealed that He is still at work, drawing us back to Jerusalem, to His Garden on Holy Mount Moriah by revealing that He is the Eternal Messiah of Israel. Roman fresco crosses were also discovered etched in the plaster inside the huge water cistern in the Garden tomb area where the first Jewish followers of Yeshua fled to hide from the Roman invasion. *It is significant that the cross is etched in the plaster in the very place where the living water is stored!* This is where *the Living Water came out of the Rock* when the Great Stone was rolled away from the mouth of the well of salvation by the Angel of the LORD. The cistern was obviously used by the very earliest Jewish Christians as a place to gather secretly to worship the LORD without the Roman intrusion. The water cistern was a safe place for believers to hide from the threat of persecution. When Yeshua was resurrected, He appeared alive to Mary Magdalene in the Garden *near the winepress and near the threshing floor* in Mount Moriah and *this is near the water cistern.* In the story of Gideon in the Bible, the angel of the LORD appeared to him in the place of the winepress and the threshing floor. The angel of the LORD also appeared and rolled the stone away from Yeshua's sepulchre in the Garden near the winepress and the threshing floor. Now that I have verified this place, I will explain how this all leads to some truly profound discoveries of the LORD.

GIDEON'S THREE SIGNS OF THE LORD GOD OF ISRAEL

Wheat Grain Threshing floor & Wine in the Grape Vineyard
Photo ©2014 KK Ballard All Rights Reserved

The story of Gideon begins when he was threshing wheat by the winepress and the angel of the LORD appeared to him there. Three times the LORD revealed specific signs to Gideon to prove that He was the LORD God of his ancestors that had saved them before. So the Rod of God, Messiah Yeshua, appeared alive near the winepress and the threshing floor on the third day. The interesting thing about this story is that Gideon could not believe that the LORD God of Israel would choose him to perform a mighty work, since Gideon's family was poor. He feared that because he was the least of his father's household, that perhaps the LORD would never choose him for anything special. The fact is, however, that no matter how poor or insignificant Gideon was in worldly terms, the LORD of Hosts had, indeed, specifically chosen him. The LORD was going to use the man who did not feel worthy to accomplish a great task for the LORD demonstrating the power of the Rod of God that reveals the Messiah. When the LORD looked upon Gideon and spoke to him, it became clear that this was the God of Israel who was speaking to him. The LORD God of Israel told Gideon, *"Surely, I will be with you to win this battle."* God always sends His Rod into battle to save! So the LORD proved His identity *three times* to Gideon. Remember that my Israeli friend tried to pass that Almond Tree *three times* and finally took the picture! Surely it was the LORD God of Israel that pulled her to that Almond Tree *the third time* and this was a sign for me that verified that I was also hearing

from the LORD God of Israel in the Old city of Jerusalem, from Holy Mount Moriah! We know that Messiah Yeshua is the LORD God of Israel in the flesh because the Messiah is hidden in every single element of the three signs of Gideon. *Sign one proves that God's Rod is the Rod of Salvation and is the Living Torah.* So Yeshua has come to deliver Gideon from his enemies in battle, just as He gave victory and salvation to the Israelite's as they fled Pharaoh's army centuries before. In order to understand the elements that the LORD revealed to me in this Bible story, you must first be familiar with the historical account of Gideon *and his interaction with the LORD God near the winepress and the threshing floor.*

Judges 6:7-40 *And it came to pass, when the children of Israel, cried unto the LORD because of the Midianites, That the LORD sent a Prophet unto the children of Israel, which said unto them, thus saith the LORD God of Israel, I brought you up from Egypt, and brought you forth out of the house of bondage; And I delivered you out of the hand of the Egyptians, and out of the hand of all that oppressed you, and drave them out from before you, and gave you their land; And I said unto you, I AM the LORD your God; fear not the gods of the Amorites, in whose land ye dwell; but ye have not obeyed My voice. And there came an angel of the LORD, and sat under an oak which was in Ophrah, that pertained unto Joash the Abiezrite; and his son Gideon threshed wheat by the winepress, to hide it from the Midianites. And the angel of the LORD appeared unto him, and said unto him, The LORD is with thee, thou mighty man of valour. And Gideon said unto him, Oh my LORD, if the LORD be with us, why then is all this befallen us? And where be all His miracles which our fathers told us of, saying, did not the LORD bring us up from Egypt? But now the LORD hath forsaken us, and delivered us into the hands of the Midianites. And the LORD looked upon him, and said, go in this thy might, and thou shalt save Israel from the hand of the Midianites; have not I sent thee? And he said unto Him, Oh my LORD, wherewith shall I save Israel? Behold, my family is poor in Manasseh, and I am the least in my father's house. And the LORD said unto him, Surely I will be with thee, and thou shalt smite the Midianites as one man. And he said unto him, If now I have found grace in thy sight, then shew me a sign that thou talkest with me. Depart not hence, I pray thee, until I come unto thee, and bring forth my present, and set it before thee. And he said, I will tarry until thou come again. And Gideon went in, and made ready a kid, and unleavened cakes of an ephah of flour; the flesh he put in a basket, and he put the broth in a pot, and brought it out unto him under the oak, and presented it. And the angel of God said unto him, Take the flesh and the unleavened cakes, and lay them upon this rock, and pour out the broth. And he did so. Then the angel of the LORD put forth the end of the staff that was in his hand, and touched the flesh and the unleavened cakes; and there rose up fire out of the rock, and consumed the flesh and the unleavened cakes. Then the angel of the LORD departed out of his sight. And when Gideon perceived that he was an angel of the LORD, Gideon said, Alas, O LORD God! For because I have seen an angel of the LORD face to face. And the LORD said unto him, Peace be unto thee; fear not; thou shalt not die. Then Gideon built an altar there unto the LORD, and called it YHVH Shalom; unto this day it is yet in Ophrah of the Abiezrites. And it came to pass the same night that the LORD said unto him, Take thy father's young bullock, even the second bullock of seven years old, and throw down the altar of Baal that thy father hath, and cut down the grove that is by it; And build an altar unto the LORD thy God upon the top of this rock, in the ordered place, and take the second bullock, and offer a burnt sacrifice with the wood of the grove which thou shalt cut down. Then Gideon took ten men of his servants, and did as the LORD had said unto him; and so it was, because he feared his father's household, and the men of the city, that he could not do it by day, that he did it by night. And when the men of the city arose early in the morning, behold, the altar of Baal was cast down, and the grove was cut down that was by it, and the second bullock was offered upon the altar that was built. And they said one to another, Who hath done this thing? And when they enquired and asked, they said, Gideon the son of Joash hath done this thing. Then the men of the city said unto Joash, Bring out thy son, that he may die; because he hath cast down the altar of Baal, and because he hath cut down the grove that was by it. And Joash said unto all that stood against him, Will ye plead for Baal? Will ye save him? He that will plead for him, let him be put to death whilst it is yet morning; if he be a god, let him plead for himself, because one hath cast down his altar. Therefore on that day he called him Jerubbaal, saying, Let Baal plead against him, because he hath thrown down his altar. Then all the Midianites and the Amalekites and the children of the east were gathered together, and went over, and pitched in the valley of Jezreel. But the Spirit of the LORD came upon Gideon, and he blew a trumpet; and Abiezer was gathered after him. And he sent messengers throughout all Manasseh; who also was gathered after him; And he sent messengers unto Asher, and unto Zebulon, and unto Naphtali; and they came up to meet them. <u>And Gideon said unto God</u>, If thou wilt save Israel by mine hand, as thou hast said, Behold, I will put a fleece of wool in the floor; and if the dew be on the fleece only, and it be dry upon all the earth beside, then shall I know that thou wilt save Israel by mine hand, as thou hast said. And it was so; for he rose up early on the morrow, and thrust the fleece together, and wringed the dew out of the fleece, a bowl full of water. And Gideon said unto God, Let not Thine anger be hot against me, and I will speak but this once; let me prove, I pray thee, but this once with the fleece; let it now be dry only upon the fleece, and upon all the ground let there be dew. And God did so that night; for it was dry upon the fleece only, and there was dew on all the ground.*

In the first sign, Gideon prepares a specific offering for the LORD. The angel of the LORD uses *the Rod and Staff* of the LORD in sign number one! In this miracle, the elements that God provided for Israel in the wilderness of Sinai are present. They are *the unleavened bread and the meat* that were presented before the LORD as an offering. Gideon prepared the unleavened bread cakes and the meat of a lamb, along with broth to be poured out. Yeshua is the Lamb, the Living Torah, the Unleavened Bread and meat from Heaven, placed in the sepulchre on the Feast of Unleavened Bread. Yeshua declared that if we eat this Heavenly Bread and meat, we will have Eternal Life. Yeshua told us that His flesh was the true meat. Gideon places the unleavened bread and the flesh of meat upon the rock, as the angel of the LORD instructed him to do. The angel of the LORD then takes the end of his Staff and he touches the unleavened bread and the meat with the Rod in his hand. When he touches the Staff of his Rod to the unleavened bread and the meat, fire comes out of the rock and consumes it. *The Rock in the story is Messiah, the Chief Cornerstone of the Heavenly Temple, quarried out of Mount Moriah, full of the fire of the consuming Holy Spirit.* The LORD God with His Rod in His hand performs signs and miracles with the fire of His Holy Spirit that comes out of one end of the Rod. The Scriptures reveal that the Rock that followed the Israelites in the wilderness was Messiah and He provided the water for them to drink because He is the Rod, the Rock, and the Living Water. *In this miracle, the fire is the Holy Spirit out of the Rod, the Word of God, and He consumes the unleavened bread and the meat that represents the LORD Messiah as the Living Torah.* After the Rod touches it and fire comes out of the rock, the fire consumes Gideon's offering and immediately the LORD departs from Gideon's sight. Gideon was instructed by the angel of the LORD to pour out the broth and he did this just as he was instructed to by the LORD. Remember it was on the eighth day that Messiah Yeshua stood in the Holy Temple on the Feast of Tabernacles and said, *"Let all who thirst come to Me,"* just as the living water from the Pool of Shiloach/Siloam was poured out upon the altar. *On the highest point of Mount Moriah, the Living Water, the Messiah was poured out upon the altar.* Gideon now understands in his heart that this is, without a doubt, the same LORD God who provided the unleavened bread and the meat in the wilderness for his ancestors and saved them in battle.

In summary, Gideon mentioned each one of the following elements in sign one, proving that this was indeed the LORD God of Israel and these are the very elements that coincidentally describe Messiah Yeshua in the Gospel accounts.

Sign 1
The Rod and Staff
The Unleavened Bread
The Flesh of Meat
The Rock
The Broth poured out on the altar as Living Water
The Fire that Consumes from the Rod –
(The Holy Spirit speaking through the Living Torah).

Unleavened Bread - Matzah
Photo ©2013
Kimberly K Ballard

After this sign was fulfilled by the LORD, Gideon then asked for a second sign. In sign number two, Gideon tells the LORD that he will put a fleece in the floor and in the morning if the dew is only upon the fleece while all around the fleece the earth is dry, then Gideon says that he will know that the LORD will save Israel by his hand. Now the Holy Spirit revealed to me that in sign number two, *the fleece represents the sheep of Israel or the LORD'S flock.* The fleece was

placed upon the threshing floor. Gideon rose up early in the morning only to find out that what he had requested from the LORD had come to pass! *He found that only the fleece was wet with dew, while all around it, the ground was dry.* So Gideon thrust together the fleece and wrung it out, filling up a bowl full of water from all the water that was upon the fleece. This sign reveals to Gideon that this is the same LORD God that provided the Water for His flock Israel to drink in the hot dry desert of the wilderness centuries before. *While the desert ground was dry all around the LORD'S flock, represented by the fleece, they still had more than enough water to drink, by the hand of the Rod of God.* The LORD showed Gideon signs and wonders because He is the Rod and the Rock that provided Living Water to quench the thirst of the *fleece* His flock, in the wilderness. *This sign also reveals that Messiah the Lamb is the fleece who provides the Living Water of Eternal life and was threshed upon the threshing floor.* Early in the morning, before the Sabbath day ended on the seventh day, Mary came to Yeshua's Garden tomb sepulchre only to find that the Great Stone had been rolled away from the mouth of the well of salvation. The Living Water had come out of the Rock in Mount Moriah! This was the beginning of Messiah Yeshua gathering His flock back to His Garden in Jerusalem. Now the *"fleece"* could drink forever from the Living Water of the well of Yeshua/salvation. At the Garden tomb, the gutters or troughs in the ground watered the vineyard near the winepress and the threshing floor. Yeshua was the Living Torah resting in the Ark at His birth, signaling that He is the Unleavened Bread, the true meat, and Living Water from Heaven. Everyone who comes to God through His Rod of salvation will live forever and will eat the true meat, the Unleavened Bread and the First Fruit from the Almond Tree of Life. Isaiah wrote that *"God has become my salvation."* In Hebrew, Isaiah wrote, *"Behold, God has become my Yeshua!"*

Now because God has become my Yeshua, therefore Isaiah wrote, *"With joy shall ye draw Water out of the wells of Salvation."*

Isaiah 12:2-6 *Behold, God is my salvation; I will trust, and not be afraid; for the LORD YHVH is my strength and my song; He also is become my salvation. Therefore with joy shall ye draw water out of the wells of salvation. And in that day shall ye say, Praise the LORD, call upon His Name, declare His doings among the people, make mention that His Name is exalted. Sing unto the LORD; for He hath done excellent things; this is known in all the earth. Cry out and shout, thou inhabitants of Zion; for great is the Holy One of Israel in the midst of thee.*

In summary, Gideon witnesses that the Rod of God, by the power of His Holy Spirit, provided water for His flock of sheep, as the Good Shepherd of Israel.

After this miracle, Gideon requested *"a third sign."* Messiah was raised to life *"the third day"* on the Feast of First Fruits. This time Gideon asked the LORD to make only the fleece stay dry, while the ground all around the fleece was wet with dew. So God performed this miracle that night exactly as Gideon asked. *God made it dry only on the fleece, while the ground all around it was wet with dew!* The Holy Spirit revealed to me that the LORD made His flock, represented by the *fleece,* to walk at night on dry ground through the midst of the Red Sea as He led them with His powerful Rod. *Literally, you could say that the fleece stayed dry that night while all around them it was wet!* The LORD performed this third sign before Gideon, to prove the third time that He was absolutely the same LORD God of his ancestors who had rescued the flock of Israel out of Egypt. It was night when Messiah Yeshua, the Rod of God, full of the Holy Spirit walked upon the water. He performed this miracle, just after He had miraculously fed His flock with the unleavened bread and the meat of fish, representing the two tablets of the Law and the five books of Moses, the Torah. *In this miracle, the Rod of God proved that He is the Living Torah and the Lamb.* The Lamb of God, is the *fleece* full of Living Water who was threshed on the LORD'S threshing floor and He provides Living Water for His flock to drink forever, in the Eternal Garden called, *"Heaven."* The Good Shepherd laid down His life for His sheep, on His own threshing floor. *In summary, Gideon witnesses the*

power of the Rod of God that protects and saves His flock through the midst of the turbulent waters and keeps them safe and dry because He is the Living Ark of Heaven. It is the Rod of the Good Shepherd that saves and feeds the flock/fleece of Israel forever. The Messiah is every element within the Ark of the Testimony of the LORD in Heaven and we are kept safe and dry in the Ark! Remember that Noah was saved in the Ark where the food and water was stored. *This little flock of Noah's family was also kept dry by the LORD, while all around them it was wet outside the ship!* The LORD is therefore the Ark where the Eternal food and water of Heaven is stored. When we enter the door of the Ark, the LORD provides our food, shelter and water.

Gideon's story continues in the book of Judges Chapter 7 and it goes on to reveal more about the LORD, as Messiah the Rod who fights for Israel and wins the victory for them. Once more, the LORD reduces the amount of men to fight against the Midianites in order to show Gideon that He is the one who will be going before Gideon in this battle to win it. In this way, it was obvious that even though Gideon was outnumbered by the enemy, *the Rod of God* was going before him to fight the battle. *It proved that if Gideon and his men won the battle, it was only won by the strength of the powerful Rod of God and not by their own strength. It was the Rod of God, the Messiah, who would win the battle for Him and save him.* Gideon rose up early in the morning and positioned himself and his men *"by the well."* This proves that the Rod of God is the well of salvation, in Hebrew *"Yeshua."*

Judges 7:1-21 *Then Jerubbaal, who is Gideon, and all the people that were with him, rose up early, and pitched beside the well of Herod; so that the host of the Midianites were on the north side of them, by the hill of Moreh, in the valley. And the LORD said unto Gideon, The people that are with thee are too many for me to give the Midianites into their hands, lest Israel vaunt themselves against Me, saying, Mine own hand hath saved me. Now therefore go to, proclaim in the ears of the people, saying, Whosoever is fearful and afraid, let him return and depart early from mount Gilead. And there returned of the people twenty and two thousand; and there remained ten thousand. And the LORD said unto Gideon, The people are yet too many; bring them down unto the water, and I will try them for thee there; and it shall be, that of whom I say unto thee, This shall go with thee, the same shall go with thee; and of whomsoever I say unto thee, This shall not go with thee, the same shall not go. So he brought down the people unto the water; and the LORD said unto Gideon, Every one that lappeth of the water with his tongue, as a dog lappeth, him shalt thou set by himself; likewise every one that boweth down upon his knees to drink. And the number of them that lapped, putting their hand to their mouth, were three hundred men; but all the rest of the people bowed down upon their knees to drink water. And the LORD said unto Gideon, By the three hundred men that lapped will I save you, and deliver the Midianites into thine hand; and let all the other people go every man unto his place. So the people took victuals in their hand, and their trumpets; and he sent all the rest of Israel every man unto his tent, and retained those three hundred men; and the host of Midian was beneath him in the valley. And it came to pass the same night, that the LORD said unto him, Arise, get thee down unto the host; for I have delivered it into thine hand. But if thou fear to go down, go thou with Phurah thy servant down to the host; And thou shalt hear what they say; and afterward shall thine hands be strengthened to go down unto the host. Then went he down with Phurah his servant unto the outside of the armed men that were in the host. And the Midianites and the Amalekites and all the children of the east lay along in the valley like grasshoppers for multitude; and their camels were without number, as the sand by the sea side for multitude. And when Gideon was come, behold, there was a man that told a dream unto his fellow, and said, Behold, I dreamed a dream, and, lo, a cake of barley bread tumbled into the host of Midian, and came unto a tent, and smote it that it fell, and overturned it, that the tent lay along. And his fellow answered and said, This is nothing else save the sword of Gideon the son of Joash, a man of Israel; for into his hand hath God delivered Midian, and all the host. And it was so, when Gideon heard the telling of the dream, and the interpretation thereof, that he worshipped, and returned into the host of Israel, and said, Arise; for the LORD hath delivered into your hand the host of Midian. And he divided the three hundred men into three companies, and he put a trumpet in every man's hand, with empty pitchers, and lamps within the pitchers. And he said unto them, Look on me, and do likewise; and, behold, when I come to the outside of the camp, it shall be that, as I do, so shall ye do. When I blow with a trumpet, I and all that are with me, then blow ye the trumpets also on every side of all the camp, and say, The sword of the LORD, and of Gideon. So Gideon, and the hundred men that were with him, came unto the outside of the camp in the beginning of the middle watch; and they had but newly set the watch; and they blew the trumpets, and brake the pitchers that were in their hands. And the three companies blew the trumpets, and brake the pitchers, and held the lamps in their left hands, and the trumpets in their right hands to blow withal; and they cried, The sword of the LORD, and of Gideon. And they stood every man in his place round about the camp; and all the host ran, and cried, and fled.*

Gideon's final signs reveal that this is the LORD God of Israel, his Messiah. Gideon encamps by the well. Messiah is the well of Salvation. The Rod, the Sceptre, the Branch is in the right hand of God who always saves and feeds His flocks with His Rod. The LORD sent the men to drink the living water and the men who drank the living water in haste were chosen to go with Him into battle. This represents the fact that they truly thirsted for the LORD. The LORD always chooses those that truly thirst for Him. The Bread that tumbled into the tent and smote it in the dream was Messiah, the Bread from Heaven. The LORD blows His trumpet, just as He did on Mount Sinai. When Messiah Yeshua returns in the rapture, in the glory cloud during Rosh HaShanah, He will blow the Last Trump. Later, He will blow the Great Trump on Yom Kippur, when He comes a second time, just as Moses brought the Word of God down a second time from Mount Sinai. The Torches of light represent the LORD as the Holy Almond Tree Menorah, full of the fire and the Eternal light of the Holy Spirit that cannot be hidden under a pitcher. The Sword of the LORD and of Gideon is the Living Torah full of flaming fire, coming out of the mouth of the LORD Messiah. Yeshua, the Rod, gives us the Eternal victory in the battle against Satan our enemy and He has already saved us. Gideon met the powerful Messiah by the winepress and the threshing floor and so did Yeshua's disciples after His miraculous resurrection!

JACOB IN THE CITY OF LUZ

In the city of Luz, Jacob went to sleep on some stones and the Rabbis teach that the stones came from the LORD'S altar. I have read that Jacob's pillar stone was kept as a relic in Constantinople and was later used in Scotland as the Royal Coronation stone of the ancient Scottish Monarchs. As Jacob slept, he had a dream and he saw a ladder reaching from the earth to Heaven. In this dream, Jacob saw angels ascending and descending on this ladder and the LORD was standing at the top of the ladder! This was the place where the LORD God was and Jacob did not know it! Jacob renamed *"Luz"* where this event took place and called it *"Beth-el,"* meaning *"House of God."* However, the original name of the city was *"Luz."* The story in Genesis tells us that this was the God of Abraham, Isaac, and Jacob that appeared in this place. I would like to share this story and point out how it further reveals the LORD as the *Almond Tree.* In the dream, Jacob saw the opened gate and door of Heaven.

Genesis 28:10-19 *And Jacob went out from Beersheba, and went toward Haran, and he lighted upon a certain place, and tarried there all night, because the sun was set; and he took of the stones of that place, and put them for his pillows, and lay down in that place to sleep. And he dreamed, and behold a ladder set up on the earth, and the top of it reached to Heaven; and behold the angels of God ascending and descending on it. And, behold, the LORD*

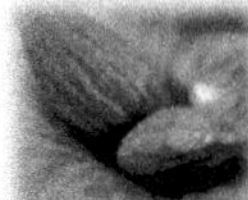

stood above it, and said, I AM the LORD God of Abraham thy father, and the God of Isaac; the land whereon thou liest, to thee will I give it, and to thy seed; And thy seed shall be as the dust of the earth, and thou shalt spread abroad to the west, and to the east, and to the north, and to the south; and in thee and in thy seed shall all families of the earth be blessed. And, behold, I AM with thee, and will keep thee in all places whither thou goest, and will bring thee again into this land; for I will not leave thee, until I have done that which I have spoken to thee of. And Jacob awaked out of his sleep, and he said, Surely the LORD is in this place; and I knew it not. And he was afraid, and said, How dreadful is this place! This is none other but the House of God, and this is the gate of Heaven. And Jacob rose up early in the morning, and took the stone that he had put for his pillows, and set it up for a pillar, and poured oil upon the top of it. And he called the name of that place Beth-el; but the name of that city was called Luz at the first.

There are two more Scriptures that reveal that *"Beth-el"* was first known as *"Luz."*

Judges 1:22-23 *And the House of Joseph they also went up against Beth-el; and the LORD was with them. And the house of Joseph sent to descry Beth-el, Now the name of the city before was Luz.*

Joshua 19:13 *And the border went over from thence toward Luz, to the side of Luz, which is Beth-el, southward; and the border descended to Atarothadar, near the hill that lieth on the south side of the nether Beth-horon.*

In this place, the LORD stood above the ladder or the staircase where the angels were ascending and descending. The LORD identified Himself as *"I AM the LORD God of Abraham thy father and the God of Isaac."* What is interesting, however, is that the text tells us that Jacob *"awaked"* out of his sleep. Remember that I told you that the word for *"Almond"* in Hebrew is *"Shaked"* and it means *"awaken" or "hasty awakening"* and *"watch."* So the truth is that when Jacob *"awakened, shaked,* then at once, *Jacob knew he had seen the LORD, the Almond Tree,* and the gate of Heaven. This remarkable revelation by the Holy Spirit was simply fantastic and I was thrilled by it! Then, as I pondered the name of the city that was *"first"* known as *"Luz,"* I knew that this name had to be quite significant. As usual, the LORD was guiding me. The name *"Luz"* itself actually refers to the *"Almond Tree"* and the LORD was in this place! This made my miracle of the Almond Tree in Jerusalem even more profound! In Spanish, *"Luz,"* means, *"light."* So I suddenly realized an astonishing truth! When Jacob, *"awakened" (Almond)* in that place, *he actually saw the Almond Tree of Life with the Shechinah glory light.* So in essence, *Jacob saw the Holy Almond Tree Menorah of Heaven!* This is the Living Testimony of Messiah Yeshua, the Almond Branch, that budded from the Almond Tree of Life! So I believe that when Jacob saw the LORD standing at the top of the staircase, he actually saw *Messiah Yeshua because He is the door and the gate of Heaven!* Now this is the reason that Yeshua told us that no one goes to the Father except through Him. Yeshua told us that He is the gate of the sheep and that His sheep must pass under the Rod of salvation to enter through the door of Heaven.

John 10:6-7 *This parable spake Yeshua unto them; but they understood not what things they were which He spake unto them. Then said Yeshua unto them again, Verily verily, I say unto you, I AM the door of the sheep.*

John 10:9 *I AM the door; by Me if any man enter in, he shall be saved, and shall go in and out, and find pasture.*

In the Gospel accounts, Messiah Yeshua specifically said that He has ascended and descended from Heaven to earth and back again!

John 3:13-17 *And no man hath ascended up to Heaven, but He that came down from Heaven, even the Son of man which is in Heaven. And as Moses lifted up the serpent in the wilderness, even so must the Son of man be lifted up; That whosoever believeth in Him should not perish, but have eternal life. For God so loved the world, that He gave His only begotten Son, that whosoever believeth in Him should not perish, but have everlasting life. For God sent not His Son into the world to condemn the world; but that the world through Him might be saved.*

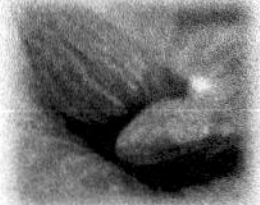

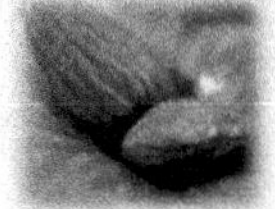

So when the Messiah descended from Heaven, the Branch of the Holy Almond Tree Menorah with the Shechinah glory light of the LORD was dwelling in our midst, and this is, again, why the Holy Menorah in the Holy Temple would no longer light after Yeshua ascended back into Heaven in the glory cloud.

John 9:5 *As long as I AM in the world, I AM the light of the world.*

Psalm 27 actually proclaims in Hebrew that *"The LORD is my light and my Yeshua!"*

Psalm 27:1 *The LORD is my light and my salvation; whom shall I fear? The LORD is the strength of my life; of whom shall I be afraid?*

In the Gospel of John, it is interesting that Yeshua reveals to Nathanael that He is the one that Jacob saw when Heaven was opened at the top of the staircase, when the angels were ascending and descending. He told Nathanael that this will happen again in the future when the curse is off the Fig Tree!

John 1:48-51 *Nathanael saith unto Him, Whence knowest thou me? Yeshua answered and said unto Him, Before that Phillip called thee, when thou wast under the fig tree, I saw thee. Nathanael answered and saith unto Him, Rabbi, Thou art the Son of God; Thou art the KING of Israel. Yeshua answered and said unto him, Because I said unto thee, I saw thee under the fig tree, believest thou? Thou shalt see greater things than these. And He saith unto Him, Verily, verily, I say unto you, Hereafter ye shall see Heaven open and the angels of God ascending and descending upon the Son of man.*

The LORD'S Rod, the Royal Sceptre of Judah, is the Son of the LORD'S own inheritance because the Royal Sceptre of the KING is the ruling power and authority of God's inheritance. Yeshua has ascended to Heaven and descended to the earth. The Messiah is the Word of God, the Living Torah, and He is our Royal shield.

Proverbs 30:4-6 *Who hath ascended up into Heaven, or descended? Who hath gathered the wind in his fists? Who hath bound the waters in a garment? Who hath established all the ends of the earth? What is His Name, and what is His Son's name, if thou canst tell? Every Word of God is pure; He is a shield unto them that put their trust in Him. Add thou not unto His Words, lest He reprove thee, and thou be found a liar.*

Of course, the Messiah is the one who *descends from Heaven* with a shout and with the sound of a trumpet in the future! Compare the next two Scriptures and you will see that the LORD God of Israel is the Messiah.

I Thessalonians 4:16 *For the LORD Himself shall descend from Heaven with a shout, with the voice of the archangel, and with the trump of God; and the dead in Messiah shall rise first.*

Psalm 47:5-7 *God is gone up with a shout, the LORD with the sound of a trumpet. Sing praises to God, sing praises; sing praises unto our KING, sing praises. For God is the KING of all the earth; sing ye praises with understanding.*

John 3:13 *And no man hath ascended up to Heaven, but He that came down from Heaven, even the Son of man which is in Heaven.*

There is one God, whose Spirit is inside Him within His heart, and this heart of God gives us a new heart so we can live forever. He teaches us the depth of true love that is unconditional. He loves each one of us that He created, and He longs for us to live with Him in His Paradise Kingdom. God is our Yeshua who has ascended on High and He descended here dwelling in the flesh to take care of the curse of death. The LORD Messiah led captivity captive and gave the gift of His Holy Spirit to His Saints. Compare the next two Scriptures.

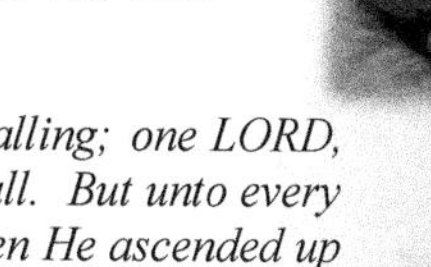

Ephesians 4:4-10 *There is one body, and one Spirit, even as ye are called in one hope of your calling; one LORD, one faith, one baptism, one God and Father of all, who is above all, and through all, and in you all. But unto every one of us is given grace according to the measure of the gift of Messiah. Wherefore He saith, When He ascended up on high, He led captivity captive, and gave gifts unto men. Now that He ascended, what is it but that He also descended first into the lower parts of the earth? He that descended is the same also that ascended up far above all Heavens, that He might fill all things.*

Psalm 68:17-20 *The chariots of God are twenty thousand, even thousands of angels; the LORD is among them, as in Sinai, in the holy place. Thou hast ascended on High, Thou hast led captivity captive; Thou hast received gifts for men; yea, for the rebellious also, that the LORD God might dwell among them. Blessed be the LORD, who daily loadeth us with benefits, even the God of our salvation. Se'lah. He that is our God is the God of salvation; and unto GOD the LORD belong the issues from death.*

Notice that the Hebrew word for *"salvation,"* which is *"Yeshua,"* in this passage is next to the word *"Selah"* that I believe refers to the Bride of the LORD, purified in the white garments of the LORD! The Hebrew word for *"ladder"* is the word *"Soolam."* The fifteenth letter in the Hebrew alphabet is *"Samech,"* and the ladder is associated with this letter that makes a closed loop. It is said to resemble a wedding ring! This brings to mind that Yeshua is the Bridegroom of Israel, who left the KINGS signet, bearing His Name at the Garden tomb as the *Alpha and Omega!*

When Jacob said *"Surely the LORD was in this place,"* He identified the LORD God with the Almond Tree of Life and with the light of His glory and that he knew not that the LORD was in this place, and when he knew it, Jacob was sore afraid. He saw the LORD at the top of the ladder, standing there as Messiah, the Bridegroom of Israel who opens the door to Heaven, to the Eternal Promised Land. So we find within the book of Genesis, the Eternal Testimony of Yeshua, the Heavenly Ark of our salvation, as it is written and sealed forever within the glorious story of Jacob in the city of Luz and for this reason, Jacob worshipped God leaning on his *Staff!*

THE IMAGE ON THE COIN

Official Tiberius Caesar Coin heads on the left & the reverse with DS Roman Senate mark on the right
Photo ©2013 Kimberly K Ballard
All Rights Reserved

One day I was driving home from the Library after studying about the LORD and all at once I noticed this coin shop. The thought suddenly came to me, *"Hey, it would be so neat to go in that shop and find a Tiberius coin from Yeshua's day!"* I had never been in this shop before and I went inside to look around. There was this large box full of coins and you could buy a certain amount of them for a dollar. I was still thinking of Yeshua as I pilfered through the box. All at once there was this really dark coin that was almost black. I lifted it out and could not believe my eyes. Although it was hard to see and read, I could see that it was an ancient Roman coin. The gentleman let me buy it and I took it home. It was quite damaged, so I cleaned it up a bit so I could read it. I was shocked that it was, in fact, a *Tiberius Caesar coin* from the time of Messiah Yeshua! It was a one of a kind coin! This was another miracle that

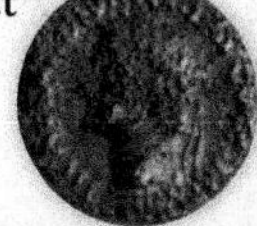

happened at the time of my Almond Tree revelation! The coin in the above photo is my Tiberius coin! No one believed that it was real except me and my Mother. Then one day, I took it to Boulder to another appraisal coin shop and they authenticated it as a true *Tiberius coin.* They said it looked like it had *water damage.* That is when the thought occurred to me, *"What if this is the very coin that Yeshua sent Simon Peter to take out of the fish's mouth for the tribute money?"* I laughed to myself and pondered it all in my heart. Incredibly, next the gentleman said, *"We have another coin you might be interested in that just came in today." I said, "What is it?"* Then he took me over to a case and pointed and said, *"It is a lepton a Pontius Pilate coin!"* I recognized the coin immediately because it was the same coin that some scientists have said was on Yeshua's burial Shroud. I could not believe it. I believe the LORD was close to me, showing me that nothing with Him is impossible, and I also wondered how this Tiberius coin wound up in the town where I live in the United States! It would be just like the LORD to give me the same coins that I laughed about that might be very significant after all from the fish's mouth! So this all inspired me to write about the coin and Messiah Yeshua!

When Messiah Yeshua was questioned by the Jews about the tribute money that they were forced to give to Caesar, Yeshua quite profoundly stated a hidden truth within His Words, and when they understood Yeshua's Words, they marveled at Him. Now Caesar considered himself to be a god and this is exactly what Pharaoh thought about himself. Caesar had put his own image and title on all the Roman coins because he claimed to be a god. The LORD God of Israel, however, always performed His mighty works with His Rod, proving that He alone is the creator of the universe who made man in His own image. He alone is the one true God and Saviour. So Yeshua asked the Jews to show Him the coin to see whose image was on it!

Matthew 22:17-22 *Tell us therefore, what thinkest thou? Is it lawful to give tribute unto Caesar, or not? But Yeshua perceived their wickedness, and said, why tempt ye Me, ye hypocrites? Shew Me the tribute money, and they brought unto Him a penny. And He saith unto them, whose is this image and superscription? They say unto Him, Caesar's. Then saith He unto them, Render therefore unto Caesar's the things which are Caesar's; and unto God the things that are God's. When they had heard these Words, they marveled, and left Him, and went their way.*

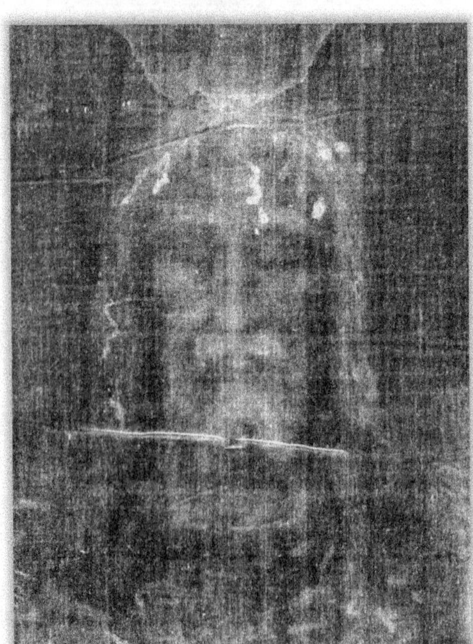

Official Shroud Face
Photograph ©1978 Barrie M. Schwortz Collection, STERA Inc., All Rights Reserved

In this story, *Yeshua the LORD* is holding the coin of the image of Caesar. Yeshua, the Royal Sceptre of God who bears the exact image of the Almighty KING, is telling them they belong to Him and to His Kingdom that lasts forever. He was telling them that they should render themselves and their hearts to Him because both men and women were made in the image of God. Even if they were forced temporarily to give this coin to an earthly ruler, it was corruptible and it would cease to exist, but Yeshua was indicating that those who were made in the image of the LORD God would live forever because His Kingdom from Heaven never ends.

Genesis 2:26-27 *And God said, Let us make man in our image, after our likeness; and let them have dominion over the fish of the sea, and over the fowl of the air, and over the cattle, and over all the earth, and over every creeping thing that creepeth upon the earth. So God created man in His own image, in the image of God created He him. Male and female created He them.*

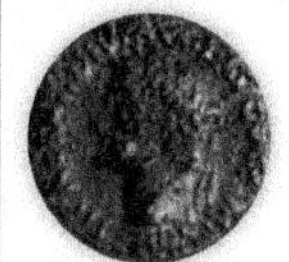

Yeshua told them that while they are on this earth, the wicked rulers will demand to have their own image placed upon the temporary things that they own. *However, the children of God that are made in His image belong to God and no one can take that away from them. When they heard it, they marveled at Yeshua's Words because Messiah Yeshua was God, the Living Torah dwelling with us and He left His image in Holy Mount Moriah on His burial Shroud, to prove that we are made in His image and that we will also bear His resurrection glory to Eternal Life.* In another passage regarding paying the tribute to Caesar, Yeshua asked them who the kings of the earth take tribute from. *"Of their own children or from strangers?"* Simon Peter said, *"Of strangers."*

Matthew 17:24-27 *And when they were come to Capernaum, they that received tribute money came to Peter, and said, Doth not your Master pay tribute? He saith, yes. And when he was come into the house, Yeshua prevented him, saying, what thinkest thou, Simon? Of whom do the Kings of the earth take custom or tribute? Of their own children, or of strangers? Peter saith unto Him, of strangers. Yeshua saith unto him, then are the children free, Notwithstanding, lest we should offend them, go thou to the sea, and cast an hook, and take up the fish that first cometh up; and when thou hast opened his mouth, thou shalt find a piece of money; that take, and give unto them for Me and thee.*

Now the interesting thing about this is that Simon Peter said that the Kings of the earth like Caesar take the tribute *from strangers and not from their own children!* Remember that during the Babylonian Exile, the Hebrews could not sing or play their harps by the willows because they were *strangers* in this place. In Hebrews 11, we learn that it was *"by faith"* that Abel, Enoch, Noah, Moses, Joseph, Abraham, Isaac, Jacob and Sara, followed and believed God. By faith, they were to receive the promise of everlasting life. Since they declared their faith to Him, the LORD said that they were declaring *"that they did not belong to this world or to its temporary kingdoms, but they belonged to the Heavenly Kingdom of God." So they were therefore called "strangers."* So in the above passage of Scripture, Yeshua asked them who the Kings of the earth take tribute from and Simon Peter said *"strangers."* In this statement, Simon Peter reveals that he and all the other Jewish people and all believers belong to God and bear His image, so they are *strangers* here. Simon Peter declares by faith, by believing in Messiah the LORD, that he has the promise of Eternal Life, to enter the Heavenly Kingdom of God. Yeshua told Simon Peter, *"Then are the children free."* In other words, because they belong to Him, they were saved by grace and had obtained *the Living Torah from Heaven,* so they were *truly free* from the bondage of this world and from its kingdoms. So the Kings of the earth take from God's children what does not belong to them. Simon Peter was declaring that he seeks a greater country where the LORD lives and dwells!

Hebrews 11:13-16 *These all died in faith, not having received the promise, but having seen them afar off, and were persuaded of them and embraced them, and confessed that they were strangers and pilgrims on the earth. For they that say such things declare plainly that they seek a country. And truly, if they had been mindful of that country from whence they came out, they might have had opportunity to have returned. But now they desire a better country, that is, an Heavenly; to be called their God; for He hath prepared for them a city.*

Yeshua told Simon Peter *"to go to the sea and cast in the hook and to take the first fish that comes up. He tells him to open its mouth to find a piece of money and give that as the tribute."* The Messiah reveals in His Words that the earthly money that bears the images of all the false gods of the kingdoms of this earth will eventually be cast into the depths of the sea where the fish live, along with corrupted worldly treasures. The LORD has prepared a great city that is called *"The Heavenly Jerusalem."* So the earthly rulers will be cast into the sea when the LORD sets up His everlasting Kingdom at the end of the age. The KING will return to destroy the wicked rulers and their kingdoms and Yeshua will set up a Righteous Kingdom on the earth. Caesar and the rich rulers lusted for the money that bears their own image, but it

will perish with all its earthly value. The LORD, however, *goes fishing with His Rod* to catch those who have been cleansed in His Living Water of the Living Torah of life, from the lust of the flesh, the lust of the eyes, and the pride of life, and they are changed and become Heavenly minded, filled with the Holy Spirit of God. They no longer live for the earthly sins and lusts because they have cast them away forever into *"Messiah, who is the body of Living Water that contains the fish for the Kingdom."* Those who belong to God are therefore called *"strangers"* on this earth because they believe by faith in the Eternal promise of the Heavenly Kingdom of God, which is their true home and country. Like Messiah Yeshua, *we bear the image of God* as children of faith. There is a prophecy in the book of Nahum that reveals what will happen to the images of all the earthly kingdoms when the Messiah comes to destroy them.

Nahum 1:14-15 *And the LORD hath given a Commandment concerning thee, that no more of thy name be sown; out of the house of thy gods will I cut off the graven image and the molten image; I will make thy grave; for thou art vile. Behold upon the mountains the feet of Him that bringeth good tidings, that publisheth peace! O Judah, keep thy solemn feasts, perform thy vows; for the wicked shall no more pass through thee; he is utterly cut off.*

The Shroud image was made by God. Messiah is the one who brings the good tidings to Israel and He is the only one that can bring Eternal peace to the earth. Any other peace is a false peace that will not last. The earthly coins and images of rulers are worthless, but in Heaven when we inherit the promise, *we will bear His glorious image* and have Eternal Life. We are *conformed to the image of Messiah, the Second perfect Adam, made in the image of God* because He is the pure Lambskin of the Living Torah, bearing the Word of God.

Romans 8:28-30 *And we know that all things work together for good to them that love God, to them who are the called according to His purpose. For whom He did foreknow, He also did predestinate to be conformed to the image of His Son, that He might be the firstborn among many brethren. Moreover whom He did predestinate, them He also called, them He also justified; and whom He justified, them He also glorified.*

Genesis 9:6 *Whoso sheddeth man's blood, by man shall his blood be shed; for in the image of God made He man.*

I John 3:1-3 *BEHOLD, what manner of love the Father hath bestowed upon us, that we should be called the sons of God; therefore the world knoweth us not, because it knew Him not. Beloved, now are we the sons of God, and it doth not yet appear what we shall be; but we know that when He shall appear, we shall be like Him; for we shall see Him as He is. And every man that hath this hope in him purifieth himself, even as He is pure.*

Simon Peter must have had great joy in his heart when Yeshua blessed him by revealing that he would also receive this promise by faith!

II Peter 3:13 *Nevertheless we, according to His promise, look for new Heavens and a new earth, where in dwelleth righteousness.*

Romans 4:13 *For the promise, that he should be the heir of the world, was not to Abraham, or to his seed, through the Law, but through the righteousness of faith.*

The Promise of Eternal Life was obtained through the righteousness of faith in *the righteousness of the Rod of God, through the Living Torah,* that is to say through the LORD God Messiah and His Eternal Testimony and Covenant. The earthly Ark held the Law given to Moses, but it is the LORD God Himself, the Messiah, who is the entire Living Torah and the Ark from Heaven that fulfills all righteousness.

Romans 10:3-11 *For they being ignorant of God's righteousness, and going about to establish their own righteousness, have not submitted themselves unto the righteousness of God. For Messiah is the end of the Law for righteousness to everyone that believeth. For Moses describeth the righteousness which is of the Law, That the man which doeth those things shall live by them. But the righteousness which is of faith speaketh on this wise, Say not in thine heart, Who shall ascend into Heaven? (that is, to bring Messiah down from above;) Or, Who shall descend into*

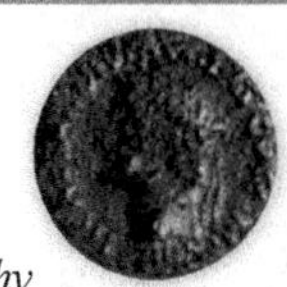

the deep? (that is, to bring up Messiah again from the dead.) But what saith it? The Word is nigh thee, even in thy mouth, and in thy heart; that is, the Word of faith, which we preach; That if thou shalt confess with thy mouth the LORD Yeshua, and shalt believe in thine heart that God hath raised Him from the dead, thou shalt be saved. For with the heart man believeth unto righteousness; and with the mouth confession is made unto salvation. For the Scripture saith, Whosoever believeth on Him shall not be ashamed.

Colossians 3:9-13 *Lie not one to another, seeing that ye have put off the old man with his deeds; And have put on the new man, which is renewed in knowledge after the image of Him that created him; Where there is neither Greek nor Jew, circumcision nor uncircumcision, Barbarian, Scythian, bond nor free; but Messiah is all, and in all. Put on therefore, as the elect of God, holy and beloved, bowels of mercies, kindness, humbleness of mind, meekness, longsuffering; Forbearing one another, and forgiving one another, if any man have a quarrel against any; even as Messiah forgave you, so also do ye.*

By faith, we must trust in this promise that through *the Messiah's righteousness* alone, we receive Eternal Life. Again I declare that the LORD God is the total fulfillment of the Ark and all it contains, and through Him we are saved, not through our own righteousness by striving in our own power to obey hundreds of self-imposed laws. The more we abide in Him, the more we resemble the KING!

THE HOLY TEMPLE'S TRUE LOCATION THE STONE PAVEMENT THE MOLTEN BRAZEN SEA AND THE ALTAR

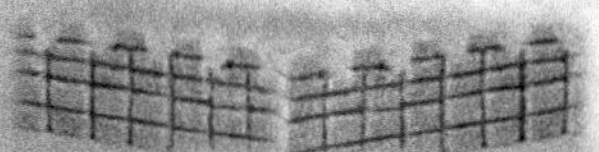
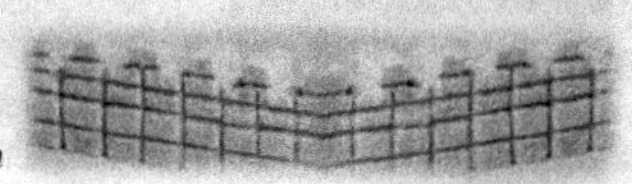

Model of the Second Temple ©2007-2014– The Temple Mount & Land of Israel Faithful Movement— Jerusalem – used with the kind permission of Gershon Salomon Edited to B&W, cropped & flipped by KK Ballard & model of the Jerusalem Western Wall & Arch Snow Photos ©2014 Kimberly K Ballard All Rights Reserved

The Jewish Apostle John wrote the description of the LORD Messiah, as He appeared in Heaven. His feet were like burnished bronze and His voice was like the sound of many waters. *When I pondered this description, I suddenly realized that the LORD is the Molten Brazen Sea in Heaven.* The Molten Brazen Sea stood in the court of the Holy Temple and it held *"living water."* It was made from molten bronze. *So Yeshua, who is the Living Water, also has the appearance of molten bronze.* Ancient bronze was known to have a composition of brass.

Revelation 1:15 *And His feet like unto fine brass, as if they burned in a furnace; and His voice as many waters.*

Revelation 2:18-19 *And unto the angel of the church in Thyatira write; These things saith the Son of God, who hath His eyes like unto a flame of fire, and His feet are like fine brass; I know thy works, and charity, and service, and faith, and thy patience, and thy works; and the last to be more than the first.*

The Molten Brazen Sea stood near the altar in the Holy Temple in Jerusalem. The Priests would wash their hands and their feet in the living water in the Brazen Sea before

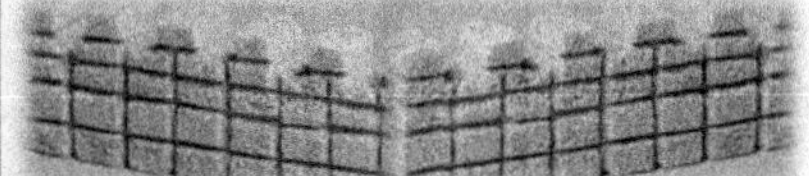
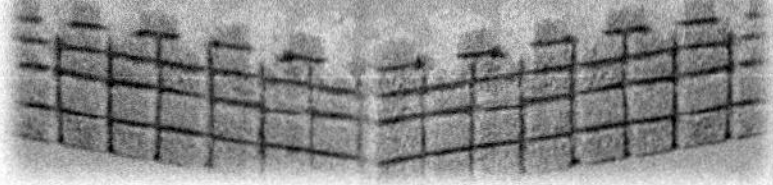

performing their sacred duties. Now it is true that highly polished bronze was buffed into a radiant and extra lustrous metal, using a special buffing method. After the bronze was buffed in this manner, it became very smooth, shiny, and reflective. The bronze was then referred to as *"burnished bronze."* In ancient times, when they did not have glass mirrors, this reflective burnished bronze was used to make mirrors for the Israelite women. A woman could see her face in the reflection, but it was like seeing a dim reflection, compared to the later glass mirrors. The ancient laver of the LORD, including its foot, was made from the burnished bronze mirrors of the Israelite women. Notice that the following passage in Exodus says that *"the foot of it was brass, of the looking glasses of the women,"* and Messiah Yeshua's *feet are like unto fine brass or burnished bronze.*

Exodus 38:8 *And he made the laver of brass, and the foot of it of brass, of the looking glasses of the women assembling, which assembled at the door of the Tabernacle of the congregation.*

Now the Molten Brazen Sea made of burnished bronze was also very reflective because it held about 3,000 baths of living water in its basin. The sapphire blue sky could be seen reflecting and floating on the surface of the living water that was in the Brazen Sea. The living water that flowed into it was water that came through a cistern from Bethlehem. Just to give you some idea of the size of the Brazen Sea, 3,000 baths is equal to about 27,000 gallons of water. The largest Biblical liquid measurement was the *"bath,"* which is said to equal about *9 gallons* of water. As the sapphire blue sky was seen floating on its surface, this was a reflection of the earth appearing as a sapphire or lapis lazuli stone. It was literally like the *liquid molten mirror telescope* that I mentioned earlier, in connection with the Shroud image. This reminds me of the Holy Spirit of the LORD moving on the surface of the waters in the beginning and turning the waters into *"living water." This reminds me of the fact that the image of Yeshua on the Shroud is only on the very surface of the linen and He is the Living Water.* It also reminds me of Yeshua walking on the surface of the Sea, revealing that He is the Rod, full of the Holy Spirit of God, whose feet in Heaven are like burnished bronze. Therefore, the description of Yeshua in Heaven reveals that He is *reflective* because His feet are like burnished bronze, as if they burned in a furnace like *molten bronze.* Yeshua is reflective, just as the Brazen Sea is reflective and under His feet was the sapphire pavement.

Now speaking of the sapphire pavement, it is interesting to note here, that there is a legend (I do not know how true it is) about sapphire that is written in the Jewish Encyclopedia, the Midrash and Talmudic sources, as well as in the Apocryphal book of Jasher. The legend says that *Moses staff (from Mount Sinai) came from the (heavenly) sapphire throne of God and it was a sapphire Rod that blossomed and bore fruit (even though the Bible clearly states that Aaron's rod was cut from the Almond tree).* The Ten Commandments were even said to be engraved in large blue sapphire gemstones and this is supposedly why the tallit fringes are blue, to remind us of God's Commandments. According to these Jewish sources, this *sapphire Rod* was in the Garden of Eden and it says that God gave it to Adam. Eventually it was supposedly passed down to Shem, Enoch and Noah. It says that God gave it to Moses and Aaron. Jacob and Joseph had it and even King David is said to have had this particular Rod when he slew Goliath. The legend says that Zipporah's father Jethro (who lived near the Mountain of God) had the Rod at some point, and stuck this *sapphire Rod* in his garden. Moses was said to be the only one that could miraculously remove it from the ground. Moses and Aaron are said to have parted the Sea with it and performed the plagues of Egypt with it. God's Name was allegedly engraved in this *sapphire Rod,* along with the following Hebrew abbreviations of the ten plagues of Egypt, דצ״ך עד״ש באח״ב *translated as, "De Za K, aDaSH, Be'aHa B."* ***(Sources; 1906 Jewish Encyclopedia.com (Aaron's Rod), ©2002-2011) AND (Jewish Source: "The Staff of Moses," ©2014 Rabbi Greg Killian @ www.betemunah.org/staff.html).*** Since this Rod consumed anyone that was not worthy to marry Jethro's daughters this, *"tree,"* that was apparently plucked out of Jethro's garden, *the sapphire Rod of*

God, is the same Living Rod mentioned in Revelation 11 with the *two witnesses* because they have the fire power from this Living Rod to consume their enemies and to create plagues with it as many times as they like! So this legend is a fascinating twist to what we already know about Aaron's Almond Rod that budded. Perhaps the Rod of God in the future in Revelation (a living Almond Rod) will miraculously have the inscription of the ten plagues upon it! Only time will tell how it will all play out, and God Himself will have to engrave it upon this Almond Rod.

Moving on now, when Yeshua walked on the surface of the water, He was revealing His identity as the LORD God of Israel, *the Living sapphire Rod of God. So when we look at God's Royal Sceptre, Messiah Yeshua, we are looking into a burnished bronze mirror that is reflecting the face of the LORD God of Israel, the Living Water of sapphire.*

So the Messiah truly bears the Name, *"The Prince of the face of the LORD God," or "The Sar HaPanim."* When we look at the face of Yeshua in His burial Shroud image, we are seeing but a mere reflection of the glorious Majestic KING in Heaven who is holding His Royal Sceptre in His right hand, so we can see a glimpse of Him in His reflective Rod. Remember that Yeshua said, *"I and the Father are one?"* Right now we are looking at the LORD through a dim reflection. We are *seeing His reflection as in a mirror* while we live on the earth, but when He appears, we shall see Him as He is, face to face, and we will no longer simply be looking at His reflection in His Royal Sceptre, which is *His Royal Standard.*

I Corinthians 13:12 *For now we see through a glass darkly; but then face to face; now I know in part; but then shall I know even as also I am known.*

All the *reflections and refractions* of the light of His Shechinah glory will *illuminate His fiery brilliance and radiance* through every sparkling precious Royal jewel of the foundation stones of the Heavenly Temple of God. His Shechinah glory light envelopes every living thing and surrounds it with His beautiful light. The light of His face exudes the joy of His countenance. The LORD has allowed us to see a glimpse of His face in the *reflection and refraction* of light that shines upon His Royal Sceptre. His glory is so great that, in our earthly state, we cannot look upon His full glory until we are changed into our incorruptible bodies, as we stand before His Divine Presence in the Heavenly Kingdom of God. When He appears in His full glory, our bodies must be transformed and changed into our glorious Eternal bodies in order to see His full Majesty. After I spoke about the *"radiance"* of the LORD in the earlier section, I said that one of the definitions of the word *"radiance"* is the word *"rapture."* So Yeshua's feet glow with the *"radiant," lustrous burnished bronze.* I realized that *the rapture* is to suddenly appear before the LORD'S Divine Presence and the moment that we are transformed in the glory cloud, we will stand before His Royal Majesty in His splendor and magnificence and see the Eternal KING of Glory in Living color. The Royal Sceptre sits at the right hand of the Majesty on High and *He is the express image of His own person!*

Hebrews 1:1-3 *God, who at sundry times and in divers manners spake in time past unto the fathers by the Prophets, Hath in these last days spoken unto us by His Son, whom He hath appointed heir of all things, by whom also He made the worlds; Who being the brightness of His glory, and the express image of His person, and upholding all things by the Word of His power, when He had by Himself purged our sins, sat down on the right hand of the Majesty on High.*

The light of His countenance that shines upon us is Messiah, who is *the image* of God.

II Corinthians 4:3-6 *But if our gospel be hid, it is hid to them that are lost; In whom the god of this world hath blinded the minds of them which believe not, lest the light of the glorious Gospel of Messiah, who is the image of God, should shine unto them. For we preach not ourselves, but Messiah Yeshua the LORD; and ourselves your servants for Yeshua's sake. For God, who commanded the light to shine out of darkness, hath shined in our hearts to give the light of the knowledge of the glory of God in the face of Yeshua Messiah.*

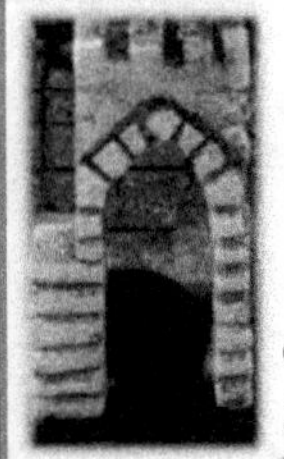

Remember that *"the light of the knowledge of the glory of God is given to us in the face of Messiah Yeshua!" The burial Shroud of Messiah Yeshua is therefore, "a photographic image manifestation" of the face of the LORD God of Israel.* Through the Shroud image, the LORD plainly manifested Himself to us, so we would never forget His Living Testimony. *This is why He left the image of His own face upon His burial Shroud to give us the knowledge of the light of the glory of God in His face during His resurrection to life when He reversed the curse of death from Eden in His Garden! This, again, is the power of the Excellency of God.*

Colossians 1:12-15 *Giving thanks unto the Father, which hath made us meet to be partakers of the inheritance of the Saints in light; Who hath delivered us from the power of darkness, and hath translated us into the Kingdom of His dear Son; In whom we have redemption through His blood, even the forgiveness of sins; Who is the image of the invisible God, the firstborn of every creature. For by Him were all things created, that are in Heaven, and that are in earth, visible and invisible, whether they be thrones, or dominions, or principalities, or powers; all things were created by Him, and for Him.*

Right now we are only beholding the glory of the LORD with open face, as in a glass.

II Corinthians 3:17-18 *Now the LORD is that Spirit; and where the Spirit of the LORD is, there is liberty. But we all, with open face beholding as in a glass the glory of the LORD, are changed into the same image from glory to glory, even as by the Spirit of the LORD.*

Now in Psalm 110, *the LORD is speaking to my LORD.* I now believe that the LORD at His right hand is *His own reflection. He proclaims that He will stretch forth His strong Sceptre to rule in the midst of His enemies!* The concept of seeing *the reflection* of the face of the LORD in His Rod, (to me) explains how Moses could not see God's face and live and yet at the same time, Moses spoke to Him face to face, as one speaks to a friend! If Moses looked at the LORD in His full glorified state, Moses would surely have died, (I believe) probably because of *the (high radiation) Gamma rays of His radiance that is like Beryl!* Moses went into *the Shechinah glory cloud,* and spoke with the LORD face to face on Mount Sinai. When the LORD revealed His Shechinah glory to Moses on the Holy Mountain just as He did at the transfiguration, I believe that the face of Moses was illuminated from the *reflection and refraction of light* from the fiery brilliance of the power of the Holy Spirit of God on the Rod. We see this phenomenon in the book of Exodus. Notice that the LORD was standing at the door!

Exodus 33:10-11 *And all the people saw the cloudy pillar stand at the Tabernacle door; and all the people rose up and worshipped, every man in his tent door. And the LORD spake unto Moses face to face, as a man speaketh unto his friend.*

As His glory passed by, Moses was speaking face to face with the LORD'S *reflection,* which is Messiah, the Royal Sceptre in the right hand of the LORD God. So the LORD God of Israel is the KING Messiah and He brings glory back to Himself. This is one LORD God, who reveals Himself, through His Spirit and through His Royal Sceptre. When Moses saw *the reflection, the LORD proclaimed the Name of the LORD,* but Moses could not see His face in its full glory and live! The LORD covered Moses with His hand, His Yad, which saved him from dying. The glory of the LORD passed by and Moses saw the back of the LORD. Notice that the LORD did this for Moses because Moses found *"grace"* in the LORD'S sight and Yeshua, the Living Torah brought us *"grace and truth!" Moses was protected in the Rock by the hand of God!*

Exodus 33:17-23 *And the LORD said unto Moses, I will do this thing also that thou hast spoken; for thou hast found grace in My sight, and I know thee by name. And he said, I beseech Thee, shew me Thy glory, And he said, I will make all My goodness pass before thee, and I will proclaim the Name of the LORD before thee; and will be gracious*

to whom I will be gracious, and will shew mercy on whom I will shew mercy. And He said, Thou canst not see My face; for there shall no man see Me, and live. And the LORD said, Behold, there is a place by Me, and thou shalt stand upon a rock; And it shall come to pass, while My glory passeth by, that I will put thee in a cleft of the rock, and will cover thee with My hand while I pass by; And I will take away mine hand and thou shalt see My back parts; but My face shall not be seen.

So the Rod came to earth as Messiah Yeshua to proclaim the Name of the LORD and to finish the work of the Divine Testimony, and now Messiah is glorified with the Father in Heaven because this is one KING with His Royal Sceptre!

John 17:1-7 *These Words spake Yeshua, and lifted up His eyes to Heaven, and said, Father, the hour is come; glorify Thy Son, that Thy Son also may glorify Thee; As Thou hast given Him power over all flesh, that He should give eternal life to as many as Thou hast given Him. And this is life eternal, that they might know Thee the only true God, and Yeshua Messiah, whom Thou hast sent. I have glorified Thee on the earth; I have finished the work which Thou gavest Me to do. And now, O Father, glorify Thou Me with Thine own self with the glory which I had with Thee before the world was. I have manifested Thy Name unto the men which Thou gavest Me out of the world; Thine they were, and Thou gavest them Me; and they have kept Thy Word. Now they have known that all things whatsoever Thou hast given Me are of Thee.*

John 8:42-43 *Yeshua said unto them, If God were your Father, ye would love Me; for I proceeded forth and came from God; neither came I of Myself, but He sent Me. Why do ye not understand My speech? Even because ye cannot hear My Word.*

In the book of Romans, *this is the mystery of Messiah that was kept secret since the world began,* but the mystery has been revealed and made manifest to us. This mystery is both obvious in the text of the Bible and it is also hidden deep within His Word.

Romans 16:25-27 *Now to Him that is of power to stablish you according to my Gospel, and the preaching of Yeshua Messiah, according to the revelation of the mystery, which was kept secret since the world began, But now is made manifest, and by the Scriptures of the Prophets, according to the Commandment of the everlasting God, made known to all Nations for the obedience of faith; To God only wise, be glory through Yeshua Messiah forever. Amen.*

Yeshua's face is *the image* of the Father (a reflection of Himself).

Matthew 11:10 *For this is He, of whom it is written, Behold, I send My messenger before Thy face, which shall prepare Thy way before Thee.*

By understanding that Messiah Yeshua is the Rod and *the reflection* of the LORD KING'S own image, we can understand Yeshua's Words in the following Scriptures.

John 10:38 *But if I do, though ye believe not Me, believe the works; that ye may know, and believe, that the Father is in Me, and I in Him.*

John 14:6-11 *Yeshua said unto Him, I AM the way, the truth, and the life; no man cometh unto the Father but by Me. If ye had known Me, ye should have known My Father also; and from henceforth ye know Him, and have seen Him. Philip saith unto Him, LORD, shew us the Father, and it sufficeth us. Yeshua saith unto him, Have I been so long time with you, and yet hast thou not known Me Philip? He that hath seen Me hath seen the Father; and how sayest thou then, Shew us the Father? Believest thou not that I AM in the Father, and the Father in Me? The Words that I speak unto you I speak not of Myself; but the Father that dwelleth in Me, He doeth the works. Believe Me that I AM in the Father, and the Father in Me; or else believe Me for the very works sake.*

Yeshua said that not everyone can see or understand this mystery of the Messiah. He said *"No one knows who the Son is, unless the LORD reveals this mystery to them."* Yeshua said that some of the Prophets and Kings of Israel had longed to look upon the mysteries of the LORD, but they never did see them! Those who heard His Words were blessed because they were able to see and hear that *Yeshua is the LORD God of Israel.*

Luke 10:22-24 *All things are delivered to Me of My Father; and no man knoweth who the Son is, but the Father; and who the Father is, but the Son, and He to whom the Son will reveal Him. And He turned Him to His disciples, and said privately, Blessed are the eyes which see the things that ye see; For I tell you, that many Prophets and Kings have desired to see those things which ye see, and have not seen them; and to hear those things which ye hear, and have not heard them.*

At some point, the LORD KING will reveal that His face is the face of Messiah to the people of Israel and He will plead with them! The two Living Cherubim Angels, *the two witnesses* will appear giving their Testimony, just before *the Living Ark* comes down from Heaven to dwell on the earth permanently.

Ezekiel 20:35 *And I will bring you into the wilderness of the people, and there will I plead with you face to face.*

In the Aaronic blessing, it is a glorious thing to have the LORD'S face shining and *reflecting* upon you. The Sceptre Messiah is also *(of course)* the *"Sar Shalom"* the Prince of Peace whose *countenance* lifts up the downtrodden and brokenhearted.

Numbers 6:24-27 *The LORD bless thee, and keep thee; The LORD make His face shine upon thee, and be gracious unto thee; The LORD lift up His countenance upon thee, and give thee peace. And they shall put My Name upon the children of Israel; and I will bless them.*

Psalm 27:8-9 *When thou saidst, Seek ye My face; my heart said unto Thee, Thy face, LORD, will I seek. Hide not Thy face far from me; put not Thy servant away in anger; Thou hast been my help; leave me not, neither forsake me, O God of my salvation.*

We would only need to *"seek God's face."* If His face was *hidden* from us, and at some point as we seek Him, His face will be revealed as the Messiah and this is definitely the case. So the Psalmist declares, *"O God of my Yeshua!"*

Deuteronomy 31:18 *And I will surely hide My face in that day for all the evils which they shall have wrought in that they are turned unto other gods.*

Psalm 10:11 *He hath said in his heart, God hath forgotten; He hideth His face; He will never see it.*

"Manifest" means *"readily perceived by the eye or the understanding, or to show plainly."* This indicates that *God was manifested in the flesh as Messiah Yeshua, so we could perceive Him with our eyes.* He plainly wanted to show Himself to us in the flesh, so we could understand Him. *"Manifest"* also means *"To prove or put beyond doubt."* The miracles of Yeshua the Rod *put beyond doubt* that He is the LORD God of Israel, *manifested in the flesh* and this is a great mystery.

I Timothy 3:16 *And without controversy great is the mystery of godliness; God was manifest in the flesh, justified in the Spirit, seen of angels, preached unto the Gentiles, believed on in the world, received up into glory.*

So John the Baptist came baptizing with *living water* to make Messiah the LORD known to Israel. *Through the miracles of Yeshua, they would come to understand that Yeshua is the reflective Molten Brazen Sea of Heaven, the Living Water that washes and purifies us.*

John 1:31 *And I knew Him not; but that He should be made manifest to Israel, therefore am I come baptizing with water.*

Now with this understanding, the LORD has spread out the sky as *a molten looking glass.* The earth is the LORD'S footstool and the floor of His throne is sapphire blue, as blue as the sky.

So this Brazen Molten Sea in the Holy Temple on the earth is only the earthly copy, *but the LORD Messiah, who is the Living Water, is the Heavenly model whose feet are like burnished bronze. The LORD is without a doubt, the Molten Brazen Sea in His Holy Heavenly Temple and because the LORD Messiah is the Living Water, He is reflecting the sky of the earth as His sapphire blue footstool.*

Job 37:18 *Hast Thou, with Him spread out the sky, which is strong, and as a molten looking glass?*

The Molten Brazen Sea is an interesting part of the Holy Temple and it was built by Hiram of Tyre for King Solomon. The description of how he made the Brazen Molten Sea is recorded in the Chronicles of the Kings. The base was made of twelve oxen. Three oxen were on each side and they faced the four directions of the compass. The twelve oxen that carried and held the living water on their backs remind me of the work of the twelve tribes of Israel who held and carried the earthly copy of the Torah, and the twelve Jewish disciples of Messiah who held and carried the Testimony of the Living Torah of the LORD, *the Living Water.* They took the LORD'S Living Testimony *to the four points of the compass of the earth,* proclaiming the LORD'S miraculous resurrection. Even though the weight of carrying it was sometimes heavy, they accomplished this task for the LORD without faltering.

This reminds me that Yeshua is the Word of God that quenches our thirst forever. Yeshua told us that this Gospel would be preached through the entire world and then the end would come. So Yeshua has washed us clean, because He is the true Molten Brazen Sea. This means, again, that the LORD, the Messiah, is the body of Living Water that is the true Tashlikh ceremony and after we have been cleansed in His baptism, the LORD will remember our sins no more. It is through Yeshua's pureness and righteousness, that we can become pure, simply because He is the Living Water and Living Torah of life. When we are cleansed in Messiah, then we can return to dwell in His Divine Presence, just as it was in the beginning and we become a Kingdom of Kings and Priests. Remember that the Priests washed in the Molten Brazen Sea and we are to immerse ourselves in His knowledge!

Revelation 1:5-6 *And from Yeshua Messiah, who is the faithful witness, and the first begotten of the dead, and the Prince of the Kings of the earth, Unto Him that loved us, and washed us from our sins in His own blood, And hath made us Kings and Priests unto God and His Father; to Him be glory and dominion forever and ever. A'men.*

Consider the Divine instructions for constructing the Molten Brazen Sea. Remember how important the number three is to the LORD concerning His Eternal resurrection Testimony and His desire that every point of the compass of the earth would learn of His glory through Messiah Yeshua.

II Chronicles 4:2-13 *Also he made a molten sea of ten cubits from brim to brim, round in compass, and five cubits the height thereof; and a line of thirty cubits did compass it round about. And under it was the similitude of oxen, which did compass it round about: ten in a cubit, compassing the sea round about. Two rows of oxen were cast, when it was cast. It stood upon twelve oxen, three looking toward the north, and three looking toward the west, and three looking toward the south, and three looking toward the east: and the sea was set above upon them, and all their hinder parts were inward. And the thickness of it was an handbreadth, and the brim of it like the work of the brim of a cup, with flowers of lilies; and it received and held three thousand baths. He made also ten lavers, and put five on the right hand, and five on the left, to wash in them: such things as they offered for the burnt offering they washed in them; but the sea was for the priests to wash in. And he made ten candlesticks of gold according to their form, and set them in the temple, five on the right hand, and five on the left. He made also ten tables, and placed them in the temple, five on the right side, and five on the left. And he made an hundred basons of gold. Furthermore he made the court of the priests, and the great court, and doors for the court, and overlaid the doors of them with brass. And he set the sea on the right side of the east end, over against the south. And Huram made the pots, and the shovels, and the basons. And Huram finished the work that he was to make for king Solomon for the house of God; To wit, the two pillars, and the pommels, and the chapiters which were on the top of the two pillars, and the*

two wreaths to cover the two pommels of the chapiters which were on the top of the pillars; And four hundred pomegranates on the two wreaths; two rows of pomegranates on each wreath, to cover the two pommels of the chapiters which were upon the pillars.

As I was doing more research on the Molten Brazen Sea, something miraculously came across my path by Divine Providence that was so astonishing and I now believe that the LORD has just revealed to me the true location where the Holy Temple of King Solomon once stood and if I am right, it is profoundly prophetic for the last days! This is a great miracle of Biblical proportions! I will now proceed to explain it!

The Molten Brazen Sea stood *between the altar and the Temple porch,* toward the south. Now there is a reference to Yeshua standing in a place called *"the stone pavement."* This happened when Yeshua stood before Pontius Pilate. This place was *a specific place that was already known as "the stone pavement"* even before Yeshua was judged there and the name of this place is also known in Aramaic as *"Gabbatha."* I found that the word *"Gabbatha"* actually means *"high elevated," "elevation," "ridge," and "ridge of the house!"* I find this to be astonishing because the Temple of Solomon (the Holy House of God) was built on the *"high elevated ridge of Holy Mount Moriah."* The threshing floor was also located here where King David built the altar to the LORD on *"the highest elevated ridge of Holy Mount Moriah,"* and this is where King Solomon later built the First Temple!

Now it is fascinating that there is a story in the Bible about King Ahaz who took down the Brazen Molten Sea from off its oxen base. The Scripture tells us that he took down the Brazen Sea and set the upper portion called the *"basin"* upon *"a stone pavement."*

II Kings 2:17 *And King Ahaz cut off the borders of the bases, and removed the laver from off them; and took down the Sea from off the brazen oxen that were under it, and put it upon a pavement of stone.*

The Molten Brazen Sea rendering ©1887 "Biblical Archaeology Volume I" By Dr. Carl Friedrich Keil, Edinburgh Scotland All Rights Reserved

My Jewish Bible called the *"Tanakh"* specifically says that *"King Ahaz set the Sea upon a stone pavement." The altar was in this "elevated place" next to the Brazen Sea.* Since the Holy Temple was located on the highest place on the rock of the ridge itself and it was built in the same location as the threshing floor of Araunah the Jebusite, this means that *"the stone pavement" where Yeshua was standing, that was already known as "Gabbatha," had to have been the same stone pavement on the high elevated ridge where King Ahaz set the basin of the Molten Brazen Sea when he removed it off its oxen base.*

The Brazen Sea itself was later destroyed by the Chaldeans, known as the Babylonians, in Riblah. All that remained of the Brazen Sea was *"the stone pavement"* that was underneath it. I believe that *"the stone pavement"* was left intact, even after the Molten Brazen Sea was destroyed from off this foundation. It was upon this same stone pavement that King Ahaz had set the basin of the Brazen Sea. The stones of the stone pavement that were underneath the altar and the Brazen Sea had to be extremely heavy stones to provide a very stable platform. It had to be made from very large, heavy thick stones that were set deep into the floor as a *permanent* foundation. Remember that these stones had to hold great weight upon them because they had to hold at least 27,000 gallons of water, as well as the heavy oxen base and the weight of the Brazen basin itself. Then to top it off, it held the weight of the heavy stones of the LORD'S altar that also sat upon this *"stone pavement."* So, needless to say, it would

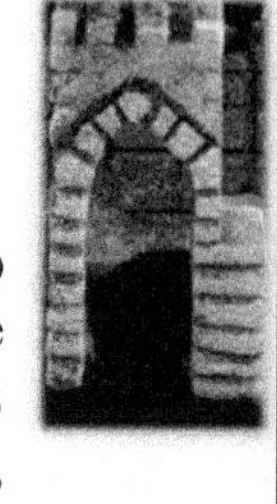

have been almost impossible to remove the original stones from the ground. The stones had to be embedded into the floor and kept in a *permanent* position in order to hold this extreme amount of weight. Now, the stones of *"the stone pavement"* where Yeshua stood when He was judged are varied from 2 to 4 feet in length and each stone is at least 15 inches or more thick, which indicates something of the depth that each stone is embedded into the floor. Each stone is also approximately 2 feet across in width. *The exciting news is that "the stone pavement" still exists today!* The Roman Soldiers of the 10th legion, who mocked the Jewish KING Yeshua, etched games on the stones of this stone pavement. They etched a scorpion, the symbol of the 10th Roman legion in it. Then next to this symbol, they etched a letter *"B"* on its side. It stands for the Greek word *"Basileus"* meaning *"King."* This particular letter *"B"* is the symbol that was used with the titles of numerous Kings and Monarchs. However, it just so happens that it was etched in *"the stone pavement" where the KING of the Jews was judged, and it was in this place, I believe, where "King Solomon" built the Holy Temple of the LORD!* In this location, there is also a crown etched on the stone pavement, along with the letter *"B,"* and both of these symbols clearly indicate that *"THE KING" was in this place!*

Now there is something else that is even more exciting than this that the LORD just suddenly revealed to me and it leads me to believe even further that *"the stone pavement"* that exists today was, indeed, the place of the Brazen Sea and the altar that stood near Solomon's porch of judgment. It is interesting that Messiah Yeshua was actually standing on this stone pavement in John 19, but if we go back to John 13 and look at Yeshua's actions, we can now comprehend exactly what He was doing with the Jewish disciples. In John 13, *Yeshua washed the Jewish disciples' feet* (Simon Peter said for Him to wash his hands and head also), and He told them that they would not understand what He was doing now, but *they would understand it later!* So later, in John 19, when Yeshua's feet stood on *"the stone pavement"* after He had washed the Jewish disciples' feet (and hands), *He was standing where the Molten Brazen Sea had once stood!* So later, they were to understand that Yeshua was the LORD God of Israel, the Living Water of the Molten Brazen Sea of Heaven, who had already washed them clean. Remember also that Yeshua's feet in Heaven are as *burnished bronze,* just like the reflective molten mirrors of the Israelite women! Yeshua was washing the feet (and hands) of His Jewish disciples, as the Living Water of Heaven and this is exactly what was done at the place of the Brazen Sea, where Yeshua was later standing! This will make more sense to us, if we read Exodus, because the LORD God of Israel stood and under His feet, there was a paved work of sapphire stone. This statement actually reveals the stone pavement that held the basin of the Living Water that reflected the sapphire blue sky but this Molten Brazen Sea is the one that is in Heaven. So under Yeshua's feet is the sapphire blue sky, as He stood upon the stone pavement.

Living Water in a jar from the place in the Jordan River where Yeshua's feet stood reflecting "A Piece of Sky" on a mirror

Exodus 24:10 *And they saw the God of Israel; and there was under His feet as it were a paved work of a sapphire stone, and as it were the body of Heaven in His clearness.*

Yeshua was, therefore, standing on the stone pavement in the place of the altar and the place of the Molten Brazen Sea that had once *"reflected the sapphire blue sky."* He did this shortly after washing the Jewish disciples' feet (and hands). So He was, in fact, revealing that He is the LORD God of Israel and the Living Water whose feet are like burnished bronze or fine brass. The interesting part of this is that Yeshua told the Jewish disciples that if He did not wash their hands and feet, then they would have no part with Him. However, once He had done this for them, He said that they were clean. So now, because the Jewish disciples had washed their hands and their feet in the Heavenly Molten Brazen Sea of Living Water, that is to say in the LORD Messiah who makes the earth His sapphire blue footstool, they could now go and perform their sacred duties for the LORD by taking the Living Torah and His Testimony throughout the entire earth, as a witness of His glory to all four directions of the compass. So they became like the oxen that carried His Eternal Testimony on their backs! Yeshua was revealing Himself as the Heavenly Molten Brazen Sea and as the exact *reflection* of the God of Israel. He was the *"body"* of Heaven in His clearness. Another exciting point to make is that Yeshua told His disciples that *"later, when it came to pass, they would believe that He was "I AM HE."* And they did after He stood on *"the stone pavement"* to be judged, in John 19!

Living Water in a jar from the place in the Jordan River where Yeshua's feet stood, reflecting "A Piece of Sky" on a mirror Photo ©2013 Kimberly K Ballard All Rights Reserved

Another remarkable detail is that when Yeshua washed the feet (and hands) of the Jewish disciples, He actually did this in *"a basin."*

John 13:3-19 *Yeshua knowing that the Father had given all things into His hands, and that He was come from God, and went to God; He riseth from supper; and laid aside His garments; and took a towel, and girded Himself. After that He poureth water into a basin, and began to wash the disciples' feet, and to wipe them with the towel where with he was girded. Then cometh He to Simon Peter; and Peter saith unto Him, LORD, dost Thou wash my feet? Yeshua answered and said unto Him, what I do thou knowest not now; but thou shalt know hereafter. Peter saith unto Him, Thou shalt never wash my feet. Yeshua answered him, If I wash thee not, thou hast no part with Me. Simon Peter saith unto Him, LORD, not my feet only, but also my hands and my head. Yeshua saith unto Him, He that is washed needeth not save to wash his feet, but is clean every whit; and ye are clean, but not all. For He knew who should betray Him; therefore said He, Ye are not all clean. So after He had washed their feet, and had taken His garments, and was set down again, He said unto them, Know ye what I have done to you? Ye call me Master and LORD; and ye say well; for so I AM. If I then, your LORD and Master, have washed your feet; ye also ought to wash one another's feet. For I have given you an example, that ye should do as I have done to you. Verily, verily, I say unto you, the servant is not greater than his LORD; neither he that is sent greater than He that sent Him. If ye know these things, happy are ye if ye do them. I speak not of you all; I know whom I have chosen; but that the Scripture may be fulfilled, He that eateth bread with Me hath lifted up his heel against Me. Now I tell you before it come, that, when it is come to pass, ye may believe that I AM HE.*

In the book of Revelation, when the New Jerusalem comes down out of Heaven and the LORD is dwelling in our midst forever, it is intriguing that there is no more Sea! I believe that this is a reference to *the Molten Brazen Sea* because the LORD is everything. He is the reflective Molten Brazen Sea of Living Water that has already cleansed us and He is the Living Torah Lamb that was offered on the altar of God. So we have washed our garments in the true Living Water and in His life blood of His Eternal Covenant of the Heavenly Ark. Therefore,

we have been purified in Him because we have cast our sins into Messiah's Heavenly *body* of Living Water, which means that we are prepared as a Bride for Him. Therefore, because He is reigning at this point in the Eternal Holy city, *"New Jerusalem,"* we have no need for the Brazen Sea anymore. The KING OF KINGS AND LORD OF LORDS is the purifying Molten Brazen Sea of Living Water and the altar of the Lamb of the Living Torah. It is finished. The LORD will now return to dwell with us again as it was in the beginning.

Revelation 21:1-5 *And I saw a new Heaven and a new earth; for the first Heaven and the first earth were passed away; and there was no more Sea. And I John saw the Holy city, New Jerusalem, coming down from God out of Heaven, prepared as a Bride adorned for her husband. And I heard a great voice out of Heaven saying, Behold, the Tabernacle of God is with men, and He will dwell with them, and they shall be His people, and God Himself shall be with them, and be their God. And God shall wipe away all tears from their eyes; and there shall be no more death, neither sorrow, nor crying, neither shall there be any more pain; for the former things are passed away. And He that sat upon the throne said, Behold, I make all things new. And He said unto me, Write; for these Words are true and faithful.*

Now incredibly, in the book of Kings, when it mentions the construction of the Brazen Sea, it also mentions *"the porch of judgment"* that Solomon built near it. It was from this place that King Solomon sat down to judge! Just outside the porch of Solomon, stood the altar and the Molten Brazen Sea. Solomon would judge from the porch that He had built from an *"elevated place on the stone pavement"* that was his throne.

I Kings 7:7 *Then he made a porch for the throne where he might judge, even the porch of judgments; and it was covered with cedar from one side of the floor to the other.*

So now when Yeshua stood on *"The stone pavement"* called *"Gabbatha,"* meaning *"high elevated place or ridge or ridge of the house,"* He was being judged by Pontius Pilate! *Therefore I believe that Yeshua was standing on the same stone pavement where Solomon judged in the porch.* This elevated stone pavement stood before the altar. Solomon's Temple stood *"on the highest ground"* and its foundation was built upon the rock, *"on the ridge" of Mount Moriah,* in the place where Abraham was sent to offer up Isaac, his son. *The place that was already known as "the stone pavement" was the place of Pilate's judgment, where Pilate sat down on the judge's seat, and it was here that Messiah Yeshua was judged on the ridge of the house or high elevated place of Holy Mount Moriah!*

John 19:13 *When Pilate heard this, he brought Yeshua out and sat down on the judge's seat at a place known as the stone pavement which in Aramaic is Gabbatha.*

King Solomon had also built a brazen scaffold that was elevated on the stone pavement, where he knelt to dedicate the First Holy Temple. The fire came down from Heaven and consumed the offering from the altar there and the Brazen Sea was near it. So I believe that the *"elevated platform"* where Solomon sat down to judge was also the scaffold. I believe this is the same platform where Pilate sat down to judge Yeshua on *"the stone pavement" because it was "elevated" and called "Gabbatha."*

Now I discovered something else that was fascinating. If the elevated brazen scaffold that King Solomon built was indeed used for judgment, it is shocking to realize that by definition, *"a scaffold"* is in fact *"an elevated platform, on which a criminal stands in judgment!"* Now this would be simply incredible, if the very spot where Solomon stood to judge called *"the brazen scaffold"* that stood in the midst of the court was the exact same location (on the firm foundation of the stone pavement), where centuries later, Pilate stood with Messiah Yeshua to judge and condemn Him as a criminal, but He was without sin as the Lamb of God *before the altar.* Yeshua was the descendant of King David and David's son had built

this elevated platform of judgment. *Therefore, Yeshua the LORD was standing where the Holy Temple will stand forever where King Solomon knelt in prayer to dedicate the First Holy Temple to God on the ridge of the house, the high elevated platform of Holy Mount Moriah known as Gabbatha!*

***II Chronicles 6:13** For Solomon had made a brazen scaffold of five cubits long, and five cubits broad, and three cubits high, and had set it in the midst of the court; and upon it he stood, and kneeled down upon his knees before all the congregation of Israel, and spread forth his hands toward Heaven*

Now incredibly, in I Kings, we find the exact location of the scaffold that Solomon stood upon when he gave the prayer dedication for the First Temple. *It was before the altar! This was the elevated stone pavement! So this means that Messiah Yeshua became the Lamb on Passover as His feet stood where the LORD'S original altar had stood for hundreds of years!* This is absolutely chilling! The Heavenly Ark stood where His throne will stand forever!

***I Kings 8:22** And Solomon stood before the altar of the LORD in the presence of all the congregation of Israel, and spread forth his hands toward Heaven.*

So Solomon was standing and *"kneeling before the altar upon the elevated platform"* to give his prayer of dedication and *"the Molten Brazen Sea was near it."* This is an extremely profound and exciting discovery from the Holy Spirit! After pondering this for a while, I decided to do more research to see if I could find any other source that might verify my hypothesis about the stone pavement. Then to my astonishment, I found a record that was kept about this stone pavement! In the year 333AD, there was a Christian pilgrim known as *"the Pilgrim of Bordeaux"* who had traveled to Jerusalem and to many other historically important sites. As he traveled, He wrote in a journal and he recorded everything that he saw. He wrote the following statement in his book and when I read it, I was astonished!

Pilgrim of Bordeaux 333AD Quote; *"And in the building itself, where stood the Temple which Solomon built, they say that the blood of Zacharias which was shed upon the stone pavement before the altar remains to this day. There are also to be seen the marks of the nails in the shoes of the Soldiers who slew him, throughout the whole enclosure, so plain that you would think they were impressed upon wax."* ***(Source: ©1898 The Pilgrim of Bordeaux 333AD ITINERARIUM BURDIGALENSE, CORPUS SCRIPTORUM ECCLES. LATINORUM, XXXVIIII, ITINERA HIEROSOLYMITANA, SAECULI IIII – VIII, ED Paul Geyer, 1898 translated by Arnold Vander Nat. 2001).***

The Pilgrim just verified that Zacharias was slain on *"the stone pavement" before the altar. Incredibly, the Pilgrim also verified that in 333 AD, this stone pavement was still in existence. It is indeed, the true location where King Solomon built the Holy Temple of God!* Now we know that this *elevated stone pavement* was the very same stone pavement where King Solomon stood before the altar to dedicate the First Holy Temple. It had to be the same stone pavement, where hundreds of years later, Messiah Yeshua stood, as He was judged and condemned as *the Lamb of God before the altar.* The marks that looked like they were impressed upon wax left in the stone pavement, from the nails in the Soldiers shoes, are still in existence and are visible to us today! In Greek, this pavement is called the *"Lithostrotos." According to this Pilgrim, "the stone pavement" where Solomon built the LORD'S Temple was not destroyed in 70 AD, but still existed in Jerusalem in 333 AD, because the Pilgrim saw it with his own eyes and he described it perfectly!*

In 70 AD, a Roman Centurion named *"Julian"* fell upon the pavement of the Temple when he was wearing the shoes embedded with thick sharp nails, just before the Temple was destroyed by Titus's army, and I believe these are the shoes that the Pilgrim mentioned.

Quote from; Flavious Josephus – "The Wars of the Jews," Book 6.1.8:81-86

"But there was one Julian, a Centurion, that came from Bithynia; a man he was of great reputation, whom I had formerly seen in that war, and one of the highest fame, both for his skill in war, his strength of body, and the courage of his soul. This man, seeing the Romans giving ground, and in a sad condition (for he stood by Titus at the Tower of Antonia), leaped out, and of himself alone put the Jews to flight when they were already conquerors, and made them retire as far as the corner of the inner court of the Temple; from him the multitude fled away in crowds as supposing that neither his strength nor his violent attacks could be those of a mere man. Accordingly he rushed through the midst of the Jews, as they were dispersed all abroad, and killed those that he caught. Nor, indeed, was there any sight that appeared more wonderful in the eyes of Caesar, or more terrible to others than this. However, he was himself pursued by fate, which it was not possible that he who was but a mortal man should escape; for as he had shoes all full of thick and sharp nails, as had every one of the other Soldiers, so when he ran on the pavement of the Temple, he slipped, and fell down upon his back with a very great noise, which was made by his armor. This made those that were running away to turn back; whereupon those Romans that were in the Tower of Antonia set up a great shout, as they were in fear for the man. But the Jews got about him in crowds, and struck at him with their spears and with their swords on all sides." ***(Source: ©1737 William Whiston Translator).***

Now putting all of this together, this has to be the reason why the stone pavement where Pontius Pilate stood to judge Yeshua *was already known as "the stone pavement" or "Gabbatha" the ridge of the house.* The LORD showed me that Pilate judged the Jewish KING where King Solomon's original judgment seat stood before the altar. Remember that the Royal emblem for the KING and the crown, were also etched into the stone pavement.

After writing all of this by the power of the Holy Spirit about the stone pavement, I discovered more connections to it that were simply astounding! The Hebrew word *"Bimah"* is *"an elevated platform on which the Torah is read after it is undressed."* This elevated platform is used today in the Synagogues and it is representative of *the ancient altar* of the Holy Temple in Jerusalem! I believe that *the Magdala Stone* is a small *Bimah* platform that Yeshua stood upon to speak the Living Torah to the Hebrews in Mary Magdalene's ancient Synagogue in Magdala! So the customs today in the Synagogue reveal that the altar and the Brazen Sea were, indeed, sitting on the elevated stone pavement or on the elevated platform near the porch of judgment and before the Holy Temple itself. When I saw this for the first time, I was absolutely shocked, because I realized that Messiah Yeshua, *the Living Torah, was standing on the elevated platform* which was the *"Bimah"* in front of Pilate, who was seated on the judgment seat in the place of the altar, and *Yeshua (the Living Torah) was undressed to be scourged on the Bimah.* It was truly incredible to see all of this coming together, and, needless to say, a shiver ran through me!

The Pilgrim of Bordeaux mentioned that Zacharias was slain on the stone pavement. Messiah Yeshua also mentioned the slaying of Zacharias, and the exact location where this took place! *It happened between the Temple and the altar.* This also reveals the exact location of *"the stone pavement"* that still bore the marks from the shoes of the Roman Centurions.

Matthew 23:34-35 *Wherefore, behold, I send unto you Prophets, and wise men, and Scribes; and some of them ye shall kill and crucify; and some of them shall ye scourge in your Synagogues, and persecute them from city to city; That upon you may come all the righteous bloodshed upon the earth, from the blood of righteous Abel unto the blood of Zacharias son of Barachias, whom ye slew between the Temple and the altar.*

Luke 11:50-51 *That the blood of all the Prophets, which was shed from the foundation of the world, may be required of this generation; From the blood of Zacharias, which perished between the altar and the Temple; verily I say unto you, It shall be required of this generation.*

Based upon Yeshua's Words, the location of *"the stone pavement"* is now very clear. *It is the same stone pavement that exists to this day, bearing the ancient marks.* When the Jewish disciples later understood that *Yeshua was standing in the place called "Gabbatha" on the high elevated stone pavement before the altar and in the place of the Molten Brazen Sea when He was judged, they finally understood that Yeshua was truly "I AM HE."* Then they understood that the LORD was fulfilling His Living Testimony and Eternal Covenant before their eyes. Where have we heard this phrase before? It is written in Isaiah about the LORD God! The Saviour is God. *He told us that we are to know and believe He is "I AM HE!" He said He is your KING!*

Isaiah 43:10-15 *Ye are My witnesses, saith the LORD, and My servant whom I have chosen; that ye may know and believe Me, and understand that I AM HE; before Me there was no God formed, neither shall there be after Me. I, even I, AM the LORD; and beside Me there is no Saviour. I have declared, and have saved, and I have shewed, when there was no strange god among you; therefore ye are My witnesses, saith the LORD, that I AM God. Yea, before the day was I AM HE; and there is none that can deliver out of My hand; I will work, and who shall let it? Thus saith the LORD, your Redeemer, the Holy One of Israel; For your sake I have sent to Babylon, and have brought down all their nobles, and the Chaldeans, whose cry is in the ships. I AM the LORD, your Holy One, the creator of Israel, your KING.*

It is fascinating that this week, just as I was editing this section of my book and reading again what I wrote about Zacharias, who was slain between the Temple and the altar, they suddenly announced on the news that they just found the tomb of Zechariah the Prophet, who was buried in the Judean hills near Jerusalem. The name *"Zechariah"* is Hebrew and it is translated into Greek as *"Zacharias."* So this was more than just an incredible coincidence! I think the fact that Zechariah wrote more than anyone other than Isaiah on the coming of the Messiah and on the end time events makes this coincidence more than profound. This is truly thrilling since I have been writing about the Messiah and talking about the end time events! *The altar itself actually symbolized peace between God and man.* Messiah Yeshua, the Prince of Peace, came to bring peace and reconciliation between God and man. When Yeshua stood before *the altar* on the stone pavement as the perfect spotless sinless Lamb of God, *the pure Living Torah sheepskin containing the Word of God,* He was taking away the *bitterness* of the curse of death in the flesh, reconciling us back to the *sweet* Garden of Heaven, which is the Eternal Promised Land. The LORD was offering us the First Fruit from the Almond Tree of Life after He was lifted up! He was bringing us the *sweetness* of Eternal salvation, through the First Fruit of the Branch!

While I continued investigating the stone pavement called *"Gabbatha,"* several Divine surprises came to me that were totally unexpected. Near the location of the altar and the Brazen Sea, I knew that there had to be an underground water source. I discovered that, indeed, there is an ancient water cistern, a pool and an ancient aqueduct, directly underneath *"the stone pavement!"* There was something about this floor that puzzled me however and as I was pondering what it meant, I realized that this was more than just a stone pavement. With the knowledge that *"Gabbatha" means "high elevated place or elevated ridge of the house,"* it suddenly came into my heart that *"the stone pavement" also had to be the threshing floor of Araunah the Jebusite.* The LORD specifically selected this location and David built the original altar in this threshing floor. Since the Pilgrim of Bordeaux said that *"the stone pavement,"* that still existed in 333 AD was *the location of the Temple of Solomon,* then we know that the threshing floor was located in this same place because it was also located upon a high elevated rock ridge on Holy Mount Moriah. Solomon built the First Temple on the threshing floor on the place where David had built the altar on the ridge. He laid *the foundations* of the Holy Temple in the rock on top of the high elevated ridge on Mount Moriah. Now I wrote about the threshing floor previously, but I had no idea at that time that I would be thinking that *"the stone pavement"* where Yeshua was judged and scourged by Pontius Pilate

was literally the threshing floor of Araunah the Jebusite. This means that Messiah Yeshua was threshed, literally, on the threshing floor of the LORD and this was the threshing floor that King David, His ancestor had purchased! The fact that a threshing floor was always located on the high elevated portion of a hill is the greatest evidence that this was the threshing floor of Araunah, if not simply for the fact that this stone pavement was called *"Gabbatha."* It was indeed high on Holy Mount Moriah where Abraham took Isaac to offer him to the LORD. On this very spot, Solomon built the Temple of the LORD. The stone pavement proved to be so much more than I expected and the LORD was revealing it all! As I continued my research, I wanted to know if there were any ancient threshing floors that were paved with stones. Surely there would be proof of this somewhere and I could verify my hypothesis about *"the stone pavement"* as the threshing floor of Araunah the Jebusite. Quite frankly, I was chilled, because after I researched for a while, I actually found photographs of a few ancient threshing floors in Greece and to my delight, they were indeed paved with stones! The animals were walking on the stone pavement over the sheaves of grain. When I saw these photographs, they looked like the stone pavement in Jerusalem! This was thrilling and I was so excited because I had already suspected that Araunah's threshing floor was *paved with stone* and was likely *the stone pavement* on which Messiah Yeshua was threshed as the grain of the First Fruits offering. I actually found this verification and evidence that some threshing floors in ancient times were indeed paved with smooth stones! They used granite, limestone, cobble stone, or other types of hard rock and laid it out as a smooth platform. Whatever the choice of stone, it only needed to be a hard type of rock that was flat and very smooth.

A type of Stone Pavement like the threshing floor of Araunah
Photo ©2013 Kimberly K Ballard All Rights Reserved

The threshing floor was always placed on the highest elevated place on the hill so the wind would catch the chaff and blow it away. The place selected for the threshing floor was made level by removing all the natural stones, pebbles, and course rocks from the area. Then after the ground was completely leveled, the dirt was beaten smooth. After the dirt was clean and level, the large smooth paving stones were laid on the ground, on the top of the smooth surface. The threshing floor was literally *a stone pavement* and the animals walked around on it, threshing the grain. The place of threshing was said to be approximately 30 to 50 feet in diameter. Some threshing floors were round, while others were rectangular or square. Now I find it interesting that not all the threshing floors were paved with stones. Some of the threshing floors had plain, hard compacted dirt floors, without any paving. *Only the very best threshing floors were paved with stones and, of course, the LORD would certainly have chosen the best threshing floor for His Eternal purposes!* A paved threshing floor was easier on the oxen who could thresh without having their hooves dragging into the dirt floor. A stone pavement made it much easier for the oxen to walk around on the smooth flat surface while threshing the grain beneath their hooves. A *stone pavement,* actually made the best type of threshing floor because the grain stayed clean and only a tiny fraction of dirt ever got into it. This really spoke to my heart because I realized that by keeping the grain clean on *the stone pavement,* this would make it *"kosher!"* It is also true that the grain could easily be swept, gathered, and winnowed with a fork on a smooth stone pavement without any dirt mixing into it. The oxen could pull the sledges easily over the grain on the smooth surface of the stone

pavement and their hooves could easily separate the hull from the grain as they walked around on the paved floor. It was the LORD who had chosen Araunah's threshing floor for His altar. A KING would have selected the very best threshing floor! So I know in my heart that the LORD chose only the best threshing floor that was located on the highest elevated ridge of Holy Mount Moriah. The oxen that were attached to the threshing sledges that King David purchased were driven by a single rider. As the oxen walked around on the stone pavement, a person sat upon the sledge. They would ride the sledge around as it was dragged repeatedly over the top of the ripe grain that was gathered and piled on the stone pavement. The sledges that I saw were made of simple wooden planks and they looked quite similar to a modern wooden snow sled without the rails. Threshing with a sledge was usually a very simple process. I saw one photograph of a donkey pulling a threshing sledge on a stone pavement, doing exactly the same work that King David's oxen would have done on the threshing floor. The underneath side of the wooden planks of the sledges were embedded with sharp stones. They would use basalt chips, flint chips, or other small sharp stones. On occasion, metal shards were sharpened and they were inserted into the bottom of the wooden planks of the threshing sledge. The flint chips and stones were said to do the least amount of damage to the grain. The sharpened stones that were embedded into the bottom of the sledge were called *"teeth."* The grain was then threshed as the sledge embedded with flint chips was repeatedly dragged across the sheaves of grain on the stone pavement, while the animals walked over it with their hooves, separating the grain from the hulls. The following description from the Bible is a fine example in the LORD'S own Words regarding this method of threshing. Notice in this passage that the LORD says, *"Thou shalt thresh the mountains,"* thus indicating that a mountain was the location of the threshing floor. The wind would blow the chaff off the threshing floor on the hill as it was winnowed with a fork off the stone pavement. ***(Source: "Threshing Board" Wikipedia (showing the threshing sledges) Copyright ©2010. en.wikipedia.org/wiki/Threshing-board) AND ("Threshing Floor," Wikipedia. Copyright ©2010-2013. en.wikipedia.org/wiki/Threshing_floor).***

Isaiah 41:15-16 *Behold, I will make thee a new sharp threshing instrument having teeth; thou shalt thresh the mountains and beat them small, and shalt make the hills as chaff. Thou shalt fan them, and the wind shall carry them away, and the whirlwind shall scatter them; and thou shalt rejoice in the LORD, and shalt glory in the Holy One of Israel.*

The next two Scriptures tell us that King David sacrificed the offerings to the LORD on the threshing floor on Holy Mount Moriah and *Yeshua became the Passover offering of the LORD on Holy Mount Moriah* in this exact location. *It was here that King Solomon built the House of the LORD.*

I Chronicles 21:28 *At that time when David saw that the LORD had answered him in the threshing floor of Araunah the Jebusite, then he sacrificed there.*

II Chronicles 3:1 *Then Solomon began to build the House of the LORD at Jerusalem in Mount Moriah, where the LORD appeared unto David his father, in the place that David had prepared in the threshing floor of Araunah the Jebusite.*

II Chronicles 7:7 *Moreover Solomon hallowed the middle of the court that was before the House of the LORD; for there he offered burnt offerings, and the fat of the peace offerings, because the brazen altar which Solomon had made was not able to receive the burnt offerings, and the meat offerings.*

It is interesting that Solomon *"hallowed"* the middle of the court, because this is the place where the LORD Messiah stood and Yeshua also told us to pray, *"Our Father who art in Heaven, hallowed be Thy Name."* So the LORD Messiah stood in the *hallowed place,* as the Molten Brazen Sea of Heaven and as the altar of the true Lamb and as the pure meat of the Living Torah! He is the *body* of the Heavenly Temple!

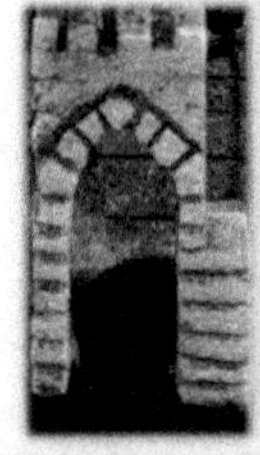

Now there was something that puzzled me about *"the stone pavement."* This had to do with the scars and marks that are impressed in the pavement like wax. The Pilgrim of Bordeaux had written that the marks were *"like they had been impressed into wax."* As I studied the stone pavement, known as *"Gabbatha,"* where Yeshua was judged, I was astonished by what I saw. On a portion of the ancient stone pavement, there were some very unusual grooves running across the top of the smooth shiny stones. The moment that I observed the marks and scars in the stone pavement, it suddenly occurred to me that the grooves could have been made by the threshing sledges as they were dragged over the grain on the stone pavement. Soon after I realized this, the next thing that the LORD revealed to me was even more astounding! In a very ancient portion of *"the stone pavement"* right above this section of the floor, there is a life size picture of Yeshua carrying His cross. As I pondered these strange grooves, it just suddenly hit me! *The stones in the floor are striated and they look identical to Matzah, the unleavened bread of the Israelites that is eaten at Passover! Then I suddenly realized that all the markings that are on the unleavened Matzah of Passover actually match the markings that are on "the stone pavement" which is the threshing floor of the grain!* This was unbelievable! It was from this particular threshing floor that the grain was taken to be used to make the unleavened bread for the Holy Temple of God! Wow, this was a great revelation! Yeshua, who had revealed Himself as the Unleavened Bread from Heaven was depicted carrying His cross, just above this special striated section of the stone pavement that bore the stripes, scars, and markings. Yeshua told us, that He is the Bread from Heaven and He was the seed grain that was threshed here in this place and then He was laid in the earth in Holy Mount Moriah in the Garden, on the Feast of Unleavened Bread. I could not believe that Yeshua's picture was standing above this special portion of *the stone pavement, bearing the Matzah stripes, marks, and scars!* This truly touched my heart. I suddenly realized the full impact of what the LORD had done for us on His threshing floor in this place! This incredible revelation came to me after I was already pondering and discovering that *"the stone pavement"* was the same place as the threshing floor of Araunah. The Matzah looked so identical in appearance to the stone pavement that I just could not believe it! When I put a picture of a piece of Passover Matzah next to a picture of *the stone pavement,* they matched perfectly! So I am now wondering if the Matzah was later patterned to look like the threshing floor of the grain for the Holy Temple of the LORD. *A single stone from the stone pavement of the threshing floor was like a single piece of Matzah or unleavened bread in its appearance.* Then I noticed that the shape of the Matzah, whether it was handmade and round or shaped into a square by a *kosher* machine, both styles of unleavened bread were shaped exactly like the ancient threshing floors that I had seen in the pictures in my research. I was so astonished by this because the LORD had revealed it to me. Now in order to fully grasp how awesome this is, you have to know about the deeper meaning of the Matzah in Jewish history. The Matzah is specifically called *"the bread of affliction."* This makes me want to cry to think of Yeshua standing on this pavement carrying the cross. It touched my heart when I comprehended for the first time *that Messiah Yeshua actually became "The bread of affliction" on "the stone pavement" of the threshing floor of the LORD! Matzah is the staff of life and Yeshua is the Staff of Life, the Rod of God.* I stopped everything and just pondered the depth of this for a while that Yeshua became the *bread of the affliction* in the place where *the stone pavement is striped and scarred,* appearing like Matzah, the unleavened bread, in the threshing floor of the LORD. Tears just streamed down my face!

Another amazing aspect to this is that Yeshua, who stood in this place being threshed as the Unleavened Bread from Heaven, is connected to the Matzah that has been made totally flat, without any leaven in it to represent *"total humility."* I just could not believe how chilling this all was because KING Yeshua humbled Himself in *extreme humility,* as the Unleavened Bread of affliction, on the threshing floor, because He was without sin. Any bread that has

leaven in it is depicted as sin. So this Heavenly Matzah, Messiah Yeshua, had no leaven or sin, as He was threshed here in total humility! The LORD gave us so much proof of His glorious Testimony and this proof is written in stone! Discovering this was not a coincidence because every detail of this was orchestrated by the LORD to prove His Divine Testimony. Now I remembered what I already wrote about the Crown of Thorns and that only a very pious and extremely humble Jewish man wears a kippah or Yarmulke with a hat over it. Yeshua may have had one smaller skull cap with a larger Crown of Thorns over that symbolizing *"total humility,"* and I wrote the above words about the bread of affliction before the LORD revealed this to me about the Crown of Thorns!

Acts 8:32-35 *The place of the Scripture which He read was this, He was led as a sheep to the slaughter and like a lamb dumb before His shearer, so opened He not His mouth; In His humiliation His judgment was taken away; and who shall declare His generation? For His life is taken from the earth. And the eunuch answered Philip, and said, I pray thee, of whom speaketh the Prophet this? Of himself, or of some other man? Then Phillip opened his mouth, and began at the same Scripture, and preached unto him Yeshua.*

Philippians 2:8-11 *And being found in fashion as a man, He humbled Himself, and became obedient unto death, even the death of the cross. Wherefore God also hath highly exalted Him, and given Him a Name which is above every Name; That at the Name of Yeshua every knee should bow, of things in Heaven, and things in earth, and things under the earth; And that every tongue should confess that Yeshua Messiah is LORD, to the glory of God the Father.*

The LORD has lifted up His Rod and exalted His own Name and everyone will bow to the KING OF KINGS, to Yeshua who rules with His righteous Royal Sceptre, because He humbled Himself in the place where the grain was threshed. *Messiah the Living Torah* was the seed grain that became the fine flour of the Eternal Unleavened Bread or Manna from Heaven that is *the Staff of Life! The Matzah is made with water and flour and nothing else, and adherence to the kosher laws is strictly followed. Yeshua is the pure fine grain of the flour of the Unleavened Bread and He is the Living Water!* As I looked at that stone pavement and visualized the Passover Matzah in it, I thought that this was just another incredible sign from the LORD. Yeshua was buried in the rock hewn tomb in God's Garden in Mount Moriah during the Feast of Unleavened Bread after He was threshed on this elevated stone pavement. So I realized that the striated pavement where Yeshua humbled Himself as *"the Bread of affliction"* was the place where He brought liberty and freedom to the captives who had been held in the bondage of the corruption of death since the days of the exile from the Garden of Eden. *Here was the picture of Yeshua carrying the cross in the place where He did carry His cross, right above this striped, striated, elevated stone pavement.* This was on the ridge of the House where the LORD will permanently set His feet!

The Matzah symbolizes *human freedom.* Actually, it symbolizes *freedom from bondage* and this corresponds to the human freedom that Yeshua brought us when He reversed the curse of death in the flesh, so we could be translated into the glorious liberty of the children of God, because the life of the flesh is in His blood of the Eternal Covenant that abides forever on the Ark of Heaven. Now we could enter His gates with thanksgiving and our bodies would be resurrected to immortality. I realized that the Matzah truly represented the Passover Lamb who clearly proved beyond doubt that He is the Bread from Heaven, who saved us from death as the *Staff* of Eternal Life.

As I gazed upon *"the stone pavement"* looking at the stripes that looked like the stripes on the unleavened Matzah of Passover, I suddenly understood Isaiah 53 in an entirely new light. The Living Torah sheepskin of the perfect Lamb of God in the flesh bore the stripes for us and healed us!

Isaiah 53:5 *But He was wounded for our transgressions, He was bruised for our iniquities; the chastisement of our peace was upon Him; and with His stripes we are healed.*

The LORD had told Israel that if they obeyed His Statutes and Commandments, things would go well for them, but if they did not, *He would visit their transgressions with the Rod and their iniquity with stripes!* So the LORD came to visit them as the powerful Rod Messiah, bearing the stripes for the transgressions and iniquities of His people!

Psalm 89:31-32 *If they break My Statutes, and keep not My Commandments; Then will I visit their transgression with the Rod, and their iniquity with stripes.*

The Matzah, whether it was round or square, was an exact picture of a threshing floor! This was the bread of affliction and it made me cry thinking of the depth of what took place in this location with Messiah Yeshua.

After having discovered this connection, I had no doubt in my mind that the Matzah represented the threshing floor that was the stone pavement of Araunah the Jebusite. It was definitely the one that King David purchased to honour the LORD! The LORD was threshed with the stripes and marks in His flesh, on His own threshing floor, so we could live with Him forever! Only the Living Torah flesh of the pure Lamb could heal us. So Messiah Yeshua's stripes healed our flesh from the sin debt and reconciled us back to the Eternal Garden to dwell with Him in Heaven! *This told me that the unleavened bread of Passover had a much deeper meaning than simply coming out of the bondage of Egypt when death passed over the Hebrews.* When Messiah Yeshua sealed His Covenant as the Lamb on Passover, He then became the Unleavened Bread of affliction. He delivered us from the bondage of the Garden of Eden and now death passes over us forever. His life blood is on the door of Heaven, so we can enter in through the gate and have life and not death!

The Matzah looked like the paved threshing floor of Araunah,
"The Stone Pavement" Photo ©2013 Kimberly K Ballard All Rights Reserved

Rabbi Yeshua is the Teacher mentioned in Isaiah that Israel will see, and He is telling us, *"This is 'the way' back to Eden, through the two Cherubim Angels! Walk in it!"* This verse speaks of Matzah, the unleavened bread of adversity, because Yeshua is the Word of God and when they hear the Word, they are to follow behind the Heavenly Ark of God in obedience.

Isaiah 30:20-21 *And though the LORD give you bread of adversity, and the water of affliction, yet shall not thy teachers be removed into a corner anymore, but thine eyes shall see thy Teachers; And thine ears shall hear a Word behind thee, saying, This is the way, walk ye in it, when ye turn to the right hand, and when ye turn to the left.*

The rules for the unleavened bread of Passover are written in Deuteronomy.

Deuteronomy 16:3 *Thou shalt eat no leavened bread with it; seven days shall thou eat unleavened bread therewith, even the bread of affliction; for thou camest forth out of the land of Egypt in haste; that thou mayest remember the day when thou camest forth out of the land of Egypt all the days of thy life.*

I Corinthians 11:23-24 *For I have received of the LORD that which also I delivered unto you, That the LORD Yeshua the same night in which He was betrayed took bread; And when He had given thanks, He brake it, and said, Take, eat; this is My body, which is broken for you; this do in remembrance of Me.*

Yeshua was arrested and cast into prison and this is when He became *the bread of affliction* for Israel and for the world, so we would not have to bear the curse of Eden, *toiling for the bread of affliction any longer ourselves.* We have been freed from this bondage! The Prince of Peace reconciled us to Himself in His Royal Garden on Holy Mount Moriah. The following Scripture is a foreshadowing the Messiah!

I Kings 22:27 *And say, Thus saith the King, Put this fellow in the prison, and feed him with bread of affliction and with water of affliction, until I come in peace.*

So Yeshua, the Rabbi of Righteousness, *was afflicted as He stood before the altar on the stone pavement,* in the place where the lambs were slain. Messiah was taken like a sheep before His shearers and put to death. Yeshua's legs were not broken on the cross, because He is the Lamb of God who takes away the sins of the world. He came in peace, but His Word would be a sword to the world.

Lamb scene Photo ©2013 Kimberly K Ballard
All Rights Reserved

Psalm 34:19-20 *Many are the afflictions of the righteous; but the LORD delivereth him out of them all. He keepeth all His bones; not one of them is broken.*

John 19:32-33 *Then came the soldiers, and brake the legs of the first, and of the other which was crucified with Him. But when they came to Yeshua, and saw that He was dead already, they brake not His legs.*

Colossians 1:20-29 *And, having made peace through the blood of His cross, by Him to reconcile all things unto Himself; by Him, I say, whether they be things in earth, or things in Heaven. And you, that were sometime alienated and enemies in your mind by wicked works, yet now hath He reconciled. In the body of His flesh through death to present you Holy and unblameable and unreproveable in His sight. If ye continue in the faith grounded and settled, and be not moved away from the hope of the Gospel, which ye have heard, and which was preached to every creature which is under Heaven; whereof I Paul am made a minister; Who now rejoice in my sufferings for you, and fill up that which is behind of the afflictions of Messiah in my flesh for His body's sake, which is the Church; Wherefore I am made a minister, according to the dispensation of God which is given to me for you, to fulfill the Word of God; Even the mystery which hath been hid from ages and from generations, but now is made manifest to His Saints; To whom God would make known what is the riches of the glory of this mystery among the Gentiles; which is Messiah in you the hope of glory; Whom we preach, warning every man, and teaching every man in all wisdom; that we may present every man perfect in Messiah Yeshua; Whereunto I also labour, striving according to His working, which worketh in me mightily.*

We were truly like prisoners bound by the evil decree of death by Satan in the Garden of Eden. Messiah tasted death for us all, so that, in Him, we could have the liberty of Eternal Life. After having discovered by the Holy Spirit, that both types of Matzah were in the exact shape of an ancient threshing floor, bearing the same markings as the stone pavement, I wept for a long time. I could not believe it. I was astonished that the LORD was revealing to me the place of Solomon's Temple! The LORD'S Word is perfect down to the smallest of details.

This brings up another point that is a small detail that the LORD revealed to me, but it is also quite significant in my mind and heart. Would you believe that something as small as a sparrow could be extremely significant? Let me explain the next part of this evidence and show

you what the LORD showed me. It just so happens that the Pool that is under *"the stone pavement"* is called the *"Struthion Pool."* This name was at one time known as *"Struthius"* which literally means *"Sparrow."* Now this would initially seem to have no real meaning, *but it did to me* and it is the final proof that I needed to show that *"the stone pavement"* was the location of the threshing floor that David purchased. As I said before, this is where He built the altar to the LORD. King David happened to mention where the Sparrow lived in one of his Psalms and it was *"at the House of God, even His altars!"* I felt that this was incredible that the water source that is directly underneath *"the stone pavement"* is called *"the Sparrow Pool"* because if David revealed *where the Sparrow lived* in his Psalm, then this Pool was likely the water source for the altar in front of the House of God that his son Solomon built! It also supplied the Living Water for the Brazen Sea. I could not believe it when I made this connection, through the Holy Spirit who revealed it to me! The Sparrow had found a place to live at the House of God the KING, at His altar and that just happens to be the name of the Pool that is under *"the stone pavement"* that is marked with the KINGS crown!

Psalm 84:3 *Yea, the sparrow hath found an House, and the swallow a nest for herself, where she may lay her young, even thine altars, O LORD of Hosts, my KING, and my God.*

It is amazing that all this time this secret was hidden in a Psalm of David. So the Pool of living water that is underneath *"the stone pavement"* where Yeshua was threshed is called *"The Sparrow Pool" even to this day!* This is profound proof that this was the location of the altar of the LORD on the stone pavement. *The little detail of the Sparrow was now revealing that this was indeed the threshing floor before the House of God that King Solomon built.* The stone pavement is complete with shallow channels in the pavement and there are *manholes* in the masonry, which are used to lower objects down into the Pool to fill them with living water. I instantly thought of the laver because it was lowered through a manhole like this by the Priests and submerged into a Pool of living water that was underneath the court between the altar and the House of God. The fact that in this place, there are manholes that exist in *"the stone pavement"* that would have allowed for *the unique pulley system that the Priests used to raise and lower the laver* to fill it with clean pure water was more than coincidental. The channels that exist in the floor today, I believe, were for the blood to drain away from the altar. It was a fact that the altar did have channels for removing the blood and cleansing it away in a purified manner and the underground Pool was the living water source for cleaning it. It is also possible that the channels were put there long before the altar of the Temple, so the grain could fall into the channels as the sledges were driven over it. The little Sparrow, I felt, was a significant detail, revealing that this was more than likely the exact location of the altar, the Molten Brazen Sea, and the House of God and this is where Yeshua was standing when He became our Passover atonement. I will tell you again that He is the Heavenly Temple that will return and set His feet here forever!

In Psalm 102, we have the word *"watch"* which is, of course *"Shaked" or "Almond"* with the word *"Sparrow"* on the House top. So the Sparrow is resting on the House of God.

Psalm 102:7 *I watch, and am as a Sparrow alone upon the House top.*

Sparrow Photo ©2013 Kimberly K Ballard

After I realized the significance of the *"Sparrow Pool,"* I remembered that Yeshua even spoke about the Sparrows and now I understand His Words because I see them in a totally

different light! Yeshua mentioned that two Sparrows were sold. This reminds me of the two tablets of the Law of Moses, the Word of God that is our meat. We will be brought to live forever at the House of God because we are more valuable than the Sparrows that live there! If we confess that *Yeshua is the Living Torah,* we will have life.

Sparrow Photo ©2013
Kimberly K Ballard All Rights Reserved

Matthew 11:29-32 *Are not two Sparrows sold for a farthing? And one of them shall not fall on the ground without your Father. But the very hairs of your head are numbered. Fear ye not therefore, ye are of more value than many Sparrows. Whosoever therefore shall confess Me before men, him will I confess also before my Father which is in Heaven.*

Yeshua then mentions five Sparrows and this reminds me of the five books of Moses, the Torah, the bread of life.

Luke 12:6-10 *Are not five Sparrows sold for two farthings, and not one of them is forgotten before God? But even the very hairs of your head are all numbered. Fear not therefore; ye are of more value than many Sparrows. Also I say unto you, Whosoever shall confess Me before men, him shall the Son of man also confess before the angels of God. And whosoever shall speak a word against the Son of man, it shall be forgiven him; but unto him that blasphemeth against the Holy Spirit it shall not be forgiven.*

The Sparrows represent the LORD'S children who have His meat, the two tablets of the Law and the Five books of Moses, which is the Bread from Heaven. Yeshua is the total sum of 7, as *the Living Torah.* He is taking care of the two Sparrows and the five Sparrows at His House, because He is our food from Heaven. Yeshua indicates that the birds will be taken care of by the LORD, and not one bird will fall, without His knowledge.

In the following Scripture, Yeshua refers to the birds of the air and He tells us that they neither sow nor reap. They do not gather into barns and He is referring to the threshing floor in this passage! He says that the Heavenly Father feeds them and we are more valuable than these little birds. If the LORD provides for the little birds, then certainly He will provide all our food from Heaven, from the Almond Tree of Life, and we shall never be in want.

Matthew 7:25-26 *Therefore I say unto you, Take no thought for your life, what ye shall eat, or what ye shall drink; nor yet for your body, what ye shall put on. Is not the life more than meat, and the body than raiment? Behold the fowls of the air; for they sow not, neither do they reap, nor gather into barns; yet your Heavenly Father feedeth them. Are ye not much better than they?*

Not one of the LORD'S Sparrows will be lost. The LORD provides us with our Heavenly House and it has been prepared for us to live in by the LORD Himself. When Yeshua spoke of the two Sparrows and the five, equaling 7, He revealed that He is the 7, the fulfillment of it all. He is the LORD'S number of completeness, as the entire Living Torah and the Law of God. We will dwell in the House of the LORD forever, just as the Sparrows did at the LORD'S altars and even at His House!

Now there was something more to this location that surprised me in my research. I have tried to show what I believe is the location of the altar and threshing floor which is *the rock ridge* upon which King Solomon built the original Holy Temple of the LORD. This brings me to my next important point.

When the Second Temple was built by King Herod, the work was described by the Jewish Historian Josephus, who made a very interesting statement!

"The Antiquities of the Jews," Flavious Josephus, Book 15 Chapter 11 Section 3

"So Herod took away the old foundations, and laid others, and erected the Temple upon them, being in length a hundred cubits, and in height twenty cubits, which [twenty], upon the sinking of their foundations, fell down; and this part it was that we resolved to raise again in the days of Nero." ***(Source: Antiquities of the Jews and Wars of the Jews by Flavious Josephus; From William Whiston, Translator 1737).***

If Herod *"took away the old foundations"* where Solomon built His Temple and He *"laid others" that did not stand, but immediately began to sink into their foundations,* this could definitely indicate that when Herod expanded the Temple Mount platform, he placed the Second Holy Temple in a different location *other than where Solomon's Temple was originally built on the rock ridge, on the highest point of Mount Moriah. Herod quite possibly laid these new foundations either beside or very near the old foundations that he took away.* The point is that Josephus wrote that the Second Temple foundations were not good and this in itself presents the basis of my next point. If the threshing floor of Araunah was built upon the highest elevation of the Mount, which was said by the Roman Church to have been located at 2443 feet, and this is where Solomon placed the First Holy Temple, *then I believe that the Romans, built the Fortress of Antonia over the top of the original Foundation Stone where Solomon's Temple had been built upon the rock and where David set up the altar.* This would, of course, also be the same location where Abraham took Isaac. It is *"the Foundation Stone"* and the rock that Adam was created from by the LORD! *Josephus tells us that this hill was very high, where the Fortress of Antonia once stood. Actually, the Fortress of Antonia stood on the highest ridge, higher than any other building!* He also states that the Hasmonean kings, long before the era of the Second Temple, built a citadel called *"The Tower" and "The Baris"* just north of the Second Temple. *It was here that the Priestly vestments were kept by the Romans during the time of the Second Temple.* I made an interesting connection to this place when I realized that Josephus also wrote *"that the Ark of Noah rested on a Mount called "Baris" and that the Ark was still visible when he was living."* Perhaps the Hasmonean kings named their Tower Baris on Holy Mount Moriah, after the landing site of Noah's Ark! *So, if the original location of Solomon's Temple was at the site of the Fortress of Antonia, you can see by looking at a satellite photo of Mount Moriah that this would place the Temple of Solomon in the center of Mount Moriah.* The Garden tomb and Golgotha are at one end of the Mount and the Temple Mount is at the other end of the Mount. Now Abraham took Isaac to the rock summit of Mount Moriah and it was here that David purchased the threshing floor and Solomon, David's son, built the First Temple. *The summit was the highest place.*

So incredibly, Josephus reveals where this rock was located and it happens to be where I thought it was located, *in the place where the stone pavement resides today.* I was able to figure this out because the Jewish Historian wrote about this *very high steep rock that was inside the Fortress of Antonia. The Roman Fortress Antonia was built upon a rock that was like a precipice!* In fact, this was just like something that the Romans would do time after time. The Romans enjoyed building over former important Jewish religious structures with buildings of their own.

Flavious Josephus, "The Wars of the Jews," Book 5, Chapter 5 Section 8

"Now, as to the Tower of Antonia, it was situated at the corner of two cloisters of the court of the Temple; of that on the west, and that on the north; it was erected upon a rock, of fifty cubits in height, and was on a great precipice; it was the work of King Herod, wherein he demonstrated his natural magnanimity. In the first place, the rock itself was covered over with smooth pieces of stone, from its foundation, both for ornament, and that anyone who would either try to get up or to go down it, might not be able to hold his feet upon it." ***(Source: Antiquities of the Jews and Wars of the Jews by Flavious Josephus; © From William Whiston, Translator 1737).***

So the Fortress of Antonia was built upon a great rock precipice that stood at an elevation that was approximately 72-75 feet high! Wow! Clearly this had to be the place of the threshing floor of Araunah and the place where *King David first set up the altar to the LORD* and this was the original Foundation Stone. If Herod did not build the Second Temple on the same foundations as the First Temple and *"laid others,"* then *it would not surprise me at all if the Romans built their military Fortress directly over the original site of Solomon's Temple and then built Herod's Temple, the Second Jewish Temple, next to the Fortress of Antonia on the*

expanded platform on a flat weak foundation that Herod laid, "whose foundation was not built upon the rock precipice." Remember that the Romans taunted the Jewish people because the Romans had *the military power* over the entire Jewish religious system at that time. *It would not be surprising then if the Romans built their military Fortress directly over the original sacred Temple site, so the Jewish people could no longer have it in their possession.* The Roman military garrison would, therefore, overlook the Temple of Herod from a higher place to intimidate the Jewish people! This would mean that the Jewish people were forced to settle for second best, while the Romans kept the best for themselves, and taunted the Jews they controlled. Remember also, that the Jewish Priestly garments were kept under lock and key *inside the Fortress and only the Jewish High Priest (who wore no shoes while performing his sacred duties)* was allowed to be escorted by the Roman Soldiers to open the sealed door in *this rock* to gain access to the Jewish Priestly vestments! *This would mean that the Gentiles were treading down the original Holy Temple site with their military personnel.* The words of Josephus became clear when he said, *"In the first place, the rock itself was covered over with smooth pieces of stone, from its foundation, both for ornament, and that anyone who would either try to get up or to go down it, might not be able to hold his feet upon it."* I ask you now? Who would be trying to walk on *the sacred rock "from its foundation,"* but the Roman Soldiers who wanted to disrespectfully put *their feet and shoes upon it,* because it was *"THE FOUNDATION STONE?"* This was the Mountain of *the Garden of Eden* and the Foundation Stone where Adam was created. In my honest opinion, *this rock was deliberately covered over with ornamental stones* to keep people from climbing up or from walking down the rock, because it was not just any rock, it was, in fact, the Holy *sacred* rock of Mount Moriah, and the rushing Living Water flows underneath this rock! There would be no reason to cover a *rock* with ornamental stones to keep people from treading upon it *with their shoes,* unless it was a very significant *"great rock precipice"* that was, indeed, *the sacred rock of the First Jewish Holy Temple of King Solomon!* Update! On December 12th 2014, the Temple Institute stated in a newsletter that *it was forbidden to wear shoes on Mount Moriah in the place of the Holy Temple. This is the one place on earth that is blessed.* This verified my revelation! The Jewish leaders greatly feared that if too many people followed Messiah Yeshua, the Romans would take away their Jewish Temple (beside the Fortress) and destroy their nation. The Romans wanted full control over the Jewish Holy site. Yeshua's disciple John wrote about this!

John 11:47-48 *Then gathered the Chief Priests and the Pharisees a council, and said, What do we? For this man doeth many miracles. If we let Him thus alone, all men will believe on Him; and the Romans shall come and take away both our place and nation.*

As I thought about this and pondered this rock precipice and its foundation where the tower had been built, I remembered some important words that Messiah Yeshua spoke. The question is, *"Do the Prophetic Words of Messiah Yeshua actually give us the location of Solomon's Temple?"* When Yeshua spoke about the *"House,"* He was always referring to *"The House of the LORD God."* Comparing Yeshua's Words to Josephus's comments, we find that Yeshua's Words are surprisingly and stunningly similar to Josephus's description of this place and the rock that resided inside the Fortress of Antonia. Yeshua spoke in parables and revealed information about the House of the LORD. Messiah Yeshua said that *"the Foundation of the House, was built upon a rock,"* and He was speaking spiritually, but many of His Prophetic Words have a deeper meaning than the interpretations that we give to them. *He is the Rock and this sacred rock is the location where His Eternal Temple will rest. Yeshua was standing in this place, as He was judged in the Fortress, at the original place of the LORD'S altar and the Molten* Brazen Sea. *Yeshua said "that the House that has its Foundations deeply laid upon a rock will not fall, but the House not built on the deep Foundation of the rock, will indeed fall."*

Luke 6:46-49 *And why call ye Me, LORD, LORD, and do not the things which I say? Whosoever cometh to Me, and heareth My sayings, and doeth them, I will shew you to whom he is like; He is like a man which built an House, and digged deep, and laid the Foundation on a rock; and when the flood arose, the stream beat vehemently upon that House, and could not shake it; for it was founded upon a rock. But he that heareth, and doeth not, is like a man that without a Foundation built an House upon the earth; against which the stream did beat vehemently, and immediately it fell; and the ruin of that House was great.*

This is why I believe the Second Temple was destroyed and this is why it fell, just as Yeshua prophetically said that it would, *because this Second House was not built upon the deep Fountains of the sacred rock of God* and therefore God brought the Roman Soldiers in to destroy the Second Temple. The time of their visitation by the LORD had come, but they did not recognize Him! If the Romans took away the sacred Foundations in the rock, this would be considered theft. Remember that when Yeshua threw out the money changers, because He was getting the leaven out of His Father's House at Passover, He called them a den of thieves and this was written in Jeremiah!

Jeremiah 7:11 *Is this House, which is called by My Name, become a den of robbers in your eyes? Behold, even I have seen it, saith the LORD.*

Luke 19:45-46 *And He went into the Temple, and began to cast out them that sold therein, and them that bought; Saying unto them, It is written, My House is the House of prayer; but ye have made it a den of thieves.*

Then to top it off, Yeshua said *"the wise man built his house upon a rock."* King Solomon has always been known as *"the wisest man who ever lived!"*

I Kings 5:7 *And it came to pass, when Hiram heard the words of Solomon, that he rejoiced greatly, and said, Blessed be the LORD this day, which hath given unto David a wise son over this great people.*

I Kings 4:29-34 *And God gave Solomon wisdom and understanding exceeding much, and largeness of heart, even as the sand that is on the sea shore. And Solomon's wisdom excelled the wisdom of all the children of the east country, and all the wisdom of Egypt. For he was wiser than all men; than Ethan the Ezrahite, and Heman, and Chalcol, and Darda, the sons of Mahol; and his fame was in all Nations round about. And he spake three thousand proverbs; and his songs were a thousand and five. And he spake of trees, from the cedar tree that is in Lebanon even unto the hyssop that springeth out of the wall; he spake also of beasts, and of fowl, and of creeping things, and of fishes. And there came of all people to hear the wisdom of Solomon, from all Kings of the earth, which had heard of his wisdom.*

So, was Yeshua revealing the location of Solomon's Temple, the House of God that was built upon a rock, when He said, *"The wise man built his house upon a rock?"* The LORD is literally the Spiritual Rock, however, His House in Jerusalem was built upon a rock that was *the Foundation Stone, and this Foundation Stone* is the one that *I believe was the great rock precipice inside the Fortress of Antonia.* It was *deliberately* covered over by the Romans with the ornamental stones so no one could walk up or down this *sacred rock from its Foundation.* It is interesting that the only thing in Jerusalem that was left standing during the destruction of Jerusalem was the Fortress of Antonia that stood on the highest elevation of Mount Moriah. *The Fortress stood higher than any other building and was deliberately built to overshadow the Second Temple that stood beside it!* Therefore, those who hear the LORD, the Messiah, and listen to Him are *like the wise man, who built his House upon a rock and this House did not fall, because it was founded on the rock.* However, those who do not listen to His Words, will not know the right place to build their House, on the High elevated rock ridge of Mount Moriah, in the place called *"Gabbatha."* If they do not hear what Messiah says, then their House will not stand.

Ancient Roman Glass from the burnt Second Holy Temple in Jerusalem Photo ©2013 Kimberly K Ballard

***Matthew 7:24-29** Therefore whosoever heareth these saying of Mine, and doeth them, I will liken him unto a wise man, which built his house upon a rock; And the rain descended, and the floods came, and the winds blew, and beat upon that House; and it fell not; for it was founded upon a rock. And every one that heareth these saying of Mine, and doeth them not, shall be likened unto a foolish man, which built his House upon the sand; And the rain descended, and the floods came, and the winds blew, and beat upon that House; and it fell; and great was the fall of it. And it came to pass, when Yeshua had ended these sayings, the people were astonished at His doctrine; For He taught them as one having Authority, and not as the Scribes.*

Yeshua was clearly speaking of the House of the LORD that would be destroyed during the Second Temple period, because it was not founded upon the rock! When King David wrote the following song, He called the LORD, *"His Rock, Fortress, High Tower, Shield, Deliverer, the Horn of Salvation, Refuge, and Saviour." Remember that in the location where the Fortress of Antonia was built was "the Rock, Fortress, High Tower, the altar having the Horns for Salvation, and the Saviour, who stood upon the stone pavement, as our Deliverer and Shield!"* All the words that David used to reveal the LORD actually unveil the true location of the LORD'S House, which is the place of the Holy Temple of the LORD God! *Ironically, this is where Yeshua stood in the Fortress of Antonia and He heard the distress and cry of His people, out of the place of His original Temple! It was in this place that floods of ungodly men made them afraid and where Messiah the LORD would become the ultimate Victor.*

***II Samuel 22:1-7** And David spake unto the LORD the words of this song in the day that the LORD had delivered him out of the hand of all his enemies, and out of the hand of Saul; And he said, The LORD is my Rock, and my Fortress, and my Deliverer; The God of my Rock; in Him will I trust; He is my Shield, and the Horn of my Salvation, my High Tower, and my Refuge, my Saviour; Thou savest me from violence. I will call on the LORD, who is worthy to be praised; so shall I be saved from mine enemies. When the waves of death compassed me, the floods of ungodly men made me afraid; The sorrows of hell compassed me about; the snares of death prevented me; In my distress I called upon the LORD, and cried to my God; and He did hear my voice out of His Temple, and my cry did enter into His ears.*

The Rock and Fortress is the LORD God. He was judged on the stone pavement to become our Saviour and our Deliverer in the place of the Rock, the High Tower, and the Fortress! It is unbelievable to see this! He heard their cry and He saved them here!

As I thought again about the stone pavement that looks like Matzah, with Messiah Yeshua pictured above it carrying His cross, I realized that this truly represents *"the Rock of offense."* So Yeshua became *"the Rock of offense"* as He stood over *"the Foundation Stone"* and this *Rock Messiah the LORD* that was quarried out of Holy Mount Moriah became the Chief Cornerstone of the permanent House of God and this is the place where Yeshua was standing over the original Foundation Stone of the Garden of Eden! Remember, He is the Heavenly Foundation Stone and we are built as living stones upon this sure Foundation that the LORD laid by Himself in the rock! Thus, we are the Heavenly Spiritual Temple, made without hands. *I truly believe that Messiah Yeshua revealed the original location of the Holy Temple of the LORD that King Solomon built, just north of the Temple Mount platform. The altar of God was placed in the north according to II Kings 16:14 and the Fortress of Antonia, the place of the altar, was on the north of Mount Moriah. Then the LORD showed me that Jeremiah the Prophet was put in stocks "by the high gate of Benjamin" and this gate was located to the right of the sheep gate, but it was by the House of the LORD. So the Benjamin gate in the far north was by the Temple of King Solomon!*

***Jeremiah 20:2** Then Pashur smote Jeremiah the Prophet, and put him in stocks that were in the high gate of Benjamin, which was by the House of the LORD.*

It is written in Isaiah that the LORD of Hosts is this stone of stumbling and Rock of offense! The LORD was hiding His face from the House of Jacob!

Isaiah 8:13-18 *Sanctify the LORD of Hosts Himself; and let Him be your fear, and let Him be your dread. And He shall be for a Sanctuary; but for a stone of stumbling and for a rock of offense to both the Houses of Israel, for a gin and for a snare to the inhabitants of Jerusalem. And many among them shall stumble, and fall, and be broken, and be snared, and be taken. Bind up the Testimony, seal the Law among My disciples. And I will wait upon the LORD, that hideth His face from the House of Jacob, and I will look for Him. Behold, I and the children whom the LORD hath given Me are for signs and for wonders in Israel from the LORD of Hosts, which dwelleth in Mount Zion.*

Romans 9:33 *As it is written, Behold, I lay in Zion a stumbling stone and rock of offence; and whosoever believeth on Him shall not be ashamed.*

Psalm 31:2-3 *Bow down Thine ear to me; deliver me speedily; be Thou my strong Rock, for an House of defence to save me. For Thou art my Rock and my Fortress; therefore for Thy Name's sake lead me, and guide me.*

Psalm 144:2 *My goodness, and my High Tower, and my Deliverer; my Shield, and He in whom I trust; who subdueth my people under me.*

Proverbs 18:10 *The Name of the LORD is a strong Tower; the righteous runneth into it, and is safe.*

Having seen all of the facts that I have presented by the power of the Holy Spirit, I find it hard to believe that the original Holy Temple was located anywhere other than in this location. I feel that the LORD gave us many clues that His Temple was built with its Foundations deeply laid in the high elevated rock ridge of Mount Moriah and this rock is not under the Dome of the Rock. There is no visible living water flowing underneath the Dome of the Rock like there is north at the Sparrow Pool, the Struthian Pool. Perhaps Solomon built his Palace where the Dome of the Rock is today. It is quite obvious to me, that when Josephus mentioned *the Foundation rock that was like a precipice inside the Fortress of Antonia* that had the ornamental stones covering it, so that no one could walk either up or down upon it, reveals that this rock had to be the summit of Mount Moriah and *the Temple was built "in" the Mount not on it. It was so sacred to the LORD, that no one was allowed to touch it.* Messiah Yeshua fulfilled the Eternal Testimony of the Heavenly Ark in this place.

II Chronicles 3:1 *Then Solomon began to build the House of the LORD at Jerusalem in Mount Moriah, where the LORD appeared unto David, his father, in the place that David had prepared in the threshing floor of Araunah the Jebusite.*

Flavious Josephus also mentioned that *"Zerubbabel built the altar where it had previously been built, in the same place where King Solomon built the altar to the LORD,"* but Herod later vastly expanded the Temple Mount area into a huge platform and built the Fortress of Antonia in the far north to overshadow his new Temple.

"The Antiquities of the Jews," Book 11 Chapter 4 Section 1 by Flavious Josephus: "He then built the altar on the same place it had formerly been built, that they might offer the appointed sacrifices upon it to God, according to the Laws of Moses."

The KING OF KINGS has blessed us with these awesome works. *The stone pavement was covered over with tons of dirt and so was the original Foundation Stone.* So it was buried and *I believe that it is still buried today and has not ever been excavated because it is waiting for the right moment in time to be revealed!*

What is profoundly interesting is that *the Struthion Pool* has also not been excavated to the north, because the Convent that is located above it cut it off. The water source for the Struthion Pool under *"the stone pavement"* has not yet been determined, but if its source is found to be from Bethlehem, this would help us to know that this was the place of the altar, the Molten Brazen Sea, and the Holy Temple of King Solomon. I was astonished to discover that before this Convent cut off the access, there was a raging source of living water flowing underneath it and the Convent did not want anymore intrusions like the small inflatable boat

that went by at one point! So they cut off the access to it, and it was in this place that the oldest section of the stone pavement was unearthed way down below the dirt level. This was the *"impressed in wax"* portion of the floor that bore the symbol of the King. A boy's school is also located over it.

I took a little break from writing and then something miraculous happened! I had to come back and write some astonishing news! Incredibly, the LORD just gave me the answer to my question, about the source of the water that flowed into the Struthion Pool called *"The Sparrow Pool!"* By complete accident, I just ran across some information about the Fortress of Antonia and discovered that the source of the water that supplied refreshment for the Roman troops in the Fortress of Antonia was indeed from Bethlehem! This was historical information! It indicated that the water that was flowing into the Fortress of Antonia, in the place where the Struthion Pool is located today, originated in Bethlehem! This was my answer! I thank the LORD for showing this to me! This had to be the place where the altar of King Solomon and King David was built on the Threshing floor. Remember that the Sparrow Pool is directly underneath the floor where the altar stood. This had to be the location of the Molten Brazen Sea that held the living water from Bethlehem! In the following excerpt it tells us that *"the hill on which the Tower of Antonia stood was the Highest of three mounds."* The altar and the threshing floor of Araunah was built on the highest elevated ridge that was later known as *"Gabbatha,"* where Yeshua was threshed, in the place of the original altar that David built. In the following excerpt we can see *that an aqueduct coming from Bethlehem did supply the Fortress of Antonia with water that was stored in 37 cisterns.*

Excerpt from: "The Temples that Jerusalem Forgot"

"From the north, it was impossible for one to see the Temple because Fort Antonia obscured the view. The hill on which the Tower of Antonia stood was the highest of the three mounds (Zion, Ophel, and Fort Antonia) on the north end of the southeast ridge. During the Hasmonaean dynasty, the Tower of Baris was expanded to become Fort Antonia. It adjoined the new city Bezetha and further obscured the Temple Mount from the north of Jerusalem. An aqueduct coming from Bethlehem supplied Fort Antonia with water that was stored in 37 cisterns for the Tenth Legion and their support personnel, which numbered approximately 10,000 men." ***(Source: ©2000 March 1, by Ernest L. Martin Ph. D.).***

Then after this statement about the Fortress of Antonia, Ernest L. Martin said:

"The Roman garrison was the dominant feature of Jerusalem, a continuous reminder to the Jews of Rome's supremacy. Further, being four and one-half times greater in area than the Temple Mount, Fort Antonia was intimidating and therefore a successful tool of psychological warfare to secure Jewish conformity to Roman authority." ***(Source: ©2000 March 1, by Ernest L. Martin Ph. D.).***

This statement verifies exactly what I said earlier. The idea was to remind the Jews of the Roman supremacy over the Holy Mountain of God and they used *the Fortress* as a tool of *"psychological warfare"* against the Jewish people. Now think about this for a minute. The greatest weapon of psychological warfare against the Jewish people would have been for Rome to have built this military Fortress over the sacred Rock of the LORD, in the place where King Solomon's Temple once stood and on the threshing floor that King David purchased from Araunah and in the place where the LORD told Abraham to go offer Isaac on Mount Moriah and where Adam was created. *So the truth is now revealed that the source of the Struthion Pool was indeed from Bethlehem and the cisterns that King Solomon built were likely the 37 cisterns that the Romans drank from in the Fortress of Antonia, as we can see in the following two excerpts about Solomon's Temple.*

1. Quote: "Solomon also provided for a sufficient water supply for the Temple by creating vast cisterns, into which water was conveyed by channels from the, "pools," near Bethlehem. One of these cisterns was the, "Great Sea," a massive cast bronze pool that stood impressively at the Temple's entrance." ***(Source: © www.newworldencyclopedia.org/entry/Solomon%27s_Temple).***

2. Quote: Solomon also provided for a sufficient water supply for the Temple by hewing in the rocky hill vast cisterns, into which water was conveyed by channels from the, "pools" near Bethlehem. One of these cisterns the, "Great Sea," was capable of containing three millions of gallons. The overflow was led off by a conduit to the Kidron. ***(Historical Source: © www.christiananswers.net/dictionary/templesolomons.html).***

The two excerpts clearly indicate that *one of the cisterns* was in fact *"the Great Sea that was a massive bronze pool that stood impressively at the Temple's entrance."* So apparently, the LORD miraculously just revealed before my eyes that this was indeed the location of *"the stone pavement" where the Molten Brazen Sea once stood, because it was filled with the living water from Bethlehem.* So Solomon's cisterns were used by the Roman Soldiers to quench their thirst! Solomon had built the pools, the cisterns, and the aqueduct, so that the water from Bethlehem ran toward Jerusalem to the Holy Temple for the purpose of performing the sacred duties of the LORD at the altar and the Molten Brazen Sea. They had to be continually filled with pure living water. The only place that had enough rushing water to supply such a vast amount of water for the Molten Brazen Sea that constantly needed to be refilled was the place of the Sparrow Pool! The altar needed that constant source of water for cleansing. I am certain now that the LORD is revealing the final proof that Herod did not build the Second Temple with its foundations *in* the rock. Herod built his *military Fortress to overshadow the Second Temple* in order to intimidate. *He built the Second Temple next to the Fortress where he hid the sacred rock and the place of Solomon's Temple under the Fortress of Antonia to psychologically intimidate the Jewish people.* Without a doubt, the Romans would have taken over the Jewish Holy Place that was absolutely the most sacred site to them and built a Roman military Fortress over it. Through this diabolical deed, the Romans had total control over the LORD'S Holy Mountain and the Jewish people had to protect the little bit of the Mount that they were given and this is why they were willing to say, *"We have no King, but Caesar!"* The Jewish Messiah was, however, threshed by the Divine predetermined plan of God on the LORD'S threshing floor and the KING OF KINGS, brought the ultimate victory to Israel! It is therefore true that Yeshua was standing in the place where the altar and the Molten Brazen Sea once stood on the high elevated platform, so the Jews would know with absolute certainty that He is *"I AM HE!"* The LORD Messiah, therefore, stood on the *Bimah* platform on display, *as the Living Torah.* I could not believe that the LORD just verified everything that I said, after I had just ended this section. *There is no doubt now that the water source under the stone pavement was from Bethlehem and so this has to be the place where Solomon built the Holy Temple.* The Benjamin Gate known as *"The Sheep Gate" was facing north" by the House of the LORD"* in Jeremiah 20:2. *Incredibly, I found on a map that this gate was between the Fortress of Antonia and the Struthion Pool! The Kings of Judah entered the Holy Temple of King Solomon through this gate! Yeshua is the KING of Judah!* The Pool of Bethesda just east of it was called *"The Sheep Pool!"* Later on in Roman History, the Roman Emperor Hadrian turned the area of the Struthion Pool and the stone pavement into a market place, in the year 135AD, after the last Jewish revolt against the Romans. Yeshua was prophesying and revealing the true location of the Holy Temple of the LORD that would soon be made into a market place when He drove out the moneychangers. Yeshua said, *"Stop making My Father's House a market place."* Yeshua was driving out corruption and leaven at that time, but Yeshua's Words had a much deeper meaning. So I believe that Yeshua was likely revealing the true location of the House of God and *THE FOUNDATION STONE! It was there in the beginning in Genesis.*

John 2:15-17 *And when He had made a scourge of small cords, He drove them all out of the Temple, and the sheep, and the oxen; and poured out the changer's money, and overthrew the tables; And said unto them that sold doves, Take these things hence; make not My Father's House an House of Merchandise. And His disciples remembered that it was written, The zeal of Thine House hath eaten me up.*

During Hadrian's occupation of Jerusalem and the Temple Mount area, he completely divided the Sparrow Pool and built arches over it. Then he added a large platform that formed a market place over the top of it all, making the place of the LORD'S House a market place! As I am completing this book, the Third Temple will be built very soon! Incredibly, Zechariah 14:9-10 proclaims *"when the LORD is KING over all the earth, the land will be lifted up and inhabited starting from Benjamin's gate!"* This is the original location of the Holy Temple of God! Glory Hallelujah! This is so thrilling! Only the LORD could have revealed this now!

Lift up thine eyes now the way toward the north…
So I lifted up mine eyes the way toward the north,
and behold northward at the gate of the altar…
Then he brought me to the door of the gate of the
LORD'S house which was toward the north…
Excerpts from Ezekiel 8:4-14

Bas Relief Imagining the Holy Temple in Heavenly Jerusalem
Dedication Malloy Photo ©2013 Kimberly K Ballard

The final proof that the Sanctuary of the Holy Temple of the LORD God of Israel was in the north is found in Ezekiel 8:4-14. The altar is often associated with the north.

THE ROYAL ARMORY RESTORING THE DAVIDIC DYNASTY

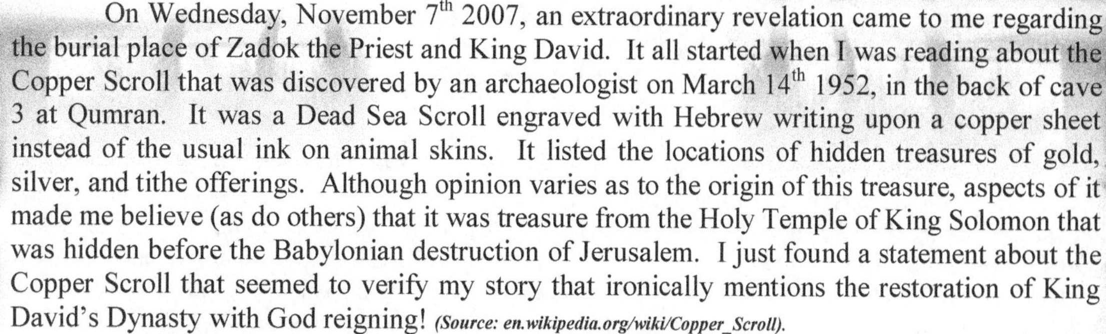

Dedication Florida Malloy Palm Trees

On Wednesday, November 7th 2007, an extraordinary revelation came to me regarding the burial place of Zadok the Priest and King David. It all started when I was reading about the Copper Scroll that was discovered by an archaeologist on March 14th 1952, in the back of cave 3 at Qumran. It was a Dead Sea Scroll engraved with Hebrew writing upon a copper sheet instead of the usual ink on animal skins. It listed the locations of hidden treasures of gold, silver, and tithe offerings. Although opinion varies as to the origin of this treasure, aspects of it made me believe (as do others) that it was treasure from the Holy Temple of King Solomon that was hidden before the Babylonian destruction of Jerusalem. I just found a statement about the Copper Scroll that seemed to verify my story that ironically mentions the restoration of King David's Dynasty with God reigning! ***(Source: en.wikipedia.org/wiki/Copper_Scroll).***

King David was buried in the city of David not on Mount Zion where his memorial tomb is today. I believe this is a deliberate diversion from the true location to hide immense treasure. Solomon was also buried in the city of David with many Kings of Judah.

I Kings 2:10 *So David slept with his fathers, and was buried in the city of David.*

I Kings 11:43 *And Solomon slept with his fathers, and was buried in the city of David his father: and Rehoboam his son reigned in his stead.*

The year 2007, when I had my Almond Tree miracle, was full of Divine revelation. I was reading about Zadok the High Priest of King David and King Solomon in my Bible at the time. In the Copper Scroll there were two treasures that actually mention Zadok. On June 4th, 2014, I sent this information to the city of David and I learned that just the night before, the city of David dedicated Solomon's anointing place at the Gihon spring where Zadok the High Priest anointed Solomon as King. So maybe the time has come to unearth this incredible blessing for Israel which in turn will bless the entire world! Here are the details of treasure's #52 and #53 from the Copper Scroll: #52 Below the Portico's Southern Corner, in the Tomb of Zadok, under the platform of the exedra, vessel's for tithe sweeping's, spoilt tithes, and inside them, figured coins." #53 In the exedra of the cliff - facing west, in front of the Garden of Zadok, under the great sealing-stone that is in its bottom; consecrated offerings. ***(Source: Copper Scroll translation, John Marco Allegro ©1960).***

To me it was obvious that these two treasures were specifically pertaining to Zadok the Priest from the time of the First Holy Temple of King Solomon in Jerusalem. The treasure was listed as being *near the tomb of Zadok in the garden of Zadok.* This puzzled me. So I said *"LORD, why would they bury important Temple treasure in a garden that is going to change over time and possibly be lost?"* Then He gave me an incredible answer that this was no ordinary garden! The Copper Scroll mentions the *exedra* in the Garden of Zadok. *After I had prayed about this garden several years went by and I was reading about the Temple and Palace of King Solomon. I printed out the information at the library so I could read it when I got home. Incredibly, near the last page when I read the description of the Armory of King*

David it said that it was an *exedra which was the same word used in the Copper Scroll about Zadok's tomb!* By definition an *exedra* is a long continuous bench that is curved where people sat for discussions. Zadok's garden was not a real garden! It was now proven to be the Armory of King David. It was ornamented with Cedar wood paneling from Lebanon, tall columns, and painted with murals inside to look like the forest of Lebanon where Solomon had obtained the Cedar wood. The Armory was like walking into a lush garden. The Armory was therefore an unmovable *"garden"* of Zadok that would always exist, where the treasure would remain buried deep in the ground, even if the upper portion of the tower was destroyed! In the Bible this Armory is called the House of the Forest of Lebanon where the Mighty men of Valour hung their shields of gold and their bucklers. It makes perfect sense to bury a mighty KING here! On June 14th 2007, I was reading the detailed information on the splendor of Solomon's palace. The following information helped me to verify that the *exedra, the portico,* was the Armory of King David. It said quote: *"He also built the House of the Forest of Lebanon; its length was one hundred cubits, its width fifty cubits, and its height thirty cubits, with four rows of cedar pillars, and cedar beams on the pillars. And it was paneled with cedar above the beams that were on forty-five pillars, fifteen to a row. There were windows with beveled frames in three rows, and window was opposite window in three tiers. And all the doorways and doorposts had rectangular frames; and window was opposite window in three tiers. He also made the Hall of Pillars: its length was fifty cubits, and its width thirty cubits; and in front of them was a portico with pillars, and a canopy was in front of them. Then he made a hall for the throne, the Hall of Judgment, where he might judge; and it was paneled with cedar from floor to ceiling. And the house where he dwelt had another court inside the hall, of like workmanship. a. The House of the Forest of Lebanon: So much magnificent cedar wood from Lebanon was used to build Solomon's palace that they called it the "House of the Forest of Lebanon." Walking in the richly paneled walls of the palace was like walking in a forest. i. The forty-five pillars set in the House of the Forest of Lebanon also gave the impression of being in a majestic forest. ii. 1 Kings 10:16-17 mentions 500 gold shields that were hung in the House of the Forest of Lebanon. Isaiah specifically called this building an Armory in Isaiah 22:8.* Now there was also a quote about Solomon's Upper Palace on page 10: *"After building the Temple, Solomon also erected a palace, a hall of justice, an Armory, and other administrative buildings on Mount Moriah. The Armory (the treasury of the Temple) was an exedra, (Hebrew, siderot, "arrangement of columns") a three-story, semi-circular building (perhaps with one long side and three shorter sides at the back rather than a truly curved back) whose roof was supported by three rows of columns, giving the appearance of its interior an effect something like that of a forest. Its rear wall continued this motif, having murals of trees. Because of this motif, the Armory was called the House of the Forest of Lebanon. It was a place for judges to meet and discuss cases."* ***(Source: www.geocities.com/theseder2/theBigE.html).***

The Chronicles of the Kings in the Bible also verify that the walls of the Royal Armory held hundreds of gold shields of the Mighty men of Valour that were later stolen from the treasures of the House of the LORD in II Chronicles 12:9-11 by Shishak king of Egypt.

II Chronicles 9:16 *And three hundred shields made he of beaten gold: three hundred shekel's of gold went into one shield. And the king put them in the house of the forest of Lebanon.*

I Kings 10:17 *And he made three hundred shields of beaten gold; three pound of gold went to one shield: and the king put them in the house of the forest of Lebanon.*

The Mighty men of Valour were famous men with superior military strength, performing mighty exploits, having courage, and extreme valour. They were the heads and chiefs of the families. A Mighty man of Valour could single-handedly take on several hundred assailants and win. They were fearless valiant knights of the Royal Sovereign King.

The Armory was built as a round tower. Military weapons and armour were hung upon the walls of the tower in neat precise rows or the weapons were arranged on the walls to form a design. This was the Royal Armory that housed the weapons of the King for his army. Now

the Armory of King David was proven to be an *exedra* just as the Copper Scroll states about Zadok's Garden. The Copper Scroll indicates that at the base of the Armory there is a great sealing stone where Zadok the Priest is buried (under the platform) with some treasures that were buried in the right pathway of its entrance. It would not surprise me if Zadok is buried in a chamber behind a rolling stone that leads to King David and his son King Solomon with the Royal treasury. When I realized that by definition the *exedra* was a curved bench (often of stone or wood) with a high back, and that it is often a semicircular *portico* with seats, and that it was used in ancient times by the High Priest for discussions, I believed that the Armory of King David was the place where Zadok the Priest held discussions of the Torah and other judicial matters before the Royal King of Judah! I had to prove it from the Bible! I asked the LORD to show me exactly why Zadok would be buried there.

As I studied Zadok carefully in the Bible, I found that he was considered to be *the most loyal of the Mighty Men of Valour of King David's men.* He stood faithfully with David after King Saul fell from God's grace. Zadok was the only one appointed to be High Priest during King Solomon's reign because Zadok alone remained faithful to Solomon. He anointed Solomon at the Gihon spring under the Divine direction of King David while the other Priest Abiathar betrayed them, and lost his position. From the Bible it was clear that the Royal Armory of King David was the place where they *hung the gold shields of the Mighty Men of Valour*. So when Zadok died, I believe *they buried the greatest of the Mighty men under the Armory of King David, at its base, under this great sealing stone, in a chamber.*

After this was revealed to me in such detail, I was then able to find the location of the Armory by carefully studying Nehemiah's wall repairs that took place after the Babylonian exile, after Solomon's Temple was destroyed. Based upon Nehemiah 3, I found where the Armory was located in the city of David. Of course the other treasures are also buried with them. Nehemiah records the workers rebuilding the walls and I had a map showing each worker on the wall that I could literally follow around each section of the wall until it reached the Royal Armory of King David. I originally wrote that I believe it is located on the Southeast side of the city of David, just before the wall angled out, that then headed to the Southeast angle of the Temple Mount. The Copper Scroll says, *"At the turning of the wall."* The Armory of King David is, therefore, located at the turning of the wall! I was trying to see if Nehemiah's wall repairs went around the city of David in a certain order around the walls, and this would eventually tell me the exact location of the Royal Armory. It turned out to be exactly where I thought it was located. Nehemiah's men repaired gates and walls starting in the north and then the repairs went west. From there the repairs went down to the southern end of the city of David. From there they went back up the eastern side and right before the wall angled out or turned, was the Armory of David. In this passage in Nehemiah 3:15-19 I saw Hashabiah (the "s" is written with an "f"), and it tells where the sepulchre of the Kings was located and the Fountain gate. Next to Hashabiah on the map it says *Ezer was at the turning part of the wall.* Actually there were one or two other people at this portion of the wall repairing it. However, it clearly states that this portion that *Ezer repaired was at the ascent to the Armory at the turning of the wall at the buttress, which is a higher part of the wall that is used to stabilize it.* Nehemiah's account verifies a 1650 map that I found. Based upon the location of the Siloam/Shiloach Pool and the Fountain gate beside it, and then going up to the Gihon Spring, one can figure out the location. The base of the Armory platform was a round sealing stone in the floor. Since the Southeast angle of the Temple Mount is buried at eighty feet as verified by Sir Charles Warren, I believe the Armory is still buried in its location at least this deep. Whatever the case may be, in the Armory of the Mighty Men, something exists today that is stunning! Now as you go south from the Fountain gate you follow it around and then travel up the eastern side. Nehemiah repaired on the left side and I followed this down to the left corner. *Since the Armory was at the turning of the wall* at the buttress, you can tell where the wall

changes and looks different. This change proves that this point of the wall is the buttress that stabilized the rest of the wall. There were stairs with an ascent leading up to the Armory. It looks like the Fullers field was below the Armory, and the Gihon spring was on its left, as well as the upper conduit. Since a huge portion of the Armory is still buried, KING DAVID and his High Priest Zadok with the Royal treasury are still there! As I followed around the Pool of Shiloach on the map, I went up the eastern wall repairs until I got to the Armory's former location. The true location of King David's tomb became obvious! King David is buried in the city of David between where the stairs descended the city, and the artificial pool known as *"The pool that was made,"* at that section of the wall of Nehemiah's wall repairs. So I believe King David is buried near the Armory or under the Armory in a chamber, which is under the *"The House of the Mighty Men!"* Now if you compare the House of Mighty men to the Song of Solomon chapter 4 in the Bible, you find these words:

Song of Solomon 4:4 *Thy neck is like the tower of David builded for an armoury, whereon there hang a thousand bucklers, all shields of mighty men.*

It makes sense that Zadok the greatest of the Mighty Men of Valour (besides King David) would have been honored with his burial at the base of the Royal Armory of the House of the Mighty Men, where He always sat to discuss judicial cases with the Law of God. So it was named *"Zadok's Garden"* which is the House of the Forest of Lebanon where he spent his entire life!

On September 13th, 2007, I found an extremely rare photo at the library in a book that was taken in 1880 when the Southeast angle of the Temple Mount was virtually untouched. In the photo I could see the remains of a large circular stone structure that could definitely have been the remains of the Armory above ground. One photo is copyrighted by Martin Gilbert 1985 from his book *"Jerusalem, Rebirth of a City."* It appears to have a pathway (ascent) leading up to its entrance. Although the Armory is in the *southeast side* of the city of David, there is a side of its entrance that faced west. I believe that Zadok is probably buried *just before the wall angled out toward* the Southeast corner of the portico of Solomon at the Armory. There are three pictures that I found. In the first photo I observed two ascents up to this stone structure. You could follow the tree line from the Kidron valley up the hill to the city of David. In another photo that was taken farther away you could see the pathway or ascent up to the Armory from tip of the city of David which ascends from the south (by the Pool of Shiloach) going directly up toward the Temple Mount. There was clearly a well worn pathway that led up to it from both directions. One of the photos I found was from a book called *"Jerusalem Revealed - Archaeology in the Holy City" 1968-1974 Copyright by the Israel Exploration Society.* It showed an excavated aerial view of the southern end of the Temple Mount where the *Priests quarters* were on the southern end of the Temple Mount which I think Nehemiah repaired directly *from the point of the Armory* and then he headed back towards the Jutting Tower near the Southeast corner.

In Antiquities of the Jews Book seven, chapter fifteen, section three, Josephus says that King David was buried with great riches. I believe this Royal treasury may be revealed by the LORD just before KING Messiah Yeshua returns to the earth to usher in the Eternal Davidic Dynasty. Yeshua is the everlasting KING of Judah! I remembered that I had put as the subtitle of my book: *"The Davidic Dynasty returns!" In Antiquities of the Jews Book 16, chapter seven, section one, a strange fire burned Herod's men who tried to steal this treasure, and Herod placed a white stone monument at the entrance to David's sepulchre to remember the fright of this terrifying event. The LORD will only allow whoever He chooses to open it.*

This treasure will be revealed at the end of the age. I believe that the Royal Armory of King David will yield great blessing with its treasury for Israel and the entire world!

THE ALMOND HARVEST SHAKING THE TREES

The Almond Tree Photo taken February 16th 2007 by LV on Holy Mount Moriah Jerusalem Israel

The Almond Tree is not only connected to the LORD'S Testimony, it is also a sign of the end times. When the Messiah comes in the future at the end of the age, He will gather His elect during what is called *"The Harvest."* In the days of the Prophet Jeremiah, *the Almond Rod appeared before him and it was to be a sign to the people for "watchfulness" from the LORD, because the LORD'S prophecy regarding Jerusalem was about to be fulfilled.* The LORD told Jeremiah that He was *"Watching over His Word to perform it."* The LORD, of course, knew all the future events that were about to take place in Jerusalem before they happened. These events did come to pass exactly as they were prophesied by His Word according to His time table. I was so excited to see that Yeshua specifically used the word for *"Almond" which is "Shaked,"* in regards to His return at the end of the age, when He said to stay *"awake and watch!"*

When Jeremiah saw the Rod of an Almond Tree, the destruction of Jerusalem was nigh at hand and *it served as a final warning from the LORD. In 2007, I saw the Rod of an Almond Tree, as the LORD manifested Himself to me in this fantastic revelation and in 2013 He actually miraculously gave me the rod of an Almond Tree!* Instantly, I made the connection to Jeremiah and I discerned that the LORD was also miraculously allowing me to see *"the Rod of an Almond Tree"* just before the final destruction at the end of the age. The LORD is once again *"Watching over His Word to perform it,"* just as He did with Jeremiah. This is a final warning to everyone on the earth to repent before the LORD Yeshua for your sins and to believe in Him and to be baptized in the living water, in the Name of the Father, Son, and Holy Spirit, so that you are sealed by the Holy Spirit for Eternal life. You want to live forever right?

When Yeshua spoke about the harvest at the end of the age, He gave signs of His return within the details of the Almond Tree Harvest. The ancient method of harvesting almonds was by beating the branches by hand with *a rod* and the almonds fell onto a tarp that was stretched out beneath the trees. The almonds were then raked and gathered into bushel baskets and the fruit was separated from the hulls. The very efficient modern method of almond harvesting is accomplished by a machine. A few Almond harvesting facts that I found can be summed up in the following explanation.

"The harvesting machine is outfitted with a mechanical arm. When the arm is extended, it clamps around the entire tree trunk and holds onto it very tightly with a firm grip. Then the harvesting machine shakes the tree with such force that the almonds quickly fly off the tree and fall to the ground, where they are left to dry in the sun for a few days. The harvesting machine can also sweep the almonds and they are gathered up together and stored inside a container. Any debris that falls to the ground with the almonds in the shaking process is sorted and separated from the almonds at this stage in the harvesting process. The final step involves

the separation of the meat of the almond from the outer hull, which is discarded. The good fruit of the almonds are kept and stored, but the hulls are thrown away."
(Source: Almond Harvesting Facts; ©2010 Almond harvesting video Bella Viva Orchards, Hughson CA All Rights Reserved).

As you can see, this method of harvesting the almond trees is quite parallel to Yeshua's Words, regarding the harvest at end of the age. The harvest that is to come is the harvest of righteous believers called the *"good fruit"* that is separated from the wicked called *"the chaff" or the "hulls!"*

One of the first things the LORD showed me in this astonishing parallel is the fact that the Rod of the Almond Tree, *Yeshua, is the arm and hand of God that will shake the universe at the end of the age when the final harvest comes.* He told us that the stars will fall from the sky. The Heavens and earth will be shaken and all the good fruit will be gathered up together in a type of container called *"His barn."* He said that His winnowing fork is in His hand and with it He will separate the good seed from the chaff, which is thrown away and burned in the fire. The details of the almond harvest indicate that after the shaking happens, the good fruit is swept up and put into God's container. The barn is actually His Heavenly Temple. This is when the LORD will gather His elect from the four winds and the righteous will be separated from the unrighteous, like the good almonds are separated from the hulls. When the almonds are growing and developing on the almond branches, the fruit grows together with the hulls until the time of the harvest and then they are separated from one another. *The hulls surround the good fruit.* With this in mind, we should now look at a few prophetic Scriptures that are associated with *"the shaking" at* the end of the age!

Isaiah 13:13 *Therefore I will shake the Heavens, and the earth shall remove out of her place, in the wrath of the LORD of Hosts, and in the day of His fierce anger.*

Isaiah 2:17-19 *And the loftiness of man shall be bowed down, and the haughtiness of men shall be made low; and the LORD alone shall be exalted in that day. And the idols He shall utterly abolish. And they shall go into the holes of the rocks, and into the caves of the earth, for fear of the LORD and for the glory of His Majesty, when He ariseth to shake terribly the earth.*

Matthew 24:29-33 *Immediately after the tribulation of those days shall the sun be darkened, and the moon shall not give her light, and the stars shall fall from Heaven, and the powers of the Heavens shall be shaken; And then shall appear the sign of the Son of man in Heaven; and then shall all the tribes of the earth mourn, and they shall see the Son of man coming in the clouds of Heaven with power and great glory. And He shall send His angels with a great sound of a trumpet, and they shall gather together His elect from the four winds, from one end of Heaven to the other. Now learn the parable of the fig tree; When his branch is yet tender, and putteth forth leaves, ye know that summer is nigh; So likewise ye, when ye shall see all these things, know that it is near, even at the doors.*

It is apparent from these Scriptures that *the great shaking of the earth and the Heavens happens first, just before the harvest* of God's elect, which is Israel. The LORD'S elect will be gathered together by the Angels at *"The Great Trumpet"* and put inside the LORD'S container *after the shaking.* So the good almonds are kept and swept up and the twigs and all the debris that falls in the shaking process, representing unbelievers, will be tossed and thrown into the fire because they are worshipping false gods and idols that originated in Babylon. The LORD has given us the choice for Eternal life now, or we can reject it and perish. We have the choice to either bear good fruit through the LORD or to bear bad fruit upon the earth. We do not produce the good fruit ourselves, it is produced as we are baptized in the Messiah and receive God's life-giving Holy Spirit. Through the LORD'S righteousness in us, then, He produces the good almonds from His Branch. Since by faith, we have kept His Commandments and statutes and have loved Him, we are considered His good almonds. By bearing good fruit for the LORD, we have stored up treasures in Heaven. We are saved through His grace by faith, by believing in Him. The good fruit is really to share with others His Living Testimony of Eternal

salvation and to live by the light of His Word, which is the Living Torah. When His light is in us, it shines out of us and His reflective light then spreads a glow of life into all the nations. This is how the world can see the glorious works and the Divine Living Testimony of the Almond Tree of life.

Now the pattern of the shaking of the Almond Trees at harvest time is evident a second time in a parallel passage in the Gospel of Mark, where Messiah Yeshua spoke about the events that were to come at the end of the age. When Yeshua spoke about *"watching"* He was saying the word for *"Shaked" or "Almond."*

Mark 13:24-37 *But in those days after that tribulation, the sun shall be darkened, and the moon shall not give her light, And the stars of Heaven shall fall, and the powers that are in Heaven shall be shaken. And then shall they see the Son of man coming in the clouds with great power and glory. And then shall He send His angels, and shall gather together His elect from the four winds, from the uttermost part of the earth to the uttermost part of Heaven. Now learn a parable of the fig tree; When her branch is yet tender, and putteth forth leaves, ye know that summer is near; So ye in like manner, when ye shall see these things come to pass, know that it is nigh, even at the doors. Verily I say unto you, that this generation shall not pass, till all these things be done. Heaven and earth shall pass away; but My Words shall not pass away. But of that day and that hour knoweth no man, no, not the angels which are in Heaven, neither the Son, but the Father. Take heed, watch and pray; for ye know not when the time is. For the Son of man is as a man taking a far journey, who left His House, and gave authority to His servants, and to every man his work, and commanded the porter to watch. Watch ye therefore; for ye know not when the Master of the house cometh, at even, or at midnight, or at the cockcrowing, or in the morning; Lest coming suddenly He find you sleeping. And what I say unto you I say unto all, Watch.*

Four times Yeshua revealed in this Scripture that He is the Almond Rod and the Word of God, the Almond Tree of Life, as He told us to *"watch"* for His return. *So the Rod of an Almond Tree has now manifested itself before the judgment comes, just exactly as it did with Jeremiah, as now His Gospel has gone to the four corners of the earth.* The Messiah was telling us again in this Scripture that *He is the arm and Rod of God that will shake the Heavens and the earth at the harvest.* Yeshua was also telling His disciples that He left the Holy Temple in Jerusalem, which is His House, and He ascended up into the Heavenly Kingdom of God until the time that He returns in the final redemption of Israel at the time of the harvest. We are to be *watchful* for His return and not to be taken by surprise. The wrath of God is poured out on the earth upon those that do not listen to His voice but take pleasure in unrighteousness. Because we are following behind the Heavenly Ark that saves us, Yeshua takes us instantly to our Heavenly destination as our Deliverer. Everyone that loves the Messiah and truly knows Him as the LORD God of Israel will not go through the shaking!

Almond in a bowl Photo ©2013 Kimberly K Ballard All Rights Reserved

Psalm 55:22 *Cast thy burden upon the LORD, and He shall sustain thee; He shall never suffer the righteous to be shaken.*

Notice in the next passage that the Fig Tree will cast off her untimely Figs when the shaking happens. This is the removal of the curse and after this happens the Fig Tree will no longer bear the curse of Eden at the arrival of Messiah Yeshua. Then the Fig Tree will bud with new life and everyone will sit under the vine and under the Fig Tree, as it was in the beginning before the curse in the LORD'S Garden in the New Heavenly Jerusalem.

Revelation 6:12-17 *And I beheld when he had opened the sixth seal, and, lo, there was a great earthquake; and the sun became black as sackcloth of hair, and the moon became as blood; And the stars of Heaven fell unto the earth, even as a fig tree casteth her untimely figs, when she is shaken of a mighty wind. And the Heaven departed as a scroll when it is rolled together; and every mountain and island were moved out of their places. And the Kings of the earth, and the great men, and the rich men, and the chief captains, and the mighty men, and every bondman, and every free man, hid themselves in the dens and in the rocks of the mountains; And said to the mountains and rocks, fall on us, and hide us from the face of Him that sitteth on the throne, and from the wrath of the Lamb; For the great day of His wrath is come; and who shall be able to stand?*

As the LORD sits on the throne of His Ark between the two Living Cherubim Angels in Heaven, the Ark is full of the LORD'S final Testimony as Messiah, the Almond Rod that budded, the Bread from Heaven, and the Rock inscribed with the Word of God. We see that the LORD will shake the earth once more in the book of Hebrews and that *His everlasting Kingdom cannot be shaken. Those who enter His glory cloud in the rapture will not be shaken.*

Hebrews 12:25-29 *See that ye refuse not Him that speaketh. For if they escaped not who refused Him that spake on earth, much more shall not we escape, if we turn away from Him that speaketh from Heaven; Whose voice then shook the earth; but now He hath promised, saying, yet once more I shake not the earth only, but also Heaven. And this Word, Yet once more, signifieth the removing of those things that are shaken, as of things that are made, that those things which cannot be shaken may remain. Wherefore we receiving a Kingdom which cannot be moved, let us have grace, whereby we may serve God acceptably with reverence and godly fear; For our God is a consuming fire.*

The *voice* of the LORD *shakes* the Heavens and the earth, since *the Living Torah* comes out of His mouth! If Zion is the city of God and it is the *Jerusalem of Heaven,* then it is interesting that Joel wrote *"the LORD shall roar out of Zion,"* meaning out of Heaven. The LORD Messiah, *the Lion of Judah,* will come from Heaven to *shake* things up but He will be the hope and strength of His people. The new moon of Rosh HaShanah is *"the sickle moon!"*

Joel 3:13-16 *Put ye in the sickle, for the harvest is ripe; come, get you down; for the press is full, the fats overflow; for their wickedness is great. Multitudes, multitudes in the valley of decision; for the day of the LORD is near in the valley of decision. The sun and the moon shall be darkened, and the stars shall withdraw their shining. The LORD also shall roar out of Zion, and utter His voice from Jerusalem; and the Heavens and the earth shall shake; but the LORD will be the hope of His people, and the strength of the children of Israel.*

Almond Hull Photo ©2013 Kimberly K Ballard All Rights Reserved

The good fruit is close to the Tree of Life, *the LORD.* He will gather and keep us. The Living Almond Tree Menorah stands firm as an Eternal Covenant, so nothing shakes Him! In the *Day of God's* wrath the hulls are swept up, discarded, and removed far away from the Almond Tree of life.

Yeshua also spoke *a parable* about the final harvest at the end of the age. The laborers that the Messiah is referring to in the parable are those that take His Living Torah Testimony to the world to reveal His Eternal Majestic glory.

Matthew 9:37-38 *Then saith He unto His disciples, The harvest truly is plenteous, but the labourers are few; Pray ye therefore the LORD of the harvest that He will send forth labourers into His harvest.*

John 3:36 *He that believeth on the Son hath everlasting life; and he that believeth not the Son shall not see life; but the wrath of God abideth on him.*

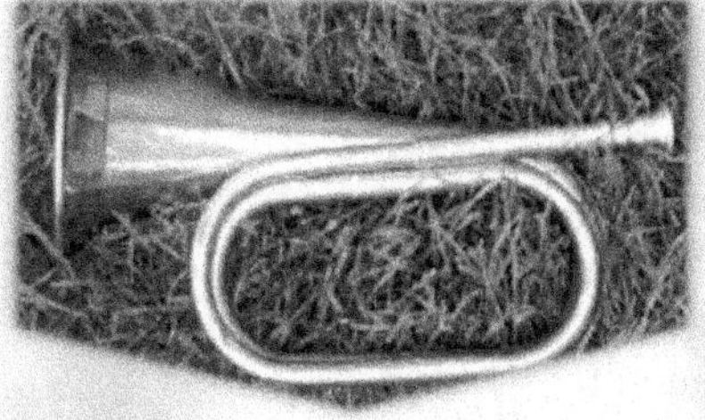
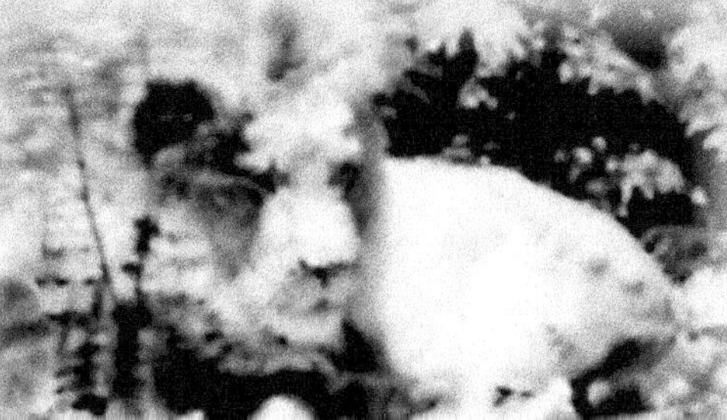
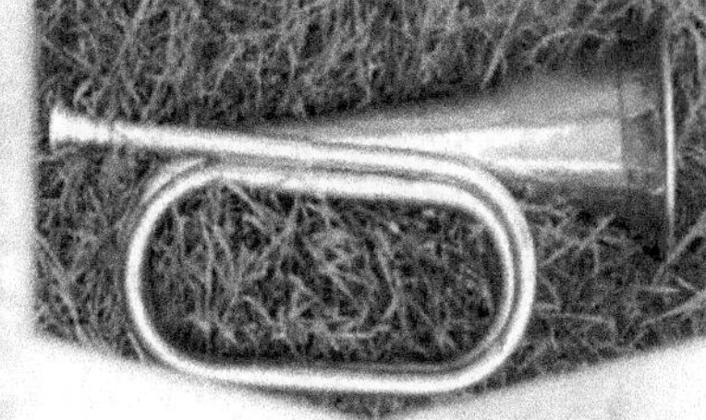

THE HARVEST ON YOM KIPPUR THE LAST DAY

Lion of Judah & Bugle, snow & harvest of corn

In the Scriptures, we find evidence that indicates when *the final harvest* will occur and I believe that this is *a different event* than *the rapture,* which occurs on Rosh HaShanah at the Last Trump. The Day of Atonement which is Yom Kippur is considered to be the Holiest day of the Biblical year. This is the time that comes after the Last Trump of Rosh HaShanah. Between Rosh HaShanah and Yom Kippur, you have the ten days of awe. This is a sober time of reflection to get right with God through repentance, so that by Yom Kippur, you are sealed in the Book of Life and you are ready to stand before the LORD God. It is a time of casting your sins into the body of living rushing water. Yom Kippur is known as *"The Great Day."* This phrase is shortened to *"The Day,"* and this is extremely significant! When we look at the Scriptures about the harvest and the shaking of the earth, we can clearly see that this day is referred to as *"The Great Day of the LORD'S wrath,"* and it is called *"the Day of the LORD." These two phrases are terms that apply only to Yom Kippur.* During Yom Kippur, the so called *"Great Trumpet"* is blown. In Matthew 24 that we just looked at, Yeshua spoke of *the Great sound of the trumpet coming after the tribulation, when the angels come to gather His elect.* In this Scripture, Yeshua spoke of the separation that will occur *when one is taken and the other is left, at the harvest.* At the end of the fast of Yom Kippur, one long blast of the shofar is blown. This happens after we have already asked the LORD to remember us for life and to be inscribed and sealed in the LORD'S Book of life.

Yom Kippur is a day of fasting and a day of repentance, before your name is sealed in the Book of life, either for good or for bad. Joel also referred to this harvest as *"The Day of the LORD,"* after the earth and the Heavens are shaken.

What I find fascinating is that the only sign that Yeshua gave to Israel that He is their Messiah is the sign of Jonah. I now believe this sign is connected to Yom Kippur because it is during Yom Kippur during the afternoon service that the entire book of Jonah is read by every Synagogue in the world. (I told you in a previous chapter that I was going to come back to this topic since it also applies to Yom Kippur!) Therefore, I believe that *Yeshua was actually giving Israel a sign,* revealing exactly when He will return as their victorious Majestic KING in the future harvest, at the end of the tribulation after the time of Jacob's trouble. When the Holy Spirit revealed this to me, I knew that the sign of Jonah dealt with more than just the three days and three nights that Yeshua spent in the tomb. *It also reveals that the Messiah will descend from Heaven to bring His Heavenly Temple to earth in Jerusalem during the Holiest day of the year and soon after this happens, we will celebrate the Feast of Tabernacles with Him. This is*

how the Feasts of the LORD actually do go in order. Yeshua was definitely giving Israel a sign to show them exactly when He will come at the harvest to gather His elect in the future, at the end of the age! *The LORD will come to remove everything that offends Him.* So hence, one is taken out and the other, the good, is left.

In the story of Jonah, the LORD had mercy upon the Gentiles, who also found favor with God because they repented for their sins and humbled their hearts before the LORD. This mercy demonstrated that the LORD is extremely gracious to anyone that comes to Him in true repentance, believing that His Word is true.

Now after the LORD revealed this to me about Yom Kippur and the sign of Jonah, I saw something else that has great significance. I believe that it is highly likely that John the Baptist came baptizing in the Jordan River before and during the High Holy Days that are meant to prepare the hearts of the people before Rosh HaShanah and before Yom Kippur to meet the LORD God. Remember that John came to prepare the way before the face of the LORD, telling the people of Israel to repent and to be baptized in the living water of the Jordan River. John was spiritually washing sins away in the living water, in the place where the Ark stood with Joshua and the Priests, to prepare the people to meet the true Living Ark of Heaven. I believe John was preaching this throughout the entire month leading up to Rosh HaShanah. He was preaching repentance, proclaiming that the Kingdom of Heaven was at hand. *Suddenly the Messiah came to the Jordan River to stand in this place and I believe that Yeshua was probably baptized on Rosh HaShanah because Heaven was opened and this is when the Holy Spirit descended in the form of a dove and rested on the Yad of God, on the Ark of the LORD'S Living Testimony.* Immediately after this event, Yeshua was led by the Holy Spirit to the wilderness. While He was in the wilderness, He did not need to eat bread, meat, or water because He is *the Living Torah* and His disciples learned this later. The LORD was *"tempted"* in all points as we are, yet without sin (Hebrews 4:5). Rabbi Simcha Pearlmutter stated something similar in his testimony, remember, when he said that Yeshua has been suffering with the Jewish people throughout history, including every death during the holocaust.

John 4:31-34 *In the meanwhile His disciples prayed Him, saying Master, eat. But He said unto them, I have meat to eat that ye know not of. Therefore said the disciples one to another, Hath any man brought Him ought to eat? Yeshua saith unto them, My meat is to do the will of Him that sent Me, and to finish His work.*

When Yeshua was tempted in the wilderness by Satan, the temptations actually revealed that Yeshua was the LORD God of Israel, the KING, the Chief Cornerstone of the Heavenly Temple and the Living Torah. **In Temptation 1.** Satan said to Yeshua, *"If Thou be the Son of God, command that these stones be made bread."* Then Yeshua replied, *"It is written, man shall not live by bread alone, but by every Word that proceedeth out of the mouth of God."* Yeshua revealed that He is the true Living Bread, the Living Torah which is the Word of God that comes out of His mouth. Yeshua is the Staff and Bread of Life and He is the Rock containing the Word of God. **In Temptation 2**. Satan took Yeshua up into the Holy city and set Him on the pinnacle of the Holy Temple in Jerusalem. Satan said to Yeshua, *"If Thou be the Son of God, cast Thyself down; for it is written, He shall give His angels charge concerning Thee; and in their hands they shall bear Thee up, lest at anytime Thou dash Thy foot against a stone."* Then Yeshua replied, *"It is written again, thou shalt not tempt the LORD thy God."* Yeshua was set on the pinnacle of the earthly Temple in Jerusalem on the corner of the Southeast angle *"above the Chief Cornerstone."* Here Yeshua reveals that *He is the Chief Cornerstone of the Heavenly Temple that will rest forever in this place.* Satan can never usurp the LORD'S throne or cast Him from it. Yeshua reveals that He is the LORD God of Israel and the Yad of God who bears us up. **In Temptation 3.** Satan takes Yeshua to an exceeding High Mountain, and shows Him all the kingdoms of the world, and the glory of them. He said to

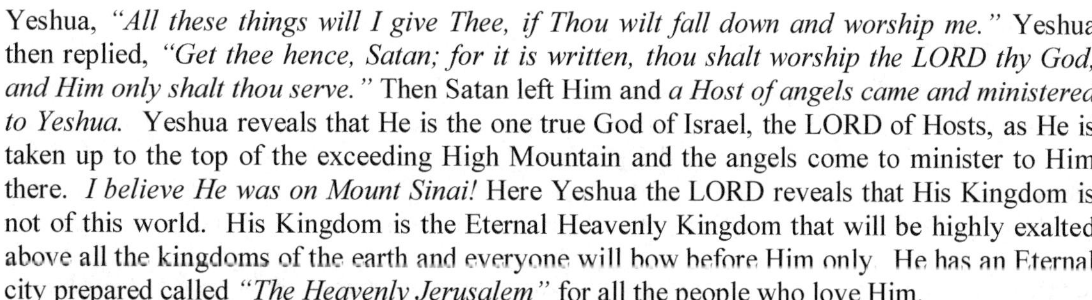
Yeshua, *"All these things will I give Thee, if Thou wilt fall down and worship me."* Yeshua then replied, *"Get thee hence, Satan; for it is written, thou shalt worship the LORD thy God, and Him only shalt thou serve."* Then Satan left Him and *a Host of angels came and ministered to Yeshua.* Yeshua reveals that He is the one true God of Israel, the LORD of Hosts, as He is taken up to the top of the exceeding High Mountain and the angels come to minister to Him there. *I believe He was on Mount Sinai!* Here Yeshua the LORD reveals that His Kingdom is not of this world. His Kingdom is the Eternal Heavenly Kingdom that will be highly exalted above all the kingdoms of the earth and everyone will bow before Him only. He has an Eternal city prepared called *"The Heavenly Jerusalem"* for all the people who love Him.

In the John 4:34 Scripture, Yeshua was speaking as the Living Torah, the Rod of the Almond Tree, when He stated that *His meat was to do the will of the one who sent Him,* and then Yeshua said, *"Look on the fields; for they are white already to harvest."* This statement is a clear indication that *Yom Kippur* is the time of the harvest *when the righteous are wearing white garments because they have clothed themselves like pure virgins to be the Bride of Messiah.* Now there are approximately *"four months"* between Shavuot/Pentecost and Yom Kippur and Messiah Yeshua mentions *four months until the harvest!*

John 4:34-36 *Yeshua saith unto them, My meat is to do the will of Him that sent Me, and to finish His work. Say not ye, There are yet four months, and then cometh the harvest? Behold, I say unto you, Lift up your eyes, and look on the fields; for they are white already to harvest. And he that reapeth receiveth wages, and gathereth fruit unto life eternal; that both he that soweth and he that reapeth may rejoice together.*

During Yom Kippur, white linen garments are worn as a sign of purity. The virgins would wear white and dance in the fields in Israel on Yom Kippur and look for a mate! So Yeshua, the Bridegroom of Israel, revealed in His parable of the ten virgins that they are to be ready for the marriage supper of the Lamb. There was a hidden meaning in the parable of the ten virgins. The five wise virgins made their garments white for the wedding day and they were prepared ahead of time. This parable uses the numbers five and five, which equals ten. There are *ten days of awe and repentance* between Rosh HaShanah and Yom Kippur. Within the ten days of awe, a person is to repent. They are to get right with the LORD and pray to be sealed in the Book of life. By the time Yom Kippur comes, their fate is sealed and they are either inscribed in the Book of life or not inscribed in the Book of life. So again, the five virgins that were wise had their names inscribed in the Book of life, but the five virgins that were not wise did not have their names inscribed in the Book of life at the time of the LORD'S return. Messiah Yeshua was telling Israel that this is the time for them to repent and get ready for His return to the earth in the final redemption.

The door of Heaven is opened from Rosh HaShanah until *"The Great Trumpet"* is blown on *Yom Kippur* and then their fate is sealed. Then the door of Heaven is shut. Remember that the foolish virgins who were not ready did not go in through the door because the door was shut! They were left outside the door, begging the LORD to let them in. They went through the great tribulation for ten days because they were not ready. This is really fascinating because Yeshua said in the book of Revelation, *"You shall have tribulation ten days."*

Revelation 2:10 *Fear none of those things which thou shalt suffer; behold, the devil shall cast some of you into prison, that ye may be tried; and ye shall have tribulation ten days; be thou faithful unto death, and I will give thee a crown of life.*

I believe that Yeshua will come at the Last Trump on Rosh HaShanah, on Tishrei 1, for His first Bride Leah, represented by the Gentile Church Bride. Then the ten days of tribulation will occur where Yeshua will work 7 years to obtain His beloved Rachel,

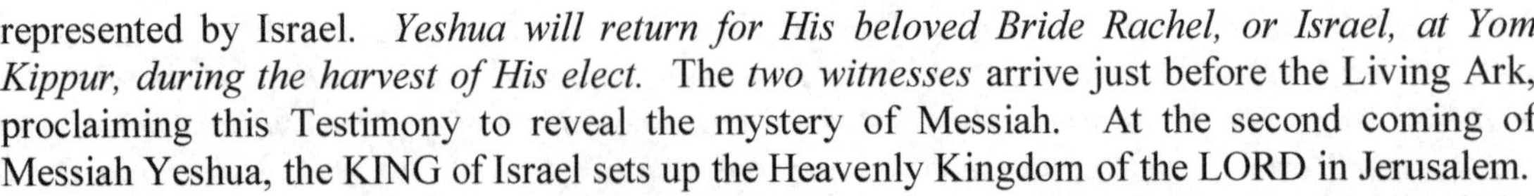

represented by Israel. *Yeshua will return for His beloved Bride Rachel, or Israel, at Yom Kippur, during the harvest of His elect.* The *two witnesses* arrive just before the Living Ark, proclaiming this Testimony to reveal the mystery of Messiah. At the second coming of Messiah Yeshua, the KING of Israel sets up the Heavenly Kingdom of the LORD in Jerusalem.

Messiah Yeshua also told the parable of the tares of the field. He explained the harvest at the end of the age and gave the details regarding the separation of the hulls and the good fruit in the harvesting of God's people. The tares worship a false god and they murder.

Matthew 13:37-43 *He answered and said unto them, He that soweth the good seed is the Son of man; The field is the world; the good seed are the children of the Kingdom; but the tares are the children of the wicked one; The enemy that sowed them is the devil; the harvest is the end of the world; and the reapers are the angels. As therefore the tares are gathered and burned in the fire; so shall it be in the end of this world. The Son of man shall send forth His angels, and they shall gather out of His Kingdom all things that offend, and them which do iniquity; And shall cast them into a furnace of fire; there shall be wailing and gnashing of teeth. Then shall the righteous shine forth as the sun in the Kingdom of their Father. Who hath ears to hear, let him hear.*

If the rapture in the cloud occurs on Rosh HaShanah at the Last Trump, the judgment would immediately fall on those left on the earth because Rosh HaShanah is also referred to as *"The Day of Judgment." On this day, the LORD will choose those who merit entrance into His Kingdom and the rest will not merit entering His gates.*

The Sickle Moon of Rosh HaShanah 2014
Photo ©2014 Sept 26th Kimberly K Ballard
All Rights Reserved

In the following verses, notice that the LORD is talking about the Saints who keep His Commandments and the faith of Messiah Yeshua and He is speaking of the dead who are blessed that have died in the LORD. Then He speaks of them entering His rest. Immediately after this we see the LORD on the cloud and *then* His wrath is poured out. Again we find the *"sickle moon"* which is the sliver of the new moon!

Revelation 14:12-20 *Here is the patience of the Saints; here are they that keep the Commandments of God, and the faith of Yeshua. And I heard a voice from Heaven saying unto me, Write, Blessed are the dead which die in the LORD from henceforth; Yea, saith the Spirit, that they may rest from their labours; and their works do follow them. And I looked, and behold a white cloud, and upon the cloud one sat like unto the Son of man, having on His head a golden crown, and in His hand a sharp sickle. And another angel came out of the Temple, crying with a loud voice to Him that sat on the cloud, Thrust in thy sickle, and reap; for the harvest of the earth is ripe. And He that sat on the cloud thrust in His sickle on the earth; and the earth was reaped. And another angel came out of the Temple which is in Heaven, he also having a sharp sickle. And another angel came out from the altar, which had power over fire; and cried with a loud cry to him that had the sharp sickle, and gather the clusters of the vine of the earth; for her grapes are fully ripe. And the angel thrust in his sickle into the earth, and gathered the vine of the earth, and cast it into the great winepress of the wrath of God. And the winepress was trodden without the city, and blood came out of the winepress, even unto the horse bridles, by the space of a thousand and six hundred furlongs.*

Proverbs 8:32-36 *Now therefore hearken unto Me, O ye children; for blessed are they that keep My ways. Hear instruction, and be wise, and refuse it not. Blessed is the man that heareth Me, watching daily at My gates, waiting at the posts of My doors. For whoso findeth Me findeth life, and shall obtain favour of the LORD. But he that sinneth against Me wrongeth his own soul; all they that hate Me love death.*

Yom Kippur is actually *"The last day"* to appeal to God and it is your last chance to change the judgment. It is *"The last day"* to repent before God, before your judgment is sealed. Ironically, on several occasions, Messiah Yeshua did mention what He would do on *"The last day!"*

John 12:48 *He that rejecteth Me, and receiveth not My Words, hath one that judgeth him; the Word that I have spoken, the same shall judge him in the last day.*

John 6:44 *No man can come to Me except the Father which hath sent me draw him; and I will raise him up at the last day.*

John 6:37-40 *All that the Father giveth Me shall come to Me; and him that cometh to Me I will in no wise cast out. For I came down from Heaven, not to do Mine own will, but the will of Him that sent Me. And this is the Father's will which hath sent Me, that of all which He hath given Me I should lose nothing, but should raise it up again at the last day. And this is the will of Him that sent Me, that every one which seeth the Son, and believeth on Him, may have everlasting life; and I will raise him up at the last day.*

Yeshua also told Martha that her brother would rise again and Martha said that she knew that her Jewish brother would rise again in the resurrection *"at the last day."*

John 11:23-26 *Yeshua saith unto her, Thy brother shall rise again. Martha saith unto Him, I know that he shall rise again in the resurrection at the last day. Yeshua said unto her, I AM the resurrection, and the life; he that believeth in Me, though he were dead, yet shall he live; And whosoever liveth and believeth in Me shall never die. Believest thou this?*

At the conclusion of Yom Kippur, there is a service called *"The Ne'ilah,"* and it refers *"To the closing of the gates." The Ark of the Torah scroll is kept open during this service. This is your last chance to repent, before the gate closes, to get right with the LORD.* Some of the prayers that are said during this service include the words, *"At the time of the closing of the Heavenly gates, forgive our iniquities."* Another one says, *"Open for us the gate, at the time of the closing of the gates."* This reminds me of the LORD shutting the door behind the wise virgins after they went into Heaven because they were ready. After they entered Heaven, the wrath was poured out upon everyone else. *The people that did not enter through the gate before it was closed were unprepared.*

Now Yeshua revealed that the great harvest would come at the end of the age, when He appeared alive after His resurrection and He told His Jewish disciples to cast their net on the right side of the ship. The disciples were in the ship all night fishing and in the morning, behold, Yeshua was standing on the shore. He called out to them and asked them if they had any *"meat,"* but the thing that is interesting is that He called them *"children."* In the wilderness, *when the LORD provided the meat, He called Israel "children!"* So in this miracle, the Word of God, the true meat, that fed the children of Israel in the wilderness, was standing on the shore, asking the children of Israel if they had any meat! Now this is interesting, first of all, because in the book of Numbers, the children of Israel were crying out to the LORD for meat. Moses made the statement, *"Shall all the fish of the sea be gathered together for them, to suffice them?"* Then the LORD said to Moses, *"Is the LORD'S hand waxed short? Thou shalt see now whether My Word shall come to pass."*

Fish in Monterey
Photo ©2014 Kimberly K Ballard
All Rights Reserved

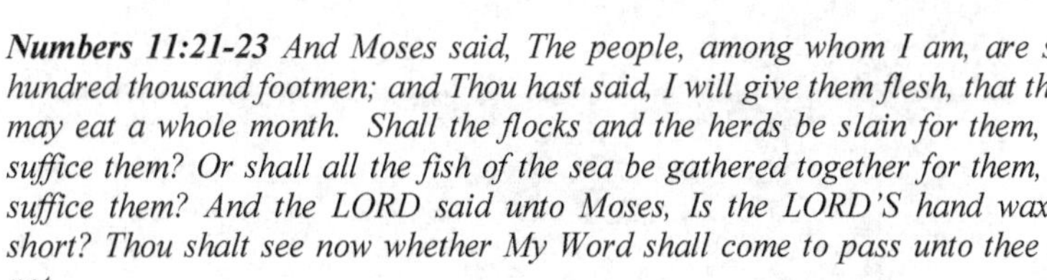

Numbers 11:21-23 *And Moses said, The people, among whom I am, are six hundred thousand footmen; and Thou hast said, I will give them flesh, that they may eat a whole month. Shall the flocks and the herds be slain for them, to suffice them? Or shall all the fish of the sea be gathered together for them, to suffice them? And the LORD said unto Moses, Is the LORD'S hand waxed short? Thou shalt see now whether My Word shall come to pass unto thee or not.*

Seagull Photo Monterey ©2014
Kimberly K Ballard All Rights Reserved

So in this miracle, the Jewish disciples suddenly understood that this was the LORD who was standing on the

shore and that He had said the same things to Moses long ago. *Yeshua was the hand of God that was causing the fish to increase because His hand was not waxed short and they were witnessing this with their own eyes!* Then the children of Israel, who were in the ship, saw that the Word of the LORD had come to pass when He miraculously gathered a multitude of fish into their nets. Yeshua first said, *"Children, have ye any meat?"* Then He revealed who He was through the miracle, showing them that all the fishes of the sea would be gathered together for them to suffice them! It is interesting that Joshua was the son of Nun and Nun means *"fish!"* Yeshua the LORD provided an abundance of fish from the sea for the children of Israel in the ship because they had fished all night and they were desperate for *meat!* Through the miracle, they realized that it was the LORD, the true meat, the Living Torah, who would now gather multitudes of people as the fishes of His catch! The Jewish disciples were obedient to Yeshua, even though they had fished all night and had yielded nothing in their nets. They threw their net over on the right side of the ship at Yeshua's Word, which reveals that Yeshua is the right hand of God, *the Living Torah.* When He miraculously filled their nets with a multitude of different fishes, the nets were breaking and the ships started to sink. *The variety of different fishes that were caught represents the different people from all the nations of the world that Yeshua would catch for His harvest. Remember that the disciples that had the net were in the ship, which is a type of Ark, and the Living Torah, the Rod of God was standing on the shore, telling them that He would help them to catch fish into the Heavenly Ark of God!*

Ocean waves crashing on rocks Monterey CA Photo ©2014 Kimberly K Ballard All Rights Reserved

Now the fact is that this was *Simon Bar Jonah the fisherman!* I talked about this to a large extent in the chapter on Yeshua's miracles, but since *the sign of Jonah profoundly pertains to Yom Kippur and the end of the age,* I had to add a few exciting details here. This was Simon the son of Jonah. *So this miracle was a sign that the harvest that is represented by the large catch of fishes in the net that was brought into the ship or into the Ark would occur at the end of the age, during Yom Kippur, which is the time when the entire book of Jonah is read.* What happened in this story after Simon Bar Jonah went fishing and the LORD filled the net on the right side of the ship? Yeshua fed them with the meat and bread that He supplied! The meat and bread represent the complete Living Torah and He was the one feeding them on the shore! This is what will happen, when the elect are taken into Heaven after the harvest. As soon as Simon Bar Jonah heard that it was the LORD, he cast himself into the sea. Remember that Jonah had said, *"Take me up, and cast me forth into the sea."*

Sailing Ship Monterey CA Photo ©2014 Kimberly K Ballard All Rights Reserved

Jonah 1:12-15 *And he said unto them, Take me up, and cast me forth into the sea; so shall the sea be calm unto you; for I know that for my sake this great tempest is upon you. Nevertheless the men rowed hard to bring it to the land; but they could not; for the sea wrought, and was tempestuous against them.*

Wherefore they cried unto the LORD, and said, We beseech Thee, O LORD, we beseech Thee, let us not perish for this man's life, and lay not upon us innocent blood; for Thou, O LORD, hast done as it pleased Thee. So they took up Jonah and cast him forth into the sea; and the sea ceased from her raging.

So there was a connection between the sign of Jonah and the harvest at the end of the age. *Simon Bar Jonah cast himself into the sea* because the LORD was standing on the shore! It was the Rod of God, the right hand of God, that caused the fish to be caught on the right side of the ship.

John 21:3-15 *Simon Peter saith unto them, I go a fishing. They say unto him, We also go with thee. They went forth, and entered into a ship immediately; and that night they caught nothing. But when the morning was now come, Yeshua stood on the shore; but the disciples knew not that it was Yeshua. Then Yeshua saith unto them, Children, have ye any meat? They answered, No. And He said unto them, Cast the net on the right side of the ship, and ye shall find. They cast therefore, and now they were not able to draw it for the multitude of fishes. Therefore that disciple whom Yeshua loved saith unto Peter, It is the LORD. Now when Simon Peter heard that it was the LORD, he girt his fisher's coat unto him, for he was naked, and did cast himself into the sea. And the other disciples came in a little ship; for they were not far from land, but as it were two hundred cubits, dragging the net with fishes. As soon then as they were come to land, they saw a fire of coals three, and fish laid thereon, and bread. Yeshua saith unto them, Bring of the fish which ye have now caught. Simon Peter went up, and drew the net to land full of great fishes, and hundred and fifty and three; and for all there were so many, yet was not the net broken. Yeshua saith unto them, Come and dine. And none of the disciples durst ask Him, Who art Thou? Knowing that it was the LORD. Yeshua then cometh, and taketh bread, and giveth them, and fish likewise. This is now the third time that Yeshua shewed Himself to His disciples, after that He was risen from the dead. So when they had dined, Yeshua saith to Simon Peter, Simon, son of Jonah, lovest thou me more than these? He saith unto Him, Yea, LORD thou knowest that I love Thee, He saith unto Him, Feed my lambs.*

Sailing Ship & Lighthouse in honour of Simon bar Jonah! Photo ©2014 Kimberly K Ballard All Rights Reserved

Yeshua was on the shore feeding *"The children of Israel"* with the bread and the fish that represent the Living Torah. This miracle happened *the third time* that Yeshua showed Himself to His disciples, after His resurrection. *Again, this is indicative of the fact that the Messiah's second coming will occur on the third day, at the end of the harvest.* The story goes on to say that Yeshua said to Simon Bar Jonah, a total of *three times,* to feed His lambs. *When He said these words, He was telling Simon Peter to go fishing for men with the Living Torah, with the Gospel of Messiah, because it is the true meat and Bread from Heaven. He also told Simon Bar Jonah, who was Jewish, to take the Gospel to the Jews first.* Remember that I said that the twelve tribes of Israel were represented in the twelve baskets that were gathered up, after the feeding of the 5,000+, from the five loaves and two fish and none of the pieces were lost! On the shore, there was a fire of *three* coals and the fish and bread were upon the fire. This is also representative of the Living Torah, full of the fire of the Holy Spirit, who will feed His people Eternally on the third day with the true meat and the true Bread from Heaven, after the harvest at the end of the age. *In this story, we can truly understand that the sign of Jonah was specifically a sign given to Israel, so they would know exactly when the LORD'S harvest would come and when the Messiah would arrive for them.* Remember Yeshua bore the First Fruit as the Living Branch of the Almond Tree on the *third day.* He is the Almond seed, our meat, just as the fruit trees on the third day of creation contained the seed that is our meat.

Joel 2:12-13 *Therefore also now, saith the LORD, turn ye even to Me with all your heart, and with fasting, and with weeping, and with mourning; And rend your heart, and not your garments, and turn unto the LORD your God; for He is gracious and merciful, slow to anger, and of great kindness, and repenteth him of the evil. Who knoweth if He will return and repent, and leave a blessing behind him; even a meat offering and a drink offering unto the LORD your God?*

If you think about the Almond tree, or any tree for that matter, the leaves of the tree sway in the wind. With the Almond Tree of life this wind is the Holy Spirit of God that moves us. I mentioned before that the pages of the Bible, the Torah, are sometimes referred to as *"leaves."* So the leaves that heal the nations are from *the Living Torah, from the Almond Tree of Life.* They are like a soothing salve to our broken hearts. We will feel the complete impact of this healing when the curse is completely removed from the earth.

Revelation 22:1-2 *And he shewed me a pure river of water of life, clear as crystal, proceeding out of the throne of God and of the Lamb. In the midst of the street of it, and on either side of the river, was there the Tree of Life, which bare twelve manner of fruits, and yielded her fruit every month; and the leaves of the Tree were for the healing of the nations.*

Genesis 1:29 *And God said, Behold, I have given you every herb bearing seed, which is upon the face of all the earth, and every tree, in the which is the fruit of a tree yielding seed; to you it shall be for meat.*

The miracle of the five loaves and the two fish add up to *the Living Torah, a perfect 7,* which is KING Messiah Yeshua. He was standing on the shore next to the body of living water as the Living Water, feeding them and revealing His identity from the book of Numbers.

The casting of Simon Bar Jonah into the sea reminds me that we are instructed to cast our sins into the sea, into the body of Messiah, the body Living Water, and the Molten Brazen Sea of the Heavenly Temple. Only the LORD God of Israel could wash our sins into the depths of the sea so they are gone forever. Only the LORD can purify us and reconcile us unto Himself.

As they dragged their heavy nets ashore, they were overflowing with multitudes of fishes. At the time of the harvest there will be multitudes upon multitudes of fishes who believe in the LORD God of Israel and they will come to Him through His Rod of salvation. Remember that I said that God used *His Rod* to catch these fish! Many of the LORD'S fish have been laid on the fire, representing the altar. This is what history records to be true, as many of the LORD'S Jewish disciples were martyred and tested, just as the Messiah was tested and just as the martyrs of the Satanic holocaust and inquisitions were tested. After the Jewish disciples, there were millions who came to the LORD through the Testimony of the Rod of God and millions of true believers have been laid under the same altar.

Revelation 6:9-11 *And when He had opened the fifth seal, I saw under the altar the souls of them that were slain for the Word of God, and for the Testimony which they held; And they cried with a loud voice, saying, How long, O LORD, holy and true, dost Thou not judge and avenge our blood on them that dwell on the earth? And white robes were given unto every one of them, that they should rest yet for a little season, until their fellow servants also and their brethren, that should be killed as they were, should be fulfilled.*

Now continuing on with the story, after the net is dragged up to the shore, the LORD tells them to *"Come and dine."* At the end of the age, when the LORD gathers His elect from the four corners of the earth, those who believe in the LORD God of Israel will sit down and dine with the LORD at the marriage supper of the Lamb. When the LORD dines with us, then He will drink the third cup of wine in the Passover Seder and this is the one that sealed His betrothal to His Bride forever as a cup of redemption. We will Tabernacle with the LORD in a permanent Heavenly Temple and not in a temporary sukkah. This is due to the fact that He represents the leafy Living Branch of the goodly Tree of Life and the First perfect Fruit that

came from the KINGS Royal Garden in Holy Mount Moriah, in Jerusalem Israel. The LORD is the 7th Heavenly Temple of perfection!

Hosea 6:1-2 *Come, and let us return to unto the LORD; for He hath torn, and He will heal us; He hath smitten, and He will bind us up. After two days will He revive us; in the third day He will raise us up, and we shall live in His sight.*

All the facts from this story reveal that the harvest of the LORD at the end of the age is during *Yom Kippur* when Israel reads the entire book of Jonah. So Messiah Yeshua revealed the time of the harvest through Simon Bar Jonah and the miracle of the fishes! Just as the prophecy in Hosea says that on the third day He would raise up Israel, Yeshua appeared on the third day, revealing these things and using Simon Bar Jonah, in the gathering of a multitude of fish. Israel has already been revived, so the third day is just around the corner because a great multitude of fish from all over the world have believed in the Name of the LORD God of Israel and have come to Him through Yeshua's Testimony. It is so stunning to see that the LORD was appearing the third day to the Jewish disciples who were fishing, so He could reveal the time of His harvest in the future through Simon Bar Jonah!

Now Yeshua also revealed the harvest at the end of the age in *the parable of the dragnet.* The parable of the dragnet is exactly parallel to the Almond Tree Harvest in every detail.

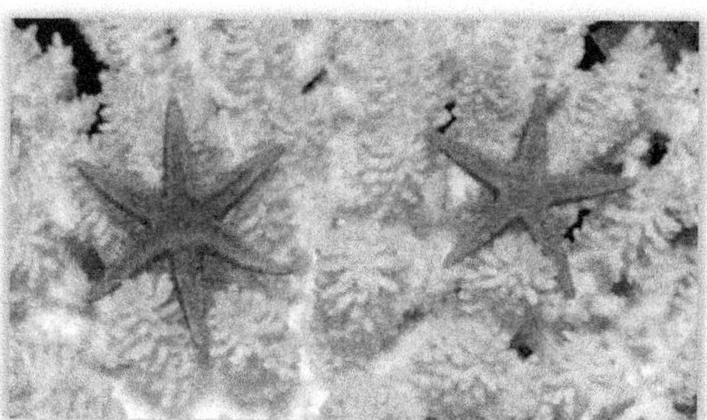

Starfish on Coral
Photo ©2014 Kimberly K Ballard All Rights Reserved

Matthew 13:47-51 *Again, the Kingdom of Heaven is like unto a net, that was cast into the sea, and gathered of every kind; Which, when it was full they drew to shore, and sat down, and gathered the good into vessels, but cast the bad away. So it will be at the end of the world; the angels shall come forth, and sever the wicked from amongst the just, And shall cast them into the furnace of fire; there shall be wailing and gnashing of teeth. Yeshua saith unto them, Have ye understood all these things? They say unto Him, Yea, LORD.*

Just as the almonds are harvested, as the goodly fruit of the trees, the LORD uses a parable about the good catch of fish of every kind that was put into a vessel. The vessel is the same as the container which is the LORD'S barn or His Heavenly Temple. The judgment of the wicked comes. The LORD will remove the wicked out and away from the just and these hulls or bad fish are thrown away and burned in the fire. Yeshua asked them if they understood this and they said to Him, *"Yea, LORD,"* thus acknowledging that they were speaking to the LORD God of Israel. When I realized that the LORD was catching fish through Simon Bar Jonah and that Jonah was a sign of Yom Kippur, I just could not believe the accuracy of the hidden truths within these Scriptures revealing the final harvest, *at the time of Yeshua's second coming for His elect.* Yeshua revealed this once again in the book of Luke. In this passage, Simon Bar Jonah calls Yeshua, *"Master."* Then Simon Bar Jonah said, *"Nevertheless at Thy Word, I will let down the net,"* his words reveal that this is the LORD God of Israel who only has to speak *the Living Torah* out of His mouth and all things are possible! When the Jewish Simon Peter saw this miracle, He fell down at Yeshua's knees because he truly realized in his humility that this was the LORD God of Israel and they were all astonished!

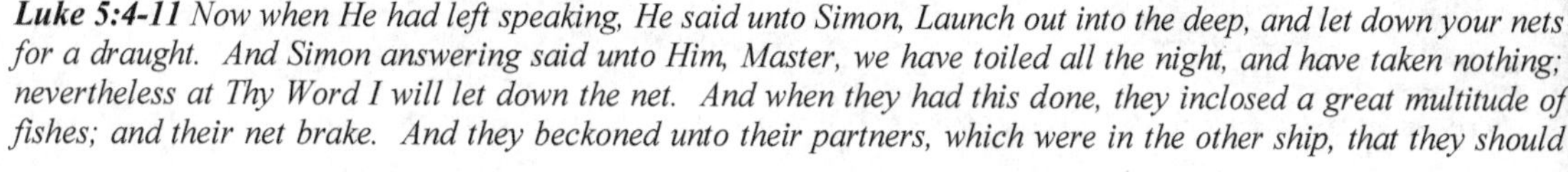

Luke 5:4-11 *Now when He had left speaking, He said unto Simon, Launch out into the deep, and let down your nets for a draught. And Simon answering said unto Him, Master, we have toiled all the night, and have taken nothing; nevertheless at Thy Word I will let down the net. And when they had this done, they inclosed a great multitude of fishes; and their net brake. And they beckoned unto their partners, which were in the other ship, that they should*

come and help them. And they came, and filled both the ships so that they began to sink. When Simon Peter saw it, he fell down at Yeshua's knees, saying, Depart from me; for I am a sinful man, O LORD. For he was astonished, and all that were with him, at the draught of the fishes which they had taken. And so was also James, and John, the sons of Zebedee, which were partners with Simon. And Yeshua said unto Simon, fear not; from henceforth thou shalt catch men. And when they had brought their ships to land, they forsook all, and followed Him.

Notice that after this astonishing miracle, *they forsook all and followed after Yeshua (Joshua) behind the Heavenly Ark!* At the end of the age it is written that *"The Messiah will end the final battle called "Armageddon."* This battle takes place in the valley of *"Megiddo"* which in ancient Hebrew means *"a fruitful place."* So the city of Armageddon was associated with *"the fruits of victory!"* ***(Source: ©1944 Hoyt Studies In the Apocalypse of John of Patmos).*** It is ironic that the Fruitful Branch, the Living Almond Rod of God, will return from Heaven to establish *"A fruitful victory"* in this place at the end of days, as He saves His beloved Israel! Yom Kippur always occurs in the fall, ten days after Rosh HaShanah or the Feast of Trumpets and then comes the Feast of Tabernacles. The LORD comes to reign then, as the Heavenly Spiritual Temple comes to earth to dwell in our midst, as our permanent dwelling and we will dine with the LORD in His permanent dwelling on the Feast of Tabernacles. This is why the Jewish disciples wanted to build three sukkahs when Moses and Elijah appeared on the Mount of the transfiguration, when they saw the LORD in His glory on Mount Sinai. The *three sukkahs* represent *the third day* when the LORD will come to dwell in the midst of Israel forever. So we are to *"watch,"* for the Almond harvest is near! *Yom Kippur is clearly the sign of Jonah when the LORD will drag up His net full of the good fishes.* Everyone that has trusted and believed in Him will go to be with Him forever. It is so exciting to finally understand what this means, by the power of the Holy Spirit. We are the almonds that bear fruit from, *"The Branch,"* and *we are the fishes that swim in the Living Water* that are gathered up in the LORD'S net to be with Him forever.

Habakkuk 2:14 *For the earth shall be filled with the knowledge of the glory of the LORD, as the waters cover the sea.*

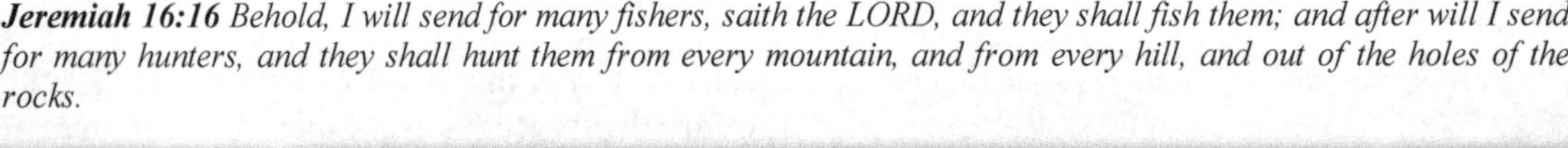

Jeremiah 16:16 *Behold, I will send for many fishers, saith the LORD, and they shall fish them; and after will I send for many hunters, and they shall hunt them from every mountain, and from every hill, and out of the holes of the rocks.*

In honour of Simon bar Jonah! Sea Turtle Monterey & Fish in reef Photos ©2014 Kimberly K Ballard All Rights Reserved

THE ALPHA & OMEGA THE FIRST AND THE LAST THE BEGINNING AND THE END!

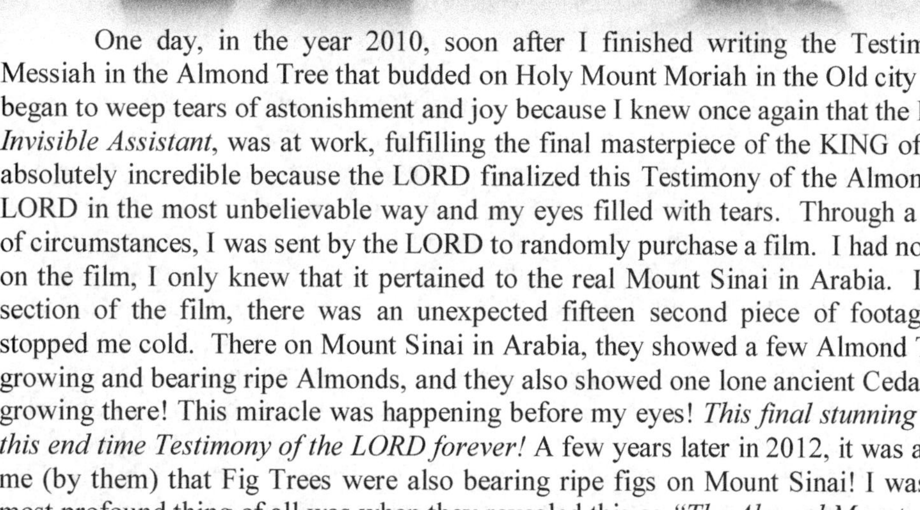

Lions & Crown in Snow & Almond Tree
Photos ©2014 Kimberly K Ballard
All Rights Reserved

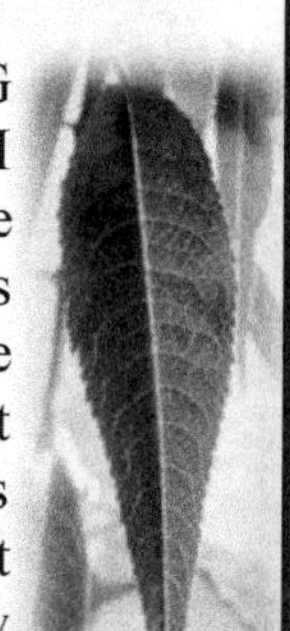

One day, in the year 2010, soon after I finished writing the Testimony of KING Messiah in the Almond Tree that budded on Holy Mount Moriah in the Old city of Jerusalem, I began to weep tears of astonishment and joy because I knew once again that the Holy Spirit, the *Invisible Assistant*, was at work, fulfilling the final masterpiece of the KING of Glory. It was absolutely incredible because the LORD finalized this Testimony of the Almond Tree and the LORD in the most unbelievable way and my eyes filled with tears. Through a miraculous set of circumstances, I was sent by the LORD to randomly purchase a film. I had no idea what was on the film, I only knew that it pertained to the real Mount Sinai in Arabia. In the very last section of the film, there was an unexpected fifteen second piece of footage that literally stopped me cold. There on Mount Sinai in Arabia, they showed a few Almond Trees that were growing and bearing ripe Almonds, and they also showed one lone ancient Cedar Tree that was growing there! This miracle was happening before my eyes! *This final stunning miracle sealed this end time Testimony of the LORD forever!* A few years later in 2012, it was also revealed to me (by them) that Fig Trees were also bearing ripe figs on Mount Sinai! I was stunned! The most profound thing of all was when they revealed this as *"The Almond Mountain,"* because of the Almond Trees growing there. *They found an almond tree growing between the rocks above the cave of Elijah!* As you can imagine, I wept in humility from the depths of my heart because the LORD had miraculously caused all of this to happen and I had already written this Testimony that went with all the same trees! No one had ever been to the real Mount Sinai to film there before this time, so there was no way of knowing this about the Almond tree, except through the Divine revelation of the Holy Spirit! I knew for certain then that the power of God had always been upon the writing of this book since I started it in 2007. I had written every detail as I was led by the Holy Spirit, before this point, for several years by blind faith alone and trust in the LORD, without ever having this knowledge, because it was not revealed yet until this film. I truly believe that the LORD gave this final gift to me, as I completed my work for Him, to forever verify and seal the story of the mystery of the Messiah! It was the LORD'S way of showing the final proof that *Yeshua is the Almond Tree of Life* and that He can bud and bear fruit where there is no life because Mount Sinai is a desolate wilderness where nothing grows at all! Now this was incredibly a complete picture and Testimony from start to finish and from beginning to end. Incredibly, I knew that Jim and Penny Caldwell who showed these things in their film clip, had actually discovered in the wilderness *"The Fig Tree of knowledge of good and evil, with the Almond Tree of Life and their trees were miraculously fruiting and somehow thriving, bearing almonds and figs on Mount Sinai in Arabia, where Moses met Yeshua!* This was an astonishing miracle and I wanted to contact them immediately to explain

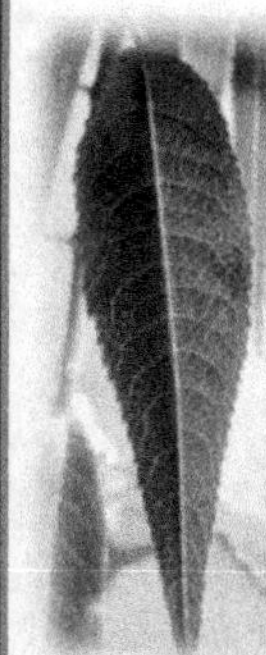

everything that was happening. I had just completed writing this book, but I could not find them until 2012 into 2013. Remember that I said that when the Fig Tree buds without the curse and you see all the trees bud, then the LORD is nigh at hand and their trees were fruiting on Mount Sinai! The LORD was bringing these stunning events together and I had so much I wanted to tell the Caldwell's! I was so thrilled! After this, I began to pensively think about the fact that my book began with my Almond Tree revelation and the miracle on Holy Mount Moriah in the Old city of Jerusalem with the budding Almond Tree in 2007, at the time of Tu B' Shevat. Then all the trees that I had written about were by Divine Providence now parallel to the trees that were discovered on Mount Sinai in Arabia by Jim and Penny Caldwell and they were truly a mirror image of each other. As I pondered this for a day or so, I questioned the LORD about why this was happening. Early the next morning, I knew that the Holy Spirit revealed the astonishing answer to me as to why this was happening now and I felt like my heart burned within me, as the LORD spoke to my heart. *My entire book and final Testimony of the LORD was all about the beautiful budding Almond Tree on Holy Mount Moriah in Jerusalem, because this is the Holy Mountain of the LORD God of Israel that brings forth liberty and freedom forever, because Messiah Yeshua was the Almond Rod that budded to life in this Holy Mount! However, the Almond Tree that was at the end of this Testimony, revealed and verified to be fruiting on Mount Sinai by Jim and Penny Caldwell, was the final evidence and Testimony of the Holy Mountain of bondage in the wilderness and Israel has been under the bondage and yoke of this Mountain for two thousand years.* All of a sudden it hit me like a bolt of lightning and I knew that the only thing between the final Testimony and evidence now revealed on Mount Sinai in Arabia that brought forth the earthly copy of the Ark and my Final Testimony of Messiah Yeshua from Holy Mount Moriah in Jerusalem that brings forth the Heavenly Ark of God, *is the Jordan River!* A chill and a shiver suddenly ran through me as I instantly understood what this meant! *This was all happening now, because we are about to cross over into the Eternal Promised Land!* Israel must cross over into the Eternal Promised Land to meet their KING face to face and to live forever! This was the answer from the Holy Spirit that was so extraordinary! Now I know that this will sound strange, but in the Caldwell's film footage, the LORD caused me to see a ghostly face in the cave of Elijah that I believe is the face of the Apostle Paul with a cross on his forehead and an inscription next to his face! Do you know how I recognized Paul's face? I just happened to have a photograph showing the face of Paul from the earliest rendering ever found and he had the same pointed beard and a cross in his forehead like a scar (like a thorn in the flesh)! When I took the picture off my door and compared the faces, I was stunned that they matched and Hebrew writing was near his face inside the cave of Elijah, across from Mount Sinai. I hope to investigate this further. I finally met Penny Caldwell through my email as I was doing final editing! The photographs that Penny and Jim so graciously allowed me to use inside my book helped to forever seal and verify this entire profound Testimony of the LORD! It is all prophetic revelation for the end of days! Remember that the LORD also caused me to see the Angel at the Garden tomb and it was very significant! Remember what the Apostle Paul wrote in the book of Galatians? *"From these two Mountains, there are two Covenants" and it is the final Covenant in Jerusalem on Holy Mount Moriah, where my Almond Tree budded in 2007, that the LORD will dwell forever as the Living Ark of the Eternal Covenant.* The LORD is the fulfillment of the Law, *the Living Torah,* and therefore, Eternal life can only come to us through Him. Mount Moriah is, therefore, the Holy Mount that brings us *Eternal freedom from the bondage of the Law in the wilderness,* where mankind worked to attain his own righteousness. Rabbi Messiah's yoke is easy and His burden is light. So Israel will only attain it when they *cross over,* following after Yeshua!

Galatians 5:1 *Stand fast therefore in the liberty wherewith Messiah hath made us free, and be not entangled again with the yoke of bondage.*

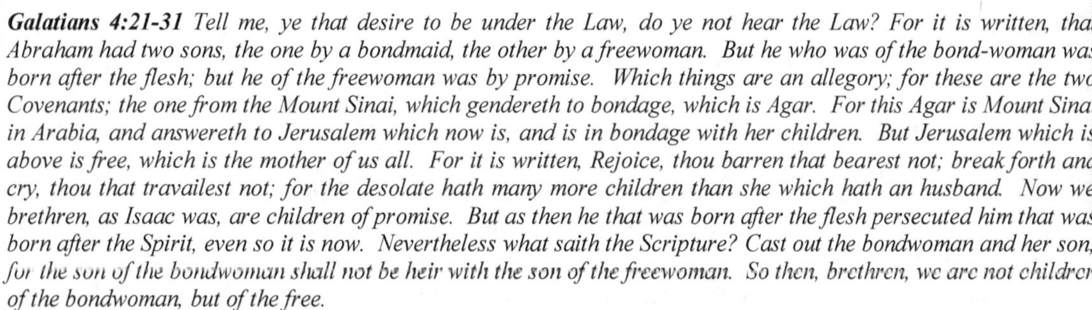
Galatians 4:21-31 *Tell me, ye that desire to be under the Law, do ye not hear the Law? For it is written, that Abraham had two sons, the one by a bondmaid, the other by a freewoman. But he who was of the bond-woman was born after the flesh; but he of the freewoman was by promise. Which things are an allegory; for these are the two Covenants; the one from the Mount Sinai, which gendereth to bondage, which is Agar. For this Agar is Mount Sinai in Arabia, and answereth to Jerusalem which now is, and is in bondage with her children. But Jerusalem which is above is free, which is the mother of us all. For it is written, Rejoice, thou barren that bearest not; break forth and cry, thou that travailest not; for the desolate hath many more children than she which hath an husband. Now we brethren, as Isaac was, are children of promise. But as then he that was born after the flesh persecuted him that was born after the Spirit, even so it is now. Nevertheless what saith the Scripture? Cast out the bondwoman and her son; for the son of the bondwoman shall not be heir with the son of the freewoman. So then, brethren, we are not children of the bondwoman, but of the free.*

So the truth is that this journey started at Mount Sinai centuries ago, but it ends in Jerusalem, in the Eternal Promised Land at God's Garden, where it really is just the beginning! My miracle Almond Tree budded to life on Holy Mount Moriah in the Old city, *in the Hebrew month of Shevat, just after Tu B' Shevat in Jerusalem Israel.* The Rosh HaShanah or New Year of Trees focuses on the budding of the Almond Tree in *Shevat.* Incredibly, it was actually *during the first of the Hebrew month of Shevat* that Moses stood on the other side of the Jordan in Moab and he began to read the book of Deuteronomy to the children of Israel. It is truly shocking when you read an overview of what is happening here in Deuteronomy during *Shevat.* This is one of the last things that the LORD revealed to me and it is strikingly profound. Incredibly the LORD brought this to my knowledge after what I wrote earlier about preparing to cross over the Jordan into the Eternal Promised Land. During the Hebrew month of *Shevat, the people of Israel were about ready to cross over the Jordan River into the Promised Land, as Joshua was about to lead them over the Jordan River, with the Ark of the LORD going before them.* Moses was standing there giving his farewell address! *Now this incredibly verified what the LORD revealed to me when I woke up, that this was all happening now, because we are about to cross over, with Yeshua taking the lead, into the Eternal Promised Land!* In the last chapter of the book of Deuteronomy, Moses is standing upon Mount Nebo and the LORD is there with him and He shows Moses the Promised Land that He will give to Israel forever. Today it has been verified by filmmaker Simon Brown of England that the Great Rolling Stone of Yeshua's tomb is standing on Mount Nebo. It is up there revealing that it has been rolled away from Holy Mount Moriah, so we can enter His rest in the Eternal Promised Land and live forever in the Heavenly Garden in Jerusalem, where we have been redeemed by the LORD! *This is the place of the Foundation Stone and the place where God gave us life!* After the LORD showed Moses the Promised Land on Mount Nebo, Moses did not enter the Promised Land. Instead he disappeared on Mount Nebo in the glory cloud and *Moses entered the Heavenly Promised Land with Yeshua,* while the children of Israel were preparing to cross over with Joshua!

When I contacted Penny Caldwell in 2012, she sent me a video interview to watch and she mentioned *"that there is a straight line from Mount Sinai to Jerusalem."* This is when I found out that they also found Fig trees bearing ripe figs in the area of Mount Sinai and I gasped in wonder! I had already written everything about the Fig tree and Messiah Yeshua, through the Divine guidance of the Holy Spirit! It was chilling! Everything was miraculously coming together as an incredible Testimony of the LORD! I suddenly realized the four L-shaped poker holes that form right angles in Yeshua's burial Shroud were like horns of the sacrificial altar. They were truly like boundary markers that set apart as *kadesh* the sacred place where God connected to humanity. He is *"the same Living God of Mount Sinai"* called *"The Mountain of fire!"* I happened to see these right angles in the floor design of the ancient Synagogue of Mary Magdalene where *Yeshua stood between Migdal and the Sea!* Those who have followed behind Yeshua will be raptured in the glory cloud, as the children of Israel

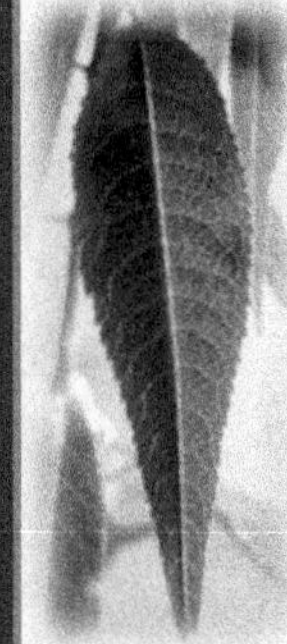
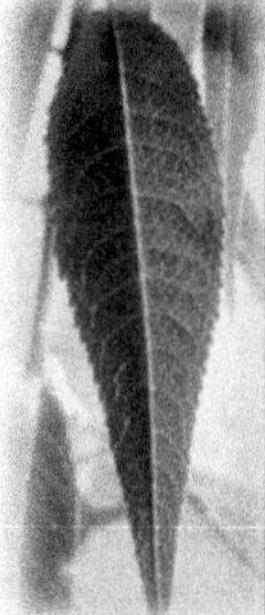

prepare to cross over for the last time with Messiah Yeshua going before them to fight the battle of Armageddon, as He fought in the day of battle. He will remove His enemies again from His Land and blow them off His threshing floor with the breath of His mouth!

In the Bible overview, it is said that *"the book of Deuteronomy creates a long pause in the advancement of the redemption story." Likewise, Yeshua the Heavenly Ark of the Covenant has given us a long pause for two thousand years, towards the advancement of the redemption story, before we can cross over into the Eternal Promised Land, following behind Yeshua after He was taken up!*

In Deuteronomy 31, Moses wrote *"The song of Moses"* just before the children of Israel crossed over the Jordan River. In the book of Revelation, in chapter 15 verse 3, those who get the victory over the beast are singing the song of Moses, the servant of God, and the song of the Lamb, just before Israel enters the Eternal Promised Land! Incredibly, during his visit to Colorado, during the Hebrew month of *Shevat,* Rabbi Richman of the Temple Institute in Jerusalem, spoke of this *new song* that they will soon be singing, but right now they do not know the words of this song because it has not yet been written. *This new song of Moses will be written when they understand the part of the song about the Lamb, when Messiah Yeshua is revealed to them as the LORD KING OF ISRAEL!* When they have this Final Testimony that proclaims that Messiah Yeshua is the LORD God of Israel, who has performed these mighty works, then they will have the right words of the song to sing! What we are witnessing, then, is historically prophetic! *Shevat* is also mentioned in the book of Zechariah. *Shevat* is the eleventh month on the Hebrew calendar and it was during *Shevat,* in the second year of Darius, *"That the Word of the LORD came unto Zechariah, the son of Berechiah, the son of Iddo the Prophet."* Zechariah wrote the prophecies about Messiah Yeshua and the Messianic era! He also wrote that people from all nations should come to Him to be saved and to worship Him as the Sovereign KING of the universe. He tells Israel that they have not listened to His Prophets. What the LORD said to Zechariah was truly profound!

Zechariah 1:14-16 *So the angel that communed with me said unto me, Cry thou, saying, Thus saith the LORD of Hosts; I AM jealous for Jerusalem and for Zion with a great jealousy. And I AM very sore displeased with the heathen that are at ease; for I was but a little displeased, and they helped forward the affliction. Therefore thus saith the LORD; I AM returned to Jerusalem with mercies; My House shall be built in it, saith the LORD of Hosts, and a line shall be stretched forth upon Jerusalem.*

Shevat is also associated with the Torah as the Living Water, because it was said by Rabbi Richman *"that at the time of the month of Shevat, the rain water that has been stored up in the sap of the trees slowly begins to flow into the branches again, causing them to come to life. For this reason, the entire month of Shevat proclaims rebirth."* Ironically in two days, on Tu B' Shevat 2014, I will send this to my publisher! Remember that the one called *"The Deliverer"* will bring about this *birth* redemption! What is incredible about this *rebirth* is that it also pertains to *the rebuilding of the Holy Temple of the LORD on Mount Moriah,* in the place of the LORD'S inheritance. The *rebirth* reminds me what I said about my birthday being on the 3rd month and the 17th day and that Aaron's rod that budded to life took place in Numbers 17. Then Yeshua budded to life the 3rd day on the 17th of Nisan. So this was all simply remarkable. Then my Israeli friend took the photograph of the Almond Tree in the Old city of Jerusalem on Mount Moriah as it was just starting to bud and flower, the 3rd time she passed it, but she happened to email it to me on the 17th of February, in 2007. To top it off, my Almond Tree miracle happened that year, in the month of *Shevat,* right after *Tu B' Shevat* that occurred on the 3rd of February, that celebrates the budding of the Almond Trees in Israel. I finished editing this book on the Testimony of the LORD in the Almond Tree, in the month of *Shevat* and exactly on the day of *Tu B' Shevat,* when the Almond Trees bud to life in Israel, after slumbering all winter! All of these miracles combined are simply astonishing! My heart was

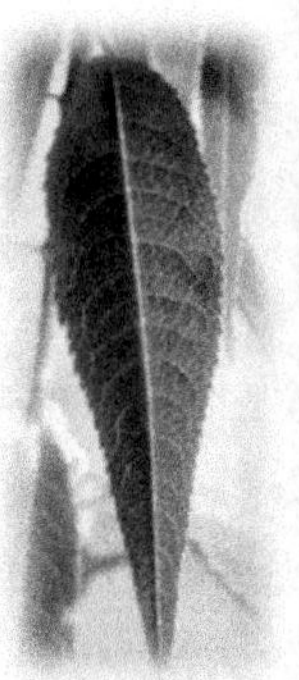

touched and blessed that my Israeli friend had photographed that Almond Tree on Mount Moriah where Yeshua budded to life as the Almond Rod of God and this was the place where the Almond Tree of Life offered us the First Fruit from the Rod that budded. We can enter the Garden of God with the Branch of the Living Torah and drink the Living Water and live forever. My beautiful Israeli friend and I knew for certain that the LORD was the *Invisible Assistant* pulling her to that Almond Tree, on the very same day that the LORD woke me up at 4AM with the Almond Tree revelation of Messiah Yeshua in 2007. To think that she opened it the next day on the 17th was so exciting. In my heart, I know that this was all part of the LORD'S Divine guidance and Providence because He was working a *Grand Finale* for the last days. What an astonishing final touch to the end of my glorious story for the LORD!

So my story began in the middle of winter and spring was just arriving in Israel. I had written that the LORD purifies us and makes us white as snow and the other day when it was 20 degrees outside, just as I completed my final editing and had just made contact with Penny Caldwell, so I could finally reveal to her that a true miracle was happening with the Almond Tree, I stopped working and walked out to my mailbox very late in the afternoon. The day before, I had swept all the snow off the driveway with a long push broom. Only the crushed tire tracks remained on the pavement. I decided to take a break and I went outside to breathe some fresh frosty air, and as I walked down the driveway, I looked up ahead and there was a cross of snow that was about 14 inches long and 12 inches wide where the snow had been swept off. It was a raised cross of snow! Wow! To me this was just another sign that the LORD was going to fulfill this pure Testimony! How incredible is this whole story? It is breathtaking! It is spectacular! Now everyone will love the KING OF KINGS with all their heart and everyone will learn of His Eternal majestic glory. At this time I also learned that the Caldwell's had their own true miracle with snow that was shaped like the star of David near Mount Sinai! It is remarkably spectacular how the LORD has performed these mighty works to bring it all together in the last days to reveal His Royal majestic glory!

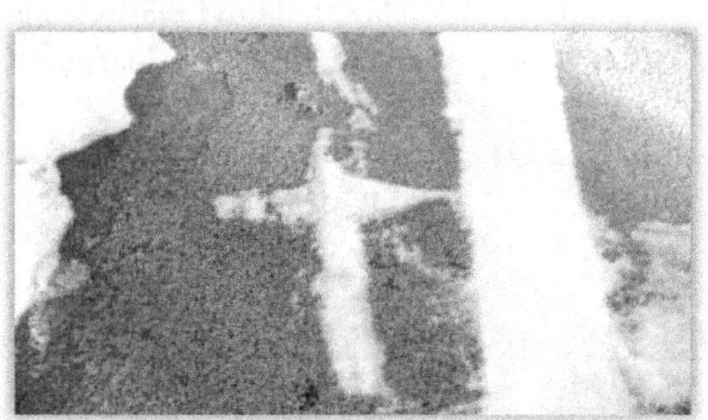

Snow Cross in my driveway where I had swept off the snow!

I have to mention that as I pondered this last miracle, it truly revealed that the LORD is the First and the Last Almond Tree of Life because He is the Rod that budded in Jerusalem in Holy Mount Moriah and He bore the ripe Fruit of almonds here, to free us from the bondage of Mount Sinai and death! It was a complete picture! It was only possible by His Majesty, the Royal Sovereign KING, who works miracles through those that love Him. After all that He has done for me, I adore Him!

Believe it or not, there was one more incredible event that happened as I was trying to decide what the LORD wanted me to do with His Royal Testimony. After the first four years of working on this book, I was contemplating publishing it and so I decided that it might be interesting to search for another Almond Tree photograph that I could put on the cover. I scrolled from page to page without really paying any attention to the numbers of the pictures. After a while, I found one Almond Tree that simply captured my imagination and for this reason, I selected this particular picture, out of many pages that I had already scrolled through. I had been seriously praying and asking the LORD to show me if this was everything that He wanted me to write in my book. I talked to the LORD and said to Him that if it was everything *"to please show me how and when He wanted me to publish this final Testimony."* As I kept praying, I earnestly cried out to the LORD, asking Him to give me some type of sign or answer. I needed to know the LORD'S will regarding publishing His Grand Finale Living Testimony.

He had entrusted this fantastic end times Testimony, full of true miracles to my care and I was finished writing it all down or so I thought, but there were more revelations that I diligently worked on, just as He guided my heart over the course of the past six years and this involved the angel at the Garden tomb and the Great Rolling Stone on Mount Nebo. After talking to the LORD about it, I clicked on this particular Almond Tree picture and it took me to a website that said, *"This is the year of the Almond Tree, Hear what God is saying, Do it!"* Then it said, *"God is watching over His Word to perform it!"* To my amazement and shock it also said, *"God's eye is upon you to fulfill His will!"* Wow! I had tears streaming down my face at this point when I read the profound words on the page and because of the fact that the LORD had finalized this Testimony through such an astonishing miracle. It was just like the LORD to answer me with such a profound clear message. I mean, seriously, how did I randomly select this particular Almond Tree and when I opened it, then it just happened to say, *"God's eye is upon you to fulfill His will,"* when I had just prayed to know God's will regarding His Almond Tree Testimony? The moral of the story is that when we seek the LORD'S will, He does hear us and He does answer us. He touched my heart so deeply with this incredible message. I love the LORD KING more than I ever imagined. The LORD guided me to that message to say, *"I want you to publish this and I AM watching over you with My eyes upon you and over My will to perform it and this is the year of the Almond Tree, so do it!"* I wept for the sheer joy of this message. Ironically, this was the same message that the LORD gave to the Prophet Jeremiah when he saw the Rod of an Almond Tree and this was a warning to the people of Israel to repent and to get right with God before the judgment!

God is calling everyone from every nation to repent and to come to Him now, before the final judgment! After my first four years of writing, the LORD gave me this final message that said, *"This is the Year of the Almond Tree."* Later that night, when I shared the message with my Mother, she was so astonished by it. We both knew that the LORD was definitely working within this project and that He was clearly telling me that the time was now, to publish this work for the glory of the LORD'S Living Testimony. I still had editing and long revisions to do for about three years from the time I got this message, so it did not happen immediately, but the LORD spoke to me through a random stranger who said, *"Hear what the LORD is saying, Do it!"* He said, *"So every time the Almond Tree bursts into blossom, it's a vivid reminder of God's sudden and rapid action to fulfill His Word and the Almond Tree's blossoms are a symbol of God's watchfulness to bring about His will and purposes in the earth!"* The most astounding thing that he said in 2010, when I ran across this blessing message was the following statement. *"This is the Hebrew year AYIN - the Hebrew letters were originally pictures and the AYIN is the picture of an eye. This is the year to know God's eye is on you."* Then he said, *"The next year (2011) is part of the AYIN season and for the next ten years."* I finished editing this book on my own in 2013 (before sending it to my publisher), which is *the third year* that rests within this ten year span of time and so it is clear that God's eye is watching over His Word to perform it and to bring His promises to pass before our eyes! After speaking to my Mother about this message that night, I said to her, *"Just out of curiosity, I wonder what page number that Almond Tree photo was on?"* So the next morning, I went to the computer to look for this Almond Tree again and hopefully, to find out where it was located. Of course! The LORD made me laugh in amazement. Here was another sign that this message was just for me because out of all the pages that I had scrolled through at random, without observing the page numbers, would you believe that this particular inspiring Almond Tree, that was bearing the final message from the LORD, happened to be located on page number 17? I could not believe it and to me this was the final Royal masterpiece of the LORD'S Living Almond Tree Testimony. This was one more perfect gift from the LORD'S heart to my heart and now I share it with all of you! I pray that you are blessed by it and I hope this changes your life and your heart forever! Israel will soon turn 70 in 2017!

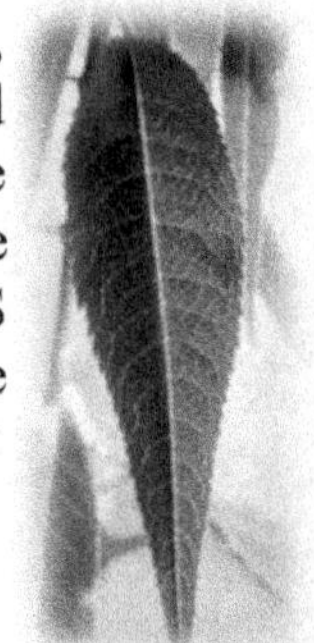

The Almond Tree has been an incredible unveiling of the LORD God of Israel, as our Messiah Yeshua! I wanted to say too, that the blessing of this final Almond message was written by Robert Heidler of Denton Texas and may the LORD bless him for it! ***(Source: ©2009 Glory of Zion International Ministries, Denton Texas, Robert Heidler).***

Now I want to tell you why it was so significant that my Israeli friend photographed the first Almond Tree that she saw budding in the Old city of Jerusalem, on Holy Mount Moriah in 2007. Obviously by now you know that my miracle of the Almond Tree did not end with Aaron's rod that budded. The Almond Tree revelation took me to places I never expected to go and now we know the LORD face to face! Now the delicate Almond petals have fully opened to our gaze and the center of the sweet Almond flower has come into full view, revealing the heart of the KING OF KINGS AND LORD OF LORDS and there it was on the Magdala Stone! The LORD is the loving righteous KING Messiah, Saviour and Redeemer of mankind. This brings us to the last element of the revelation of the Almond Tree that I received from the LORD. If you have not been excited by what you have read so far, then you must see this final statement that absolutely takes my breath away because the LORD is hidden within every single detail of the Almond Tree of Life! The LORD Yeshua, *the Living Torah* that spoke to the Apostle Paul *in Hebrew* from Heaven, *makes the end known from the beginning,* because *Hebrews* always begin reading a book from the back to the front, to the beginning and thus He created the universe. Now the best way to complete this book is to reveal the final secret of the LORD'S Eternal Testimony and here it is!

THE ALMOND TREE IN ISRAEL
IS THE FIRST TREE TO BLOOM
AND THE LAST TO BE HARVESTED
THE LORD SAID,
"I AM THE FIRST AND THE LAST!"

My miracle Almond Tree in Jerusalem on Holy Mount Moriah in the Old city was *the first* Almond Tree budding and flowering, and *the last* Almond Tree on Mount Sinai that was revealed to me at the end of this book, that Jim and Penny Caldwell discovered, was ripe and ready to harvest! Now I understand why Messiah Yeshua's Testimony and Eternal Covenant is the Almond Branch from the Almond Tree of Life because He is, *"The First and the Last!"* The LORD is, indeed, *the Holy Almond Tree Menorah,* full of never ending light! I was completely astonished by this fact because it is so powerful! When this connection came to my heart, I just could not believe it! Again I shed tears when I realized how deeply the Creator of the universe encoded Himself into every detail of His creation and specifically, in the beautiful Almond Tree of His Eternal Testimony. From the moment that the LORD gave me the first revelation in the month of *Shevat* and just after *Tu B' Shevat* on February 16th 2007, until the very final editing, completed in the month of *Shevat,* exactly on the day of *Tu B' Shevat 2013,* when the Almond Trees in Israel bud to life again, the LORD has revealed Himself to me in every single little detail and aspect of the Almond Tree from beginning to end. *The First and the Last is the Almond Tree of Life* and my Israeli friend photographed *"The First Almond Tree that came to life on Holy Mount Moriah!"* So I thought that this was a fitting way to end this wonderful Testimony of the LORD. *We are God's witnesses and we have seen His marvelous works and Majestic glory with our own eyes! We have seen the rod of an Almond Tree!*

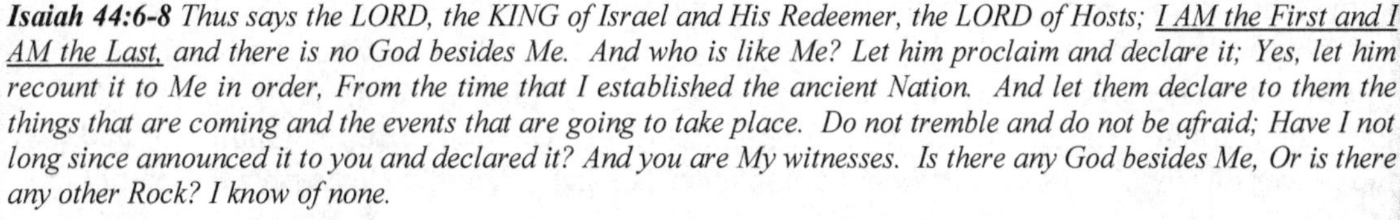

Isaiah 44:6-8 *Thus says the LORD, the KING of Israel and His Redeemer, the LORD of Hosts; I AM the First and I AM the Last, and there is no God besides Me. And who is like Me? Let him proclaim and declare it; Yes, let him recount it to Me in order, From the time that I established the ancient Nation. And let them declare to them the things that are coming and the events that are going to take place. Do not tremble and do not be afraid; Have I not long since announced it to you and declared it? And you are My witnesses. Is there any God besides Me, Or is there any other Rock? I know of none.*

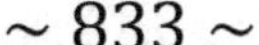

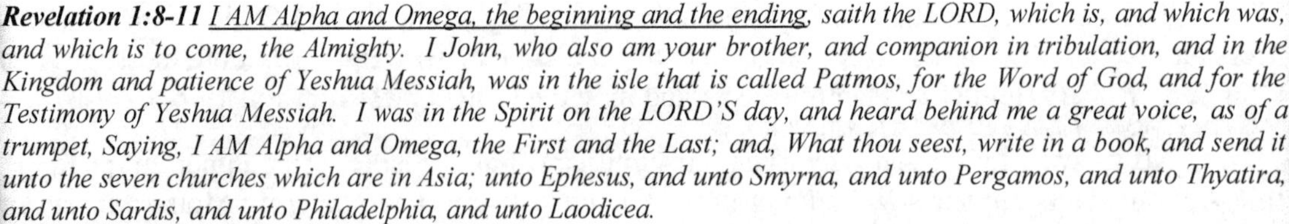

Revelation 1:8-11 *I AM Alpha and Omega, the beginning and the ending, saith the LORD, which is, and which was, and which is to come, the Almighty. I John, who also am your brother, and companion in tribulation, and in the Kingdom and patience of Yeshua Messiah, was in the isle that is called Patmos, for the Word of God, and for the Testimony of Yeshua Messiah. I was in the Spirit on the LORD'S day, and heard behind me a great voice, as of a trumpet, Saying, I AM Alpha and Omega, the First and the Last; and, What thou seest, write in a book, and send it unto the seven churches which are in Asia; unto Ephesus, and unto Smyrna, and unto Pergamos, and unto Thyatira, and unto Sardis, and unto Philadelphia, and unto Laodicea.*

Revelation 21:6-7 *And He said to me, It is done, I AM the Alpha and the Omega, the beginning and the end. I will give to the one who thirsts from the spring of the Water of Life without cost. He who overcomes shall inherit these things, and I will be his God and he will be My son.*

Revelation 22:13-14 *I AM Alpha and Omega, the beginning and the end, the First and the Last. Blessed are they that do His Commandments, that they may have right to the Tree of Life, and may enter in through the gates into the city.*

Revelation 2:8 *And unto the angel of the church in Smyrna write; These things saith the First and the Last, which was dead, and is alive.*

The LORD inscribed His everlasting Living Testimony and Covenant of the heart, with *the Living Torah* upon our hearts forever and the Almond that has heart health benefits to prolong life! The KING of glory prolongs our lives forever, as His Living Water and life blood flows like a never ending stream of life into our hearts.

Proverbs 11:30 *The fruit of the righteous is a Tree of Life; and he that winneth souls is wise.*

Whoever keeps this hope of Messiah the LORD within their heart will be like a Tree planted by rivers of Living Water!

Jeremiah 17:7-8 *Blessed is the man that trusteth in the LORD, and whose hope the LORD is. For he shall be as a tree planted by the waters, and that spreadeth out her roots by the river, and shall not see when heat cometh, but her leaf shall be green; and shall not be careful in the year of drought, neither shall cease from yielding fruit.*

Psalm 1:1-4 *Blessed is the man that walketh not in the counsel of the ungodly, nor standeth in the way of sinners, nor sitteth in the seat of the scornful. But his delight is in the Law of the LORD; and in His Law doth he meditate day and night. And he shall be like a tree planted by the rivers of water, that bringeth forth his fruit in his season; his leaf also shall not wither; and whatsoever he doeth shall prosper. The ungodly are not so; but are like the chaff which the wind driveth away.*

Now I end my book by going back to the beginning to the Almond Tree of Life! When Mary Magdalene became the first woman to eat the First Fruit from the Almond Tree of Life and then she went to tell *the men* to come to the Garden to partake of this Fruit, KING Yeshua reversed the curse in His Garden and now we can live forever with the LORD, *"As it was at first, in the beginning."* The *"first"* book of the Bible, which is Genesis is *"The beginning,"* and no one knew who God was in the beginning. The *"last"* book of the Bible is the ending and it is *"The Revelation" that Messiah Yeshua is the LORD God of Israel. In Revelation 10:7 when the voice of the seventh angel shall begin to sound, the mystery of God is finished as He declared to his servants the prophets. This revelation of Yeshua is the mystery of God and it is the Testimony of the two witnesses in the days when they prophecy, which by definition can be a message in written form!* The Revelation reveals God from the beginning, so that we will know who God is in the end. In the beginning, we were dwelling with the LORD in the Garden and now in Revelation, the LORD reveals His face to us, as the one who purchased us with a price because He loved us so much that He made the way for us to return to live in His glorious Paradise Garden. The *Living Almond Tree* is a faithful Testimony from beginning to end. By the power of *His Living Almond Rod,* we can enter His gates into the Heavenly Garden of God.

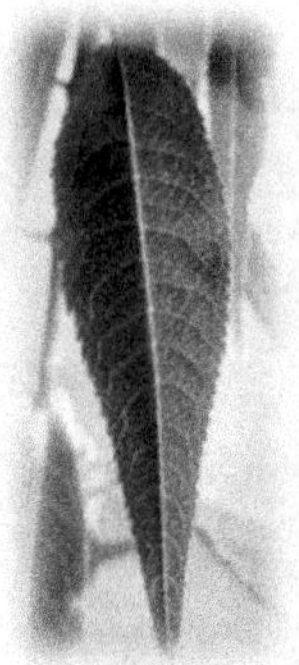

The disciple named John gave us one final amazing clue! John said that Messiah Yeshua performed so many miracles that if they were written down, that he supposed that the world itself could not contain the books that should be written. Now I understand John. He said this because Yeshua created the entire universe and everything in it. So the world could not contain the books that would tell of the LORD'S Living Encyclopedia to the Creation of the entire universe! *YESHUA IS HIS ROYAL MAJESTY, THE GREAT ROYAL SOVEREIGN, THE ETERNAL KING OF KINGS AND MIGHTY LORD OF LORDS! FOREVER YOU WILL REIGN MY KING OF EVERLASTING GLORY! The Kingdoms of this world are now Yours!*

John 21:24-25 *This is the disciple which testifieth of these things, and wrote these things; and we know that his Testimony is true. And there are also many other things which Yeshua did, the which, if they should be written every one, I suppose that even the world itself could not contain the books that should be written. Amen.*

THE END!

However, the End is really just the Beginning!

The Way Back to the Garden is through KING Messiah Yeshua,
The Heavenly Ark of the Covenant, containing the Living Almond Rod of God that budded!

Revelation 22:20-21 *He which Testifieth these things saith, Surely I come quickly, A'men. Even so, come, LORD Yeshua. The grace of our LORD Yeshua Messiah be with you all, Amen.*

THE FIRST AND THE LAST IS THE ALMOND TREE OF LIFE
<u>THE BEGINNING AND THE END</u>
<u>THESE ARE THE DAYS OF THE WITNESS OF MOSES & ELIJAH!</u>

Enter through His Gate into the Eternal Kingdom!

Official Photograph of "The Magdala Stone," taken in October 2009
Courtesy of and ©2009 Magdala Center Excavations Israel

The Excavations of the Ancient Synagogue of Magdala
Official Photograph taken in December 2009
Courtesy of and ©2009 Magdala Center Excavations Israel

Official Aerial Photograph
©2013 by David Silverman & Yuval Nadel
for Magdala Center Excavations Israel

The Excavation photos of the Ancient Synagogue of Mary Magdalene, where Yeshua arrived in, "The Jesus Boat" & gave the sign of Jonah, to reveal the time of His return from Heaven. I noticed that the L-shaped right angles on the Shroud of Turin are also on the pavement here in the corners of the floor & in the corners of the circular design in this Synagogue. The right angles symbolize the four horns of the sacrificial altar. A horn denotes the power of the light of the Living Torah of truth depicted in Messiah Yeshua (salvation) the Living Almond tree Menorah.

"THE JESUS BOAT"

"The Jesus Boat," That carried the Living Torah
so He could speak the Word of Eternal Life to Israel.
It was excavated between Magdala and Ginosar Israel
Official Photographs ©2013 The Yigal Allon Center, Ginosar Israel

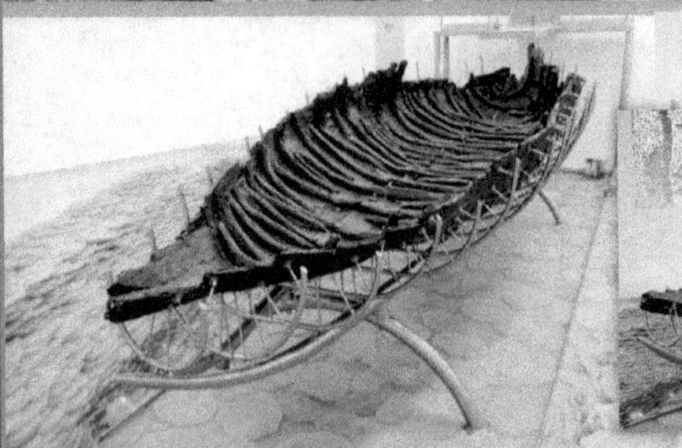

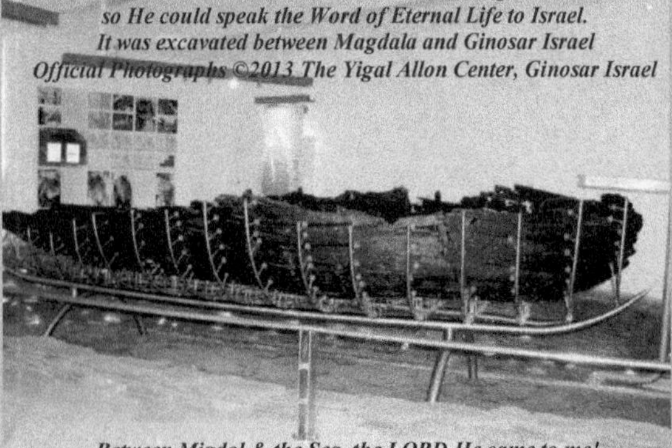

Official Photographs of, "The Jesus Boat"
©2013 The Yigal Allon Center, Ginosar Israel

Between Migdol & the Sea, the LORD He came to me!
The fishes shall tell you the hand of the LORD hath wrought this!

The Fig Tree discovered fruiting on the lower north flank of the Real Mount Sinai in Arabia Official Photo ©1992 Jim and Penny Caldwell, All Rights Reserved - My book verifies through Divine Providence & through many miracles with the Almond Tree of Life & The Fig Tree of the Knowledge of Good and Evil, that Jim & Penny truly found the real Mount Sinai in Arabia!

Here is the sign of the coming of the LORD! Luke 21:29 And He spake to them a parable; Behold the fig tree and all the trees; When they now shoot forth, ye see and know of your own selves that summer is now nigh at hand. So likewise ye, when ye see these things come to pass, know ye that the Kingdom of God is nigh at hand. Verily I say unto you, This generation shall not pass away, till all be fulfilled.

Official Photo of the Burnt peak of Mount Sinai – Incredibly, The Almond Mountain in the Wilderness of Arabia, where Jim & Penny Caldwell miraculously found their fruiting Almond Trees, Cedar & Fig Discovered in 1992 Photo ©1992 Jim and Penny Caldwell, All Rights Reserved

The Official Photo of the Split Rock of Horeb Discovered in 1992 Photo ©1992 Jim and Penny Caldwell All Rights Reserved

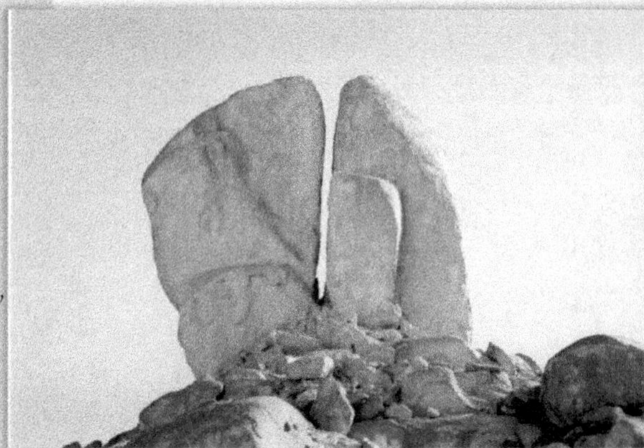

Behold, the Ark of the Covenant of the LORD of all the earth passeth over before you into Jordan.

Revelation 15:3-5 And they sing the song of Moses the servant of God, and the song of the Lamb, saying, Great and marvelous are they works, LORD God Almighty; just and true are Thy ways, Thou KING of Saints, who shall not fear Thee, O LORD, and glorify Thy Name? For Thou only are holy; for all Nations shall come and worship before Thee; for Thy judgments are made manifest. And after that I looked, and behold, the Temple of the Tabernacle of the Testimony in Heaven was opened.

Preparing to cross over the Jordan River into the Eternal Promised Land Palm Trees & River Photos ©2013 Kimberly K Ballard All Rights Reserved

♫ A New Song of Moses includes the Lamb. ♫
It is a blend of Exodus 15 and Revelation 15

I will sing unto the LORD, for He hath triumphed gloriously; Great and marvelous are they works, LORD God Almighty; just and true are Thy ways, Thou KING of Saints, who shall not fear Thee, O LORD, and glorify Thy Name? For Thou only are holy; for all nations shall come and worship before Thee; for Thy judgments are made manifest. The LORD is my strength and song, and He is become my Yeshua: He is my God, and I will prepare Him an habitation; my father's God, and I will exalt Him. The LORD is a man of war: the LORD is His Name. And I heard the angel of the waters say, Thou art righteous, O LORD, which art, and wast, and shalt be, because Thou hast judged thus. For they have shed the blood of Saints and Prophets, and Thou hast given them blood to drink; for they are worthy. And I heard another out of the altar say, Even so, LORD God Almighty, true and righteous are Thy judgments. Thy right hand, O LORD, is become glorious in power: Thy right hand, O LORD hath dashed in pieces the enemy. And in the greatness of Thine Excellency Thou hast overthrown them that rose up against Thee: Thou sentest forth Thy wrath, which consumed them as stubble. And He gathered them together into a place called in the Hebrew tongue Armageddon. The enemy said, I will pursue, I will overtake, I will divide the spoil; my lust shall be satisfied upon them: I will draw my sword and my hand shall destroy them. These shall make war with the Lamb, and the Lamb shall overcome them; for He is Lord of lords, and King of kings: and they that are with Him are called, and chosen, and faithful. And I heard a loud voice saying in Heaven, Now is come salvation, and strength, and the Kingdom of our God; and the power of His Messiah; for the accuser of our brethren is cast down, which accused them before our God day and night. And they overcame him by the blood of the Lamb, and by the Word of their Testimony; and they loved not their lives unto the death. Rejoice over her, thou Heaven, and ye holy Apostles and Prophets; for God hath avenged you on her. Fear and dread shall fall upon them; by the greatness of Thine arm they shall be as still as a stone; till Thy people pass over, O LORD, till the people pass over, which Thou hast purchased. Thou shalt bring them in, and plant them in the mountain of Thine inheritance, in the place, O LORD which Thou hast made for Thee to dwell in, in the Sanctuary, O LORD, which Thy hands have established. The LORD shall reign forever and ever. And the seventh angel sounded; and there were great voices in Heaven, saying, The kingdoms of this world are become the Kingdoms of our Lord, and of His Messiah; and He shall reign forever and ever.

"The Little Prince," Resting under my Sukkah tree!

The Official Letter from Montpelier Virginia with the Cedar cones

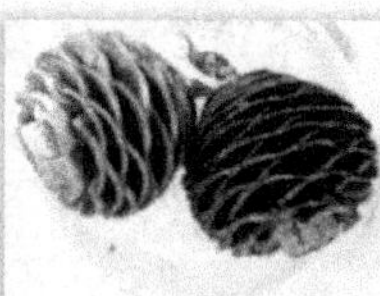

The Snow white Dove

Official Shroud Face of Messiah Yeshua

Messiah Yeshua producing the sweetness of the resurrection glory! God's Living Almond Rod that budded to life, bearing the First Fruit from the Eternal Almond Tree of Life, in the Heavenly Ark of the Covenant!

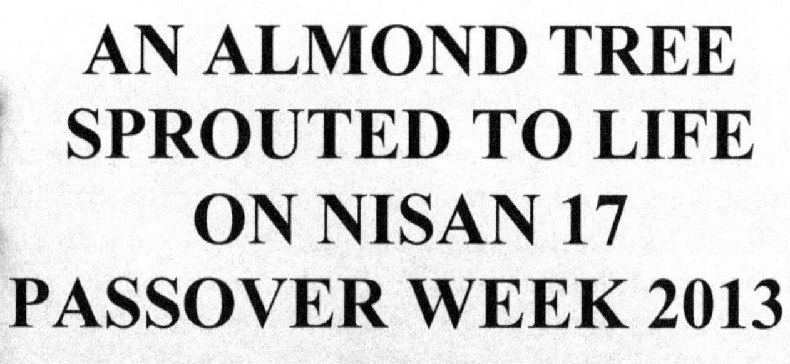

AN ALMOND TREE SPROUTED TO LIFE ON NISAN 17 PASSOVER WEEK 2013!

This is an incredible update! An astonishing miracle has come to pass this week during Passover 2013. I was in the process of designing my book cover in late March 2013 and Passover was quickly approaching. I only had a few days left to accomplish it due to a time constraint and so unfortunately, beyond my control, it held over into the beginning of Passover. I finally had to quit working on it, even if I could not save all my hard work. Now remember that I said previously that I planted seeds on *Tu B' Shevat* this year, Israel's New Year of Trees. I planted some Almond seeds, Cedar of Lebanon seeds, and fruit tree seeds on January 26, 2013, on the Rosh HaShanah of Trees. Now my book about the miracle of the Almond Tree was nearing publication and after some frustration with not being able to save my book cover, after a little over two months had passed or precisely 8 weeks and five days after Tu B' Shevat, I had just celebrated Passover on the evening of March 25th which was Nisan 14, the day that Messiah Yeshua was crucified as the Lamb of God and I remembered Him in the Passover Seder. I even ate the Lamb's Ear Maror that I wrote about in this book and it tasted a bit like parsley! I did not see anything happening with either the Almond seeds or Cedar seeds and I said to the seeds, *"Come on, it is time to sprout, Passover is here!"* When Nisan 14 arrived on March 25th and for two days afterwards still nothing at all was happening with the seeds. I prayed to the LORD about it and wondered whether He was still with me on this project because I seemed to be running into so many problems with not being able to save my finished book cover. Then on Nisan 17, which was March 28th, which as you know by now is the most important day of Yeshua's resurrection, I came into the room in the morning and noticed that the soil appeared to be lifting up a little in one of the packs of seeds and I wondered whether or not something was happening with one of the Almond seeds, but since so many weeks had passed from Tu B' Shevat, I just thought that I was imagining it, so I did not get up close to it to check. Later on in the evening, when it was nearing 10:30 pm, I went to sleep for a few hours, but I woke up well before dawn when it was still dark and silent outside. I was thinking about Yeshua's resurrection. So I got up and went to look out the glass door to see what it looked like outside and then it struck me *that three days and three nights had just passed and that Yeshua would have been raised to life within this time frame, as the Rod of an Almond Tree.* As I looked out through the glass, I was pondering the women coming to the Garden tomb before dawn while it was still dark and silent outside, just like it was now on the third day of Passover. I then said softly, *"LORD this is exactly the time that you came to life,"* and I was touched thinking of that Biblical scene happening almost 2,000 years ago. Then I went back to sleep, saying a little prayer that included having my seeds sprout. As it became morning on Nisan 18 on March 29th I came upstairs. It was now the fourth day of Passover and today was my Mother's birthday and it was *"Good Friday."* So sometime between Nisan 17 and Nisan 18 or the third into the fourth day of Passover, one Almond Tree was raised to life in its container! *It had been exactly three days and exactly three nights from Passover!* Just to be sure, I double checked the

Biblical calendar and this was absolutely correct! There were suddenly these Almond leaves mounding up and rising up out of the soil in the container! I was so shocked and I was thrilled beyond belief! I was so happy that tears rolled down my checks, as I realized the powerful connection of this little sprout to Messiah Yeshua and my book! I had tried since 2007 to plant Almond seeds with no success, but this time one sprouted. This was my final sign that this Testimony was about to go forth to the world! I could hardly comprehend the timing of this astonishing and fantastic miracle. I believe the LORD performed this miracle just for me to show me that He is still working in this project, even though I could not save my book cover in time for Passover week. Later I found out that my entire book cover was saved and every element had worked! The next day, on March 30th I came up to look at the newly sprouted Almond Tree and I could not believe that the trunk of the tree was already one inch tall! This was the fourth day of Pesach. On the fifth day of Pesach or Passover week, which was March 31st, the leaves of the tree were opening up and it was almost two inches tall already!

On the sixth day of Pesach, the Shroud of Yeshua was exhibited in Italy and I watched the exhibition on the internet. This morning, my Almond Tree was putting forth leaves from the trunk of the tree, the third day after it sprouted to life. On the seventh day of Passover, which was April 1st, it was the fourth day after the tree sprouted and it grew to just over 2 inches tall and two leaves were coming out of the trunk of the Almond Tree. If there was ever one last proof of this entire Testimony of the LORD, this miracle was another blessing before my book went into print! So I looked up what was happening during this Holy Week on Nisan 17 and Nisan 18 specifically. It is customary to read Isaiah 61 which talks about *"The Favorable year of the LORD!"* It is also customary to read Psalm 89. This speaks about the LORD as *"My Father, my God, the Rock and my Saviour."* It is also customary on this day to read Revelation 1:5-8. This speaks about *"Messiah Yeshua, the faithful witness and the first born of the dead, who has freed us from our sins with His life blood."* Here, He is called *"The Ruler of the King's of the earth."* Then Luke 4:16-21 is also read, which refers to Isaiah 61 and again speaks of *"The Favorable Year of the LORD!"* In the evening on Nisan 17, which was March 28th on Thursday, the Exodus passage that is read on this day speaks about *"Passover, the Lamb and eating the Unleavened Bread."* The Psalm 116 passage that is read speaks of *"Lifting up the cup of salvation and the LORD delivering us from death."* They read I Corinthians 11:23-26 and it speaks about *"Yeshua's body represented in the Unleavened Bread that was broken for us and the cup of the New Covenant in His life blood that we remember His death during Passover or Pesach until He comes."* John 13 is also read and it speaks about *"Yeshua washing the Jewish disciples' feet (and hands), so they were cleansed in the Molten Brazen Sea, the Basin that is the LORD."* All of these Scriptures are read on the third day of Pesach in the Church. On Nisan 18, it is customary to read about *the Passover of atonement* in the offering from Numbers 28. In the Church on this day it is customary to read about *the LORD'S Passion on this Good Friday.* The Scriptures include, Isaiah 52, Psalm 31, Hebrews 4, and John 18. When my new little Almond Tree reached six days old, it was already nearing 3 inches tall on Wednesday, April 3rd 2013. This is the first Almond Tree I have ever seen in person and touched in my entire life. *Now I can say with confidence, that I was given the Rod of an Almond Tree by the LORD Yeshua, as a Living Testimony to show His glory!*

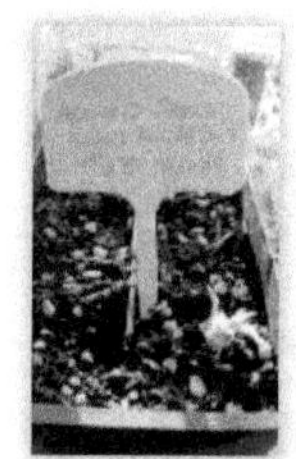

Day 1 My Almond Tree Sprouted to life on Thurs. Nisan 17, 3 days and 3 nights after Passover, on the Third Day of Passover week, exactly when Yeshua came to life as the Almond Branch from the Almond Tree of Life and it appeared like this in the morning on Passover day 4, Nisan 18 on March 29th 2013 Photo 6:55 PM on Good Friday & it also happened to be my Mother's Birthday 2013. It is an astounding miracle that came to me, as I was working on my book cover to finish it! It is the day of the celebration of Yeshua's Passion!

Day 2 March 30th 2013 11:13AM on Nisan 19 Passover week day 5 Saturday Sabbath Day, Almond Tree over an inch tall!

Day 3 after sprouting to life, the Almond Tree on Sunday March 31st 2013 10:36 AM on Nisan 20, The Tree is growing fast on Holy Passover week day 6!

Day 4 after sprouting as it appeared on Monday April 1st 2013 3:39PM on Holy Passover week day 7

Day 14 after sprouting as my Almond Tree appeared on Thursday April 11th 2013

Day 17 taken Sunday April 14th 2013 5:53PM

Day 21 after sprouting as it appeared on Thursday April 18th 2013 6:45PM

Day 24 - 4 inches tall. This photograph was taken on Sunday April 21, 2013

Day 33 Transplanted on April 24th 2013 Pesach Sheni This day was, "The Second Passover"

Day 44 May 5th 2013

Day 47 May 8th 2013

Pentecost May 15th 2013 49th day from Passover Day 54 after sprouting

Pentecost May 16th 2013 50 days after Passover Almond 6.5 inches tall!

My Miracle Almond Rod lifted up to Heaven on May 27 2013 Almost 7 inches tall!

My Miracle Passover Almond Tree in this photo was 17 inches tall on Sept. 27th 2013. In this photograph, it was standing in the rain during the Colorado Flood. After such severe drought, I had lifted it up to Heaven and prayed for rain. A rare and devastating flood came and the drought ended in seven days. Over the next year it put forth branches, grew the height of the garage ceiling, and I was able to use many photos of it in my book on all the earlier pages!

My Miracle Passover Almond Tree, Flight Clouds & Doves

On January 14th 2014, two days before Tu B' Shevat my Almond Tree was 5' 3" tall! The first Branch came out of my Almond Tree in the seventh month! The Branch grew at a perfect right angle to the trunk like an arm.

My Almond Tree grew tall the summer of 2014! A spring picture taken April 2nd 2015 at center. Top pictures taken in the fall on September 20th 2014 On April 2nd 2015 just before Passover my miracle Almond Tree was almost 9 feet tall! Photos ©2014 & ©2015 Kimberly K Ballard All Rights Reserved

BIBLIOGRAPHY

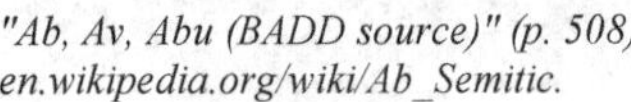

"Ab, Av, Abu (BADD source)" (p. 508) en.wikipedia.org/wiki/Ab_Semitic.

"Acacia Albida" (p. 621) Encyclopaedia Britannica, Copyright 2012 Inc., www.britannica.com/EBchecked/topic/12961/Albida-acacia.

"Acacia Albida" (p. 620) The Jewish Virtual Library, Copyright 2008, The Gale Group, ©2012 The American-Israel Cooperative Enterprise. http://www.jewishvirtuallibrary.org/jsource/judaica/ejud_0002_0016_0_15852.html.

Acacia Plant (Acacia Seyal Facts) (p. 628) ©2007 — All Rights Reserved. http://www.acaciaplant.net.

Acacia Seyal (p. 628) - Duke, James A. Purdue University Center for New Crops & Plants Products. Copyright 1983. www.hort.purdue.edu/newcrop/duke_energy/Acacia_seyal.html.

Acacia Tortilis Facts (p. 613-14) - Modzelevich, Martha. "Flowers In Israel" - Copyright 2005-2011. http://www.flowersinisrael.com/Acaciatortilis_page.htm.

"Accessory fruit" - "False Fruit" (p. 386) - en.wikipedia.org/wiki/Accessory_fruit. 2010.

"Adam & the shortening of days after Tishrei" (p. 535) - jewishencyclopedia.com/articles/758-adam.

Almond Harvesting (p. 813-14); You Tube; Orchards, Bella Viva, Hughson CA. www.youtube.com/user/BellaVivaOrchards. Copyright 2011 All Rights Reserved. http://www.youtube.com/watch?v=f2CMxHPi9j0.

Almonds and heart health: Janecky, Cheryl. Ezine Articles, Copyright 2009, February 20th. http://ezinearticles.com/?Defy-Death---Snack-Yourself-Into-a-Healthy-Heart-With-Almonds&id=2018013.

"Almond Trees" by Davis wiki (a wiki spot). Copyright 2013. http://daviswiki.org/Almond_Trees.

—. "Almond" Wikipedia. 2009-2013. http://en.wikipedia.org/wiki/Almond.

Alphabet (Aleph-Bet 101) (pp 288, 511, 691) Sources: Judaism. Jewish Virtual Library, "Hebrew, Hebrew Copyright 2008 The Gale Group & Copyright 2013 The American-Israeli Cooperative Enterprise.http://www.jewishvirtuallibrary.org/jsource/Judaism/alephbet.html.

"Ancient Hebrew letter Shin" (p. 566) - Benner, Jeff A. Copyright 1999-2013. http://www.ancient-hebrew.org/3_sin.html.

Andrew the Apostle (p. 697) Copyright 2011 http://www.patriarchate.org/patriarchate/former-patriarchs/Andrew-apostle.

Aqueducts & threshing floor (p. 489): bible.ca/archeaology/bible-archeology-jerusalem-temple-mount-threshing-floor-aqueduct.htm.

"Ark of the Covenant was a Giant Capacitor" (pp 548, 559) Mark, Strauss. - filed to "Mad Science" Text Source: io9.com/the-engineer-who-said-the-ark-of-the-covenant-was-a-gia-1598583115. 2014 July 1.

Armstrong, W.P. Fig Fruit (p. 381) ©2010, March 5 http://www.waynesword.palomar.edu/pljune99.htm.

"Army Standards - The Roman Empire" (p. 227) ©2008. http://www.roman-empire.net/army/leg-standards.html.

"Astrophotography" (p. 551) ©2010-2011 All Rights Reserved www.en.wikipedia.org/wiki/Astrophotograpy.

Authority, Israeli Antiquities (p. 680) "The Leon Levy Dead Sea Scrolls Digital Library" Copyright 2012 http://www.deadseascrolls.org.il/.

"Babylon" Gate of Heaven (p. 475) - en.wikipedia.org/wiki/Babylon.

"Baca" (p. 689) www.biblehub.com/topical/b/baca.htm (accessed 2010-2012).

"BADD meaning" (p. 508) - starling.rinet.ru/cgi-bin/response.cgi?root=config&morpho=0&basename=/data/semham/semet&first=1741.

Bagatti, P. B., & MILIK, J. T. (p. 454) "Pubblicazioni Dello Studium Biblicum Franciscanum N. 13 "GLI SCAVI DEL "DOMINUS FLEVIT" Parte I LA Necropoli Del Periodo Romano. Copyright 1958. http://www.jamestabor.com.

BBC News - "Jordan Cave may be oldest Church" (p. 699) McGrath, Matt. BBC Science Correspondent. BBC News - http://www.news.bbc.co.uk/2/hi/science/nature/7446812.stm

Beryl Stone (p. 760) Tech, Cal. "Colors From Ionizing Radiation" Copyright 2011, April 12th. www.minerals.gps.caltech.edu/COLOR_Causes/Radiate/index.html.

Biltz, Mark (p. 692) Senior Pastor of El Shaddai Ministries in Tacoma, Washington USA. Copyright 2012. http://www.elshaddaiministries.us.

Blau, Ludwig & Kohler, Kaufmann. The Jewish Encyclopedia.com. Copyright 2002. www.thejewishencyclopedia.com (accessed 2010-2012).

Bordeaux Pilgrim excerpts (pp 790-795): "The Pilgrim of Bordeaux" 333AD ITINERARIUM BURDIGALENSE, CORPUS SCRIPTORUM ECCLES.LATINORUM, XXXVIIII, ITINERA HIEROSOLYMITANA, SAECULI IIII - VIII,. Geyer, Paul (ed.) Translated by Vander Nat., Arnold. Copyright 1898, 2001 translation, online Copyright 2005. http://www.homepages.luc.edu/~avande1/jerusalem/sources/bordeauxJerus.htm.

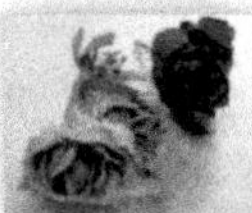

British Royal Monarchy: Household, The Royal. "The Official Website of The Royal British Monarchy of HRH Queen Elizabeth II" (pp 583, 600, 611) - Copyright Crown 2012, 2011. http://www.royal.gov.uk/MonarchUK/Symbols/TheCrownJewels.aspx.

"Cedar of Lebanon" (p. 738) - Haskell, Tony - Somerset Gardens Trust – Autumn 1998 - extracts from "The Forest Trees of Britain" by the Rev CA Johns BA, FLS dated 1894. - Compiled by Tony Haskell. "The Association of Gardens Trusts, "The Cedar of Lebanon - Cedrus libani"." Extract from Sharpe's London Magazine, London England.

"Charmer" (p. 478) - unintelligable languages pg 295 Jewish definition from: "A Book of Jewish Concepts" - Philip, Birnbaum, Revised Edition." Hebrew Publishing Co. New York, 1964, 1975.

"Chuppah" (p. 439) - en.wikipedia.org/wiki/Chuppah.

"Condenser - Electrical" (p. 548) - Encyclopedia Britannica, Inc. ©1960 William Benton, Publisher Chicago: London: Toronto.

Copper Scroll translations: Allegro, John Marco ©1960.

Copper Scroll (p 809)-en.wikipedia.org/wiki/Copper_Scroll

—. "Corona Discharge" (p. 305) Copyright 2011. http://www.en.wikipedia.org/wiki/Corona_discharge.

"Crown of Thorns" - Father, A Passionist. "The Mystery of the Crown of Thorns" (p. 702) Copyright 2011, Preserving Christian Publications, Inc., Albany, NY. http://www.catholictradition.org/Passion/crown-thorns3.htm.

Crown - The Jewish Priestly Tzizt (p. 598) - ©2007 All Rights Reserved. http://www.templeinstitute.org.

Danin, Dr. Avinoam, Professor Emeritus of Botany at The Hebrew University Jerusalem Israel" (pp 381, 383, 388) Flora of Israel Online, The Hebrew University of Jerusalem". Copyright 2006+. http://www.flora.huji.ac.il.

Dictionary, Random House College. Random House College Dictionary. fifth Edition. Translated by Random House College Dictionary. Nashville Tennessee: Random House Publishing, 1975.

—. "Dorcas Gazelle" (pp 621-622) Wikipedia. Copyright 2010. http://en.wikipedia.org/wiki/Dorcas_Gazelle.

Dye: "Historical Dye colors" (p. 593) - en.wikipedia.org/wiki/Natural_dye. 2009.

Dye for the Priestly Garments (p. 598); The Temple Institute - Tola' at Shani scarlet dye, Tekhelet blue & Royal purple dye, Copyright ©2007 All Rights Reserved. http://www.templeinstitute.org.

"Egyptian Statue of Sekema on auction at Christies" (p. 605) - news.yahoo.com/egypt-challenges-sale-valuable-ancient-statue-104733054.html#.

"Ein Karem - Mary drank from visiting Elisabeth" (p. 597) - tiuli.com/track_info.asp?lng=engotrack_id=91.

—. "Electrical Conductor" (p. 542) Copyright 2011. http://www.wikipedia.org/wiki/Electrical_conductor.

—. "Electrical Photographic Corona Discharge" (p. 542), Wikipedia. Copyright 2010. http://www.en.wikipedia.org/wiki/Corona_discharge.

—. "Electromagnetic Radiation" (pp 541-6, 549, 553, 760) ©2011 www.en.wikipedia.org/wiki/Electromagnetic_radiation

—. "Electromagnetic Spectrum" (p. 541), Copyright 2007. www.en.wikipedia.org/wiki/Electromagnetic_spectrum.

"Electrostatic Painting" (p. 546) Copyright 2012. http://www.ehow.com/how-does_5565360_electrostatic-painting-works.html.

Encyclopedia, Fruits. "Fruits Encyclopedia, Worlds Best Sources of Fruits information". Copyright 2013. http://www.fruitsencyclopedia.com/almonds.html.

Encyclopedia, International Standard Bible: Beecher, Willis J. - Copyright 2010.

Encyclopedia, New World - "Temple of Jerusalem". Copyright 2008, September 26th. www.newworldencyclopedia.org/entry/Solomon%27s_Temple & www.newworldencyclopedia.org/entry/Temple_of_Jerusalem

—. "Erhu," (Musical Instrument made from Sandalwood) (p. 230) ©2013. http://www.en.wikipedia.org/wiki/Erhu.

Exodus Crossing Site (p. 174) - Caldwell, Jim and Penny - splitrockresearch.org.

Exodus crossing Site (p. 174) - Dr, Moller, Lennart. theexoduscase.org.

Exodus Crossing Site Map (p. 174): bibleatlas.org/full/mount_paran.htm (Map of the Gulf of Aqaba - a branch of the Red Sea).

—. "Ferrocerium" (p. 560) Copyright 2010. http://www.en.wikipedia.org/wiki/Ferrocerium.

—. Fig Tree (p. 383), Copyright 2011. http://www.en.wikipedia.org/wiki/Fig_trees.

—. Fig Wasp and Syconium (pp 381, 383), Copyright 2011. http://www.simple.wikipedia.org/wiki/Fig and Fig Wasp and Syconium.

Flax Growing Facts - Mills, Irish Linen (p. 595) - "Irish Linen - The Fabric of Ireland," Copyright 2010. http://www.irishlinenmills.com/History/history.htm.

"Fountain of Mary" (p. 597) - (biblehistory.com/ibh/Israel+Monuments/Pools+And+Fountains/Fountain+of+the+Virgin) AND "Fountain of the Virgin" (p. 597) - en.wikipedia.org/wiki/Fountain_of_the_Virgin.

"Four Species" (of the Lulav) & "Myrtle" (pp 748-749) Jewish Virtual Library, Copyright 2008 The Gale Group Copyright 2012 The American-Israel Cooperative Enterprise. http://www.jewishvirtuallibrary.org/jsource/judaica/ejud_0002_0007_0_06640.html AND http://www.jewishvirtuallibrary.org/jsource/judaica/ejud_0002_0014_0_14422.html.

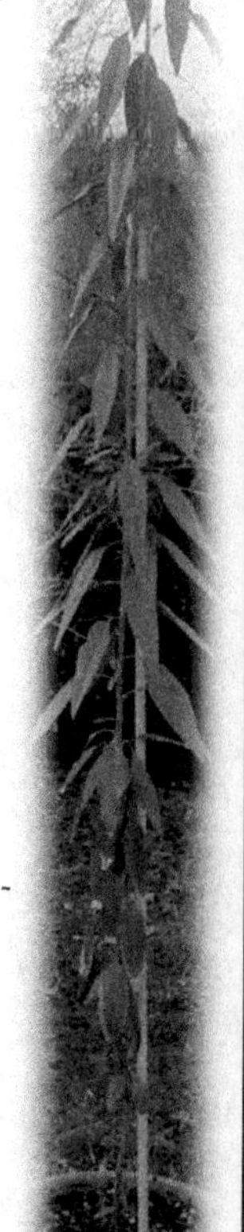

Garden Tomb excavations - Condor, Captain. "Survey of Western Palestine" (p. 513), Jerusalem Volume, p. 432, Source; Jerusalem, Bethany, and Bethlehem, p. 166). Copyright 1881.

Garden Tomb: "The Garden Tomb" (p. 693), Tvedtnes, John A. Newspaper and proceedings of the Society for Early Historic Archaeology. April, 1982-1983. 4-11.

"Gihon" (p. 597) - Easton's Bible Dictionary 1897 Public Domain from biblestudytools.com/dictionary/gihon/.

"Gihon" (p.597) - "Fountain of Mary" - classic.net.bible.org/dictionary.php?Word=GIHON.

—. "Guzheng" (Musical Instrument made of Sandalwood) (p. 230), ©2013 www.enwikipedia.org/wiki/Guzheng.

Heidler, Robert - Glory of Zion International Ministries, Denton TX (The Year of the Almond Tree) (p. 833), ©2009

"History of the City of Rome The Middle Ages" (p. 701) - Gregorovius, Ferdinand. - Translated by Anne Hamilton From the fourth German Edition. London England: George Bell & Sons, Copyright 1894 (Public Domain)

"Holy Half Shekel Coin" (p. 182) - begedivri.com.

"Holy Spirit as a Dove" (p. 414) - (Ben Zoma interpretation c. 100), (Hag. 15a), (Talmud, Berachot 3a), (Shab. 31a; Sanh.96a) - jewishencyclopedia.com/articles/7833-holy-spirit & (jewishencyclopedia.com/articles/13537 shekinah)

Hunt, June. Hope For The Heart Ministries (p. 624), Dallas, Texas ©2010. http://www.hopefortheheart.org.

"In a Vision, in a Mirror" quote (p. 551): Shoshan-Simon, Moshe Dr. "The Israel Koschitzsky Virtual Beit Midrash," From; "Reading Midrash Aggada," Shiur -#12; Mirror Images Vayikra Rabba 1:14-15

"Invisibility Cloak" (p. 555) - ©2013 June 6 - www.technologyreview.com/view/515776/human-scale-invisibility-cloak-unveiled/.

"Invisibility Cloak" (pp 554-5), ©2014 Aug. 10, Volume XV Issue II of "Illumin," A review of engineering in everyday life by Emily Sylvester-illumin.usc.edu/printer/211/the-prospects-of-invisibility-cloaks-bending-the-laws-of-light/.

"Jacob's Well" (p. 498) - biblehistory.com/links.php?cat=40&sub=680.

"Jacob's Well" (p. 498), en.wikipedia.org/wiki/Jacob's_Well

James Madison's Montpelier (pp 773-9), ©2009 www.montpelier.org/

Jerusalem: Blank, Wayne. "A History of Jerusalem, Titus and the Zealots". Copyright 2012, February 4th. http://www.keyway.ca/htm2012/20120204.htm.

Jerusalem, Rebirth of a City. (p. 812) ©1985 Martin Gilbert

"Jerusalem Revealed (p. 812) - Archaeology in the Holy City" ©1968-1974 by the Israel Exploration Society.

Josephus, Flavious. "Antiquities of the Jews." The Complete Works, by A.M. Translated by William Whiston. Nashville, Tennessee: Thomas Nelson, Inc., 1737, Copyright 1998.

Judaica, Encyclopaedia - H.B. Tristram, Natural History of the Bible (18775), Tevu'ot ha-Areẓ (1900) J. Schwarz, Flora Loew, Arbeit und Sitte in Palaestina, 7 vols. in 8 (1928–42) G. Dalman, Plants of the Bible (1952) H.N. and A.L. Moldenke, and J. Feliks.

Judaica, Encyclopedia- Loew, Flora, 2 (1924), 257–74, Plants of the Bible (1952), 316 (index), S.V. H.N. and A.L. Moldenke, and Olam ha-Ẓome'aḥ ha-Mikra'i (19682), 99–101. ADD. BIBLIOGRAPHY: Feliks, Ha-Ẓome'aḥ, 51. J. Feliks.

Justice and Mercy (p. 821) - M. Arzt, (1963), 271–86, Perushim ve-Ḥiddushim ba-Yerushalmi, 3 (1941), 67–108 L. Ginzberg, in: HUCA, 6 (1929), 12–37 Morgenstern, and World of Prayer, 2 (1963), 262–7. E. Munk. Jewish Virtual Library, "Ne'ilat She'arim ("Closing of the Gates"), the symbolic closing of the heavenly gates, On the Day of Atonement. Copyright © 2008 The Gale Group. All Rights Reserved -©2013 The American-Israeli Cooperative Enterprise www.jewishvirtuallibrary.org/jsource/judaica/ejud_0002_0015_0_14668.html.

"Kaparot" (Kaparos) - judaism.about.com/od/holidays/a/kaparot-kaparos-Yomkippur-Customs.

"Karpas" (p. 622) - Wecker, Menachem. My Jewish Learning, "Joseph & the Technicolor Dreamcoat" (Rashi cites references to karpas (wool) in Esther 1:6 and to a k'tonet pasim, a woolen coat, in Samuel 2, 13:18. (A midrash that Rashi cites claims the word is an acronym for Joseph's troubles). Copyright 2013. http://www.myjewishlearning.com/culture/2/Theatre_and_Dance/Theatre/America/joseph-dreamcoat.shtml.

"Kippah or Yarmulke" (pp 617-18) Segal, Rabbi Ronen Levi Yitzchak (AKA Ronennachman770). You tube - ©2010 http://www.youtube.com/watch?v=NgJwLboehbQ & www.youtube.com/results?search_query=ronennachmann770+Kippah+or+Yarmulke.

Kosherkippot (pp 617-18) You Tube "How to buy a Kippah" - The Frik Kippah on a mannequin. ©2011, September 1. http://www.youtube.com/watch?v=MPwOvUuPjbw Link: http://www.milechai.com/kippot/index.html.

Legion XXIV (p. 226) - Imperial Standards - Imperial Aquila-Signums-Vexillium-Imago-Draco-Standards. ©2010. http://www.legionxxiv.org/signum/.

Leon Levy Dead Sea Scroll Project (p. 680) ©2012 ***video transcribed by KKB at:*** *www.deadseascrolls.org.il/about-the-project/a-note-from-the-iaa-director (Israeli Antiquities Authority)*

Letter from King Philip of the Romans, Listing the relics stolen by Abbot Martin during the Sack of Constantinople in 1204 (pp 686-687), Crusades-Encyclopedia, "Historia Constantinopolitana". Vols. Gunther, ch. xxiv, in Riant: Exuviae, Vol. 1, p. 120 ff. von Pairis', Gunther.

"Light Spectrum" (p. 541, 549) - Encyclopaedia Britannica Inc. ©2011. http://www.britannica.com.

—. "Liquid Molten Mirror Telescopes" (p. 552), ©2010-11 http://www.en.wikipedia.org/wiki/Liquid-mirror_telescope.

—. Malaysia facts regarding precious gemstones, peacocks, sandlewood, exotic flora of the world (p. 229-30) - ©2013. http://www.en.wikipedia.org/wiki/Malaysia.

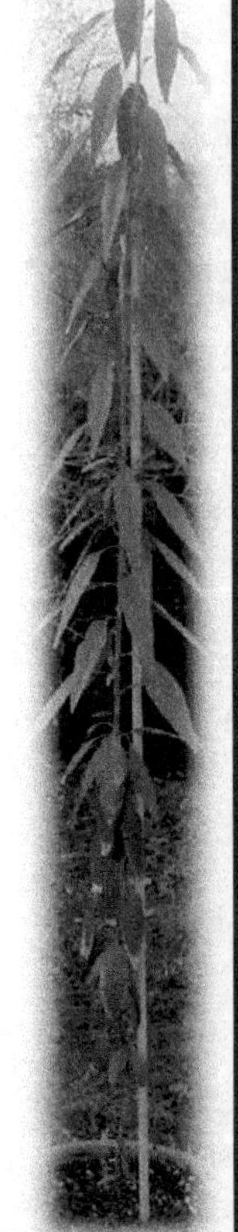

Mark Twain (p. 377), 1867 printed 1881 London England jewishvirtuallibrary.org/jsourc/Quote/TwainJews.html.

"Maror" (p. 482) - Source, and Encyclopaedia, Loew, Flora (1928), Moldenke, A.L., Plants of the Bible (1952) Judaica. Jewish Virtual Library - Copyright 2008 The Gale Group All Rights Reserved & Copyright 2011 The American-Israeli Cooperative Enterprise. http://www.jewishvirtuallibrary.org/jsource/judaica/ejud_0002_0013_0_13332.htm.

Martin, Ernest L., PH. D. "The Temples that Jerusalem Forgot" (p. 806) - (Excerpts about the Fortress of Antonia and the water cisterns). Copyright 2000, March 1.

McCurdy, J. Frederic & Kohler, Kaufmann & Gottheil, Richard (p. 667) The Jewish Encyclopedia.com. ©2002. http://www.thejewishencyclopedia.com (2010-2012).

"Meaning of 666 - Greek chi-xi-stigma" (p. 171) - www.biblestudytools.com/lexicons/greek/nas/chi-xi-stigma.html.

"Meaning of 666"(p. 171) - www.youtube.com/watch?v=vFw2Kr13mng.

"Meaning of Z"l for Ronen Nachmann Z"l" (p. 618) - en.wikipedia.org/wiki/Z"l.

Medieval Sourcebook; The Fourth Crusade 1204 (p. 687); Collected Sources". Copyright 1997, December - Paul Halsall. http://www.fordham.edu/halsall/source/4cde.asp. University of Pennsylvania, [n.d.] 189?), 1-18. "FordHam University, The Jesuit University of New York,"

"Meleke" (p. 457) - ehow.com/list_7629853_types-limestone.html. ©2011.

"Meleke Limestone in Jerusalem" (p. 458) - en.wikipedia.org/wiki/Jerusalem_stone.

"Meleke Limestone" (p. 458) - soft when quarried - thefullwiki.org/Meleke.

Military, Ancient (p. 227): Smith, William, LLD., Wayte, William. Marindin, G.E. "Signa Militaria," A Dictionary of Greek and Roman Antiquities. Albemarle Stree, London: Murray, John, Copyright 1890 All Rights Reserved.

—. "Molten Sea" (p. 552) ©2012 en.wikipedia.org/wiki/Molten_Sea.

Moses' actions - Biblica - "Introductions to the books of the Bible." "Deuteronomy" The NIV study Bible. Copyright 2002. http://www.biblica.com/niv/study-bible/deuteronomy/

"Moses liberator (p. 504) - brought nation together" - jewish encyclopedia.com/articles/11049-moses.

—. Mount Ophir (p. 229), ©2013 en.wikipedia.org/wiki/Mount_Ophir.

"Mussaf" - en.wikipedia.org/wiki/Mussaf.

"Mussaf Prayer - Kingliness, Zichronot - Rememberances, shofar blasts, Torah Mount Sinai" (p. 493) - www.theholidayspot.com/rosh_hashana/prayer.htm.

"Mussaf Prayers (pp 494, 497), Rabbi Simcha Pearlmutter, Rabbi testimony of Jesus, Yeshua, Messiah" - Full Text: jerusalemcalling.org/Rabbi_Simcha_Pearlmutter.htm.

"Mussaf prayers Rosh HaShanah" (p. 494) - ualberta.ca/~yreshef/shabbat/roshprayers.html.

"Mussaf Prayer of Rosh HaShanah in English" (p. 493), Copyright 2012-2013. NetGlimpse.com. Rosh Hashanah Prayers - http://www.netglimse.com/holidays/rosh_hashanah/rosh_hashanah_prayers_prayers,_mussaf_prayer_of_rosh_hashanah_in_english.

"Mussaf Prayer of Rosh HaShanah - Zichronot Rememberances" (p. 493) Sources: Ohr Kodesh Congregation in Chevy Chase, MD. Jewish Virtual Library, Copyright 2008 The Gale Group and Copyright 2013 The American-Israeli Cooperative Enterprise. http://www.jewishvirtuallibrary.org/jsource/Judaism/RoshHashanahMorningServices.html.

—. Mustard Plant Cruciferae Facts (p. 363), Copyright 2011. http://www.britannica.com.

—. "Myrrh & frankincense," (p. 658), Wikipedia ©2011. http://en.wikipedia.org/wiki/Myrrh & http://en.wikipedia.org/wiki/Frankincense.

—. "Natural Dye" (p. 593), Copyright 2009. http://www.en.wikipedia.org/wiki/Natural_dye.

Onesimus (p. 693), Copyright 2011. http://www.ec-patr.org/list/index.php?lang=en&id=3.

Onesimus (p. 693), Copyright 2011. http://www.patriarchate.org/patriarchate/former-patriarchs/Onesimus.

—. Onesimus (p. 693), Copyright 2011. http://www.en.wikipedia.org/wiki/Onesimus.

—. Parthenocarpy - (pp 388-9), Greek Karpos Facts ©2010. http://www.en.wikipedia.org/wiki/Parthenocarpy.

"Parthenocarpy" (pp 388-9) - (Greek word meaning - Parthenos & Karpos virgin fruit). Copyright 2010 Lewis, Helen. Mastering Horticulture: http://www.masteringhorticulture.blogspot.com/2010/10/parthenocarpy.html.

"Parthenocarpy" (pp 388-9), The Free Dictionary.com ©2011. http://www.thefreedictionary.com/parthenocarpy.

—. Pistacia lentiscus (p. 690), Copyright 2011. http://www.en.wikipedia.org/wiki/Pistacia_lentiscus/.

Polycarp (p. 698), Copyright 2011. http://www.patriarchate.org/patriarchate/former-patriarchs/Polycarp-i.

Priestly Garments - Linen, 6 ply thread, (pp 288, 594), Golden Girdle/High Priest - The Temple Institute, Jerusalem Israel Copyright 2007 All Rights Reserved. http://www.templeinstitute.org.

Rabbi, Pearlmutter Simcha. "Part Six of Nine- Rabbi Simcha Pearlmutter, Rabbi testimony of Jesus, Yeshua, Messiah" - Full Text: (pp 180-181, 432-433, 443, 497). jerusalemcalling.org/Rabbi_Simcha_Pearlmutter.htm.

Reich, Ronny. "BAS Library, Biblical Archaeology Society - "Caiaphas Name inscribed on bone boxes" (p.455), "Biblical Archaeology Review (BAR Magazine), September-October, Copyright 1992.

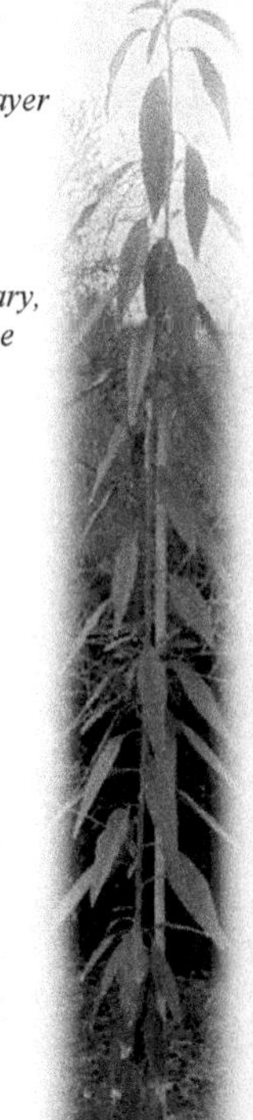

"Rod like Conductors and Lightning Rod" (p. 544), Random House Inc. The Random House College Dictionary Revised Edition. Random House, Inc., Copyright 1975.

Roman Early History Reference Crown (p. 631) ©2012. http://www.perpetuacatholic.info/index.php?p=1.17.

—. "Roman Frescos" (p. 766), Copyright 2011. http://www.en.wikipedia.org/wiki/Fresco.

"Rooster" (p. 438) - en.wikipedia.org/wiki/Gallic_rooster.

"Rooster" (p. 437), Rabbi Sinclair, Julian, "Thanking the Rooster" theJC.com (The Jewish Chronicle) 2014, June 1.

Rosh HaSha nah (p. 430) - Chumney, Eddie - Hebraic Heritage Ministries. "Heaven is opened on Rosh HaShanah - The Seven Festivals of the Messiah." (mayimhayim.org/Festivals/Feast7.htm)

Rosh HaShanah information (p. 637), Zalman, Eisenstock. "Open the gates on Rosh HaShanah" - www.jewishmag.com/158mag/rosh_hashanah_elul/rosh_hashanah_elul.htm. September 2011 Edition of the Jewish Magazine.

"Rosh HaShanah - The Hidden Day" (p. 444, 536) - mayimhayim.org/Festivals/Feast7.htm.

Rosh HaShanah (p. 640), "Three books, life, death, and suspended until Yom Kippur" - myjewishlearning.com - B. Rosh HaShanah 16 B.

"Royal Sceptre of King Tut" (p. 604) - eyeonart.net/history/ancient/egypt/tut.htm.

Sash - Binder for Scroll of the Law (p. 682) - www.jewishencyclopedia.com/articles/13358-scroll-of-the-law

Sceptre (p. 585), "The Royal Sceptre of Charles V" ©2007. http://wwwen.wikipedia.org/wiki/Crown_Jewels_of_France

"Serpentine" (Mineral) (p. 460-463, 712) - Encyclopaedia Britannica, Classic Edition, ©1911 Public Domain.

"Shechem" (p. 605) - bibleatlas.org/shechem.htm.

"Shechem" (p. 480, 498) - Faust's Bible Dictionary (Also called: Sichem, Sychem, and Sychar) - bible-history.com/links.php?cat=40&sub=680.

"Shiloah" (p. 597) - bibleapps.com/s/shiloah.htm.

"Shiloah" (p. 597) jewishencyclopedia.com/articles/13578-shiloah.

Shroud (p. 622) - Lemberg, Mechthild Flury (Textile Historian for the Shroud of Turin). The Invisible Mending of the Shroud, the Theory and the Reality. http://shroud.com/pdfs/n65part5.pdf.

Shroud (p. 623) - Lupia, John N. Regina Caeli Press - The Ancient Jewish Shroud At Turin (Tallit). Copyright 2010. http://www.reginacaelipress.com.

Shroud & Relics (p. 688) - Military Records, Historical Byzantine from 985AD, Stephenson, Paul (commentary by). (References & quotes from the tenth century regarding the swaddling clothes & God-bearing winding sheet of the LORD). Translated by McGeer, E., in Byzantine authors, preoccupations, literary activities & translations of the - harangues. Vols. Studia Anselmiana 110 (1993), pp. 107-17, for references to texts and editions. Copyright translation, Paul Stephenson, 28 December 2003 & Revised November 2006; July 2010, Copyright 2003, 2005, 2010.

Shroud of Turin & Sudarium facts (pp 623, 680) - Schwortz, Barrie M. & "The Shroud Sent to Louis IX of France by Baldwin II, The Latin Emporer at Constantinople." AND "Pathologist Analysis on the Shroud of Turin" "The Shroud of Turin Website. April 17, Copyright 2011. http://www.shroud.com/pdf/n56part5.pdf.

Shroud (p. 623) - van der Hoeven, A.A.M. "The Turin Shroud as John Mark's Temple Garment" - Copyright 2012, September 27. http://www.jesusking.info/John Mark's garment.pdf.

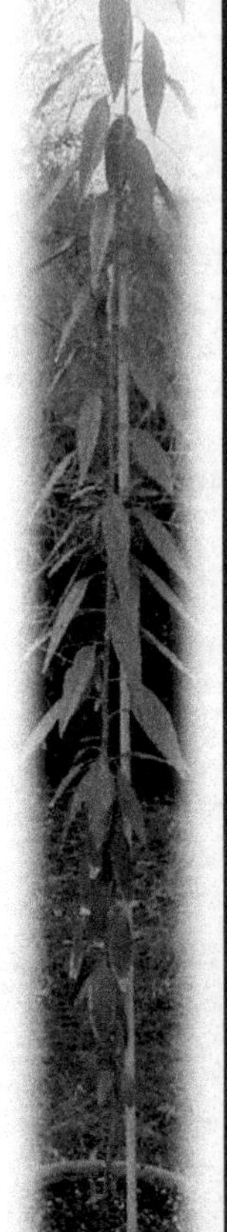

"Signet Ring of Seti I found in Egyptian coffin in Israel" - (p. 603) - foxnews.com/science/2014/04/09/israeli-archaeologists-uncover-3300-year-old-coffin-gold-signet/.

"Sin" the cresent moon-god (p. 171) - en.wikipedia.org/wiki/Sin_%28mythology%29.

"Sin" the moon-god (revelation of the man of sin) (p. 171) - en.wikipedia.org/wiki/Sin_(mythology)

"Sin" (p. 171) -www.britannica.com/EBchecked/topic/545523/Sin.

Sinai in Arabia (pp 203, 207, 211, 521) - Caldwell, Jim & Penny - Split Rock Research ©1992-2015 All Rights Reserved. http://splitrockresearch.org/content/Welcome/

Solomon's Palace and the Armory (p. 810), Copyright 2007. http://www. geocities.com/theseder2/theBigE.html.

—. Solomon's Pools (p. 489), Copyright 2011. http://www.en.wikipedia.org/wiki/Solomon's_Pools.

"Solomon's Temple" (p. 807), Christiananswers.net. Bible Encyclopedia, WebBible Encyclopedia - Copyright 2008 n.d. All Rights Reserved. http://christiananswers.net/dictionary/templesolomons.html.

Soons, Dr. Petrus (p. 553), Shroud3d.com - 3D Imaging Shroud Wave Fringes - ©2010 http://www.shroud3d.com/.

"Sound of Jerusalem gold bell of the High Priest from the Second Temple Period" (p. 590) - youtube.com/watch?v=xjx9tP3yTRI.

—. Spacetime (p. 722), Copyright 2012. http://www.en.wikipedia.org/wiki/Spacetime

—. Stachys (p. 483-486), Copyright 2011. http://www.en.wikipedia.org/wiki/Stachys.

—. Stachys The Apostle (p. 483-486), Copyright 2011. http://www.en.wikipedia.org/wiki/Stachys_the_Apostle.

Stachys The Apostle (p. 483-486), Copyright 2011. www.patriarchate.org/patriarchate/formerpatriarchs/stachys.

"St Andrews in Scotland" (p. 696) - en.wikipedia/org/wiki/St_Andrews.

—. "Static Electricity - Electrostatic Discharge," (p. 545), ©2011. http://www.en.wikipedia.org/wiki/Static_electricity.

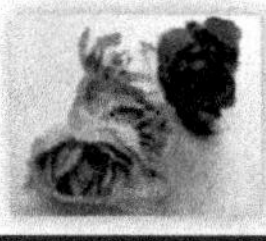

Strong, James, LL.D., S.T.D. The New Strong's Exhaustive Concordance of Bible, Including Greek and Hebrew Lexicon/Dictionaries. Thomas Nelson, ©1995 USA.

"Studies In the Apocalypse of John of Patmos (p. 826)- A Non-interpretive and Literary Approach to the Last Book of the English Bible". Hoyt, Edyth Armstrong - Ann Arbor: Edward Brothers 1956, Copyright 1944.

Sudarium (p. 675), Guscin, Mark, B.A. M.Phil. "The Sudarium of Oviedo, It's History and Relationship to the Shroud of Turin". Copyright 1997 All Rights Reserved. http://www.shroud.com/guscin.htm.

Sudarium (p. 680), Schwortz, Barrie M. - http://www.shroud.com

Swaddling cloth (p. 597) - "Mary washed Yeshua's swaddling cloth in Fountain of Mary" - en.wikipedia/org/wiki/Fountain_of_the_Virgin.

"Talmud Bavli Yoma 39b" (p. 715), Quote from: Rabbi Jonathan Cahn, "Hope of the World"- Copyright 2011. www.hopeoftheworld.org (To view the Talmud online http://www.sacred-texts.com/jud/talmud.htm).

Talmud (p. 646), Hadaf, Kollel Iyun of Yerushalayim. The Dafyomi Advancement Forum, The Internet Center for the Study of Talmud - Insights Into The Daily Daf - Rosh HaShanah 25. http://www.dafyomi.co.il/rhashanah/insites/rh-dt-025.htm (accessed 2011-2012).

—. Tarshish (p. 229), Copyright 2013. http://www.en.wikipedia.org/wiki/Tarshish.

Tefillin (p. 243, 566) - Finkelstein, Joel Rabbi. Part of a series given by Rabbi Joel Finkelstein of ASBEE, The Marcos and Adira Katz YuTorah Online. ©2012, January 17 Copyright Yeshiva University. Video title: "How to put on Tefillin" www.yourtube.com/watch?v=3UFCu8BRaQU Website: www.yotorah.org/lectures/lecture.cfm/762533/.

Telescope Facts (p. 549-550), Copyright 2011-2012. http://www.amazing-space.stsci.edu/resources/explorations/groudup/lesson/eras/early-refractors/page2.php.

Temple of Peace (p. 701) - Dewing, H. B. Translation by. Procopius with an English translation in seven volumes III History of the Wars, books V and VI London, First Printed in Great Britain: William Heinemann ltd Cambridge, Massachusetts Harvard University Press, ©1919.

—. "Temple of Peace, Forum of Vespasian" (p. 701), ©2011. www.en.wikipedia.org/wiki/Temple_of_Peace, _Rome#Temple_of_Peace.

"Temple of Peace Forum of Vespasian (p. 701) - ROMA, CENTRO STORICO a FORI IMPERIALI Basilica di Massenzio, Tempio dell Pace e Fori Imperiali: scavi archeologici per le stazioni della metropolitana C nel Centro Storico." Arch. Morganti, Giuseppe (21-07-2004). (Decr.16/12/1997 - Roma Capitale 1998, Cod. b4.1). http://www.flickr.com/photos/imperial_fora_of_rome/sets/72157594587104523/.

Temple of Peace or Forum of Vespasian - Rome Reborn. (p. 701), Virginia, The Rectors and Visitors of the University of. Copyright ©2008 All Rights Reserved. http://www.romereborn.frischerconsulting.com/ge/TS-070-PA.html.

The American Heritage Dictionary of the English Language, Fourth Edition "Definitions of the words; Taffeta & Wimple". Houghton Mifflin Company, Copyright 2000 (updated 2009) All Rights Reserved.

"The Annals of the World" by James USSHER., Pierce, Larry & Marion. P.O. Box 726, Green Forest, AR 72638: Master Books, Inc., (First printing October 2003 & Fourth printing December 2004), Copyright 2003.

The Authorized King James Version of the Bible. Humphrey Milford, Amen House, E.C.4 - New York 35 West 32nd Street. Oxford England: Printed at the University Press London 1897, 1897.

The Dead Sea Scrolls: A New Translation - Wise, Michael, Abegg Jr, Martin & Cook, Edward. San Francisco: Harper, An Imprint of HarperCollins Publishers, Inc., Copyright 1996 All Rights Reserved. (pp 228, 716).

"The Fourth Crusade" (p. 687), Translations and Reprints from the Original Sources in European History, Dana Carlton Munro, ed. and tr., vol. III, no. 1 (University of Pennsylvania,1907), pp. 13-14.
Original found in Robert de Clari, ch. lxxiilxxiii, in Hopf: Chro. "The Sack of Constantinople by the Crusaders". http://www.shsu.edu/~his_nep/1204.html.

The Jewish Encyclopedia.com of Rabbinical Literature. Copyright 2002. http://www.thejewishencyclopedia.com/view.jsp?artid=709&letter=A#ixzz1ljfQv8Mv (accessed 2011).

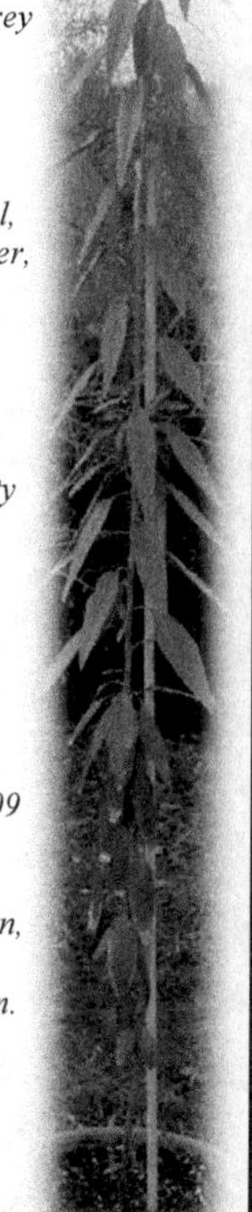

"The Works of Tacitus" (p. 693-694) - Church, Alfred John, Brodribb, William Jackson - Translated by.. Copyright 1864-1877. http://www.sacred-texts.com/cla/tac/index.htm.

—."Threshing Board" (p. 794), Wikipedia (threshing sledges) ©2010. en.wikipedia.org/wiki/Threshing-board.

—. "Threshing Floor," (p. 794), Wikipedia ©2010-2013. http://en.wikipedia.org/wiki/Threshing_floor.

—. "Tish B' Av" (The Ninth of Av) (p. 507), Wikipedia. ©2011-2013. http://en.wikipedia.org/wiki/Tisha_B%27Av.

"Torah Binder" (p. 670) - Brooklyn Museum, https://www.brooklynmuseum.org/opencollection/objects/5114/Torah_Binder.

Torah Binder (p. 676), Reed Magazine, "The Art of Teaching, The Teaching of Art" page 3 Torah Binder of Geraldine Ondrizek. Copyright 2011. http://www.academic.reed.edu/art/faculty/ondrizek/installations/M168/Page9.html & (Torah Binder excerpt) http://www.reed.edu/reed_magazine/winter2007/features/art_teaching/3.html.

"Torah Binder" (p. 686) (Swaddling cloth). The Jewish Museum, NY USA. The Jewish Museum, glossary, ©2011-2013. http://www.thejewishmuseum.org/glossary.

"Torah Binders" (p. 673), The Czech Memorial Scrolls Museum, Archive of the Jewish Museum in Prague ©2011-2013. www.Czechmemorialscrolltrust.org/binders.htm.

"Torah Binder used to swaddle in the bris ceremony, used as funeral shroud at life's end.". (p. 684), Weisberg, Ruth.- Ruth Weisberg Unfurled Source for; Skirball Cultural Center, Los Angeles. AND other death sources.

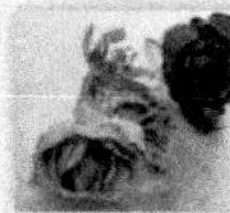

Torah on the web - Copyright 1997-2012 by Yeshivat Har Etzion. http://www.vbm-torah.org/archive/midrash69/12midrash.htm.

"Torah Ornaments" (p. 673) - Copyright 2013: www.jewishvirtuallibrary.org/jsource/judaica/ejud_0002_0020_0_19950.html. (Regarding Torah Binders/wimple).

Webster, Noah. Webster's New Twentieth Century Dictionary, Unabridged Second Edition. Cleveland and New York USA: The World Publishing Company, © 1973.

—. "Wimpel" (p. 670), Copyright 2011. http://en.wikipedia.org/wiki/Wimpel.

Wimpel (p. 670), "The Jewish Wimpel". Copyright 2011. http://www.jewishwimpel.com/about_the_wimpel.html.

"Wimpeln, or Ashkenazic binders, birth of a male child. (pp 673,684), Wonderful illuminated letters (painted or embroidered) with animals often described the wish that the boy be raised to a life of Torah, Chuppah (wedding) and good deeds." Kolel.org. Copyright 2011. http://www.kolel.org/torahstory/module1/mantles.html.

Wimple, Mappa, bris blessing - "The German-Jewish Wimpel: Wrapped Wishes, Nearly Forgotten". Singer, Matt. Matt Singer's Blog, Copyright 2009, October 23. http://personal.psu.edu/mfs197/blogs/matt_singers_blog/2009/10/the-german-jewish-wimpel-wrapped-wishes-nearly-forgotten.html.

"World's Oldest Cypress Doors," (p. 701), Storage, William. - The Door Panels of Santa Sabina. ©2006-2012 All Rights Reserved. http://www.digitalimages.net/Gallery/Scenic/Rome/Churches/Ancient/ancient.html#SanClemente.

Wyatt Archaeological Research- Wyattmuseum.com (pp 714, 727)

"Yentl" (pp 294, 382, 496) - Movie based upon the book titled "Yentl the Yeshiva boy" by Isaac Bashevis Singer, The Movie "Yentl" Screenplay- Jack Rosenthal - Screenplay - Barbra Streisand & Directed by Barbra Streisand. Produced by Executive- Larry DeWaay - Producer- Barbra Streisand - Co-Producer- Rusty LeMorande. Yentl Performed by Barbra Streisand. MGM Distribution Company, Domestic Theatrical Distributor, Copyright 1983.

Doves came as soon as I finished Editing & Condensing this book on September 14, 2014 Photo ©2014 Kimberly K Ballard All Rights Reserved

Drum, Winged Dove & Crown & Percussion Roses
Photos ©2013 Kimberly K Ballard All Rights Reserved

INDEX

A

B

C

D

E

F

G

H

I

J

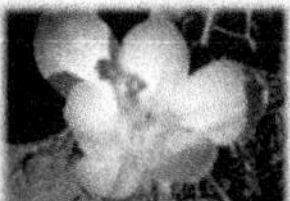
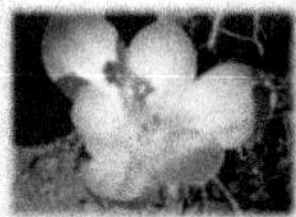

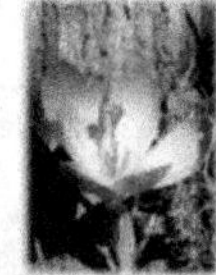

About the Author

Official Photograph of Kimberly K Ballard

Kimberly K Ballard is an avid Bible researcher. She is deeply interested in the Historic, Prophetic and Archaeological Hebrew Messiah of Israel. She is a diligent student of the Bible in its entirety and has written the astonishing details that are compiled within this book, as they were revealed to her over a six year span of time, by the power of the LORD'S Holy Spirit.

Kimberly studied Professional Classical Music at Colorado State University in the mid 1980's. As a Percussion Performance Major, she was a long time University Orchestra member and served as the Timpanist and as a Percussionist in the University Symphony Orchestra, under the direction and appointment of NYC Juilliard Graduate Violin Professor, Wilfred A. Schwartz. She also performed on call, in the Professional Fort Collins Symphony Orchestra in Fort Collins Colorado, under Maestro Wilfred A. Schwartz. She studied Percussion Performance under the tutelage of Marion Lowe, Principal Symphony Percussionist and then Graduate Student Professor. Kimberly performed with the University Marimba Ensemble, Percussion Ensemble, for Theater Productions and for World renowned guest Composers, Symphony Timpanists and Professional Musicians and performed in the MENC, Music Educators National Conference/National Association for Music Education. She was also a drum student of Mr. Dave Goodman, currently Music Executive for Disney. Kimberly studied Jazz and Classical Voice at CSU and Latin Conga's in Boulder Colorado. Today Kimberly is an aspiring Music Composer, Arranger, Recording and Producing original Music in her private home studio using Percussion, Piano and voice. She has also played guitar and flute. A CD of her Music was released in 2006 and aired on a Messianic Radio Station and is still sold by an Independent Music Company. She is the Author of this book!

Dedication – My father is buried at the base of this giant tree in Dallas Texas. I came up from his roots. This book fulfills a promise that I made to him.

My Percussion Briefcase with Mallets that I carried daily – my life!

Jordan River at Qasr el-Yahud. Opposite & a little south of Jericho. It would be somewhere near here that the crossing of Joshua 3 took place. This photo looks to the north. Photo ©2014 Leon Mauldin All Rights Reserved – bleon1.wordpress.com/

Till Thy people pass over, O LORD,
till the people pass over, which Thou hast purchased

My Living Nisan 17 Almond Rod of God lifted up (side)

Dreaming of the Third Temple – A schematic model of the Third Temple itself AND Model of the Second Temple in Jerusalem Israel (top)

Lifting up my Almond Rod of the Testimony at sunset on November 21st 2014

My Almond Tree as it budded on January 21st 2015 the first day of Shevat!

CPSIA information can be obtained
at www.ICGtesting.com
Printed in the USA
BVHW011727040819
554906BV00017BA/11/P

9 781941 173114